Ivan Turgenev, Novels and

In this book:
Fathers and Children
Translated by Constance Garnett

A Nobleman's Nest
Translator: Isabel F. Hapgood

Smoke
Translator: Constance Black Garnett

Rudin
Translator: Constance Garnett

The Torrents of Spring
Translator: Constance Garnett

The Jew And Other Stories
Translator:
Constance Garnett

The Diary of a Superfluous Man and Other Stories
Translator: Constance Garnett

Ivan Sergeyevich Turgenev (1818 – 1883) was a Russian novelist, short story writer, and playwright. Turgenev was one of the master of Russian Realism, and his novel Fathers and Sons (1862) is regarded as one of the major works of 19th-century fiction.

During the period of 1853-62 Turgenev wrote some of his finest stories as well as the first four of his novels: Rudin (1856), A Nest of the Gentry (1859), and Fathers and Sons (1862).

In this book:
Fathers and Children
Translated by Constance Garnett

A Nobleman's Nest
Translator: Isabel F. Hapgood

Smoke
Translator: Constance Black Garnett

Rudin
Translator: Constance Garnett

The Torrents of Spring
Translator: Constance Garnett

The Jew And Other Stories
Translator:
Constance Garnett

The Diary of a Superfluous Man and Other Stories
Translator: Constance Garnett

Fathers and Children

CHAPTER I

'Well, Piotr, not in sight yet?' was the question asked on May the 20th, 1859, by a gentleman of a little over forty, in a dusty coat and checked trousers, who came out without his hat on to the low steps of the posting station at S——. He was addressing his servant, a chubby young fellow, with whitish down on his chin, and little, lack-lustre eyes.

The servant, in whom everything—the turquoise ring in his ear, the streaky hair plastered with grease, and the civility of his movements—indicated a man of the new, improved generation, glanced with an air of indulgence along the road, and made answer:

'No, sir; not in sight.'

'Not in sight?' repeated his master.

'No, sir,' responded the man a second time.

His master sighed, and sat down on a little bench. We will introduce him to the reader while he sits, his feet tucked under him, gazing thoughtfully round.

His name was Nikolai Petrovitch Kirsanov. He had, twelve miles from the posting station, a fine property of two hundred souls, or, as he expressed it—since he had arranged the division of his land with the peasants, and started 'a farm'—of nearly five thousand acres. His father, a general in the army, who served in 1812, a coarse, half-educated, but not ill-natured man, a typical Russian, had been in harness all his life, first in command of a brigade, and then of a division, and lived constantly in the provinces, where, by virtue of his rank, he played a fairly important part. Nikolai Petrovitch was born in the south of Russia like his elder brother, Pavel, of whom more hereafter. He was educated at home till he was fourteen, surrounded by cheap tutors, free-and-easy but toadying adjutants, and all the usual regimental and staff set. His mother, one of the Kolyazin family, as a girl called Agathe, but as a general's wife Agathokleya Kuzminishna Kirsanov, was one of those military ladies who take their full share of the duties and dignities of office. She wore gorgeous caps and rustling silk dresses; in church she was the first to advance to the cross; she talked a great deal in a loud voice, let her children kiss her hand in the morning, and gave them her blessing at night—in fact, she got everything out of life she could. Nikolai Petrovitch, as a general's son—though so far from being distinguished by courage that he even deserved to be called 'a funk'—was intended, like his brother Pavel, to enter the army; but he broke his leg on the very day when the news of his commission came, and, after being two months in bed, retained a slight limp to the end of his days. His father gave him up as a bad job, and let him go into the civil service. He took him to Petersburg directly he was eighteen, and placed him in the university. His brother happened about the same time to be made an officer in the Guards. The young men started living together in one set of rooms, under the remote supervision of a cousin on their mother's side, Ilya Kolyazin, an official of high rank. Their father returned to his division and his wife, and only rarely sent his sons large sheets of grey paper, scrawled over in a bold clerkly hand. At the bottom of these sheets stood in letters, enclosed carefully in scroll-work, the words, 'Piotr Kirsanov, General-Major.' In 1835 Nikolai Petrovitch left the university, a graduate, and in the same year General Kirsanov was put on to the retired list after an unsuccessful review, and came to Petersburg with his wife to live. He was about to take a house in the Tavrichesky Gardens, and had joined the English club, but he died suddenly of an apoplectic fit. Agathokleya Kuzminishna soon followed him; she could not accustom herself to a dull life in the capital; she was consumed by the ennui of existence away from the regiment. Meanwhile Nikolai Petrovitch had already, in his parents' lifetime and to their no slight chagrin, had time to fall in love with the daughter of his landlord, a petty official, Prepolovensky. She was a pretty and, as it is called, 'advanced' girl; she used to read the serious articles in the 'Science' column of the journals. He married her directly the term of mourning was over; and leaving the civil service in which his father had by favour procured him a post, was perfectly blissful with his Masha, first in a country villa near the Lyesny Institute, afterwards in town in a pretty little flat with a clean staircase and a draughty drawing-room, and then in the country, where he settled finally, and where in a short time a son, Arkady, was born to him. The young couple lived very happily and peacefully; they were scarcely ever apart; they read together, sang and played duets together on the piano; she tended her

flowers and looked after the poultry-yard; he sometimes went hunting, and busied himself with the estate, while Arkady grew and grew in the same happy and peaceful way. Ten years passed like a dream. In 1847 Kirsanov's wife died. He almost succumbed to this blow; in a few weeks his hair was grey; he was getting ready to go abroad, if possible to distract his mind ... but then came the year 1848. He returned unwillingly to the country, and, after a rather prolonged period of inactivity, began to take an interest in improvements in the management of his land. In 1855 he brought his son to the university; he spent three winters with him in Petersburg, hardly going out anywhere, and trying to make acquaintance with Arkady's young companions. The last winter he had not been able to go, and here we have him in the May of 1859, already quite grey, stoutish, and rather bent, waiting for his son, who had just taken his degree, as once he had taken it himself.
The servant, from a feeling of propriety, and perhaps, too, not anxious to remain under the master's eye, had gone to the gate, and was smoking a pipe. Nikolai Petrovitch bent his head, and began staring at the crumbling steps; a big mottled fowl walked sedately towards him, treading firmly with its great yellow legs; a muddy cat gave him an unfriendly look, twisting herself coyly round the railing. The sun was scorching; from the half-dark passage of the posting station came an odour of hot rye-bread. Nikolai Petrovitch fell to dreaming. 'My son ... a graduate ... Arkasha ...' were the ideas that continually came round again and again in his head; he tried to think of something else, and again the same thoughts returned. He remembered his dead wife.... 'She did not live to see it!' he murmured sadly. A plump, dark-blue pigeon flew into the road, and hurriedly went to drink in a puddle near the well. Nikolai Petrovitch began looking at it, but his ear had already caught the sound of approaching wheels.
'It sounds as if they're coming sir,' announced the servant, popping in from the gateway.
Nikolai Petrovitch jumped up, and bent his eyes on the road. A carriage appeared with three posting-horses harnessed abreast; in the carriage he caught a glimpse of the blue band of a student's cap, the familiar outline of a dear face.
'Arkasha! Arkasha!' cried Kirsanov, and he ran waving his hands.... A few instants later, his lips were pressed to the beardless, dusty, sunburnt-cheek of the youthful graduate.

CHAPTER II

'Let me shake myself first, daddy,' said Arkady, in a voice tired from travelling, but boyish and clear as a bell, as he gaily responded to his father's caresses; 'I am covering you with dust.'
'Never mind, never mind,' repeated Nikolai Petrovitch, smiling tenderly, and twice he struck the collar of his son's cloak and his own greatcoat with his hand. 'Let me have a look at you; let me have a look at you,' he added, moving back from him, but immediately he went with hurried steps towards the yard of the station, calling, 'This way, this way; and horses at once.'
Nikolai Petrovitch seemed far more excited than his son; he seemed a little confused, a little timid. Arkady stopped him.
'Daddy,' he said, 'let me introduce you to my great friend, Bazarov, about whom I have so often written to you. He has been so good as to promise to stay with us.'
Nikolai Petrovitch went back quickly, and going up to a tall man in a long, loose, rough coat with tassels, who had only just got out of the carriage, he warmly pressed the ungloved red hand, which the latter did not at once hold out to him.
'I am heartily glad,' he began, 'and very grateful for your kind intention of visiting us.... Let me know your name, and your father's.'
'Yevgeny Vassilyev,' answered Bazarov, in a lazy but manly voice; and turning back the collar of his rough coat, he showed Nikolai Petrovitch his whole face. It was long and lean, with a broad forehead, a nose flat at

the base and sharper at the end, large greenish eyes, and drooping whiskers of a sandy colour; it was lighted up by a tranquil smile, and showed self-confidence and intelligence.

'I hope, dear Yevgeny Vassilyitch, you won't be dull with us,' continued Nikolai Petrovitch.

Bazarov's thin lips moved just perceptibly, though he made no reply, but merely took off his cap. His long, thick hair did not hide the prominent bumps on his head.

'Then, Arkady,' Nikolai Petrovitch began again, turning to his son, 'shall the horses be put to at once? or would you like to rest?'

'We will rest at home, daddy; tell them to harness the horses.'

'At once, at once,' his father assented. 'Hey, Piotr, do you hear? Get things ready, my good boy; look sharp.'

Piotr, who as a modernised servant had not kissed the young master's hand, but only bowed to him from a distance, again vanished through the gateway.

'I came here with the carriage, but there are three horses for your coach too,' said Nikolai Petrovitch fussily, while Arkady drank some water from an iron dipper brought him by the woman in charge of the station, and Bazarov began smoking a pipe and went up to the driver, who was taking out the horses; 'there are only two seats in the carriage, and I don't know how your friend' ...

'He will go in the coach,' interposed Arkady in an undertone. 'You must not stand on ceremony with him, please. He's a splendid fellow, so simple—you will see.'

Nikolai Petrovitch's coachman brought the horses round.

'Come, hurry up, bushy beard!' said Bazarov, addressing the driver.

'Do you hear, Mityuha,' put in another driver, standing by with his hands thrust behind him into the opening of his sheepskin coat, 'what the gentleman called you? It's a bushy beard you are too.'

Mityuha only gave a jog to his hat and pulled the reins off the heated shaft-horse.

'Look sharp, look sharp, lads, lend a hand,' cried Nikolai Petrovitch; 'there'll be something to drink our health with!'

In a few minutes the horses were harnessed; the father and son were installed in the carriage; Piotr climbed up on to the box; Bazarov jumped into the coach, and nestled his head down into the leather cushion; and both the vehicles rolled away.

CHAPTER III

'So here you are, a graduate at last, and come home again,' said Nikolai Petrovitch, touching Arkady now on the shoulder, now on the knee. 'At last!'

'And how is uncle? quite well?' asked Arkady, who, in spite of the genuine, almost childish delight filling his heart, wanted as soon as possible to turn the conversation from the emotional into a commonplace channel.

'Quite well. He was thinking of coming with me to meet you, but for some reason or other he gave up the idea.'

'And how long have you been waiting for me?' inquired Arkady.

'Oh, about five hours.'

'Dear old dad!'

Arkady turned round quickly to his father, and gave him a sounding kiss on the cheek. Nikolai Petrovitch gave vent to a low chuckle.

'I have got such a capital horse for you!' he began. 'You will see. And your room has been fresh papered.'

'And is there a room for Bazarov?'

'We will find one for him too.'

'Please, dad, make much of him. I can't tell you how I prize his friendship.'

'Have you made friends with him lately?'

'Yes, quite lately.'
'Ah, that's how it is I did not see him last winter. What does he study?'
'His chief subject is natural science. But he knows everything. Next year he wants to take his doctor's degree.'
'Ah! he's in the medical faculty,' observed Nikolai Petrovitch, and he was silent for a little. 'Piotr,' he went on, stretching out his hand, 'aren't those our peasants driving along?'
Piotr looked where his master was pointing. Some carts harnessed with unbridled horses were moving rapidly along a narrow by-road. In each cart there were one or two peasants in sheepskin coats, unbuttoned.
'Yes, sir,' replied Piotr.
'Where are they going,—to the town?'
'To the town, I suppose. To the gin-shop,' he added contemptuously, turning slightly towards the coachman, as though he would appeal to him. But the latter did not stir a muscle; he was a man of the old stamp, and did not share the modern views of the younger generation.
'I have had a lot of bother with the peasants this year,' pursued Nikolai Petrovitch, turning to his son. 'They won't pay their rent. What is one to do?'
'But do you like your hired labourers?'
'Yes,' said Nikolai Petrovitch between his teeth. 'They're being set against me, that's the mischief; and they don't do their best. They spoil the tools. But they have tilled the land pretty fairly. When things have settled down a bit, it will be all right. Do you take an interest in farming now?'
'You've no shade; that's a pity,' remarked Arkady, without answering the last question.
'I have had a great awning put up on the north side over the balcony,' observed Nikolai Petrovitch; 'now we can have dinner even in the open air.'
'It'll be rather too like a summer villa.... Still, that's all nonsense. What air though here! How delicious it smells! Really I fancy there's nowhere such fragrance in the world as in the meadows here! And the sky too.'
Arkady suddenly stopped short, cast a stealthy look behind him, and said no more.
'Of course,' observed Nikolai Petrovitch, 'you were born here, and so everything is bound to strike you in a special——'
'Come, dad, that makes no difference where a man is born.'
'Still——'
'No; it makes absolutely no difference.'
Nikolai Petrovitch gave a sidelong glance at his son, and the carriage went on a half-a-mile further before the conversation was renewed between them.
'I don't recollect whether I wrote to you,' began Nikolai Petrovitch, 'your old nurse, Yegorovna, is dead.'
'Really? Poor thing! Is Prokofitch still living?'
'Yes, and not a bit changed. As grumbling as ever. In fact, you won't find many changes at Maryino.'
'Have you still the same bailiff?'
'Well, to be sure there is a change there. I decided not to keep about me any freed serfs, who have been house servants, or, at least, not to intrust them with duties of any responsibility.' (Arkady glanced towards Piotr.) *'Il est libre, en effet,'* observed Nikolai Petrovitch in an undertone; 'but, you see, he's only a valet. Now I have a bailiff, a townsman; he seems a practical fellow. I pay him two hundred and fifty roubles a year. But,' added Nikolai Petrovitch, rubbing his forehead and eyebrows with his hand, which was always an indication with him of inward embarrassment, 'I told you just now that you would not find changes at Maryino.... That's not quite correct. I think it my duty to prepare you, though....'
He hesitated for an instant, and then went on in French.
'A severe moralist would regard my openness, as improper; but, in the first place, it can't be concealed, and secondly, you are aware I have always had peculiar ideas as regards the relation of father and son. Though, of course, you would be right in blaming me. At my age.... In short ... that ... that girl, about whom you have probably heard already ...'
'Fenitchka?' asked Arkady easily.
Nikolai Petrovitch blushed. 'Don't mention her name aloud, please.... Well ... she is living with me now. I have installed her in the house ... there were two little rooms there. But that can all be changed.'
'Goodness, daddy, what for?'
'Your friend is going to stay with us ... it would be awkward ...'
'Please don't be uneasy on Bazarov's account. He's above all that.'
'Well, but you too,' added Nikolai Petrovitch. 'The little lodge is so horrid—that's the worst of it.'
'Goodness, dad,' interposed Arkady, 'it's as if you were apologising; I wonder you're not ashamed.'

'Of course, I ought to be ashamed,' answered Nikolai Petrovitch, flushing more and more.
'Nonsense, dad, nonsense; please don't!' Arkady smiled affectionately. 'What a thing to apologise for!' he thought to himself, and his heart was filled with a feeling of condescending tenderness for his kind, soft-hearted father, mixed with a sense of secret superiority. 'Please, stop,' he repeated once more, instinctively revelling in a consciousness of his own advanced and emancipated condition.
Nikolai Petrovitch glanced at him from under the fingers of the hand with which he was still rubbing his forehead, and there was a pang in his heart.... But at once he blamed himself for it.
'Here are our meadows at last,' he said after a long silence.
'And that in front is our forest, isn't it?' asked Arkady.
'Yes. Only I have sold the timber. This year they will cut it down.'
'Why did you sell it?'
'The money was needed; besides, that land is to go to the peasants.'
'Who don't pay you their rent?'
'That's their affair; besides, they will pay it some day.'
'I am sorry about the forest,' observed Arkady, and he began to look about him.
The country through which they were driving could not be called picturesque. Fields upon fields stretched all along to the very horizon, now sloping gently upwards, then dropping down again; in some places woods were to be seen, and winding ravines, planted with low, scanty bushes, recalling vividly the representation of them on the old-fashioned maps of the times of Catherine. They came upon little streams too with hollow banks; and tiny lakes with narrow dykes; and little villages, with low hovels under dark and often tumble-down roofs, and slanting barns with walls woven of brushwood and gaping doorways beside neglected threshing-floors; and churches, some brick-built, with stucco peeling off in patches, others wooden, with crosses fallen askew, and overgrown grave-yards. Slowly Arkady's heart sunk. To complete the picture, the peasants they met were all in tatters and on the sorriest little nags; the willows, with their trunks stripped of bark, and broken branches, stood like ragged beggars along the roadside; cows lean and shaggy and looking pinched up by hunger, were greedily tearing at the grass along the ditches. They looked as though they had just been snatched out of the murderous clutches of some threatening monster; and the piteous state of the weak, starved beasts in the midst of the lovely spring day, called up, like a white phantom, the endless, comfortless winter with its storms, and frosts, and snows.... 'No,' thought Arkady, 'this is not a rich country; it does not impress one by plenty or industry; it can't, it can't go on like this, reforms are absolutely necessary ... but how is one to carry them out, how is one to begin?'
Such were Arkady's reflections; ... but even as he reflected, the spring regained its sway. All around was golden green, all—trees, bushes, grass—shone and stirred gently in wide waves under the soft breath of the warm wind; from all sides flooded the endless trilling music of the larks; the peewits were calling as they hovered over the low-lying meadows, or noiselessly ran over the tussocks of grass; the rooks strutted among the half-grown short spring-corn, standing out black against its tender green; they disappeared in the already whitening rye, only from time to time their heads peeped out amid its grey waves. Arkady gazed and gazed, and his reflections grew slowly fainter and passed away.... He flung off his cloak and turned to his father, with a face so bright and boyish, that the latter gave him another hug.
'We're not far off now,' remarked Nikolai Petrovitch; 'we have only to get up this hill, and the house will be in sight. We shall get on together splendidly, Arkasha; you shall help me in farming the estate, if only it isn't a bore to you. We must draw close to one another now, and learn to know each other thoroughly, mustn't we!'
'Of course,' said Arkady; 'but what an exquisite day it is to-day!'
'To welcome you, my dear boy. Yes, it's spring in its full loveliness. Though I agree with Pushkin—do you remember in Yevgeny Onyegin—

ıe how sad thy coming is
ıg, spring, sweet time of
t ...'

'Arkady!' called Bazarov's voice from the coach, 'send me a match; I've nothing to light my pipe with.'
Nikolai Petrovitch stopped, while Arkady, who had begun listening to him with some surprise, though with sympathy too, made haste to pull a silver matchbox out of his pocket, and sent it to Bazarov by Piotr.

'Will you have a cigar?' shouted Bazarov again.
'Thanks,' answered Arkady.
Piotr returned to the carriage, and handed him with the match-box a thick black cigar, which Arkady began to smoke promptly, diffusing about him such a strong and pungent odour of cheap tobacco, that Nikolai Petrovitch, who had never been a smoker from his youth up, was forced to turn away his head, as imperceptibly as he could for fear of wounding his son.
A quarter of an hour later, the two carriages drew up before the steps of a new wooden house, painted grey, with a red iron roof. This was Maryino, also known as New-Wick, or, as the peasants had nicknamed it, Poverty Farm.

CHAPTER IV

No crowd of house-serfs ran out on to the steps to meet the gentlemen; a little girl of twelve years old made her appearance alone. After her there came out of the house a young lad, very like Piotr, dressed in a coat of grey livery, with white armorial buttons, the servant of Pavel Petrovitch Kirsanov. Without speaking, he opened the door of the carriage, and unbuttoned the apron of the coach. Nikolai Petrovitch with his son and Bazarov walked through a dark and almost empty hall, from behind the door of which they caught a glimpse of a young woman's face, into a drawing-room furnished in the most modern style.
'Here we are at home,' said Nikolai Petrovitch, taking off his cap, and shaking back his hair. 'That's the great thing; now we must have supper and rest.'
'A meal would not come amiss, certainly,' observed Bazarov, stretching, and he dropped on to a sofa.
'Yes, yes, let us have supper, supper directly.' Nikolai Petrovitch with no apparent reason stamped his foot. 'And here just at the right moment comes Prokofitch.'
A man about sixty entered, white-haired, thin, and swarthy, in a cinnamon-coloured dress-coat with brass buttons, and a pink neckerchief. He smirked, went up to kiss Arkady's hand, and bowing to the guest retreated to the door, and put his hands behind him.
'Here he is, Prokofitch,' began Nikolai Petrovitch; 'he's come back to us at last.... Well, how do you think him looking?'
'As well as could be,' said the old man, and was grinning again, but he quickly knitted his bushy brows. 'You wish supper to be served?' he said impressively.
'Yes, yes, please. But won't you like to go to your room first, Yevgeny Vassilyitch?'
'No, thanks; I don't care about it. Only give orders for my little box to be taken there, and this garment, too,' he added, taking off his frieze overcoat.
'Certainly. Prokofitch, take the gentleman's coat.' (Prokofitch, with an air of perplexity, picked up Bazarov's 'garment' in both hands, and holding it high above his head, retreated on tiptoe.) 'And you, Arkady, are you going to your room for a minute?'
'Yes, I must wash,' answered Arkady, and was just moving towards the door, but at that instant there came into the drawing-room a man of medium height, dressed in a dark English suit, a fashionable low cravat, and kid shoes, Pavel Petrovitch Kirsanov. He looked about forty-five: his close-cropped, grey hair shone with a dark lustre, like new silver; his face, yellow but free from wrinkles, was exceptionally regular and pure in line, as though carved by a light and delicate chisel, and showed traces of remarkable beauty; specially fine were his clear, black, almond-shaped eyes. The whole person of Arkady's uncle, with its aristocratic elegance, had preserved the gracefulness of youth and that air of striving upwards, away from earth, which for the most part is lost after the twenties are past.
Pavel Petrovitch took out of his trouser pocket his exquisite hand with its long tapering pink nails, a hand which seemed still more exquisite from the snowy whiteness of the cuff, buttoned with a single, big opal, and

gave it to his nephew. After a preliminary handshake in the European style, he kissed him thrice after the Russian fashion, that is to say, he touched his cheek three times with his perfumed moustaches, and said, 'Welcome.'
Nikolai Petrovitch presented him to Bazarov; Pavel Petrovitch greeted him with a slight inclination of his supple figure, and a slight smile, but he did not give him his hand, and even put it back into his pocket.
'I had begun to think you were not coming to-day,' he began in a musical voice, with a genial swing and shrug of the shoulders, as he showed his splendid white teeth. 'Did anything happen on the road.'
'Nothing happened,' answered Arkady; 'we were rather slow. But we're as hungry as wolves now. Hurry up Prokofitch, dad; and I'll be back directly.'
'Stay, I'm coming with you,' cried Bazarov, pulling himself up suddenly from the sofa. Both the young men went out.
'Who is he?' asked Pavel Petrovitch.
'A friend of Arkasha's; according to him, a very clever fellow.'
'Is he going to stay with us?'
'Yes.'
'That unkempt creature?'
'Why, yes.'
Pavel Petrovitch drummed with his finger tips on the table. 'I fancy Arkady *s'est dégourdi,'* he remarked. 'I'm glad he has come back.'
At supper there was little conversation. Bazarov especially said nothing, but he ate a great deal. Nikolai Petrovitch related various incidents in what he called his career as a farmer, talked about the impending government measures, about committees, deputations, the necessity of introducing machinery, etc. Pavel Petrovitch paced slowly up and down the dining-room (he never ate supper), sometimes sipping at a wineglass of red wine, and less often uttering some remark or rather exclamation, of the nature of 'Ah! aha! hm!' Arkady told some news from Petersburg, but he was conscious of a little awkwardness, that awkwardness, which usually overtakes a youth when he has just ceased to be a child, and has come back to a place where they are accustomed to regard him and treat him as a child. He made his sentences quite unnecessarily long, avoided the word 'daddy,' and even sometimes replaced it by the word 'father,' mumbled, it is true, between his teeth; with an exaggerated carelessness he poured into his glass far more wine than he really wanted, and drank it all off. Prokofitch did not take his eyes off him, and kept chewing his lips. After supper they all separated at once.
'Your uncle's a queer fish,' Bazarov said to Arkady, as he sat in his dressing-gown by his bedside, smoking a short pipe. 'Only fancy such style in the country! His nails, his nails—you ought to send them to an exhibition!'
'Why of course, you don't know,' replied Arkady. 'He was a great swell in his own day, you know. I will tell you his story one day. He was very handsome, you know, used to turn all the women's heads.'
'Oh, that's it, is it? So he keeps it up in memory of the past. It's a pity there's no one for him to fascinate here though. I kept staring at his exquisite collars. They're like marble, and his chin's shaved simply to perfection. Come, Arkady Nikolaitch, isn't that ridiculous?'
'Perhaps it is; but he's a splendid man, really.'
'An antique survival! But your father's a capital fellow. He wastes his time reading poetry, and doesn't know much about farming, but he's a good-hearted fellow.'
'My father's a man in a thousand.'
'Did you notice how shy and nervous he is?'
Arkady shook his head as though he himself were not shy and nervous.
'It's something astonishing,' pursued Bazarov, 'these old idealists, they develop their nervous systems till they break down ... so balance is lost. But good-night. In my room there's an English washstand, but the door won't fasten. Anyway that ought to be encouraged—an English washstand stands for progress!'
Bazarov went away, and a sense of great happiness came over Arkady. Sweet it is to fall asleep in one's own home, in the familiar bed, under the quilt worked by loving hands, perhaps a dear nurse's hands, those kind, tender, untiring hands. Arkady remembered Yegorovna, and sighed and wished her peace in heaven.... For himself he made no prayer.
Both he and Bazarov were soon asleep, but others in the house were awake long after. His son's return had agitated Nikolai Petrovitch. He lay down in bed, but did not put out the candles, and his head propped on his hand, he fell into long reveries. His brother was sitting long after midnight in his study, in a wide armchair

before the fireplace, on which there smouldered some faintly glowing embers. Pavel Petrovitch was not undressed, only some red Chinese slippers had replaced the kid shoes on his feet. He held in his hand the last number of *Galignani*, but he was not reading; he gazed fixedly into the grate, where a bluish flame flickered, dying down, then flaring up again.... God knows where his thoughts were rambling, but they were not rambling in the past only; the expression of his face was concentrated and surly, which is not the way when a man is absorbed solely in recollections. In a small back room there sat, on a large chest, a young woman in a blue dressing jacket with a white kerchief thrown over her dark hair, Fenitchka. She was half listening, half dozing, and often looked across towards the open door through which a child's cradle was visible, and the regular breathing of a sleeping baby could be heard.

CHAPTER V

The next morning Bazarov woke up earlier than any one and went out of the house. 'Oh, my!' he thought, looking about him, 'the little place isn't much to boast of!' When Nikolai Petrovitch had divided the land with his peasants, he had had to build his new manor-house on four acres of perfectly flat and barren land. He had built a house, offices, and farm buildings, laid out a garden, dug a pond, and sunk two wells; but the young trees had not done well, very little water had collected in the pond, and that in the wells tasted brackish. Only one arbour of lilac and acacia had grown fairly well; they sometimes had tea and dinner in it. In a few minutes Bazarov had traversed all the little paths of the garden; he went into the cattle-yard and the stable, routed out two farm-boys, with whom he made friends at once, and set off with them to a small swamp about a mile from the house to look for frogs.
'What do you want frogs for, sir?' one of the boys asked him.
'I'll tell you what for,' answered Bazarov, who possessed the special faculty of inspiring confidence in people of a lower class, though he never tried to win them, and behaved very casually with them; 'I shall cut the frog open, and see what's going on in his inside, and then, as you and I are much the same as frogs, only that we walk on legs, I shall know what's going on inside us too.'
'And what do you want to know that for?'
'So as not to make a mistake, if you're taken ill, and I have to cure you.'
'Are you a doctor then?'
'Yes.'
'Vaska, do you hear, the gentleman says you and I are the same as frogs, that's funny!'
'I'm afraid of frogs,' observed Vaska, a boy of seven, with a head as white as flax, and bare feet, dressed in a grey smock with a stand-up collar.
'What is there to be afraid of? Do they bite?'
'There, paddle into the water, philosophers,' said Bazarov.
Meanwhile Nikolai Petrovitch too had waked up, and gone in to see Arkady, whom he found dressed. The father and son went out on to the terrace under the shelter of the awning; near the balustrade, on the table, among great bunches of lilacs, the samovar was already boiling. A little girl came up, the same who had been the first to meet them at the steps on their arrival the evening before. In a shrill voice she said—
'Fedosya Nikolaevna is not quite well, she cannot come; she gave orders to ask you, will you please to pour out tea yourself, or should she send Dunyasha?'
'I will pour out myself, myself,' interposed Nikolai Petrovitch hurriedly. 'Arkady, how do you take your tea, with cream, or with lemon?'
'With cream,' answered Arkady; and after a brief silence, he uttered interrogatively, 'Daddy?'
Nikolai Petrovitch in confusion looked at his son.
'Well?' he said.

Arkady dropped his eyes.
'Forgive me, dad, if my question seems unsuitable to you,' he began, 'but you yourself, by your openness yesterday, encourage me to be open ... you will not be angry ...?'
'Go on.'
'You give me confidence to ask you.... Isn't the reason, Fen ... isn't the reason she will not come here to pour out tea, because I'm here?'
Nikolai Petrovitch turned slightly away.
'Perhaps,' he said, at last, 'she supposes ... she is ashamed.'
Arkady turned a rapid glance on his father.
'She has no need to be ashamed. In the first place, you are aware of my views' (it was very sweet to Arkady to utter that word); 'and secondly, could I be willing to hamper your life, your habits in the least thing? Besides, I am sure you could not make a bad choice; if you have allowed her to live under the same roof with you, she must be worthy of it; in any case, a son cannot judge his father,—least of all, I, and least of all such a father who, like you, has never hampered my liberty in anything.'
Arkady's voice had been shaky at the beginning; he felt himself magnanimous, though at the same time he realised he was delivering something of the nature of a lecture to his father; but the sound of one's own voice has a powerful effect on any man, and Arkady brought out his last words resolutely, even with emphasis.
'Thanks, Arkasha,' said Nikolai Petrovitch thickly, and his fingers again strayed over his eyebrows and forehead. 'Your suppositions are just in fact. Of course, if this girl had not deserved.... It is not a frivolous caprice. It's not easy for me to talk to you about this; but you will understand that it is difficult for her to come here, in your presence, especially the first day of your return.'
'In that case I will go to her,' cried Arkady, with a fresh rush of magnanimous feeling, and he jumped up from his seat. 'I will explain to her that she has no need to be ashamed before me.'
Nikolai Petrovitch too got up.
'Arkady,' he began, 'be so good ... how can ... there ... I have not told you yet ...'
But Arkady did not listen to him, and ran off the terrace. Nikolai Petrovitch looked after him, and sank into his chair overcome by confusion. His heart began to throb. Did he at that moment realise the inevitable strangeness of the future relations between him and his son? Was he conscious that Arkady would perhaps have shown him more respect if he had never touched on this subject at all? Did he reproach himself for weakness?—it is hard to say; all these feelings were within him, but in the state of sensations—and vague sensations—while the flush did not leave his face, and his heart throbbed.
There was the sound of hurrying footsteps, and Arkady came on to the terrace. 'We have made friends, dad!' he cried, with an expression of a kind of affectionate and good-natured triumph on his face. 'Fedosya Nikolaevna is not quite well to-day really, and she will come a little later. But why didn't you tell me I had a brother? I should have kissed him last night, as I have kissed him just now.'
Nikolai Petrovitch tried to articulate something, tried to get up and open his arms. Arkady flung himself on his neck.
'What's this? embracing again?' sounded the voice of Pavel Petrovitch behind them.
Father and son were equally rejoiced at his appearance at that instant; there are positions, genuinely affecting, from which one longs to escape as soon as possible.
'Why should you be surprised at that?' said Nikolai Petrovitch gaily. 'Think what ages I have been waiting for Arkasha. I've not had time to get a good look at him since yesterday.'
'I'm not at all surprised,' observed Pavel Petrovitch; 'I feel not indisposed to be embracing him myself.'
Arkady went up to his uncle, and again felt his cheeks caressed by his perfumed moustache. Pavel Petrovitch sat down to the table. He wore an elegant morning suit in the English style, and a gay little fez on his head. This fez and the carelessly tied little cravat carried a suggestion of the freedom of country life, but the stiff collars of his shirt—not white, it is true, but striped, as is correct in morning dress—stood up as inexorably as ever against his well-shaved chin.
'Where's your new friend?' he asked Arkady.
'He's not in the house; he usually gets up early and goes off somewhere. The great thing is, we mustn't pay any attention to him; he doesn't like ceremony.'
'Yes, that's obvious.' Pavel Petrovitch began deliberately spreading butter on his bread. 'Is he going to stay long with us?'
'Perhaps. He came here on the way to his father's.'
'And where does his father live?'

'In our province, sixty-four miles from here. He has a small property there. He was formerly an army doctor.'
'Tut, tut, tut! To be sure, I kept asking myself, "Where have I heard that name, Bazarov?" Nikolai, do you remember, in our father's division there was a surgeon Bazarov?'
'I believe there was.'
'Yes, yes, to be sure. So that surgeon was his father. Hm!' Pavel Petrovitch pulled his moustaches. 'Well, and what is Mr. Bazarov himself?' he asked, deliberately.
'What is Bazarov?' Arkady smiled. 'Would you like me, uncle, to tell you what he really is?'
'If you will be so good, nephew.'
'He's a nihilist.'
'Eh?' inquired Nikolai Petrovitch, while Pavel Petrovitch lilted a knife in the air with a small piece of butter on its tip, and remained motionless.
'He's a nihilist,' repeated Arkady.
'A nihilist,' said Nikolai Petrovitch. 'That's from the Latin, *nihil, nothing*, as far as I can judge; the word must mean a man who ... who accepts nothing?'
'Say, "who respects nothing,"' put in Pavel Petrovitch, and he set to work on the butter again.
'Who regards everything from the critical point of view,' observed Arkady.
'Isn't that just the same thing?' inquired Pavel Petrovitch.
'No, it's not the same thing. A nihilist is a man who does not bow down before any authority, who does not take any principle on faith, whatever reverence that principle may be enshrined in.'
'Well, and is that good?' interrupted Pavel Petrovitch.
'That depends, uncle. Some people it will do good to, but some people will suffer for it.'
'Indeed. Well, I see it's not in our line. We are old-fashioned people; we imagine that without principles, taken as you say on faith, there's no taking a step, no breathing. *Vous avez changé tout cela*. God give you good health and the rank of a general, while we will be content to look on and admire, worthy ... what was it?'
'Nihilists,' Arkady said, speaking very distinctly.
'Yes. There used to be Hegelists, and now there are nihilists. We shall see how you will exist in void, in vacuum; and now ring, please, brother Nikolai Petrovitch; it's time I had my cocoa.'
Nikolai Petrovitch rang the bell and called, 'Dunyasha!' But instead of Dunyasha, Fenitchka herself came on to the terrace. She was a young woman about three-and-twenty, with a white soft skin, dark hair and eyes, red, childishly-pouting lips, and little delicate hands. She wore a neat print dress; a new blue kerchief lay lightly on her plump shoulders. She carried a large cup of cocoa, and setting it down before Pavel Petrovitch, she was overwhelmed with confusion: the hot blood rushed in a wave of crimson over the delicate skin of her pretty face. She dropped her eyes, and stood at the table, leaning a little on the very tips of her fingers. It seemed as though she were ashamed of having come in, and at the same time felt that she had a right to come.
Pavel Petrovitch knitted his brows severely, while Nikolai Petrovitch looked embarrassed.
'Good morning, Fenitchka,' he muttered through his teeth.
'Good morning,' she replied in a voice not loud but resonant, and with a sidelong glance at Arkady, who gave her a friendly smile, she went gently away. She walked with a slightly rolling gait, but even that suited her.
For some minutes silence reigned on the terrace. Pavel Petrovitch sipped his cocoa; suddenly he raised his head. 'Here is Sir Nihilist coming towards us,' he said in an undertone.
Bazarov was in fact approaching through the garden, stepping over the flower-beds. His linen coat and trousers were besmeared with mud; clinging marsh weed was twined round the crown of his old round hat; in his right hand he held a small bag; in the bag something alive was moving. He quickly drew near the terrace, and said with a nod, 'Good morning, gentlemen; sorry I was late for tea; I'll be back directly; I must just put these captives away.'
'What have you there—leeches?' asked Pavel Petrovitch.
'No, frogs.'
'Do you eat them—or keep them?'
'For experiment,' said Bazarov indifferently, and he went off into the house.
'So he's going to cut them up,' observed Pavel Petrovitch. 'He has no faith in principles, but he has faith in frogs.'
Arkady looked compassionately at his uncle; Nikolai Petrovitch shrugged his shoulders stealthily. Pavel Petrovitch himself felt that his epigram was unsuccessful, and began to talk about husbandry and the new

bailiff, who had come to him the evening before to complain that a labourer, Foma, 'was deboshed,' and quite unmanageable. 'He's such an Æsop,' he said among other things; 'in all places he has protested himself a worthless fellow; he's not a man to keep his place; he'll walk off in a huff like a fool.'

CHAPTER VI

Bazarov came back, sat down to the table, and began hastily drinking tea. The two brothers looked at him in silence, while Arkady stealthily watched first his father and then his uncle.

'Did you walk far from here?' Nikolai Petrovitch asked at last.

'Where you've a little swamp near the aspen wood. I started some half-dozen snipe; you might slaughter them; Arkady.'

'Aren't you a sportsman then?'

'No.'

'Is your special study physics?' Pavel Petrovitch in his turn inquired.

'Physics, yes; and natural science in general.'

'They say the Teutons of late have had great success in that line.'

'Yes; the Germans are our teachers in it,' Bazarov answered carelessly.

The word Teutons instead of Germans, Pavel Petrovitch had used with ironical intention; none noticed it however.

'Have you such a high opinion of the Germans?' said Pavel Petrovitch, with exaggerated courtesy. He was beginning to feel a secret irritation. His aristocratic nature was revolted by Bazarov's absolute nonchalance. This surgeon's son was not only not overawed, he even gave abrupt and indifferent answers, and in the tone of his voice there was something churlish, almost insolent.

'The scientific men there are a clever lot.'

'Ah, ah. To be sure, of Russian scientific men you have not such a flattering opinion, I dare say?'

'That is very likely.'

'That's very praiseworthy self-abnegation,' Pavel Petrovitch declared, drawing himself up, and throwing his head back. 'But how is this? Arkady Nikolaitch was telling us just now that you accept no authorities? Don't you believe in *them?'*

'And how am I accepting them? And what am I to believe in? They tell me the truth, I agree, that's all.'

'And do all Germans tell the truth?' said Pavel Petrovitch, and his face assumed an expression as unsympathetic, as remote, as if he had withdrawn to some cloudy height.

'Not all,' replied Bazarov, with a short yawn. He obviously did not care to continue the discussion.

Pavel Petrovitch glanced at Arkady, as though he would say to him, 'Your friend's polite, I must say.' 'For my own part,' he began again, not without some effort, 'I am so unregenerate as not to like Germans. Russian Germans I am not speaking of now; we all know what sort of creatures they are. But even German Germans are not to my liking. In former days there were some here and there; they had—well, Schiller, to be sure, Goethe ... my brother—he takes a particularly favourable view of them.... But now they have all turned chemists and materialists ...'

'A good chemist is twenty times as useful as any poet,' broke in Bazarov.

'Oh, indeed,' commented Pavel Petrovitch, and, as though falling asleep, he faintly raised his eyebrows. 'You don't acknowledge art then, I suppose?'

'The art of making money or of advertising pills!' cried Bazarov, with a contemptuous laugh.

'Ah, ah. You are pleased to jest, I see. You reject all that, no doubt? Granted. Then you believe in science only?'

'I have already explained to you that I don't believe in anything; and what is science—science in the abstract? There are sciences, as there are trades and crafts; but abstract science doesn't exist at all.'

'Very good. Well, and in regard to the other traditions accepted in human conduct, do you maintain the same negative attitude?'

'What's this, an examination?' asked Bazarov.

Pavel Petrovitch turned slightly pale.... Nikolai Petrovitch thought it his duty to interpose in the conversation.

'We will converse on this subject with you more in detail some day, dear Yevgeny Vassilyitch; we will hear your views, and express our own. For my part, I am heartily glad you are studying the natural sciences. I have heard that Liebig has made some wonderful discoveries in the amelioration of soils. You can be of assistance to me in my agricultural labours; you can give me some useful advice.'

'I am at your service, Nikolai Petrovitch; but Liebig's miles over our heads! One has first to learn the a b c, and then begin to read, and we haven't set eyes on the alphabet yet.'

'You are certainly a nihilist, I see that,' thought Nikolai Petrovitch. 'Still, you will allow me to apply to you on occasion,' he added aloud. 'And now I fancy, brother, it's time for us to be going to have a talk with the bailiff.'

Pavel Petrovitch got up from his seat.

'Yes,' he said, without looking at any one; 'it's a misfortune to live five years in the country like this, far from mighty intellects! You turn into a fool directly. You may try not to forget what you've been taught, but—in a snap!—they'll prove all that's rubbish, and tell you that sensible men have nothing more to do with such foolishness, and that you, if you please, are an antiquated old fogey. What's to be done? Young people, of course, are cleverer than we are!'

Pavel Petrovitch turned slowly on his heels, and slowly walked away; Nikolai Petrovitch went after him.

'Is he always like that?' Bazarov coolly inquired of Arkady directly the door had closed behind the two brothers.

'I must say, Yevgeny, you weren't nice to him,' remarked Arkady. 'You have hurt his feelings.'

'Well, am I going to consider them, these provincial aristocrats! Why, it's all vanity, dandy habits, fatuity. He should have continued his career in Petersburg, if that's his bent. But there, enough of him! I've found a rather rare species of a water-beetle, *Dytiscus marginatus;*do you know it? I will show you.'

'I promised to tell you his story,' began Arkady.

'The story of the beetle?'

'Come, don't, Yevgeny. The story of my uncle. You will see he's not the sort of man you fancy. He deserves pity rather than ridicule.'

'I don't dispute it; but why are you worrying over him?'

'One ought to be just, Yevgeny.'

'How does that follow?'

'No; listen ...'

And Arkady told him his uncle's story. The reader will find it in the following chapter.

CHAPTER VII

Pavel Petrovitch Kirsanov was educated first at home, like his younger brother, and afterwards in the Corps of Pages. From childhood he was distinguished by remarkable beauty; moreover he was self-confident, somewhat ironical, and had a rather biting humour; he could not fail to please. He began to be seen everywhere, directly he had received his commission as an officer. He was much admired in society, and he indulged every whim, even every caprice and every folly, and gave himself airs, but that too was attractive in him. Women went out of their senses over him; men called him a coxcomb, and were secretly jealous of him.

He lived, as has been related already, in the same apartments as his brother, whom he loved sincerely, though he was not at all like him. Nikolai Petrovitch was a little lame, he had small, pleasing features of a rather melancholy cast, small, black eyes, and thin, soft hair; he liked being lazy, but he also liked reading, and was timid in society.

Pavel Petrovitch did not spend a single evening at home, prided himself on his ease and audacity (he was just bringing gymnastics into fashion among young men in society), and had read in all some five or six French books. At twenty-eight he was already a captain; a brilliant career awaited him. Suddenly everything was changed.

At that time, there was sometimes seen in Petersburg society a woman who has even yet not been forgotten. Princess R——. She had a well-educated, well-bred, but rather stupid husband, and no children. She used suddenly to go abroad, and suddenly return to Russia, and led an eccentric life in general. She had the reputation of being a frivolous coquette, abandoned herself eagerly to every sort of pleasure, danced to exhaustion, laughed and jested with young men, whom she received in the dim light of her drawing-room before dinner; while at night she wept and prayed, found no peace in anything, and often paced her room till morning, wringing her hands in anguish, or sat, pale and chill, over a psalter. Day came, and she was transformed again into a grand lady; again she went out, laughed, chattered, and simply flung herself headlong into anything which could afford her the slightest distraction. She was marvellously well-proportioned, her hair coloured like gold and heavy as gold hung below her knees, but no one would have called her a beauty; in her whole face the only good point was her eyes, and even her eyes were not good—they were grey, and not large—but their glance was swift and deep, unconcerned to the point of audacity, and thoughtful to the point of melancholy—an enigmatic glance. There was a light of something extraordinary in them, even while her tongue was lisping the emptiest of inanities. She dressed with elaborate care. Pavel Petrovitch met her at a ball, danced a mazurka with her, in the course of which she did not utter a single rational word, and fell passionately in love with her. Being accustomed to make conquests, in this instance, too, he soon attained his object, but his easy success did not damp his ardour. On the contrary, he was in still more torturing, still closer bondage to this woman, in whom, even at the very moment when she surrendered herself utterly, there seemed always something still mysterious and unattainable, to which none could penetrate. What was hidden in that soul—God knows! It seemed as though she were in the power of mysterious forces, incomprehensible even to herself; they seemed to play on her at will; her intellect was not powerful enough to master their caprices. Her whole behaviour presented a series of inconsistencies; the only letters which could have awakened her husband's just suspicions, she wrote to a man who was almost a stranger to her, whilst her love had always an element of melancholy; with a man she had chosen as a lover, she ceased to laugh and to jest, she listened to him, and gazed at him with a look of bewilderment. Sometimes, for the most part suddenly, this bewilderment passed into chill horror; her face took a wild, death-like expression; she locked herself up in her bedroom, and her maid, putting her ear to the keyhole, could hear her smothered sobs. More than once, as he went home after a tender interview, Kirsanov felt within him that heartrending, bitter vexation which follows on a total failure.

'What more do I want?' he asked himself, while his heart was heavy. He once gave her a ring with a sphinx engraved on the stone.

'What's that?' she asked; 'a sphinx?'

'Yes,' he answered, 'and that sphinx is you.'

'I?' she queried, and slowly raising her enigmatical glance upon him. 'Do you know that's awfully flattering?' she added with a meaningless smile, while her eyes still kept the same strange look.

Pavel Petrovitch suffered even while Princess R—— loved him; but when she grew cold to him, and that happened rather quickly, he almost went out of his mind. He was on the rack, and he was jealous; he gave her no peace, followed her about everywhere; she grew sick of his pursuit of her, and she went abroad. He resigned his commission in spite of the entreaties of his friends and the exhortations of his superiors, and followed the princess; four years he spent in foreign countries, at one time pursuing her, at another time intentionally losing sight of her. He was ashamed of himself, he was disgusted with his own lack of spirit ... but nothing availed. Her image, that incomprehensible, almost meaningless, but bewitching image, was deeply rooted in his heart. At Baden he once more regained his old footing with her; it seemed as though she had never loved him so passionately ... but in a month it was all at an end: the flame flickered up for the last time and went out for ever. Foreseeing inevitable separation, he wanted at least to remain her friend, as though friendship with such a woman was possible.... She secretly left Baden, and from that time steadily avoided Kirsanov. He returned to Russia, and tried to live his former life again; but he could not get back into the old groove. He wandered from place to place like a man possessed; he still went into society; he still retained the habits of a man of the world; he could boast of two or three fresh conquests; but he no longer expected anything much of himself or of others, and he undertook nothing. He grew old and grey; spending all his evenings at the club, jaundiced and bored, and arguing in bachelor society became a necessity for him—a bad sign, as we all know. Marriage, of course, he did not even think of. Ten years passed in this way; they passed by colourless and fruitless—and quickly, fearfully quickly. Nowhere does time fly past as in Russia; in prison they say it flies even faster. One day at dinner at the club, Pavel Petrovitch heard of the death of the Princess R——. She had died at Paris in a state bordering on insanity.

He got up from the table, and a long time he paced about the rooms of the club, or stood stockstill near the card-players, but he did not go home earlier than usual. Some time later he received a packet addressed to him; in it was the ring he had given the princess. She had drawn lines in the shape of a cross over the sphinx and sent him word that the solution of the enigma—was the cross.

This happened at the beginning of the year 1848, at the very time when Nikolai Petrovitch came to Petersburg, after the loss of his wife. Pavel Petrovitch had scarcely seen his brother since the latter had settled in the country; the marriage of Nikolai Petrovitch had coincided with the very first days of Pavel Petrovitch's acquaintance with the princess. When he came back from abroad, he had gone to him with the intention of staying a couple of months with him, in sympathetic enjoyment of his happiness, but he had only succeeded in standing a week of it. The difference in the positions of the two brothers was too great. In 1848, this difference had grown less; Nikolai Petrovitch had lost his wife, Pavel Petrovitch had lost his memories; after the death of the princess he tried not to think of her. But to Nikolai, there remained the sense of a well-spent life, his son was growing up under his eyes; Pavel, on the contrary, a solitary bachelor, was entering upon that indefinite twilight period of regrets that are akin to hopes, and hopes that are akin to regrets, when youth is over, while old age has not yet come.

This time was harder for Pavel Petrovitch than for another man; in losing his past, he lost everything.

'I will not invite you to Maryino now,' Nikolai Petrovitch said to him one day, (he had called his property by that name in honour of his wife); 'you were dull there in my dear wife's time, and now I think you would be bored to death.'

'I was stupid and fidgety then,' answered Pavel Petrovitch; 'since then I have grown quieter, if not wiser. On the contrary, now, if you will let me, I am ready to settle with you for good.'

For all answer Nikolai Petrovitch embraced him; but a year and a half passed after this conversation, before Pavel Petrovitch made up his mind to carry out his intention. When he was once settled in the country, however, he did not leave it, even during the three winters which Nikolai Petrovitch spent in Petersburg with his son. He began to read, chiefly English; he arranged his whole life, roughly speaking, in the English style, rarely saw the neighbours, and only went out to the election of marshals, where he was generally silent, only occasionally annoying and alarming land-owners of the old school by his liberal sallies, and not associating with the representatives of the younger generation. Both the latter and the former considered him 'stuck up'; and both parties respected him for his fine aristocratic manners; for his reputation for successes in love; for the fact that he was very well dressed and always stayed in the best room in the best hotel; for the fact that he generally dined well, and had once even dined with Wellington at Louis Philippe's table; for the fact that he always took everywhere with him a real silver dressing-case and a portable bath; for the fact that he always smelt of some exceptionally 'good form' scent; for the fact that he played whist in masterly fashion, and always lost; and lastly, they respected him also for his incorruptible honesty. Ladies considered him enchantingly romantic, but he did not cultivate ladies' acquaintance....

'So you see, Yevgeny,' observed Arkady, as he finished his story, 'how unjustly you judge of my uncle! To say nothing of his having more than once helped my father out of difficulties, given him all his money—the property, perhaps you don't know, wasn't divided—he's glad to help any one, among other things he always sticks up for the peasants; it's true, when he talks to them he frowns and sniffs eau de cologne.' ...

'His nerves, no doubt,' put in Bazarov.

'Perhaps; but his heart is very good. And he's far from being stupid. What useful advice he has given me especially ... especially in regard to relations with women.'

'Aha! a scalded dog fears cold water, we know that!'

'In short,' continued Arkady, 'he's profoundly unhappy, believe me; it's a sin to despise him.'

'And who does despise him?' retorted Bazarov. 'Still, I must say that a fellow who stakes his whole life on one card—a woman's love—and when that card fails, turns sour, and lets himself go till he's fit for nothing, is not a man, but a male. You say he's unhappy; you ought to know best; to be sure, he's not got rid of all his

fads. I'm convinced that he solemnly imagines himself a superior creature because he reads that wretched *Galignani*, and once a month saves a peasant from a flogging.'
'But remember his education, the age in which he grew up,' observed Arkady.
'Education?' broke in Bazarov. 'Every man must educate himself, just as I've done, for instance.... And as for the age, why should I depend on it? Let it rather depend on me. No, my dear fellow, that's all shallowness, want of backbone! And what stuff it all is, about these mysterious relations between a man and woman? We physiologists know what these relations are. You study the anatomy of the eye; where does the enigmatical glance you talk about come in there? That's all romantic, nonsensical, æsthetic rot. We had much better go and look at the beetle.'
And the two friends went off to Bazarov's room, which was already pervaded by a sort of medico-surgical odour, mingled with the smell of cheap tobacco.

CHAPTER VIII

Pavel Petrovitch did not long remain present at his brother's interview with his bailiff, a tall, thin man with a sweet consumptive voice and knavish eyes, who to all Nikolai Petrovitch's remarks answered, 'Certainly, sir,' and tried to make the peasants out to be thieves and drunkards. The estate had only recently been put on to the new reformed system, and the new mechanism worked, creaking like an ungreased wheel, warping and cracking like homemade furniture of unseasoned wood. Nikolai Petrovitch did not lose heart, but often he sighed, and was gloomy; he felt that the thing could not go on without money, and his money was almost all spent. Arkady had spoken the truth; Pavel Petrovitch had more than once helped his brother; more than once, seeing him struggling and cudgelling his brains, at a loss which way to turn, Pavel Petrovitch moved deliberately to the window, and with his hands thrust into his pockets, muttered between his teeth, *'mais je puis vous de l'argent,'* and gave him money; but to-day he had none himself, and he preferred to go away. The petty details of agricultural management worried him; besides, it constantly struck him that Nikolai Petrovitch, for all his zeal and industry, did not set about things in the right way, though he would not have been able to point out precisely where Nikolai Petrovitch's mistake lay. 'My brother's not practical enough,' he reasoned to himself; 'they impose upon him.' Nikolai Petrovitch, on the other hand, had the highest opinion of Pavel Petrovitch's practical ability, and always asked his advice. 'I'm a soft, weak fellow, I've spent my life in the wilds,' he used to say; 'while you haven't seen so much of the world for nothing, you see through people; you have an eagle eye.' In answer to which Pavel Petrovitch only turned away, but did not contradict his brother.
Leaving Nikolai Petrovitch in his study, he walked along the corridor, which separated the front part of the house from the back; when he had reached a low door, he stopped in hesitation, then pulling his moustaches, he knocked at it.
'Who's there? Come in,' sounded Fenitchka's voice.
'It's I,' said Pavel Petrovitch, and he opened the door.
Fenitchka jumped up from the chair on which she was sitting with her baby, and giving him into the arms of a girl, who at once carried him out of the room, she put straight her kerchief hastily.
'Pardon me, if I disturb you,' began Pavel Petrovitch, not looking at her; 'I only wanted to ask you ... they are sending into the town to-day, I think ... please let them buy me some green tea.'
'Certainly,' answered Fenitchka; 'how much do you desire them to buy?'
'Oh, half a pound will be enough, I imagine. You have made a change here, I see,' he added, with a rapid glance round him, which glided over Fenitchka's face too. 'The curtains here,' he explained, seeing she did not understand him.

'Oh, yes, the curtains; Nikolai Petrovitch was so good as to make me a present of them; but they have been put up a long while now.'

'Yes, and it's a long while since I have been to see you. Now it is very nice here.'

'Thanks to Nikolai Petrovitch's kindness,' murmured Fenitchka.

'You are more comfortable here than in the little lodge you used to have?' inquired Pavel Petrovitch urbanely, but without the slightest smile.

'Certainly, it's more comfortable.'

'Who has been put in your place now?'

'The laundry-maids are there now.'

'Ah!'

Pavel Petrovitch was silent. 'Now he is going,' thought Fenitchka; but he did not go, and she stood before him motionless.

'What did you send your little one away for?' said Pavel Petrovitch at last. 'I love children; let me see him.'

Fenitchka blushed all over with confusion and delight. She was afraid of Pavel Petrovitch; he had scarcely ever spoken to her.

'Dunyasha,' she called; 'will you bring Mitya, please.' (Fenitchka did not treat any one in the house familiarly.) 'But wait a minute, he must have a frock on,' Fenitchka was going towards the door.

'That doesn't matter,' remarked Pavel Petrovitch.

'I will be back directly,' answered Fenitchka, and she went out quickly.

Pavel Petrovitch was left alone, and he looked round this time with special attention. The small low-pitched room in which he found himself was very clean and snug. It smelt of the freshly painted floor and of camomile. Along the walls stood chairs with lyre-shaped backs, bought by the late general on his campaign in Poland; in one corner was a little bedstead under a muslin canopy beside an iron-clamped chest with a convex lid. In the opposite corner a little lamp was burning before a big dark picture of St. Nikolai the wonder-worker; a tiny porcelain egg hung by a red ribbon from the protruding gold halo down to the saint's breast; by the windows greenish glass jars of last year's jam carefully tied down could be seen; on their paper covers Fenitchka herself had written in big letters 'Gooseberry'; Nikolai Petrovitch was particularly fond of that preserve. On a long cord from the ceiling a cage hung with a short-tailed siskin in it; he was constantly chirping and hopping about, the cage was constantly shaking and swinging, while hempseeds fell with a light tap on to the floor. On the wall just above a small chest of drawers hung some rather bad photographs of Nikolai Petrovitch in various attitudes, taken by an itinerant photographer; there too hung a photograph of Fenitchka herself, which was an absolute failure; it was an eyeless face wearing a forced smile, in a dingy frame, nothing more could be made out; while above Fenitchka, General Yermolov, in a Circassian cloak, scowled menacingly upon the Caucasian mountains in the distance, from beneath a little silk shoe for pins which fell right on to his brows.

Five minutes passed; bustling and whispering could be heard in the next room. Pavel Petrovitch took up from the chest of drawers a greasy book, an odd volume of Masalsky's *Musketeer*, and turned over a few pages.... The door opened, and Fenitchka came in with Mitya in her arms. She had put on him a little red smock with embroidery on the collar, had combed his hair and washed his face; he was breathing heavily, his whole body working, and his little hands waving in the air, as is the way with all healthy babies; but his smart smock obviously impressed him, an expression of delight was reflected in every part of his little fat person. Fenitchka had put her own hair too in order, and had arranged her kerchief; but she might well have remained as she was. And really is there anything in the world more captivating than a beautiful young mother with a healthy baby in her arms?

'What a chubby fellow!' said Pavel Petrovitch graciously, and he tickled Mitya's little double chin with the tapering nail of his forefinger. The baby stared at the siskin, and chuckled.

'That's uncle,' said Fenitchka, bending her face down to him and slightly rocking him, while Dunyasha quietly set in the window a smouldering perfumed stick, putting a halfpenny under it.

'How many months old is he?' asked Pavel Petrovitch.

'Six months; it will soon be seven, on the eleventh.'

'Isn't it eight, Fedosya Nikolaevna?' put in Dunyasha, with some timidity.

'No, seven; what an idea!' The baby chuckled again, stared at the chest, and suddenly caught hold of his mother's nose and mouth with all his five little fingers. 'Saucy mite,' said Fenitchka, not drawing her face away.

'He's like my brother,' observed Pavel Petrovitch.

'Who else should he be like?' thought Fenitchka.

'Yes,' continued Pavel Petrovitch, as though speaking to himself; 'there's an unmistakable likeness.' He looked attentively, almost mournfully, at Fenitchka.

'That's uncle,' she repeated, in a whisper this time.

'Ah! Pavel! so you're here!' was heard suddenly the voice of Nikolai Petrovitch.

Pavel Petrovitch turned hurriedly round, frowning; but his brother looked at him with such delight, such gratitude, that he could not help responding to his smile.

'You've a splendid little cherub,' he said, and looking at his watch, 'I came in here to speak about some tea.'

And, assuming an expression of indifference, Pavel Petrovitch at once went out of the room.

'Did he come of himself?' Nikolai Petrovitch asked Fenitchka.

'Yes; he knocked and came in.'

'Well, and has Arkasha been in to see you again?'

'No. Hadn't I better move into the lodge, Nikolai Petrovitch?'

'Why so?'

'I wonder whether it wouldn't be best just for the first.'

'N ... no,' Nikolai Petrovitch brought out hesitatingly, rubbing his forehead. 'We ought to have done it before.... How are you, fatty?' he said, suddenly brightening, and going up to the baby, he kissed him on the cheek; then he bent a little and pressed his lips to Fenitchka's hand, which lay white as milk upon Mitya's little red smock.

'Nikolai Petrovitch! what are you doing?' she whispered, dropping her eyes, then slowly raising them. Very charming was the expression of her eyes when she peeped, as it were, from under her lids, and smiled tenderly and a little foolishly.

Nikolai Petrovitch had made Fenitchka's acquaintance in the following manner. He had once happened three years before to stay a night at an inn in a remote district town. He was agreeably struck by the cleanness of the room assigned to him, the freshness of the bed-linen. Surely the woman of the house must be a German? was the idea that occurred to him; but she proved to be a Russian, a woman of about fifty, neatly dressed, of a good-looking, sensible countenance and discreet speech. He entered into conversation with her at tea; he liked her very much. Nikolai Petrovitch had at that time only just moved into his new home, and not wishing to keep serfs in the house, he was on the look-out for wage-servants; the woman of the inn on her side complained of the small number of visitors to the town, and the hard times; he proposed to her to come into his house in the capacity of housekeeper; she consented. Her husband had long been dead, leaving her an only daughter, Fenitchka. Within a fortnight Arina Savishna (that was the new housekeeper's name) arrived with her daughter at Maryino and installed herself in the little lodge. Nikolai Petrovitch's choice proved a successful one. Arina brought order into the household. As for Fenitchka, who was at that time seventeen, no one spoke of her, and scarcely any one saw her; she lived quietly and sedately, and only on Sundays Nikolai Petrovitch noticed in the church somewhere in a side place the delicate profile of her white face. More than a year passed thus.

One morning, Arina came into his study, and bowing low as usual, she asked him if he could do anything for her daughter, who had got a spark from the stove in her eye. Nikolai Petrovitch, like all stay-at-home people, had studied doctoring and even compiled a homoeopathic guide. He at once told Arina to bring the patient to him. Fenitchka was much frightened when she heard the master had sent for her; however, she followed her mother. Nikolai Petrovitch led her to the window and took her head in his two hands. After thoroughly examining her red and swollen eye, he prescribed a fomentation, which he made up himself at once, and tearing his handkerchief in pieces, he showed her how it ought to be applied. Fenitchka listened to all he had to say, and then was going. 'Kiss the master's hand, silly girl,' said Arina. Nikolai Petrovitch did not give her his hand, and in confusion himself kissed her bent head on the parting of her hair. Fenitchka's eye was soon well again, but the impression she had made on Nikolai Petrovitch did not pass away so quickly. He was for ever haunted by that pure, delicate, timidly raised face; he felt on the palms of his hands that soft hair, and saw those innocent, slightly parted lips, through which pearly teeth gleamed with moist brilliance in the sunshine. He began to watch her with great attention in church, and tried to get into conversation with her. At first she was shy of him, and one day meeting him at the approach of evening in a narrow footpath through a field of rye, she ran into the tall thick rye, overgrown with cornflowers and wormwood, so as not to meet him face to face. He caught sight of her little head through a golden network of ears of rye, from which she was peeping out like a little animal, and called affectionately to her—

'Good-evening, Fenitchka! I don't bite.'

'Good-evening,' she whispered, not coming out of her ambush.
By degrees she began to be more at home with him, but was still shy in his presence, when suddenly her mother, Arina, died of cholera. What was to become of Fenitchka? She inherited from her mother a love for order, regularity, and respectability; but she was so young, so alone. Nikolai Petrovitch was himself so good and considerate.... It's needless to relate the rest....
'So my brother came in to see you?' Nikolai Petrovitch questioned her. 'He knocked and came in?'
'Yes.'
'Well, that's a good thing. Let me give Mitya a swing.'
And Nikolai Petrovitch began tossing him almost up to the ceiling, to the huge delight of the baby, and to the considerable uneasiness of the mother, who every time he flew up stretched her arms up towards his little bare legs.
Pavel Petrovitch went back to his artistic study, with its walls covered with handsome bluish-grey hangings, with weapons hanging upon a variegated Persian rug nailed to the wall; with walnut furniture, upholstered in dark green velveteen, with a *renaissance*bookcase of old black oak, with bronze statuettes on the magnificent writing-table, with an open hearth. He threw himself on the sofa, clasped his hands behind his head, and remained without moving, looking with a face almost of despair at the ceiling. Whether he wanted to hide from the very walls that which was reflected in his face, or for some other reason, he got up, drew the heavy window curtains, and again threw himself on the sofa.

CHAPTER IX

On the same day Bazarov made acquaintance with Fenitchka. He was walking with Arkady in the garden, and explaining to him why some of the trees, especially the oaks, had not done well.
'You ought to have planted silver poplars here by preference, and spruce firs, and perhaps limes, giving them some loam. The arbour there has done well,' he added, 'because it's acacia and lilac; they're accommodating good fellows, those trees, they don't want much care. But there's some one in here.'
In the arbour was sitting Fenitchka, with Dunyasha and Mitya. Bazarov stood still, while Arkady nodded to Fenitchka like an old friend.
'Who's that?' Bazarov asked him directly they had passed by. 'What a pretty girl!'
'Whom are you speaking of?'
'You know; only one of them was pretty.'
Arkady, not without embarrassment, explained to him briefly who Fenitchka was.
'Aha!' commented Bazarov; 'your father's got good taste, one can see. I like him, your father, ay, ay! He's a jolly fellow. We must make friends though,' he added, and turned back towards the arbour.
'Yevgeny!' Arkady cried after him in dismay; 'mind what you are about, for mercy's sake.'
'Don't worry yourself,' said Bazarov; 'I know how to behave myself—I'm not a booby.'
Going up to Fenitchka, he took off his cap.
'Allow me to introduce myself,' he began, with a polite bow. 'I'm a harmless person, and a friend of Arkady Nikolaevitch's.'
Fenitchka got up from the garden seat and looked at him without speaking.
'What a splendid baby!' continued Bazarov; 'don't be uneasy, my praises have never brought ill-luck yet. Why is it his cheeks are so flushed? Is he cutting his teeth?'
'Yes,' said Fenitchka; 'he has cut four teeth already, and now the gums are swollen again.'
'Show me, and don't be afraid, I'm a doctor.'
Bazarov took the baby up in his arms, and to the great astonishment both of Fenitchka and Dunyasha the child made no resistance, and was not frightened.

'I see, I see.... It's nothing, everything's as it should be; he will have a good set of teeth. If anything goes wrong, tell me. And are you quite well yourself?'
'Quite, thank God.'
'Thank God, indeed—that's the great thing. And you?' he added, turning to Dunyasha.
Dunyasha, a girl very prim in the master's house, and a romp outside the gates, only giggled in answer.
'Well, that's all right. Here's your gallant fellow.'
Fenitchka received the baby in her arms.
'How good he was with you!' she commented in an undertone.
'Children are always good with me.' answered Bazarov; 'I have a way with them.'
'Children know who loves them,' remarked Dunyasha.
'Yes, they certainly do,' Fenitchka said. 'Why, Mitya will not go to some people for anything.'
'Will he come to me?' asked Arkady, who, after standing in the distance for some time, had gone up to the arbour.
He tried to entice Mitya to come to him, but Mitya threw his head back and screamed, to Fenitchka's great confusion.
'Another day, when he's had time to get used to me,' said Arkady indulgently, and the two friends walked away.
'What's her name?' asked Bazarov.
'Fenitchka ... Fedosya,' answered Arkady.
'And her father's name? One must know that too.'
'Nikolaevna.'
'*Bene*. What I like in her is that she's not too embarrassed. Some people, I suppose, would think ill of her for it. What nonsense! What is there to embarrass her? She's a mother—she's all right.'
'She's all right,' observed Arkady,—'but my father.'
'And he's right too,' put in Bazarov.
'Well, no, I don't think so.'
'I suppose an extra heir's not to your liking?'
'I wonder you're not ashamed to attribute such ideas to me!' retorted Arkady hotly; 'I don't consider my father wrong from that point of view; I think he ought to marry her.'
'Hoity-toity!' responded Bazarov tranquilly. 'What magnanimous fellows we are! You still attach significance to marriage; I did not expect that of you.'
The friends walked a few paces in silence.
'I have looked at all your father's establishment,' Bazarov began again. 'The cattle are inferior, the horses are broken down; the buildings aren't up to much, and the workmen look confirmed loafers; while the superintendent is either a fool, or a knave, I haven't quite found out which yet.'
'You are rather hard on everything to-day, Yevgeny Vassilyevitch.'
'And the dear good peasants are taking your father in to a dead certainty. You know the Russian proverb, "The Russian peasant will cheat God Himself."'
'I begin to agree with my uncle,' remarked Arkady; 'you certainly have a poor opinion of Russians.'
'As though that mattered! The only good point in a Russian is his having the lowest possible opinion of himself. What does matter is that two and two make four, and the rest is all foolery.'
'And is nature foolery?' said Arkady, looking pensively at the bright-coloured fields in the distance, in the beautiful soft light of the sun, which was not yet high up in the sky.
'Nature, too, is foolery in the sense you understand it. Nature's not a temple, but a workshop, and man's the workman in it.'
At that instant, the long drawn notes of a violoncello floated out to them from the house. Some one was playing Schubert's *Expectation*with much feeling, though with an untrained hand, and the melody flowed with honey sweetness through the air.
'What's that?' cried Bazarov in amazement.
'It's my father.'
'Your father plays the violoncello?'
'Yes.'
'And how old is your father?'
'Forty-four.'
Bazarov suddenly burst into a roar of laughter.

'What are you laughing at?'
'Upon my word, a man of forty-four, a *paterfamilias* in this out-of-the-way district, playing on the violoncello!'
Bazarov went on laughing; but much as he revered his master, this time Arkady did not even smile.

CHAPTER X

About a fortnight passed by. Life at Maryino went on its accustomed course, while Arkady was lazy and enjoyed himself, and Bazarov worked. Every one in the house had grown used to him, to his careless manners, and his curt and abrupt speeches. Fenitchka, in particular, was so far at home with him that one night she sent to wake him up; Mitya had had convulsions; and he had gone, and, half joking, half-yawning as usual, he stayed two hours with her and relieved the child. On the other hand Pavel Petrovitch had grown to detest Bazarov with all the strength of his soul; he regarded him as stuck-up, impudent, cynical, and vulgar; he suspected that Bazarov had no respect for him, that he had all but a contempt for him—him, Pavel Kirsanov!
Nikolai Petrovitch was rather afraid of the young 'nihilist,' and was doubtful whether his influence over Arkady was for the good; but he was glad to listen to him, and was glad to be present at his scientific and chemical experiments. Bazarov had brought with him a microscope, and busied himself for hours together with it. The servants, too, took to him, though he made fun of them; they felt, all the same, that he was one of themselves, not a master. Dunyasha was always ready to giggle with him, and used to cast significant and stealthy glances at him when she skipped by like a rabbit; Piotr, a man vain and stupid to the last degree, for ever wearing an affected frown on his brow, a man whose whole merit consisted in the fact that he looked civil, could spell out a page of reading, and was diligent in brushing his coat—even he smirked and brightened up directly Bazarov paid him any attention; the boys on the farm simply ran after the 'doctor' like puppies. The old man Prokofitch was the only one who did not like him; he handed him the dishes at table with a surly face, called him a 'butcher' and 'an upstart,' and declared that with his great whiskers he looked like a pig in a stye. Prokofitch in his own way was quite as much of an aristocrat as Pavel Petrovitch.
The best days of the year had come—the first days of June. The weather kept splendidly fine; in the distance, it is true, the cholera was threatening, but the inhabitants of that province had had time to get used to its visits. Bazarov used to get up very early and go out for two or three miles, not for a walk—he couldn't bear walking without an object—but to collect specimens of plants and insects. Sometimes he took Arkady with him.
On the way home an argument usually sprang up, and Arkady was usually vanquished in it, though he said more than his companion.
One day they had lingered rather late; Nikolai Petrovitch went to meet them in the garden, and as he reached the arbour he suddenly heard the quick steps and voices of the two young men. They were walking on the other side of the arbour, and could not see him.
'You don't know my father well enough,' said Arkady.
'Your father's a nice chap,' said Bazarov, 'but he's behind the times; his day is done.'
Nikolai Petrovitch listened intently.... Arkady made no answer.
The man whose day was done remained two minutes motionless, and stole slowly home.
'The day before yesterday I saw him reading Pushkin,' Bazarov was continuing meanwhile. 'Explain to him, please, that that's no earthly use. He's not a boy, you know; it's time to throw up that rubbish. And what an idea to be a romantic at this time of day! Give him something sensible to read.'
'What ought I to give him?' asked Arkady.
'Oh, I think Büchner's *Stoff und Kraft* to begin with.'

'I think so too,' observed Arkady approving, *'Stoff und Kraft* is written in popular language....'

'So it seems,' Nikolai Petrovitch said the same day after dinner to his brother, as he sat in his study, 'you and I are behind the times, our day's over. Well, well. Perhaps Bazarov is right; but one thing I confess, makes me feel sore; I did so hope, precisely now, to get on to such close intimate terms with Arkady, and it turns out I'm left behind, and he has gone forward, and we can't understand one another.'

'How has he gone forward? And in what way is he so superior to us already?' cried Pavel Petrovitch impatiently. 'It's that high and mighty gentleman, that nihilist, who's knocked all that into his head. I hate that doctor fellow; in my opinion, he's simply a quack; I'm convinced, for all his tadpoles, he's not got very far even in medicine.'

'No, brother, you mustn't say that; Bazarov is clever, and knows his subject.'

'And his conceit's something revolting,' Pavel Petrovitch broke in again.

'Yes,' observed Nikolai Petrovitch, 'he is conceited. But there's no doing without that, it seems; only that's what I did not take into account. I thought I was doing everything to keep up with the times; I have started a model farm; I have done well by the peasants, so that I am positively called a "Red Radical" all over the province; I read, I study, I try in every way to keep abreast with the requirements of the day—and they say my day's over. And, brother, I begin to think that it is.'

'Why so?'

'I'll tell you why. This morning I was sitting reading Pushkin.... I remember, it happened to be *The Gipsies* ... all of a sudden Arkady came up to me, and, without speaking, with such a kindly compassion on his face, as gently as if I were a baby, took the book away from me, and laid another before me—a German book ... smiled, and went away, carrying Pushkin off with him.'

'Upon my word! What book did he give you?'

'This one here.'

And Nikolai Petrovitch pulled the famous treatise of Büchner, in the ninth edition, out of his coat-tail pocket.

Pavel Petrovitch turned it over in his hands. 'Hm!' he growled. 'Arkady Nikolaevitch is taking your education in hand. Well, did you try reading it?'

'Yes, I tried it.'

'Well, what did you think of it?'

'Either I'm stupid, or it's all—nonsense. I must be stupid, I suppose.'

'Haven't you forgotten your German?' queried Pavel Petrovitch.

'Oh, I understand the German.'

Pavel Petrovitch again turned the book over in his hands, and glanced from under his brows at his brother. Both were silent.

'Oh, by the way,' began Nikolai Petrovitch, obviously wishing to change the subject, 'I've got a letter from Kolyazin.'

'Matvy Ilyitch?'

'Yes. He has come to——to inspect the province. He's quite a bigwig now; and writes to me that, as a relation, he should like to see us again, and invites you and me and Arkady to the town.'

'Are you going?' asked Pavel Petrovitch.

'No; are you?'

'No, I shan't go either. Much object there would be in dragging oneself over forty miles on a wild-goose chase. *Mathieu* wants to show himself in all his glory. Damn him! he will have the whole province doing him homage; he can get on without the likes of us. A grand dignity, indeed, a privy councillor! If I had stayed in the service, if I had drudged on in official harness, I should have been a general-adjutant by now. Besides, you and I are behind the times, you know.'

'Yes, brother; it's time, it seems, to order a coffin and cross one's arms on ones breast,' remarked Nikolai Petrovitch, with a sigh.

'Well, I'm not going to give in quite so soon,' muttered his brother. 'I've got a tussle with that doctor fellow before me, I feel sure of that.'

A tussle came off that same day at evening tea. Pavel Petrovitch came into the drawing-room, all ready for the fray, irritable and determined. He was only waiting for an excuse to fall upon the enemy; but for a long while an excuse did not present itself. As a rule, Bazarov said little in the presence of the 'old Kirsanovs' (that was how he spoke of the brothers), and that evening he felt out of humour, and drank off cup after cup of tea without a word. Pavel Petrovitch was all aflame with impatience; his wishes were fulfilled at last.

The conversation turned on one of the neighbouring landowners. 'Rotten aristocratic snob,' observed Bazarov indifferently. He had met him in Petersburg.
'Allow me to ask you,' began Pavel Petrovitch, and his lips were trembling, 'according to your ideas, have the words "rotten" and "aristocrat" the same meaning?'
'I said "aristocratic snob,"' replied Bazarov, lazily swallowing a sip of tea.
'Precisely so; but I imagine you have the same opinion of aristocrats as of aristocratic snobs. I think it my duty to inform you that I do not share that opinion. I venture to assert that every one knows me for a man of liberal ideas and devoted to progress; but, exactly for that reason, I respect aristocrats—real aristocrats. Kindly remember, sir' (at these words Bazarov lifted his eyes and looked at Pavel Petrovitch), 'kindly remember, sir,' he repeated, with acrimony—'the English aristocracy. They do not abate one iota of their rights, and for that reason they respect the rights of others; they demand the performance of what is due to them, and for that reason they perform their own duties. The aristocracy has given freedom to England, and maintains it for her.'
'We've heard that story a good many times,' replied Bazarov; 'but what are you trying to prove by that?'
'I am tryin' to prove by that, sir' (when Pavel Petrovitch was angry he intentionally clipped his words in this way, though, of course, he knew very well that such forms are not strictly grammatical. In this fashionable whim could be discerned a survival of the habits of the times of Alexander. The exquisites of those days, on the rare occasions when they spoke their own language, made use of such slipshod forms; as much as to say, 'We, of course, are born Russians, at the same time we are great swells, who are at liberty to neglect the rules of scholars'); 'I am tryin' to prove by that, sir, that without the sense of personal dignity, without self-respect—and these two sentiments are well developed in the aristocrat—there is no secure foundation for the social ... *bien public* ... the social fabric. Personal character, sir—that is the chief thing; a man's personal character must be firm as a rock, since everything is built on it. I am very well aware, for instance, that you are pleased to consider my habits, my dress, my refinements, in fact, ridiculous; but all that proceeds from a sense of self-respect, from a sense of duty—yes, indeed, of duty. I live in the country, in the wilds, but I will not lower myself. I respect the dignity of man in myself.'
'Let me ask you, Pavel Petrovitch,' commented Bazarov; 'you respect yourself, and sit with your hands folded; what sort of benefit does that do to the *bien public?* If you didn't respect yourself, you'd do just the same.'
Pavel Petrovitch turned white. 'That's a different question. It's absolutely unnecessary for me to explain to you now why I sit with folded hands, as you are pleased to express yourself. I wish only to tell you that aristocracy is a principle, and in our days none but immoral or silly people can live without principles. I said that to Arkady the day after he came home, and I repeat it now. Isn't it so, Nikolai?'
Nikolai Petrovitch nodded his head.
'Aristocracy, Liberalism, progress, principles,' Bazarov was saying meanwhile; 'if you think of it, what a lot of foreign ... and useless words! To a Russian they're good for nothing.'
'What is good for something according to you? If we listen to you, we shall find ourselves outside humanity, outside its laws. Come—the logic of history demands ...'
'But what's that logic to us? We call get on without that too.'
'How do you mean?'
'Why, this. You don't need logic, I hope, to put a bit of bread in your mouth when you're hungry. What's the object of these abstractions to us?'
Pavel Petrovitch raised his hands in horror.
'I don't understand you, after that. You insult the Russian people. I don't understand how it's possible not to acknowledge principles, rules! By virtue of what do you act then?'
'I've told you already, uncle, that we don't accept any authorities,' put in Arkady.
'We act by virtue of what we recognise as beneficial,' observed Bazarov. 'At the present time, negation is the most beneficial of all—and we deny——'
'Everything?'
'Everything!'
'What? not only art and poetry ... but even ... horrible to say ...'
'Everything,' repeated Bazarov, with indescribable composure.
Pavel Petrovitch stared at him. He had not expected this; while Arkady fairly blushed with delight.
'Allow me, though,' began Nikolai Petrovitch. 'You deny everything; or, speaking more precisely, you destroy everything.... But one must construct too, you know.'

'That's not our business now.... The ground wants clearing first.'
'The present condition of the people requires it,' added Arkady, with dignity; 'we are bound to carry out these requirements, we have no right to yield to the satisfaction of our personal egoism.'
This last phrase obviously displeased Bazarov; there was a flavour of philosophy, that is to say, romanticism about it, for Bazarov called philosophy, too, romanticism, but he did not think it necessary to correct his young disciple.
'No, no!' cried Pavel Petrovitch, with sudden energy. 'I'm not willing to believe that you, young men, know the Russian people really, that you are the representatives of their requirements, their efforts! No; the Russian people is not what you imagine it. Tradition it holds sacred; it is a patriarchal people; it cannot live without faith ...'
'I'm not going to dispute that,' Bazarov interrupted. 'I'm even ready to agree that in that you're right.'
'But if I am right ...'
'And, all the same, that proves nothing.'
'It just proves nothing,' repeated Arkady, with the confidence of a practised chess-player, who has foreseen an apparently dangerous move on the part of his adversary, and so is not at all taken aback by it.
'How does it prove nothing?' muttered Pavel Petrovitch, astounded. 'You must be going against the people then?'
'And what if we are?' shouted Bazarov. 'The people imagine that, when it thunders, the prophet Ilya's riding across the sky in his chariot. What then? Are we to agree with them? Besides, the people's Russian; but am I not Russian too?'
'No, you are not Russian, after all you have just been saying! I can't acknowledge you as Russian.'
'My grandfather ploughed the land,' answered Bazarov with haughty pride. 'Ask any one of your peasants which of us—you or me—he'd more readily acknowledge as a fellow-countryman. You don't even know how to talk to them.'
'While you talk to him and despise him at the same time.'
'Well, suppose he deserves contempt. You find fault with my attitude, but how do you know that I have got it by chance, that it's not a product of that very national spirit, in the name of which you wage war on it?'
'What an idea! Much use in nihilists!'
'Whether they're of use or not, is not for us to decide. Why, even you suppose you're not a useless person.'
'Gentlemen, gentlemen, no personalities, please!' cried Nikolai Petrovitch, getting up.
Pavel Petrovitch smiled, and laying his hand on his brother's shoulder, forced him to sit down again.
'Don't be uneasy,' he said; 'I shall not forget myself, just through that sense of dignity which is made fun of so mercilessly by our friend—our friend, the doctor. Let me ask,' he resumed, turning again to Bazarov; 'you suppose, possibly, that your doctrine is a novelty? That is quite a mistake. The materialism you advocate has been more than once in vogue already, and has always proved insufficient ...'
'A foreign word again!' broke in Bazarov. He was beginning to feel vicious, and his face assumed a peculiar coarse coppery hue. 'In the first place, we advocate nothing; that's not our way.'
'What do you do, then?'
'I'll tell you what we do. Not long ago we used to say that our officials took bribes, that we had no roads, no commerce, no real justice ...'
'Oh, I see, you are reformers—that's what that's called, I fancy. I too should agree to many of your reforms, but ...'
'Then we suspected that talk, perpetual talk, and nothing but talk, about our social diseases, was not worth while, that it all led to nothing but superficiality and pedantry; we saw that our leading men, so-called advanced people and reformers, are no good; that we busy ourselves over foolery, talk rubbish about art, unconscious creativeness, parliamentarism, trial by jury, and the deuce knows what all; while, all the while, it's a question of getting bread to eat, while we're stifling under the grossest superstition, while all our enterprises come to grief, simply because there aren't honest men enough to carry them on, while the very emancipation our Government's busy upon will hardly come to any good, because peasants are glad to rob even themselves to get drunk at the gin-shop.'
'Yes,' interposed Pavel Petrovitch, 'yes; you were convinced of all this, and decided not to undertake anything seriously, yourselves.'
'We decided not to undertake anything,' repeated Bazarov grimly. He suddenly felt vexed with himself for having, without reason, been so expansive before this gentleman.
'But to confine yourselves to abuse?'

'To confine ourselves to abuse.'
'And that is called nihilism?'
'And that's called nihilism,' Bazarov repeated again, this time with peculiar rudeness.
Pavel Petrovitch puckered up his face a little. 'So that's it!' he observed in a strangely composed voice. 'Nihilism is to cure all our woes, and you, you are our heroes and saviours. But why do you abuse others, those reformers even? Don't you do as much talking as every one else?'
'Whatever faults we have, we do not err in that way,' Bazarov muttered between his teeth.
'What, then? Do you act, or what? Are you preparing for action?'
Bazarov made no answer. Something like a tremor passed over Pavel Petrovitch, but he at once regained control of himself.
'Hm! ... Action, destruction ...' he went on. 'But how destroy without even knowing why?'
'We shall destroy, because we are a force,' observed Arkady.
Pavel Petrovitch looked at his nephew and laughed.
'Yes, a force is not to be called to account,' said Arkady, drawing himself up.
'Unhappy boy!' wailed Pavel Petrovitch, he was positively incapable of maintaining his firm demeanour any longer. 'If you could only realise what it is you are doing for your country. No; it's enough to try the patience of an angel! Force! There's force in the savage Kalmuck, in the Mongolian; but what is it to us? What is precious to us is civilisation; yes, yes, sir, its fruits are precious to us. And don't tell me those fruits are worthless; the poorest dauber, *un barbouilleur*, the man who plays dance music for five farthings an evening, is of more use than you, because they are the representatives of civilisation, and not of brute Mongolian force! You fancy yourselves advanced people, and all the while you are only fit for the Kalmuck's hovel! Force! And recollect, you forcible gentlemen, that you're only four men and a half, and the others are millions, who won't let you trample their sacred traditions under foot, who will crush you and walk over you!'
'If we're crushed, serve us right,' observed Bazarov. 'But that's an open question. We are not so few as you suppose.'
'What? You seriously suppose you will come to terms with a whole people?'
'All Moscow was burnt down, you know, by a farthing dip,' answered Bazarov.
'Yes, yes. First a pride almost Satanic, then ridicule—that, that's what it is attracts the young, that's what gains an ascendancy over the inexperienced hearts of boys! Here's one of them sitting beside you, ready to worship the ground under your feet. Look at him! (Arkady turned away and frowned.) And this plague has spread far already. I have been told that in Rome our artists never set foot in the Vatican. Raphael they regard as almost a fool, because, if you please, he's an authority; while they're all the while most disgustingly sterile and unsuccessful, men whose imagination does not soar beyond 'Girls at a Fountain,' however they try! And the girls even out of drawing. They are fine fellows to your mind, are they not?'
'To my mind,' retorted Bazarov, 'Raphael's not worth a brass farthing; and they're no better than he.'
'Bravo! bravo! Listen, Arkady ... that's how young men of to-day ought to express themselves! And if you come to think of it, how could they fail to follow you! In old days, young men had to study; they didn't want to be called dunces, so they had to work hard whether they liked it or not. But now, they need only say, "Everything in the world is foolery!" and the trick's done. Young men are delighted. And, to be sure, they were simply geese before, and now they have suddenly turned nihilists.'
'Your praiseworthy sense of personal dignity has given way,' remarked Bazarov phlegmatically, while Arkady was hot all over, and his eyes were flashing. 'Our argument has gone too far; it's better to cut it short, I think. I shall be quite ready to agree with you,' he added, getting up, 'when you bring forward a single institution in our present mode of life, in family or in social life, which does not call for complete and unqualified destruction.'
'I will bring forward millions of such institutions,' cried Pavel Petrovitch—'millions! Well—the Mir, for instance.'
A cold smile curved Bazarov's lips. 'Well, as regards the Mir,' he commented; 'you had better talk to your brother. He has seen by now, I should fancy, what sort of thing the Mir is in fact—its common guarantee, its sobriety, and other features of the kind.'
'The family, then, the family as it exists among our peasants!' cried Pavel Petrovitch.
'And that subject, too, I imagine, it will be better for yourselves not to go into in detail. Don't you realise all the advantages of the head of the family choosing his daughters-in-law? Take my advice, Pavel Petrovitch,

allow yourself two days to think about it; you're not likely to find anything on the spot. Go through all our classes, and think well over each, while I and Arkady will ...'
'Will go on turning everything into ridicule,' broke in Pavel Petrovitch.
'No, will go on dissecting frogs. Come, Arkady; good-bye for the present, gentlemen!'
The two friends walked off. The brothers were left alone, and at first they only looked at one another.
'So that,' began Pavel Petrovitch, 'so that's what our young men of this generation are! They are like that—our successors!'
'Our successors!' repeated Nikolai Petrovitch, with a dejected smile. He had been sitting on thorns, all through the argument, and had done nothing but glance stealthily, with a sore heart, at Arkady. 'Do you know what I was reminded of, brother? I once had a dispute with our poor mother; she stormed, and wouldn't listen to me. At last I said to her, "Of course, you can't understand me; we belong," I said, "to two different generations." She was dreadfully offended, while I thought, "There's no help for it. It's a bitter pill, but she has to swallow it." You see, now, our turn has come, and our successors can say to us, "You are not of our generation; swallow your pill."'
'You are beyond everything in your generosity and modesty,' replied Pavel Petrovitch. 'I'm convinced, on the contrary, that you and I are far more in the right than these young gentlemen, though we do perhaps express ourselves in old-fashioned language, *vieilli*, and have not the same insolent conceit.... And the swagger of the young men nowadays! You ask one, "Do you take red wine or white?" "It is my custom to prefer red!" he answers in a deep bass, with a face as solemn as if the whole universe had its eyes on him at that instant....'
'Do you care for any more tea?' asked Fenitchka, putting her head in at the door; she had not been able to make up her mind to come into the drawing-room while there was the sound of voices in dispute there.
'No, you can tell them to take the samovar,' answered Nikolai Petrovitch, and he got up to meet her. Pavel Petrovitch said *'bon soir'* to him abruptly, and went away to his study.

CHAPTER XI

Half an hour later Nikolai Petrovitch went into the garden to his favourite arbour. He was overtaken by melancholy thoughts. For the first time he realised clearly the distance between him and his son; he foresaw that every day it would grow wider and wider. In vain, then, had he spent whole days sometimes in the winter at Petersburg over the newest books; in vain had he listened to the talk of the young men; in vain had he rejoiced when he succeeded in putting in his word too in their heated discussions. 'My brother says we are right,' he thought, 'and apart from all vanity, I do think myself that they are further from the truth than we are, though at the same time I feel there is something behind them we have not got, some superiority over us.... Is it youth? No; not only youth. Doesn't their superiority consist in there being fewer traces of the slaveowner in them than in us?'
Nikolai Petrovitch's head sank despondently, and he passed his hand over his face.
'But to renounce poetry?' he thought again; 'to have no feeling for art, for nature ...'
And he looked round, as though trying to understand how it was possible to have no feeling for nature. It was already evening; the sun was hidden behind a small copse of aspens which lay a quarter of a mile from the garden; its shadow stretched indefinitely across the still fields. A peasant on a white nag went at a trot along the dark, narrow path close beside the copse; his whole figure was clearly visible even to the patch on his shoulder, in spite of his being in the shade; the horse's hoofs flew along bravely. The sun's rays from the farther side fell full on the copse, and piercing through its thickets, threw such a warm light on the aspen trunks that they looked like pines, and their leaves were almost a dark blue, while above them rose a pale blue sky, faintly tinged by the glow of sunset. The swallows flew high; the wind had quite died away, belated bees hummed slowly and drowsily among the lilac blossom; a swarm of midges hung like a cloud over a

solitary branch which stood out against the sky. 'How beautiful, my God!' thought Nikolai Petrovitch, and his favourite verses were almost on his lips; he remembered Arkady's *Stoff und Kraft*—and was silent, but still he sat there, still he gave himself up to the sorrowful consolation of solitary thought. He was fond of dreaming; his country life had developed the tendency in him. How short a time ago, he had been dreaming like this, waiting for his son at the posting station, and what a change already since that day; their relations that were then undefined, were defined now—and how defined! Again his dead wife came back to his imagination, but not as he had known her for many years, not as the good domestic housewife, but as a young girl with a slim figure, innocently inquiring eyes, and a tight twist of hair on her childish neck. He remembered how he had seen her for the first time. He was still a student then. He had met her on the staircase of his lodgings, and, jostling by accident against her, he tried to apologise, and could only mutter, *'Pardon, monsieur,'* while she bowed, smiled, and suddenly seemed frightened, and ran away, though at the bend of the staircase she had glanced rapidly at him, assumed a serious air, and blushed. Afterwards, the first timid visits, the half-words, the half-smiles, and embarrassment; and melancholy, and yearnings, and at last that breathing rapture.... Where had it all vanished? She had been his wife, he had been happy as few on earth are happy.... 'But,' he mused, 'these sweet first moments, why could one not live an eternal, undying life in them?'

He did not try to make his thought clear to himself; but he felt that he longed to keep that blissful time by something stronger than memory; he longed to feel his Marya near him again to have the sense of her warmth and breathing, and already he could fancy that over him....

'Nikolai Petrovitch,' came the sound of Fenitchka's voice close by him; 'where are you?'

He started. He felt no pang, no shame. He never even admitted the possibility of comparison between his wife and Fenitchka, but he was sorry she had thought of coming to look for him. Her voice had brought back to him at once his grey hairs, his age, his reality....

The enchanted world into which he was just stepping, which was just rising out of the dim mists of the past, was shaken—and vanished.

'I'm here,' he answered; 'I'm coming, run along.' 'There it is, the traces of the slave owner,' flashed through his mind. Fenitchka peeped into the arbour at him without speaking, and disappeared; while he noticed with astonishment that the night had come on while he had been dreaming. Everything around was dark and hushed. Fenitchka's face had glimmered so pale and slight before him. He got up, and was about to go home; but the emotion stirred in his heart could not be soothed at once, and he began slowly walking about the garden, sometimes looking at the ground at his feet, and then raising his eyes towards the sky where swarms of stars were twinkling. He walked a great deal, till he was almost tired out, while the restlessness within him, a kind of yearning, vague, melancholy restlessness, still was not appeased. Oh, how Bazarov would have laughed at him, if he had known what was passing within him then! Arkady himself would have condemned him. He, a man forty-four years old, an agriculturist and a farmer, was shedding tears, causeless tears; this was a hundred times worse than the violoncello.

Nikolai Petrovitch continued walking, and could not make up his mind to go into the house, into the snug peaceful nest, which looked out at him so hospitably from all its lighted windows; he had not the force to tear himself away from the darkness, the garden, the sense of the fresh air in his face, from that melancholy, that restless craving.

At a turn in the path, he was met by Pavel Petrovitch. 'What's the matter with you?' he asked Nikolai Petrovitch; 'you are as white as a ghost; you are not well; why don't you go to bed?'

Nikolai Petrovitch explained to him briefly his state of feeling and moved away. Pavel Petrovitch went to the end of the garden, and he too grew thoughtful, and he too raised his eyes toward the heavens. But in his beautiful dark eyes, nothing was reflected but the light of the stars. He was not born an idealist, and his fastidiously dry and sensuous soul, with its French tinge of cynicism was not capable of dreaming....

'Do you know what?' Bazarov was saying to Arkady the same night. 'I've got a splendid idea. Your father was saying to-day that he'd had an invitation from your illustrious relative. Your father's not going; let us be off to X——; you know the worthy man invites you too. You see what fine weather it is; we'll stroll about and look at the town. We'll have five or six days' outing, and enjoy ourselves.'

'And you'll come back here again?'

'No; I must go to my father's. You know, he lives about twenty-five miles from X——. I've not seen him for a long while, and my mother too; I must cheer the old people up. They've been good to me, especially my father; he's awfully funny. I'm their only one too.'

'And will you be long with them?'

'I don't suppose so. It will be dull, of course.'
'And you'll come to us on your way back?'
'I don't know ... I'll see. Well, what do you say? Shall we go?'
'If you like,' observed Arkady languidly.
In his heart he was highly delighted with his friend's suggestion, but he thought it a duty to conceal his feeling. He was not a nihilist for nothing!
The next day he set off with Bazarov to X——. The younger part of the household at Maryino were sorry at their going; Dunyasha even cried ... but the old folks breathed more easily.

CHAPTER XII

The town of X—— to which our friends set off was in the jurisdiction of a governor who was a young man, and at once a progressive and a despot, as often happens with Russians. Before the end of the first year of his government, he had managed to quarrel not only with the marshal of nobility, a retired officer of the guards, who kept open house and a stud of horses, but even with his own subordinates. The feuds arising from this cause assumed at last such proportions that the ministry in Petersburg had found it necessary to send down a trusted personage with a commission to investigate it all on the spot. The choice of the authorities fell upon Matvy Ilyitch Kolyazin, the son of the Kolyazin, under whose protection the brothers Kirsanov had once found themselves. He, too, was a 'young man'; that is to say, he had not long passed forty, but he was already on the high road to becoming a statesman, and wore a star on each side of his breast—one, to be sure, a foreign star, not of the first magnitude. Like the governor, whom he had come down to pass judgment upon, he was reckoned a progressive; and though he was already a bigwig, he was not like the majority of bigwigs. He had the highest opinion of himself; his vanity knew no bounds, but he behaved simply, looked affable, listened condescendingly, and laughed so good-naturedly, that on a first acquaintance he might even be taken for 'a jolly good fellow.' On important occasions, however, he knew, as the saying is, how to make his authority felt. 'Energy is essential,' he used to say then, *'l'énergie est la première qualité d'un homme d'état;'* and for all that, he was usually taken in, and any moderately experienced official could turn him round his finger. Matvy Ilyitch used to speak with great respect of Guizot, and tried to impress every one with the idea that he did not belong to the class of *routiniers* and high-and-dry bureaucrats, that not a single phenomenon of social life passed unnoticed by him.... All such phrases were very familiar to him. He even followed, with dignified indifference, it is true, the development of contemporary literature; so a grown-up man who meets a procession of small boys in the street will sometimes walk after it. In reality, Matvy Ilyitch had not got much beyond those political men of the days of Alexander, who used to prepare for an evening party at Madame Svyetchin's by reading a page of Condillac; only his methods were different, more modern. He was an adroit courtier, a great hypocrite, and nothing more; he had no special aptitude for affairs, and no intellect, but he knew how to manage his own business successfully; no one could get the better of him there, and, to be sure, that's the principal thing.
Matvy Ilyitch received Arkady with the good-nature, we might even call it playfulness, characteristic of the enlightened higher official. He was astonished, however, when he heard that the cousins he had invited had remained at home in the country. 'Your father was always a queer fellow,' he remarked, playing with the tassels of his magnificent velvet dressing-gown, and suddenly turning to a young official in a discreetly buttoned-up uniform, he cried, with an air of concentrated attention, 'What?' The young man, whose lips were glued together from prolonged silence, got up and looked in perplexity at his chief. But, having nonplussed his subordinate, Matvy Ilyitch paid him no further attention. Our higher officials are fond as a rule of nonplussing their subordinates; the methods to which they have recourse to attain that end are rather various. The following means, among others, is in great vogue, *'is quite a favourite,'* as the English say; a

high official suddenly ceases to understand the simplest words, assuming total deafness. He will ask, for instance, What's to-day?'

He is respectfully informed, 'To-day's Friday, your Ex-s-s-s-lency.'

'Eh? What? What's that? What do you say?' the great man repeats with intense attention.

'To-day's Friday, your Ex—s—s—lency.'

'Eh? What? What's Friday? What Friday?'

'Friday, your Ex—s—s—s—lency, the day of the week.'

'What, do you pretend to teach me, eh?'

Matvy Ilyitch was a higher official all the same, though he was reckoned a liberal.

'I advise you, my dear boy, to go and call on the Governor,' he said to Arkady; 'you understand, I don't advise you to do so because I adhere to old-fashioned ideas of the necessity of paying respect to authorities, but simply because the Governor's a very decent fellow; besides, you probably want to make acquaintance with the society here.... You're not a bear, I hope? And he's giving a great ball the day after to-morrow.'

'Will you be at the ball?' inquired Arkady.

'He gives it in my honour,' answered Matvy Ilyitch, almost pityingly. 'Do you dance?'

'Yes; I dance, but not well.'

'That's a pity! There are pretty girls here, and it's a disgrace for a young man not to dance. Again, I don't say that through any old-fashioned ideas; I don't in the least imagine that a man's wit lies in his feet, but Byronism is ridiculous, *il a fait son temps.'*

'But, uncle, it's not through Byronism, I ...'

'I will introduce you to the ladies here; I will take you under my wing,' interrupted Matvy Ilyitch, and he laughed complacently. 'You'll find it warm, eh?'

A servant entered and announced the arrival of the superintendent of the Crown domains, a mild-eyed old man, with deep creases round his mouth, who was excessively fond of nature, especially on a summer day, when, in his words, 'every little busy bee takes a little bribe from every little flower.' Arkady withdrew.

He found Bazarov at the tavern where they were staying, and was a long while persuading him to go with him to the Governor's. 'Well, there's no help for it,' said Bazarov at last. 'It's no good doing things by halves. We came to look at the gentry; let's look at them!'

The Governor received the young men affably, but he did not ask them to sit down, nor did he sit down himself. He was in an everlasting fuss and hurry; in the morning he used to put on a tight uniform and an excessively stiff cravat; he never ate or drank enough; he was for ever making arrangements. He invited Kirsanov and Bazarov to his ball, and within a few minutes invited them a second time, regarding them as brothers, and calling them Kisarov.

They were on their way home from the Governor's, when suddenly a short man, in a Slavophil national dress, leaped out of a trap that was passing them, and crying, 'Yevgeny Vassilyitch!' dashed up to Bazarov.

'Ah! it's you, Herr Sitnikov,' observed Bazarov, still stepping along on the pavement; 'by what chance did you come here?'

'Fancy, absolutely by chance,' he replied, and returning to the trap, he waved his hand several times, and shouted, 'Follow, follow us! My father had business here,' he went on, hopping across the gutter, 'and so he asked me.... I heard to-day of your arrival, and have already been to see you....' (The friends did, in fact, on returning to their room, find there a card, with the corners turned down, bearing the name of Sitnikov, on one side in French, on the other in Slavonic characters.) 'I hope you are not coming from the Governor's?'

'It's no use to hope; we come straight from him.'

'Ah! in that case I will call on him too.... Yevgeny Vassilyitch, introduce me to your ... to the ...'

'Sitnikov, Kirsanov,' mumbled Bazarov, not stopping.

'I am greatly flattered,' began Sitnikov, walking sidewise, smirking, and hurriedly pulling off his really over-elegant gloves. 'I have heard so much.... I am an old acquaintance of Yevgeny Vassilyitch, and, I may say—his disciple. I am indebted to him for my regeneration....'

Arkady looked at Bazarov's disciple. There was an expression of excitement and dulness imprinted on the small but pleasant features of his well-groomed face; his small eyes, that seemed squeezed in, had a fixed and uneasy look, and his laugh, too, was uneasy—a sort of short, wooden laugh.

'Would you believe it,' he pursued, 'when Yevgeny Vassilyitch for the first time said before me that it was not right to accept any authorities, I felt such enthusiasm ... as though my eyes were opened! Here, I thought, at last I have found a man! By the way, Yevgeny Vassilyitch, you positively must come to know a lady here,

who is really capable of understanding you, and for whom your visit would be a real festival; you have heard of her, I suppose?'
'Who is it?' Bazarov brought out unwillingly.
'Kukshina, *Eudoxie*, Evdoksya Kukshin. She's a remarkable nature, *émancipée* in the true sense of the word, an advanced woman. Do you know what? We'll all go together to see her now. She lives only two steps from here. We will have lunch there. I suppose you have not lunched yet?'
'No; not yet.'
'Well, that's capital. She has separated, you understand, from her husband; she is not dependent on any one.'
'Is she pretty?' Bazarov cut in.
'N-no, one couldn't say that.'
'Then, what the devil are you asking us to see her for?'
'Fie; you must have your joke.... She will give us a bottle of champagne.'
'Oh, that's it. One can see the practical man at once. By the way, is your father still in the gin business?'
'Yes,' said Sitnikov, hurriedly, and he gave a shrill spasmodic laugh. 'Well? Will you come?'
'I don't really know.'
'You wanted to see people, go along,' said Arkady in an undertone.
'And what do you say to it, Mr. Kirsanov?' Sitnikov put in. 'You must come too; we can't go without you.'
'But how can we burst in upon her all at once?'
'That's no matter. Kukshina's a brick!'
'There will be a bottle of champagne?' asked Bazarov.
'Three!' cried Sitnikov; 'that I answer for.'
'What with?'
'My own head.'
'Your father's purse would be better. However, we are coming.'

CHAPTER XIII

The small gentleman's house in the Moscow style, in which Avdotya Nikitishna, otherwise Evdoksya, Kukshin, lived, was in one of the streets of X——, which had been lately burnt down; it is well known that our provincial towns are burnt down every five years. At the door, above a visiting card nailed on all askew, there was a bell-handle to be seen, and in the hall the visitors were met by some one, not exactly a servant, nor exactly a companion, in a cap—unmistakable tokens of the progressive tendencies of the lady of the house. Sitnikov inquired whether Avdotya Nikitishna was at home.
'Is that you, *Victor?'* sounded a shrill voice from the adjoining room. 'Come in.'
The woman in the cap disappeared at once.
'I'm not alone,' observed Sitnikov, with a sharp look at Arkady and Bazarov as he briskly pulled off his overcoat, beneath which appeared something of the nature of a coachman's velvet jacket.
'No matter,' answered the voice. *'Entrez.'*
The young men went in. The room into which they walked was more like a working study than a drawing-room. Papers, letters, fat numbers of Russian journals, for the most part uncut, lay at random on the dusty tables; white cigarette ends lay scattered in every direction. On a leather-covered sofa, a lady, still young, was half reclining. Her fair hair was rather dishevelled; she wore a silk gown, not perfectly tidy, heavy bracelets on her short arms, and a lace handkerchief on her head. She got up from the sofa, and carelessly drawing a velvet cape trimmed with yellowish ermine over her shoulders, she said languidly, 'Good-morning, *Victor,'* and pressed Sitnikov's hand.
'Bazarov, Kirsanov,' he announced abruptly in imitation of Bazarov.

'Delighted,' answered Madame Kukshin, and fixing on Bazarov a pair of round eyes, between which was a forlorn little turned-up red nose, 'I know you,' she added, and pressed his hand too.
Bazarov scowled. There was nothing repulsive in the little plain person of the emancipated woman; but the expression of her face produced a disagreeable effect on the spectator. One felt impelled to ask her, 'What's the matter; are you hungry? Or bored? Or shy? What are you in a fidget about?' Both she and Sitnikov had always the same uneasy air. She was extremely unconstrained, and at the same time awkward; she obviously regarded herself as a good-natured, simple creature, and all the while, whatever she did, it always struck one that it was not just what she wanted to do; everything with her seemed, as children say, done on purpose, that's to say, not simply, not naturally.
'Yes, yes, I know you, Bazarov,' she repeated. (She had the habit—peculiar to many provincial and Moscow ladies—of calling men by their surnames from the first day of acquaintance with them.) 'Will you have a cigar?'
'A cigar's all very well,' put in Sitnikov, who by now was lolling in an armchair, his legs in the air; 'but give us some lunch. We're awfully hungry; and tell them to bring us up a little bottle of champagne.'
'Sybarite,' commented Evdoksya, and she laughed. (When she laughed the gum showed above her upper teeth.) 'Isn't it true, Bazarov; he's a Sybarite?'
'I like comfort in life,' Sitnikov brought out, with dignity. 'That does not prevent my being a Liberal.'
'No, it does; it does prevent it!' cried Evdoksya. She gave directions, however, to her maid, both as regards the lunch and the champagne.
'What do you think about it?' she added, turning to Bazarov. 'I'm persuaded you share my opinion.'
'Well, no,' retorted Bazarov; 'a piece of meat's better than a piece of bread even from the chemical point of view.'
'You are studying chemistry? That is my passion. I've even invented a new sort of composition myself.'
'A composition? You?'
'Yes. And do you know for what purpose? To make dolls' heads so that they shouldn't break. I'm practical, too, yon see. But everything's not quite ready yet. I've still to read Liebig. By the way, have you read Kislyakov's article on Female Labour, in the *Moscow Gazette?*Read it please. You're interested in the woman question, I suppose? And in the schools too? What does your friend do? What is his name?'
Madame Kukshin shed her questions one after another with affected negligence, not waiting for an answer; spoilt children talk so to their nurses.
'My name's Arkady Nikolaitch Kirsanov,' said Arkady, 'and I'm doing nothing.'
Evdoksya giggled. 'How charming! What, don't you smoke? Victor, do you know, I'm very angry with you.'
'What for?'
'They tell me you've begun singing the praises of George Sand again. A retrograde woman, and nothing else! How can people compare her with Emerson! She hasn't an idea on education, nor physiology, nor anything. She'd never, I'm persuaded, heard of embryology, and in these days—what can be done without that?' (Evdoksya even threw up her hands.) 'Ah, what a wonderful article Elisyevitch has written on that subject! He's a gentleman of genius.' (Evdoksya constantly made use of the word 'gentleman' instead of the word 'man.') 'Bazarov, sit by me on the sofa. You don't know, perhaps, I'm awfully afraid of you.'
'Why so? Allow me to ask.'
'You're a dangerous gentleman; you're such a critic. Good God! yes! why, how absurd, I'm talking like some country lady. I really am a country lady, though. I manage my property myself; and only fancy, my bailiff Erofay's a wonderful type, quite like Cooper's Pathfinder; something in him so spontaneous! I've come to settle here finally; it's an intolerable town, isn't it? But what's one to do?'
'The town's like every town,' Bazarov remarked coolly.
'All its interests are so petty, that's what's so awful! I used to spend the winters in Moscow ... but now my lawful spouse, Monsieur Kukshin's residing there. And besides, Moscow nowadays ... there, I don't know—it's not the same as it was. I'm thinking of going abroad; last year I was on the point of setting off.'
'To Paris, I suppose?' queried Bazarov.
'To Paris and to Heidelberg.'
'Why to Heidelberg?'
'How can you ask? Why, Bunsen's there!'
To this Bazarov could find no reply.
'Pierre Sapozhnikov ... do you know him?'
'No, I don't.'

'Not know *Pierre* Sapozhnikov ... he's always at Lidia Hestatov's.'
'I don't know her either.'
'Well, it was he undertook to escort me. Thank God, I'm independent; I've no children.... What was that I said: *thank God!* It's no matter though.'
Evdoksya rolled a cigarette up between her fingers, which were brown with tobacco stains, put it to her tongue, licked it up, and began smoking. The maid came in with a tray.
'Ah, here's lunch! Will you have an appetiser first? Victor, open the bottle; that's in your line.'
'Yes, it's in my line,' muttered Sitnikov, and again he gave vent to the same convulsive laugh.
'Are there any pretty women here?' inquired Bazarov, as he drank off a third glass.
'Yes, there are,' answered Evdoksya; 'but they're all such empty-headed creatures. *Mon amie,* Odintsova, for instance, is nice-looking. It's a pity her reputation's rather doubtful.... That wouldn't matter, though, but she's no independence in her views, no width, nothing ... of all that. The whole system of education wants changing. I've thought a great deal about it, our women are very badly educated.'
'There's no doing anything with them,' put in Sitnikov; 'one ought to despise them, and I do despise them fully and completely!' (The possibility of feeling and expressing contempt was the most agreeable sensation to Sitnikov; he used to attack women in especial, never suspecting that it was to be his fate a few months later to be cringing before his wife merely because she had been born a princess Durdoleosov.) 'Not a single one of them would be capable of understanding our conversation; not a single one deserves to be spoken of by serious men like us!'
'But there's not the least need for them to understand our conversation,' observed Bazarov.
'Whom do you mean?' put in Evdoksya.
'Pretty women.'
'What? Do you adopt Proudhon's ideas, then?'
Bazarov drew himself up haughtily. 'I don't adopt any one's ideas; I have my own.'
'Damn all authorities!' shouted Sitnikov, delighted to have a chance of expressing himself boldly before the man he slavishly admired.
'But even Macaulay,' Madame Kukshin was beginning ...
'Damn Macaulay,' thundered Sitnikov. 'Are you going to stand up for the silly hussies?'
'For silly hussies, no, but for the rights of women, which I have sworn to defend to the last drop of my blood.'
'Damn!'—but here Sitnikov stopped. 'But I don't deny them,' he said.
'No, I see you're a Slavophil.'
'No, I'm not a Slavophil, though, of course ...'
'No, no, no! You are a Slavophil. You're an advocate of patriarchal despotism. You want to have the whip in your hand!'
'A whip's an excellent thing,' remarked Bazarov; 'but we've got to the last drop.'
'Of what?' interrupted Evdoksya.
'Of champagne, most honoured Avdotya Nikitishna, of champagne—not of your blood.'
'I can never listen calmly when women are attacked,' pursued Evdoksya. 'It's awful, awful. Instead of attacking them, you'd better read Michelet's book, *De l'amour*. That's exquisite! Gentlemen, let us talk of love,' added Evdoksya, letting her arm fall languidly on the rumpled sofa cushion.
A sudden silence followed. 'No, why should we talk of love,' said Bazarov; 'but you mentioned just now a Madame Odintsov ... That was what you called her, I think? Who is that lady?'
'She's charming, charming!' piped Sitnikov. 'I will introduce you. Clever, rich, a widow. It's a pity, she's not yet advanced enough; she ought to see more of our Evdoksya. I drink to your health, *Evdoxie!* Let us clink glasses! *Et toc, et toc, et tin-tin-tin! Et toc, et toc, et tin-tin-tin!!!'*
'Victor, you're a wretch.'
The lunch dragged on a long while. The first bottle of champagne was followed by another, a third, and even a fourth.... Evdoksya chattered without pause; Sitnikov seconded her. They had much discussion upon the question whether marriage was a prejudice or a crime, and whether men were born equal or not, and precisely what individuality consists in. Things came at last to Evdoksya, flushed from the wine she had drunk, tapping with her flat finger-tips on the keys of a discordant piano, and beginning to sing in a hoarse voice, first gipsy songs, and then Seymour Schiff's song, 'Granada lies slumbering'; while Sitnikov tied a scarf round his head, and represented the dying lover at the words—

thy lips to min

Arkady could not stand it at last. 'Gentlemen, it's getting something like Bedlam,' he remarked aloud. Bazarov, who had at rare intervals put in an ironical word in the conversation—he paid more attention to the champagne—gave a loud yawn, got up, and, without taking leave of their hostess, he walked off with Arkady. Sitnikov jumped up and followed them.

'Well, what do you think of her?' he inquired, skipping obsequiously from right to left of them. 'I told you, you see, a remarkable personality! If we only had more women like that! She is, in her own way, an expression of the highest morality.'

'And is that establishment of your governor's an expression of the highest morality too?' observed Bazarov, pointing to a ginshop which they were passing at that instant.

Sitnikov again went off into a shrill laugh. He was greatly ashamed of his origin, and did not know whether to feel flattered or offended at Bazarov's unexpected familiarity.

CHAPTER XIV

A few days later the ball at the Governor's took place. Matvy Ilyitch was the real 'hero of the occasion.' The marshal of nobility declared to all and each that he had come simply out of respect for him; while the Governor, even at the ball, even while he remained perfectly motionless, was still 'making arrangements.' The affability of Matvy Ilyitch's demeanour could only be equalled by its dignity. He was gracious to all, to some with a shade of disgust, to others with a shade of respect; he was all bows and smiles *'en vrai chevalier français'* before the ladies, and was continually giving vent to a hearty, sonorous, unshared laugh, such as befits a high official. He slapped Arkady on the back, and called him loudly 'nephew'; vouchsafed Bazarov—who was attired in a rather old evening coat—a sidelong glance in passing—absent but condescending—and an indistinct but affable grunt, in which nothing could be distinguished but 'I ...' and 'very much'; gave Sitnikov a finger and a smile, though with his head already averted; even to Madame Kukshin, who made her appearance at the ball with dirty gloves, no crinoline, and a bird of Paradise in her hair, he said *'enchanté.'*. There were crowds of people, and no lack of dancing men; the civilians were for the most part standing close along the walls, but the officers danced assiduously, especially one of them who had spent six weeks in Paris, where he had mastered various daring interjections of the kind of—*'zut,' 'Ah, fichtr-re,' 'pst, pst, mon bibi,'* and such. He pronounced them to perfection with genuine Parisian*chic,* and at the same time he said *'si j'aurais'* for *'si j'avais,' 'absolument'* in the sense of 'absolutely,' expressed himself, in fact, in that Great Russo-French jargon which the French ridicule so when they have no reason for assuring us that we speak French like angels,*'comme des anges.'*

Arkady, as we are aware, danced badly, while Bazarov did not dance at all; they both took up their position in a corner; Sitnikov joined himself on to them, with an expression of contemptuous scorn on his face, and giving vent to spiteful comments, he looked insolently about him, and seemed to be really enjoying himself. Suddenly his face changed, and turning to Arkady, he said, with some show of embarrassment it seemed, 'Odintsova is here!'

Arkady looked round, and saw a tall woman in a black dress standing at the door of the room. He was struck by the dignity of her carriage. Her bare arms lay gracefully beside her slender waist; gracefully some light sprays of fuchsia drooped from her shining hair on to her sloping shoulders; her clear eyes looked out from under a rather overhanging white brow, with a tranquil and intelligent expression—tranquil it was precisely, not pensive—and on her lips was a scarcely perceptible smile. There was a kind of gracious and gentle force about her face.

'Do you know her?' Arkady asked Sitnikov.

'Intimately. Would you like me to introduce you?'

'Please ... after this quadrille.'

Bazarov's attention, too, was directed to Madame Odintsov.

'That's a striking figure,' he remarked. 'Not like the other females.'

After waiting till the end of the quadrille, Sitnikov led Arkady up to Madame Odintsov; but he hardly seemed to be intimately acquainted with her; he was embarrassed in his sentences, while she looked at him in some surprise. But her face assumed an expression of pleasure when she heard Arkady's surname. She asked him whether he was not the son of Nikolai Petrovitch.

'Yes.'

'I have seen your father twice, and have heard a great deal about him,' she went on; 'I am glad to make your acquaintance.'

At that instant some adjutant flew up to her and begged for a quadrille. She consented.

'Do you dance then?' asked Arkady respectfully.

'Yes, I dance. Why do you suppose I don't dance? Do you think I am too old?'

'Really, how could I possibly.... But in that case, let me ask you for a mazurka.'

Madame Odintsov smiled graciously. 'Certainly,' she said, and she looked at Arkady not exactly with an air of superiority, but as married sisters look at very young brothers. Madame Odintsov was a little older than Arkady—she was twenty-nine—but in her presence he felt himself a schoolboy, a little student, so that the difference in age between them seemed of more consequence. Matvy Ilyitch approached her with a majestic air and ingratiating speeches. Arkady moved away, but he still watched her; he could not take his eyes off her even during the quadrille. She talked with equal ease to her partner and to the grand official, softly turned her head and eyes, and twice laughed softly. Her nose—like almost all Russian noses—was a little thick; and her complexion was not perfectly clear; Arkady made up his mind, for all that, that he had never before met such an attractive woman. He could not get the sound of her voice out of his ears; the very folds of her dress seemed to hang upon her differently from all the rest—more gracefully and amply—and her movements were distinguished by a peculiar smoothness and naturalness.

Arkady felt some timidity in his heart when at the first sounds of the mazurka he began to sit it out beside his partner; he had prepared to enter into a conversation with her, but he only passed his hand through his hair, and could not find a single word to say. But his timidity and agitation did not last long; Madame Odintsov's tranquillity gained upon him too; before a quarter of an hour had passed he was telling her freely about his father, his uncle, his life in Petersburg and in the country. Madame Odintsov listened to him with courteous sympathy, slightly opening and closing her fan; his talk was broken off when partners came for her; Sitnikov, among others, twice asked her. She came back, sat down again, took up her fan, and her bosom did not even heave more rapidly, while Arkady fell to chattering again, filled through and through by the happiness of being near her, talking to her, looking at her eyes, her lovely brow, all her sweet, dignified, clever face. She said little, but her words showed a knowledge of life; from some of her observations Arkady gathered that this young woman had already felt and thought much....

'Who is that you were standing with?' she asked him, 'when Mr. Sitnikov brought you to me?'

'Did you notice him?' Arkady asked in his turn. 'He has a splendid face, hasn't he? That's Bazarov, my friend.' Arkady fell to discussing 'his friend.' He spoke of him in such detail, and with such enthusiasm, that Madame Odintsov turned towards him and looked attentively at him. Meanwhile, the mazurka was drawing to a close. Arkady felt sorry to part from his partner; he had spent nearly an hour so happily with her! He had, it is true, during the whole time continually felt as though she were condescending to him, as though he ought to be grateful to her ... but young hearts are not weighed down by that feeling.

The music stopped. *'Merci,'* said Madame Odintsov, getting up. 'You promised to come and see me; bring your friend with you. I shall be very curious to see the man who has the courage to believe in nothing.'

The Governor came up to Madame Odintsov, announced that supper was ready, and, with a careworn face, offered her his arm. As she went away, she turned to give a last smile and bow to Arkady. He bowed low, looked after her (how graceful her figure seemed to him, draped in the greyish lustre of the black silk!), and thinking, 'This minute she has forgotten my existence,' was conscious of an exquisite humility in his soul.

'Well?' Bazarov questioned him, directly he had gone back to him in the corner. 'Did you have a good time? A gentleman has just been talking to me about that lady; he said, "She's—oh, fie! fie!" but I fancy the fellow was a fool. What do you think, what is she?—oh, fie! fie!'

'I don't quite understand that definition,' answered Arkady.

'Oh, my! What innocence!'

'In that case, I don't understand the gentleman you quote. Madame Odintsov is very sweet, no doubt, but she behaves so coldly and severely, that....'
'Still waters ... you know!' put in Bazarov. 'That's just what gives it piquancy. You like ices, I expect?'
'Perhaps,' muttered Arkady. 'I can't give an opinion about that. She wishes to make your acquaintance, and has asked me to bring you to see her.'
'I can imagine how you've described me! But you did very well. Take me. Whatever she may be—whether she's simply a provincial lioness, or "advanced" after Kukshina's fashion—any way she's got a pair of shoulders such as I've not set eyes on for a long while.'
Arkady was wounded by Bazarov's cynicism, but—as often happens—he reproached his friend not precisely for what he did not like in him ...
'Why are you unwilling to allow freethinking in women?' he said in a low voice.
'Because, my boy, as far as my observations go, the only freethinkers among women are frights.'
The conversation was cut short at this point. Both the young men went away immediately after supper. They were pursued by a nervously malicious, but somewhat faint-hearted laugh from Madame Kukshin; her vanity had been deeply wounded by neither of them having paid any attention to her. She stayed later than any one at the ball, and at four o'clock in the morning she was dancing a polka-mazurka with Sitnikov in the Parisian style. This edifying spectacle was the final event of the Governor's ball.

CHAPTER XV

'Let's see what species of mammalia this specimen belongs to,' Bazarov said to Arkady the following day, as they mounted the staircase of the hotel in which Madame Odintsov was staying. 'I scent out something wrong here.'
'I'm surprised at you!' cried Arkady. 'What? You, you, Bazarov, clinging to the narrow morality, which ...'
'What a funny fellow you are!' Bazarov cut him short, carelessly. 'Don't you know that "something wrong" means "something right" in my dialect and for me? It's an advantage for me, of course. Didn't you tell me yourself this morning that she made a strange marriage, though, to my mind, to marry a rich old man is by no means a strange thing to do, but, on the contrary, very sensible. I don't believe the gossip of the town; but I should like to think, as our cultivated Governor says, that it's well-grounded.'
Arkady made no answer, and knocked at the door of the apartments. A young servant in livery, conducted the two friends in to a large room, badly furnished, like all rooms in Russian hotels, but filled with flowers. Soon Madame Odintsov herself appeared in a simple morning dress. She seemed still younger by the light of the spring sunshine. Arkady presented Bazarov, and noticed with secret amazement that he seemed embarrassed, while Madame Odintsov remained perfectly tranquil, as she had been the previous day. Bazarov himself was conscious of being embarrassed, and was irritated by it. 'Here's a go!—frightened of a petticoat!' he thought, and lolling, quite like Sitnikov, in an easy-chair, he began talking with an exaggerated appearance of ease, while Madame Odintsov kept her clear eyes fixed on him.
Anna Sergyevna Odintsov was the daughter of Sergay Nikolaevitch Loktev, notorious for his personal beauty, his speculations, and his gambling propensities, who after cutting a figure and making a sensation for fifteen years in Petersburg and Moscow, finished by ruining himself completely at cards, and was forced to retire to the country, where, however, he soon after died, leaving a very small property to his two daughters—Anna, a girl of twenty, and Katya, a child of twelve. Their mother, who came of an impoverished line of princes—the H——s— had died at Petersburg when her husband was in his heydey. Anna's position after her father's death was very difficult. The brilliant education she had received in Petersburg had not fitted her for putting up with the cares of domestic life and economy,—for an obscure existence in the country. She knew positively no one in the whole neighbourhood, and there was no one she could consult.

Her father had tried to avoid all contact with the neighbours; he despised them in his way, and they despised him in theirs. She did not lose her head, however, and promptly sent for a sister of her mother's Princess Avdotya Stepanovna H——, a spiteful and arrogant old lady, who, on installing herself in her niece's house, appropriated all the best rooms for her own use, scolded and grumbled from morning till night, and would not go a walk even in the garden unattended by her one serf, a surly footman in a threadbare pea-green livery with light blue trimming and a three-cornered hat. Anna put up patiently with all her aunt's whims, gradually set to work on her sister's education, and was, it seemed, already getting reconciled to the idea of wasting her life in the wilds.... But destiny had decreed another fate for her. She chanced to be seen by Odintsov, a very wealthy man of forty-six, an eccentric hypochondriac, stout, heavy, and sour, but not stupid, and not ill-natured; he fell in love with her, and offered her his hand. She consented to become his wife, and he lived six years with her, and on his death settled all his property upon her. Anna Sergyevna remained in the country for nearly a year after his death; then she went abroad with her sister, but only stopped in Germany; she got tired of it, and came back to live at her favourite Nikolskoe, which was nearly thirty miles from the town of X——. There she had a magnificent, splendidly furnished house and a beautiful garden, with conservatories; her late husband had spared no expense to gratify his fancies. Anna Sergyevna went very rarely to the town, generally only on business, and even then she did not stay long. She was not liked in the province; there had been a fearful outcry at her marriage with Odintsov, all sorts of fictions were told about her; it was asserted that she had helped her father in his cardsharping tricks, and even that she had gone abroad for excellent reasons, that it had been necessary to conceal the lamentable consequences ... 'You understand?' the indignant gossips would wind up. 'She has gone through the fire,' was said of her; to which a noted provincial wit usually added: 'And through all the other elements?' All this talk reached her; but she turned a deaf ear to it; there was much independence and a good deal of determination in her character.

Madame Odintsov sat leaning back in her easy-chair, and listened with folded hands to Bazarov. He, contrary to his habit, was talking a good deal, and obviously trying to interest her—again a surprise for Arkady. He could not make up his mind whether Bazarov was attaining his object. It was difficult to conjecture from Anna Sergyevna's face what impression was being made on her; it retained the same expression, gracious and refined; her beautiful eyes were lighted up by attention, but by quiet attention. Bazarov's bad manners had impressed her unpleasantly for the first minutes of the visit like a bad smell or a discordant sound; but she saw at once that he was nervous, and that even flattered her. Nothing was repulsive to her but vulgarity, and no one could have accused Bazarov of vulgarity. Arkady was fated to meet with surprises that day. He had expected that Bazarov would talk to a clever woman like Madame Odintsov about his opinions and his views; she had herself expressed a desire to listen to the man 'who dares to have no belief in anything'; but, instead of that, Bazarov talked about medicine, about homoeopathy, and about botany. It turned out that Madame Odintsov had not wasted her time in solitude; she had read a good many excellent books, and spoke herself in excellent Russian. She turned the conversation upon music; but noticing that Bazarov did not appreciate art, she quietly brought it back to botany, even though Arkady was just launching into a discourse upon the significance of national melodies. Madame Odintsov treated him as though he were a younger brother; she seemed to appreciate his good-nature and youthful simplicity—and that was all. For over three hours, a lively conversation was kept up, ranging freely over various subjects.

The friends at last got up and began to take leave. Anna Sergyevna looked cordially at them, held out her beautiful, white hand to both, and, after a moment's thought, said with a doubtful but delightful smile. 'If you are not afraid of being dull, gentlemen, come and see me at Nikolskoe.'

'Oh, Anna Sergyevna,' cried Arkady, 'I shall think it the greatness happiness ...'

'And you, Monsieur Bazarov?'

Bazarov only bowed, and a last surprise was in store for Arkady; he noticed that his friend was blushing.

'Well?' he said to him in the street; 'are you still of the same opinion—that she's ...'

'Who can tell? See how correct she is!' retorted Bazarov; and after a brief pause he added, 'She's a perfect grand-duchess, a royal personage. She only needs a train on behind, and a crown on her head.'

'Our grand-duchesses don't talk Russian like that,' remarked Arkady.

'She's seen ups and downs, my dear boy; she's known what it is to be hard up!'

'Any way, she's charming,' observed Arkady.

'What a magnificent body!' pursued Bazarov. 'Shouldn't I like to see it on the dissecting-table.'

'Hush, for mercy's sake, Yevgeny! that's beyond everything.'

'Well, don't get angry, you baby. I meant it's first-rate. We must go to stay with her.'

'When?'

'Well, why not the day after to-morrow. What is there to do here? Drink champagne with Kukshina. Listen to your cousin, the Liberal dignitary?... Let's be off the day after to-morrow. By the way, too—my father's little place is not far from there. This Nikolskoe's on the S—— road, isn't it?'
'Yes.'
'Optime, why hesitate? leave that to fools and prigs! I say, what a splendid body!'
Three days later the two friends were driving along the road to Nikolskoe. The day was bright, and not too hot, and the sleek posting-horses trotted smartly along, switching their tied and plaited tails. Arkady looked at the road, and not knowing why, he smiled.
'Congratulate me,' cried Bazarov suddenly, 'to-day's the 22nd of June, my guardian angel's day. Let's see how he will watch over me. To-day they expect me home,' he added, dropping his voice.... 'Well, they can go on expecting.... What does it matter!'

CHAPTER XVI

The country-house in which Anna Sergyevna lived stood on an exposed hill at no great distance from a yellow stone church with a green roof, white columns, and a fresco over the principal entrance representing the 'Resurrection of Christ' in the 'Italian' style. Sprawling in the foreground of the picture was a swarthy warrior in a helmet, specially conspicuous for his rotund contours. Behind the church a long village stretched in two rows, with chimneys peeping out here and there above the thatched roofs. The manor-house was built in the same style as the church, the style known among us as that of Alexander; the house too was painted yellow, and had a green roof, and white columns, and a pediment with an escutcheon on it. The architect had designed both buildings with the approval of the deceased Odintsov, who could not endure—as he expressed it—idle and arbitrary innovations. The house was enclosed on both sides by the dark trees of an old garden; an avenue of lopped pines led up to the entrance.
Our friends were met in the hall by two tall footmen in livery; one of them at once ran for the steward. The steward, a stout man in a black dress coat, promptly appeared and led the visitors by a staircase covered with rugs to a special room, in which two bedsteads were already prepared for them with all necessaries for the toilet. It was clear that order reigned supreme in the house; everything was clean, everywhere there was a peculiar delicate fragrance, just as there is in the reception rooms of ministers.
'Anna Sergyevna asks you to come to her in half-an-hour,' the steward announced; 'will there be orders to give meanwhile?'
'No orders,' answered Bazarov; 'perhaps you will be so good as to trouble yourself to bring me a glass of vodka.'
'Yes, sir,' said the steward, looking in some perplexity, and he withdrew, his boots creaking as he walked.
'What *grand genre!'* remarked Bazarov. 'That's what it's called in your set, isn't it? She's a grand-duchess, and that's all about it.'
'A nice grand-duchess,' retorted Arkady, 'at the very first meeting she invited such great aristocrats as you and me to stay with her.'
'Especially me, a future doctor, and a doctor's son, and a village sexton's grandson.... You know, I suppose, I'm the grandson of a sexton? Like the great Speransky,' added Bazarov after a brief pause, contracting his lips. 'At any rate she likes to be comfortable; oh, doesn't she, this lady! Oughtn't we to put on evening dress?'
Arkady only shrugged his shoulders ... but he too was conscious of a little nervousness.
Half-an-hour later Bazarov and Arkady went together into the drawing-room. It was a large lofty room, furnished rather luxuriously but without particularly good taste. Heavy expensive furniture stood in the ordinary stiff arrangement along the walls, which were covered with cinnamon-coloured paper with gold flowers on it; Odintsov had ordered the furniture from Moscow through a friend and agent of his, a spirit

merchant. Over a sofa in the centre of one wall hung a portrait of a faded light-haired man—and it seemed to look with displeasure at the visitors. 'It must be the late lamented,' Bazarov whispered to Arkady, and turning up his nose, he added, 'Hadn't we better bolt ...?' But at that instant the lady of the house entered. She wore a light barège dress; her hair smoothly combed back behind her ears gave a girlish expression to her pure and fresh face.

'Thank you for keeping your promise,' she began. 'You must stay a little while with me; it's really not bad here. I will introduce you to my sister; she plays the piano well. That is a matter of indifference to you, Monsieur Bazarov; but you, I think, Monsieur Kirsanov, are fond of music. Besides my sister I have an old aunt living with me, and one of our neighbours comes in sometimes to play cards; that makes up all our circle. And now let us sit down.'

Madame Odintsov delivered all this little speech with peculiar precision, as though she had learned it by heart; then she turned to Arkady. It appeared that her mother had known Arkady's mother, and had even been her confidante in her love for Nikolai Petrovitch. Arkady began talking with great warmth of his dead mother; while Bazarov fell to turning over albums. 'What a tame cat I'm getting!' he was thinking to himself.

A beautiful greyhound with a blue collar on, ran into the drawing-room, tapping on the floor with his paws, and after him entered a girl of eighteen, black-haired and dark-skinned, with a rather round but pleasing face, and small dark eyes. In her hands she held a basket filled with flowers.

'This is my Katya,' said Madame Odintsov, indicating her with a motion of her head. Katya made a slight curtsey, placed herself beside her sister, and began picking out flowers. The greyhound, whose name was Fifi, went up to both of the visitors, in turn wagging his tail, and thrusting his cold nose into their hands.

'Did you pick all that yourself?' asked Madame Odintsov.

'Yes,' answered Katya.

'Is auntie coming to tea?'

'Yes.'

When Katya spoke, she had a very charming smile, sweet, timid, and candid, and looked up from under her eyebrows with a sort of humorous severity. Everything about her was still young and undeveloped; the voice, and the bloom on her whole face, and the rosy hands, with white palms, and the rather narrow shoulders.... She was constantly blushing and getting out of breath.

Madame Odintsov turned to Bazarov. 'You are looking at pictures from politeness, Yevgeny Vassilyitch,' she began. That does not interest you. You had better come nearer to us, and let us have a discussion about something.'

Bazarov went closer. 'What subject have you decided upon for discussion?' he said.

'What you like. I warn you, I am dreadfully argumentative.'

'You?'

'Yes. That seems to surprise you. Why?'

'Because, as far as I can judge, you have a calm, cool character, and one must be impulsive to be argumentative.'

'How can you have had time to understand me so soon? In the first place, I am impatient and obstinate—you should ask Katya; and secondly, I am very easily carried away.'

Bazarov looked at Anna Sergyevna. 'Perhaps; you must know best. And so you are inclined for a discussion—by all means. I was looking through the views of the Saxon mountains in your album, and you remarked that that couldn't interest me. You said so, because you suppose me to have no feeling for art, and as a fact I haven't any; but these views might be interesting to me from a geological standpoint, for the formation of the mountains, for instance.'

'Excuse me; but as a geologist, you would sooner have recourse to a book, to a special work on the subject, and not to a drawing.'

'The drawing shows me at a glance what would be spread over ten pages in a book.'

Anna Sergyevna was silent for a little.

'And so you haven't the least artistic feeling?' she observed, putting her elbow on the table, and by that very action bringing her face nearer to Bazarov. 'How can you get on without it?'

'Why, what is it wanted for, may I ask?'

'Well, at least to enable one to study and understand men.'

Bazarov smiled. 'In the first place, experience of life does that; and in the second, I assure you, studying separate individuals is not worth the trouble. All people are like one another, in soul as in body; each of us has brain, spleen, heart, and lungs made alike; and the so-called moral qualities are the same in all; the slight variations are of no importance. A single human specimen is sufficient to judge of all by. People are like trees in a forest; no botanist would think of studying each individual birch-tree.'

Katya, who was arranging the flowers, one at a time in a leisurely fashion, lifted her eyes to Bazarov with a puzzled look, and meeting his rapid and careless glance, she crimsoned up to her ears. Anna Sergyevna shook her head.

'The trees in a forest,' she repeated. 'Then according to you there is no difference between the stupid and the clever person, between the good-natured and ill-natured?'

'No, there is a difference, just as between the sick and the healthy. The lungs of a consumptive patient are not in the same condition as yours and mine, though they are made on the same plan. We know approximately what physical diseases come from; moral diseases come from bad education, from all the nonsense people's heads are stuffed with from childhood up, from the defective state of society; in short, reform society, and there will be no diseases.'

Bazarov said all this with an air, as though he were all the while thinking to himself, 'Believe me or not, as you like, it's all one to me!' He slowly passed his fingers over his whiskers, while his eyes strayed about the room.

'And you conclude,' observed Anna Sergyevna, 'that when society is reformed, there will be no stupid nor wicked people?'

'At any rate, in a proper organisation of society, it will be absolutely the same whether a man is stupid or clever, wicked or good.'

'Yes, I understand; they will all have the same spleen.'

'Precisely so, madam.'

Madame Odintsov turned to Arkady. 'And what is your opinion, Arkady Nikolaevitch?'

'I agree with Yevgeny,' he answered.

Katya looked up at him from under her eyelids.

'You amaze me, gentlemen,' commented Madame Odintsov, 'but we will have more talk together. But now I hear my aunt coming to tea; we must spare her.'

Anna Sergyevna's aunt, Princess H——, a thin little woman with a pinched-up face, drawn together like a fist, and staring ill-natured-looking eyes under a grey front, came in, and, scarcely bowing to the guests, she dropped into a wide velvet covered arm-chair, upon which no one but herself was privileged to sit. Katya put a footstool under her feet; the old lady did not thank her, did not even look at her, only her hands shook under the yellow shawl, which almost covered her feeble body. The Princess liked yellow; her cap, too, had bright yellow ribbons.

'How have you slept, aunt?' inquired Madame Odintsov, raising her voice.

'That dog in here again,' the old lady muttered in reply, and noticing Fifi was making two hesitating steps in her direction, she cried, 'Ss——ss!'

Katya called Fifi and opened the door for him.

Fifi rushed out delighted, in the expectation of being taken out for a walk; but when he was left alone outside the door, he began scratching and whining. The princess scowled. Katya was about to go out....

'I expect tea is ready,' said Madame Odintsov.

'Come gentlemen; aunt, will you go in to tea?'

The princess got up from her chair without speaking and led the way out of the drawing-room. They all followed her in to the dining-room. A little page in livery drew back, with a scraping sound, from the table, an arm-chair covered with cushions, devoted to the princess's use; she sank into it; Katya in pouring out the tea handed her first a cup emblazoned with a heraldic crest. The old lady put some honey in her cup (she considered it both sinful and extravagant to drink tea with sugar in it, though she never spent a farthing herself on anything), and suddenly asked in a hoarse voice, 'And what does Prince Ivan write?'

No one made her any reply. Bazarov and Arkady soon guessed that they paid no attention to her though they treated her respectfully.

'Because of her grand family,' thought Bazarov....

After tea, Anna Sergyevna suggested they should go out for a walk; but it began to rain a little, and the whole party, with the exception of the princess, returned to the drawing-room. The neighbour, the devoted card-player, arrived; his name was Porfiry Platonitch, a stoutish, greyish man with short, spindly legs, very polite and ready to be amused. Anna Sergyevna, who still talked principally with Bazarov, asked him whether he'd like to try a contest with them in the old-fashioned way at preference? Bazarov assented, saying 'that he ought to prepare himself beforehand for the duties awaiting him as a country doctor.'

'You must be careful,' observed Anna Sergyevna; 'Porfiry Platonitch and I will beat you. And you, Katya,' she added, 'play something to Arkady Nikolaevitch; he is fond of music, and we can listen, too.'
Katya went unwillingly to the piano; and Arkady, though he certainly was fond of music, unwillingly followed her; it seemed to him that Madame Odintsov was sending him away, and already, like every young man at his age, he felt a vague and oppressive emotion surging up in his heart, like the forebodings of love.
Katya raised the top of the piano, and not looking at Arkady, she said in a low voice—
'What am I to play you?'
'What you like,' answered Arkady indifferently.
'What sort of music do you like best?' repeated Katya, without changing her attitude.
'Classical,' Arkady answered in the same tone of voice.
'Do you like Mozart?'
'Yes, I like Mozart.'
Katya pulled out Mozart's Sonata-Fantasia in C minor. She played very well, though rather over correctly and precisely. She sat upright and immovable, her eyes fixed on the notes, and her lips tightly compressed, only at the end of the sonata her face glowed, her hair came loose, and a little lock fell on to her dark brow. Arkady was particularly struck by the last part of the sonata, the part in which, in the midst of the bewitching gaiety of the careless melody, the pangs of such mournful, almost tragic suffering, suddenly break in.... But the ideas stirred in him by Mozart's music had no reference to Katya. Looking at her, he simply thought, 'Well, that young lady doesn't play badly, and she's not bad-looking either.'
When she had finished the sonata, Katya without taking her hands from the keys, asked, 'Is that enough?' Arkady declared that he could not venture to trouble her again, and began talking to her about Mozart; he asked her whether she had chosen that sonata herself, or some one had recommended it to her. But Katya answered him in monosyllables; she withdrew into herself, went back into her shell. When this happened to her, she did not very quickly come out again; her face even assumed at such times an obstinate, almost stupid expression. She was not exactly shy, but diffident, and rather overawed by her sister, who had educated her, and who had no suspicion of the fact. Arkady was reduced at last to calling Fifi to him, and with an affable smile patting him on the head to give himself an appearance of being at home.
Katya set to work again upon her flowers.
Bazarov meanwhile was losing and losing. Anna Sergyevna played cards in masterly fashion; Porfiry Platonitch, too, could hold his own in the game. Bazarov lost a sum which, though trifling in itself, was not altogether pleasant for him. At supper Anna Sergyevna again turned the conversation on botany.
'We will go for a walk to-morrow morning,' she said to him; 'I want you to teach me the Latin names of the wild flowers and their species.'
'What use are the Latin names to you?' asked Bazarov.
'Order is needed in everything,' she answered.
'What an exquisite woman Anna Sergyevna is!' cried Arkady, when he was alone with his friend in the room assigned to them.
'Yes,' answered Bazarov, 'a female with brains. Yes, and she's seen life too.'
'In what sense do you mean that, Yevgeny Vassilyitch?'
'In a good sense, a good sense, my dear friend, Arkady Nikolaevitch! I'm convinced she manages her estate capitally too. But what's splendid is not her, but her sister.'
'What, that little dark thing?'
'Yes, that little dark thing. She now is fresh and untouched, and shy and silent, and anything you like. She's worth educating and developing. You might make something fine out of her; but the other's—a stale loaf.'
Arkady made no reply to Bazarov, and each of them got into bed with rather singular thoughts in his head.
Anna Sergyevna, too, thought of her guests that evening. She liked Bazarov for the absence of gallantry in him, and even for his sharply defined views. She found in him something new, which she had not chanced to meet before, and she was curious.
Anna Sergyevna was a rather strange creature. Having no prejudices of any kind, having no strong convictions even, she never gave way or went out of her way for anything. She had seen many things very clearly; she had been interested in many things, but nothing had completely satisfied her; indeed, she hardly desired complete satisfaction. Her intellect was at the same time inquiring and indifferent; her doubts were never soothed to forgetfulness, and they never grew strong enough to distract her. Had she not been rich and independent, she would perhaps have thrown herself into the struggle, and have known passion. But life was easy for her, though she was bored at times, and she went on passing day after day with deliberation, never in

a hurry, placid, and only rarely disturbed. Dreams sometimes danced in rainbow colours before her eyes even, but she breathed more freely when they died away, and did not regret them. Her imagination indeed overstepped the limits of what is reckoned permissible by conventional morality; but even then her blood flowed as quietly as ever in her fascinatingly graceful, tranquil body. Sometimes coming out of her fragrant bath all warm and enervated, she would fall to musing on the nothingness of life, the sorrow, the labour, the malice of it.... Her soul would be filled with sudden daring, and would flow with generous ardour, but a draught would blow from a half-closed window, and Anna Sergyevna would shrink into herself, and feel plaintive and almost angry, and there was only one thing she cared for at that instant—to get away from that horrid draught.

Like all women who have not succeeded in loving, she wanted something, without herself knowing what. Strictly speaking, she wanted nothing; but it seemed to her that she wanted everything. She could hardly endure the late Odintsov (she had married him from prudential motives, though probably she would not have consented to become his wife if she had not considered him a good sort of man), and had conceived a secret repugnance for all men, whom she could only figure to herself as slovenly, heavy, drowsy, and feebly importunate creatures. Once, somewhere abroad, she had met a handsome young Swede, with a chivalrous expression, with honest blue eyes under an open brow; he had made a powerful impression on her, but it had not prevented her from going back to Russia.

'A strange man this doctor!' she thought as she lay in her luxurious bed on lace pillows under a light silk coverlet.... Anna Sergyevna had inherited from her father a little of his inclination for splendour. She had fondly loved her sinful but good-natured father, and he had idolised her, used to joke with her in a friendly way as though she were an equal, and to confide in her fully, to ask her advice. Her mother she scarcely remembered.

'This doctor is a strange man!' she repeated to herself. She stretched, smiled, clasped her hands behind her head, then ran her eyes over two pages of a stupid French novel, dropped the book—and fell asleep, all pure and cold, in her pure and fragrant linen.

The following morning Anna Sergyevna went off botanising with Bazarov directly after lunch, and returned just before dinner; Arkady did not go off anywhere, and spent about an hour with Katya. He was not bored with her; she offered of herself to repeat the sonata of the day before; but when Madame Odintsov came back at last, when he caught sight of her, he felt an instantaneous pang at his heart. She came through the garden with a rather tired step; her cheeks were glowing and her eyes shining more brightly than usual under her round straw hat. She was twirling in her fingers the thin stalk of a wildflower, a light mantle had slipped down to her elbows, and the wide gray ribbons of her hat were clinging to her bosom. Bazarov walked behind her, self-confident and careless as usual, but the expression of his face, cheerful and even friendly as it was, did not please Arkady. Muttering between his teeth, 'Good-morning!' Bazarov went away to his room, while Madame Odintsov shook Arkady's hand abstractedly, and also walked past him.

'Good-morning!' thought Arkady ... 'As though we had not seen each other already to-day!'

CHAPTER XVII

Time, it is well known, sometimes flies like a bird, sometimes crawls like a worm; but man is wont to be particularly happy when he does not even notice whether it passes quickly or slowly. It was in that way Arkady and Bazarov spent a fortnight at Madame Odintsov's. The good order she had established in her house and in her life partly contributed to this result. She adhered strictly to this order herself, and forced others to submit to it. Everything during the day was done at a fixed time. In the morning, precisely at eight o'clock, all the party assembled for tea; from morning-tea till lunch-time every one did what he pleased, the hostess herself was engaged with her bailiff (the estate was on the rent-system), her steward, and her head housekeeper. Before dinner the party met again for conversation or reading; the evening was devoted to walking, cards, and music; at half-past ten Anna Sergyevna retired to her own room, gave her orders for the following day, and went to bed. Bazarov did not like this measured, somewhat ostentatious punctuality in daily life, 'like moving along rails,' he pronounced it to be; the footmen in livery, the decorous stewards, offended his democratic sentiments. He declared that if one went so far, one might as well dine in the English style at once—in tail-coats and white ties. He once spoke plainly upon the subject to Anna Sergyevna. Her attitude was such that no one hesitated to speak his mind freely before her. She heard him out; and then her comment was, 'From your point of view, you are right—and perhaps, in that respect, I am too much of a lady; but there's no living in the country without order, one would be devoured by ennui,' and she continued to go her own way. Bazarov grumbled, but the very reason life was so easy for him and Arkady at Madame Odintsov's was that everything in the house 'moved on rails.' For all that, a change had taken place in both the young men since the first days of their stay at Nikolskoe. Bazarov, in whom Anna Sergyevna was obviously interested, though she seldom agreed with him, began to show signs of an unrest, unprecedented in him; he was easily put out of temper, and unwilling to talk, he looked irritated, and could not sit still in one place, just as though he were possessed by some secret longing; while Arkady, who had made up his mind conclusively that he was in love with Madame Odintsov, had begun to yield to a gentle melancholy. This melancholy did not, however, prevent him from becoming friendly with Katya; it even impelled him to get into friendly, affectionate terms with her. '*She* does not appreciate me? So be it!... But here is a good creature, who does not repulse me,' he thought, and his heart again knew the sweetness of magnanimous emotions. Katya vaguely realised that he was seeking a sort of consolation in her company, and did not deny him or herself the innocent pleasure of a half-shy, half-confidential friendship. They did not talk to each other in Anna Sergyevna's presence; Katya always shrank into herself under her sister's sharp eyes; while Arkady, as befits a man in love, could pay attention to nothing else when near the object of his passion; but he was happy with Katya alone. He was conscious that he did not possess the power to interest Madame Odintsov; he was shy and at a loss when he was left alone with her, and she did not know what to say to him, he was too young for her. With Katya, on the other hand, Arkady felt at home; he treated her condescendingly, encouraged her to express the impressions made on her by music, reading novels, verses, and other such trifles, without noticing or realising that these trifles were what interested him too. Katya, on her side, did not try to drive away melancholy. Arkady was at his ease with Katya, Madame Odintsov with Bazarov, and thus it usually came to pass that the two couples, after being a little while together, went off on their separate ways, especially during the walks. Katya adored nature, and Arkady loved it, though he did not dare to acknowledge it; Madame Odintsov was, like Bazarov, rather indifferent to the beauties of nature. The almost continual separation of the two friends was not without its consequences; the relations between them began to change. Bazarov gave up talking to Arkady about Madame Odintsov, gave up even abusing her 'aristocratic ways'; Katya, it is true, he praised as before, and only advised him to restrain her sentimental tendencies, but his praises were hurried, his advice dry, and in general he talked less to Arkady than before ... he seemed to avoid him, seemed ill at ease with him.

Arkady observed it all, but he kept his observations to himself.

The real cause of all this 'newness' was the feeling inspired in Bazarov by Madame Odintsov, a feeling which tortured and maddened him, and which he would at once have denied, with scornful laughter and cynical abuse, if any one had ever so remotely hinted at the possibility of what was taking place in him. Bazarov had a great love for women and for feminine beauty; but love in the ideal, or, as he expressed it, romantic sense, he called lunacy, unpardonable imbecility; he regarded chivalrous sentiments as something of the nature of deformity or disease, and had more than once expressed his wonder that Toggenburg and all the minnesingers and troubadours had not been put into a lunatic asylum. 'If a woman takes your fancy,' he used to say, 'try and gain your end; but if you can't—well, turn your back on her—there are lots of good fish in the sea.' Madame Odintsov had taken his fancy; the rumours about her, the freedom and independence of her ideas, her unmistakable liking for him, all seemed to be in his favour, but he soon saw that with her he would not 'gain his ends,' and to turn his back on her he found, to his own bewilderment, beyond his power. His blood was on fire directly if he merely thought of her; he could easily have mastered his blood, but something else was taking root in him, something he had never admitted, at which he had always jeered, at which all his pride revolted. In his conversations with Anna Sergyevna he expressed more strongly than ever his calm contempt for everything idealistic; but when he was alone, with indignation he recognised idealism in himself. Then he would set off to the forest and walk with long strides about it, smashing the twigs that came in his way, and cursing under his breath both her and himself; or he would get into the hay-loft in the

barn, and, obstinately closing his eyes, try to force himself to sleep, in which, of course, he did not always succeed. Suddenly his fancy would bring before him those chaste hands twining one day about his neck, those proud lips responding to his kisses, those intellectual eyes dwelling with tenderness—yes, with tenderness—on his, and his head went round, and he forgot himself for an instant, till indignation boiled up in him again. He caught himself in all sorts of 'shameful' thoughts, as though he were driven on by a devil mocking him. Sometimes he fancied that there was a change taking place in Madame Odintsov too; that there were signs in the expression of her face of something special; that, perhaps ... but at that point he would stamp, or grind his teeth, and clench his fists.
Meanwhile Bazarov was not altogether mistaken. He had struck Madame Odintsov's imagination; he interested her, she thought a great deal about him. In his absence, she was not dull, she was not impatient for his coming, but she always grew more lively on his appearance; she liked to be left alone with him, and she liked talking to him, even when he irritated her or offended her taste, her refined habits. She was, as it were, eager at once to sound him and to analyse herself.
One day walking in the garden with her, he suddenly announced, in a surly voice, that he intended going to his father's place very soon.... She turned white, as though something had given her a pang, and such a pang, that she wondered and pondered long after, what could be the meaning of it. Bazarov had spoken of his departure with no idea of putting her to the test, of seeing what would come of it; he never 'fabricated.' On the morning of that day he had an interview with his father's bailiff, who had taken care of him when he was a child, Timofeitch. This Timofeitch, a little old man of much experience and astuteness, with faded yellow hair, a weather-beaten red face, and tiny tear-drops in his shrunken eyes, unexpectedly appeared before Bazarov, in his shortish overcoat of stout greyish-blue cloth, girt with a strip of leather, and in tarred boots.
'Hullo, old man; how are you?' cried Bazarov.
'How do you do, Yevgeny Vassilyitch?' began the little old man, and he smiled with delight, so that his whole face was all at once covered with wrinkles.
'What have you come for? They sent for me, eh?'
'Upon my word, sir, how could we?' mumbled Timofeitch. (He remembered the strict injunctions he had received from his master on starting.) 'We were sent to the town on business, and we'd heard news of your honour, so here we turned off on our way, that's to say—to have a look at your honour ... as if we could think of disturbing you!'
'Come, don't tell lies!' Bazarov cut him short. 'Is this the road to the town, do you mean to tell me?' Timofeitch hesitated, and made no answer. 'Is my father well?'
'Thank God, yes.'
'And my mother?'
'Anna Vlasyevna too, glory be to God.'
'They are expecting me, I suppose?'
The little old man held his tiny head on one side.
'Ah, Yevgeny Vassilyitch, it makes one's heart ache to see them; it does really.'
'Come, all right, all right! shut up! Tell them I'm coming soon.'
'Yes, sir,' answered Timofeitch, with a sigh.
As he went out of the house, he pulled his cap down on his head with both hands, clambered into a wretched-looking racing droshky, and went off at a trot, but not in the direction of the town.
On the evening of the same day, Madame Odintsov was sitting in her own room with Bazarov, while Arkady walked up and down the hall listening to Katya's playing. The princess had gone upstairs to her own room; she could not bear guests as a rule, and 'especially this new riff-raff lot,' as she called them. In the common rooms she only sulked; but she made up for it in her own room by breaking out into such abuse before her maid that the cap danced on her head, wig and all. Madame Odintsov was well aware of all this.
'How is it you are proposing to leave us?' she began; 'how about your promise?'
Bazarov started. 'What promise?'
'Have you forgotten? You meant to give me some lessons in chemistry.'
'It can't be helped! My father expects me; I can't loiter any longer. However, you can read Pelouse et Frémy, *Notions générales de Chimie;* it's a good book, and clearly written. You will find everything you need in it.'
'But do you remember; you assured me a book cannot take the place of ... I've forgotten how you put it, but you know what I mean ... do you remember?'
'It can't be helped!' repeated Bazarov.

'Why go away?' said Madame Odintsov, dropping her voice.
He glanced at her. Her head had fallen on to the back of her easy-chair, and her arms, bare to the elbow, were folded on her bosom. She seemed paler in the light of the single lamp covered with a perforated paper shade. An ample white gown hid her completely in its soft folds; even the tips of her feet, also crossed, were hardly seen.
'And why stay?' answered Bazarov.
Madame Odintsov turned her head slightly. 'You ask why. Have you not enjoyed yourself with me? Or do you suppose you will not be missed here?'
'I am sure of it.'
Madame Odintsov was silent a minute. 'You are wrong in thinking that. But I don't believe you. You could not say that seriously.' Bazarov still sat immovable. 'Yevgeny Vassilyitch, why don't you speak?'
'Why, what am I to say to you? People are not generally worth being missed, and I less than most.'
'Why so?'
'I'm a practical, uninteresting person. I don't know how to talk.'
'You are fishing, Yevgeny Vassilyitch.'
'That's not a habit of mine. Don't you know yourself that I've nothing in common with the elegant side of life, the side you prize so much?'
Madame Odintsov bit the corner of her handkerchief.
'You may think what you like, but I shall be dull when you go away.'
'Arkady will remain,' remarked Bazarov. Madame Odintsov shrugged her shoulders slightly. 'I shall be dull,' she repeated.
'Really? In any case you will not feel dull for long.'
'What makes you suppose that?'
'Because you told me yourself that you are only dull when your regular routine is broken in upon. You have ordered your existence with such unimpeachable regularity that there can be no place in it for dulness or sadness ... for any unpleasant emotions.'
'And do you consider I am so unimpeachable ... that's to say, that I have ordered my life with such regularity?'
'I should think so. Here's an example; in a few minutes it will strike ten, and I know beforehand that you will drive me away.'
'No; I'm not going to drive you away, Yevgeny Vassilyitch. You may stay. Open that window.... I feel half-stifled.'
Bazarov got up and gave a push to the window. It flew up with a loud crash.... He had not expected it to open so easily; besides, his hands were shaking. The soft, dark night looked in to the room with its almost black sky, its faintly rustling trees, and the fresh fragrance of the pure open air.
'Draw the blind and sit down,' said Madame Odintsov; 'I want to have a talk with you before you go away. Tell me something about yourself; you never talk about yourself.'
'I try to talk to you upon improving subjects, Anna Sergyevna.'
'You are very modest.... But I should like to know something about you, about your family, about your father, for whom you are forsaking us.'
'Why is she talking like that?' thought Bazarov.
'All that's not in the least interesting,' he uttered aloud, 'especially for you; we are obscure people....'
'And you regard me as an aristocrat?'
Bazarov lifted his eyes to Madame Odintsov.
'Yes,' he said, with exaggerated sharpness.
She smiled. 'I see you know me very little, though you do maintain that all people are alike, and it's not worth while to study them. I will tell you my life some time or other ... but first you tell me yours.'
'I know you very little,' repeated Bazarov. 'Perhaps you are right; perhaps, really, every one is a riddle. You, for instance; you avoid society, you are oppressed by it, and you have invited two students to stay with you. What makes you, with your intellect, with your beauty, live in the country?'
'What? What was it you said?' Madame Odintsov interposed eagerly. 'With my ... beauty?'
Bazarov scowled. 'Never mind that,' he muttered; 'I meant to say that I don't exactly understand why you have settled in the country?'
'You don't understand it.... But you explain it to yourself in some way?'

'Yes ... I assume that you remain continually in the same place because you indulge yourself, because you are very fond of comfort and ease, and very indifferent to everything else.'

Madame Odintsov smiled again. 'You would absolutely refuse to believe that I am capable of being carried away by anything?'

Bazarov glanced at her from under his brows.

'By curiosity, perhaps; but not otherwise.'

'Really? Well, now I understand why we are such friends; you are just like me, you see.'

'We are such friends ...' Bazarov articulated in a choked voice.

'Yes!... Why, I'd forgotten you wanted to go away.'

Bazarov got up. The lamp burnt dimly in the middle of the dark, luxurious, isolated room; from time to time the blind was shaken, and there flowed in the freshness of the insidious night; there was heard its mysterious whisperings. Madame Odintsov did not move in a single limb; but she was gradually possessed by concealed emotion.

It communicated itself to Bazarov. He was suddenly conscious that he was alone with a young and lovely woman....

'Where are you going?' she said slowly.

He answered nothing, and sank into a chair.

'And so you consider me a placid, pampered, spoiled creature,' she went on in the same voice, never taking her eyes off the window. 'While I know so much about myself, that I am unhappy.'

'You unhappy? What for? Surely you can't attach any importance to idle gossip?'

Madame Odintsov frowned. It annoyed her that he had given such a meaning to her words.

'Such gossip does not affect me, Yevgeny Vassilyitch, and I am too proud to allow it to disturb me. I am unhappy because ... I have no desires, no passion for life. You look at me incredulously; you think that's said by an "aristocrat," who is all in lace, and sitting in a velvet armchair. I don't conceal the fact: I love what you call comfort, and at the same time I have little desire to live. Explain that contradiction as best you can. But all that's romanticism in your eyes.'

Bazarov shook his head. 'You are in good health, independent, rich; what more would you have? What do you want?'

'What do I want,' echoed Madame Odintsov, and she sighed, 'I am very tired, I am old, I feel as if I have had a very long life. Yes, I am old,' she added, softly drawing the ends of her lace over her bare arms. Her eyes met Bazarov's eyes, and she faintly blushed. 'Behind me I have already so many memories: my life in Petersburg, wealth, then poverty, then my father's death, marriage, then the inevitable tour in due order.... So many memories, and nothing to remember, and before me, before me—a long, long road, and no goal.... I have no wish to go on.'

'Are you so disillusioned?' queried Bazarov.

'No, but I am dissatisfied,' Madame Odintsov replied, dwelling on each syllable. 'I think if I could interest myself strongly in something....'

'You want to fall in love,' Bazarov interrupted her, 'and you can't love; that's where your unhappiness lies.'

Madame Odintsov began to examine the sleeve of her lace.

'Is it true I can't love?' she said.

'I should say not! Only I was wrong in calling that an unhappiness. On the contrary, any one's more to be pitied when such a mischance befalls him.'

'Mischance, what?'

'Falling in love.'

'And how do you come to know that?'

'By hearsay,' answered Bazarov angrily.

'You're flirting,' he thought; 'you're bored, and teasing me for want of something to do, while I ...' His heart really seemed as though it were being torn to pieces.

'Besides, you are perhaps too exacting,' he said, bending his whole frame forward and playing with the fringe of the chair.

'Perhaps. My idea is everything or nothing. A life for a life. Take mine, give up thine, and that without regret or turning back. Or else better have nothing.'

'Well?' observed Bazarov; 'that's fair terms, and I'm surprised that so far you ... have not found what you wanted.'

'And do you think it would be easy to give oneself up wholly to anything whatever?'

'Not easy, if you begin reflecting, waiting and attaching value to yourself, prizing yourself, I mean; but to give oneself up without reflection is very easy.'
'How can one help prizing oneself? If I am of no value, who could need my devotion?'
'That's not my affair; that's the other's business to discover what is my value. The chief thing is to be able to devote oneself.'
Madame Odintsov bent forward from the back of her chair. 'You speak,' she began, 'as though you had experienced all that.'
'It happened to come up, Anna Sergyevna; all that, as you know, is not in my line.'
'But you could devote yourself?'
'I don't know. I shouldn't like to boast.'
Madame Odintsov said nothing, and Bazarov was mute. The sounds of the piano floated up to them from the drawing-room.
'How is it Katya is playing so late?' observed Madame Odintsov.
Bazarov got up. 'Yes, it is really late now; it's time for you to go to bed.'
'Wait a little; why are you in a hurry?... I want to say one word to you.'
'What is it?'
'Wait a little,' whispered Madame Odintsov. Her eyes rested on Bazarov; it seemed as though she were examining him attentively.
He walked across the room, then suddenly went up to her, hurriedly said 'Good-bye,' squeezed her hand so that she almost screamed, and was gone. She raised her crushed fingers to her lips, breathed on them, and suddenly, impulsively getting up from her low chair, she moved with rapid steps towards the door, as though she wished to bring Bazarov back.... A maid came into the room with a decanter on a silver tray. Madame Odintsov stood still, told her she could go, and sat down again, and again sank into thought. Her hair slipped loose and fell in a dark coil down her shoulders. Long after the lamp was still burning in Anna Sergyevna's room, and for long she stayed without moving, only from time to time chafing her hands, which ached a little from the cold of the night.
Bazarov went back two hours later to his bed-room with his boots wet with dew, dishevelled and ill-humoured. He found Arkady at the writing-table with a book in his hands, his coat buttoned up to the throat.
'You're not in bed yet?' he said, in a tone, it seemed, of annoyance.
'You stopped a long while with Anna Sergyevna this evening,' remarked Arkady, not answering him.
'Yes, I stopped with her all the while you were playing the piano with Katya Sergyevna.'
'I did not play ...' Arkady began, and he stopped. He felt the tears were coming into his eyes, and he did not like to cry before his sarcastic friend.

CHAPTER XVIII

The following morning when Madame Odintsov came down to morning tea, Bazarov sat a long while bending over his cup, then suddenly he glanced up at her.... She turned to him as though he had struck her a blow, and he fancied that her face was a little paler since the night before. She quickly went off to her own room, and did not appear till lunch. It rained from early morning; there was no possibility of going for a walk. The whole company assembled in the drawing-room. Arkady took up the new number of a journal and began reading it aloud. The princess, as was her habit, tried to express her amazement in her face, as though he were doing something improper, then glared angrily at him; but he paid no attention to her.
'Yevgeny Vassilyitch' said Anna Sergyevna, 'come to my room.... I want to ask you.... You mentioned a textbook yesterday ...'

She got up and went to the door. The princess looked round with an expression that seemed to say, 'Look at me; see how shocked I am!' and again glared at Arkady; but he raised his voice, and exchanging glances with Katya, near whom he was sitting, he went on reading.
Madame Odintsov went with rapid steps to her study. Bazarov followed her quickly, not raising his eyes, and only with his ears catching the delicate swish and rustle of her silk gown gliding before him. Madame Odintsov sank into the same easy-chair in which she had sat the previous evening, and Bazarov took up the same position as before.
'What was the name of that book?' she began, after a brief silence.
'Pelouse et Frémy, *Notions générales,'* answered Bazarov. 'I might though recommend you also Ganot, *Traité élémentaire de physique éxpérimentale*. In that book the illustrations are clearer, and in general it's a text-book.'
Madame Odintsov stretched out her hand. 'Yevgeny Vassilyitch, I beg your pardon, but I didn't invite you in here to discuss text-books. I wanted to continue our conversation of last night. You went away so suddenly.... It will not bore you ...'
'I am at your service, Anna Sergyevna. But what were we talking about last night?'
Madame Odintsov flung a sidelong glance at Bazarov.
'We were talking of happiness, I believe. I told you about myself. By the way, I mentioned the word "happiness." Tell me why it is that even when we are enjoying music, for instance, or a fine evening, or a conversation with sympathetic people, it all seems an intimation of some measureless happiness existing apart somewhere rather than actual happiness—such, I mean, as we ourselves are in possession of? Why is it? Or perhaps you have no feeling like that?'
'You know the saying, "Happiness is where we are not,"' replied Bazarov; 'besides, you told me yesterday you are discontented. I certainly never have such ideas come into my head.'
'Perhaps they seem ridiculous to you?'
'No; but they don't come into my head.'
'Really? Do you know, I should very much like to know what you do think about?'
'What? I don't understand.'
'Listen; I have long wanted to speak openly to you. There's no need to tell you—you are conscious of it yourself—that you are not an ordinary man; you are still young—all life is before you. What are you preparing yourself for? What future is awaiting you? I mean to say—what object do you want to attain? What are you going forward to? What is in your heart? in short, who are you? What are you?'
'You surprise me, Anna Sergyevna. You are aware that I am studying natural science, and who I ...'
'Well, who are you?'
'I have explained to you already that I am going to be a district doctor.'
Anna Sergyevna made a movement of impatience.
'What do you say that for? You don't believe it yourself. Arkady might answer me in that way, but not you.'
'Why, in what is Arkady ...'
'Stop! Is it possible you could content yourself with such a humble career, and aren't you always maintaining yourself that you don't believe in medicine? You—with your ambition—a district doctor! You answer me like that to put me off, because you have no confidence in me. But, do you know, Yevgeny Vassilyitch, that I could understand you; I have been poor myself, and ambitious, like you; I have been perhaps through the same trials as you.'
'That is all very well, Anna Sergyevna, but you must pardon me for ... I am not in the habit of talking freely about myself at any time as a rule, and between you and me there is such a gulf ...'
'What sort of gulf? You mean to tell me again that I am an aristocrat? No more of that, Yevgeny Vassilyitch; I thought I had proved to you ...'
'And even apart from that,' broke in Bazarov, 'what could induce one to talk and think about the future, which for the most part does not depend on us? If a chance turns up of doing something—so much the better; and if it doesn't turn up—at least one will be glad one didn't gossip idly about it beforehand.'
'You call a friendly conversation idle gossip?... Or perhaps you consider me as a woman unworthy of your confidence? I know you despise us all.'
'I don't despise you, Anna Sergyevna, and you know that.'
'No, I don't know anything ... but let us suppose so. I understand your disinclination to talk of your future career; but as to what is taking place within you now ...'

'Taking place!' repeated Bazarov, 'as though I were some sort of government or society! In any case, it is utterly uninteresting; and besides, can a man always speak of everything that "takes place" in him?'

'Why, I don't see why you can't speak freely of everything you have in your heart.'

'Can *you?'* asked Bazarov.

'Yes,' answered Anna Sergyevna, after a brief hesitation.

Bazarov bowed his head. 'You are more fortunate than I am.'

Anna Sergyevna looked at him questioningly. 'As you please,' she went on, 'but still something tells me that we have not come together for nothing; that we shall be great friends. I am sure this—what should I say, constraint, reticence in you will vanish at last.'

'So you have noticed reticence ... as you expressed it ... constraint?'

'Yes.'

Bazarov got up and went to the window. 'And would you like to know the reason of this reticence? Would you like to know what is passing within me?'

'Yes,' repeated Madame Odintsov, with a sort of dread she did not at the time understand.

'And you will not be angry?'

'No.'

'No?' Bazarov was standing with his back to her. 'Let me tell you then that I love you like a fool, like a madman.... There, you've forced it out of me.'

Madame Odintsov held both hands out before her; but Bazarov was leaning with his forehead pressed against the window pane. He breathed hard; his whole body was visibly trembling. But it was not the tremor of youthful timidity, not the sweet alarm of the first declaration that possessed him; it was passion struggling in him, strong and painful—passion not unlike hatred, and perhaps akin to it.... Madame Odintsov felt both afraid and sorry for him.

'Yevgeny Vassilyitch!' she said, and there was the ring of unconscious tenderness in her voice.

He turned quickly, flung a searching look on her, and snatching both her hands, he drew her suddenly to his breast.

She did not at once free herself from his embrace, but an instant later, she was standing far away in a corner, and looking from there at Bazarov. He rushed at her ...

'You have misunderstood me,' she whispered hurriedly, in alarm. It seemed if he had made another step she would have screamed.... Bazarov bit his lips, and went out.

Half-an-hour after, a maid gave Anna Sergyevna a note from Bazarov; it consisted simply of one line: 'Am I to go to-day, or can I stop till to-morrow?'

'Why should you go? I did not understand you—you did not understand me,' Anna Sergyevna answered him, but to herself she thought: 'I did not understand myself either.'

She did not show herself till dinner-time, and kept walking to and fro in her room, stopping sometimes at the window, sometimes at the looking-glass, and slowly rubbing her handkerchief over her neck, on which she still seemed to feel a burning spot. She asked herself what had induced her to 'force' Bazarov's words, his confidence, and whether she had suspected nothing ... 'I am to blame,' she decided aloud, 'but I could not have foreseen this.' She fell to musing, and blushed crimson, remembering Bazarov's almost animal face when he had rushed at her....

'Oh?' she uttered suddenly aloud, and she stopped short and shook back her curls.... She caught sight of herself in the glass; her head thrown back, with a mysterious smile on the half-closed, half-opened eyes and lips, told her, it seemed, in a flash something at which she herself was confused....

'No,' she made up her mind at last. 'God knows what it would lead to; he couldn't be played with; peace is anyway the best thing in the world.'

Her peace of mind was not shaken; but she felt gloomy, and even shed a few tears once though she could not have said why—certainly not for the insult done her. She did not feel insulted; she was more inclined to feel guilty. Under the influence of various vague emotions, the sense of life passing by, the desire of novelty, she had forced herself to go up to a certain point, forced herself to look behind herself, and had seen behind her not even an abyss, but what was empty ... or revolting.

CHAPTER XIX

Great as was Madame Odintsov's self-control, and superior as she was to every kind of prejudice, she felt awkward when she went into the dining-room to dinner. The meal went off fairly successfully, however. Porfiry Platonovitch made his appearance and told various anecdotes; he had just come back from the town. Among other things, he informed them that the governor had ordered his secretaries on special commissions to wear spurs, in case he might send them off anywhere for greater speed on horseback. Arkady talked in an undertone to Katya, and diplomatically attended to the princess's wants. Bazarov maintained a grim and obstinate silence. Madame Odintsov looked at him twice, not stealthily, but straight in the face, which was bilious and forbidding, with downcast eyes, and contemptuous determination stamped on every feature, and thought: 'No ... no ... no.' ... After dinner, she went with the whole company into the garden, and seeing that Bazarov wanted to speak to her, she took a few steps to one side and stopped. He went up to her, but even then did not raise his eyes, and said hoarsely—

'I have to apologise to you, Anna Sergyevna. You must be in a fury with me.'

'No, I'm not angry with you, Yevgeny Vassilyitch,' answered Madame Odintsov; 'but I am sorry.'

'So much the worse. Any way, I'm sufficiently punished. My position, you will certainly agree, is most foolish. You wrote to me, "Why go away?" But I cannot stay, and don't wish to. To-morrow I shall be gone.'

'Yevgeny Vassilyitch, why are you ...'

'Why am I going away?'

'No; I didn't mean to say that.'

'There's no recalling the past, Anna Sergyevna ... and this was bound to come about sooner or later. Consequently I must go. I can only conceive of one condition upon which I could remain; but that condition will never be. Excuse my impertinence, but you don't love me, and you never will love me, I suppose?'

Bazarov's eyes glittered for an instant under their dark brows.

Anna Sergyevna did not answer him. 'I'm afraid of this man,' flashed through her brain.

'Good-bye, then,' said Bazarov, as though he guessed her thought, and he went back into the house.

Anna Sergyevna walked slowly after him, and calling Katya to her, she took her arm. She did not leave her side till quite evening. She did not play cards, and was constantly laughing, which did not at all accord with her pale and perplexed face. Arkady was bewildered, and looked on at her as all young people look on—that's to say, he was constantly asking himself, 'What is the meaning of that?' Bazarov shut himself up in his room; he came back to tea, however. Anna Sergyevna longed to say some friendly word to him, but she did not know how to address him....

An unexpected incident relieved her from her embarrassment; a steward announced the arrival of Sitnikov.

It is difficult to do justice in words to the strange figure cut by the young apostle of progress as he fluttered into the room. Though, with his characteristic impudence, he had made up his mind to go into the country to visit a woman whom he hardly knew, who had never invited him; but with whom, according to information he had gathered, such talented and intimate friends were staying, he was nevertheless trembling to the marrow of his bones; and instead of bringing out the apologies and compliments he had learned by heart beforehand, he muttered some absurdity about Evdoksya Kukshin having sent him to inquire after Anna Sergyevna's health, and Arkady Nikolaevitch's too, having always spoken to him in the highest terms.... At this point he faltered and lost his presence of mind so completely that he sat down on his own hat. However, since no one turned him out, and Anna Sergyevna even presented him to her aunt and her sister, he soon recovered himself and began to chatter volubly. The introduction of the commonplace is often an advantage in life; it relieves over-strained tension, and sobers too self-confident or self-sacrificing emotions by recalling its close kinship with them. With Sitnikov's appearance everything became somehow duller and simpler; they all even ate a more solid supper, and retired to bed half-an-hour earlier than usual.

'I might now repeat to you,' said Arkady, as he lay down in bed, to Bazarov, who was also undressing, what you once said to me, 'Why are you so melancholy? One would think you had fulfilled some sacred duty.' For some time past a sort of pretence of free-and-easy banter had sprung up between the two young men, which is always an unmistakable sign of secret displeasure or unexpressed suspicions.

'I'm going to my father's to-morrow,' said Bazarov.

Arkady raised himself and leaned on his elbow. He felt both surprised, and for some reason or other pleased. 'Ah!' he commented, 'and is that why you're sad?'

Bazarov yawned. 'You'll get old if you know too much.'

'And Anna Sergyevna?' persisted Arkady.

'What about Anna Sergyevna?'

'I mean, will she let you go?'

'I'm not her paid man.'

Arkady grew thoughtful, while Bazarov lay down and turned with his face to the wall.

Some minutes went by in silence. 'Yevgeny?' cried Arkady suddenly.

'Well?'

'I will leave with you to-morrow too.'

Bazarov made no answer.

'Only I will go home,' continued Arkady. 'We will go together as far as Hohlovsky, and there you can get horses at Fedot's. I should be delighted to make the acquaintance of your people, but I'm afraid of being in their way and yours. You are coming to us again later, of course?'

'I've left all my things with you,' Bazarov said, without turning round.

'Why doesn't he ask me why I am going, and just as suddenly as he?' thought Arkady. 'In reality, why am I going, and why is he going?' he pursued his reflections. He could find no satisfactory answer to his own question, though his heart was filled with some bitter feeling. He felt it would be hard to part from this life to which he had grown so accustomed; but for him to remain alone would be rather odd. 'Something has passed between them,' he reasoned to himself; 'what good would it be for me to hang on after he's gone? She's utterly sick of me; I'm losing the last that remained to me.' He began to imagine Anna Sergyevna to himself, then other features gradually eclipsed the lovely image of the young widow.

'I'm sorry to lose Katya too!' Arkady whispered to his pillow, on which a tear had already fallen.... All at once he shook back his hair and said aloud—

'What the devil made that fool of a Sitnikov turn up here?'

Bazarov at first stirred a little in his bed, then he uttered the following rejoinder: 'You're still a fool, my boy, I see. Sitnikovs are indispensable to us. I—do you understand? I need dolts like him. It's not for the gods to bake bricks, in fact!'...

'Oho!' Arkady thought to himself, and then in a flash all the fathomless depths of Bazarov's conceit dawned upon him. 'Are you and I gods then? at least, you're a god; am not I a dolt then?'

'Yes,' repeated Bazarov; 'you're still a fool.'

Madame Odintsov expressed no special surprise when Arkady told her the next day that he was going with Bazarov; she seemed tired and absorbed. Katya looked at him silently and seriously; the princess went so far as to cross herself under her shawl so that he could not help noticing it. Sitnikov, on the other hand, was completely disconcerted. He had only just come in to lunch in a new and fashionable get-up, not on this occasion of a Slavophil cut; the evening before he had astonished the man told off to wait on him by the amount of linen he had brought with him, and now all of a sudden his comrades were deserting him! He took a few tiny steps, doubled back like a hunted hare at the edge of a copse, and abruptly, almost with dismay, almost with a wail, announced that he proposed going too. Madame Odintsov did not attempt to detain him.

'I have a very comfortable carriage,' added the luckless young man, turning to Arkady; 'I can take you, while Yevgeny Vassilyitch can take your coach, so it will be even more convenient.'

'But, really, it's not at all in your way, and it's a long way to my place.'

'That's nothing, nothing; I've plenty of time; besides, I have business in that direction.'

'Gin-selling?' asked Arkady, rather too contemptuously.

But Sitnikov was reduced to such desperation that he did not even laugh as usual. 'I assure you, my carriage is exceedingly comfortable,' he muttered; 'and there will be room for all.'

'Don't wound Monsieur Sitnikov by a refusal,' commented Anna Sergyevna.

Arkady glanced at her, and bowed his head significantly.

The visitors started off after lunch. As she said good-bye to Bazarov, Madame Odintsov held out her hand to him, and said, 'We shall meet again, shan't we?'

'As you command,' answered Bazarov.

'In that case, we shall.'
Arkady was the first to descend the steps; he got into Sitnikov's carriage. A steward tucked him in respectfully, but he could have killed him with pleasure, or have burst into tears.
Bazarov took his seat in the coach. When they reached Hohlovsky, Arkady waited till Fedot, the keeper of the posting-station, had put in the horses, and going up to the coach, he said, with his old smile, to Bazarov, 'Yevgeny, take me with you; I want to come to you.'
'Get in,' Bazarov brought out through his teeth.
Sitnikov, who had been walking to and fro round the wheels of his carriage, whistling briskly, could only gape when he heard these words; while Arkady coolly pulled his luggage out of the carriage, took his seat beside Bazarov, and bowing politely to his former fellow-traveller, he called, 'Whip up!' The coach rolled away, and was soon out of sight.... Sitnikov, utterly confused, looked at his coachman, but the latter was flicking his whip about the tail of the off horse. Then Sitnikov jumped into the carriage, and growling at two passing peasants, 'Put on your caps, idiots!' he drove to the town, where he arrived very late, and where, next day, at Madame Kukshin's, he dealt very severely with two 'disgusting stuck-up churls.'
When he was seated in the coach by Bazarov, Arkady pressed his hand warmly, and for a long while he said nothing. It seemed as though Bazarov understood and appreciated both the pressure and the silence. He had not slept all the previous night, and had not smoked, and had eaten scarcely anything for several days. His profile, already thinner, stood out darkly and sharply under his cap, which was pulled down to his eyebrows.
'Well, brother,' he said at last, 'give us a cigarette. But look, I say, is my tongue yellow?'
'Yes, it is,' answered Arkady.
'Hm ... and the cigarette's tasteless. The machine's out of gear.'
'You look changed lately certainly,' observed Arkady.
'It's nothing! we shall soon be all right. One thing's a bother—my mother's so tender-hearted; if you don't grow as round as a tub, and eat ten times a day, she's quite upset. My father's all right, he's known all sorts of ups and downs himself. No, I can't smoke,' he added, and he flung the cigarette into the dust of the road.
'Do you think it's twenty miles?' asked Arkady.
'Yes. But ask this sage here.' He indicated the peasant sitting on the box, a labourer of Fedot's.
But the sage only answered, 'Who's to know—miles hereabout aren't measured,' and went on swearing in an undertone at the shaft horse for 'kicking with her head-piece,' that is, shaking with her head down.
'Yes, yes,' began Bazarov; 'it's a lesson to you, my young friend, an instructive example. God knows, what rot it is? Every man hangs on a thread, the abyss may open under his feet any minute, and yet he must go and invent all sorts of discomforts for himself, and spoil his life.'
'What are you alluding to?' asked Arkady.
'I'm not alluding to anything; I'm saying straight out that we've both behaved like fools. What's the use of talking about it! Still, I've noticed in hospital practice, the man who's furious at his illness—he's sure to get over it.'
'I don't quite understand you,' observed Arkady; 'I should have thought you had nothing to complain of.'
'And since you don't quite understand me, I'll tell you this—to my mind, it's better to break stones on the highroad than to let a woman have the mastery of even the end of one's little finger. That's all ...' Bazarov was on the point of uttering his favourite word, 'romanticism,' but he checked himself, and said, 'rubbish. You don't believe me now, but I tell you; you and I have been in feminine society, and very nice we found it; but to throw up society like that is for all the world like a dip in cold water on a hot day. A man hasn't time to attend to such trifles; a man ought not to be tame, says an excellent Spanish proverb. Now, you, I suppose, my sage friend,' he added, turning to the peasant sitting on the box—'you've a wife?'
The peasant showed both the friends his dull blear-eyed face.
'A wife? Yes. Every man has a wife.'
'Do you beat her?'
'My wife? Everything happens sometimes. We don't beat her without good reason!'
'That's excellent. Well, and does she beat you?'
The peasant gave a tug at the reins. 'That's a strange thing to say, sir. You like your joke.'... He was obviously offended.
'You hear, Arkady Nikolaevitch! But we have taken a beating ... that's what comes of being educated people.'
Arkady gave a forced laugh, while Bazarov turned away, and did not open his mouth again the whole journey.

The twenty miles seemed to Arkady quite forty. But at last, on the slope of some rising ground, appeared the small hamlet where Bazarov's parents lived. Beside it, in a young birch copse, could be seen a small house with a thatched roof.
Two peasants stood with their hats on at the first hut, abusing each other. 'You're a great sow,' said one; 'and worse than a little sucking pig.'
'And your wife's a witch,' retorted the other.
'From their unconstrained behaviour,' Bazarov remarked to Arkady, 'and the playfulness of their retorts, you can guess that my father's peasants are not too much oppressed. Why, there he is himself coming out on the steps of his house. They must have heard the bells. It's he; it's he—I know his figure. Ay, ay! how grey he's grown though, poor chap!'

CHAPTER XX

Bazarov leaned out of the coach, while Arkady thrust his head out behind his companion's back, and caught sight on the steps of the little manor-house of a tall, thinnish man with dishevelled hair, and a thin hawk nose, dressed in an old military coat not buttoned up. He was standing, his legs wide apart, smoking a long pipe and screwing up his eyes to keep the sun out of them.
The horses stopped.
'Arrived at last,' said Bazarov's father, still going on smoking though the pipe was fairly dancing up and down between his fingers. 'Come, get out; get out; let me hug you.'
He began embracing his son ... 'Enyusha, Enyusha,' was heard a trembling woman's voice. The door was flung open, and in the doorway was seen a plump, short, little old woman in a white cap and a short striped jacket. She moaned, staggered, and would certainly have fallen, had not Bazarov supported her. Her plump little hands were instantly twined round his neck, her head was pressed to his breast, and there was a complete hush. The only sound heard was her broken sobs.
Old Bazarov breathed hard and screwed his eyes up more than ever.
'There, that's enough, that's enough, Arisha! give over,' he said, exchanging a glance with Arkady, who remained motionless in the coach, while the peasant on the box even turned his head away; 'that's not at all necessary, please give over.'
'Ah, Vassily Ivanitch,' faltered the old woman, 'for what ages, my dear one, my darling, Enyusha,' ... and, not unclasping her hands, she drew her wrinkled face, wet with tears and working with tenderness, a little away from Bazarov, and gazed at him with blissful and comic-looking eyes, and again fell on his neck.
'Well, well, to be sure, that's all in the nature of things,' commented Vassily Ivanitch, 'only we'd better come indoors. Here's a visitor come with Yevgeny. You must excuse it,' he added, turning to Arkady, and scraping with his foot; 'you understand, a woman's weakness; and well, a mother's heart ...'
His lips and eyebrows too were twitching, and his beard was quivering ... but he was obviously trying to control himself and appear almost indifferent.
'Let's come in, mother, really,' said Bazarov, and he led the enfeebled old woman into the house. Putting her into a comfortable armchair, he once more hurriedly embraced his father and introduced Arkady to him.
'Heartily glad to make your acquaintance,' said Vassily Ivanovitch, 'but you mustn't expect great things; everything here in my house is done in a plain way, on a military footing. Arina Vlasyevna, calm yourself, pray; what weakness! The gentleman our guest will think ill of you.'
'My dear sir,' said the old lady through her tears, 'your name and your father's I haven't the honour of knowing....'
'Arkady Nikolaitch,' put in Vassily Ivanitch solemnly, in a low voice.

'You must excuse a silly old woman like me.' The old woman blew her nose, and bending her head to right and to left, carefully wiped one eye after the other. 'You must excuse me. You see, I thought I should die, that I should not live to see my da .. arling.'
'Well, here we have lived to see him, madam,' put in Vassily Ivanovitch. 'Tanyushka,' he turned to a bare-legged little girl of thirteen in a bright red cotton dress, who was timidly peeping in at the door, 'bring your mistress a glass of water—on a tray, do you hear?—and you, gentlemen,' he added, with a kind of old-fashioned playfulness, 'let me ask you into the study of a retired old veteran.'
'Just once more let me embrace you, Enyusha,' moaned Arina Vlasyevna. Bazarov bent down to her. 'Why, what a handsome fellow you have grown!'
'Well, I don't know about being handsome,' remarked Vassily Ivanovitch, 'but he's a man, as the saying is, *ommfay*. And now I hope, Arina Vlasyevna, that having satisfied your maternal heart, you will turn your thoughts to satisfying the appetites of our dear guests, because, as you're aware, even nightingales can't be fed on fairy tales.'
The old lady got up from her chair. 'This minute, Vassily Ivanovitch, the table shall be laid. I will run myself to the kitchen and order the samovar to be brought in; everything shall be ready, everything. Why, I have not seen him, not given him food or drink these three years; is that nothing?'
'There, mind, good mother, bustle about; don't put us to shame; while you, gentlemen, I beg you to follow me. Here's Timofeitch come to pay his respects to you, Yevgeny. He, too, I daresay, is delighted, the old dog. Eh, aren't you delighted, old dog? Be so good as to follow me.'
And Vassily Ivanovitch went bustling forward, scraping and flapping with his slippers trodden down at heel. His whole house consisted of six tiny rooms. One of them—the one to which he led our friends—was called the study. A thick-legged table, littered over with papers black with the accumulation of ancient dust as though they had been smoked, occupied all the space between the two windows; on the walls hung Turkish firearms, whips, a sabre, two maps, some anatomical diagrams, a portrait of Hoffland, a monogram woven in hair in a blackened frame, and a diploma under glass; a leather sofa, torn and worn into hollows in parts, was placed between two huge cupboards of birch-wood; on the shelves books, boxes, stuffed birds, jars, and phials were huddled together in confusion; in one corner stood a broken galvanic battery.
'I warned you, my dear Arkady Nikolaitch,' began Vassily Ivanitch, 'that we live, so to say, bivouacking....'
'There, stop that, what are you apologising for?' Bazarov interrupted. 'Kirsanov knows very well we're not Croesuses, and that you have no butler. Where are we going to put him, that's the question?'
'To be sure, Yevgeny; I have a capital room there in the little lodge; he will be very comfortable there.'
'Have you had a lodge put up then?'
'Why, where the bath-house is,' put in Timofeitch.
'That is next to the bathroom,' Vassily Ivanitch added hurriedly. 'It's summer now ... I will run over there at once, and make arrangements; and you, Timofeitch, meanwhile bring in their things. You, Yevgeny, I shall of course offer my study. *Suum cuique.'*
'There you have him! A comical old chap, and very good-natured,' remarked Bazarov, directly Vassily Ivanitch had gone. 'Just such a queer fish as yours, only in another way. He chatters too much.'
'And your mother seems an awfully nice woman,' observed Arkady.
'Yes, there's no humbug about her. You'll see what a dinner she'll give us.'
'They didn't expect you to-day, sir; they've not brought any beef?' observed Timofeitch, who was just dragging in Bazarov's box.
'We shall get on very well without beef. It's no use crying for the moon. Poverty, they say, is no vice.'
'How many serfs has your father?' Arkady asked suddenly.
'The estate's not his, but mother's; there are fifteen serfs, if I remember.'
'Twenty-two in all,' Timofeitch added, with an air of displeasure.
The flapping of slippers was heard, and Vassily Ivanovitch reappeared. 'In a few minutes your room will be ready to receive you,' he cried triumphantly. Arkady ... Nikolaitch? I think that is right? And here is your attendant,' he added, indicating a short-cropped boy, who had come in with him in a blue full-skirted coat with ragged elbows and a pair of boots which did not belong to him. 'His name is Fedka. Again, I repeat, even though my son tells me not to, you mustn't expect great things. He knows how to fill a pipe, though. You smoke, of course?'
'I generally smoke cigars,' answered Arkady.
'And you do very sensibly. I myself give the preference to cigars, but in these solitudes it is exceedingly difficult to obtain them.'

'There, that's enough humble pie,' Bazarov interrupted again. 'You'd much better sit here on the sofa and let us have a look at you.'

Vassily Ivanovitch laughed and sat down. He was very like his son in face, only his brow was lower and narrower, and his mouth rather wider, and he was for ever restless, shrugging up his shoulder as though his coat cut him under the armpits, blinking, clearing his throat, and gesticulating with his fingers, while his son was distinguished by a kind of nonchalant immobility.

'Humble-pie!' repeated Vassily Ivanovitch. 'You must not imagine, Yevgeny, I want to appeal, so to speak, to our guest's sympathies by making out we live in such a wilderness. Quite the contrary, I maintain that for a thinking man nothing is a wilderness. At least, I try as far as possible not to get rusty, so to speak, not to fall behind the age.'

Vassily Ivanovitch drew out of his pocket a new yellow silk handkerchief, which he had had time to snatch up on the way to Arkady's room, and flourishing it in the air, he proceeded: 'I am not now alluding to the fact that, for example, at the cost of sacrifices not inconsiderable for me, I have put my peasants on the rent-system and given up my land to them on half profits. I regarded that as my duty; common sense itself enjoins such a proceeding, though other proprietors do not even dream of it; I am alluding to the sciences, to culture.'

'Yes; I see you have here *The Friend of Health* for 1855,' remarked Bazarov.

'It's sent me by an old comrade out of friendship,' Vassily Ivanovitch made haste to answer; 'but we have, for instance, some idea even of phrenology,' he added, addressing himself principally, however, to Arkady, and pointing to a small plaster head on the cupboard, divided into numbered squares; 'we are not unacquainted even with Schenlein and Rademacher.'

'Why do people still believe in Rademacher in this province?' asked Bazarov.

Vassily Ivanovitch cleared his throat. 'In this province.... Of course, gentlemen, you know best; how could we keep pace with you? You are here to take our places. In my day, too, there was some sort of a Humouralist school, Hoffmann, and Brown too with his vitalism—they seemed very ridiculous to us, but, of course, they too had been great men at one time or other. Some one new has taken the place of Rademacher with you; you bow down to him, but in another twenty years it will be his turn to be laughed at.'

'For your consolation I will tell you,' observed Bazarov, 'that nowadays we laugh at medicine altogether, and don't bow down to any one.'

'How's that? Why, you're going to be a doctor, aren't you?'

'Yes, but the one fact doesn't prevent the other.'

Vassily Ivanovitch poked his third finger into his pipe, where a little smouldering ash was still left. 'Well, perhaps, perhaps—I am not going to dispute. What am I? A retired army-doctor, *volla-too;* now fate has made me take to farming. I served in your grandfather's brigade,' he addressed himself again to Arkady; 'yes, yes, I have seen many sights in my day. And I was thrown into all kinds of society, brought into contact with all sorts of people! I myself, the man you see before you now, have felt the pulse of Prince Wittgenstein and of Zhukovsky! They were in the southern army, in the fourteenth, you understand' (and here Vassily Ivanovitch pursed his mouth up significantly). 'Well, well, but my business was on one side; stick to your lancet, and let everything else go hang! Your grandfather was a very honourable man, a real soldier.'

'Confess, now, he was rather a blockhead,' remarked Bazarov lazily.

'Ah, Yevgeny, how can you use such an expression! Do consider.... Of course, General Kirsanov was not one of the ...'

'Come, drop him,' broke in Bazarov; 'I was pleased as I was driving along here to see your birch copse; it has shot up capitally.'

Vassily Ivanovitch brightened up. 'And you must see what a little garden I've got now! I planted every tree myself. I've fruit, and raspberries, and all kinds of medicinal herbs. However clever you young gentlemen may be, old Paracelsus spoke the holy truth: *in herbis verbis et lapidibus*.... I've retired from practice, you know, of course, but two or three times a week it will happen that I'm brought back to my old work. They come for advice—I can't drive them away. Sometimes the poor have recourse to me for help. And indeed there are no doctors here at all. There's one of the neighbours here, a retired major, only fancy, he doctors the people too. I asked the question, "Has he studied medicine?" And they told me, "No, he's not studied; he does it more from philanthropy."... Ha! ha! ha! from philanthropy! What do you think of that? Ha! ha! ha!'

'Fedka, fill me a pipe!' said Bazarov rudely.

'And there's another doctor here who just got to a patient,' Vassily Ivanovitch persisted in a kind of desperation, 'when the patient had gone *ad patres;* the servant didn't let the doctor speak; you're no longer wanted, he told him. He hadn't expected this, got confused, and asked, "Why, did your master hiccup before his death?" "Yes." "Did he hiccup much?" "Yes." "Ah, well, that's all right," and off he set back again. Ha! ha! ha!'

The old man was alone in his laughter; Arkady forced a smile on his face. Bazarov simply stretched. The conversation went on in this way for about an hour; Arkady had time to go to his room, which turned out to be the anteroom attached to the bathroom, but was very snug and clean. At last Tanyusha came in and announced that dinner was ready.

Vassily Ivanovitch was the first to get up. 'Come, gentlemen. You must be magnanimous and pardon me if I've bored you. I daresay my good wife will give you more satisfaction.'

The dinner, though prepared in haste, turned out to be very good, even abundant; only the wine was not quite up to the mark; it was almost black sherry, bought by Timofeitch in the town at a well-known merchant's, and had a faint coppery, resinous taste, and the flies were a great nuisance. On ordinary days a serf-boy used to keep driving them away with a large green branch; but on this occasion Vassily Ivanovitch had sent him away through dread of the criticism of the younger generation. Arina Vlasyevna had had time to dress: she had put on a high cap with silk ribbons and a pale blue flowered shawl. She broke down again directly she caught sight of her Enyusha, but her husband had no need to admonish her; she made haste to wipe away her tears herself, for fear of spotting her shawl. Only the young men ate anything; the master and mistress of the house had dined long ago. Fedka waited at table, obviously encumbered by having boots on for the first time; he was assisted by a woman of a masculine cast of face and one eye, by name Anfisushka, who performed the duties of housekeeper, poultry-woman, and laundress. Vassily Ivanovitch walked up and down during the whole of dinner, and with a perfectly happy, positively beatific countenance, talked about the serious anxiety he felt at Napoleon's policy, and the intricacy of the Italian question. Arina Vlasyevna took no notice of Arkady. She did not press him to eat; leaning her round face, to which the full cherry-coloured lips and the little moles on the cheeks and over the eyebrows gave a very simple good-natured expression, on her little closed fist, she did not take her eyes off her son, and kept constantly sighing; she was dying to know for how long he had come, but she was afraid to ask him.

'What if he says for two days,' she thought, and her heart sank. After the roast Vassily Ivanovitch disappeared for an instant, and returned with an opened half-bottle of champagne. 'Here,' he cried, 'though we do live in the wilds, we have something to make merry with on festive occasions!' He filled three champagne glasses and a little wineglass, proposed the health of 'our inestimable guests,' and at once tossed off his glass in military fashion; while he made Arina Vlasyevna drink her wineglass to the last drop. When the time came in due course for preserves, Arkady, who could not bear anything sweet, thought it his duty, however, to taste four different kinds which had been freshly made, all the more as Bazarov flatly refused them and began at once smoking a cigarette. Then tea came on the scene with cream, butter, and cracknels; then Vassily Ivanovitch took them all into the garden to admire the beauty of the evening. As they passed a garden seat he whispered to Arkady—

'At this spot I love to meditate, as I watch the sunset; it suits a recluse like me. And there, a little farther off, I have planted some of the trees beloved of Horace.'

'What trees?' asked Bazarov, overhearing.

'Oh ... acacias.'

Bazarov began to yawn.

'I imagine it's time our travellers were in the arms of Morpheus,' observed Vassily Ivanovitch.

'That is, it's time for bed,' Bazarov put in. 'That's a correct idea. It is time, certainly.'

As he said good-night to his mother, he kissed her on the forehead, while she embraced him, and stealthily behind his back she gave him her blessing three times. Vassily Ivanovitch conducted Arkady to his room, and wished him 'as refreshing repose as I enjoyed at your happy years.' And Arkady did as a fact sleep excellently in his bath-house; there was a smell of mint in it, and two crickets behind the stove rivalled each other in their drowsy chirping. Vassily Ivanovitch went from Arkady's room to his study, and perching on the sofa at his son's feet, he was looking forward to having a chat with him; but Bazarov at once sent him away, saying he was sleepy, and did not fall asleep till morning. With wide open eyes he stared vindictively into the darkness; the memories of childhood had no power over him; and besides, he had not yet had time to get rid of the impression of his recent bitter emotions. Arina Vlasyevna first prayed to her heart's content, then she had a long, long conversation with Anfisushka, who stood stock-still before her mistress, and fixing her solitary eye upon her, communicated in a mysterious whisper all her observations and conjectures in regard to Yevgeny Vassilyevitch. The old lady's head was giddy with happiness and wine and tobacco smoke; her husband tried to talk to her, but with a wave of his hand gave it up in despair.

Arina Vlasyevna was a genuine Russian gentlewoman of the olden times; she ought to have lived two centuries before, in the old Moscow days. She was very devout and emotional; she believed in fortune-telling, charms, dreams, and omens of every possible kind; she believed in the prophecies of crazy people, in house-spirits, in wood-spirits, in unlucky meetings, in the evil eye, in popular remedies, she ate specially prepared salt on Holy Thursday, and believed that the end of the world was at hand; she believed that if on Easter Sunday the lights did not go out at vespers, then there would be a good crop of buckwheat, and that a mushroom will not grow after it has been looked on by the eye of man; she believed that the devil likes to be where there is water, and that every Jew has a blood-stained patch on his breast; she was afraid of mice, of snakes, of frogs, of sparrows, of leeches, of thunder, of cold water, of draughts, of horses, of goats, of red-haired people, and black cats, and she regarded crickets and dogs as unclean beasts; she never ate veal, doves, crayfishes, cheese, asparagus, artichokes, hares, nor water-melons, because a cut water-melon suggested the head of John the Baptist, and of oysters she could not speak without a shudder; she was fond of eating—and fasted rigidly; she slept ten hours out of the twenty-four—and never went to bed at all if Vassily Ivanovitch had so much as a headache; she had never read a single book except*Alexis or the Cottage in the Forest;* she wrote one, or at the most two letters in a year, but was great in housewifery, preserving, and jam-making, though with her own hands she never touched a thing, and was generally disinclined to move from her place. Arina Vlasyevna was very kindhearted, and in her way not at all stupid. She knew that the world is divided into masters whose duty it is to command, and simple folk whose duty it is to serve them—and so she felt no repugnance to servility and prostrations to the ground; but she treated those in subjection to her kindly and gently, never let a single beggar go away empty-handed, and never spoke ill of any one, though she was fond of gossip. In her youth she had been pretty, had played the clavichord, and spoken French a little; but in the course of many years' wanderings with her husband, whom she had married against her will, she had grown stout, and forgotten music and French. Her son she loved and feared unutterably; she had given up the management of the property to Vassily Ivanovitch—and now did not interfere in anything; she used to groan, wave her handkerchief, and raise her eyebrows higher and higher with horror directly her old husband began to discuss the impending government reforms and his own plans. She was apprehensive, and constantly expecting some great misfortune, and began to weep directly she remembered anything sorrowful.... Such women are not common nowadays. God knows whether we ought to rejoice!

CHAPTER XXI

On getting up Arkady opened the window, and the first object that met his view was Vassily Ivanovitch. In an Oriental dressing-gown girt round the waist with a pocket-handkerchief he was industriously digging in his garden. He perceived his young visitor, and leaning on his spade, he called, 'The best of health to you! How have you slept?'

'Capitally,' answered Arkady.

'Here am I, as you see, like some Cincinnatus, marking out a bed for late turnips. The time has come now—and thank God for it!—when every one ought to obtain his sustenance with his own hands; it's useless to reckon on others; one must labour oneself. And it turns out that Jean Jacques Rousseau is right. Half an hour ago, my dear young gentleman, you might have seen me in a totally different position. One peasant woman, who complained of looseness—that's how they express it, but in our language, dysentery—I ... how can I express it best? I administered opium, and for another I extracted a tooth. I proposed an anæsthetic to her ... but she would not consent. All that I do *gratis—anamatyer (en amateur).* I'm used to it, though; you see, I'm a plebeian, *homo novus*—not one of the old stock, not like my spouse.... Wouldn't you like to come this way into the shade, to breathe the morning freshness a little before tea?'

Arkady went out to him.

'Welcome once again,' said Vassily Ivanovitch, raising his hand in a military salute to the greasy skull-cap which covered his head. 'You, I know, are accustomed to luxury, to amusements, but even the great ones of this world do not disdain to spend a brief space under a cottage roof.'

'Good heavens,' protested Arkady, 'as though I were one of the great ones of this world! And I'm not accustomed to luxury.'

'Pardon me, pardon me,' rejoined Vassily Ivanovitch with a polite simper. 'Though I am laid on the shelf now, I have knocked about the world too—I can tell a bird by its flight. I am something of a psychologist too in my own way, and a physiognomist. If I had not, I will venture to say, been endowed with that gift, I should have come to grief long ago; I should have stood no chance, a poor man like me. I tell you without flattery, I am sincerely delighted at the friendship I observe between you and my son. I have just seen him; he got up as he usually does—no doubt you are aware of it—very early, and went a ramble about the neighbourhood. Permit me to inquire—have you known my son long?'

'Since last winter.'

'Indeed. And permit me to question you further—but hadn't we better sit down? Permit me, as a father, to ask without reserve, What is your opinion of my Yevgeny?'

'Your son is one of the most remarkable men I have ever met,' Arkady answered emphatically.

Vassily Ivanovitch's eyes suddenly grew round, and his cheeks were suffused with a faint flush. The spade fell out of his hand.

'And so you expect,' he began ...

'I'm convinced,' Arkady put in, 'that your son has a great future before him; that he will do honour to your name. I've been certain of that ever since I first met him.'

'How ... how was that?' Vassily Ivanovitch articulated with an effort. His wide mouth was relaxed in a triumphant smile, which would not leave it.

'Would you like me to tell you how we met?'

'Yes ... and altogether....'

Arkady began to tell his tale, and to talk of Bazarov with even greater warmth, even greater enthusiasm than he had done on the evening when he danced a mazurka with Madame Odintsov.

Vassily Ivanovitch listened and listened, blinked, and rolled his handkerchief up into a ball in both his hands, cleared his throat, ruffled up his hair, and at last could stand it no longer; he bent down to Arkady and kissed him on his shoulder. 'You have made me perfectly happy,' he said, never ceasing to smile. 'I ought to tell you, I ... idolise my son; my old wife I won't speak of—we all know what mothers are!—but I dare not show my feelings before him, because he doesn't like it. He is averse to every kind of demonstration of feeling; many people even find fault with him for such firmness of character, and regard it as a proof of pride or lack of feeling, but men like him ought not to be judged by the common standard, ought they? And here, for example, many another fellow in his place would have been a constant drag on his parents; but he, would you believe it? has never from the day he was born taken a farthing more than he could help, that's God's truth!'

'He is a disinterested, honest man,' observed Arkady.

'Exactly so; he is disinterested. And I don't only idolise him, Arkady Nikolaitch, I am proud of him, and the height of my ambition is that some day there will be the following lines in his biography: "The son of a simple army-doctor, who was, however, capable of divining his greatness betimes, and spared nothing for his education ..."' The old man's voice broke.

Arkady pressed his hand.

'What do you think,' inquired Vassily Ivanovitch, after a short silence, 'will it be in the career of medicine that he will attain the celebrity you anticipate for him?'

'Of course, not in medicine, though even in that department he will be one of the leading scientific men.'

'In what then, Arkady Nikolaitch?'

'It would he hard to say now, but he will be famous.'

'He will be famous!' repeated the old man, and he sank into a reverie.

'Arina Vlasyevna sent me to call you in to tea,' announced Anfisushka, coming by with an immense dish of ripe raspberries.

Vassily Ivanovitch started. 'And will there be cooled cream for the raspberries?'

'Yes.'

'Cold now, mind! Don't stand on ceremony, Arkady Nikolaitch; take some more. How is it Yevgeny doesn't come?'

'I'm here,' was heard Bazarov's voice from Arkady's room.

Vassily Ivanovitch turned round quickly. 'Aha! you wanted to pay a visit to your friend; but you were too late, *amice,* and we have already had a long conversation with him. Now we must go in to tea, mother summons us. By the way, I want to have a little talk with you.'
'What about?'
'There's a peasant here; he's suffering from icterus....
'You mean jaundice?'
'Yes, a chronic and very obstinate case of icterus. I have prescribed him centaury and St. John's wort, ordered him to eat carrots, given him soda; but all that's merely palliative measures; we want some more decided treatment. Though you do laugh at medicine, I am certain you can give me practical advice. But we will talk of that later. Now come in to tea.'
Vassily Ivanovitch jumped up briskly from the garden seat, and hummed from *Robert le Diable*—

ule, the rule we set ours
ve, to live for pleasure!'

'Singular vitality!' observed Bazarov, going away from the window.
It was midday. The sun was burning hot behind a thin veil of unbroken whitish clouds. Everything was hushed; there was no sound but the cocks crowing irritably at one another in the village, producing in every one who heard them a strange sense of drowsiness and ennui; and somewhere, high up in a tree-top, the incessant plaintive cheep of a young hawk. Arkady and Bazarov lay in the shade of a small haystack, putting under themselves two armfuls of dry and rustling, but still greenish and fragrant grass.
'That aspen-tree,' began Bazarov, 'reminds me of my childhood; it grows at the edge of the clay-pits where the bricks were dug, and in those days I believed firmly that that clay-pit and aspen-tree possessed a peculiar talismanic power; I never felt dull near them. I did not understand then that I was not dull, because I was a child. Well, now I'm grown up, the talisman's lost its power.'
'How long did you live here altogether?' asked Arkady.
'Two years on end; then we travelled about. We led a roving life, wandering from town to town for the most part.'
'And has this house been standing long?'
'Yes. My grandfather built it—my mother's father.'
'Who was he—your grandfather?'
'Devil knows. Some second-major. He served with Suvorov, and was always telling stories about the crossing of the Alps—inventions probably.'
'You have a portrait of Suvorov hanging in the drawing-room. I like these dear little houses like yours; they're so warm and old-fashioned; and there's always a special sort of scent about them.'
'A smell of lamp-oil and clover,' Bazarov remarked, yawning. 'And the flies in those dear little houses.... Faugh!'
'Tell me,' began Arkady, after a brief pause, 'were they strict with you when you were a child?'
'You can see what my parents are like. They're not a severe sort.'
'Are you fond of them, Yevgeny?'
'I am, Arkady.'
'How fond they are of you!'
Bazarov was silent for a little. 'Do you know what I'm thinking about?' he brought out at last, clasping his hands behind his head.
'No. What is it?'
'I'm thinking life is a happy thing for my parents. My father at sixty is fussing around, talking about "palliative" measures, doctoring people, playing the bountiful master with the peasants—having a festive time, in fact; and my mother's happy too; her day's so chockful of duties of all sorts, and sighs and groans that she's no time even to think of herself; while I ...'
'While you?'
'I think; here I lie under a haystack.... The tiny space I occupy is so infinitely small in comparison with the rest of space, in which I am not, and which has nothing to do with me; and the period of time in which it is my lot to live is so petty beside the eternity in which I have not been, and shall not be.... And in this atom,

this mathematical point, the blood is circulating, the brain is working and wanting something.... Isn't it loathsome? Isn't it petty?'

'Allow me to remark that what you're saying applies to men in general.'

'You are right,' Bazarov cut in. 'I was going to say that they now—my parents, I mean—are absorbed and don't trouble themselves about their own nothingness; it doesn't sicken them ... while I ... I feel nothing but weariness and anger.'

'Anger? why anger?'

'Why? How can you ask why? Have you forgotten?'

'I remember everything, but still I don't admit that you have any right to be angry. You're unlucky, I'll allow, but ...'

'Pooh! then you, Arkady Nikolaevitch, I can see, regard love like all modern young men; cluck, cluck, cluck you call to the hen, but if the hen comes near you, you run away. I'm not like that. But that's enough of that. What can't be helped, it's shameful to talk about.' He turned over on his side. 'Aha! there goes a valiant ant dragging off a half-dead fly. Take her, brother, take her! Don't pay attention to her resistance; it's your privilege as an animal to be free from the sentiment of pity—make the most of it—not like us conscientious self-destructive animals!'

'You shouldn't say that, Yevgeny! When have you destroyed yourself?'

Bazarov raised his head. 'That's the only thing I pride myself on. I haven't crushed myself, so a woman can't crush me. Amen! It's all over! You shall not hear another word from me about it.'

Both the friends lay for some time in silence.

'Yes,' began Bazarov, 'man's a strange animal. When one gets a side view from a distance of the dead-alive life our "fathers" lead here, one thinks, What could be better? You eat and drink, and know you are acting in the most reasonable, most judicious manner. But if not, you're devoured by ennui. One wants to have to do with people if only to abuse them.'

'One ought so to order one's life that every moment in it should be of significance,' Arkady affirmed reflectively.

'I dare say! What's of significance is sweet, however mistaken; one could make up one's mind to what's insignificant even. But pettiness, pettiness, that's what's insufferable.'

'Pettiness doesn't exist for a man so long as he refuses to recognise it.'

'H'm ... what you've just said is a common-place reversed.'

'What? What do you mean by that term?'

'I'll tell you; saying, for instance, that education is beneficial, that's a common-place; but to say that education is injurious, that's a common-place turned upside down. There's more style about it, so to say, but in reality it's one and the same.'

'And the truth is—where, which side?'

'Where? Like an echo I answer, Where?'

'You're in a melancholy mood to-day, Yevgeny.'

'Really? The sun must have softened my brain, I suppose, and I can't stand so many raspberries either.'

'In that case, a nap's not a bad thing,' observed Arkady.

'Certainly; only don't look at me; every man's face is stupid when he's asleep.'

'But isn't it all the same to you what people think of you?'

'I don't know what to say to you. A real man ought not to care; a real man is one whom it's no use thinking about, whom one must either obey or hate.'

'It's funny! I don't hate anybody,' observed Arkady, after a moment's thought.

'And I hate so many. You are a soft-hearted, mawkish creature; how could you hate any one?... You're timid; you don't rely on yourself much.'

'And you,' interrupted Arkady, 'do you expect much of yourself? Have you a high opinion of yourself?'

Bazarov paused. 'When I meet a man who can hold his own beside me,' he said, dwelling on every syllable, 'then I'll change my opinion of myself. Yes, hatred! You said, for instance, to-day as we passed our bailiff Philip's cottage—it's the one that's so nice and clean—well, you said, Russia will come to perfection when the poorest peasant has a house like that, and every one of us ought to work to bring it about.... And I felt such a hatred for this poorest peasant, this Philip or Sidor, for whom I'm to be ready to jump out of my skin, and who won't even thank me for it ... and why should he thank me? Why, suppose he does live in a clean house, while the nettles are growing out of me,—well what do I gain by it?'

'Hush, Yevgeny ... if one listened to you to-day one would be driven to agreeing with those who reproach us for want of principles.'
'You talk like your uncle. There are no general principles—you've not made out that even yet! There are feelings. Everything depends on them.'
'How so?'
'Why, I, for instance, take up a negative attitude, by virtue of my sensations; I like to deny—my brain's made on that plan, and that's all about it! Why do I like chemistry? Why do you like apples?—by virtue of our sensations. It's all the same thing. Deeper than that men will never penetrate. Not every one will tell you that, and, in fact, I shan't tell you so another time.'
'What? and is honesty a matter of the senses?'
'I should rather think so.'
'Yevgeny!' Arkady was beginning in a dejected voice ...
'Well? What? Isn't it to your taste?' broke in Bazarov. 'No, brother. If you've made up your mind to mow down everything, don't spare your own legs. But we've talked enough metaphysics. "Nature breathes the silence of sleep," said Pushkin.'
'He never said anything of the sort,' protested Arkady.
'Well, if he didn't, as a poet he might have—and ought to have said it. By the way, he must have been a military man.'
'Pushkin never was a military man!'
'Why, on every page of him there's, "To arms! to arms! for Russia's honour!"'
'Why, what stories you invent! I declare, it's positive calumny.'
'Calumny? That's a mighty matter! What a word he's found to frighten me with! Whatever charge you make against a man, you may be certain he deserves twenty times worse than that in reality.'
'We had better go to sleep,' said Arkady, in a tone of vexation.
'With the greatest pleasure,' answered Bazarov. But neither of them slept. A feeling almost of hostility had come over both the young men. Five minutes later, they opened their eyes and glanced at one another in silence.
'Look,' said Arkady suddenly, 'a dry maple leaf has come off and is falling to the earth; its movement is exactly like a butterfly's flight. Isn't it strange? Gloom and decay—like brightness and life.'
'Oh, my friend, Arkady Nikolaitch!' cried Bazarov, 'one thing I entreat of you; no fine talk.'
'I talk as best I can.... And, I declare, its perfect despotism. An idea came into my head; why shouldn't I utter it?'
'Yes; and why shouldn't I utter my ideas? I think that fine talk's positively indecent.'
'And what is decent? Abuse?'
'Ha! ha! you really do intend, I see, to walk in your uncle's footsteps. How pleased that worthy imbecile would have been if he had heard you!'
'What did you call Pavel Petrovitch?'
'I called him, very justly, an imbecile.'
'But this is unbearable!' cried Arkady.
'Aha! family feeling spoke there,' Bazarov commented coolly. 'I've noticed how obstinately it sticks to people. A man's ready to give up everything and break with every prejudice; but to admit that his brother, for instance, who steals handkerchiefs, is a thief—that's too much for him. And when one comes to think of it: my brother, mine—and no genius ... that's an idea no one can swallow.'
'It was a simple sense of justice spoke in me and not in the least family feeling,' retorted Arkady passionately. 'But since that's a sense you don't understand, since you haven't that sensation, you can't judge of it.'
'In other words, Arkady Kirsanov is too exalted for my comprehension. I bow down before him and say no more.'
'Don't, please, Yevgeny; we shall really quarrel at last.'
'Ah, Arkady! do me a kindness. I entreat you, let us quarrel for once in earnest....'
'But then perhaps we should end by ...'
'Fighting?' put in Bazarov. 'Well? Here, on the hay, in these idyllic surroundings, far from the world and the eyes of men, it wouldn't matter. But you'd be no match for me. I'll have you by the throat in a minute.'
Bazarov spread out his long, cruel fingers.... Arkady turned round and prepared, as though in jest, to resist.... But his friend's face struck him as so vindictive—there was such menace in grim earnest in the smile that distorted his lips, and in his glittering eyes, that he felt instinctively afraid.

'Ah! so this is where you have got to!' the voice of Vassily Ivanovitch was heard saying at that instant, and the old army-doctor appeared before the young men, garbed in a home-made linen pea-jacket, with a straw hat, also home-made, on his head. 'I've been looking everywhere for you.... Well, you've picked out a capital place, and you're excellently employed. Lying on the "earth, gazing up to heaven." Do you know, there's a special significance in that?'
'I never gaze up to heaven except when I want to sneeze,' growled Bazarov, and turning to Arkady he added in an undertone. 'Pity he interrupted us.'
'Come, hush!' whispered Arkady, and he secretly squeezed his friend's hand. But no friendship can long stand such shocks.
'I look at you, my youthful friends,' Vassily Ivanovitch was saying meantime, shaking his head, and leaning his folded arms on a rather cunningly bent stick of his own carving, with a Turk's figure for a top,—'I look, and I cannot refrain from admiration. You have so much strength, such youth and bloom, such abilities, such talents! Positively, a Castor and Pollux!'
'Get along with you—going off into mythology!' commented Bazarov. 'You can see at once that he was a great Latinist in his day! Why, I seem to remember, you gained the silver medal for Latin prose—didn't you?'
'The Dioscuri, the Dioscuri!' repeated Vassily Ivanovitch.
'Come, shut up, father; don't show off.'
'Once in a way it's surely permissible,' murmured the old man. 'However, I have not been seeking for you, gentlemen, to pay you compliments; but with the object, in the first place, of announcing to you that we shall soon be dining; and secondly, I wanted to prepare you, Yevgeny.... You are a sensible man, you know the world, and you know what women are, and consequently you will excuse.... Your mother wished to have a Te Deum sung on the occasion of your arrival. You must not imagine that I am inviting you to attend this thanksgiving—it is over indeed now; but Father Alexey ...'
'The village parson?'
'Well, yes, the priest; he ... is to dine ... with us.... I did not anticipate this, and did not even approve of it ... but it somehow came about ... he did not understand me.... And, well ... Arina Vlasyevna ... Besides, he's a worthy, reasonable man.'
'He won't eat my share at dinner, I suppose?' queried Bazarov.
Vassily Ivanovitch laughed. 'How you talk!'
'Well, that's all I ask. I'm ready to sit down to table with any man.'
Vassily Ivanovitch set his hat straight. 'I was certain before I spoke,' he said, 'that you were above any kind of prejudice. Here am I, an old man at sixty-two, and I have none.' (Vassily Ivanovitch did not dare to confess that he had himself desired the thanksgiving service. He was no less religious than his wife.) 'And Father Alexey very much wanted to make your acquaintance. You will like him, you'll see. He's no objection even to cards, and he sometimes—but this is between ourselves ... positively smokes a pipe.'
'All right. We'll have a round of whist after dinner, and I'll clean him out.'
'He! he! he! We shall see! That remains to be seen.'
'I know you're an old hand,' said Bazarov, with a peculiar emphasis.
Vassily Ivanovitch's bronzed cheeks were suffused with an uneasy flush.
'For shame, Yevgeny.... Let bygones be bygones. Well, I'm ready to acknowledge before this gentleman I had that passion in my youth; and I have paid for it too! How hot it is, though! Let me sit down with you. I shan't be in your way, I hope?'
'Oh, not at all,' answered Arkady.
Vassily Ivanovitch lowered himself, sighing, into the hay. 'Your present quarters remind me, my dear sirs,' he began, 'of my military bivouacking existence, the ambulance halts, somewhere like this under a haystack, and even for that we were thankful.' He sighed. 'I had many, many experiences in my life. For example, if you will allow me, I will tell you a curious episode of the plague in Bessarabia.'
'For which you got the Vladimir cross?' put in Bazarov. 'We know, we know.... By the way, why is it you're not wearing it?'
'Why, I told you that I have no prejudices,' muttered Vassily Ivanovitch (he had only the evening before had the red ribbon unpicked off his coat), and he proceeded to relate the episode of the plague. 'Why, he's fallen asleep,' he whispered all at once to Arkady, pointing to Yevgeny, and winking good-naturedly. 'Yevgeny! get up,' he went on aloud. 'Let's go in to dinner.'
Father Alexey, a good-looking stout man with thick, carefully-combed hair, with an embroidered girdle round his lilac silk cassock, appeared to be a man of much tact and adaptability. He made haste to be the first

to offer his hand to Arkady and Bazarov, as though understanding beforehand that they did not want his blessing, and he behaved himself in general without constraint. He neither derogated from his own dignity, nor gave offence to others; he vouchsafed a passing smile at the seminary Latin, and stood up for his bishop; drank two small glasses of wine, but refused a third; accepted a cigar from Arkady, but did not proceed to smoke it, saying he would take it home with him. The only thing not quite agreeable about him was a way he had of constantly raising his hand with care and deliberation to catch the flies on his face, sometimes succeeding in smashing them. He took his seat at the green table, expressing his satisfaction at so doing in measured terms, and ended by winning from Bazarov two roubles and a half in paper money; they had no idea of even reckoning in silver in the house of Arina Vlasyevna.... She was sitting, as before, near her son (she did not play cards), her cheek, as before, propped on her little fist; she only got up to order some new dainty to be served. She was afraid to caress Bazarov, and he gave her no encouragement, he did not invite her caresses; and besides, Vassily Ivanovitch had advised her not to 'worry' him too much. 'Young men are not fond of that sort of thing,' he declared to her. (It's needless to say what the dinner was like that day; Timofeitch in person had galloped off at early dawn for beef; the bailiff had gone off in another direction for turbot, gremille, and crayfish; for mushrooms alone forty-two farthings had been paid the peasant women in copper); but Arina Vlasyevna's eyes, bent steadfastly on Bazarov, did not express only devotion and tenderness; in them was to be seen sorrow also, mingled with awe and curiosity; there was to be seen too a sort of humble reproachfulness.

Bazarov, however, was not in a humour to analyse the exact expression of his mother's eyes; he seldom turned to her, and then only with some short question. Once he asked her for her hand 'for luck'; she gently laid her soft, little hand on his rough, broad palm.

'Well,' she asked, after waiting a little, 'has it been any use?'

'Worse luck than ever,' he answered, with a careless laugh.

'He plays too rashly,' pronounced Father Alexey, as it were compassionately, and he stroked his beard.

'Napoleon's rule, good Father, Napoleon's rule,' put in Vassily Ivanovitch, leading an ace.

'It brought him to St. Helena, though,' observed Father Alexey, as he trumped the ace.

'Wouldn't you like some currant tea, Enyusha?' inquired Arina Vlasyevna.

Bazarov merely shrugged his shoulders.

'No!' he said to Arkady the next day. I'm off from here to-morrow. I'm bored; I want to work, but I can't work here. I will come to your place again; I've left all my apparatus there too. In your house one can at any rate shut oneself up. While here my father repeats to me, "My study is at your disposal—nobody shall interfere with you," and all the time he himself is never a yard away. And I'm ashamed somehow to shut myself away from him. It's the same thing too with mother. I hear her sighing the other side of the wall, and if one goes in to her, one's nothing to say to her.'

'She will be very much grieved,' observed Arkady, 'and so will he.'

'I shall come back again to them.'

'When?'

'Why, when on my way to Petersburg.'

'I feel sorry for your mother particularly.'

'Why's that? Has she won your heart with strawberries, or what?'

Arkady dropped his eyes. 'You don't understand your mother, Yevgeny. She's not only a very good woman, she's very clever really. This morning she talked to me for half-an-hour, and so sensibly, interestingly.'

'I suppose she was expatiating upon me all the while?'

'We didn't talk only about you.'

'Perhaps; lookers-on see most. If a woman can keep up half-an-hour's conversation, it's always a hopeful sign. But I'm going, all the same.'

'It won't be very easy for you to break it to them. They are always making plans for what we are to do in a fortnight's time.'

'No; it won't be easy. Some demon drove me to tease my father to-day; he had one of his rent-paying peasants flogged the other day, and quite right too—yes, yes, you needn't look at me in such horror—he did quite right, because he's an awful thief and drunkard; only my father had no idea that I, as they say, was cognisant of the facts. He was greatly perturbed, and now I shall have to upset him more than ever.... Never mind! Never say die! He'll get over it!'

Bazarov said, 'Never mind'; but the whole day passed before he could make up his mind to inform Vassily Ivanovitch of his intentions. At last, when he was just saying good-night to him in the study, he observed, with a feigned yawn—

'Oh ... I was almost forgetting to tell you.... Send to Fedot's for our horses to-morrow.'

Vassily Ivanovitch was dumbfounded. 'Is Mr. Kirsanov leaving us, then?'

'Yes; and I'm going with him.'

Vassily Ivanovitch positively reeled. 'You are going?'

'Yes ... I must. Make the arrangements about the horses, please.'

'Very good....' faltered the old man; 'to Fedot's ... very good ... only ... only.... How is it?'

'I must go to stay with him for a little time. I will come back again later.'

'Ah! For a little time ... very good.' Vassily Ivanovitch drew out his handkerchief, and, blowing his nose, doubled up almost to the ground. 'Well ... everything shall be done. I had thought you were to be with us ... a little longer. Three days.... After three years, it's rather little; rather little, Yevgeny!'

'But, I tell you, I'm coming back directly. It's necessary for me to go.'

'Necessary.... Well! Duty before everything. So the horses shall be in readiness. Very good. Arina and I, of course, did not anticipate this. She has just begged some flowers from a neighbour; she meant to decorate the room for you.' (Vassily Ivanovitch did not even mention that every morning almost at dawn he took counsel with Timofeitch, standing with his bare feet in his slippers, and pulling out with trembling fingers one dog's-eared rouble note after another, charged him with various purchases, with special reference to good things to eat, and to red wine, which, as far as he could observe, the young men liked extremely.) 'Liberty ... is the great thing; that's my rule.... I don't want to hamper you ... not ...'

He suddenly ceased, and made for the door.

'We shall soon see each other again, father, really.'

But Vassily Ivanovitch, without turning round, merely waved his hand and was gone. When he got back to his bedroom he found his wife in bed, and began to say his prayers in a whisper, so as not to wake her up. She woke, however. 'Is that you, Vassily Ivanovitch?' she asked.

'Yes, mother.'

'Have you come from Enyusha? Do you know, I'm afraid of his not being comfortable on that sofa. I told Anfisushka to put him on your travelling mattress and the new pillows; I should have given him our feather-bed, but I seem to remember he doesn't like too soft a bed....'

'Never mind, mother; don't worry yourself. He's all right. Lord, have mercy on me, a sinner,' he went on with his prayer in a low voice. Vassily Ivanovitch was sorry for his old wife; he did not mean to tell her over night what a sorrow there was in store for her.

Bazarov and Arkady set off the next day. From early morning all was dejection in the house; Anfisushka let the tray slip out of her hands; even Fedka was bewildered, and was reduced to taking off his boots. Vassily Ivanitch was more fussy than ever; he was obviously trying to put a good face on it, talked loudly, and stamped with his feet, but his face looked haggard, and his eyes were continually avoiding his son. Arina Vlasyevna was crying quietly; she was utterly crushed, and could not have controlled herself at all if her husband had not spent two whole hours early in the morning exhorting her. When Bazarov, after repeated promises to come back certainly not later than in a month's time, tore himself at last from the embraces detaining him, and took his seat in the coach; when the horses had started, the bell was ringing, and the wheels were turning round, and when it was no longer any good to look after them, and the dust had settled, and Timofeitch, all bent and tottering as he walked, had crept back to his little room; when the old people were left alone in their little house, which seemed suddenly to have grown shrunken and decrepit too, Vassily Ivanovitch, after a few more moments of hearty waving of his handkerchief on the steps, sank into a chair, and his head dropped on to his breast. 'He has cast us off; he has forsaken us,' he faltered; 'forsaken us; he was dull with us. Alone, alone!' he repeated several times. Then Arina Vlasyevna went up to him, and, leaning her grey head against his grey head, said, 'There's no help for it, Vasya! A son is a separate piece cut off. He's like the falcon that flies home and flies away at his pleasure; while you and I are like funguses in the hollow of a tree, we sit side by side, and don't move from our place. Only I am left you unchanged for ever, as you for me.'

Vassily Ivanovitch took his hands from his face and clasped his wife, his friend, as warmly as he had never clasped in youth; she comforted him in his grief.

CHAPTER XXII

In silence, only rarely exchanging a few insignificant words, our friends travelled as far as Fedot's. Bazarov was not altogether pleased with himself. Arkady was displeased with him. He was feeling, too, that causeless melancholy which is only known to very young people. The coachman changed the horses, and getting up on to the box, inquired, 'To the right or to the left?'

Arkady started. The road to the right led to the town, and from there home; the road to the left led to Madame Odintsov's.

He looked at Bazarov.

'Yevgeny,' he queried; 'to the left?'

Bazarov turned away. 'What folly is this?' he muttered.

'I know it's folly,' answered Arkady.... 'But what does that matter? It's not the first time.'

Bazarov pulled his cap down over his brows. 'As you choose,' he said at last. 'Turn to the left,' shouted Arkady.

The coach rolled away in the direction of Nikolskoe. But having resolved on the folly, the friends were even more obstinately silent than before, and seemed positively ill-humoured.

Directly the steward met them on the steps of Madame Odintsov's house, the friends could perceive that they had acted injudiciously in giving way so suddenly to a passing impulse. They were obviously not expected. They sat rather a long while, looking rather foolish, in the drawing-room. Madame Odintsov came in to them at last. She greeted them with her customary politeness, but was surprised at their hasty return; and, so far as could be judged from the deliberation of her gestures and words, she was not over pleased at it. They made haste to announce that they had only called on their road, and must go on farther, to the town, within four hours. She confined herself to a light exclamation, begged Arkady to remember her to his father, and sent for her aunt. The princess appeared very sleepy, which gave her wrinkled old face an even more ill-natured expression. Katya was not well; she did not leave her room. Arkady suddenly realised that he was at least as anxious to see Katya as Anna Sergyevna herself. The four hours were spent in insignificant discussion of one thing and another; Anna Sergyevna both listened and spoke without a smile. It was only quite at parting that her former friendliness seemed, as it were, to revive.

'I have an attack of spleen just now,' she said; 'but you must not pay attention to that, and come again—I say this to both of you—before long.'

Both Bazarov and Arkady responded with a silent bow, took their seats in the coach, and without stopping again anywhere, went straight home to Maryino, where they arrived safely on the evening of the following day. During the whole course of the journey neither one nor the other even mentioned the name of Madame Odintsov; Bazarov, in particular, scarcely opened his mouth, and kept staring in a side direction away from the road, with a kind of exasperated intensity.

At Maryino every one was exceedingly delighted to see them. The prolonged absence of his son had begun to make Nikolai Petrovitch uneasy; he uttered a cry of joy, and bounced about on the sofa, dangling his legs, when Fenitchka ran to him with sparkling eyes, and informed him of the arrival of the 'young gentlemen'; even Pavel Petrovitch was conscious of some degree of agreeable excitement, and smiled condescendingly as he shook hands with the returned wanderers. Talk, questions followed; Arkady talked most, especially at supper, which was prolonged long after midnight. Nikolai Petrovitch ordered up some bottles of porter which had only just been sent from Moscow, and partook of the festive beverage till his cheeks were crimson, and he kept laughing in a half-childish, half-nervous little chuckle. Even the servants were infected by the general gaiety. Dunyasha ran up and down like one possessed, and was continually slamming doors; while Piotr was, at three o'clock in the morning, still attempting to strum a Cossack waltz on the guitar. The strings gave forth a sweet and plaintive sound in the still air; but with the exception of a small preliminary flourish, nothing came of the cultured valet's efforts; nature had given him no more musical talent than all the rest of the world.

But meanwhile things were not going over harmoniously at Maryino, and poor Nikolai Petrovitch was having a bad time of it. Difficulties on the farm sprang up every day—senseless, distressing difficulties. The troubles with the hired labourers had become insupportable. Some asked for their wages to be settled, or for an increase of wages, while others made off with the wages they had received in advance; the horses fell sick; the harness fell to pieces as though it were burnt; the work was carelessly done; a threshing machine that had been ordered from Moscow turned out to be useless from its great weight, another was ruined the first time it was used; half the cattle sheds were burnt down through an old blind woman on the farm going in windy weather with a burning brand to fumigate her cow ... the old woman, it is true, maintained that the whole mischief could be traced to the master's plan of introducing newfangled cheeses and milk-products. The overseer suddenly turned lazy, and began to grow fat, as every Russian grows fat when he gets a snug berth. When he caught sight of Nikolai Petrovitch in the distance, he would fling a stick at a passing pig, or threaten a half-naked urchin, to show his zeal, but the rest of the time he was generally asleep. The peasants who had been put on the rent system did not bring their money at the time due, and stole the forest-timber; almost every night the keepers caught peasants' horses in the meadows of the 'farm,' and sometimes forcibly bore them off. Nikolai Petrovitch would fix a money fine for damages, but the matter usually ended after the horses had been kept a day or two on the master's forage by their returning to their owners. To crown all, the peasants began quarrelling among themselves; brothers asked for a division of property, their wives could not get on together in one house; all of a sudden the squabble, as though at a given signal, came to a head, and at once the whole village came running to the counting-house steps, crawling to the master often drunken and with battered face, demanding justice and judgment; then arose an uproar and clamour, the shrill wailing of the women mixed with the curses of the men. Then one had to examine the contending parties, and shout oneself hoarse, knowing all the while that one could never anyway arrive at a just decision.... There were not hands enough for the harvest; a neighbouring small owner, with the most benevolent countenance, contracted to supply him with reapers for a commission of two roubles an acre, and cheated him in the most shameless fashion; his peasant women demanded unheard-of sums, and the corn meanwhile went to waste; and here they were not getting on with the mowing, and there the Council of Guardians threatened and demanded prompt payment, in full, of interest due....

'I can do nothing!' Nikolai Petrovitch cried more than once in despair. 'I can't flog them myself; and as for calling in the police captain, my principles don't allow of it, while you can do nothing with them without the fear of punishment!'

'Du calme, du calme,' Pavel Petrovitch would remark upon this, but even he hummed to himself, knitted his brows, and tugged at his moustache.

Bazarov held aloof from these matters, and indeed as a guest it was not for him to meddle in other people's business. The day after his arrival at Maryino, he set to work on his frogs, his infusoria, and his chemical experiments, and was for ever busy with them. Arkady, on the contrary, thought it his duty, if not to help his father, at least to make a show of being ready to help him. He gave him a patient hearing, and once offered him some advice, not with any idea of its being acted upon, but to show his interest. Farming details did not arouse any aversion in him; he used even to dream with pleasure of work on the land, but at this time his brain was swarming with other ideas. Arkady, to his own astonishment, thought incessantly of Nikolskoe; in former days he would simply have shrugged his shoulders if any one had told him that he could ever feel dull under the same roof as Bazarov—and that roof his father's! but he actually was dull and longed to get away. He tried going long walks till he was tired, but that was no use. In conversation with his father one day, he found out that Nikolai Petrovitch had in his possession rather interesting letters, written by Madame Odintsov's mother to his wife, and he gave him no rest till he got hold of the letters, for which Nikolai Petrovitch had to rummage in twenty drawers and boxes. Having gained possession of these half-crumbling papers, Arkady felt, as it were, soothed, just as though he had caught a glimpse of the goal towards which he ought now to go. 'I mean that for both of you,' he was constantly whispering—she had added that herself! 'I'll go, I'll go, hang it all!' But he recalled the last visit, the cold reception, and his former embarrassment, and timidity got the better of him. The 'go-ahead' feeling of youth, the secret desire to try his luck, to prove his powers in solitude, without the protection of any one whatever, gained the day at last. Before ten days had passed after his return to Maryino, on the pretext of studying the working of the Sunday schools, he galloped off to the town again, and from there to Nikolskoe. Urging the driver on without intermission, he flew along, like a young officer riding to battle; and he felt both frightened and light-hearted, and was breathless with impatience. 'The great thing is—one mustn't think,' he kept repeating to himself. His driver happened to be a lad of spirit; he halted before every public house, saying, 'A drink or not a drink?' but, to make up for it, when he had drunk he did not spare his horses. At last the lofty roof of the familiar house came in sight.... 'What am I to do?' flashed through Arkady's head. 'Well, there's no turning back now!' The three horses galloped in unison; the driver whooped and whistled at them. And now the bridge was groaning under the hoofs and wheels, and now the avenue of lopped pines seemed running to meet them.... There was a glimpse of a woman's pink dress against the dark green, a young face from under the light fringe of a parasol.... He recognised Katya, and she recognised him. Arkady told the driver to stop the galloping horses, leaped out of the carriage, and went up to her. 'It's you!' she cried, gradually flushing all over; 'let us go to my sister, she's here in the garden; she will be pleased to see you.'

Katya led Arkady into the garden. His meeting with her struck him as a particularly happy omen; he was delighted to see her, as though she were of his own kindred. Everything had happened so splendidly; no steward, no formal announcement. At a turn in the path he caught sight of Anna Sergyevna. She was standing with her back to him. Hearing footsteps, she turned slowly round.

Arkady felt confused again, but the first words she uttered soothed him at once. 'Welcome back, runaway!' she said in her even, caressing voice, and came to meet him, smiling and frowning to keep the sun and wind out of her eyes. 'Where did you pick him up, Katya?'

'I have brought you something, Anna Sergyevna,' he began, 'which you certainly don't expect.'

'You have brought yourself; that's better than anything.'

CHAPTER XXIII

Having seen Arkady off with ironical compassion, and given him to understand that he was not in the least deceived as to the real object of his journey, Bazarov shut himself up in complete solitude; he was overtaken by a fever for work. He did not dispute now with Pavel Petrovitch, especially as the latter assumed an excessively aristocratic demeanour in his presence, and expressed his opinions more in inarticulate sounds than in words. Only on one occasion Pavel Petrovitch fell into a controversy with the *nihilist* on the subject of the question then much discussed of the rights of the nobles of the Baltic province; but suddenly he stopped of his own accord, remarking with chilly politeness, 'However, we cannot understand one another; I, at least, have not the honour of understanding you.'

'I should think not!' cried Bazarov. 'A man's capable of understanding anything—how the æther vibrates, and what's going on in the sun—but how any other man can blow his nose differently from him, that he's incapable of understanding.'

'What, is that an epigram?' observed Pavel Petrovitch inquiringly, and he walked away.

However, he sometimes asked permission to be present at Bazarov's experiments, and once even placed his perfumed face, washed with the very best soap, near the microscope to see how a transparent infusoria swallowed a green speck, and busily munched it with two very rapid sort of clappers which were in its throat. Nikolai Petrovitch visited Bazarov much oftener than his brother; he would have come every day, as he expressed it, to 'study,' if his worries on the farm had not taken off his attention. He did not hinder the young man in his scientific researches; he used to sit down somewhere in a corner of the room and look on attentively, occasionally permitting himself a discreet question. During dinner and supper-time he used to try to turn the conversation upon physics, geology, or chemistry, seeing that all other topics, even agriculture, to say nothing of politics, might lead, if not to collisions, at least to mutual unpleasantness. Nikolai Petrovitch surmised that his brother's dislike for Bazarov was no less. An unimportant incident, among many others, confirmed his surmises. The cholera began to make its appearance in some places in the neighbourhood, and even 'carried off' two persons from Maryino itself. In the night Pavel Petrovitch happened to have rather severe symptoms. He was in pain till the morning, but did not have recourse to Bazarov's skill. And when he met him the following day, in reply to his question, 'Why he had not sent for him?' answered, still quite pale, but scrupulously brushed and shaved, 'Why, I seem to recollect you said yourself you didn't believe in medicine.' So the days went by. Bazarov went on obstinately and grimly working ... and meanwhile there was in Nikolai Petrovitch's house one creature to whom, if he did not open his heart, he at least was glad to talk.... That creature was Fenitchka.

He used to meet her for the most part early in the morning, in the garden, or the farmyard; he never used to go to her room to see her, and she had only once been to his door to inquire—ought she to let Mitya have his bath or not? It was not only that she confided in him, that she was not afraid of him—she was positively freer and more at her ease in her behaviour with him than with Nikolai Petrovitch himself. It is hard to say how it came about; perhaps it was because she unconsciously felt the absence in Bazarov of all gentility, of all that superiority which at once attracts and overawes. In her eyes he was both an excellent doctor and a simple man. She looked after her baby without constraint in his presence; and once when she was suddenly attacked with giddiness and headache—she took a spoonful of medicine from his hand. Before Nikolai Petrovitch she kept, as it were, at a distance from Bazarov; she acted in this way not from hypocrisy, but from a kind of feeling of propriety. Pavel Petrovitch she was more afraid of than ever; for some time he had begun to watch her, and would suddenly make his appearance, as though he sprang out of the earth behind her back, in his English suit, with his immovable vigilant face, and his hands in his pockets. 'It's like a bucket of cold water on one,' Fenitchka complained to Dunyasha, and the latter sighed in response, and thought of another 'heartless' man. Bazarov, without the least suspicion of the fact, had become the*cruel tyrant* of her heart.

Fenitchka liked Bazarov; but he liked her too. His face was positively transformed when he talked to her; it took a bright, almost kind expression, and his habitual nonchalance was replaced by a sort of jesting attentiveness. Fenitchka was growing prettier every day. There is a time in the life of young women when they suddenly begin to expand and blossom like summer roses; this time had come for Fenitchka. Dressed in a delicate white dress, she seemed herself slighter and whiter; she was not tanned by the sun; but the heat, from which she could not shield herself, spread a slight flush over her cheeks and ears, and, shedding a soft indolence over her whole body, was reflected in a dreamy languor in her pretty eyes. She was almost unable to work; her hands seem to fall naturally into her lap. She scarcely walked at all, and was constantly sighing and complaining with comic helplessness.

'You should go oftener to bathe,' Nikolai Petrovitch told her. He had made a large bath covered in with an awning in one of his ponds which had not yet quite disappeared.

'Oh, Nikolai Petrovitch! But by the time one gets to the pond, one's utterly dead, and, coming back, one's dead again. You see, there's no shade in the garden.'

'That's true, there's no shade,' replied Nikolai Petrovitch, rubbing his forehead.

One day at seven o'clock in the morning Bazarov, returning from a walk, came upon Fenitchka in the lilac arbour, which was long past flowering, but was still thick and green. She was sitting on the garden seat, and had as usual thrown a white kerchief over her head; near her lay a whole heap of red and white roses still wet with dew. He said good morning to her.

'Ah! Yevgeny Vassilyitch!' she said, and lifted the edge of her kerchief a little to look at him, in doing which her arm was left bare to the elbow.

'What are you doing here?' said Bazarov, sitting down beside her. 'Are you making a nosegay?'

'Yes, for the table at lunch. Nikolai Petrovitch likes it.'

'But it's a long while yet to lunch time. What a heap of flowers!'

'I gathered them now, for it will be hot then, and one can't go out. One can only just breathe now. I feel quite weak with the heat. I'm really afraid whether I'm not going to be ill.'

'What an idea! Let me feel your pulse.' Bazarov took her hand, felt for the evenly-beating pulse, but did not even begin to count its throbs. 'You'll live a hundred years!' he said, dropping her hand.

'Ah, God forbid!' she cried.

'Why? Don't you want a long life?'

'Well, but a hundred years! There was an old woman near us eighty-five years old—and what a martyr she was! Dirty and deaf and bent and coughing all the time; nothing but a burden to herself. That's a dreadful life!'

'So it's better to be young?'

'Well, isn't it?'

'But why is it better? Tell me!'

'How can you ask why? Why, here I now, while I'm young, I can do everything—go and come and carry, and needn't ask any one for anything.... What can be better?'

'And to me it's all the same whether I'm young or old.'

'How do you mean—it's all the same? It's not possible what you say.'

'Well, judge for yourself, Fedosya Nikolaevna, what good is my youth to me. I live alone, a poor lonely creature ...'

'That always depends on you.'

'It doesn't at all depend on me! At least, some one ought to take pity on me.'

Fenitchka gave a sidelong look at Bazarov, but said nothing. 'What's this book you have?' she asked after a short pause.

'That? That's a scientific book, very difficult.'

'And are you still studying? And don't you find it dull? You know everything already I should say.'

'It seems not everything. You try to read a little.'

'But I don't understand anything here. Is it Russian?' asked Fenitchka, taking the heavily bound book in both hands. 'How thick it is!'

'Yes, it's Russian.'

'All the same, I shan't understand anything.'

'Well, I didn't give it you for you to understand it. I wanted to look at you while you were reading. When you read, the end of your little nose moves so nicely.'

Fenitchka, who had set to work to spell out in a low voice the article on 'Creosote' she had chanced upon, laughed and threw down the book ... it slipped from the seat on to the ground.

'Nonsense!'

'I like it too when you laugh,' observed Bazarov.

'I like it when you talk. It's just like a little brook babbling.'

Fenitchka turned her head away. 'What a person you are to talk!' she commented, picking the flowers over with her finger. 'And how can you care to listen to me? You have talked with such clever ladies.'

'Ah, Fedosya Nikolaevna! believe me; all the clever ladies in the world are not worth your little elbow.'

'Come, there's another invention!' murmured Fenitchka, clasping her hands.

Bazarov picked the book up from the ground.

'That's a medical book; why do you throw it away?'

'Medical?' repeated Fenitchka, and she turned to him again. 'Do you know, ever since you gave me those drops—do you remember?—Mitya has slept so well! I really can't think how to thank you; you are so good, really.'

'But you have to pay doctors,' observed Bazarov with a smile. 'Doctors, you know yourself, are grasping people.'

Fenitchka raised her eyes, which seemed still darker from the whitish reflection cast on the upper part of her face, and looked at Bazarov. She did not know whether he was joking or not.

'If you please, we shall be delighted.... I must ask Nikolai Petrovitch ...'

'Why, do you think I want money?' Bazarov interposed. 'No; I don't want money from you.'

'What then?' asked Fenitchka.

'What?' repeated Bazarov. 'Guess!'

'A likely person I am to guess!'

'Well, I will tell you; I want ... one of those roses.'

Fenitchka laughed again, and even clapped her hands, so amusing Bazarov's request seemed to her. She laughed, and at the same time felt flattered. Bazarov was looking intently at her.

'By all means,' she said at last; and, bending down to the seat, she began picking over the roses. 'Which will you have—a red one or a white one?'

'Red, and not too large.'

She sat up again. 'Here, take it,' she said, but at once drew back her outstretched hand, and, biting her lips, looked towards the entrance of the arbour, then listened.

'What is it?' asked Bazarov. 'Nikolai Petrovitch?'

'No ... Mr. Kirsanov has gone to the fields ... besides, I'm not afraid of him ... but Pavel Petrovitch ... I fancied ...'

'What?'

'I fancied he was coming here. No ... it was no one. Take it.' Fenitchka gave Bazarov the rose.

'On what grounds are you afraid of Pavel Petrovitch?'
'He always scares me. And I know you don't like him. Do you remember, you always used to quarrel with him? I don't know what your quarrel was about, but I can see you turn him about like this and like that.'
Fenitchka showed with her hands how in her opinion Bazarov turned Pavel Petrovitch about.
Bazarov smiled. 'But if he gave me a beating,' he asked, 'would you stand up for me?'
'How could I stand up for you? but no, no one will get the better of you.'
'Do you think so? But I know a hand which could overcome me if it liked.'
'What hand?'
'Why, don't you know, really? Smell, how delicious this rose smells you gave me.'
Fenitchka stretched her little neck forward, and put her face close to the flower.... The kerchief slipped from her head on to her shoulders; her soft mass of dark, shining, slightly ruffled hair was visible.
'Wait a minute; I want to smell it with you,' said Bazarov. He bent down and kissed her vigorously on her parted lips.
She started, pushed him back with both her hands on his breast, but pushed feebly, and he was able to renew and prolong his kiss.
A dry cough was heard behind the lilac bushes. Fenitchka instantly moved away to the other end of the seat. Pavel Petrovitch showed himself, made a slight bow, and saying with a sort of malicious mournfulness, 'You are here,' he retreated. Fenitchka at once gathered up all her roses and went out of the arbour. 'It was wrong of you, Yevgeny Vassilyevitch,' she whispered as she went. There was a note of genuine reproach in her whisper.
Bazarov remembered another recent scene, and he felt both shame and contemptuous annoyance. But he shook his head directly, ironically congratulated himself 'on his final assumption of the part of the gay Lothario,' and went off to his own room.
Pavel Petrovitch went out of the garden, and made his way with deliberate steps to the copse. He stayed there rather a long while; and when he returned to lunch, Nikolai Petrovitch inquired anxiously whether he were quite well—his face looked so gloomy.
'You know, I sometimes suffer with my liver,' Pavel Petrovitch answered tranquilly.

CHAPTER XXIV

Two hours later he knocked at Bazarov's door.
'I must apologise for hindering you in your scientific pursuits,' he began, seating himself on a chair in the window, and leaning with both hands on a handsome walking-stick with an ivory knob (he usually walked without a stick), 'but I am constrained to beg you to spare me five minutes of your time ... no more.'
'All my time is at your disposal,' answered Bazarov, over whose face there passed a quick change of expression directly Pavel Petrovitch crossed the threshold.
'Five minutes will be enough for me. I have come to put a single question to you.'
'A question? What is it about?'
'I will tell you, if you will kindly hear me out. At the commencement of your stay in my brother's house, before I had renounced the pleasure of conversing with you, it was my fortune to hear your opinions on many subjects; but so far as my memory serves, neither between us, nor in my presence, was the subject of single combats and duelling in general broached. Allow me to hear what are your views on that subject?'
Bazarov, who had risen to meet Pavel Petrovitch, sat down on the edge of the table and folded his arms.
'My view is,' he said, 'that from the theoretical standpoint, duelling is absurd; from the practical standpoint, now—it's quite a different matter.'

'That is, you mean to say, if I understand you right, that whatever your theoretical views on duelling, you would not in practice allow yourself to be insulted without demanding satisfaction?'

'You have guessed my meaning absolutely.'

'Very good. I am very glad to hear you say so. Your words relieve me from a state of incertitude.'

'Of uncertainty, you mean to say.'

'That is all the same! I express myself so as to be understood; I ... am not a seminary rat. Your words save me from a rather deplorable necessity. I have made up my mind to fight you.'

Bazarov opened his eyes wide. 'Me?'

'Undoubtedly.'

'But what for, pray?'

'I could explain the reason to you,' began Pavel Petrovitch, 'but I prefer to be silent about it. To my idea your presence here is superfluous; I cannot endure you; I despise you; and if that is not enough for you ...'

Pavel Petrovitch's eyes glittered ... Bazarov's too were flashing.

'Very good,' he assented. 'No need of further explanations. You've a whim to try your chivalrous spirit upon me. I might refuse you this pleasure, but—so be it!'

'I am sensible of my obligation to you,' replied Pavel Petrovitch; 'and may reckon then on your accepting my challenge without compelling me to resort to violent measures.'

'That means, speaking without metaphor, to that stick?' Bazarov remarked coolly. 'That is precisely correct. It's quite unnecessary for you to insult me. Indeed, it would not be a perfectly safe proceeding. You can remain a gentleman.... I accept your challenge, too, like a gentleman.'

'That is excellent,' observed Pavel Petrovitch, putting his stick in the corner. 'We will say a few words directly about the conditions of our duel; but I should like first to know whether you think it necessary to resort to the formality of a trifling dispute, which might serve as a pretext for my challenge?'

'No; it's better without formalities.'

'I think so myself. I presume it is also out of place to go into the real grounds of our difference. We cannot endure one another. What more is necessary?'

'What more, indeed?' repeated Bazarov ironically.

'As regards the conditions of the meeting itself, seeing that we shall have no seconds—for where could we get them?'

'Exactly so; where could we get them?'

'Then I have the honour to lay the following proposition before you: The combat to take place early to-morrow, at six, let us say, behind the copse, with pistols, at a distance of ten paces....'

'At ten paces? that will do; we hate one another at that distance.'

'We might have it eight,' remarked Pavel Petrovitch.

'We might.'

'To fire twice; and, to be ready for any result, let each put a letter in his pocket, in which he accuses himself of his end.'

'Now, that I don't approve of at all,' observed Bazarov. 'There's a slight flavour of the French novel about it, something not very plausible.'

'Perhaps. You will agree, however, that it would be unpleasant to incur a suspicion of murder?'

'I agree as to that. But there is a means of avoiding that painful reproach. We shall have no seconds, but we can have a witness.'

'And whom, allow me to inquire?'

'Why, Piotr.'

'What Piotr?'

'Your brother's valet. He's a man who has attained to the acme of contemporary culture, and he will perform his part with all the *comilfo (comme il faut)* necessary in such cases.'

'I think you are joking, sir.'

'Not at all. If you think over my suggestion, you will be convinced that it's full of common-sense and simplicity. You can't hide a candle under a bushel; but I'll undertake to prepare Piotr in a fitting manner, and bring him on to the field of battle.'

'You persist in jesting still,' Pavel Petrovitch declared, getting up from his chair. 'But after the courteous readiness you have shown me, I have no right to pretend to lay down.... And so, everything is arranged.... By the way, perhaps you have no pistols?'

'How should I have pistols, Pavel Petrovitch? I'm not in the army.'

'In that case, I offer you mine. You may rest assured that it's five years now since I shot with them.'
'That's a very consoling piece of news.'
Pavel Petrovitch took up his stick.... 'And now, my dear sir, it only remains for me to thank you and to leave you to your studies. I have the honour to take leave of you.'
'Till we have the pleasure of meeting again, my dear sir,' said Bazarov, conducting his visitor to the door.
Pavel Petrovitch went out, while Bazarov remained standing a minute before the door, and suddenly exclaimed, 'Pish, well, I'm dashed! how fine, and how foolish! A pretty farce we've been through! Like trained dogs dancing on their hind-paws. But to decline was out of the question; why, I do believe he'd have struck me, and then ...' (Bazarov turned white at the very thought; all his pride was up in arms at once)—'then it might have come to my strangling him like a cat.' He went back to his microscope, but his heart was beating, and the composure necessary for taking observations had disappeared. 'He caught sight of us to-day,' he thought; 'but would he really act like this on his brother's account? And what a mighty matter is it—a kiss? There must be something else in it. Bah! isn't he perhaps in love with her himself? To be sure, he's in love; it's as clear as day. What a complication! It's a nuisance!' he decided at last; 'it's a bad job, look at it which way you will. In the first place, to risk a bullet through one's brains, and in any case to go away; and then Arkady ... and that dear innocent pussy, Nikolai Petrovitch. It's a bad job, an awfully bad job.'
The day passed in a kind of peculiar stillness and languor. Fenitchka gave no sign of her existence; she sat in her little room like a mouse in its hole. Nikolai Petrovitch had a careworn air. He had just heard that blight had begun to appear in his wheat, upon which he had in particular rested his hopes. Pavel Petrovitch overwhelmed every one, even Prokofitch, with his icy courtesy. Bazarov began a letter to his father, but tore it up, and threw it under the table.
'If I die,' he thought, 'they will find it out; but I'm not going to die. No, I shall struggle along in this world a good while yet.' He gave Piotr orders to come to him on important business the next morning directly it was light. Piotr imagined that he wanted to take him to Petersburg with him. Bazarov went late to bed, and all night long he was harassed by disordered dreams.... Madame Odintsov kept appearing in them, now she was his mother, and she was followed by a kitten with black whiskers, and this kitten seemed to be Fenitchka; then Pavel Petrovitch took the shape of a great wood, with which he had yet to fight. Piotr waked him up at four o'clock; he dressed at once, and went out with him.
It was a lovely, fresh morning; tiny flecked clouds hovered overhead in little curls of foam on the pale clear blue; a fine dew lay in drops on the leaves and grass, and sparkled like silver on the spiders' webs; the damp, dark earth seemed still to keep traces of the rosy dawn; from the whole sky the songs of larks came pouring in showers. Bazarov walked as far as the copse, sat down in the shade at its edge, and only then disclosed to Piotr the nature of the service he expected of him. The refined valet was mortally alarmed; but Bazarov soothed him by the assurance that he would have nothing to do but stand at a distance and look on, and that he would not incur any sort of responsibility. 'And meantime,' he added, 'only think what an important part you have to play!' Piotr threw up his hands, looked down, and leaned against a birch-tree, looking green with terror.
The road from Maryino skirted the copse; a light dust lay on it, untouched by wheel or foot since the previous day. Bazarov unconsciously stared along this road, picked and gnawed a blade of grass, while he kept repeating to himself, 'What a piece of foolery!' The chill of the early morning made him shiver twice.... Piotr looked at him dejectedly, but Bazarov only smiled; he was not afraid.
The tramp of horses' hoofs was heard along the road.... A peasant came into sight from behind the trees. He was driving before him two horses hobbled together, and as he passed Bazarov he looked at him rather strangely, without touching his cap, which it was easy to see disturbed Piotr, as an unlucky omen. 'There's some one else up early too,' thought Bazarov; 'but he at least has got up for work, while we ...'
'Fancy the gentleman's coming,' Piotr faltered suddenly.
Bazarov raised his head and saw Pavel Petrovitch. Dressed in a light check jacket and snow-white trousers, he was walking rapidly along the road; under his arm he carried a box wrapped up in green cloth.
'I beg your pardon, I believe I have kept you waiting,' he observed, bowing first to Bazarov, then to Piotr, whom he treated respectfully at that instant, as representing something in the nature of a second. 'I was unwilling to wake my man.'
'It doesn't matter,' answered Bazarov; 'we've only just arrived ourselves.'
'Ah! so much the better!' Pavel Petrovitch took a look round. 'There's no one in sight; no one hinders us. We can proceed?'
'Let us proceed.'

'You do not, I presume, desire any fresh explanations?'

'No, I don't.'

'Would you like to load?' inquired Pavel Petrovitch, taking the pistols out of the box.

'No; you load, and I will measure out the paces. My legs are longer,' added Bazarov with a smile. 'One, two, three.'

'Yevgeny Vassilyevitch,' Piotr faltered with an effort (he shaking as though he were in a fever), 'say what you like, I am going farther off.'

'Four ... five.... Good. Move away, my good fellow, move away; you may get behind a tree even, and stop up your ears, only don't shut your eyes; and if any one falls, run and pick him up. Six ... seven ... eight....' Bazarov stopped. 'Is that enough?' he said, turning to Pavel Petrovitch; 'or shall I add two paces more?'

'As you like,' replied the latter, pressing down the second bullet.

'Well, we'll make it two paces more.' Bazarov drew a line on the ground with the toe of his boot. 'There's the barrier then. By the way, how many paces may each of us go back from the barrier? That's an important question too. That point was not discussed yesterday.'

'I imagine, ten,' replied Pavel Petrovitch, handing Bazarov both pistols. 'Will you be so good as to choose?'

'I will be so good. But, Pavel Petrovitch, you must admit our combat is singular to the point of absurdity. Only look at the countenance of our second.'

'You are disposed to laugh at everything,' answered Pavel Petrovitch. 'I acknowledge the strangeness of our duel, but I think it my duty to warn you that I intend to fight seriously. *A bon entendeur, salut!'*

'Oh! I don't doubt that we've made up our minds to make away with each other; but why not laugh too and unite *utile dulci?* You talk to me in French, while I talk to you in Latin.'

'I am going to fight in earnest,' repeated Pavel Petrovitch, and he walked off to his place. Bazarov on his side counted off ten paces from the barrier, and stood still.

'Are you ready?' asked Pavel Petrovitch.

'Perfectly.'

'We can approach one another.'

Bazarov moved slowly forward, and Pavel Petrovitch, his left hand thrust in his pocket, walked towards him, gradually raising the muzzle of his pistol.... 'He's aiming straight at my nose,' thought Bazarov, 'and doesn't he blink down it carefully, the ruffian! Not an agreeable sensation though. I'm going to look at his watch chain.'

Something whizzed sharply by his very ear, and at the same instant there was the sound of a shot. 'I heard it, so it must be all right,' had time to flash through Bazarov's brain. He took one more step, and without taking aim, pressed the spring.

Pavel Petrovitch gave a slight start, and clutched at his thigh. A stream of blood began to trickle down his white trousers.

Bazarov flung aside the pistol, and went up to his antagonist. 'Are you wounded?' he said.

'You had the right to call me up to the barrier,' said Pavel Petrovitch, 'but that's of no consequence. According to our agreement, each of us has the right to one more shot.'

'All right, but, excuse me, that'll do another time,' answered Bazarov, catching hold of Pavel Petrovitch, who was beginning to turn pale. 'Now, I'm not a duellist, but a doctor, and I must have a look at your wound before anything else. Piotr! come here, Piotr! where have you got to?'

'That's all nonsense.... I need no one's aid,' Pavel Petrovitch declared jerkily, 'and ... we must ... again ...' He tried to pull at his moustaches, but his hand failed him, his eyes grew dim, and he lost consciousness.

'Here's a pretty pass! A fainting fit! What next!' Bazarov cried unconsciously, as he laid Pavel Petrovitch on the grass. 'Let's have a look what's wrong.' He pulled out a handkerchief, wiped away the blood, and began feeling round the wound.... 'The bone's not touched,' he muttered through his teeth; 'the ball didn't go deep; one muscle, *vastus externus,* grazed. He'll be dancing about in three weeks!... And to faint! Oh, these nervous people, how I hate them! My word, what a delicate skin!'

'Is he killed?' the quaking voice of Piotr came rustling behind his back.

Bazarov looked round. 'Go for some water as quick as you can, my good fellow, and he'll outlive us yet.'

But the modern servant seemed not to understand his words, and he did not stir. Pavel Petrovitch slowly opened his eyes. 'He will die!' whispered Piotr, and he began crossing himself.

'You are right ... What an imbecile countenance!' remarked the wounded gentleman with a forced smile.

'Well, go for the water, damn you!' shouted Bazarov.

'No need.... It was a momentary *vertigo*.... Help me to sit up ... there, that's right.... I only need something to bind up this scratch, and I can reach home on foot, or you can send a droshky for me. The duel, if you are willing, shall not be renewed. You have behaved honourably ... to-day, to-day—observe.'
'There's no need to recall the past,' rejoined Bazarov; 'and as regards the future, it's not worth while for you to trouble your head about that either, for I intend being off without delay. Let me bind up your leg now; your wound's not serious, but it's always best to stop bleeding. But first I must bring this corpse to his senses.'
Bazarov shook Piotr by the collar, and sent him for a droshky.
'Mind you don't frighten my brother,' Pavel Petrovitch said to him; 'don't dream of informing him.'
Piotr flew off; and while he was running for a droshky, the two antagonists sat on the ground and said nothing. Pavel Petrovitch tried not to look at Bazarov; he did not want to be reconciled to him in any case; he was ashamed of his own haughtiness, of his failure; he was ashamed of the whole position he had brought about, even while he felt it could not have ended in a more favourable manner. 'At any rate, there will be no scandal,' he consoled himself by reflecting, 'and for that I am thankful.' The silence was prolonged, a silence distressing and awkward. Both of them were ill at ease. Each was conscious that the other understood him. That is pleasant to friends, and always very unpleasant to those who are not friends, especially when it is impossible either to have things out or to separate.
'Haven't I bound up your leg too tight?' inquired Bazarov at last.
'No, not at all; it's capital,' answered Pavel Petrovitch; and after a brief pause, he added, 'There's no deceiving my brother; we shall have to tell him we quarrelled over politics.'
'Very good,' assented Bazarov. 'You can say I insulted all anglomaniacs.'
'That will do capitally. What do you imagine that man thinks of us now?' continued Pavel Petrovitch, pointing to the same peasant, who had driven the hobbled horses past Bazarov a few minutes before the duel, and going back again along the road, took off his cap at the sight of the 'gentlefolk.'
'Who can tell!' answered Bazarov; 'it's quite likely he thinks nothing. The Russian peasant is that mysterious unknown about whom Mrs. Radcliffe used to talk so much. Who is to understand him! He doesn't understand himself!'
'Ah! so that's your idea!' Pavel Petrovitch began; and suddenly he cried, 'Look what your fool of a Piotr has done! Here's my brother galloping up to us!'
Bazarov turned round and saw the pale face of Nikolai Petrovitch, who was sitting in the droshky. He jumped out of it before it had stopped, and rushed up to his brother.
'What does this mean?' he said in an agitated voice. 'Yevgeny Vassilyitch, pray, what is this?'
'Nothing,' answered Pavel Petrovitch; 'they have alarmed you for nothing. I had a little dispute with Mr. Bazarov, and I have had to pay for it a little.'
'But what was it all about, mercy on us!'
'How can I tell you? Mr. Bazarov alluded disrespectfully to Sir Robert Peel. I must hasten to add that I am the only person to blame in all this, while Mr. Bazarov has behaved most honourably. I called him out.'
'But you're covered with blood, good Heavens!'
'Well, did you suppose I had water in my veins? But this blood-letting is positively beneficial to me. Isn't that so, doctor? Help me to get into the droshky, and don't give way to melancholy. I shall be quite well to-morrow. That's it; capital. Drive on, coachman.'
Nikolai Petrovitch walked after the droshky; Bazarov was remaining where he was....
'I must ask you to look after my brother,' Nikolai Petrovitch said to him, 'till we get another doctor from the town.'
Bazarov nodded his head without speaking. In an hour's time Pavel Petrovitch was already lying in bed with a skilfully bandaged leg. The whole house was alarmed; Fenitchka fainted. Nikolai Petrovitch kept stealthily wringing his hands, while Pavel Petrovitch laughed and joked, especially with Bazarov; he had put on a fine cambric night-shirt, an elegant morning wrapper, and a fez, did not allow the blinds to be drawn down, and humorously complained of the necessity of being kept from food.
Towards night, however, he began to be feverish; his head ached. The doctor arrived from the town. (Nikolai Petrovitch would not listen to his brother, and indeed Bazarov himself did not wish him to; he sat the whole day in his room, looking yellow and vindictive, and only went in to the invalid for as brief a time as possible; twice he happened to meet Fenitchka, but she shrank away from him with horror.) The new doctor advised a cooling diet; he confirmed, however, Bazarov's assertion that there was no danger. Nikolai Petrovitch told him his brother had wounded himself by accident, to which the doctor responded, 'Hm!' but having twenty-

five silver roubles slipped into his hand on the spot, he observed, 'You don't say so! Well, it's a thing that often happens, to be sure.'

No one in the house went to bed or undressed. Nikolai Petrovitch kept going in to his brother on tiptoe, retreating on tiptoe again; the latter dozed, moaned a little, told him in French, *Couchez-vous,* and asked for drink. Nikolai Petrovitch sent Fenitchka twice to take him a glass of lemonade; Pavel Petrovitch gazed at her intently, and drank off the glass to the last drop. Towards morning the fever had increased a little; there was slight delirium. At first Pavel Petrovitch uttered incoherent words; then suddenly he opened his eyes, and seeing his brother near his bed bending anxiously over him, he said, 'Don't you think, Nikolai, Fenitchka has something in common with Nellie?'

'What Nellie, Pavel dear?'

'How can you ask? Princess R——. Especially in the upper part of the face. *C'est de la même famille.'*

Nikolai Petrovitch made no answer, while inwardly he marvelled at the persistence of old passions in man. 'It's like this when it comes to the surface,' he thought.

'Ah, how I love that light-headed creature!' moaned Pavel Petrovitch, clasping his hands mournfully behind his head. 'I can't bear any insolent upstart to dare to touch ...' he whispered a few minutes later.

Nikolai Petrovitch only sighed; he did not even suspect to whom these words referred.

Bazarov presented himself before him at eight o'clock the next day. He had already had time to pack, and to set free all his frogs, insects, and birds.

'You have come to say good-bye to me?' said Nikolai Petrovitch, getting up to meet him.

'Yes.'

'I understand you, and approve of you fully. My poor brother, of course, is to blame; and he is punished for it. He told me himself that he made it impossible for you to act otherwise. I believe that you could not avoid this duel, which ... which to some extent is explained by the almost constant antagonism of your respective views.' (Nikolai Petrovitch began to get a little mixed up in his words.) 'My brother is a man of the old school, hot-tempered and obstinate.... Thank God that it has ended as it has. I have taken every precaution to avoid publicity.'

'I'm leaving you my address, in case there's any fuss,' Bazarov remarked casually.

'I hope there will be no fuss, Yevgeny Vassilyitch.... I am very sorry your stay in my house should have such a ... such an end. It is the more distressing to me through Arkady's ...'

'I shall be seeing him, I expect,' replied Bazarov, in whom 'explanations' and 'protestations' of every sort always aroused a feeling of impatience; 'in case I don't, I beg you to say good-bye to him for me, and accept the expression of my regret.'

'And I beg ...' answered Nikolai Petrovitch. But Bazarov went off without waiting for the end of his sentence.

When he heard of Bazarov's going, Pavel Petrovitch expressed a desire to see him, and shook his hand. But even then he remained as cold as ice; he realised that Pavel Petrovitch wanted to play the magnanimous. He did not succeed in saying good-bye to Fenitchka; he only exchanged glances with her at the window. Her face struck him as looking dejected. 'She'll come to grief, perhaps,' he said to himself.... 'But who knows? she'll pull through somehow, I dare say!' Piotr, however, was so overcome that he wept on his shoulder, till Bazarov damped him by asking if he'd a constant supply laid on in his eyes; while Dunyasha was obliged to run away into the wood to hide her emotion. The originator of all this woe got into a light cart, smoked a cigar, and when at the third mile, at the bend in the road, the Kirsanovs' farm, with its new house, could be seen in a long line, he merely spat, and muttering, 'Cursed snobs!' wrapped himself closer in his cloak.

Pavel Petrovitch was soon better; but he had to keep his bed about a week. He bore his captivity, as he called it, pretty patiently, though he took great pains over his toilette, and had everything scented with eau-de-cologne. Nikolai Petrovitch used to read him the journals; Fenitchka waited on him as before, brought him lemonade, soup, boiled eggs, and tea; but she was overcome with secret dread whenever she went into his room. Pavel Petrovitch's unexpected action had alarmed every one in the house, and her more than any one; Prokofitch was the only person not agitated by it; he discoursed upon how gentlemen in his day used to fight, but only with real gentlemen; low curs like that they used to order a horsewhipping in the stable for their insolence.

Fenitchka's conscience scarcely reproached her; but she was tormented at times by the thought of the real cause of the quarrel; and Pavel Petrovitch too looked at her so strangely ... that even when her back was turned, she felt his eyes upon her. She grew thinner from constant inward agitation, and, as is always the way, became still more charming.

One day—the incident took place in the morning—Pavel Petrovitch felt better and moved from his bed to the sofa, while Nikolai Petrovitch, having satisfied himself he was better, went off to the threshing-floor. Fenitchka brought him a cup of tea, and setting it down on a little table, was about to withdraw. Pavel Petrovitch detained her.
'Where are you going in such a hurry, Fedosya Nikolaevna?' he began; 'are you busy?'
'... I have to pour out tea.'
'Dunyasha will do that without you; sit a little while with a poor invalid. By the way, I must have a little talk with you.'
Fenitchka sat down on the edge of an easy-chair, without speaking.
'Listen,' said Pavel Petrovitch, tugging at his moustaches; 'I have long wanted to ask you something; you seem somehow afraid of me?'
'I?'
'Yes, you. You never look at me, as though your conscience were not at rest.'
Fenitchka crimsoned, but looked at Pavel Petrovitch. He impressed her as looking strange, and her heart began throbbing slowly.
'Is your conscience at rest?' he questioned her.
'Why should it not be at rest?' she faltered.
'Goodness knows why! Besides, whom can you have wronged? Me? That is not likely. Any other people in the house here? That, too, is something incredible. Can it be my brother? But you love him, don't you?'
'I love him.'
'With your whole soul, with your whole heart?'
'I love Nikolai Petrovitch with my whole heart.'
'Truly? Look at me, Fenitchka.' (It was the first time he had called her that name.) 'You know, it's a great sin telling lies!'
'I am not telling lies, Pavel Petrovitch. Not love Nikolai Petrovitch—I shouldn't care to live after that.'
'And will you never give him up for any one?'
'For whom could I give him up?'
'For whom indeed! Well, how about that gentleman who has just gone away from here?'
Fenitchka got up. 'My God, Pavel Petrovitch, what are you torturing me for? What have I done to you? How can such things be said?'...
'Fenitchka,' said Pavel Petrovitch, in a sorrowful voice, 'you know I saw ...'
'What did you see?'
'Well, there ... in the arbour.'
Fenitchka crimsoned to her hair and to her ears. 'How was I to blame for that?' she articulated with an effort.
Pavel Petrovitch raised himself up. 'You were not to blame? No? Not at all?'
'I love Nikolai Petrovitch, and no one else in the world, and I shall always love him!' cried Fenitchka with sudden force, while her throat seemed fairly breaking with sobs. 'As for what you saw, at the dreadful day of judgment I will say I'm not to blame, and wasn't to blame for it, and I would rather die at once if people can suspect me of such a thing against my benefactor, Nikolai Petrovitch.'
But here her voice broke, and at the same time she felt that Pavel Petrovitch was snatching and pressing her hand.... She looked at him, and was fairly petrified. He had turned even paler than before; his eyes were shining, and what was most marvellous of all, one large solitary tear was rolling down his cheek.
'Fenitchka!' he was saying in a strange whisper; 'love him, love my brother! Don't give him up for any one in the world; don't listen to any one else! Think what can be more terrible than to love and not be loved! Never leave my poor Nikolai!'
Fenitchka's eyes were dry, and her terror had passed away, so great was her amazement. But what were her feelings when Pavel Petrovitch, Pavel Petrovitch himself, put her hand to his lips and seemed to pierce into it without kissing it, and only heaving convulsive sighs from time to time....
'Goodness,' she thought, 'isn't it some attack coming on him?'...
At that instant his whole ruined life was stirred up within him.
The staircase creaked under rapidly approaching footsteps.... He pushed her away from him, and let his head drop back on the pillow. The door opened, and Nikolai Petrovitch entered, cheerful, fresh, and ruddy. Mitya, as fresh and ruddy as his father, in nothing but his little shirt, was frisking on his shoulder, catching the big buttons of his rough country coat with his little bare toes.

Fenitchka simply flung herself upon him, and clasping him and her son together in her arms, dropped her head on his shoulder. Nikolai Petrovitch was surprised; Fenitchka, the reserved and staid Fenitchka, had never given him a caress in the presence of a third person.

'What's the matter?' he said, and, glancing at his brother, he gave her Mitya. 'You don't feel worse?' he inquired, going up to Pavel Petrovitch.

He buried his face in a cambric handkerchief. 'No ... not at all ... on the contrary, I am much better.'

'You were in too great a hurry to move on to the sofa. Where are you going?' added Nikolai Petrovitch, turning round to Fenitchka; but she had already closed the door behind her. 'I was bringing in my young hero to show you, he's been crying for his uncle. Why has she carried him off? What's wrong with you, though? Has anything passed between you, eh?'

'Brother!' said Pavel Petrovitch solemnly.

Nikolai Petrovitch started. He felt dismayed, he could not have said why himself.

'Brother,' repeated Pavel Petrovitch, 'give me your word that you will carry out my one request.'

'What request? Tell me.'

'It is very important; the whole happiness of your life, to my idea, depends on it. I have been thinking a great deal all this time over what I want to say to you now.... Brother, do your duty, the duty of an honest and generous man; put an end to the scandal and bad example you are setting—you, the best of men!'

'What do you mean, Pavel?'

'Marry Fenitchka.... She loves you; she is the mother of your son.'

Nikolai Petrovitch stepped back a pace, and flung up his hands. 'Do you say that, Pavel? you whom I have always regarded as the most determined opponent of such marriages! You say that? Don't you know that it has simply been out of respect for you that I have not done what you so rightly call my duty?'

'You were wrong to respect me in that case,' Pavel Petrovitch responded, with a weary smile. 'I begin to think Bazarov was right in accusing me of snobbishness. No dear brother, don't let us worry ourselves about appearances and the world's opinion any more; we are old folks and humble now; it's time we laid aside vanity of all kinds. Let us, just as you say, do our duty; and mind, we shall get happiness that way into the bargain.'

Nikolai Petrovitch rushed to embrace his brother.

'You have opened my eyes completely!' he cried. 'I was right in always declaring you the wisest and kindest-hearted fellow in the world, and now I see you are just as reasonable as you are noble-hearted.'

'Quietly, quietly,' Pavel Petrovitch interrupted him; 'don't hurt the leg of your reasonable brother, who at close upon fifty has been fighting a duel like an ensign. So, then, it's a settled matter; Fenitchka is to be my *... belle soeur.'*

'My dearest Pavel! But what will Arkady say?'

'Arkady? he'll be in ecstasies, you may depend upon it! Marriage is against his principles, but then the sentiment of equality in him will be gratified. And, after all, what sense have class distinctions *au dix-neuvième siècle?'*

'Ah, Pavel, Pavel! let me kiss you once more! Don't be afraid, I'll be careful.'

The brothers embraced each other.

'What do you think, should you not inform her of your intention now?' queried Pavel Petrovitch.

'Why be in a hurry?' responded Nikolai Petrovitch. 'Has there been any conversation between you?'

'Conversation between us? *Quelle idée!'*

'Well, that is all right then. First of all, you must get well, and meanwhile there's plenty of time. We must think it over well, and consider ...'

'But your mind is made up, I suppose?'

'Of course, my mind is made up, and I thank you from the bottom of my heart. I will leave you now; you must rest; any excitement is bad for you.... But we will talk it over again. Sleep well, dear heart, and God bless you!'

'What is he thanking me like that for?' thought Pavel Petrovitch, when he was left alone. 'As though it did not depend on him! I will go away directly he is married, somewhere a long way off—to Dresden or Florence, and will live there till I——'

Pavel Petrovitch moistened his forehead with eau de cologne, and closed his eyes. His beautiful, emaciated head, the glaring daylight shining full upon it, lay on the white pillow like the head of a dead man.... And indeed he was a dead man.

CHAPTER XXV

At Nikolskoe Katya and Arkady were sitting in the garden on a turf seat in the shade of a tall ash tree; Fifi had placed himself on the ground near them, giving his slender body that graceful curve, which is known among dog-fanciers as 'the hare bend.' Both Arkady and Katya were silent; he was holding a half-open book in his hands, while she was picking out of a basket the few crumbs of bread left in it, and throwing them to a small family of sparrows, who with the frightened impudence peculiar to them were hopping and chirping at her very feet. A faint breeze stirring in the ash leaves kept slowly moving pale-gold flecks of sunlight up and down over the path and Fifi's tawny back; a patch of unbroken shade fell upon Arkady and Katya; only from time to time a bright streak gleamed on her hair. Both were silent, but the very way in which they were silent, in which they were sitting together, was expressive of confidential intimacy; each of them seemed not even to be thinking of his companion, while secretly rejoicing in his presence. Their faces, too, had changed since we saw them last; Arkady looked more tranquil, Katya brighter and more daring.

'Don't you think,' began Arkady, 'that the ash has been very well named in Russian *yasen;* no other tree is so lightly and brightly transparent *(yasno)* against the air as it is.'

Katya raised her eyes to look upward, and assented, 'Yes'; while Arkady thought, 'Well, she does not reproach me for *talking finely.'*

'I don't like Heine,' said Katya, glancing towards the book which Arkady was holding in his hands, 'either when he laughs or when he weeps; I like him when he's thoughtful and melancholy.'

'And I like him when he laughs,' remarked Arkady.

'That's the relics left in you of your old satirical tendencies.' ('Relics!' thought Arkady—'if Bazarov had heard that?') 'Wait a little; we shall transform you.'

'Who will transform me? You?'

'Who?—my sister; Porfiry Platonovitch, whom you've given up quarrelling with; auntie, whom you escorted to church the day before yesterday.'

'Well, I couldn't refuse! And as for Anna Sergyevna, she agreed with Yevgeny in a great many things, you remember?'

'My sister was under his influence then, just as you were.'

'As I was? Do you discover, may I ask, that I've shaken off his influence now?'

Katya did not speak.

'I know,' pursued Arkady, 'you never liked him.'

'I can have no opinion about him.'

'Do you know, Katerina Sergyevna, every time I hear that answer I disbelieve it.... There is no man that every one of us could not have an opinion about! That's simply a way of getting out of it.'

'Well, I'll say, then, I don't.... It's not exactly that I don't like him, but I feel that he's of a different order from me, and I am different from him ... and you too are different from him.'

'How's that?'

'How can I tell you.... He's a wild animal, and you and I are tame.'

'Am I tame too?'

Katya nodded.

Arkady scratched his ear. 'Let me tell you, Katerina Sergyevna, do you know, that's really an insult?'

'Why, would you like to be a wild——'

'Not wild, but strong, full of force.'

'It's no good wishing for that.... Your friend, you see, doesn't wish for it, but he has it.'

'Hm! So you imagine he had a great influence on Anna Sergyevna?'

'Yes. But no one can keep the upper hand of her for long,' added Katya in a low voice.

'Why do you think that?'
'She's very proud.... I didn't mean that ... she values her independence a great deal.'
'Who doesn't value it?' asked Arkady, and the thought flashed through his mind, 'What good is it?' 'What good is it?' it occurred to Katya to wonder too. When young people are often together on friendly terms, they are constantly stumbling on the same ideas.
Arkady smiled, and, coming slightly closer to Katya, he said in a whisper, 'Confess that you are a little afraid of her.'
'Of whom?'
'Her,' repeated Arkady significantly.
'And how about you?' Katya asked in her turn.
'I am too, observe I said, I am *too.'*
Katya threatened him with her finger. 'I wonder at that,' she began; 'my sister has never felt so friendly to you as just now; much more so than when you first came.'
'Really!'
'Why, haven't you noticed it? Aren't you glad of it?'
Arkady grew thoughtful.
'How have I succeeded in gaining Anna Sergyevna's good opinion? Wasn't it because I brought her your mother's letters?'
'Both that and other causes, which I shan't tell you.'
'Why?'
'I shan't say.'
'Oh! I know; you're very obstinate.'
'Yes, I am.'
'And observant.'
Katya gave Arkady a sidelong look. 'Perhaps so; does that irritate you? What are you thinking of?'
'I am wondering how you have come to be as observant as in fact you are. You are so shy so reserved; you keep every one at a distance.'
'I have lived a great deal alone; that drives one to reflection. But do I really keep every one at a distance?'
Arkady flung a grateful glance at Katya.
'That's all very well,' he pursued; 'but people in your position—I mean in your circumstances—don't often have that faculty; it is hard for them, as it is for sovereigns, to get at the truth.'
'But, you see, I am not rich.'
Arkady was taken aback, and did not at once understand Katya. 'Why, of course, the property's all her sister's!' struck him suddenly; the thought was not unpleasing to him. 'How nicely you said that!' he commented.
'What?'
'You said it nicely, simply, without being ashamed or making a boast of it. By the way, I imagine there must always be something special, a kind of pride of a sort in the feeling of any man, who knows and says he is poor.'
'I have never experienced anything of that sort, thanks to my sister. I only referred to my position just now because it happened to come up.'
'Well; but you must own you have a share of that pride I spoke of just now.'
'For instance?'
'For instance, you—forgive the question—you wouldn't marry a rich man, I fancy, would you?'
'If I loved him very much.... No, I think even then I wouldn't marry him.'
'There! you see!' cried Arkady, and after a short pause he added, 'And why wouldn't you marry him?'
'Because even in the ballads unequal matches are always unlucky.'
'You want to rule, perhaps, or ...'
'Oh, no! why should I? On the contrary, I am ready to obey; only inequality is intolerable. To respect one's self and obey, that I can understand, that's happiness; but a subordinate existence ... No, I've had enough of that as it is.'
'Enough of that as it is,' Arkady repeated after Katya. 'Yes, yes,' he went on, 'you're not Anna Sergyevna's sister for nothing; you're just as independent as she is; but you're more reserved. I'm certain you wouldn't be the first to give expression to your feeling, however strong and holy it might be ...'
'Well, what would you expect?' asked Katya.

'You're equally clever; and you've as much, if not more, character than she.'
'Don't compare me with my sister, please,' interposed Katya hurriedly; 'that's too much to my disadvantage. You seem to forget my sister's beautiful and clever, and ... you in particular, Arkady Nikolaevitch, ought not to say such things, and with such a serious face too.'
'What do you mean by "you in particular"—and what makes you suppose I am joking?'
'Of course, you are joking.'
'You think so? But what if I'm persuaded of what I say? If I believe I have not put it strongly enough even?'
'I don't understand you.'
'Really? Well, now I see; I certainly took you to be more observant than you are.'
'How?'
Arkady made no answer, and turned away, while Katya looked for a few more crumbs in the basket, and began throwing them to the sparrows; but she moved her arm too vigorously, and they flew away, without stopping to pick them up.
'Katerina Sergyevna!' began Arkady suddenly; 'it's of no consequence to you, probably; but, let me tell you, I put you not only above your sister, but above every one in the world.'
He got up and went quickly away, as though he were frightened at the words that had fallen from his lips.
Katya let her two hands drop together with the basket on to her lap, and with bent head she stared a long while after Arkady. Gradually a crimson flush came faintly out upon her cheeks; but her lips did not smile and her dark eyes had a look of perplexity and some other, as yet undefined, feeling.
'Are you alone?' she heard the voice of Anna Sergyevna near her; 'I thought you came into the garden with Arkady.'
Katya slowly raised her eyes to her sister (elegantly, even elaborately dressed, she was standing in the path and tickling Fifi's ears with the tip of her open parasol), and slowly replied, 'Yes, I'm alone.'
'So I see,' she answered with a smile; 'I suppose he has gone to his room.'
'Yes.'
'Have you been reading together?'
'Yes.'
Anna Sergyevna took Katya by the chin and lifted her face up.
'You have not been quarrelling, I hope?'
'No,' said Katya, and she quietly removed her sister's hand.
'How solemnly you answer! I expected to find him here, and meant to suggest his coming a walk with me. That's what he is always asking for. They have sent you some shoes from the town; go and try them on; I noticed only yesterday your old ones are quite shabby. You never think enough about it, and you have such charming little feet! Your hands are nice too ... though they're large; so you must make the most of your little feet. But you're not vain.'
Anna Sergyevna went farther along the path with a light rustle of her beautiful gown; Katya got up from the grass, and, taking Heine with her, went away too—but not to try on her shoes.
'Charming little feet!' she thought, as she slowly and lightly mounted the stone steps of the terrace, which were burning with the heat of the sun; 'charming little feet you call them.... Well, he shall be at them.'
But all at once a feeling of shame came upon her, and she ran swiftly upstairs.
Arkady had gone along the corridor to his room; a steward had overtaken him, and announced that Mr. Bazarov was in his room.
'Yevgeny!' murmured Arkady, almost with dismay; 'has he been here long?'
'Mr. Bazarov arrived this minute, sir, and gave orders not to announce him to Anna Sergyevna, but to show him straight up to you.'
'Can any misfortune have happened at home?' thought Arkady, and running hurriedly up the stairs, he at once opened the door. The sight of Bazarov at once reassured him, though a more experienced eye might very probably have discerned signs of inward agitation in the sunken, though still energetic face of the unexpected visitor. With a dusty cloak over his shoulders, with a cap on his head, he was sitting at the window; he did not even get up when Arkady flung himself with noisy exclamations on his neck.
'This is unexpected! What good luck brought you?' he kept repeating, bustling about the room like one who both imagines himself and wishes to show himself delighted. 'I suppose everything's all right at home; every one's well, eh?'
'Everything's all right, but not every one's well,' said Bazarov. 'Don't be a chatterbox, but send for some kvass for me, sit down, and listen while I tell you all about it in a few, but, I hope, pretty vigorous sentences.'

Arkady was quiet while Bazarov described his duel with Pavel Petrovitch. Arkady was very much surprised, and even grieved, but he did not think it necessary to show this; he only asked whether his uncle's wound was really not serious; and on receiving the reply that it was most interesting, but not from a medical point of view, he gave a forced smile, but at heart he felt both wounded and as it were ashamed. Bazarov seemed to understand him.

'Yes, my dear fellow,' he commented, 'you see what comes of living with feudal personages. You turn a feudal personage yourself, and find yourself taking part in knightly tournaments. Well, so I set off for my father's,' Bazarov wound up, 'and I've turned in here on the way ... to tell you all this, I should say, if I didn't think a useless lie a piece of foolery. No, I turned in here—the devil only knows why. You see, it's sometimes a good thing for a man to take himself by the scruff of the neck and pull himself up, like a radish out of its bed; that's what I've been doing of late.... But I wanted to have one more look at what I'm giving up, at the bed where I've been planted.'

'I hope those words don't refer to me,' responded Arkady with some emotion; 'I hope you don't think of giving me up?'

Bazarov turned an intent, almost piercing look upon him.

'Would that be such a grief to you? It strikes me *you* have given me up already, you look so fresh and smart.... Your affair with Anna Sergyevna must be getting on successfully.'

'What do you mean by my affair with Anna Sergyevna?'

'Why, didn't you come here from the town on her account, chicken? By the way, how are those Sunday schools getting on? Do you mean to tell me you're not in love with her? Or have you already reached the stage of discretion?'

'Yevgeny, you know I have always been open with you; I can assure you, I will swear to you, you're making a mistake.'

'Hm! That's another story,' remarked Bazarov in an undertone. 'But you needn't be in a taking, it's a matter of absolute indifference to me. A sentimentalist would say, "I feel that our paths are beginning to part," but I will simply say that we're tired of each other.'

'Yevgeny ...'

'My dear soul, there's no great harm in that. One gets tired of much more than that in this life. And now I suppose we'd better say good-bye, hadn't we? Ever since I've been here I've had such a loathsome feeling, just as if I'd been reading Gogol's effusions to the governor of Kalouga's wife. By the way, I didn't tell them to take the horses out.'

'Upon my word, this is too much!'

'Why?'

'I'll say nothing of myself; but that would be discourteous to the last degree to Anna Sergyevna, who will certainly wish to see you.'

'Oh, you're mistaken there.'

'On the contrary, I am certain I'm right,' retorted Arkady. 'And what are you pretending for? If it comes to that, haven't you come here on her account yourself?'

'That may be so, but you're mistaken any way.'

But Arkady was right. Anna Sergyevna desired to see Bazarov, and sent a summons to him by a steward. Bazarov changed his clothes before going to her; it turned out that he had packed his new suit so as to be able to get it out easily.

Madame Odintsov received him not in the room where he had so unexpectedly declared his love to her, but in the drawing-room. She held her finger tips out to him cordially, but her face betrayed an involuntary sense of tension.

'Anna Sergyevna,' Bazarov hastened to say, 'before everything else I must set your mind at rest. Before you is a poor mortal, who has come to his senses long ago, and hopes other people too have forgotten his follies. I am going away for a long while; and though, as you will allow, I'm by no means a very soft creature, it would be anything but cheerful for me to carry away with me the idea that you remember me with repugnance.'

Anna Sergyevna gave a deep sigh like one who has just climbed up a high mountain, and her face was lighted up by a smile. She held out her hand a second time to Bazarov, and responded to his pressure.

'Let bygones be bygones,' she said. 'I am all the readier to do so because, speaking from my conscience, I was to blame then too for flirting or something. In a word, let us be friends as before. That was a dream, wasn't it? And who remembers dreams?'

'Who remembers them? And besides, love ... you know, is a purely imaginary feeling.'
'Really? I am very glad to hear that.'
So Anna Sergyevna spoke, and so spoke Bazarov; they both supposed they were speaking the truth. Was the truth, the whole truth, to be found in their words? They could not themselves have said, and much less could the author. But a conversation followed between them precisely as though they completely believed one another.
Anna Sergyevna asked Bazarov, among other things, what he had been doing at the Kirsanovs'. He was on the point of telling her about his duel with Pavel Petrovitch, but he checked himself with the thought that she might imagine he was trying to make himself interesting, and answered that he had been at work all the time.
'And I,' observed Anna Sergyevna, 'had a fit of depression at first, goodness knows why; I even made plans for going abroad, fancy!... Then it passed off, your friend Arkady Nikolaitch came, and I fell back into my old routine, and took up my real part again.'
'What part is that, may I ask?'
'The character of aunt, guardian, mother—call it what you like. By the way, do you know I used not quite to understand your close friendship with Arkady Nikolaitch; I thought him rather insignificant. But now I have come to know him better, and to see that he is clever.... And he's young, he's young ... that's the great thing ... not like you and me, Yevgeny Vassilyitch.'
'Is he still as shy in your company?' queried Bazarov.
'Why, was he?' ... Anna Sergyevna began, and after a brief pause she went on: 'He has grown more confiding now; he talks to me. He used to avoid me before. Though, indeed, I didn't seek his society either. He's more friends with Katya.'
Bazarov felt irritated. 'A woman can't help humbugging, of course!' he thought. 'You say he used to avoid you,' he said aloud, with a chilly smile; 'but it is probably no secret to you that he was in love with you?'
'What! he too?' fell from Anna Sergyevna's lips.
'He too,' repeated Bazarov, with a submissive bow. 'Can it be you didn't know it, and I've told you something new?'
Anna Sergyevna dropped her eyes. 'You are mistaken, Yevgeny Vassilyitch.'
'I don't think so. But perhaps I ought not to have mentioned it.' 'And don't you try telling me lies again for the future,' he added to himself.
'Why not? But I imagine that in this too you are attributing too much importance to a passing impression. I begin to suspect you are inclined to exaggeration.'
'We had better not talk about it, Anna Sergyevna.'
'Oh, why?' she retorted; but she herself led the conversation into another channel. She was still ill at ease with Bazarov, though she had told him, and assured herself that everything was forgotten. While she was exchanging the simplest sentences with him, even while she was jesting with him, she was conscious of a faint spasm of dread. So people on a steamer at sea talk and laugh carelessly, for all the world as though they were on dry land; but let only the slightest hitch occur, let the least sign be seen of anything out of the common, and at once on every face there comes out an expression of peculiar alarm, betraying the constant consciousness of constant danger.
Anna Sergyevna's conversation with Bazarov did not last long. She began to seem absorbed in thought, answered abstractedly, and suggested at last that they should go into the hall, where they found the princess and Katya. 'But where is Arkady Nikolaitch?' inquired the lady of the house; and on hearing that he had not shown himself for more than an hour, she sent for him. He was not very quickly found; he had hidden himself in the very thickest part of the garden, and with his chin propped on his folded hands, he was sitting lost in meditation. They were deep and serious meditations, but not mournful. He knew Anna Sergyevna was sitting alone with Bazarov, and he felt no jealousy, as once he had; on the contrary, his face slowly brightened; he seemed to be at once wondering and rejoicing, and resolving on something.

CHAPTER XXVI

The deceased Odintsov had not liked innovations, but he had tolerated 'the fine arts within a certain sphere,' and had in consequence put up in his garden, between the hothouse and the lake, an erection after the fashion of a Greek temple, made of Russian brick. Along the dark wall at the back of this temple or gallery were placed six niches for statues, which Odintsov had proceeded to order from abroad. These statues were to represent Solitude, Silence, Meditation, Melancholy, Modesty, and Sensibility. One of them, the goddess of Silence, with her finger on her lip, had been sent and put up; but on the very same day some boys on the farm had broken her nose; and though a plasterer of the neighbourhood undertook to make her a new nose 'twice as good as the old one,' Odintsov ordered her to be taken away, and she was still to be seen in the corner of the threshing barn, where she had stood many long years, a source of superstitious terror to the peasant women. The front part of the temple had long ago been overgrown with thick bushes; only the pediments of the columns could be seen above the dense green. In the temple itself it was cool even at mid-day. Anna Sergyevna had not liked visiting this place ever since she had seen a snake there; but Katya often came and sat on the wide stone seat under one of the niches. Here, in the midst of the shade and coolness, she used to read and work, or to give herself up to that sensation of perfect peace, known, doubtless, to each of us, the charm of which consists in the half-unconscious, silent listening to the vast current of life that flows for ever both around us and within us.

The day after Bazarov's arrival Katya was sitting on her favourite stone seat, and beside her again was sitting Arkady. He had besought her to come with him to the 'temple.'

There was about an hour still to lunch-time; the dewy morning had already given place to a sultry day. Arkady's face retained the expression of the preceding day; Katya had a preoccupied look. Her sister had, directly after their morning tea, called her into her room, and after some preliminary caresses, which always scared Katya a little, she had advised her to be more guarded in her behaviour with Arkady, and especially to avoid solitary talks with him, as likely to attract the notice of her aunt and all the household. Besides this, even the previous evening Anna Sergyevna had not been herself; and Katya herself had felt ill at ease, as though she were conscious of some fault in herself. As she yielded to Arkady's entreaties, she said to herself that it was for the last time.

'Katerina Sergyevna,' he began with a sort of bashful easiness, 'since I've had the happiness of living in the same house with you, I have discussed a great many things with you; but meanwhile there is one, very important ... for me ... one question, which I have not touched upon up till now. You remarked yesterday that I have been changed here,' he went on, at once catching and avoiding the questioning glance Katya was turning upon him. 'I have changed certainly a great deal, and you know that better than any one else—you to whom I really owe this change.'

'I?... Me?...' said Katya.

'I am not now the conceited boy I was when I came here,' Arkady went on. 'I've not reached twenty-three for nothing; as before, I want to be useful, I want to devote all my powers to the truth; but I no longer look for my ideals where I did; they present themselves to me ... much closer to hand. Up till now I did not understand myself; I set myself tasks which were beyond my powers.... My eyes have been opened lately, thanks to one feeling.... I'm not expressing myself quite clearly, but I hope you understand me.'

Katya made no reply, but she ceased looking at Arkady.

'I suppose,' he began again, this time in a more agitated voice, while above his head a chaffinch sang its song unheeding among the leaves of the birch—'I suppose it's the duty of every one to be open with those ... with those people who ... in fact, with those who are near to him, and so I ... I resolved ...'

But here Arkady's eloquence deserted him; he lost the thread, stammered, and was forced to be silent for a moment. Katya still did not raise her eyes. She seemed not to understand what he was leading up to in all this, and to be waiting for something.

'I foresee I shall surprise you,' began Arkady, pulling himself together again with an effort, 'especially since this feeling relates in a way ... in a way, notice ... to you. You reproached me, if you remember, yesterday with a want of seriousness,' Arkady went on, with the air of a man who has got into a bog, feels that he is sinking further and further in at every step, and yet hurries onwards in the hope of crossing it as soon as possible; 'that reproach is often aimed ... often falls ... on young men even when they cease to deserve it; and if I had more self-confidence ...' ('Come, help me, do help me!' Arkady was thinking, in desperation; but, as before, Katya did not turn her head.) 'If I could hope ...'

'If I could feel sure of what you say,' was heard at that instant the clear voice of Anna Sergyevna.

Arkady was still at once, while Katya turned pale. Close by the bushes that screened the temple ran a little path. Anna Sergyevna was walking along it escorted by Bazarov. Katya and Arkady could not see them, but they heard every word, the rustle of their clothes, their very breathing. They walked on a few steps, and, as though on purpose, stood still just opposite the temple.

'You see,' pursued Anna Sergyevna, 'you and I made a mistake; we are both past our first youth, I especially so; we have seen life, we are tired; we are both—why affect not to know it?—clever; at first we interested each other, curiosity was aroused ... and then ...'

'And then I grew stale,' put in Bazarov.

'You know that was not the cause of our misunderstanding. But, however, it was to be, we had no need of one another, that's the chief point; there was too much ... what shall I say? ... that was alike in us. We did not realise it all at once. Now, Arkady ...'

'So you need him?' queried Bazarov.

'Hush, Yevgeny Vassilyitch. You tell me he is not indifferent to me, and it always seemed to me he liked me. I know that I might well be his aunt, but I don't wish to conceal from you that I have come to think more often of him. In such youthful, fresh feeling there is a special charm ...'

'The word *fascination* is most usual in such cases,' Bazarov interrupted; the effervescence of his spleen could be heard in his choked though steady voice. 'Arkady was mysterious over something with me yesterday, and didn't talk either of you or your sister.... That's a serious symptom.'

'He is just like a brother with Katya,' commented Anna Sergyevna, 'and I like that in him, though, perhaps, I ought not to have allowed such intimacy between them.'

'That idea is prompted by ... your feelings as a sister?' Bazarov brought out, drawling.

'Of course ... but why are we standing still? Let us go on. What a strange talk we are having, aren't we? I could never have believed I should talk to you like this. You know, I am afraid of you ... and at the same time I trust you, because in reality you are so good.'

'In the first place, I am not in the least good; and in the second place, I have lost all significance for you, and you tell me I am good.... It's like a laying a wreath of flowers on the head of a corpse.'

'Yevgeny Vassilyitch, we are not responsible ...' Anna Sergyevna began; but a gust of wind blew across, set the leaves rustling, and carried away her words. 'Of course, you are free ...' Bazarov declared after a brief pause. Nothing more could be distinguished; the steps retreated ... everything was still.

Arkady turned to Katya. She was sitting in the same position, but her head was bent still lower. 'Katerina Sergyevna,' he said with a shaking voice, and clasping his hands tightly together, 'I love you for ever and irrevocably, and I love no one but you. I wanted to tell you this, to find out your opinion of me, and to ask for your hand, since I am not rich, and I feel ready for any sacrifice.... You don't answer me? You don't believe me? Do you think I speak lightly? But remember these last days! Surely for a long time past you must have known that everything—understand me—everything else has vanished long ago and left no trace? Look at me, say one word to me ... I love ... I love you ... believe me!'

Katya glanced at Arkady with a bright and serious look, and after long hesitation, with the faintest smile, she said, 'Yes.'

Arkady leapt up from the stone seat. 'Yes! You said Yes, Katerina Sergyevna! What does that word mean? Only that I do love you, that you believe me ... or ... or ... I daren't go on ...'

'Yes,' repeated Katya, and this time he understood her. He snatched her large beautiful hands, and, breathless with rapture, pressed them to his heart. He could scarcely stand on his feet, and could only repeat, 'Katya, Katya ...' while she began weeping in a guileless way, smiling gently at her own tears. No one who has not seen those tears in the eyes of the beloved, knows yet to what a point, faint with shame and gratitude, a man may be happy on earth.

The next day, early in the morning, Anna Sergyevna sent to summon Bazarov to her boudoir, and with a forced laugh handed him a folded sheet of notepaper. It was a letter from Arkady; in it he asked for her sister's hand.

Bazarov quickly scanned the letter, and made an effort to control himself, that he might not show the malignant feeling which was instantaneously aflame in his breast.

'So that's how it is,' he commented; 'and you, I fancy, only yesterday imagined he loved Katerina Sergyevna as a brother. What are you intending to do now?'

'What do you advise me?' asked Anna Sergyevna, still laughing.

'Well, I suppose,' answered Bazarov, also with a laugh, though he felt anything but cheerful, and had no more inclination to laugh than she had; 'I suppose you ought to give the young people your blessing. It's a good match in every respect; Kirsanov's position is passable, he's the only son, and his father's a good-natured fellow, he won't try to thwart him.'

Madame Odintsov walked up and down the room. By turns her face flushed and grew pale. 'You think so,' she said. 'Well, I see no obstacles ... I am glad for Katya ... and for Arkady Nikolaevitch too. Of course, I will wait for his father's answer. I will send him in person to him. But it turns out, you see, that I was right yesterday when I told you we were both old people.... How was it I saw nothing? That's what amazes me!' Anna Sergyevna laughed again, and quickly turned her head away.

'The younger generation have grown awfully sly,' remarked Bazarov, and he too laughed. 'Good-bye,' he began again after a short silence. 'I hope you will bring the matter to the most satisfactory conclusion; and I will rejoice from a distance.'

Madame Odintsov turned quickly to him. 'You are not going away? Why should you not stay *now?* Stay ... it's exciting talking to you ... one seems walking on the edge of a precipice. At first one feels timid, but one gains courage as one goes on. Do stay.'

'Thanks for the suggestion, Anna Sergyevna, and for your flattering opinion of my conversational talents. But I think I have already been moving too long in a sphere which is not my own. Flying fishes can hold out for a time in the air; but soon they must splash back into the water; allow me, too, to paddle in my own element.'

Madame Odintsov looked at Bazarov. His pale face was twitching with a bitter smile. 'This man did love me!' she thought, and she felt pity for him, and held out her hand to him with sympathy.

But he too understood her. 'No!' he said, stepping back a pace. 'I'm a poor man, but I've never taken charity so far. Good-bye, and good luck to you.'

'I am certain we are not seeing each other for the last time,' Anna Sergyevna declared with an unconscious gesture.

'Anything may happen!' answered Bazarov, and he bowed and went away.

'So you are thinking of making yourself a nest?' he said the same day to Arkady, as he packed his box, crouching on the floor. 'Well, it's a capital thing. But you needn't have been such a humbug. I expected something from you in quite another quarter. Perhaps, though, it took you by surprise yourself?'

'I certainly didn't expect this when I parted from you,' answered Arkady; 'but why are you a humbug yourself, calling it "a capital thing," as though I didn't know your opinion of marriage.'

'Ah, my dear fellow,' said Bazarov, 'how you talk! You see what I'm doing; there seems to be an empty space in the box, and I am putting hay in; that's how it is in the box of our life; we would stuff it up with anything rather than have a void. Don't be offended, please; you remember, no doubt, the opinion I have always had of Katerina Sergyevna. Many a young lady's called clever simply because she can sigh cleverly; but yours can hold her own, and, indeed, she'll hold it so well that she'll have you under her thumb—to be sure, though, that's quite as it ought to be.' He slammed the lid to, and got up from the floor. 'And now, I say again, good-bye, for it's useless to deceive ourselves—we are parting for good, and you know that yourself ... you have acted sensibly; you're not made for our bitter, rough, lonely existence. There's no dash, no hate in you, but you've the daring of youth and the fire of youth. Your sort, you gentry, can never get beyond refined submission or refined indignation, and that's no good. You won't fight—and yet you fancy yourselves gallant chaps—but we mean to fight. Oh well! Our dust would get into your eyes, our mud would bespatter you, but yet you're not up to our level, you're admiring yourselves unconsciously, you like to abuse yourselves; but we're sick of that—we want something else! we want to smash other people! You're a capital fellow; but you're a sugary, liberal snob for all that—*ay volla-too,* as my parent is fond of saying.'

'You are parting from me for ever, Yevgeny,' responded Arkady mournfully; 'and have you nothing else to say to me?'

Bazarov scratched the back of his head. 'Yes, Arkady, yes, I have other things to say to you, but I'm not going to say them, because that's sentimentalism—that means, mawkishness. And you get married as soon as you can; and build your nest, and get children to your heart's content. They'll have the wit to be born in a better time than you and me. Aha! I see the horses are ready. Time's up! I've said good-bye to every one.... What now? embracing, eh?'

Arkady flung himself on the neck of his former leader and friend, and the tears fairly gushed from his eyes.

'That's what comes of being young!' Bazarov commented calmly. 'But I rest my hopes on Katerina Sergyevna. You'll see how quickly she'll console you! Good-bye, brother!' he said to Arkady when he had got into the light cart, and, pointing to a pair of jackdaws sitting side by side on the stable roof, he added, 'That's for you! follow that example.'

'What does that mean?' asked Arkady.

'What? Are you so weak in natural history, or have you forgotten that the jackdaw is a most respectable family bird? An example to you!... Good-bye!'

The cart creaked and rolled away.

Bazarov had spoken truly. In talking that evening with Katya, Arkady completely forgot about his former teacher. He already began to follow her lead, and Katya was conscious of this, and not surprised at it. He was to set off the next day for Maryino, to see Nikolai Petrovitch. Anna Sergyevna was not disposed to put any constraint on the young people, and only on account of the proprieties did not leave them by themselves for too long together. She magnanimously kept the princess out of their way; the latter had been reduced to a state of tearful frenzy by the news of the proposed marriage. At first Anna Sergyevna was afraid the sight of their happiness might prove rather trying to herself, but it turned out quite the other way; this sight not only did not distress her, it interested her, it even softened her at last. Anna Sergyevna felt both glad and sorry at this. 'It is clear that Bazarov was right,' she thought; 'it has been curiosity, nothing but curiosity, and love of ease, and egoism ...'

'Children,' she said aloud, 'what do you say, is love a purely imaginary feeling?'

But neither Katya nor Arkady even understood her. They were shy with her; the fragment of conversation they had involuntarily overheard haunted their minds. But Anna Sergyevna soon set their minds at rest; and it was not difficult for her—she had set her own mind at rest.

CHAPTER XXVII

Bazarov's old parents were all the more overjoyed by their son's arrival, as it was quite unexpected. Arina Vlasyevna was greatly excited, and kept running backwards and forwards in the house, so that Vassily Ivanovitch compared her to a 'hen partridge'; the short tail of her abbreviated jacket did, in fact, give her something of a birdlike appearance. He himself merely growled and gnawed the amber mouthpiece of his pipe, or, clutching his neck with his fingers, turned his head round, as though he were trying whether it were properly screwed on, then all at once he opened his wide mouth and went off into a perfectly noiseless chuckle.

'I've come to you for six whole weeks, governor,' Bazarov said to him. 'I want to work, so please don't hinder me now.'

'You shall forget my face completely, if you call that hindering you!' answered Vassily Ivanovitch.

He kept his promise. After installing his son as before in his study, he almost hid himself away from him, and he kept his wife from all superfluous demonstrations of tenderness. 'On Enyusha's first visit, my dear soul,' he said to her, 'we bothered him a little; we must be wiser this time.' Arina Vlasyevna agreed with her husband, but that was small compensation since she saw her son only at meals, and was now absolutely afraid to address him. 'Enyushenka,' she would say sometimes—and before he had time to look round, she was nervously fingering the tassels of her reticule and faltering, 'Never mind, never mind, I only——' and afterwards she would go to Vassily Ivanovitch and, her cheek in her hand, would consult him: 'If you could only find out, darling, which Enyusha would like for dinner to-day—cabbage-broth or beetroot-soup?'—'But why didn't you ask him yourself?'—'Oh, he will get sick of me!' Bazarov, however, soon ceased to shut himself up; the fever of work fell away, and was replaced by dreary boredom or vague restlessness. A strange weariness began to show itself in all his movements; even his walk, firm, bold and strenuous, was changed. He gave up walking in solitude, and began to seek society; he drank tea in the drawing-room, strolled about the kitchen-garden with Vassily Ivanovitch, and smoked with him in silence; once even asked after Father Alexey. Vassily Ivanovitch at first rejoiced at this change, but his joy was not long-lived. 'Enyusha's breaking my heart,' he complained in secret to his wife; 'it's not that he's discontented or angry—that would be nothing; he's sad, he's sorrowful—that's what's so terrible. He's always silent. If he'd only abuse us; he's growing thin, he's lost his colour.'—'Mercy on us, mercy on us!' whispered the old woman; 'I would put an amulet on his neck, but, of course, he won't allow it.' Vassily Ivanovitch several times attempted in the most circumspect manner to question Bazarov about his work, about his health, and about Arkady.... But Bazarov's replies were reluctant and casual; and, once noticing that his father was trying gradually to lead up to something in conversation, he said to him in a tone of vexation: 'Why do you always seem to be walking round me on tiptoe? That way's worse than the old one.'—'There, there, I meant nothing!' poor Vassily Ivanovitch answered hurriedly. So his diplomatic hints remained fruitless. He hoped to awaken his son's sympathy one day by beginning *à propos* of the approaching emancipation of the peasantry, to talk about progress; but the latter responded indifferently: 'Yesterday I was walking under the fence, and I heard the peasant boys here, instead of some old ballad, bawling a street song. That's what progress is.'

Sometimes Bazarov went into the village, and in his usual bantering tone entered into conversation with some peasant: 'Come,' he would say to him, 'expound your views on life to me, brother; you see, they say all the strength and future of Russia lies in your hands, a new epoch in history will be started by you—you give us our real language and our laws.'

The peasant either made no reply, or articulated a few words of this sort, 'Well, we'll try ... because, you see, to be sure....'

'You explain to me what your *mir* is,' Bazarov interrupted; 'and is it the same *mir* that is said to rest on three fishes?'

'That, little father, is the earth that rests on three fishes,' the peasant would declare soothingly, in a kind of patriarchal, simple-hearted sing-song; 'and over against ours, that's to say, the *mir*, we know there's the master's will; wherefore you are our fathers. And the stricter the master's rule, the better for the peasant.'

After listening to such a reply one day, Bazarov shrugged his shoulders contemptuously and turned away, while the peasant sauntered slowly homewards.

'What was he talking about?' inquired another peasant of middle age and surly aspect, who at a distance from the door of his hut had been following his conversation with Bazarov.—'Arrears? eh?'

'Arrears, no indeed, mate!' answered the first peasant, and now there was no trace of patriarchal singsong in his voice; on the contrary, there was a certain scornful gruffness to be heard in it: 'Oh, he clacked away about something or other; wanted to stretch his tongue a bit. Of course, he's a gentleman; what does he understand?'

'What should he understand!' answered the other peasant, and jerking back their caps and pushing down their belts, they proceeded to deliberate upon their work and their wants. Alas! Bazarov, shrugging his shoulders contemptuously, Bazarov, who knew how to talk to peasants (as he had boasted in his dispute with Pavel Petrovitch), did not in his self-confidence even suspect that in their eyes he was all the while something of the nature of a buffooning clown.

He found employment for himself at last, however. One day Vassily Ivanovitch bound up a peasant's wounded leg before him, but the old man's hands trembled, and he could not manage the bandages; his son helped him, and from time to time began to take a share in his practice, though at the same time he was constantly sneering both at the remedies he himself advised and at his father, who hastened to make use of them. But Bazarov's jeers did not in the least perturb Vassily Ivanovitch; they were positively a comfort to him. Holding his greasy dressing-gown across his stomach with two fingers, and smoking his pipe, he used to listen with enjoyment to Bazarov; and the more malicious his sallies, the more good-humouredly did his delighted father chuckle, showing every one of his black teeth. He used even to repeat these sometimes flat or pointless retorts, and would, for instance, for several days constantly without rhyme or reason, reiterate, 'Not a matter of the first importance!' simply because his son, on hearing he was going to matins, had made use of that expression. 'Thank God! he has got over his melancholy!' he whispered to his wife; 'how he gave it to me to-day, it was splendid!' Moreover, the idea of having such an assistant excited him to ecstasy, filled him with pride. 'Yes, yes,' he would say to some peasant woman in a man's cloak, and a cap shaped like a horn, as he handed her a bottle of Goulard's extract or a box of white ointment, 'you ought to be thanking God, my good woman, every minute that my son is staying with me; you will be treated now by the most scientific, most modern method. Do you know what that means? The Emperor of the French, Napoleon, even, has no better doctor.' And the peasant woman, who had come to complain that she felt so sort of queer all over (the exact meaning of these words she was not able, however, herself to explain), merely bowed low and rummaged in her bosom, where four eggs lay tied up in the corner of a towel.

Bazarov once even pulled out a tooth for a passing pedlar of cloth; and though this tooth was an average specimen, Vassily Ivanovitch preserved it as a curiosity, and incessantly repeated, as he showed it to Father Alexey, 'Just look, what a fang! The force Yevgeny has! The pedlar seemed to leap into the air. If it had been an oak, he'd have rooted it up!'

'Most promising!' Father Alexey would comment at last, not knowing what answer to make, and how to get rid of the ecstatic old man.

One day a peasant from a neighbouring village brought his brother to Vassily Ivanovitch, ill with typhus. The unhappy man, lying flat on a truss of straw, was dying; his body was covered with dark patches, he had long ago lost consciousness. Vassily Ivanovitch expressed his regret that no one had taken steps to procure medical aid sooner, and declared there was no hope. And, in fact, the peasant did not get his brother home again; he died in the cart.

Three days later Bazarov came into his father's room and asked him if he had any caustic.

'Yes; what do you want it for?'

'I must have some ... to burn a cut.'

'For whom?'

'For myself.'

'What, yourself? Why is that? What sort of a cut? Where is it?'

'Look here, on my finger. I went to-day to the village, you know, where they brought that peasant with typhus fever. They were just going to open the body for some reason or other, and I've had no practice of that sort for a long while.'

'Well?'

'Well, so I asked the district doctor about it; and so I dissected it.'

Vassily Ivanovitch all at once turned quite white, and, without uttering a word, rushed to his study, from which he returned at once with a bit of caustic in his hand. Bazarov was about to take it and go away.

'For mercy's sake,' said Vassily Ivanovitch, 'let me do it myself.'

Bazarov smiled. 'What a devoted practitioner!'

'Don't laugh, please. Show me your finger. The cut is not a large one. Do I hurt?'

'Press harder; don't be afraid.'

Vassily Ivanovitch stopped. 'What do you think, Yevgeny; wouldn't it be better to burn it with hot iron?'

'That ought to have been done sooner; the caustic even is useless, really, now. If I've taken the infection, it's too late now.'

'How ... too late ...' Vassily Ivanovitch could scarcely articulate the words.

'I should think so! It's more than four hours ago.'

Vassily Ivanovitch burnt the cut a little more. 'But had the district doctor no caustic?'

'No.'

'How was that, good Heavens? A doctor not have such an indispensable thing as that!'

'You should have seen his lancets,' observed Bazarov as he walked away.

Up till late that evening, and all the following day, Vassily Ivanovitch kept catching at every possible excuse to go into his son's room; and though far from referring to the cut—he even tried to talk about the most irrelevant subjects—he looked so persistently into his face, and watched him in such trepidation, that Bazarov lost patience and threatened to go away. Vassily Ivanovitch gave him a promise not to bother him, the more readily as Arina Vlasyevna, from whom, of course, he kept it all secret, was beginning to worry him as to why he did not sleep, and what had come over him. For two whole days he held himself in, though he did not at all like the look of his son, whom he kept watching stealthily, ... but on the third day, at dinner, he could bear it no longer. Bazarov sat with downcast looks, and had not touched a single dish.

'Why don't you eat, Yevgeny?' he inquired, putting on an expression of the most perfect carelessness. 'The food, I think, is very nicely cooked.'

'I don't want anything, so I don't eat.'

'Have you no appetite? And your head?' he added timidly; 'does it ache?'

'Yes. Of course, it aches.'

Arina Vlasyevna sat up and was all alert.

'Don't be angry, please, Yevgeny,' continued Vassily Ivanovitch; 'won't you let me feel your pulse?'

Bazarov got up. 'I can tell you without feeling my pulse; I'm feverish.'

'Has there been any shivering?'

'Yes, there has been shivering too. I'll go and lie down, and you can send me some lime-flower tea. I must have caught cold.'

'To be sure, I heard you coughing last night,' observed Arina Vlasyevna.

'I've caught cold,' repeated Bazarov, and he went away.

Arina Vlasyevna busied herself about the preparation of the decoction of lime-flowers, while Vassily Ivanovitch went into the next room and clutched at his hair in silent desperation.

Bazarov did not get up again that day, and passed the whole night in heavy, half-unconscious torpor. At one o'clock in the morning, opening his eyes with an effort, he saw by the light of a lamp his father's pale face bending over him, and told him to go away. The old man begged his pardon, but he quickly came back on tiptoe, and half-hidden by the cupboard door, he gazed persistently at his son. Arina Vlasyevna did not go to bed either, and leaving the study door just open a very little, she kept coming up to it to listen 'how Enyusha was breathing,' and to look at Vassily Ivanovitch. She could see nothing but his motionless bent back, but even that afforded her some faint consolation. In the morning Bazarov tried to get up; he was seized with giddiness, his nose began to bleed; he lay down again. Vassily Ivanovitch waited on him in silence; Arina Vlasyevna went in to him and asked him how he was feeling. He answered, 'Better,' and turned to the wall. Vassily Ivanovitch gesticulated at his wife with both hands; she bit her lips so as not to cry, and went away. The whole house seemed suddenly darkened; every one looked gloomy; there was a strange hush; a shrill cock was carried away from the yard to the village, unable to comprehend why he should be treated so. Bazarov still lay, turned to the wall. Vassily Ivanovitch tried to address him with various questions, but they fatigued Bazarov, and the old man sank into his armchair, motionless, only cracking his finger-joints now and then. He went for a few minutes into the garden, stood there like a statue, as though overwhelmed with unutterable bewilderment (the expression of amazement never left his face all through), and went back again to his son, trying to avoid his wife's questions. She caught him by the arm at last and passionately, almost menacingly, said, 'What is wrong with him?' Then he came to himself, and forced himself to smile at her in reply; but to his own horror, instead of a smile, he found himself taken somehow by a fit of laughter. He had sent at daybreak for a doctor. He thought it necessary to inform his son of this, for fear he should be angry. Bazarov suddenly turned over on the sofa, bent a fixed dull look on his father, and asked for drink.

Vassily Ivanovitch gave him some water, and as he did so felt his forehead. It seemed on fire.

'Governor,' began Bazarov, in a slow, drowsy voice; 'I'm in a bad way; I've got the infection, and in a few days you'll have to bury me.'

Vassily Ivanovitch staggered back, as though some one had aimed a blow at his legs.

'Yevgeny!' he faltered; 'what do you mean!... God have mercy on you! You've caught cold!'

'Hush!' Bazarov interposed deliberately. 'A doctor can't be allowed to talk like that. There's every symptom of infection; you know yourself.'

'Where are the symptoms ... of infection Yevgeny?... Good Heavens!'

'What's this?' said Bazarov, and, pulling up his shirtsleeve, he showed his father the ominous red patches coming out on his arm.

Vassily Ivanovitch was shaking and chill with terror.

'Supposing,' he said at last, 'even supposing ... if even there's something like ... infection ...'

'Pyæmia,' put in his son.

'Well, well ... something of the epidemic ...'

'Pyæmia,' Bazarov repeated sharply and distinctly; 'have you forgotten your text-books?'

'Well, well—as you like.... Anyway, we will cure you!'

'Come, that's humbug. But that's not the point. I didn't expect to die so soon; it's a most unpleasant incident, to tell the truth. You and mother ought to make the most of your strong religious belief; now's the time to put it to the test.' He drank off a little water. 'I want to ask you about one thing ... while my head is still under my control. To-morrow or next day my brain, you know, will send in its resignation. I'm not quite certain even now whether I'm expressing myself clearly. While I've been lying here, I've kept fancying red dogs were running round me, while you were making them point at me, as if I were a woodcock. Just as if I were drunk. Do you understand me all right?'

'I assure you, Yevgeny, you are talking perfectly correctly.'

'All the better. You told me you'd sent for the doctor. You did that to comfort yourself ... comfort me too; send a messenger ...'

'To Arkady Nikolaitch?' put in the old man.

'Who's Arkady Nikolaitch?' said Bazarov, as though in doubt.... 'Oh, yes! that chicken! No, let him alone; he's turned jackdaw now. Don't be surprised; that's not delirium yet. You send a messenger to Madame Odintsov, Anna Sergyevna; she's a lady with an estate.... Do you know?' (Vassily Ivanovitch nodded.) 'Yevgeny Bazarov, say, sends his greetings, and sends word he is dying. Will you do that?'
'Yes, I will do it.... But is it a possible thing for you to die, Yevgeny?... Think only! Where would divine justice be after that?'
'I know nothing about that; only you send the messenger.'
'I'll send this minute, and I'll write a letter myself.'
'No, why? Say I sent greetings; nothing more is necessary. And now I'll go back to my dogs. Strange! I want to fix my thoughts on death, and nothing comes of it. I see a kind of blur ... and nothing more.'
He turned painfully back to the wall again; while Vassily Ivanovitch went out of the study, and struggling as far as his wife's bedroom, simply dropped down on to his knees before the holy pictures.
'Pray, Arina, pray for us!' he moaned; 'our son is dying.'
The doctor, the same district doctor who had had no caustic, arrived, and after looking at the patient, advised them to persevere with a cooling treatment, and at that point said a few words of the chance of recovery.
'Have you ever chanced to see people in my state *not* set off for Elysium?' asked Bazarov, and suddenly snatching the leg of a heavy table that stood near his sofa, he swung it round, and pushed it away. 'There's strength, there's strength,' he murmured; 'everything's here still, and I must die!... An old man at least has time to be weaned from life, but I ... Well, go and try to disprove death. Death will disprove you, and that's all! Who's crying there?' he added, after a short pause—'Mother? Poor thing! Whom will she feed now with her exquisite beetroot-soup? You, Vassily Ivanovitch, whimpering too, I do believe! Why, if Christianity's no help to you, be a philosopher, a Stoic, or what not! Why, didn't you boast you were a philosopher?'
'Me a philosopher!' wailed Vassily Ivanovitch, while the tears fairly streamed down his cheeks.
Bazarov got worse every hour; the progress of the disease was rapid, as is usually the way in cases of surgical poisoning. He still had not lost consciousness, and understood what was said to him; he was still struggling. 'I don't want to lose my wits,' he muttered, clenching his fists; 'what rot it all is!' And at once he would say, 'Come, take ten from eight, what remains?' Vassily Ivanovitch wandered about like one possessed, proposed first one remedy, then another, and ended by doing nothing but cover up his son's feet. 'Try cold pack ... emetic ... mustard plasters on the stomach ... bleeding,' he would murmur with an effort. The doctor, whom he had entreated to remain, agreed with him, ordered the patient lemonade to drink, and for himself asked for a pipe and something 'warming and strengthening'—that's to say, brandy. Arina Vlasyevna sat on a low stool near the door, and only went out from time to time to pray. A few days before, a looking-glass had slipped out of her hands and been broken, and this she had always considered an omen of evil; even Anfisushka could say nothing to her. Timofeitch had gone off to Madame Odintsov's.
The night passed badly for Bazarov.... He was in the agonies of high fever. Towards morning he was a little easier. He asked for Arina Vlasyevna to comb his hair, kissed her hand, and swallowed two gulps of tea. Vassily Ivanovitch revived a little.
'Thank God!' he kept declaring; 'the crisis is coming, the crisis is at hand!'
'There, to think now!' murmured Bazarov; 'what a word can do! He's found it; he's said "crisis," and is comforted. It's an astounding thing how man believes in words. If he's told he's a fool, for instance, though he's not thrashed, he'll be wretched; call him a clever fellow, and he'll be delighted if you go off without paying him.'
This little speech of Bazarov's, recalling his old retorts, moved Vassily Ivanovitch greatly.
'Bravo! well said, very good!' he cried, making as though he were clapping his hands.
Bazarov smiled mournfully.
'So what do you think,' he said; 'is the crisis over, or coming?'
'You are better, that's what I see, that's what rejoices me,' answered Vassily Ivanovitch.
'Well, that's good; rejoicings never come amiss. And to her, do you remember? did you send?'
'To be sure I did.'
The change for the better did not last long. The disease resumed its onslaughts. Vassily Ivanovitch was sitting by Bazarov. It seemed as though the old man were tormented by some special anguish. He was several times on the point of speaking—and could not.
'Yevgeny!' he brought out at last; 'my son, my one, dear son!'
This unfamiliar mode of address produced an effect on Bazarov. He turned his head a little, and, obviously trying to fight against the load of oblivion weighing upon him, he articulated: 'What is it, father?'

'Yevgeny,' Vassily Ivanovitch went on, and he fell on his knees before Bazarov, though the latter had closed his eyes and could not see him. 'Yevgeny, you are better now; please God, you will get well, but make use of this time, comfort your mother and me, perform the duty of a Christian! What it means for me to say this to you, it's awful; but still more awful ... for ever and ever, Yevgeny ... think a little, what ...'
The old man's voice broke, and a strange look passed over his son's face, though he still lay with closed eyes.
'I won't refuse, if that can be any comfort to you,' he brought out at last; 'but it seems to me there's no need to be in a hurry. You say yourself I am better.'
'Oh, yes, Yevgeny, better certainly; but who knows, it is all in God's hands, and in doing the duty ...'
'No, I will wait a bit,' broke in Bazarov. 'I agree with you that the crisis has come. And if we're mistaken, well! they give the sacrament to men who're unconscious, you know.'
'Yevgeny, I beg.'
'I'll wait a little. And now I want to go to sleep. Don't disturb me.' And he laid his head back on the pillow.
The old man rose from his knees, sat down in the armchair, and, clutching his beard, began biting his own fingers ...
The sound of a light carriage on springs, that sound which is peculiarly impressive in the wilds of the country, suddenly struck upon his hearing. Nearer and nearer rolled the light wheels; now even the neighing of the horses could be heard.... Vassily Ivanovitch jumped up and ran to the little window. There drove into the courtyard of his little house a carriage with seats for two, with four horses harnessed abreast. Without stopping to consider what it could mean, with a rush of a sort of senseless joy, he ran out on to the steps.... A groom in livery was opening the carriage doors; a lady in a black veil and a black mantle was getting out of it ...
'I am Madame Odintsov,' she said. 'Yevgeny Vassilvitch is still living? You are his father? I have a doctor with me.'
'Benefactress!' cried Vassily Ivanovitch, and snatching her hand, he pressed it convulsively to his lips, while the doctor brought by Anna Sergyevna, a little man in spectacles, of German physiognomy, stepped very deliberately out of the carriage. 'Still living, my Yevgeny is living, and now he will be saved! Wife! wife!... An angel from heaven has come to us....'
'What does it mean, good Lord!' faltered the old woman, running out of the drawing-room; and, comprehending nothing, she fell on the spot in the passage at Anna Sergyevna's feet, and began kissing her garments like a mad woman.
'What are you doing!' protested Anna Sergyevna; but Arina Vlasyevna did not heed her, while Vassily Ivanovitch could only repeat, 'An angel! an angel!'
'Wo ist der Kranke? and where is the patient?' said the doctor at last, with some impatience.
Vassily Ivanovitch recovered himself. 'Here, here, follow me, würdigster Herr Collega,' he added through old associations.
'Ah!' articulated the German, grinning sourly.
Vassily Ivanovitch led him into the study. 'The doctor from Anna Sergyevna Odintsov,' he said, bending down quite to his son's ear, 'and she herself is here.'
Bazarov suddenly opened his eyes. 'What did you say?'
'I say that Anna Sergyevna is here, and has brought this gentleman, a doctor, to you.'
Bazarov moved his eyes about him. 'She is here.... I want to see her.'
'You shall see her, Yevgeny; but first we must have a little talk with the doctor. I will tell him the whole history of your illness since Sidor Sidoritch' (this was the name of the district doctor) 'has gone, and we will have a little consultation.'
Bazarov glanced at the German. 'Well, talk away quickly, only not in Latin; you see, I know the meaning of *jam moritur.'*
'*Der Herr scheint des Deutschen mächtig zu sein*,' began the new follower of Æsculapius, turning to Vassily Ivanovitch.
'*Ich ... gabe* ... We had better speak Russian,' said the old man.
'Ah, ah! so that's how it is.... To be sure ...' And the consultation began.
Half-an-hour later Anna Sergyevna, conducted by Vassily Ivanovitch, came into the study. The doctor had had time to whisper to her that it was hopeless even to think of the patient's recovery.
She looked at Bazarov ... and stood still in the doorway, so greatly was she impressed by the inflamed, and at the same time deathly face, with its dim eyes fastened upon her. She felt simply dismayed, with a sort of cold

and suffocating dismay; the thought that she would not have felt like that if she had really loved him flashed instantaneously through her brain.

'Thanks,' he said painfully, 'I did not expect this. It's a deed of mercy. So we have seen each other again, as you promised.'

'Anna Sergyevna has been so kind,' began Vassily Ivanovitch ...

'Father, leave us alone. Anna Sergyevna, you will allow it, I fancy, now?'

With a motion of his head, he indicated his prostrate helpless frame.

Vassily Ivanovitch went out.

'Well, thanks,' repeated Bazarov. 'This is royally done. Monarchs, they say, visit the dying too.'

'Yevgeny Vassilyitch, I hope——'

'Ah, Anna Sergyevna, let us speak the truth. It's all over with me. I'm under the wheel. So it turns out that it was useless to think of the future. Death's an old joke, but it comes fresh to every one. So far I'm not afraid ... but there, senselessness is coming, and then it's all up!——' he waved his hand feebly. 'Well, what had I to say to you ... I loved you! there was no sense in that even before, and less than ever now. Love is a form, and my own form is already breaking up. Better say how lovely you are! And now here you stand, so beautiful ...'

Anna Sergyevna gave an involuntary shudder.

'Never mind, don't be uneasy.... Sit down there.... Don't come close to me; you know, my illness is catching.'

Anna Sergyevna swiftly crossed the room, and sat down in the armchair near the sofa on which Bazarov was lying.

'Noble-hearted!' he whispered. 'Oh, how near, and how young, and fresh, and pure ... in this loathsome room!... Well, good-bye! live long, that's the best of all, and make the most of it while there is time. You see what a hideous spectacle; the worm half-crushed, but writhing still. And, you see, I thought too: I'd break down so many things, I wouldn't die, why should I! there were problems to solve, and I was a giant! And now all the problem for the giant is how to die decently, though that makes no difference to any one either.... Never mind; I'm not going to turn tail.'

Bazarov was silent, and began feeling with his hand for the glass. Anna Sergyevna gave him some drink, not taking off her glove, and drawing her breath timorously.

'You will forget me,' he began again; 'the dead's no companion for the living. My father will tell you what a man Russia is losing.... That's nonsense, but don't contradict the old man. Whatever toy will comfort the child ... you know. And be kind to mother. People like them aren't to be found in your great world if you look by daylight with a candle.... I was needed by Russia.... No, it's clear, I wasn't needed. And who is needed? The shoemaker's needed, the tailor's needed, the butcher ... gives us meat ... the butcher ... wait a little, I'm getting mixed.... There's a forest here ...'

Bazarov put his hand to his brow.

Anna Sergyevna bent down to him. 'Yevgeny Vassilyitch, I am here ...'

He at once took his hand away, and raised himself.

'Good-bye,' he said with sudden force, and his eyes gleamed with their last light. 'Good-bye.... Listen ... you know I didn't kiss you then.... Breathe on the dying lamp, and let it go out ...'

Anna Sergyevna put her lips to his forehead.

'Enough!' he murmured, and dropped back on to the pillow. 'Now ... darkness ...'

Anna Sergyevna went softly out. 'Well?' Vassily Ivanovitch asked her in a whisper.

'He has fallen asleep,' she answered, hardly audibly. Bazarov was not fated to awaken. Towards evening he sank into complete unconsciousness, and the following day he died. Father Alexey performed the last rites of religion over him. When they anointed him with the last unction, when the holy oil touched his breast, one eye opened, and it seemed as though at the sight of the priest in his vestments, the smoking censers, the light before the image, something like a shudder of horror passed over the death-stricken face. When at last he had breathed his last, and there arose a universal lamentation in the house, Vassily Ivanovitch was seized by a sudden frenzy. 'I said I should rebel,' he shrieked hoarsely, with his face inflamed and distorted, shaking his fist in the air, as though threatening some one; 'and I rebel, I rebel!' But Arina Vlasyevna, all in tears, hung upon his neck, and both fell on their faces together. 'Side by side,' Anfisushka related afterwards in the servants' room, 'they dropped their poor heads like lambs at noonday ...'

But the heat of noonday passes, and evening comes and night, and then, too, the return to the kindly refuge, where sleep is sweet for the weary and heavy laden....

CHAPTER XXVIII

Six months had passed by. White winter had come with the cruel stillness of unclouded frosts, the thick-lying, crunching snow, the rosy rime on the trees, the pale emerald sky, the wreaths of smoke above the chimneys, the clouds of steam rushing out of the doors when they are opened for an instant, with the fresh faces, that look stung by the cold, and the hurrying trot of the chilled horses. A January day was drawing to its close; the cold evening was more keen than ever in the motionless air, and a lurid sunset was rapidly dying away. There were lights burning in the windows of the house at Maryino; Prokofitch in a black frockcoat and white gloves, with a special solemnity, laid the table for seven. A week before in the small parish church two weddings had taken place quietly, and almost without witnesses—Arkady and Katya's, and Nikolai Petrovitch and Fenitchka's; and on this day Nikolai Petrovitch was giving a farewell dinner to his brother, who was going away to Moscow on business. Anna Sergyevna had gone there also directly after the ceremony was over, after making very handsome presents to the young people.

Precisely at three o'clock they all gathered about the table. Mitya was placed there too; with him appeared a nurse in a cap of glazed brocade. Pavel Petrovitch took his seat between Katya and Fenitchka; the 'husbands' took their places beside their wives. Our friends had changed of late; they all seemed to have grown stronger and better looking; only Pavel Petrovitch was thinner, which gave even more of an elegant and 'grand seigneur' air to his expressive features.... And Fenitchka too was different. In a fresh silk gown, with a wide velvet head-dress on her hair, with a gold chain round her neck, she sat with deprecating immobility, respectful towards herself and everything surrounding her, and smiled as though she would say, 'I beg your pardon; I'm not to blame.' And not she alone—all the others smiled, and also seemed apologetic; they were all a little awkward, a little sorry, and in reality very happy. They all helped one another with humorous attentiveness, as though they had all agreed to rehearse a sort of artless farce. Katya was the most composed of all; she looked confidently about her, and it could be seen that Nikolai Petrovitch was already devotedly fond of her. At the end of dinner he got up, and, his glass in his hand, turned to Pavel Petrovitch.

'You are leaving us ... you are leaving us, dear brother,' he began; 'not for long, to be sure; but still, I cannot help expressing what I ... what we ... how much I ... how much we.... There, the worst of it is, we don't know how to make speeches. Arkady, you speak.'

'No, daddy, I've not prepared anything.'

'As though I were so well prepared! Well, brother, I will simply say, let us embrace you, wish you all good luck, and come back to us as quickly as you can!'

Pavel Petrovitch exchanged kisses with every one, of course not excluding Mitya; in Fenitchka's case, he kissed also her hand, which she had not yet learned to offer properly, and drinking off the glass which had been filled again, he said with a deep sigh, 'May you be happy, my friends! *Farewell!'* This English finale passed unnoticed; but all were touched.

'To the memory of Bazarov,' Katya whispered in her husband's ear, as she clinked glasses with him. Arkady pressed her hand warmly in response, but he did not venture to propose this toast aloud.

The end, would it seem? But perhaps some one of our readers would care to know what each of the characters we have introduced is doing in the present, the actual present. We are ready to satisfy him.

Anna Sergyevna has recently made a marriage, not of love but of good sense, with one of the future leaders of Russia, a very clever man, a lawyer, possessed of vigorous practical sense, a strong will, and remarkable fluency—still young, good-natured, and cold as ice. They live in the greatest harmony together, and will live perhaps to attain complete happiness ... perhaps love. The Princess K—— is dead, forgotten the day of her death. The Kirsanovs, father and son, live at Maryino; their fortunes are beginning to mend. Arkady has become zealous in the management of the estate, and the 'farm' now yields a fairly good income. Nikolai Petrovitch has been made one of the mediators appointed to carry out the emancipation reforms, and works with all his energies; he is for ever driving about over his district; delivers long speeches (he maintains the opinion that the peasants ought to be 'brought to comprehend things,' that is to say, they ought to be reduced to a state of quiescence by the constant repetition of the same words); and yet, to tell the truth, he does not give complete satisfaction either to the refined gentry, who talk with *chic,* or depression of the *emancipation* (pronouncing it as though it were French), nor of the uncultivated gentry, who unceremoniously curse 'the damned *'mancipation.'* He is too soft-hearted for both sets. Katerina Sergyevna has a son, little Nikolai, while Mitya runs about merrily and talks fluently. Fenitchka, Fedosya Nikolaevna, after her husband and Mitya, adores no one so much as her daughter-in-law, and when the latter is at the piano, she would gladly spend the whole day at her side.

A passing word of Piotr. He has grown perfectly rigid with stupidity and dignity, but he too is married, and received a respectable dowry with his bride, the daughter of a market-gardener of the town, who had refused two excellent suitors, only because they had no watch; while Piotr had not only a watch—he had a pair of kid shoes.

In the Brühl Terrace in Dresden, between two and four o'clock—the most fashionable time for walking—you may meet a man about fifty, quite grey, and looking as though he suffered from gout, but still handsome, elegantly dressed, and with that special stamp, which is only gained by moving a long time in the higher strata of society. That is Pavel Petrovitch. From Moscow he went abroad for the sake of his health, and has settled for good at Dresden, where he associates most with English and Russian visitors. With English people he behaves simply, almost modestly, but with dignity; they find him rather a bore, but respect him for being, as they say, *'a perfect gentleman.'* With Russians he is more free and easy, gives vent to his spleen, and makes fun of himself and them, but that is done by him with great amiability, negligence, and propriety. He holds Slavophil views; it is well known that in the highest society this is regarded as *très distingué!* He reads nothing in Russian, but on his writing table there is a silver ashpan in the shape of a peasant's plaited shoe. He is much run after by our tourists. Matvy Ilyitch Kolyazin, happening to be in temporary opposition, paid him a majestic visit; while the natives, with whom, however, he is very little seen, positively grovel before him. No one can so readily and quickly obtain a ticket for the court chapel, for the theatre, and such things as *der Herr Baron von Kirsanoff.* He does everything good-naturedly that he can; he still makes some little noise in the world; it is not for nothing that he was once a great society lion;—but life is a burden to him ... a heavier burden than he suspects himself. One need but glance at him in the Russian church, when, leaning against the wall on one side, he sinks into thought, and remains long without stirring, bitterly compressing his lips, then suddenly recollects himself, and begins almost imperceptibly crossing himself....

Madame Kukshin, too, went abroad. She is in Heidelberg, and is now studying not natural science, but architecture, in which, according to her own account, she has discovered new laws. She still fraternises with students, especially with the young Russians studying natural science and chemistry, with whom Heidelberg is crowded, and who, astounding the naïve German professors at first by the soundness of their views of things, astound the same professors no less in the sequel by their complete inefficiency and absolute idleness. In company with two or three such young chemists, who don't know oxygen from nitrogen, but are filled with scepticism and self-conceit, and, too, with the great Elisyevitch, Sitnikov roams about Petersburg, also getting ready to be great, and in his own conviction continues the 'work' of Bazarov. There is a story that some one recently gave him a beating; but he was avenged upon him; in an obscure little article, hidden in an obscure little journal, he has hinted that the man who beat him was a coward. He calls this irony. His father bullies him as before, while his wife regards him as a fool ... and a literary man.

There is a small village graveyard in one of the remote corners of Russia. Like almost all our graveyards, it presents a wretched appearance; the ditches surrounding it have long been overgrown; the grey wooden crosses lie fallen and rotting under their once painted gables; the stone slabs are all displaced, as though some one were pushing them up from behind; two or three bare trees give a scanty shade; the sheep wander unchecked among the tombs.... But among them is one untouched by man, untrampled by beast, only the birds perch upon it and sing at daybreak. An iron railing runs round it; two young fir-trees have been planted, one at each end. Yevgeny Bazarov is buried in this tomb. Often from the little village not far off, two quite feeble old people come to visit it—a husband and wife. Supporting one another, they move to it with heavy steps; they go up to the railing, fall down, and remain on their knees, and long and bitterly they weep, and yearn and intently gaze at the dumb stone, under which their son is lying; they exchange some brief word, wipe away the dust from the stone, set straight a branch of a fir-tree, and pray again, and cannot tear themselves from this place, where they seem to be nearer to their son, to their memories of him.... Can it be that their prayers, their tears are fruitless? Can it be that love, sacred, devoted love, is not all-powerful? Oh, no! However passionate, sinning, and rebellious the heart hidden in the tomb, the flowers growing over it peep serenely at us with their innocent eyes; they tell us not of eternal peace alone, of that great peace of 'indifferent' nature; tell us too of eternal reconciliation and of life without end.

A Nobleman's Nest

I

The brilliant, spring day was inclining toward the evening, tiny rose-tinted cloudlets hung high in the heavens, and seemed not to be floating past, but retreating into the very depths of the azure.

In front of the open window of a handsome house, in one of the outlying streets of O * * * the capital of a Government, sat two women; one fifty years of age, the other seventy years old, and already aged.

The former was named Márya Dmítrievna Kalítin. Her husband, formerly the governmental procurator, well known in his day as an active official—a man of energetic and decided character, splenetic and stubborn—had died ten years previously. He had received a fairly good education, had studied at the university, but, having been born in a poverty-stricken class of society, he had early comprehended the necessity of opening up a way for himself, and of accumulating money. Márya Dmítrievna had married him for love; he was far from uncomely in appearance, he was clever, and, when he chose, he could be very amiable. Márya Dmítrievna (her maiden name had been Péstoff) had lost her parents in early childhood, had spent several years in Moscow, in a government educational institute, and, on returning thence, had lived fifty versts from O * * *, in her native village, Pokróvskoe, with her aunt and her elder brother. This brother soon removed to Petersburg on service, and kept his sister and his aunt on short commons, until his sudden death put an end to his career. Márya Dmítrievna inherited Pokróvskoe, but did not live there long; during the second year after her marriage to Kalítin, who succeeded in conquering her heart in the course of a few days, Pokróvskoe was exchanged for another estate, much more profitable, but ugly and without a manor-house, and, at the same time, Kalítin acquired a house in the town of O * * *, and settled down there permanently with his wife. A large garden was attached to the house; on one side, it joined directly on to the open fields, beyond the town. Kalítin,—who greatly disliked the stagnation of the country,—had evidently made up his mind, that there was no reason for dragging out existence on the estate. Márya Dmítrievna, many a time, in her own mind regretted her pretty Pokróvskoe, with its merry little stream, its broad meadows, and verdant groves; but she opposed her husband in nothing, and worshipped his cleverness and knowledge of the world. But when, after fifteen years of married life, he died, leaving a son and two daughters, Márya Dmítrievna had become so wonted to her house, and to town life, that she herself did not wish to leave O * * *.

In her youth, Márya Dmítrievna had enjoyed the reputation of being a pretty blonde, and at the age of fifty her features were not devoid of attraction, although they had become somewhat swollen and indefinite in outline. She was more sentimental than kind, and even in her mature age she had preserved the habits of her school-days; she indulged herself, was easily irritated, and even wept when her ways were interfered with; on the other hand, she was very affectionate and amiable, when all her wishes were complied with, and when no one contradicted her. Her house was one of the most agreeable in the town. Her fortune was very considerable, not so much her inherited fortune, as that acquired by her husband. Both her daughters lived with her; her son was being educated at one of the best government institutions in Petersburg.

The old woman, who was sitting by the window with Márya Dmítrievna, was that same aunt, her father's sister, with whom she had spent several years, in days gone by, at Pokróvskoe. Her name was Márfa Timoféevna Péstoff. She bore the reputation of being eccentric, had an independent character, told the entire truth to every one, straight in the face, and, with the most scanty resources, bore herself as though she possessed thousands. She had not been able to endure the deceased Kalítin, and as soon as her niece married him, she retired to her tiny estate, where she lived for ten whole years in the hen-house of a peasant. Márya Dmítrievna was afraid of her. Black-haired and brisk-eyed even in her old age, tiny, sharp-nosed Márfa Timoféevna walked quickly, held herself upright, and talked rapidly and intelligibly, in a shrill, ringing voice. She always wore a white cap and a white jacket.

"What art thou doing that for?—" she suddenly inquired of Márya Dmítrievna.—"What art thou sighing about, my mother?"

"Because," said the other.—"What wonderfully beautiful clouds!"

"So, thou art sorry for them, is that it?"

Márya Dmítrievna made no reply.

"Isn't that Gedeónovsky coming yonder?"—said Márfa Timoféevna, briskly moving her knitting-needles (she was knitting a huge, motley-hued scarf). "He might keep thee company in sighing,—or, if not, he might tell us some lie or other."

"How harshly thou always speakest about him! Sergyéi Petróvitch is an—estimable man."
"Estimable!" repeated the old woman reproachfully.
"And how devoted he was to my dead husband!" remarked Márya Dmítrievna;—"to this day, I cannot think of it with indifference."
"I should think not! he pulled him out of the mire by his ears,"—growled Márfa Timoféevna, and her knitting-needles moved still more swiftly in her hands.
"He looks like such a meek creature,"—she began again,—"his head is all grey, but no sooner does he open his mouth, than he lies or calumniates. And he's a State Councillor, to boot! Well, he's a priest's son: and there's nothing more to be said!"
"Who is without sin, aunty? Of course, he has that weakness. Sergyéi Petróvitch received no education,—of course he does not speak French; but, say what you will, he is an agreeable man."
"Yes, he's always licking thy hand. He doesn't talk French,—what a calamity! I'm not strong on the French 'dialect' myself. 'T would be better if he did not speak any language at all: then he wouldn't lie. But there he is, by the way—speak of the devil,—" added Márfa Timoféevna, glancing into the street.—"There he strides, thine agreeable man. What a long-legged fellow, just like a stork."
Márya Dmítrievna adjusted her curls. Márfa Timoféevna watched her with a grin.
"Hast thou not a grey hair there, my mother? Thou shouldst scold thy Paláshka. Why doesn't she see it?"
"Oh, aunty, you're always so...." muttered Márya Dmítrievna, with vexation, and drummed on the arm of her chair with her fingers.
"Sergyéi Petróvitch Gedeónovsky!" squeaked a red-cheeked page-lad, springing in through the door.

II

There entered a man of lofty stature, in a neat coat, short trousers, grey chamois-skin gloves, and two neckties—one black, on top, and the other white, underneath. Everything about him exhaled decorum and propriety, beginning with his good-looking face and smoothly brushed temple-curls, and ending with his boots, which had neither heels nor squeak. He bowed first to the mistress of the house, then to Márfa Timoféevna, and slowly drawing off his gloves, took Márya Dmítrievna's hand. After kissing it twice in succession, with respect, he seated himself, without haste, in an arm-chair, and said with a smile, as he rubbed the very tips of his fingers:
"And is Elizavéta Mikhaílovna well?"
"Yes,"—replied Márya Dmítrievna,—"she is in the garden."
"And Eléna Mikhaílovna?"
"Lyénotchka is in the garden also. Is there anything new?"
"How could there fail to be, ma'am, how could there fail to be,"—returned the visitor, slowly blinking his eyes, and protruding his lips. "Hm! ... now, here's a bit of news, if you please, and a very astounding bit: Lavrétzky, Feódor Ivánitch, has arrived."
"Fédya?"—exclaimed Márfa Timoféevna.—"But come now, my father, art not thou inventing that?"
"Not in the least, ma'am, I saw him myself."
"Well, that's no proof."
"He has recovered his health finely,"—went on Gedeónovsky, pretending not to hear Márfa Timoféevna's remark:—"he has grown broader in the shoulders, and the rosy colour covers the whole of his cheeks."
"He has recovered his health,"—ejaculated Márya Dmítrievna, with pauses:—"that means, that he had something to recover from?"
"Yes, ma'am,"—returned Gedeónovsky:—"Any other man, in his place, would have been ashamed to show himself in the world."
"Why so?"—interrupted Márfa Timoféevna;—"what nonsense is this? A man returns to his native place—what would you have him do with himself? And as if he were in any way to blame!"
"The husband is always to blame, madam, I venture to assure you, when the wife behaves badly."
"Thou sayest that, my good sir, because thou hast never been married thyself." Gedeónovsky smiled in a constrained way.
"Permit me to inquire," he asked, after a brief pause,—"for whom is that very pretty scarf destined?"
Márfa Timoféevna cast a swift glance at him.
"It is destined"—she retorted,—"for the man who never gossips, nor uses craft, nor lies, if such a man exists in the world. I know Fédya well; his sole fault is, that he was too indulgent to his wife. Well, he married for love, and nothing good ever comes of those love-marriages,"—added the old woman, casting a sidelong

glance at Márya Dmítrievna, and rising.—"And now, dear little father, thou mayest whet thy teeth on whomsoever thou wilt, only not on me; I'm going away, I won't interfere."—And Márfa Timoféevna withdrew.

"There, she is always like that,"—said Márya Dmítrievna, following her aunt with her eyes:—"Always!"

"It's her age! There's no help for it, ma'am!" remarked Gedeónovsky.—"There now, she permitted herself to say: 'the man who does not use craft.' But who doesn't use craft nowadays? it's the spirit of the age. One of my friends, a very estimable person, and, I must tell you, a man of no mean rank, was wont to say: that 'nowadays, a hen approaches a grain of corn craftily—she keeps watching her chance to get to it from one side.' But when I look at you, my lady, you have a truly angelic disposition; please to favour me with your snow-white little hand."

Márya Dmítrievna smiled faintly, and extended her plump hand, with the little finger standing out apart, to Gedeónovsky. He applied his lips to it, and she moved her arm-chair closer to him, and bending slightly toward him, she asked in a low tone:

"So, you have seen him? Is he really—all right, well, cheerful?"

"He is cheerful, ma'am; all right, ma'am," returned Gedeónovsky, in a whisper.

"And you have not heard where his wife is now?"

"She has recently been in Paris, ma'am; now, I hear, she has removed to the kingdom of Italy."

"It is dreadful, really,—Fédya's position; I do not know how he can endure it. Accidents do happen, with every one, in fact; but he, one may say, has been advertised all over Europe."

Gedeónovsky sighed.

"Yes, ma'am; yes, ma'am. Why, she, they say, has struck up acquaintance with artists, and pianists, and, as they call it in their fashion, with lions and wild beasts. She has lost her shame, completely...."

"It is very, very sad,"—said Márya Dmítrievna:—"on account of the relationship; for you know, Sergyéi Petróvitch, he's my nephew, once removed."

"Of course, ma'am; of course, ma'am. How could I fail to be aware of everything which relates to your family? Upon my word, ma'am!"

"Will he come to see us,—what do you think?"

"We must assume that he will, ma'am; but I hear, that he is going to his country estate."

Márya Dmítrievna cast her eyes heavenward.

"Akh, Sergyéi Petróvitch, when I think of it, how circumspectly we women must behave!"

"There are different sorts of women, Márya Dmítrievna. Unfortunately, there are some of fickle character ... well, and it's a question of age, also; then, again, the rules have not been inculcated in their childhood." (Sergyéi Petróvitch pulled a checked blue handkerchief out of his pocket, and began to unfold it).—"Such women exist, of course," (Sergyéi Petróvitch raised a corner of the handkerchief to his eyes, one after the other),—"but, generally speaking, if we take into consideration, that is.... There is an unusual amount of dust in town," he concluded.

"*Maman, maman*"—screamed a pretty little girl of eleven, as she rushed into the room:—"Vladímir Nikoláitch is coming to our house on horseback!"

Márya Dmítrievna rose; Sergyéi Petróvitch also rose and bowed:—"Our most humble salute to Eléna Mikhaílovna," he said, and withdrawing into a corner, out of propriety, he began to blow his long and regularly-formed nose.

"What a splendid horse he has!—" went on the little girl.—"He was at the gate just now, and told Liza and me, that he would ride up to the porch."

The trampling of hoofs became audible; and a stately horseman, on a fine brown steed, made his appearance in the street, and halted in front of the open window.

III

"Good afternoon, Márya Dmítrievna!"—exclaimed the horseman, in a ringing, agreeable voice.—"How do you like my new purchase?"

Márya Dmítrievna went to the window.

"Good afternoon, *Woldemar*! Akh, what a magnificent horse! From whom did you buy it?"

"From the remount officer.... He asked a high price, the robber!"

"What is its name?"

"Orlando.... But that's a stupid name; I want to change it.... *Eh bien, eh bien, mon garçon*.... What a turbulent beast!" The horse snorted, shifted from foot to foot, and tossed his foaming muzzle.

"Pat him, Lénotchka, have no fears...."
The little girl stretched her hand out of the window, but Orlando suddenly reared up, and leaped aside. The rider did not lose control, gripped the horse with his knees, gave him a lash on the neck with his whip, and, despite his opposition, placed him once more in front of the window.
"*Prenez garde! prenez garde!*"—Márya Dmítrievna kept repeating.
"Pat him, Lyénotchka,"—returned the rider,—"I will not permit him to be wilful."
Again the little girl stretched forth her hand, and timidly touched the quivering nostrils of Orlando, who trembled incessantly and strained at the bit.
"Bravo!"—exclaimed Márya Dmítrievna,—"and now, dismount, and come in."
The horseman turned his steed round adroitly, gave him the spurs, and after dashing along the street at a brisk gallop, rode into the yard. A minute later, he ran in through the door of the anteroom into the drawing-room, flourishing his whip; at the same moment, on the threshold of another door, a tall, graceful, black-haired girl of nineteen—Márya Dmítrievna's eldest daughter, Liza—made her appearance.

IV

The young man, with whom we have just made the reader acquainted, was named Vladímir Nikoláitch Pánshin. He served in Petersburg, as an official for special commissions, in the Ministry of the Interior. He had come to the town of O * * * to execute a temporary governmental commission, and was under the command of Governor-General Zonnenberg, to whom he was distantly related. Pánshin's father, a staff-captain of cavalry on the retired list, a famous gambler, a man with a crumpled visage and a nervous twitching of the lips, had passed his whole life in the society of people of quality, had frequented the English Clubs in both capitals, and bore the reputation of an adroit, not very trustworthy, but charming and jolly fellow. In spite of his adroitness, he found himself almost constantly on the very verge of indigence, and left behind him to his only son a small and impaired fortune. On the other hand, he had, after his own fashion, taken pains with his education: Vladímir Nikoláitch spoke French capitally, English well, and German badly; but it is permissible to let fall a German word in certain circumstances—chiefly humorous,—"*c'est même très chic*," as the Petersburg Parisians express themselves. Vladímir Nikoláitch already understood, at the age of fifteen, how to enter any drawing-room whatever without embarrassment, how to move about in it agreeably, and to withdraw at the proper time. Pánshin's father had procured for his son many influential connections; as he shuffled the cards between two rubbers, or after a successful capture of all the tricks, he let slip no opportunity to drop a nice little word about his "Volódka" to some important personage who was fond of social games. On his side, Vladímir Nikoláitch, during his stay in the university, whence he emerged with the rank of actual student, made acquaintance with several young men of quality, and became a frequenter of the best houses. He was received gladly everywhere; he was extremely good-looking, easy in his manners, entertaining, always well and ready for everything; where it was requisite, he was respectful; where it was possible, he was insolent, a capital companion, *un charmant garçon*. The sacred realm opened out before him. Pánshin speedily grasped the secret of the science of society; he understood how to imbue himself with genuine respect for its decrees; he understood how, with half-bantering gravity, to busy himself with nonsense and assume the appearance of regarding everything serious as trivial; he danced exquisitely, he dressed in English style. In a short time he became renowned as one of the most agreeable and adroit young men in Petersburg. Pánshin was, in reality, very adroit,—no less so than his father: but he was, also, very gifted. He could do everything: he sang prettily, he drew dashingly, he wrote verses, he acted very far from badly on the stage. He had only just passed his twenty-eighth birthday, but he was already Junior Gentleman of the Emperor's bedchamber, and had a very tolerable rank. Pánshin firmly believed in himself, in his brains, in his penetration; he advanced boldly and cheerfully, at full swing; his life flowed along as on oil. He was accustomed to please everybody, old and young, and imagined that he was a judge of people, especially of women: he did know well their everyday weaknesses. As a man not a stranger to art, he felt within him both fervour, and some enthusiasm, and rapture, and in consequence of this he permitted himself various deviations from the rules: he caroused, he picked up acquaintance with persons who did not belong to society, and, in general, maintained a frank and simple demeanour; but in soul he was cold and cunning, and in the midst of the wildest carouse his clever little brown eye was always on guard, and watching; this bold, this free young man could never forget himself and get completely carried away. To his honour it must be said, that he never bragged of his conquests. He had hit upon Márya Dmítrievna's house immediately on his arrival in O * * *, and had promptly made himself entirely at home there. Márya Dmítrievna fairly adored him.

Pánshin amiably saluted all who were in the room, shook hands with Márya Dmítrievna and Lizavéta Mikhaílovna, lightly tapped Gedeónovsky on the shoulder, and whirling round on his heels, caught Lyénotchka by the head, and kissed her on the brow.
"And you are not afraid to ride such a vicious horse?"—Márya Dmítrievna asked him.
"Good gracious! it is a very peaceable beast; but I'll tell you what I am afraid of: I'm afraid to play preference with Sergyéi Petróvitch; last night, at the Byelenítzyns', he won my last farthing."
Gedeónovsky laughed a shrill and servile laugh: he fawned on the brilliant young official from Petersburg, the pet of the governor. In his conversations with Márya Dmítrievna, he frequently alluded to Pánshin's remarkable capacities. "For why should not I praise him?" he argued. "The young man is making a success in the highest sphere of life, discharges his service in an exemplary manner, and is not the least bit proud." Moreover, even in Petersburg Pánshin was considered an energetic official: he got through an immense amount of work; he alluded to it jestingly, as is befitting a fashionable man who attaches no particular importance to his labours, but he was "an executor." The higher officials love such subordinates; he never had the slightest doubt himself, that, if he so wished, he could become a Minister in course of time.
"You are pleased to say that I beat you at cards,"—remarked Gedeónovsky:—"but who was it that won twelve rubles from me last week? and besides...."
"Villain, villain," Pánshin interrupted him, with a caressing but almost disdainful carelessness, and without paying any further attention to him, he stepped up to Liza.
"I have not been able to find the overture of 'Oberon' here," he began:—"Mme. Byelenítzyn was merely boasting, that she had all the classical music,—as a matter of fact, she has nothing except polkas and waltzes; but I have already written to Moscow, and within a week I shall have that overture. By the way,"—he continued,—"I wrote a new romance yesterday; the words also are my own. Would you like to have me sing it for you? I do not know how it has turned out; Mme. Byelenítzyn thought it extremely charming, but her words signify nothing,—I wish to know your opinion. However, I think it will be better later on...."
"Why later on?"—interposed Márya Dmítrievna:—"Why not now?"
"I obey, ma'am,"—said Pánshin, with a certain bright, sweet smile, which was wont to appear on his face, and suddenly to vanish,—pushed forward a chair with his knee, seated himself at the piano, and after striking several chords, he began to sing, clearly enunciating the words, the following romance:

noon floats high above the earth
l the clouds so pale;
rom the crest of the sea surge moveth
gic ray.
ea of my soul hath acknowledged thee
: its moon,
t is moved,—in joy and in sorrow,—
ee alone.
the anguish of love, the anguish of dumb aspira
oul is full;
'er pain.... But thou from agitation art as free
at moon.

Pánshin sang the second couplet with peculiar expression and force; the surging of the waves could be heard in the tempestuous accompaniment. After the words: "I suffer pain...." he heaved a slight sigh, dropped his eyes, and lowered his voice,—*morendo*. When he had finished, Liza praised the motive, Márya Dmítrievna said: "It is charming;"—while Gedeónovsky even shouted: "Ravishing! both poetry and harmony are equally ravishing!..." Lyénotchka, with childish adoration, gazed at the singer. In a word, the composition of the youthful dilettante pleased all present extremely; but outside of the door of the drawing-room, in the anteroom, stood an elderly man, who had just arrived, to whom, judging by the expression of his downcast face and the movement of his shoulders, Pánshin's romance, charming as it was, afforded no pleasure. After waiting a while, and whisking the dust from his boots with a coarse handkerchief, this man suddenly screwed up his eyes, pressed his lips together grimly, bent his back, which was already sufficiently bowed without that, and slowly entered the drawing-room.
"Ah! Christofór Feódoritch, good afternoon!"—Pánshin was the first of all to exclaim, and sprang hastily from his seat.—"I had no suspicion that you were here,—I could not, on any account, have made up my mind to sing my romance in your presence. I know that you do not care for frivolous music."

"I vas not listening," remarked the newcomer, in imperfect Russian, and having saluted all, he remained awkwardly standing in the middle of the room.

"Have you come, Monsieur Lemm,"—said Márya Dmítrievna,—"to give a music lesson to Liza?"

"No, not to Lisaféta Mikhaílovna, but to Eléna Mikhaílovna."

"Ah! Well,—very good. Lyénotchka, go upstairs with Monsieur Lemm."

The old man was on the point of following the little girl, but Pánshin stopped him.

"Do not go away after the lesson, Christofór Feódoritch,"—he said:—"Lizavéta Mikhaílovna and I will play a Beethoven sonata for four hands."

The old man muttered something, but Pánshin went on in German, pronouncing his words badly:

"Lizavéta Mikhaílovna has shown me the spiritual cantata which you presented to her—'tis a very fine thing! Please do not think that I am incapable of appreciating serious music,—quite the contrary: it is sometimes tiresome, but, on the other hand, it is very beneficial."

The old man crimsoned to his very ears, cast a sidelong glance at Liza, and hastily left the room.

Márya Dmítrievna requested Pánshin to repeat the romance; but he declared, that he did not wish to wound the ears of the learned German, and proposed to Liza that they should occupy themselves with the Beethoven sonata. Then Márya Dmítrievna sighed, and in her turn, proposed to Gedeónovsky that he should take a stroll in the garden with her.—"I wish,"—she said, "to talk and take counsel with you still further, over our poor Fédya." Gedeónovsky grinned, bowed, took up—with two fingers, his hat, and his gloves neatly laid on its brim, and withdrew, in company with Márya Dmítrievna. Pánshin and Liza were left alone in the room; she fetched the sonata, and opened it; both seated themselves, in silence, at the piano.—From above, the faint sounds of scales, played by Lyénotchka's uncertain little fingers, were wafted to them.

V

Christopher-Theodore-Gottlieb Lemm was born in the year 1786, in the kingdom of Saxony, in the town of Chemnitz, of poor musicians. His father played the French horn, his mother the harp; he himself, at the age of five, was already practising on three different instruments. At eight years of age he became an orphan, and at the age of ten he began to earn a bit of bread for himself by his art. For a long time he led a wandering life, played everywhere—in inns, at fairs, and at peasant weddings and at balls; at last, he got into an orchestra, and rising ever higher and higher, he attained to the post of director. He was rather a poor executant; but he possessed a thorough knowledge of music. At the age of twenty-eight he removed to Russia. He was imported by a great gentleman, who himself could not endure music, but maintained an orchestra as a matter of pride. Lemm lived seven years with him, in the capacity of musical conductor, and left him with empty hands; the gentleman was ruined, and wished to give him a note of hand, but afterward refused him even this,—in a word, did not pay him a farthing. People advised him to leave the country: but he was not willing to return home in poverty from Russia, from great Russia, that gold-mine of artists; he decided to remain, and try his luck. For the space of twenty years he did try his luck: he sojourned with various gentry, he lived in Moscow and in the capitals of various governments, he suffered and endured a great deal, he learned to know want, he floundered like a fish on the ice; but the idea of returning to his native land never abandoned him in the midst of all these calamities to which he was subjected; it alone upheld him. But it did not suit Fate to render him happy with this last and first joy: at the age of fifty, ill, prematurely infirm, he got stranded in the town of O * * * and there remained for good, having finally lost all hope of quitting the Russia which he detested, and managing, after a fashion, to support his scanty existence by giving lessons. Lemm's external appearance did not predispose one in his favour. He was small of stature, round-shouldered, with shoulder-blades which projected crookedly, and a hollow chest, with huge, flat feet, with pale-blue nails on the stiff, unbending fingers of his sinewy, red hands; he had a wrinkled face, sunken cheeks, and tightly-compressed lips, that he was incessantly moving as though chewing, which, added to his customary taciturnity, produced an almost malevolent impression; his grey hair hung in elf-locks over his low brow; his tiny, motionless eyes smouldered like coals which had just been extinguished; he walked heavily, swaying his clumsy body from side to side at every step. Some of his movements were suggestive of the awkward manner in which an owl in a cage plumes itself when it is conscious that it is being watched, though it itself hardly sees anything with its huge, yellow, timorously and dozily blinking eyes. Confirmed, inexorable grief had laid upon the poor musician its ineffaceable seal, had distorted and disfigured his already ill-favoured figure; but for any one who knew enough not to stop at first impressions, something unusual was visible in this half-wrecked being. A worshipper of Bach and Handel, an expert in his profession, gifted with a lively imagination, and with that audacity of thought which is accessible only to the German race, Lemm, in course of time—who knows?—might have entered the ranks of the great composers of his native land, if life had led him differently; but he had not been born under a fortunate star! He had written a great deal in his day—and he had not succeeded in seeing a single one of his compositions published; he had not understood how to set about the matter in the proper way, to cringe opportunely, to bustle at the right moment. Once, long, long ago, one of his admirers and friends, also a German and also poor, had published two of his sonatas at his own expense,—and the whole edition remained in the cellars of the musical shops; they had vanished dully, without leaving a trace, as though some one had flung them into the river by night. At last Lemm gave up in despair; moreover, his years were making themselves felt: he had begun to grow rigid, to stiffen, as his fingers stiffened also. Alone, with an aged cook, whom he had taken from the almshouse (he had never been married), he lived on in O * * *, in a tiny house, not far from the Kalítin residence; he walked a great deal, read the Bible and collections of Protestant psalms, and Shakespeare in Schlegel's translation. It was long since he had composed anything; but, evidently, Liza, his best pupil, understood how to arouse him: he had written for her the cantata to which Pánshin had alluded. He had taken the words for this cantata from the psalms; several verses he had composed himself; it was to be sung by two choruses,—the chorus of the happy, and the chorus of the unhappy; both became reconciled, in the end, and sang together: "O merciful God, have mercy upon us sinners, and purge out of us by fire all evil thoughts and earthly hopes!"—On the title-page, very carefully written, and even drawn, stood the following: "Only the Just are Right. A Spiritual Cantata. Composed and dedicated to Miss Elizavéta Kalítin, my beloved pupil, by her teacher, C. T. G. Lemm." The words: "Only the Just are Right," and "Elizavéta Kalítin," were surrounded by rays. Below was added: "For you alone,"—"Für Sie allein."—Therefore Lemm had crimsoned and had cast a sidelong glance at Liza; it pained him greatly when Pánshin spoke of his cantata in his presence.

VI

Pánshin struck the opening chords of the sonata loudly, and with decision (he was playing the second hand), but Liza did not begin her part. He stopped, and looked at her. Liza's eyes, fixed straight upon him, expressed displeasure; her lips were not smiling, her whole face was stern, almost sad.

"What is the matter with you?"—he inquired.

"Why did not you keep your word?" said she.—"I showed you Christofór Feódoritch's cantata on condition that you would not mention it to him."

"Pardon me, Lizavéta Mikhaílovna, it was a slip of the tongue."

"You have wounded him—and me also. Now he will not trust me any more."

"What would you have me do, Lizavéta Mikhaílovna! From my earliest childhood, I have never been able to endure the sight of a German: something simply impels me to stir him up."

"Why do you say that, Vladímir Nikoláitch! This German is a poor, solitary, broken man—and you feel no pity for him? You want to stir him up? Pánshin was disconcerted.

"You are right, Lizavéta Mikhaílovna,"—he said. "My eternal thoughtlessness is responsible for the whole thing. No, do not say a word; I know myself well. My thoughtlessness has done me many an ill turn. Thanks to it, I have won the reputation of an egoist."

Pánshin paused for a moment. No matter how he began a conversation, he habitually wound up by speaking of himself, and he did it in a charming, soft, confidential, almost involuntary way.

"And here in your house,"—he went on:—"your mother likes me, of course,—she is so kind; you ... however, I do not know your opinion of me; but your aunt, on the contrary, cannot bear me. I must have offended her, also, by some thoughtless, stupid remark. For she does not like me, does she?"

"No," said Liza, with some hesitation:—"you do not please her."

Pánshin swept his fingers swiftly over the keys; a barely perceptible smile flitted across his lips.

"Well, and you?"—he said:—"Do I seem an egoist to you also?"

"I know you very slightly,"—returned Liza:—"but I do not consider you an egoist; on the contrary, I ought to feel grateful to you...."

"I know, I know, what you mean to say,"—Pánshin interrupted her, and again ran his fingers over the keys:—"for the music, for the books which I bring you, for the bad drawings with which I decorate your album, and so forth and so on. I can do all that—and still be an egoist. I venture to think, that you are not bored in my company, and that you do not regard me as a bad man, but still you assume, that I—how in the world shall I express it?—would not spare my own father or friend for the sake of a jest."

"You are heedless and forgetful, like all worldly people,"—said Liza:—"that is all."

Pánshin frowned slightly.
"Listen," he said:—"let us not talk any more about me; let us play our sonata. One thing only I will ask of you,"—he said, as with his hand he smoothed out the leaves of the bound volume which stood on the music-rack:—"think what you will of me, call me an egoist even,—so be it! but do not call me a worldly man: that appellation is intolerable to me.... *Anch'io son pittore.* I also am an artist,—and I will immediately prove it to you in action. Let us begin."
"We will begin, if you please,"—said Liza.
The first adagio went quite successfully, although Pánshin made more than one mistake. He played his own compositions and those which he had practised very prettily, but he read music badly. On the other hand, the second part of the sonata—a rather brisk allegro—did not go at all: at the twentieth measure, Pánshin, who had got two measures behind, could hold out no longer, and pushed back his chair with a laugh.
"No!"—he exclaimed:—"I cannot play to-day; it is well that Lemm does not hear us: he would fall down in a swoon."
Liza rose, shut the piano, and turned to Pánshin.
"What shall we do now?"—she asked.
"I recognise you in that question! You cannot possibly sit with folded hands. Come, if you like, let us draw, before it has grown completely dark. Perhaps the other muse,—the muse of drawing ... what's her name? I've forgotten ... will be more gracious to me. Where is your album? Do you remember?—my landscape there is not finished."
Liza went into the next room for her album, and Pánshin, when he was left alone, pulled a batiste handkerchief from his pocket, polished his nails, and gazed somewhat askance at his hands. They were very handsome and white; on the thumb of the left hand he wore a spiral gold ring. Liza returned; Pánshin seated himself near the window, and opened the album.
"Aha!"—he exclaimed:—"I see that you have begun to copy my landscape—and that is fine. Very good! Only here—give me a pencil—the shadows are not put on thickly enough.... Look."
And Pánshin, with a bold sweep, prolonged several long strokes. He constantly drew one and the same landscape: in the foreground were large, dishevelled trees, in the distance, a meadow, and saw-toothed mountains on the horizon. Liza looked over his shoulder at his work.
"In drawing, and in life in general,"—said Pánshin, bending his head now to the right, now to the left:—"lightness and boldness are the principal thing."
At that moment, Lemm entered the room, and, with a curt inclination, was on the point of departing; but Pánshin flung aside the album and pencil, and barred his way.
"Whither are you going, my dear Christofór Feódoritch? Are not you going to stay and drink tea?"
"I must go home,"—said Lemm in a surly voice:—"my head aches."
"Come, what nonsense!—stay. You and I will have a dispute over Shakespeare."
"My head aches,"—repeated the old man.
"We tried to play a Beethoven sonata without you,"—went on Pánshin, amiably encircling his waist with his arm, and smiling brightly:—"but we couldn't make it go at all. Just imagine, I couldn't play two notes in succession correctly."
"You vould haf done better to sing your romantz,"—retorted Lemm, pushing aside Pánshin's arm, and left the room.
Liza ran after him. She overtook him on the steps.
"Christofór Feódoritch, listen,"—she said to him in German, as she accompanied him to the gate, across the close-cropped green grass of the yard:—"I am to blame toward you—forgive me."
Lemm made no reply.
"I showed your cantata to Vladímir Nikoláitch; I was convinced that he would appreciate it,—and it really did please him greatly."
Lemm halted.
"Zat is nozing,"—he said in Russian, and then added in his native tongue:—"but he cannot understand anything; how is it that you do not perceive that?—he is a dilettante—and that's all there is to it!"
"You are unjust to him,"—returned Liza:—"he understands everything, and can do nearly everything himself."
"Yes, everything is second-class, light-weight, hasty work. That pleases, and he pleases, and he is content with that—well, and bravo! But I am not angry; that cantata and I—we are old fools; I am somewhat ashamed, but that does not matter."

"Forgive me, Christofór Feódoritch,"—said Liza again.
"It does not mattair, it does not mattair," he repeated again in Russian:—"you are a goot girl ... but see yonder, some vun is coming to your house. Good-bye. You are a fery goot girl."
And Lemm, with hasty strides, betook himself toward the gate, through which was entering a gentleman with whom he was not acquainted, clad in a grey coat and a broad-brimmed straw hat. Courteously saluting him (he bowed to all newcomers in the town of O * * *; he turned away from his acquaintances on the street—that was the rule which he had laid down for himself), Lemm passed him, and disappeared behind the hedge. The stranger looked after him in amazement, and, exchanging a glance with Liza, advanced straight toward her.

VII

"You do not recognise me,"—he said, removing his hat,—"but I recognise you, although eight years have passed since I saw you last. You were a child then. I am Lavrétzky. Is your mother at home? Can I see her?"
"Mamma will be very glad,"—replied Liza:—"she has heard of your arrival."
"Your name is Elizavéta, I believe?"—said Lavrétzky, as he mounted the steps of the porch.
"Yes."
"I remember you well; you had a face, at that time, such as one does not forget; I used to bring you bonbons then."
Liza blushed and thought, "What a strange man he is!" Lavrétzky paused for a minute in the anteroom. Liza entered the drawing-room, where Pánshin's voice and laughter were resounding; he had imparted some gossip of the town to Márya Dmítrievna and Gedeónovsky, who had already returned from the garden, and was himself laughing loudly at what he had narrated. At the name of Lavrétzky, Márya Dmítrievna started in utter trepidation, turned pale, and advanced to meet him.
"How do you do, how do you do, my dear *cousin*!"—she exclaimed, in a drawling and almost tearful voice:—"how glad I am to see you!"
"How do you do, my kind cousin,"—returned Lavrétzky; and shook her proffered hand in a friendly way:—"how does the Lord show mercy on you?"
"Sit down, sit down, my dear Feódor Ivánitch. Akh, how delighted I am! Permit me, in the first place, to present to you my daughter Liza...."
"I have already introduced myself to Lizavéta Mikhaílovna,"—Lavrétzky interrupted her.
"Monsieur Pánshin.... Sergyéi Petróvitch Gedeónovsky.... But pray sit down! I look at you, and I simply cannot believe my eyes. How is your health?"
"As you see, I am blooming. And you, cousin,—I don't want to cast the evil eye on you—you have not grown thin during these eight years."
"Just think, what a long time it is since we saw each other,"—remarked Márya Dmítrievna, dreamily.—"Whence come you now? Where have you left ... that is, I meant to say"—she hastily caught herself up—"I meant to say, are you to be with us long?"
"I have just come from Berlin,"—returned Lavrétzky,—"and to-morrow I set out for my estate—probably to remain there a long time."
"Of course, you will live at Lavríki?"
"No, not at Lavríki, but I have a tiny village about twenty-five versts from here; I am going there."
"The village which you inherited from Glafíra Petróvna?"
"The same."
"Good gracious, Feódor Ivánitch! You have a splendid house at Lavríki!"
Lavrétzky scowled slightly.
"Yes ... but in that little estate there is a small wing; and, for the present, I need nothing more. That place is the most convenient for me just now."
Márya Dmítrievna again became so perturbed, that she even straightened herself up, and flung her hands apart. Pánshin came to her assistance, and entered into conversation with Lavrétzky. Márya Dmítrievna recovered her composure, leaned back in her chair, and only interjected a word from time to time; but, all the while, she gazed so compassionately at her visitor, she sighed so significantly, and shook her head so mournfully, that the latter, at last, could endure it no longer, and asked her, quite sharply: was she well?
"Thank God, yes,"—replied Márya Dmítrievna,—"why?"
"Because it seemed to me that you were not quite yourself."

Márya Dmítrievna assumed a dignified and somewhat offended aspect.—"If that's the way you take it,"—she said to herself,—"I don't care in the least; evidently, my good man, nothing affects thee any more than water does a goose; any one else would have pined away with grief, but it swells thee up more than ever." Márya Dmítrievna did not stand on ceremony with herself; she expressed herself more elegantly aloud.

As a matter of fact, Lavrétzky did not resemble a victim of fate. His rosy-cheeked, purely-Russian face, with its large, white brow, rather thick nose, and broad, regular lips, fairly overflowed with native health, with strong, durable force. He was magnificently built,—and his blond hair curled all over his head, like a young man's. Only in his eyes, which were blue and prominent and fixed, was there to be discerned something which was not revery, nor yet weariness, and his voice sounded rather too even.

In the meantime, Pánshin had continued to keep up the conversation. He turned it on the profits of sugar-refining, concerning which two French pamphlets had recently made their appearance, and with calm modesty undertook to set forth their contents, but without saying one word about them.

"Why, here's Fédya!" suddenly rang out Márfa Timoféevna's voice in the adjoining room, behind the half-closed door:—"Actually, Fédya!" And the old woman briskly entered the room. Before Lavrétzky could rise from his chair, she clasped him in her embrace.—"Come, show thyself, show thyself,"—she said, moving back from his face.—"Eh! What a splendid fellow thou art! Thou hast grown older, but hast not grown in the least less comely, really! But why art thou kissing my hands,—kiss me myself, if my wrinkled cheeks are not repulsive to thee. Can it be, that thou didst not ask after me: 'Well, tell me, is aunty alive?' Why, thou wert born into my arms, thou rogue! Well, never mind that; why shouldst thou have remembered me? Only, thou art a sensible fellow, to have come. Well, my mother,"—she added, addressing Márya Dmítrievna,—"hast thou given him any refreshments?"

"I want nothing,"—said Lavrétzky, hastily.

"Come, drink some tea, at least, my dear little father. O Lord my God! He has come, no one knows whence, and they don't give him a cup of tea! Go, Liza, and see about it, as quickly as possible. I remember that, as a little fellow, he was a dreadful glutton, and he must be fond of eating even now."

"My respects, Márfa Timoféevna,"—said Pánshin, approaching the angry old woman from one side, and bowing low.

"Excuse me, sir,"—retorted Márfa Timoféevna,—"I did not notice you for joy.—Thou hast grown to resemble thy mother, the darling,"—she went on, turning again to Lavrétzky:—"only, thy nose was and remains like thy father's. Well—and art thou to be long with us?"

"I am going away to-morrow, aunty."

"Whither?"

"Home, to Vasílievskoe."

"To-morrow?"

"Yes."

"Well, if it must be to-morrow, it must. God be with thee,—thou knowest best. Only, see here, thou must come to say farewell."—The old woman tapped him on the cheek.—"I did not think I should live to see thee; and that not because I was preparing to die; no—I am good for another ten years, probably: all we Péstoffs are tenacious of life; thy deceased grandfather used to call us double-lived; but the Lord only knew how much longer thou wouldst ramble about abroad. Well, but thou art a dashing fine fellow, a fine fellow; thou canst still lift ten puds in one hand as of yore, I suppose? Thy deceased father, excuse me, was cranky in some respects, but he did well when he hired a Swiss for thee; thou rememberest, how thou and he had fistfights; that's called gymnastics, isn't it?—But why have I been cackling thus? I have only been keeping Mr. Panshín" (she never called him Pánshin, as she ought) "from arguing. But we had better drink tea; let us go and drink it on the terrace, my dear; our cream—is not like what you get in your Londons and Parises. Let us go, let us go, and do thou, Fédiusha, give me thy arm. O! how thick it is! There's no danger of falling with thee."

All rose and betook themselves to the terrace, with the exception of Gedeónovsky, who quietly departed. During the entire duration of Lavrétzky's conversation with the mistress of the house, Pánshin, and Márfa Timoféevna, he had sat in a corner, attentively blinking, and sticking out his lips, in childish curiosity: he now hastened to carry the news about the new visitor throughout the town.

On that same day, at eleven o'clock in the evening, this is what was going on at Mme. Kalítin's house. Down-stairs, on the threshold of the drawing-room, Vladímir Nikoláitch, having seized a favourable moment, was saying farewell to Liza, and telling her, as he held her hand: "You know who it is that attracts me hither; you know why I am incessantly coming to your house; what is the use of words, when everything is so plain?" Liza made him no reply, and without a smile, and with eyebrows slightly elevated, and blushing, she stared at the floor, but did not withdraw her hand; and up-stairs, in Márfa Timoféevna's chamber, by the light of the shrine-lamp, which hung in front of the dim, ancient holy pictures, Lavrétzky was sitting in an arm-chair, with his elbows on his knees, and his face in his hands; the old woman, standing before him, was silently stroking his hair, from time to time. He spent more than an hour with her, after taking leave of the mistress of the house; he said almost nothing to his kind old friend, and she did not interrogate him.... And what was the use of talking, what was there to interrogate him about? She understood everything as it was, and she sympathised with everything wherewith his heart was full to overflowing.

VIII

Feódor Ivánovitch Lavrétzky (we must ask the reader's permission to break the thread of our narrative for a time) was descended from an ancient family of the nobility. The ancestral founder of the Lavrétzkys had come out of Prussia during the princely reign of Vasíly the Blind, and had been granted two hundred quarters of land, on Byezhétsk Heights. Many of his descendants were members of various branches of the public service, and sat under princes and distinguished personages in distant governorships, but not one of them ever rose above the rank of table-decker at the Court of the Tzars, or acquired any considerable fortune. The most opulent and noteworthy of all the Lavrétzkys had been Feódor Ivánitch's great-grandfather, Andréi, a harsh, insolent, clever, and crafty man. Down to the day of which we are speaking, the fame of his arbitrary violence, of his fiendish disposition, his mad lavishness, and unquenchable thirst had not died out. He had been very stout and lofty of stature, swarthy of visage, and beardless; he lisped, and appeared to be sleepy; but the more softly he spoke, the more did every one around him tremble. He obtained for himself a wife to match. Goggle-eyed, with hawk-like nose, with a round, sallow face, a gipsy by birth, quick-tempered and revengeful, she was not a whit behind her husband, who almost starved her to death, and whom she did not survive, although she was eternally snarling at him.

Andréi's son, Piótr, Feódor's grandfather, did not resemble his father: he was a simple squire of the steppes, decidedly hare-brained, a swashbuckler and dawdler, rough but not malicious, hospitable, and fond of dogs. He was more than thirty years old when he inherited from his father two thousand souls in capital order; but he speedily dispersed them, sold a part of his estate, and spoiled his house-servants. Petty little people, acquaintances and non-acquaintances, crawled from all sides, like black-beetles, to his spacious, warm, and slovenly mansion; all these ate whatever came to hand, but ate their fill, drank themselves drunk, and carried off what they could, lauding and magnifying the amiable host; and the host, when he was not in a good humour, also magnified his guests—as drones and blackguards—but he was bored without them. Piótr Andréitch's wife was a meek person: he took her from a neighbouring family, at his father's choice and command; her name was Anna Pávlovna. She never interfered with anything, received visitors cordially, and was fond of going out herself, although powdering her hair, according to her own words, was death to her. They put a felt hood on your head, she was wont to narrate in her old age, combed your hair all up on top, smeared it with tallow, sprinkled on flour, stuck in iron pins,—and you could not wash yourself afterward; but to go visiting without powder was impossible—people would take offence;—torture!—She was fond of driving after trotters, was ready to play cards from morning until night, and always covered up with her hand the few farthings of winnings set down to her when her husband approached the card-table; but she gave her dowry and all her money to him, and required no accounting for its use. She bore him two children: a son, Iván, Feódor's father, and a daughter, Glafíra.

Iván was not brought up at home, but at the house of a wealthy old aunt, Princess Kubenskóy; she had designated him as her heir (had it not been for that, his father would not have let him go); she dressed him like a doll, hired every sort of teacher for him, provided him with a governor, a Frenchman, a former abbé, a disciple of Jean-Jacques Rousseau, a certain M. Courtin de Vaucelles, an adroit and subtle intriguer,—the most *fine fleur* of the emigration, as she expressed it,—and ended by marrying this "fine-fleur" when she was almost seventy years of age; she transferred to his name her entire fortune, and soon afterward, rouged, scented with amber, *à la Richelieu*, surrounded by small negroes, slender-legged dogs, and screeching parrots, she died on a crooked little couch of the time of Louis XV, with an enamelled snuff-box, the work of Petitot, in her hands,—and died, deserted by her husband: the sneaking M. Courtin had preferred to retire to Paris with her money.

Iván was only in his twentieth year when this blow (we are speaking of the Princess's marriage, not of her death) descended upon him; he did not wish to remain in his aunt's house, where from a wealthy heir he had suddenly been converted into a parasite; in Petersburg, the society in which he had been reared, was closed to him; to service, beginning with the lowest ranks, difficult and dark, he felt repugnance (all this took place at the very beginning of the reign of the Emperor Alexander). He was compelled, perforce, to return to the country, to his father. Dirty, poor, tattered did his native nest appear to him: the dulness and soot of existence on the steppes offended him at every step; he was tormented with boredom; on the other hand, every one in the house, with the exception of his mother, looked upon him with unfriendly eyes. His father did not like his habits of the capital; his dress-suits, frilled shirts, books, his flute, his cleanliness, in which, not without reason, they scented his fastidiousness; he was constantly complaining and grumbling at his son.—"Nothing here suits him," he was wont to say: "at table he is dainty, he does not eat, he cannot endure the odour of the servants, the stifling atmosphere; the sight of drunken men disturbs him, and you mustn't dare to fight in his presence, either; he will not enter government service: he's frail in health, forsooth; phew, what an effeminate creature! And all because Voltaire sticks in his head!"

The old man cherished a particular dislike for Voltaire, and for the "fanatic" Diderot, although he had never read a single line of their writings: reading was not in his line. Piótr Andréitch was not mistaken: Diderot and Voltaire really were sticking in his son's head, and not they only,—but Rousseau and Raynal and Helvetius, and many other writers of the same sort, were sticking in his head,—but only in his head. Iván Petróvitch's former tutor, the retired abbé and encyclopedist, had contented himself with pouring the whole philosophy of the XVIII century into his pupil in a mass, and the latter went about brimful of it; it gained lodgment within him, without mingling with his blood, without penetrating into his soul, without making itself felt as a firm conviction.... And could convictions be demanded of a young fellow of fifty years ago, when we have not even yet grown up to them? He also embarrassed the visitors to his father's house: he loathed them, and they feared him; and with his sister, Glafíra, who was twelve years older than he, he did not get on at all.

This Glafíra was a strange being; homely, hunchbacked, gaunt, with stern, staring eyes and thin, tightly compressed lips; in face, voice, and quick, angular movements, she recalled her grandmother, the gipsy, the wife of Andréi. Persistent, fond of power, she would not even hear of marriage. The return of Iván Petróvitch did not please her; so long as the Princess Kubenskóy had kept him with her, she had cherished the hope of receiving at least half of the parental estate: she resembled her grandmother in her avarice. Moreover, Glafíra was envious of her brother: he was so cultivated, he spoke French so well, with a Parisian accent, while she was scarcely able to say: "*bon jour*," and "*comment vous portez vous*?" To tell the truth, her parents did not understand any French at all,—but that did not render it any the more pleasant for her.

Iván Petróvitch did not know what to do with himself for tedium and melancholy; he spent nearly a year in the country, and it seemed to him like ten years.—Only with his mother did he relieve his heart, and he was wont to sit, by the hour, in her low-ceiled rooms, listening to the simple prattle of the good woman, and gorging himself with preserves. It so happened, that among Anna Pávlovna's maids there was one very pretty girl, with clear, gentle eyes and delicate features, named Malánya, both clever and modest. She pleased Iván Petróvitch at first sight, and he fell in love with her: he fell in love with her timid walk, her shy answers, her soft voice, her gentle smile; with every passing day she seemed to him more charming. And she became attached to Iván Petróvitch with her whole soul, as only Russian girls can become attached—and gave herself to him.

In the country manor-house of a landed proprietor, no secret can be kept long: every one soon knew of the bond between the young master and Malánya; the tidings of this connection at last reached Piótr Andréitch himself. At any other time, he would, in all probability, have paid no heed to such an insignificant matter; but he had long been in a rage with his son, and rejoiced at the opportunity to put to shame the Petersburg philosopher and dandy. Tumult, shrieks, and uproar arose: Malánya was locked up in the lumber-room; Iván Petróvitch was summoned to his parent. Anna Pávlovna also hastened up at the outcry. She made an effort to pacify her husband, but Piótr Andréitch no longer listened to anything. Like a vulture he pounced upon his son, upbraided him with immorality, with impiety, with hypocrisy; incidentally, he vented on him all his accumulated wrath against the Princess Kubenskóy, and overwhelmed him with insulting epithets. At first, Iván Petróvitch held his peace, and stood firm, but when his father took it into his head to threaten him with a disgraceful chastisement, he lost patience. "The fanatic Diderot has come on the stage again," he thought,—"so just wait, I'll put him in action; I'll astonish you all."

Thereupon, in a quiet voice, although trembling in every limb, Iván Petróvitch announced to his father, that there was no necessity for upbraiding him with immorality, that, although he did not intend to justify his fault, yet he was ready to rectify it, and that the more willingly because he felt himself superior to all prejudices—in short, he was ready to marry Malánya. By uttering these words, Iván Petróvitch did, undoubtedly, attain his object: he astounded Piótr Andréitch to such a degree, that the latter stared with all his eyes, and was rendered dumb for a moment; but he immediately recovered himself, and just as he was, clad in a short coat lined with squirrel-skin, and with slippers on his bare feet, he flung himself with clenched fists upon Iván Petróvitch, who that day, as though expressly, had his hair dressed *à la Titus*, and had donned a new blue English dress-coat, boots with tassels, and dandified chamois trousers, skin-tight. Anna Pávlovna shrieked at the top of her voice, and covered her face with her hands, but her son ran through the whole house, sprang out into the yard, rushed into the vegetable garden, across the garden, flew out upon the highway, and kept running, without looking behind him, until, at last, he ceased to hear behind him the heavy tramp of his father's footsteps, and his violent, broken shouts.... "Stop, rascal!" he roared,—"stop! I'll curse thee!"

Iván Petróvitch hid himself in the house of a neighbouring peasant proprietor, while Piótr Andréitch returned home utterly exhausted and perspiring, and announcing almost before he had recovered his breath, that he would deprive his son of his blessing and his heritage, ordered all his idiotic books to be burned, and the maid Malánya to be sent forthwith to a distant village. Kind people turned up, who sought out Iván Petróvitch and informed him of all. Mortified, enraged, he vowed that he would take revenge on his father; and that very night, lying in wait for the peasant cart in which Malánya was being carried off, he rescued her by force, galloped off with her to the nearest town, and married her. He was supplied with money by a neighbour, an eternally intoxicated and extremely good-natured retired naval officer, a passionate lover of every sort of noble adventure, as he expressed it. On the following day, Iván Petróvitch wrote a caustically-cold and courteous letter to Piótr Andréitch, and betook himself to an estate where dwelt his second cousin, Dmítry Péstoff, and his sister, Márfa Timoféevna, already known to the reader. He told them everything, announced that he intended to go to Petersburg to seek a place, and requested them to give shelter to his wife, for a time at least. At the word "wife" he fell to weeping bitterly, and, despite his city breeding and his philosophy, he prostrated himself humbly, after the fashion of a Russian beggar, before the feet of his relatives, and even beat his brow against the floor. The Péstoffs, kind and compassionate people, gladly acceded to his request; he spent three weeks with them, in secret expectation of a reply from his father; but no reply came,—and none could come. Piótr Andréitch, on learning of his son's marriage, had taken to his bed, and had forbidden the name of Iván Petróvitch to be mentioned in his presence; but his mother, without the knowledge of her husband, borrowed five hundred rubles from the ecclesiastical supervisor of the diocese, and sent them to him, together with a small holy picture for his wife; she was afraid to write, but she gave orders that Iván Petróvitch was to be told, by the lean peasant her envoy, who managed to walk sixty versts in the course of twenty-four hours, that he must not grieve too much, that, God willing, everything would come right, and his father would convert wrath into mercy; that she, also, would have preferred a different daughter-in-law, but that, evidently, God had so willed it, and she sent her maternal blessing to Malánya Sergyéevna. The lean little peasant received a ruble, requested permission to see his new mistress, to whom he was related as co-sponsor at a baptism, kissed her hand, and hastened off homeward.

And Iván Petróvitch set off for Petersburg with a light heart. The unknown future awaited him; poverty, perhaps, menaced him, but he had bidden farewell to the life in the country which he detested, and, most important of all, he had not betrayed his teachers, he really had "put in action" and justified in fact Rousseau, Diderot, and *la déclaration des droits de l'homme*. A sense of duty accomplished, of triumph, of pride, filled his soul; and his separation from his wife did not greatly alarm him; the necessity of living uninterruptedly with his wife would have perturbed him more. That affair was ended; he must take up other affairs. In Petersburg, contrary to his own expectation, fortune smiled on him: Princess Kubenskóy—whom Monsieur Courtin had already succeeded in abandoning, but who had not yet succeeded in dying,—by way, in some measure, of repairing the injury which she had done to her nephew, recommended him to the good graces of all her friends, and gave him five thousand rubles,—almost her last farthing,—and a Lepíkovsky watch with his coat of arms in a garland of cupids. Three months had not elapsed, when he had already obtained a place in the Russian mission to London, and he went to sea on the first English ship which sailed (there was no thought of steamers in those days). A few months later, he received a letter from Péstoff. The kind-hearted squire congratulated Iván Petróvitch on the birth of a son, who had made his appearance in the world, in the village of Pokróvskoe, on August 20, 1807, and was named Feódor, in honour of the holy martyr, Feódor the Strategist. Owing to her extreme weakness, Malánya Sergyéevna added only a few lines; but those few lines astonished Iván Petróvitch: he was not aware that Márfa Timoféevna had taught his wife to read and write. However, Iván Petróvitch did not give himself up for long to the sweet agitation of paternal emotions: he was paying court to one of the most famous Phrynes or Laïses of the period (classical appellations were still flourishing at that epoch); the peace of Tilsit had just been concluded, and everybody was making haste to enjoyment, everything was whirling round in a sort of mad whirlwind. He had very little money; but he played luckily at cards, he picked up acquaintances, he took part in all the merrymakings,—in a word, he was dashing along under full sail.

IX

It was long before old Lavrétzky could forgive his son for his marriage; if, after the lapse of half a year, Iván Petróvitch had presented himself in contrition, and had flung himself at his feet, he would, probably, have pardoned him, after first scolding him roundly, and administering a few taps with his crutch, by way of inspiring awe; but Iván Petróvitch was living abroad, and, evidently, cared not a rap.—"Hold your tongue! Don't dare!" Piótr Andréitch kept repeating to his wife, as soon as she tried to incline him to mercy: "He ought to pray to God for me forever, the pup, for not having laid my curse upon him; my late father would have slain him with his own hands, the good-for-nothing, and he would have done right." At such terrible speeches, Anna Pávlovna merely crossed herself furtively. As for Iván Petróvitch's wife, Piótr Andréitch, at first, would not allow her to be mentioned, and even in reply to a letter of Péstoff, wherein the latter alluded to his daughter-in-law, he gave orders to say to him, that he knew nothing whatever about any daughter-in-law of his, and that it was prohibited by the laws to harbour runaway maids, on which point he regarded it as his duty to warn him; but later on, when he learned of the birth of a grandson, he softened, gave orders that inquiries should be made on the sly concerning the health of the young mother, and sent her, also as though it did not come from him, a little money. Fédya had not reached his first birthday, when Anna Pávlovna was seized with a fatal illness. A few days before her end, when she could no longer leave her bed, she declared to her husband, in the presence of the priest, that she wished to see and bid farewell to her daughter-in-law, and to bestow her blessing on her grandchild. The afflicted old man soothed her, and immediately sent his own equipage for his daughter-in-law, for the first time calling her Malánya Sergyéevna. She came with her son and with Márfa Timoféevna, who would not let her go alone on any terms, and would not have allowed her to be affronted. Half dead with terror, Malánya entered Piótr Andréitch's study. The nurse carried Fédya after her. Piótr Andréitch gazed at her in silence; she approached to kiss his hand; her quivering lips hardly met in a noiseless kiss.

"Well, new-ground, undried noblewoman,"—he said at last:—"how do you do; let us go to the mistress."

He rose and bent over Fédya; the baby smiled, and stretched out his little, white arms. The old man was completely upset.

"Okh," he said,—"thou orphan! Thou hast plead thy father's cause with me; I will not abandon thee, my birdling!"

As soon as Malánya Sergyéevna entered the bedchamber of Anna Pávlovna, she knelt down near the door. Anna Pávlovna beckoned her to the bed, embraced her, blessed her son; then, turning her countenance, ravaged by disease, to her husband, she tried to speak....

"I know, I know what entreaty thou desirest to make,"—said Piótr Andréitch:—"do not worry: she shall stay with us, and I will pardon Vánka for her sake."

Anna Pávlovna, with an effort, grasped her husband's hand, and pressed it to her lips. On that same evening she died.

Piótr Andréitch kept his word. He informed his son, that, for the sake of his mother's dying hour, for the sake of baby Feódor, he restored to him his blessing, and would keep Malánya Sergyéevna in his own house. Two rooms were set apart for her use in the entresol, he introduced her to his most respected visitor, one-eyed Brigadier Skuryókhin, and to his wife; he presented her with two maids and a page-boy for errands. Márfa Timoféevna bade her farewell; she detested Glafíra, and quarrelled with her thrice in the course of one day.

At first the poor woman found her situation painful and awkward; but afterward, she learned to bear things patiently, and became accustomed to her father-in-law. He, also, became accustomed to her, he even grew to love her, although he almost never spoke to her, although in his caresses a certain involuntary disdain toward her was perceptible. Malánya Sergyéevna had most of all to endure from her sister-in-law. Glafíra, already during her mother's lifetime, had succeeded in getting gradually the entire house into her hands: every one, beginning with her father, was subject to her; not a lump of sugar was given out without her permission; she would have consented to die, rather than to share the power with any other mistress of the house! Her brother's marriage had angered her even more than it had Piótr Andréitch: she took it upon herself to teach the upstart a lesson, and from the very first hour Malánya Sergyéevna became her slave.

And how could she contend with the self-willed, arrogant Glafíra, she who was mild, constantly agitated, and terrified, and also weak in health? Not a day passed, that Glafíra did not remind her of her former position, did not praise her for not forgetting her place. Malánya Sergyéevna would gladly have reconciled herself to these reminders and praises, however bitter they might be ... but they took Fédya away from her: that was what broke her heart. Under the pretext that she was not competent to take charge of his education, she was hardly permitted to see him; Glafíra took this matter upon herself; the child passed under her full control. Malánya Sergyéevna began, out of grief, to entreat Iván Petróvitch, in her letters, to come home as speedily as possible; Piótr Andréitch himself wished to see his son; but he merely wrote in reply, thanking his father about his wife, and for the money sent, and promising to come soon,—and did not come. The year '12 recalled him, at last, to his fatherland from abroad.

On meeting again, for the first time, after their six years' separation, the father and son exchanged embraces, and did not allude, by so much as a word, to their former dissensions; they were not in the mood for it then: all Russia had risen against the enemy, and both of them felt that Russian blood was flowing in their veins. Piótr Andréitch, at his own expense, clothed an entire regiment of soldiers. But the war came to an end, the danger passed; again Iván Petróvitch began to feel bored, again he longed for far-away places, for the world to which he had grown fast, and where he felt himself at home. Malánya Sergyéevna could not hold him back; she counted for too little with him. Even her hopes had not been realised: her husband, also, deemed it much more fitting that Fédya's education should be entrusted to Glafíra. Iván Petróvitch's poor wife could not withstand this blow, could not endure this second parting: without a murmur, in a few days she expired. During the whole course of her life, she had never been able to offer resistance, and she did not combat her malady. She could no longer speak, the shadows of the tomb had already descended upon her face, but her features, as of old, expressed patient perplexity, and the steadfast gentleness of submission; with the same dumb humility she gazed at Glafíra, and, like Anna Pávlovna on her deathbed, she kissed the hand of Piótr Andréitch, and pressed her lips to Glafíra's hand also, entrusting to her, Glafíra, her only son. Thus ended its earthly career a kind and gentle being, torn, God alone knows why, from its native soil and immediately flung aside, like an uprooted sapling, with its roots to the sun; it faded away, it vanished, without a trace, that being, and no one mentioned it. Those who grieved for Malánya Sergyéevna were her maid and Piótr Andréitch. The old man missed her silent presence. "Forgive—farewell, my patient one!" he whispered, as he made her the parting reverence in church. He wept as he threw a handful of earth into the grave.

He did not long survive her—not more than five years. In the winter of 1819, he died peacefully in Moscow, whither he had removed with Glafíra and his grandson, and left orders in his will, that he should be buried by the side of Anna Pávlovna and "Malásha." Iván Petróvitch was in Paris at the time, for his pleasure; he had resigned from the service soon after 1815. On hearing of his father's death, he decided to return to Russia. It was necessary to consider the organisation of the estate ... and Fédya, according to Glafíra's letter, had reached the age of twelve years, and the time had arrived for occupying himself seriously with the boy's education.

X

Iván Petróvitch returned to Russia an Anglomaniac. His closely-clipped hair, starched neckcloth, long-skirted, yellowish-gray overcoat with a multitude of capes, his sour expression of visage, a certain harshness and also indifference of demeanour, his manner of talking through his teeth, a wooden, abrupt laugh, the absence of smiles, a conversation exclusively political and politico-economical, a passion for bloody roast beef and port wine,—everything about him fairly reeked of Great Britain; he seemed thoroughly imbued with her spirit. But—strange to say! while he had turned into an Anglomaniac, Iván Petróvitch had simultaneously become a patriot; at all events, he called himself a patriot, although he was but badly acquainted with Russia, was not wedded to a single Russian habit, and expressed himself queerly in Russian: in ordinary conversation, his speech was clumsy and pithless, studded all over with Gallicisms; but no sooner did the discussion touch upon important topics, than Iván Petróvitch instantly brought out such expressions as: "to show new proofs of self-zeal," "that doth not agree with the nature of the circumstances," and so forth. Iván Petróvitch brought with him several manuscript plans touching the organisation and amelioration of the empire; he was extremely dissatisfied with everything he saw,—the absence of system, in particular, stirred up his bile. On meeting his sister, he announced to her, with his very first words, that he intended to introduce radical reforms, that henceforth everything on his estate should proceed upon a new system. Glafíra Petróvna made no reply to Iván Petróvitch, but merely set her teeth, and said to herself: "And what is to become of me?"—But when she reached the country estate, in company with her brother and her nephew, she speedily regained her composure. In the house, several changes actually took place: the female hangers-on and drones were subjected to instant expulsion; among their number two old women suffered, one who was blind and the other crippled with paralysis, also a decrepit Major of the Otchakóff period, who, on account of his truly astonishing voracity, was fed on nothing but black bread and lentils. A decree was also issued, that the former guests were not to be received: they were superseded by a distant neighbour, a fair-haired, scrofulous baron, a very well educated and very stupid man. New furniture from Moscow made its appearance; cuspidors, and bells, and wash-stands were introduced and they began to serve the noon breakfast differently; foreign wines took the place of vódka and homemade liqueurs; new liveries were made for the servants; the motto, "in recto virtus," was added to the family coat of arms.... But, in reality, Glafíra's power was not diminished: all the disbursements and purchases depended on her, as before; the imported Alsatian valet made an attempt to vie with her—and lost his place, in spite of the fact that his master took his side. So far as the management, the administration, of the estates was concerned (Glafíra Petróvna entered into all these matters), despite Iván Petróvitch's frequently expressed intention "to infuse new life into this chaos," everything remained as of yore, except that, here and there, the quit-rents were augmented, and the husbandry-service became more oppressive, and the peasants were forbidden to apply directly to Iván Petróvitch. The patriot heartily despised his fellow-citizens. Iván Petróvitch's system was applied, in its full force, to Fédya only: his education actually was subjected to "radical reform"; his father had exclusive charge of it.

XI

Up to the time of Iván Petróvitch's return from abroad, Fédya had been, as we have already said, in the hands of Glafíra Petróvna. He was less than eight years of age when his mother died, he had not seen her every day, and he had loved her passionately: the memory of her, of her pale and gentle face, her melancholy glances and timid caresses, had forever imprinted itself upon his heart; but he dimly comprehended her position in the house; he was conscious that between him and her there existed a barrier which she dared not and could not overthrow. He shunned his father, and Iván Petróvitch never petted him; his grandfather occasionally stroked his head, and permitted him to kiss his hand, but he called him and considered him a little fool. After the death of Malánya Sergyéevna, his aunt took him in hand definitively. Fédya feared her,—feared her bright, keen eyes, her sharp voice; he dared not utter a sound in her presence; it sometimes happened that when he had merely fidgeted on his chair, she would scream out: "Where art thou going? sit still!" On Sundays, after the Liturgy, he was permitted to play,—that is to say, he was given a thick book, a mysterious book, the work of a certain Maxímovitch-Ambódik, entitled: "Symbols and Emblems." This book contained about a thousand in part very puzzling pictures, with equally puzzling explanations in five languages. Cupid, with a plump, naked body, played a great part in these pictures. To one of them, labelled "Saffron and Rainbow," was appended the explanation: "The action of this is great ..."; opposite another, which represented "A Heron flying with a violet blossom in his mouth," stood the inscription: "All of them are known unto thee." Cupid and a bear licking its cub was designated as: "Little by little." Fédya contemplated these pictures; he was familiar with the most minute details of them all; some of them—always the same ones—set him to thinking and excited his imagination; he knew no other diversions. When the time came to teach him languages and music, Glafíra Petróvna hired, for a paltry sum, an elderly spinster, a Swede, with frightened, hare-like eyes, who spoke French and German indifferently, played the piano after a fashion, and, in addition, knew how to salt cucumbers in first-class style. In the society of this instructress, of his aunt, and of an old chambermaid, Vasílievna, Fédya passed four whole years. He used to sit in the corner with his "Emblems"—and sit ... and sit ... while the low-ceiled room smelled of geraniums, a solitary tallow candle burned dimly, a cricket chirped monotonously, as though it were bored, the little clock ticked hastily on the wall, a mouse stealthily scratched and gnawed behind the wall-hangings, and the three old maids, like the Parcæ, moved their knitting-needles silently and swiftly to and fro, the shadows cast by their hands now flitted, again quivered strangely in the semi-darkness, and strange thoughts, also half-dark, swarmed in the child's head. No one would have called Fédya an interesting child: he was quite pallid, but fat, awkwardly built, and clumsy,—"a regular peasant," according to Glafíra Petróvna's expression; the pallor would speedily have disappeared from his face if he had been permitted to go out of doors more frequently. He studied tolerably well, although he frequently idled; he never wept; on the other hand, at times a fierce obstinacy came over him; then no one could do anything with him. Fédya loved none of the persons around him.... Woe to the heart which loves not in its youth!

Thus did Iván Petróvitch find him, and without loss of time he set to work to apply his system to him.—"I want to make a man of him first of all, *un homme*,"—he said to Glafíra Petróvna:—"and not only a man, but a Spartan." Iván Petróvitch began the execution of his intention by dressing his son in Highland garb: the lad of twelve began to go about with bare knees, and with a cock's feather in his crush-cap; the Swede was superseded by a young Swiss man, who had learned gymnastics to perfection; music, as an occupation unworthy of a man, was banished forever; the natural sciences, international law, mathematics, the carpenter's trade after the advice of Jean-Jacques Rousseau, and heraldry, for the maintenance of knightly sentiments—these were the things wherewith the future "man" was to occupy himself; he was waked at four o'clock in the morning, was immediately drenched with cold water, and made to run around a tall pillar, at the end of a rope; he ate once a day, one dish, rode on horseback, practised firing a cross-bow; on every convenient opportunity he exercised his strength of will, after the model of his parent, and every evening he noted down in a special book an account of the past day and his impressions; and Iván Petróvitch, on his side, wrote him precepts in French, in which he called him *mon fils*, and addressed him as *vous*. In Russian Fédya called his father "thou," but he dared not sit down in his presence. The "system" bewildered the boy, introduced confusion into his head, squeezed it; but, on the other hand, the new mode of life acted beneficially on his health: at first he caught a fever, but soon recovered, and became a fine, dashing fellow. His father was proud of him, and called him, in his strange jargon: "A son of nature, my product." When Fédya reached the age of sixteen, Iván Petróvitch regarded it as his duty to instil into him betimes scorn for the fair sex,—and the youthful Spartan, with timidity in his soul, with the first down upon his lips, full of vigour, strength, and blood, attempted to appear indifferent, cold, and harsh.

Meanwhile, time passed and passed. Iván Petróvitch spent the greater part of the year at Lavríki (that was the name of his paternal estate), and in the winters he went alone to Moscow, stopped at an inn, diligently frequented the club, orated and set forth his plans in drawing-rooms, and conducted himself more like an Anglomaniac, a grumbler, and a statesman than ever. But the year 1825 arrived, and brought with it much woe. Iván Petróvitch's intimate friends and acquaintances were subjected to severe trials. Iván Petróvitch made haste to retreat to his country estate, and locked himself up in his house. Another year elapsed, and Iván Petróvitch suddenly grew feeble, weakened, declined, his health deserted him. A free-thinker—he took to going to church, and to ordering services of prayer; a European—he began to steam himself at the bath, to dine at two o'clock, to go to bed at nine, to fall asleep to the chatter of the aged butler; a statesman—he burned all his plans, all his correspondence, trembled before the governor, and fidgeted in the presence of the rural chief of police; a man with a will of iron—he whimpered and complained when an abscess broke out on him, when he was served with a plate of cold soup. Glafíra Petróvna again reigned over everything in the house; again clerks, village bailiffs, common peasants, began to creep through the back entrance to the "ill-tempered old hag,"—that was what the house-servants called her. The change in Iván Petróvitch gave his son a great shock; he was already in his nineteenth year, and had begun to reason and to free himself from the weight of the hand which oppressed him. He had noticed, even before this, a discrepancy between his father's words and deeds, between his broad and liberal theories and his harsh, petty despotism; but he had not anticipated such a sudden break. The inveterate egoist suddenly revealed himself at full length. Young Lavrétzky was getting ready to go to Moscow, to prepare himself for the university,—when an unforeseen, fresh calamity descended upon the head of Iván Petróvitch: he became blind, and that hopelessly, in one day.

Not trusting in the skill of Russian physicians, he began to take measures to obtain permission to go abroad. It was refused. Then he took his son with him, and for three whole years he roamed over Russia, from one doctor to another, incessantly journeying from town to town and driving the physicians, his son, his servants, to despair by his pusillanimity and impatience. He returned to Lavríki a perfect rag, a tearful and capricious child. Bitter days ensued, every one endured much at his hands. Iván Petróvitch calmed down only while he was eating his dinner; he had never eaten so greedily, nor so much; all the rest of the time he never gave himself or others any peace. He prayed, grumbled at fate, railed at himself, reviled politics, his system,—reviled everything which he had made his boast and upon which he had prided himself, everything which he had held up as an example for his son; he insisted that he believed in nothing, and then prayed again; he could not bear to be left alone for a single moment, and demanded from the members of his household, that they should sit uninterruptedly, day and night, beside his arm-chair, and amuse him with stories, which he incessantly interrupted with the exclamation: "You are inventing the whole of it—what trash!"

Glafíra Petróvna had a particularly hard time; he positively could not get along without her—and to the end she complied with all the invalid's whims, although sometimes she could not make up her mind on the instant to answer him, lest the sound of her voice should betray her inward wrath. In this manner he lingered on two years, and died in the beginning of May, when he had been carried out upon the balcony, in the sunshine. "Gláshka, Gláshka! the bouillon, the bouillon, you old foo ..." lisped his stiffening tongue, and without finishing the last word, it became silent forever. Glafíra Petróvna, who had just snatched the cup of bouillon from the hands of the butler, stopped short, stared her brother in the face, crossed herself slowly and broadly, and withdrew in silence; and his son, who was present, said nothing, either, but leaned against the railing of the balcony, and gazed for a long time into the garden, all fragrant and verdant, all glittering in the rays of the golden sun of spring. He was twenty-three years old; how terribly, how imperceptibly fast those three and twenty years had sped past!... Life was opening before him.

XII

After having buried his father, and entrusted to the immutable Glafíra Petróvna the management of the farming and the oversight over the clerks, young Lavrétzky betook himself to Moscow, whither he was drawn by an obscure but powerful sentiment. He recognised the defects of his education, and intended to repair omissions, so far as possible. During the last five years, he had read a great deal, and had seen some things; many thoughts had been seething in his brain; any professor might have envied him some of his knowledge, but, at the same time, he did not know much with which every gymnasium lad has long been familiar. The Anglomaniac had played his son an evil trick; his whimsical education had borne its fruits. For long years, he had abased himself before his father without a question; but when, at last, he had divined him, the deed was done, the habits had become rooted. He did not know how to make acquaintance with people: at twenty-three years of age, with an indomitable thirst for love in his shame-stricken heart, he did not dare to look a single woman in the eye. With his clear, solid but somewhat heavy sense, with his inclination to stubbornness, contemplation, and indolence, he ought, from his earliest years, to have been cast into the whirlpool of life, but he had been kept in an artificial isolation.... And now the charmed circle was broken, yet he continued to stand in one spot, locked up, tightly compressed in himself. It was ridiculous, at his age, to don a student's uniform; but he was not afraid of ridicule: his Spartan training had served its turn to this extent at least, that it had developed in him scorn for other people's remarks,—and so, unabashed, he donned the uniform of a student. He entered the physico-mathematical department. Healthy, rosy-cheeked, with a well-grown beard, taciturn, he produced a strange impression upon his comrades; they did not suspect that in this surly man, who punctually drove to the lectures in a roomy country sledge and pair, there was concealed almost a child. He seemed to them some sort of wise pedant; they did not need him and did not seek his society, he avoided them. In the course of the first two years which he spent at the university, he came into close contact with only one student, from whom he took lessons in Latin. This student, Mikhalévitch by name, an enthusiast and a poet, sincerely loved Lavrétzky, and quite innocently became the cause of an important change in his fate.

One day, at the theatre (Motchálоff was then at the height of his fame, and Lavrétzky never missed a performance), he saw a young girl in a box of the *bel-étage*,—and, although no woman ever passed his surly figure without causing his heart to quiver, it never yet had beaten so violently. With her elbows resting on the velvet of the box, the young girl sat motionless; alert, young life sparkled in every feature of her pretty, round, dark-skinned face; an elegant mind was expressed in the beautiful eyes which gazed attentively and softly from beneath slender brows, in the swift smile of her expressive lips, in the very attitude of her head, her arms, her neck; she was charmingly dressed. Beside her sat a wrinkled, sallow woman, forty-five years of age, with a toothless smile on her constrainedly-anxious and empty countenance, and in the depths of the box an elderly man was visible, wearing an ample coat and a tall neckcloth, with an expression of feeble stateliness and a certain obsequious suspicion in his little eyes, with dyed moustache and side-whiskers, an insignificant, huge forehead, and furrowed cheeks,—a retired General, by all the signs. Lavrétzky could not take his eyes from the young girl who had startled him; all at once, the door of the box opened, and Mikhalévitch entered. The appearance of that man, almost his sole acquaintance in all Moscow,—his appearance in the company of the only young girl who had engrossed his whole attention, seemed to Lavrétzky strange and significant. As he continued to gaze at the box, he noticed that all the persons in it treated Mikhalévitch like an old friend. The performance on the stage ceased to interest Lavrétzky; Motchálоff himself, although that evening he was "in high feather," did not produce upon him the customary impression. In one very pathetic passage, Lavrétzky involuntarily glanced at his beauty: she was bending her whole body forward, her cheeks were aflame; under the influence of his persistent gaze, her eyes, which were riveted on the stage, turned slowly, and rested upon him.... All night long, those eyes flitted before his vision. At last, the artificially erected dam had given way: he trembled and burned, and on the following day he betook himself to Mikhalévitch. From him he learned, that the beauty's name was Varvára Pávlovna Koróbyn; that the old man and woman who had sat with her in the box were her father and mother, and that he himself, Mikhalévitch, had made their acquaintance a year previously, during his stay in the suburbs of Moscow, "on contract service" (as tutor) with Count N. The enthusiast expressed himself in the most laudatory manner concerning Varvára Pávlovna—"My dear fellow," he exclaimed, with the impetuous harmony in his voice which was peculiar to him,—"that young girl is an amazing, a talented being, an artist in the genuine sense of the word, and extremely amiable to boot."—Perceiving from Lavrétzky's question what an impression Varvára Pávlovna had produced upon him, he himself proposed to introduce him to her, adding that he was quite at home in their house; that the General was not at all a proud man, and the mother was so stupid that she all but sucked a rag. Lavrétzky blushed, muttered something unintelligible, and fled. For five whole days he wrestled with his timidity; on the sixth day the young Spartan donned a new uniform, and placed himself at the disposition of Mikhalévitch, who being his own valet, confined himself to brushing his hair,—and the two set out for the Koróbyns'.

XIII

The father of Varvára Pávlovna, Pável Petróvitch Koróbyn, Major-General on the retired list, had spent his whole life in Petersburg, in the service; had borne the reputation, in his youth, of being an accomplished dancer and officer of the line; found himself, owing to poverty, the adjutant of two or three ill-favoured Generals; married the daughter of one of them, receiving twenty-five thousand rubles as her dowry; acquired, in its finest details, the love of drills and reviews; toiled, and toiled hard, for his livelihood, and at last, at the end of twenty years, attained to the rank of General, and received a regiment. It was time for him to rest, and without delay to establish his prosperity on a firm basis; this was what he calculated on doing, but he managed the matter somewhat incautiously: he hit upon a new method of putting the coin of the realm into circulation,—the method proved to be a capital one, but he did not get out in season: a complaint was made against him; a more than unpleasant, an ugly scandal ensued. The General managed to wriggle out of the scandal, after a fashion, but his career was ruined: he was advised to resign. He hung about in Petersburg for a couple of years longer in the hope that some snug little place would get stranded on him: but the place did not strand on him, and his daughter came out of the government school, and his expenses increased every day.... Repressing his wrath, he decided to remove to Moscow for the sake of economy, hired a tiny, low-roofed house on Old Stable Street, with a coat of arms a fathom tall on the roof, and began to live the life of a Moscow General on the retired list, spending 2750 rubles a year. Moscow is a hospitable town, glad to welcome everybody who comes along, and more particularly, Generals; Pável Petróvitch's heavy figure, which yet was not lacking in military mien, speedily began to make its appearance in the best drawing-rooms of Moscow. His bald nape, with tufts of dyed hair, and the dirty ribbon of the order of St. Anna on a neckcloth the hue of the raven's wing, began to be well known to all the easily bored and pallid young men who morosely hovered around the gambling-tables while dancing was in progress. Pável Petróvitch understood how to place himself in society; he talked little, but, by force of old habit, through his nose,—of course, not with individuals belonging to the higher ranks; he played cards cautiously, at home he ate sparingly, but when visiting he ate for six. Concerning his wife, there is hardly anything to say: her name was Kallíope Kárlovna; a tear oozed from her left eye, by virtue of which Kallíope Kárlovna (she was, moreover, of German extraction) regarded herself as a woman of sentiment; she lived in constant fear of something, never seemed to have had quite enough to eat, and wore tight velvet gowns, a turban, and dull bracelets of hollow metal. Varvára Pávlovna, the only daughter of Pável Petróvitch and Kallíope Kárlovna, had just passed her seventeenth birthday when she came out of the * * * Institute, where she had been considered, if not the greatest beauty, certainly the cleverest girl and the best musician, and where she had received the *chiffre*; [1]she was not yet nineteen when Lavrétzky beheld her for the first time.

XIV

The legs of the Spartan gave way beneath him when Mikhalévitch conducted him into the rather shabbily furnished drawing-room of the Koróbyns, and presented him to the master and mistress of the house. But the feeling of timidity which had taken possession of him promptly disappeared: in the General the kindliness of nature innate in all Russians was greatly increased by that special sort of courtesy which is peculiar to all besmirched people; the Generaless soon disappeared, somehow; as for Varvára Pávlovna, she was so calm and self-possessedly amiable, that any one would immediately have felt himself at home in her presence; moreover, from the whole of her enchanting person, from her smiling eyes, from her innocently-sloping shoulders and faintly-rosy hands, from her light and, at the same time, rather languid gait, from the very sound of her voice, which was low and sweet,—there breathed forth an insinuating charm, as intangible as a delicate perfume, a soft and as yet modest intoxication, something which it is difficult to express in words, but which touched and excited,—and, of course, excited something which was not timidity. Lavrétzky turned the conversation on the theatre, on the performance of the preceding evening; she immediately began, herself, to speak of Motcháloff, and did not confine herself merely to exclamations and sighs, but uttered several just and femininely-penetrating remarks concerning his acting. Mikhalévitch alluded to music; without any affectation she seated herself at the piano, and played with precision several mazurkas by Chopin, which had only just come into fashion. The dinner-hour arrived; Lavrétzky made a motion to depart, but they kept him; at table, the General treated him to good claret, for which the General's lackey had galloped in a cab to Depré's. Late at night, Lavrétzky returned home, and sat for a long time, without undressing, his eyes covered with his hand, in dumb enchantment. It seemed to him, that only now had he come to understand why life was worth living; all his hypotheses, his intentions, all that nonsense and rubbish, vanished instantaneously; his whole soul was merged in one sentiment, in one desire, in the desire for happiness, possession, love, the sweet love of woman. From that day forth, he began to go often to the Koróbyns'. Six months later, he declared himself to Varvára Pávlovna, and offered her his hand. His proposal was accepted; the General had long since, almost on the eve of his first visit, inquired of Mikhalévitch how many serfs he, Lavrétzky, had; and Varvára Pávlovna also, who, during the whole period of the young man's courtship and even at the moment of his declaration, had preserved her habitual tranquillity and clearness of soul,—Varvára Pávlovna also was well aware that her lover was rich; and Kallíope Kárlovna said to herself: "Meine Tochter macht eine schöne Partie"—and bought herself a new turban.

XV

So his proposal was accepted, but on certain conditions. In the first place, Lavrétzky must immediately leave the university: who marries a student? and what a dreadful idea,—for a landed proprietor, rich, and twenty-six years old, to take lessons like a school-boy! In the second place, Varvára Pávlovna took upon herself the labour of ordering and purchasing the trousseau, even of choosing the bridegroom's gifts. She had a great deal of practical sense, much taste, much love for comfort, and a great knack for securing for herself that comfort. This knack particularly astonished Lavrétzky when, immediately after the wedding, he and his wife set out in a commodious carriage, which she had bought, for Lavríki. How everything which surrounded him had been planned, foreseen, provided for by Varvára Pávlovna! What charming travelling requisites, what fascinating toilet-boxes and coffeepots, made their appearance in divers snug nooks, and how prettily Varvára Pávlovna herself boiled the coffee in the mornings! But Lavrétzky was not then in a mood for observation: he was in a beatific state, he was intoxicating himself with happiness; he gave himself up to it like a child.... And he was as innocent as a child, that young Alcides. Not in vain did witchery exhale from the whole being of his young wife; not in vain did she promise to the senses the secret luxury of unknown delights; she fulfilled more than she had promised. On arriving at Lavríki, in the very hottest part of the summer, she found the house dirty and dark, the servants ridiculous and antiquated, but she did not find it necessary even to hint at this to her husband. If she had been making preparations to settle down at Lavríki, she would have made over everything about it, beginning, of course, with the house; but the idea of remaining in that God-forsaken corner of the steppes never entered her mind for one moment; she lived in it, as though camping out, gently enduring all the inconveniences and making amusing jests over them. Márfa Timoféevna came to see her nursling; Varvára Pávlovna took a great liking for her, but she did not take a liking for Varvára Pávlovna. Neither did the new mistress of the house get on well with Glafíra Petróvna; she would have left her in peace, but old Koróbyn wanted to feather his nest from his son-in-law's affairs; "it was no shame, even for a General," said he, "to manage the estate of so near a relative." It must be assumed that Pável Petróvitch would not have disdained to busy himself with the estate of an entire stranger. Varvára Pávlovna conducted her attack in a very artful manner: without thrusting herself forward, and still, to all appearances, wholly absorbed in the felicity of the honeymoon, in quiet country life, in music and reading, she little by little drove Glafíra Petróvna to such a state, that one morning the latter rushed like a madwoman into Lavrétzky's study, and, hurling her bunch of keys on the table, announced that it was beyond her power to occupy herself with the housekeeping, and that she did not wish to remain in the country. Having been properly prepared in advance, Lavrétzky immediately consented to her departure.—Glafíra Petróvna had not expected this. "Very well," said she, and her eyes grew dark,—"I see that I am not wanted here! I know who it is that is driving me hence—from my native nest. But do thou remember my words, nephew: thou shalt never be able to build thyself a nest anywhere, thou must wander all thy life. That is my legacy to thee."—That very day she departed to her own little estate, and a week later General Koróbyn arrived, and with agreeable melancholy in his gaze and movements, took the management of the entire estate into his hands.

In September, Varvára Petróvna carried her husband off to Petersburg. She spent two winters in Petersburg (they removed to Tzárskoe Seló for the summer), in a beautiful, light, elegantly furnished apartment; they made many acquaintances in middle-class and even in the higher circles of society, they went out and received a great deal, and gave most charming musical and dancing parties. Varvára Pávlovna attracted guests as a flame attracts moths. Such a dissipated life did not altogether please Feódor Ivánitch. His wife advised him to enter the service; owing to his father's old memories, and his own conceptions, he would not serve, but to please his wife he remained in Petersburg. But he speedily divined that no one prevented his isolating himself, that it was not for nothing that he had the quietest and most comfortable study in all Petersburg, that his solicitous wife was even ready to help him to isolate himself,—and from that time forth all went splendidly. Once more he took up his own education, which, in his opinion, was unfinished, once more he began to read, he even began to study the English language. It was strange to see his mighty, broad-shouldered figure, eternally bent over his writing-table, his full, hairy, ruddy face half concealed by the pages of a dictionary or an exercise-book. Every morning he spent in work, dined capitally (Varvára Pávlovna was an excellent housewife), and in the evening he entered an enchanting, fragrant, brilliant world, all populated with young, merry faces,—and the central point of that world was also the zealous hostess, his wife. She gladdened him with the birth of a son, but the poor boy did not live long: he died in the spring, and in the summer, by the advice of the physicians, Lavrétzky took his wife abroad, to the baths. Diversion was indispensable to her, after such a bereavement, and her health required a warm climate. They spent the summer and autumn in Germany and Switzerland, and in the winter, as might have been expected, they went to Paris. In Paris Varvára Pávlovna blossomed out like a rose, and managed to build a little nest for herself as promptly and as adroitly as in Petersburg. She found an extremely pretty apartment, in one of the quiet but fashionable Paris streets; she made her husband such a dressing-gown as he had never owned before; she hired a trim maid, a capital cook, a smart footman; she got an enchanting carriage, a charming little piano. A week had not passed before she crossed a street, wore her shawl, opened her parasol, and put on her gloves in a style equal to that of the purest-blooded Parisienne. And she soon provided herself with acquaintances. At first, only Russians went to her house, then Frenchmen began to make their appearance, very amiable, courteous, unmarried, with beautiful manners and euphonious family names; they all talked fast and much, bowed with easy grace, and screwed up their eyes in a pleasing way; all of them had white teeth which gleamed beneath rosy lips,—and how they did understand the art of smiling! Every one of them brought his friends, and "la belle Madame de Lavretzki" soon became known from the Chaussée d'Antin to the Rue de Lille. In those days (this took place in 1836), that tribe of feuilleton and chronicle writers, which now swarm everywhere, like ants in an ant-hill which has been cut open, had not multiplied; but even then, a certain M——r Jules presented himself in Varvára Pávlovna's salon, a gentleman of insignificant appearance, with a scandalous reputation, insolent and base, like all duellists and beaten men. This M—r Jules was extremely repulsive to Varvára Pávlovna, but she received him because he scribbled for various journals, and incessantly alluded to her, calling her now *"Mme. de L * * * tzki,"* now "*Mme. de * * * cette grande dame Russe si distinguée, qui demeure rue de P.*"; narrating to all the world, that is to say, to a few hundred subscribers, who cared nothing whatever about "*Mme. de L * * * tzki*," how that pretty and charming lady was a real Frenchwoman in mind (*une vraie française par l'esprit*),—there is no higher encomium for the French,—what a remarkable musician she was, and how wonderfully she waltzed (Varvára Pávlovna, in reality, did waltz in such a manner as to draw all hearts after the hem of her light, fluttering gown) ... in a word, he spread her fame throughout the world,—and assuredly that is agreeable, say what you will. Mlle. Mars had already left the stage, and Mlle. Rachel had not yet made her appearance; nevertheless, Varvára Pávlovna diligently frequented the theatres. She went into ecstasies over Italian music, and laughed at the ruins of Odra, yawned decorously at the Comédie Française, and wept at the acting of Mme. Dorval in some ultra-romantic melodrama or other; but, chief of all, Liszt played a couple of times at her house, and was so nice, so simple—it was delightful! In such pleasant sensations passed a winter, at the end of which Varvára Pávlovna was even presented at Court. Feódor Ivánitch, on his side, was not bored, although life, at times, weighed heavily on his shoulders,—heavily, because it was empty. He read the newspapers, he listened to lectures at the Sorbonne and the Collège de France, he kept track of the debates in parliament, he undertook the translation of a well-known scientific work on irrigation. "I am not wasting time,"—he said to himself,—"all this is useful; but next winter I must, without fail, return to Russia and set to work." It is difficult to say, whether he was clearly conscious in what that work consisted, and God knows whether he would have succeeded in returning to Russia for the winter,—in the meantime, he went with his wife to Baden-Baden.... An unexpected event destroyed all his plans.

XVI

One day, on entering Varvára Pávlovna's boudoir in her absence, Lavrétzky beheld on the floor a tiny, carefully-folded scrap of paper. He mechanically picked it up, mechanically unfolded it, and read the following, written in French:

"Dear angel Betsy! (I cannot possibly bring myself to call thee Barbe or Varvára). I waited in vain for thee at the corner of the Boulevard; come to-morrow, at half-past one, to our little apartment. Thy good fatty (*ton gros bonhomme de mari*) generally buries himself in his books at that hour; again we will sing the song of your poet Puskin (*de votre poète Pouskine*) which thou hast taught me: 'Old husband, menacing husband!'—A thousand kisses on thy hands and feet! I await thee."

"ERNEST."

Lavrétzky did not, on the instant, understand what sort of thing it was he had read; he perused it a second time—and his head reeled, the floor swayed beneath his feet, like the deck of a steamer when it is pitching—he cried out, and sobbed and wept simultaneously.

He lost his senses. He had so blindly trusted his wife, that the possibility of deception, of treachery, had never presented itself to his mind. That Ernest, that lover of his wife's was a fair-haired, good-looking boy of three and twenty, with a small snub nose and thin moustache, almost the most insignificant of all her admirers. Several minutes passed, half an hour passed; Lavrétzky still stood, crushing the fatal missive in his hand and staring senselessly at the floor; through a sort of dark whirlwind, visions of pale faces flitted before him; his heart sank within him, in anguish; it seemed to him that he was falling, falling, falling ... and that there was no end to it. The light, familiar rustle of a silken robe aroused him from his state of stupefaction; Varvára Pávlovna, in bonnet and shawl, had hastily returned from her stroll. Lavrétzky trembled all over, and rushed out of the room; he felt that at that moment he was capable of tearing her to pieces, of beating her until she was half dead, in peasant fashion, of strangling her with his hands. The astonished Varvára Pávlovna tried to stop him; he could only whisper: "Betsy"—and fled from the house.

Lavrétzky took a carriage, and ordered the man to drive him out of town. The entire remainder of the day, and the whole night long until the morning, he roamed about, incessantly halting and wringing his hands: now he raged, again it seemed rather ridiculous to him, even rather amusing. In the morning he was chilled through, and entered a wretched suburban inn, asked for a room, and seated himself on a chair by the window. A convulsive yawning seized hold upon him. He could hardly stand on his feet, his body was exhausted,—but he was conscious of no fatigue,—yet fatigue claimed its rights: he sat and stared, and understood nothing; he did not understand what had happened to him, why he found himself alone, with benumbed limbs, with a bitterness in his mouth, with a stone on his breast, in a bare, strange room; he did not understand what had made her, Várya, give herself to that Frenchman, and how she had been able, knowing herself to be unfaithful, to be as calm, amiable, and confiding toward him as before! "I understand nothing!" whispered his parched lips. "Who will guarantee me now, that in Petersburg...." And he did not finish the question, and yawned again, quivering and writhing all over. The bright and the dark memories tormented him equally; it suddenly occurred to him, that a few days previously, in his presence and in that of Ernest, she had seated herself at the piano and had sung: "Old husband, menacing husband!" He recalled the expression of her face, the strange glitter of her eyes, and the flush on her cheeks,—and he rose from his chair; he wanted to go and to say to them: "You have made a mistake in trifling with me; my great-grandfather used to hang the peasants up by the ribs, and my grandfather himself was a peasant"—and kill them both. Then, all of a sudden, it seemed to him, that everything which was taking place with him was a dream, and not even a dream, but merely some nonsense or other: that all he had to do was to shake himself, to look about him.... He did look about him, and as the hawk buries his claws in the bird he has captured, anguish pierced more and more deeply into his heart. To crown all, Lavrétzky was hoping at the end of a few months to become a father.... The past, the future, his whole life was poisoned. He returned, at last, to Paris, put up at a hotel, and sent Varvára Pávlovna the note of M—r Ernest, with the following letter:

"The accompanying document will explain everything to you. I will say to you, by the way, that I did not recognise you: you, always such a precise person, to drop such an important paper!" (This phrase poor Lavrétzky had prepared and cherished for the space of several hours.) "I can see you no more; I assume that you, also, cannot wish to meet me. I have assigned fifteen thousand francs a year to you; I cannot give more. Send your address to the office of the estate. Do what you will, live where you please. I wish you happiness. No answer is necessary."

Lavrétzky wrote to his wife, that no answer was necessary ... but he waited, he thirsted for an answer, an explanation of this incomprehensible, this incredible affair. Varvára Pávlovna, that very day, sent him a long letter in French. It made an end of him; his last doubts vanished,—and he felt ashamed that he had still cherished doubts. Varvára Pávlovna did not defend herself: she merely wished to see him, she entreated him not to condemn her irrevocably. The letter was cold and constrained, although the traces of tears were visible here and there. Lavrétzky uttered a bitter laugh, and bade the messenger say that it was all very good. Three days later, he had quitted Paris: but he went, not to Russia, but to Italy. He himself did not know why he had chosen Italy, in particular; in reality, it made no difference to him whither he went,—provided it were not home. He sent instructions to his peasant-steward in regard to his wife's pension, ordered him, at the same time, to take all matters pertaining to the estate instantly out of the hands of General Koróbyn, without awaiting the surrender of the accounts, and to make arrangements for the departure of His Excellency from Lavríki; he formed a vivid picture to himself, of the consternation, the fruitless haughtiness of the ejected General, and, with all his grief, he felt a certain malicious satisfaction. Then he invited Glafíra Petróvna, in a letter also, to return to Lavríki, and sent her a power of attorney. Glafíra Petróvna did not return to Lavríki, and herself published in the newspapers that she had destroyed the power of attorney, which was quite superfluous. Hiding himself in a small Italian town, it was a long time still before Lavrétzky could force himself not to watch his wife. He learned from the newspapers, that she had quitted Paris, as it was supposed, for Baden-Baden: her name soon made its appearance in an article written by that same M'sieu Jules. In this article, a sort of friendly condolence pierced through the customary playfulness; Feódor Ivánitch's soul was in a very ugly state when he read that article. Later on, he learned that a daughter had been born to him; at the end of a couple of months, he was informed by his peasant-steward, that Varvára Pávlovna had demanded the first third of her allowance. Then more and more evil reports began to arrive; at last, a tragicomic tale made the rounds—creating a sensation—of the newspapers, wherein his wife played an unenviable part. All was at an end: Varvára Pávlovna had become "a celebrity."

Lavrétzky ceased to follow her career; but he was not able speedily to conquer himself. At times, he was seized with such a longing for his wife, that it seemed to him, he would give everything—he would even, if necessary ... forgive her—if only he might again hear her caressing voice, again feel her hand in his hand. But time went on, and not in vain. He was not born to be a martyr; his healthy nature asserted its rights. Much became clear to him; the very blow which had assailed him, no longer seemed to him unforeseen; he understood his wife,—one understands a person who is near to one, when parted from him. Again he was able to occupy himself, to work, although with far less zeal than of yore: scepticism, for which the way had been prepared by the experiences of life, by his education, definitively took possession of his soul. He became extremely indifferent to everything. Four years elapsed, and he felt himself strong enough to return to his native land, to meet his own people. Without halting either in Petersburg or Moscow, he arrived in the town of O * * * where we took leave of him, and whither we now beg the indulgent reader to return with us.

XVII

On the morning following the day which we have described, at nine o'clock, Lavrétzky ascended the porch of the Kalítin house. Liza emerged to meet him, in hat and gloves.

"Where are you going?" he asked her.

"To church. To-day is Sunday."

"And do you really care to go to the Liturgy?"

Liza said nothing, but gazed at him in amazement.

"Pardon me, please,"—said Lavrétzky,—"I ... I did not mean to say that. I came to say good-bye to you: I am going to my country place an hour hence."

"It is not far from here, is it?"—inquired Liza.

"Twenty-five versts."
Lyénotchka made her appearance on the threshold of the door, accompanied by a maid.
"See that you do not forget us,"—said Liza, and descended the steps.
"And do not you forget me. And see here,"—he added,—"you are going to church: pray for me also, by the way."
Liza paused and turned toward him.
"Certainly,"—she said, looking him straight in the face:—"I will pray for you. Come along, Lyénotchka."
Lavrétzky found Márya Dmítrievna alone in the drawing-room. An odour of eau de cologne and mint emanated from her. She had a headache, according to her own account, and she had passed a restless night. She welcomed him with her customary languid amiability, and gradually got to talking.
"What an agreeable young man Vladímir Nikoláitch is," she inquired:—"is he not?"
"What Vladímir Nikoláitch?"
"Why, Pánshin, you know,—the one who was here yesterday evening. He took an immense liking to you; I will tell you, as a secret,*mon cher cousin*, he is simply beside himself over my Liza. What do you think of that? He comes of a good family, he discharges his service splendidly, he is clever, well, and a Junior Gentleman of the Bedchamber, and if it be God's will.... I, on my side, as a mother, shall be very glad. It is a great responsibility, of course: up to the present time, whether it be for good or evil, you see, I am always, everywhere, entirely alone: I have reared my children, I have taught them, I have done everything ... and now I have ordered a governess from Mme. Bolius...."
Márya Dmítrievna launched out into a description of her toils, her efforts, and her maternal feelings. Lavrétzky listened to her in silence, and twirled his hat in his hands. His cold, heavy gaze disconcerted the loquacious lady.
"And how do you like Liza?"—she asked.
"Lizavéta Mikhaílovna is an extremely beautiful girl,"—replied Lavrétzky, rose, bowed, and went to Márfa Timoféevna. Márya Dmítrievna gazed after him with displeasure, and said to herself: "What a dolt, what a peasant! Well, now I understand why his wife could not remain faithful to him."
Márfa Timoféevna was sitting in her own room, surrounded by her suite. It consisted of five beings, almost equally near to her heart: a fat-jowled trained bullfinch, which she loved because he had ceased to whistle and draw water; a tiny, very timorous and peaceable dog, Róska; an angry cat Matrós (Sailor); a black-visaged nimble little girl of nine, with huge eyes and a sharp little nose, who was named Schúrotchka; and an elderly woman, fifty years of age, in a white cap, and a light brown, bob-tailed jacket over a dark gown, by name Nastásya Kárpovna Ogárkoff. Schúrotchka was of the petty burgher class, a full orphan. Márfa Timoféevna had taken charge of her out of pity, as she had of Róska: she had picked up both the dog and the girl in the street; both were thin and hungry, both were being drenched by the autumnal rain, no one had hunted up Róska, and Schúrotchka's uncle, a drunken shoemaker, who had not enough to eat himself, and who did not feed his niece, though he beat her over the head with his last, gladly surrendered her to Márfa Timoféevna. With Nastásya Kárpovna, Márfa Timoféevna had made acquaintance on a pilgrimage, in a monastery; she herself had gone up to her in church (Márfa Timoféevna liked her because, to use her own words, "she prayed tastily"), had herself begun the conversation, and had invited her to come to her for a cup of tea. From that day forth, she had never parted with her. Nastásya Kárpovna was a woman of the merriest and gentlest disposition, a childless widow, member of a poverty-stricken family of the petty nobility; she had a round, grey head, soft white hands, a soft face, with large, kindly features, and a rather ridiculous snub nose; she fairly worshipped Márfa Timoféevna, and the latter loved her greatly, although she jeered at her tender heart: Nastásya Kárpovna felt a weakness for all young people, and involuntarily blushed like a girl at the most innocent jest. Her entire capital consisted of twelve hundred paper rubles; she lived at the expense of Márfa Timoféevna, but on equal terms with her: Márfa Timoféevna would not have tolerated servility.
"Ah, Fédya!" she began, as soon as she caught sight of him:—"last night, thou didst not see my family: admire it. We are all assembled for tea; this is our second, feast-day tea. Thou mayest pet all: only Schúrotchka will not allow thee, and the cat scratches. Art thou going away to-day?"
"Yes,"—Lavrétzky seated himself on a narrow little chair.—"I have already said farewell to Márya Dmítrievna. I have also seen Lizavéta Mikhaílovna."
"Call her Liza, my father,—why should she be Mikhaílovna to thee! And sit still, or thou wilt break Schúrotchka's chair."
"She has gone to church,"—pursued Lavrétzky. "Is she pious?"
"Yes, Fédya,—very. More than thou and I, Fédya."

"But are not you pious?"—remarked Nastásya Kárpovna, in a whisper. "And to-day: you did not get to the early Liturgy, but you will go to the later one."
"Not a bit of it—thou wilt go alone: I am lazy, my mother,"—retorted Márfa Timoféevna,—"I am pampering myself greatly with my tea."—She called Nastásya *thou*, although she lived on equal terms with her,—she was not a Péstoff for nothing: three Péstoffs are recorded with distinction in the Book of Remembrance of Iván Vasílievitch, the Terrible; Márfa Timoféevna knew it.
"Tell me, please,"—began Lavrétzky again:—"Márya Dmítrievna has just been talking about that ... what's his name ... Pánshin. What sort of a person is he?"
"What a chatterbox, the Lord forgive her!"—grumbled Márfa Timoféevna:—"I suppose she imparted to you, as a secret, what a fine suitor has turned up. She might do her whispering with her priest's son; but no, that is not enough for her. But there's nothing in it, as yet, and thank God for that! but she's babbling already."
"Why 'thank God'?"—asked Lavrétzky.
"Why, because the young fellow does not please me; and what is there to rejoice about?"
"He does not please you?"
"Yes, he cannot fascinate everybody. It's enough that Nastásya Kárpovna here should be in love with him."
The poor widow was thoroughly startled.
"What makes you say that, Márfa Timoféevna? You do not fear God!"—she exclaimed, and a blush instantly suffused her face and neck.
"And he certainly knows the rogue,"—Márfa Timoféevna interrupted her:—"he knows how to captivate her: he presented her with a snuff-box. Fédya, ask her to give thee a pinch of snuff; thou wilt see what a splendid snuff-box it is: on the lid is depicted a hussar on horseback. Thou hadst better not defend thyself, my mother."
Nastásya Kárpovna merely repelled the suggestion with a wave of her hands.
"Well,"—inquired Lavrétzky,—"and is Liza not indifferent to him?"
"Apparently, she likes him,—however, the Lord only knows. Another man's soul, thou knowest, is a dark forest, much more the soul of a young girl. Now, there's Schúrotchka's soul—try to dissect that! Why has she been hiding herself, and yet does not go away, ever since thou camest?"
Schúrotchka snorted with suppressed laughter and ran out of the room, and Lavrétzky rose from his seat.
"Yes,"—he said slowly:—"a maiden's soul is not to be divined."
He began to take leave.
"Well? Shall we see thee again soon?"—asked Márfa Timoféevna.
"That's as it may happen, aunty; it is not far off."
"Yes, but thou art going to Vasílievskoe. Thou wilt not live at Lavríki:—well, that is thy affair; only, go and salute the tomb of thy mother, and the tomb of thy grandmother too, by the bye. Thou hast acquired all sorts of learning yonder abroad, and who knows, perchance they will feel it in their graves that thou hast come to them. And don't forget, Fédya, to have a requiem service celebrated for Glafíra Petróvna also; here's a silver ruble for thee. Take it, take it, I want to pay for having a requiem service for her. During her lifetime I did not like her, but there's no denying it, the woman had plenty of character. She was a clever creature; and she did not wrong thee, either. And now go, with God's blessing, or thou wilt grow weary of me."
And Márfa Timoféevna embraced her nephew.
"And Liza shall not marry Pánshin,—don't worry about that; that's not the sort of husband she deserves."
"Why, I am not worrying in the least," replied Lavrétzky, and withdrew.

XVIII

Four hours later, he was driving homeward. His tarantás rolled swiftly along the soft country road. There had been a drought for a fortnight; a thin milky cloud was diffused through the air, and veiled the distant forests; it reeked with the odour of burning. A multitude of small, dark cloudlets, with indistinctly delineated edges, were creeping across the pale-blue sky; a fairly strong wind was whisking along in a dry, uninterrupted stream, without dispelling the sultriness. Leaning his head against a cushion, and folding his arms on his breast, Lavrétzky gazed at the strips of ploughed land, in fan-shape, which flew past, at the willow-trees slowly flitting by, at the stupid crows and daws gazing with dull suspicion askance at the passing equipage, at the long strips of turf between the cultivated sections, overgrown with artemisia, wormwood, and wild tansy; he gazed ... and that fresh, fertile nakedness and wildness of the steppe, that verdure, those long hillocks, the ravines with stubby oak bushes, the grey hamlets, the flexible birch-trees,—this whole Russian picture, which he had not seen for a long time, wafted into his soul sweet and, at the same time, painful sensations, weighed on his breast with a certain agreeable oppression. His thoughts slowly roved about; their outlines were as indistinct and confused as the outlines of those lofty cloudlets, which, also, seemed to be roving. He recalled his childhood, his mother; he remembered how she died, how they had carried him to her, and how she, pressing his head to her bosom, had begun to sing feebly over him, but had cast a glance at Glafíra Petróvna—and had relapsed into silence. He recalled his father, at first alert, dissatisfied with every one, and with a brazen voice,—then blind, tearful, and with a dirty grey beard; he recalled how, one day, at table, after drinking an extra glass of wine, and spilling the sauce over his napkin, he had suddenly burst out laughing, and had begun, winking his sightless eyes and flushing crimson, to tell stories of his conquests; he recalled Varvára Pávlovna,—and involuntarily screwed up his eyes, as a man does from momentary inward pain, and shook his head. Then his thoughts came to a pause on Liza.

"Here," he thought, "is a new being, who is only just entering upon life. A splendid young girl, what will become of her? She is comely. A pale, fresh face, such serious eyes and lips, and an honest and innocent gaze. It is a pity that she seems to be somewhat enthusiastic. A splendid figure, and she walks so lightly, and her voice is soft. I greatly like to see her pause suddenly, listen attentively, without a smile, and then meditate, and toss back her hair. Really, it strikes me that Pánshin is not worthy of her. But what is there wrong about him? She will traverse the road which all traverse. I had better take a nap." And Lavrétzky closed his eyes.

He could not get to sleep, but plunged into the dreamy stupor of the road. Images of the past, as before, arose in leisurely fashion, floated through his soul, mingling and entangling themselves with other scenes. Lavrétzky, God knows why, began to think about Robert Peel ... about French history ... about how he would win a battle if he were a general; he thought he heard shots and shrieks.... His head sank to one side, he opened his eyes.... The same fields, the same views of the steppe; the polished shoes of the trace-horse flashed in turn through the billowing dust; the shirt of the postilion, yellow, with red gussets at the armpits, puffed out in the wind.... "A pretty way to return to my native land"—flashed through Lavrétzky's head; and he shouted: "Faster!" wrapped himself up in his cloak, and leaned back harder against his pillow. The tarantás gave a jolt: Lavrétzky sat upright, and opened his eyes wide. Before him, on a hillock, a tiny hamlet lay outspread; a little to the right, a small, ancient manor-house was to be seen, with closed shutters and a crooked porch; all over the spacious yard, from the very gates, grew nettles, green and thick as hemp; there, also, stood a small oaken store-house, still sound. This was Vasílievskoe.

The postilion turned up to the gate, and brought the horses to a standstill; Lavrétzky's footman rose on the box, and, as though preparing to spring down, shouted: "Hey!" A hoarse, dull barking rang out, but not even the dog showed himself; the lackey again prepared to leap down, and again shouted: "Hey!" The decrepit barking was renewed, and, a moment later, a man ran out into the yard, no one could tell whence,—a man in a nankeen kaftan, with a head as white as snow; shielding his eyes with his hand, he stared at the tarantás, suddenly slapped himself on both thighs, at first danced about a little on one spot, then ran to open the gate. The tarantás drove into the yard, the wheels rustling against the nettles, and halted in front of the porch. The white-headed man, very nimble, to all appearances, was already standing, with his feet planted very wide apart and very crooked, on the last step; and having unbuttoned the apron, convulsively held up the leather and aided the master to descend to the earth, and then kissed his hand.

"Good-day, good-day, brother,"—said Lavrétzky,—"I think thy name is Antón? Thou art still alive?"

The old man bowed in silence, and ran to fetch the keys. While he was gone, the postilion sat motionless, bending sideways and gazing at the locked door; but Lavrétzky's lackey remained standing as he had sprung down, in a picturesque pose, with one hand resting on the box. The old man brought the keys, and quite unnecessarily writhing like a serpent, raising his elbows on high, he unlocked the door, stepped aside, and again bowed to his girdle.

"Here I am at home, here I have got back,"—said Lavrétzky to himself, as he entered the tiny anteroom, while the shutters were opened, one after the other, with a bang and a squeak, and the daylight penetrated into the deserted rooms.

XIX

The tiny house where Lavrétzky had arrived, and where, two years previously, Glafíra Petróvna had breathed her last, had been built in the previous century, out of sturdy pine lumber; in appearance it was decrepit, but was capable of standing another fifty years or more. Lavrétzky made the round of all the rooms, and, to the great discomfiture of the aged, languid flies, with white dust on their backs, who were sitting motionless under the lintels of the doors, he ordered all the windows to be opened; no one had opened them since the death of Glafíra Petróvna. Everything in the house remained as it had been: the small, spindle-legged couches in the drawing-room, covered with glossy grey material, worn through and flattened down, vividly recalled the days of Katherine II; in the drawing-room, also, stood the mistress's favourite chair, with a tall, straight back, against which, even in her old age, she had not leaned. On the principal wall hung an ancient portrait of Feódor's great-grandfather, Andréi Lavrétzky; the dark, sallow face was barely discernible against the warped and blackened background; the small, vicious eyes gazed surlily from beneath pendent, swollen lids; the black hair, devoid of powder, rose in a brush over the heavy, deeply-seamed brow. On the corner of the portrait hung a wreath of dusty immortelles. "Glafíra Petróvna herself was pleased to weave it," announced Antón. In the bedchamber rose a narrow bed, under a tester of ancient, striped material, of very excellent quality; a mountain of faded pillows, and a thin quilted coverlet, lay on the bed, and by the head of the bed hung an image of the Presentation in the Temple of the All-Holy Birthgiver of God, the very same image to which the old spinster, as she lay dying alone and forgotten by every one, had pressed for the last time, her lips which were already growing cold. The toilet-table, of inlaid wood with brass trimmings and a crooked mirror with tarnished gilding, stood by the window. Alongside the bedroom was the room for the holy pictures, a tiny chamber, with bare walls and a heavy shrine of images in the corner; on the floor lay a small, threadbare rug, spotted with wax; Glafíra Petróvna had been wont to make her prostrations upon it. Antón went off with Lavrétzky's lackey to open the stable and carriage-house; in his stead, there presented herself an old woman, almost of the same age as he, with a kerchief bound round her head, down to her very brows; her head trembled, and her eyes gazed dully, but expressed zeal, and a long-established habit of serving with assiduity, and, at the same time, a certain respectful commiseration. She kissed Lavrétzky's hand, and paused at the door, in anticipation of orders. He positively was unable to recall her name; he could not even remember whether he had ever seen her. It turned out that her name was Apraxyéya; forty years before, that same Glafíra Petróvna had banished her from the manor-house service, and had ordered her to attend to the fowls; however, she said little,—as though she had outlived her mind,—and only looked on cringingly. In addition to these two old people, and three potbellied brats in long shirts, Antón's great-grandchildren, there dwelt in the service-rooms of the manor a one-armed little old peasant, who was exempt from compulsory service; he made a drumming noise like a woodcock when he spoke, and was not capable of doing anything. Not much more useful than he was the decrepit dog, who had welcomed Lavrétzky's home-coming with his bark: it had already been fastened up for ten years with a heavy chain, bought by order of Glafíra Petróvna, and was barely in a condition to move and drag its burden. After inspecting the house, Lavrétzky went out into the park, and was satisfied with it. It was all overgrown with tall grass, burdock, and gooseberry and raspberry bushes; but there was much shade in it: there were many old linden-trees, which surprised the beholder by their huge size and the strange arrangement of their branches; they had been too closely planted, and at some time or other—a hundred years before—had been pollarded. The park ended in a small, clear pond, with a rim of tall, reddish reeds. The traces of human life fade away very quickly: Glafíra Petróvna's farm had not succeeded in running wild, but it already seemed plunged in that tranquil dream wherewith everything on earth doth dream, where the restless infection of people does not exist. Feódor Ivánitch also strolled through the village; the women stared at him from the thresholds of their cottages, each with her cheek propped on one hand; the peasant men saluted him from afar; the children ran away; the dogs barked indifferently. At last he felt hungry, but he did not expect his servants and cook until toward evening; the cart with provisions from Lavríki had not yet arrived,—he was compelled to appeal to Antón. Antón immediately arranged matters: he caught an old hen, cut its throat, and plucked it; Apraxyéya rubbed and scrubbed it for a long time, and washed it, like linen, before she placed it in the stew-pan; when, at last, it was cooked, Antón put on the table-cloth and set the table, placed in front of the plate a blackened salt-cellar of plated ware on three feet, and a small faceted carafe with a round glass stopper and a narrow neck; then he announced to Lavrétzky, in a chanting voice, that the meal was ready,—and took up his post behind his chair, having wound a napkin around his right fist, and disseminating some strong, ancient odour, which resembled the odour of cypress wood. Lavrétzky tasted the soup, and came upon the hen; its skin was all covered with big pimples, a thick tendon ran down each leg, its flesh had a flavour of charcoal and lye. When he had finished his dinner, Lavrétzky said that he would like some tea, if.... "This very moment, sir, I will serve it, sir,"—interrupted the old man,—and he kept his promise. A pinch of tea was hunted up, wrapped in a scrap of red paper, a small but very mettlesome and noisy samovár was searched out, also sugar, in very tiny bits, that seemed to have been melted around the edges. Lavrétzky drank his tea out of a large cup; he remembered that cup in his childhood: playing-cards were depicted on it, only visitors drank out of it,—and he now drank out of it, like a visitor. Toward evening, his servants arrived; Lavrétzky did not wish to sleep in his aunt's bed; he gave orders that a bed should be made up for him in the dining-room. Extinguishing the candle, he stared about him for a long time, and meditated on cheerless thoughts; he experienced the sensation familiar to every man who chances to pass the night, for the first time, in a place which has long been uninhabited; it seemed to him that the darkness which surrounded him on all sides could not accustom itself to the new inhabitant, that the very walls of the house were waxing indignant. At last he sighed, drew the coverlet up over him, and fell asleep. Antón remained afoot longer than the rest; for a long time he whispered with Apraxyéya, groaned in a low tone, and crossed himself a couple of times. Neither of them expected that the master would settle down among them at Vasílievskoe, when, near at hand, he owned such a magnificent estate, with a capitally-organised manor-house; they did not even suspect that it was precisely that manor-house which was repugnant to Lavrétzky: it evoked in him oppressive memories. After having whispered his fill, Antón took his staff, and beat upon the board at the store-house which had long been hanging silent, and immediately lay down for a nap in the yard, without covering up his grey head with anything. The May night was tranquil and caressing—and the old man slumbered sweetly.

XX

The next morning Lavrétzky rose quite early, had a talk with the overseer, visited the threshing-floor, ordered the chain to be removed from the watch-dog, who only barked a little, but did not even move away from his kennel;—and on his return home, sank into a sort of peaceful torpor, from which he did not emerge all day. "I have sunk down to the very bottom of the river now," he said to himself more than once. He sat by the window, made no movement, and seemed to be listening to the current of tranquil life which surrounded him, to the infrequent noises of the country solitudes. Yonder, somewhere beyond the nettles, some one began to sing, in the shrillest of voices; a gnat seemed to be chiming in with the voice. Now it ceased, but the gnat still squeaked on; athwart the energetic, insistently-plaintive buzzing of the flies resounded the booming of a fat bumble-bee, which kept bumping its head against the ceiling; a cock on the road began to crow, hoarsely prolonging the last note; a peasant cart rumbled past; the gate toward the village creaked. "Well?" suddenly quavered a woman's voice.—"Okh, thou my dear little sweetheart," said Antón to a little girl of two years, whom he was dandling in his arms. "Fetch some kvas," repeats the same female voice,—and all at once a deathlike silence ensues; nothing makes any noise, nothing stirs; the breeze does not flutter a leaf; the swallows dart along near the ground, one after the other, without a cry, and sadness descends upon the soul from their silent flight.—"Here I am, sunk down to the bottom of the river," Lavrétzky says to himself again.—"And life is at all times tranquil, leisurely here," he thinks:—"whoever enters its circle must become submissive: here there is nothing to agitate one's self about, nothing to disturb; here success awaits only him who lays out his path without haste, as the husbandman lays the furrow with his plough." And what strength there is all around, what health there is in this inactive calm! Yonder now, under the window, a sturdy burdock is making its way out from among the thick grass; above it, the lovage is stretching forth its succulent stalk, the Virgin's-tears toss still higher their rosy tendrils; and yonder, further away, in the fields, the rye is gleaming, and the oats are beginning to shoot up their stalks, and every leaf on every tree, every blade of grass on its stalk, spreads itself out to its fullest extent. "My best years have been spent on the love of a woman," Lavrétzky pursued his meditations:—"may the irksomeness here sober me, may it soothe me, prepare me so that I may understand how to do my work without haste"; and again he began to lend an ear to the silence, expecting nothing,—and, at the same time, as it were incessantly expecting something: the silence enfolds him on all sides, the sun glides quietly across the calm blue sky, a cloud floats gently in its wake; it seems as though they know whither and why they are floating. At that same moment, in other spots on earth, life was seething, bustling, roaring; here the same life was flowing on inaudibly, like water amid marsh-grass; and until the very evening, Lavrétzky could not tear himself from the contemplation of that life fleeting, flowing onward; grief for the past melted in his soul like snows of springtime,—and, strange to say!—never had the feeling of his native land been so deep and strong within him.

XXI

In the course of a fortnight, Feódor Ivánitch brought Glafíra Petróvna's little house into order; cleaned up the yard, the garden; comfortable furniture was brought to him from Lavríki, wine, books, newspapers from the town; horses made their appearance in the stables; in a word, Feódor Ivánitch provided himself with everything that was necessary and began to live—not exactly like a country squire, nor yet exactly like a recluse. His days passed monotonously, but he was not bored, although he saw no one; he occupied himself

diligently and attentively with the farming operations, he rode about the neighbourhood on horseback, he read. He read but little, however: it was more agreeable for him to listen to the tales of old Antón. As a rule, Lavrétzky would seat himself with a pipe of tobacco and a cup of cold tea near the window; Antón would stand near the door, with his hands clasped behind him, and begin his leisurely stories of olden times,—of those fabulous times—when the oats and barley were sold not by measures but by huge sacks, at two or three kopéks the sack; when in all directions, even close to the town, stretched impenetrable forests, untouched steppes. "And now," wailed the old man, who was already over eighty years of age:—"they have felled and ploughed up everything until there is no place to drive through." Antón, also, related many things concerning his mistress Glafíra Petróvna: how sagacious and economical she had been; how a certain gentleman, a youthful neighbour, had attempted to gain her good-will, had taken to calling frequently,—and how she had been pleased, for his benefit, even to don her cap with rose-purple ribbons, and her yellow gown of tru-tru levantine; but how, later on, having flown into a rage with her neighbour, on account of the unseemly question: "What might your capital amount to, madam?" she had given orders that he should not be admitted, and how she had then commanded, that everything, down to the very smallest scrap, should be given to Feódor Ivánitch after her death. And, in fact, Lavrétzky found all his aunt's effects intact, not excepting the festival cap, with the rose-purple ribbons, and the gown of yellow tru-tru levantine. The ancient papers and curious documents, which Lavrétzky had counted upon, proved not to exist, with the exception of one tattered little old book, in which his grandfather, Piótr Andréitch, had jotted down, now—"Celebration in the city of Saint Petersburg of the peace concluded with the Turkish Empire by his Illustriousness Prince Alexánder Alexándrovitch Prozoróvsky"; now a recipe for a decoction for the chest, with the comment: "This instruction was given to Generaless Praskóvya Feódorovna Saltykóff, by Feódor Avkséntievitch, Archpriest of the Church of the Life-giving Trinity"; again, some item of political news, like the following: "In the '*Moscow News*,' it is announced that Premier-Major Mikhaíl Petróvitch Kolýtcheff has died. Was not he the son of Piótr Vasílievitch Kolýtcheff?" Lavrétzky also found several ancient calendars and dream-books, and the mystical works of Mr. Ambódik; many memories were awakened in him by the long-forgotten but familiar "Symbols and Emblems." In Glafíra Petróvna's toilet-table Lavrétzky found a small packet, tied with black ribbon, and sealed with black wax, thrust into the remotest recesses of the drawer. In the packet, face to face, lay a pastel portrait of his father in his youth, with soft curls tumbling over his brow, with long, languid eyes, and mouth half opened,—and the almost effaced portrait of a pale woman in a white gown, with a white rose in her hand,—his mother. Glafíra Petróvna had never permitted her own portrait to be made.—
"Dear little father Feódor Ivánitch,"—Antón was wont to say to Lavrétzky:—"although I did not then have my residence in the manor-house of the masters, yet I remember your great-grandfather, Andréi Afanásievitch,—that I do; I was eighteen years of age when he died. Once I met him in the garden,—my very hamstrings shook; but he did nothing, only inquired my name,—and sent me to his chamber for a pocket-handkerchief. He was a real gentleman, there's no gainsaying that,—and he recognised no superior over him. For I must inform you, that your great-grandfather had a wonderful amulet,—a monk from Mount Athos gave him that amulet. And that monk said to him: 'I give thee this for thine affability, Boyárin; wear it—and fear not fate.' Well, and of course, dear little father, you know, what sort of times those were; what the master took a notion to do, that he did. Once in a while, some one, even one of the gentry, would take it into his head to thwart him; but no sooner did he look at him, than he would say: 'You're sailing in shoal water'—that was his favourite expression. And he lived, your great-grandfather of blessed memory, in a tiny wooden mansion; but what property he left behind him, what silver, and all sorts of supplies,—all the cellars were filled to the brim! He was a master. That little carafe, which you were pleased to praise,—belonged to him: he drank vódka from it. And then your grandfather, Piótr Ivánitch, built himself a stone mansion; but he acquired no property; with him everything went at sixes and sevens; and he lived worse than his papa, and got no pleasure for himself,—but wasted all the money, and there was none to pay for requiems for his soul; he left not even a silver spoon behind him, so it was lucky that Glafíra Petróvna brought things into order."
"And is it true,"—Lavrétzky interrupted him,—"that she was called an ill-tempered old hag?"
"Why, surely, some did call her that!"—returned Antón, in displeasure.

"WELL, little father,"—the old man one day summoned the courage to ask;—"and how about our young mistress; where is she pleased to have her residence?"
"I have separated from my wife,"—said Lavrétzky, with an effort:—"please do not inquire about her."
"I obey, sir,"—replied the old man, sadly.

After the lapse of three weeks, Lavrétzky rode into O * * * on horseback, to the Kalítins', and passed the evening with them. Lemm was there; Lavrétzky conceived a great liking for him. Although, thanks to his father, he did not play on any instrument, yet he was passionately fond of music,—intelligent, classical music. Pánshin was not at the Kalítins' that evening. The Governor had sent him off somewhere, out of town. Liza played alone, and with great precision; Lemm grew animated, excited, rolled a piece of paper into a baton, and beat time. Márya Dmítrievna laughed, at first, as she watched him, and then went off to bed; as she said, Beethoven was too agitating for her nerves. At midnight, Lavrétzky escorted Lemm to his lodgings, and sat with him until three o'clock in the morning. Lemm talked a great deal; his bent shoulders straightened up, his eyes opened widely and sparkled; his very hair stood upright above his brow. It was such a very long time since any one had taken an interest in him, but Lavrétzky evidently did take an interest, and interrogated him solicitously and attentively. This touched the old man; he ended by showing his visitor his music, he even played and sang to him, with his ghost of a voice, several selections from his compositions,—among others, the whole of Schiller's ballad "Fridolin," which he had set to music. Lavrétzky lauded it, made him repeat portions of it, and invited him to visit him for a few days. Lemm, who was escorting him to the street, immediately accepted, and shook his hand warmly; but when he was left alone, in the cool, damp air of the day which was just beginning to dawn, he glanced around him, screwed up his eyes, writhed, and went softly to his tiny chamber, like a guilty creature: "Ich bin wohl nicht klug" (I'm not in my right mind),—he muttered, as he lay down on his hard, short bed. He tried to assert that he was ill when, a few days later, Lavrétzky came for him in a calash; but Feódor Ivánitch went to him, in his room, and persuaded him. The circumstance which operated most powerfully of all on Lemm was, that Lavrétzky had ordered a piano to be sent to his country-house from the town: a piano for his—Lemm's—use. Together they went to the Kalítins', and spent the evening, but not so agreeably as on the former occasion. Pánshin was there, had a great deal to narrate about his journey, and very amusingly mimicked and illustrated in action the country squires he had seen; Lavrétzky laughed, but Lemm did not emerge from his corner, maintained silence, quietly quivered all over like a spider, looked glum and dull, and grew animated only when Lavrétzky began to take his leave. Even when he was seated in the calash, the old man continued to be shy and to fidget; but the quiet, warm air, the light breeze, the delicate shadows, the perfume of the grass, of the birch buds, the peaceful gleam of the starry, moonless heaven, the energetic hoof-beats and snorting of the horses, all the charms of the road, of spring, of night,—descended into the heart of the poor German, and he himself was the first to address Lavrétzky.

XXII

He began to talk of music, of Liza, then again of music. He seemed, somehow, to utter his words more slowly when he spoke of Liza. Lavrétzky turned the conversation on his compositions, and, half in jest, proposed to write a libretto for him.

"H'm, a libretto!"—rejoined Lemm:—"no, that is beyond me: I have not that animation, that play of fancy, which is indispensable for an opera; I have already lost my powers.... But if I could still do something,—I would be satisfied with a romance; of course, I should like some good words...."

He relapsed into silence, and sat for a long time motionless, with his eyes raised heavenward.

"For example," he said at last:—"something of this sort: 'Ye stars, O ye pure stars'?"...

Lavrétzky turned his face slightly toward him and began to stare at him.

"'Ye stars, ye pure stars,'"—repeated Lemm.... "'Ye gaze alike upon the just and upon the guilty ... but only the innocent of heart,'—or something of that sort ... 'understand you,' that is to say, no,—'love you.' However, I am not a poet ... how should I be! But something in that style, something lofty."

Lemm pushed his hat back on the nape of his neck; in the delicate gloom of the light night, his face seemed whiter and more youthful.

"'And ye also,'"—he went on, with a voice which gradually grew quieter:—"'ye know who loves, who knows how to love, for ye are pure, ye, alone, can comfort.'... No, that's not right yet! I am not a poet,"—he said:—"but something of that sort...."

"I regret that I am not a poet,"—remarked Lavrétzky.

"Empty visions!" retorted Lemm, and huddled in the corner of the calash. He closed his eyes, as though preparing to go to sleep.

Several moments elapsed.... Lavrétzky listened.... "'Stars, pure stars, love,'"—the old man was whispering.

"Love,"—Lavrétzky repeated to himself, became thoughtful, and his soul grew heavy within him.

"You have written some very beautiful music for 'Fridolin,' Christofór Feódoritch,"—he said aloud:—"and what think you; did that Fridolin, after the Count had led him to his wife, become her lover—hey?"
"That is what you think,"—returned Lemm: "because, probably, experience...." He suddenly fell silent, and turned away in confusion. Lavrétzky laughed in a constrained way, turned away also, and began to stare along the road.
The stars had already begun to pale, and the sky was grey, when the calash rolled up to the porch of the little house at Vasílievskoe. Lavrétzky conducted his guest to the chamber which had been assigned to him, returned to his study, and sat down by the window. In the park, a nightingale was singing its last lay before the dawn. Lavrétzky remembered that a nightingale had been singing in the Kalítins' garden also; he recalled, too, the tranquil movement of Liza's eyes when, at the first sounds of it, they had turned toward the dark window. He began to think of her, and his heart grew calm within him. "Pure little star,"—he said to himself, in a low tone:—"pure stars,"—he added, with a smile, and calmly lay down to sleep.
But Lemm sat, for a long time, on his bed, with a book of music-paper on his knees. It seemed as though a strange, sweet melody were about to visit him: he was already burning and growing agitated, he already felt the lassitude and sweetness of its approach ... but it did not come.
"I am not a poet, and not a musician!"—he whispered at last....
And his weary head sank back heavily on the pillow.

XXIII

On the following morning, host and guest drank tea in the garden, under an ancient linden-tree.
"Maestro!"—said Lavrétzky, among other things:—"you will soon have to compose a triumphal cantata."
"On what occasion?"
"On the occasion of the marriage of Mr. Pánshin to Liza. Did you notice how he was paying court to her last evening? It seems as though everything were going smoothly with them."
"That shall not be!" exclaimed Lemm.
"Why not?"
"Because it is impossible. However,"—he added, after a pause:—"everything is possible in this world. Especially here, with you, in Russia."
"Let us leave Russia out of the question for the present; but what evil do you see in that marriage?"
"All is evil, all. Lizavéta Mikhaílovna is an upright, serious maiden, with exalted sentiments,—but he ... he is a di-let-tante, in one word."
"But surely she loves him?"
Lemm rose from the bench.
"No, she does not love him, that is to say, she is very pure in heart, and does not know herself what 'love' means. Madam von Kalítin tells her, that he is a nice young man, and she listens to Madam von Kalítin, because she is still a perfect child, although she is nineteen years of age: she says her prayers in the morning, she says her prayers in the evening,—and that is very praiseworthy; but she does not love him. She can love only the fine, but he is not fine; that is, his soul is not fine."
Lemm uttered this whole speech coherently and with fervour, pacing back and forth, with short strides, in front of the tea-table, and with his eyes flitting over the ground.
"My dearest Maestro!"—exclaimed Lavrétzky all at once:—"it strikes me, that you are in love with my cousin yourself."
Lemm came to a sudden halt.
"Please,"—he began in an uncertain voice:—"do not jest thus with me. I am not a lunatic."
Lavrétzky felt sorry for the old man; he entreated his forgiveness. After tea, Lemm played him his cantata, and at dinner, being instigated thereto by Lavrétzky himself, he again began to talk about Liza. Lavrétzky listened to him with attention and curiosity.
"What think you, Christofór Feódoritch,"—he said at last—"everything appears to be in order with us now, the garden is in full bloom.... Shall not we invite her here for the day, together with her mother and my old aunt,—hey? Would that be agreeable to you?"
Lemm bent his head over his plate.
"Invite her,"—he said, almost inaudibly.
"And Pánshin need not be asked?"
"He need not,"—replied the old man, with a half-childlike smile.
Two days later, Feódor Ivánitch set out for the town, to the Kalítins.

XXIV

He found them all at home, but he did not immediately announce to them his intention: he wished, first, to have a talk alone with Liza. Chance aided him: they were left alone together in the drawing-room. They fell into conversation: she had succeeded in getting used to him,—and, in general, she was not shy of any one. He listened to her, looked her straight in the face, and mentally repeated Lemm's words, and agreed with him. It sometimes happens, that two persons who are already acquainted, but not intimate, suddenly and swiftly draw near to each other in the course of a few minutes,—and the consciousness of this approach is immediately reflected in their glances, in their friendly, quiet smiles, in their very movements. Precisely this is what took place with Lavrétzky and Liza. "So that's what he is like," she thought, gazing caressingly at him; "so that's what thou art like," he said to himself also. And therefore, he was not greatly surprised when she, not without a slight hesitation, however, announced to him, that she had long had it in her heart to say something to him, but had been afraid of annoying him.

"Have no fear; speak out,"—he said, and halted in front of her.

Liza raised her clear eyes to his.

"You are so kind,"—she began, and, at the same time, she said to herself:—"'yes, he really is kind' ... you will pardon me, but I ought not to speak of this to you ... but how could you ... why did you separate from your wife?"

Lavrétzky shuddered, glanced at Liza, and seated himself beside her.

"My child," he began,—"please do not touch that wound; your hands are tender, but nevertheless I shall suffer pain."

"I know,"—went on Liza, as though she had not heard him:—"she is culpable toward you, I do not wish to defend her; but how is it possible to put asunder that which God has joined together?"

"Our convictions on that point are too dissimilar, Lizavéta Mikhaílovna,"—said Lavrétzky, rather sharply;—"we shall not understand each other."

Liza turned pale; her whole body quivered slightly; but she did not hold her peace.

"You ought to forgive,"—she said softly:—"if you wish to be forgiven."

"Forgive!"—Lavrétzky caught her up:—"Ought not you first to know for whom you are pleading? Forgive that woman, take her back into my house,—her,—that empty, heartless creature! And who has told you, that she wishes to return to me? Good heavens, she is entirely satisfied with her position.... But what is the use of talking about it! Her name ought not to be uttered by you. You are too pure, you are not even in a position to understand what sort of a being she is."

"Why vilify her?"—said Liza, with an effort. The trembling of her hands became visible. "It was you yourself who abandoned her, Feódor Ivánitch."

"But I tell you,"—retorted Lavrétzky, with an involuntary outburst of impatience:—"that you do not know what sort of a creature she is!"

"Then why did you marry her?"—whispered Liza, and dropped her eyes.

Lavrétzky sprang up hastily from his seat.

"Why did I marry? I was young and inexperienced then; I was deceived, I was carried away by a beautiful exterior. I did not know women, I did not know anything. God grant that you may make a happier marriage! But, believe me, it is impossible to vouch for anything."

"And I may be just as unhappy,"—said Liza (her voice began to break): "but, in that case, I must submit; I do not know how to talk, but if we do not submit...."

Lavrétzky clenched his fists and stamped his foot.

"Be not angry; forgive me!"—ejaculated Liza, hastily.

At that moment, Márya Dmítrievna entered. Liza rose, and started to leave the room.

"Stop!"—Lavrétzky unexpectedly called after her. "I have a great favour to ask of your mother and of you: make me a visit to celebrate my new home. You know, I have set up a piano; Lemm is staying with me; the lilacs are now in bloom; you will get a breath of the country air, and can return the same day,—do you accept?"

Liza glanced at her mother, and Márya Dmítrievna assumed an air of suffering, but Lavrétzky, without giving her a chance to open her mouth, instantly kissed both her hands. Márya Dmítrievna, who was always susceptible to endearments, and had not expected such amiability from "the dolt," was touched to the soul, and consented. While she was considering what day to appoint, Lavrétzky approached Liza, and, still greatly agitated, furtively whispered to her: "Thank you, you are a good girl, I am to blame."... And her pale face flushed crimson with a cheerful—bashful smile; her eyes also smiled,—up to that moment, she had been afraid that she had offended him.

"May Vladímir Nikoláitch go with us?"—asked Márya Dmítrievna.

"Certainly,"—responded Lavrétzky:—"but would it not be better if we confined ourselves to our own family circle?"

"Yes, certainly, but you see...." Márya Dmítrievna began. "However, as you like," she added.

It was decided to take Lyénotchka and Schúrotchka. Márfa Timoféevna declined to make the journey.

"It is too hard for me, my dear,"—she said,—"my old bones ache: and I am sure there is no place at your house where I can spend the night; and I cannot sleep in a strange bed. Let these young people do the gallivanting."

Lavrétzky did not succeed in being alone again with Liza; but he looked at her in such a way, that she felt at ease, and rather ashamed, and sorry for him. On taking leave of her, he pressed her hand warmly; when she was left alone, she fell into thought.

XXV

When Lavrétzky reached home, he was met on the threshold of the drawing-room by a tall, thin man, in a threadbare blue coat, with frowzy grey side-whiskers, a long, straight nose, and small, inflamed eyes. This was Mikhalévitch, his former comrade at the university. Lavrétzky did not recognise him at first, but embraced him warmly as soon as he mentioned his name. They had not seen each other since the Moscow days. There was a shower of exclamations, of questions; long-smothered memories came forth into the light of day. Hurriedly smoking pipe after pipe, drinking down tea in gulps, and flourishing his long arms, Mikhalévitch narrated his adventures to Lavrétzky; there was nothing very cheerful about them, he could not boast of success in his enterprises,—but he laughed incessantly, with a hoarse, nervous laugh. A month previously, he had obtained a situation in the private counting-house of a wealthy distiller, about three hundred versts from the town of O * * *, and, on learning of Lavrétzky's return from abroad, he had turned aside from his road, in order to see his old friend. Mikhalévitch talked as abruptly as in his younger days, was as noisy and effervescent as ever. Lavrétzky was about to allude to his circumstances, but Mikhalévitch interrupted him, hastily muttering: "I've heard, brother, I've heard about it,—who could have anticipated it?"—and immediately turned the conversation into the region of general comments.

"I, brother,"—he said:—"must leave thee to-morrow; to-day, thou must excuse me—we will go to bed late—I positively must find out what are thy opinions, convictions, what sort of a person thou hast become, what life has taught thee." (Mikhalévitch still retained the phraseology of the '30s.) "So far as I myself am concerned, I have changed in many respects, brother: the billows of life have fallen upon my breast,—who the dickens was it that said that?—although, in important, essential points, I have not changed; I believe, as of yore, in the good, in the truth; but I not only believe,—I am now a believer, yes—I am a believer, a religious believer. Hearken, thou knowest that I write verses; there is no poetry in them, but there is truth. I will recite to thee my last piece: in it I have given expression to my most sincere convictions. Listen."—Mikhalévitch began to recite a poem; it was rather long, and wound up with the following lines:

> ıew feeling I have surrendered myself with all my l
> e become like a child in soul:
> [have burned all that I worshipped.
> e worshipped all that I burned."

As he declaimed these last two lines, Mikhalévitch was on the verge of tears; slight convulsive twitchings, the signs of deep feeling—flitted across his broad lips, his ugly face lighted up. Lavrétzky listened and listened to him; the spirit of contradiction began to stir within him: the ever-ready, incessantly-seething enthusiasm of the Moscow student irritated him. A quarter of an hour had not elapsed, before a dispute flared up between them, one of those interminable disputes, of which only Russians are capable. After a separation of many years' duration, spent in two widely-different spheres, understanding clearly neither other people's thoughts nor their own,—cavilling at words and retorting with mere words, they argued about the most abstract subjects,—and argued as though it were a matter of life and death to both of them: they shouted and yelled so, that all the people in the house took fright, and poor Lemm, who, from the moment of Mikhalévitch's arrival, had locked himself up in his room, became bewildered, and began, in a confused way, to be afraid.

"But what art thou after this? disillusioned?"—shouted Mikhalévitch at one o'clock in the morning.

"Are there any such disillusioned people?"—retorted Lavrétzky:—"they are all poor and ill,—and I'll pick thee up with one hand, shall I?"
"Well, if not a *disillusioned* man, then a *sceptuik*, and that is still worse." (Mikhalévitch's pronunciation still smacked of his native Little Russia.) "And what right hast thou to be a sceptic? Thou hast had bad luck in life, granted; that was no fault of thine: thou wert born with a passionate, loving soul, and thou wert forcibly kept away from women: the first woman that came in thy way was bound to deceive thee."
"And she did deceive me,"—remarked Lavrétzky, gloomily.
"Granted, granted; I was the instrument of fate there,—but what nonsense am I talking?—there's no fate about it; it's merely an old habit of expressing myself inaccurately. But what does that prove?"
"It proves, that they dislocated me in my childhood."
"But set thy joints! to that end thou art a human being, a man; thou hast no need to borrow energy! But, at any rate, is it possible, is it permissible, to erect a private fact, so to speak, into a general law, into an immutable law?"
"Where is the rule?"—interrupted Lavrétzky,—"I do not admit...."
"Yes, it is thy rule, thy rule," Mikhalévitch interrupted him in his turn....
"Thou art an egoist, that's what thou art!"—he thundered, an hour later:—"thou hast desired thine own personal enjoyment, thou hast desired happiness in life, thou hast desired to live for thyself alone...."
"What dost thou mean by personal enjoyment?"
"And everything has deceived thee; everything has crumbled away beneath thy feet."
"What is personal enjoyment,—I ask thee?"
"And it was bound to crumble. For thou hast sought support where it was not to be found, for thou hast built thy house on a quicksand...."
"Speak more plainly, without metaphors, because I do not understand thee."
"Because,—laugh if it pleases thee,—because there is no faith in thee, no warmth of heart; mind, merely a farthing mind; thou art simply a pitiful, lagging Voltairian—that's what thou art!"
"Who—I am a Voltairian?"
"Yes, just the same sort as thy father was, and dost not suspect it thyself."
"After that,"—cried Lavrétzky,—"I have a right to say that thou art a fanatic!"
"Alas!"—returned Mikhalévitch, with contrition:—"unhappily, as yet I have in no way earned so lofty an appellation...."
"Now I have discovered what to call thee,"—shouted this same Mikhalévitch, at three o'clock in the morning;—"thou art not a sceptic, not a disillusioned man, not a Voltairian,—thou art a trifler, and thou art an evil-minded trifler, a conscious trifler, not an ingenuous trifler. Ingenuous triflers lie around on the oven and do nothing, because they do not know how to do anything; and they think of nothing. But thou art a thinking man,—and thou liest around; thou mightest do something—and thou dost nothing; thou liest with thy well-fed belly upward and sayest: 'It is proper to lie thus, because everything that men do is nonsense, and twaddle which leads to nothing.'"
"But what makes thee think that I trifle,"—insisted Lavrétzky:—"why dost thou assume such thoughts on my part?"
"And more than that, all of you, all the people of your sort,"—pursued the obstreperous Mikhalévitch:—"are erudite triflers. You know on what foot the German limps, you know what is bad about the English and the French,—and your knowledge comes to your assistance, justifies your shameful laziness, your disgusting inactivity. Some men will even pride themselves, and say, 'What a clever fellow I am!—I lie around, but the others, the fools, bustle about.' Yes!—And there are such gentlemen among us,—I am not saying this with reference to thee, however,—who pass their whole lives in a sort of stupor of tedium, grow accustomed to it, sit in it like ... like a mushroom in sour cream," Mikhalévitch caught himself up, and burst out laughing at his own comparison.—"Oh, that stupor of tedium is the ruin of the Russians! The repulsive trifler, all his life long, is getting ready to work...."
"Come, what art thou calling names for?"—roared Lavrétzky, in his turn.—"Work ... act ... Tell me, rather, what to do, but don't call names, you Poltáva Demosthenes!"
"Just see what a freak he has taken! I'll not tell thee that, brother; every one must know that himself," retorted Demosthenes, ironically.—"A landed proprietor, a nobleman—and he doesn't know what to do! Thou hast no faith, or thou wouldst know; thou hast no faith—and there is no revelation."
"Give me a rest, at any rate, you devil: give me a chance to look around me,"—entreated Lavrétzky.

"Not a minute, not a second of respite!"—retorted Mikhalévitch, with an imperious gesture of the hand.—"Not one second!—Death does not wait, and life ought not to wait."...
"And when, where did men get the idea of becoming triflers?"—he shouted, at four o'clock in the morning, but his voice had now begun to be rather hoarse: "among us! now! in Russia! when on every separate individual a duty, a great obligation is incumbent toward God, toward the nation, toward himself! We are sleeping, but time is passing on; we are sleeping...."
"Permit me to observe to thee,"—said Lavrétzky,—"that we are not sleeping at all, now, but are, rather, preventing others from sleeping. We are cracking our throats like cocks. Hark, isn't that the third cock-crow?"
This sally disconcerted and calmed down Mikhalévitch. "Farewell until to-morrow,"—he said, with a smile,—and thrust his pipe into his tobacco-pouch. "Farewell until to-morrow," repeated Lavrétzky. But the friends conversed for an hour longer. However, their voices were no longer raised, and their speeches were quiet, sad, and kind.
Mikhalévitch departed on the following day, in spite of all Lavrétzky's efforts to detain him. Feódor Ivánitch did not succeed in persuading him to remain; but he talked with him to his heart's content. It came out, that Mikhalévitch had not a penny in the world. Already, on the preceding evening, Lavrétzky, with compassion, had observed in him all the signs and habits of confirmed poverty; his boots were broken, a button was missing from the back of his coat, his hands were guiltless of gloves, down was visible in his hair; on his arrival, it had not occurred to him to ask for washing materials, and at supper he ate like a shark, tearing the meat apart with his hands, and cracking the bones noisily with his strong, black teeth. It appeared, also, that the service had been of no benefit to him, that he had staked all his hopes on the revenue-farmer, who had engaged him simply with the object of having in his counting-house "an educated man." In spite of all this, Mikhalévitch was not dejected, and lived on as a cynic, an idealist, a poet, sincerely rejoicing and grieving over the lot of mankind, over his own calling,—and troubled himself very little as to how he was to keep himself from dying with hunger. Mikhalévitch had not married, but had been in love times without number, and wrote verses about all his lady-loves; with especial fervour did he sing the praises of one mysterious "panna" with black and curling locks.... Rumours were in circulation, it is true, to the effect that the "panna" in question was a plain Jewess, well known to many cavalry officers ... but, when you come to think of it,—does that make any difference?
Mikhalévitch did not get on well with Lemm: his vociferous speeches, his harsh manners, frightened the German, who was not used to such things.... An unfortunate wretch always scents another unfortunate wretch from afar, but rarely makes up to him in old age,—and this is not in the least to be wondered at: he has nothing to share with him,—not even hopes.
Before his departure, Mikhalévitch had another long talk with Lavrétzky, prophesied perdition to him, if he did not come to a sense of his errors, entreated him to occupy himself seriously with the existence of his peasants, set himself up as an example, saying, that he had been purified in the furnace of affliction,—and immediately thereafter, several times mentioned himself as a happy man, compared himself to the birds of heaven, the lilies of the field....
"A black lily, at any rate,"—remarked Lavrétzky.
"Eh, brother, don't put on any of your aristocratic airs,"—retorted Mikhalévitch, good-naturedly:—"but thank God, rather, that in thy veins flows honest, plebeian blood. But I perceive, that thou art now in need of some pure, unearthly being, who shall wrest thee from this apathy of thine."
"Thanks, brother,"—said Lavrétzky:—"I have had enough of those unearthly beings."
"Shut up, *cuinuik!*"—exclaimed Mikhalévitch.
"Cynic,"—Lavrétzky corrected him.
"Just so, *cuinuik*,"—repeated Mikhalévitch, in no wise disconcerted.
Even as he took his seat in the tarantás, to which his flat, yellow, strangely light trunk was carried forth, he continued to talk; wrapped up in some sort of a Spanish cloak with a rusty collar, and lion's paws in place of clasps, he still went on setting forth his views as to the fate of Russia, and waving his swarthy hand through the air, as though he were sowing the seeds of its future welfare. At last the horses started.... "Bear in mind my last three words,"—he shouted, thrusting his whole body out of the tarantás, and balancing himself:—"religion, progress, humanity!... Farewell!" His head, with its cap pulled down to the very eyes, vanished. Lavrétzky remained standing alone on the porch and staring down the road until the tarantás disappeared from his sight. "But I think he probably is right,"—he said to himself, as he reentered the house:—"probably

I am a trifler." Many of Mikhalévitch's words had sunk indelibly into his soul, although he had disputed and had not agreed with him. If only a man be kindly, no one can repulse him.

XXVI

Two days later, Márya Dmítrievna arrived with all her young people at Vasílievskoe, in accordance with her promise. The little girls immediately ran out into the garden, while Márya Dmítrievna languidly traversed the rooms, and languidly praised everything. Her visit to Lavrétzky she regarded as a token of great condescension, almost in the light of a good deed. She smiled affably when Antón and Apraxyéya, after the ancient custom of house-serfs, came to kiss her hand,—and in an enervated voice, through her nose, she asked them to give her some tea. To the great vexation of Antón, who had donned white knitted gloves, the newly-arrived lady was served with tea not by him, but by Lavrétzky's hired valet, who, according to the assertion of the old man, knew nothing whatever about proper forms. On the other hand, Antón reasserted his rights at dinner: firm as a post he stood behind Márya Dmítrievna's chair—and yielded his place to no one. The long-unprecedented arrival of visitors at Vasílievskoe both agitated and rejoiced the old man: it pleased him to see, that his master knew nice people. However, he was not the only one who was excited on that day: Lemm, also, was excited. He put on a short, snuff-coloured frock-coat, with a sharp-pointed collar, bound his neckerchief tightly, and incessantly coughed and stepped aside, with an agreeable and courteous mien. Lavrétzky noted, with satisfaction, that the close relations between himself and Liza still continued: no sooner did she enter, than she offered him her hand, in friendly wise. After dinner, Lemm drew forth, from the back pocket of his coat, into which he had been constantly thrusting his hand, a small roll of music, and pursing up his lips, he silently laid it on the piano. It was a romance, which he had composed on the preceding day to old-fashioned German words, in which the stars were alluded to. Liza immediately seated herself at the piano and began to decipher the romance.... Alas, the music turned out to be complicated, and disagreeably strained; it was obvious that the composer had attempted to express some passionate, profound sentiment, but nothing had come of it: so the attempt remained merely an attempt. Lavrétzky and Liza both felt this,—and Lemm understood it: he said not a word, put his romance back in his pocket, and in reply to Liza's proposal to play it over again, he merely said significantly, with a shake of his head: "Enough—for the present!"—bent his shoulders, shrank together, and left the room.

Toward evening, they all went fishing together. The pond beyond the garden contained a quantity of carp and loach. They placed Márya Dmítrievna in an arm-chair near the bank, in the shade, spread a rug under her feet, and gave her the best hook; Antón, in the quality of an old and expert fisherman, offered his services. He assiduously spitted worms on the hook, slapped them down with his hand, spat on them, and even himself flung the line and hook, bending forward with his whole body. That same day, Márya Dmítrievna expressed herself to Feódor Ivánitch, with regard to him, in the following phrase, in the French language of girls' institutes: "*Il n'y a plus maintenant de ces gens comme ça comme autrefois.*" Lemm, with the two little girls, went further away, to the dam; Lavrétzky placed himself beside Liza. The fish bit incessantly, the carp which were caught were constantly flashing their sides, now gold, now silver, in the air; the joyous exclamations of the little girls were unceasing; Márya Dmítrievna herself gave vent to a couple of shrill, feminine shrieks. Lavrétzky and Liza caught fewer than the others; this, probably, resulted from the fact that they paid less attention than the rest to their fishing, and allowed their floats to drift close inshore. The tall, reddish reeds rustled softly around them, in front of them the motionless water gleamed softly, and their conversation was soft also. Liza stood on a small raft; Lavrétzky sat on the inclined trunk of a willow; Liza wore a white gown, girt about the waist with a broad ribbon, also white in hue; her straw hat was hanging from one hand, with the other, she supported, with some effort, the curved fishing-rod. Lavrétzky gazed at the pure, rather severe profile, at her hair tucked behind her ears, at her soft cheeks, which were as sunburned as those of a child,—and said to himself: "O how charmingly thou standest on my pond!" Liza did not turn toward him, but stared at the water,—and half smiled, half screwed up her eyes. The shadow of a linden-tree near at hand fell upon both of them.

"Do you know,"—began Lavrétzky:—"I have been thinking a great deal about my last conversation with you, and have come to the conclusion, that you are extraordinarily kind."

"I did not mean it in that way at all ..." Liza began,—and was overcome with shame.

"You are kind,"—repeated Lavrétzky. "I am a rough man, but I feel that every one must love you. There's Lemm now, for example: he is simply in love with you."

Liza's brows quivered, rather than contracted; this always happened with her when she heard something disagreeable.

"I felt very sorry for him to-day,"—Lavrétzky resumed:—"with his unsuccessful romance. To be young, and be able to do a thing—that can be borne; but to grow old, and not have the power—is painful. And the offensive thing about it is, that you are not conscious when your powers begin to wane. It is difficult for an old man to endure these shocks!... Look out, the fish are biting at your hook.... They say,"—added Lavrétzky, after a brief pause,—"that Vladímir Nikoláitch has written a very pretty romance."

"Yes,"—replied Liza;—"it is a trifle, but it is not bad."

"And what is your opinion,"—asked Lavrétzky:—"is he a good musician?"

"It seems to me that he has great talent for music; but up to the present time he has not cultivated it as he should."

"Exactly. And is he a nice man?"

Liza laughed, and cast a quick glance at Feódor Ivánitch.

"What a strange question!"—she exclaimed, drawing up her hook, and flinging it far out again.

"Why is it strange?—I am asking you about him as a man who has recently come hither, as your relative."

"As a relative?"

"Yes. I believe I am a sort of uncle to you."

"Vladímir Nikoláitch has a kind heart,"—said Liza:—"he is clever; mamma is very fond of him."

"And do you like him?"

"He is a nice man: why should not I like him?"

"Ah!"—said Lavrétzky, and relapsed into silence. A half-mournful, half-sneering expression flitted across his face. His tenacious gaze discomfited Liza, but she continued to smile. "Well, God grant them happiness!"—he muttered, at last, as though to himself, and turned away his head.

Liza blushed.

"You are mistaken, Feódor Ivánitch,"—she said:—"there is no cause for your thinking.... But do not you like Vladímir Nikoláitch?"

"I do not."

"Why?"

"It seems to me, that he has no heart."

The smile vanished from Liza's face.

"You have become accustomed to judge people harshly,"—she said, after a long silence.

"I think not. What right have I to judge others harshly, when I myself stand in need of indulgence? Or have you forgotten that a lazy man is the only one who does not laugh at me?... Well,"—he added:—"and have you kept your promise?"

"What promise?"

"Have you prayed for me?"

"Yes, I have prayed, and I do pray for you every day. But please do not speak lightly of that."

Lavrétzky began to assure Liza, that such a thing had never entered his head, that he entertained a profound respect for all convictions; then he entered upon a discussion of religion, its significance in the history of mankind, the significance of Christianity....

"One must be a Christian,"—said Liza, not without a certain effort:—"not in order to understand heavenly things ... yonder ... earthly things, but because every man must die."

Lavrétzky, with involuntary surprise, raised his eyes to Liza's, and encountered her glance.

"What a word you have uttered!"—said he.

"The word is not mine,"—she replied.

"It is not yours.... But why do you speak of death?"

"I do not know. I often think about it."

"Often?"

"Yes."

"One would not say so, to look at you now: you have such a merry, bright face, you are smiling...."

"Yes, I am very merry now,"—returned Liza ingenuously.

Lavrétzky felt like seizing both her hands, and clasping them tightly.

"Liza, Liza!"—called Márya Dmítrievna,—"come hither, look! What a carp I have caught!"

"Immediately, *maman*,"—replied Liza, and went to her, but Lavrétzky remained on his willow-tree.

"I talk with her as though I were not a man whose life is finished," he said to himself. As she departed, Liza had hung her hat on a bough; with a strange, almost tender sentiment, Lavrétzky gazed at the hat, at its long, rather crumpled ribbons. Liza speedily returned to him, and again took up her stand on the raft.

"Why do you think that Vladímir Nikoláitch has no heart?"—she inquired, a few moments later.

"I have already told you, that I may be mistaken; however, time will show."

Liza became thoughtful. Lavrétzky began to talk about his manner of life at Vasílievskoe, about Mikhalévitch, about Antón; he felt impelled to talk to Liza, to communicate to her everything that occurred to his soul: she was so charming, she listened to him so attentively; her infrequent comments and replies seemed to him so simple and wise. He even told her so.

Liza was amazed.

"Really?"—she said;—"why, I have always thought that I, like my maid Nástya, had no words of my own. One day she said to her betrothed: 'Thou must find it tiresome with me; thou always sayest such fine things to me, but I have no words of my own.'"

"And thank God for that!" thought Lavrétzky.

XXVII

In the meantime, evening drew on, and Márya Dmítrievna expressed a desire to return home. The little girls were, with difficulty, torn away from the pond, and made ready. Lavrétzky announced his intention to escort his guests half way, and ordered his horse to be saddled. As he seated Márya Dmítrievna in the carriage, he remembered Lemm; but the old man was nowhere to be found. He had disappeared as soon as the angling was over. Antón slammed to the carriage door, with a strength remarkable for his years, and grimly shouted: "Drive on, coachman!" The carriage rolled off. On the back seat sat Márya Dmítrievna and Liza; on the front seat, the little girls and the maid. The evening was warm and still, and the windows were lowered on both sides. Lavrétzky rode at a trot by Liza's side of the carriage, with his hand resting on the door,—he had dropped the reins on the neck of his steed, which was trotting smoothly,—and from time to time exchanged a few words with the young girl. The sunset glow vanished; night descended, and the air grew even warmer. Márya Dmítrievna soon fell into a doze; the little girls and the maid also dropped off to sleep. The carriage rolled swiftly and smoothly onward; Liza leaned forward; the moon, which had just risen, shone on her face, the fragrant night breeze blew on her cheeks and neck. She felt at ease. Her hand lay on the door of the carriage, alongside of Lavrétzky's hand. And he, also, felt at ease: he was being borne along through the tranquil nocturnal warmth, never taking his eyes from the kind young face, listening to the youthful voice, which was ringing even in a whisper, saying simple, kindly things; he did not even notice that he had passed the half-way point. He did not wish to awaken Márya Dmítrievna, pressed Liza's hand lightly, and said:—"We are friends, now, are we not?" She nodded, he drew up his horse. The carriage rolled on, gently swaying and lurching: Lavrétzky proceeded homeward at a footpace. The witchery of the summer night took possession of him; everything around him seemed so unexpectedly strange, and, at the same time, so long, so sweetly familiar; far and near,—and things were visible at a long distance, although the eye did not comprehend much of what it beheld,—everything was at rest; young, blossoming life made itself felt in that very repose. Lavrétzky's horse walked briskly, swaying regularly to right and left; its huge black shadow kept pace alongside; there was something mysteriously pleasant in the tramp of its hoofs, something cheerful and wondrous in the resounding call of the quail. The stars were hidden in a sort of brilliant smoke; the moon, not yet at the full, shone with a steady gleam; its light flooded the blue sky in streams, and fell like a stain of smoky gold upon the thin cloudlets which floated past; the crispness of the air called forth a slight moisture in the eyes, caressingly enveloped all the limbs, poured in an abundant flood into the breast. Lavrétzky enjoyed himself, and rejoiced at his enjoyment. "Come, life is still before us," he thought:—"it has not been completely ruined yet by...." He did not finish his sentence, and say who or what had ruined it.... Then he began to think of Liza, that it was hardly likely that she loved Pánshin; that had he met her under different circumstances,—God knows what might have come of it; that he understood Lemm, although she had no "words of her own." Yes, but that was not true: she had words of her own.... "Do not speak lightly of that," recurred to Lavrétzky's memory. He rode for a long time, with drooping head, then he straightened himself up, and slowly recited:

> I have burned all that I worshi
> ɜ worshipped all that I burned..

but immediately gave his horse a cut with the whip, and rode at a gallop all the rest of the way home.

As he alighted from his horse, he cast a last glance around him, with an involuntary, grateful smile. Night, the speechless, caressing night, lay upon the hills and in the valleys; from afar, from its fragrant depths, God knows whence,—whether from heaven or earth,—emanated a soft, quiet warmth. Lavrétzky wafted a last salutation to Liza, and ran up the steps.

The following day passed rather languidly. Rain fell from early morning; Lemm cast furtive glances from beneath his eyebrows, and pursed up his lips more and more tightly, as though he had vowed to himself never to open them again. On lying down to sleep, Lavrétzky had taken to bed with him a whole pile of French newspapers, which had already been lying on his table for two weeks, with their wrappers unbroken. He set to work idly to strip off the wrappers, and glance through the columns of the papers, which, however, contained nothing new. He was on the point of throwing them aside,—when, all of a sudden, he sprang out of bed as though he had been stung. In the feuilleton of one of the papers, M'sieu Jules, already known to us, imparted to his readers "a sad bit of news": "The charming, bewitching native of Moscow," he wrote, "one of the queens of fashion, the ornament of Parisian salons, Madame de Lavretzki, had died almost instantaneously,—and this news, unhappily only too true, had only just reached him, M. Jules. He was,"—he continued,—"he might say, a friend of the deceased...."

Lavrétzky dressed himself, went out into the garden, and until morning dawned, he paced back and forth in one and the same alley.

XXVIII

On the following morning, at tea, Lemm requested Lavrétzky to furnish him with horses, that he might return to town. "It is time that I should set about my work,—that is to say, my lessons," remarked the old man:—"but here I am only wasting time in vain." Lavrétzky did not immediately reply to him: he seemed preoccupied. "Very well,"—he said at last;—"I will accompany you myself."—Without any aid from the servants, grunting and fuming, Lemm packed his small trunk, and tore up and burned several sheets of music-paper. The horses were brought round. As he emerged from his study, Lavrétzky thrust into his pocket the newspaper of the day before. During the entire journey, Lemm and Lavrétzky had very little to say to each other: each of them was engrossed with his own thoughts, and each was delighted that the other did not disturb him. And they parted rather coldly,—which, by the way, frequently happens between friends in Russia. Lavrétzky drove the old man to his tiny house: the latter alighted, got out his trunk, and without offering his hand to his friend (he held his trunk in front of his chest with both hands), without even looking at him,—he said in Russian: "Good-bye, sir!"—"Good-bye,"—repeated Lavrétzky, and ordered his coachman to drive him to his own lodgings. (He had hired a lodging in the town of O * * * in case he might require it.) After writing several letters and dining in haste, Lavrétzky took his way to the Kalítins. In their drawing-room he found no one but Pánshin, who informed him that Márya Dmítrievna would be down directly, and immediately entered into conversation with him, with the most cordial amiability. Up to that day, Pánshin had treated Lavrétzky, not exactly in a patronizing way, yet condescendingly; but Liza, in telling Pánshin about her jaunt of the day before, had expressed herself to the effect that Lavrétzky was a very fine and clever man; that was enough: the "very fine" man must be captivated. Pánshin began with compliments to Lavrétzky, with descriptions of the raptures with which, according to his statement, Márya Dmítrievna's whole family had expressed themselves about Vasílievskoe, and then, according to his wont, passing adroitly to himself, he began to talk about his own occupations, his views of life, of the world, of the government service;—he said a couple of words about the future of Russia, about the proper way of keeping the governors in hand; thereupon, merrily jeered at himself, and added, that, among other things, he had been commissioned in Petersburg—"*de populariser l'idée du cadastre*." He talked for quite a long time, with careless self-confidence solving all difficulties, and juggling with the most weighty administrative and political questions, as a sleight-of-hand performer juggles with his balls. The expressions: "This is what I would do, if I were the government"; "You, as a clever man, will immediately agree with me"—were never absent from his tongue. Lavrétzky listened coldly to Pánshin's idle chatter: he did not like this handsome, clever, and unconstrainedly elegant man, with his brilliant smile, courteous voice, and searching eyes. Pánshin speedily divined, with the swift comprehension of other people's sentiments which was peculiar to him, that he was not affording his interlocutor any particular pleasure, and made his escape, under a plausible pretext, deciding in his own mind that Lavrétzky might be a very fine man, but that he was not sympathetic, was "*aigri*," and, "*en somme*," rather ridiculous.—Márya Dmítrievna made her appearance accompanied by Gedeónovsky; then Márfa Timoféevna entered with Liza; after them followed the other members of the household; then came that lover of music, Mme. Byelenítzyn, a small, thin lady, with an almost childish, fatigued and handsome little face, in a rustling black gown, with a motley-hued fan, and heavy gold bracelets; her husband also came, a rosy-cheeked, plump man, with huge feet and hands, with white eyelashes, and an impassive smile on his thick lips; in company his wife never spoke to him, but at home, in moments of tenderness, she was wont to call him "her little pig"; Pánshin returned: the rooms became very full of people and very noisy. Such a throng of people was not to Lavrétzky's liking; Mme. Byelenítzyn particularly enraged him by constantly staring at him through her lorgnette. He would have withdrawn at once, had it not been for Liza: he wished to say two words to her in private, but for a long time he was not able to seize a convenient moment, and contented himself with watching her in secret joy; never had her face seemed to him more noble and charming. She appeared to great advantage from the proximity of Mme. Byelenítzyn. The latter was incessantly fidgeting about on her chair, shrugging her narrow little shoulders, laughing, in an enervated way, and screwing up her eyes, then suddenly opening them very wide. Liza sat quietly, her gaze was direct, and she did not laugh at all. The hostess sat down to play cards with Márfa Timoféevna, Mme. Byelenítzyn, and Gedeónovsky, who played very slowly, was constantly making mistakes, blinking his eyes, and mopping his face with his handkerchief. Pánshin assumed a melancholy mien, expressed himself with brevity, with great significance and mournfulness,—for all the world like an artist who has not had his say,—but despite the entreaties of Mme. Byelenítzyn, who was having a violent flirtation with him, he would not consent to sing his romance: Lavrétzky embarrassed him. Feódor Ivánitch also said little; the peculiar expression of his face had startled Liza, as soon as he entered the room: she immediately felt that he had something to communicate to her, but, without herself knowing why, she was afraid to interrogate him. At last, as she passed into the hall to pour tea, she involuntarily turned her head in his direction. He immediately followed her.

"What is the matter with you?"—she said, as she placed the teapot on the samovár.

"Have you noticed it?"

"You are not the same to-day as I have seen you heretofore."

Lavrétzky bent over the table.

"I wanted,"—he began,—"to tell you a certain piece of news, but now it is not possible.—However, read what is marked with pencil in this feuilleton,"—he added, giving her the copy of the newspaper which he had brought with him.—"I beg that you will keep this secret; I will call on you to-morrow morning."

Liza was surprised.... Pánshin made his appearance on the threshold of the door: she put the newspaper in her pocket.

"Have you read Obermann, Lizavéta Mikhaílovna?"—Pánshin asked her meditatively.

Liza gave him a superficial answer, left the hall, and went up-stairs. Lavrétzky returned to the drawing-room, and approached the card-table. Márfa Timoféevna, with her cap-ribbons untied, and red in the face, began to complain to him about her partner, Gedeónovsky, who, according to her, did not know how to lead.

"Evidently,"—she said,—"playing cards is quite a different thing from inventing fibs."

Her partner continued to blink and mop his face. Liza entered the drawing-room, and seated herself in a corner; Lavrétzky looked at her, she looked at him,—and something like dread fell upon them both. He read surprise and a sort of secret reproach in her face. Long as he might to talk to her, he could not do it; to remain in the same room with her, a guest among strangers, was painful to him: he decided to go away. As he took leave of her, he managed to repeat that he would come on the morrow, and he added that he trusted in her friendship.

"Come,"—she replied, with the same amazement on her face.

Pánshin brightened up after Lavrétzky's departure; he began to give advice to Gedeónovsky, banteringly paid court to Mme. Byelenítzyn, and, at last, sang his romance. But he talked with Liza and gazed at her as before: significantly and rather sadly.

And again, Lavrétzky did not sleep all night long. He did not feel sad, he was not excited, he had grown altogether calm; but he could not sleep. He did not even recall the past; he simply gazed at his life: his heart beat strongly and evenly, the hours flew past, but he did not even think of sleeping. At times, only, did the thought come to the surface in his mind: "But that is not true, it is all nonsense,"—and he paused, lowered his head, and began again to gaze at his life.

XXIX

Márya Dmítrievna did not receive Lavrétzky with any excess of cordiality, when he presented himself on the following day. "Well, you are making yourself pretty free of the house,"—she said to herself. Personally, he did not greatly please her, and, in addition, Pánshin, under whose influence she was, had sung his praises in a very sly and careless manner on the preceding evening. As she did not look upon him in the light of a guest, and did not consider it necessary to trouble herself about a relative almost a member of the family, half an hour had not elapsed before he was strolling down an alley in the garden with Liza. Lyénotchka and Schúrotchka were frolicking a short distance away, among the flower-beds.

Liza was composed, as usual, but paler than usual. She took from her pocket and handed to Lavrétzky the sheet of newspaper, folded small.

"This is dreadful!"—said she.

Lavrétzky made no reply.

"But perhaps it is not yet true,"—added Liza.

"That is why I asked you not to mention it to any one."

Liza walked on a little way.

"Tell me,"—she began:—"you are not grieved? Not in the least?"

"I do not know myself what my feelings are,"—replied Lavrétzky.

"But, assuredly, you used to love her?"

"Yes, I did."

"Very much?"

"Very much."

"And you are not grieved by her death?"

"It is not now that she has died to me."

"What you say is sinful.... Do not be angry with me. You call me your friend: a friend may say anything. To tell the truth, I feel terrified.... Your face was so malign yesterday.... Do you remember, how you were complaining of her, not long ago?—and perhaps, already, at that very time, she was no longer alive. This is terrible. It is exactly as though it had been sent to you as a chastisement."

Lavrétzky laughed bitterly.

"Do you think so?... At all events, I am free now."

Liza gave a slight start.

"Stop, do not talk like that. Of what use to you is your freedom? You must not think about that now, but about forgiveness...."

"I forgave her long ago,"—interrupted Lavrétzky, with a wave of the hand.

"No, not that,"—returned Liza, and blushed. "You did not understand me rightly. You must take means to obtain forgiveness...."

"Who is there to forgive me?"

"Who?—God. Who else but God can forgive us?"

Lavrétzky caught her hand.

"Akh, Lizavéta Mikhaílovna, believe me,"—he exclaimed:—"I have been sufficiently punished as it is. I have already atoned for everything, believe me."

"You cannot know that,"—said Liza in a low voice. "You have forgotten;—not very long ago,—when you were talking to me,—you were not willing to forgive her...."

The two walked silently down the alley.

"And how about your daughter?"—Liza suddenly inquired, and halted.

Lavrétzky started.

"Oh, do not worry yourself! I have already despatched letters to all the proper places. The future of my daughter, as you call ... as you say ... is assured. Do not disquiet yourself."

Liza smiled sadly.

"But you are right,"—went on Lavrétzky:—"what can I do with my freedom? Of what use is it to me?"

"When did you receive that newspaper?"—said Liza, making no reply to his question.

"The day after your visit."

"And is it possible ... is it possible that you did not even weep?"

"No. I was stunned; but where were the tears to come from? Weep over the past,—but, you see, it is entirely extirpated in my case!... Her behaviour itself did not destroy my happiness, but merely proved to me that it had never existed. What was there to cry about? But, who knows?—perhaps I should have been more grieved if I had received this news two weeks earlier...."

"Two weeks?"—returned Liza. "But what has happened in those two weeks?"

Lavrétzky made no answer, and Liza suddenly blushed more furiously than before.

"Yes, yes, you have guessed it,"—interposed Lavrétzky:—"in the course of those two weeks I have learned what a pure woman's soul is like, and my past has retreated still further from me."
Liza became confused, and softly walked toward the flower-garden, to Lyénotchka and Schúrotchka.
"And I am glad that I have shown you this newspaper,"—said Lavrétzky, as he followed her:—"I have already contracted the habit of concealing nothing from you, and I hope that you will repay me with the same confidence."
"Do you think so?"—said Liza, and stopped short. "In that case, I ought to ... but no! That is impossible."
"What is it? Speak, speak!"
"Really, it seems to me that I ought not.... However," added Liza, and turned to Lavrétzky with a smile:—"what is half-frankness worth?—Do you know? I received a letter to-day."
"From Pánshin?"
"Yes, from him.... How did you know?"
"He asks your hand?"
"Yes,"—uttered Liza, and looked seriously in Lavrétzky's eyes.
Lavrétzky, in his turn, gazed seriously at Liza.
"Well, and what reply have you made to him?"—he said at last.
"I do not know what reply to make,"—replied Liza, and dropped her clasped hands.
"What? Surely, you like him?"
"Yes, he pleases me; he seems to be a nice man...."
"You said the same thing to me, in those very same words, three days ago. What I want to know is, whether you love him with that strong, passionate feeling which we are accustomed to call love?"
"As *you* understand it,—no."
"You are not in love with him?"
"No. But is that necessary?"
"Of course it is!"
"Mamma likes him,"—pursued Liza:—"he is amiable; I have nothing against him."
"Still, you are wavering?"
"Yes ... and perhaps,—your words may be the cause of it. Do you remember what you said day before yesterday? But that weakness...."
"Oh, my child!"—suddenly exclaimed Lavrétzky—and his voice trembled:—"do not argue artfully, do not designate as weakness the cry of your heart, which does not wish to surrender itself without love. Do not take upon yourself that terrible responsibility toward a man whom you do not love and to whom you do not wish to belong...."
"I am listening,—I am taking nothing upon myself ..." Liza was beginning.
"Listen to your heart; it alone will tell you the truth,"—Lavrétzky interrupted her.... "Experience, reasoning—all that is stuff and nonsense! Do not deprive yourself of the best, the only happiness on earth."
"Is it you, Feódor Ivánitch, who are speaking thus? You, yourself, married for love—and were you happy?"
Lavrétzky wrung his hands.
"Akh, do not talk to me of that! You cannot even understand all that a young, untried, absurdly educated lad can mistake for love!... Yes, and in short, why calumniate one's self? I just told you, that I had not known happiness ... no! I was happy!"
"It seems to me, Feódor Ivánitch,"—said Liza, lowering her voice (when she did not agree with her interlocutor, she always lowered her voice; and, at the same time, she became greatly agitated):—"happiness on earth does not depend upon us...."
"It does, it does depend upon us, believe me," (he seized both her hands; Liza turned pale, and gazed at him almost in terror, but with attention):—"if only we have not ruined our own lives. For some people, a love-marriage may prove unhappy; but not for you, with your calm temperament, with your clear soul! I entreat you, do not marry without love, from a sense of duty, of renunciation, or anything else.... That, also, is want of faith, that is calculation,—and even worse. Believe me,—I have a right to speak thus: I have paid dearly for that right. And if your God...."
At that moment, Lavrétzky noticed that Lyénotchka and Schúrotchka were standing beside Liza, and staring at him with dumb amazement. He released Liza's hands, said hastily: "Pray pardon me,"—and walked toward the house.
"I have only one request to make of you,"—he said, returning to Liza:—"do not decide instantly, wait, think over what I have said to you. Even if you have not believed me, if you have made up your mind to a marriage

of reason,—even in that case, you ought not to marry Mr. Pánshin: he cannot be your husband.... Promise me, will you not, not to be in a hurry?"

Liza tried to answer Lavrétzky, but did not utter a word,—not because she had made up her mind "to be in a hurry"; but because her heart was beating too violently, and a sensation resembling fear had stopped her breath.

XXX

As he was leaving the Kalítins' house, Lavrétzky encountered Pánshin; they saluted each other coldly. Lavrétzky went home to his apartment, and locked himself in. He experienced a sensation such as he had, in all probability, never experienced before. Had he remained long in that state of "peaceful numbness"? had he long continued to feel, as he had expressed it, "at the bottom of the river"? What had altered his position? what had brought him out, to the surface? the most ordinary, inevitable though always unexpected of events;—death? Yes: but he did not think so much about the death of his wife, about his freedom, as,—what sort of answer would Liza give to Pánshin? He was conscious that, in the course of the last three days, he had come to look upon her with different eyes; he recalled how, on returning home, and thinking about her in the silence of the night, he had said to himself: "If...." That "if," wherein he had alluded to the past, to the impossible, had come to pass, although not in the way he had anticipated,—but this was little in itself. "She will obey her mother," he thought, "she will marry Pánshin; but even if she refuses him,—is it not all the same to me?" As he passed in front of the mirror, he cast a cursory glance at his face, and shrugged his shoulders.

The day sped swiftly by in these reflections; evening arrived. Lavrétzky wended his way to the Kalítins. He walked briskly, but approached their house with lingering steps. In front of the steps stood Pánshin's drozhky. "Come,"—thought Lavrétzky,—"I will not be an egoist," and entered the house. Inside he met no one, and all was still in the drawing-room; he opened the door, and beheld Márya Dmítrievna, playing picquet with Pánshin. Pánshin bowed to him in silence, and the mistress of the house uttered a little scream:—"How unexpected!"—and frowned slightly. Lavrétzky took a seat by her side, and began to look over her cards.

"Do you know how to play picquet?"—she asked him, with a certain dissembled vexation, and immediately announced that she discarded.

Pánshin reckoned up ninety, and politely and calmly began to gather up the tricks, with a severe and dignified expression on his countenance. That is the way in which diplomats should play; probably, that is the way in which he was wont to play in Petersburg, with some powerful dignitary, whom he desired to impress with a favourable opinion as to his solidity and maturity. "One hundred and one, one hundred and two, hearts; one hundred and three,"—rang out his measured tone, and Lavrétzky could not understand what note resounded in it: reproach or self-conceit.

"Is Márfa Timoféevna to be seen?"—he asked, observing that Pánshin, still with great dignity, was beginning to shuffle the cards. Not a trace of the artist was, as yet, to be observed in him.

"Yes, I think so. She is in her own apartments, up-stairs,"—replied Márya Dmítrievna:—"you had better inquire."

Lavrétzky went up-stairs, and found Márfa Timoféevna at cards also: she was playing *duratchkí* (fools) with Nastásya Kárpovna. Róska barked at him; but both the old ladies welcomed him cordially, and Márfa Timoféevna, in particular, seemed to be in high spirits.

"Ah! Fédya! Pray come in,"—she said:—"sit down, my dear little father. We shall be through our game directly. Wouldst thou like some preserves? Schúrotchka, get him a jar of strawberries. Thou dost not want it? Well, then sit as thou art; but as for smoking—thou must not: I cannot bear thy tobacco, and, moreover, it makes Matrós sneeze."

Lavrétzky made haste to assert that he did not care to smoke.

"Hast thou been down-stairs?"—went on the old woman:—"whom didst thou see there? Is Pánshin still on hand, as usual? And didst thou see Liza? No? She intended to come hither.... Yes, there she is; speak of an angel...."

Liza entered the room and, on perceiving Lavrétzky, she blushed.

"I have run in to see you for a minute, Márfa Timoféevna," she began....

"Why for a minute?"—returned the old woman. "What makes all you young girls such restless creatures? Thou seest, that I have a visitor: chatter to him, entertain him."

Liza seated herself on the edge of a chair, raised her eyes to Lavrétzky,—and felt that it was impossible not to give him to understand how her interview with Pánshin had ended. But how was that to be done? She felt both ashamed and awkward. She had not been acquainted with him long, with that man who both went rarely to church and bore with so much indifference the death of his wife,—and here she was already imparting her secrets to him.... He took an interest in her, it is true; she, herself, trusted him, and felt attracted to him; but, nevertheless, she felt ashamed, as though a stranger had entered her pure, virgin chamber.

Márfa Timoféevna came to her assistance.

"If thou wilt not entertain him,"—she began, "who will entertain him, poor fellow? I am too old for him, he is too clever for me, and for Nastásya Kárpovna he is too old, you must give her nothing but very young men."

"How can I entertain Feódor Ivánitch?"—said Liza.—"If he likes, I will play something for him on the piano,"—she added, irresolutely.

"Very good indeed: that's my clever girl,"—replied Márfa Timoféevna,—"Go down-stairs, my dear people; when you are through, come back; for I have been left the 'fool,' and I feel insulted, and want to win back."

Liza rose: Lavrétzky followed her. As they were descending the staircase, Liza halted.

"They tell the truth,"—she began:—"when they say that the hearts of men are full of contradictions. Your example ought to frighten me, to render me distrustful of marriage for love, but I...."

"You have refused him?"—interrupted Lavrétzky.

"No; but I have not accepted him. I told him everything, everything that I felt, and asked him to wait. Are you satisfied?"—she added, with a swift smile,—and lightly touching the railing with her hand, she ran down the stairs.

"What shall I play for you?"—she asked, as she raised the lid of the piano.

"Whatever you like,"—replied Lavrétzky, and seated himself in such a position that he could watch her.

Liza began to play, and, for a long time, never took her eyes from her fingers. At last, she glanced at Lavrétzky, and stopped short: so wonderful and strange did his face appear to her.

"What is the matter with you?"—she asked.

"Nothing,"—he replied:—"all is very well with me; I am glad for you, I am glad to look at you,—go on."

"It seems to me,"—said Liza, a few moments later:—"that if he really loved me, he would not have written that letter; he ought to have felt that I could not answer him now."

"That is of no importance,"—said Lavrétzky:—"the important point is, that you do not love him."

"Stop,—what sort of a conversation is this! I keep having visions of your dead wife, and you are terrible to me!"

"My Lizéta plays charmingly, does she not, Valdemar?"—Márya Dmítrievna was saying to Pánshin at the same moment.

"Yes,"—replied Pánshin;—"very charmingly."

Márya Dmítrievna gazed tenderly at her young partner; but the latter assumed a still more important and careworn aspect, and announced fourteen kings.

XXXI

Lavrétzky was not a young man; he could not long deceive himself as to the sentiments with which Liza had inspired him; he became definitively convinced, on that day, that he had fallen in love with her. This conviction brought no great joy to him. "Is it possible," he thought, "that at the age of five and thirty I have nothing better to do than to put my soul again into the hands of a woman? But Liza is not like *that one*; she would not require from me shameful sacrifices; she would not draw me away from my occupations; she herself would encourage me to honourable, severe toil, and we would advance together toward a fine goal. Yes," he wound up his meditations:—"all that is good, but the bad thing is, that she will not in the least wish to marry me. It was not for nothing that she told me, that I am terrible to her. On the other hand, she does not love that Pánshin either.... A poor consolation!"

Lavrétzky rode out to Vasílievskoe; but he did not remain four days,—it seemed so irksome to him there. He was tortured, also, by expectancy: the information imparted by M—r. Jules required confirmation, and he had received no letters. He returned to the town, and sat out the evening at the Kalítins'. It was easy for him to see, that Márya Dmítrievna had risen in revolt against him; but he succeeded in appeasing her somewhat by losing fifteen rubles to her at picquet,—and he spent about half an hour alone with Liza, in spite of the fact that her mother, no longer ago than the day before, had advised her not to be too familiar with a man "*qui a un si grand ridicule*." He found a change in her: she seemed, somehow, to have become more thoughtful, she upbraided him for his absence, and asked him—would he not go to church on the following morning (the next day was Sunday)?

"Go,"—she said to him, before he had succeeded in replying:—"we will pray together for the repose of *her* soul."—Then she added, that she did not know what she ought to do,—she did not know whether she had the right to make Pánshin wait any longer for her decision.
"Why?"—asked Lavrétzky.
"Because,"—said she: "I am already beginning to suspect what that decision will be."
She declared that her head ached, and went off to her own room up-stairs, irresolutely offering Lavrétzky the tips of her fingers.
The next day, Lavrétzky went to the morning service. Liza was already in the church when he arrived. She observed him, although she did not turn toward him. She prayed devoutly; her eyes sparkled softly, her head bent and rose softly. He felt that she was praying for him also,—and a wonderful emotion filled his soul. He felt happy, and somewhat conscience-stricken. The decorously-standing congregation, the familiar faces, the melodious chanting, the odour of the incense, the long, slanting rays of light from the windows, the very gloom of the walls and vaulted roof,—all spoke to his ear. He had not been in a church for a long time, he had not appealed to God for a long time: and even now, he did not utter any words of prayer,—he did not even pray without words, but for a moment, at least, if not in body, certainly with all his mind, he prostrated himself and bowed humbly to the very earth. He recalled how, in his childhood, he had prayed in church on every occasion until he became conscious of some one's cool touch on his brow; "this," he had been accustomed to say to himself at that time, "is my guardian-angel accepting me, laying upon me the seal of the chosen." He cast a glance at Liza.... "Thou hast brought me hither," he thought:—"do thou also touch me, touch my soul." She continued to pray in the same calm manner as before; her face seemed to him joyful, and he was profoundly moved once more; he entreated for that other soul—peace, for his own—pardon....
They met in the porch; she greeted him with cheerful and amiable dignity. The sun brilliantly illuminated the young grass in the churchyard, and the motley-hued gowns and kerchiefs of the women; the bells of the neighbouring churches were booming aloft; the sparrows were chirping in the hedgerows. Lavrétzky stood with head uncovered, and smiled; a light breeze lifted his hair, and the tips of the ribbons on Liza's hat. He put Liza into her carriage, distributed all his small change to the poor, and softly wended his way homeward.

XXXII

Difficult days arrived for Feódor Ivánitch. He found himself in a constant fever. Every morning he went to the post-office, with excitement broke the seals of his letters and newspapers,—and nowhere did he find anything which might have confirmed or refuted the fateful rumour. Sometimes he became repulsive even to himself: "Why am I thus waiting,"—he said to himself, "like a crow for blood, for the sure news of my wife's death?" He went to the Kalítins' every day; but even there he was no more at his ease: the mistress of the house openly sulked at him, received him with condescension; Pánshin treated him with exaggerated courtesy; Lemm had become misanthropic, and hardly even bowed to him,—and, chief of all, Liza seemed to avoid him. But when she chanced to be left alone with him, in place of her previous trustfulness, confusion manifested itself in her: she did not know what to say to him, and he himself felt agitation. In the course of a few days, Liza had become quite different from herself as he had previously known her: in her movements, her voice, in her very laugh, a secret trepidation was perceptible, an unevenness which had not heretofore existed. Márya Dmítrievna, like the genuine egoist she was, suspected nothing; but Márfa Timoféevna began to watch her favourite. Lavrétzky more than once reproached himself with having shown to Liza the copy of the newspaper which he had received: he could not fail to recognise the fact, that in his spiritual condition there was an element which was perturbing to pure feeling. He also assumed that the change in Liza had been brought about by her conflict with herself, by her doubts: what answer should she give to Pánshin? One day she brought him a book, one of Walter Scott's novels, which she herself had asked of him.
"Have you read this book?"—he asked.
"No; I do not feel in a mood for books now,"—she replied, and turned to go.
"Wait a minute: I have not been alone with you for a long time. You seem to be afraid of me."
"Yes."
"Why so, pray?"
"I do not know."
Lavrétzky said nothing for a while.
"Tell me,"—he began:—"you have not yet made up your mind?"
"What do you mean by that?"—she said, without raising her eyes.
"You understand me...."

Liza suddenly flushed up.
"Ask me no questions about anything,"—she ejaculated, with vivacity:—"I know nothing, I do not even know myself...." And she immediately beat a retreat.
On the following day, Lavrétzky arrived at the Kalítins' after dinner, and found all preparations made to have the All-Night Vigil service held there. In one corner of the dining-room, on a square table, covered with a clean cloth, small holy pictures in gold settings, with tiny, dull brilliants in their halos, were already placed, leaning against the wall. An old man-servant, in a grey frock-coat and slippers, walked the whole length of the room in a deliberate manner, and without making any noise with his heels, and placed two wax tapers in slender candlesticks in front of the holy images, crossed himself, made a reverence, and softly withdrew. The unlighted drawing-room was deserted. Lavrétzky walked down the dining-room, and inquired—was it not some one's Name-day? He was answered, in a whisper, that it was not, but that the Vigil service had been ordered at the desire of Lizavéta Mikhaílovna and Márfa Timoféevna; that the intention had been to bring thither the wonder-working *ikóna*, but it had gone to a sick person, thirty versts distant. There soon arrived, also, in company with the chanters, the priest, a man no longer young, with a small bald spot, who coughed loudly in the anteroom; the ladies all immediately trooped in single file from the boudoir, and approached to receive his blessing; Lavrétzky saluted him in silence; and he returned the salute in silence. The priest stood still for a short time, then cleared his throat again, and asked in a low tone, with a bass voice:
"Do you command me to proceed?"
"Proceed, bátiushka,"—replied Márya Dmítrievna.
He began to vest himself; the chanter obsequiously asked for a live coal; the incense began to diffuse its fragrance. The maids and lackeys emerged from the anteroom and halted in a dense throng close to the door. Róska, who never came down-stairs, suddenly made his appearance in the dining-room: they began to drive him out, and he became confused, turned around and sat down; a footman picked him up and carried him away. The Vigil service began. Lavrétzky pressed himself into a corner; his sensations were strange, almost melancholy; he himself was not able clearly to make out what he felt. Márya Dmítrievna stood in front of them all, before an arm-chair; she crossed herself with enervated carelessness, in regular lordly fashion,—now glancing around her, again suddenly casting her eyes upward: she was bored. Márfa Timoféevna seemed troubled; Nastásya Kárpovna kept prostrating herself, and rising with a sort of modest, soft rustle; Liza took up her stand, and never stirred from her place, never moved; from the concentrated expression of her countenance, it was possible to divine that she was praying assiduously and fervently. When she kissed the cross, at the end of the service, she also kissed the priest's large, red hand. Márya Dmítrievna invited him to drink tea; he took off his stole, assumed a rather secular air, and passed into the drawing-room with the ladies. A not over animated conversation began. The priest drank four cups of tea, incessantly mopping his bald spot with his handkerchief, and narrated, among other things, that merchant Avóshnikoff had contributed seven hundred rubles to gild the "cupola" of the church, and he also imparted a sure cure for freckles. Lavrétzky tried to seat himself beside Liza, but she maintained a severe, almost harsh demeanour, and never once glanced at him; she appeared to be deliberately refraining from noticing him; a certain cold, dignified rapture had descended upon her. For some reason or other, Lavrétzky felt inclined to smile uninterruptedly, and say something amusing; but there was confusion in his heart, and he went away at last, secretly perplexed.... He felt that there was something in Liza into which he could not penetrate.
On another occasion, Lavrétzky, as he sat in the drawing-room, and listened to the insinuating but heavy chatter of Gedeónovsky, suddenly turned round, without himself knowing why he did so, and caught a deep, attentive, questioning gaze in Liza's eyes.... It was riveted on him, that puzzling gaze, afterward. Lavrétzky thought about it all night long. He had not fallen in love in boyish fashion, it did not suit him to sigh and languish, neither did Liza arouse that sort of sentiment; but love has its sufferings at every age,—and he underwent them to the full.

XXXIII

One day, according to his custom, Lavrétzky was sitting at the Kalítins'. A fatiguingly-hot day had been followed by so fine an evening, that Márya Dmítrievna, despite her aversion to the fresh air, had ordered all the windows and doors into the garden to be opened, and had announced that she would not play cards, that it was a sin to play cards in such weather, and one must enjoy nature. Pánshin was the only visitor. Tuned up by the evening, and unwilling to sing before Lavrétzky, yet conscious of an influx of artistic emotions, he turned to poetry: he recited well, but with too much self-consciousness, and with unnecessary subtleties, several of Lérmontoff's poems (at that time, Púshkin had not yet become fashionable again)—and, all at once, as though ashamed of his expansiveness, he began, apropos of the familiar "Thought," to upbraid and reprove the present generation; in that connection, not missing the opportunity to set forth, how he would turn everything around in his own way, if the power were in his hands. "Russia," said he,—"has lagged behind Europe; she must catch up with it. People assert, that we are young—that is nonsense; and moreover, that we possess no inventive genius: X ... himself admits that we have not even invented a mouse-trap. Consequently, we are compelled, willy-nilly, to borrow from others. 'We are ill,'—says Lérmontoff,—I agree with him; but we are ill because we have only half converted ourselves into Europeans; that is where we have made our mistake, and that is what we must be cured of." ("*Le cadastre*,"—thought Lavrétzky).—"The best heads among us,"—he went on,—"*les meilleurs têtes*—have long since become convinced of this; all nations are, essentially, alike; only introduce good institutions, and there's an end of the matter. One may even conform to the existing national life; that is our business, the business of men ..." (he came near saying: "of statesmen") "who are in the service; but, in case of need, be not uneasy: the institutions will transform that same existence." Márya Dmítrievna, with emotion, backed up Pánshin. "What a clever man this is,"—she thought,—"talking in my house!" Liza said nothing, as she leaned against a window-frame; Lavrétzky also maintained silence; Márfa Timoféevna, who was playing cards in the corner with her friend, muttered something to herself. Pánshin strode up and down the room, and talked eloquently, but with a secret spite: he seemed to be scolding not the whole race, but certain individuals of his acquaintance. In the Kalítins' garden, in a large lilac-bush, dwelt a nightingale, whose first evening notes rang forth in the intervals of this eloquent harangue; the first stars lighted up in the rosy sky, above the motionless crests of the lindens. Lavrétzky rose, and began to reply to Pánshin; an argument ensued. Lavrétzky defended the youth and independence of Russia; he surrendered himself, his generation as sacrifice,—but upheld the new men, their convictions, and their desires; Pánshin retorted in a sharp and irritating way, declared that clever men must reform everything, and went so far, at last, that, forgetting his rank of Junior Gentleman of the Imperial Bedchamber, and his official career, he called Lavrétzky a "laggard conservative," he even hinted,—in a very remote way, it is true,—at his false position in society. Lavrétzky did not get angry, did not raise his voice (he remembered that Mikhalévitch also had called him a laggard—only, a Voltairian)—and calmly vanquished Pánshin on every point. He demonstrated to him the impossibility of leaps and supercilious reforms, unjustified either by a knowledge of the native land or actual faith in an ideal, even a negative ideal; he cited, as an example, his own education, and demanded, first of all, a recognition of national truth and submission to it,—that submission without which even boldness against falsehood is impossible; he did not evade, in conclusion, the reproach—merited, in his opinion—of frivolous waste of time and strength.

"All that is very fine!"—exclaimed the enraged Pánshin, at last:—"Here, you have returned to Russia,—what do you intend to do?"

"Till the soil,"—replied Lavrétzky:—"and try to till it as well as possible."

"That is very praiseworthy, there's no disputing that,"—rejoined Pánshin:—"and I have been told, that you have already had great success in that direction; but you must admit, that not every one is fitted for that sort of occupation...."

"*Une nature poétique*,"—began Márya Dmítrievna,—"of course, cannot till the soil ... *et puis*, you are called, Vladímir Nikoláitch, to do everything *en grand*."

This was too much even for Pánshin: he stopped short, and the conversation stopped short also. He tried to turn it on the beauty of the starry sky, on Schubert's music—but, for some reason, it would not run smoothly; he ended, by suggesting to Márya Dmítrievna, that he should play picquet with her.—"What! on such an evening?"—she replied feebly; but she ordered the cards to be brought.

Pánshin, with a crackling noise, tore open the fresh pack, while Liza and Lavrétzky, as though in pursuance of an agreement, both rose, and placed themselves beside Márfa Timoféevna. They both, suddenly, felt so very much at ease that they were even afraid to be left alone together,—and, at the same time, both felt that the embarrassment which they had experienced during the last few days had vanished, never more to return. The old woman stealthily patted Lavrétzky on the cheek, slyly screwed up her eyes, and shook her head several times, remarking in a whisper: "Thou hast got the best of the clever fellow, thanks." Everything in the room became still; the only sound was the faint crackling of the wax candles, and, now and then, the tapping of hands on the table, and an exclamation, or the reckoning of the spots,—and the song, mighty, resonant to the verge of daring, of the nightingale, poured in a broad stream through the window, in company with the dewy coolness.

XXXIV

Liza had not uttered a single word during the course of the dispute between Lavrétzky and Pánshin, but had attentively followed it, and had been entirely on Lavrétzky's side. Politics possessed very little interest for her; but the self-confident tone of the fashionable official (he had never, hitherto, so completely expressed himself) had repelled her; his scorn of Russia had wounded her. It had never entered Liza's head, that she was a patriot; but she was at her ease with Russian people; the Russian turn of mind gladdened her; without any affectation, for hours at a time, she chatted with the overseer of her mother's estate, when he came to town, and talked with him as with an equal, without any lordly condescension. Lavrétzky felt all this: he would not have undertaken to reply to Pánshin alone; he had been talking for Liza only. They said nothing to each other, even their eyes met but rarely; but both understood that they had come very close together that evening, understood that they loved and did not love the same things. On only one point did they differ; but Liza secretly hoped to bring him to God. They sat beside Márfa Timoféevna, and appeared to be watching her play; and they really were watching it,—but, in the meanwhile, their hearts had waxed great in their bosoms, and nothing escaped them: for them the nightingale was singing, the stars were shining, and the trees were softly whispering, lulled both by slumber and by the softness of the summer, and by the warmth. Lavrétzky surrendered himself wholly to the billow which was bearing him onward,—and rejoiced; but no word can express that which took place in the young girl's pure soul: it was a secret to herself; so let it remain for all others. No one knows, no one has seen, and no one ever will see, how that which is called into life and blossom pours forth and matures grain in the bosom of the earth.

The clock struck ten. Márfa Timoféevna went off to her rooms up-stairs, with Nastásya Kárpovna; Lavrétzky and Liza strolled through the room, halted in front of the open door to the garden, gazed into the dark distance, then at each other—and smiled; they would have liked, it appeared, to take each other by the hand, and talk their fill. They returned to Márya Dmítrievna and Pánshin, whose picquet had become protracted. The last "king" came to an end at length, and the hostess rose, groaning, and sighing, from the cushion-garnished arm-chair; Pánshin took his hat, kissed Márya Dmítrievna's hand, remarked that nothing now prevented other happy mortals from going to bed, or enjoying the night, but that he must sit over stupid papers until the morning dawned, bowed coldly to Liza (he had not expected that in reply to his offer of marriage, she would ask him to wait,—and therefore he was sulking at her)—and went away. Lavrétzky followed him. At the gate they parted; Pánshin aroused his coachman by poking him with the tip of his cane in the neck, seated himself in his drozhky, and drove off. Lavrétzky did not feel like going home; he walked out beyond the town, into the fields. The night was tranquil and bright, although there was no moon; Lavrétzky roamed about on the dewy grass for a long time; he came by accident upon a narrow path; he walked along it. It led him to a long fence, to a wicket-gate; he tried, without himself knowing why, to push it open: it creaked softly, and opened, as though it had been awaiting the pressure of his hand; Lavrétzky found himself in a garden, advanced a few paces along an avenue of lindens, and suddenly stopped short in amazement: he recognised the garden of the Kalítins.

He immediately stepped into a black blot of shadow which was cast by a thick hazel-bush, and stood for a long time motionless, wondering and shrugging his shoulders.

"This has not happened for nothing," he thought.

Everything was silent round about; not a sound was borne to him from the direction of the house. He cautiously advanced. Lo, at the turn in the avenue, the whole house suddenly gazed at him with its dark front; only in two of the upper windows were lights twinkling: in Liza's room, a candle was burning behind a white shade, and in Márfa Timoféevna's bedroom a shrine-lamp was glowing with a red gleam in front of the holy pictures, reflecting itself in an even halo in the golden settings; down-stairs, the door leading out on the balcony yawned broadly, as it stood wide open. Lavrétzky seated himself on a wooden bench, propped his head on his hand, and began to gaze at the door and the window. Midnight struck in the town; in the house, the small clocks shrilly rang out twelve; the watchman beat with a riffle of taps on the board. Lavrétzky thought of nothing, expected nothing; it was pleasant to him to feel himself near Liza, to sit in her garden on the bench, where she also had sat more than once.... The light disappeared in Liza's room.

"Good night, my dear girl," whispered Lavrétzky, as he continued to sit motionless, and without taking his eyes from the darkened window.

Suddenly a light appeared in one of the windows of the lower storey, passed to a second, a third.... Some one was walking through the rooms with a candle. "Can it be Liza? Impossible!"... Lavrétzky half rose to his feet. A familiar figure flitted past, and Liza made her appearance in the drawing-room. In a white gown, with her hair hanging loosely on her shoulders, she softly approached a table, bent over it, set down the candle, and searched for something; then, turning her face toward the garden, she approached the open door, and, all white, light, graceful, paused on the threshold. A quiver ran through Lavrétzky's limbs.

"Liza!"—burst from his lips, in barely audible tones.

She started, and began to stare into the darkness.

"Liza!"—repeated Lavrétzky more loudly, and emerged from the shadow of the avenue.

Liza, in alarm, stretched forth her head, and staggered backward. He called her for the third time, and held out his arms toward her. She left the door, and advanced into the garden.

"Is it you?"—she said.—"Are you here?"

"It is I ... I ... listen to me,"—whispered Lavrétzky, and, grasping her hand, he led her to the bench.

She followed him without resistance; her pale face, her impassive eyes, all her movements, were expressive of unutterable amazement. Lavrétzky seated her on the bench, and himself took up his stand in front of her.

"I had no thought of coming hither,"—he began:—"I came hither by chance.... I ... I ... I love you,"—he said, with involuntary terror.

Liza slowly glanced at him; apparently, she had only that moment comprehended where she was, and that she was with him. She tried to rise, but could not, and covered her face with her hands.

"Liza,"—said Lavrétzky:—"Liza,"—he repeated, and bowed down at her feet....

Her shoulders began to quiver slightly, the fingers of her pale hands were pressed more tightly to her face.

"What is the matter with you?"—Lavrétzky uttered, and caught the sound of soft sobbing. His heart turned cold.... He understood the meaning of those tears. "Can it be that you love me?"—he whispered, and touched her knee.

"Rise," he heard her voice:—"rise, Feódor Ivánitch. What is this that you and I are doing?"

He rose, and seated himself by her side on the bench. She was no longer weeping, but was gazing attentively at him with her wet eyes.

"I am frightened: what are we doing?"—she repeated.

"I love you,"—he said again:—"I am ready to give the whole of my life to you."

Again she shuddered, as though something had stung her, and raised her gaze heavenward.

"All this is in God's power,"—she said.

"But do you love me, Liza? Shall we be happy?"

She dropped her eyes; he softly drew her to him, and her head sank upon his shoulder.... He turned her head a little to one side, and touched her pale lips.

Half an hour later, Lavrétzky was standing before the wicket. He found it locked, and was obliged to leap across the fence. He returned to the town, and walked through the sleeping streets. A sensation of great, of unexpected happiness filled his soul; all doubts had died within him. "Vanish, past, dark spectre," he thought: "she loves me, she will be mine." All at once, it seemed to him that in the air, over his head, wondrous, triumphant sounds rang out; the sounds rolled on still more magnificently; in a chanting, mighty flood they streamed on,—and in them, so it seemed, all his happiness was speaking and singing. He glanced around him: the sounds were floating from two upper windows of a tiny house.

"Lemm!"—cried Lavrétzky, and ran to the house.—"Lemm! Lemm!"—he repeated loudly.

The sounds died away, and the figure of the old man in his dressing-gown, with breast bare, and hair dishevelled, made its appearance at the window.

"Aha!"—he said, with dignity:—"is that you?"

"Christofór Feódoritch! what splendid music! For God's sake, let me in."

The old man, without uttering a word, with a majestic movement of the arm flung the door-key out of the window into the street. Lavrétzky briskly ran up-stairs, entered the room, and was on the point of rushing at Lemm, but the latter imperiously motioned him to a chair; he said, abruptly, in Russian: "Sit down and listen!" seated himself at the piano, gazed proudly and sternly about him, and began to play. It was long since Lavrétzky had heard anything of the sort: a sweet, passionate melody, which gripped the heart from its very first notes; it was all beaming and languishing with inspiration, with happiness, with beauty; it swelled and melted away; it touched everything which exists on earth of precious, mysterious, holy; it breathed forth deathless sadness, and floated away to die in heaven. Lavrétzky straightened himself up and stood there, cold and pale with rapture. Those sounds fairly sank into his soul, which had only just been shaken with the bliss of love; they themselves were flaming with love. "Repeat it,"—he whispered, as soon as the last chord resounded. The old man cast upon him an eagle glance, struck his breast with his hand, and saying deliberately, in his native language:—"I made that, for I am a great musician,"—he again played his wonderful composition. There was no candle in the room; the light of the rising moon fell aslant through the window; the sensitive air trembled resonantly; the pale, little room seemed a sanctuary, and the head of the old man rose high and inspired in the silvery semi-darkness. Lavrétzky approached and embraced him. At first, Lemm did not respond to his embrace, he even repulsed it with his elbow; for a long time, without moving a single limb, he continued to gaze forth, as before, sternly, almost roughly, and only bellowed a couple of times: "Aha!" At last his transfigured face grew calm, relaxed, and, in reply to Lavrétzky's warm congratulations, he first smiled a little, then fell to weeping, feebly sobbing like a child.

"This is marvellous,"—he said:—"that precisely you should now have come; but I know—I know all."

"You know all?"—ejaculated Lavrétzky, in confusion.

"You have heard me,"—returned Lemm:—"have not you understood that I know all?"

Lavrétzky could not get to sleep until the morning: all night long, he sat on his bed. And Liza did not sleep: she prayed.

XXXV

The reader knows how Lavrétzky had grown up and developed; let us say a few words about Liza's bringing up. She was ten years old when her father died; but he had paid little heed to her. Overwhelmed with business, constantly absorbed in increasing his property, splenetic, harsh, impatient, he furnished money unsparingly for teachers, tutors, clothing, and the other wants of the children; but he could not endure, as he expressed it, "to dandle the squalling brats,"—and he had no time to dandle them: he worked, toiled over his business, slept little, occasionally played cards, worked again; he compared himself to a horse harnessed to a threshing-machine. "My life has rushed by fast," he said on his deathbed, with a proud smile on his parched lips. Márya Dmítrievna, in reality, troubled herself about Liza hardly more than did the father, although she had boasted to Lavrétzky that she alone had reared her children; she had dressed Liza like a doll, in the presence of visitors had patted her on the head, and called her, to her face, a clever child and a darling—and that was all: any regular care wearied the lazy gentlewoman. During her father's lifetime, Liza had been in the hands of a governess, Mlle. Moreau, from Paris, and after his death she had passed into the charge of Márfa Timoféevna. The reader is acquainted with Márfa Timoféevna; but Mlle. Moreau was a tiny, wrinkled creature, with birdlike ways and a tiny, birdlike mind. In her youth she had led a very dissipated life, and in her riper years she had but two passions left—for dainties and for cards. When she was gorged, was not playing cards, and not chattering, her face instantly assumed an almost deathlike expression: she would sit, and gaze, and breathe, and it was evident that no thought was passing through her head. It was not even possible to call her good-natured: there are also birds which are not good-natured. Whether it was in consequence of her frivolously-spent youth, or of the Paris air, which she had breathed since her childhood,—she harboured within her a certain cheap, general scepticism, which is usually expressed by the words: "*tout ça c'est des bêtises*." She talked an irregular, but purely Parisian jargon, did not gossip, was not capricious,—and what more could be desired in a governess? On Liza she had little influence; all the more powerful upon her was the influence of her nurse, Agáfya Vlásievna.

The lot of this woman was remarkable. She sprang from a peasant family; at the age of sixteen, they married her to a peasant; but there was a sharp distinction between her and her sister-peasant women. For twenty years her father had been the village elder, had accumulated a good deal of money, and had petted her. She was a wonderful beauty, the most dashingly-elegant peasant maid in all the country round about, clever, a good talker, daring. Her master, Dmítry Péstoff, the father of Márya Dmítrievna, a modest, quiet man, caught sight of her one day at the threshing, talked with her, and fell passionately in love with her.

Soon afterward, she became a widow; Péstoff, although he was a married man, took her into his house, and clothed her in the style of a house-servant. Agáfya immediately accommodated herself to her new position, exactly as though she had never lived in any other way. Her skin became white, she grew plump; her arms, under their muslin sleeves, became "like fine wheat flour," like those of a cook; the samovár stood constantly on her table; she would wear nothing but velvet and silk, she slept on a feather-bed of down. This blissful life lasted for the space of five years; but Dmítry Péstoff died: his widow, a good-natured gentlewoman, desirous of sparing her husband's memory, was not willing to behave dishonourably toward her rival, the more so, as Agáfya had never forgotten herself before her; but she married her to the cow-herd, and sent her out of her sight. Three years passed. Once, on a hot summer day, the lady of the manor went to her dairy. Agáfya treated her to such splendid cold cream, bore herself so modestly, and was so neat in person, and so cheerful and satisfied with everything, that her mistress announced to her her pardon, and permitted her to come to the manor-house; and six months later, she had become so attached to her, that she promoted her to the post of housekeeper, and entrusted the entire management to her. Again Agáfya came into power, again she grew plump and white-skinned; her mistress had complete confidence in her. In this manner, five more years elapsed. Again misfortune fell upon Agáfya. Her husband, whom she had had raised to the post of footman, took to drink, began to disappear from the house, and wound up by stealing six of the family's silver spoons, and hiding them—until a convenient opportunity—in his wife's chest. This was discovered. He was again degraded to the rank of cow-herd, and a sentence of disgrace was pronounced upon Agáfya; she was not banished from the house, but she was reduced from the place of housekeeper to that of seamstress, and ordered to wear a kerchief on her head, instead of a cap. To the amazement of all, Agáfya accepted the blow which had overtaken her with humble submission. She was then over thirty years of age, all her children had died, and her husband did not long survive. The time had arrived for her to come to a sense of her position; she did so. She became very taciturn and devout, never missed a single Matins service, nor a single Liturgy, and gave away all her fine clothes. Fifteen years she spent quietly, peacefully, with dignity, quarrelling with no one, yielding to every one. If any one spoke rudely to her,—she merely bowed, and returned thanks for the lesson. Her mistress had forgiven her long since, had removed the ban from her, and had given her a cap from her own head; but she herself refused to remove her kerchief, and always went about in a dark-hued gown; and after the death of her mistress, she became still more quiet and humble. A Russian easily conceives fear and affection; but it is difficult to win his respect: it is not soon given, nor to every one. Every one in the house respected Agáfya; no one even recalled her former sins, as though they had been buried in the earth, along with the old master.

When Kalítin became the husband of Márya Dmítrievna, he wished to entrust the housekeeping to Agáfya; but she declined, "because of the temptation"; he roared at her, she made him a lowly reverence, and left the room. The clever Kalítin understood people; and he also understood Agáfya, and did not forget her. On removing his residence to the town, he appointed her, with her own consent, as nurse to Liza, who had just entered her fifth year.

At first, Liza was frightened by the serious and stern face of her new nurse; but she speedily became accustomed to her, and conceived a strong affection for her. She herself was a serious child; her features recalled the clear-cut, regular face of Kalítin; only, she had not her father's eyes; hers beamed with a tranquil attention and kindness which are rare in children. She did not like to play with dolls, her laughter was neither loud nor long, she bore herself with decorum. She was not often thoughtful, and was never so without cause; after remaining silent for a time, she almost always ended by turning to some one of her elders, with a question which showed that her brain was working over a new impression. She very early ceased to lisp, and already in her fourth year she spoke with perfect distinctness. She was afraid of her father; her feeling toward her mother was undefined,—she did not fear her, neither did she fondle her; but she did not fondle Agáfya either, although she loved only her alone. Agáfya and she were never separated. It was strange to see them together. Agáfya, all in black, with a dark kerchief on her head, with a face thin and transparent as wax, yet still beautiful and expressive, would sit upright, engaged in knitting a stocking; at her feet, in a little arm-chair, sat Liza, also toiling over some sort of work, or, with her bright eyes uplifted gravely, listening to what Agáfya was relating to her, and Agáfya did not tell her fairy-stories; in a measured, even voice, she would narrate the life of the Most-pure Virgin, the lives of the hermits, the saints of God, of the holy martyrs; she would tell Liza how the holy men lived in the deserts, how they worked out their salvation, endured hunger and want,—and, fearing not kings, confessed Christ; how the birds of heaven brought them food, and the wild beasts obeyed them; how on those spots where their blood fell, flowers sprang up.—"Yellow violets?"—one day asked Liza, who was very fond of flowers.... Agáfya talked gravely and meekly to Liza, as though she felt that it was not for her to utter such lofty and sacred words. Liza listened to her—and the image of the Omnipresent, Omniscient God penetrated into her soul with a certain sweet power, filled her with pure, devout awe, and Christ became for her a person close to her, almost a relative: and Agáfya taught her to pray. Sometimes she woke Liza early, at daybreak, hastily dressed her, and surreptitiously took her to Matins: Liza followed her on tiptoe, hardly breathing; the chill and semi-obscurity of the dawn, the freshness and emptiness of the streets, the very mysteriousness of these unexpected absences, the cautious return to the house, to bed,—all this mingling of the forbidden, the strange, the holy, agitated the little girl, penetrated into the very depths of her being. Agáfya never condemned anybody, and did not scold Liza for her pranks. When she was displeased over anything, she simply held her peace; and Liza understood that silence; with the swift perspicacity of a child, she also understood very well when Agáfya was displeased with other people—with Márya Dmítrievna herself, or with Kalítin. Agáfya took care of Liza for a little more than three years; she was replaced by Mlle. Moreau; but the frivolous Frenchwoman, with her harsh manners and her exclamation:

"*tout ça c'est des bêtises*,"—could not erase from Liza's heart her beloved nurse: the seeds which had been sown had struck down roots too deep. Moreover, Agáfya, although she had ceased to have charge of Liza, remained in the house, and often saw her nursling, who confided in her as before.

But Agáfya could not get along with Márfa Timoféevna, when the latter came to live in the Kalítin house. The stern dignity of the former "peasant woman" did not please the impatient and self-willed old woman. Agáfya begged permission to go on a pilgrimage, and did not return. Dark rumours circulated, to the effect that she had withdrawn to a convent of Old Ritualists. But the traces left by her in Liza's soul were not effaced. As before, the latter went to the Liturgy as to a festival, prayed with delight, with a certain repressed and bashful enthusiasm, which secretly amazed Márya Dmítrievna not a little, although she put no constraint upon Liza, but merely endeavoured to moderate her zeal, and did not permit her to make an excessive number of prostrations: that was not lady-like manners, she said. Liza studied well,—that is to say, assiduously; God had not endowed her with particularly brilliant capacities, with a great mind; she acquired nothing without labour. She played well on the piano; but Lemm alone knew what it cost her. She read little; she had no "words of her own," but she had thoughts of her own, and she went her own way. It was not for nothing that she resembled her father: he, also, had not been wont to ask others what he should do. Thus she grew up—quietly, at leisure; thus she attained her nineteenth year. She was very pretty, without herself being aware of the fact. An unconscious, rather awkward grace revealed itself in her every movement; her voice rang with the silvery sound of unaffected youth, the slightest sensation of pleasure evoked a winning smile on her lips, imparted a deep gleam and a certain mysterious caress to her sparkling eyes. Thoroughly imbued with the sense of duty, with the fear of wounding any one whatsoever, with a kind and gentle heart, she loved every one in general, and no one in particular; God alone she loved with rapture, timidly, tenderly. Lavrétzky was the first to break in upon her tranquil inner life.

Such was Liza.

XXXVI

At twelve o'clock on the following day, Lavrétzky set out for the Kalítins'. On the way thither, he met Pánshin, who galloped past him on horseback, with his hat pulled down to his very eyebrows. At the Kalítins', Lavrétzky was not admitted,—for the first time since he had known them. Márya Dmítrievna was "lying down,"—so the lackey announced; "they" had a headache. Neither Márfa Timoféevna nor Lizavéta Mikhaílovna was at home. Lavrétzky strolled along the garden, in anxious hope of meeting Liza, but saw no one. He returned a couple of hours later, and received the same answer, in connection with which the lackey bestowed a sidelong glance upon him. It seemed to Lavrétzky impolite to intrude himself upon them for a third time that day—and he decided to drive out to Vasílievskoe, where, without reference to this, he had business to attend to. On the way he constructed various plans, each more beautiful than the other; but in his aunt's hamlet, sadness fell upon him; he entered into conversation with Antón; the old man, as though expressly, had nothing but cheerless thoughts in his mind. He narrated to Lavrétzky, how Glafíra Petróvna, before her death, had bitten her own hand,—and, after a short pause, he added: "Every man, master—dear little father, is given to devouring himself." It was already late when Lavrétzky set out on the return journey. The sounds of the preceding day took possession of him, the image of Liza arose in his soul in all its gentle transparency; he melted at the thought that she loved him,—and drove up to his little town-house in a composed and happy frame of mind.

The first thing which struck him on entering the anteroom was the scent of patchouli, which was very repulsive to him; several tall trunks and coffers were standing there. The face of the valet who ran forth to receive him seemed to him strange. Without accounting to himself for his impressions, he crossed the threshold of the drawing-room.... From the couch there rose to greet him a lady in a black gown with flounces, and raising a batiste handkerchief to her pale face, she advanced several paces, bent her carefully-dressed head,—and fell at his feet.... Then only did he recognise her: the lady was—his wife.

It took his breath away.... He leaned against the wall.

"Theodore, do not drive me away!"—she said in French, and her voice cut his heart like a knife.

He glanced at her without comprehending, yet he immediately noticed that she had grown pale and thin.

"Theodore,"—she went on, from time to time raising her eyes, and cautiously wringing her wondrously-beautiful fingers, with rosy, polished nails:—"Theodore, I am to blame toward you, deeply to blame,—I will say more, I am a criminal; but do you listen to me; repentance tortures me, I have become a burden to myself, I could not longer endure my position; how many times have I meditated returning to you, but I feared your wrath;—I have decided to break every connection with the past ... *puis, j'ai été si malade*,—I have been so ill,"—she added, and passed her hand across her brow and her cheek,—"I have taken advantage of the rumour of my death which had got into circulation, I have abandoned everything; without halting, day and night I have hastened hither; I have hesitated, for a long time, to present myself before you, my judge—*paraître devant vous, mon juge*,—but, at last, I made up my mind, remembering your invariable kindness, to come to you; I learned your address in Moscow. Believe me," she continued, softly rising from the floor, and seating herself on the very edge of an arm-chair:—"I have often meditated death, and I would have summoned up sufficient courage to take my life—akh, life is now an intolerable burden to me!—but the thought of my daughter, of my Ádotchka, held me back; she is here, she is asleep in the adjoining room, poor child! She is weary,—you shall see her: she, at least, is not guilty toward you,—and I am so unhappy, so unhappy!"—exclaimed Mme. Lavrétzky, and burst into tears.

Lavrétzky came to himself, at last; he separated himself from the wall, and moved toward the door.

"You are going away?"—said his wife, in despair:—"oh, this is cruel!—Without saying one word to me, without even one reproach.... This scorn is killing me, this is terrible!"

Lavrétzky stopped short.

"What is it that you wish to hear from me?"—he uttered, in a toneless voice.

"Nothing, nothing,"—she caught him up with vivacity:—"I know that I have no right to demand anything;—I am not a fool, believe me;—I do not hope, I do not dare to hope for your forgiveness;—I only venture to entreat you, that you will give me directions what I am to do, where I am to live?—I will fulfil your command, whatever it may be, like a slave."

"I have no commands to give you,"—returned Lavrétzky, in the same voice:—"you know, that everything is at an end between us ... and now more than ever.—You may live where you see fit;—and if your allowance is insufficient...."

"Akh, do not utter such dreadful words,"—Varvára Pávlovna interrupted him:—"spare me, if only ... if only for the sake of that angel...." And, as she said these words, Varvára Pávlovna flew headlong into the next room, and immediately returned with a tiny, very elegantly dressed little girl in her arms. Heavy, ruddy-gold curls fell over her pretty, rosy little face, over her large, black, sleepy eyes; she smiled, and blinked at the light, and clung with her chubby hand to her mother's neck.

"*Ada, vois, c'est ton père*,"—said Varvára Pávlovna, pushing the curls aside from her eyes, and giving her a hearty kiss:—"*prie le avec moi*."

"*C'est ça, papa?*"—lisped the little girl, brokenly.

"*Oui, mon enfant, n'est ce pas, que tu l'aimes?*"

But this was too much for Lavrétzky.

"In what melodrama is it that there is precisely such a scene?"—he muttered, and left the room.

Varvára Pávlovna stood for a while rooted to the spot, slightly shrugged her shoulders, carried the little girl into the other room, undressed her, and put her to bed. Then she got a book, sat down near the lamp, waited for about an hour, and, at last, lay down on the bed herself.

"*Eh bien, madame?*"—inquired her maid, a Frenchwoman, whom she had brought from Paris, as she removed her corsets.

"*Eh bien, Justine*,"—she replied;—"he has aged greatly, but it strikes me that he is as good-natured as ever.—Give me my gloves for the night, prepare my high-necked grey gown for to-morrow; and do not forget the mutton chops for Ada.... Really, it will be difficult to obtain them here; but we must make the effort."

"*À la guerre, comme à la guerre*,"—responded Justine, and put out the light.

XXXVII

For more than two hours Lavrétzky roamed about the streets of the town. The night which he had spent in the suburbs of Paris recurred to his mind. His heart swelled to bursting within him, and in his head, which was empty, and, as it were, stunned, the same set of thoughts kept swirling,—dark, wrathful, evil thoughts. "She is alive, she is here," he whispered, with constantly augmenting amazement. He felt that he had lost Liza. Bile choked him; this blow had struck him too suddenly. How could he so lightly have believed the absurd gossip of a feuilleton, a scrap of paper? "Well, and if I had not believed it, what difference would that have made? I should not have known that Liza loves me; she herself would not have known it." He could not banish from himself the form, the voice, the glances of his wife ... and he cursed himself, cursed everything in the world.

Worn out, he arrived toward morning at Lemm's. For a long time, he could produce no effect with his knocking; at last, the old man's head, in a nightcap, made its appearance in the window, sour, wrinkled, no longer bearing the slightest resemblance to that inspiredly-morose head which, four and twenty hours previously, had gazed on Lavrétzky from the full height of its artistic majesty.

"What do you want?"—inquired Lemm:—"I cannot play every night; I have taken a decoction."—But, evidently, Lavrétzky's face was very strange: the old man made a shield for his eyes out of his hands, stared at his nocturnal visitor, and admitted him.

Lavrétzky entered the room, and sank down on a chair; the old man halted in front of him, with the skirts of his motley-hued, old dressing-gown tucked up, writhing and mumbling with his lips.

"My wife has arrived,"—said Lavrétzky, raising his head, and suddenly breaking into an involuntary laugh.

Lemm's face expressed surprise, but he did not even smile, and only wrapped himself more closely in his dressing-gown.

"You see, you do not know,"—went on Lavrétzky:—"I imagined ... I read in a newspaper, that she was no longer alive."

"O—o, you read that a short time ago?"—asked Lemm.

"Yes."

"O—o,"—repeated the old man, and elevated his eyebrows.—"And she has arrived?"

"Yes. She is now at my house; but I ... I am an unhappy man."

And again he broke into a laugh.

"You are an unhappy man,"—repeated Lemm, slowly.

"Christofór Feódoritch,"—began Lavrétzky:—"will you undertake to deliver a note?"

"H'm. May I inquire, to whom?"

"To Liza...."

"Ah,—yes, yes, I understand. Very well. But when must the note be delivered?"

"To-morrow, as early as possible."

"H'm. I can send Katrina, my cook. No, I will go myself."

"And will you bring me the answer?"

"Yes, I will."

Lemm sighed.

"Yes, my poor young friend; you really are—an unhappy man."

Lavrétzky wrote a couple of words to Liza: he informed her of his wife's arrival, begged her to appoint a meeting,—and flung himself on the narrow divan, face to the wall; and the old man lay down on the bed, and tossed about for a long time, coughing and taking sips of his decoction.

Morning came: they both rose. With strange eyes they gazed at each other. Lavrétzky wanted to kill himself at that moment. The cook, Katrina, brought them some bad coffee. The clock struck eight. Lemm put on his hat, and saying that he had a lesson to give at the Kalítins' at nine, but that he would find a decent pretext, set out. Lavrétzky again flung himself on the little couch, and again, from the depths of his soul, a sorrowful laugh welled up. He thought of how his wife had driven him out of his house; he pictured to himself Liza's position, closed his eyes, and threw his hands behind his head. At last Lemm returned, and brought him a scrap of paper, on which Liza had scrawled with pencil the following words: "We cannot see each other to-day; perhaps—to-morrow evening. Farewell." Lavrétzky quietly and abstractedly thanked Lemm, and went to his own house.

He found his wife at breakfast; Ada, all curls, in a white frock with blue ribbons, was eating a mutton chop. Varvára Pávlovna immediately rose, as soon as Lavrétzky entered the room, and approached him, with humility depicted on her face. He requested her to follow him to his study, locked the door behind him, and began to stride to and fro; she sat down, laid one hand modestly on the other, and began to watch him with her still beautiful, although slightly painted eyes.

For a long time Lavrétzky did not speak: he felt that he could not control himself; he perceived clearly, that Varvára Pávlovna was not in the least afraid of him, but was assuming the air of being on the very verge of falling into a swoon.

"Listen, madam,"—he began, at last, breathing heavily at times, grinding his teeth:—"there is no necessity for our dissembling with each other; I do not believe in your repentance; and even if it were genuine, it is impossible for me to become reconciled to you, to live with you again."

Varvára Pávlovna compressed her lips and narrowed her eyes. "This is disgust,"—she thought:—"of course! I am no longer even a woman to him."

"It is impossible,"—repeated Lavrétzky, and buttoned up his coat to the throat.—"I do not know why you have taken it into your head to come hither: probably, you have no money left."
"Alas! you are insulting me,"—whispered Varvára Pávlovna.
"However that may be,—you are, unhappily, my wife, nevertheless. I cannot turn you out ... and this is what I have to propose to you. You may set out, this very day, if you like, for Lavríki, and live there; the house is good, as you know; you will receive all that is necessary, in addition to your allowance.... Do you agree?"
Varvára Pávlovna raised her embroidered handkerchief to her eyes.
"I have already told you,"—she said, her lips twitching nervously:—"that I shall agree to anything whatever you may see fit to do with me: on this occasion, nothing is left for me to do, except to ask you: will you permit me, at least, to thank you for your magnanimity?"
"No gratitude, I beg of you; it is better so,"—hastily returned Lavrétzky.—"Accordingly,"—he went on, approaching the door:—"I may count upon...."
"To-morrow I shall be at Lavríki,"—said Varvára Pávlovna, respectfully rising from her seat.—"But, Feódor Ivánitch" (she no longer called him Theodore)....
"What do you want?"
"I know that I have, as yet, in no way earned my forgiveness; may I hope, at least, in time...."
"Ekh, Varvára Pávlovna,"—Lavrétzky interrupted her:—"you are a clever woman, and as I am not a fool, I know that that is quite unnecessary for you. And I forgave you long ago; but there was always a gulf between us."
"I shall know how to submit,"—replied Varvára Pávlovna, and bowed her head. "I have not forgotten my fault; I should not be surprised to learn that you were even delighted at the news of my death,"—she added gently, pointing slightly with her hand at the copy of the newspaper which lay on the table, forgotten by Lavrétzky.
Feódor Ivánitch shuddered: the feuilleton was marked with a pencil. Varvára Pávlovna gazed at him with still greater humility. She was very pretty at that moment. Her grey Paris gown gracefully clothed her willowy form, which was almost that of a girl of seventeen; her slender, delicate neck encircled with a white collar, her bosom which rose and fell evenly, her arms devoid of bracelets and rings,—her whole figure, from her shining hair to the tip of her barely revealed little boot, was so elegant....
Lavrétzky swept an angry glance over her, came near exclaiming: "Brava!" came near smiting her in the temple with his fist—and left the room. An hour later, he had already set out for Vasílievskoe, and two hours later, Varvára Pávlovna gave orders that the best carriage in town should be engaged, donned a simple straw hat with a black veil, and a modest mantle, entrusted Ada to Justine, and set out for the Kalítins: from the inquiries instituted by her servant she had learned that her husband was in the habit of going to them every day.

XXXVIII

The day of the arrival of Lavrétzky's wife in town of O * * *, a cheerless day for him, was also a painful day for Liza. She had not succeeded in going down-stairs and bidding her mother "good morning," before the trampling of a horse's hoofs resounded under the window, and with secret terror she beheld Pánshin riding into the yard: "He has presented himself thus early for a definitive explanation,"—she thought—and she was not mistaken; after spending a while in the drawing-room, he suggested that she should go with him into the garden, and demanded her decision as to his fate. Liza summoned up her courage, and informed him that she could not be his wife. He listened to her to the end, as he stood with his side toward her, and his hat pulled down on his brows; courteously, but in an altered tone, he asked her: was that her last word, and had he, in any way, given her cause for such a change in her ideas? then he pressed his hand to his eyes, sighed briefly and abruptly, and removed his hand from his face.
"I have not wished to follow the beaten path,"—he said, in a dull voice,—"I have wished to find my companion after the inclination of the heart; but, evidently, that was not destined to be. Farewell, dream!"—He bowed profoundly to Liza, and returned to the house.
She hoped that he would immediately take his departure; but he went into Márya Dmítrievna's boudoir, and sat with her for about an hour. As he went away, he said to Liza: "*Votre mère vous appelle; adieu à jamais* ..." mounted his horse, and set off from the very porch at full gallop. Liza went in to Márya Dmítrievna, and found her in tears: Pánshin had communicated to her his misfortune.
"Why hast thou killed me? Why hast thou killed me?"—in this wise did the mortified widow begin her complaints.—"Whom else didst thou want? What! is not he a suitable husband for thee? A Junior Gentleman

of the Emperor's Bedchamber! not *interessant*! He might marry any Maid of Honour he chose in Petersburg. And I—I had been hoping so! And hast thou changed long toward him? What has sent this cloud drifting hither—it did not come of itself! Can it be that ninny? A pretty counsellor thou hast found!

"And he, my dear one,"—pursued Márya Dmítrievna:—"how respectful, how attentive, even in his own grief! He has promised not to abandon me. Akh, I shall not survive this! Akh, I have got a deadly headache. Send Palásha to me. Thou wilt be the death of me, if thou dost not change thy mind,—dost thou hear?" And calling her an ingrate a couple of times, Márya Dmítrievna sent Liza away.

She went to her own room. But before she had time to recover her breath from her explanation with Pánshin and her mother, another thunderstorm broke over her, and this time from a quarter whence she had least expected it. Márfa Timoféevna entered her room, and immediately slammed the door behind her. The old woman's face was pale, her cap was awry, her eyes were flashing, her hands and lips were trembling. Liza was amazed: never before had she seen her sensible and reasonable aunt in such a state.

"Very fine, madam,"—began Márfa Timoféevna, in a tremulous and broken whisper: "very fine indeed! From whom hast thou learned this, my mother?... Give me water; I cannot speak."

"Calm yourself, aunty; what is the matter with you?"—said Liza, giving her a glass of water.—"Why, you yourself did not favour Mr. Pánshin."

Márfa Timoféevna set down the glass.

"I cannot drink: I shall knock out my last remaining teeth. What dost thou mean by Panshín? What has Panshín to do with it? Do thou tell me, rather, who taught thee to appoint rendezvous by night—hey? my mother?"

Liza turned pale.

"Please do not think of excusing thyself,"—continued Márfa Timoféevna.—"Schúrotchka herself saw all, and told me. I have forbidden her to chatter, but she does not lie."

"I have made no excuses, aunty,"—said Liza, in a barely audible voice.

"Ah, ah! Now, see here, my mother; didst thou appoint a meeting with him, with that old sinner, that quiet man?"

"No."

"Then how did it come about?"

"I went down-stairs, to the drawing-room, for a book; he was in the garden, and called me."

"And thou wentest? Very fine. And thou lovest him, dost thou not?"

"I do,"—replied Liza, in a tranquil voice.

"Gracious heavens! she loves him!"—Márfa Timoféevna tore off her cap.—"She loves a married man! Hey? she loves!"

"He told me,"—began Liza....

"What did he tell thee, the darling, wha-at was it?"

"He told me that his wife was dead."

Márfa Timoféevna crossed herself.—"The kingdom of heaven be hers,"—she whispered:—"she was a frivolous woman—God forgive her. So that's how it is: then he's a widower. Yes, I see that he is equal to anything. He killed off his first wife, and now he's after another. Thou art a sly one, art thou not? Only, this is what I have to say to thee, niece: in my time, when I was young, girls were severely punished for such capers. Thou must not be angry with me, my mother; only fools get angry at the truth. I have given orders that he is not to be admitted to-day. I am fond of him, but I shall never forgive him for this. A widower, forsooth! Give me some water.... But thou art my brave girl, for sending Panshín off with a long face; only, do not sit out nights with that goat's breed,—with men,—do not grieve me, an old woman! For I am not always amiable—I know how to bite, also!... A widower!"

Márfa Timoféevna departed, but Liza sat down in the corner and began to cry. She felt bitter in soul; she had not deserved such humiliation. Her love had not announced its presence by cheerfulness; this was the second time she had wept since the night before. That new, unexpected feeling had barely come to life in her heart when she had had to pay so heavily for it, when strange hands had roughly touched her private secret! She felt ashamed, and pained, and bitter: but there was neither doubt nor terror in her,—and Lavrétzky became all the dearer to her. She had hesitated as long as she did not understand herself; but after that meeting—she could hesitate no longer; she knew that she loved,—and had fallen in love honourably, not jestingly, she had become strongly attached, for her whole life; she felt that force could not break that bond.

XXXIX

Márya Dmítrievna was greatly perturbed when the arrival of Varvára Pávlovna was announced to her; she did not even know whether to receive her; she was afraid of offending Feódor Ivánitch. At last, curiosity carried the day. "What of it?"—she said to herself,—"why, she is a relative also,"—and seating herself in her arm-chair, she said to the lackey: "Ask her in!" Several minutes elapsed; the door opened, Varvára Pávlovna approached Márya Dmítrievna swiftly, with barely audible footsteps, and, without giving her a chance to rise from her chair, almost went down on her knees before her.

"Thank you, aunty,"—she began in a touched and gentle voice, in Russian: "thank you! I had not hoped for such condescension on your part; you are as kind as an angel."

As she uttered these words, Varvára Pávlovna unexpectedly took possession of one of Márya Dmítrievna's hands, and pressing it lightly in her pale-lilac gloves, obsequiously raised it to her full, rosy lips. Márya Dmítrievna completely lost her head, on beholding such a beautiful, charmingly-dressed woman, almost on her knees at her feet; she did not know what to do: she did not wish to withdraw her hand, she wished to give her a seat, and to say something amiable to her; she ended by rising, and kissing Varvára Pávlovna on her smooth, fragrant brow. Varvára Pávlovna was perfectly dumfounded by this kiss.

"Good morning,—*bon jour*,"—said Márya Dmítrievna:—"of course, I had no idea, ... however, of course, I am delighted to see you. You understand, my dear,—it is not for me to sit in judgment between wife and husband."

"My husband is wholly in the right,"—Varvára Pávlovna interrupted her:—"I alone am to blame."

"That is a very praiseworthy sentiment,"—returned Márya Dmítrievna:—"very. Have you been here long? Have you seen him? But sit down, pray."

"I arrived yesterday,"—replied Varvára Pávlovna, meekly seating herself on a chair; "I have seen Feódor Ivánitch, I have talked with him."

"Ah! Well, and how does he take it?"

"I was afraid that my sudden arrival would arouse his wrath,"—went on Varvára Pávlovna:—"but he did not deprive me of his presence."

"That is to say, he did not.... Yes, yes, I understand,"—ejaculated Márya Dmítrievna.—"He is only rather rough in appearance, but his heart is soft."

"Feódor Ivánitch has not forgiven me; he would not listen to me.... But he was so kind as to appoint Lavríki for my place of residence."

"Ah! A very fine estate!"

"I set out thither to-morrow, in compliance with his will; but I considered it my duty to call on you first."

"I am very, very grateful to you, my dear. One must never forget one's relatives. And, do you know, I am astonished that you speak Russian so well. *C'est étonnant!*"

Varvára Pávlovna sighed.

"I have spent too much time abroad, Márya Dmítrievna, I know that; but my heart has always been Russian, and I have not forgotten my native land."

"Exactly so, exactly so; that is the best of all. Feódor Ivánitch, however, did not in the least expect you.... Yes; believe my experience;*la patrie avant tout*. Akh, please show me,—what a charming mantle that is you have on!"

"Do you like it?"—Varvára Pávlovna promptly dropped it from her shoulders.—"It is a very simple thing, from Madame Baudran."

"That is instantly perceptible. From Madame Baudran.... How charming, and what taste! I am convinced that you have brought with you a mass of the most entrancing things. I should like to look them over."

"My entire toilette is at your service, my dearest aunt. If you will permit, I can give your maid some points. I have a maid-servant from Paris,—a wonderful seamstress."

"You are very kind, my dear. But, really, I am ashamed."

"Ashamed! ..." repeated Varvára Pávlovna, reproachfully.—"If you wish to make me happy,—command me, as though I belonged to you."

Márya Dmítrievna thawed.

"*Vous êtes charmante*," she said.—"But why do not you take off your bonnet, your gloves?"

"What? You permit?"—asked Varvára Pávlovna, clasping her hands, as though with emotion.

"Of course; for you will dine with us, I hope. I ... I will introduce you to my daughter."—Márya Dmítrievna became slightly confused. "Well! here goes!"—she said to herself.—"She is not quite well to-day."

"Oh, *ma tante*, how kind you are!"—exclaimed Varvára Pávlovna, and raised her handkerchief to her eyes.

A page announced the arrival of Gedeónovsky. The old chatterbox entered, made his bows, and smiled. Márya Dmítrievna presented him to her visitor. He came near being discomfited at first; but Varvára Pávlovna treated him with such coquettish respect, that his ears began to burn, and fibs, scandals, amiable remarks trickled out of his mouth like honey. Varvára Pávlovna listened to him with a repressed smile, and became rather talkative herself. She modestly talked about Paris, about her travels, about Baden; twice she made Márya Dmítrievna laugh, and on each occasion she heaved another little sigh, as though she were mentally reproaching herself for her ill-timed mirth; she asked permission to bring Ada; removing her gloves, she showed, with her smooth hands washed with soap *à la guimauve*, how and where flounces, ruches, lace, and knots of ribbon were worn; she promised to bring a phial of the new English perfume, Victoria's Essence, and rejoiced like a child when Márya Dmítrievna consented to accept it as a gift; she wept at the remembrance of the feeling she had experienced when, for the first time, she had heard the Russian bells;—"so profoundly did they stagger my very heart,"—she said.

At that moment, Liza entered.

From the morning, from the very moment when, chilled with terror, she had perused Lavrétzky's note, Liza had been preparing herself to meet his wife; she had a presentiment that she should see her, by way of punishment to her own criminal hopes, as she called them. She had made up her mind not to shun her. The sudden crisis in her fate had shaken her to the very foundations; in the course of about two hours her face had grown haggard; but she did not shed a tear. "It serves me right!"—she said to herself, with difficulty and agitation suppressing in her soul certain bitter, spiteful impulses, which alarmed even herself:—"Come, I must go down!"—she thought, as soon as she heard of Mme. Lavrétzky's arrival, and she went.... For a long time she stood outside the door of the drawing-room, before she could bring herself to open it; with the thought: "I am to blame toward her,"—she crossed the threshold, and forced herself to look at her, forced herself to smile. Varvára Pávlovna advanced to meet her as soon as she saw her, and made a slight but nevertheless respectful inclination before her.—"Allow me to introduce myself,"—she began, in an insinuating voice:—"your *maman*is so indulgent toward me, that I hope you will also be ... kind." The expression on Varvára Pávlovna's face, as she uttered this last word, her sly smile, her cold and at the same time soft glance, the movement of her arms and shoulders, her very gown, her whole being, aroused in Liza such a feeling of repulsion, that she could make her no answer, and with an effort she offered her hand. "This young lady despises me,"—thought Varvára Pávlovna, as she warmly pressed Liza's cold fingers, and, turning to Márya Dmítrievna, she said in an undertone: "*Mais elle est délicieuse!*" Liza flushed faintly, insult was audible to her in this exclamation; but she made up her mind not to trust her impressions, and seated herself by the window, at her embroidery-frame. Even there, Varvára Pávlovna did not leave her in peace: she went up to her, began to praise her taste, her art.... Liza's heart beat violently and painfully, she could hardly control herself, she could hardly sit still on her chair. It seemed to her that Varvára Pávlovna knew everything, and, secretly triumphing, was jeering at her. Fortunately for her, Gedeónovsky entered into conversation with Varvára Pávlovna, and distracted her attention. Liza bent over her embroidery-frame, and stealthily watched her. "*He* loved that woman,"—she said to herself. But she immediately banished from her head the thought of Lavrétzky: she was afraid of losing control over herself, she felt that her head was softly whirling. Márya Dmítrievna began to talk about music.

"I have heard, my dear,"—she began:—"that you are a wonderful performer."

"It is a long time since I have played,"—replied Varvára Pávlovna, as she seated herself, in a leisurely manner, at the piano, and ran her fingers in a dashing way over the keys.—"Would you like to have me play?"

"Pray do."

Varvára Pávlovna played a brilliant and difficult étude of Herz in a masterly style. She had a great deal of strength and execution.

"A sylph!"—exclaimed Gedeónovsky.

"Remarkable!"—assented Márya Dmítrievna.—"Well, Varvára Pávlovna, I must confess,"—she said, calling her, for the first time, by her name:—"you have amazed me; you might even give concerts. We have an old musician here, a German, an eccentric fellow, very learned; he gives Liza lessons; he will simply go out of his mind over you."

"Lizavéta Mikhaílovna is also a musician?"—inquired Varvára Pávlovna, turning her head slightly in her direction.

"Yes, she plays quite well, and loves music; but what does that signify, in comparison with you? But there is a young man here; you ought to make his acquaintance. He is—an artist in soul, and composes very prettily. He is the only one who can fully appreciate you."

"A young man?"—said Varvára Pávlovna.—"Who is he? Some poor fellow?"

"Good gracious,—he's our chief cavalier, and not among us only—*et à Pétersbourg*. A Junior Gentleman of the Bedchamber, received in the best society. You certainly must have heard of him,—Pánshin, Vladímir Nikoláitch. He is here on a government commission ... a future Minister, upon my word!"

"And an artist?"

"An artist in soul, and such a charming fellow. You shall see him. He has been at my house very frequently of late; I have invited him for this evening; I hope that he will come,"—added Márya Dmítrievna, with a gentle sigh and a sidelong bitter smile.

Liza understood the significance of that smile; but she cared nothing for it.

"And is he young?"—repeated Varvára Pávlovna, lightly modulating from one key to another.

"He is eight and twenty—and of the most happy personal appearance. *Un jeune homme accompli*, upon my word."

"A model young man, one may say,"—remarked Gedeónovsky.

Varvára Pávlovna suddenly began to play a noisy Strauss waltz, which started with such a mighty and rapid trill as made even Gedeónovsky start; in the very middle of the waltz, she abruptly changed into a mournful motif, and wound up with the aria from "Lucia": "Fra poco."... She had reflected that merry music was not compatible with her situation. The aria from "Lucia," with emphasis on the sentimental notes, greatly affected Márya Dmítrievna.

"What soul!"—she said, in a low tone, to Gedeónovsky.

"A sylph!"—repeated Gedeónovsky, and rolled his eyes heavenward.

Dinner-time arrived. Márfa Timoféevna came down-stairs when the soup was already standing on the table. She treated Varvára Pávlovna very coolly, replying with half-words to her amiabilities, and not looking at her. Varvára Pávlovna herself speedily comprehended that she could do nothing with the old woman, and ceased to address her; on the other hand, Márya Dmítrievna became more affectionate than ever with her guest: her aunt's discourtesy enraged her. However, Varvára Pávlovna was not the only person at whom Márfa Timoféevna refused to look: she never cast a glance at Liza, either, although her eyes fairly flashed. She sat like a stone image, all sallow, pale, with tightly compressed lips—and ate nothing. Liza seemed to be composed; and, as a matter of fact, all had become more tranquil in her soul; a strange insensibility, the insensibility of the man condemned to death, had come upon her. At dinner Varvára Pávlovna talked little: she seemed to have become timid once more, and spread over her face an expression of modest melancholy. Gedeónovsky alone enlivened the conversation with his tales, although he kept casting cowardly glances at Márfa Timoféevna, and a cough and tickling in the throat seized upon him every time that he undertook to lie in her presence,—but she did not hinder him, she did not interrupt him. After dinner it appeared that Varvára Pávlovna was extremely fond of preference; this pleased Márya Dmítrievna to such a degree, that she even became greatly affected, and thought to herself:—"But what a fool Feódor Ivánitch must be: he was not able to appreciate such a woman!"

She sat down to play cards with her and Gedeónovsky, while Márfa Timoféevna led Liza off to her own rooms up-stairs, saying that she looked ill, that her head must be aching.

"Yes, she has a frightful headache,"—said Márya Dmítrievna, turning to Varvára Pávlovna, and rolling up her eyes.—"I myself have such sick-headaches...." Liza entered her aunt's room and dropped on a chair, exhausted. Márfa Timoféevna gazed at her for a long time, in silence, knelt down softly in front of her—and began, in the same speechless manner, to kiss her hands, in turn. Liza leaned forward, blushed, and fell to weeping, but did not raise Márfa Timoféevna, did not withdraw her hands: she felt that she had not the right to withdraw them, had not the right to prevent the old woman showing her contrition, her sympathy, asking her pardon for what had taken place on the day before; and Márfa Timoféevna could not have done with kissing those poor, pale, helpless hands—and silent tears streamed from her eyes and from Liza's eyes; and the cat Matrós purred in the wide arm-chair beside the ball of yarn and the stocking, the elongated flame of the shrine-lamp quivered gently and flickered in front of the holy picture,—in the adjoining room, behind the door, stood Nastásya Kárpovna, and also stealthily wiped her eyes, with a checked handkerchief rolled up into a ball.

XL

And, in the meantime, down-stairs in the drawing-room preference was in progress; Márya Dmítrievna won, and was in high spirits. A footman entered, and announced the arrival of Pánshin.
Márya Dmítrievna dropped her cards, and fidgeted about in her chair; Varvára Pávlovna looked at her with a half-smile, then directed her gaze to the door. Pánshin made his appearance, in a black frock-coat, with a tall English collar, buttoned up to the throat. "It was painful for me to obey, but you see I have come." That was what his freshly-shaved, unsmiling face expressed.
"Goodness, *Woldemar*,"—exclaimed Márya Dmítrievna:—"you always used to enter without being announced!"
Pánshin replied to Márya Dmítrievna merely with a look, bowed courteously to her, but did not kiss her hand. She introduced him to Varvára Pávlovna; he retreated a pace, bowed to her with equal courtesy, but with a shade of elegance and deference, and seated himself at the card-table. The game of preference soon came to an end. Pánshin inquired after Lizavéta Mikhaílovna, learned that she did not feel quite well, and expressed his regrets; then he entered into conversation with Varvára Pávlovna, weighing and chiselling clearly every word, in diplomatic fashion, respectfully listening to her replies to the very end. But the importance of his diplomatic tone had no effect on Varvára Pávlovna, did not communicate itself to her. Quite the contrary: she gazed into his face with merry attention, talked in a free-and-easy way, and her delicate nostrils quivered slightly, as though with suppressed laughter. Márya Dmítrievna began to extol her talent; Pánshin inclined his head as politely as his collar permitted, declared that "he was convinced of it in advance,"—and turned the conversation almost on Metternich himself. Varvára Pávlovna narrowed her velvety eyes, and saying, in a low tone: "Why, you also are an artist yourself, *un confrère*,"—added in a still lower tone: "*Venez!*"—and nodded her head in the direction of the piano. That one carelessly dropped word: "*Venez!*"—instantaneously, as though by magic, altered Pánshin's entire aspect. His careworn mien vanished; he smiled, became animated, unbuttoned his coat, and repeating: "What sort of an artist am I, alas! But you, I hear, are a genuine artist"—wended his way, in company with Varvára Pávlovna, to the piano.
"Make him sing his romance:—'When the moon floats,'"—exclaimed Márya Dmítrievna.
"Do you sing?"—said Varvára Pávlovna, illuminating him with a bright, swift glance.—"Sit down."
Pánshin began to decline.
"Sit down,"—she repeated, insistently tapping the back of the chair.
He sat down, coughed, pulled open his collar, and sang his romance.
"*Charmant!*"—said Varvára Pávlovna:—"you sing beautifully, *vous avez du style*,—sing it again."
She walked round the piano, and took up her stand directly opposite Pánshin. He sang his romance again, imparting a melodramatic quiver to his voice. Varvára Pávlovna gazed intently at him, with her elbows propped on the piano, and her white hands on a level with her lips. Pánshin finished.
"*Charmant, charmante idée*,"—said she, with the calm confidence of an expert.—"Tell me, have you written anything for the female voice, for a mezzo-soprano?"
"I hardly write anything,"—replied Pánshin;—"you see, I only do this sort of thing in the intervals between business affairs ... but do you sing?"
"Yes."
"Oh! do sing something for us,"—said Márya Dmítrievna.
Varvára Pávlovna pushed back her hair from her flushed cheeks with her hand, and shook her head.
"Our voices ought to go well together,"—she said, turning to Pánshin:—"let us sing a duet. Do you know 'Son geloso,' or 'La ci darem,' or 'Mira la bianca luna'?"
"I used to sing 'Mira la bianca luna,'"—replied Pánshin:—"but I have forgotten it long ago."
"Never mind, we will try it over in an undertone. Let me come."
Varvára Pávlovna sat down at the piano. Pánshin stood beside her. They sang the duet in an undertone, Varvára Pávlovna correcting him several times; then they sang it aloud, then they repeated it twice: "Mira la bianca lu...u...una." Varvára Pávlovna's voice had lost its freshness, but she managed it very adroitly. Pánshin was timid at first, and sang rather out of tune, but later on he warmed up, and if he did not sing faultlessly, at least he wriggled his shoulders, swayed his whole body, and elevated his hand now and then, like a genuine singer. Varvára Pávlovna played two or three little things of Thalberg's, and coquettishly "recited" a French ariette. Márya Dmítrievna no longer knew how to express her delight; several times she was on the point of sending for Liza; Gedeónovsky, also, found no words and merely rocked his head,—but all of a sudden he yawned, and barely succeeded in concealing his mouth with his hand. This yawn did not escape Varvára Pávlovna; she suddenly turned her back to the piano, said: "*Assez de musique, comme ça*; let us chat,"—and folded her hands. "*Oui, assez de musique*,"—merrily repeated Pánshin—and struck up a conversation with

her,—daring, light, in the French language. "Exactly as in the best Parisian salon,"—thought Márya Dmítrievna, as she listened to their evasive and nimble speeches. Pánshin felt perfectly contented; his eyes sparkled, he smiled; at first, he passed his hand over his face, contracted his brows, and sighed spasmodically when he chanced to meet the glances of Márya Dmítrievna; but later on, he entirely forgot her, and surrendered himself completely to the enjoyment of the half-fashionable, half-artistic chatter. Varvára Pávlovna showed herself to be a great philosopher: she had an answer ready for everything, she did not hesitate over anything, she doubted nothing; it could be seen that she had talked much and often with clever persons of various sorts. All her thoughts, all her feelings, circled about Paris. Pánshin turned the conversation on literature: it appeared that she, as well as he, read only French books: Georges Sand excited her indignation; Balzac she admired, although he fatigued her; in Sue and Scribe she discerned great experts of the heart; she adored Dumas and Féval; in her soul she preferred Paul de Kock to the whole of them, but, of course, she did not even mention his name. To tell the truth, literature did not interest her greatly. Varvára Pávlovna very artfully avoided everything which could even distantly recall her position; there was not a hint about love in her remarks: on the contrary, they were rather distinguished by severity toward the impulses of passion, by disenchantment, by meekness. Pánshin retorted; she disagreed with him ... but, strange to say!—at the very time when words of condemnation, often harsh, were issuing from her lips, the sound of those words caressed and enervated, and her eyes said ... precisely what those lovely eyes said, it would be difficult to state; but their speech was not severe, not clear, yet sweet. Pánshin endeavoured to understand their mysterious significance, endeavoured to talk with his own eyes, but he was conscious that he was not at all successful; he recognised the fact that Varvára Pávlovna, in her quality of a genuine foreign lioness, stood above him, and therefore he was not in full control of himself. Varvára Pávlovna had a habit, while talking, of lightly touching the sleeve of her interlocutor; these momentary touches greatly agitated Vladímir Nikoláitch. Varvára Pávlovna possessed the art of getting on easily with every one; two hours had not elapsed before it seemed to Pánshin that he had known her always, and Liza, that same Liza, whom he loved, nevertheless, to whom he had offered his hand on the preceding day,—vanished as in a mist. Tea was served; the conversation became still more unconstrained. Márya Dmítrievna rang for her page, and ordered him to tell Liza to come down-stairs if her head felt better. Pánshin, on hearing Liza's name, set to talking about self-sacrifice, about who was the more capable of sacrifice—man or woman? Márya Dmítrievna immediately became agitated, began to assert that woman is the more capable, declared that she would prove it in two words, got entangled, and wound up by a decidedly infelicitous comparison. Varvára Pávlovna picked up a music-book, half-concealed herself with it, and leaning over in the direction of Pánshin, nibbling at a biscuit, with a calm smile on her lips and in her glance, she remarked, in an undertone: "*Elle n'a pas inventé la poudre, la bonne dame.*" Pánshin was somewhat alarmed and amazed at Varvára Pávlovna's audacity; but he did not understand how much scorn for him, himself, was concealed in that unexpected sally, and, forgetting the affection and the devotion of Márya Dmítrievna, forgetting the dinners wherewith she had fed him, the money which she had lent him,—he, with the same little smile, the same tone, replied (unlucky wight!): "*Je crois bien,*"—and not even: "*Je crois bien,*" but:—"*Je crois ben!*"

Varvára Pávlovna cast a friendly glance at him, and rose. Liza had entered; in vain had Márfa Timoféevna sought to hold her back: she had made up her mind to endure the trial to the end. Varvára Pávlovna advanced to meet her, in company with Pánshin, on whose face the former diplomatic expression had again made its appearance.

"How is your health?"—he asked Liza.

"I feel better now, thank you,"—she replied.

"We have been having a little music here; it is a pity that you did not hear Varvára Pávlovna. She sings superbly, *un artiste consommée*."

"Come here, *ma chérie*,"—rang out Márya Dmítrievna's voice.

Varvára Pávlovna instantly, with the submissiveness of a little child, went up to her, and seated herself on a small tabouret at her feet. Márya Dmítrievna had called her for the purpose of leaving her daughter alone with Pánshin, if only for a moment: she still secretly cherished the hope that the girl would come to her senses. Moreover, a thought had occurred to her, to which she desired to give immediate expression.

"Do you know,"—she whispered to Varvára Pávlovna:—"I want to make an effort to reconcile you with your husband: I do not guarantee success, but I will try. You know that he has great respect for me."

Varvára Pávlovna slowly raised her eyes to Márya Dmítrievna, and clasped her hands prettily.

"You would be my saviour, *ma tante*,"—she said, in a mournful voice:—"I do not know how to thank you for all your affection; but I am too guilty toward Feódor Ivánitch; he cannot forgive me."

"But is it possible that you ... really ..." began Márya Dmítrievna, with curiosity.
"Do not ask me,"—Varvára Pávlovna interrupted her, and dropped her eyes.—"I was young, giddy.... However, I do not wish to defend myself."
"Well, nevertheless, why not make the effort? Do not despair,"—returned Márya Dmítrievna, and was on the point of patting her on the shoulder, but glanced at her face—and grew timid. "She is a modest, modest creature,"—she thought,—"and exactly like a young girl still."
"Are you ill?"—Pánshin was saying, meanwhile, to Liza.
"Yes, I am not very well."
"I understand you,"—he said, after a rather prolonged silence.—"Yes, I understand you."
"How so?"
"I understand you,"—significantly repeated Pánshin, who simply did not know what to say.
Liza became confused, and then said to herself: "So be it!" Pánshin assumed a mysterious air, and fell silent, gazing severely to one side.
"But the clock has struck eleven, I think,"—remarked Márya Dmítrievna.
The guests understood the hint, and began to take their leave. Varvára Pávlovna was made to promise that she would come to dinner on the morrow, and bring Ada; Gedeónovsky, who had almost fallen asleep as he sat in one corner, offered to escort her home. Pánshin solemnly saluted every one, and at the steps, as he put Varvára Pávlovna into her carriage, he pressed her hand and shouted after her: "*Au revoir!*" Gedeónovsky seated himself by her side; all the way home, she amused herself by placing the tip of her foot on his foot, as though by accident; he became confused, and paid her compliments; she giggled and made eyes at him when the light from a street-lantern fell on the carriage. The waltz which she had herself played, rang in her head, and excited her; wherever she happened to find herself, all she had to do was to imagine to herself lights, a ball-room, the swift whirling to the sounds of music—and her soul went fairly aflame, her eyes darkened strangely, a smile hovered over her lips, something gracefully-bacchic was disseminated all over her body. On arriving at home, Varvára Pávlovna sprang lightly from the carriage,—only fashionable lionesses know how to spring out in that way,—turned to Gedeónovsky, and suddenly burst into a ringing laugh, straight in his face.
"A charming person,"—thought the State Councillor, as he wended his way homeward to his lodgings, where his servant was awaiting him with a bottle of eau de Cologne:—"it is well that I am a staid man ... only, what was she laughing at?"
Márfa Timoféevna sat all night long by Liza's pillow.

XLI

Lavrétzky spent a day and a half at Vasílievskoe, and during nearly the whole of that time he wandered about the neighbourhood. He could not remain long in one place: anguish gnawed him; he experienced all the torture of incessant, impetuous, and impotent impulses. He recalled the feeling which had taken possession of his soul on the day following his arrival in the country; he recalled his intentions at that time, and waxed very angry with himself. What could have torn him away from that which he recognised as his duty, the sole task of his future? The thirst for happiness—once more, the thirst for happiness!—"Obviously, Mikhalévitch is right," he thought. "Thou hast wished once more to taste of happiness in life,"—he said to himself,—"thou hast forgotten what a luxury, what an unmerited mercy it is when it has visited a man even once. It was not complete, thou wilt say? But put forth thy claims to complete, genuine happiness! Look about thee: who of those around thee is blissful, who enjoys himself? Yonder, a peasant is driving to the reaping; perchance, he is satisfied with his lot.... What of that? Wouldst thou change with him? Remember thy mother: how insignificantly small were her demands, and what lot fell to her share? Thou hast, evidently, only been bragging before Pánshin, when thou saidst to him, that thou hadst come to Russia in order to till the earth; thou hast come in order to run after the girls in thine old age. The news of thy freedom came, and thou didst discard everything, thou didst forget everything, thou didst run like a little boy after a butterfly."... Liza's image uninterruptedly presented itself before his thoughts; with an effort he drove it away, as he did also another importunate image, other imperturbably-crafty, beautiful, and detested features. Old Antón noticed that his master was not himself; after heaving several sighs outside the door, and several more on the threshold, he made up his mind to approach him, and advised him to drink something warm. Lavrétzky shouted at him, ordered him to leave the room, but afterward begged his pardon; but this caused Antón to grow still more disconsolate. Lavrétzky could not sit in the drawing-room; he felt as though his great-grandfather Andréi were gazing scornfully from the canvas at his puny descendant.—"Ekh, look out for thyself! thou art sailing in shoal water!" his lips, pursed up on one side, seemed to be saying. "Can it be,"—he thought,—"that I shall not be able to conquer myself,—that I shall give in to this—nonsense?" (The severely-wounded in war always call their wounds "nonsense." If a man could not deceive himself,—he could not live on the earth.) "Am I really a miserable little boy? Well, yes: I have beheld close by, I have almost held in my hand, the possibility of happiness for my whole life—it has suddenly vanished; and in a lottery, if you turn the wheel just a little further, a poor man might become a rich one. If it was not to be, it was not to be,—and that's the end of the matter. I'll set to work, with clenched teeth, and I will command myself to hold my tongue; luckily, it is not the first time I have had to take myself in hand. And why did I run away, why am I sitting here, with my head thrust into a bush, like an ostrich? To be afraid to look catastrophe in the face—is nonsense!—Antón!"—he called loudly,—"order the tarantás to be harnessed up immediately. Yes,"—he meditated once more,—"I must command myself to hold my tongue, I must keep a tight rein on myself."...

With such arguments did Lavrétzky strive to alleviate his grief; but it was great and powerful; and even Apraxyéya, who had outlived not so much her mind as every feeling, even Apraxyéya shook her head, and sorrowfully followed him with her eyes, when he seated himself in the tarantás, in order to drive to the town. The horses galloped off; he sat motionless and upright, and stared impassively ahead along the road.

XLII

Liza had written to Lavrétzky on the day before, that he was to come to their house in the evening; but he first went up to his own quarters. He did not find either his wife or his daughter at home; from the servants he learned that she had gone with her to the Kalítins'. This news both startled and enraged him. "Evidently, Varvára Pávlovna is determined not to give me a chance to live,"—he thought, with the excitement of wrath in his heart. He began to stride to and fro, incessantly thrusting aside with his feet and hands the child's toys, the books, and the feminine appurtenances which came in his way; he summoned Justine, and ordered her to remove all that "rubbish."—"*Oui, monsieur,*"—said she, with a grimace, and began to put the room in order, gracefully bending, and giving Lavrétzky to understand, by every movement, that she regarded him as an unlicked bear. With hatred he watched her worn but still "piquant," sneering, Parisian face, her white cuffs, her silken apron, and light cap. He sent her away, at last, and after long wavering (Varvára Pávlovna still did not return) he made up his mind to betake himself to the Kalítins',—not to Márya Dmítrievna—(not, on any account, would he have entered her drawing-room, that drawing-room where his wife was), but to Márfa Timoféevna; he remembered that a rear staircase from the maids' entrance led straight to her rooms. This is what Lavrétzky did. Chance favoured him: in the yard he met Schúrotchka; she conducted him to Márfa Timoféevna. He found her, contrary to her wont, alone; she was sitting in a corner, with hair uncovered, bowed over, with her hands clasped in her lap. On perceiving Lavrétzky, the old woman was greatly alarmed, rose briskly to her feet, and began to walk hither and yon in the room, as though in search of her cap.

"Ah, here thou art, here thou art,"—she began, avoiding his gaze, and bustling about—"well, how do you do? Come, what now? What is to be done? Where wert thou yesterday? Well, she has come,—well, yes. Well, we must just ... somehow or other."

Lavrétzky dropped into a chair.

"Come, sit down, sit down,"—went on the old woman.—"Thou hast come straight up-stairs. Well, yes, of course. What? thou art come to look at me? Thanks."

The old woman was silent for a while; Lavrétzky did not know what to say to her; but she understood him.

"Liza ... yes, Liza was here just now,"—went on Márfa Timoféevna, tying and untying the cords of her reticule. "She is not quite well. Schúrotchka, where art thou? Come hither, my mother, why canst thou not sit still? And I have a headache. It must be from *that*—from the singing and from the music."

"From what singing, aunty?"

"Why, of course, they keep singing—what do you call it?—duets. And always in Italian: *tchi-tchi*, and *tcha-tcha*, regular magpies. They begin to drag the notes out, and it's just like tugging at your soul. Pánshin and that wife of yours. And all that has come about so quickly; already they are on the footing of relatives, they do not stand on ceremony. However, I will say this much: even a dog seeks a refuge; no harm will come to her, so long as people don't turn her out."

"Nevertheless, I must confess that I did not expect this,"—replied Lavrétzky:—"it must have required great boldness."

"No, my dear soul, that is not boldness; it is calculation. The Lord be with her—I want nothing to do with her! They tell me that thou art sending her to Lavríki,—is it true?"

"Yes, I am placing that estate at the disposal of Varvára Pávlovna."

"Has she asked for money?"

"Not yet."

"Well, it will not be long before she does. But I have only just taken a good look at thee. Art thou well?"

"Yes."

"Schúrotchka,"—suddenly cried Márfa Timoféevna:—"go, and tell Lizavéta Mikhaílovna—that is to say, no, ask her ... she's down-stairs, isn't she?"

"Yes, ma'am."

"Well, yes; then ask her: 'Where did she put my book?' She knows."

"I obey, ma'am."

Again the old woman began to bustle about, and to open the drawers of her commode. Lavrétzky sat motionless on his chair.

Suddenly light footsteps became audible on the stairs—and Liza entered. Lavrétzky rose to his feet, and bowed; Liza halted by the door.

"Liza, Lízotchka,"—said Márfa Timoféevna hastily;—"where is my book, where didst thou put my book?"

"What book, aunty?"

"Why, my book; good heavens! However, I did not call thee.... Well, it makes no difference. What are you doing there—down-stairs? See here, Feódor Ivánitch has come.—How is thy head?"

"It is all right."

"Thou art always saying: 'It is all right.' What's going on with you down-stairs,—music again?"

"No—they are playing cards."

"Yes, of course, she is up to everything. Schúrotchka, I perceive that thou wishest to have a run in the garden. Go along."

"Why, no, Márfa Timoféevna...."

"Don't argue, if you please. Go! Nastásya Kárpovna has gone into the garden alone: stay with her. Respect the old woman."—Schúrotchka left the room.—"Why, where is my cap? Really, now, where has it got to?"

"Pray let me look for it,"—said Liza.

"Sit down, sit down; my own legs haven't given out yet. I must have left it yonder, in my bedroom."

And, casting a sidelong glance at Lavrétzky, Márfa Timoféevna left the room. She was on the point of leaving the door open, but suddenly turned round toward it, and shut it.

Liza leaned against the back of her chair, and gently lifted her hands to her face; Lavrétzky remained standing, as he was.

"This is how we were to meet again,"—he said, at last.

Liza took her hands from her face.

"Yes,"—she said dully:—"we were promptly punished."

"Punished?"—said Lavrétzky. "But what were you punished for?"

Liza raised her eyes to him. They expressed neither grief nor anxiety: they looked smaller and dimmer. Her face was pale; her slightly parted lips had also grown pale.

Lavrétzky's heart shuddered with pity and with love.

"You wrote to me: 'All is at an end,'"—he whispered:—"Yes, all is at an end—before it has begun."

"We must forget all that,"—said Liza:—"I am glad that you came; I wanted to write to you, but it is better thus. Only, we must make use, as promptly as possible, of these minutes. It remains for both of us to do our duty. You, Feódor Ivánitch, ought to become reconciled to your wife."

"Liza!"

"I implore you to do it; in that way alone can we expiate ... everything which has taken place. Think it over—and you will not refuse me."

"Liza, for God's sake,—you are demanding the impossible. I am ready to do everything you command; but become reconciled to her*now*!... I agree to everything, I have forgotten everything; but I cannot force my heart to.... Have mercy, this is cruel!"

"I do not require from you ... what you think; do not live with her, if you cannot; but become reconciled,"—replied Liza, and again raised her hand to her eyes.—"Remember your little daughter; do this for me."

"Very well,"—said Lavrétzky, through his teeth:—"I will do it; let us assume that thereby I am fulfilling my duty. Well, and you—in what does your duty consist?"

"I know what it is."
Lavrétzky suddenly started.
"Surely, you are not preparing to marry Pánshin?"—he asked.
Liza smiled almost imperceptibly.
"Oh, no!"—she said.
"Akh, Liza, Liza!"—cried Lavrétzky:—"how happy we might have been!"
Again Liza glanced at him.
"Now you see yourself, Feódor Ivánitch, that happiness does not depend upon us, but upon God."
"Yes, because you...."
The door of the adjoining room opened swiftly, and Márfa Timoféevna entered, with her cap in her hand.
"I have found it at last,"—she said, taking up her stand between Lavrétzky and Liza.—"I had mislaid it myself. That's what it is to be old, alack! However, youth is no better. Well, and art thou going to Lavríki thyself, with thy wife?"—she added, addressing Feódor Ivánitch.
"With her, to Lavríki?—I do not know,"—he said, after a pause.
"Thou art not going down-stairs?"
"Not to-day."
"Well, very good, as it pleases thee; but I think thou shouldst go down-stairs, Liza. Akh, gracious goodness!—and I have forgotten to give the bullfinch his food. Just wait, I'll be back directly...."
And Márfa Timoféevna ran out of the room, without putting on her cap.
Lavrétzky went quickly up to Liza.
"Liza,"—he began in a beseeching voice:—"we are parting forever, my heart is breaking,—give me your hand in farewell."
Liza raised her head. Her weary, almost extinct gaze rested on him....
"No,"—she said, and drew back the hand which she had already put forward—"no. Lavrétzky"—(she called him thus, for the first time)—"I will not give you my hand. To what end? Go away, I entreat you. You know that I love you,"—she added, with an effort:—"but no ... no."
And she raised her handkerchief to her eyes.
The door creaked.... The handkerchief slipped off Liza's knees. Lavrétzky caught it before it fell to the floor, hastily thrust it into his side pocket, and, turning round, his eyes met those of Márfa Timoféevna.
"Lízotchka, I think thy mother is calling thee,"—remarked the old woman.
Liza immediately rose, and left the room.
Márfa Timoféevna sat down again in her corner. Lavrétzky began to take leave of her.
"Fédya,"—she suddenly said.
"What, aunty?"
"Art thou an honourable man?"
"What?"
"I ask thee: art thou an honourable man?"
"I hope so."
"H'm. But give me thy word of honour that thou art an honourable man."
"Certainly.—But why?"
"I know why. Yes, and thou also, my benefactor, if thou wilt think it over well,—for thou art not stupid,—wilt understand thyself why I ask this of thee. And now, farewell, my dear. Thanks for thy visit; and remember the word that has been spoken, Fédya, and kiss me. Okh, my soul, it is hard for thee, I know: but then, life is not easy for any one. That is why I used to envy the flies; here, I thought, is something that finds life good; but once, in the night, I heard a fly grieving in the claws of a spider,—no, I thought, a thundercloud hangs over them also. What is to be done, Fédya? but remember thy word, nevertheless.—Go."
Lavrétzky emerged from the back entrance, and was already approaching the gate ... when a lackey overtook him.
"Márya Dmítrievna ordered me to ask you to be so good as to come to her,"—he announced to Lavrétzky.
"Say to her, my good fellow, that I cannot at present ..." began Feódor Ivánitch.
"She ordered me to entreat you urgently,"—went on the lackey:—"she ordered me to say, that she is at home."
"But have the visitors gone?"—asked Lavrétzky.
"Yes, sir,"—returned the lackey, and grinned.
Lavrétzky shrugged his shoulders, and followed him.

XLIII

Márya Dmítrievna was sitting alone, in her boudoir, in a sofa-chair, and sniffing eau de Cologne; a glass of orange-flower water was standing beside her, on a small table. She was excited, and seemed to be timorous. Lavrétzky entered.

"You wished to see me,"—he said, saluting her coldly.

"Yes,"—returned Márya Dmítrievna, and drank a little of the water. "I heard that you went straight up-stairs to aunty; I gave orders that you should be requested to come to me: I must have a talk with you. Sit down, if you please."—Márya Dmítrievna took breath.—"You know,"—she went on:—"that your wife has arrived?"

"That fact is known to me,"—said Lavrétzky.

"Well, yes,—that is, I meant to say, she came to me, and I received her; that is what I wish to have an explanation about with you now, Feódor Ivánitch. I, thank God, have won universal respect, I may say, and I would not do anything improper for all the world. Although I foresaw that it would be disagreeable to you, still, I could not make up my mind to refuse her, Feódor Ivánitch; she is my relative—through you: put yourself in my place—what right had I to turn her out of my house?—You agree with me?"

"There is no necessity for your agitating yourself, Márya Dmítrievna,"—returned Lavrétzky: "you have behaved very well indeed; I am not in the least angry. I have not the slightest intention of depriving Varvára Pávlovna of the right to see her acquaintances; I only refrained from entering your apartments to-day because I wished to avoid meeting her,—that was all."

"Akh, how delighted I am to hear that from you, Feódor Ivánitch,"—exclaimed Márya Dmítrievna:—"however, I always expected this from your noble sentiments. But that I should feel agitated, is not wonderful: I am a woman and a mother. And your wife ... of course, I cannot judge between her and you—I told her so myself; but she is such an amiable lady, that she cannot cause anything but pleasure."

Lavrétzky laughed, and played with his hat.

"And this is what I wished to say to you, Feódor Ivánitch,"—went on Márya Dmítrievna, moving a little nearer to him:—"if you had only seen how modestly, how respectfully she behaves!—Really, it is touching. But if you had heard how she speaks of you! 'I am wholly culpable with regard to him,' she says; 'I did not know how to appreciate him,' she says; 'he is an angel,' she says, 'not a man.' Truly, she did say that, 'an angel.' She is so penitent.... I never beheld such penitence, I give you my word!"

"Well, Márya Dmítrievna,"—said Lavrétzky:—"permit me to ask you a question: I am told that Varvára Pávlovna has been singing for you; did she sing during her repentance—or how?"...

"Akh, aren't you ashamed to talk like that! She sang and played merely with the object of giving me pleasure, because I begged, almost commanded her to do so. I perceive that she is distressed—so distressed, I wonder how I can divert her. And I had heard that she had such a fine talent.—Upon my word, Feódor Ivánitch, she is a completely crushed, overwhelmed woman—ask Sergyéi Petróvitch if she is not, *tout à fait*,—what have you to say to that?"

Lavrétzky simply shrugged his shoulders.

"And then, what a little angel that Ada of your is, what a darling!—How pretty she is, how clever! how well she talks French; and she understands Russian—she called me *tyótenka* [aunty]. And do you know, as for being shy, like nearly all children of her age,—there is no shyness about her. She is awfully like you, Feódor Ivánitch. Her eyes, her brows ... well, she's you all over again, your perfect image. I am not very fond of such small children, I must confess; but I have simply lost my heart to your little daughter."

"Márya Dmítrievna,"—exclaimed Lavrétzky, suddenly:—"allow me to ask you why you are pleased to say all this to me?"

"Why?"—again Márya Dmítrievna sniffed at her eau de Cologne, and sipped her water:—"I say it, Feódor Ivánitch, because ... you see, I am a relative, I take the closest interest in you.... I know that you have the very kindest of hearts. Hearken to me, *mon cousin*,—I am a woman of experience, and I am not talking at random: forgive, forgive your wife."—Márya Dmítrievna's eyes suddenly filled with tears.—"Reflect: youth, inexperience ... well, perhaps, a bad example—she had not the sort of a mother who might have put her on the right road. Forgive her, Feódor Ivánitch; she has been sufficiently punished."

Tears trickled down Márya Dmítrievna's cheeks; she did not wipe them away: she loved to weep. Lavrétzky sat as on hot coals. "My God,"—he thought,—"what sort of torture, what sort of a day has fallen to my lot!"

"You do not answer,"—began Márya Dmítrievna again:—"what am I to understand by that?—is it possible that you can be so cruel? No, I will not believe that. I feel that my words have convinced you. Feódor

Ivánitch, God will reward you for your kindness of heart, and you will now receive your wife from my hands...."

Lavrétzky involuntarily rose from his chair; Márya Dmítrievna also rose, and stepping briskly behind a screen, led forth Varvára Pávlovna. Pale, half-fainting, with eyes cast down, she seemed to have renounced every thought, every impulse of her own—to have placed herself wholly in the hands of Márya Dmítrievna.

Lavrétzky retreated a pace.

"You were here?"—he exclaimed.

"Do not blame her,"—said Márya Dmítrievna, hastily;—"she did not wish to remain on any account whatever, but I ordered her to stay, and placed her there behind the screen. She assured me that it would only make you more angry; but I would not listen to her; I know you better than she does. Receive your wife from my hands; go, Várya, be not afraid, fall at your husband's feet" (she tugged at her hand)—"and my blessing on you!..."

"Wait, Márya Dmítrievna,"—Lavrétzky interrupted her, in a dull, but quivering voice:—"you are, probably, fond of sentimental scenes," (Lavrétzky was not mistaken: Márya Dmítrievna had retained from her boarding-school days a passion for a certain theatricalness); "they amuse you; but others suffer from them. However, I will not discuss the matter with you; in *this* scene you are not the principal actor. What do *you* want of me, madam?"—he added, addressing his wife. "Have not I done for you all that I could? Do not retort, that you have not plotted this meeting; I shall not believe you,—and you know that I cannot believe you. What, then, do you want? You are clever,—you never do anything without an object. You must understand that I am not capable of living with you as I used to live; not because I am angry with you, but because I have become a different man. I told you that on the day after your return, and you yourself, at that moment, acquiesced with me in your own soul. But you wish to reinstate yourself in public opinion; it is not enough for you to live in my house, you want to live under one roof with me,—is not that the truth?"

"I want you to forgive me,"—said Varvára Pávlovna, without raising her eyes.

"She wants you to forgive her,"—repeated Márya Dmítrievna.

"And not for my own sake, but for Ada's,"—whispered Varvára Pávlovna.

"Not for her sake, but for Ada's,"—repeated Márya Dmítrievna.

"Very good. You wish that?"—ejaculated Lavrétzky, with an effort. "As you like, I agree to that."

Varvára Pávlovna cast a swift glance at him, and Márya Dmítrievna cried out:—"Well, God be praised"—and again tugged at Varvára Pávlovna's hand. "Now receive from me...."

"Wait, I tell you,"—Lavrétzky interrupted her. "I consent to live with you, Varvára Pávlovna,"—he continued:—"That is to say, I will take you to Lavríki, and I will live with you as long as my strength holds out, and then I shall go away,—and return now and then. You see, I do not wish to deceive you; but do not demand anything more. You yourself would smile, were I to comply with the desire of your respected relative, and press you to my heart, and assure you that ... there had been no past, that the felled tree could burst into blossom once more. But I perceive that I must submit. You will not understand that word; ... it matters not. I repeat, I will live with you ... or, no, I cannot promise that ... I will join you, I will regard you again as my wife...."

"But give her your hand on that, at least,"—said Márya Dmítrievna, whose tears were long since dried up.

"Up to the present moment, I have not deceived Varvára Pávlovna,"—returned Lavrétzky;—"she will believe me as it is. I will take her to Lavríki;—and recollect, Varvára Pávlovna: our compact will be regarded as broken just as soon as you leave that place. And now, permit me to withdraw."

He bowed to both ladies, and hastily quitted the room.

"You are not taking her with you,"—called Márya Dmítrievna after him.... "Let him alone,"—Varvára Pávlovna whispered to her, and immediately threw her arms round her, began to utter thanks, to kiss her hands, and to call her her saviour.

Márya Dmítrievna accepted her caresses with condescension; but in her secret soul she was pleased neither with Lavrétzky nor with Varvára Pávlovna, nor with the whole scene which she had planned. There had turned out to be very little sentimentality; Varvára Pávlovna, in her opinion, should have flung herself at her husband's feet.

"How was it that you did not understand me?"—she commented:—"why, I told you: 'fall at his feet.'"

"It was better thus, dear aunty; do not disturb yourself—everything is all right,"—insisted Varvára Pávlovna.

"Well, and he is as cold as ice,"—remarked Márya Dmítrievna. "Even if you did not weep, why, I fairly overflowed before him. He means to shut you up in Lavríki. The idea,—and you cannot even come to see me! All men are unfeeling,"—she said, in conclusion, and shook her head significantly.

"On the other hand, women know how to value kindness and magnanimity,"—said Varvára Pávlovna, and softly dropping on her knees before Márya Dmítrievna, she embraced the latter's corpulent form with her arms, and pressed her face against her. That face wore a quiet smile, but Márya Dmítrievna's tears were flowing again.

And Lavrétzky went home, locked himself up in his valet's room, flung himself on the divan, and lay there until the morning.

XLIV

The next day was Sunday. The chiming of the bells for the early Liturgy did not awaken Lavrétzky—he had not closed an eye all night long—but it did remind him of another Sunday, when, at the wish of Liza, he had gone to church. He hastily rose; a certain secret voice told him that he would see her there again to-day. He noiselessly quitted the house, ordered Varvára Pávlovna to be informed that he would return to dinner, and with great strides wended his way thither, whither the monotonously-mournful chiming summoned him. He arrived early: there was hardly any one in the church; a chanter in the choir was reading the Hours; his voice, occasionally broken by a cough, boomed on in measured cadence, now rising, now falling. Lavrétzky took up his stand not far from the entrance. The prayerfully inclined arrived one by one, paused, crossed themselves, bowed on all sides; their footsteps resounded in the emptiness and silence, distinctly re-echoing from the arches overhead. A decrepit little old woman, in an ancient hooded cloak, knelt down beside Lavrétzky, and began to pray assiduously; her yellow, toothless, wrinkled face expressed intense emotion; her red eyes gazed fixedly upward at the holy picture on the ikonostásis; her bony hand kept incessantly emerging from under her cloak, and slowly but vigorously made a great, sweeping sign of the cross. A peasant, with a thick beard and a surly face, tousled and dishevelled, entered the church, went down at once on both knees, and immediately set to crossing himself, hastily flinging back his head and shaking it after every prostration. Such bitter woe was depicted on his countenance, and in all his movements, that Lavrétzky made up his mind to approach and ask him what was the matter. The peasant started back timidly and roughly, and looked at him.... "My son is dead,"—he said, in hasty accents—and again began to prostrate himself to the floor. "What can take the place, for them, of the consolation of the church?"—Lavrétzky thought,—and tried to pray himself; but his heart had grown heavy and hard, and his thoughts were far away. He was still expecting Liza—but Liza did not come. The church began to fill with people; still she did not come. The Liturgy began, the deacon had already read the Gospel, the bell had pealed for the hymn "Worthy"; Lavrétzky moved a little,—and suddenly caught sight of Liza. She had arrived before him, but he had not descried her; crowded into the space between the wall and the choir, she neither glanced around nor moved. Lavrétzky did not take his eyes from her until the very end of the Liturgy: he was bidding her farewell. The congregation began to disperse, but she still stood on; she seemed to be awaiting Lavrétzky's departure. At last, she crossed herself for the last time, and went away, without looking round; she had only a maid with her. Lavrétzky followed her out of the church, and overtook her in the street; she was walking very rapidly, with her head bowed and her veil lowered over her face.

"Good morning, Lizavéta Mikhaílovna,"—said he, loudly, with forced ease:—"may I accompany you?"

She said nothing; he walked along by her side.

"Are you satisfied with me?"—he asked her, lowering his voice.—"You have heard what took place last night?"

"Yes, yes,"—she said in a whisper:—"you did well."

And she walked on faster than ever.

"You are satisfied?"

Liza only nodded her head.

"Feódor Ivánitch,"—she began, in a composed, but weak voice:—"I have wanted to ask you: do not come to our house again; go away as speedily as possible; we can see each other later on,—sometime, a year hence. But now, do this for me; comply with my request, for God's sake."

"I am ready to obey you in all things, Lizavéta Mikhaílovna; but is it possible that we are to part thus? will you not say a single word to me?"

"Feódor Ivánitch, here you are now, walking by my side. But you are already far away from me. And not you alone, but also...."

"Finish, I entreat you!"—exclaimed Lavrétzky:—"what is it that you mean to say?"
"You will hear, perhaps ... but whatever happens, forget ... no, do not forget me,—remember me."
"I forget you!..."
"Enough; farewell. Do not follow me."
"Liza ..."—Lavrétzky was beginning.
"Farewell, farewell!"—she repeated, dropped her veil still lower, and advanced almost at a run.
Lavrétzky gazed after her, and dropping his head, went back down the street. He hit upon Lemm, who was also walking along, with his hat pulled down on his nose, and staring at the ground under his feet.
They stared at each other in silence.
"Well, what have you to say?"—said Lavrétzky at last.
"What have I to say?"—returned Lemm surlily:—"I have nothing to say. Everything is dead, and we are dead. (Alles ist todt und wir sind todt.) You are going to the right, I think?"
"Yes."
"Then I go to the left. Good-bye."
On the following morning, Feódor Ivánitch and his wife set out for Lavríki. She drove in front, in the carriage, with Ada and Justine; he came behind, in his tarantás. The pretty little girl never quitted the carriage-window during the whole journey; she was surprised at everything: at the peasants, the peasant women, the wells, the shaft-arches, the carriage-bells, at the multitude of jackdaws; Justine shared her surprise. Varvára Pávlovna laughed at their comments and exclamations.... She was in high spirits; before their departure from the town of O * * * she had had an explanation with her husband.
"I understand your position,"—she had said to him,—and he, from the expression of her clever eyes, was able to conclude that she did fully understand his position,—"but you must do me the justice, at least, to say that I am easy to live with; I shall not obtrude myself upon you, embarrass you; I wanted to assure Ada's future. I need nothing further."
"Yes, and you have attained your object,"—said Feódor Ivánitch.
"My sole idea now is to shut myself up in the wilds; I shall forever remember your good deed in my prayers...."
"Faugh!... enough of that,"—he interrupted her.
"And I shall know how to respect your independence, and your repose,"—she completed her phrase, which she had prepared in advance.
Lavrétzky had made her a low bow. Varvára Pávlovna understood that her husband, in his soul, was grateful to her.
On the second day, toward the evening, they reached Lavríki; a week later, Lavrétzky set off for Moscow, leaving his wife five thousand rubles for her expenses—and the day after Lavrétzky's departure, Pánshin, whom Varvára Pávlovna had begged not to forget her in her isolation, made his appearance. She gave him the warmest sort of a welcome, and until late into the night the lofty rooms of the house and the very garden rang with the sounds of music, singing, and merry French speeches. Pánshin visited Varvára Pávlovna for three days; when he took leave of her, and warmly pressed her beautiful hands, he promised to return very soon—and he kept his promise.

XLV

Liza had a separate little room, on the second story of her mother's house, small, clean, bright, with a white bed, pots of flowers in the corners and in front of the holy pictures, with a tiny writing-table, a case of books, and a crucifix on the wall. This little chamber was called the nursery; Liza had been born in it. On returning to it from church, where she had seen Lavrétzky, she put everything in order, even more carefully than usual, wiped the dust off everything, looked over and tied up with ribbons her note-books and the letters of her friends, locked all the drawers, watered the plants, and touched every flower with her hand. She did all this without haste, without noise, with a certain touched and tranquil solicitude on her face. She halted, at last, in the middle of the room, slowly looked around her, and stepping up to the table over which hung the crucifix, she knelt down, laid her head on her clasped hands, and remained motionless.
Márfa Timoféevna entered, and found her in this position. Liza did not notice her entrance. The old woman went outside the door, on tiptoe, and gave vent to several loud coughs. Liza rose quickly to her feet, and wiped her eyes, in which glittered clear tears which had not fallen.

"I see that thou hast been arranging thy little cell again,"—said Márfa Timoféevna, and bent low over a pot containing a young rose-bush:—"what a splendid perfume it has!"

Liza gazed thoughtfully at her aunt.

"What a word you have uttered!"—she whispered.

"What sort of a word, what word?"—interposed the old woman, vivaciously;—"what dost thou mean?—This is dreadful,"—she said, suddenly tearing off her cap, and seating herself on Liza's bed:—"this is beyond my strength! today is the fourth day that I seem to be seething in a kettle; I can no longer pretend that I notice nothing,—I cannot see thee growing pale, withering away, weeping,—I cannot, I cannot!"

"Why, what is the matter with you, aunty?"—said Liza:—"I am all right...."

"All right?"—exclaimed Márfa Timoféevna:—"tell that to others, but not to me! All right! But who was it that was on her knees just now? whose eyelashes are still wet with tears? All right! Why, look at thyself, what hast thou done to thy face, what has become of thine eyes?—All right! As though I did not know all!"

"It will pass off, aunty; give me time."

"It will pass off, but when? O Lord God, my Master! is it possible that thou didst love him so? why, he is an old man, Lízotchka. Well, I do not dispute that he is a good man, he does not bite; but what does that signify? we are all good people: the world is large, there will always be plenty of that sort."

"I tell you, that it will all pass off, it is all over already."

"Listen, Lízotchka, to what I have to say to thee,"—said Márfa Timoféevna, suddenly, making Liza sit down beside her on the bed, and adjusting now her hair, now her kerchief.—"It only seems to you, while it is fresh, that your grief is beyond remedy. Ekh, my darling, for death alone there is no remedy! Only say to thyself: 'I won't give in—so there now!' and afterward thou wilt be amazed thyself—how soon, how well, it will pass off. Only have patience."

"Aunty,"—replied Liza:—"it is already past, all is over already."

"Past—over—forsooth! Why, even thy little nose has grown pointed, and thou sayest: 'It is over—it is over!'"

"Yes, it is over, aunty, if you will only help me,"—cried Liza, with sudden animation, and threw herself on Márfa Timoféevna's neck.—"Dear aunty, be my friend, help me; do not be angry, understand me."

"Why, what is this, what is this, my mother? Don't frighten me, please; I shall scream in another minute; don't look at me like that: tell me quickly what thou meanest?"

"I ... I want ..." Liza hid her face in Márfa Timoféevna's bosom.... "I want to enter a convent,"—she said, in a dull tone.

The old woman fairly leaped on the bed.

"Cross thyself, my mother, Lízotchka; come to thy senses: God be with thee, what dost thou mean?"—she stammered at last: "lie down, my darling, sleep a little: this comes from lack of sleep, my dear."

Liza raised her head, her cheeks were burning.

"No, aunty,"—she articulated, "do not speak like that. I have made up my mind, I have prayed, I have asked counsel of God; all is ended, my life with you is ended. Such a lesson is not in vain; and it is not the first time I have thought of this. Happiness was not suited to me; even when I cherished hopes of happiness, my heart was always heavy. I know everything, my own sins and the sins of others, and how papa acquired his wealth; I know everything. All that must be atoned for by prayer—atoned for by prayer. I am sorry for all of you—I am sorry for mamma, for Lyénotchka; but there is no help for it; I feel that I cannot live here; I have already taken leave of everything, I have made my reverence to everything in the house for the last time; something is calling me hence; I am weary; I want to shut myself up forever. Do not hold me back, do not dissuade me; help me, or I will go away alone."

Márfa Timoféevna listened in terror to her niece.

"She is ill, she is raving,"—she thought:—"I must send for a doctor; but for which? Gedeónovsky was praising some one the other day; he's always lying,—but, perhaps, he told the truth that time." But when she became convinced that Liza was not ill, and was not raving, when to all her objections Liza steadfastly made one and the same reply, Márfa Timoféevna became seriously frightened and grieved.—"But thou dost not know, my darling,"—she began to try to prevail upon her;—"what sort of a life they lead in convents! Why, my own one, they will feed thee with green hemp-oil; they will put on thee coarse, awfully coarse linen; they will make thee go about cold; thou canst not endure all that, Lízotchka. All that is the traces of Agáfya in thee; it was she who led thee astray. Why, she began by living her life, living a gay life; do thou live thy life also. Let me, at least, die in peace, and then do what thou wilt. And who ever heard of any one going into a convent, all on account of such a goat's beard—the Lord forgive me!—on account of a man? Come, if thy heart is so heavy, go away on a journey, pray to a saint, have a prayer-service said, but don't put the black cowl on thy head, my dear little father, my dear little mother...."

And Márfa Timoféevna began to weep bitterly.

Liza comforted her, wiped away her tears, but remained inflexible. In her despair, Márfa Timoféevna tried to resort to threats: she would tell Liza's mother everything; but even that was of no avail. Only as a concession to the old woman's urgent entreaties, did Liza consent to defer the fulfilment of her intention for six months; in return, Márfa Timoféevna was compelled to give her her word that she would help her, and obtain the permission of Márya Dmítrievna if, at the end of six months, she had not changed her mind.

With the advent of the first cold weather, Varvára Pávlovna, despite her promise to shut herself up in the depths of the country, after providing herself with money, removed to Petersburg, where she hired a modest but pretty apartment, which had been found for her by Pánshin, who had quitted the Government of O * * * before her. During the latter part of his sojourn in O * * * he had completely fallen out of favour with Márya Dmítrievna; he had suddenly ceased to call upon her and hardly ever quitted Lavríki. Varvára Pávlovna had enslaved him, precisely that,—enslaved him; no other word will express her unlimited, irrevocable, irresponsible power over him.

Lavrétzky passed the winter in Moscow, but in the spring of the following year the news reached him that Liza had entered the B * * * convent, in one of the most remote corners of Russia.

EPILOGUE

Eight years have passed. Spring has come again.... But first, let us say a few words about the fate of Mikhalévitch, Pánshin, Mme. Lavrétzky—and take our leave of them. Mikhalévitch, after long peregrinations, has finally hit upon his real vocation: he has obtained the post of head inspector in a government institution. He is very well satisfied with his lot, and his pupils "adore" him, although they mimic him. Pánshin has advanced greatly in rank, and already has a directorship in view; he walks with his back somewhat bent: it must be the cross of the Order of Vladímir, which has been conferred upon him, that drags him forward. The official in him has, decidedly, carried the day over the artist; his still youthful face has turned quite yellow, his hair has grown thin, and he no longer sings or draws, but secretly occupies himself with literature: he has written a little comedy, in the nature of "a proverb,"—and, as every one who writes nowadays "shows up" some one or something, he has shown up in it a coquette, and he reads it surreptitiously to two or three ladies who are favourably disposed toward him. But he has not married, although many fine opportunities of so doing have presented themselves: for this Varvára Pávlovna is responsible. As for her, she lives uninterruptedly in Paris, as of yore: Feódor Ivánitch has given her a bill of exchange on himself, and bought himself free from her,—from the possibility of a second, unexpected invasion. She has grown old and fat, but it is still pretty and elegant. Every person has his own ideal: Varvára Pávlovna has found hers—in the dramatic productions of Dumas fils. She assiduously frequents the theatre where consumptive and sentimental ladies of the frail class are put on the stage; to be Mme. Doche seems to her the very apex of human felicity; one day, she declared that she desired no better lot for her daughter. It is to be hoped that fate will deliver Mademoiselle Ada from such felicity: from a rosy, plump child, she has turned into a weak-chested, pale-faced young girl; her nerves are already deranged. The number of Varvára Pávlovna's admirers has decreased; but they have not transferred their allegiance: she will, in all probability, retain several of them to the end of her life. The most ardent of them, of late, has been a certain Zakurdálo-Skubýrnikoff, one of the retired dandies of the Guards, a man of eight and thirty, of remarkably robust build. The Frenchmen who frequent Mme. Lavrétzky's salon call him "*le gros taureau de l'Ukraïne*"; Varvára Pávlovna never invites him to her fashionable evening gatherings, but he enjoys her favour in the fullest measure.

So ... eight years have passed. Again the sky is breathing forth the beaming happiness of spring; again it is smiling upon the earth and upon men; again, beneath its caress, everything has burst into blossom, into love and song. The town of O * * * has undergone very little change in the course of those eight years; but Márya Dmítrievna's house seems to have grown young: its recently painted walls shine as in welcome, and the panes of the open windows are crimsoning and glittering in the rays of the setting sun. Through these windows, out upon the street, are wafted the sounds of ringing young voices, of incessant laughter; the whole house seems bubbling with life, and overflowing the brim with merriment. The mistress of the house herself has long since gone to her grave: Márya Dmítrievna died two years after Liza's profession as a nun; and Márfa Timoféevna did not long survive her niece; they rest side by side in the town cemetery. Nastásya Kárpovna, also, is dead; the faithful old woman went, every week, for the space of several years, to pray over

the ashes of her friend.... Her time came, and her bones also were laid in the damp earth. But Márya Dmítrievna's house has not passed into the hands of strangers, has not left her family; the nest has not been destroyed: Lyénotchka, who has become a stately, beautiful young girl, and her betrothed, a fair-haired officer of hussars; Márya Dmítrievna's son, who has just been married in Petersburg, and has come with his young wife to spend the spring in O * * *; his wife's sister, an Institute-girl of sixteen, with brilliantly scarlet cheeks and clear eyes; Schúrotchka, who has also grown up and become pretty—these are the young folks who are making the walls of the Kalítin house re-echo with laughter and chatter. Everything about it has been changed, everything has been brought into accord with the new inhabitants. Beardless young house-servants, who grin and jest, have taken the places of the former sedate old servitors; where overgrown Róska was wont to stroll, two setters are chasing madly about, and leaping over the divans; the stable has been filled with clean-limbed amblers, high-spirited shaft-horses, fiery trace-horses[1] with braided manes, and riding-horses from the Don; the hours for breakfast, dinner, and supper have become mixed up and confused; according to the expression of the neighbours, "an unprecedented state of affairs" has been established.
On the evening of which we are speaking, the inhabitants of the Kalítin house (the oldest of them, Lyénotchka's betrothed, was only four and twenty) were engaged in a far from complicated, but, judging from their vigorous laughter, a very amusing game: they were running through the rooms, and catching each other; the dogs, also, were running and barking, and the canaries which hung in cages in front of the windows vied with each other in singing at the tops of their voices, increasing the uproar of ringing volleys of noise with their furious chirping. While this deafening diversion was at its very height, a mud-stained tarantás drove up to the gate, and a man of forty-five, clad in travelling garb, descended from it, and stopped short in amazement. He stood motionless for some time, swept an attentive glance over the house, passed through the gate into the yard, and slowly ascended the steps. There was no one in the anteroom to receive him; but the door of the "hall" flew wide open; through it, all flushed, bounced Schúrotchka, and instantly, in pursuit of her, with ringing laughter, rushed the whole youthful band. She came to a sudden halt and fell silent at the sight of the stranger; but the clear eyes fastened upon him were as caressing as ever, the fresh faces did not cease to smile. Márya Dmítrievna's son stepped up to the visitor, and courteously asked him what he wished.
"I am Lavrétzky,"—said the visitor.
A vigorous shout rang out in response—and not because all these young people were so extremely delighted at the arrival of the distant, almost forgotten relative, but simply because they were ready to make an uproar and rejoice on every convenient opportunity. They immediately surrounded Lavrétzky: Lyénotchka, in the quality of an old acquaintance, was the first to introduce herself, and to assure him that, in another moment, she certainly would have recognised him, and then she presented all the rest of the company, calling each one of them, including her betrothed, by his pet name. The whole throng moved through the dining-room to the drawing-room. The hangings in both rooms were different, but the furniture remained the same; Lavrétzky recognised the piano; even the same embroidery-frame was standing in the window, in the same position—and almost with the same unfinished bit of embroidery as eight years previously. They made him sit down in a comfortable easy-chair; all seated themselves decorously around him. Questions, exclamations, stories showered down without cessation.
"But it is a long time since we have seen you,"—remarked Lyénotchka, ingenuously:—"and we have not seen Varvára Pávlovna either."
"I should think so!"—interposed her brother, hurriedly. "I carried thee off to Petersburg, but Feódor Ivánitch lived in the country all the time."
"Yes, and mamma has died since, you know."
"And Márfa Timoféevna,"—said Schúrotchka.
"And Nastásya Kárpovna,"—rejoined Lyénotchka.—"And M'sieu Lemm...."
"What? And is Lemm dead also?"—asked Lavrétzky.
"Yes,"—replied young Kalítin:—"he went away from here to Odessa—they say that some one decoyed him thither; and there he died."
"You do not know—whether he left any music behind him?"
"I don't know,—it is hardly probable."
All fell silent, and exchanged glances. A cloud of sadness had descended upon all the young faces.
"And Matróska is alive,"—suddenly remarked Lyénotchka.
"And Gedeónovsky is alive,"—added her brother.
At the name of Gedeónovsky a vigorous peal of laughter rang out in unison.

"Yes, he is alive, and lies just as he always did,"—went on Márya Dmítrievna's son:—"and just imagine, that naughty child there" (and he pointed at his wife's sister, the Institute-girl) "put pepper in his snuff-box yesterday."
"How he did sneeze!" exclaimed Lyénotehka:—and again a peal of irrepressible laughter rang out.
"We received news of Liza recently,"—said young Kalítin,—and again everything grew still round about:—"things are well with her,—her health is now improving somewhat."
"Is she still in the same convent?"—asked Lavrétzky, not without an effort.
"Yes, still in the same place."
"Does she write to you?"
"No, never; the news reaches us through other people."—A sudden, profound silence ensued. "The angel of silence has flown past," all said to themselves.
"Would not you like to go into the garden?"—Kalítin turned to Lavrétzky:—"it is very pretty now, although we have rather neglected it."
Lavrétzky went out into the garden, and the first thing that struck his eyes was the bench on which he had once spent with Liza a few happy moments, never to be repeated; it had grown black and crooked; but he recognised it, and his soul was seized by that feeling which has no peer in sweetness and in sorrow,—the feeling of living grief for vanished youth, for happiness which it once possessed. In company with the young people, he strolled through the alleys: the linden-trees had not grown much older and taller during the last eight years, but their shade had become more dense; on the other hand, all the shrubs had sprung upward, the raspberry-bushes had waxed strong, the hazel copse had become entirely impenetrable, and everywhere there was an odour of thickets, forest, grass, and lilacs.
"What a good place this would be to play at puss-in-the-corner,"—suddenly cried Lyénotchka, as they entered a small, verdant glade, hemmed in by lindens:—"by the way, there are five of us."
"And hast thou forgotten Feódor Ivánitch?"—her brother observed to her.... "Or art thou not reckoning in thyself?"
Lyénotchka blushed faintly.
"But is it possible that Feódor Ivánitch, at his age, can..."—she began.
"Please play,"—interposed Lavrétzky, hastily:—"pay no heed to me. It will be all the more agreeable to me if I know that I am not embarrassing you. And there is no need for you to bother about me; we old fellows have occupations of which you, as yet, know nothing, and which no diversion can replace: memories."
The young people listened to Lavrétzky with courteous and almost mocking respect,—exactly as though their teacher were reading them a lesson,—and suddenly all of them flew away from him, and ran over the glade; four of them took up their stand near the trees, one stood in the centre,—and the fun began.
But Lavrétzky returned to the house, went into the dining-room, approached the piano, and touched one of the keys: a faint, but pure sound rang out, and secretly trembled in his heart: with that note began that inspired melody wherewith, long ago, on that same blissful night, Lemm, the dead Lemm, had led him to such raptures. Then Lavrétzky passed into the drawing-room, and did not emerge from it for a long time: in that room, where he had so often seen Liza, her image rose up before him more vividly than ever; it seemed to him, that he felt around him the traces of her presence; but his grief for her was exhausting and not light: there was in it none of the tranquillity which death inspires. Liza was still living somewhere, dully, far away; he thought of her as among the living, but did not recognise the young girl whom he had once loved in that pale spectre swathed in the conventual garment, surrounded by smoky clouds of incense. Lavrétzky would not have recognised himself, had he been able to contemplate himself as he mentally contemplated Liza. In the course of those eight years the crisis had, at last, been effected in his life; that crisis which many do not experience, but without which it is not possible to remain an honourable man to the end: he had really ceased to think of his own happiness, of selfish aims. He had calmed down, and—why should the truth be concealed?—he had aged, not alone in face and body, he had aged in soul; to preserve the heart youthful to old age, as some say, is difficult, and almost absurd: he may feel content who has not lost faith in good, steadfastness of will, desire for activity.... Lavrétzky had a right to feel satisfied: he had become a really fine agriculturist, he had really learned to till the soil, and he had toiled not for himself alone; in so far as he had been able, he had freed from care and established on a firm foundation the existence of his serfs.
Lavrétzky emerged from the house into the garden: he seated himself on the familiar bench—and in that dear spot, in the face of the house, where he had, on the last occasion, stretched out his hands in vain to the fatal cup in which seethes and sparkles the wine of delight,—he, a solitary, homeless wanderer,—to the sounds of the merry cries of the younger generation which had already superseded him,—took a survey of his life. His

heart was sad, but not heavy and not very sorrowful: he had nothing which he had need to regret or be ashamed of. "Play on, make merry, grow on, young forces,"—he thought, and there was no bitterness in his meditations:—"life lies before you, and it will be easier for you to live: you will not be compelled, as we have been, to seek your road, to struggle, to fall, and to rise to your feet again amid the gloom; we have given ourselves great trouble, that we might remain whole,—and how many of us have failed in that!—but you must do deeds, work,—and the blessing of old fellows like me be upon you. But all that remains for me, after to-day, after these emotions, is to make my final reverence to you, and, although with sadness, yet without envy, without any dark feelings, to say, in view of the end, in view of God who is awaiting me: 'Long live solitary old age! Burn thyself out, useless life!'"

Lavrétzky rose softly, and softly went away; no one noticed him, no one detained him; the merry cries resounded more loudly than ever in the garden behind the green, dense wall of lofty lindens. He seated himself in his tarantás, and ordered the coachman to drive home, and not to press the horses hard.

"And the end?" perchance some dissatisfied reader will say. "And what became of Lavrétzky? of Liza?" But what can one say about people who are still alive, but who have already departed from the earthly arena,—why revert to them? They say that Lavrétzky paid a visit to that distant convent where Liza had hidden herself—and saw her. In going from one choir to the other, she passed close to him—passed with the even, hurriedly-submissive gait of a nun—and did not cast a glance at him; only the lashes of the eye which was turned toward him trembled almost imperceptibly, and her haggard face was bowed a little lower than usual—and the fingers of her clasped hands, interlaced with her rosary, were pressed more tightly to one another. What did they both think,—what did they both feel? Who knows? Who shall say? There are moments in life, there are feelings ... we can only indicate them,—and pass by.

Smoke

I

On the 10th of August 1862, at four o'clock in the afternoon, a great number of people were thronging before the well-known *Konversation* in Baden-Baden. The weather was lovely; everything around—the green trees, the bright houses of the gay city, and the undulating outline of the mountains—everything was in holiday mood, basking in the rays of the kindly sunshine; everything seemed smiling with a sort of blind, confiding delight; and the same glad, vague smile strayed over the human faces too, old and young, ugly and beautiful alike. Even the blackened and whitened visages of the Parisian demi-monde could not destroy the general impression of bright content and elation, while their many-coloured ribbons and feathers and the sparks of gold and steel on their hats and veils involuntarily recalled the intensified brilliance and light fluttering of birds in spring, with their rainbow-tinted wings. But the dry, guttural snapping of the French jargon, heard on all sides could not equal the song of birds, nor be compared with it.

Everything, however, was going on in its accustomed way. The orchestra in the Pavilion played first a medley from the Traviata, then one of Strauss's waltzes, then 'Tell her,' a Russian song, adapted for instruments by an obliging conductor. In the gambling saloons, round the green tables, crowded the same familiar figures, with the same dull, greedy, half-stupefied, half-exasperated, wholly rapacious expression, which the gambling fever lends to all, even the most aristocratic, features. The same well-fed and ultra-fashionably dressed Russian landowner from Tambov with wide staring eyes leaned over the table, and with uncomprehending haste, heedless of the cold smiles of the croupiers themselves, at the very instant of the cry '*rien ne va plus*,' laid with perspiring hand golden rings of *louis d'or* on all the four corners of the roulette, depriving himself by so doing of every possibility of gaining anything, even in case of success. This did not in the least prevent him the same evening from affirming the contrary with disinterested indignation to Prince Kokó, one of the well-known leaders of the aristocratic opposition, the Prince Kokó, who in Paris at the salon of the Princess Mathilde, so happily remarked in the presence of the Emperor: '*Madame, le principe de la propriété est profondément ébranlé en Russie*.' At the Russian tree, *à l'arbre Russe*, our dear fellow-countrymen and countrywomen were assembled after their wont. They approached haughtily and carelessly in fashionable style, greeted each other with dignity and elegant ease, as befits beings who find themselves at the topmost pinnacle of contemporary culture. But when they had met and sat down together, they were absolutely at a loss for anything to say to one another, and had to be content with a pitiful interchange of inanities, or with the exceedingly indecent and exceedingly insipid old jokes of a hopelessly stale French wit, once a journalist, a chattering buffoon with Jewish shoes on his paltry little legs, and a contemptible little beard on his mean little visage. He retailed to them, *à ces princes russes*, all the sweet absurdities from the old comic almanacs *Charivari* and *Tintamarre*, and they, *ces princes russes*, burst into grateful laughter, as though forced in spite of themselves to recognise the crushing superiority of foreign wit, and their own hopeless incapacity to invent anything amusing. Yet here were almost all the '*fine fleur*' of our society, 'all the high-life and mirrors of fashion.' Here was Count X., our incomparable dilettante, a profoundly musical nature, who so divinely recites songs on the piano, but cannot in fact take two notes correctly without fumbling at random on the keys, and sings in a style something between that of a poor gypsy singer and a Parisian hairdresser. Here was our enchanting Baron Q., a master in every line: literature, administration, oratory, and card-sharping. Here, too, was Prince Y., the friend of religion and the people, who in the blissful epoch when the spirit-trade was a monopoly, had made himself betimes a huge fortune by the sale of vodka adulterated with belladonna; and the brilliant General O. O., who had achieved the subjugation of something, and the pacification of something else, and who is nevertheless still a nonentity, and does not know what to do with himself. And R. R. the amusing fat man, who regards himself as a great invalid and a great wit, though he is, in fact, as strong as a bull, and as dull as a post.... This R. R. is almost the only man in our day who has preserved the traditions of the dandies of the forties, of the epoch of the 'Hero of our Times,' and the Countess Vorotinsky. He has preserved, too, the special gait with the swing on the heels, and *le culte de la pose* (it cannot even be put into words in Russian), the unnatural deliberation of movement, the sleepy dignity of expression, the immovable, offended-looking countenance, and the habit of interrupting other people's remarks with a yawn, gazing at his own finger-nails, laughing through his nose, suddenly shifting his hat from the back of his head on to his eyebrows, etc. Here, too, were people in government circles, diplomats, big-wigs with European names, men of wisdom and intellect, who imagine that the Golden Bull was an edict of the Pope, and that the English poor-tax is a tax levied on the poor. And here, too, were the hot-blooded, though tongue-tied, devotees of the *dames aux camellias*, young society dandies, with superb partings down the back of their heads, and splendid drooping whiskers, dressed in real London costumes, young bucks whom one would fancy there was nothing to hinder from becoming as vulgar as the illustrious French wit above mentioned. But no! our home products are not in fashion it seems; and Countess S., the celebrated arbitress of fashion and *grand genre*, by spiteful tongues nicknamed 'Queen of the Wasps,' and 'Medusa in a mob-cap,' prefers, in the absence of the French wit, to consort with the Italians, Moldavians, American spiritualists, smart secretaries of foreign embassies, and Germans of effeminate, but prematurely circumspect, physiognomy, of whom the place is full. The example of the Countess is followed by the Princess Babette, she in whose arms Chopin died (the ladies in Europe in whose arms he expired are to be reckoned by thousands); and the Princess Annette, who would have been perfectly captivating, if the simple village washerwoman had not suddenly peeped out in her at times, like a smell of cabbage wafted across the most delicate perfume; and Princess Pachette, to whom the following mischance had occurred: her husband had fallen into a good berth, and all at once, *Dieu sait pourquoi*, he had thrashed the provost and stolen 20,000 roubles of public money; and the laughing Princess Zizi; and the tearful Princess Zozo. They all left their compatriots on one side, and were merciless in their treatment of them. Let us too leave them on one side, these charming ladies, and walk away from the renowned tree near which they sit in such costly but somewhat tasteless costumes, and God grant them relief from the boredom consuming them!

II

A few paces from the 'Russian tree,' at a little table in front of Weber's coffee-house, there was sitting a good-looking man, about thirty, of medium height, thin and dark, with a manly and pleasant face. He sat bending forward with both arms leaning on his stick, with the calm and simple air of a man to whom the idea had not occurred that any one would notice him or pay any attention to him. His large expressive golden-brown eyes were gazing deliberately about him, sometimes screwed up to keep the sunshine out of them, and then watching fixedly some eccentric figure that passed by him while a childlike smile faintly stirred his fine moustache and lips, and his prominent short chin. He wore a roomy coat of German cut, and a soft grey hat hid half of his high forehead. At the first glance he made the impression of an honest, sensible, rather self-confident young man such as there are many in the world. He seemed to be resting from prolonged labours and to be deriving all the more simple-minded amusement from the scene spread out before him because his thoughts were far away, and because they moved too, those thoughts, in a world utterly unlike that which surrounded him at the moment. He was a Russian; his name was Grigory Mihalovitch Litvinov.

We have to make his acquaintance, and so it will be well to relate in a few words his past, which presents little of much interest or complexity.

He was the son of an honest retired official of plebeian extraction, but he was educated, not as one would naturally expect, in the town, but in the country. His mother was of noble family, and had been educated in a government school. She was a good-natured and very enthusiastic creature, not devoid of character, however. Though she was twenty years younger than her husband, she remodelled him, as far as she could, drew him out of the petty official groove into the landowner's way of life, and softened and refined his harsh and stubborn character. Thanks to her, he began to dress with neatness, and to behave with decorum; he came to respect learned men and learning, though, of course, he never took a single book in his hand; he gave up swearing, and tried in every way not to demean himself. He even arrived at walking more quietly and speaking in a subdued voice, mostly of elevated subjects, which cost him no small effort. 'Ah! they ought to be flogged, and that's all about it!' he sometimes thought to himself, but aloud he pronounced: 'Yes, yes, that's so ... of course; it is a great question.' Litvinov's mother set her household too upon a European footing; she addressed the servants by the plural 'you' instead of the familiar 'thou,' and never allowed any one to gorge himself into a state of lethargy at her table. As regards the property belonging to her, neither she nor her husband was capable of looking after it at all. It had been long allowed to run to waste, but there was plenty of land, with all sorts of useful appurtenances, forest-lands and a lake, on which there had once stood a factory, which had been founded by a zealous but unsystematic owner, and had flourished in the hands of a scoundrelly merchant, and gone utterly to ruin under the superintendence of a conscientious German manager. Madame Litvinov was contented so long as she did not dissipate her fortune or contract debts. Unluckily she could not boast of good health, and she died of consumption in the very year that her son entered the Moscow university. He did not complete his course there owing to circumstances of which the reader will hear more later on, and went back to his provincial home, where he idled away some time without work and without ties, almost without acquaintances. Thanks to the disinclination for active service of the local gentry, who were, however, not so much penetrated by the Western theory of the evils of 'absenteeism,' as by the home-grown conviction that 'one's own shirt is the nearest to one's skin,' he was drawn for military service in 1855, and almost died of typhus in the Crimea, where he spent six months in a mud-hut on the shore of the Putrid Sea, without ever seeing a single ally. After that, he served, not of course without unpleasant experiences, on the councils of the nobility, and after being a little time in the country, acquired a passion for farming. He realised that his mother's property, under the indolent and feeble management of his infirm old father, did not yield a tenth of the revenue it might yield, and that in experienced and skilful hands it might be converted into a perfect gold mine. But he realised, too, that experience and skill were just what he lacked—and he went abroad to study agriculture and technology—to learn them from the first rudiments. More than four years he had spent in Mecklenburg, in Silesia, and in Carlsruhe, and he had travelled in Belgium and in England. He had worked conscientiously and accumulated information;- he had not acquired it easily; but he had persevered through his difficulties to the end, and now with confidence in himself, in his future, and in his usefulness to his neighbours, perhaps even to the whole countryside, he was preparing to return home, where he was summoned with despairing prayers and entreaties in every letter from his father, now completely bewildered by the emancipation, the re-division of lands, and the terms of redemption—by the new régime in short. But why was he in Baden?

Well, he was in Baden because he was from day to day expecting the arrival there of his cousin and betrothed, Tatyana Petrovna Shestov. He had known her almost from childhood, and had spent the spring and summer with her at Dresden, where she was living with her aunt. He felt sincere love and profound respect for his young kinswoman, and on the conclusion of his dull preparatory labours, when he was preparing to enter on a new field, to begin real, unofficial duties, he proposed to her as a woman dearly loved, a comrade and a friend, to unite her life with his—for happiness and for sorrow, for labour and for rest, 'for better, for worse' as the English say. She had consented, and he had returned to Carlsruhe, where his books, papers and properties had been left.... But why was he at Baden, you ask again?

Well, he was at Baden, because Tatyana's aunt, who had brought her up, Kapitolina Markovna Shestov, an old unmarried lady of fifty-five, a most good-natured, honest, eccentric soul, a free thinker, all aglow with the fire of self-sacrifice and abnegation, an *esprit fort* (she read Strauss, it is true she concealed the fact from her niece) and a democrat, sworn opponent of aristocracy and fashionable society, could not resist the temptation of gazing for once on this aristocratic society in such a fashionable place as Baden.... Kapitolina Markovna wore no crinoline and had her white hair cut in a round crop, but luxury and splendour had a secret fascination for her, and it was her favourite pastime to rail at them and express her contempt of them. How could one refuse to gratify the good old lady? But Litvinov was so quiet and simple, he gazed so self-confidently about him, because his life lay so clearly mapped out before him, because his career was defined, and because he was proud of this career, and rejoiced in it as the work of his own hands.

III

'Hullo! hullo! here he is!' he suddenly heard a squeaky voice just above his ear, and a plump hand slapped him on the shoulder. He lifted his head, and perceived one of his few Moscow acquaintances, a certain Bambaev, a good-natured but good-for-nothing fellow. He was no longer young, he had a flabby nose and soft cheeks, that looked as if they had been boiled, dishevelled greasy locks, and a fat squat person. Everlastingly short of cash, and everlastingly in raptures over something, Rostislav Bambaev wandered, aimless but exclamatory, over the face of our long-suffering mother-earth.

'Well, this is something like a meeting!' he repeated, opening wide his sunken eyes, and drawing down his thick lips, over which the straggling dyed moustaches seemed strangely out of place. 'Ah, Baden! All the world runs here like black-beetles! How did you come here, Grisha?'

There was positively no one in the world Bambaev did not address by his Christian name.

'I came here three days ago.'

'From where?'

'Why do you ask?'

'Why indeed? But stop, stop a minute, Grisha. You are, perhaps, not aware who has just arrived here! Gubaryov himself, in person! That's who's here! He came yesterday from Heidelberg. You know him of course?'

'I have heard of him.'

'Is that all? Upon my word! At once, this very minute we will haul you along to him. Not know a man like that! And by the way here's Voroshilov.... Stop a minute, Grisha, perhaps you don't know him either? I have the honour to present you to one another. Both learned men! He's a phœnix indeed! Kiss each other!'

And uttering these words, Bambaev turned to a good-looking young man standing near him with a fresh and rosy, but prematurely demure face. Litvinov got up, and, it need hardly be said, did not kiss him, but exchanged a cursory bow with the phœnix, who, to judge from the severity of his demeanour, was not overpleased at this unexpected introduction.

'I said a phœnix, and I will not go back from my word,' continued Bambaev; 'go to Petersburg, to the military school, and look at the golden board; whose name stands first there? The name of Voroshilov, Semyon Yakovlevitch! But, Gubaryov, Gubaryov, my dear fellow! It's to him we must fly! I absolutely worship that man! And I'm not alone, every one's at his feet! Ah, what a work he is writing, O—O—O!...'

'What is his work about?' inquired Litvinov.

'About everything, my dear boy, after the style of Buckle, you know ... but more profound, more profound.... Everything will be solved and made clear in it.'

'And have you read this work yourself?'

'No, I have not read it, and indeed it's a secret, which must not be spread about; but from Gubaryov one may expect everything, everything! Yes!' Bambaev sighed and clasped his hands. 'Ah, if we had two or three intellects like that growing up in Russia, ah, what mightn't we see then, my God! I tell you one thing, Grisha; whatever pursuit you may have been engaged in in these latter days—and I don't even know what your pursuits are in general—whatever your convictions may be—I don't know them either—from him, Gubaryov, you will find something to learn. Unluckily, he is not here for long. We must make the most of him; we must go. To him, to him!'

A passing dandy with reddish curls and a blue ribbon on his low hat, turned round and stared through his eyeglass with a sarcastic smile at Bambaev. Litvinov felt irritated.

'What are you shouting for?' he said; 'one would think you were hallooing dogs on at a hunt! I have not had dinner yet.'

'Well, think of that! we can go at once to Weber's ... the three of us ... capital! You have the cash to pay for me?' he added in an undertone.

'Yes, yes; only, I really don't know——'

'Leave off, please; you will thank me for it, and he will be delighted. Ah, heavens!' Bambaev interrupted himself. 'It's the finale from Ernani they're playing. How delicious!... *A som ... mo Carlo....* What a fellow I am, though! In tears in a minute. Well, Semyon Yakovlevitch! Voroshilov! shall we go, eh?'

Voroshilov, who had remained all the while standing with immovable propriety, still maintaining his former haughty dignity of demeanour, dropped his eyes expressively, frowned, and muttered something between his teeth ... But he did not refuse; and Litvinov thought, 'Well, we may as well do it, as I've plenty of time on my hands.' Bambaev took his arm, but before turning towards the café he beckoned to Isabelle the renowned flower-girl of the Jockey Club: he had conceived the idea of buying a bunch of flowers of her. But the aristocratic flower-girl did not stir; and, indeed, what should induce her to approach a gentleman without gloves, in a soiled fustian jacket, streaky cravat, and boots trodden down at heel, whom she had not even seen in Paris? Then Voroshilov in his turn beckoned to her. To him she responded, and he, taking a tiny bunch of violets from her basket, flung her a florin. He thought to astonish her by his munificence, but not an eyelash on her face quivered, and when he had turned away, she pursed up her mouth contemptuously. Voroshilov was dressed very fashionably, even exquisitely, but the experienced eye of the Parisian girl noted at once in his get-up and in his bearing, in his very walk, which showed traces of premature military drill, the absence of genuine, pure-blooded 'chic.'

When they had taken their seats in the principal dining-hall at Weber's, and ordered dinner, our friends fell into conversation. Bambaev discoursed loudly and hotly upon the immense importance of Gubaryov, but soon he ceased speaking, and, gasping and chewing noisily, drained off glass after glass. Voroshilov ate and drank little, and as it were reluctantly, and after questioning Litvinov as to the nature of his interests, fell to giving expression to his own opinions—not so much on those interests, as on questions of various kinds in general.... All at once he warmed up, and set off at a gallop like a spirited horse, boldly and decisively assigning to every syllable, every letter, its due weight, like a confident cadet going up for his 'final' examination, with vehement, but inappropriate gestures. At every instant, since no one interrupted him, he became more eloquent, more emphatic; it seemed as though he were reading a dissertation or lecture. The names of the most recent scientific authorities—with the addition of the dates of the birth or death of each of them—the titles of pamphlets that had only just appeared, and names, names, names ... fell in showers together from his tongue, affording himself intense satisfaction, reflected in his glowing eyes. Voroshilov, seemingly, despised everything old, and attached value only to the cream of culture, the latest, most advanced points of science; to mention, however inappropriately, a book of some Doctor Zauerbengel on Pennsylvanian prisons, or yesterday's articles in the *Asiatic Journal* on the Vedas and Puranas (he pronounced it *Journal* in the English fashion, though he certainly did not know English) was for him a real joy, a felicity. Litvinov listened and listened to him, and could not make out what could be his special line. At one moment his talk was of the part played by the Celtic race in history; then he was carried away to the ancient world, and discoursed upon the Æginetan marbles, harangued with great warmth on the sculptor living earlier than Phidias, Onetas, who was, however, transformed by him into Jonathan, which lent his whole discourse a half-Biblical, half-American flavour; then he suddenly bounded away to political economy and called Bastiat a fool or a blockhead, 'as bad as Adam Smith and all the physiocrats.' 'Physiocrats,' murmured Bambaev after him ... 'aristocrats?' Among other things Voroshilov called forth an expression of bewilderment on Bambaev's face by a criticism, dropped casually in passing, of Macaulay, as an old-fashioned writer, superseded by modern historical science; as for Gneist, he declared he need scarcely refer to him, and he shrugged his shoulders. Bambaev shrugged his shoulders too. 'And all this at once, without any inducement, before strangers, in a café'—Litvinov reflected, looking at the fair hair, clear eyes, and white teeth of his new acquaintance (he was specially embarrassed by those large sugar-white teeth, and those hands with their inappropriate gesticulations), 'and he doesn't once smile; and with it all, he would seem to be a nice lad, and absolutely inexperienced.' Voroshilov began to calm down at last, his voice, youthfully resonant and shrill as a young cock's, broke a little.... Bambaev seized the opportunity to declaim verses and again nearly burst into tears, which scandalised one table near them, round which was seated an English family, and set another tittering; two Parisian *cocottes* were dining at this second table with a creature who resembled an ancient baby in a wig. The waiter brought the bill; the friends paid it.

'Well,' cried Bambaev, getting heavily up from his chair, 'now for a cup of coffee, and quick march. There she is, our Russia,' he added, stopping in the doorway, and pointing almost rapturously with his soft red hand to Voroshilov and Litvinov.... 'What do you think of her?...'

'Russia, indeed,' thought Litvinov; and Voroshilov, whose face had by now regained its concentrated expression, again smiled condescendingly, and gave a little tap with his heels.

Within five minutes they were all three mounting the stairs of the hotel where Stepan Nikolaitch Gubaryov was staying.... A tall slender lady, in a hat with a short black veil, was coming quickly down the same staircase. Catching sight of Litvinov she turned suddenly round to him, and stopped still as though struck by amazement. Her face flushed instantaneously, and then as quickly grew pale under its thick lace veil; but Litvinov did not observe her, and the lady ran down the wide steps more quickly than before.

IV

'Grigory Litvinov, a brick, a true Russian heart. I commend him to you,' cried Bambaev, conducting Litvinov up to a short man of the figure of a country gentleman, with an unbuttoned collar, in a short jacket, grey morning trousers and slippers, standing in the middle of a light, and very well-furnished room; 'and this,' he added, addressing himself to Litvinov, 'is he, the man himself, do you understand? Gubaryov, then, in a word.'

Litvinov stared with curiosity at 'the man himself.' He did not at first sight find in him anything out of the common. He saw before him a gentleman of respectable, somewhat dull exterior, with a broad forehead, large eyes, full lips, a big beard, and a thick neck, with a fixed gaze, bent sidelong and downwards. This gentleman simpered, and said, 'Mmm ... ah ... very pleased,...' raised his hand to his own face, and at once turning his back on Litvinov, took a few paces upon the carpet, with a slow and peculiar shuffle, as though he were trying to slink along unseen. Gubaryov had the habit of continually walking up and down, and constantly plucking and combing his beard with the tips of his long hard nails. Besides Gubaryov, there was also in the room a lady of about fifty, in a shabby silk dress, with an excessively mobile face almost as yellow as a lemon, a little black moustache on her upper lip, and eyes which moved so quickly that they seemed as though they were jumping out of her head; there was too a broad-shouldered man sitting bent up in a corner.

‘Well, honoured Matrona Semyonovna,’ began Gubaryov, turning to the lady, and apparently not considering it necessary to introduce Litvinov to her, ‘what was it you were beginning to tell us?’

The lady (her name was Matrona Semyonovna Suhantchikov—she was a widow, childless, and not rich, and had been travelling from country to country for two years past) began with peculiar exasperated vehemence:

‘Well, so he appears before the prince and says to him: “Your Excellency,” he says, “in such an office and such a position as yours, what will it cost you to alleviate my lot? You,” he says, “cannot but respect the purity of my ideas! And is it possible,” he says, “in these days to persecute a man for his ideas?” And what do you suppose the prince did, that cultivated dignitary in that exalted position?’

‘Why, what did he do?’ observed Gubaryov, lighting a cigarette with a meditative air.

The lady drew herself up and held out her bony right hand, with the first finger separated from the rest.

‘He called his groom and said to him, “Take off that man’s coat at once, and keep it yourself. I make you a present of that coat!”’

‘And did the groom take it?’ asked Bambaev, throwing up his arms.

‘He took it and kept it. And that was done by Prince Barnaulov, the well-known rich grandee, invested with special powers, the representative of the government. What is one to expect after that!’

The whole frail person of Madame Suhantchikov was shaking with indignation, spasms passed over her face, her withered bosom was heaving convulsively under her flat corset; of her eyes it is needless to speak, they were fairly leaping out of her head. But then they were always leaping, whatever she might be talking about.

‘A crying shame, a crying shame!’ cried Bambaev. ‘No punishment could be bad enough!’

‘Mmm.... Mmm.... From top to bottom it’s all rotten,’ observed Gubaryov, without raising his voice, however. ‘In that case punishment is not ... that needs ... other measures.’

‘But is it really true?’ commented Litvinov.

‘Is it true?’ broke in Madame Suhantchikov. ‘Why, that one can’t even dream of doubting ... can’t even d-d-d-ream of it.’ She pronounced these words with such energy that she was fairly shaking with the effort. ‘I was told of that by a very trustworthy man. And you, Stepan Nikolaitch, know him—Elistratov, Kapiton. He heard it himself from eyewitnesses, spectators of this disgraceful scene.’

‘What Elistratov?’ inquired Gubaryov. ‘The one who was in Kazan?’

‘Yes. I know, Stepan Nikolaitch, a rumour was spread about him that he took bribes there from some contractors or distillers. But then who is it says so? Pelikanov! And how can one believe Pelikanov, when every one knows he is simply—a spy!’

‘No, with your permission, Matrona Semyonovna,’ interposed Bambaev, ‘I am friends with Pelikanov, he is not a spy at all.’

‘Yes, yes, that’s just what he is, a spy!’

‘But wait a minute, kindly——’

‘A spy, a spy!’ shrieked Madame Suhantchikov.

‘No, no, one minute, I tell you what,’ shrieked Bambaev in his turn.

‘A spy, a spy,’ persisted Madame Suhantchikov.

‘No, no! There’s Tentelyev now, that’s a different matter,’ roared Bambaev with all the force of his lungs.

Madame Suhantchikov was silent for a moment.

‘I know for a fact about that gentleman,’ he continued in his ordinary voice, ‘that when he was summoned before the secret police, he grovelled at the feet of the Countess Blazenkrampff and kept whining, “Save me, intercede for me!” But Pelikanov never demeaned himself to baseness like that.’

‘Mm ... Tentelyev ...’ muttered Gubaryov, ‘that ... that ought to be noted.’

Madame Suhantchikov shrugged her shoulders contemptuously.

‘They’re one worse than another,’ she said, ‘but I know a still better story about Tentelyev. He was, as every one knows, a most horrible despot with his serfs, though he gave himself out for an emancipator. Well, he was once at some friend’s house in Paris, and suddenly in comes Madame Beecher Stowe—you know, *Uncle Tom’s Cabin*. Tentelyev, who’s an awfully pushing fellow, began asking the host to present him; but directly she heard his name. “What?” she said, “he presumes to be introduced to the author of *Uncle Tom?*” And she gave him a slap on the cheek! “Go away!” she says, “at once!” And what do you think? Tentelyev took his hat and slunk away, pretty crestfallen.’

M[rs]. Beecher Stowe.

'Come, I think that's exaggerated,' observed Bambaev. '"Go away" she certainly did say, that's a fact, but she didn't give him a smack!'

'She did, she did!' repeated Madam Suhantchikov with convulsive intensity: 'I am not talking idle gossip. And you are friends with men like that!'

'Excuse me, excuse me, Matrona Semyonovna, I never spoke of Tentelyev as a friend of mine; I was speaking of Pelikanov.'

'Well, if it's not Tentelyev, it's another. Mihnyov, for example.'

'What did he do then?' asked Bambaev, already showing signs of alarm.

'What? Is it possible you don't know? He exclaimed on the Poznesensky Prospect in the hearing of all the world that all the liberals ought to be in prison; and what's more, an old schoolfellow came to him, a poor man of course, and said, "Can I come to dinner with you?" And this was his answer. "No, impossible; I have two counts dining with me to-day ... get along with you!-
-"'

'But that's slander, upon my word!' vociferated Bambaev.

'Slander? ... slander? In the first place, Prince Vahrushkin, who was also dining at your Mihnyov's——'

'Prince Vahrushkin,' Gubaryov interpolated severely, 'is my cousin; but I don't allow him to enter my house.... So there is no need to mention him even.'

'In the second place,' continued Madame Suhantchikov, with a submissive nod in Gubaryov's direction, 'PraskovyaYakovlovna told me so herself.'

'You have hit on a fine authority to quote! Why, she and Sarkizov are the greatest scandal-mongers going.'

'I beg your pardon, Sarkizov is a liar, certainly. He filched the very pall of brocade off his dead father's coffin. I will never dispute that; but Praskovya Yakovlovna—there's no comparison! Remember how magnanimously she parted from her husband! But you, I know, are always ready——'

'Come, enough, enough, Matrona Semyonovna,' said Bambaev, interrupting her, 'let us give up this tittle-tattle, and take a loftier flight. I am not new to the work, you know. Have you read *Mlle. de la Quintinie?* That's something charming now! And quite- in accord with your principles at the same time!'

'I never read novels now,' was Madame Suhantchikov's dry and sharp reply.

'Why?'

'Because I have not the time now; I have no thoughts now but for one thing, sewing machines.'

'What machines?' inquired Litvinov.

'Sewing, sewing; all women ought to provide themselves with sewing-machines, and form societies; in that way they will all be enabled to earn their living, and will become independent at once. In no other way can they ever be emancipated. That is an important, most important social question. I had such an argument about it with Boleslav Stadnitsky. Boleslav Stadnitsky is a marvellous nature, but he looks at these things in an awfully frivolous spirit. He does nothing but laugh. Idiot!'

'All will in their due time be called to account, from all it will be exacted,' pronounced Gubaryov deliberately, in a tone half-professorial, half-prophetic.

'Yes, yes,' repeated Bambaev, 'it will be exacted, precisely so, it will be exacted. But, Stepan Nikolaitch,' he added, dropping his voice, 'how goes the great work?'

'I am collecting materials,' replied Gubaryov,- knitting his brows; and, turning to Litvinov, whose head began to swim from the medley of unfamiliar names, and the frenzy of backbiting, he asked him what subjects he was interested in.

Litvinov satisfied his curiosity.

'Ah! to be sure, the natural sciences. That is useful, as training; as training, not as an end in itself. The end at present should be ... mm ... should be ... different. Allow me to ask what views do you hold?'

'What views?'

'Yes, that is, more accurately speaking, what are your political views?'

Litvinov smiled.

'Strictly speaking, I have no political views.'

The broad-shouldered man sitting in the corner raised his head quickly at these words and looked attentively at Litvinov.

'How is that?' observed Gubaryov with peculiar gentleness. 'Have you not yet reflected on the subject, or have you grown weary of it?'

'How shall I say? It seems to me that for us Russians, it is too early yet to have political views or to imagine that we have them. Observe that I attribute to the word "political" the meaning which belongs to it by right, and that——'

'Aha! he belongs to the undeveloped,' Gubaryov interrupted him, with the same gentleness, and going up to Voroshilov, he asked him: 'Had he read the pamphlet he had given him?'

Voroshilov, to Litvinov's astonishment, had not uttered a word ever since his entrance, but had only knitted his brows and rolled his eyes (as a rule he was either speechifying or else perfectly dumb). He now expanded his chest in soldierly fashion, and with a tap of his heels, nodded assent.

'Well, and how was it? Did you like it?'

'As regards the fundamental principles, I liked it; but I did not agree with the inferences.'

'Mmm ... Andrei Ivanitch praised that pamphlet, however. You must expand your doubts to me later.'

'You desire it in writing?'

Gubaryov was obviously surprised; he had not expected this; however, after a moment's thought, he replied:

'Yes, in writing. By the way, I will ask you to explain to me your views also ... in regard to ... in regard to associations.'

'Associations on Lassalle's system, do you desire, or on the system of Schulze-Delitzsch?'

'Mmm ... on both. For us Russians, you understand, the financial aspect of the matter is specially important. Yes, and the *artel* ... as the germ.... All that, one must take note of. One must go deeply into it. And the question, too, of the land to be apportioned to the peasants....'

'And you, Stepan Nikolaitch, what is your view as to the number of acres suitable?' inquired Voroshilov, with reverential delicacy in his voice.

'Mmm ... and the commune?' articulated Gubaryov, deep in thought, and biting a tuft of his beard he stared at the table-leg. 'The commune!... Do you understand. That is a grand word! Then what is the significance of these conflagrations? these ... these government measures against Sunday-schools, reading-rooms, journals? And the refusal of the peasants to sign the charters regulating their position in the future? And finally, what of what is happening in Poland? Don't you see that ... mmm ... that we ... we have to unite with the people ... find out ... find out their views——' Suddenly a heavy, almost a wrathful emotion seemed to take possession of Gubaryov; he even grew black in the face and breathed heavily, but still did not raise his eyes, and continued to gnaw at his beard. 'Can't you see——'

'Yevseyev is a wretch!' Madame Suhantchikov burst out noisily all of a sudden. Bambaev had been relating something to her in a voice lowered out of respect for their host. Gubaryov turned round swiftly on his heels, and again began limping about the room.

Fresh guests began to arrive; towards the end of the evening a good many people were assembled. Among them came, too, Mr. Yevseyev whom Madame Suhantchikov had vilified so cruelly. She entered into conversation with him very cordially, and asked him to escort her home; there arrived too a certain Pishtchalkin, an ideal mediator, one of those men of precisely whom perhaps Russia stands in need—a man, that is, narrow, of little information, and no great gifts, but conscientious, patient, and honest; the peasants of his district almost worshipped him, and he regarded himself very respectfully as a creature genuinely deserving of esteem. A few officers, too, were there, escaped for a brief furlough to Europe, and rejoicing—though of course warily, and ever mindful of their colonel in the background of their brains—in the opportunity of dallying a little with intellectual—even rather dangerous—people; two lanky students from Heidelberg came hurrying in, one looked about him very contemptuously, the other giggled spasmodically ... both were very ill at ease; after them a Frenchman—a so-called *petit jeune homme*—poked his nose in; a nasty, silly, pitiful little creature, ... who enjoyed some repute among his fellow *commis-voyageurs* on the theory that Russian countesses had fallen in love with him; for his own part, his reflections were centred more upon getting a supper gratis; the last to appear was Tit Bindasov, in appearance a rollicking German student, in reality a skinflint, in words a terrorist, by vocation a police-officer, a friend of Russian merchants' wives and Parisian *cocottes;* bald, toothless, and drunken; he arrived very red and sodden, affirming that he had lost his last farthing to that blackguard Benazet; in reality, he had won sixteen guldens.... In short, there were a number of people. Remarkable—really remarkable—was the respect with which all these people treated Gubaryov as a preceptor or chief; they laid their ideas before him, and submitted them to his judgment; and he replied by muttering, plucking at his beard, averting his eyes, or by some disconnected, meaningless words, which were at once seized upon as the utterances of the loftiest wisdom. Gubaryov himself seldom interposed in the discussions; but the others strained their lungs to the utmost to make up for it. It happened more than once that three or four were shouting-3 for ten minutes together, and all were content and understood. The conversation lasted till after midnight, and was as usual distinguished by the number and variety of the subjects discussed. Madame Suhantchikov talked about Garibaldi, about a certain Karl Ivanovitch, who had been flogged by the serfs of his own household, about Napoleon III., about women's work, about a merchant, Pleskatchov, who had designedly caused the death of twelve work-women, and had received a medal for it with the inscription 'for public services'; about the proletariat, about the Georgian Prince Tchuktcheulidzov, who had shot his wife with a cannon, and about the future of Russia. Pishtchalkin, too, talked of the future of Russia, and of the spirit monopoly, and of the significance of nationalities, and of how he hated above everything what was vulgar. There was an outburst all of a sudden from Voroshilov; in a single breath, almost choking himself, he mentioned Draper, Virchow, Shelgunov, Bichat, Helmholtz, Star, St. Raymund, Johann Müller the physiologist, and Johann Müller the historian—obviously confounding them—Taine, Renan, Shtchapov; and then Thomas Nash, Peele, Greene.... 'What sort of queer fish may they be?' Bambaev muttered bewildered, Shakespeare's predecessors having the same relation-3 to him as the ranges of the Alps to Mont Blanc. Voroshilov replied cuttingly, and he too touched on the future of Russia. Bambaev also spoke of the future of Russia, and even depicted it in glowing colours: but he was thrown into special raptures over the thought of Russian music, in which he saw something. 'Ah! great indeed!' and in confirmation he began humming a song of Varlamov's, but was soon interrupted by a general shout, 'He is singing the *Miserere* from the*Trovatore*, and singing it excruciatingly too.' One little officer was reviling Russian literature in the midst of the hubbub; another was quoting verses from *Sparks;* but Tit Bindasov went even further; he declared that all these swindlers ought to have their teeth knocked out, ... and that's all about it, but he did not particularise who were the swindlers alluded to. The smoke from the cigars became stifling; all were hot and exhausted, every one was hoarse, all eyes were growing dim, and the perspiration stood out in drops on every face. Bottles of iced beer were brought in and drunk off instantaneously. 'What was I saying?' remarked one; 'and with whom was I disputing, and about what?' inquired another. And among all the uproar and the smoke, Gubaryov walked indefatigably up and down as before, swaying from side to side and twitching at his beard;-3 now listening, turning an ear to some controversy, now putting in a word of his own; and every one was forced to feel that he, Gubaryov, was the source of it all, that he was the master here, and the most eminent personality....

Litvinov, towards ten o'clock, began to have a terrible headache, and, taking advantage of a louder outburst of general excitement, went off quietly unobserved. Madame Suhantchikov had recollected a fresh act of injustice of Prince Barnaulov; he had all but given orders to have some one's ears bitten off.

The fresh night air enfolded Litvinov's flushed face caressingly, the fragrant breeze breathed on his parched lips. 'What is it,' he thought as he went along the dark avenue, 'that I have been present at? Why were they met together? What were they shouting, scolding, and making such a pother about? What was it all for?' Litvinov shrugged his shoulders, and turning into Weber's, he picked up a newspaper and asked for an ice. The newspaper was taken up with a discussion on the Roman question, and the ice turned out to be very nasty. He was already preparing to go home, when suddenly an unknown person in a wide-brimmed hat drew near, and saying in Russian: 'I hope I am not in your way?' sat down at his table. Only then, after a closer glance at-3 the stranger, Litvinov recognised him as the broad-shouldered gentleman hidden away in a corner at Gubaryov's, who had stared at him with such attention when the conversation had turned on political views. During the whole evening this gentleman had not once opened his mouth, and now, sitting down near Litvinov, and taking off his hat, he looked at him with an expression of friendliness and some embarrassment.

-3

V

'Mr. Gubaryov, at whose rooms I had the pleasure of meeting you to-day,' he began, 'did not introduce me to you; so that, with your leave, I will now introduce myself—Potugin, retired councillor. I was in the department of finances in St. Petersburg. I hope you do not think it strange.... I am not in the habit as a rule of making friends so abruptly ... but with you....'

Potugin grew rather mixed, and he asked the waiter to bring him a little glass of kirsch-wasser. 'To give me courage,' he added with a smile.

Litvinov looked with redoubled interest at the last of all the new persons with whom it had been his lot to be brought into contact that day. His thought was at once, 'He is not the same as those.'

Certainly he was not. There sat before him, drumming with delicate fingers on the edge of the table, a broad-shouldered man, with an ample frame on short legs, a downcast head of curly hair, with very intelligent and very mournful eyes under bushy brows, a thick well-cut mouth, bad teeth, and that purely Russian nose to which is assigned the epithet 'potato'; a man of awkward, even odd exterior; at least, he was certainly not of a common type. He was carelessly dressed; his old-fashioned coat hung on him like a sack, and his cravat was twisted awry. His sudden friendliness, far from striking Litvinov as intrusive, secretly flattered him; it was impossible not to see that it was not a common practice with this man to attach himself to strangers. He made a curious impression on Litvinov; he awakened in him respect and liking, and a kind of involuntary compassion.

'I am not in your way then?' he repeated in a soft, rather languid and faint voice, which was marvellously in keeping with his whole personality.

'No, indeed,' replied Litvinov; 'quite the contrary, I am very glad.'

'Really? Well, then, I am glad too. I have heard a great deal about you; I know what you are engaged in, and what your plans are. It's a good work. That's why you were silent this evening.'

'Yes; you too said very little, I fancy,' observed Litvinov.

Potugin sighed. 'The others said enough and to spare. I listened. Well,' he added, after a moment's pause, raising his eyebrows with a rather humorous expression, 'did you like our building of the Tower of Babel?'

'That's just what it was. You have expressed it capitally. I kept wanting to ask those gentlemen what they were in such a fuss about.'

Potugin sighed again.

'That's the whole point of it, that they don't know that themselves. In former days the expression used about them would have been: "they are the blind instruments of higher ends"; well, nowadays we make use of sharper epithets. And take note that I am not in the least intending to blame them; I will say more, they are all ... that is, almost all, excellent people. Of Madame Suhantchikov, for instance, I know for certain much that is good; she gave away the last of her fortune to two poor nieces. Even admitting that the desire of doing something picturesque, of showing herself off, was not without its influence on her, still you will agree that it was a remarkable act of self-sacrifice in a woman not herself well-off! Of Mr. Pishtchalkin there is no need to speak even; the peasants of his district will certainly in time present him with a silver bowl like a pumpkin, and perhaps even a holy picture representing his patron saint, and though he will tell them in his speech of thanks that he does not deserve such an honour, he won't tell the truth there; he does deserve it. Mr. Bambaev, your friend, has a wonderfully good heart; it's true that it's with him as with the poet Yazikov, who they say used to sing the praises of Bacchic revelry, sitting over a book and sipping water; his enthusiasm is completely without a special object, still it is enthusiasm; and Mr. Voroshilov, too, is the most good-natured fellow; like all his sort, all men who've taken the first prizes at school, he's an *aide-de-camp* of the sciences, and he even holds his tongue sententiously, but then he is so young. Yes, yes, they are all excellent people, and when you come to results, there's nothing to show for it; the ingredients are all first-rate, but the dish is not worth eating.'

Litvinov listened to Potugin with growing astonishment: every phrase, every turn of his slow but self-confident speech betrayed both the power of speaking and the desire to speak.

Potugin did, in fact, like speaking, and could speak well; but, as a man in whom life had succeeded in wearing away vanity, he waited with philosophic calm for a good opportunity, a meeting with a kindred spirit.

'Yes, yes,' he began again, with the special dejected but not peevish humour peculiar to him, 'it is all very strange. And there is something else I want you to note. Let a dozen Englishmen, for example, come together, and they will at once begin to talk of the sub-marine telegraph, or the tax on paper, or a method of tanning rats' skins,—of something, that's to say, practical and definite; a dozen Germans, and of course Schleswig-Holstein and the unity of Germany will be brought on the scene; given a dozen Frenchmen, and the conversation will infallibly turn upon amorous adventures, however much you try to divert them from the subject; but let a dozen Russians meet together, and instantly there springs up the question—you had an opportunity of being convinced of the fact this evening—the question of the significance and the future of Russia, and in terms so general, beginning with creation, without facts or conclusions. They worry and worry away at that unlucky subject, as children chew away at a bit of india-rubber—neither for pleasure nor profit, as the saying is. Well, then, of course the rotten West comes in for its share. It's a curious thing, it beats us at every point, this West—but yet we declare that it's rotten! And if only we had a genuine contempt for it,' pursued Potugin, 'but that's really all cant and humbug. We can do well enough as far as abuse goes, but the opinion of the West is the only thing we value, the opinion, that's to say, of the Parisian loafers.... I know a man—a good fellow, I fancy—the father of a family, and no longer young; he was thrown into deep dejection for some days because in a Parisian restaurant he had asked for *une portion de biftek aux pommes de terre*, and a real Frenchman thereupon shouted: *Garçon! biftek pommes!* My friend was ready to die with shame, and after that he shouted everywhere, *Biftek pommes!* and taught others to do the same. The very *cocottes* are surprised at the reverential trepidation with which our young barbarians enter their shameful drawing-rooms. "Good God!" they are thinking, "is this really where I am, with no less a person than Anna Deslions herself!"'

'Tell me, pray,' continued Litvinov, 'to what do you ascribe the influence Gubaryov undoubtedly has over all about him? Is it his talent, his abilities?'

'No, no; there is nothing of that sort about him....'

'His personal character is it, then?'

'Not that either, but he has a strong will. We Slavs, for the most part, as we all know,-4 are badly off for that commodity, and we grovel before it. It is Mr. Gubaryov's will to be a ruler, and every one has recognised him as a ruler. What would you have? The government has freed us from the dependence of serfdom—and many thanks to it! but the habits of slavery are too deeply ingrained in us; we cannot easily be rid of them. We want a master in everything and everywhere; as a rule this master is a living person, sometimes it is some so-called tendency which gains authority over us.... At present, for instance, we are all the bondslaves of natural science.... Why, owing to what causes, we take this bondage upon us, that is a matter difficult to see into; but such seemingly is our nature. But the great thing is, that we should have a master. Well, here he is amongst us; that means he is ours, and we can afford to despise everything else! Simply slaves! And our pride is slavish, and slavish too is our humility. If a new master arises—it's all over with the old one. Then it was Yakov, and now it is Sidor; we box Yakov's ears and kneel to Sidor! Call to mind how many tricks of that sort have been played amongst us! We talk of scepticism as our special characteristic; but even in our scepticism we are not like a free man fighting with a sword, but like a lackey hitting out with his fist, and-4 very likely he is doing even that at his master's bidding. Then, we are a soft people too; it's not difficult to keep the curb on us. So that's the way Mr. Gubaryov has become a power among us; he has chipped and chipped away at one point, till he has chipped himself into success. People see that he is a man who has a great opinion of himself, who believes in himself, and commands. That's the great thing, that he can command; it follows that he must be right, and we ought to obey him. All our sects, our Onuphrists and Akulinists, were founded exactly in that way. He who holds the rod is the corporal.'

Potugin's cheeks were flushed and his eyes grew dim; but, strange to say, his speech, cruel and even malicious as it was, had no touch of bitterness, but rather of sorrow, genuine and sincere sorrow.

'How did you come to know Gubaryov?' asked Litvinov.

'I have known him a long while. And observe, another peculiarity among us; a certain writer, for example, spent his whole life in inveighing in prose and verse against drunkenness, and attacking the system of the drink monopoly, and lo and behold! he went and bought two spirit distilleries and opened a hundred drink-shops—and it made no difference!-4Any other man might have been wiped off the face of the earth, but he was not even reproached for it. And here is Mr. Gubaryov; he is a Slavophil and a democrat and a socialist and anything you like, but his property has been and is still managed by his brother, a master of the old style, one of those who were famous for their fists. And the very Madame Suhantchikov, who makes Mrs. Beecher Stowe box Tentelyev's ears, is positively in the dust before Gubaryov's feet. And you know the only thing he has to back him is that he reads clever books, and always gets at the pith of them. You could see for yourself to-day what sort of gift he has for expression; and thank God, too, that he does talk little, and keeps in his shell. For when he is in good spirits, and lets himself go, then it's more than even I, patient as I am, can stand. He begins by coarse joking and telling filthy anecdotes ... yes, really, our majestic Mr. Gubaryov tells filthy anecdotes, and guffaws so revoltingly over them all the time.'

'Are you so patient?' observed Litvinov. 'I should have supposed the contrary. But let me ask your name and your father's name?'

Potugin sipped a little kirsch-wasser.

'My name is Sozont.... Sozont Ivanitch. They gave me that magnificent name in honour of a kinsman, an archimandrite, to whom I am-4 indebted for nothing else. I am, if I may venture so to express myself, of most reverend stock. And as for your doubts about my patience, they are quite groundless: I am very patient. I served for twenty-two years under the authority of my own uncle, an actual councillor of state, Irinarh Potugin. You don't know him?'

'No.'

'I congratulate you. No, I am patient. "But let us return to our first head," as my esteemed colleague, who was burned alive some centuries ago, the protopope Avvakum, used to say. I am amazed, my dear sir, at my fellow-countrymen. They are all depressed, they all walk with downcast heads, and at the same time they are all filled with hope, and on the smallest excuse they lose their heads and fly off into ecstasies. Look at the Slavophils even, among whom Mr. Gubaryov reckons himself: they are most excellent people, but there is the same mixture of despair and exultation, they too live in the future tense. Everything will be, will be, if you please. In reality there is nothing done, and Russia for ten whole centuries has created nothing of its own, either in government, in law, in science, in art, or even in handicraft.... But wait a little, have patience; it is all coming. And why is it coming; give us leave to inquire? Why, because we, to be sure, the cultured classes are all worthless; but the people.... Oh, the great people! You see that peasant's smock? That is the source that everything is to come from. All the other idols have broken down; let us have faith in the smock-frock. Well, but suppose the smock-frock fails us? No, it will not fail. Read Kohanovsky, and cast your eyes up to heaven! Really, if I were a painter, I would paint a picture of this sort: a cultivated man standing before a peasant, doing him homage: heal me, dear master-peasant, I am perishing of disease; and a peasant doing homage in his turn to the cultivated man: teach me, dear master-gentleman, I am perishing from ignorance. Well, and of course, both are standing still. But what we ought to do is to feel really humble for a little—not only in words—and to borrow from our elder brothers what they have invented already before us and better than us! Waiter, *noch ein Gläschen Kirsch!* You mustn't think I'm a drunkard, but alcohol loosens my tongue.'

'After what you have just said,' observed Litvinov with a smile, 'I need not even inquire to which party you belong, and what is your opinion about Europe. But let me make one observation to you. You say that we ought to borrow from our elder brothers: but how can we borrow without consideration of the conditions of climate and of soil, the local and national peculiarities? My father, I recollect, ordered from Butenop a cast-iron thrashing machine highly recommended; the machine was very good, certainly—but what happened? For five long years it remained useless in the barn, till it was replaced by a wooden American one—far more suitable to our ways and habits, as the American machines are as a rule. One cannot borrow at random, Sozont Ivanitch.'

Potugin lifted his head.

'I did not expect such a criticism as that from you, excellent Grigory Mihalovitch,' he began, after a moment's pause. 'Who wants to make you borrow at random? Of course you steal what belongs to another man, not because it is some one else's, but because it suits you; so it follows that you consider, you make a selection. And as for results, pray don't let us be unjust to ourselves; there will be originality enough in them by virtue of those very local, climatic, and other conditions which you mention. Only lay good food before it, and the natural stomach will digest it in its own way; and in time, as the organism gains in vigour, it will give it a sauce of its own. Take our language even as an instance. Peter the Great deluged it with thousands of foreign words, Dutch, French, and German; those words expressed ideas with which the Russian people had to be familiarised; without scruple or ceremony Peter poured them wholesale by bucketsful into us. At first, of course, the result was something of a monstrous product; but later there began precisely that process of digestion to which I have alluded. The ideas had been introduced and assimilated; the foreign forms evaporated gradually, and the language found substitutes for them from within itself; and now your humble servant, the most mediocre stylist, will undertake to translate any page you like out of Hegel—yes, indeed, out of Hegel—without making use of a single word not Slavonic. What has happened with the language, one must hope will happen in other departments. It all turns on the question: is it a nature of strong vitality? and our nature—well, it will stand the test; it has gone through greater trials than that. Only nations in a state of nervous debility, feeble nations, need fear for their health and their independence, just as it is only weak-minded people who are capable of falling into triumphant rhapsodies over the fact that we are Russians. I am very careful over my health, but I don't go into ecstasies over it: I should be ashamed.'

'That is all very true, Sozont Ivanitch,' observed Litvinov in his turn; 'but why inevitably expose ourselves to such tests? You say yourself that at first the result was monstrous! Well, what if that monstrous product had persisted? Indeed it has persisted, as you know yourself.'

'Only not in the language—and that means a great deal! And it is our people, not I, who have done it; I am not to blame because they are destined to go through a discipline of this kind. "The Germans have developed in a normal way," cry the Slavophils, "let us too have a normal development!" But how are you to get it when the very first historical step taken by our race—the summoning of a prince from over the sea to rule over them—is an irregularity, an abnormality, which is repeated in every one of us down to the present day; each of us, at least once in his life, has certainly said to something foreign, not Russian: "Come, rule and reign over me!" I am ready, of course, to agree that when we put a foreign substance into our own body we cannot tell for certain what it is we are putting there, bread or poison; yet it is a well-known thing that you can never get from bad to good through what is better, but always through a worse state of transition, and poison too is useful in medicine. It is only fit for fools or knaves to point with triumph to the poverty of the peasants after the-5 emancipation, and the increase of drunkenness since the abolition of the farming of the spirit-tax.... Through worse to better!'

Potugin passed his hand over his face. 'You asked me what was my opinion of Europe,' he began again: 'I admire her, and am devoted to her principles to the last degree, and don't in the least think it necessary to conceal the fact. I have long—no, not long—for some time ceased to be afraid to give full expression to my convictions—and I saw that you too had no hesitation in informing Mr. Gubaryov of your own way of thinking. Thank God I have given up paying attention to the ideas and points of view and habits of the man I am conversing with. Really, I know of nothing worse than that quite superfluous cowardice, that cringing desire to be agreeable, by virtue of which you may see an important dignitary among us trying to ingratiate himself with some little student who is quite insignificant in his eyes, positively playing down to him, with all sorts of tricks and devices. Even if we admit that the dignitary may do it out of desire for popularity, what induces us common folk to shuffle and degrade ourselves. Yes, yes, I am a Westerner, I am devoted to Europe: that's to say, speaking more accurately, I am devoted to culture—the culture at which they make fun so-5 wittily among us just now—and to civilisation—yes, yes, that is a better word—and I love it with my whole heart and believe in it, and I have no other belief, and never shall have. That word, ci-vi-li-sa-tion (Potugin pronounced each syllable with full stress and emphasis), is intelligible, and pure, and holy, and all the other ideals, nationality, glory, or what you like—they smell of blood.... Away with them!'

'Well, but Russia, Sozont Ivanitch, your country—you love it?'

Potugin passed his hand over his face. 'I love her passionately and passionately hate her.'

Litvinov shrugged his shoulders.

'That's stale, Sozont Ivanitch, that's a commonplace.'

'And what of it? So that's what you're afraid of! A commonplace! I know many excellent commonplaces. Here, for example, Law and Liberty is a well-known commonplace. Why, do you consider it's better as it is with us, lawlessness and bureaucratic tyranny? And, besides, all those phrases by which so many young heads are turned: vile bourgeoisie,*souveraineté du peuple*, right to labour, aren't they commonplaces too? And as for love, inseparable from hate....'

'Byronism,' interposed Litvinov, 'the romanticism of the thirties.'

-5

'Excuse me, you're mistaken; such a mingling of emotions was first mentioned by Catullus, the Roman poet Catullus,[1] two thousand years ago. I have read that, for I know a little Latin, thanks to my clerical origin, if so I may venture to express myself. Yes, indeed, I both love and hate my Russia, my strange, sweet, nasty, precious country. I have left her just now. I want a little fresh air after sitting for twenty years on a clerk's high stool in a government office; I have left Russia, and I am happy and contented here; but I shall soon go back again: I feel that. It's a beautiful land of gardens—but our wild berries will not grow here.'

'You are happy and contented, and I too like the place,' said Litvinov, 'and I came here to study; but that does not prevent me from seeing things like that.'

He pointed to two *cocottes* who passed by, attended by a little group of members of the Jockey Club, grimacing and lisping, and to the gambling saloon, full to overflowing in spite of the lateness of the hour.

'And who told you I am blind to that?' Potugin broke in. 'But pardon my saying it, your remark reminds me of the triumphant-5 allusions made by our unhappy journalists at the time of the Crimean war, to the defects in the English War Department, exposed in the *Times*. I am not an optimist myself, and all humanity, all our life, all this comedy with tragic issues presents itself to me in no roseate colours: but why fasten upon the West what is perhaps ingrained in our very human nature? That gambling hall is disgusting, certainly; but is our home-bred card-sharping any lovelier, think you? No, my dear Grigory Mihalovitch, let us be more humble, more retiring. A good pupil sees his master's faults, but he keeps a respectful silence about them; these very faults are of use to him, and set him on the right path. But if nothing will satisfy you but sharpening your teeth on the unlucky West, there goes Prince Kokó at a gallop, he will most likely lose in a quarter of an hour over the green table the hardly earned rent wrung from a hundred and fifty families; his nerves are upset, for I saw him at Marx's to-day turning over a pamphlet of Vaillot.... He will be a capital person for you to talk to!'

'But, please, please,' said Litvinov hurriedly, seeing that Potugin was getting up from his place, 'I know Prince Kokó very little, and besides, of course, I greatly prefer talking to you.'

'Thanks very much,' Potugin interrupted-5 him, getting up and making a bow; 'but I have already had a good deal of conversation with you; that's to say, really, I have talked alone, and you have probably noticed yourself that a man is always as it were ashamed and awkward when he has done all the talking, especially so on a first meeting, as if to show what a fine fellow one is. Good-bye for the present. And I repeat I am very glad to have made your acquaintance.'

'But wait a minute, Sozont Ivanitch, tell me at least where you live, and whether you intend to remain here long.'

Potugin seemed a little put out.

'I shall remain about a week in Baden. We can meet here though, at Weber's or at Marx's, or else I will come to you.'

'Still I must know your address.'

'Yes. But you see I am not alone.'

'You are married?' asked Litvinov suddenly.

'No, good heavens! ... what an absurd idea! But I have a girl with me.'...

'Oh!' articulated Litvinov, with a face of studied politeness, as though he would ask pardon, and he dropped his eyes.

'She is only six years old,' pursued Potugin. 'She's an orphan ... the daughter of a lady ... a good friend of mine. So we had better meet here. Good-bye.'

-5

He pulled his hat over his curly head, and disappeared quickly. Twice there was a glimpse of him under the gas-lamps in the rather meanly lighted road that leads into the Lichtenthaler Allee.

-5

VI

'A strange man!' thought Litvinov, as he turned into the hotel where he was staying; 'a strange man! I must see more of him!' He went into his room; a letter on the table caught his eye. 'Ah! from Tanya!' he thought, and was overjoyed at once; but the letter was from his country place, from his father. Litvinov broke the thick heraldic seal, and was just setting to work to read it ... when he was struck by a strong, very agreeable, and familiar fragrance, and saw in the window a great bunch of fresh heliotrope in a glass of water. Litvinov bent over them not without amazement, touched them, and smelt them.... Something seemed to stir in his memory, something very remote ... but what, precisely, he could not discover. He rang for the servant and asked him where these flowers had come from. The man replied that they had been brought by a lady who would not give her name, but said that 'Herr Zlitenhov' would be sure to guess who she was by the-6 flowers. Again something stirred in Litvinov's memory. He asked the man what the lady looked like, and the servant informed him that she was tall and grandly dressed and had a veil over her face. 'A Russian countess most likely,' he added.

'What makes you think that?' asked Litvinov.

'She gave me two guldens,' responded the servant with a grin.

Litvinov dismissed him, and for a long while after he stood in deep thought before the window; at last, however, with a wave of his hand, he began again upon the letter from the country. His father poured out to him his usual complaints, asserting that no one would take their corn, even for nothing, that the people had got quite out of all habits of obedience, and that probably the end of the world was coming soon. 'Fancy,' he wrote, among other things, 'my last coachman, the Kalmuck boy, do you remember him? has been bewitched, and the fellow would certainly have died, and I should have had none to drive me, but, thank goodness, some kind folks suggested and advised to send the sick man to Ryazan, to a priest, well-known as a master against witchcraft: and his cure has actually succeeded as well as possible, in confirmation of which I lay before you the-6 letter of the good father as a document.' Litvinov ran through this document with curiosity. In it was set forth: 'that the serving-man Nicanor Dmitriev was beset with a malady which could not be touched by the medical faculty; and this malady was the work of wicked people; but he himself, Nicanor, was the cause of it, since he had not fulfilled his promise to a certain girl, and therefore by the aid of others she had made him unfit for anything, and if I had not appeared to aid him in these circumstances, he would surely have perished utterly, like a worm; but I, trusting in the All-seeing Eye, have become a stay to him in his life; and how I accomplished it, that is a mystery; I beg your excellency not to countenance a girl who has such wicked arts, and even to chide her would be no harm, or she may again work him a mischief.'

Litvinov fell to musing over this document; it brought him a whiff of the desert, of the steppes, of the blind darkness of the life mouldering there, and it seemed a marvellous thing that he should be reading such a letter in Baden, of all places. Meanwhile it had long struck midnight; Litvinov went to bed and put out his light. But he could not get to sleep; the faces he had seen, the talk he had heard, kept coming back and revolving,-6 strangely interwoven and entangled in his burning head, which ached from the fumes of tobacco. Now he seemed to hear Gubaryov's muttering, and fancied his eyes with their dull, persistent stare fastened on the floor; then suddenly those eyes began to glow and leap, and he recognised Madame Suhantchikov, and listened to her shrill voice, and involuntarily repeated after her in a whisper, 'she did, she did, slap his face.' Then the clumsy figure of Potugin passed before him; and for the tenth, and the twentieth time he went over every word he had uttered; then, like a jack in the box, Voroshilov jumped up in his trim coat, which fitted him like a new uniform; and Pishtchalkin gravely and sagaciously nodded his well-cut and truly well-intentioned head; and then Bindasov bawled and swore, and Bambaev fell into tearful transports.... And above all—this scent, this persistent, sweet, heavy scent gave him no rest, and grew more and more powerful in the darkness, and more and more importunately it reminded him of something which still eluded his grasp.... The idea occurred to Litvinov that the scent of flowers at night in a bedroom was injurious, and he got up, and groping his way to the nosegay, carried it into the next room; but even from there the oppressive fragrance penetrated to-6 him on his pillow and under the counterpane, and he tossed in misery from side to side. A slight delirium had already begun to creep over him; already the priest, 'the master against witchcraft' had twice run across his road in the guise of a very playful hare with a beard and a pig-tail, and Voroshilov was trilling before him, sitting in a huge general's plumed cock-hat like a nightingale in a bush.... When suddenly he jumped up in bed, and clasping his hands, cried, 'Can it be she? it can't be!'

But to explain this exclamation of Litvinov's we must beg the indulgent reader to go back a few years with us.

-6

VII

Early in the fifties, there was living in Moscow, in very straitened circumstances, almost in poverty, the numerous family of the Princes Osinin. These were real princes—not Tartar-Georgians, but pure-blooded descendants of Rurik. Their name is often to be met with in our chronicles under the first grand princes of Moscow, who created a united Russia. They possessed wide acres and many domains. Many a time they were rewarded for 'service and blood and disablement.' They sat in the Council of Boyars. One of them even rose to a very high position. But they fell under the ban of the empire through the plots of enemies 'on a charge of witchcraft and evil philtres,' and they were ruined 'terribly and beyond recall.' They were deprived of their rank, and banished to remote parts; the Osinins fell and had never risen again, had never attained to power again. The ban was taken off in time, and they were even reinstated in their Moscow house and belongings,-6 but it was of no avail. Their family was impoverished, 'run to seed'; it did not revive under Peter, nor under Catherine; and constantly dwindling and growing humbler, it had by now reckoned private stewards, managers of wine-shops, and ward police-inspectors among its members. The family of Osinins, of whom we have made mention, consisted of a husband and wife and five children. It was living near the Dogs' Place, in a one-storied little wooden house, with a striped portico looking on to the street, green lions on the gates, and all the other pretensions of nobility, though it could hardly make both ends meet, was constantly in debt at the green-grocer's, and often sitting without firewood or candles in the winter. The prince himself was a dull, indolent man, who had once been a handsome dandy, but had gone to seed completely. More from regard for his wife, who had been a maid-of-honour, than from respect for his name, he had been presented with one of those old-fashioned Moscow posts that have a small salary, a queer-sounding name, and absolutely no duties attached. He never meddled in anything, and did nothing but smoke from morning till night, breathing heavily, and always wrapped in a dressing-gown. His wife was a sickly irritable woman, for ever worried over domestic trifles—over getting her children-6 placed in government schools, and keeping up her Petersburg connections; she could never accustom herself to her position and her remoteness from the Court.

Litvinov's father had made acquaintance with the Osinins during his residence at Moscow, had had occasion to do them some services, and had once lent them three hundred roubles; and his son often visited them while he was a student; his lodging happened to be at no great distance from their house. But he was not drawn to them simply as near neighbours, nor tempted by their comfortless way of living. He began to be a frequent visitor at their house after he had fallen in love with their eldest daughter Irina.

She had then completed her seventeenth year; she had only just left school, from which her mother withdrew her through a disagreement with the principal. This disagreement arose from the fact that Irina was to have delivered at a public function some verses in French, complimentary to the curator, and just before the performance her place was filled by another girl, the daughter of a very rich spirit-contractor. The princess could not stomach this affront; and indeed Irina herself never forgave the principal for this act of injustice; she had been dreaming beforehand of how she would rise before the eyes of every one, attracting universal attention, and would deliver her speech, and how Moscow would talk about her afterwards!... And, indeed, Moscow would have talked about her afterwards. She was a tall, slim girl, with a somewhat hollow chest and narrow unformed shoulders, with a skin of a dead-white, rare at her age, and pure and smooth as china, with thick fair hair; there were darker tresses mingled in a very original way with the light ones. Her features—exquisitely, almost too perfectly, correct—had not yet quite lost the innocent expression that belongs to childhood; the languid curves of her lovely neck, and her smile—half-indifferent, half-weary—betrayed the nervous temperament of a delicate girl; but in the lines of those fine, faintly-smiling lips, of that small, falcon, slightly-narrow nose, there was something wilful and passionate, something dangerous for herself and others. Astounding, really astounding were her eyes, dark grey with greenish lights, languishing, almond-shaped as an Egyptian goddess's, with shining lashes and bold sweep of eyebrow. There was a strange look in those eyes; they seemed looking out intently and thoughtfully—looking out from some unknown depth and distance. At school, Irina had been reputed one of the best pupils for intelligence and abilities, but of uneven temper, fond of power, and headstrong; one class-mistress prophesied that her passions would be her ruin—'*vos passions vous perdront*', on the other hand, another class-mistress censured her for coldness and want of feeling, and called her '*une jeune fille sans cœur*.' Irina's companions thought her proud and reserved: her brothers and sisters stood a little in awe of her: her mother had no confidence in her: and her father felt ill at ease when she fastened her mysterious eyes upon him. But she inspired a feeling of involuntary respect in both her father and her mother, not so much through her qualities, as from a peculiar, vague sense of expectations which she had, in some undefined way, awakened in them.

'You will see, Praskovya Danilovna,' said the old prince one day, taking his pipe out of his mouth, 'our chit of an Irina will give us all a lift in the world yet.'

The princess got angry, and told her husband that he made use of '*des expressions insupportables*'; afterwards, however, she fell to musing over his words, and repeated through her teeth:

'Well ... and it would be a good thing if we did get a lift.'

Irina enjoyed almost unlimited freedom in her parents' house; they did not spoil her, they even avoided her a little, but they did not thwart her, and that was all she wanted.... Sometimes—during some too humiliating scene—when some tradesman would come and keep shouting, to be heard over the whole court, that he was sick of coming after his money, or their own servants would begin abusing their masters to their face, with 'fine princes you are, to be sure; you may whistle for your supper, and go hungry to bed'—Irina would not stir a muscle; she would sit unmoved, an evil smile on her dark face; and her smile alone was more bitter to her parents than any reproaches, and they felt themselves guilty—guilty, though guiltless—towards this being on whom had been bestowed, as it seemed, from her very birth, the right to wealth, to luxury, and to homage.

Litvinov fell in love with Irina from the moment he saw her (he was only three years older than she was), but for a long while he failed to obtain not only a response, but even a hearing. Her manner to him was even overcast with a shade of something like hostility; he did in fact wound her pride, and she concealed the wound, and could never forgive it. He was too young and too modest at that time to understand what might be concealed under this hostile, almost contemptuous severity. Often, forgetful of lectures and exercises, he would sit and sit in the Osinins' cheerless drawing-room, stealthily watching Irina, his heart slowly and painfully throbbing and suffocating him; and she would seem angry or bored, would get up and walk about the room, look coldly at him as though he were a table or chair, shrug her shoulders, and fold her arms. Or for a whole evening, even when talking with Litvinov, she would purposely avoid looking at him, as though denying him even that grace. Or she would at last take up a book and stare at it, not reading, but frowning and biting her lips. Or else she would suddenly ask her father or brother aloud: 'What's the German for patience?' He tried to tear himself away from the enchanted circle in which he suffered and struggled impotently like a bird in a trap; he went away from Moscow for a week. He nearly went out of his mind with misery and dulness; he returned quite thin and ill to the Osinins'.... Strange to say, Irina too had grown perceptibly thinner during those days; her face had grown pale, her cheeks were wan.... But she met him with still greater coldness, with almost malignant indifference; as though he had intensified that secret wound he had dealt at her pride.... She tortured him in this way for two months. Then everything was transformed in one day. It was as though love had broken into flame with the heat, or had dropped down from a storm-cloud. One day—long will he remember that day—he was once more sitting in the Osinins' drawing-room at the window, and was looking mechanically into the street. There was vexation and weariness in his heart, he despised himself, and yet he could not move from his place.... He thought that if a river ran there under the window, he would throw himself in, with a shudder of fear, but without a regret. Irina placed herself not far from him, and was somehow strangely silent and motionless. For some days now she had not talked to him at all, or to any one else; she kept sitting, leaning on her elbows, as though she were in perplexity, and only rarely she looked slowly round. This cold torture was at last more than Litvinov could bear; he got up, and without saying good-bye, he began to look for his hat. 'Stay,' sounded suddenly, in a soft whisper. Litvinov's heart throbbed, he did not at once recognise Irina's voice; in that one word, there was a ring of something that had never been in it before. He lifted his head and was stupefied; Irina was looking fondly—yes, fondly at him. 'Stay,' she repeated; 'don't go. I want to be with you.' Her voice sank still lower. 'Don't go.... I wish it.' Understanding nothing, not fully conscious what he was doing, he drew near her, stretched out his hands.... She gave him both of hers at once, then smiling, flushing hotly, she turned away, and still smiling, went out of the room. She came back a few minutes later with her youngest sister, looked at him again with the same prolonged tender gaze, and made him sit near her.... At first she could say nothing; she only sighed and blushed; then she began, timidly as it were, to question him about his pursuits, a thing she had never done before. In the evening of the same day, she tried several times to beg his forgiveness for not having done him justice before, assured him she had now become quite different, astonished him by a sudden outburst of republicanism (he had at that time a positive hero-worship for Robespierre, and did not presume to criticise Marat aloud), and only a week later he knew that she loved him. Yes; he long remembered that first day ... but he did not forget those that came after either—those days, when still forcing himself to doubt, afraid to believe in it, he saw clearly, with transports of rapture, almost of dread, bliss un-hoped for coming to life, growing, irresistibly carrying everything before it, reaching him at last. Then followed the radiant moments of first love—moments which are not destined to be, and could not fittingly be, repeated in the same life. Irina became all at once as docile as a lamb, as soft as silk, and boundlessly kind; she began giving lessons to her younger sisters—not on the piano, she was no musician, but in French and English; she read their school-books with them, and looked after the housekeeping; everything was amusing and interesting to her; she would sometimes chatter incessantly, and sometimes sink into speechless tenderness; she made all sorts of plans, and was lost in endless anticipations of what she would do when she was married to Litvinov (they never doubted that their marriage would come to pass), and how together they would ... 'Work?' prompted Litvinov.... 'Yes; work,' repeated Irina, 'and read ... but travel before all things.' She particularly wanted to leave Moscow as soon as possible, and when Litvinov reminded her that he had not yet finished his course of study at the university, she always replied, after a moment's thought, that it was quite possible to finish his studies at Berlin or ... somewhere or other. Irina was very little reserved in the expression of her feelings, and so her relations with Litvinov did not long remain a secret from the prince and princess. Rejoice they could not; but, taking all circumstances into consideration, they saw no necessity for putting a veto on it at once. Litvinov's fortune was considerable....

'But his family, his family!' ... protested the princess. 'Yes, his family, of course,' replied the prince; but at least he's not quite a plebeian; and, what's the principal point, Irina, you know, will not listen to us. Has there ever been a time when she did not do what she chose? *Vous connaissez sa violence!* Besides, there is nothing fixed definitely yet.' So reasoned the prince, but mentally he added, however: 'Madame Litvinov—is that all? I had expected something else.' Irina took complete possession of her future *fiancé*, and indeed he himself eagerly surrendered himself into her hands. It was as if he had fallen into a rapid river, and had lost himself.... And bitter and sweet it was to him, and he regretted nothing and heeded nothing. To reflect on the significance and the duties of marriage, or whether he, so hopelessly enslaved, could be a good husband, and what sort of wife Irina would make, and whether their relations to one another were what they should be—was more than he could bring himself to. His blood was on fire, he could think of nothing, only—to follow her, be with her, for the future without end, and then—let come what may!

But in spite of the complete absence of opposition on Litvinov's side, and the wealth of impulsive tenderness on Irina's, they did not get on quite without any misunderstandings and quarrels. One day he ran to her straight from the university in an old coat and ink-stained hands. She rushed to meet him with her accustomed fond welcome; suddenly she stopped short.

'You have no gloves,' she said abruptly, and added directly after: 'Fie! what a student you are!'

'You are too particular, Irina,' remarked Litvinov.

'You are a regular student,' she repeated. '*Vous n'êtes pas distingué*'; and turning her back on him she went out of the room. It is true that an hour later she begged him to forgive her.... As a rule she readily censured herself and accused herself to him; but, strange to say, she often almost with tears blamed herself for evil propensities which she had not, and obstinately denied her real defects. Another time he found her in tears, her head in her hands, and her hair in disorder; and when, all in agitation, he asked her the cause of her grief, she pointed with her finger at her own bosom without speaking. Litvinov gave an involuntary shiver. 'Consumption!' flashed through his brain, and he seized her hand.

'Are you ill, Irina?' he articulated in a shaking voice. (They had already begun on great occasions to call each other by their first names.) 'Let me go at once for a doctor.'

But Irina did not let him finish; she stamped with her foot in vexation.

'I am perfectly well ... but this dress ... don't you understand?'

'What is it? ... this dress,' he repeated in bewilderment.

'What is it? Why, that I have no other, and that it is old and disgusting, and I am obliged to put on this dress every day ... even when you—Grisha—Grigory, come here.... You will leave off loving me, at last, seeing me so slovenly!'

'For goodness sake, Irina, what are you saying? That dress is very nice.... It is dear to me too because I saw you for the first time in it, darling.'

Irina blushed.

'Do not remind me, if you please, Grigory Mihalovitch, that I had no other dress even then.'

'But I assure you, Irina Pavlovna, it suits you so exquisitely.'

'No, it is horrid, horrid,' she persisted, nervously pulling at her long, soft curls. 'Ugh, this poverty, poverty and squalor! How is one to escape from this sordidness! How get out of this squalor!'

Litvinov did not know what to say, and slightly turned away from her.

All at once Irina jumped up from her chair, and laid both her hands on his shoulders.

'But you love me, Grisha? You love me?' she murmured, putting her face close to him, and her eyes, still filled with tears, sparkled with the light of happiness, 'You love me, dear, even in this horrid dress?'

Litvinov flung himself on his knees before her.

'Ah, love me, love me, my sweet, my saviour,' she whispered, bending over him.

So the days flew, the weeks passed, and though as yet there had been no formal declaration, though Litvinov still deferred his demand for her hand, not, certainly, at his own desire, but awaiting directions from Irina (she remarked sometimes that they were both ridiculously young, and they must add at least a few weeks more to their years), still everything was moving to a conclusion, and the future as it came nearer grew more and more clearly defined, when suddenly an event occurred, which scattered all their dreams and plans like light roadside dust.

VIII

That winter the court visited Moscow. One festivity followed another; in its turn came the customary great ball in the Hall of Nobility. The news of this ball, only, it is true, in the form of an announcement in the *Political Gazette*, reached even the little house in Dogs' Place. The prince was the first to be roused by it; he decided at once that he must not fail to go and take Irina, that it would be unpardonable to let slip the opportunity of seeing their sovereigns, that for the old nobility this constituted indeed a duty in its own way. He defended his opinion with a peculiar warmth, not habitual in him; the princess agreed with him to some extent, and only sighed over the expense; but a resolute opposition was displayed by Irina. 'It is not necessary, I will not go,' she replied to all her parents' arguments. Her obstinacy reached such proportions that the old prince decided at last to beg Litvinov to try to persuade her, by reminding her among other reasons that it was not proper for a young girl to avoid society, that she ought to 'have this experience,' that no one ever saw her anywhere, as it was. Litvinov undertook to lay these 'reasons' before her. Irina looked steadily and scrutinisingly at him, so steadily and scrutinisingly that he was confused, and then, playing with the ends of her sash, she said calmly:

'Do you desire it, you?'

'Yes.... I suppose so,' replied Litvinov hesitatingly. 'I agree with your papa.... Indeed, why should you not go ... to see the world, and show yourself,' he added with a short laugh.

'To show myself,' she repeated slowly. 'Very well then, I will go.... Only remember, it is you yourself who desired it.'

'That's to say, I——.' Litvinov was beginning.

'You yourself have desired it,' she interposed. 'And here is one condition more; you must promise me that you will not be at this ball.'

'But why?'

'I wish it to be so.'

Litvinov unclasped his hands.

'I submit ... but I confess I should so have enjoyed seeing you in all your grandeur, witnessing the sensation you are certain to make.... How proud I should be of you!' he added with a sigh.

Irina laughed.

'All the grandeur will consist of a white frock, and as for the sensation.... Well, any way, I wish it.'

'Irina, darling, you seem to be angry?'

Irina laughed again.

'Oh, no! I am not angry. Only, Grisha....' (She fastened her eyes on him, and he thought he had never before seen such an expression in them.) 'Perhaps, it must be,' she added in an undertone.

'But, Irina, you love me, dear?'

'I love you,' she answered with almost solemn gravity, and she clasped his hand firmly like a man.

All the following days Irina was busily occupied over her dress and her coiffure; on the day before the ball she felt unwell, she could not sit still, and twice she burst into tears in solitude; before Litvinov she wore the same uniform smile.... She treated him, however, with her old tenderness, but carelessly, and was constantly looking at herself in the glass. On the day of the ball she was silent and pale, but collected. At nine o'clock in the evening Litvinov came to look at her. When she came to meet him in a white tarlatan gown, with a spray of small blue flowers in her slightly raised hair, he almost uttered a cry; she seemed to him so lovely and stately beyond what was natural to her years. 'Yes, she has grown up since this morning!' he thought, 'and how she holds herself! That's what race does!' Irina stood before him, her hands hanging loose, without smiles or affectation, and looked resolutely, almost boldly, not at him, but away into the distance straight before her.

'You are just like a princess in a story book,' said Litvinov at last. 'You are like a warrior before the battle, before victory.... You did not allow me to go to this ball,' he went on, while she remained motionless as before, not because she was not listening to him, but because she was following another inner voice, 'but you will not refuse to accept and take with you these flowers?'

He offered her a bunch of heliotrope. She looked quickly at Litvinov, stretched out her hand, and suddenly seizing the end of the spray which decorated her hair, she said:

'Do you wish it, Grisha? Only say the word, and I will tear off all this, and stop at home.'

Litvinov's heart seemed fairly bursting. Irina's hand had already snatched the spray....

'No, no, what for?' he interposed hurriedly, in a rush of generous and magnanimous feeling, 'I am not an egoist.... Why should I restrict your freedom ... when I know that your heart——'

'Well, don't come near me, you will crush my dress,' she said hastily.

Litvinov was disturbed.

'But you will take the nosegay?' he asked.

'Of course; it is very pretty, and I love that scent. *Merci*—I shall keep it in memory——'

'Of your first coming out,' observed Litvinov, 'your first triumph.'

Irina looked over her shoulder at herself in the glass, scarcely bending her figure.

'And do I really look so nice? You are not partial?'

Litvinov overflowed in enthusiastic praises. Irina was already not listening to him, and holding the flowers up to her face, she was again looking away into the distance with her strange, as it were, overshadowed, dilated eyes, and the ends of her delicate ribbons stirred by a faint current of air rose slightly behind her shoulders like wings.

The prince made his appearance, his hair well becurled, in a white tie, and a shabby black evening coat, with the medal of nobility on a Vladimir ribbon in his buttonhole. After him came the princess in a china silk dress of antique cut, and with the anxious severity under which mothers try to conceal their agitation, set her daughter to rights behind, that is to say, quite needlessly shook out the folds of her gown. An antiquated hired coach with seats for four, drawn by two shaggy hacks, crawled up to the steps, its wheels grating over the frozen mounds of unswept snow, and a decrepit groom in a most unlikely-looking livery came running out of the passage, and with a sort of desperate courage announced that the carriage was ready.... After giving a blessing for the night to the children left at home, and enfolding themselves in their fur wraps, the prince and princess went out to the steps; Irina in a little cloak, too thin and too short—how she hated the little cloak at that moment!—followed them in silence. Litvinov escorted them outside, hoping for a last look from Irina, but she took her seat in the carriage without turning her head.

About midnight he walked under the windows of the Hall of Nobility. Countless lights of huge candelabra shone with brilliant radiance through the red curtains; and the whole square, blocked with carriages, was ringing with the insolent, festive, seductive strains of a waltz of Strauss'.

The next day at one o'clock, Litvinov betook himself to the Osinins'. He found no one at home but the prince, who informed him at once that Irina had a headache, that she was in bed, and would not get up till the evening, that such an indisposition was however little to be wondered at after a first ball.

'*C'est très naturel, vous savez, dans les jeunes filles*,' he added in French, somewhat to Litvinov's surprise; the latter observed at the same instant that the prince was not in his dressing-gown as usual, but was wearing a coat. 'And besides,' continued Osinin, 'she may well be a little upset after the events of yesterday!'

'Events?' muttered Litvinov.

'Yes, yes, events, events, *de vrais événements*. You cannot imagine, Grigory Mihalovitch, *quel succès elle a eu!*The whole court noticed her! Prince Alexandr Fedorovitch said that her place was not here, and that she reminded him of Countess Devonshire. You know ... that ... celebrated.... And old Blazenkrampf declared in the hearing of all, that Irina was *la reine du bal*, and desired to be introduced to her; he was introduced to me too, that's to say, he told me that he remembered me a hussar, and asked me where I was holding office now. Most entertaining man that Count, and such an *adorateur du beau sexe!* But that's not all; my princess ... they gave her no peace either: Natalya Nikitishna herself conversed with her ... what more could we have? Irina danced *avec tous les meilleurs cavaliers;* they kept bringing them up to me.... I positively lost count of them. Would you believe it, they were all flocking about us in crowds; in the mazurka they did nothing but seek her out. One foreign diplomatist, hearing she was a Moscow girl, said to the Tsar: '*Sire*,' he said, '*décidément c'est Moscou qui est le centre de votre empire!*' and another diplomatist added: '*C'est une vraie révolution, Sire—révélation* or *révolution* ... something of that sort. Yes, yes, it was. I tell you it was something extraordinary.'

'Well, and Irina Pavlovna herself?' inquired Litvinov, whose hands and feet had grown cold hearing the prince's speech, 'did she enjoy herself, did she seem pleased?'

'Of course she enjoyed herself; how could she fail to be pleased? But, as you know, she's not to be seen through at a glance! Every one was saying to me yesterday: it is really surprising! *jamais on ne dirait que mademoiselle votre fille est a son premier bal*. Count Reisenbach among the rest ... you know him most likely.'

'No, I don't know him at all, and have never heard of him.'

'My wife's cousin.'

'I don't know him.'

'A rich man, a chamberlain, living in Petersburg, in the swim of things; in Livonia every one is in his hands. Hitherto he has neglected us ... but there, I don't bear him ill-will for that. *J'ai l'humeur facile, comme vous savez*. Well, that's the kind of man he is. He sat near Irina, conversed with her for a quarter of an hour, not more, and said afterwards to my princess: "*Ma cousine*," he says, "*votre fille est une perle; c'est une perfection*, every one is congratulating me on such a niece...." And afterwards I look round—and he had gone up to a ... a very great personage, and was talking, and kept looking at Irina ... and the personage was looking at her too.'...

'And so Irina Pavlovna will not appear all day?' Litvinov asked again.

'Quite so; her head aches very badly. She told me to greet you from her, and thank you for your flowers, *qu'on a trouvé charmant*. She needs rest.... The princess has gone out on a round of visits ... and I myself ... you see....'

The prince cleared his throat, and began to fidget as though he were at a loss what to add further. Litvinov took his hat, and saying he did not want to disturb him, and would call again later to inquire after her health, he went away.

-8

A few steps from the Osinins' house he saw an elegant carriage for two persons standing before the police sentry-box. A groom in livery, equally elegant, was bending negligently from the box, and inquiring of the Finnish police-sergeant whereabouts Prince Pavel Vassilyevitch Osinin lived. Litvinov glanced at the carriage; in it sat a middle-aged man of bloated complexion, with a wrinkled and haughty face, a Greek nose, and an evil mouth, muffled in a sable wrap, by all outward signs a very great man indeed.

-8

IX

Litvinov did not keep his promise of returning later; he reflected that it would be better to defer his visit till the following day. When he went into the too familiar drawing-room at about twelve o'clock, he found there the two youngest princesses, Viktorinka and Kleopatrinka. He greeted them, and then inquired, 'Was Irina Pavlovna better, and could he see her?'

'Irinotchka has gone away with mammy,' replied Viktorinka; she lisped a little, but was more forward than her sister.

'How ... gone away?' repeated Litvinov, and there was a sort of still shudder in the very bottom of his heart. 'Does she not, does she not look after you about this time, and give you your lessons?'

'Irinotchka will not give us any lessons any more now,' answered Viktorinka. 'Not any more now,' Kleopatrinka repeated after her.

'Is your papa at home?' asked Litvinov.

-8

'Papa is not at home,' continued Viktorinka, 'and Irinotchka is not well; all night long she was crying and crying....'

'Crying?'

'Yes, crying ... Yegorovna told me, and her eyes are so red, they are quite in-inflamed....'

Litvinov walked twice up and down the room shuddering as though with cold, and went back to his lodging. He experienced a sensation like that which gains possession of a man when he looks down from a high tower; everything failed within him, and his head was swimming slowly with a sense of nausea. Dull stupefaction, and thoughts scurrying like mice, vague terror, and the numbness of expectation, and curiosity—strange, almost malignant—and the weight of crushed tears in his heavy laden breast, on his lips the forced empty smile, and a meaningless prayer—addressed to no one.... Oh, how bitter it all was, and how hideously degrading! 'Irina does not want to see me,' was the thought that was incessantly revolving in his brain; 'so much is clear; but why is it? What can have happened at that ill-fated ball? And how is such a change possible all at once? So suddenly....' People always see death coming suddenly, but they can never get accustomed to its suddenness, they feel it senseless.-9 'She sends no message for me, does not want to explain herself to me....'

'Grigory Mihalitch,' called a strained voice positively in his ear.

Litvinov started, and saw before him his servant with a note in his hand. He recognised Irina's writing.... Before he had broken the seal, he had a foreknowledge of woe, and bent his head on his breast and hunched his shoulders, as though shrinking from the blow.

He plucked up courage at last, and tore open the envelope all at once. On a small sheet of notepaper were the following lines:

'Forgive me, Grigory Mihalitch. All is over between us; I am going away to Petersburg. I am dreadfully unhappy, but the thing is done. It seems my fate ... but no, I do not want to justify myself. My presentiments have been realised. Forgive me, forget me; I am not worthy of you.—Irina. Be magnanimous: do not try to see me.'

Litvinov read these five lines, and slowly dropped on to the sofa, as though some one had dealt him a blow on the breast. He dropped the note, picked it up, read it again, whispered 'to Petersburg,' and dropped it again; that was all. There even came upon him a sense of peace; he even, with his hands thrown behind him, smoothed the pillow under his head.-9 'Men wounded to death don't fling themselves about,' he thought, 'as it has come, so it has gone. All this is natural enough: I always expected it....' (He was lying to himself; he had never expected anything like it.) 'Crying?... Was she crying?... What was she crying for? Why, she did not love me! But all that is easily understood and in accordance with her character. She—she is not worthy of me.... That's it!' (He laughed bitterly.) 'She did not know herself what power was latent in her,—well, convinced of it in her effect at the ball, was it likely she would stay with an insignificant student?—all that's easily understood.'

But then he remembered her tender words, her smile, and those eyes, those never to be forgotten eyes, which he would never see again, which used to shine and melt at simply meeting his eyes; he recalled one swift, timorous, burning kiss—and suddenly he fell to sobbing, sobbing convulsively, furiously, vindictively; turned over on his face, and choking and stifling with frenzied satisfaction as though thirsting to tear himself to pieces with all around him, he turned his hot face in the sofa pillow, and bit it in his teeth.

Alas! the gentleman whom Litvinov had seen the day before in the carriage was no other than the cousin of the Princess Osinin, the rich chamberlain, Count Reisenbach. Noticing the sensation produced by Irina on certain personages of the highest rank, and instantaneously reflecting what advantages might *mit etwas Accuratesse* be derived from the fact, the count made his plan at once like a man of energy and a skilful courtier. He decided to act swiftly, in Napoleonic style. 'I will take that original girl into my house,' was what he meditated, 'in Petersburg; I will make her my heiress, devil take me, of my whole property even; as I have no children. She is my niece, and my countess is dull all alone.... It's always more agreeable to have a pretty face in one's drawing-room.... Yes, yes; ... that's it; *es ist eine Idee, es ist eine Idee!*' He would have to dazzle, bewilder, and impress the parents. 'They've not enough to eat'—the count pursued his reflection when he was in the carriage and on his way to Dogs' Place—'so, I warrant, they won't be obstinate. They're not such over-sentimental folks either. I might give them a sum of money down into the bargain. And she? She will consent. Honey is sweet—she had a taste of it last night. It's a whim on my part, granted; let them profit by it, ... the fools. I shall say to them one thing and another ... and you must decide—otherwise I shall adopt another—an orphan—which would be still more suitable. Yes or no—twenty-four hours I fix for the term—*und damit Punctum.*'

And with these very words on his lips, the count presented himself before the prince, whom he had forewarned of his visit the evening before at the ball. On the result of this visit it seems hardly worth while to enlarge further. The count was not mistaken in his prognostications: the prince and princess were in fact not obstinate, and accepted the sum of money; and Irina did in fact consent before the allotted term had expired. It was not easy for her to break off her relations with Litvinov; she loved him; and after sending him her note, she almost kept her bed, weeping continually, and grew thin and wan. But for all that, a month later the princess carried her off to Petersburg, and established her at the count's; committing her to the care of the countess, a very kind-hearted woman, but with the brain of a hen, and something of a hen's exterior.

Litvinov threw up the university, and went home to his father in the country. Little by little his wound healed. At first he had no news of Irina, and indeed he avoided all conversation that touched on Petersburg and Petersburg society. Later on, by degrees, rumours—not evil exactly, but curious—began to circulate about her; gossip began to be busy about her. The name of the young Princess Osinin, encircled in splendour, impressed with quite a special stamp, began to be more and more frequently mentioned even in provincial circles. It was pronounced with curiosity, respect, and envy, as men at one time used to mention the name of the Countess Vorotinsky. At last the news came of her marriage. But Litvinov hardly paid attention to these last tidings; he was already betrothed to Tatyana.

Now, the reader can no doubt easily understand exactly what it was Litvinov recalled when he cried, 'Can it be she?' and therefore we will return to Baden and take up again the broken thread of our story.

X

Litvinov fell asleep very late, and did not sleep long; the sun had only just risen when he got out of bed. The summits of dark mountains visible from his windows stood out in misty purple against the clear sky. 'How cool it must be there under the trees!' he thought; and he dressed in haste, and looked with indifference at the bouquet which had opened more luxuriantly after the night; he took a stick and set off towards the 'Old Castle' on the famous 'Cliffs.' Invigorating and soothing was the caressing contact of the fresh morning about him. He drew long breaths, and stepped out boldly; the vigorous health of youth was throbbing in every vein; the very earth seemed springy under his light feet. With every step he grew more light-hearted, more happy; he walked in the dewy shade in the thick sand of the little paths, beside the fir-trees that were fringed with the vivid green of the spring shoots at the end of every twig. 'How jolly it is!' he kept repeating to himself. Suddenly he heard the sound of familiar voices; he looked ahead and saw Voroshilov and Bambaev coming to meet him. The sight of them jarred upon him; he rushed away like a school-boy avoiding his teacher, and hid himself behind a bush.... 'My Creator!' he prayed, 'mercifully remove my countrymen!' He felt that he would not have grudged any money at the moment if only they did not see him.... And they actually did not see him: the Creator was merciful to him. Voroshilov, in his self-confident military voice, was holding forth to Bambaev on the various phases of Gothic architecture, and Bambaev only grunted approvingly; it was obvious that Voroshilov had been dinning his phrases into him a long while, and the good-natured enthusiast was beginning to be bored. Compressing his lips and craning his neck, Litvinov listened a long while to their retreating footsteps; for a long time the accents of instructive discourse—now guttural, now nasal—reached his ears; at last, all was still again. Litvinov breathed freely, came out of his ambush, and walked on.

For three hours he wandered about the mountains. Sometimes he left the path, and jumped from rock to rock, slipping now and then on the smooth moss; then he would sit-9 down on a fragment of the cliff under an oak or a beech, and muse on pleasant fancies to the never-ceasing gurgle of the little rills over-grown with ferns, the soothing rustle of the leaves, and the shrill notes of a solitary blackbird. A light and equally pleasant drowsiness began to steal over him, it seemed to approach him caressingly, and he dropped asleep ... but suddenly he smiled and looked round; the gold and green of the forest, and the moving foliage beat down softly on his eyes—and again he smiled and again closed them. He began to want breakfast, and he made his way towards the old castle where for a few kreutzers he could get a glass of good milk and coffee. But he had hardly had time to establish himself at one of the little white-painted tables set on the platform before the castle, when the heavy tramping of horses was heard, and three open carriages drove up, out of which stepped a rather numerous company of ladies and gentlemen.... Litvinov at once recognised them as Russians, though they were all talking French ... just because they were all talking French. The ladies' dresses were marked by a studied elegance; the gentlemen wore close-fitting coats with waists—which is not altogether usual nowadays—grey trousers of fancy material, and very glossy town hats. A narrow black cravat closely-9 fettered the neck of each of these gentlemen, and something military was apparent in their whole deportment. They were, in fact, military men; Litvinov had chanced upon a picnic party of young generals—persons of the highest society, of weight and importance. Their importance was clearly expressed in everything: in their discreet nonchalance, in their amiably condescending smiles, in the intense indifference of their expression, the effeminate little movements of their shoulders, the swing of the figure, and the crook of the knees; it was expressed, too, in the sound of their voices, which seemed to be affably and fastidiously thanking a subservient multitude. All these officers were superlatively washed and shaved, and thoroughly saturated with that genuine aroma of nobility and the Guards, compounded of the best cigar smoke, and the most marvellous patchouli. They all had the hands too of noblemen—white and large, with nails firm as ivory; their moustaches seemed positively polished, their teeth shone, and their skin—rosy on their cheeks, bluish on their chins—was most delicate and fine. Some of the young generals were frivolous, others were serious; but the stamp of the best breeding was on all of them. Each of them seemed to be deeply conscious of his own dignity, and the importance of his-9own future part in the government, and conducted himself with severity and ease, with a faint shade of that carelessness, that 'deuce-take-it' air, which comes out so naturally during foreign travel. The party seated themselves with much noise and ostentation, and called the obsequious waiters. Litvinov made haste to drink off his glass of milk, paid for it, and putting his hat on, was just making off past the party of generals....

'Grigory Mihalitch,' he heard a woman's voice. 'Don't you recognise me?'

He stopped involuntarily. That voice ... that voice had too often set his heart beating in the past.... He turned round and saw Irina.

She was sitting at a table, her arms folded on the back of a chair drawn up near; with her head bent on one side and a smile on her face, she was looking at him cordially, almost with delight.

Litvinov knew her at once, though she had changed since he saw her that last time ten years ago, though she had been transformed from a girl into a woman. Her slim figure had developed and reached its perfection, the lines of her once narrow shoulders now recalled the goddesses that stand out on the ceilings of ancient Italian palaces. But her eyes remained the same, and it seemed to Litvinov that they were looking at him just as in those days in the little house in Moscow.

'Irina Pavlovna,' he uttered irresolutely.

'You know me? How glad I am! how glad——'

She stopped short, slightly blushing, and drew herself up.

'This is a very pleasant meeting,' she continued now in French. 'Let me introduce you to my husband. *Valérien, Monsieur Litvinov, un ami d'enfance;* Valerian Vladimirovitch Ratmirov, my husband.'

One of the young generals, almost the most elegant of all, got up from his seat, and with excessive courtesy bowed to Litvinov, while the rest of his companions faintly knitted their brows, or rather each of them withdrew for an instant into himself, as though protesting betimes against any contact with an extraneous civilian, and the other ladies taking part in the picnic thought fit to screw up their eyes a little and simper, and even to assume an air of perplexity.

'Have you—er—been long in Baden?' asked General Ratmirov, with a dandified air utterly un-Russian. He obviously did not know what to talk about with the friend of his wife's childhood.

'No, not long!' replied Litvinov.

'And do you intend to stay long?' pursued the polite general.

'I have not made up my mind yet.'

'Ah! that is very delightful ... very.'

The general paused. Litvinov, too, was speechless. Both held their hats in their hands and bending forward with a grin, gazed at the top of each other's heads.

'*Deux gendarmes un beau dimanche*,' began humming—out of tune of course, we have never come across a Russian nobleman who did not sing out of tune—a dull-eyed and yellow-faced general, with an expression of constant irritability on his face, as though he could not forgive himself for his own appearance. Among all his companions he alone had not the complexion of a rose.

'But why don't you sit down, Grigory Mihalitch,' observed Irina at last.

Litvinov obeyed and sat down.

'*I say, Valérien, give me some fire*,' remarked in English another general, also young, but already stout, with fixed eyes which seemed staring into the air, and thick silky whiskers, into which he slowly plunged his snow-white fingers. Ratmirov gave him a silver matchbox.

'*Avez vous des papiros?*' asked one of the ladies, with a lisp.

'*De vrais papelitos, comtesse.*'

'*Deux gendarmes un beau dimanche*,' the dull-eyed general hummed again, with intense exasperation.

'You must be sure to come and see us,' Irina was saying to Litvinov meantime; 'we are staying at the Hôtel de l'Europe. From four to six I am always at home. We have not seen each other for such a long time.'

Litvinov looked at Irina; she did not drop her eyes.

'Yes, Irina Pavlovna, it is a long time—ever since we were at Moscow.'

'At Moscow, yes, at Moscow,' she repeated abruptly. 'Come and see me, we will talk and recall old times. Do you know, Grigory Mihalitch, you have not changed much.'

'Really? But you have changed, Irina Pavlovna.'

'I have grown older.'

'No, I did not mean that.'

'*Irène?*' said a lady in a yellow hat and with yellow hair in an interrogative voice after some preliminary whispering and giggling with the officer sitting near her. '*Irène?*'

'I am older,' pursued Irina, without answering the lady, 'but I am not changed. No, no, I am changed in nothing.'

'*Deux gendarmes un beau dimanche!*' was heard again. The irritable general only remembered the first line of the well-known ditty.

'It still pricks a little, your excellency,' observed the stout general with the whiskers, with a loud and broad intonation, apparently quoting from some amusing story, well-known to the whole *beau monde*, and, with a short wooden laugh he again fell to staring into the air. All the rest of the party laughed too.

'What a sad dog you are, Boris!' observed Ratmirov in an undertone. He spoke in English and pronounced even the name 'Boris' as if it were English.

'*Irène?*' the lady in the yellow hat said inquiringly for the third time. Irina turned sharply round to her.

'*Eh bien? quoi? que me voulez-vous?*'

'*Je vous dirai plus tard*,' replied the lady, mincing. With a very unattractive exterior, she was for ever mincing and grimacing. Some wit said of her that she '*minaudait dans le vide*,' 'grimaced upon the desert air.'

Irina frowned and shrugged her shoulders impatiently. '*Mais que fait donc Monsieur Verdier? Pourquoi ne vient-il pas?*' cried one lady with that prolonged drawl which is the peculiarity of the Great Russian accent, and is so insupportable to French ears.

'Ah, voo, ah, voo, mossoo Verdew, mossoo Verdew,' sighed another lady, whose birthplace was Arzamass.

'*Tranquillisez-vous, mesdames*,' interposed Ratmirov. '*Monsieur Verdier m'a promis de venir se mettre à vos pieds.*'

'He, he, he!'—The ladies fluttered their fans.

The waiter brought some glasses of beer.

'*Baierisch-Bier?*' inquired the general with whiskers, assuming a bass voice, and affecting astonishment—'*Guten Morgen.*'

'Well? Is Count Pavel still there?' one young general inquired coldly and listlessly of another.

'Yes,' replied the other equally coldly, '*Mais c'est provisoire*. *Serge*, they say, will be put in his place.'

'Aha!' filtered the first through his teeth.

'Ah, yes,' filtered the second.

'I can't understand,' began the general who had hummed the song, 'I can't understand what induced Paul to defend himself—to bring forward all sorts of reasons. Certainly, he crushed the merchant pretty well, *il lui a fait rendre gorge* ... well, and what of it? He may have had his own motives.'

'He was afraid ... of being shown up in the newspapers,' muttered some one.

The irritable general grew hot.

'Well, it is too much! Newspapers! Shown up! If it depended on me, I would not let anything be printed in those papers but the taxes on meat or bread, and announcements of sales of boots or furs.'

'And gentlemen's properties up for auction,' put in Ratmirov.

'Possibly under present circumstances.... What a conversation, though, in Baden *au Vieux-Château*.'

'*Mais pas du tout! pas du tout!*' replied the lady in the yellow hat, '*j'adore les questions politiques*.'

'*Madame a raison*,' interposed another general with an exceedingly pleasant and girlish-looking face. 'Why should we avoid those questions ... even in Baden?'

As he said these words he looked urbanely at Litvinov and smiled condescendingly. 'A man of honour ought never under any circumstances to disown his convictions. Don't you think so?'

'Of course,' rejoined the irritable general, darting a look at Litvinov, and as it were indirectly attacking him, 'but I don't see the necessity....'

'No, no,' the condescending general interposed with the same mildness, 'your friend, Valerian Vladimirovitch, just referred to the sale of gentlemen's estates. Well? Is not that a fact?'

'But it's impossible to sell them nowadays; nobody wants them!' cried the irritable general.

'Perhaps ... perhaps. For that very reason we ought to proclaim that fact ... that sad fact at every step. We are ruined ... very good; we are beggared ... there's no disputing about that; but we, the great owners, we still represent a principle ... *un principe*. To preserve that principle is our duty. *Pardon, madame*, I think you dropped your handkerchief. When some, so to say, darkness has come over even the highest minds, we ought submissively to point out (the general held out his finger) with the finger of a citizen the abyss to which everything is tending. We ought to warn, we ought to say with respectful firmness, 'turn back, turn back.... That is what we ought to say.'

'There's no turning back altogether, though,' observed Ratmirov moodily.

The condescending general only grinned.

'Yes, altogether, altogether, *mon très cher*. The further back the better.'

The general again looked courteously at Litvinov. The latter could not stand it.

'Are we to return as far as the Seven Boyars, your excellency?'

'Why not? I express my opinion without hesitation; we must undo ... yes ... undo all that has been done.'

'And the emancipation of the serfs.'

'And the emancipation ... as far as that is possible. *On est patriote ou on ne l'est pas.* "And freedom?" they say to me. Do you suppose that freedom is prized by the people? Ask them——'

'Just try,' broke in Litvinov, 'taking that freedom away again.'

'*Comment nommez-vous ce monsieur?*' whispered the general to Ratmirov.

'What are you discussing here?' began the stout general suddenly. He obviously played the part of the spoilt child of the party. 'Is it all about the newspapers? About penny-a-liners? Let me tell you a little anecdote of what happened to me with a scribbling fellow—such a lovely thing. I was told he had written a libel on me. Well, of course, I at once had him brought before me. They brought me the penny-a-liner.

'"How was it," said I, "my dear chap, you came to write this libel? Was your patriotism too much for you?" "Yes, it was too much," says he. "Well," says I, "and do you like money?" "Yes," says he. Then, gentlemen, I gave him the knob of my cane to sniff at. "And do you like that, my angel?" "No," says he, "I don't like that." "But sniff it as you ought," says I, "my hands are clean." "I don't like it," says he, "and that's all." "But I like it very much, my angel," says I, "though not for myself. Do you understand that allegory, my treasure?" "Yes," says he. "Then mind and be a good boy for the future, and now here's a rouble sterling for you; go away and be grateful to me night and day," and so the scribbling chap went off.'

The general burst out laughing and again every one followed his example—every one except Irina, who did not even smile and looked darkly at the speaker.

The condescending general slapped Boris on the shoulder.

'That's all your invention, O friend of my bosom.... You threatening any one with a stick.... You haven't got a stick.*C'est pour faire rire ces dames.* For the sake of a good story. But that's not the point. I said just now that we must turn back completely. Understand me. I am not hostile to so-called progress, but all these universities and seminaries, and popular schools, these students, priests' sons, and commoners, all these small fry, *tout ce fond du sac, la petite propriété, pire que le prolétariat* (the general uttered this in a languishing, almost faint voice) *voilà ce qui m'effraie*... that's where one ought to draw the line, and make other people draw it too.' (Again he gave Litvinov a genial glance.) 'Yes, one must draw the line. Don't forget that among us no one makes any demand, no one is asking for anything. Local government, for instance—who asks for that? Do you ask for it? or you, or you? or you, *mesdames?*You rule not only yourselves but all of us, you know.' (The general's handsome face was lighted up by a smile of amusement.) 'My dear friends, why should we curry favour with the multitude. You like democracy, it flatters you, and serves your ends ... but you know it's a double weapon. It is better in the old way, as before ... far more secure. Don't deign to reason with the herd, trust in the aristocracy, in that alone is power.... Indeed it will be better. And progress ... I certainly have nothing against progress. Only don't give us lawyers and sworn juries and elective officials ... only don't touch discipline, discipline before all things—you may build bridges, and quays, and hospitals, and why not light the streets with gas?'

'Petersburg has been set on fire from one end to the other, so there you have your progress!' hissed the irritable general.

'Yes, you're a mischievous fellow, I can see,' said the stout general, shaking his head lazily; 'you would do for a chief-prosecutor, but in my opinion *avec Orphée aux enfers le progrès a dit son dernier mot.*'

'*Vous dites toujours des bêtises,*' giggled the lady from Arzamass.

The general looked dignified.

'*Je ne suis jamais plus sérieux, madame, que quand je dis des bêtises.*'

'Monsieur Verdier has uttered that very phrase several times already,' observed Irina in a low voice.

'*De la poigne et des formes,*' cried the stout general, '*de la poigne surtout.* And to translate into Russian: be civil but don't spare your fists.'

'Ah, you're a rascal, an incorrigible rascal,' interposed the condescending general. '*Mesdames*, don't listen to him, please. A barking dog does not bite. He cares for nothing but flirtation.'

'That's not right, though, Boris,' began Ratmirov, after exchanging a glance with his wife, 'it's all very well to be mischievous, but that's going too far. Progress is a phenomenon of social life, and this is what we must not forget; it's a symptom. It's what we must watch.'

'All right, I say,' observed the stout general, wrinkling up his nose; 'we all know you are aiming at the ministry.'

'Not at all ... the ministry indeed! But really one can't refuse to recognise things.'

Boris plunged his fingers again into his whiskers, and stared into the air.

'Social life is very important, because in the development of the people, in the destinies, so to speak, of the country——'

'*Valérien,*' interrupted Boris reprovingly, '*il y a des dames ici.* I did not expect this of you, or do you want to get on to a committee?'

'But they are all closed now, thank God,' put in the irritable general, and he began humming again '*Deux gendarmes un beau dimanche.*'

Ratmirov raised a cambric handkerchief to his nose and gracefully retired from the discussion; the condescending general repeated 'Rascal! rascal!' but Boris turned to the lady who 'grimaced upon the desert air' and without lowering his voice, or a change in the expression of his face, began to ply her with questions as to when 'she would reward his devotion,' as though he were desperately in love with her and suffering tortures on her account.

At every moment during this conversation Litvinov felt more and more ill at ease. His pride, his clean plebeian pride, was fairly in revolt.

What had he, the son of a petty official, in common with these military aristocrats of Petersburg? He loved everything they hated; he hated everything they loved; he was only too vividly conscious of it, he felt it in every part of his being. Their jokes he thought dull, their tone intolerable, every gesture false; in the very smoothness of their speeches he detected a note of revolting contemptuousness—and yet he was, as it were, abashed before them, before these creatures, these enemies. 'Ugh! how disgusting! I am in their way, I am ridiculous to them,' was the thought that kept revolving in his head. 'Why am I stopping? Let me escape at once, at once.' Irina's presence could not retain him; she, too, aroused melancholy emotions in him. He got up from his seat and began to take leave.

'You are going already?' said Irina, but after a moment's reflection she did not press him to stay, and only extracted a promise from him that he would not fail to come and see her. General Ratmirov took leave of him with the same refined courtesy, shook hands with him and accompanied him to the end of the platform.... But Litvinov had scarcely had time to turn round the first bend in the road when he heard a general roar of laughter behind him. This laughter had no reference to him, but was occasioned by the long-expected Monsieur Verdier, who suddenly made his appearance on the platform, in a Tyrolese hat, and blue blouse, riding a donkey, but the blood fairly rushed into Litvinov's cheeks, and he felt intense bitterness: his tightly compressed lips seemed as though drawn by wormwood. 'Despicable, vulgar creatures,' he muttered, without reflecting that the few minutes he had spent in their company had not given him sufficient ground for such severe criticism. And this was the world into which Irina had fallen, Irina, once his Irina! In this world she moved, and lived, and reigned; for it, she had sacrificed her personal dignity, the noblest feelings of her heart.... It was clearly as it should be; it was clear that she had deserved no better fate! How glad he was that she had not thought of questioning him about his intentions! He might have opened his heart before 'them' in 'their' presence.... 'For nothing in the world! never!' murmured Litvinov, inhaling deep draughts of the fresh air and descending the road towards Baden almost at a run. He thought of his betrothed, his sweet, good, sacred Tatyana, and how pure, how noble, how true she seemed to him. With what unmixed tenderness he recalled her features, her words, her very gestures ... with what impatience he looked forward to her return.

The rapid exercise soothed his nerves. Returning home he sat down at the table and took up a book; suddenly he let it fall, even with a shudder.... What had happened to him? Nothing had happened, but Irina ... Irina.... All at once his meeting with her seemed something marvellous, strange, extraordinary. Was it possible? he had met, he had talked with the same Irina.... And why was there no trace in her of that hateful worldliness which was so sharply stamped upon all these others. Why did he fancy that she seemed, as it were, weary, or sad, or sick of her position? She was in their camp, but she was not an enemy. And what could have impelled her to receive him joyfully, to invite him to see her?

Litvinov started. 'O Tanya, Tanya!' he cried passionately, 'you are my guardian angel, you only, my good genius. I love you only and will love you for ever. And I will not go to see *her*. Forget her altogether! Let her amuse herself with her generals.' Litvinov set to his book again.

XI

Litvinov took up his book again, but he could not read. He went out of the house, walked a little, listened to the music, glanced in at the gambling, returned again to his room, and tried again to read—still without success. The time seemed to drag by with peculiar dreariness. Pishtchalkin, the well-intentioned peaceable mediator, came in and sat with him for three hours. He talked, argued, stated questions, and discoursed intermittently, first of elevated, and then of practical topics, and succeeded in diffusing around him such an atmosphere of dulness that poor Litvinov was ready to cry. In raising dulness—agonising, chilling, helpless, hopeless dulness—to a fine art, Pishtchalkin was absolutely unrivalled even among persons of the highest morality, who are notoriously masters in that line. The mere sight of his well-cut and well-brushed head, his clear lifeless eyes, his benevolent nose, produced an involuntary despondency, and his deliberate, drowsy, lazy tone seemed to have been created only to state with conviction and lucidity such sententious truths as that twice two makes four and not five or three, that water is liquid, and benevolence laudable; that to the private individual, no less than to the state, and to the state no less than to the private individual, credit is absolutely indispensable for financial operations. And with all this he was such an excellent man! But such is the sentence the fates have passed on Russia; among us, good men are dull. Pishtchalkin retreated at last; he was replaced by Bindasov, who, without any beating about the bush, asked Litvinov with great effrontery for a loan of a hundred guldens, and the latter gave it him, in spite of the fact that Bindasov was not only unattractive, but even repulsive to him, that he knew for certain that he would never get his money back; and was, besides, himself in need of it. What made him give him the money then, the reader will inquire. Who can tell! That is another Russian weakness. Let the reader lay his hand on his heart and remember how many acts in his own life have had absolutely no other reason. And Bindasov did not even thank Litvinov; he asked for a glass of red Baden wine, and without wiping his lips departed, loudly and offensively tramping with his boots. And how vexed Litvinov was with himself already, as he watched the red nape of the retreating sharper's neck! Before evening he received a letter from Tatyana in which she informed him that as her aunt was not well, she could not come to Baden for five or six days. This news had a depressing influence on Litvinov; it increased his vexation, and he went to bed early in a disagreeable frame of mind. The following day turned out no better, if not worse, than the preceding. From early morning Litvinov's room was filled with his own countrymen; Bambaev, Voroshilov, Pishtchalkin, the two officers, the two Heidelberg students, all crowded in at once, and yet did not go away right up till dinner time, though they had soon said all they had to say and were obviously bored. They simply did not know what to do with themselves, and having got into Litvinov's lodgings they 'stuck' there, as they say. First they discussed the fact that Gubaryov had gone back to Heidelberg, and that they would have to go after him; then they philosophised a little, and touched on the Polish question; then they advanced to reflections on gambling and *cocottes*, and fell to repeating scandalous anecdotes; at last the conversation sank into a discussion of all sorts of 'strong men' and monsters of obesity and gluttony. First, they trotted out all the ancient stories of Lukin, of the deacon who ate no less than thirty-three herrings for a wager, of the Uhlan colonel, Ezyedinov, renowned for his corpulence, and of the soldier who broke the shin-bone on his own forehead; then followed unadulterated lying. Pishtchalkin himself related with a yawn that he knew a peasant woman in Little Russia, who at the time of her death had proved to weigh half a ton and some pounds, and a landowner who had eaten three geese and a sturgeon for luncheon; Bambaev suddenly fell into an ecstatic condition, and declared he himself was able to eat a whole sheep, 'with seasoning' of course; and Voroshilov burst out with something about a comrade, an athletic cadet, so grotesque that every one was reduced to silence, and after looking at each other, they took up their hats, and the party broke up. Litvinov, when he was left alone, tried to occupy himself, but he felt just as if his head was full of smouldering soot; he could do nothing that was of any use, and the evening too was wasted. The next morning he was just preparing for lunch, when some one knocked at his door. 'Good Lord,' thought Litvinov, 'one of yesterday's dear friends again,' and not without some trepidation he pronounced:

'*Herein!*'

The door opened slowly and in walked Potugin. Litvinov was exceedingly delighted to see him.

'This is nice!' he began, warmly shaking hands with his unexpected visitor, 'this is good of you! I should certainly have looked you up myself, but you would not tell me where you live. Sit down, please, put down your hat. Sit down.'

Potugin made no response to Litvinov's warm welcome, and remained standing in the middle of the room, shifting from one leg to the other; he only laughed a little and shook his head. Litvinov's cordial reception obviously touched him, but there was some constraint in the expression of his face.

'There's ... some little misunderstanding,' he began, not without hesitation. 'Of course, it would always be ... a pleasure ... to me ... but I have been sent ... especially to you.'

'That's to say, do you mean,' commented Litvinov in an injured voice, 'that you would not have come to me of your own accord?'

'Oh, no, ... indeed! But I ... I should, perhaps, not have made up my mind to intrude on you to-day, if I had not been asked to come to you. In fact, I have a message for you.'

'From whom, may I ask?'

'From a person you know, from Irina Pavlovna Ratmirov. You promised three days ago to go and see her and you have not been.'

Litvinov stared at Potugin in amazement.

'You know Madame Ratmirov?'

'As you see.'

'And you know her well?'

'I am to a certain degree a friend of hers.'

Litvinov was silent for a little.

'Allow me to ask you,' he began at last, 'do you know why Irina Pavlovna wants to see me?'

Potugin went up to the window.

'To a certain degree I do. She was, as far as I can judge, very pleased at meeting you,—well,—and she wants to renew your former relations.'

'Renew,' repeated Litvinov. 'Excuse my indiscretion, but allow me to question you a little more. Do you know what was the nature of those relations?'

'Strictly speaking ... no, I don't know. But I imagine,' added Potugin, turning suddenly to Litvinov and looking affectionately at him, 'I imagine that they were of some value. Irina Pavlovna spoke very highly of you, and I was obliged to promise her I would bring you. Will you come?'

'When?'

'Now ... at once.'

Litvinov merely made a gesture with his hand.

'Irina Pavlovna,' pursued Potugin, 'supposes that the ... how can I express it ... the environment, shall we say, in which you found her the other day, was not likely to be particularly attractive to you; but she told me to tell you, that the devil is not so black as he is fancied.'

'Hm.... Does that saying apply strictly to the environment?'

'Yes ... and in general.'

'Hm.... Well, and what is your opinion, Sozont Ivanitch, of the devil?'

'I think, Grigory Mihalitch, that he is in any case not what he is fancied.'

'Is he better?'

'Whether better or worse it's hard to say, but certainly he is not the same as he is fancied. Well, shall we go?'

'Sit here a little first. I must own that it still seems rather strange to me.'

'What seems strange, may I make bold to inquire?'

'In what way can you have become a friend of Irina Pavlovna?'

Potugin scanned himself.

'With my appearance, and my position in society, it certainly does seem rather incredible; but you know—Shakespeare has said already, "There are more things in heaven and earth, Horatio, etc." Life too is not to be trifled with. Here is a simile for you; a tree stands before you when there is no wind; in what way can a leaf on a lower branch touch a leaf on an upper branch? It's impossible. But when the storm rises it is all changed ... and the two leaves touch.'

'Aha! So there were storms?'

'I should think so! Can one live without them? But enough of philosophy. It's time to go.'

Litvinov was still hesitating.

'O good Lord!' cried Potugin with a comic face, 'what are young men coming to nowadays! A most charming lady invites them to see her, sends messengers after them on purpose, and they raise difficulties. You ought to be ashamed, my dear sir, you ought to be ashamed. Here's your hat. Take it and "Vorwärts," as our ardent friends the Germans say.'

Litvinov still stood irresolute for a moment, but he ended by taking his hat and going out of the room with Potugin.

XII

They went to one of the best hotels in Baden and asked for Madame Ratmirov. The porter first inquired their names, and then answered at once that '*die Frau Fürstin ist zu Hause*,' and went himself to conduct them up the staircase and knock at the door of the apartment and announce them. '*Die Frau Fürstin*' received them promptly: she was alone, her husband had gone off to Carlsruhe for an interview with a great official, an influential personage who was passing through that town.

Irina was sitting at a small table, embroidering on canvas when Potugin and Litvinov crossed the threshold. She quickly flung her embroidery aside, pushed away the little table and got up; an expression of genuine pleasure overspread her face. She wore a morning dress, high at the neck; the superb lines of her shoulders and arms could be seen through the thin stuff; her carelessly-coiled hair had come loose and fell low on her slender neck. Irina flung a swift glance at Potugin, murmured '*merci*,' and holding out her hand to Litvinov reproached him amicably for forgetfulness.

'And you such an old friend!' she added.

Litvinov was beginning to apologise. '*C'est bien, c'est bien*,' she assented hurriedly and, taking his hat from him, with friendly insistence made him sit down. Potugin, too, was sitting down, but got up again directly, and saying that he had an engagement he could not put off, and that he would come in again after dinner, he proceeded to take leave. Irina again flung him a rapid glance, and gave him a friendly nod, but she did not try to keep him, and directly he had vanished behind the portière, she turned with eager impatience to Litvinov.

'Grigory Mihalitch,' she began, speaking Russian in her soft musical voice, 'here we are alone at last, and I can tell you how glad I am at our meeting, because it ... it gives me a chance...' (Irina looked him straight in the face) 'of asking your forgiveness.'

Litvinov gave an involuntary start. He had not expected so swift an attack. He had not expected she would herself turn the conversation upon old times.

'Forgiveness ... for what?' ... he muttered.

Irina flushed.

'For what? ... you know for what,' she said, and she turned slightly away. 'I wronged you, Grigory Mihalitch ... though, of course, it was my fate' (Litvinov was reminded of her letter) 'and I do not regret it ... it would be in any case too late; but, meeting you so unexpectedly, I said to myself that we absolutely must become friends, absolutely ... and I should feel it deeply, if it did not come about ... and it seems to me for that we must have an explanation, without putting it off, and once for all, so that afterwards there should be no ... *gêne*, no awkwardness, once for all, Grigory Mihalitch; and that you must tell me you forgive me, or else I shall imagine you feel ... *de la rancune. Voilà!* It is perhaps a great piece of fatuity on my part, for you have probably forgotten everything long, long ago, but no matter, tell me, you have forgiven me.'

Irina uttered this whole speech without taking breath, and Litvinov could see that there were tears shining in her eyes ... yes, actually tears.

'Really, Irina Pavlovna,' he began hurriedly, 'how can you beg my pardon, ask forgiveness?... That is all past and buried, and I can only feel astounded that, in the midst of all the splendour which surrounds you, you have stillpreserved a recollection of the obscure companions of your youth....'

'Does it astound you?' said Irina softly.

'It touches me,' Litvinov went on, 'because I could never have imagined——'

'You have not told me you have forgiven me, though,' interposed Irina.

'I sincerely rejoice at your happiness, Irina Pavlovna. With my whole heart I wish you all that is best on earth....'

'And you will not remember evil against me?'

'I will remember nothing but the happy moments for which I was once indebted to you.'

Irina held out both hands to him; Litvinov clasped them warmly, and did not at once let them go.... Something that long had not been, secretly stirred in his heart at that soft contact. Irina was again looking straight into his face; but this time she was smiling.... And he for the first time gazed directly and intently at her.... Again he recognised the features once so precious, and those deep eyes, with their marvellous lashes, and the little mole on her cheek, and the peculiar growth of her hair on her forehead, and her habit of somehow sweetly and humorously curving her lips and faintly twitching her eyebrows, all, all he recognised.... But how beautiful she had grown! What fascination, what power in her fresh, woman's body! And no rouge, no touching up, no powder, nothing false on that fresh pure face.... Yes, this was a beautiful woman. A mood of musing came upon Litvinov.... He was still looking at her, but his thoughts were far away.... Irina perceived it.

'Well, that is excellent,' she said aloud; 'now my conscience is at rest then, and I can satisfy my curiosity.'

'Curiosity,' repeated Litvinov, as though puzzled.

'Yes, yes ... I want above all things to know what you have been doing all this time, what plans you have; I want to know all, how, what, when ... all, all. And you will have to tell me the truth, for I must warn you, I have not lost sight of you ... so far as I could.'

'You did not lose sight of me, you ... there ... in Petersburg?'

'In the midst of the splendour which surrounded me, as you expressed it just now. Positively, yes, I did not. As for that splendour we will talk about that again; but now you must tell me, you must tell me so much, at such length, no one will disturb us. Ah, how delightful it will be,' added Irina, gaily sitting down and arranging herself at her ease in an armchair. 'Come, begin.'

'Before telling my story, I have to thank you,' began Litvinov.

'What for?'

'For the bouquet of flowers, which made its appearance in my room.'

'What bouquet? I know nothing about it.'

'What?'

'I tell you I know nothing about it.... But I am waiting.... I am waiting for your story.... Ah, what a good fellow that Potugin is to have brought you!'

Litvinov pricked up his ears.

'Have you known this Mr. Potugin long?' he queried.

'Yes, a long while ... but tell me your story.'

'And do you know him well?'

'Oh, yes!' Irina sighed. 'There are special reasons.... You have heard, of course, of Eliza Byelsky.... Who died, you know, the year before last, such a dreadful death?... Ah, to be sure, I'd forgotten you don't know all our scandals.... It is well, it is well indeed, that you don't know them. *O quelle chance!* at last, at last, a man, a live man, who knows nothing of us! And to be able to talk Russian with him, bad Russian of course, but still Russian, not that everlasting, mawkish, sickening French patter of Petersburg.'

'And Potugin, you say, was connected with—'

'It's very painful for me even to refer to it,' Irina broke in. 'Eliza was my greatest friend at school, and afterwards in Petersburg we saw each other continually. She confided all her secrets to me, she was very unhappy, she suffered much. Potugin behaved splendidly in the affair, with true chivalry. He sacrificed himself. It was only then I learnt to appreciate him! But we have drifted away again. I am waiting for your story, Grigory Mihalitch.'

'But my story cannot interest you the least, Irina Pavlovna.'

'That's not your affair.'

'Think, Irina Pavlovna, we have not seen each other for ten years, ten whole years. How much water has flowed by since then.'

'Not water only! not water only!' she repeated with a peculiar bitter expression; 'that's just why I want to hear what you are going to tell me.'

'And beside I really don't know where to begin.'

'At the beginning. From the very time when you ... when I went away to Petersburg. You left Moscow then.... Do you know I have never been back to Moscow since!'

'Really?'

'It was impossible at first; and afterwards when I was married——.'

'Have you been married long?'

'Four years.'

'Have you no children?'

'No,' she answered drily.

Litvinov was silent for a little.

'And did you go on living at that, what was his name, Count Reisenbach's, till your marriage?'

Irina looked steadily at him, as though she were trying to make up her mind why he asked that question.

'No,' ... was her answer at last.

'I suppose, your parents.... By the way, I haven't asked after them. Are they——'

'They are both well.'

'And living at Moscow as before?'

'At Moscow as before.'

'And your brothers and sisters?'

'They are all right; I have provided for all of them.'

'Ah!' Litvinov glanced up from under his brows at Irina. 'In reality, Irina Pavlovna, it's not I who ought to tell my story, but you, if only——' He suddenly felt embarrassed and stopped.

Irina raised her hands to her face and turned her wedding-ring round upon her finger.

'Well? I will not refuse,' she assented at last. 'Some day ... perhaps.... But first you ... because, do you see, though I tried to follow you up, I know scarcely anything of you; while of me ... well, of me you have heard enough certainly. Haven't you? I suppose you have heard of me, tell me?'

'You, Irina Pavlovna, occupied too conspicuous a place in the world, not to be the subject of talk ... especially in the provinces, where I have been and where every rumour is believed.'

'And do you believe the rumours? And of what kind were the rumours?'

'To tell the truth, Irina Pavlovna, such rumours very seldom reached me. I have led a very solitary life.'

'How so? why, you were in the Crimea, in the militia?'

'You know that too?'

'As you see. I tell you, you have been watched.'

Again Litvinov felt puzzled.

'Why am I to tell you what you know without me?' said Litvinov in an undertone.

'Why ... to do what I ask you. You see I ask you, Grigory Mihalitch.'

Litvinov bowed his head and began ... began in rather a confused fashion to recount in rough outline to Irina his uninteresting adventures. He often stopped and looked inquiringly at Irina, as though to ask whether he had told enough. But she insistently demanded the continuation of his narrative and pushing her hair back behind her ears, her elbows on the arm of her chair, she seemed to be catching every word with strained attention. Looking at her from one side and following the expression on her face, any one might perhaps have imagined she did not hear what Litvinov was saying at all, but was only deep in meditation.... But it was not of Litvinov she was meditating, though he grew confused and red under her persistent gaze. A whole life was rising up before her, a very different one, not his life, but her own.

Litvinov did not finish his story, but stopped short under the influence of an unpleasant sense of growing inner discomfort. This time Irina said nothing to him, and did not urge him to go on, but pressing her open hand to her eyes, as though she were tired, she leaned slowly back in her chair, and remained motionless. Litvinov waited for a little; then, reflecting that his visit had already lasted more than two hours, he was stretching out his hand for his hat, when suddenly in an adjoining room there was the sound of the rapid creak of thin kid boots, and preceded by the same exquisite aristocratic perfume, there entered Valerian Vladimirovitch Ratmirov.

Litvinov rose and interchanged bows with the good-looking general, while Irina, with no sign of haste, took her hand from her face, and looking coldly at her husband, remarked in French, 'Ah! so you've come back! But what time is it?'

'Nearly four, *ma chère amie*, and you not dressed yet—the princess will be expecting us,' answered the general; and with an elegant bend of his tightly-laced figure in Litvinov's direction, he added with the almost effeminate playfulness of intonation characteristic of him, 'It's clear an agreeable visitor has made you forgetful of time.'

The reader will permit us at this point to give him some information about General Ratmirov. His father was the natural ... what do you suppose? You are not wrong—but we didn't mean to say that ... the natural son of an illustrious personage of the reign of Alexander I. and of a pretty little French actress. The illustrious personage brought his son forward in the world, but left him no fortune, and the son himself (the father of our hero) had not time to grow rich; he died before he had risen above the rank of a colonel in the police. A year before his death he had married a handsome young widow who had happened to put herself under his protection. His son by the widow, Valerian Alexandrovitch, having got into the Corps of Pages by favour, attracted the notice of the authorities, not so much by his success in the sciences, as by his fine bearing, his fine manners, and his good behaviour (though he had been exposed to all that pupils in the government military schools were inevitably exposed to in former days) and went into the Guards. His career was a brilliant one, thanks to the discreet gaiety of his disposition, his skill in dancing, his excellent seat on horseback when an orderly at reviews, and lastly, by a kind of special trick of deferential familiarity with his superiors, of tender, attentive almost clinging subservience, with a flavour of vague liberalism, light as air.... This liberalism had not, however, prevented him from flogging fifty peasants in a White Russian village, where he had been sent to put down a riot. His personal appearance was most prepossessing and singularly youthful-looking; smooth-faced and rosy-checked, pliant and persistent, he made the most of his amazing success with women; ladies of the highest rank and mature age simply went out of their senses over him. Cautious from habit, silent from motives of prudence, General Ratmirov moved constantly in the highest society, like the busy bee gathering honey even from the least attractive flowers—and without morals, without information of any kind, but with the reputation of being good at business; with an insight into men, and a ready comprehension of the exigencies of the moment, and above all, a never-swerving desire for his own advantage, he saw at last all paths lying open before him....

Litvinov smiled constrainedly, while Irina merely shrugged her shoulders.

'Well,' she said in the same cold tone, 'did you see the Count?'

'To be sure I saw him. He told me to remember him to you.'

'Ah! is he as imbecile as ever, that patron of yours?'

General Ratmirov made no reply. He only smiled to himself, as though lenient to the over-hastiness of a woman's judgment. With just such a smile kindly-disposed grown-up people respond to the nonsensical whims of children.

'Yes,' Irina went on, 'the stupidity of your friend the Count is too striking, even when one has seen a good deal of the world.'

'You sent me to him yourself,' muttered the general, and turning to Litvinov he asked him in Russian, 'Was he getting any benefit from the Baden waters?'

'I am in perfect health, I'm thankful to say,' answered Litvinov.

'That's the greatest of blessings,' pursued the general, with an affable grimace; 'and indeed one doesn't, as a rule, come to Baden for the waters; but the waters here are very effectual, *je veux dire, efficaces;* and any one who suffers, as I do for instance, from a nervous cough——'

Irina rose quickly. 'We will see each other again, Grigory Mihalitch, and I hope soon,' she said in French, contemptuously cutting short her husband's speech, 'but now I must go and dress. That old princess is insufferable with her everlasting *parties de plaisir*, of which nothing comes but boredom.'

'You're hard on every one to-day,' muttered her husband, and he slipped away into the next room.

Litvinov was turning towards the door.... Irina stopped him.

'You have told me everything,' she said, 'but the chief thing you concealed.'

'What's that?'

'You are going to be married, I'm told?'

Litvinov blushed up to his ears.... As a fact, he had intentionally not referred to Tanya; but he felt horribly vexed, first, that Irina knew about his marriage, and, secondly, that she had, as it were, convicted him of a desire to conceal it from her. He was completely at a loss what to say, while Irina did not take her eyes off him.

'Yes, I am going to be married,' he said at last, and at once withdrew.

Ratmirov came back into the room.

'Well, why aren't you dressed?' he asked.

'You can go alone; my head aches.'

'But the princess....'

Irina scanned her husband from head to foot in one look, turned her back upon him, and went away to her boudoir.

XIII

Litvinov felt much annoyed with himself, as though he had lost money at roulette, or failed to keep his word. An inward voice told him that he—on the eve of marriage, a man of sober sense, not a boy—ought not to have given way to the promptings of curiosity, nor the allurements of recollection. 'Much need there was to go!' he reflected. 'On her side simply flirtation, whim, caprice.... She's bored, she's sick of everything, she clutched at me ... as some one pampered with dainties will suddenly long for black bread ... well, that's natural enough.... But why did I go? Can I feel anything but contempt for her?' This last phrase he could not utter even in thought without an effort.... 'Of course, there's no kind of danger, and never could be,' he pursued his reflections. 'I know whom I have to deal with. But still one ought not to play with fire.... I'll never set my foot in her place again.' Litvinov dared not, or could not as yet, confess to himself how beautiful Irina had seemed to him, how powerfully she had worked upon his feelings.

Again the day passed dully and drearily. At dinner, Litvinov chanced to sit beside a majestic *belhomme*, with dyed moustaches, who said nothing, and only panted and rolled his eyes ... but, being suddenly taken with a hiccup, proved himself to be a fellow-countryman, by at once exclaiming, with feeling, in Russian, 'There, I said I ought not to eat melons!' In the evening, too, nothing happened to compensate for a lost day; Bindasov, before Litvinov's very eyes, won a sum four times what he had borrowed from him, but, far from repaying his debt, he positively glared in his face with a menacing air, as though he were prepared to borrow more from him just because he had been a witness of his winnings. The next morning he was again invaded by a host of his compatriots; Litvinov got rid of them with difficulty, and setting off to the mountains, he first came across Irina—he pretended not to recognise her, and passed quickly by—and then Potugin. He was about to begin a conversation with Potugin, but the latter did not respond to him readily. He was leading by the hand a smartly dressed little girl, with fluffy, almost white curls, large black eyes, and a pale, sicklylittle face, with that peculiar peremptory and impatient expression characteristic of spoiled children. Litvinov spent two hours in the mountains, and then went back homewards along the Lichtenthaler Allee.... A lady, sitting on a bench, with a blue veil over her face, got up quickly, and came up to him.... He recognised Irina.

'Why do you avoid me, Grigory Mihalitch?' she said, in the unsteady voice of one who is boiling over within.

Litvinov was taken aback. 'I avoid you, Irina Pavlovna?'

'Yes, you ... you——'

Irina seemed excited, almost angry.

'You are mistaken, I assure you.'

'No, I am not mistaken. Do you suppose this morning—when we met, I mean—do you suppose I didn't see that you knew me? Do you mean to say you did not know me? Tell me.'

'I really ... Irina Pavlovna——'

'Grigory Mihalitch, you're a straightforward man, you have always told the truth; tell me, tell me, you knew me, didn't you? you turned away on purpose?'

Litvinov glanced at Irina. Her eyes shone with a strange light, while her cheeks and lips were of a deathly pallor under the thick net of her veil. In the expression of her face, in the very sound of her abruptly jerked-out whisper, there was something so irresistibly mournful, beseeching ... Litvinov could not pretend any longer.

'Yes ... I knew you,' he uttered not without effort.

Irina slowly shuddered, and slowly dropped her hands.

'Why did you not come up to me?' she whispered.

'Why ... why!' Litvinov moved on one side, away from the path, Irina followed him in silence. 'Why?' he repeated once more, and suddenly his face was aflame, and he felt his chest and throat choking with a passion akin to hatred. 'You ... you ask such a question, after all that has passed between us? Not now, of course, not now; but there ... there ... in Moscow.'

'But, you know, we decided; you know, you promised——' Irina was beginning.

'I have promised nothing! Pardon the harshness of my expressions, but you ask for the truth—so think for yourself: to what but a caprice—incomprehensible, I confess, to me—to what but a desire to try how much power you still have over me, can I attribute your ... I don't know what to call it ... your persistence? Our paths have lain so far apart! I have forgotten it all, I've lived through all that suffering long ago, I've become a different man completely; you are married—happy, at least, in appearance—you fill an envied position in the world; what's the object, what's the use of our meeting? What am I to you? what are you to me? We cannot even understand each other now; there is absolutely nothing in common between us now, neither in the past nor in the present! Especially ... especially in the past!'

Litvinov uttered all this speech hurriedly, jerkily, without turning his head. Irina did not stir, except from time to time she faintly stretched her hands out to him. It seemed as though she were beseeching him to stop and listen to her, while, at his last words, she slightly bit her lower lip, as though to master the pain of a sharp, rapid wound.

'Grigory Mihalitch,' she began at last, in a calmer voice; and she moved still further away from the path, along which people from time to time passed.

Litvinov in his turn followed her.

'Grigory Mihalitch, believe me, if I could imagine I had one hair's-breadth of power over you left, I would be the first to avoid you. If I have not done so, if I made up my mind, in spite of my ... of the wrong I did you in the past, to renew my acquaintance with you, it was because ... because——'

'Because what?' asked Litvinov, almost rudely.

‘Because,’ Irina declared with sudden force—‘it’s too insufferable, too unbearably stifling for me in society, in the envied position you talk about; because meeting you, a live man, after all these dead puppets—you have seen samples of them three days ago, there *au Vieux Château*,—I rejoice over you as an oasis in the desert, while you suspect me of flirting, and despise me and repulse me on the ground that I wronged you—as indeed I did—but far more myself!’

‘You chose your lot yourself, Irina Pavlovna,’ Litvinov rejoined sullenly, as before not turning his head.

‘I chose it myself, yes ... and I don’t complain, I have no right to complain,’ said Irina hurriedly; she seemed to derive a secret consolation from Litvinov’s very harshness. ‘I know that you must think ill of me, and I won’t justify myself; I only want to explain my feeling to you, I want to convince you I am in no flirting humour now.... Me flirting with you! Why, there is no sense in it.... When I saw you, all that was good, that was young in me, revived ... that time when I had not yet chosen my lot, everything that lies behind in that streak of brightness behind those ten years....’

‘Come, really, Irina Pavlovna! So far as I am aware, the brightness in your life began precisely with the time we separated....’

Irina put her handkerchief to her lips.

‘That’s very cruel, what you say, Grigory Mihalitch; but I can’t feel angry with you. Oh, no, that was not a bright time, it was not for happiness I left Moscow; I have known not one moment, not one instant of happiness ... believe me, whatever you have been told. If I were happy, could I talk to you as I am talking now.... I repeat to you, you don’t know what these people are.... Why, they understand nothing, feel for nothing; they’ve no intelligence even, *ni esprit ni intelligence*, nothing but tact and cunning; why, in reality, music and poetry and art are all equally remote from them.... You will say that I was rather indifferent to all that myself; but not to the same degree, Grigory Mihalitch ... not to the same degree! It’s not a woman of the world before you now, you need only look at me—not a society queen.... That’s what they call us, I believe ... but a poor, poor creature, really deserving of pity. Don’t wonder at my words.... I am beyond feeling pride now! I hold out my hand to you as a beggar, will you understand, just as a beggar.... I ask for charity,’ she added suddenly, in an involuntary, irrepressible outburst, ‘I ask for charity, and you——’

Her voice broke. Litvinov raised his head and looked at Irina; her breathing came quickly, her lips were quivering. Suddenly his heart beat fast, and the feeling of hatred vanished.

‘You say that our paths have lain apart,’ Irina went on. ‘I know you are about to marry from inclination, you have a plan laid out for your whole life; yes, that’s all so, but we have not become strangers to one another, Grigory Mihalitch; we can still understand each other. Or do you imagine I have grown altogether dull—altogether debased in the mire? Ah, no, don’t think that, please! Let me open my heart, I beseech you—there—even for the sake of those old days, if you are not willing to forget them. Do so, that our meeting may not have come to pass in vain; that would be too bitter; it would not last long in any case.... I don’t know how to say it properly, but you will understand me, because I ask for little, so little ... only a little sympathy, only that you should not repulse me, that you should let me open my heart——’

Irina ceased speaking, there were tears in her voice. She sighed, and timidly, with a kind of furtive, searching look, gazed at Litvinov, held out her hand to him....

Litvinov slowly took the hand and faintly pressed it.

‘Let us be friends,’ whispered Irina.

‘Friends,’ repeated Litvinov dreamily.

‘Yes, friends ... or if that is too much to ask, then let us at least be friendly.... Let us be simply as though nothing had happened.’

‘As though nothing had happened,...’ repeated Litvinov again. ‘You said just now, Irina Pavlovna, that I was unwilling to forget the old days.... But what if I can’t forget them?’

A blissful smile flashed over Irina’s face, and at once disappeared, to be replaced by a harassed, almost scared expression.

‘Be like me, Grigory Mihalitch, remember only what was good in them; and most of all, give me your word.... Your word of honour....’

‘Well?’

‘Not to avoid me ... not to hurt me for nothing. You promise? tell me!’

‘Yes.’

‘And you will dismiss all evil thoughts of me from your mind.’

‘Yes ... but as for understanding you—I give it up.’

'There's no need of that ... wait a little, though, you will understand. But you will promise?'

'I have said yes already.'

'Thanks. You see I am used to believe you. I shall expect you to-day, to-morrow, I will not go out of the house. And now I must leave you. The Grand Duchess is coming along the avenue.... She's caught sight of me, and I can't avoid going up to speak to her.... Good-bye till we meet.... Give me your hand, *vite, vite*. Till we meet.'

And warmly pressing Litvinov's hand, Irina walked towards a middle-aged person of dignified appearance, who was coming slowly along the gravel path, escorted by two other ladies, and a strikingly handsome groom in livery.

'*Eh bonjour, chère Madame*,' said the personage, while Irina curtseyed respectfully to her. '*Comment allez-vous aujourd'hui? Venez un peu avec moi.*'

'*Votre Altesse a trop de bonté*,' Irina's insinuating voice was heard in reply.

XIV

Litvinov let the Grand Duchess and all her suite get out of sight, and then he too went along the avenue. He could not make up his mind clearly what he was feeling; he was conscious both of shame and dread, while his vanity was flattered.... The unexpected explanation with Irina had taken him utterly by surprise; her rapid burning words had passed over him like a thunder-storm. 'Queer creatures these society women,' he thought; 'there's no consistency in them ... and how perverted they are by the surroundings in which they go on living, while they're conscious of its hideousness themselves!'... In reality he was not thinking this at all, but only mechanically repeating these hackneyed phrases, as though he were trying to ward off other more painful thoughts. He felt that he must not think seriously just now, that he would probably have to blame himself, and he moved with lagging steps, almost forcing himself to pay attention to everything that happened to meet him.... He suddenly found himself before a seat, caught sight of some one's legs in front of it, and looked upwards from them.... The legs belonged to a man, sitting on the seat, and reading a newspaper; this man turned out to be Potugin. Litvinov uttered a faint exclamation. Potugin laid the paper down on his knees, and looked attentively, without a smile, at Litvinov; and Litvinov also attentively, and also without a smile, looked at Potugin.

'May I sit by you?' he asked at last.

'By all means, I shall be delighted. Only I warn you, if you want to have a talk with me, you mustn't be offended with me—I'm in a most misanthropic humour just now, and I see everything in an exaggeratedly repulsive light.'

'That's no matter, Sozont Ivanitch,' responded Litvinov, sinking down on the seat, 'indeed it's particularly appropriate.... But why has such a mood come over you?'

'I ought not by rights to be ill-humoured,' began Potugin. 'I've just read in the paper a project for judicial reforms in Russia, and I see with genuine pleasure that we've got some sense at last, and they're not as usual on the pretext of independence, nationalism, or originality, proposing to tack a little home-made tag of our own on to the clearstraightforward logic of Europe; but are taking what's good from abroad intact. A single adaptation in its application to the peasants' sphere is enough.... There's no doing away with communal ownership!... Certainly, certainly, I ought not to be ill-humoured; but to my misfortune I chanced upon a Russian "rough diamond," and had a talk with him, and these rough diamonds, these self-educated geniuses, would make me turn in my grave!'

'What do you mean by a rough diamond?' asked Litvinov.

'Why, there's a gentleman disporting himself here, who imagines he's a musical genius. "I have done nothing, of course," he'll tell you. "I'm a cipher, because I've had no training, but I've incomparably more melody and more ideas in me than in Meyerbeer." In the first place, I say: why have you had no training? and secondly, that, not to talk of Meyerbeer, the humblest German flute-player, modestly blowing his part in the humblest German orchestra, has twenty times as many ideas as all our untaught geniuses; only the flute-player keeps his ideas to himself, and doesn't trot them out with a flourish in the land of Mozarts and Haydns; while our friend the rough diamond has only to strum some little waltz or song, and at once you see him with his hands in his trouser pocket and a sneer of contempt on his lips: I'm a genius, he says. And in painting it's just the same, and in everything else. Oh, these natural geniuses, how I hate them! As if every one didn't know that it's only where there's no real science fully assimilated, and no real art, that there's this flaunting affectation of them. Surely it's time to have done with this flaunting, this vulgar twaddle, together with all hackneyed phrases such as "no one ever dies of hunger in Russia," "nowhere is there such fast travelling as in Russia," "we Russians could bury all our enemies under our hats." I'm for ever hearing of the richness of the Russian nature, their unerring instinct, and of Kulibin.... But what is this richness, after all, gentlemen? Half-awakened mutterings or else half-animal sagacity. Instinct, indeed! A fine boast. Take an ant in a forest and set it down a mile from its ant-hill, it will find its way home; man can do nothing like it; but what of it? do you suppose he's inferior to the ant? Instinct, be it ever so unerring, is unworthy of man; sense, simple, straightforward, common sense—that's our heritage, our pride; sense won't perform any such tricks, but it's that that everything rests upon. As for Kulibin, who without any knowledge of mechanics succeeded in making some very bad watches, why, I'd have those watches set up in the pillory, and say: see, good people, this is the way *not* to do it. Kulibin's not to blame for it, but his work's rubbish. To admire Telushkin's boldness and cleverness because he climbed on to the Admiralty spire is well enough; why not admire him? But there's no need to shout that he's made the German architects look foolish, that they're no good, except at making money.... He's not made them look foolish in the least; they had to put a scaffolding round the spire afterwards, and repair it in the usual way. For mercy's sake, never encourage the idea in Russia that anything can be done without training. No; you may have the brain of a Solomon, but you must study, study from the A B C. Or else hold your tongue, and sit still, and be humble! Phoo! it makes one hot all over!'

Potugin took off his hat and began fanning himself with his handkerchief.

'Russian art,' he began again. 'Russian art, indeed!... Russian impudence and conceit, I know, and Russian feebleness too, but Russian art, begging your pardon, I've never come across. For twenty years on end they've been doing homage to that bloated nonentity Bryullov, and fancying that we have founded a school of our own, and even that it will be better than all others.... Russian art, ha, ha, ha! ho, ho!'

'Excuse me, though, Sozont Ivanitch,' remarked Litvinov, 'would you refuse to recognise Glinka too, then?'

Potugin scratched his head.

'The exception, you know, only proves the rule, but even in that instance we could not dispense with bragging. If we'd said, for example, that Glinka was really a remarkable musician, who was only prevented by circumstances—outer and inner—from becoming the founder of the Russian opera, none would have disputed it; but no, that was too much to expect! They must at once raise him to the dignity of commander-in-chief, of grand-marshal, in the musical world, and disparage other nations while they were about it; they have nothing to compare with him, they declare, then quote you some marvellous home-bred genius whose compositions are nothing but a poor imitation of second-rate foreign composers, yes, second-rate ones, for they're the easiest to imitate. Nothing to compare with him? Oh, poor benighted barbarians, for whom standards in art are non-existent, and artists are something of the same species as the strong man Rappo: there's a foreign prodigy, they say, can lift fifteen stone in one hand, but our man can lift thirty! Nothing to compare with us, indeed! I will venture to tell you some thing I remember, and can't get out of my head. Last spring I visited the Crystal Palace near London; in that Palace, as you're aware, there's a sort of exhibition of everything that has been devised by the ingenuity of man—an encyclopædia of humanity one might call it. Well, I walked to and fro among the machines and implements and statues of great men; and all the while I thought, if it were decreed that some nation or other should disappear from the face of the earth, and with it everything that nation had invented, should disappear from the Crystal Palace, our dear mother, Holy Russia, could go and hide herself in the lower regions, without disarranging a single nail in the place: everything might remain undisturbed where it is; for even the *samovar*, the woven bast shoes, the yoke-bridle, and the knout—these are our famous products—were not invented by us. One could not carry out the same experiment on the Sandwich islanders; those islanders have made some peculiar canoes and javelins of their own; their absence would be noticed by visitors. It's a libel! it's too severe, you say perhaps.... But I say, first, I don't know how to roar like any sucking dove; and secondly, it's plain that it's not only the devil no one dares to look straight in the face, for no one dares to look straight at himself, and it's not only children who like being soothed to sleep. Our older inventions came to us from the East, our later ones we've borrowed, and half spoiled, from the West, while we still persist in talking about the independence of Russian art! Some bold spirits have even discovered an original Russian science; twice two makes four with us as elsewhere, but the result's obtained more ingeniously, it appears.'

'But wait a minute, Sozont Ivanitch,' cried Litvinov. 'Do wait a minute! You know we send something to the universal exhibitions, and doesn't Europe import something from us.'

'Yes, raw material, raw products. And note, my dear sir: this raw produce of ours is generally only good by virtue of other exceedingly bad conditions; our bristles, for instance, are large and strong, because our pigs are poor; our hides are stout and thick because our cows are thin; our tallow's rich because it's boiled down with half the flesh.... But why am I enlarging on that to you, though; you are a student of technology, to be sure, you must know all that better than I do. They talk to me of our inventive faculty! The inventive faculty of the Russians! Why our worthy farmers complain bitterly and suffer loss because there's no satisfactory machine for drying grain in existence, to save them from the necessity of putting their sheaves in ovens, as they did in the days of Rurik; these ovens are fearfully wasteful—just as our bast shoes and our Russian mats are,—and they are constantly getting on fire. The farmers complain, but still there's no sign of a drying-machine. And why is there none? Because the German farmer doesn't need them; he can thrash his wheat as it is, so he doesn't bother to invent one, and we ... are not capable of doing it! Not capable—and that's all about it! Try as we may! From this day forward I declare whenever I come across one of those rough diamonds, these self-taught geniuses, I shall say: "Stop a minute, my worthy friend! Where's that drying-machine? let's have it!" But that's beyond them! Picking up some old cast-off shoe, dropped ages ago by St. Simon or Fourier, and sticking it on our heads and treating it as a sacred relic—that's what we're capable of; or scribbling an article on the historical and contemporary significance of the proletariat in the principal towns of France—that we can do too; but I tried once, asking a writer and political economist of that sort—rather like your friend, Mr. Voroshilov—to mention twenty towns in France, and what do you think came of that? Why the economist in despair at last mentioned Mont-Fermeuil as one of the French towns, remembering it probably from some novel of Paul de Kock's. And that reminds me of the following anecdote. I was one day strolling through a wood with a dog and a gun——'

'Are you a sportsman then?' asked Litvinov.

'I shoot a little. I was making my way to a swamp in search of snipe; I'd been told of the swamp by other sportsmen. I saw sitting in a clearing before a hut a timber merchant's clerk, as fresh and smooth as a peeled nut, he was sitting there, smiling away—what at, I can't say. So I asked him: "Whereabouts was the swamp, and were there many snipe in it?" "To be sure, to be sure," he sang out promptly, and with an expression of face as though I'd given him a rouble; "the swamp's first-rate, I'm thankful to say; and as for all kinds of wild fowl,—my goodness, they're to be found there in wonderful plenty." I set off, but not only found no wild fowl, the swamp itself had been dry for a long time. Now tell me, please, why is the Russian a liar? Why does the political economist lie, and why the lie about the wild fowl too?'

Litvinov made no answer, but only sighed sympathetically.

'But turn the conversation with the same political economist,' pursued Potugin, 'on the most abstruse problems of social science, keeping to theory, without facts...!—he takes flight like a bird, a perfect eagle. I did once succeed, though, in catching one of those birds. I used a pretty snare, though an obvious one, as you shall see if you please. I was talking with one of our latter-day "new young men" about various questions, as they call them. Well, he got very hot, as they always do. Marriage among other things he attacked with really childish exasperation. I brought forward one argument after another.... I might as well have talked to a stone wall! I saw I should never get round him like that. And then I had a happy thought! "Allow me to submit to you," I began,—one must always talk very respectfully to these "new young men"—"I am really surprised at you, my dear sir; you are studying natural science, and your attention has never up till now been caught by the fact that all carnivorous and predatory animals—wild beasts and birds—all who have to go out in search of prey, and to exert themselves to obtain animal food for themselves and their young ... and I suppose you would include man in the category of such animals?" "Of course, I should," said the "new young man," "man is nothing but a carnivorous animal." "And predatory?" I added. "And predatory," he declared. "Well said," I observed. "Well, then I am surprised you've never noticed that such animals live in monogamy." The "new young man" started. "How so?" "Why, it is so. Think of the lion, the wolf, the fox, the vulture, the kite; and, indeed, would you condescend to suggest how they could do otherwise. It's hard work enough for the two together to get a living for their offspring." My "new young man" grew thoughtful. "Well," says he, "in that case the animal is not a rule for man." Thereupon I called him an idealist, and wasn't he hurt at that! He almost cried. I had to comfort him by promising not to tell of him to his friends. To deserve to be called an idealist is no laughing matter! The main point in which our latter-day young people are out in their reckoning is this. They fancy that the time for the old, obscure, underground work is over, that it was all very well for their old-fashioned fathers to burrow like moles, but that's too humiliating a part for us, we will take action in the light of day, we will take action.... Poor darlings! why your children even won't take action; and don't you care to go back to burrowing, burrowing underground again in the old tracks?'

A brief silence followed.

'I am of opinion, my dear sir,' began Potugin again, 'that we are not only indebted to civilisation for science, art, and law, but that even the very feeling for beauty and poetry is developed and strengthened under the influence of the same civilisation, and that the so-called popular, simple, unconscious creation is twaddling and rubbishy. Even in Homer there are traces of a refined and varied civilisation; love itself is enriched by it. The Slavophils would cheerfully hang me for such a heresy, if they were not such chicken-hearted creatures; but I will stick up for my own ideas all the same; and however much they press Madame Kohanovsky and "The swarm of bees at rest" upon me,—I can't stand the odour of that *triple extrait de mougik Russe*, as I don't belong to the highest society, which finds it absolutely necessary to assure itself from time to time that it has not turned quite French, and for whose exclusive benefit this literature *en cuir de Russie* is manufactured. Try reading the raciest, most "popular" passages from the "Bees" to a common peasant—a real one; he'll think you're repeating him a new spell against fever or drunkenness. I repeat, without civilisation there's not even poetry. If you want to get a clear idea of the poetic ideal of the uncivilisedRussian, you should turn up our ballads, our legends. To say nothing of the fact that love is always presented as the result of witchcraft, of sorcery, and produced by some philtre, to say nothing of our so-called epic literature being the only one among all the European and Asiatic literatures—the only one, observe, which does not present any typical pair of lovers—unless you reckon Vanka-Tanka as such; and of the Holy Russian knight always beginning his acquaintance with his destined bride by beating her "most pitilessly" on her white body, because "the race of women is puffed up"! all that I pass over; but I should like to call your attention to the artistic form of the young hero, the *jeune premier*, as he was depicted by the imagination of the primitive, uncivilised Slav. Just fancy him a minute; the *jeune premier* enters; a cloak he has worked himself of sable, back-stitched along every seam, a sash of seven-fold silk girt close about his armpits, his fingers hidden away under his hanging sleevelets, the collar of his coat raised high above his head, from before, his rosy face no man can see, nor, from behind, his little white neck; his cap is on one ear, while on his feet are boots of morocco, with points as sharp as a cobbler's awl, and the heels peaked like nails. Round the points an egg can be rolled, and a sparrow can fly under the heels. And the young hero advances with that peculiar mincing gait by means of which our Alcibiades, Tchivilo Plenkovitch, produced such a striking, almost medical, effect on old women and young girls, the same gait which we see in our loose-limbed waiters, that cream, that flower of Russian dandyism, that *ne plus ultra* of Russian taste. This I maintain without joking; a sack-like gracefulness, that's an artistic ideal. What do you think, is it a fine type? Does it present many materials for painting, for sculpture? And the beauty who fascinates the young hero, whose "face is as red as the blood of the hare"?... But I think you're not listening to me?'

Litvinov started. He had not, in fact, heard what Potugin was saying; he kept thinking, persistently thinking of Irina, of his last interview with her....

'I beg your pardon, Sozont Ivanitch,' he began, 'but I'm going to attack you again with my former question about ... about Madame Ratmirov.'

Potugin folded up his newspaper and put it in his pocket.

'You want to know again how I came to know her?'

'No, not exactly. I should like to hear your opinion ... on the part she played in Petersburg. What was that part, in reality?'

'I really don't know what to say to you, Grigory Mihalitch; I was brought into rather intimate terms with Madame Ratmirov ... but quite accidentally, and not for long. I never got an insight into her world, and what took place in it remained unknown to me. There was some gossip before me, but as you know, it's not only in democratic circles that slander reigns supreme among us. Besides I was not inquisitive. I see though,' he added, after a short silence, 'she interests you.'

'Yes; we have twice talked together rather openly. I ask myself, though, is she sincere?'

Potugin looked down. 'When she is carried away by feeling, she is sincere, like all women of strong passions. Pride too, sometimes prevents her from lying.'

'Is she proud? I should rather have supposed she was capricious.'

'Proud as the devil; but that's no harm.'

'I fancy she sometimes exaggerates....'

'That's nothing either, she's sincere all the same. Though after all, how can you expect truth? The best of those society women are rotten to the marrow of their bones.'

'But, Sozont Ivanitch, if you remember, you called yourself her friend. Didn't you drag me almost by force to go and see her?'

'What of that? she asked me to get hold of you; and I thought, why not? And I really am her friend. She has her good qualities: she's very kind, that is to say, generous, that's to say she gives others what she has no sort of need of herself. But of course you must know her at least as well as I do.'

'I used to know Irina Pavlovna ten years ago; but since then——'

'Ah, Grigory Mihalitch, why do you say that? Do you suppose any one's character changes? Such as one is in one's cradle, such one is still in one's tomb. Or perhaps it is' (here Potugin bowed his head still lower) 'perhaps, you're afraid of falling into her clutches? that's certainly ... But of course one is bound to fall into some woman's clutches.'

Litvinov gave a constrained laugh. 'You think so?'

'There's no escape. Man is weak, woman is strong, opportunity is all-powerful, to make up one's mind to a joyless life is hard, to forget oneself utterly is impossible ... and on one side is beauty and sympathy and warmth and light,—how is one to resist it? Why, one runs like a child to its nurse. Ah, well, afterwards to be sure comes cold and darkness and emptiness ... in due course. And you end by being strange to everything, by losing comprehension of everything. At first you don't understand how love is possible; afterwards one won't understand how life is possible.'

Litvinov looked at Potugin, and it struck him that he had never yet met a man more lonely, more desolate ... more unhappy. This time he was not shy, he was not stiff; downcast and pale, his head on his breast, and his hands on his knees, he sat without moving, merely smiling his dejected smile. Litvinov felt sorry for the poor, embittered, eccentric creature.

'Irina Pavlovna mentioned among other things,' he began in a low voice, 'a very intimate friend of hers, whose name if I remember was Byelsky, or Dolsky....'

Potugin raised his mournful eyes and looked at Litvinov.

'Ah!' he commented thickly.... 'She mentioned ... well, what of it? It's time, though,' he added with a rather artificial yawn, 'for me to be getting home—to dinner. Good-bye.'

He jumped up from the seat and made off quickly before Litvinov had time to utter a word.... His compassion gave way to annoyance—annoyance with himself, be it understood. Want of consideration of any kind was foreign to his nature; he had wished to express his sympathy for Potugin, and it had resulted in something like a clumsy insinuation. With secret dissatisfaction in his heart, he went back to his hotel.

'Rotten to the marrow of her bones,' he thought a little later ... 'but proud as the devil! She, that woman who is almost on her knees to me, proud? proud and not capricious?'

Litvinov tried to drive Irina's image out of his head, but he did not succeed. For this very reason he did not think of his betrothed; he felt to-day this haunting image would not give up its place. He made up his mind to await without further anxiety the solution of all this 'strange business'; the solution could not be long in coming, and Litvinov had not the slightest doubt it would turn out to be most innocent and natural. So he fancied, but meanwhile he was not only haunted by Lina's image—every word she had uttered kept recurring in its turn to his memory.

The waiter brought him a note: it was from the same Irina:

'If you have nothing to do this evening, come to me; I shall not be alone; I shall have guests, and you will get a closer view of our set, our society. I want you very much to see something of them; I fancy they will show themselves in all their brilliance. You ought to know what sort of atmosphere I am breathing. Come; I shall be glad to see you, and you will not be bored. (Irina had spelt the Russian incorrectly here.) Prove to me that our explanation to-day has made any sort of misunderstanding between us impossible for ever.—Yours devotedly, I.

Litvinov put on a frock coat and a white tie, and set off to Irina's. 'All this is of no importance,' he repeated mentally on the way, 'as for looking at *them* ... why shouldn't I have a look at them? It will be curious.' A few days before, these very people had aroused a different sensation in him; they had aroused his indignation.

He walked with quickened steps, his cap pulled down over his eyes, and a constrained smile on his lips, while Bambaev, sitting before Weber's café, and pointing him out from a distance to Voroshilov and Pishtchalkin, cried excitedly: 'Do you see that man? He's a stone! he's a rock! he's a flint!!!'

XV

Litvinov found rather many guests at Irina's. In a corner at a card-table were sitting three of the generals of the picnic: the stout one, the irascible one, and the condescending one. They were playing whist with dummy, and there is no word in the language of man to express the solemnity with which they dealt, took tricks, led clubs and led diamonds ... there was no doubt about their being statesmen now! These gallant generals left to mere commoners, *aux bourgeois*, the little turns and phrases commonly used during play, and uttered only the most indispensable syllables; the stout general however permitted himself to jerk off between two deals: '*Ce satané as de pique!*' Among the visitors Litvinov recognised ladies who had been present at the picnic; but there were others there also whom he had not seen before. There was one so ancient that it seemed every instant as though she would fall to pieces: she shrugged her bare, gruesome, dingy grey shoulders, and, covering her mouth with her fan, leered languishingly with her absolutely death-like eyes upon Ratmirov; he paid her much attention; she was held in great honour in the highest society, as the last of the Maids of Honour of the Empress Catherine. At the window, dressed like a shepherdess, sat Countess S., 'the Queen of the Wasps,' surrounded by young men. Among them the celebrated millionaire and beau Finikov was conspicuous for his supercilious deportment, his absolutely flat skull, and his expression of soulless brutality, worthy of a Khan of Bucharia, or a Roman Heliogabalus. Another lady, also a countess, known by the pet name of *Lise*, was talking to a long-haired, fair, and pale spiritualistic medium. Beside them was standing a gentleman, also pale and long-haired, who kept laughing in a meaning way. This gentleman also believed in spiritualism, but added to that an interest in prophecy, and, on the basis of the Apocalypse and the Talmud, was in the habit of foretelling all kinds of marvellous events. Not a single one of these events had come to pass; but he was in no wise disturbed by that fact, and went on prophesying as before. At the piano, the musical genius had installed himself, the rough diamond, who had stirred Potugin to such indignation; he was striking chords with a careless hand, *d'une main distraite*, and kept staring vaguely about him. Irina was sitting on a sofa between Prince Kokó and Madame H., once a celebrated beauty and wit, who had long ago become a repulsive old crone, with the odour of sanctity and evaporated sinfulness about her. On catching sight of Litvinov, Irina blushed and got up, and when he went up to her, she pressed his hand warmly. She was wearing a dress of black crépon, relieved by a few inconspicuous gold ornaments; her shoulders were a dead white, while her face, pale too, under the momentary flood of crimson overspreading it, was breathing with the triumph of beauty, and not of beauty alone; a hidden, almost ironical happiness was shining in her half-closed eyes, and quivering about her lips and nostrils....

Ratmirov approached Litvinov and after exchanging with him his customary civilities, unaccompanied however by his customary playfulness, he presented him to two or three ladies: the ancient ruin, the Queen of the Wasps, Countess Liza ... they gave him a rather gracious reception. Litvinov did not belong to their set; but he was good-looking, extremely so, indeed, and the expressive features of his youthful face awakened their interest. Only he did not know how to fasten that interest upon himself; he was unaccustomed to society and was conscious of some embarrassment, added to which the stout general stared at him persistently. 'Aha! lubberly civilian! free-thinker!' that fixed heavy stare seemed to be saying: 'down on your knees to us; crawl to kiss our hands!' Irina came to Litvinov's aid. She managed so adroitly that he got into a corner near the door, a little behind her. As she addressed him, she had each time to turn round to him, and every time he admired the exquisite curve of her splendid neck, he drank in the subtle fragrance of her hair. An expression of gratitude, deep and calm, never left her face; he could not help seeing that gratitude and nothing else was what those smiles, those glances expressed, and he too was all aglow with the same emotion, and he felt shame, and delight and dread at once ... and at the same time she seemed continually as though she would ask, 'Well? what do you think of them?' With special clearness Litvinov heard this unspoken question whenever any one of the party was guilty of some vulgar phrase or act, and that occurred more than once during the evening. Once she did not even conceal her feelings, and laughed aloud.

Countess Liza, a lady of superstitious bent, with an inclination for everything extraordinary, after discoursing to her heart's content with the spiritualist upon Home, turning tables, self-playing concertinas, and so on, wound up by asking him whether there were animals which could be influenced by mesmerism.

'There is one such animal any way,' Prince Kokó declared from some way off. 'You know Melvanovsky, don't you? They put him to sleep before me, and didn't he snore, he, he!'

'You are very naughty, *mon prince;* I am speaking of real animals, *je parle des bêtes.*'

'*Mais moi aussi, madame, je parle d'une bête....*'

'There are such,' put in the spiritualist; 'for instance—crabs; they are very nervous, and are easily thrown into a cataleptic state.'

The countess was astounded. 'What? Crabs! Really? Oh, that's awfully interesting! Now, that I should like to see, M'sieu Luzhin,' she added to a young man with a face as stony as a new doll's, and a stony collar (he prided himself on the fact that he had bedewed the aforesaid face and collar with the sprays of Niagara and the Nubian Nile, though he remembered nothing of all his travels, and cared for nothing but Russian puns...). 'M'sieu Luzhin, if you would be so good, do bring us a crab quick.'

M'sieu Luzhin smirked. 'Quick must it be, or quickly?' he queried.

The countess did not understand him. '*Mais oui*, a crab,' she repeated, '*une écrevisse*.'

'Eh? what is it? a crab? a crab?' the Countess S. broke in harshly. The absence of M. Verdier irritated her; she could not imagine why Irina had not invited that most fascinating of Frenchmen. The ancient ruin, who had long since ceased understanding anything—moreover she was completely deaf—only shook her head.

'*Oui, oui, vous allez voir*, M'sieu Luzhin, please....'

The young traveller bowed, went out, and returned quickly. A waiter walked behind him, and grinning from ear to ear, carried in a dish, on which a large black crab was to be seen.

'*Voici, madame*,' cried Luzhin; 'now we can proceed to the operation on cancer. Ha, ha, ha!' (Russians are always the first to laugh at their own witticisms.)

'He, he, he!' Count Kokó did his duty condescendingly as a good patriot, and patron of all national products.

(We beg the reader not to be amazed and indignant; who can say confidently for himself that sitting in the stalls of the Alexander Theatre, and infected by its atmosphere, he has not applauded even worse puns?)

'*Merci, merci*,' said the countess. '*Allons, allons, Monsieur Fox, montrez nous ça.*'

The waiter put the dish down on a little round table. There was a slight movement among the guests; several heads were craned forward; only the generals at the card-table preserved the serene solemnity of their pose. The spiritualist ruffled up his hair, frowned, and, approaching the table, began waving his hands in the air; the crab stretched itself, backed, and raised its claws. The spiritualist repeated and quickened his movements; the crab stretched itself as before.

'*Mais que doit-elle donc faire?*' inquired the countess.

'*Elle doâ rester immobile et se dresser sur sa quiou*,' replied Mr. Fox, with a strong American accent, and he brandished his fingers with convulsive energy over the dish; but the mesmerism had no effect, the crab continued to move. The spiritualist declared that he was not himself, and retired with an air of displeasure from the table. The countess began to console him, by assuring him that similar failures occurred sometimes even with Mr. Home.... Prince Kokó confirmed her words. The authority on the Apocalypse and the Talmud stealthily went up to the table, and making rapid but vigorous thrusts with his fingers in the direction of the crab, he too tried his luck, but without success; no symptom of catalepsy showed itself. Then the waiter was called, and told to take away the crab, which he accordingly did, grinning from ear to ear, as before; he could be heard exploding outside the door.... There was much laughter afterwards in the kitchen *über diese Russen*. The self-taught genius, who had gone on striking notes during the experiments with the crab, dwelling on melancholy chords, on the ground that there was no knowing what influence music might have—the self-taught genius played his invariable waltz, and, of course, was deemed worthy of the most flattering applause. Pricked on by rivalry, Count H., our incomparable dilettante (see Chapter I.), gave a little song of his own composition, cribbed wholesale from Offenbach. Its playful refrain to the words: '*Quel œuf? quel bœuf?*' set almost all the ladies' heads swinging to right and to left; one went so far as to hum the tune lightly, and the irrepressible, inevitable word, '*Charmant! charmant!*' was fluttering on every one's lips. Irina exchanged a glance with Litvinov, and again the same secret, ironical expression quivered about her lips.... But a little later it was still more strongly marked, there was even a shade of malice in it, when Prince Kokó, that representative and champion of the interests of the nobility, thought fit to propound his views to the spiritualist, and, of course, gave utterance before long to his famous phrase about the shock to the principle of property, accompanied naturally by an attack on democrats. The spiritualist's American blood was stirred; he began to argue. The prince, as his habit was, at once fell to shouting at the top of his voice; instead of any kind of argument he repeated incessantly: '*C'est absurde! cela n'a pas le sens commun!*' The millionaire Finikov began saying insulting things, without much heed to whom they referred; the Talmudist's piping notes and even the Countess S.'s jarring voice could be heard.... In fact, almost the same incongruous uproar arose as at Gubaryov's; the only difference was that here there was no beer nor tobacco-smoke, and every one was better dressed. Ratmirov tried to restore tranquillity (the generals manifested their displeasure, Boris's exclamation could be heard, '*Encore cette satanée politique!*'), but his efforts were not successful, and at that point, a high official of the stealthily inquisitorial type, who was present, and undertook to present *le résumé en peu de mots*, sustained a defeat: in fact he so hummed and hawed, so repeated himself, and was so obviously incapable of listening to or taking in the answers he received, and so unmistakably failed to perceive himself what precisely constituted *la question* that no other result could possibly have been anticipated. And then too Irina was slily provoking the disputants and setting them against one another, constantly exchanging glances and slight signs with Litvinov as she did so.... But he was sitting like one spell-bound, he was hearing nothing, and waiting for nothing but for those splendid eyes to sparkle again, that pale, tender, mischievous, exquisite face to flash upon him again.... It ended by the ladies growing restive, and requesting that the dispute should cease.... Ratmirov entreated the dilettante to sing his song again, and the self-taught genius once more played his waltz....

Litvinov stayed till after midnight, and went away later than all the rest. The conversation had in the course of the evening touched upon a number of subjects, studiously avoiding anything of the faintest interest; the generals, after finishing their solemn game, solemnly joined in it: the influence of these statesmen was at once apparent. The conversation turned upon notorieties of the Parisian demi-monde, with whose names and talents every one seemed intimately acquainted, on Sardou's latest play, on a novel of About's, on Patti in the *Traviata*. Some one proposed a game of 'secretary,' *au secrétaire;* but it was not a success. The answers given were pointless, and often not free from grammatical mistakes; the stout general related that he had once in answer to the question: *Qu'est-ce que l'amour?*replied, *Une colique remontée au cœur*, and promptly went off into his wooden guffaw; the ancient ruin with a mighty effort struck him with her fan on the arm; a flake of plaster was shaken off her forehead by this rash action. The old crone was beginning a reference to the Slavonic principalities and the necessity of orthodox propaganda on the Danube, but, meeting with no response, she subsided with a hiss. In reality they talked more about Home than anything else; even the 'Queen of the Wasps' described how hands had once crept about her, and how she had seen them, and put her own ring on one of them. It was certainly a triumph for Irina: even if Litvinov had paid more attention to what was being said around him, he still could not have gleaned one single sincere saying, one single clever thought, one single new fact from all their disconnected and lifeless babble. Even in their cries and exclamations, there was no note of real feeling, in their slander no real heat. Only at rare intervals under the mask of assumed patriotic indignation, or of assumed contempt and indifference, the dread of possible losses could be heard in a plaintive whimper, and a few names, which will not be forgotten by posterity, were pronounced with gnashing of teeth ... And not a drop of living water under all this noise and wrangle! What stale, what unprofitable nonsense, what wretched trivialities were absorbing all these heads and hearts, and not for that one evening, not in society only, but at home too, every hour and every day, in all the depth and breadth of their existence! And what ignorance, when all is said! What lack of understanding of all on which human life is built, all by which life is made beautiful!

On parting from Litvinov, Irina again pressed his hand and whispered significantly, 'Well? Are you pleased? Have you seen enough? Do you like it?' He made her no reply, but merely bowed low in silence.

Left alone with her husband, Irina was just going to her bedroom.... He stopped her.

'*Je vous ai beaucoup admirée ce soir, madame*,' he observed, smoking a cigarette, and leaning against the mantelpiece, '*vous vous êtes parfaitement moquée de nous tous*.'

'*Pas plus cette fois-ci que les autres*,' she answered indifferently.

'How do you mean me to understand you?' asked Ratmirov.

'As you like.'

'Hm. *C'est clair.*' Ratmirov warily, like a cat, knocked off the ash of the cigarette with the tip of the long nail of his little finger. 'Oh, by the way! This new friend of yours—what the dickens is his name?—Mr. Litvinov—doubtless enjoys the reputation of a very clever man.'

At the name of Litvinov, Irina turned quickly round.

'What do you mean to say?'

The general smiled.

'He keeps very quiet ... one can see he's afraid of compromising himself.'

Irina too smiled; it was a very different smile from her husband's.

'Better keep quiet than talk ... as some people talk.'

'*Attrapé!*' answered Ratmirov with feigned submissiveness. 'Joking apart, he has a very interesting face. Such a ... concentrated expression ... and his whole bearing.... Yes....' The general straightened his cravat, and bending his head stared at his own moustache. 'He's a republican, I imagine, of the same sort as your other friend, Mr. Potugin; that's another of your clever fellows who are dumb.'

Irina's brows were slowly raised above her wide open clear eyes, while her lips were tightly pressed together and faintly curved.

'What's your object in saying that, Valerian Vladimiritch,' she remarked, as though sympathetically. 'You are wasting your arrows on the empty air.... We are not in Russia, and there is no one to hear you.'

Ratmirov was stung.

'That's not merely my opinion, Irina Pavlovna,' he began in a voice suddenly guttural; 'other people too notice that that gentleman has the air of a conspirator.'

'Really? who are these other people?'

'Well, Boris for instance——'

'What? was it necessary for him too to express his opinion?'

Irina shrugged her shoulders as though shrinking from the cold, and slowly passed the tips of her fingers over them.

'Him ... yes, him. Allow me to remark, Irina Pavlovna, that you seem angry; and you know if one is angry——'

'Am I angry? Oh, what for?'

'I don't know; possibly you have been disagreeably affected by the observation I permitted myself to make in reference to——'

Ratmirov stammered.

'In reference to?' Irina repeated interrogatively. 'Ah, if you please, no irony, and make haste. I'm tired and sleepy.'

She took a candle from the table. 'In reference to——?'

'Well, in reference to this same Mr. Litvinov; since there's no doubt now that you take a great interest in him.'

Irina lifted the hand in which she was holding the candlestick, till the flame was brought on a level with her husband's face, and attentively, almost with curiosity, looking him straight in the face, she suddenly burst into laughter.

'What is it?' asked Ratmirov scowling.

Irina went on laughing.

'Well, what is it?' he repeated, and he stamped his foot.

He felt insulted, wounded, and at the same time against his will he was impressed by the beauty of this woman, standing so lightly and boldly before him ... she was tormenting him. He saw everything, all her charms—even the pink reflection of the delicate nails on her slender finger-tips, as they tightly clasped the dark bronze of the heavy candlestick—even that did not escape him ... while the insult cut deeper and deeper into his heart. And still Irina laughed.

'What? you? you jealous?' she brought out at last, and turning her back on her husband she went out of the room. 'He's jealous!' he heard outside the door, and again came the sound of her laugh.

Ratmirov looked moodily after his wife; he could not even then help noticing the bewitching grace of her figure, her movements, and with a violent blow, crushing the cigarette on the marble slab of the mantelpiece, he flung it to a distance. His cheeks had suddenly turned white, a spasm passed over the lower half of his face, and with a dull animal stare his eyes strayed about the floor, as though in search of something.... Every semblance of refinement had vanished from his face. Such an expression it must have worn when he was flogging the White Russian peasants.

Litvinov had gone home to his rooms, and sitting down to the table he had buried his head in both hands, and remained a long while without stirring. He got up at last, opened a box, and taking out a pocket-book, he drew out of an inner pocket a photograph of Tatyana. Her face gazed out mournfully at him, looking ugly and old, as photographs usually do. Litvinov's betrothed was a girl of Great Russian blood, a blonde, rather plump, and with the features of her face rather heavy, but with a wonderful expression of kindness and goodness in her intelligent, clear brown eyes, with a serene, white brow, on which it seemed as though a sunbeam always rested. For a long time Litvinov did not take his eyes from the photograph, then he pushed it gently away and again clutched his head in both hands. 'All is at an end!' he whispered at last, 'Irina! Irina!'

Only now, only at that instant, he realised that he was irrevocably, senselessly, in love with her, that he had loved her since the very day of that first meeting with her at the Old Castle, that he had never ceased to love her. And yet how astounded, how incredulous, how scornful, he would have been, had he been told so a few hours back!

'But Tanya, Tanya, my God! Tanya! Tanya!' he repeated in contrition; while Irina's shape fairly rose before his eyes in her black almost funereal garb, with the radiant calm of victory on her marble white face.

XVI

Litvinov did not sleep all night, and did not undress. He was very miserable. As an honest and straightforward man, he realised the force of obligations, the sacredness of duty, and would have been ashamed of any double dealing with himself, his weakness, his fault. At first he was overcome by apathy; it was long before he could throw off the gloomy burden of a single half-conscious, obscure sensation; then terror took possession of him at the thought that the future, his almost conquered future, had slipped back into the darkness, that his home, the solidly-built home he had only just raised, was suddenly tottering about him....

He began reproaching himself without mercy, but at once checked his own vehemence. 'What feebleness!' he thought. 'It's no time for self-reproach and cowardice; now I must act. Tanya is my betrothed, she has faith in my love, my honour, we are bound together for life, and cannot, must not, be put asunder.' He vividly pictured to himself all Tanya's qualities, mentally he picked them out and reckoned them up; he was trying to call up feeling and tenderness in himself. 'One thing's left for me,' he thought again, 'to run away, to run away directly, without waiting for her arrival, to hasten to meet her; whether I suffer, whether I am wretched with Tanya—that's not likely—but in any case to think of that, to take that into consideration is useless; I must do my duty, if I die for it! But you have no right to deceive her,' whispered another voice within him. 'You have no right to hide from her the change in your feelings; it may be that when she knows you love another woman, she will not be willing to become your wife? Rubbish! rubbish!' he answered, 'that's all sophistry, shameful double-dealing, deceitful conscientiousness; I have no right not to keep my word, that's the thing. Well, so be it.... Then I must go away from here, without seeing the other....'

But at that point Litvinov's heart throbbed with anguish, he turned cold, physically cold, a momentary shiver passed over him, his teeth chattered weakly. He stretched and yawned, as though he were in a fever. Without dwelling longer on his last thought, choking back that thought, turning away from it, he set himself to marvelling and wondering in perplexity how he could again ... again love that corrupt worldly creature, all of whose surroundings were so hateful, so repulsive to him. He tried to put to himself the question: 'What nonsense, do you really love her?' and could only wring his hands in despair. He was still marvelling and wondering, and suddenly there rose up before his eyes, as though from a soft fragrant mist, a seductive shape, shining eyelashes were lifted, and softly and irresistibly the marvellous eyes pierced him to the heart and a voice was singing with sweetness in his ears, and resplendent shoulders, the shoulders of a young queen, were breathing with voluptuous freshness and warmth....

Towards morning a determination was at last fully formed in Litvinov's mind. He decided to set off that day to meet Tatyana, and seeing Irina for the last time, to tell her, since there was nothing else for it, the whole truth, and to part from her for ever.

He set in order and packed his things, waited till twelve o'clock, and started to go to her. But at the sight of her half-curtained windows Litvinov's heart fairly failed him ... he could not summon up courage to enter the hotel. He walked once or twice up and down Lichtenthaler Allee. 'A very good day to Mr. Litvinov!' he suddenly heard an ironical voice call from the top of a swiftly-moving 'dogcart.' Litvinov raised his eyes and saw General Ratmirov sitting beside Prince M., a well-known sportsman and fancier of English carriages and horses. The prince was driving, the general was leaning over on one side, grinning, while he lifted his hat high above his head. Litvinov bowed to him, and at the same instant, as though he were obeying a secret command, he set off at a run towards Irina's.

She was at home. He sent up his name; he was at once received. When he went in, she was standing in the middle of the room. She was wearing a morning blouse with wide open sleeves; her face, pale as the day before, but not fresh as it had been then, expressed weariness; the languid smile with which she welcomed her visitor emphasised that expression even more clearly. She held out her hand to him in a friendly way, but absent-mindedly.

'Thanks for coming,' she began in a plaintive voice, and she sank into a low chair. 'I am not very well this morning; I spent a bad night. Well, what have you to say about last night? Wasn't I right?'

Litvinov sat down.

'I have come to you, Irina Pavlovna,' he began.

She instantly sat up and turned round; her eyes simply fastened upon Litvinov.

'What is it,' she cried. 'You're pale as death, you're ill. What's the matter with you?'

Litvinov was confused.

'With me, Irina Pavlovna?'

'Have you had bad news? Some misfortune has happened, tell me, tell me——'

Litvinov in his turn looked at Irina.

'I have had no bad news,' he brought out not without effort, 'but a misfortune has certainly happened, a great misfortune ... and it has brought me to you.'

'A misfortune? What is it?'

'Why ... that——'

Litvinov tried to go on ... and could not. He only pinched his hands together so that his fingers cracked. Irina was bending forward and seemed turned to stone.

'Oh! I love you!' broke at last with a low groan from Litvinov's breast, and he turned away, as though he would hide his face.

'What, Grigory Mihalitch, you' ... Irina too could not finish her sentence, and leaning back in her chair, she put both her hands to her eyes. 'You ... love me.'

'Yes ... yes ... yes,' he repeated with bitterness, turning his head further and further away.

Everything was silent in the room; a butterfly that had flown in was fluttering its wings and struggling between the curtain and the window.

The first to speak was Litvinov.

'That, Irina Pavlovna,' he began, 'that is the misfortune, which ... has befallen me, which I ought to have foreseen and avoided, if I had not now just as in the Moscow days been carried off my feet at once. It seems fate is pleased to force me once again through you to suffer tortures, which one would have thought should not be repeated again.... It was not without cause I struggled.... I tried to struggle; but of course there's no escaping one's fate. And I tell you all this to put an end at once to this ... this tragic farce,' he added with a fresh outburst of shame and bitterness.

Litvinov was silent again; the butterfly was struggling and fluttering as before. Irina did not take her hands from her face.

'And you are not mistaken?' her whisper sounded from under those white, bloodless-looking hands.

'I am not mistaken,' answered Litvinov in a colourless voice. 'I love you, as I have never loved any one but you. I am not going to reproach you; that would be too foolish; I'm not going to tell you that perhaps nothing of all this would have happened if you yourself had behaved differently with me.... Of course, I alone am to blame, my self-confidence has been my ruin; I am deservedly punished, and you could not have anticipated it. Of course you did not consider that it would have been far less dangerous for me if you had not been so keenly alive to your wrong ... your supposed wrong to me; and had not wished to make up for it ... but what's done can't be undone. I only wanted to make clear my position to you; it's hard enough as it is.... But at least there will be, as you say, no misunderstanding, while the openness of my confession will soften, I hope, the feeling of offence which you cannot but feel.'

Litvinov spoke without raising his eyes, but even if he had glanced at Irina, he could not have seen what was passing in her face, as she still as before kept her hands over her eyes. But what was passing over her face meanwhile would probably have astounded him; both alarm and delight were apparent on it, and a kind of blissful helplessness and agitation; her eyes hardly glimmered under their overhanging lids, and her slow, broken breathing was chill upon her lips, that were parted as though with thirst....

Litvinov was silent, waiting for a response, some sound.... Nothing!

'There is one thing left for me,' he began again, 'to go away; I have come to say good-bye to you.'

Irina slowly dropped her hands on to her knees.

'But I remember, Grigory Mihalitch,' she began; 'that ... that person of whom you spoke to me, she was to have come here? You are expecting her?'

'Yes; but I shall write to her ... she will stop somewhere on the way ... at Heidelberg, for instance.'

'Ah! Heidelberg.... Yes.... It's nice there.... But all this must upset your plans. Are you perfectly certain, Grigory Mihalitch, that you are not exaggerating, *et que ce n'est pas une fausse alarme?*'

Irina spoke softly, almost coldly, with short pauses, looking away towards the window. Litvinov made no answer to her last question.

'Only, why did you talk of offence?' she went on. 'I am not offended ... oh, no! and if one or other of us is to blame, in any case it's not you; not you alone.... Remember our last conversations, and you will be convinced that it's not you who are to blame.'

'I have never doubted your magnanimity,' Litvinov muttered between his teeth, 'but I should like to know, do you approve of my intention?'

'To go away?'

'Yes.'

Irina continued to look away.

'At the first moment, your intention struck me as premature ... but now I have thought over what you have said ... and if you are really not mistaken, then I suppose that you ought to go away. It will be better so ... better for us both.'

Irina's voice had grown lower and lower, and her words too came more and more slowly.

'General Ratmirov, certainly, might notice,' Litvinov was beginning....

Irina's eyes dropped again, and something strange quivered about her lips, quivered and died away.

'No; you did not understand me,' she interrupted him. 'I was not thinking of my husband. Why should I? And there is nothing to notice. But I repeat, separation is necessary for us both.'

Litvinov picked up his hat, which had fallen on the ground.

'Everything is over,' he thought, 'I must go. And so it only remains for me to say good-bye to you, Irina Pavlovna,' he said aloud, and suddenly felt a pang, as though he were preparing to pronounce his own sentence on himself. 'It only remains for me to hope that you will not remember evil against me, and ... and that if we ever——'

Irina again cut him short.

'Wait a little, Grigory Mihalitch, don't say good-bye to me yet. That would be too hurried.'

Something wavered in Litvinov, but the burning pain broke out again and with redoubled violence in his heart.

'But I can't stay,' he cried. 'What for? Why prolong this torture?'

'Don't say good-bye to me yet,' repeated Irina. 'I must see you once more.... Another such dumb parting as in Moscow again—no, I don't want that. You can go now, but you must promise me, give me your word of honour that you won't go away without seeing me once more.'

'You wish that?'

'I insist on it. If you go away without saying good-bye to me, I shall never forgive it, do you hear, never! Strange!' she added as though to herself, 'I cannot persuade myself that I am in Baden.... I keep feeling that I am in Moscow.... Go now.'

Litvinov got up.

'Irina Pavlovna,' he said, 'give me your hand.'

Irina shook her head.

'I told you that I don't want to say good-bye to you....'

'I don't ask it for that.'

Irina was about to stretch out her hand, but she glanced at Litvinov for the first time since his avowal, and drew it back.

'No, no,' she whispered, 'I will not give you my hand. No ... no. Go now.'

Litvinov bowed and went away. He could not tell why Irina had refused him that last friendly handshake.... He could not know what she feared.

He went away, and Irina again sank into the armchair and again covered her face.

XVII

Litvinov did not return home; he went up to the hills, and getting into a thick copse, he flung himself face downwards on the earth, and lay there about an hour. He did not suffer tortures, did not weep; he sank into a kind of heavy, oppressive stupor. Never had he felt anything like it; it was an insufferably aching and gnawing sensation of emptiness, emptiness in himself, his surroundings, everywhere.... He thought neither of Irina nor of Tatyana. He felt one thing only: a blow had fallen and life was sundered like a cord, and all of him was being drawn along in the clutches of something chill and unfamiliar. Sometimes it seemed to him that a whirlwind had swooped down upon him, and he had the sensation of its swift whirling round and the irregular beating of its dark wings. But his resolution did not waver. To remain in Baden ... that could not even be considered. In thought he had already gone, he was already sitting in the rattling, snorting train, hurrying, hurrying into the dumb, dead distance. He got up at last, and leaning his head against a tree, stayed motionless; only with one hand, he all unconsciously snatched and swung in rhythm the topmost frond of a fern. The sound of approaching footsteps drew him out of his stupor: two charcoal-burners were making their way down the steep path with large sacks on their shoulders. 'It's time!' whispered Litvinov, and he followed the charcoal-burners to the town, turned into the railway station, and sent off a telegram to Tatyana's aunt, Kapitolina Markovna. In this telegram he informed her of his immediate departure, and appointed as a meeting-place, Schrader's hotel in Heidelberg.

'Make an end, make an end at once,' he thought; 'it's useless putting it off till to-morrow.' Then he went to the gambling saloon, stared with dull curiosity at the faces of two or three gamblers, got a back view of Bindasov's ugly head in the distance, noticed the irreproachable countenance of Pishtchalkin, and after waiting a little under the colonnade, he set off deliberately to Irina's. He was not going to her through the force of sudden, involuntary temptation; when he made up his mind to go away, he also made up his mind to keep his word and see her once more.He went into the hotel unobserved by the porter, ascended the staircase, not meeting any one, and without knocking at the door, he mechanically pushed it open and went into the room.

In the room, in the same armchair, in the same dress, in precisely the same attitude as three hours before, was sitting Irina.... It was obvious that she had not moved from the place, had not stirred all that time. She slowly raised her head, and seeing Litvinov, she trembled all over and clutched the arm of the chair. 'You frightened me,' she whispered.

Litvinov looked at her with speechless bewilderment. The expression of her face, her lustreless eyes, astounded him.

Irina gave a forced smile and smoothed her ruffled hair. 'Never mind.... I really don't know.... I think I must have fallen asleep here.'

'I beg your pardon, Irina Pavlovna,' began Litvinov. 'I came in unannounced.... I wanted to do what you thought fit to require of me. So as I am going away to-day——'

'To-day? But I thought you told me that you meant first to write a letter——'

'I have sent a telegram.'

'Ah! you found it necessary to make haste. And when are you going? What time, I mean?'

'At seven o'clock this evening.'

'Ah! at seven o'clock! And you have come to say good-bye?'

'Yes, Irina Pavlovna, to say good-bye.'

Irina was silent for a little.

'I ought to thank you, Grigory Mihalitch, it was probably not easy for you to come here.'

'No, Irina Pavlovna, it was anything but easy.'

'Life is not generally easy, Grigory Mihalitch; what do you think about it?'

'It depends, Irina Pavlovna.'

Irina was silent again for a little; she seemed sunk in thought.

'You have proved your affection for me by coming,' she said at last, 'I thank you. And I fully approve of your decision to put an end to everything as soon as possible ... because any delay ... because ... because I, even I whom you have reproached as a flirt, called an actress ... that, I think, was what you called me?...'

Irina got up swiftly, and, sitting down in another chair, stooped down and pressed her face and arms on the edge of the table.

'Because I love you ...' she whispered between her clasped fingers.

Litvinov staggered, as though some one had dealt him a blow in the chest. Irina turned her head dejectedly away from him, as though she in her turn wanted to hide her face from him, and laid it down on the table.

'Yes, I love you ... I love you ... and you know it.'

'I? I know it?' Litvinov said at last; 'I?'

'Well, now you see,' Irina went on, 'that you certainly must go, that delay's impossible ... both for you, and for me delay's impossible. It's dangerous, it's terrible ... good-bye!' she added, rising impulsively from her chair, 'good-bye!'

She took a few steps in the direction of the door of her boudoir, and putting her hand behind her back, made a hurried movement in the air, as though she would find and press the hand of Litvinov; but he stood like a block of wood, at a distance.... Once more she said, 'Good-bye, forget me,' and without looking round she rushed away.

Litvinov remained alone, and yet still could not come to himself. He recovered himself at last, went quickly to the boudoir door, uttered Irina's name once, twice, three times.... He had already his hand on the lock.... From the hotel stairs rose the sound of Ratmirov's sonorous voice.

Litvinov pulled down his hat over his eyes, and went out on to the staircase. The elegant general was standing before the Swiss porter's box and explaining to him in bad German that he wanted a hired carriage for the whole of the next day. On catching sight of Litvinov, he again lifted his hat unnaturally high, and again wished him 'a very good-day'; he was obviously jeering at him, but Litvinov had no thoughts for that. He hardly responded to Ratmirov's bow, and, making his way to his lodging, he stood still before his already packed and closed trunk. His head was turning round and his heart vibrating like a harp-string. What was to be done now? And could he have foreseen this?

Yes, he had foreseen it, however unlikely it seemed. It had stunned him like a clap of thunder, yet he had foreseen it, though he had not courage even to acknowledge it. Besides he knew nothing now for certain. Everything was confusion and turmoil within him; he had lost the thread of his own thoughts. He remembered Moscow, he remembered how then too 'it' had come upon him like a sudden tempest. He was breathless; rapture, but a rapture comfortless and hopeless, oppressed and tore his heart. For nothing in the world would he have consented that the words uttered by Irina should not have actually been uttered by her.... But then? those words could not for all that change the resolution he had taken. As before, it did not waver; it stood firm like an anchor. Litvinov had lost the thread of his own thoughts ... yes; but his will still remained to him, and he disposed of himself as of another man dependent on him. He rang for the waiter, asked him for the bill, bespoke a place in the evening omnibus; designedly he cut himself off all paths of retreat. 'If I die for it after!' he declared, as he had in the previous sleepless night; that phrase seemed especially to his taste. 'Then even if I die for it!' he repeated, walking slowly up and down the room, and only at rare intervals, unconsciously, he shut his eyes and held his breath, while those words, those words of Irina's forced their way into his soul, and set it aflame. 'It seems you won't love twice,' he thought; 'another life came to you, you let it come into yours—never to be rid of that poison to the end, you will never break those bonds! Yes; but what does that prove? Happiness?... Is it possible? You love her, granted ... and she ... she loves you....'

But at this point again he had to pull himself up. As a traveller on a dark night, seeing before him a light, and afraid of losing the path, never for an instant takes his eyes off it, so Litvinov continually bent all the force of his attention on a single point, a single aim. To reach his betrothed, and not precisely even his betrothed (he was trying not to think of her) but to reach a room in the Heidelberg hotel, that was what stood immovably before him, a guiding light. What would be later, he did not know, nor did he want to know.... One thing was beyond doubt, he would not come back. 'If I die first!' he repeated for the tenth time, and he glanced at his watch.

A quarter-past six! How long still to wait! He paced once more up and down. The sun was nearly setting, the sky was crimson above the trees, and the pink flush of twilight lay on the narrow windows of his darkening room. Suddenly Litvinov fancied the door had been opened quickly and softly behind him and as quickly closed again.... He turned round; at the door, muffled in a dark cloak, was standing a woman....

'Irina,' he cried, and clapped his hands together in amazement.... She raised her head and fell upon his breast.

Two hours later he was sitting in his room on the sofa. His box stood in the corner, open and empty, and on the table in the midst of things flung about in disorder, lay a letter from Tatyana, just received by him. She wrote to him that she had decided to hasten her departure from Dresden, since her aunt's health was completely restored, and that if nothing happened to delay them, they would both be in Baden the following day at twelve o'clock, and hoped that he would come to meet them at the station. Apartments had already been taken for them by Litvinov in the same hotel in which he was staying.

The same evening he sent a note to Irina, and the following morning he received a reply from her. 'Sooner or later,' she wrote, 'it must have been. I tell you again what I said yesterday: my life is in your hands, do with me what you will. I do not want to hamper your freedom, but let me say, that if necessary, I will throw up everything, and follow you to the ends of the earth. We shall see each other to-morrow, of course.—Your Irina.'

The last two words were written in a large, bold, resolute hand.

XVIII

Among the persons assembled on the 18th of August at twelve o'clock on the platform at the railway station was Litvinov. Not long before, he had seen Irina: she was sitting in an open carriage with her husband and another gentleman, somewhat elderly. She caught sight of Litvinov, and he perceived that some obscure emotion flitted over her eyes; but at once she hid herself from him with her parasol.

A strange transformation had taken place in him since the previous day—in his whole appearance, his movements, the expression of his face; and indeed he felt himself a different man. His self-confidence had vanished, and his peace of mind had vanished too, and his respect for himself; of his former spiritual condition nothing was left. Recent ineffaceable impressions obscured all the rest from him. Some sensation unknown before had come, strong, sweet—and evil; the mysterious guest had made its way to the innermost shrine and taken possession and lain down in it, in silence, but in all its magnitude, like the owner in a new house. Litvinov was no longer ashamed, he was afraid; at the same time a desperate hardihood had sprung up in him; the captured, the vanquished know well this mixture of opposing feelings; the thief too knows something of it after his first robbery. Litvinov had been vanquished, vanquished suddenly ... and what had become of his honesty?

The train was a few minutes late. Litvinov's suspense passed into agonising torture; he could not stop still in one place, and, pale all over, moved about jostling in the crowd. 'My God,' he thought, 'if I only had another twenty-four hours.'... The first look at Tanya, the first look of Tanya ... that was what filled him with terror ... that was what he had to live through directly.... And afterwards? Afterwards ... come, what may come!... He now made no more resolutions, he could not answer for himself now. His phrase of yesterday flashed painfully through his head.... And this was how he was meeting Tanya....

A prolonged whistle sounded at last, a heavy momentarily increasing rumble was heard, and, slowly rolling round a bend in the line, the train came into sight. The crowd hurried to meet it, and Litvinov followed it, dragging his feet like a condemned man. Faces, ladies' hats began to appear out of the carriages, at one window a white handkerchief gleamed.... Kapitolina Markovna was waving to him.... It was over; she had caught sight of Litvinov and he recognised her. The train stood still; Litvinov rushed to the carriage door, and opened it; Tatyana was standing near her aunt, smiling brightly and holding out her hand.

He helped them both to get out, uttered a few words of welcome, unfinished and confused, and at once bustled about, began taking their tickets, their travelling bags, and rugs, ran to find a porter, called a fly; other people were bustling around them. He was glad of their presence, their fuss, and loud talk. Tatyana moved a little aside, and, still smiling, waited calmly for his hurried arrangements to be concluded. Kapitolina Markovna, on the other hand, could not keep still; she could not believe that she was at last at Baden.

She suddenly cried, 'But the parasols? Tanya, where are our parasols?' all unconscious that she was holding them fast under her arm; then she began taking a loud and prolonged farewell of another lady with whom she had made friends on the journey from Heidelberg to Baden. This lady was no other than our old friend Madame Suhantchikov. She had gone away to Heidelberg to do obeisance to Gubaryov, and was returning with 'instructions.' Kapitolina Markovna wore a rather peculiar striped mantle and a round travelling hat of a mushroom-shape, from under which her short white hair fell in disorder; short and thin, she was flushed with travelling and kept talking Russian in a shrill and penetrating voice.... She was an object of attention at once.

Litvinov at last put her and Tatyana into a fly, and placed himself opposite them. The horses started. Then followed questionings, renewed handshaking, interchanging of smiles and welcomes.... Litvinov breathed freely; the first moment had passed off satisfactorily. Nothing in him, apparently, had struck or bewildered Tanya; she was smiling just as brightly and confidently, she was blushing as charmingly, and laughing as goodnaturedly. He brought himself at last to take a look at her; not a stealthy cursory glance, but a direct steady look at her, hitherto his own eyes had refused to obey him. His heart throbbed with involuntary emotion: the serene expression of that honest, candid face gave him a pang of bitter reproach. 'So you are here, poor girl,' he thought, 'you whom I have so longed for, so urged to come, with whom I had hoped to spend my life to the end, you have come, you believed in me ... while I ... while I.'... Litvinov's head sank; but Kapitolina Markovna gave him no time for musing; she was pelting him with questions.

'What is that building with columns? Where is it the gambling's done? Who is that coming along? Tanya, Tanya, look, what crinolines! And who can that be? I suppose they are mostly French creatures from Paris here? Mercy, what a hat! Can you get everything here just as in Paris? But, I expect, everything's awfully dear, eh? Ah, I've made the acquaintance of such a splendid, intellectual woman! You know her, Grigory

Mihalitch; she told me she had met you at some Russian's, who's a wonderfully intellectual person too. She promised to come and see us. How she does abuse all these aristocrats—it's simply superb! What is that gentleman with grey moustaches? The Prussian king? Tanya, Tanya, look, that's the Prussian king. No? not the Prussian king, the Dutch ambassador, did you say? I can't hear, the wheels rattle so. Ah, what exquisite trees!'

'Yes, exquisite, aunt,' Tanya assented, 'and how green everything is here, how bright and gay! Isn't it, Grigory Mihalitch?'

'Oh, very bright and gay' ... he answered through his teeth.

The carriage stopped at last before the hotel. Litvinov conducted the two travellers to the room taken for them, promised to come back within an hour, and went to his own room. Directly he entered it, he fell again under the spell which had been lulled for a while. Here, in that room, since the day before, Irina reigned supreme; everything was eloquent of her, the very air seemed to have kept secret traces of her visit.... Again Litvinov felt himself her slave. He drew out her handkerchief, hidden in his bosom, pressed it to his lips, and burning memories flowed in subtle poison through his veins. He realised that there was no turning back, no choosing now; the sorrowful emotion aroused in him by Tatyana melted away like snow in the fire, and remorse died down ... died down so completely that his uneasiness even was soothed, and the possibility—present to his intellect—of hypocrisy no longer revolted him.... Love, Irina's love, that was now his truth, his bond, his conscience.... The sensible Litvinov did not even ponder how to get out of a position, the horror and hideousness of which he bore lightly, as if it did not concern him.

The hour had not yet passed when a waiter came to Litvinov from the newly arrived ladies; they begged him to come to them in the public drawing-room. He followed the messenger, and found them already dressed and in their hats. They both expressed a desire to go out at once to see Baden, as the weather was so fine. Kapitolina Markovna especially seemed burning with impatience; she was quite cast down when she heard that the hour of the fashionable promenade before the Konversation Hall had not yet arrived. Litvinov gave her his arm, and the ceremony of sight-seeing began. Tatyana walked beside her aunt, looking about her with quiet interest; Kapitolina Markovna pursued her inquiries. The sight of the roulette, the dignified croupiers, whom—had she met them in any other place—she would certainly have taken for ministers, the quickly moving scoops, the heaps of gold and silver on the green cloth, the old women gambling, and the painted *cocottes* reduced Kapitolina Markovna to a sort of speechless stupor; she altogether forgot that she ought to feel moral indignation, and could only gaze and gaze, giving a start of surprise at every new sight.... The whiz of the ivory ball into the bottom of the roulette thrilled her to the marrow of her bones, and it was only when she was again in the open air that, drawing a long breath, she recovered energy enough to denounce games of chance as an immoral invention of aristocracy. A fixed, unpleasant smile had made its appearance on Litvinov's lips; he had spoken abruptly and lazily, as though he were annoyed or bored.... But now he turned round towards Tatyana, and was thrown into secret confusion; she was looking attentively at him, with an expression as though she were asking herself what sort of an impression was being made on her. He made haste to nod his head to her, she responded with the same gesture, and again looked at him questioningly, with a sort of strained effort, as though he were standing much further off than he really was. Litvinov led his ladies away from the Konversation Hall, and passing the 'Russian tree,' under which two Russian ladies were already sitting, he went towards Lichtenthaler Allee. He had hardly entered the avenue when he saw Irina in the distance.

She was walking towards him with her husband and Potugin. Litvinov turned white as a sheet; he did not slacken his pace, however, and when he was on a level with her, he made a bow without speaking. She too bowed to him, politely, but coldly, and taking in Tatyana in a rapid glance, she glided by.... Ratmirov lifted his hat high, Potugin muttered something.

'Who is that lady?' Tatyana asked suddenly. Till that instant she had hardly opened her lips.

'That lady?' repeated Litvinov, 'that lady? That is a Madame Ratmirov.'

'Is she Russian?'

'Yes.'

'Did you make her acquaintance here?'

'No; I have known her a long while.'

'How beautiful she is!'

'Did you notice her dress?' put in Kapitolina Markovna. 'Ten families might live for a whole year on the cost of her lace alone. Was that her husband with her?' she inquired turning to Litvinov.

'Yes.'

'He must be awfully rich, I suppose?'

'Really I don't know; I don't think so.'

'What is his rank?'

'He's a general.'

'What eyes she has!' said Tatyana, 'and what a strange expression in them: pensive and penetrating at the same time.... I have never seen such eyes.'

Litvinov made no answer; he fancied that he felt again Tatyana's questioning glance bent on his face, but he was wrong, she was looking at her own feet, at the sand of the path.

'Mercy on us! Who is that fright?' cried Kapitolina Markovna suddenly, pointing to a low jaunting-car in which a red-haired pug-nosed woman lay lolling impudently, in an extraordinarily gorgeous costume and lilac stockings.

'That fright! why, that's the celebrated Ma'mselle Cora.'

'Who?'

'Ma'mselle Cora ... a Parisian ... notoriety.'

'What? That pug? Why, but she's hideous!'

'It seems that's no hindrance.'

Kapitolina Markovna could only lift her hands in astonishment.

'Well, this Baden of yours!' she brought out at last. 'Can one sit down on a seat here? I'm rather tired.'

'Of course you can, Kapitolina Markovna.... That's what the seats are put here for.'

'Well, really, there's no knowing! But there in Paris, I'm told, there are seats, too, along the boulevards; but it's not proper to sit on them.'

Litvinov made no reply to Kapitolina Markovna; only at that moment he realised that two paces away was the very spot where he had had that explanation with Irina, which had decided everything. Then he recalled that he had noticed a small rosy spot on her cheek to-day....

Kapitolina Markovna sank down on to the seat, Tatyana sat down beside her. Litvinov remained on the path; between Tatyana and him—or was it only his fancy?—something seemed to have happened ... unconsciously and gradually.

'Ah, she's a wretch, a perfect wretch!' Kapitolina Markovna declared, shaking her head commiseratingly; 'why, with the price of *her* get-up, you could keep not ten, but a hundred families. Did you see under her hat, on *her* red hair, there were diamonds? Upon my word, diamonds in the day-time!'

'Her hair's not red,' remarked Litvinov; 'she dyes it red—that's the fashion now.'

Again Kapitolina Markovna could only lift her hands; she was positively dumbfounded.

'Well,' she said at last, 'where we were, in Dresden, things had not got to such a scandalous pitch yet. It's a little further from Paris, anyway, that's why. Don't you think that's it, Grigory Mihalitch, eh?'

'Don't I think so?' answered Litvinov. While he thought to himself, 'What on earth is she talking of?' 'I? Of course ... of course....'

But at this point the sound of slow footsteps was heard, and Potugin approached the seat.

'Good-morning, Grigory Mihalitch,' he began, smiling and nodding.

Litvinov grasped him by the hand at once.

'Good-morning, good-morning, Sozont Ivanitch. I fancy I passed you just now with ... just now in the avenue?'

'Yes, it was me.'

Potugin bowed respectfully to the ladies sitting on the seat.

'Let me introduce you, Sozont Ivanitch. Old friends and relatives of mine, who have only just arrived in Baden. Potugin, Sozont Ivanitch, a countryman of ours, also staying in Baden.'

Both ladies rose a little. Potugin renewed his bows.

'It's quite a levée here,' Kapitolina Markovna began in a delicate voice; the kind-hearted old lady was easily intimidated, but she tried before all to keep up her dignity. 'Every one regards it as an agreeable duty to stay here.'

'Baden is an agreeable place, certainly,' answered Potugin, with a sidelong look at Tatyana; 'a very agreeable place, Baden.'

'Yes; but it's really too aristocratic, so far as I can form an opinion. You see we have been staying all this time in Dresden ... a very interesting town; but here there's positively a levée.'

'She's pleased with the word,' thought Potugin. 'You are perfectly right in that observation,' he said aloud; 'but then the scenery here is exquisite, and the site of the place is something one cannot often find. Your fellow-traveller especially is sure to appreciate that. Are you not, madam?' he added, addressing himself this time directly to Tatyana.

Tatyana raised her large, clear eyes to Potugin. It seemed as though she were perplexed. What was wanted of her, and why had Litvinov introduced her, on the first day of her arrival, to this unknown man, who had, though, a kind and clever face, and was looking at her with cordial and friendly eyes.

'Yes,' she said at last, 'it's very nice here.'

'You ought to visit the old castle,' Potugin went on; 'I especially advise a drive to——'

'The Saxon Switzerland——' Kapitolina Markovna was beginning.

The blare of wind instruments floated up the avenue; it was the Prussian military band from Rastadt (in 1862 Rastadt was still an allied fortress), beginning its weekly concert in the pavilion. Kapitolina Markovna got up.

'The music!' she said; 'the music *à la Conversation!...* We must go there. It's four o'clock now ... isn't it? Will the fashionable world be there now?'

'Yes,' answered Potugin: 'this is the most fashionable time, and the music is excellent.'

'Well, then, don't let us linger. Tanya, come along.'

'You allow me to accompany you?' asked Potugin, to Litvinov's considerable astonishment; it was not possible for it even to enter his head that Irina had sent Potugin.

Kapitolina Markovna simpered.

'With the greatest pleasure—M'sieu ... M'sieu——'

'Potugin,' he murmured, and he offered her his arm.

Litvinov gave his to Tatyana, and both couples walked towards the Konversation Hall.

Potugin went on talking with Kapitolina Markovna. But Litvinov walked without uttering a word; yet twice, without any cause, he smiled, and faintly pressed Tatyana's arm against his. There was a falsehood in those demonstrations, to which she made no response, and Litvinov was conscious of the lie. They did not express a mutual confidence in the close union of two souls given up to one another; they were a temporary substitute—for words which he could not find. That unspoken something which was beginning between them grew and gained strength. Once more Tatyana looked attentively, almost intently, at him.

It was the same before the Konversation Hall at the little table round which they all four seated themselves, with this sole difference, that, in the noisy bustle of the crowd, the clash and roar of the music, Litvinov's silence seemed more comprehensible. Kapitolina Markovna became quite excited; Potugin hardly had time to answer her questions, to satisfy her curiosity. Luckily for him, there suddenly appeared in the mass of moving figures the lank person and everlastingly leaping eyes of Madame Suhantchikov. Kapitolina Markovna at once recognised her, invited her to their table, made her sit down, and a hurricane of words arose.

Potugin turned to Tatyana, and began a conversation with her in a soft, subdued voice, his face bent slightly down towards her with a very friendly expression; and she, to her own surprise, answered him easily and freely; she was glad to talk with this stranger, this outsider, while Litvinov sat immovable as before, with the same fixed and unpleasant smile on his lips.

Dinner-time came at last. The music ceased, the crowd thinned. Kapitolina Markovna parted from Madame Suhantchikov on the warmest terms. She had conceived an immense respect for her, though she did say afterwards to her niece, that 'this person is really too severe; but then she does know everything and everybody; and we must really get sewing-machines directly the wedding festivities are over.' Potugin took leave of them; Litvinov conducted his ladies home. As they were going into the hotel, he was handed a note; he moved aside and hurriedly tore open the envelope. On a tiny scrap of vellum paper were the following words, scribbled in pencil: 'Come to me this evening at seven, for one minute, I entreat you.—Irina.' Litvinov thrust the note into his pocket, and, turning round, put on his smile again ... to whom? why? Tatyana was standing with her back to him. They dined at the common table of the hotel. Litvinov was sitting between Kapitolina Markovna and Tatyana, and he began talking, telling anecdotes and pouring out wine for himself and the ladies, with a strange, sudden joviality. He conducted himself in such a free and easy manner, that a French infantry officer from Strasbourg, sitting opposite, with a beard and moustaches *à la* Napoleon III., thought it admissible to join in the conversation, and even wound up by a toast *à la santé des belles Moscovites!* After dinner, Litvinov escorted the two ladies to their room, and after standing a little while at the window with a scowl on his face, he suddenly announced that he had to go out for a short time on business, but would be back without fail by the evening. Tatyana said nothing; she turned pale and dropped her eyes. Kapitolina Markovna was in the habit of taking a nap after dinner; Tatyana was well aware that Litvinov knew of this habit of her aunt's; she had expected him to take advantage of it, to remain with her, for he had not been alone with her, nor spoken frankly to her, since her arrival. And now he was going out! What was she to make of it? And, indeed, his whole behaviour all along....

Litvinov withdrew hurriedly, not waiting for remonstrances; Kapitolina Markovna lay down on the sofa, and with one or two sighs and groans, fell into a serene sleep; while Tatyana moved away into a corner, and sat down in a low chair, folding her arms tightly across her bosom.

XIX

Litvinov went quickly up the staircase of the *Hôtel de l'Europe;* a little girl of thirteen, with a sly little face of Kalmuck cast, who had apparently been on the look-out for him, stopped him, saying in Russian: 'Come this way, please; Irina Pavlovna will be here directly.' He looked at her in perplexity. She smiled, repeated: 'Come along, come along,' and led him to a small room, facing Irina's bedroom, and filled with travelling trunks and portmanteaus, then at once disappeared, closing the door very softly. Litvinov had not time to look about him, before the door was quickly opened, and before him in a pink ball-dress, with pearls in her hair and on her neck, stood Irina. She simply rushed at him, clutched him by both hands, and for a few instants was speechless; her eyes were shining, and her bosom heaving as though she had run up to a height.

'I could not receive ... you there,' she began in a hurried whisper: 'we are just going to a dinner party, but I wanted above everything to see you.... That is your betrothed, I suppose, with whom I met you to-day?'

'Yes, that was my betrothed,' said Litvinov, with emphasis on the word 'was.'

'And so I wanted to see you for one minute, to tell you that you must consider yourself absolutely free, that everything that happened yesterday ought not to affect your plans....'

'Irina!' cried Litvinov, 'why are you saying this?' He uttered these words in a loud voice. There was the note in them of unbounded passion. Irina involuntarily closed her eyes for a minute.

'Oh, my sweet one!' she went on in a whisper still more subdued, but with unrestrained emotion, 'you don't know how I love you, but yesterday I only paid my debt, I made up for the past.... Ah! I could not give you back my youth, as I would, but I have laid no obligations on you, I have exacted no promise of any sort of you, my sweet! Do what you will, you are free as air, you are bound in no way, understand that, understand that!'

'But I can't live without you, Irina,' Litvinov interrupted, in a whisper now; 'I am yours for ever and always, since yesterday.... I can only breathe at your feet....'

He stooped down all in a tremble to kiss her hands. Irina gazed at his bent head.

'Then let me say,' she said, 'that I too am ready for anything, that I too will consider no one, and nothing. As you decide, so it shall be. I, too, am for ever yours ... yours.'

Some one tapped warily at the door. Irina stooped, whispered once more, 'Yours ... good-bye!' Litvinov felt her breath on his hair, the touch of her lips. When he stood up, she was no longer in the room, but her dress was rustling in the corridor, and from the distance came the voice of Ratmirov: '*Eh bien? Vous ne venez pas?*'

Litvinov sat down on a high chest, and hid his face. A feminine fragrance, fresh and delicate, clung about him.... Irina had held his hand in her hands. 'It's too much, too much,' was his thought. The little girl came into the room, and smiling again in response to his agitated glance, said:

'Kindly come, now——'

He got up, and went out of the hotel. It was no good even to think of returning home: he had to regain his balance first. His heart was beating heavily and unevenly; the earth seemed faintly reeling under his feet. Litvinov turned again along the Lichtenthaler Allee. He realised that the decisive moment had come, that to put it off longer, to dissemble, to turn away, had become impossible, that an explanation with Tatyana had become inevitable; he could imagine how she was sitting there, never stirring, waiting for him ... he could foresee what he would say to her; but how was he to act, how was he to begin? He had turned his back on his upright, well-organised, orderly future; he knew that he was flinging himself headlong into a gulf ... but that did not confound him. The thing was done, but how was he to face his judge? And if only his judge would come to meet him—an angel with a flaming sword; that would be easier for a sinning heart ... instead of which he had himself to plunge the knife in.... Infamous! But to turn back, to abandon that other, to take advantage of the freedom offered him, recognised as his.... No! better to die! No, he would have none of such loathsome freedom ... but would humble himself in the dust, and might those eyes look down on him with love....

'Grigory Mihalitch,' said a melancholy voice, and some one's hand was laid heavily upon Litvinov.

He looked round in some alarm and recognised Potugin.

'I beg your pardon, Grigory Mihalitch,' began the latter with his customary humility, 'I am disturbing you perhaps, but, seeing you in the distance, I thought.... However if you're not in the humour....'

'On the contrary I'm delighted,' Litvinov muttered between his teeth.

Potugin walked beside him.

'What a lovely evening!' he began, 'so warm! Have you been walking long?'

'No, not long.'

'Why do I ask though; I've just seen you come out of the *Hôtel de l'Europe*.'

'Then you've been following me?'

'Yes.'

'You have something to say to me?'

'Yes,' Potugin repeated, hardly audibly.

Litvinov stopped and looked at his uninvited companion. His face was pale, his eyes moved restlessly; his contorted features seemed overshadowed by old, long-standing grief.

'What do you specially want to say to me?' Litvinov said slowly, and he moved forward.

'Ah, with your permission ... directly. If it's all the same to you, let us sit down here on this seat. It will be most convenient.'

'Why, this is something mysterious,' Litvinov declared, seating himself near him. 'You don't seem quite yourself, Sozont Ivanitch.'

'No; I'm all right; and it's nothing mysterious either. I specially wanted to tell you ... the impression made on me by your betrothed ... she is betrothed to you, I think?... well, anyway, by the girl to whom you introduced me to-day. I must say that in the course of my whole existence I have never met a more attractive creature. A heart of gold, a really angelic nature.'

Potugin uttered all these words with the same bitter and mournful air, so that even Litvinov could not help noticing the incongruity between his expression of face and his speech.

'You have formed a perfectly correct estimate of Tatyana Petrovna,' Litvinov began, 'though I can't help being surprised, first that you should be aware of the relation in which I stand to her; and secondly, that you should have understood her so quickly. She really has an angelic nature; but allow me to ask, did you want to talk to me about this?'

'It's impossible not to understand her at once,' Potugin replied quickly, as though evading the last question. 'One need only take one look into her eyes. She deserves every possible happiness on earth, and enviable is the fate of the man whose lot it is to give her that happiness! One must hope he may prove worthy of such a fate.'

Litvinov frowned slightly.

'Excuse me, Sozont Ivanitch,' he said, 'I must confess our conversation strikes me as altogether rather original.... I should like to know, does the hint contained in your words refer to me?'

Potugin did not at once answer Litvinov; he was visibly struggling with himself.

'Grigory Mihalitch,' he began at last, 'either I am completely mistaken in you, or you are capable of hearing the truth, from whomsoever it may come, and in however unattractive a form it may present itself. I told you just now, that I saw where you came from.'

'Why, from the *Hôtel de l'Europe*. What of that?'

'I know, of course, whom you have been to see there.'

'What?'

'You have been to see Madame Ratmirov.'

'Well, I have been to see her. What next?'

'What next?... You, betrothed to Tatyana Petrovna, have been to see Madame Ratmirov, whom you love ... and who loves you.'

Litvinov instantly got up from the seat; the blood rushed to his head.

'What's this?' he cried at last, in a voice of concentrated exasperation: 'stupid jesting, spying? Kindly explain yourself.'

Potugin turned a weary look upon him.

'Ah! don't be offended at my words. Grigory Mihalitch, me you cannot offend. I did not begin to talk to you for that, and I'm in no joking humour now.'

'Perhaps, perhaps. I'm ready to believe in the excellence of your intentions; but still I may be allowed to ask you by what right you meddle in the private affairs, in the inner life, of another man, a man who is nothing to you; and what grounds you have for so confidently giving out your own ... invention for the truth?'

'My invention! If I had imagined it, it should not have made you angry; and as for my right, well I never heard before that a man ought to ask himself whether he had the right to hold out a hand to a drowning man.'

'I am humbly grateful for your tender solicitude,' cried Litvinov passionately, 'but I am not in the least in need of it, and all the phrases about the ruin of inexperienced young men wrought by society women, about the immorality of fashionable society, and so on, I look upon merely as stock phrases, and indeed in a sense I positively despise them; and so I beg you to spare your rescuing arm, and to let me drown in peace.'

Potugin again raised his eyes to Litvinov. He was breathing hard, his lips were twitching.

'But look at me, young man,' broke from him at last, and he clapped himself on the breast: 'can you suppose I have anything in common with the ordinary, self-satisfied moralist, a preacher? Don't you understand that simply from interest in you, however strong it might be, I would never have let fall a word, I would never have given you grounds for reproaching me with what I hate above all things—indiscretion, intrusiveness? Don't you see that this is something of a different kind altogether, that before you is a man crushed, utterly obliterated by the very passion, from the results of which he would save you, and ... and for the same woman!'

Litvinov stepped back a pace.

'Is it possible? What did you say?... You ... you ... Sozont Ivanitch? But Madame Byelsky ... that child?'

'Ah, don't cross-examine me.... Believe me! That is a dark terrible story, and I'm not going to tell you it. Madame Byelsky I hardly knew, that child is not mine, but I took it all upon myself ... because ... *she* wished it, because it was necessary for *her*. Why am I here in your hateful Baden? And, in fact, could you suppose, could you for one instant imagine, that I'd have brought myself to caution you out of sympathy for you? I'm sorry for that sweet, good girl, your*fiancée*, but what have I to do with your future, with you both?... But I am afraid for her ... for her.'

'You do me great honour, Mr. Potugin,' began Litvinov, 'but since, according to you, we are both in the same position, why is it you don't apply such exhortations to yourself, and ought I not to ascribe your apprehensions to another feeling?'

'That is to jealousy, you mean? Ah, young man, young man, it's shameful of you to shuffle and make pretences, it's shameful of you not to realise what a bitter sorrow is speaking to you now by my lips! No, I am not in the same position as you! I, I am old, ridiculous, an utterly harmless old fool—but you! But there's no need to talk about it! You would not for one second agree to accept the position I fill, and fill with gratitude! Jealousy? A man is not jealous who has never had even a drop of hope, and this is not the first time it has been my lot to endure this feeling. I am only afraid ... afraid for her, understand that. And could I have guessed when she sent me to you that the feeling of having wronged you—she owned to feeling that—would carry her so far?'

'But excuse me, Sozont Ivanitch, you seem to know....'

'I know nothing, and I know everything! I know,' he added, turning away, 'I know where she was yesterday. But there's no holding her back now; like a stone set rolling, she must roll on to the bottom. I should be a great idiot indeed, if I imagined my words could hold you back at once ... you, when a woman like that.... But that's enough of this. I couldn't restrain myself, that's my whole excuse. And after all how can one know, and why not try? Perhaps, you will think again; perhaps, some word of mine will go to your heart, you will not care to ruin her and yourself, and that innocent sweet creature.... Ah! don't be angry, don't stamp about! What have I to fear? Why should I mince matters? It's not jealousy speaking in me, not anger.... I'm ready to fall at your feet, to beseech you.... Good-bye, though. You needn't be afraid, all this will be kept secret. I wished for your good.'

Potugin strode off along the avenue and quickly vanished in the now falling darkness. Litvinov did not detain him.

'A terrible dark story....' Potugin had said to Litvinov, and would not tell it.... Let us pass it over with a few words only.

Eight years before, it had happened to him to be sent by his department to Count Reisenbach as a temporary clerk. It was in the summer. Potugin used to drive to his country villa with papers, and be whole days there at a time. Irina was then living at the count's. She was never haughty with people in a humbler station, at least she never treated them superciliously, and the countess more than once reproved her for her excessive Moscow familiarity. Irina soon detected a man of intelligence in the humble clerk, attired in the stiffly buttoned frockcoat that was his uniform. She used often and eagerly to talk to him ... while he ... he fell in love with her passionately, profoundly, secretly.... Secretly! So *he* thought. The summer passed; the count no longer needed any outside assistance. Potugin lost sight of Irina but could not forget her. Three years after, he utterly unexpectedly received an invitation, through a third person, to go to see a lady slightly known to him. This lady at first was reluctant to speak out, but after exacting an oath from him to keep everything he was going to hear absolutely secret, she proposed to him ... to marry a girl, who occupied a conspicuous position in society, and for whom marriage had become a necessity. The lady scarcely ventured to hint at the principal personage, and then promised Potugin money ... a large sum of money. Potugin was not offended, astonishment stifled all feeling of anger in him; but, of course, he point-blank declined. Then the lady handed him a note—from Irina. 'You are a generous, noble man,' she wrote, 'and I know you would do anything for me; I beg of you this sacrifice. You will save one who is very dear to me. In saving her, you will save me too.... Do not ask me how. I could never have brought myself to any one with such an entreaty, but to you I hold out my hands and say to you, do it for my sake.' Potugin pondered, and said that for Irina Pavlovna, certainly he was ready to do a great deal; but he should like to hear her wishes from her own lips. The interview took place the same evening; it did not last long, and no one knew of it, except the same lady. Irina was no longer living at Count Reisenbach's.

'What made you think of me, of all people?' Potugin asked her.

She was beginning to expatiate on his noble qualities, but suddenly she stopped....

'No,' she said, 'you must be told the truth. I know, I know that you love me; so that was why I made up my mind ...' and then she told him everything.

Eliza Byelsky was an orphan; her relations did not like her, and reckoned on her inheritance ... ruin was facing her. In saving her, Irina was really doing a service to him who was responsible for it all, and who was himself nowstanding in a very close relation to Irina.... Potugin, without speaking, looked long at Irina, and consented. She wept, and flung herself all in tears on his neck. And he too wept ... but very different were their tears. Everything had already been made ready for the secret marriage, a powerful hand removed all obstacles.... But illness came ... and then a daughter was born, and then the mother ... poisoned herself. What was to be done with the child? Potugin received it into his charge, received it from the same hands, from the hands of Irina.

A terrible dark story.... Let us pass on, readers, pass on!

Over an hour more passed before Litvinov could bring himself to go back to his hotel. He had almost reached it when he suddenly heard steps behind him. It seemed as though they were following him persistently, and walking faster when he quickened his pace. When he moved under a lamp-post Litvinov turned round and recognised General Ratmirov. In a white tie, in a fashionable overcoat, flung open, with a row of stars and crosses on a golden chain in the buttonhole of his dresscoat, the general was returning from dinner, alone. His eyes, fastened with insolent persistence on Litvinov, expressed such contempt and such hatred, his whole deportment was suggestive of such intense defiance, that Litvinov thought it his duty, stifling his wrath, to go to meet him, to face a 'scandal.' But when he was on a level with Litvinov, the general's face suddenly changed, his habitual playful refinement reappeared upon it, and his hand in its pale lavender glove flourished his glossy hat high in the air. Litvinov took off his in silence, and each went on his way.

'He has noticed something, for certain!' thought Litvinov.

'If only it were ... any one else!' thought the general.

Tatyana was playing picquet with her aunt when Litvinov entered their room.

'Well, I must say, you're a pretty fellow!' cried Kapitolina Markovna, and she threw down her cards. 'Our first day, and he's lost for the whole evening! Here we've been waiting and waiting, and scolding and scolding....'

'I said nothing, aunt,' observed Tatyana.

'Well, you're meekness itself, we all know! You ought to be ashamed, sir! and you betrothed too!'

Litvinov made some sort of excuse and sat down to the table.

'Why have you left off your game?' he asked after a brief silence.

'Well, that's a nice question! We've been playing cards from sheer dulness, not knowing what to do with ourselves ... but now you've come.'

'If you would care to hear the evening music,' observed Litvinov, 'I should be delighted to take you.'

Kapitolina Markovna looked at her niece.

'Let us go, aunt, I am ready,' she said, 'but wouldn't it be better to stay at home?'

'To be sure! Let us have tea in our own old Moscow way, with the samovar, and have a good chat. We've not had a proper gossip yet.'

Litvinov ordered tea to be sent up, but the good chat did not come off. He felt a continual gnawing of conscience; whatever he said, it always seemed to him that he was telling lies and Tatyana was seeing through it. Meanwhile there was no change to be observed in her; she behaved just as unconstrainedly ... only her look never once rested upon Litvinov, but with a kind of indulgent timorousness glided over him, and she was paler than usual.

Kapitolina Markovna asked her whether she had not a headache.

Tatyana was at first about to say no, but after a moment's thought, she said, 'Yes, a little.'

'It's the journey,' suggested Litvinov, and he positively blushed with shame.

'Yes, the journey,' repeated Tatyana, and her eyes again glided over him.

'You ought to rest, Tanya darling.'

'Yes, I will go to bed soon, aunt.'

On the table lay a *Guide des Voyageurs;* Litvinov fell to reading aloud the description of the environs of Baden.

'Quite so,' Kapitolina Markovna interrupted, 'but there's something we mustn't forget. I'm told linen is very cheap here, so we must be sure to buy some for the trousseau.'

Tatyana dropped her eyes.

'We have plenty of time, aunt. You never think of yourself, but you really ought to get yourself some clothes. You see how smart every one is here.'

'Eh, my love! what would be the good of that? I'm not a fine lady! It would be another thing if I were such a beauty as your friend, Grigory Mihalitch, what was her name?'

'What friend?'

'Why, that we met to-day.'

'Oh, she!' said Litvinov, with feigned indifference, and again he felt disgust and shame. 'No!' he thought, 'to go on like this is impossible.'

He was sitting by his betrothed, while a few inches from her in his side pocket, was Irina's handkerchief.

Kapitolina Markovna went for a minute into the other room.

'Tanya ...' said Litvinov, with an effort. It was the first time that day he had called her by that name.

She turned towards him.

'I ... I have something very important to say to you.'

'Oh! really? when? directly?'

'No, to-morrow.'

'Oh! to-morrow. Very well.'

Litvinov's soul was suddenly filled with boundless pity. He took Tatyana's hand and kissed it humbly, like a sinner; her heart throbbed faintly and she felt no happiness.

In the night, at two o'clock, Kapitolina Markovna, who was sleeping in the same room with her niece, suddenly lifted up her head and listened.

'Tanya,' she said, 'you are crying?'

Tatyana did not at once answer.

'No, aunt,' sounded her gentle voice, 'I've caught a cold.'

XX

'Why did I say that to her?' Litvinov thought the next morning as he sat in his room at the window. He shrugged his shoulders in vexation: he had said that to Tatyana simply to cut himself off all way of retreat. In the window lay a note from Irina: she asked him to see her at twelve. Potugin's words incessantly recurred to his mind, they seemed to reach him with a faint ill-omened sound as of a rumbling underground. He was angry with himself, but could not get rid of them anyhow. Some one knocked at the door.

'*Wer da?*' asked Litvinov.

'Ah! you're at home! open!' he heard Bindasov's hoarse bass.
The door handle creaked.
Litvinov turned white with exasperation.
'I'm not at home,' he declared sharply.
'Not at home? That's a good joke!'
'I tell you—not at home, get along.'

'That's civil! And I came to ask you for a little loan,' grumbled Bindasov.
He walked off, however, tramping on his heels as usual.
Litvinov was all but dashing out after him, he felt such a longing to throttle the hateful ruffian. The events of the last few days had unstrung his nerves; a little more, and he would have burst into tears. He drank off a glass of cold water, locked up all the drawers in the furniture, he could not have said why, and went to Tatyana's.
He found her alone. Kapitolina Markovna had gone out shopping. Tatyana was sitting on the sofa, holding a book in both hands. She was not reading it, and scarcely knew what book it was. She did not stir, but her heart was beating quickly in her bosom, and the little white collar round her neck quivered visibly and evenly.
Litvinov was confused.... However, he sat down by her, said good-morning, smiled at her; she too smiled at him without speaking. She had bowed to him when he came in, bowed courteously, not affectionately, and she did not glance at him. He held out his hand to her; she gave him her chill fingers, but at once freed them again, and took up the book. Litvinov felt that to begin the conversation with unimportant subjects would be insulting Tatyana; she after her custom made no demands, but everything in her said plainly, 'I am waiting, I am waiting.'... He must fulfil his promise. But though almost the whole night he had thought of nothing else, he had not prepared even the first introductory words, and absolutely did not know in what way to break this cruel silence.
'Tanya,' he began at last, 'I told you yesterday that I have something important to say to you. I am ready, only I beg you beforehand not to be angry against me, and to rest assured that my feelings for you....'
He stopped. He caught his breath. Tatyana still did not stir, and did not look at him; she only clutched the book tighter than ever.
'There has always been,' Litvinov went on, without finishing the sentence he had begun, 'there has always been perfect openness between us; I respect you too much to be a hypocrite with you; I want to prove to you that I know how to value the nobleness and independence of your nature, even though ... though of course....'
'Grigory Mihalitch,' began Tatyana in a measured voice while a deathly pallor overspread her whole face, 'I will come to your assistance, you no longer love me, and you don't know how to tell me so.'
Litvinov involuntarily shuddered.
'Why?' ... he said, hardly intelligibly, 'why could you suppose?... I really don't understand....'
'What! isn't it the truth? Isn't it the truth?—tell me, tell me.'
Tatyana turned quite round to Litvinov; her face, with her hair brushed back from it, approached his face, and her eyes, which for so long had not looked at him, seemed to penetrate into his eyes.
'Isn't it the truth?' she repeated.
He said nothing, did not utter a single sound. He could not have lied at that instant, even if he had known she would believe him, and that his lie would save her; he was not even able to bear her eyes upon him. Litvinov said nothing, but she needed no answer, she read the answer in his very silence, in those guilty downcast eyes—and she turned away again and dropped the book.... She had been still uncertain till that instant, and Litvinov understood that; he understood that she had been still uncertain—and how hideous, actually hideous was all that he was doing.
He flung himself on his knees before her.
'Tanya,' he cried, 'if only you knew how hard it is for me to see you in this position, how awful to me to think that it's I ... I! My heart is torn to pieces, I don't know myself, I have lost myself, and you, and everything.... Everything is shattered, Tanya, everything! Could I dream that I ... I should bring such a blow upon you, my best friend, my guardian angel?... Could I dream that we should meet like this, should spend such a day as yesterday!...'
Tatyana was trying to get up and go away. He held her back by the border of her dress.
'No, listen to me a minute longer. You see I am on my knees before you, but I have not come to beg your forgiveness; you cannot, you ought not to forgive me. I have come to tell you that your friend is ruined, that

he is falling into the pit, and would not drag you down with him.... But save me ... no! even you cannot save me. I should push you away, I am ruined, Tanya, I am ruined past all help.'

Tatyana looked at Litvinov.

'You are ruined?' she said, as though not fully understanding him. 'You are ruined?'

'Yes, Tanya, I am ruined. All the past, all that was precious, everything I have lived for up till now, is ruined for me; everything is wretched, everything is shattered, and I don't know what awaits me in the future. You said just now that I no longer loved you.... No, Tanya, I have not ceased to love you, but a different, terrible, irresistible passion has come upon me, has overborne me. I fought against it while I could....'

Tatyana got up, her brows twitched, her pale face darkened. Litvinov too rose to his feet.

'You love another woman,' she began, 'and I guess who she is.... We met her yesterday, didn't we?... Well, I see what is left for me to do now. Since you say yourself this passion is unalterable' ... (Tatyana paused an instant, possibly she had still hoped Litvinov would not let this last word pass unchallenged, but he said nothing), 'it only remains for me to give you back ... your word.'

Litvinov bent his head, as though submissively receiving a well-deserved blow.

'You have every right to be angry with me,' he said. 'You have every right to reproach me for feebleness ... for deceit.'

Tatyana looked at him again.

'I have not reproached you, Litvinov, I don't blame you. I agree with you: the bitterest truth is better than what went on yesterday. What sort of a life could ours have been now!'

'What sort of a life will mine be now!' echoed mournfully in Litvinov's soul.

Tatyana went towards the door of the bedroom.

'I will ask you to leave me alone for a little time, Grigory Mihalitch—we will see each other again, we will talk again. All this has been so unexpected I want to collect myself a little ... leave me alone ... spare my pride. We shall see each other again.'

And uttering these words, Tatyana hurriedly withdrew and locked the door after her.

Litvinov went out into the street like a man dazed and stunned; in the very depths of his heart something dark and bitter lay hid, such a sensation must a man feel who has murdered another; and at the same time he felt easier as though he had at last flung off a hated load. Tatyana's magnanimity had crushed him, he felt vividly all that he had lost ... and yet? with his regret was mingled irritation; he yearned towards Irina as to the sole refuge left him, and felt bitter against her. For some time Litvinov's feelings had been every day growing more violent and more complex; this complexity tortured him, exasperated him, he was lost in this chaos. He thirsted for one thing; to get out at last on to the path, whatever it might be, if only not to wander longer in this incomprehensible half-darkness. Practical people of Litvinov's sort ought never to be carried away by passion, it destroys the very meaning of their lives.... But nature cares nothing for logic, our human logic; she has her own, which we do not recognise and do not acknowledge till we are crushed under its wheel.

On parting from Tatyana, Litvinov held one thought in his mind, to see Irina; he set off indeed to see her. But the general was at home, so at least the porter told him, and he did not care to go in, he did not feel himself capable of hypocrisy, and he moved slowly off towards the Konversation Hall. Litvinov's incapacity for hypocrisy was evident that day to both Voroshilov and Pishtchalkin, who happened to meet him; he simply blurted out to the former that he was empty as a drum; to the latter that he bored every one to extinction; it was lucky indeed that Bindasov did come across him; there would certainly have been a '*grosser Scandal*.' Both the young men were stupefied; Voroshilov went so far as to ask himself whether his honour as an officer did not demand satisfaction? But like Gogol's lieutenant, Pirogov, he calmed himself with bread and butter in a café. Litvinov caught sight in the distance of Kapitolina Markovna running busily from shop to shop in her striped mantle.... He felt ashamed to face the good, absurd, generous old lady. Then he recalled Potugin, their conversation yesterday.... Then something was wafted to him, something intangible and unmistakable: if a falling shadow shed a fragrance, it could not be more elusive, but he felt at once that it was Irina near him, and in fact she appeared a few paces from him, arm-in-arm with another lady; their eyes met at once. Irina probably noticed something peculiar in the expression of Litvinov's face; she stopped before a shop, in which a number of tiny wooden clocks of Black Forest make were exhibited, and summoning him by a motion of her head, she pointed to one of these clocks, and calling upon him to admire a charming clock-face with a painted cuckoo above it, she said, not in a whisper, but as though finishing a phrase begun, in her ordinary tone of voice, much less likely to attract the attention of outsiders, 'Come in an hour's time, I shall be alone.'

But at this moment the renowned lady-killer Monsieur Verdier swooped down upon her, and began to fall into ecstasies over the colour, *feuille morte*, of her gown and the low-crowned Spanish hat she wore tilted almost down to her eyebrows.... Litvinov vanished in the crowd.

XXI

'Grigory,' Irina was saying to him two hours later, as she sat beside him on the sofa, and laid both hands on his shoulder, 'what is the matter with you? Tell me now quickly, while we're alone.'

'The matter with me?' said Litvinov. 'I am happy, happy, that's what's the matter with me.'

Irina looked down, smiled, sighed.

'That's not an answer to my question, my dear one.'

Litvinov grew thoughtful.

'Well, let me tell you then ... since you insist positively on it' (Irina opened her eyes wide and trembled slightly), 'I have told everything to-day to my betrothed.'

'What, everything? You mentioned me?'

Litvinov fairly threw up his arms.

'Irina, for God's sake, how could such an idea enter your head! that I——'

'There, forgive me ... forgive me. What did you say?'

'I told her that I no longer loved her.'

'She asked why?'

'I did not disguise the fact that I loved another woman, and that we must part.'

'Ah ... and what did she do? Agreed?'

'O Irina! what a girl she is! She was all self-sacrifice, all generosity!'

'I've no doubt, I've no doubt ... there was nothing else for her to do, though.'

'And not one reproach, not one hard word to me, who have spoiled her whole life, deceived her, pitilessly flung her over....'

Irina scrutinised her finger nails.

'Tell me, Grigory ... did she love you?'

'Yes, Irina, she loved me.'

Irina was silent a minute, she straightened her dress.

'I must confess,' she began, 'I don't quite understand what induced you to explain matters to her.'

'What induced me, Irina! Would you have liked me to lie, to be a hypocrite to her, that pure soul? or did you suppose——'

'I supposed nothing,' Irina interrupted. 'I must admit I have thought very little about her. I don't know how to think of two people at once.'

'That is, you mean——'

'Well, and so what then? Is she going away, that pure soul?' Irina interrupted a second time.

'I know nothing,' answered Litvinov. 'I am to see her again. But she will not stay.'

'Ah! *bon voyage!*'

'No, she will not stay. But I'm not thinking of her either now, I am thinking of what you said to me, what you have promised me.'

Irina looked up at him from under her eyelids.

'Ungrateful one! aren't you content yet?'

'No, Irina, I'm not content. You have made me happy, but I'm not content, and you understand me.'

'That is, I——'

'Yes, you understand me. Remember your words, remember what you wrote to me. I can't share you with others; no, no, I can't consent to the pitiful rôle of secret lover; not my life alone, this other life too I have flung at your feet, I have renounced everything, I have crushed it all to dust, without compunction and beyond recall; but in return I trust, I firmly believe, that you too will keep your promise, and unite your lot with mine for ever.'

'You want me to run away with you? I am ready....' (Litvinov bent down to her hands in ecstasy.) 'I am ready. I will not go back from my word. But have you yourself thought over all the difficulties—have you made preparations?'

'I? I have not had time yet to think over or prepare anything, but only say yes, let me act, and before a month is over....'

'A month! we start for Italy in a fortnight.'

'A fortnight, then, is enough for me. O Irina, you seem to take my proposition coldly; perhaps it seems unpractical to you, but I am not a boy, I am not used to comforting myself with dreams, I know what a tremendous step this is, I know what a responsibility I am taking on myself; but I can see no other course. Think of it, I must break every tie with the past, if only not to be a contemptible liar in the eyes of the girl I have sacrificed for you!'

Irina drew herself up suddenly and her eyes flashed.

'Oh, I beg your pardon, Grigory Mihalitch! If I decide, if I run away, then it will at least be with a man who does it for my sake, for my sake simply, and not in order that he may not degrade himself in the good opinion of a phlegmatic young person, with milk and water, *du lait coupé* instead of blood, in her veins! And I must tell you too, it's the first time, I confess, that it's been my lot to hear that the man I honour with my regard is deserving of commiseration,playing a pitiful part! I know a far more pitiful part, the part of a man who doesn't know what is going on in his own heart!'

Litvinov drew himself up in his turn.

'Irina,' he was beginning——

But all at once she clapped both hands to her forehead, and with a convulsive motion, flinging herself on his breast, she embraced him with force beyond a woman's.

'Forgive me, forgive me,' she began, with a shaking voice, 'forgive me, Grigory! You see how corrupted I am, how horrid I am, how jealous and wicked! You see how I need your aid, your indulgence! Yes, save me, drag me out of this mire, before I am quite ruined! Yes, let us run away, let us run away from these people, from this society to some far off, fair, free country! Perhaps your Irina will at last be worthier of the sacrifices you are making for her! Don't be angry with me, forgive me, my sweet, and know that I will do everything you command, I will go anywhere you will take me!'

Litvinov's heart was in a turmoil. Irina clung closer than before to him with all her youthful supple body. He bent over her fragrant, disordered tresses, and in an intoxication of gratitude and ecstasy, he hardly dared to caress them with his hand, he hardly touched them with his lips.

'Irina, Irina,' he repeated,—'my angel....'

She suddenly raised her head, listened....

'It's my husband's step, ... he has gone into his room,' she whispered, and, moving hurriedly away, she crossed over to another armchair. Litvinov was getting up.... 'What are you doing?' she went on in the same whisper; 'you must stay, he suspects you as it is. Or are you afraid of him?' She did not take her eyes off the door. 'Yes, it's he; he will come in here directly. Tell me something, talk to me.' Litvinov could not at once recover himself and was silent. 'Aren't you going to the theatre to-morrow?' she uttered aloud. 'They're giving *Le Verre d'Eau*, an old-fashioned piece, and Plessy is awfully affected.... We're as though we were in a perfect fever,' she added, dropping her voice. 'We can't do anything like this; we must think things over well. I ought to warn you that all my money is in his hands; *mais j'ai mes bijoux*. We'll go to Spain, would you like that?' She raised her voice again. 'Why is it all actresses get so fat? Madeleine Brohan for instance.... Do talk, don't sit so silent. My head is going round. But you, you must not doubt me.... I will let you know where to come to-morrow. Only it was a mistake to have told that young lady.... *Ah, mais c'est charmant!*' she cried suddenly and with a nervous laugh, she tore the lace edge of her handkerchief.

'May I come in?' asked Ratmirov from the other room.

'Yes ... yes.'

The door opened, and in the doorway appeared the general. He scowled on seeing Litvinov; however, he bowed to them, that is to say, he bent the upper portion of his person.

'I did not know you had a visitor,' he said: '*je vous demande pardon de mon indiscrétion*. So you still find Baden entertaining, M'sieu—Litvinov?'

Ratmirov always uttered Litvinov's surname with hesitation, every time, as though he had forgotten it, and could not at once recall it.... In this way, as well as by the lofty flourish of his hat in saluting him, he meant to insult his pride.

'I am not bored here, *m'sieu le général*.'

'Really? Well, I find Baden fearfully boring. We are soon going away, are we not, Irina Pavlovna? *Assez de Bade comme ça*. By the way, I've won you five hundred francs to-day.'

Irina stretched out her hand coquettishly.

'Where are they? Please let me have them for pin-money.'

'You shall have them, you shall have them.... You are going, M'sieu—Litvinov?'

'Yes, I am going, as you see.'

Ratmirov again bent his body.

'Till we meet again!'

'Good-bye, Grigory Mihalitch,' said Irina. 'I will keep my promise.'

'What is that? May I be inquisitive?' her husband queried.

Irina smiled.

'No, it was only ... something we've been talking of. *C'est à propos du voyage ... où il vous plaira.* You know—Stael's book?'

'Ah! ah! to be sure, I know. Charming illustrations.'

Ratmirov seemed on the best of terms with his wife; he called her by her pet name in addressing her.

XXII

'Better not think now, really,' Litvinov repeated, as he strode along the street, feeling that the inward riot was rising up again in him. 'The thing's decided. She will keep her promise, and it only remains for me to take all necessary steps.... Yet she hesitates, it seems.'... He shook his head. His own designs struck even his own imagination in a strange light; there was a smack of artificiality, of unreality about them. One cannot dwell long upon the same thoughts; they gradually shift like the bits of glass in a kaleidoscope ... one peeps in, and already the shapes before one's eyes are utterly different. A sensation of intense weariness overcame Litvinov.... If he could for one short hour but rest!... But Tanya? He started, and, without reflecting even, turned submissively homewards, merely struck by the idea, that this day was tossing him like a ball from one to the other.... No matter; he must make an end. He went back to his hotel, and with the same submissiveness, insensibility, numbness, without hesitation or delay, he went to see Tatyana.

He was met by Kapitolina Markovna. From the first glance at her, he knew that she knew about it all; the poor maiden lady's eyes were swollen with weeping, and her flushed face, fringed with her dishevelled white locks, expressed dismay and an agony of indignation, sorrow, and boundless amazement. She was on the point of rushing up to Litvinov, but she stopped short, and, biting her quivering lip, she looked at him as though she would supplicate him, and kill him, and assure herself that it was a dream, a senseless, impossible thing, wasn't it?

'Here you ... you are come,' she began.... The door from the next room opened instantaneously, and with a light tread Tatyana came in; she was of a transparent pallor, but she was quite calm.

She gently put one arm round her aunt and made her sit down beside her.

'You sit down too, Grigory Mihalitch,' she said to Litvinov, who was standing like one distraught at the door. 'I am very glad to see you once more. I have informed auntie of your decision, our common decision; she fully shares it and approves of it.... Without mutual love there can be no happiness, mutual esteem alone is not enough' (at the word 'esteem' Litvinov involuntarily looked down) 'and better to separate now, than to repent later. Isn't it, aunt?'

'Yes, of course,' began Kapitolina Markovna, 'of course, Tanya darling, the man who does not know how to appreciate you ... who could bring himself——'

'Aunt, aunt,' Tatyana interrupted, 'remember what you promised me. You always told me yourself: truth, Tatyana, truth before everything—and independence. Well, truth's not always sweet, nor independence either; or else where would be the virtue of it?'

She kissed Kapitolina Markovna on her white hair, and turning to Litvinov, she went on:

'We propose, aunt and I, leaving Baden.... I think it will be more comfortable so for all of us.'

'When do you think of going?' Litvinov said thickly. He remembered that Irina had said the very same words to him not long before.

Kapitolina Markovna was darting forward, but Tatyana held her back, with a caressing touch on her shoulder.

'Probably soon, very soon.'

'And will you allow me to ask where you intend going?' Litvinov said in the same voice.

'First to Dresden, then probably to Russia.'

'But what can you want to know that for now, Grigory Mihalitch?' ... cried Kapitolina Markovna.

‘Aunt, aunt,’ Tatyana interposed again. A brief silence followed.

‘Tatyana Petrovna,’ began Litvinov, ‘you know how agonisingly painful and bitter my feelings must be at this instant.’

Tatyana got up.

‘Grigory Mihalitch,’ she said, ‘we will not talk about that ... if you please, I beg you for my sake, if not for your own. I have known you long enough, and I can very well imagine what you must be feeling now. But what’s the use of talking, of touching a sore’ (she stopped; it was clear she wanted to stem the emotion rushing upon her, to swallow the rising tears; she succeeded)—‘why fret a sore we cannot heal? Leave that to time. And now I have to ask a service of you, Grigory Mihalitch; if you will be so good, I will give you a letter directly: take it to the post yourself, it is rather important, but aunt and I have no time now.... I shall be much obliged to you. Wait a minute.... I will bring it directly....’

In the doorway Tatyana glanced uneasily at Kapitolina Markovna; but she was sitting with such dignity and decorum, with such a severe expression on her knitted brows and tightly compressed lips, that Tatyana merely gave her a significant nod and went out.

But scarcely had the door closed behind her, when every trace of dignity and severity instantaneously vanished from Kapitolina Markovna’s face; she got up, ran on tiptoe up to Litvinov, and all hunched together and trying to look him in the face, she began in a quaking tearful whisper:

‘Good God,’ she said, ‘Grigory Mihalitch, what does it mean? is it a dream or what? *You* give up Tanya, you tired of her, you breaking your word! You doing this, Grigory Mihalitch, you on whom we all counted as if you were a stone wall! You? you? you, Grisha?’... Kapitolina Markovna stopped. ‘Why, you will kill her, Grigory Mihalitch,’ she went on, without waiting for an answer, while her tears fairly coursed in fine drops over her cheeks. ‘You mustn’t judge by her bearing up now, you know her character! She never complains; she does not think of herself, so others must think of her! She keeps saying to me, “Aunt, we must save our dignity!” but what’s dignity, when I foresee death, death before us?’... Tatyana’s chair creaked in the next room. ‘Yes, I foresee death,’ the old lady went on still more softly. ‘And how can such a thing have come about? Is it witchcraft, or what? It’s not long since you were writing her the tenderest letters. And in fact can an honest man act like this? I’m a woman, free, as you know, from prejudice of any sort, *esprit fort*, and I have given Tanya too the same sort of education, she too has a free mind....’

‘Aunt!’ came Tatyana’s voice from the next room.

‘But one’s word of honour is a duty, Grigory Mihalitch, especially for people of your, of my principles! If we’re not going to recognise duty, what is left us? This cannot be broken off in this way, at your whim, without regard to what may happen to another! It’s unprincipled ... yes, it’s a crime; a strange sort of freedom!’

‘Aunt, come here please,’ was heard again.

‘I’m coming, my love, I’m coming....’ Kapitolina Markovna clutched at Litvinov’s hand.—‘I see you are angry, Grigory Mihalitch.’... (‘Me! me angry?’ he wanted to exclaim, but his tongue was dumb.) ‘I don’t want to make you angry—oh, really, quite the contrary! I’ve come even to entreat you; think again while there is time; don’t destroy her, don’t destroy your own happiness, she will still trust you, Grisha, she will believe in you, nothing is lost yet; why, she loves you as no one will ever love you! Leave this hateful Baden-Baden, let us go away together, only throw off this enchantment, and, above all, have pity, have pity——’

‘Aunt!’ called Tatyana, with a shade of impatience in her voice.

But Kapitolina Markovna did not hear her.

‘Only say “yes,”’ she repeated to Litvinov; ‘and I will still make everything smooth.... You need only nod your head to me, just one little nod like this.’

Litvinov would gladly, he felt, have died at that instant; but the word ‘yes’ he did not utter, and he did not nod his head.

Tatyana reappeared with a letter in her hand. Kapitolina Markovna at once darted away from Litvinov, and, averting her face, bent low over the table, as though she were looking over the bills and papers that lay on it.

Tatyana went up to Litvinov.

‘Here,’ she said, ‘is the letter I spoke of.... You will go to the post at once with it, won’t you?’

Litvinov raised his eyes.... Before him, really, stood his judge. Tatyana struck him as taller, slenderer; her face, shining with unwonted beauty, had the stony grandeur of a statue’s; her bosom did not heave, and her gown, of one colour and straight as a Greek chiton, fell in the long, unbroken folds of marble drapery to her feet, which were hidden by it. Tatyana was looking straight before her, only at Litvinov; her cold, calm gaze, too, was the gaze of a statue. He read his sentence in it; he bowed, took a letter from the hand held out so immovably to him, and silently withdrew.

Kapitolina Markovna ran to Tatyana; but the latter turned off her embraces and dropped her eyes; a flush of colour spread over her face, and with the words, 'and now, the sooner the better,' she went into the bedroom. Kapitolina Markovna followed her with hanging head.

The letter, entrusted to Litvinov by Tatyana, was addressed to one of her Dresden friends—a German lady—who let small furnished apartments. Litvinov dropped the letter into the post-box, and it seemed to him as though with that tiny scrap of paper he was dropping all his past, all his life into the tomb. He went out of the town, and strolled a long time by narrow paths between vineyards; he could not shake off the persistent sensation of contempt for himself, like the importunate buzzing of flies in summer: an unenviable part, indeed, he had played in the last interview.... And when he went back to his hotel, and after a little time inquired about the ladies, he was told that immediately after he had gone out, they had given orders to be driven to the railway station, and had departed by the mail train—to what destination was not known. Their things had been packed and their bills paid ever since the morning. Tatyana had asked Litvinov to take her letter to the post, obviously with the object of getting him out of the way. He ventured to ask the hall-porter whether the ladies had left any letters for him, but the porter replied in the negative, and looked amazed even; it was clear that this sudden exit from rooms taken for a week struck him too as strange and dubious. Litvinov turned his back on him, and locked himself up in his room.

He did not leave it till the following day: the greater part of the night he was sitting at the table, writing, and tearing what he had written.... The dawn was already beginning when he finished his task—it was a letter to Irina.

XXIII

This was what was in this letter to Irina:

'My betrothed went away yesterday; we shall never see each other again.... I do not know even for certain where she is going to live. With her, she takes all that till now seemed precious and desirable to me; all my previous ideas, my plans, my intentions, have gone with her; my labours even are wasted, my work of years ends in nothing, all my pursuits have no meaning, no applicability; all that is dead; myself, my old self, is dead and buried since yesterday. I feel, I see, I know this clearly ... far am I from regretting this. Not to lament of it, have I begun upon this to you.... As though I could complain when you love me, Irina! I wanted only to tell you that, of all this dead past, all those hopes and efforts, turned to smoke and ashes, there is only one thing left living, invincible, my love for you. Except that love, nothing is left for me; to say it is the sole thing precious to me, would be too little; I live wholly in that love; that love is my whole being; in it are my future, my career, my vocation, my country! You know me, Irina; you know that fine talk of any sort is foreign to my nature, hateful to me, and however strong the words in which I try to express my feelings, you will have no doubts of their sincerity, you will not suppose them exaggerated. I'm not a boy, in the impulse of momentary ecstasy, lisping unreflecting vows to you, but a man of matured age—simply and plainly, almost with terror, telling you what he has recognised for unmistakable truth. Yes, your love has replaced everything for me—everything, everything! Judge for yourself: can I leave this my *all* in the hands of another? can I let him dispose of you? You—you will belong to him, my whole being, my heart's blood will belong to him—while I myself ... where am I? what am I? An outsider—an onlooker ... looking on at my own life! No, that's impossible, impossible! To share, to share in secret that without which it's useless, impossible to live ... that's deceit and death. I know how great a sacrifice I am asking of you, without any sort of right to it; indeed, what can give one a right to sacrifice? But I am not acting thus from egoism: an egoist would find it easier and smoother not to raise this question at all. Yes, my demands are difficult, and I am not surprised that they alarm you. The people among whom you have to live are hateful to you, you are sick of society, but are you strong enough to throw up that society? to trample on the success it has crowned you with? to rouse public opinion against you—the opinion of these hateful people? Ask yourself, Irina, don't take a burden upon you greater than you can bear. I don't want to reproach you; but remember: once already you could not hold out against temptation. I can give you so little in return for all you are losing. Hear my last word: if you don't feel capable to-morrow, to-day even, of leaving all and following me—you see how boldly I speak, how little I spare myself,—if you are frightened at the uncertainty of the future, and estrangement and solitude and the censure of men, if you cannot rely on yourself, in fact, tell me so openly and without delay, and I will go away; I shall go with a broken heart, but I shall bless you for your truthfulness. But if you really, my beautiful, radiant queen, love a man so petty, so obscure as I, and are really ready to share his fate,—well, then, give me your hand, and let us set off together on our difficult way! Only understand, my decision is unchanging; either all or nothing. It's unreasonable ... but I could not do otherwise—I cannot, Irina! I love you too much.—Yours, G. L.'

Litvinov did not much like this letter himself; it did not quite truly and exactly express what he wanted to say; it was full of awkward expressions, high flown or bookish, and doubtless it was not better than many of the other letters he had torn up; but it was the last, the chief point was thoroughly stated anyway, and harassed, and worn out, Litvinov did not feel capable of dragging anything else out of his head. Besides he did not possess the faculty of putting his thought into literary form, and like all people with whom it is not habitual, he took great trouble over the style. His first letter was probably the best; it came warmer from the heart. However that might be, Litvinov despatched his missive to Irina.

She replied in a brief note:

'Come to me to-day,' she wrote to him: '*he* has gone away for the whole day. Your letter has greatly disturbed me. I keep thinking, thinking ... and my head is in a whirl. I am very wretched, but you love me, and I am happy. Come. Yours, I.'

She was sitting in her boudoir when Litvinov went in. He was conducted there by the same little girl of thirteen who on the previous day had watched for him on the stairs. On the table before Irina was standing an open, semi-circular, cardboard box of lace: she was carelessly turning over the lace with one hand, in the other she was holding Litvinov's letter. She had only just left off crying; her eyelashes were wet, and her eyelids swollen; on her cheeks could be seen the traces of undried tears not wiped away. Litvinov stood still in the doorway; she did not notice his entrance.

'You are crying?' he said wonderingly.

She started, passed her hand over her hair and smiled.

'Why are you crying?' repeated Litvinov. She pointed in silence to the letter. 'So you were ... over that,' he articulated haltingly.

'Come here, sit down,' she said, 'give me your hand. Well, yes, I was crying ... what are you surprised at? Is that nothing?' she pointed again to the letter.

Litvinov sat down.

'I know it's not easy, Irina, I tell you so indeed in my letter ... I understand your position. But if you believe in the value of your love for me, if my words have convinced you, you ought, too, to understand what I feel now at the sight of your tears. I have come here, like a man on his trial, and I await what is to be my sentence? Death or life? Your answer decides everything. Only don't look at me with those eyes.... They remind me of the eyes I saw in old days in Moscow.'

Irina flushed at once, and turned away, as though herself conscious of something evil in her gaze.

'Why do you say that, Grigory? For shame! You want to know my answer ... do you mean to say you can doubt it? You are troubled by my tears ... but you don't understand them. Your letter, dearest, has set me thinking. Here you write that my love has replaced everything for you, that even your former studies can never now be put into practice; but I ask myself, can a man live for love alone? Won't it weary him at last, won't he want an active career, and won't he cast the blame on what drew him away from active life? That's the thought that dismays me, that's what I am afraid of, and not what you imagine.'

Litvinov looked intently at Irina, and Irina intently looked at him, as though each would penetrate deeper and further into the soul of the other, deeper and further than word can reach, or word betray.

'You are wrong in being afraid of that,' began Litvinov. 'I must have expressed myself badly. Weariness? Inactivity? With the new impetus your love will give me? O Irina, in your love there's a whole world for me, and I can't yet foresee myself what may develop from it.'

Irina grew thoughtful.

'Where are we going?' she whispered.

'Where? We will talk of that later. But, of course, then ... then you agree? you agree, Irina?'

She looked at him. 'And you will be happy?'

'O Irina!'

'You will regret nothing? Never?'

She bent over the cardboard box, and again began looking over the lace in it.

'Don't be angry with me, dear one, for attending to this trash at such a moment.... I am obliged to go to a ball at a certain lady's, these bits of finery have been sent me, and I must choose to-day. Ah! I am awfully wretched!' she cried suddenly, and she laid her face down on the edge of the box. Tears began falling again from her eyes.... She turned away; the tears might spoil the lace.

'Irina, you are crying again,' Litvinov began uneasily.

'Ah, yes, again,' Irina interposed hurriedly. 'O Grigory, don't torture me, don't torture yourself!... Let us be free people! What does it matter if I do cry! And indeed do I know myself why my tears are flowing? You know, you have heard my decision, you believe it will not be changed. That I agree to ... What was it you said?... to all or nothing ... what more would you have? Let us be free! Why these mutual chains? We are alone together now, you love me. I love you; is it possible we have nothing to do but wringing our thoughts out of each other? Look at me, I don't want to talk about myself, I have never by one word hinted that for me perhaps it was not so easy to set at nought my duty as a wife ... and, of course, I don't deceive myself, I know I am a criminal, and that *he* has a right to kill me. Well, what of it? Let us be free, I say. To-day is ours—a life-time's ours.'

She got up from the arm-chair and looked at Litvinov with her head thrown back, faintly smiling and moving her eyebrows, while with one arm bare to the elbow she pushed back from her face a long tress on which a few tears glistened. A rich scarf slipped from the table and fell on the floor at Irina's feet. She trampled contemptuously on it. 'Or don't you like me, to-day? Have I grown ugly since yesterday? Tell me, have you often seen a prettier hand? And this hair? Tell me, do you love me?'

She clasped him in both arms, held his head close to her bosom, her comb fell out with a ringing sound, and her falling hair wrapped him in a soft flood of fragrance.

XXIV

Litvinov walked up and down his room in the hotel, his head bowed in thought. He had now to pass from theory to practice, to devise ways and means for flight, for moving to unknown countries.... But, strange to say, he was not pondering so much upon ways and means as upon whether actually, beyond doubt, the decision had been reached on which he had so obstinately insisted? Had the ultimate, irrevocable word been uttered? But Irina to be sure had said to him at parting, 'Act, act, and when every thing is ready, only let me know.' That was final! Away with all doubts.... He must proceed to action. And Litvinov proceeded—in the meantime—to calculation. Money first of all. Litvinov had, he found, in ready money one thousand three hundred and twenty-eight guldens, in French money, two thousand eight hundred and fifty-five francs; the sum was trifling, but it was enough for the first necessities, and then he must at once write to his father to send him all he could; he would have to sell the forest part of the land. But on what pretext?... Well, a pretext would be found. Irina had spoken, it's true, of her *bijoux*, but that must not be taken into his reckoning; that, who knows, might come in for a rainy day. He had besides a good Geneva watch, for which he might get ... well, say, four hundred francs. Litvinov went to a banker's, and with much circumlocution introduced the question whether it was possible, in case of need, to borrow money; but bankers at Baden are wary old foxes, and in response to such circumlocutions they promptly assume a drooping and blighted air, for all the world like a wild flower whose stalk has been severed by the scythe; some indeed laugh outright in your face, as though appreciating an innocent joke on your part. Litvinov, to his shame, even tried his luck at roulette, even, oh ignominy! put a thaler on the number thirty, corresponding with his own age. He did this with a view to augmenting and rounding off his capital; and if he did not augment it, he certainly did round off his capital by losing the odd twenty-eight guldens. There was a second question, also not an unimportant one; that was the passport. But for a woman a passport is not quite so obligatory, and there are countries where it is not required at all, Belgium, for instance, and England; besides, one might even get some other passport, not Russian. Litvinov pondered very seriously on all this; his decision was firm, absolutely unwavering, and yet all the time against his will, overriding his will, something not serious, almost humorous came in, filtered through his musings, as though the very enterprise were a comic business, and no one ever did elope with any one in reality, but only in plays and novels, and perhaps somewhere in the provinces, in some of those remote districts, where, according to the statements of travellers, people are literally sick continually from *ennui*. At that point Litvinov recalled how an acquaintance of his, a retired cornet, Batsov, had eloped with a merchant's daughter in a staging sledge with bells and three horses, having as a preliminary measure made the parents drunk, and adopted the same precaution as well with the bride, and how, as it afterwards turned out, he was outwitted and within an ace of a thrashing into the bargain. Litvinov felt exceedingly irritated with himself for such inappropriate reminiscences, and then with the recollection of Tatyana, her sudden departure, all that grief and suffering and shame, he felt only too acutely that the affair he was arranging was deadly earnest, and how right he had been when he had told Irina that his honour even left no other course open.... And again at the mere name something of flame turned with sweet ache about his heart and died away again.

The tramp of horses' hoofs sounded behind him.... He moved aside.... Irina overtook him on horseback; beside her rode the stout general. She recognised Litvinov, nodded to him, and lashing her horse with a sidestroke of her whip, she put him into a gallop, and suddenly dashed away at headlong speed. Her dark veil fluttered in the wind....

'*Pas si vite! Nom de Dieu! pas si vite!*' cried the general, and he too galloped after her.

XXV

The next morning Litvinov had only just come home from seeing the banker, with whom he had had another conversation on the playful instability of our exchange, and the best means of sending money abroad, when the hotel porter handed him a letter. He recognised Irina's handwriting, and without breaking the seal—a presentiment of evil, Heaven knows why, was astir in him—he went into his room. This was what he read (the letter was in French):

'My dear one, I have been thinking all night of your plan.... I am not going to shuffle with you. You have been open with me, and I will be open with you; I *cannot* run away with you, I *have not the strength* to do it. I feel how I am wronging you; my second sin is greater than the first, I despise myself, my cowardice, I cover myself with reproaches, but I cannot change myself. In vain I tell myself that I have destroyed your happiness, that you have the right now to regard me as a frivolous flirt, that I myself drew you on, that I have given you solemn promises.... I am full of horror, of hatred for myself, but I can't do otherwise, I can't, I can't. I don't want to justify myself, I won't tell you I was carried away myself ... all that's of no importance; but I want to tell you, and to say it again and yet again, I am yours, yours for ever, do with me as you will when you will, free from all obligation, from all responsibility! I am yours.... But run away, throw up everything ... no! no! no! I besought you to save me, I hoped to wipe out everything, to burn up the past as in a fire ... but I see there is no salvation for me; I see the poison has gone too deeply into me; I see one cannot breathe this atmosphere for years with impunity. I have long hesitated whether to write you this letter, I dread to think what decision you may come to, I trust only to your love for me. But I felt it would be dishonest on my part to hide the truth from you—especially as perhaps you have already begun to take the first steps for carrying out our project. Ah! it was lovely but impracticable. O my dear one, think me a weak, worthless woman, despise, but don't abandon me, don't abandon your Irina!... To leave this life I have not the courage, but live it without you I cannot either. We soon go back to Petersburg, come there, live there, we will find occupation for you, your labours in the past shall not be thrown away, you shall find good use for them ... only live near me, only love me; such as I am, with all my weaknesses and my vices, and believe me, no heart will ever be so tenderly devoted to you as the heart of your Irina. Come soon to me, I shall not have an instant's peace until I see you.—Yours, yours, yours, I.'

The blood beat like a sledge-hammer in Litvinov's head, then slowly and painfully sank to his heart, and was chill as a stone in it. He read through Irina's letter, and just as on that day at Moscow he fell in exhaustion on the sofa, and stayed there motionless. A dark abyss seemed suddenly to have opened on all sides of him, and he stared into this darkness in senseless despair. And so again, again deceit, no, worse than deceit, lying and baseness.... And life shattered, everything torn up by its roots utterly, and the sole thing which he could cling to—the last prop in fragments too! 'Come after us to Petersburg,' he repeated with a bitter inward laugh, 'we will find you occupation.... Find me a place as a head clerk, eh? and who are *we?* Here there's a hint of her past. Here we have the secret, hideous something I know nothing of, but which she has been trying to wipe out, to burn as in a fire. Here we have that world of intrigues, of secret relations, of shameful stories of Byelskys and Dolskys.... And what a future, what a lovely part awaiting me! To live close to her, visit her, share with her the morbid melancholy of the lady of fashion who is sick and weary of the world, but can't live outside its circle, be the friend of the house of course, of his Excellency ... until ... until the whim changes and the plebeian lover loses his piquancy, and is replaced by that fat general or Mr. Finikov—that's possible and pleasant, and I dare say useful.... She talks of a good use for my talents?... but the other project's impracticable, impracticable....' In Litvinov's soul rose, like sudden gusts of wind before a storm, momentary impulses of fury.... Every expression in Irina's letter roused his indignation, her very assertions of her unchanging feelings affronted him. 'She can't let it go like that,' he cried at last, 'I won't allow her to play with my life so mercilessly.'

Litvinov jumped up, snatched his hat. But what was he to do? Run to her? Answer her letter? He stopped short, and his hands fell.

'Yes; what was to be done?'

Had he not himself put this fatal choice to her? It had not turned out as he had wished ... there was that risk about every choice. She had changed her mind, it was true; she herself had declared at first that she would throw up everything and follow him; that was true too; but she did not deny her guilt, she called herself a weak woman; she did not want to deceive him, she had been deceived in herself.... What answer could be made to that? At any rate she was not hypocritical, she was not deceiving him ... she was open, remorselessly open. There was nothing forced her to speak out, nothing to prevent her from soothing him with promises, putting things off, and keeping it all in uncertainty till her departure ... till her departure with her husband for Italy? But she had ruined his life, ruined two lives.... What of that?

But as regards Tatyana, she was not guilty; the guilt was his, his, Litvinov's alone, and he had no right to shake off the responsibility his own sin had laid with iron yoke upon him.... All this was so; but what was left him to do now?

Again he flung himself on the sofa and again in gloom, darkly, dimly, without trace, with devouring swiftness, the minutes raced past....

'And why not obey her?' flashed through his brain. 'She loves me, she is mine, and in our very yearning towards each other, in this passion, which after so many years has burst upon us, and forced its way out with such violence, is there not something inevitable, irresistible, like a law of nature? Live in Petersburg ... and shall I be the first to be put in such a position? And how could we be in safety together?...'

And he fell to musing, and Irina's shape, in the guise in which it was imprinted for ever in his late memories, softly rose before him.... But not for long.... He mastered himself, and with a fresh outburst of indignation drove away from him both those memories and that seductive image.

'You give me to drink from that golden cup,' he cried, 'but there is poison in the draught, and your white wings are besmirched with mire.... Away! Remain here with you after the way I ... I drove away my betrothed ... a deed of infamy, of infamy!' He wrung his hands with anguish, and another face with the stamp of suffering on its still features, with dumb reproach in its farewell eyes, rose from the depths....

And for a long time Litvinov was in this agony still; for a long time, his tortured thought, like a man fever-stricken, tossed from side to side.... He grew calm at last; at last he came to a decision. From the very first instant he had a presentiment of this decision; ... it had appeared to him at first like a distant, hardly perceptible point in the midst of the darkness and turmoil of his inward conflict; then it had begun to move nearer and nearer, till it ended by cutting with icy edge into his heart.

Litvinov once more dragged his box out of the corner, once more he packed all his things, without haste, even with a kind of stupid carefulness, rang for the waiter, paid his bill, and despatched to Irina a note in Russian to the following purport:

'I don't know whether you are doing me a greater wrong now than then; but I know this present blow is infinitely heavier.... It is the end. You tell me, "I cannot"; and I repeat to you, "I cannot ..." do what you want. I cannot and I don't want to. Don't answer me. You are not capable of giving me the only answer I would accept. I am going away to-morrow early by the first train. Good-bye, may you be happy! We shall in all probability not see each other again.'

Till night-time Litvinov did not leave his room; God knows whether he was expecting anything. About seven o'clock in the evening a lady in a black mantle with a veil on her face twice approached the steps of his hotel. Moving a little aside and gazing far away into the distance, she suddenly made a resolute gesture with her hand, and for the third time went towards the steps....

'Where are you going, Irina Pavlovna?' she heard a voice utter with effort behind her.

She turned with nervous swiftness.... Potugin ran up to her.

She stopped short, thought a moment, and fairly flung herself towards him, took his arm, and drew him away.

'Take me away, take me away,' she repeated breathlessly.

'What is it, Irina Pavlovna?' he muttered in bewilderment.

'Take me away,' she reiterated with redoubled force, 'if you don't want me to remain for ever ... there.'

Potugin bent his head submissively, and hurriedly they went away together.

The following morning early Litvinov was perfectly ready for his journey—into his room walked ... Potugin.

He went up to him in silence, and in silence shook his hand. Litvinov, too, said nothing. Both of them wore long faces, and both vainly tried to smile.

'I came to wish you a good journey,' Potugin brought out at last.

'And how did you know I was going to-day?' asked Litvinov.

Potugin looked on the floor around him.... 'I became aware of it ... as you see. Our last conversation took in the end such a strange turn.... I did not want to part from you without expressing my sincere good feeling for you.'

'You have good feeling for me now ... when I am going away?'

Potugin looked mournfully at Litvinov. 'Ah, Grigory Mihalitch, Grigory Mihalitch,' he began with a short sigh, 'it's no time for that with us now, no time for delicacy or fencing. You don't, so far as I have been able to perceive, take much interest in our national literature, and so, perhaps, you have no clear conception of Vaska Buslaev?'

'Of whom?'

'Of Vaska Buslaev, the hero of Novgorod ... in Kirsch-Danilov's collection.'

'What Buslaev?' said Litvinov, somewhat puzzled by the unexpected turn of the conversation. 'I don't know.'

'Well, never mind. I only wanted to draw your attention to something. Vaska Buslaev, after he had taken away his Novgorodians on a pilgrimage to Jerusalem, and there, to their horror, bathed all naked in the holy river Jordan, for he believed not "in omen nor in dream, nor in the flight of birds," this logical Vaska Buslaev climbed up Mount Tabor, and on the top of this mountain there lies a great stone, over which men of every kind have tried in vain to jump.... Vaska too ventured to try his luck. And he chanced upon a dead head, a human skull in his road; he kicked it away with his foot. So the skull said to him; "Why do you kick me? I knew how to live, and I know how to roll in the dust—and it will be the same with you." And in fact, Vaska jumps over the stone, and he did quite clear it, but he caught his heel and broke his skull. And in this place, I must by the way observe that it wouldn't be amiss for our friends, the Slavophils, who are so fond of kicking dead heads and decaying nationalities underfoot to ponder over that legend.'

'But what does all that mean?' Litvinov interposed impatiently at last. 'Excuse me, it's time for me....'

'Why, this,' answered Potugin, and his eyes beamed with such affectionate warmth as Litvinov had not even expected of him, 'this, that you do not spurn a dead human head, and for your goodness, perhaps you may succeed inleaping over the fatal stone. I won't keep you any longer, only let me embrace you at parting.'

'I'm not going to try to leap over it even,' Litvinov declared, kissing Potugin three times, and the bitter sensations filling his soul were replaced for an instant by pity for the poor lonely creature.

'But I must go, I must go ...' he moved about the room.

'Can I carry anything for you?' Potugin proffered his services.

'No, thank you, don't trouble, I can manage....'

He put on his cap, took up his bag. 'So you say,' he queried, stopping in the doorway, 'you have seen her?'

'Yes, I've seen her.'

'Well ... tell me about her.'

Potugin was silent a moment. 'She expected you yesterday ... and to-day she will expect you.'

'Ah! Well, tell her.... No, there's no need, no need of anything. Good-bye.... Good-bye!'

'Good-bye, Grigory Mihalitch.... Let me say one word more to you. You still have time to listen to me; there's more than half an hour before the train starts. You are returning to Russia.... There you will ... in time ... get to work.... Allow an old chatterbox—for, alas, I am a chatterbox, and nothing more—to give you advice for your journey. Every time it is your lot to undertake any piece of work, ask yourself: Are you serving the cause of civilisation, in the true and strict sense of the word; are you promoting one of the ideals of civilisation; have your labours that educating, Europeanising character which alone is beneficial and profitable in our day among us? If it is so, go boldly forward, you are on the right path, and your work is a blessing! Thank God for it! You are not alone now. You will not be a "sower in the desert"; there are plenty of workers ... pioneers ... even among us now.... But you have no ears for this now. Good-bye, don't forget me!'

Litvinov descended the staircase at a run, flung himself into a carriage, and drove to the station, not once looking round at the town where so much of his personal life was left behind. He abandoned himself, as it were, to the tide; it snatched him up and bore him along, and he firmly resolved not to struggle against it ... all other exercise of independent will he renounced.

He was just taking his seat in the railway carriage.

'Grigory Mihalitch ... Grigory....' he heard a supplicating whisper behind him.

He started.... Could it be Irina? Yes; it was she. Wrapped in her maid's shawl, a travelling hat on her dishevelled hair, she was standing on the platform, and gazing at him with worn and weary eyes.

'Come back, come back, I have come for you,' those eyes were saying. And what, what were they not promising? She did not move, she had not power to add a word; everything about her, even the disorder of her dress, everything seemed entreating forgiveness....

Litvinov was almost beaten, scarcely could he keep from rushing to her.... But the tide to which he had surrendered himself reasserted itself.... He jumped into the carriage, and turning round, he motioned Irina to a place beside him. She understood him. There was still time. One step, one movement, and two lives made one for ever would have been hurried away into the uncertain distance.... While she wavered, a loud whistle sounded and the train moved off.

Litvinov sank back, while Irina moved staggering to a seat, and fell on it, to the immense astonishment of a supernumerary diplomatic official who chanced to be lounging about the railway station. He was slightly acquaintedwith Irina, and greatly admired her, and seeing that she lay as though overcome by faintness, he imagined that she had '*une attaque de nerfs*,' and therefore deemed it his duty, the duty *d'un galant chevalier*, to go to her assistance. But his astonishment assumed far greater proportions when, at the first word addressed to her, she suddenly got up, repulsed his proffered arm, and hurrying out into the street, had in a few instants vanished in the milky vapour of fog, so characteristic of the climate of the Black Forest in the early days of autumn.

XXVI

We happened once to go into the hut of a peasant-woman who had just lost her only, passionately loved son, and to our considerable astonishment we found her perfectly calm, almost cheerful. 'Let her be,' said her husband, to whom probably our astonishment was apparent, 'she is gone numb now.' And Litvinov had in the same way 'gone numb.' The same sort of calm came over him during the first few hours of the journey. Utterly crushed, hopelessly wretched as he was, still he was at rest, at rest after the agonies and sufferings of the last few weeks, after all the blows which had fallen one after another upon his head. They had been the more shattering for him that he was little fitted by nature for such tempests. Now he really hoped for nothing, and tried not to remember, above all not to remember. He was going to Russia ... he had to go somewhere; but he was making no kind of plans regarding his own personality. He did notrecognise himself, he did not comprehend his own actions, he had positively lost his real identity, and, in fact, he took very little interest in his own identity. Sometimes it seemed to him that he was taking his own corpse home, and only the bitter spasms of irremediable spiritual pain passing over him from time to time brought him back to a sense of still being alive. At times it struck him as incomprehensible that a man—a man!—could let a woman, let love, have such power over him ... 'Ignominious weakness!' he muttered, and shook back his cloak, and sat up more squarely; as though to say, the past is over, let's begin fresh ... a moment, and he could only smile bitterly and wonder at himself. He fell to looking out of the window. It was grey and damp; there was no rain, but the fog still hung about; and low clouds trailed across the sky. The wind blew facing the train; whitish clouds of steam, some singly, others mingled with other darker clouds of smoke, whirled in endless file past the window at which Litvinov was sitting. He began to watch this steam, this smoke. Incessantly mounting, rising and falling, twisting and hooking on to the grass, to the bushes as though in sportive antics, lengthening out, and hiding away, clouds upon clouds flew by ... they were for ever changing andstayed still the same in their monotonous, hurrying, wearisome sport! Sometimes the wind changed, the line bent to right or left, and suddenly the whole mass vanished, and at once reappeared at the opposite window; then again the huge tail was flung out, and again it veiled Litvinov's view of the vast plain of the Rhine. He gazed and gazed, and a strange reverie came over him.... He was alone in the compartment; there was no one to disturb him. 'Smoke, smoke,' he repeated several times; and suddenly it all seemed as smoke to him, everything, his own life, Russian life—everything human, especially everything Russian. All smoke and steam, he thought; all seems for ever changing, on all sides new forms, phantoms flying after phantoms, while in reality it is all the same and the same again; everything hurrying, flying towards something, and everything vanishing without a trace, attaining to nothing; another wind blows, and all is dashing in the opposite direction, and there again the same untiring, restless—and useless gambols! He remembered much that had taken place with clamour and flourish before his eyes in the last few years ... 'Smoke,' he whispered, 'smoke'; he remembered the hot disputes, the wrangling, the clamour at Gubaryov's, and in other sets of men, of high and low degree, advanced and reactionist, old and young ... 'Smoke,' he repeated, 'smoke and steam'; he remembered, too, the fashionable picnic, and he remembered various opinions and speeches of other political personages—even all Potugin's sermonising ... 'Smoke, smoke, nothing but smoke.' And what of his own struggles and passions and agonies and dreams? He could only reply with a gesture of despair.

And meanwhile the train dashed on and on; by now Rastadt, Carlsruhe, and Bruchsal had long been left far behind; the mountains on the right side of the line swerved aside, retreated into the distance, then moved up again, but not so high, and more thinly covered with trees.... The train made a sharp turn ... and there was Heidelberg. The carriage rolled in under the cover of the station; there was the shouting of newspaper-boys, selling papers of all sorts, even Russian; passengers began bustling in their seats, getting out on to the platform, but Litvinov did not leave his corner, and still sat on with downcast head. Suddenly some one called him by name; he raised his eyes; Bindasov's ugly phiz was thrust in at the window; and behind him—or was he dreaming, no, it was really so—all the familiar Baden faces;there was Madame Suhantchikov, there was Voroshilov, and Bambaev too; they all rushed up to him, while Bindasov bellowed:

'But where's Pishtchalkin? We were expecting him; but it's all the same, hop out, and we'll be off to Gubaryov's.'

'Yes, my boy, yes, Gubaryov's expecting us,' Bambaev confirmed, making way for him, 'hop out.'

Litvinov would have flown into a rage, but for a dead load lying on his heart. He glanced at Bindasov and turned away without speaking.

'I tell you Gubaryov's here,' shrieked Madame Suhantchikov, her eyes fairly starting out of her head.

Litvinov did not stir a muscle.

'Come, do listen, Litvinov,' Bambaev began at last, 'there's not only Gubaryov here, there's a whole phalanx here of the most splendid, most intellectual young fellows, Russians—and all studying the natural sciences, all of the noblest convictions! Really you must stop here, if it's only for them. Here, for instance, there's a certain ... there, I've forgotten his surname, but he's a genius! simply!'

'Oh, let him be, let him be, Rostislav Ardalionovitch,' interposed Madame Suhantchikov, 'let him be! You see what sort of a fellow he is; and all his family are the same. He has an aunt; at first she struck me as a sensible woman, but the day before yesterday I went to see her here—she had only just before gone to Baden and was back here again before you could look round—well, I went to see her; began questioning her.... Would you believe me, I couldn't get a word out of the stuck-up thing. Horrid aristocrat!'

Poor Kapitolina Markovna an aristocrat! Could she ever have anticipated such a humiliation?

But Litvinov still held his peace, turned away, and pulled his cap over his eyes. The train started at last.

'Well, say something at parting at least, you stonyhearted man!' shouted Bambaev, 'this is really too much!'

'Rotten milksop!' yelled Bindasov. The carriages were moving more and more rapidly, and he could vent his abuse with impunity. 'Niggardly stick-in-the-mud.'

Whether Bindasov invented this last appellation on the spot, or whether it had come to him second-hand, it apparently gave great satisfaction to two of the noble young fellows studying natural science, who happened to be standing by, for only a few days later it appeared in the Russian periodical sheet, published at that time at Heidelberg under the title: *A tout venant je crache!*[2] or, 'We don't care a hang for anybody!'

But Litvinov repeated again, 'Smoke, smoke, smoke! Here,' he thought, 'in Heidelberg now are over a hundred Russian students; they're all studying chemistry, physics, physiology—they won't even hear of anything else ... but in five or six years' time there won't be fifteen at the lectures by the same celebrated professors; the wind will change, the smoke will be blowing ... in another quarter ... smoke ... smoke...!'[3]

Towards nightfall he passed by Cassel. With the darkness intolerable anguish pounced like a hawk upon him, and he wept, burying himself in the corner of the carriage. For a long time his tears flowed, not easing his heart, but torturing him with a sort of gnawing bitterness; while at the same time, in one of the hotels of Cassel, Tatyana was lying in bed feverishly ill.

Kapitolina Markovna was sitting beside her. 'Tanya,' she was saying, 'for God's sake, let me send a telegram to Grigory Mihalitch, do let me, Tanya!'

'No, aunt,' she answered; 'you mustn't; don't be frightened, give me some water; it will soon pass.'

And a week later she did, in fact, recover, and the two friends continued their journey.

XXVII

Stopping neither at Petersburg nor at Moscow, Litvinov went back to his estate. He was dismayed when he saw his father; the latter was so weak and failing. The old man rejoiced to have his son, as far as a man can rejoice who is just at the close of life; he at once gave over to him the management of everything, which was in great disorder, and lingering on a few weeks longer, he departed from this earthly sphere. Litvinov was left alone in his ancient little manor-house, and with a heavy heart, without hope, without zeal, and without money, he began to work the land. Working the land is a cheerless business, as many know too well; we will not enlarge on how distasteful it seemed to Litvinov. As for reforms and innovations, there was, of course, no question even of them; the practical application of the information he had gathered abroad was put off for an indefinite period; poverty forced him to make shift from day to day, to consent to all sorts of compromises—both material and moral. The new had 'begun ill,' the old had lost all power; ignorance jostled up against dishonesty; the whole agrarian organisation was shaken and unstable as quagmire bog, and only one great word, 'freedom,' was wafted like the breath of God over the waters. Patience was needed before all things, and a patience not passive, but active, persistent, not without tact and cunning at times.... For Litvinov, in his frame of mind, it was doubly hard. He had but little will to live left in him.... Where was he to get the will to labour and take trouble?

But a year passed, after it another passed, the third was beginning. The mighty idea was being realised by degrees, was passing into flesh and blood, the young shoot had sprung up from the scattered seed, and its foes, both open and secret, could not stamp it out now. Litvinov himself, though he had ended by giving up the greater part of his land to the peasants on the half-profit system, that's to say, by returning to the wretched primitive methods, had yet succeeded in doing something; he had restored the factory, set up a tiny farm with five free hired labourers—he had had at different times fully forty—and had paid his principal private debts.... And his spirit had gained strength; he had begun to be like the old Litvinov again. It's true, a deeply buried melancholy never left him, and he was too quiet for his years; he shut himself up in a narrow circle and broke off all his old connections ... but the deadly indifference had passed, and among the living he moved and acted as a living man again. The last traces, too, had vanished of the enchantment in which he had been held; all that had passed at Baden appeared to him dimly as in a dream.... And Irina? even she had paled and vanished too, and Litvinov only had a faint sense of something dangerous behind the mist that gradually enfolded her image. Of Tatyana news reached him from time to time; he knew that she was living with her aunt on her estate, a hundred and sixty miles from him, leading a quiet life, going out little, and scarcely receiving any guests—cheerful and well, however. It happened on one fine May day, that he was sitting in his study, listlessly turning over the last number of a Petersburg paper; a servant came to announce the arrival of an old uncle. This uncle happened to be a cousin of Kapitolina Markovna and had been recently staying with her. He had bought an estate in Litvinov's vicinity and was on his way thither. He stayed twenty-four hours with his nephew and told him a great deal about Tatyana's manner of life. The next day after his departure Litvinov sent her a letter, the first since their separation. He begged for permission to renew her acquaintance, at least by correspondence, and also desired to learn whether he must for ever give up all idea of some day seeing her again? Not without emotion he awaited the answer ... the answer came at last. Tatyana responded cordially to his overture. 'If you are disposed to pay us a visit,' she finished up, 'we hope you will come; you know the saying, "even the sick are easier together than apart."' Kapitolina Markovna joined in sending her regards. Litvinov was as happy as a child; it was long since his heart had beaten with such delight over anything. He felt suddenly light and bright.... Just as when the sun rises and drives away the darkness of night, a light breeze flutters with the sun's rays over the face of the reviving earth. All that day Litvinov kept smiling, even while he went about his farm and gave his orders. He at once began making arrangements for the journey, and a fortnight later he was on his way to Tatyana.

XXVIII

He drove rather slowly by cross tracks, without any special adventures; only once the tire of a hind wheel broke; a blacksmith hammered and welded it, swearing both at the tire and at himself, and positively flung up the job; luckily it turned out that among us one can travel capitally even with a tire broken, especially on the 'soft,' that's to say on the mud. On the other hand, Litvinov did come upon some rather curious chance-meetings. At one place he found a Board of Mediators sitting, and at the head of it Pishtchalkin, who made on him the impression of a Solon or a Solomon, such lofty wisdom characterised his remarks, and such boundless respect was shown him both by landowners and peasants.... In exterior, too, he had begun to resemble a sage of antiquity; his hair had fallen off the crown of his head, and his full face had completely set in a sort of solemn jelly of positively blatant virtue. He expressed his pleasure atLitvinov's arrival in—'if I may make bold to use so ambitious an expression, my own district,' and altogether seemed fairly overcome by an excess of excellent intentions. One piece of news he did, however, succeed in communicating, and that was about Voroshilov; the hero of the Golden Board had re-entered military service, and had already had time to deliver a lecture to the officers of his regiment on Buddhism or Dynamism, or something of the sort—Pishtchalkin could not quite remember. At the next station it was a long while before the horses were in readiness for Litvinov; it was early dawn, and he was dozing as he sat in his coach. A voice, that struck him as familiar, waked him up; he opened his eyes.... Heavens! wasn't it Gubaryov in a grey pea-jacket and full flapping pyjamas standing on the steps of the posting hut, swearing?... No, it wasn't Mr. Gubaryov.... But what a striking resemblance!... Only this worthy had a mouth even wider, teeth even bigger, the expression of his dull eyes was more savage and his nose coarser, and his beard thicker, and the whole countenance heavier and more repulsive.

'Scou-oundrels, scou-oundrels!' he vociferated slowly and viciously, his wolfish mouth gaping wide. 'Filthy louts.... Here you have ... vaunted freedom indeed ... and can't get horses ... scou-oundrels!'

'Scou-oundrels, scou-oundrels!' thereupon came the sound of another voice from within, and at the same moment there appeared on the steps—also in a grey smoking pea-jacket and pyjamas—actually, unmistakably, the real Gubaryov himself, Stepan Nikolaevitch Gubaryov. 'Filthy louts!' he went on in imitation of his brother (it turned out that the first gentleman was his elder brother, the man of the old school, famous for his fists, who had managed his estate). 'Flogging's what they want, that's it; a tap or two on the snout, that's the sort of freedom for them.... Self-government indeed.... I'd let them know it.... But where is that M'sieu Roston?... What is he thinking about?... It's his business, the lazy scamp ... to see we're not put to inconvenience.'

'Well, I told you, brother,' began the elder Gubaryov, 'that he was a lazy scamp, no good in fact! But there, for the sake of old times, you ... M'sieu Roston, M'sieu Roston!... Where have you got to?'

'Roston! Roston!' bawled the younger, the great Gubaryov. 'Give a good call for him, do brother Dorimedont Nikolaitch!'

'Well, I am shouting for him, Stepan Nikolaitch! M'sieu Roston!'

'Here I am, here I am, here I am!' was heard a hurried voice, and round the corner of the hut skipped Bambaev.

Litvinov fairly gasped. On the unlucky enthusiast a shabby braided coat, with holes in the elbows, dangled ruefully; his features had not exactly changed, but they looked pinched and drawn together; his over-anxious little eyes expressed a cringing timorousness and hungry servility; but his dyed whiskers stood out as of old above his swollen lips. The Gubaryov brothers with one accord promptly set to scolding him from the top of the steps; he stopped, facing them below, in the mud, and with his spine curved deprecatingly, he tried to propitiate them with a little nervous smile, kneading his cap in his red fingers, shifting from one foot to the other, and muttering that the horses would be here directly.... But the brothers did not cease, till the younger at last cast his eyes upon Litvinov. Whether he recognised Litvinov, or whether he felt ashamed before a stranger, anyway he turned abruptly on his heels like a bear, and gnawing his beard, went into the station hut; his brother held his tongue at once, and he too, turning like a bear, followed him in. The great Gubaryov, evidently, had not lost his influence even in his own country.

Bambaev was slowly moving after the brothers.... Litvinov called him by his name. He looked round, lifted up his head, and recognising Litvinov, positively flew at him with outstretched arms; but when he had run up to the carriage, he clutched at the carriage door, leaned over it, and began sobbing violently.

'There, there, Bambaev,' protested Litvinov, bending over him and patting him on the shoulder.

But he went on sobbing. 'You see ... you see ... to what....' he muttered brokenly.

'Bambaev!' thundered the brothers from the hut.

Bambaev raised his head and hurriedly wiped his tears.

'Welcome, dear heart,' he whispered, 'welcome and farewell!... You hear, they are calling me.'

'But what chance brought you here?' inquired Litvinov, 'and what does it all mean? I thought they were calling a Frenchman....'

'I am their ... house-steward, butler,' answered Bambaev, and he pointed in the direction of the hut. 'And I'm turned Frenchman for a joke. What could I do, brother? You see, I'd nothing to eat, I'd lost my last farthing, and so one's forced to put one's head under the yoke. One can't afford to be proud.'

'But has he been long in Russia? and how did he part from his comrades?'

'Ah, my boy, that's all on the shelf now.... The wind's changed, you see.... Madame Suhantchikov, Matrona Semyonovna, he simply kicked out. She went to Portugal in her grief.'

'To Portugal? How absurd!'

'Yes, brother, to Portugal, with two Matronovtsys.'

'With whom?'

'The Matronovtsys; that's what the members of her party are called.'

'Matrona Semyonovna has a party of her own? And is it a numerous one?'

'Well, it consists of precisely those two. And he will soon have been back here six months. Others have got into difficulties, but he was all right. He lives in the country with his brother, and you should just hear him now....'

'Bambaev!'

'Coming, Stepan Nikolaitch, coming. And you, dear old chap, are flourishing, enjoying yourself! Well, thank God for that! Where are you off to now?... There, I never thought, I never guessed.... You remember Baden? Ah, that was a place to live in! By the way, you remember Bindasov too? Only fancy, he's dead. He turned exciseman, and was in a row in a public-house; he got his head broken with a billiard-cue. Yes, yes, hard times have come now! But still I say, Russia ... ah, our Russia! Only look at those two geese; why, in the whole of Europe there's nothing like them! The genuine Arzamass breed!'

And with this last tribute to his irrepressible desire for enthusiasm, Bambaev ran off to the station hut, where again, seasoned with opprobrious epithets, his name was shouted.

Towards the close of the same day, Litvinov was nearly reaching Tatyana's village. The little house where his former betrothed lived stood on the slope of a hill, above a small river, in the midst of a garden recently planted. The house, too, was new, lately built, and could be seen a long way off across the river and the open country. Litvinov caught sight of it more than a mile and a half off, with its sharp gable, and its row of little windows, gleaming red in the evening sun. At starting from the last station he was conscious of a secret agitation; now he was in a tremor simply—a happy tremor, not unmixed with dread. 'How will they meet me?' he thought, 'how shall I present myself?'... To turn off his thoughts with something, he began talking with his driver, a steady peasant with a grey beard, who charged him, however, for twenty-five miles, when the distance was not twenty. He asked him, did he know the Shestov ladies?

'The Shestov ladies? To be sure! Kind-hearted ladies, and no doubt about it! They doctor us too. It's the truth I'm telling you. Doctors they are! People go to them from all about. Yes, indeed. They fairly crawl to them. If any one, take an example, falls sick, or cuts himself or anything, he goes straight to them and they'll give him a lotion directly, or powders, or a plaster, and it'll be all right, it'll do good. But one can't show one's gratitude, we won't consent to that, they say; it's not for money. They've set up a school too.... Not but what that's a foolish business!'

While the driver talked, Litvinov never took his eyes off the house.... Out came a woman in white on to the balcony, stood a little, stood and then disappeared.... 'Wasn't it she?' His heart was fairly bounding within him. 'Quicker, quicker!' he shouted to the driver; the latter urged on the horses. A few instants more ... and the carriage rolled in through the opened gates.... And on the steps Kapitolina Markovna was already standing, and beside herself with joy, was clapping her hands crying, 'I heard him, I knew him first! It's he! it's he!... I knew him!'

Litvinov jumped out of the carriage, without giving the page who ran up time to open the door, and hurriedly embracing Kapitolina Markovna, dashed into the house, through the hall, into the dining-room.... Before him, all shamefaced, stood Tatyana. She glanced at him with her kind caressing eyes (she was a little thinner, but it suited her), and gave him her hand. But he did not take her hand, he fell on his knees before her. She had not at all expected this and did not know what to say, what to do.... The tears started into her eyes. She was frightened, but her whole face beamed with delight.... 'Grigory Mihalitch, what is this, Grigory Mihalitch?' she said ... while he still kissed the hem of her dress ... and with a thrill of tenderness he recalled that at Baden he had been in the same way on his knees before her.... But then—and now!

'Tanya!' he repeated, 'Tanya! you have forgiven me, Tanya!'

'Aunt, aunt, what is this?' cried Tatyana turning to Kapitolina Markovna as she came in.

'Don't hinder him, Tanya,' answered the kind old lady. 'You see the sinner has repented.'

But it is time to make an end; and indeed there is nothing to add; the reader can guess the rest by himself.... But what of Irina?

She is still as charming, in spite of her thirty years; young men out of number fall in love with her, and would fall in love with her even more, if ... if....

Reader, would you care to pass with us for a few instants to Petersburg into one of the first houses there? Look; before you is a spacious apartment, we will not say richly—that is too low an expression—but grandly, imposingly, inspiringly decorated. Are you conscious of a certain flutter of servility? Know that you have entered a temple, a temple consecrated to the highest propriety, to the loftiest philanthropy, in a word, to things unearthly.... A kind of mystic, truly mystic, hush enfolds you. The velvet hangings on the doors, the velvet curtains on the window, the bloated, spongy rug on the floor, everything as it were destined and fitted beforehand for subduing, for softening all coarse sounds and violent sensations. The carefully hung lamps inspire well-regulated emotions; a discreet fragrance is diffused in the close air; even the samovar on the table hisses in a restrained and modest manner. The lady of the house, an important personage in the Petersburg world, speaks hardly audibly; she always speaks as though there were some one dangerously ill, almost dying in the room; the other ladies, following her example, faintly whisper; while her sister, pouring out tea, moves her lips so absolutely without sound that a young man sitting before her, who has been thrown by chance into the temple of decorum, is positively at a loss to know what she wants of him, while she for the sixth time breathes to him, '*Voulez-vous une tasse de thé?*' In the corners are to be seen young, good-looking men; their glances are brightly, gently ingratiating; unruffled gentleness, tinged with obsequiousness, is apparent in their faces; a number of the stars and crosses of distinction gleam softly on their breasts. The conversation is always gentle; it turns on religious and patriotic topics, the Mystic Drop, F. N. Glinka, the missions in the East, the monasteries and brotherhoods in White Russia. At times, with muffled tread over the soft carpets, move footmen in livery; their huge calves, cased in tight silk stockings, shake noiselessly at every step; the respectful motion of the solid muscles only augments the general impression of decorum, of solemnity, of sanctity.

It is a temple, a temple!

'Have you seen Madame Ratmirov to-day?' one great lady queries softly.

'I met her to-day at Lise's,' the hostess answers with her Æolian note. 'I feel so sorry for her.... She has a satirical intellect ... *elle n'a pas la foi.*'

'Yes, yes,' repeats the great lady ... 'that I remember, Piotr Ivanitch said about her, and very true it is, *qu'elle a ... qu'elle a* an ironical intellect.'

'*Elle n'a pas la foi,*' the hostess's voice exhaled like the smoke of incense,—'*C'est une âme égarée.* She has an ironical mind.'

And that is why the young men are not all without exception in love with Irina.... They are afraid of her ... afraid of her 'ironical intellect.' That is the current phrase about her; in it, as in every phrase, there is a grain of truth. And not only the young men are afraid of her; she is feared by grown men too, and by men in high places, and even by the grandest personages. No one can so truly and artfully scent out the ridiculous or petty side of a character, no one else has the gift of stamping it mercilessly with the never-forgotten word.... And the sting of that word is all the sharper that it comes from lovely, sweetly fragrant lips.... It's hard to say what passes in that soul; but in the crowd of her adorers rumour does not recognise in any one the position of a favoured suitor.

Irina's husband is moving rapidly along the path which among the French is called the path of distinction. The stout general has shot past him; the condescending one is left behind. And in the same town in which Irina lives, lives also our friend Sozont Potugin; he rarely sees her, and she has no special necessity to keep up any connection with him.... The little girl who was committed to his care died not long ago.

Rudin

I

IT was a quiet summer morning. The sun stood already pretty high in the clear sky but the fields were still sparkling with dew; a fresh breeze blew fragrantly from the scarce awakened valleys and in the forest, still damp and hushed, the birds were merrily carolling their morning song. On the ridge of a swelling upland, which was covered from base to summit with blossoming rye, a little village was to be seen. Along a narrow by-road to this little village a young woman was walking in a white muslin gown, and a round straw hat, with a parasol in her hand. A page boy followed her some distance behind.

She moved without haste and as though she were enjoying the walk. The high nodding rye all round her moved in long softly rustling waves, taking here a shade of silvery green and there a ripple of red; the larks were trilling overhead. The young woman had come from her own estate, which was not more than a mile from the village to which she was turning her steps. Her name was Alexandra Pavlovna Lipin. She was a widow, childless, and fairly well off, and lived with her brother, a retired cavalry officer, Sergei Pavlitch Volintsev. He was unmarried and looked after her property.

Alexandra Pavlovna reached the village and, stopping at the last hut, a very old and low one, she called up the boy and told him to go in and ask after the health of its mistress. He quickly came back accompanied by a decrepit old peasant with a white beard.

'Well, how is she?' asked Alexandra Pavlovna.

'Well, she is still alive,' began the old man.

'Can I go in?'

'Of course; yes.'

Alexandra Pavlovna went into the hut. It was narrow, stifling, and smoky inside. Some one stirred and began to moan on the stove which formed the bed. Alexandra Pavlovna looked round and discerned in the half darkness the yellow wrinkled face of the old woman tied up in a checked handkerchief. Covered to the very throat with a heavy overcoat she was breathing with difficulty, and her wasted hands were twitching.

Alexandra Pavlovna went close up to the old woman and laid her fingers on her forehead; it was burning hot.

'How do you feel, Matrona?' she inquired, bending over the bed.

'Oh, oh!' groaned the old woman, trying to make her out, 'bad, very bad, my dear! My last hour has come, my darling!'

'God is merciful, Matrona; perhaps you will be better soon. Did you take the medicine I sent you?'

The old woman groaned painfully, and did not answer. She had hardly heard the question.

'She has taken it,' said the old man who was standing at the door.

Alexandra Pavlovna turned to him.

'Is there no one with her but you?' she inquired.

'There is the girl—her granddaughter, but she always keeps away. She won't sit with her; she's such a gad-about. To give the old woman a drink of water is too much trouble for her. And I am old; what use can I be?'

'Shouldn't she be taken to me—to the hospital?'

'No. Why take her to the hospital? She would die just the same. She has lived her life; it's God's will now seemingly. She will never get up again. How could she go to the hospital? If they tried to lift her up, she would die.'

'Oh!' moaned the sick woman, 'my pretty lady, don't abandon my little orphan; our master is far away, but you——'

She could not go on, she had spent all her strength in saying so much.

'Do not worry yourself,' replied Alexandra Pavlovna, 'everything shall be done. Here is some tea and sugar I have brought you. If you can fancy it you must drink some. Have you a samovar, I wonder?' she added, looking at the old man.

'A samovar? We haven't a samovar, but we could get one.'

'Then get one, or I will send you one. And tell your granddaughter not to leave her like this. Tell her it's shameful.'

The old man made no answer but took the parcel of tea and sugar with both hands.

'Well, good-bye, Matrona!' said Alexandra Pavlovna, 'I will come and see you again; and you must not lose heart but take your medicine regularly.'

The old woman raised her head and drew herself a little towards Alexandra Pavlovna.

'Give me your little hand, dear lady,' she muttered.

Alexandra Pavlovna did not give her hand; she bent over her and kissed her on the forehead.

'Take care, now,' she said to the old man as she went out, 'and give her the medicine without fail, as it is written down, and give her some tea to drink.'

Again the old man made no reply, but only bowed.

Alexandra Pavlovna breathed more freely when she came out into the fresh air. She put up her parasol and was about to start homewards, when suddenly there appeared round the corner of a little hut a man about thirty, driving a low racing droshky and wearing an old overcoat of grey linen, and a foraging cap of the same. Catching sight of Alexandra Pavlovna he at once stopped his horse and turned round towards her. His broad and colourless face with its small light grey eyes and almost white moustache seemed all in the same tone of colour as his clothes.

'Good-morning!' he began, with a lazy smile; 'what are you doing here, if I may ask?'

'I have been visiting a sick woman... And where have you come from, Mihailo Mihailitch?'

The man addressed as Mihailo Mihailitch looked into her eyes and smiled again.

'You do well,' he said, 'to visit the sick, but wouldn't it be better for you to take her into the hospital?'

'She is too weak; impossible to move her.'

'But don't you intend to give up your hospital?'

'Give it up? Why?'

'Oh, I thought so.'

'What a strange notion! What put such an idea into your head?'

'Oh, you are always with Madame Lasunsky now, you know, and seem to be under her influence. And in her words—hospitals, schools, and all that sort of things, are mere waste of time—useless fads. Philanthropy ought to be entirely personal, and education too, all that is the soul's work... that's how she expresses herself, I believe. From whom did she pick up that opinion I should like to know?'

Alexandra Pavlovna laughed.

'Darya Mihailovna is a clever woman, I like and esteem her very much; but she may make mistakes, and I don't put faith in everything she says.'

'And it's a very good thing you don't,' rejoined Mihailo Mihailitch, who all the while remained sitting in his droshky, 'for she doesn't put much faith in what she says herself. I'm very glad I met you.'

'Why?'

'That's a nice question! As though it wasn't always delightful to meet you? To-day you look as bright and fresh as this morning.'

Alexandra Pavlovna laughed again.

'What are you laughing at?'

'What, indeed! If you could see with what a cold and indifferent face you brought out your compliment! I wonder you didn't yawn over the last word!'

'A cold face.... You always want fire; but fire is of no use at all. It flares and smokes and goes out.'

'And warms,'... put in Alexandra Pavlovna.

'Yes... and burns.'

'Well, what if it does burn! That's no great harm either! It's better anyway than——'

'Well, we shall see what you will say when you do get nicely burnt one day,' Mihailo Mihailitch interrupted her in a tone of vexation and made a cut at the horse with the reins, 'Good-bye.'

'Mihailo Mihailitch, stop a minute!' cried Alexandra Pavlovna, 'when are you coming to see us?'

'To-morrow; my greetings to your brother.'

And the droshky rolled away.

Alexandra Pavlovna looked after Mihailo Mihailitch.

'What a sack!' she thought. Sitting huddled up and covered with dust, his cap on the back of his head and tufts of flaxen hair straggling from beneath it, he looked strikingly like a huge sack of flour.

Alexandra Pavlovna turned tranquilly back along the path homewards. She was walking with downcast eyes. The tramp of a horse near made her stop and raise her head.... Her brother had come on horseback to meet her; beside him was walking a young man of medium height, wearing a light open coat, a light tie, and a light grey hat, and carrying a cane in his hand. He had been smiling for a long time at Alexandra Pavlovna, even though he saw that she was absorbed in thought and noticing nothing, and when she stopped he went up to her and in a tone of delight, almost of emotion, cried:

'Good-morning, Alexandra Pavlovna, good-morning!'

'Ah! Konstantin Diomiditch! good-morning!' she replied. 'You have come from Darya Mihailovna?'

'Precisely so, precisely so,' rejoined the young man with a radiant face, 'from Darya Mihailovna. Darya Mihailovna sent me to you; I preferred to walk.... It's such a glorious morning, and the distance is only three miles. When I arrived, you were not at home. Your brother told me you had gone to Semenovka; and he was just going out to the fields; so you see I walked with him to meet you. Yes, yes. How very delightful!'

The young man spoke Russian accurately and grammatically but with a foreign accent, though it was difficult to determine exactly what accent it was. In his features there was something Asiatic. His long hook nose, his large expressionless prominent eyes, his thick red lips, and retreating forehead, and his jet black hair,—everything about him suggested an Oriental extraction; but the young man gave his surname as Pandalevsky and spoke of Odessa as his birthplace, though he was brought up somewhere in White Russia at the expense of a rich and benevolent widow.

Another widow had obtained a government post for him. Middle-aged ladies were generally ready to befriend Konstantin Diomiditch; he knew well how to court them and was successful in coming across them. He was at this very time living with a rich lady, a landowner, Darya Mihailovna Lasunsky, in a position between that of a guest and of a dependant. He was very polite and obliging, full of sensibility and secretly given to sensuality, he had a pleasant voice, played well on the piano, and had the habit of gazing intently into the eyes of any one he was speaking to. He dressed very neatly, and wore his clothes a very long time, shaved his broad chin carefully, and arranged his hair curl by curl.

Alexandra Pavlovna heard his speech to the end and turned to her brother.

'I keep meeting people to-day; I have just been talking to Lezhnyov.'

'Oh, Lezhnyov! was he driving somewhere?'

'Yes, and fancy; he was in a racing droshky, and dressed in a kind of linen sack, all covered with dust.... What a queer creature he is!'

'Perhaps so; but he's a capital fellow.'

'Who? Mr. Lezhnyov?' inquired Pandalevsky, as though he were surprised.

'Yes, Mihailo Mihailitch Lezhnyov,' replied Volintsev. 'Well, good-bye; it's time I was off to the field; they are sowing your buckwheat. Mr. Pandalevsky will escort you home.' And Volintsev rode off at a trot.

'With the greatest of pleasure!' cried Konstantin Diomiditch, offering Alexandra Pavlovna his arm.

She took it and they both turned along the path to her house.

Walking with Alexandra Pavlovna on his arm seemed to afford Konstantin Diomiditch great delight; he moved with little steps, smiling, and his Oriental eyes were even be-dimmed by a slight moisture, though this indeed was no rare occurrence with them; it did not mean much for Konstantin Diomiditch to be moved and dissolve into tears. And who would not have been pleased to have on his arm a pretty, young and graceful woman? Of Alexandra Pavlovna the whole of her district was unanimous in declaring that she was charming, and the district was not wrong. Her straight, ever so slightly tilted nose would have been enough alone to drive any man out of his senses, to say nothing of her velvety dark eyes, her golden brown hair, the dimples in her smoothly curved cheeks, and her other beauties. But best of all was the sweet expression of her face; confiding, good and gentle, it touched and attracted at the same time. Alexandra Pavlovna had the glance and the smile of a child; other ladies found her a little simple.... Could one wish for anything more?

'Darya Mihailovna sent you to me, did you say?' she asked Pandalevsky.

'Yes; she sent me,' he answered, pronouncing the letter *s* like the English *th*. 'She particularly wishes and told me to beg you very urgently to be so good as to dine with her to-day. She is expecting a new guest whom she particularly wishes you to meet.'

'Who is it?'

'A certain Muffel, a baron, a gentleman of the bed-chamber from Petersburg. Darya Mihailovna made his acquaintance lately at the Prince Garin's, and speaks of him in high terms as an agreeable and cultivated young man. His Excellency the baron is interested, too, in literature, or more strictly speaking——ah! what an exquisite butterfly! pray look at it!——more strictly speaking, in political economy. He has written an essay on some very interesting question, and wants to submit it to Darya Mihailovna's criticism.'

'An article on political economy?'

'From the literary point of view, Alexandra Pavlovna, from the literary point of view. You are well aware, I suppose, that in that line Darya Mihailovna is an authority. Zhukovsky used to ask her advice, and my benefactor, who lives at Odessa, that benevolent old man, Roxolan Mediarovitch Ksandrika——No doubt you know the name of that eminent man?'

'No; I have never heard of him.'

'You never heard of such a man? surprising! I was going to say that Roxolan Mediarovitch always had the very highest opinion of Darya Mihailovna's knowledge of Russian!

'Is this baron a pedant then?' asked Alexandra Pavlovna.

'Not in the very least. Darya Mihailovna says, on the contrary, that you see that he belongs to the best society at once. He spoke of Beethoven with such eloquence that even the old prince was quite delighted by it. That, I own, I should like to have heard; you know that is in my line. Allow me to offer you this lovely wild-flower.'

Alexandra Pavlovna took the flower, and when she had walked a few steps farther, let it drop on the path. They were not more than two hundred paces from her house. It had been recently built and whitewashed, and looked out hospitably with its wide light windows from the thick foliage of the old limes and maples.

'So what message do you give me for Darya Mihailovna?' began Pandalevsky, slightly hurt at the fate of the flower he had given her. 'Will you come to dinner? She invites your brother too.'

'Yes; we will come, most certainly. And how is Natasha?'

'Natalya Alexyevna is well, I am glad to say. But we have already passed the road that turns off to Darya Mihailovna's. Allow me to bid you good-bye.'

Alexandra Pavlovna stopped. 'But won't you come in?' she said in a hesitating voice.

'I should like to, indeed, but I am afraid it is late. Darya Mihailovna wishes to hear a new etude of Thalberg's, so I must practise and have it ready. Besides, I am doubtful, I must confess, whether my visit could afford you any pleasure.'

'Oh, no! why?'

Pandalevsky sighed and dropped his eyes expressively.

'Good-bye, Alexandra Pavlovna!' he said after a slight pause; then he bowed and turned back.

Alexandra Pavlovna turned round and went home.

Konstantin Diomiditch, too, walked homewards. All softness had vanished at once from his face; a self-confident, almost hard expression came into it. Even his walk was changed; his steps were longer and he trod more heavily. He had walked about two miles, carelessly swinging his cane, when all at once he began to smile again: he saw by the roadside a young, rather pretty peasant girl, who was driving some calves out of an oat-field. Konstantin Diomiditch approached the girl as warily as a cat, and began to speak to her. She said nothing at first, only blushed and laughed, but at last she hid her face in her sleeve, turned away, and muttered:

'Go away, sir; upon my word...'

Konstantin Diomiditch shook his finger at her and told her to bring him some cornflowers.

'What do you want with cornflowers?—to make a wreath?' replied the girl; 'come now, go along then.'

'Stop a minute, my pretty little dear,' Konstantin Diomiditch was beginning.

'There now, go along,' the girl interrupted him, 'there are the young gentlemen coming.'

Konstantin Diomiditch looked round. There really were Vanya and Petya, Darya Mihailovna's sons, running along the road; after them walked their tutor, Bassistoff, a young man of two-and-twenty, who had only just left college. Bassistoff was a well-grown youth, with a simple face, a large nose, thick lips, and small pig's eyes, plain and awkward, but kind, good, and upright. He dressed untidily and wore his hair long—not from affectation, but from laziness; he liked eating and he liked sleeping, but he also liked a good book, and an earnest conversation, and he hated Pandalevsky from the depths of his soul.

Darya Mihailovna's children worshipped Bassistoff, and yet were not in the least afraid of him; he was on a friendly footing with all the rest of the household, a fact which was not altogether pleasing to its mistress, though she was fond of declaring that for her social prejudices did not exist.

'Good-morning, my dears,' began Konstantin Diomiditch, 'how early you have come for your walk to-day! But I,' he added, turning to Bassistoff, 'have been out a long while already; it's my passion—to enjoy nature.'

'We saw how you were enjoying nature,' muttered Bassistoff.

'You are a materialist, God knows what you are imagining! I know you.' When Pandalevsky spoke to Bassistoff or people like him, he grew slightly irritated, and pronounced the letter *s* quite clearly, even with a slight hiss.

'Why, were you asking your way of that girl, am I to suppose?' said Bassistoff, shifting his eyes to right and to left.

He felt that Pandalevsky was looking him straight in the face, and this fact was exceedingly unpleasant to him. 'I repeat, a materialist and nothing more.'

'You certainly prefer to see only the prosaic side in everything.'

'Boys!' cried Bassistoff suddenly, 'do you see that willow at the corner? let's see who can get to it first. One! two! three! and away!'

The boys set off at full speed to the willow. Bassistoff rushed after them.

'What a lout!' thought Pandalevsky, 'he is spoiling those boys. A perfect peasant!'

And looking with satisfaction at his own neat and elegant figure, Konstantin Diomiditch struck his coat-sleeve twice with his open hand, pulled up his collar, and went on his way. When he had reached his own room, he put on an old dressing-gown and sat down with an anxious face to the piano.

II

Darya Mihailovna's house was regarded as almost the first in the whole province. It was a huge stone mansion, built after designs of Rastrelli in the taste of last century, and in a commanding position on the summit of a hill, at whose base flowed one of the principal rivers of central Russia. Darya Mihailovna herself was a wealthy and distinguished lady, the widow of a privy councillor. Pandalevsky said of her, that she knew all Europe and all Europe knew her! However, Europe knew her very little; even at Petersburg she had not played a very prominent part; but on the other hand at Moscow every one knew her and visited her. She belonged to the highest society, and was spoken of as a rather eccentric woman, not wholly good-natured, but excessively clever. In her youth she had been very pretty. Poets had written verses to her, young men had been in love with her, distinguished men had paid her homage. But twenty-five or thirty years had passed since those days and not a trace of her former charms remained. Every one who saw her now for the first time was impelled to ask himself, if this woman—skinny, sharp-nosed, and yellow-faced, though still not old in years—could once have been a beauty, if she was really the same woman who had been the inspiration of poets.... And every one marvelled inwardly at the mutability of earthly things. It is true that Pandalevsky discovered that Darya Mihailovna had preserved her magnificent eyes in a marvellous way; but we have seen that Pandalevsky also maintained that all Europe knew her.

Darya Mihailovna went every summer to her country place with her children (she had three: a daughter of seventeen, Natalya, and two sons of nine and ten years old). She kept open house in the country, that is, she received men, especially unmarried ones; provincial ladies she could not endure. But what of the treatment she received from those ladies in return?

Darya Mihailovna, according to them, was a haughty, immoral, and insufferable tyrant, and above all—she permitted herself such liberties in conversation, it was shocking! Darya Mihailovna certainly did not care to stand on ceremony in the country, and in the unconstrained frankness of her manners there was perceptible a slight shade of the contempt of the lioness of the capital for the petty and obscure creatures who surrounded her. She had a careless, and even a sarcastic manner with her own set; but the shade of contempt was not there.

By the way, reader, have you observed that a person who is exceptionally nonchalant with his inferiors, is never nonchalant with persons of a higher rank? Why is that? But such questions lead to nothing.

When Konstantin Diomiditch, having at last learnt by heart the *etude* of Thalberg, went down from his bright and cheerful room to the drawing-room, he already found the whole household assembled. The salon was already beginning. The lady of the house was reposing on a wide couch, her feet gathered up under her, and a new French pamphlet in her hand; at the window behind a tambour frame, sat on one side the daughter of Darya Mihailovna, on the other, Mlle. Boncourt, the governess, a dry old maiden lady of sixty, with a false front of black curls under a parti-coloured cap and cotton wool in her ears; in the corner near the door was huddled Bassistoff reading a paper, near him were Petya and Vanya playing draughts, and leaning by the stove, his hands clasped behind his back, was a gentleman of low stature, with a swarthy face covered with bristling grey hair, and fiery black eyes—a certain African Semenitch Pigasov.

This Pigasov was a strange person. Full of acerbity against everything and every one—especially against women—he was railing from morning to night, sometimes very aptly, sometimes rather stupidly, but always with gusto. His ill-humour almost approached puerility; his laugh, the sound of his voice, his whole being seemed steeped in venom. Darya Mihailovna gave Pigasov a cordial reception; he amused her with his sallies. They were certainly absurd enough. He took delight in perpetual exaggeration. For example, if he were told of any disaster, that a village had been struck by lightning, or that a mill had been carried away by floods, or that a peasant had cut his hand with an axe, he invariably asked with concentrated bitterness, 'And what's her name?' meaning, what is the name of the woman responsible for this calamity, for according to his convictions, a woman was the cause of every misfortune, if you only looked deep enough into the matter. He once threw himself on his knees before a lady he hardly knew at all, who had been effusive in her hospitality to him and began tearfully, but with wrath written on his face, to entreat her to have compassion on him, saying that he had done her no harm and never would come to see her for the future. Once a horse had bolted with one of Darya Mihailovna's maids, thrown her into a ditch and almost killed her. From that time Pigasov never spoke of that horse except as the 'good, good horse,' and he even came to regard the hill and the ditch as specially picturesque spots. Pigasov had failed in life and had adopted this whimsical craze. He came of poor parents. His father had filled various petty posts, and could scarcely read and write, and did not trouble himself about his son's education; he fed and clothed him and nothing more. His mother spoiled him, but she died early. Pigasov educated himself, sent himself to the district school and then to the gymnasium, taught himself French, German, and even Latin, and, leaving the gymnasiums with an excellent certificate, went to Dorpat, where he maintained a perpetual struggle with poverty, but succeeded in completing his three years' course. Pigasov's abilities did not rise above the level of mediocrity; patience and perseverance were his strong points, but the most powerful sentiment in him was ambition, the desire to get into good society, not to be inferior to others in spite of fortune. He had studied diligently and gone to the Dorpat University from ambition. Poverty exasperated him, and made him watchful and cunning. He expressed himself with originality; from his youth he had adopted a special kind of stinging and exasperated eloquence. His ideas did not rise above the common level; but his way of speaking made him seem not only a clever, but even a very clever, man. Having taken his degree as candidate, Pigasov decided to devote himself to the scholastic profession; he understood that in any other career he could not possibly be the equal of his associates. He tried to select them from a higher rank and knew how to gain their good graces; even by flattery, though he was always abusing them. But to do this he had not, to speak plainly, enough raw material. Having educated himself through no love for study, Pigasov knew very little thoroughly. He broke down miserably in the public disputation, while another student who had shared the same room with him, and who was constantly the subject of his ridicule, a man of very limited ability who had received a careful and solid education, gained a complete triumph. Pigasov was infuriated by this failure, he threw all his books and manuscripts into the fire and went into a government office. At first he did not get on badly, he made a fair official, not very active, extremely self-confident and bold, however; but he wanted to make his way more quickly, he made a false step, got into trouble, and was obliged to retire from the service. He spent three years on the property he had bought himself and suddenly married a wealthy half-educated woman who was captivated by his unceremonious and sarcastic manners. But Pigasov's character had become so soured and irritable that family life was unendurable to him. After living with him a few years, his wife went off secretly to Moscow and sold her estate to an enterprising speculator; Pigasov had only just finished building a house on it. Utterly crushed by this last blow, Pigasov began a lawsuit with his wife, but gained nothing by it. After this he lived in solitude, and went to see his neighbours, whom he abused behind their backs and even to their faces, and who welcomed him with a kind of constrained half-laugh, though he did not inspire them with any serious dread. He never took a book in his hand. He had about a hundred serfs; his peasants were not badly off.

'Ah! *Constantin*,' said Darya Mihailovna, when Pandalevsky came into the drawing-room, 'is *Alexandrine* coming?'

'Alexandra Pavlovna asked me to thank you, and they will be extremely delighted,' replied Konstantin Diomiditch, bowing affably in all directions, and running his plump white hand with its triangular cut nails through his faultlessly arranged hair.

'And is Volintsev coming too?'

'Yes.'

'So, according to you, African Semenitch,' continued Darya Mihailovna, turning to Pigasov, 'all young ladies are affected?'

Pigasov's mouth twitched, and he plucked nervously at his elbow.

'I say,' he began in a measured voice—in his most violent moods of exasperation he always spoke slowly and precisely. 'I say that young ladies, in general—of present company, of course, I say nothing.'

'But that does not prevent your thinking of them,' put in Darya Mihailovna.

'I say nothing of them,' repeated Pigasov. 'All young ladies, in general, are affected to the most extreme point—affected in the expression of their feelings. If a young lady is frightened, for instance, or pleased with anything, or distressed, she is certain first to throw her person into some such elegant attitude (and Pigasov threw his figure into an unbecoming pose and spread out his hands) and then she shrieks—ah! or she laughs or cries. I did once though (and here Pigasov smiled complacently) succeed in eliciting a genuine, unaffected expression of emotion from a remarkably affected young lady!'

'How did you do that?'

Pigasov's eyes sparkled.

'I poked her in the side with an aspen stake, from behind. She did shriek, and I said to her, "Bravo, bravo! that's the voice of nature, that was a genuine shriek! Always do like that for the future!"'

Every one in the room laughed.

'What nonsense you talk, African Semenitch,' cried Darya Mihailovna. 'Am I to believe that you would poke a girl in the side with a stake!'

'Yes, indeed, with a stake, a very big stake, like those that are used in the defence of a fort.'

'*Mais c'est un horreur ce que vous dites la, Monsieur*,' cried Mlle. Boncourt, looking angrily at the boys, who were in fits of laughter.

'Oh, you mustn't believe him,' said Darya Mihailovna. 'Don't you know him?'

But the offended French lady could not be pacified for a long while, and kept muttering something to herself.

'You need not believe me,' continued Pigasov coolly, 'but I assure you I told the simple truth. Who should know if not I? After that perhaps you won't believe that our neighbour, Madame Tchepuz, Elena Antonovna, told me herself, mind *herself*, that she had murdered her nephew?'

'What an invention!'

'Wait a minute, wait a minute! Listen and judge for yourselves. Mind, I don't want to slander her, I even like her as far as one can like a woman. She hasn't a single book in her house except a calendar, and she can't read except aloud, and that exercise throws her into a violent perspiration, and she complains then that her eyes feel bursting out of her head.... In short, she's a capital woman, and her servant girls grow fat. Why should I slander her?'

'You see,' observed Darya Mihailovna, 'African Semenitch has got on his hobbyhorse, now he will not be off it to-night.'

'My hobby! But women have three at least, which they are never off, except, perhaps, when they're asleep.'

'What three hobbies are those?'

'Reproof, reproach, recrimination.'

'Do you know, African Semenitch,' began Darya Mihailovna, 'you cannot be so bitter against women for nothing. Some woman or other must have——'

'Done me an injury, you mean?' Pigasov interrupted.

Darya Mihailovna was rather embarrassed; she remembered Pigasov's unlucky marriage, and only nodded.

'One woman certainly did me an injury,' said Pigasov, 'though she was a good, very good one.'

'Who was that?'

'My mother,' said Pigasov, dropping his voice.

'Your mother? What injury could she have done you?'

'She brought me into the world.'

Darya Mihailovna frowned.

'Our conversation,' she said, 'seems to have taken a gloomy turn. *Constantin*, play us Thalberg's new *etude*. I daresay the music will soothe African Semenitch. Orpheus soothed savage beasts.'

Konstantin Diomiditch took his seat at the piano, and played the etude very fairly well. Natalya Alexyevna at first listened attentively, then she bent over her work again.

'*Merci, c'est charmant*,' observed Darya Mihailovna, 'I love Thalberg. *Il est si distingue*. What are you thinking of, African Semenitch?'

'I thought,' began African Semenitch slowly, 'that there are three kinds of egoists; the egoists who live themselves and let others live; the egoists who live themselves and don't let others live; and the egoists who don't live themselves and don't let others live. Women, for the most part, belong to the third class.'

'That's polite! I am very much astonished at one thing, African Semenitch; your confidence in your convictions; of course you can never be mistaken.'

'Who says so? I make mistakes; a man, too, may be mistaken. But do you know the difference between a man's mistakes and a woman's? Don't you know? Well, here it is; a man may say, for example, that twice two makes not four, but five, or three and a half; but a woman will say that twice two makes a wax candle.'

'I fancy I've heard you say that before. But allow me to ask what connection had your idea of the three kinds of egoists with the music you have just been hearing?'

'None at all, but I did not listen to the music.'

'Well, "incurable I see you are, and that is all about it,"' answered Darya Mihailovna, slightly altering Griboyedov's line. 'What do you like, since you don't care for music? Literature?'

'I like literature, only not our contemporary literature.'

'Why?'

'I'll tell you why. I crossed the Oka lately in a ferry boat with a gentleman. The ferry got fixed in a narrow place; they had to drag the carriages ashore by hand. This gentleman had a very heavy coach. While the ferrymen were straining themselves to drag the coach on to the bank, the gentleman groaned so, standing in the ferry, that one felt quite sorry for him.... Well, I thought, here's a fresh illustration of the system of division of labour! That's just like our modern literature; other people do the work, and it does the groaning.'

Darya Mihailovna smiled.

'And that is called expressing contemporary life,' continued Pigasov indefatigably, 'profound sympathy with the social question and so on. ... Oh, how I hate those grand words!'

'Well, the women you attack so—they at least don't use grand words.'

Pigasov shrugged his shoulders.

'They don't use them because they don't understand them.'

Darya Mihailovna flushed slightly.

'You are beginning to be impertinent, African Semenitch!' she remarked with a forced smile.

There was complete stillness in the room.

'Where is Zolotonosha?' asked one of the boys suddenly of Bassistoff.

'In the province of Poltava, my dear boy,' replied Pigasov, 'in the centre of Little Russia.' (He was glad of an opportunity of changing the conversation.) 'We were talking of literature,' he continued, 'if I had money to spare, I would at once become a Little Russian poet.'

'What next? a fine poet you would make!' retorted Darya Mihailovna. 'Do you know Little Russian?'

'Not a bit; but it isn't necessary.'

'Not necessary?'

'Oh no, it's not necessary. You need only take a sheet of paper and write at the top "A Ballad," then begin like this, "Heigho, alack, my destiny!" or "the Cossack Nalivaiko was sitting on a hill and then on the mountain, under the green tree the birds are singing, grae, voropae, gop, gop!" or something of that kind. And the thing's done. Print it and publish it. The Little Russian will read it, drop his head into his hands and infallibly burst into tears—he is such a sensitive soul!'

'Good heavens!' cried Bassistoff. 'What are you saying? It's too absurd for anything. I have lived in Little Russia, I love it and know the language... "grae, grae, voropae" is absolute nonsense.'

'It may be, but the Little Russian will weep all the same. You speak of the "language."... But is there a Little Russian language? Is it a language, in your opinion? an independent language? I would pound my best friend in a mortar before I'd agree to that.'

Bassistoff was about to retort.

'Leave him alone!' said Darya Mihailovna, 'you know that you will hear nothing but paradoxes from him.'

Pigasov smiled ironically. A footman came in and announced the arrival of Alexandra Pavlovna and her brother.

Darya Mihailovna rose to meet her guests.

'How do you do, Alexandrine?' she began, going up to her, 'how good of you to come!... How are you, Sergei Pavlitch?'

Volintsev shook hands with Darya Mihailovna and went up to Natalya Alexyevna.

'But how about that baron, your new acquaintance, is he coming to-day?' asked Pigasov.

'Yes, he is coming.'

'He is a great philosopher, they say; he is just brimming over with Hegel, I suppose?'

Darya Mihailovna made no reply, and making Alexandra Pavlovna sit down on the sofa, established herself near her.

'Philosophies,' continued Pigasov, 'are elevated points of view! That's another abomination of mine; these elevated points of view. And what can one see from above? Upon my soul, if you want to buy a horse, you don't look at it from a steeple!'

'This baron was going to bring you an essay?' said Alexandra Pavlovna.

'Yes, an essay,' replied Darya Mihailovna, with exaggerated carelessness, 'on the relation of commerce to manufactures in Russia. ... But don't be afraid; we will not read it here.... I did not invite you for that. *Le baron est aussi aimable que savant*. And he speaks Russian beautifully! *C'est un vrai torrent... il vous entraine*!

'He speaks Russian so beautifully,' grumbled Pigasov, 'that he deserves a eulogy in French.'

'You may grumble as you please, African Semenitch.... It's in keeping with your ruffled locks.... I wonder, though, why he does not come. Do you know what, *messieurs et mesdames*' added Darya Mihailovna, looking round, 'we will go into the garden. There is still nearly an hour to dinner-time and the weather is glorious.'

All the company rose and went into the garden.

Darya Mihailovna's garden stretched right down to the river. There were many alleys of old lime-trees in it, full of sunlight and shade and fragrance and glimpses of emerald green at the ends of the walks, and many arbours of acacias and lilacs.

Volintsev turned into the thickest part of the garden with Natalya and Mlle. Boncourt. He walked beside Natalya in silence. Mlle. Boncourt followed a little behind.

'What have you been doing to-day?' asked Volintsev at last, pulling the ends of his handsome dark brown moustache.

In features he resembled his sister strikingly; but there was less movement and life in his expression, and his soft beautiful eyes had a melancholy look.

'Oh! nothing,' answered Natalya, 'I have been listening to Pigasov's sarcasms, I have done some embroidery on canvas, and I've been reading.'

'And what have you been reading?'

'Oh! I read—a history of the Crusades,' said Natalya, with some hesitation.

Volintsev looked at her.

'Ah!' he ejaculated at last, 'that must be interesting.'

He picked a twig and began to twirl it in the air. They walked another twenty paces.

'What is this baron whom your mother has made acquaintance with?' began Volintsev again.

'A Gentleman of the Bedchamber, a new arrival; *maman* speaks very highly of him.'

'Your mother is quick to take fancies to people.'

'That shows that her heart is still young,' observed Natalya.

'Yes. I shall soon bring you your mare. She is almost quite broken in now. I want to teach her to gallop, and I shall manage it soon.'

'*Merci*!... But I'm quite ashamed. You are breaking her in yourself ... and they say it's so hard!'

'To give you the least pleasure, you know, Natalya Alexyevna, I am ready... I... not in such trifles——'

Volintsev grew confused.

Natalya looked at him with friendly encouragement, and again said '*merci*!'

'You know,' continued Sergei Pavlitch after a long pause, 'that not such things.... But why am I saying this? you know everything, of course.'

At that instant a bell rang in the house.

'Ah! *la cloche du diner*!' cried Mlle. Boncourt, '*rentrons*.'

'*Quel dommage*,' thought the old French lady to herself as she mounted the balcony steps behind Volintsev and Natalya, '*quel dommage que ce charmant garcon ait si peu de ressources dans la conversation*,' which may be translated, 'you are a good fellow, my dear boy, but rather a fool.'

The baron did not arrive to dinner. They waited half-an-hour for him. Conversation flagged at the table. Sergei Pavlitch did nothing but gaze at Natalya, near whom he was sitting, and zealously filled up her glass with water. Pandalevsky tried in vain to entertain his neighbour, Alexandra Pavlovna; he was bubbling over with sweetness, but she hardly refrained from yawning.

Bassistoff was rolling up pellets of bread and thinking of nothing at all; even Pigasov was silent, and when Darya Mihailovna remarked to him that he had not been very polite to-day, he replied crossly, 'When am I polite? that's not in my line;' and smiling grimly he added, 'have a little patience; I am only kvas, you know, *du simple* Russian kvas; but your Gentleman of the Bedchamber——'

'Bravo!' cried Darya Mihailovna, 'Pigasov is jealous, he is jealous already!'

But Pigasov made her no rejoinder, and only gave her a rather cross look.

Seven o'clock struck, and they were all assembled again in the drawing-room.

'He is not coming, clearly,' said Darya Mihailovna.

But, behold, the rumble of a carriage was heard: a small tarantass drove into the court, and a few instants later a footman entered the drawing-room and gave Darya Mihailovna a note on a silver salver. She glanced through it, and turning to the footman asked:

'But where is the gentleman who brought this letter?'

'He is sitting in the carriage. Shall I ask him to come up?'

'Ask him to do so.'

The man went out.

'Fancy, how vexatious!' continued Darya Mihailovna, 'the baron has received a summons to return at once to Petersburg. He has sent me his essay by a certain Mr. Rudin, a friend of his. The baron wanted to introduce him to me—he speaks very highly of him. But how vexatious it is! I had hoped the baron would stay here for some time.'

'Dmitri Nikolaitch Rudin,' announced the servant

III

A man of about thirty-five entered, of a tall, somewhat stooping figure, with crisp curly hair and swarthy complexion, an irregular but expressive and intelligent face, a liquid brilliance in his quick, dark blue eyes, a straight, broad nose, and well-curved lips. His clothes were not new, and were somewhat small, as though he had outgrown them.

He walked quickly up to Darya Mihailovna, and with a slight bow told her that he had long wished to have the honour of an introduction to her, and that his friend the baron greatly regretted that he could not take leave of her in person.

The thin sound of Rudin's voice seemed out of keeping with his tall figure and broad chest.

'Pray be seated... very delighted,' murmured Darya Mihailovna, and, after introducing him to the rest of the company, she asked him whether he belonged to those parts or was a visitor.

'My estate is in the T—— province,' replied Rudin, holding his hat on his knees. 'I have not been here long. I came on business and stayed for a while in your district town.'

'With whom?'

'With the doctor. He was an old chum of mine at the university.'

'Ah! the doctor. He is highly spoken of. He is skilful in his work, they say. But have you known the baron long?'

'I met him last winter in Moscow, and I have just been spending about a week with him.'

'He is a very clever man, the baron.'

'Yes.'

Darya Mihailovna sniffed at her little crushed-up handkerchief steeped in *eau de cologne*.

'Are you in the government service?' she asked.

'Who? I?'

'Yes.'

'No. I have retired.'

There followed a brief pause. The general conversation was resumed.

'If you will allow me to be inquisitive,' began Pigasov, turning to Rudin, 'do you know the contents of the essay which his excellency the baron has sent?'

'Yes, I do.'

'This essay deals with the relations to commerce—or no, of manufactures to commerce in our country.... That was your expression, I think, Darya Mihailovna?'

'Yes, it deals with'... began Darya Mihailovna, pressing her hand to her forehead.

'I am, of course, a poor judge of such matters,' continued Pigasov, 'but I must confess that to me even the title of the essay seems excessively (how could I put it delicately?) excessively obscure and complicated.'

'Why does it seem so to you?'

Pigasov smiled and looked across at Darya Mihailovna.

'Why, is it clear to you?' he said, turning his foxy face again towards Rudin.

'To me? Yes.'

'H'm. No doubt you must know better.'

'Does your head ache?' Alexandra Pavlovna inquired of Darya Mihailovna.

'No. It is only my—*c'est nerveux*.'

'Allow me to inquire,' Pigasov was beginning again in his nasal tones, 'your friend, his excellency Baron Muffel—I think that's his name?'

'Precisely.'

'Does his excellency Baron Muffel make a special study of political economy, or does he only devote to that interesting subject the hours of leisure left over from his social amusements and his official duties?'

Rudin looked steadily at Pigasov.

'The baron is an amateur on this subject,' he replied, growing rather red, 'but in his essay there is much that is interesting and just.'

'I am not able to dispute it with you; I have not read the essay. But I venture to ask—the work of your friend Baron Muffel is no doubt founded more upon general propositions than upon facts?'

'It contains both facts and propositions founded upon the facts.'

'Yes, yes. I must tell you that, in my opinion—and I've a right to give my opinion, on occasion; I spent three years at Dorpat... all these, so-called general propositions, hypotheses, these systems—excuse me, I am a provincial, I speak the truth bluntly—are absolutely worthless. All that's only theorising—only good for misleading people. Give us facts, sir, and that's enough!'

'Really!' retorted Rudin, 'why, but ought not one to give the significance of the facts?'

'General propositions,' continued Pigasov, 'they're my abomination, these general propositions, theories, conclusions. All that's based on so-called convictions; every one is talking about his convictions, and attaches importance to them, prides himself on them. Ah!'

And Pigasov shook his fist in the air. Pandalevsky laughed.

'Capital!' put in Rudin, 'it follows that there is no such thing as conviction according to you?'

'No, it doesn't exist.'

'Is that your conviction?'

'Yes.'

'How do you say that there are none then? Here you have one at the very first turn.'

All in the room smiled and looked at one another.

'One minute, one minute, but——,' Pigasov was beginning.

But Darya Mihailovna clapped her hands crying, 'Bravo, bravo, Pigasov's beaten!' and she gently took Rudin's hat from his hand.

'Defer your delight a little, madam; there's plenty of time!' Pigasov began with annoyance. 'It's not sufficient to say a witty word, with a show of superiority; you must prove, refute. We had wandered from the subject of our discussion.'

'With your permission,' remarked Rudin, coolly, 'the matter is very simple. You do not believe in the value of general propositions—you do not believe in convictions?'

'I don't believe in them, I don't believe in anything!'

'Very good. You are a sceptic.'

'I see no necessity for using such a learned word. However——'

'Don't interrupt!' interposed Darya Mihailovna.

'At him, good dog!' Pandalevsky said to himself at the same instant, and smiled all over.

'That word expresses my meaning,' pursued Rudin. 'You understand it; why not make use of it? You don't believe in anything. Why do you believe in facts?'

'Why? That's good! Facts are matters of experience, every one knows what facts are. I judge of them by experience, by my own senses.'

'But may not your senses deceive you? Your senses tell you that the sun goes round the earth,... but perhaps you don't agree with Copernicus? You don't even believe in him?'

Again a smile passed over every one's face, and all eyes were fastened on Rudin. 'He's by no means a fool,' every one was thinking.

'You are pleased to keep on joking,' said Pigasov. 'Of course that's very original, but it's not to the point.'

'In what I have said hitherto,' rejoined Rudin, 'there is, unfortunately, too little that's original. All that has been well known a very long time, and has been said a thousand times. That is not the pith of the matter.'

'What is then?' asked Pigasov, not without insolence.

In discussions he always first bantered his opponent, then grew cross, and finally sulked and was silent.

'Here it is,' continued Rudin. 'I cannot help, I own, feeling sincere regret when I hear sensible people attack——'

'Systems?' interposed Pigasov.

'Yes, with your leave, even systems. What frightens you so much in that word? Every system is founded on a knowledge of fundamental laws, the principles of life——'

'But there is no knowing them, no discovering them.'

'One minute. Doubtless they are not easy for every one to get at, and to make mistakes is natural to man. However, you will certainly agree with me that Newton, for example, discovered some at least of these fundamental laws? He was a genius, we grant you; but the grandeur of the discoveries of genius is that they become the heritage of all. The effort to discover universal principles in the multiplicity of phenomena is one of the radical characteristics of human thought, and all our civilisation——'

'That's what you're driving at!' Pigasov broke in in a drawling tone. 'I am a practical man and all these metaphysical subtleties I don't enter into and don't want to enter into.'

'Very good! That's as you prefer. But take note that your very desire to be exclusively a practical man is itself your sort of system—your theory.'

'Civilisation you talk about!' blurted in Pigasov; 'that's another admirable notion of yours! Much use in it, this vaunted civilisation! I would not give a brass farthing for your civilisation!'

'But what a poor sort of argument, African Semenitch!' observed Darya Mihailovna, inwardly much pleased by the calmness and perfect good-breeding of her new acquaintance. '*Cest un homme comme il faut*,' she thought, looking with well-disposed scrutiny at Rudin; 'we must be nice to him!' Those last words she mentally pronounced in Russian.

'I will not champion civilisation,' continued Rudin after a short pause, 'it does not need my championship. You don't like it, every one to his own taste. Besides, that would take us too far. Allow me only to remind you of the old saying, "Jupiter, you are angry; therefore you are in the wrong." I meant to say that all those onslaughts upon systems—general propositions—are especially distressing, because together with these systems men repudiate knowledge in general, and all science and faith in it, and consequently also faith in themselves, in their own powers. But this faith is essential to men; they cannot exist by their sensations alone they are wrong to fear ideas and not to trust in them. Scepticism is always characterised by barrenness and impotence.'

'That's all words!' muttered Pigasov.

'Perhaps so. But allow me to point out to you that when we say "that's all words!" we often wish ourselves to avoid the necessity of saying anything more substantial than mere words.'

'What?' said Pigasov, winking his eyes.

'You understood what I meant,' retorted Rudin, with involuntary, but instantly repressed impatience. 'I repeat, if man has no steady principle in which he trusts, no ground on which he can take a firm stand, how can he form a just estimate of the needs, the tendencies and the future of his country? How can he know what he ought to do, if——'

'I leave you the field,' ejaculated Pigasov abruptly, and with a bow he turned away without looking at any one.

Rudin stared at him, and smiled slightly, saying nothing.

'Aha! he has taken to flight!' said Darya Mihailovna. 'Never mind, Dmitri...! I beg your pardon,' she added with a cordial smile, 'what is your paternal name?'

'Nikolaitch.'

'Never mind, my dear Dmitri Nikolaitch, he did not deceive any of us. He wants to make a show of not wishing to argue any more. He is conscious that he cannot argue with you. But you had better sit nearer to us and let us have a little talk.'

Rudin moved his chair up.

'How is it we have not met till now?' was Darya Mihailovna's question. 'That is what surprises me. Have you read this book? *C'est de Tocqueville, vous savez*?'

And Darya Mihailovna held out the French pamphlet to Rudin.

Rudin took the thin volume in his hand, turned over a few pages of it, and laying it down on the table, replied that he had not read that particular work of M. de Tocqueville, but that he had often reflected on the question treated by him. A conversation began to spring up. Rudin seemed uncertain at first, and not disposed to speak out freely; his words did not come readily, but at last he grew warm and began to speak. In a quarter of an hour his voice was the only sound in the room, All were crowding in a circle round him.

Only Pigasov remained aloof, in a corner by the fireplace. Rudin spoke with intelligence, with fire and with judgment; he showed much learning, wide reading. No one had expected to find in him a remarkable man. His clothes were so shabby, so little was known of him. Every one felt it strange and incomprehensible that such a clever man should have suddenly made his appearance in the country. He seemed all the more wonderful and, one may even say, fascinating to all of them, beginning with Darya Mihailovna. She was pluming herself on having discovered him, and already at this early date was dreaming of how she would introduce Rudin into the world. In her quickness to receive impressions there was much that was almost childish, in spite of her years. Alexandra Pavlovna, to tell the truth, understood little of all that Rudin said, but was full of wonder and delight; her brother too was admiring him. Pandalevsky was watching Darya Mihailovna and was filled with envy. Pigasov thought, 'If I have to give five hundred roubles I will get a nightingale to sing better than that!' But the most impressed of all the party were Bassistoff and Natalya. Scarcely a breath escaped Bassistoff; he sat the whole time with open mouth and round eyes and listened—listened as he had never listened to any one in his life—while Natalya's face was suffused by a crimson flush, and her eyes, fastened unwaveringly on Rudin, were both dimmed and shining.

'What splendid eyes he has!' Volintsev whispered to her.

'Yes, they are.'

'It's only a pity his hands are so big and red.'

Natalya made no reply.

Tea was brought in. The conversation became more general, but still by the sudden unanimity with which every one was silent, directly Rudin opened his mouth, one could judge of the strength of the impression he had produced. Darya Mihailovna suddenly felt inclined to tease Pigasov. She went up to him and said in an undertone, 'Why don't you speak instead of doing nothing but smile sarcastically? Make an effort, challenge him again,' and without waiting for him to answer, she beckoned to Rudin.

'There's one thing more you don't know about him,' she said to him, with a gesture towards Pigasov,—'he is a terrible hater of women, he is always attacking them; pray, show him the true path.'

Rudin involuntarily looked down upon Pigasov; he was a head and shoulders taller. Pigasov almost withered up with fury, and his sour face grew pale.

'Darya Mihailovna is mistaken,' he said in an unsteady voice, 'I do not only attack women; I am not a great admirer of the whole human species.'

'What can have given you such a poor opinion of them?' inquired Rudin.

Pigasov looked him straight in the face.

'The study of my own heart, no doubt, in which I find every day more and more that is base. I judge of others by myself. Possibly this too is erroneous, and I am far worse than others, but what am I to do? it's a habit!'

'I understand you and sympathise with you!' was Rudin's rejoinder. 'What generous soul has not experienced a yearning for self-humiliation? But one ought not to remain in that condition from which there is no outlet beyond.'

'I am deeply indebted for the certificate of generosity you confer on my soul,' retorted Pigasov. 'As for my condition, there's not much amiss with it, so that even if there were an outlet from it, it might go to the deuce, I shouldn't look for it!'

'But that means—pardon the expression—to prefer the gratification of your own pride to the desire to be and live in the truth.'

'Undoubtedly,' cried Pigasov, 'pride—that I understand, and you, I expect, understand, and every one understands; but truth, what is truth? Where is it, this truth?'

'You are repeating yourself, let me warn you,' remarked Darya Mihailovna.

Pigasov shrugged his shoulders.

'Well, where's the harm if I do? I ask: where is truth? Even the philosophers don't know what it is. Kant says it is one thing; but Hegel—no, you're wrong, it's something else.'

'And do you know what Hegel says of it?' asked Rudin, without raising his voice.

'I repeat,' continued Pigasov, flying into a passion, 'that I cannot understand what truth means. According to my idea, it doesn't exist at all in the world, that is to say, the word exists but not the thing itself.'

'Fie, fie!' cried Darya Mihailovna, 'I wonder you're not ashamed to say so, you old sinner! No truth? What is there to live for in the world after that?'

'Well, I go so far as to think, Darya Mihailovna,' retorted Pigasov, in a tone of annoyance, 'that it would be much easier for you, in any case, to live without truth than without your cook, Stepan, who is such a master hand at soups! And what do you want with truth, kindly tell me? you can't trim a bonnet with it!'

'A joke is not an argument,' observed Darya Mihailovna, 'especially when you descend to personal insult.'

'I don't know about truth, but I see speaking it does not answer,' muttered Pigasov, and he turned angrily away.

And Rudin began to speak of pride, and he spoke well. He showed that man without pride is worthless, that pride is the lever by which the earth can be moved from its foundations, but that at the same time he alone deserves the name of man who knows how to control his pride, as the rider does his horse, who offers up his own personality as a sacrifice to the general good.

'Egoism,' so he ended, 'is suicide. The egoist withers like a solitary barren tree; but pride, ambition, as the active effort after perfection, is the source of all that is great.... Yes! a man must prune away the stubborn egoism of his personality to give it the right of self-expression.'

'Can you lend me a pencil?' Pigasov asked Bassistoff.

Bassistoff did not at once understand what Pigasov had asked him.

'What do you want a pencil for?' he said at last

'I want to write down Mr. Rudin's last sentence. If one doesn't write it down, one might forget it, I'm afraid! But you will own, a sentence like that is such a handful of trumps.'

'There are things which it is a shame to laugh at and make fun of, African Semenitch!' said Bassistoff warmly, turning away from Pigasov.

Meanwhile Rudin had approached Natalya. She got up; her face expressed her confusion. Volintsev, who was sitting near her, got up too.

'I see a piano,' began Rudin, with the gentle courtesy of a travelling prince; 'don't you play on it?'

'Yes, I play,' replied Natalya, 'but not very well. Here is Konstantin Diomiditch plays much better than I do.'

Pandalevsky put himself forward with a simper. 'You should not say that, Natalya Alexyevna; your playing is not at all inferior to mine.'

'Do you know Schubert's "Erlkonig"?' asked Rudin.

'He knows it, he knows it!' interposed Darya Mihailovna. 'Sit down, Konstantin. You are fond of music, Dmitri Nikolaitch?'

Rudin only made a slight motion of the head and ran his hand through his hair, as though disposing himself to listen. Pandalevsky began to play.

Natalya was standing near the piano, directly facing Rudin. At the first sound his face was transfigured. His dark blue eyes moved slowly about, from time to time resting upon Natalya. Pandalevsky finished playing.

Rudin said nothing and walked up to the open window. A fragrant mist lay like a soft shroud over the garden; a drowsy scent breathed from the trees near. The stars shed a mild radiance. The summer night was soft—and softened all. Rudin gazed into the dark garden, and looked round.

'That music and this night,' he began, 'reminded me of my student days in Germany; our meetings, our serenades.'

'You have been in Germany then?' said Darya Mihailovna.

'I spent a year at Heidelberg, and nearly a year at Berlin.'

'And did you dress as a student? They say they wear a special dress there.'

'At Heidelberg I wore high boots with spurs, and a hussar's jacket with braid on it, and I let my hair grow to my shoulders. In Berlin the students dress like everybody else.'

'Tell us something of your student life,' said Alexandra Pavlovna.

Rudin complied. He was not altogether successful in narrative. There was a lack of colour in his descriptions. He did not know how to be humorous. However, from relating his own adventures abroad, Rudin soon passed to general themes, the special value of education and science, universities, and university life generally. He sketched in a large and comprehensive picture in broad and striking lines. All listened to him with profound attention. His eloquence was masterly and attractive, not altogether clear, but even this want of clearness added a special charm to his words.

The exuberance of his thought hindered Rudin from expressing himself definitely and exactly. Images followed upon images; comparisons started up one after another—now startlingly bold, now strikingly true. It was not the complacent effort of the practised speaker, but the very breath of inspiration that was felt in his impatient improvising. He did not seek out his words; they came obediently and spontaneously to his lips, and each word seemed to flow straight from his soul, and was burning with all the fire of conviction. Rudin was the master of almost the greatest secret—the music of eloquence. He knew how in striking one chord of the heart to set all the others vaguely quivering and resounding. Many of his listeners, perhaps, did not understand very precisely what his eloquence was about; but their bosoms heaved, it seemed as though veils were lifted before their eyes, something radiant, glorious, seemed shimmering in the distance.

All Rudin's thoughts seemed centred on the future; this lent him something of the impetuous dash of youth... Standing at the window, not looking at any one in special, he spoke, and inspired by the general sympathy and attention, the presence of young women, the beauty of the night, carried along by the tide of his own emotions, he rose to the height of eloquence, of poetry.... The very sound of his voice, intense and soft, increased the fascination; it seemed as though some higher power were speaking through his lips, startling even to himself.... Rudin spoke of what lends eternal significance to the fleeting life of man.

'I remember a Scandinavian legend,' thus he concluded, 'a king is sitting with his warriors round the fire in a long dark barn. It was night and winter. Suddenly a little bird flew in at the open door and flew out again at the other. The king spoke and said that this bird is like man in the world; it flew in from darkness and out again into darkness, and was not long in the warmth and light.... "King," replies the oldest of the warriors, "even in the dark the bird is not lost, but finds her nest." Even so our life is short and worthless; but all that is great is accomplished through men. The consciousness of being the instrument of these higher powers ought to outweigh all other joys for man; even in death he finds his life, his nest.'

Rudin stopped and dropped his eyes with a smile of involuntary embarrassment.

'*Vous etes un poete*,' was Darya Mihailovna's comment in an undertone. And all were inwardly agreeing with her—all except Pigasov. Without waiting for the end of Rudin's long speech, he quietly took his hat and as he went out whispered viciously to Pandalevsky who was standing near the door:

'No! Fools are more to my taste.'

No one, however, tried to detain him or even noticed his absence.

The servants brought in supper, and half an hour later, all had taken leave and separated. Darya Mihailovna begged Rudin to remain the night. Alexandra Pavlovna, as she went home in the carriage with her brother, several times fell to exclaiming and marvelling at the extraordinary cleverness of Rudin. Volintsev agreed with her, though he observed that he sometimes expressed himself somewhat obscurely—that is to say, not altogether intelligibly, he added,—wishing, no doubt, to make his own thought clear, but his face was gloomy, and his eyes, fixed on a corner of the carriage, seemed even more melancholy than usual.

Pandalevsky went to bed, and as he took off his daintily embroidered braces, he said aloud 'A very smart fellow!' and suddenly, looking harshly at his page, ordered him out of the room. Bassistoff did not sleep the whole night and did not undress—he was writing till morning a letter to a comrade of his in Moscow; and Natalya, too, though she undressed and lay down in her bed, had not an instant's sleep and never closed her eyes. With her head propped on her arm, she gazed fixedly into the darkness; her veins were throbbing feverishly and her bosom often heaved with a deep sigh.

IV

The next morning Rudin had only just finished dressing when a servant came to him with an invitation from Darya Mihailovna to come to her boudoir and drink tea with her. Rudin found her alone. She greeted him very cordially, inquired whether he had passed a good night, poured him out a cup of tea with her own hands, asked him whether there was sugar enough in it, offered him a cigarette, and twice again repeated that she was surprised that she had not met him long before. Rudin was about to take a seat some distance away; but Darya Mihailovna motioned him to an easy chair, which stood near her lounge, and bending a little towards him began to question him about his family, his plans and intentions. Darya Mihailovna spoke carelessly and listened with an air of indifference; but it was perfectly evident to Rudin that she was laying herself out to please him, even to flatter him. It was not for nothing that she had arranged this morning interview, and had dressed so simply yet elegantly *a la Madame Recamier*! But Darya Mihailovna soon left off questioning him. She began to tell him about herself, her youth, and the people she had known. Rudin gave a sympathetic attention to her lucubrations, though—a curious fact—whatever personage Darya Mihailovna might be talking about, she always stood in the foreground, she alone, and the personage seemed to be effaced, to slink away in the background, and to disappear. But to make up for that, Rudin learnt in full detail precisely what Darya Mihailovna had said to a certain distinguished statesman, and what influence she had had on such and such a celebrated poet. To judge from Darya Mihailovna's accounts, one might fancy that all the distinguished men of the last five-and-twenty years had dreamt of nothing but how they could make her acquaintance, and gain her good opinion. She spoke of them simply, without particular enthusiasm or admiration, as though they were her daily associates, calling some of them queer fellows. As she talked of them, like a rich setting round a worthless stone, their names ranged themselves in a brilliant circlet round the principal name—around Darya Mihailovna.

Rudin listened, smoking a cigarette, and said little. He could speak well and liked speaking; carrying on a conversation was not in his line, though he was also a good listener. All men—if only they had not been intimidated by him to begin with—opened their hearts with confidence in his presence; he followed the thread of another man's narrative so readily and sympathetically. He had a great deal of good-nature—that special good-nature of which men are full, who are accustomed to feel themselves superior to others. In arguments he seldom allowed his antagonist to express himself fully, he crushed him by his eager, vehement and passionate dialectic.

Darya Mihailovna expressed herself in Russian. She prided herself on her knowledge of her own language, though French words and expressions often escaped her. She intentionally made use of simple popular terms of speech; but not always successfully. Rudin's ear was not outraged by the strange medley of language on Darya Mihailovna's lips, indeed he hardly had an ear for it.

Darya Mihailovna was exhausted at last and letting her head fall on the cushions of her easy-chair she fixed her eyes on Rudin and was silent.

'I understand now,' began Rudin, speaking slowly, 'I understand why you come every summer into the country. This period of rest is essential for you; the peace of the country after your life in the capital refreshes and strengthens you. I am convinced that you must be profoundly sensitive to the beauties of nature.'

Darya Mihailovna gave Rudin a sidelong look.

'Nature—yes—yes—of course.... I am passionately fond of it; but do you know, Dmitri Nikolaitch, even in the country one cannot do without society. And here there is practically none. Pigasov is the most intelligent person here.'

'The cross old gentleman who was here last night?' inquired Rudin.

'Yes.... In the country though, even he is of use—he sometimes makes one laugh.'

'He is by no means stupid,' returned Rudin, 'but he is on the wrong path. I don't know whether you will agree with me, Darya Mihailovna, but in negation—in complete and universal negation—there is no salvation to be found? Deny everything and you will easily pass for a man of ability; it's a well-known trick. Simple-hearted people are quite ready to conclude that you are worth more than what you deny. And that's often an error. In the first place, you can pick holes in anything; and secondly, even if you are right in what you say, it's the worse for you; your intellect, directed by simple negation, grows colourless and withers up. While you gratify your vanity, you are deprived of the true consolations of thought; life—the essence of life—evades your petty and jaundiced criticism, and you end by scolding and becoming ridiculous. Only one who loves has the right to censure and find fault.'

'Voila, Monsieur Pigasov enterre,' observed Darya Mihailovna. 'What a genius you have for defining a man! But Pigasov certainly would not have even understood you. He loves nothing but his own individuality.'

'And he finds fault with that so as to have the right to find fault with others,' Rudin put in.

Darya Mihailovna laughed.

'"He judges the sound," as the saying is, "the sound by the sick." By the way, what do you think of the baron?'

'The baron? He is an excellent man, with a good heart and a knowledge ... but he has no character... and he will remain all his life half a savant, half a man of the world, that is to say, a dilettante, that is to say, to speak plainly,—neither one thing nor the other. ... But it's a pity!'

'That was my own idea,' observed Darya Mihailovna. 'I read his article.... *Entre nous... cela a assez peu de fond!*'

'Who else have you here?' asked Rudin, after a pause.

Darya Mihailovna knocked off the ash of her cigarette with her little finger.

'Oh, there is hardly any one else. Madame Lipin, Alexandra Pavlovna, whom you saw yesterday; she is very sweet—but that is all. Her brother is also a capital fellow—*un parfait honnete homme*. The Prince Garin you know. Those are all. There are two or three neighbours besides, but they are really good for nothing. They either give themselves airs or are unsociable, or else quite unsuitably free and easy. The ladies, as you know, I see nothing of. There is one other of our neighbours said to be a very cultivated, even a learned, man, but a dreadfully queer creature, a whimsical character.*Alexandrine*, knows him, and I fancy is not indifferent to him.... Come, you ought to talk to her, Dmitri Nikolaitch; she's a sweet creature. She only wants developing.'

'I liked her very much,' remarked Rudin.

'A perfect child, Dmitri Nikolaitch, an absolute baby. She has been married, *mais c'est tout comme*.... If I were a man, I should only fall in love with women like that.'

'Really?'

'Certainly. Such women are at least fresh, and freshness cannot be put on.'

'And can everything else?' Rudin asked, and he laughed—a thing which rarely happened with him. When he laughed his face assumed a strange, almost aged appearance, his eyes disappeared, his nose was wrinkled up.

'And who is this queer creature, as you call him, to whom Madame Lipin is not indifferent?' he asked.

'A certain Lezhnyov, Mihailo Mihailitch, a landowner here.'

Rudin seemed astonished; he raised his head.

'Lezhnyov—Mihailo Mihailitch?' he questioned. 'Is he a neighbour of yours?'

'Yes. Do you know him?'

Rudin did not speak for a minute.

'I used to know him long ago. He is a rich man, I suppose?' he added, pulling the fringe on his chair.

'Yes, he is rich, though he dresses shockingly, and drives in a racing droshky like a bailiff. I have been anxious to get him to come here; he is spoken of as clever; I have some business with him.... You know I manage my property myself.'

Rudin bowed assent.

'Yes; I manage it myself,' Darya Mihailovna continued. 'I don't introduce any foreign crazes, but prefer what is our own, what is Russian, and, as you see, things don't seem to do badly,' she added, with a wave of her hand.

'I have always been persuaded,' observed Rudin urbanely, 'of the absolutely mistaken position of those people who refuse to admit the practical intelligence of women.'

Darya Mihailovna smiled affably.

'You are very good to us,' was her comment 'But what was I going to say? What were we speaking of? Oh, yes; Lezhnyov: I have some business with him about a boundary. I have several times invited him here, and even to-day I am expecting him; but there's no knowing whether he'll come... he's such a strange creature.'

The curtain before the door was softly moved aside and the steward came in, a tall man, grey and bald, in a black coat, a white cravat, and a white waistcoat.

'What is it?' inquired Darya Mihailovna, and, turning a little towards Rudin, she added in a low voice, '*n'est ce pas, comme il ressemble a Canning?*'

'Mihailo Mihailitch Lezhnyov is here,' announced the steward. 'Will you see him?'

'Good Heavens!' exclaimed Darya Mihailovna, 'speak of the devil——ask him up.'

The steward went away.

'He's such an awkward creature. Now he has come, it's at the wrong moment; he has interrupted our talk.'

Rudin got up from his seat, but Darya Mihailovna stopped him.

'Where are you going? We can discuss the matter as well before you. And I want you to analyse him too, as you did Pigasov. When you talk, *vous gravez comme avec un burin*. Please stay.' Rudin was going to protest, but after a moment's thought he sat down.

Mihailo Mihailitch, whom the reader already knows, came into the room. He wore the same grey overcoat, and in his sunburnt hands he carried the same old foraging cap. He bowed tranquilly to Darya Mihailovna, and came up to the tea-table.

'At last you have favoured me with a visit, Monsieur Lezhnyov!' began Darya Mihailovna. 'Pray sit down. You are already acquainted, I hear,' she continued, with a gesture in Rudin's direction.

Lezhnyov looked at Rudin and smiled rather queerly.

'I know Mr. Rudin,' he assented, with a slight bow.

'We were together at the university,' observed Rudin in a low voice, dropping his eyes.

'And we met afterwards also,' remarked Lezhnyov coldly.

Darya Mihailovna looked at both in some perplexity and asked Lezhnyov to sit down He sat down.

'You wanted to see me,' he began, 'on the subject of the boundary?'

'Yes; about the boundary. But I also wished to see you in any case. We are near neighbours, you know, and all but relations.'

'I am much obliged to you,' returned Lezhnyov. 'As regards the boundary, we have perfectly arranged that matter with your manager; I have agreed to all his proposals.'

'I knew that. But he told me that the contract could not be signed without a personal interview with you.'

'Yes; that is my rule. By the way, allow me to ask: all your peasants, I believe, pay rent?'

'Just so.'

'And you trouble yourself about boundaries! That's very praiseworthy.'

Lezhnyov did not speak for a minute.

'Well, I have come for a personal interview,' he said at last.

Darya Mihailovna smiled.

'I see you have come. You say that in such a tone.... You could not have been very anxious to come to see me.'

'I never go anywhere,' rejoined Lezhnyov phlegmatically.

'Not anywhere? But you go to see Alexandra Pavlovna.'

'I am an old friend of her brother's.'

'Her brother's! However, I never wish to force any one.... But pardon me, Mihailo Mihailitch, I am older than you, and I may be allowed to give you advice; what charm do you find in such an unsociable way of living? Or is my house in particular displeasing to you? You dislike me?'

'I don't know you, Darya Mihailovna, and so I can't dislike you. You have a splendid house; but I will confess to you frankly I don't like to have to stand on ceremony. And I haven't a respectable suit, I haven't any gloves, and I don't belong to your set.'

'By birth, by education, you belong to it, Mihailo Mihailitch! *vous etes des notres*.'

'Birth and education are all very well, Darya Mihailovna; that's not the question.'

'A man ought to live with his fellows, Mihailo Mihailitch! What pleasure is there in sitting like Diogenes in his tub?'

'Well, to begin with, he was very well off there, and besides, how do you know I don't live with my fellows?'

Darya Mihailovna bit her lip.

'That's a different matter! It only remains for me to express my regret that I have not the honour of being included in the number of your friends.'

'Monsieur Lezhnyov,' put in Rudin, 'seems to carry to excess a laudable sentiment—the love of independence.'

Lezhnyov made no reply, he only looked at Rudin. A short silence followed.

'And so,' began Lezhnyov, getting up, 'I may consider our business as concluded, and tell your manager to send me the papers.'

'You may,... though I confess you are so uncivil I ought really to refuse you.'

'But you know this rearrangement of the boundary is far more in your interest than in mine.'

Darya Mihailovna shrugged her shoulders.

'You will not even have luncheon here?' she asked.

'Thank you; I never take luncheon, and I am in a hurry to get home.'

Darya Mihailovna got up.

'I will not detain you,' she said, going to the window. 'I will not venture to detain you.'

Lezhnyov began to take leave.

'Good-bye, Monsieur Lezhnyov! Pardon me for having troubled you.'

'Oh, not at all!' said Lezhnyov, and he went away.

'Well, what do you say to that?' Darya Mihailovna asked of Rudin. 'I had heard he was eccentric, but really that was beyond everything!'

'His is the same disease as Pigasov's,' observed Rudin, 'the desire of being original. One affects to be a Mephistopheles—the other a cynic. In all that, there is much egoism, much vanity, but little truth, little love. Indeed, there is even calculation of a sort in it. A man puts on a mask of indifference and indolence so that some one will be sure to think. "Look at that man; what talents he has thrown away!" But if you come to look at him more attentively, there is no talent in him whatever.'

'*Et de deux!*' was Darya Mihailovna's comment. 'You are a terrible man at hitting people off. One can hide nothing from you.'

'Do you think so?' said Rudin.... 'However,' he continued, 'I ought not really to speak about Lezhnyov; I loved him, loved him as a friend... but afterwards, through various misunderstandings...'

'You quarrelled?'

'No. But we parted, and parted, it seems, for ever.'

'Ah, I noticed that the whole time of his visit you were not quite yourself.... But I am much indebted to you for this morning. I have spent my time extremely pleasantly. But one must know where to stop. I will let you go till lunch time and I will go and look after my business. My secretary, you saw him—Constantin, *c'est lui qui est mon secretaire*—must be waiting for me by now. I commend him to you; he is an excellent, obliging young man, and quite enthusiastic about you. *Au revoir, cher* Dmitri Nikolaitch! How grateful I am to the baron for having made me acquainted with you!'

And Darya Mihailovna held out her hand to Rudin. He first pressed it, then raised it to his lips and went away to the drawing-room and from there to the terrace. On the terrace he met Natalya.

V

Darya Mihailovna's daughter, Natalya Alexyevna, at a first glance might fail to please. She had not yet had time to develop; she was thin, and dark, and stooped slightly. But her features were fine and regular, though too large for a girl of seventeen. Specially beautiful was her pure, smooth forehead above fine eyebrows, which seemed broken in the middle. She spoke little, but listened to others, and fixed her eyes on them as though she were forming her own conclusions. She would often stand with listless hands, motionless and deep in thought; her face at such moments showed that her mind was at work within.... A scarcely perceptible smile would suddenly appear on her lips and vanish again; then she would slowly raise her large dark eyes. '*Qu'a-vez-vous?*' Mlle, Boncourt would ask her, and then she would begin to scold her, saying that it was improper for a young girl to be absorbed and to appear absent-minded. But Natalya was not absent-minded; on the contrary, she studied diligently; she read and worked eagerly. Her feelings were strong and deep, but reserved; even as a child she seldom cried, and now she seldom even sighed and only grew slightly pale when anything distressed her. Her mother considered her a sensible, good sort of girl, calling her in a joke '*mon honnete homme de fille*' but had not a very high opinion of her intellectual abilities. 'My Natalya happily is cold,' she used to say, 'not like me—and it is better so. She will be happy.' Darya Mihailovna was mistaken. But few mothers understand their daughters.

Natalya loved Darya Mihailovna, but did not fully confide in her.

'You have nothing to hide from me,' Darya Mihailovna said to her once, 'or else you would be very reserved about it; you are rather a close little thing.'

Natalya looked her mother in the face and thought, 'Why shouldn't I be reserved?'

When Rudin met her on the terrace she was just going indoors with Mlle, Boncourt to put on her hat and go out into the garden. Her morning occupations were over. Natalya was not treated as a school-girl now. Mlle, Boncourt had not given her lessons in mythology and geography for a long while; but Natalya had every morning to read historical books, travels, or other instructive works with her. Darya Mihailovna selected them, ostensibly on a special system of her own. In reality she simply gave Natalya everything which the French bookseller forwarded her from Petersburg, except, of course, the novels of Dumas Fils and Co. These novels Darya Mihailovna read herself. Mlle, Boncourt looked specially severely and sourly through her spectacles when Natalya was reading historical books; according to the old French lady's ideas all history was filled with *impermissible* things, though for some reason or other of all the great men of antiquity she herself knew only one—Cambyses, and of modern times—Louis XIV. and Napoleon, whom she could not endure. But Natalya read books too, the existence of which Mlle, Boncourt did not suspect; she knew all Pushkin by heart.

Natalya flushed slightly at meeting Rudin.

'Are you going for a walk?' he asked her.

'Yes. We are going into the garden.'

'May I come with you?'

Natalya looked at Mlle, Boncourt

'*Mais certainement, monsieur; avec plaisir*,' said the old lady promptly.

Rudin took his hat and walked with them.

Natalya at first felt some awkwardness in walking side by side with Rudin on the same little path; afterwards she felt more at ease. He began to question her about her occupations and how she liked the country. She replied not without timidity, but without that hasty bashfulness which is so often taken for modesty. Her heart was beating.

'You are not bored in the country?' asked Rudin, taking her in with a sidelong glance.

'How can one be bored in the country? I am very glad we are here. I am very happy here.'

'You are happy—that is a great word. However, one can understood it; you are young.'

Rudin pronounced this last phrase rather strangely; either he envied Natalya or he was sorry for her.

'Yes! youth!' he continued, 'the whole aim of science is to reach consciously what is bestowed on youth for nothing.'

Natalya looked attentively at Rudin; she did not understand him.

'I have been talking all this morning with your mother,' he went on; 'she is an extraordinary woman. I understand why all our poets sought her friendship. Are you fond of poetry?' he added, after a pause.

'He is putting me through an examination,' thought Natalya, and aloud: 'Yes, I am very fond of it.'

'Poetry is the language of the gods. I love poems myself. But poetry is not only in poems; it is diffused everywhere, it is around us. Look at those trees, that sky on all sides there is the breath of beauty, and of life, and where there is life and beauty, there is poetry also.'

'Let us sit down here on this bench,' he added. 'Here—so. I somehow fancy that when you are more used to me (and he looked her in the face with a smile) 'we shall be friends, you and I. What do you think?'

'He treats me like a school-girl,' Natalya reflected again, and, not knowing what to say, she asked him whether he intended to remain long in the country.

'All the summer and autumn, and perhaps the winter too. I am a very poor man, you know; my affairs are in confusion, and, besides, I am tired now of wandering from place to place. The time has come to rest.'

Natalya was surprised.

'Is it possible you feel that it is time for you to rest?' she asked him timidly.

Rudin turned so as to face Natalya.

'What do you mean by that?'

'I mean,' she replied in some embarrassment, 'that others may rest; but you... you ought to work, to try to be useful. Who, if not you——'

'I thank you for your flattering opinion,' Rudin interrupted her. 'To be useful... it is easy to say!' (He passed his hand over his face.) 'To be useful!' he repeated. 'Even if I had any firm conviction, how could I be useful?—even if I had faith in my own powers, where is one to find true, sympathetic souls?'

And Rudin waved his hand so hopelessly, and let his head sink so gloomily, that Natalya involuntarily asked herself, were those really his—those enthusiastic words full of the breath of hope, she had heard the evening before.

'But no,' he said, suddenly tossing back his lion-like mane, 'that is all folly, and you are right. I thank you, Natalya Alexyevna, I thank you truly.' (Natalya absolutely did not know what he was thanking her for.) 'Your single phrase has recalled to me my duty, has pointed out to me my path.... Yes, I must act. I must not bury my talent, if I have any; I must not squander my powers on talk alone—empty, profitless talk—on mere words,' and his words flowed in a stream. He spoke nobly, ardently, convincingly, of the sin of cowardice and indolence, of the necessity of action. He lavished reproaches on himself, maintained that to discuss beforehand what you mean to do is as unwise as to prick with a pin the swelling fruit, that it is only a vain waste of strength and sap. He declared that there was no noble idea which would not gain sympathy, that the only people who remained misunderstood were those who either did not know themselves what they wanted, or were not worthy to be understood. He spoke at length, and ended by once more thanking Natalya Alexyevna, and utterly unexpectedly pressed her hand, exclaiming. 'You are a noble, generous creature!'

This outburst horrified Mlle, Boncourt, who in spite of her forty years' residence in Russia understood Russian with difficulty, and was only moved to admiration by the splendid rapidity and flow of words on Rudin's lips. In her eyes, however, he was something of the nature of a virtuoso or artist; and from people of that kind, according to her notions, it was impossible to demand a strict adherence to propriety.

She got up and drew her skirts with a jerk around her, observed to Natalya that it was time to go in, especially as M. Volinsoff (so she spoke of Volintsev) was to be there to lunch.

'And here he is,' she added, looking up one of the avenues which led to the house, and in fact Volintsev appeared not far off.

He came up with a hesitating step, greeted all of them from a distance, and with an expression of pain on his face he turned to Natalya and said:

'Oh, you are having a walk?'

'Yes,' answered Natalya, 'we were just going home.'

'Ah!' was Volintsev's reply. 'Well, let us go,' and they all walked towards the house.

'How is your sister?' Rudin inquired, in a specially cordial tone, of Volintsev. The evening before, too, he had been very gracious to him.

'Thank you; she is quite well. She will perhaps be here to-day.... I think you were discussing something when I came up?'

'Yes; I have had a conversation with Natalya Alexyevna. She said one thing to me which affected me strongly.'

Volintsev did not ask what the one thing was, and in profound silence they all returned to Darya Mihailovna's house.

Before dinner the party was again assembled in the drawing-room. Pigasov, however, did not come. Rudin was not at his best; he did nothing but press Pandalevsky to play Beethoven. Volintsev was silent and stared at the floor. Natalya did not leave her mother's side, and was at times lost in thought, and then bent over her work. Bassistoff did not take his eyes off Rudin, constantly on the alert for him to say something brilliant. About three hours were passed in this way rather monotonously. Alexandra Pavlovna did not come to dinner, and when they rose from table Volintsev at once ordered his carriage to be ready, and slipped away without saying good-bye to any one.

His heart was heavy. He had long loved Natalya, and was repeatedly resolving to make her an offer.... She was kindly disposed to him,—but her heart remained unmoved; he saw that clearly. He did not hope to inspire in her a tenderer sentiment, and was only waiting for the time when she should be perfectly at home with him and intimate with him. What could have disturbed him? what change had he noticed in these two days? Natalya had behaved to him exactly the same as before....

Whether it was that some idea had come upon him that he perhaps did not know Natalya's character at all—that she was more a stranger to him than he had thought,—or jealousy had begun to work in him, or he had some dim presentiment of ill... anyway, he suffered, though he tried to reason with himself.

When he came in to his sister's room, Lezhnyov was sitting with her.

'Why have you come back so early?' asked Alexandra Pavlovna.

'Oh! I was bored.'

'Was Rudin there?'

'Yes.'

Volintsev flung down his cap and sat down. Alexandra Pavlovna turned eagerly to him.

'Please, Serezha, help me to convince this obstinate man (she signified Lezhnyov) that Rudin is extraordinarily clever and eloquent.'

Volintsev muttered something.

'But I am not disputing at all with you,' Lezhnyov began. 'I have no doubt of the cleverness and eloquence of Mr. Rudin; I only say that I don't like him.'

'But have you seen him?' inquired Volintsev.

'I saw him this morning at Darya Mihallovna's. You know he is her first favourite now. The time will come when she will part with him—Pandalevsky is the only man she will never part with—but now he is supreme. I saw him, to be sure! He was sitting there,—and she showed me off to him, "see, my good friend, what queer fish we have here!" But I am not a prize horse, to be trotted out on show, so I took myself off.'

'But how did you come to be there?'

'About a boundary; but that was all nonsense; she simply wanted to have a look at my physiognomy. She's a fine lady,—that's explanation enough!'

'His superiority is what offends you—that's what it is!' began Alexandra Pavlovna warmly, 'that's what you can't forgive. But I am convinced that besides his cleverness he must have an excellent heart as well. You should see his eyes when he——'

'"Of purity exalted speaks,"' quoted Lezhnyov.

'You make me angry, and I shall cry. I am heartily sorry I did not go to Darya Mihailovna's, but stopped with you. You don't deserve it. Leave off teasing me,' she added, in an appealing voice, 'You had much better tell me about his youth.'

'Rudin's youth?'

'Yes, of course. Didn't you tell me you knew him well, and had known him a long time?'

Lezhnyov got up and walked up and down the room.

'Yes,' he began, 'I do know him well. You want me to tell you about his youth? Very well. He was born in T——, and was the son of a poor landowner, who died soon after. He was left alone with his mother. She was a very good woman, and she idolised him; she lived on nothing but oatmeal, and every penny she had she spent on him. He was educated in Moscow, first at the expense of some uncle, and afterwards, when he was grown up and fully fledged, at the expense of a rich prince whose favour he had courted—there, I beg your pardon, I won't do it again—with whom he had made friends. Then he went to the university. At the university I got to know him and we became intimate friends. I will tell you about our life in those days some other time, I can't now. Then he went abroad....'

Lezhnyov continued to walk up and down the room; Alexandra Pavlovna followed him with her eyes.

'While he was abroad,' he continued, 'Rudin wrote very rarely to his mother, and paid her altogether only one visit for ten days.... The old lady died without him, cared for by strangers; but up to her death she never took her eyes off his portrait. I went to see her when I was staying in T——. She was a kind and hospitable woman; she always used to feast me on cherry jam. She loved her Mitya devotedly. People of the Petchorin type tell us that we always love those who are least capable of feeling love themselves; but it's my idea that all mothers love their children especially when they are absent. Afterwards I met Rudin abroad. Then he was connected with a lady, one of our countrywomen, a bluestocking, no longer young, and plain, as a bluestocking is bound to be. He lived a good while with her, and at last threw her over—or no, I beg pardon,—she threw him over. It was then that I too threw him over. That's all.'

Lezhnyov ceased speaking, passed his hand over his brow, and dropped into a chair as if he were exhausted.

'Do you know, Mihailo Mihailitch,' began Alexandra Pavlovna, 'you are a spiteful person, I see; indeed you are no better than Pigasov. I am convinced that all you have told me is true, that you have not made up anything, and yet in what an unfavourable light you have put it all! The poor old mother, her devotion, her solitary death, and that lady—What does it all amount to? You know that it's easy to put the life of the best of men in such colours—and without adding anything, observe—that every one would be shocked! But that too is slander of a kind!'

Lezhnyov got up and again walked about the room.

'I did not want to shock you at all, Alexandra Pavlovna,' he brought out at last, 'I am not given to slander. However,' he added, after a moment's thought, 'in reality there is a foundation of fact in what you said. I did not mean to slander Rudin; but—who knows! very likely he has had time to change since those days—very possibly I am unjust to him.'

'Ah! you see. So promise me that you will renew your acquaintance with him, and will get to know him thoroughly and then report your final opinion of him to me.'

'As you please. But why are you so quiet, Sergei Pavlitch?'

Volintsev started and raised his head, as though he had just waked up.

'What can I say? I don't know him. Besides, my head aches to-day.'

'Yes, you look rather pale this evening,' remarked Alexandra Pavlovna; 'are you unwell?'

'My head aches,' repeated Volintsev, and he went away.

Alexandra Pavlovna and Lezhnyov looked after him, and exchanged glances, though they said nothing. What was passing in Volintsev's heart was no mystery to either of them.

VI

More than two months had passed; during the whole of that period Rudin had scarcely been away from Darya Mihailovna's house. She could not get on without him. To talk to him about herself and to listen to his eloquence became a necessity for her. He would have taken his leave on one occasion, on the ground that all his money was spent; she gave him five hundred roubles. He borrowed two hundred roubles more from Volintsev. Pigasov visited Darya Mihailovna much less frequently than before; Rudin crushed him by his presence. And indeed it was not only Pigasov who was conscious of an oppression.

'I don't like that prig,' Pigasov used to say, 'he expresses himself so affectedly like a hero of a romance. If he says "I," he stops in rapt admiration, "I, yes, I!" and the phrases he uses are all so drawn-out; if you sneeze, he will begin at once to explain to you exactly why you sneezed and did not cough. If he praises you, it's just as if he were creating you a prince. If he begins to abuse himself, he humbles himself into the dust—come, one thinks, he will never dare to face the light of day after that. Not a bit of it! It only cheers him up, as if he'd treated himself to a glass of grog.'

Pandalevsky was a little afraid of Rudin, and cautiously tried to win his favour. Volintsev had got on to curious terms with him. Rudin called him a knight-errant, and sang his praises to his face and behind his back; but Volintsev could not bring himself to like him and always felt an involuntary impatience and annoyance when Rudin devoted himself to enlarging on his good points in his presence. 'Is he making fun of me?' he thought, and he felt a throb of hatred in his heart. He tried to keep his feelings in check, but in vain; he was jealous of him on Natalya's account. And Rudin himself, though he always welcomed Volintsev with effusion, though he called him a knight-errant, and borrowed money from him, did not feel exactly friendly towards him. It would be difficult to define the feelings of these two men when they pressed each other's hands like friends and looked into each other's eyes.

Bassistoff continued to adore Rudin, and to hang on every word he uttered. Rudin paid him very little attention. Once he spent a whole morning with him, discussing the weightiest problems of life, and awakening his keenest enthusiasm, but afterwards he took no further notice of him. Evidently it was only a phrase when he said that he was seeking for pure and devoted souls. With Lezhnyov, who began to be a frequent visitor at the house, Rudin did not enter into discussion; he seemed even to avoid him. Lezhnyov, on his part, too, treated him coldly. He did not, however, report his final conclusions about him, which somewhat disquieted Alexandra Pavlovna. She was fascinated by Rudin, but she had confidence in Lezhnyov. Every one in Darya Mihailovna's house humoured Rudin's fancies; his slightest preferences were carried out He determined the plans for the day. Not a single *partie de plaisir* was arranged without his co-operation.

He was not, however, very fond of any kind of impromptu excursion or picnic, and took part in them rather as grown-up people take part in children's games, with an air of kindly, but rather wearied, friendliness. He took interest in everything else, however. He discussed with Darya Mihailovna her plans for the estate, the education of her children, her domestic arrangements, and her affairs generally; he listened to her schemes, and was not bored by petty details, and, in his turn, proposed reforms and made suggestions. Darya Mihailovna agreed to them in words—and that was all. In matters of business she was really guided by the advice of her bailiff—an elderly, one-eyed Little Russian, a good-natured and crafty old rogue. 'What is old is fat, what is new is thin,' he used to say, with a quiet smile, winking his solitary eye.

Next to Darya Mihailovna, it was Natalya to whom Rudin used to talk most often and at most length. He used privately to give her books, to confide his plans to her, and to read her the first pages of the essays and other works he had in his mind. Natalya did not always fully grasp the significance of them.

But Rudin did not seem to care much about her understanding, so long as she listened to him. His intimacy with Natalya was not altogether pleasing to Darya Mihailovna. 'However,' she thought, 'let her chatter away with him in the country. She amuses him as a little girl now. There is no great harm in it, and, at any rate, it will improve her mind. At Petersburg I will soon put a stop to it.'

Darya Mihailovna was mistaken. Natalya did not chatter to Rudin like a school-girl; she eagerly drank in his words, she tried to penetrate to their full significance; she submitted her thoughts, her doubts to him; he became her leader, her guide. So far, it was only the brain that was stirred, but in the young the brain is not long stirred alone. What sweet moments Natalya passed when at times in the garden on the seat, in the transparent shade of the aspen tree, Rudin began to read Goethe's *Faust*, Hoffman, or Bettina's letters, or Novalis, constantly stopping and explaining what seemed obscure to her. Like almost all Russian girls, she spoke German badly, but she understood it well, and Rudin was thoroughly imbued with German poetry, German romanticism and philosophy, and he drew her after him into these forbidden lands. Unimagined splendours were revealed there to her earnest eyes from the pages of the book which Rudin held on his knee; a stream of divine visions, of new, illuminating ideas, seemed to flow in rhythmic music into her soul, and in her heart, moved with the high delight of noble feeling, slowly was kindled and fanned into a flame the holy spark of enthusiasm.

'Tell me, Dmitri Nikolaitch,' she began one day, sitting by the window at her embroidery-frame, 'shall you be in Petersburg in the winter?'

'I don't know,' replied Rudin, as he let the book he had been glancing through fall upon his knee; 'if I can find the means, I shall go.'

He spoke dejectedly; he felt tired, and had done nothing all day.

'I think you are sure to find the means.'

Rudin shook his head.

'You think so!'

And he looked away expressively.

Natalya was on the point of replying, but she checked herself.

'Look.' began Rudin, with a gesture towards the window, 'do you see that apple-tree? It is broken by the weight and abundance of its own fruit. True emblem of genius.'

'It is broken because it had no support,' replied Natalya

'I understand you, Natalya Alexyevna, but it is not so easy for a man to find such a support.'

'I should think the sympathy of others... in any case isolation always....'

Natalya was rather confused, and flushed a little.

'And what will you do in the country in the winter?' she added hurriedly.

'What shall I do? I shall finish my larger essay—you know it—on "Tragedy in Life and in Art." I described to you the outline of it the day before yesterday, and shall send it to you.'

'And you will publish it?'

'No.'

'No? For whose sake will you work then?'

'And if it were for you?'

Natalya dropped her eyes.

'It would be far above me.'

'What, may I ask, is the subject of the essay?' Bassistoff inquired modestly. He was sitting a little distance away.

'"Tragedy in Life and in Art,"' repeated Rudin. 'Mr. Bassistoff too will read it. But I have not altogether settled on the fundamental motive. I have not so far worked out for myself the tragic significance of love.'

Rudin liked to talk of love, and frequently did so. At first, at the word 'love,' Mlle, Boncourt started, and pricked up her eyes like an old war-horse at the sound of the trumpet; but afterwards she had grown used to it, and now only pursed up her lips and took snuff at intervals.

'It seems to me,' said Natalya timidly, 'that the tragic in love is unrequited love.'

'Not at all!' replied Rudin; 'that is rather the comic side of love. ... The question must be put in an altogether different way... one must attack it more deeply.... Love!' he pursued, 'all is mystery in love; how it comes, how it develops, how it passes away. Sometimes it comes all at once, undoubting, glad as day; sometimes it smoulders like fire under ashes, and only bursts into a flame in the heart when all is over; sometimes it winds its way into the heart like a serpent, and suddenly slips out of it again.... Yes, yes; it is the great problem. But who does love in our days? Who is so bold as to love?'

And Rudin grew pensive.

'Why is it we have not seen Sergei Pavlitch for so long?' he asked suddenly.

Natalya blushed, and bent her head over her embroidery frame.

'I don't know,' she murmured.

'What a splendid, generous fellow he is!' Rudin declared, standing up. 'It is one of the best types of a Russian gentleman.'

Mlle, Boncourt gave him a sidelong look out of her little French eyes.

Rudin walked up and down the room.

'Have you noticed,' he began, turning sharply round on his heels, 'that on the oak—and the oak is a strong tree—the old leaves only fall off when the new leaves begin to grow?'

'Yes,' answered Natalya slowly, 'I have noticed it'

'That is what happens to an old love in a strong heart; it is dead already, but still it holds its place; only another new love can drive it out.'

Natalya made no reply.

'What does that mean?' she was thinking.

Rudin stood still, tossed his hair back, and walked away.

Natalya went to her own room. She sat a long while on her little bed in perplexity, pondering over Rudin's last words. All at once she clasped her hands and began to weep bitterly. What she was weeping for—who can tell? She herself could not tell why her tears were falling so fast. She dried them; but they flowed afresh, like water from a long-pent-up source.

On this same day Alexandra Pavlovna had a conversation with Lezhnyov about Rudin. At first he bore all her attacks in silence; but at last she succeeded in rousing him into talk.

'I see,' she said to him, 'you dislike Dmitri Nikolaitch, as you did before. I purposely refrained from questioning you till now; but now you have had time to make up your mind whether there is any change in him, and I want to know why you don't like him.'

'Very well,' answered Lezhnyov with his habitual phlegm, 'since your patience is exhausted; only look here, don't get angry.'

'Come, begin, begin.'

'And let me have my say to the end.'

'Of course, of course; begin.'

'Very well,' said Lezhnyov, dropping lazily on to the sofa; 'I admit that I certainly don't like Rudin. He is a clever fellow.'

'I should think so.'

'He is a remarkably clever man, though in reality essentially shallow.'

'It's easy to say that.'

'Though essentially shallow,' repeated Lezhnyov; 'but there's no great harm in that; we are all shallow. I will not even quarrel with him for being a tyrant at heart, lazy, ill-informed!'

Alexandra Pavlovna clasped her hands.

'Rudin—ill-informed!' she cried.

'Ill-informed!' repeated Lezhnyov in precisely the same voice, 'that he likes to live at other people's expanse, to cut a good figure, and so forth—all that's natural enough. But what's wrong is, that he is as cold as ice.'

'He cold! that fiery soul cold!' interrupted Alexandra Pavlovna.

'Yes, cold as ice, and he knows it, and pretends to be fiery. What's bad,' pursued Lezhnyov, gradually growing warm, 'he is playing a dangerous game—not dangerous for him, of course; he does not risk a farthing, not a straw on it—but others stake their soul.'

'Whom and what are you talking of? I don't understand you,' said Alexandra Pavlovna.

'What's bad, he isn't honest. He's a clever man, certainly; he ought to know the value of his own words, and he brings them out as if they were worth something to him. I don't dispute that he's a fine speaker, but not in the Russian style. And indeed, after all, fine speaking is pardonable in a boy, but at his years it is disgraceful to take pleasure in the sound of his own voice, and to show off!'

'I think, Mihailo Mihailitch, it's all the same for those who hear him, whether he is showing off or not.'

'Excuse me, Alexandra Pavlovna, it is not all the same. One man says a word to me and it thrills me all over, another may say the same thing, or something still finer—and I don't prick up my ears. Why is that?'

'You don't, perhaps,' put in Alexandra Pavlovna.

'I don't,' retorted Lezhnyov, 'though perhaps my ears are long enough. The point is, that Rudin's words seem to remain mere words, and never to pass into deeds—and meanwhile even words may trouble a young heart, may be the ruin of it.'

'But whom do you mean, Mihailo Mihailitch?'

Lezhnyov paused.

'Do you want to know whom I mean, Natalya Alexyevna?'

Alexandra Pavlovna was taken aback for a moment, but she began to smile the instant after.

'Really,' she began, 'what queer ideas you always have! Natalya is still a child; and besides, if there were anything in what you say, do you suppose Darya Mihailovna——'

'Darya Mihailovna is an egoist to begin with, and lives for herself; and then she is so convinced of her own skill in educating her children that it does not even enter her head to feel uneasy about them. Nonsense! how is it possible: she has but to give one nod, one majestic glance—and all is over, all is obedience again. That's what that lady imagines; she fancies herself a female Maecenas, a learned woman, and God knows what, but in fact she is nothing more than a silly, worldly old woman. But Natalya is not a baby; believe me, she thinks more, and more profoundly too, than you and I do. And that her true, passionate, ardent nature must fall in with an actor, a flirt like this! But of course that's in the natural order of things.'

'A flirt! Do you mean that he is a flirt?'

'Of course he is. And tell me yourself, Alexandra Pavlovna, what is his position in Darya Mihailovna's house? To be the idol, the oracle of the household, to meddle in the arrangements, all the gossip and petty trifles of the house—is that a dignified position for a man to be in?'

Alexandra Pavlovna looked at Lezhnyov in surprise.

'I don't know you, Mihailo Mihailitch,' she began to say. 'You are flushed and excited. I believe there must be something else hidden under this.'

'Oh, so that's it! Tell a woman the truth from conviction, and she will never rest easy till she has invented some petty outside cause quite beside the point which has made you speak in precisely that manner and no other.'

Alexandra Pavlovna began to get angry.

'Bravo, Monsieur Lezhnyov! You begin to be as bitter against women as Mr. Pigasov; but you may say what you like, penetrating as you are, it's hard for me to believe that you understand every one and everything. I think you are mistaken. According to your ideas, Rudin is a kind of Tartuffe.'

'No, the point is, that he is not even a Tartuffe. Tartuffe at least knew what he was aiming at; but this fellow, for all his cleverness——'

'Well, well, what of him? Finish your sentence, you unjust, horrid man!'

Lezhnyov got up.

'Listen, Alexandra Pavlovna,' he began, 'it is you who are unjust, not I. You are cross with me for my harsh criticism of Rudin; I have the right to speak harshly of him! I have paid dearly enough, perhaps, for that privilege. I know him well: I lived a long while with him. You remember I promised to tell you some time about our life at Moscow. It is clear that I must do so now. But will you have the patience to hear me out?'

'Tell me, tell me!'

'Very well, then.'

Lezhnyov began walking with measured steps about the room, coming to a standstill at times with his head bent.

'You know, perhaps,' he began, 'or perhaps you don't know, that I was left an orphan at an early age, and by the time I was seventeen I had no one in authority over me. I lived at my aunt's at Moscow, and did just as I liked. As a boy I was rather silly and conceited, and liked to brag and show off. After my entrance at the university I behaved like a regular schoolboy, and soon got into a scrape. I won't tell you about it; it's not worth while. But I told a lie about it, and rather a shameful lie. It all came out, and I was put to open shame. I lost my head and cried like a child. It happened at a friend's rooms before a lot of fellow-students. They all began to laugh at me, all except one student, who, observe, had been more indignant with me than any, so long as I had been obstinate and would not confess my deceit. He took pity on me, perhaps; anyway, he took me by the arm and led me away to his lodging.'

'Was that Rudin?' asked Alexandra Pavlovna.

'No, it was not Rudin... it was a man... he is dead now... he was an extraordinary man. His name was Pokorsky. To describe him in a few words is beyond my powers, but directly one begins to speak of him, one does not want to speak of any one else. He had a noble, pure heart, and an intelligence such as I have never met since. Pokorsky lived in a little, low-pitched room, in an attic of an old wooden house. He was very poor, and supported himself somehow by giving lessons. Sometimes he had not even a cup of tea to offer to his friends, and his only sofa was so shaky that it was like being on board ship. But in spite of these discomforts a great many people used to go to see him. Every one loved him; he drew all hearts to him. You would not believe what sweetness and happiness there was in sitting in his poor little room! It was in his room I met Rudin. He had already parted from his prince before then.'

'What was there so exceptional in this Pokorsky?' asked Alexandra Pavlovna.

'How can I tell you? Poetry and truth—that was what drew all of us to him. For all his clear, broad intellect he was as sweet and simple as a child. Even now I have his bright laugh ringing in my ears, and at the same time he

Burnt his midnight lamp
Before the holy and the true,

as a dear half-cracked fellow, the poet of our set, expressed it.'

'And how did he talk?' Alexandra Pavlovna questioned again.

'He talked well when he was in the mood, but not remarkably so. Rudin even then was twenty times as eloquent as he.'

Lezhnyov stood still and folded his arms.

'Pokorsky and Rudin were very unlike. There was more flash and brilliance about Rudin, more fluency, and perhaps more enthusiasm. He appeared far more gifted than Pokorsky, and yet all the while he was a poor creature by comparison. Rudin was excellent at developing any idea, he was capital in argument, but his ideas did not come from his own brain; he borrowed them from others, especially from Pokorsky. Pokorsky was quiet and soft—even weak in appearance—and he was fond of women to distraction, and fond of dissipation, and he would never take an insult from any one. Rudin seemed full of fire, and courage, and life, but at heart he was cold and almost a coward, until his vanity was touched, then he would not stop at anything. He always tried to get an ascendency over people, but he got it in the name of general principles and ideas, and certainly had a great influence over many. To tell the truth, no one loved him; I was the only one, perhaps, who was attached to him. They submitted to his yoke, but all were devoted to Pokorsky. Rudin never refused to argue and discuss with any one he met. He did not read very much, though far more anyway than Pokorsky and all the rest of us; besides, he had a well-arranged intellect, and a prodigious memory, and what an effect that has on young people! They must have generalisations, conclusions, incorrect if you like, perhaps, but still conclusions! A perfectly sincere man never suits them. Try to tell young people that you cannot give them the whole truth, and they will not listen to you. But you mustn't deceive them either. You want to half believe yourself that you are in possession of the truth. That was why Rudin had such a powerful effect on all of us. I told you just now, you know, that he had not read much, but he read philosophical books, and his brain was so constructed that he extracted at once from what he had read all the general principles, penetrated to the very root of the thing, and then made deductions from it in all directions—consecutive, brilliant, sound ideas, throwing up a wide horizon to the soul. Our set consisted then—it's only fair to say—of boys, and not well-informed boys. Philosophy, art, science, and even life itself were all mere words to us—ideas if you like, fascinating and magnificent ideas, but disconnected and isolated. The general connection of those ideas, the general principle of the universe we knew nothing of, and had had no contact with, though we discussed it vaguely, and tried to form an idea of it for ourselves. As we listened to Rudin, we felt for the first time as if we had grasped it at last, this general connection, as if a veil had been lifted at last! Even admitting he was not uttering an original thought—what of that! Order and harmony seemed to be established in all we knew; all that had been disconnected seemed to fall into a whole, to take shape and grow like a building before our eyes, all was full of light and inspiration everywhere.... Nothing remained meaningless and undesigned, in everything wise design and beauty seemed apparent, everything took a clear and yet mystic significance; every isolated event of life fell into harmony, and with a kind of holy awe and reverence and sweet emotion we felt ourselves to be, as it were, the living vessels of eternal truth, her instruments destined for some great... Doesn't it all seem very ridiculous to you?'

'Not the least!' replied Alexandra Pavlovna slowly; 'why should you think so? I don't altogether understand you, but I don't think it ridiculous.'

'We have had time to grow wiser since then, of course,' Lezhnyov continued, 'all that may seem childish to us now.... But, I repeat, we all owed a great deal to Rudin then. Pokorsky was incomparably nobler than he, no question about it; Pokorsky breathed fire and strength into all of us; but he was often depressed and silent. He was nervous and not robust; but when he did stretch his wings—good heavens!—what a flight! up to the very height of the blue heavens! And there was a great deal of pettiness in Rudin, handsome and stately as he was; he was a gossip, indeed, and he loved to have a hand in everything, arranging and explaining everything. His fussy activity was inexhaustible—he was a diplomatist by nature. I speak of him as I knew him then. But unluckily he has not altered. On the other hand, his ideals haven't altered at five-and-thirty! It's not every one who can say that of himself!'

'Sit down,' said Alexandra Pavlovna, 'why do you keep moving about like a pendulum?'

'I like it better,' answered Lezhnyov. 'Well, after I had come into Pokorsky's set, I may tell you, Alexandra Pavlovna, I was quite transformed; I grew humble and anxious to learn; I studied, and was happy and reverent—in a word, I felt just as though I had entered a holy temple. And really, when I recall our gatherings, upon my word there was much that was fine, even touching, in them. Imagine a party of five or six lads gathered together, one tallow candle burning. The tea was dreadful stuff, and the cake was stale, very stale; but you should have seen our faces, you should have heard our talk! Eyes were sparkling with enthusiasm, cheeks flushed, and hearts beating, while we talked of God, and truth, of the future of humanity, and poetry ... often what we said was absurd, and we were in ecstasies over nonsense; but what of that?... Pokorsky sat with crossed legs, his pale cheek on his hand, and his eyes seemed to shed light. Rudin stood in the middle of the room and spoke, spoke splendidly, for all the world like the young Demosthenes by the resounding sea; our poet, Subotin of the dishevelled locks, would now and then throw out some abrupt exclamation as though in his sleep, while Scheller, a student forty years old, the son of a German pastor, who had the reputation among us of a profound thinker, thanks to his eternal, inviolable silence, held his peace with more rapt solemnity than usual; even the lively Shtchitof, the Aristophanes of our reunions, was subdued and did no more than smile, while two or three novices listened with reverent transports.... And the night seemed to fly by on wings. It was already the grey morning when we separated, moved, happy, aspiring and sober (there was no question of wine among us at such times) with a kind of sweet weariness in our souls... and one even looked up at the stars with a kind of confidence, as though they had become nearer and more comprehensible. Ah! that was a glorious time, and I can't bear to believe that it was altogether wasted! And it was not wasted—not even for those whose lives were sordid afterwards. How often have I chanced to come across such old college friends! You would think the man had sunk altogether to the brute, but one had only to utter Pokorsky's name before him and every trace of noble feeling in him was stirred at once; it was like uncorking a forgotten phial of fragrance in some dark and dirty room.'

Lezhnyov stopped; his colourless face was flushed.

'And what was the cause of your quarrel with Rudin?' said Alexandra Pavlovna, looking wonderingly at Lezhnyov.

'I did not quarrel with him, but I parted from him when I came to know him thoroughly abroad. But I might well have quarrelled with him in Moscow, he did me a bad turn there.'

'What was that?'

'It was like this. I—how can I tell you?—it does not accord very well with my appearance, but I was always much given to falling in love.'

'You?'

'Yes, I was indeed. That's a curious idea, isn't it? But, anyway, it was so. Well, so I fell in love in those days with a very pretty young girl.... But why do you look at me like that? I could tell you something about myself a great deal more extraordinary than that!'

'And what is that something, if I may know?'

'Oh, just this. In those Moscow days I used to have a tryst at nights—with whom, would you imagine? with a young lime-tree at the bottom of my garden. I used to embrace its slender and graceful trunk, and I felt as though I were embracing all nature, and my heart melted and expanded as though it really were taking in the whole of nature. That's what I was then. And do you think, perhaps, I didn't write verses? Why, I even composed a whole drama in imitation of Manfred. Among the characters was a ghost with blood on his breast, and not his own blood, observe, but the blood of all humanity.... Yes, yes, you need not wonder at that. But I was beginning to tell you about my love affair. I made the acquaintance of a girl——'

'And you gave up your trysts with the lime-tree?' inquired Alexandra Pavlovna.

'Yes; I gave them up. This girl was a sweet, good creature, with clear, lively eyes and a ringing voice.'

'You give an excellent description of her,' commented Alexandra Pavlovna with a smile.

'You are such a severe critic,' retorted Lezhnyov. 'Well, this girl lived with her old father.... But I will not enter into details; I will only tell you that this girl was so kind-hearted, if you only asked her for half a cup of tea she would give it you brimming over! Two days after first meeting her I was wild over her, and on the seventh day I could hold out no longer, and confessed it in full to Rudin. At that time I was completely under his influence, and his influence, I will tell you frankly, was beneficial in many things. He was the first person who did not treat me with contempt, but tried to lick me into shape. I loved Pokorsky passionately, and felt a kind of awe before his purity of soul, but I came closer to Rudin. When he heard about my love, he fell into an indescribable ecstasy, congratulated me, embraced me, and at once fell to disserting and enlarging upon all the dignity of my new position. I pricked up my ears.... Well, you know how he can talk. His words had an extraordinary effect on me. I at once assumed an amazing consequence in my own eyes, and I put on a serious exterior and left off laughing. I remember I used even to go about at that time with a kind of circumspection, as though I had a sacred chalice within me, full of a priceless liquid, which I was afraid of spilling over.... I was very happy, especially as I found favour in her eyes. Rudin wanted to make my beloved's acquaintance, and I myself almost insisted on presenting him.'

'Ah! I see, I see now what it is,' interrupted Alexandra Pavlovna. 'Rudin cut you out with your charmer, and you have never been able to forgive him.... I am ready to take a wager I am right!'

'You would lose your wager, Alexandra Pavlovna; you are wrong. Rudin did not cut me out; he did not even try to cut me out; but, all the same, he put an end to my happiness, though, looking at it in cool blood, I am ready to thank him for it now. But I nearly went out of my mind at the time. Rudin did not in the least wish to injure me—quite the contrary! But through his cursed habit of pinning every emotion—his own and other people's—with a phrase, as one pins butterflies in a case, he set to making clear to ourselves our relations to one another, and how we ought to treat each other, and arbitrarily compelled us to take stock of our feelings and ideas, praised us and blamed us, even entered into a correspondence with us—fancy! Well, he succeeded in completely disconcerting us! I should hardly, even then, have married the young lady (I had so much sense still left), but, at least, we might have spent some months happily a *la Paul et Virginie*; but now came strained relations, misunderstandings of every kind. It ended by Rudin, one fine morning, arriving at the conviction that it was his sacred duty as a friend to acquaint the old father with everything—and he did so.'

'Is it possible?' cried Alexandra Pavlovna.

'Yes, and did it with my consent, observe. That's where the wonder comes in!... I remember even now what a chaos my brain was in; everything was simply turning round—things looked as they do in a camera obscura—white seemed black and black white; falsehood was truth, and a whim was duty.... Ah! even now I feel shame at the recollection of it! Rudin—he never flagged—not a bit of it! He soared through all sorts of misunderstandings and perplexities, like a swallow over a pond.'

'And so you parted from the girl?' asked Alexandra Pavlovna, naively bending her head on one side, and raising her eyebrows.

'We parted—and it was a horrible parting—outrageously awkward and public, quite unnecessarily public.... I wept myself, and she wept, and I don't know what passed.... It seemed as though a kind of Gordian knot had been tied. It had to be cut, but it was painful! However, everything in the world is ordered for the best. She has married an excellent man, and is well off now.'

'But confess, you have never been able to forgive Rudin, all the same,' Alexandra Pavlovna was beginning.

'Not at all!' interposed Lezhnyov, 'why, I cried like a child when he was going abroad. Still, to tell the truth, even then there was the germ in my heart. And when I met him later abroad... well, by that time I had grown older.... Rudin struck me in his true light.'

'What was it exactly you discovered in him?'

'Why, all I have been telling you the last hour. But enough of him. Perhaps everything will turn out all right. I only wanted to show you that, if I do judge him hardly, it is not because I don't know him. ... As far as concerns Natalya Alexyevna, I won't say any more, but you should observe your brother.'

'My brother! Why?'

'Why, look at him. Do you really notice nothing?'

Alexandra Pavlovna looked down.

'You are right,' she assented. 'Certainly—my brother—for some time he has not been himself.... But do you really think——'

'Hush! I think he is coming,' whispered Lezhnyov. 'But Natalya is not a child, believe me, though unluckily she is as inexperienced as a child. You will see, that girl will astonish us all.'

'In what way?'

'Oh! in this way.... Do you know it's precisely girls like that who drown themselves, take poison, and so forth? Don't be misled by her looking so calm. Her passions are strong, and her character—my goodness!'

'Come! I think you are indulging in a flight of fancy now. To a phlegmatic person like you, I suppose even I seem a volcano?'

'Oh, no!' answered Lezhnyov, with a smile. 'And as for character—you have no character at all, thank God!'

'What impertinence is that?'

'That? It's the highest compliment, believe me.'

Volintsev came in and looked suspiciously at Lezhnyov and his sister. He had grown thin of late. They both began to talk to him, but he scarcely smiled in response to their jests, and looked, as Pigasov once said of him, like a melancholy hare. But there has certainly never been a man in the world who, at some time in his life, has not looked worse than that. Volintsev felt that Natalya was drifting away from him, and with her it seemed as if the earth was giving way under his feet.

VII

The next day was Sunday, and Natalya got up late. The day before she had been very silent all day; she was secretly ashamed of her tears, and she slept very badly. Sitting half-dressed at her little piano, at times she played some chords, hardly audibly for fear of waking Mlle. Boncourt, and then let her forehead fall on the cold keys and remained a long while motionless. She kept thinking, not of Rudin himself, but of some word he had uttered, and she was wholly buried in her own thought. Sometimes she recollected Volintsev. She knew that he loved her. But her mind did not dwell on him more than an instant.... She felt a strange agitation. In the morning she dressed hurriedly and went down, and after saying good-morning to her mother, seized an opportunity and went out alone into the garden.... It was a hot day, bright and sunny in spite of occasional showers of rain. Slight vapoury clouds sailed smoothly over the clear sky, scarcely obscuring the sun, and at times a downpour of rain fell suddenly in sheets, and was as quickly over. The thickly falling drops, flashing like diamonds, fell swiftly with a kind of dull thud; the sunshine glistened through their sparkling drops; the grass, that had been rustling in the wind, was still, thirstily drinking in the moisture; the drenched trees were languidly shaking all their leaves; the birds were busily singing, and it was pleasant to hear their twittering chatter mingling with the fresh gurgle and murmur of the running rain-water. The dusty roads were steaming and slightly spotted by the smart strokes of the thick drops. Then the clouds passed over, a slight breeze began to stir, and the grass began to take tints of emerald and gold. The trees seemed more transparent with their wet leaves clinging together. A strong scent arose from all around.

The sky was almost cloudless again when Natalya came into the garden. It was full of sweetness and peace—that soothing, blissful peace in which the heart of man is stirred by a sweet languor of undefined desire and secret emotion.

Natalya walked along a long line of silver poplars beside the pond; suddenly, as if he had sprung out of the earth, Rudin stood before her. She was confused. He looked her in the face.

'You are alone?' he inquired.

'Yes, I am alone,' replied Natalya, 'but I was going back directly. It is time I was home.'

'I will go with you.'

And he walked along beside her.

'You seem melancholy,' he said.

'I—I was just going to say that I thought you were out of spirits.'

'Very likely—it is often so with me. It is more excusable in me than in you.'

'Why? Do you suppose I have nothing to be melancholy about?'

'At your age you ought to find happiness in life.'

Natalya walked some steps in silence.

'Dmitri Nikolaitch!' she said.

'Well?'

'Do you remember—the comparison you made yesterday—do you remember—of the oak?'

'Yes, I remember. Well?'

Natalya stole a look at Rudin.

'Why did you—what did you mean by that comparison?'

Rudin bent his head and fastened his eyes on the distance.

'Natalya Alexyevna!' he began with the intense and pregnant intonation peculiar to him, which always made the listener believe that Rudin was not expressing even the tenth part of what he held locked in his heart—'Natalya Alexyevna! you may have noticed that I speak little of my own past. There are some chords which I do not touch upon at all. My heart—who need know what has passed in it? To expose that to view has always seemed sacrilege to me. But with you I cast aside reserve; you win my confidence.... I cannot conceal from you that I too have loved and have suffered like all men.... When and how? it's useless to speak of that; but my heart has known much bliss and much pain....'

Rudin made a brief pause.

'What I said to you yesterday,' he went on, 'might be applied in a degree to me in my present position. But again it is useless to speak of this. That side of life is over for me now. What remains for me is a tedious and fatiguing journey along the parched and dusty road from point to point... When I shall arrive—whether I arrive at all—God knows.... Let us rather talk of you.'

'Can it be, Dmitri Nikolaitch,' Natalya interrupted him, 'you expect nothing from life?'

'Oh, no! I expect much, but not for myself.... Usefulness, the content that comes from activity, I shall never renounce; but I have renounced happiness. My hopes, my dreams, and my own happiness have nothing in common. Love'—(at this word he shrugged his shoulders)—'love is not for me; I am not worthy of it; a woman who loves has a right to demand the whole of a man, and I can never now give the whole of myself. Besides, it is for youth to win love; I am too old. How could I turn any one's head? God grant I keep my own head on my shoulders.'

'I understand,' said Natalya, 'that one who is bent on a lofty aim must not think of himself; but cannot a woman be capable of appreciating such a man? I should have thought, on the contrary, that a woman would be sooner repelled by an egoist.... All young men—the youth you speak of—all are egoists, they are all occupied only with themselves, even when they love. Believe me, a woman is not only able to value self-sacrifice; she can sacrifice herself.'

Natalya's cheeks were slightly flushed and her eyes shining. Before her friendship with Rudin she would never have succeeded in uttering such a long and ardent speech.

'You have heard my views on woman's mission more than once,' replied Rudin with a condescending smile. 'You know that I consider that Joan of Arc alone could have saved France.... but that's not the point. I wanted to speak of you. You are standing on the threshold of life.... To dwell on your future is both pleasant and not unprofitable.... Listen: you know I am your friend; I take almost a brother's interest in you. And so I hope you will not think my question indiscreet; tell me, is your heart so far quite untouched?'

Natalya grew hot all over and said nothing, Rudin stopped, and she stopped too.

'You are not angry with me?' he asked.

'No,' she answered, 'but I did not expect——'

'However,' he went on, 'you need not answer me. I know your secret.'

Natalya looked at him almost with dismay.

'Yes, yes, I know who has won your heart. And I must say that you could not have made a better choice. He is a splendid man; he knows how to value you; he has not been crushed by life—he is simple and pure-hearted in soul... he will make your happiness.'

'Of whom are you speaking, Dmitri Niklaitch?'

'Is it possible you don't understand? Of Volintsev, of course. What? isn't it true?'

Natalya turned a little away from Rudin. She was completely overwhelmed.

'Do you imagine he doesn't love you? Nonsense! he does not take his eyes off you, and follows every movement of yours; indeed, can love ever be concealed? And do not you yourself look on him with favour? So far as I can observe, your mother, too, likes him.... Your choice——'

'Dmitri Nikolaitch,' Natalya broke in, stretching out her hand in her confusion towards a bush near her, 'it is so difficult, really, for me to speak of this; but I assure you... you are mistaken.'

'I am mistaken!' repeated Rudin. 'I think not. I have not known you very long, but I already know you well. What is the meaning of the change I see in you? I see it clearly. Are you just the same as when I met you first, six weeks ago? No, Natalya Alexyevna, your heart is not free.'

'Perhaps not,' answered Natalya, hardly audibly, 'but all the same you are mistaken.'

'How is that?' asked Rudin.

'Let me go! don't question me!' replied Natalya, and with swift steps she turned towards the house.

She was frightened herself by the feelings of which she was suddenly conscious in herself.

Rudin overtook her and stopped her.

'Natalya Alexyevna,' he said, 'this conversation cannot end like this; it is too important for me too.... How am I to understand you?'

'Let me go!' repeated Natalya.

'Natalya Alexyevna, for mercy's sake!'

Rudin's face showed his agitation. He grew pale.

'You understand everything, you must understand me too!' said Natalya; she snatched away her hand and went on, not looking round.

'Only one word!' cried Rudin after her

She stood still, but did not turn round.

'You asked me what I meant by that comparison yesterday. Let me tell you, I don't want to deceive you. I spoke of myself, of my past,—and of you.'

'How? of me?'

'Yes, of you; I repeat, I will not deceive you. You know now what was the feeling, the new feeling I spoke of then.... Till to-day I should not have ventured...'

Natalya suddenly hid her face in her hands, and ran towards the house.

She was so distracted by the unexpected conclusion of her conversation with Rudin, that she ran past Volintsev without even noticing him. He was standing motionless with his back against a tree. He had arrived at the house a quarter of an hour before, and found Darya Mihailovna in the drawing-room; and after exchanging a few words got away unobserved and went in search of Natalya. Led by a lover's instinct, he went straight into the garden and came upon her and Rudin at the very instant when she snatched her hand away from him. Darkness seemed to fall upon his eyes. Gazing after Natalya, he left the tree and took two strides, not knowing whither or wherefore. Rudin saw him as he came up to him. Both looked each other in the face, bowed, and separated in silence.

'This won't be the end of it,' both were thinking.

Volintsev went to the very end of the garden. He felt sad and sick; a load lay on his heart, and his blood throbbed in sudden stabs at intervals. The rain began to fall a little again. Rudin turned into his own room. He, too, was disturbed; his thoughts were in a whirl. The trustful, unexpected contact of a young true heart is agitating for any one.

At table everything went somehow wrong. Natalya, pale all over, could scarcely sit in her place and did not raise her eyes. Volintsev sat as usual next her, and from time to time began to talk in a constrained way to her. It happened that Pigasov was dining at Darya Mihailovna's that day. He talked more than any one at table. Among other things he began to maintain that men, like dogs, can be divided into the short-tailed and the long-tailed. People are short-tailed, he said, either from birth or through their own fault. The short-tailed are in a sorry plight; nothing succeeds with them—they have no confidence in themselves. But the man who has a long furry tail is happy. He may be weaker and inferior to the short-tailed; but he believes in himself; he displays his tail and every one admires it. And this is a fit subject for wonder; the tail, of course, is a perfectly useless part of the body, you admit; of what use can a tail be? but all judge of their abilities by their tail. 'I myself,' he concluded with a sigh, 'belong to the number of the short-tailed, and what is most annoying, I cropped my tail myself.'

'By which you mean to say,' commented Rudin carelessly, 'what La Rochefoucauld said long before you: Believe in yourself and others will believe in you. Why the tail was brought in, I fail to understand.'

'Let every one,' Volintsev began sharply and with flashing eyes, 'let every one express himself according to his fancy. Talk of despotism! ... I consider there is none worse than the despotism of so-called clever men; confound them!'

Everyone was astonished at this outbreak from Volintsev; it was received in silence. Rudin tried to look at him, but he could not control his eyes, and turned away smiling without opening his lips.

'Aha! so you too have lost your tail!' thought Pigasov; and Natalya's heart sank in terror. Darya Mihailovna gave Volintsev a long puzzled stare and at last was the first to speak; she began to describe an extraordinary dog belonging to a minister So-and-So.

Volintsev went away soon after dinner. As he bade Natalya good-bye he could not resist saying to her:

'Why are you confused, as though you had done wrong? You cannot have done wrong to any one!'

Natalya did not understand at all, and could only gaze after him. Before tea Rudin went up to her, and bending over the table as though he were examining the papers, whispered:

'It is all like a dream, isn't it? I absolutely must see you alone—if only for a minute.' He turned to Mlle, Boncourt 'Here,' he said to her, 'this is the article you were looking for,' and again bending towards Natalya, he added in a whisper, 'Try to be near the terrace in the lilac arbour about ten o'clock; I will wait for you.'

Pigasov was the hero of the evening. Rudin left him in possession of the field. He afforded Darya Mihailovna much entertainment; first he told a story of one of his neighbours who, having been henpecked by his wife for thirty years, had grown so womanish that one day in crossing a little puddle when Pigasov was present, he put out his hand and picked up the skirt of his coat, as women do with their petticoats. Then he turned to another gentleman who to begin with had been a freemason, then a hypochondriac, and then wanted to be a banker.

'How were you a freemason, Philip Stepanitch?' Pigasov asked him.

'You know how; I wore the nail of my little finger long.'

But what most diverted Darya Mihailovna was when Pigasov set off on a dissertation upon love, and maintained that even he had been sighed for, that one ardent German lady had even given him the nickname of her 'dainty little African' and her 'hoarse little crow.' Darya Mihailovna laughed, but Pigasov spoke the truth; he really was in a position to boast of his conquests. He maintained that nothing could be easier than to make any woman you chose fall in love with you; you only need repeat to her for ten days in succession that heaven is on her lips and bliss in her eyes, and that the rest of womankind are all simply rag-bags beside her; and on the eleventh day she will be ready to say herself that there is heaven on her lips and bliss in her eyes, and will be in love with you. Everything comes to pass in the world; so who knows, perhaps Pigasov was right?

At half-past nine Rudin was already in the arbour. The stars had come out in the pale, distant depths of the heaven; there was still a red glow where the sun had set, and there the horizon seemed brighter and clearer; a semi-circular moon shone golden through the black network of the weeping birch-tree. The other trees stood like grim giants, with thousands of chinks looking like eyes, or fell into compact masses of darkness. Not a leaf was stirring; the topmost branches of the lilacs and acacias seemed to stretch upwards into the warm air, as though listening for something. The house was a dark mass now; patches of red light showed where the long windows were lighted up. It was a soft and peaceful evening, but under this peace was felt the secret breath of passion.

Rudin stood, his arms folded on his breast, and listened with strained attention. His heart beat violently, and involuntarily he held his breath. At last he caught the sound of light, hurrying footsteps, and Natalya came into the arbour.

Rudin rushed up to her, and took her hands. They were cold as ice.

'Natalya Alexyevna!' he began, in an agitated whisper, 'I wanted to see you.... I could not wait till to-morrow. I must tell you what I did not suspect—what I did not realise even this morning. I love you!'

Natalya's hands trembled feebly in his.

'I love you!' he repeated, 'and how could I have deceived myself so long? How was it I did not guess long ago that I love you? And you? Natalya Alexyevna, tell me!'

Natalya could scarcely draw her breath.

'You see I have come here,' she uttered, at last

'No, say that you love me!'

'I think—yes,' she whispered.

Rudin pressed her hands still more warmly, and tried to draw her to him.

Natalya looked quickly round.

'Let me go—I am frightened.... I think some one is listening to us.... For God's sake, be on your guard. Volintsev suspects.'

'Never mind him! You saw I did not even answer him to-day.... Ah, Natalya Alexyevna, how happy I am! Nothing shall sever us now!'

Natalya looked into his eyes.

'Let me go,' she whispered; 'it's time.'

'One instant,' began Rudin.

'No, let me go, let me go.'

'You seem afraid of me.'

'No, but it's time.'

'Repeat, then, at least once more.'...

'You say you are happy?' asked Natalya.

'I? No man in the world is happier than I am! Can you doubt it?'

Natalya lifted up her head. Very beautiful was her pale, noble, young face, transformed by passion, in the mysterious shadows of the arbour, in the faint light reflected from the evening sky.

'I tell you then,' she said, 'I will be yours.'

'Oh, my God!' cried Rudin.

But Natalya made her escape, and was gone.

Rudin stood still a little while, then walked slowly out of the arbour. The moon threw a light on his face; there was a smile on his lips.

'I am happy,' he uttered in a half whisper. 'Yes, I am happy,' he repeated, as though he wanted to convince himself.

He straightened his tall figure, shook back his locks, and walked quickly into the garden, with a happy gesture of his hands.

Meanwhile the bushes of the lilac arbour moved apart, and Pandalevsky appeared. He looked around warily, shook his head, pursed up his mouth, and said, significantly, 'So that's how it is. That must be brought to Darya Mihailovna's knowledge.' And he vanished.

VIII

On his return home, Volintsev was so gloomy and dejected, he gave his sister such listless answers, and so quickly locked himself up in his room, that she decided to send a messenger to Lezhnyov. She always had recourse to him in times of difficulty. Lezhnyov sent her word that he would come in the next day.

Volintsev was no more cheerful in the morning. After tea he was starting to superintend the work on the estate, but he stayed at home instead, lay on the sofa, and took up a book—a thing he did not often do. Volintsev had no taste for literature, and poetry simply alarmed him. 'This is as incomprehensible as poetry,' he used to say, and, in confirmation of his words, he used to quote the following lines from a Russian poet:—

'And till his gloomy lifetime's close
Nor reason nor experience proud
Will crush nor crumple Destiny's
Ensanguined forget-me-nots.'

Alexandra Pavlovna kept looking uneasily at her brother, but she did not worry him with questions. A carriage drew up at the steps.

'Ah!' she thought, 'Lezhnyov, thank goodness!'

A servant came in and announced the arrival of Rudin.

Volintsev flung his book on the floor, and raised his head. 'Who has come?' he asked.

'Rudin, Dmitri Nikolaitch,' repeated the man. Volintsev got up.

'Ask him in,' he said, 'and you, sister,' he added, turning to Alexandra Pavlovna, 'leave us alone.'

'But why?' she was beginning.

'I have a good reason,' he interrupted, passionately. 'I beg you to leave us.'

Rudin entered. Volintsev, standing in the middle of the room, received him with a chilly bow, without offering his hand.

'Confess you did not expect me,' began Rudin, and he laid his hat down by the window His lips were slightly twitching. He was ill at ease, but tried to conceal his embarrassment.

'I did not expect you, certainly,' replied Volintsev, 'after yesterday. I should have more readily expected some one with a special message from you.'

'I understand what you mean,' said Rudin, taking a seat, 'and am very grateful for your frankness. It is far better so. I have come myself to you, as to a man of honour.'

'Cannot we dispense with compliments?' observed Volintsev.

'I want to explain to you why I have come.'

'We are acquainted; why should you not come? Besides, this is not the first time you have honoured me with a visit.'

'I came to you as one man of honour to another,' repeated Rudin, 'and I want now to appeal to your sense of justice.... I have complete confidence in you.'

'What is the matter?' said Volintsev, who all this time was still standing in his original position, staring sullenly at Rudin, and sometimes pulling the ends of his moustache.

'If you would kindly... I came here to make an explanation, certainly, but all the same it cannot be done off-hand.'

'Why not?'

'A third person is involved in this matter.'

'What third person?'

'Sergei Pavlitch, you understand me?'

'Dmitri Nikolaitch, I don't understand you in the least.'

'You prefer——'

'I prefer you should speak plainly!' broke in Volintsev.

He was beginning to be angry in earnest.

Rudin frowned.

'Permit... we are alone... I must tell you—though you certainly are aware of it already (Volintsev shrugged his shoulders impatiently)—I must tell you that I love Natalya Alexyevna, and I have the right to believe that she loves me.'

Volintsev turned white, but made no reply. He walked to the window and stood with his back turned.

'You understand, Sergei Pavlitch,' continued Rudin, 'that if I were not convinced...'

'Upon my word!' interrupted Volintsev, 'I don't doubt it in the least.... Well! so be it! Good luck to you! Only I wonder what the devil induced you to come with this news to me.... What have I to do with it? What is it to me whom you love, or who loves you? It simply passes my comprehension.'

Volintsev continued to stare out of the window. His voice sounded choked.

Rudin got up.

'I will tell you, Sergei Pavlitch, why I decided to come to you, why I did not even think I had the right to hide from you our—our mutual feelings. I have too profound an esteem for you—that is why I have come; I did not want... we both did not wish to play a part before you. Your feeling for Natalya Alexyevna was known to me.... Believe me, I have no illusions about myself; I know how little I deserve to supplant you in her heart, but if it was fated this should be, is it made any better by pretence, hypocrisy, and deceit? Is it any better to expose ourselves to misunderstandings, or even to the possibilities of such a scene as took place yesterday at dinner? Sergei Pavlitch, tell me yourself, is it?'

Volintsev folded his arms on his chest, as though he were trying to hold himself in.

'Sergei Pavlitch!' Rudin continued, 'I have given you pain, I feel it—but understand us—understand that we had no other means of proving our respect to you, of proving that we know how to value your honour and uprightness. Openness, complete openness with any other man would have been misplaced; but with you it took the form of duty. We are happy to think our secret is in your hands.'

Volintsev gave vent to a forced laugh.

'Many thanks for your confidence in me!' he exclaimed, 'though, pray observe, I neither wished to know your secret, nor to tell you mine, though you treat it as if it were your property. But excuse me, you speak as though for two. Does it follow I am to suppose that Natalya Alexyevna knows of your visit, and the object of it?'

Rudin was a little taken aback.

'No, I did not communicate my intention to Natalya Alexyevna; but I know she would share my views.'

'That's all very fine indeed,' Volintsev began after a short pause, drumming on the window pane with his fingers, 'though I must confess it would have been far better if you had had rather less respect for me. I don't care a hang for your respect, to tell you the truth; but what do you want of me now?'

'I want nothing—or—no! I want one thing; I want you not to regard me as treacherous or hypocritical, to understand me... I hope that now you cannot doubt of my sincerity... I want us, Sergei Pavlitch, to part as friends... you to give me your hand as you once did.'

And Rudin went up to Volintsev.

'Excuse me, my good sir,' said Volintsev, turning round and stepping back a few paces, 'I am ready to do full justice to your intentions, all that's very fine, I admit, very exalted, but we are simple people, we do not gild our gingerbread, we are not capable of following the flight of great minds like yours.... What you think sincere, we regard as impertinent and disingenuous and indiscreet.... What is clear and simple to you, is involved and obscure to us.... You boast of what we conceal.... How are we to understand you! Excuse me, I can neither regard you as a friend, nor will I give you my hand.... That is petty, perhaps, but I am only a petty person.'

Rudin took his hat from the window seat.

'Sergei Pavlitch!' he said sorrowfully, 'goodbye; I was mistaken in my expectations. My visit certainly was rather a strange one... but I had hoped that you... (Volintsev made a movement of impatience). ... Excuse me, I will say no more of this. Reflecting upon it all, I see indeed, you are right, you could not have behaved otherwise. Good-bye, and allow me, at least once more, for the last time, to assure you of the purity of my intentions.... I am convinced of your discretion.'

'That is too much!' cried Volintsev, shaking with anger, 'I never asked for your confidence; and so you have no right whatever to reckon on my discretion!'

Rudin was about to say something, but he only waved his hands, bowed and went away, and Volintsev flung himself on the sofa and turned his face to the wall.

'May I come in?' Alexandra Pavlovna's voice was heard saying at the door.

Volintsev did not answer at once, and stealthily passed his hand over his face. 'No, Sasha,' he said, in a slightly altered voice, 'wait a little longer.'

Half an hour later, Alexandra Pavlovna again came to the door.

'Mihailo Mihailitch is here,' she said, 'will you see him?'

'Yes,' answered Volintsev, 'let them show him up here.'

Lezhnyov came in.

'What, aren't you well?' he asked, seating himself in a chair near the sofa.

Volintsev raised himself, and, leaning on his elbow gazed a long, long while into his friend's face, and then repeated to him his whole conversation with Rudin word for word. He had never before given Lezhnyov a hint of his sentiments towards Natalya, though he guessed they were no secret to him.

'Well, brother, you have surprised me!' Lezhnyov said, as soon as Volintsev had finished his story. 'I expected many strange things from him, but this is——Still I can see him in it.'

'Upon my honour!' cried Volintsev, in great excitement, 'it is simply insolence! Why, I almost threw him out of the window. Did he want to boast to me or was he afraid? What was the object of it? How could he make up his mind to come to a man——?'

Volintsev clasped his hands over his head and was speechless.

'No, brother, that's not it,' replied Lezhnyov tranquilly; 'you won't believe me, but he really did it from a good motive. Yes, indeed. It was generous, do you see, and candid, to be sure, and it would offer an opportunity of speechifying and giving vent to his fine talk, and, of course, that's what he wants, what he can't live without. Ah! his tongue is his enemy. Though it's a good servant to him too.'

'With what solemnity he came in and talked, you can't imagine!'

'Well, he can't do anything without that. He buttons his great-coat as if he were fulfilling a sacred duty. I should like to put him on a desert island and look round a corner to see how he would behave there. And he discourses on simplicity!'

'But tell me, my dear fellow,' asked Volintsev, 'what is it, philosophy or what?'

'How can I tell you? On one side it is philosophy, I daresay, and on the other something altogether different It is not right to put every folly down to philosophy.'

Volintsev looked at him.

'Wasn't he lying then, do you imagine?'

'No, my son, he wasn't lying. But, do you know, we've talked enough of this. Let's light our pipes and call Alexandra Pavlovna in here. It's easier to talk when she's with us and easier to be silent. She shall make us some tea.'

'Very well,' replied Volintsev. 'Sasha, come in,' he cried aloud.

Alexandra Pavlovna came in. He grasped her hand and pressed it warmly to his lips.

Rudin returned in a curious and mingled frame of mind. He was annoyed with himself, he reproached himself for his unpardonable precipitancy, his boyish impulsiveness. Some one has justly said: there is nothing more painful than the consciousness of having just done something stupid.

Rudin was devoured by regret.

'What evil genius drove me,' he muttered between his teeth, 'to call on that squire! What an idea it was! Only to expose myself to insolence!'

But in Darya Mihailovna's house something extraordinary had been happening. The lady herself did not appear the whole morning, and did not come in to dinner; she had a headache, declared Pandalevsky, the only person who had been admitted to her room. Natalya, too, Rudin scarcely got a glimpse of: she sat in her room with Mlle. Boncourt When she met him at the dinner-table she looked at him so mournfully that his heart sank. Her face was changed as though a load of sorrow had descended upon her since the day before. Rudin began to be oppressed by a vague presentiment of trouble. In order to distract his mind in some way he occupied himself with Bassistoff, had much conversation with him, and found him an ardent, eager lad, full of enthusiastic hopes and still untarnished faith. In the evening Darya Mihailovna appeared for a couple of hours in the drawing-room. She was polite to Rudin, but kept him somehow at a distance, and smiled and frowned, talking through her nose, and in hints more than ever. Everything about her had the air of the society lady of the court. She had seemed of late rather cooler to Rudin. 'What is the secret of it?' he thought, with a sidelong look at her haughtily-lifted head.

He had not long to wait for the solution of the enigma. As he was returning at twelve o'clock at night to his room, along a dark corridor, some one suddenly thrust a note into his hand. He looked round; a girl was hurrying away in the distance, Natalya's maid, he fancied. He went into his room, dismissed the servant, tore open the letter, and read the following lines in Natalya's handwriting:—

'Come to-morrow at seven o'clock in the morning, not later, to Avduhin pond, beyond the oak copse. Any other time will be impossible. It will be our last meeting, all will be over, unless... Come. We must make our decision.—P.S. If I don't come, it will mean we shall not see each other again; then I will let you know.'

Rudin turned the letter over in his hands, musing upon it, then laid it under his pillow, undressed, and lay down. For a long while he could not get to sleep, and then he slept very lightly, and it was not yet five o'clock when he woke up.

IX

The Avduhin pond, near which Natalya had fixed the place of meeting, had long ceased to be a pond. Thirty years before it had burst through its banks and it had been given up since then. Only by the smooth flat surface of the hollow, once covered with slimy mud, and the traces of the banks, could one guess that it had been a pond. A farm-house had stood near it. It had long ago passed away. Two huge pine-trees preserved its memory; the wind was for ever droning and sullenly murmuring in their high gaunt green tops. There were mysterious tales among the people of a fearful crime supposed to have been committed under them; they used to tell, too, that not one of them would fall without bringing death to some one; that a third had once stood there, which had fallen in a storm and crushed a girl.

The whole place near the old pond was supposed to be haunted; it was a barren wilderness, dark and gloomy, even on a sunny day—it seemed darker and gloomier still from the old, old forest of dead and withered oak-trees which was near it. A few huge trees lifted their grey heads above the low undergrowth of bushes like weary giants. They were a sinister sight; it seemed as though wicked old men had met together bent on some evil design. A narrow path almost indistinguishable wandered beside it. No one went near the Avduhin pond without some urgent reason. Natalya intentionally chose this solitary place. It was not more than half-a-mile from Darya Mihailovna's house.

The sun had already risen some time when Rudin reached the Avduhin pond, but it was not a bright morning. Thick clouds of the colour of milk covered the whole sky, and were driven flying before the whistling, shrieking wind. Rudin began to walk up and down along the bank, which was covered with clinging burdocks and blackened nettles. He was not easy in his mind. These interviews, these new emotions had a charm for him, but they also troubled him, especially after the note of the night before. He felt that the end was drawing near, and was in secret perplexity of spirit, though none would have imagined it, seeing with what concentrated determination he folded his arms across his chest and looked around him. Pigasov had once said truly of him, that he was like a Chinese idol, his head was constantly overbalancing him. But with the head alone, however strong it may be, it is hard for a man to know even what is passing in himself.... Rudin, the clever, penetrating Rudin, was not capable of saying certainly whether he loved Natalya, whether he was suffering, and whether he would suffer at parting from her. Why then, since he had not the least disposition to play the Lovelace—one must do him that credit—had he turned the poor girl's head? Why was he awaiting her with a secret tremor? To this the only answer is that there are none so easily carried away as those who are without passion.

He walked on the bank, while Natalya was hurrying to him straight across country through the wet grass.

'Natalya Alexyevna, you'll get your feet wet!' said her maid Masha, scarcely able to keep up with her.

Natalya did not hear and ran on without looking round.

'Ah, supposing they've seen us!' cried Masha; 'indeed it's surprising how we got out of the house... and ma'mselle may wake up... It's a mercy it's not far.... Ah, the gentleman's waiting already,' she added, suddenly catching sight of Rudin's majestic figure, standing out picturesquely on the bank; 'but what does he want to stand on that mound for—he ought to have kept in the hollow.'

Natalya stopped.

'Wait here, Masha, by the pines,' she said, and went on to the pond.

Rudin went up to her; he stopped short in amazement. He had never seen such an expression on her face before. Her brows were contracted, her lips set, her eyes looked sternly straight before her.

'Dmitri Nikolaitch,' she began, 'we have no time to lose. I have come for five minutes. I must tell you that my mother knows everything. Mr. Pandalevsky saw us the day before yesterday, and he told her of our meeting. He was always mamma's spy. She called me in to her yesterday.'

'Good God!' cried Rudin, 'this is terrible.... What did your mother say?'

'She was not angry with me, she did not scold me, but she reproached me for my want of discretion.'

'That was all?'

'Yes, and she declared she would sooner see me dead than your wife!'

'Is it possible she said that?'

'Yes; and she said too that you yourself did not want to marry me at all, that you had only been flirting with me because you were bored, and that she had not expected this of you; but that she herself was to blame for having allowed me to see so much of you... that she relied on my good sense, that I had very much surprised her... and I don't remember now all she said to me.'

Natalya uttered all this in an even, almost expressionless voice.

'And you, Natalya Alexyevna, what did you answer?' asked Rudin.

'What did I answer?' repeated Natalya.... 'What do you intend to do now?'

'Good God, good God!' replied Rudin, 'it is cruel! So soon... such a sudden blow!... And is your mother in such indignation?'

'Yes, yes, she will not hear of you.'

'It is terrible! You mean there is no hope?

'None.'

'Why should we be so unhappy! That abominable Pandalevsky!... You ask me, Natalya Alexyevna, what I intend to do? My head is going round—I cannot take in anything... I can feel nothing but my unhappiness... I am amazed that you can preserve such self-possession!'

'Do you think it is easy for me?' said Natalya.

Rudin began to walk along the bank. Natalya did not take her eyes off him.

'Your mother did not question you?' he said at last.

'She asked me whether I love you.'

'Well... and you?'

Natalya was silent a moment. 'I told the truth.'

Rudin took her hand.

'Always, in all things generous, noble-hearted! Oh, the heart of a girl—it's pure gold! But did your mother really declare her decision so absolutely on the impossibility of our marriage?'

'Yes, absolutely. I have told you already; she is convinced that you yourself don't think of marrying me.'

'Then she regards me as a traitor! What have I done to deserve it?' And Rudin clutched his head in his hands.

'Dmitri Nikolaitch!' said Natalya, 'we are losing our time. Remember I am seeing you for the last time. I came here not to weep and lament—you see I am not crying—I came for advice.'

'And what advice can I give you, Natalya Alexyevna?'

'What advice? You are a man; I am used to trusting to you, I shall trust you to the end. Tell me, what are your plans?'

'My plans.... Your mother certainly will turn me out of the house.'

'Perhaps. She told me yesterday that she must break off all acquaintance with you.... But you do not answer my question?'

'What question?'

'What do you think we must do now?'

'What we must do?' replied Rudin; 'of course submit.'

'Submit,' repeated Natalya slowly, and her lips turned white.

'Submit to destiny,' continued Rudin. 'What is to be done? I know very well how bitter it is, how painful, how unendurable. But consider yourself, Natalya Alexyevna; I am poor. It is true I could work; but even if I were a rich man, could you bear a violent separation from your family, your mother's anger?... No, Natalya Alexyevna; it is useless even to think of it. It is clear it was not fated for us to live together, and the happiness of which I dreamed is not for me!'

All at once Natalya hid her face in her hands and began to weep. Rudin went up to her.

'Natalya Alexyevna! dear Natalya!' he said with warmth, 'do not cry, for God's sake, do not torture me, be comforted.'

Natalya raised her head.

'You tell me to be comforted,' she began, and her eyes blazed through her tears; 'I am not weeping for what you suppose—I am not sad for that; I am sad because I have been deceived in you.... What! I come to you for counsel, and at such a moment!—and your first word is, submit! submit! So this is how you translate your talk of independence, of sacrifice, which...'

Her voice broke down.

'But, Natalya Alexyevna,' began Rudin in confusion, 'remember—I do not disown my words—only——'

'You asked me,' she continued with new force, 'what I answered my mother, when she declared she would sooner agree to my death than my marriage to you; I answered that I would sooner die than marry any other man... And you say, "Submit!" It must be that she is right; you must, through having nothing to do, through being bored, have been playing with me.'

'I swear to you, Natalya Alexyevna—I assure you,' maintained Rudin.

But she did not listen to him.

'Why did you not stop me? Why did you yourself—or did you not reckon upon obstacles? I am ashamed to speak of this—but I see it is all over now.'

'You must be calm, Natalya Alexyevna,' Rudin was beginning; 'we must think together what means——'

'You have so often talked of self-sacrifice,' she broke in, 'but do you know, if you had said to me to-day at once, "I love you, but I cannot marry you, I will not answer for the future, give me your hand and come with me"—do you know, I would have come with you; do you know, I would have risked everything? But there's all the difference between word and deed, and you were afraid now, just as you were afraid the day before yesterday at dinner of Volintsev.'

The colour rushed to Rudin's face. Natalya's unexpected energy had astounded him; but her last words wounded his vanity.

'You are too angry now, Natalya Alexyevna,' he began; 'you cannot realise how bitterly you wound me. I hope that in time you will do me justice; you will understand what it has cost me to renounce the happiness which you have said yourself would have laid upon me no obligations. Your peace is dearer to me than anything in the world, and I should have been the basest of men, if I could have taken advantage——'

'Perhaps, perhaps,' interrupted Natalya, 'perhaps you are right; I don't know what I am saying. But up to this time I believed in you, believed in every word you said.... For the future, pray keep a watch upon your words, do not fling them about at hazard. When I said to you, "I love you," I knew what that word meant; I was ready for everything.... Now I have only to thank you for a lesson—and to say good-bye.'

'Stop, for God's sake, Natalya Alexyevna, I beseech you. I do not deserve your contempt, I swear to you. Put yourself in my position. I am responsible for you and for myself. If I did not love you with the most devoted love—why, good God! I should have at once proposed you should run away with me.... Sooner or later your mother would forgive us—and then... But before thinking of my own happiness——'

He stopped. Natalya's eyes fastened directly upon him put him to confusion.

'You try to prove to me that you are an honourable man, Dmitri Nikolaitch,' she said. 'I do not doubt that. You are not capable of acting from calculation; but did I want to be convinced of that? did I come here for that?'

'I did not expect, Natalya Alexyevna——'

'Ah! you have said it at last! Yes, you did not expect all this—you did not know me. Do not be uneasy... you do not love me, and I will never force myself on any one.'

'I love you!' cried Rudin.

Natalya drew herself up.

'Perhaps; but how do you love me? Remember all your words, Dmitri Nikolaitch. You told me: "Without complete equality there is no love."... You are too exalted for me; I am no match for you.... I am punished as I deserve. There are duties before you more worthy of you. I shall not forget this day.... Good-bye.'

'Natalya Alexyevna, are you going? Is it possible for us to part like this?'

He stretched out his hand to her. She stopped. His supplicating voice seemed to make her waver.

'No,' she uttered at last. 'I feel that something in me is broken. ... I came here, I have been talking to you as if it were in delirium; I must try to recollect. It must not be, you yourself said, it will not be. Good God, when I came out here, I mentally took a farewell of my home, of my past—and what? whom have I met here?—a coward... and how did you know I was not able to bear a separation from my family? "Your mother will not consent... It is terrible!" That was all I heard from you, that you, you, Rudin?—No! good-bye.... Ah! if you had loved me, I should have felt it now, at this moment.... No, no, goodbye!'

She turned swiftly and ran towards Masha, who had begun to be uneasy and had been making signs to her a long while.

'It is *you* who are afraid, not I!' cried Rudin after Natalya.

She paid no attention to him, and hastened homewards across the fields. She succeeded in getting back to her bedroom; but she had scarcely crossed the threshold when her strength failed her, and she fell senseless into Masha's arms.

But Rudin remained a long while still standing on the bank. At last he shivered, and with slow steps made his way to the little path and quietly walked along it. He was deeply ashamed... and wounded. 'What a girl!' he thought, 'at seventeen!... No, I did not know her!... She is a remarkable girl. What strength of will!... She is right; she deserves another love than what I felt for her. I felt for her?' he asked himself. 'Can it be I already feel no more love for her? So this is how it was all to end! What a pitiful wretch I was beside her!'

The slight rattle of a racing droshky made Rudin raise his head. Lezhnyov was driving to meet him with his invariable trotting pony. Rudin bowed to him without speaking, and as though struck with a sudden thought, turned out of the road and walked quickly in the direction of Darya Mihailovna's house.

Lezhnyov let him pass, looked after him, and after a moment's thought he too turned his horse's head round, and drove back to Volintsev's, where he had spent the night. He found him asleep, and giving orders he should not be waked, he sat down on the balcony to wait for some tea and smoked a pipe.

X

Volintsev got up at ten o'clock. When he heard that Lezhnyov was sitting in the balcony, he was much surprised, and sent to ask him to come to him.

'What has happened?' he asked him. 'I thought you meant to drive home?'

'Yes; I did mean to, but I met Rudin.... He was wandering about the country with such a distracted countenance. So I turned back at once.'

'You came back because you met Rudin?'

'That's to say,—to tell the truth, I don't know why I came back myself, I suppose because I was reminded of you; I wanted to be with you, and I have plenty of time before I need go home.'

Volintsev smiled bitterly.

'Yes; one cannot think of Rudin now without thinking of me.... Boy!' he cried harshly, 'bring us some tea.'

The friends began to drink tea. Lezhnyov talked of agricultural matters,—of a new method of roofing barns with paper....

Suddenly Volintsev leaped up from his chair and struck the table with such force that the cups and saucers rang.

'No!' he cried, 'I cannot bear this any longer! I will call out this witty fellow, and let him shoot me,—at least I will try to put a bullet through his learned brains!'

'What are you talking about? Upon my word!' grumbled Lezhnyov, 'how can you scream like that? I dropped my pipe.... What's the matter with you?'

'The matter is, that I can't hear his name and keep calm; it sets all my blood boiling!'

'Hush, my dear fellow, hush! aren't you ashamed?' rejoined Lezhnyov, picking up his pipe from the ground. 'Leave off! Let him alone!'

'He has insulted me,' pursued Volintsev, walking up and down the room. 'Yes! he has insulted me. You must admit that yourself. At first I was not sharp enough; he took me by surprise; and who could have expected this? But I will show him that he cannot make a fool of me. ... I will shoot him, the damned philosopher, like a partridge.'

'Much you will gain by that, indeed! I won't speak of your sister now. I can see you're in a passion... how could you think of your sister! But in relation to another individual—what! do you imagine, when you've killed the philosopher, you can improve your own chances?'

Volintsev flung himself into a chair.

'Then I must go away somewhere! For here my heart is simply being crushed by misery; only I can find no place to go.'

'Go away... that's another matter! That I am ready to agree to. And do you know what I should suggest? Let us go together—to the Caucasus, or simply to Little Russia to eat dumplings. That's a capital idea, my dear fellow!'

'Yes; but whom shall we leave my sister with?'

'And why should not Alexandra Pavlovna come with us? Upon my soul, it will be splendid. As for looking after her—yes, I'll undertake that! There will be no difficulty in getting anything we want: if she likes, I will arrange a serenade under her window every night; I will sprinkle the coachmen with*eau de cologne* and strew flowers along the roads. And we shall both be simply new men, my dear boy; we shall enjoy ourselves so, we shall come back so fat that we shall be proof against the darts of love!'

'You are always joking, Misha!'

'I'm not joking at all. It was a brilliant idea of yours.'

'No; nonsense!' Volintsev shouted again. 'I want to fight him, to fight him!...'

'Again! What a rage you are in!'

A servant entered with a letter in his hand.

'From whom?' asked Lezhnyov.

'From Rudin, Dmitri Nikolaitch. The Lasunsky's servant brought it.'

'From Rudin?' repeated Volintsev, 'to whom?'

'To you.'

'To me!... give it me!'

Volintsev seized the letter, quickly tore it open, and began to read. Lezhnyov watched him attentively; a strange, almost joyful amazement was expressed on Volintsev's face; he let his hands fall by his side.

'What is it?' asked Lezhnyov.

'Read it,' Volintsev said in a low voice, and handed him the letter.

Lezhnyov began to read. This is what Rudin wrote:

'SIR—

'I am going away from Darya Mihailovna's house to-day, and leaving it for ever. This will certainly be a surprise to you, especially after what passed yesterday. I cannot explain to you what exactly obliges me to act in this way; but it seems to me for some reason that I ought to let you know of my departure. You do not like me, and even regard me as a bad man. I do not intend to justify myself; time will justify me. In my opinion it is even undignified in a man and quite unprofitable to try to prove to a prejudiced man the injustice of his prejudice. Whoever wishes to understand me will not blame me, and as for any one who does not wish, or cannot do so,—his censure does not pain me. I was mistaken in you. In my eyes you remain as before a noble and honourable man, but I imagined you were able to be superior to the surroundings in which you were brought up. I was mistaken. What of that? It is not the first, nor will it be the last time. I repeat to you, I am going away. I wish you all happiness. Confess that this wish is completely disinterested, and I hope that now you will be happy. Perhaps in time you will change your opinion of me. Whether we shall ever meet again, I don't know, but in any case I remain your sincere well-wisher,

'D. R.

'P.S. The two hundred roubles I owe you I will send directly I reach my estate in T—— province. Also I beg you not to speak to Darya Mihailovna of this letter.

'P.P.S. One last, but important request more; since I am going away, I hope you will not allude before Natalya Alexyevna to my visit to you.'

'Well, what do you say to that?' asked Volintsev, directly Lezhnyov had finished the letter.

'What is one to say?' replied Lezhnyov, 'Cry "Allah! Allah!" like a Mussulman and sit gaping with astonishment—that's all one can do.... Well, a good riddance! But it's curious: you see he thought it his *duty* to write you this letter, and he came to see you from a sense of *duty*... these gentlemen find a duty at every step, some duty they owe... or some debt,' added Lezhnyov, pointing with a smile to the postscript.

'And what phrases he rounds off!' cried Volintsev. 'He was mistaken in me. He expected I would be superior to my surroundings. What a rigmarole! Good God! it's worse than poetry!'

Lezhnyov made no reply, but his eyes were smiling. Volintsev got up.

'I want to go to Darya Mihailovna's,' he announced. 'I want to find out what it all means.'

'Wait a little, my dear boy; give him time to get off. What's the good of running up against him again? He is to vanish, it seems. What more do you want? Better go and lie down and get a little sleep; you have been tossing about all night, I expect. But everything will be smooth for you.'

'What leads you to that conclusion?'

'Oh, I think so. There, go and have a nap; I will go and see your sister. I will keep her company.'

'I don't want to sleep in the least. What's the object of my going to bed? I had rather go out to the fields,' said Volintsev, putting on his out-of-door coat.

'Well, that's a good thing too. Go along, and look at the fields....'

And Lezhnyov betook himself to the apartments of Alexandra Pavlovna. He found her in the drawing-room. She welcomed him effusively. She was always pleased when he came; but her face still looked sorrowful. She was uneasy about Rudin's visit the day before.

'You have seen my brother?' she asked Lezhnyov. 'How is he to-day?'

'All right, he has gone to the fields.'

Alexandra Favlovna did not speak for a minute.

'Tell me, please,' she began, gazing earnestly at the hem of her pocket-handkerchief, 'don't you know why...'

'Rudin came here?' put in Lezhnyov. 'I know, he came to say good-bye.'

Alexandra Pavlovna lifted up her head.

'What, to say good-bye!'

'Yes. Haven't you heard? He is leaving Darya Mihailovna's.'

'He is leaving?'

'For ever; at least he says so.'

'But pray, how is one to explain it, after all?...'

'Oh, that's a different matter! To explain it is impossible, but it is so. Something must have happened with them. He pulled the string too tight—and it has snapped.'

'Mihailo Mihailitch!' began Alexandra Pavlovna, 'I don't understand; you are laughing at me, I think....'

'No indeed! I tell you he is going away, and he even let his friends know by letter. It's just as well, I daresay, from one point of view; but his departure has prevented one surprising enterprise from being carried out that I had begun to talk to your brother about.'

'What do you mean? What enterprise?'

'Why, I proposed to your brother that we should go on our travels, to distract his mind, and take you with us. To look after you especially I would take on myself....'

'That's capital!' cried Alexandra Pavlovna. 'I can fancy how you would look after me. Why, you would let me die of hunger.'

'You say so, Alexandra Pavlovna, because you don't know me. You think I am a perfect blockhead, a log; but do you know I am capable of melting like sugar, of spending whole days on my knees?'

'I should like to see that, I must say!'

Lezhnyov suddenly got up. 'Well, marry me, Alexandra Pavlovna, and you will see all that'

Alexandra Pavlovna blushed up to her ears.

'What did you say, Mihailo Mihailitch?' she murmured in confusion.

'I said what it has been for ever so long,' answered Lezhnyov, 'on the tip of my tongue to say a thousand times over. I have brought it out at last, and you must act as you think best. But I will go away now, so as not to be in your way. If you will be my wife... I will walk away... if you don't dislike the idea, you need only send to call me in; I shall understand....'

Alexandra Pavlovna tried to keep Lezhnyov, but he went quickly away, and going into the garden without his cap, he leaned on a little gate and began looking about him.

'Mihailo Mihailitch!' sounded the voice of a maid-servant behind him, 'please come in to my lady. She sent me to call you.'

Mihailo Mihailitch turned round, took the girl's head in both his hands, to her great astonishment, and kissed her on the forehead, then he went in to Alexandra Pavlovna.

XI

On returning home, directly after his meeting with Lezhnyov, Rudin shut himself up in his room, and wrote two letters; one to Volintsev (already known to the reader) and the other to Natalya. He sat a very long time over this second letter, crossed out and altered a great deal in it, and, copying it carefully on a fine sheet of note-paper, folded it up as small as possible, and put it in his pocket. With a look of pain on his face he paced several times up and down his room, sat down in the chair before the window, leaning on his arm; a tear slowly appeared upon his eyelashes. He got up, buttoned himself up, called a servant and told him to ask Darya Mihailovna if he could see her.

The man returned quickly, answering that Darya Mihailovna would be delighted to see him. Rudin went to her.

She received him in her study, as she had that first time, two months before. But now she was not alone; with her was sitting Pandalevsky, unassuming, fresh, neat, and agreeable as ever.

Darya Mihailovna met Rudin affably, and Rudin bowed affably to her; but at the first glance at the smiling faces of both, any one of even small experience would have understood that something of an unpleasant nature had passed between them, even if it had not been expressed. Rudin knew that Darya Mihailovna was angry with him. Darya Mihailovna suspected that he was now aware of all that had happened.

Pandalevsky's disclosure had greatly disturbed her. It touched on the worldly pride in her. Rudin, a poor man without rank, and so far without distinction, had presumed to make a secret appointment with her daughter—the daughter of Darya Mihailovna Lasunsky.

'Granting he is clever, he is a genius!' she said, 'what does that prove? Why, any one may hope to be my son-in-law after that?'

'For a long time I could not believe my eyes.' put in Pandalevsky. 'I am surprised at his not understanding his position!'

Darya Mihailovna was very much agitated, and Natalya suffered for it

She asked Rudin to sit down. He sat down, but not like the old Rudin, almost master of the house, not even like an old friend, but like a guest, and not even a very intimate guest. All this took place in a single instant... so water is suddenly transformed into solid ice.

'I have come to you, Darya Mihailovna,' began Rudin, 'to thank you for your hospitality. I have had some news to-day from my little estate, and it is absolutely necessary for me to set off there to-day.'

Darya Mihailovna looked attentively at Rudin.

'He has anticipated me; it must be because he has some suspicion,' she thought. 'He spares one a disagreeable explanation. So much the better. Ah! clever people for ever!'

'Really?' she replied aloud. 'Ah! how disappointing! Well, I suppose there's no help for it. I shall hope to see you this winter in Moscow. We shall soon be leaving here.'

'I don't know, Darya Mihailovna, whether I shall succeed in getting to Moscow, but, if I can manage it, I shall regard it as a duty to call on you.'

'Aha, my good sir!' Pandalevsky in his turn reflected; 'it's not long since you behaved like the master here, and now this is how you have to express yourself!'

'Then I suppose you have unsatisfactory news from your estate?' he articulated, with his customary ease.

'Yes,' replied Rudin drily.

'Some failure of crops, I suppose?'

'No; something else. Believe me, Darya Mihailovna,' added Rudin, 'I shall never forget the time I have spent in your house.'

'And I, Dmitri Nikolaitch, shall always look back upon our acquaintance with you with pleasure. When must you start?'

'To-day, after dinner.'

'So soon!... Well, I wish you a successful journey. But, if your affairs do not detain you, perhaps you will look us up again here.'

'I shall scarcely have time,' replied Rudin, getting up. 'Excuse me,' he added; 'I cannot at once repay you my debt, but directly I reach my place——'

'Nonsense, Dmitri Nikolaitch!' Darya Mihailovna cut him short. 'I wonder you're not ashamed to speak of it!... What o'clock is it?' she asked.

Pandalevsky drew a gold and enamel watch out of his waistcoat pocket, and looked at it carefully, bending his rosy cheek over his stiff, white collar.

'Thirty-three minutes past two,' he announced.

'It is time to dress,' observed Darya Mihailovna. 'Good-bye for the present, Dmitri Nikolaitch!'

Rudin got up. The whole conversation between him and Darya Mihailovna had a special character. In the same way actors repeat their parts, and diplomatic dignitaries interchange their carefully-worded phrases.

Rudin went away. He knew by now through experience that men and women of the world do not even break with a man who is of no further use to them, but simply let him drop, like a kid glove after a ball, like the paper that has wrapped up sweets, like an unsuccessful ticket for a lottery.

He packed quickly, and began to await with impatience the moment of his departure. Every one in the house was very much surprised to hear of his intentions; even the servants looked at him with a puzzled air. Bassistoff did not conceal his sorrow. Natalya evidently avoided Rudin. She tried not to meet his eyes. He succeeded, however, in slipping his note into her hand. After dinner Darya Mihailovna repeated once more that she hoped to see him before they left for Moscow, but Rudin made her no reply. Pandalevsky addressed him more frequently than any one. More than once Rudin felt a longing to fall upon him and give him a slap on his rosy, blooming face. Mlle. Boncourt often glanced at Rudin with a peculiarly stealthy expression in her eyes; in old setter dogs one may sometimes see the same expression.

'Aha!' she seemed to be saying to herself, 'so you're caught!'

At last six o'clock struck, and Rudin's carriage was brought to the door. He began to take a hurried farewell of all. He had a feeling of nausea at his heart. He had not expected to leave this house like this; it seemed as though they were turning him out. 'What a way to do it all! and what was the object of being in such a hurry? Still, it is better so.' That was what he was thinking as he bowed in all directions with a forced smile. For the last time he looked at Natalya, and his heart throbbed; her eyes were bent upon him in sad, reproachful farewell.

He ran quickly down the steps, and jumped into his carriage. Bassistoff had offered to accompany him to the next station, and he took his seat beside him.

'Do you remember,' began Rudin, directly the carriage had driven from the courtyard into the broad road bordered with fir-trees, 'do you remember what Don Quixote says to his squire when he is leaving the court of the duchess? "Freedom," he says, "my friend Sancho, is one of the most precious possessions of man, and happy is he to whom Heaven has given a bit of bread, and who need not be indebted to any one!" What Don Quixote felt then, I feel now.... God grant, my dear Bassistoff, that you too may some day experience this feeling!'

Bassistoff pressed Rudin's hand, and the honest boy's heart beat violently with emotion. Till they reached the station Rudin spoke of the dignity of man, of the meaning of true independence. He spoke nobly, fervently, and justly, and when the moment of separation had come, Bassistoff could not refrain from throwing himself on his neck and sobbing. Rudin himself shed tears too, but he was not weeping because he was parting from Bassistoff. His tears were the tears of wounded vanity.

Natalya had gone to her own room, and there she read Rudin's letter.

'Dear Natalya Alexyevna,' he wrote her, 'I have decided to depart. There is no other course open to me. I have decided to leave before I am told plainly to go. By my departure all difficulties will be put an end to, and there will be scarcely any one who will regret me. What else did I expect?... It is always so, but why am I writing to you?

'I am parting from you probably for ever, and it would be too painful to me to leave you with a worse recollection of me than I deserve. This is why I am writing to you. I do not want either to justify myself or to blame any one whatever except myself; I want, as far as possible, to explain myself.... The events of the last days have been so unexpected, so sudden....

'Our interview to-day will be a memorable lesson to me. Yes, you are right; I did not know you, and I thought I knew you! In the course of my life I have had to do with people of all kinds. I have known many women and young girls, but in you I met for the first time an absolutely true and upright soul. This was something I was not used to, and I did not know how to appreciate you fittingly. I felt an attraction to you from the first day of our acquaintance; you may have observed it. I spent with you hour after hour without learning to know you; I scarcely even tried to know you—and I could imagine that I loved you! For this sin I am punished now.

'Once before I loved a woman, and she loved me. My feeling for her was complex, like hers for me; but, as she was not simple herself, it was all the better for her. Truth was not told to me then, and now I did not recognise it when it was offered me.... I have recognised it at last, when it is too late.... What is past cannot be recalled.... Our lives might have become united, and they never will be united now. How can I prove to you that I might have loved you with real love—the love of the heart, not of the fancy—when I do not know myself whether I am capable of such love?

'Nature has given me much. I know it, and I will not disguise it from you through false modesty, especially now at a moment so bitter, so humiliating for me.... Yes, Nature has given me much, but I shall die without doing anything worthy of my powers, without leaving any trace behind me. All my wealth is dissipated idly; I do not see the fruits of the seeds I sow. I am wanting in something. I cannot say myself exactly what it is I am wanting in.... I am wanting, certainly, in something without which one cannot move men's hearts, or wholly win a woman's heart; and to sway men's minds alone is precarious, and an empire ever unprofitable. A strange, almost farcical fate is mine; I would devote myself—eagerly and wholly to some cause,—and I cannot devote myself. I shall end by sacrificing myself to some folly or other in which I shall not even believe.... Alas! at thirty-five to be still preparing for something!...

'I have never spoken so openly of myself to any one before—this is my confession.

'But enough of me. I should like to speak of you, to give you some advice; I can be no use to you further.... You are still young; but as long as you live, always follow the impulse of your heart, do not let it be subordinated to your mind or the mind of others. Believe me, the simpler, the narrower the circle in which life is passed the better; the great thing is not to open out new sides, but that all the phases of life should reach perfection in their own time. "Blessed is he who has been young in his youth." But I see that this advice applies far more to myself than to you.

'I confess, Natalya Alexyevna, I am very unhappy. I never deceived myself as to the nature of the feeling which I inspired in Darya Mihailovna; but I hoped I had found at least a temporary home.... Now I must take the chances of the rough world again. What will replace for me your conversation, your presence, your attentive and intelligent face?... I myself am to blame; but admit that fate seems to have designed a jest at my expense. A week ago I did not even myself suspect that I loved you. The day before yesterday, that evening in the garden, I for the first time heard from your lips,... but why remind you of what you said then? and now I am going away to-day. I am going away disgraced, after a cruel explanation with you, carrying with me no hope.... And you do not know yet to what a degree I am to blame as regards you... I have such a foolish lack of reserve, such a weak habit of confiding. But why speak of this? I am leaving you for ever!'

(Here Rudin had related to Natalya his visit to Volintsev, but on second thoughts he erased all that part, and added the second postscript to his letter to Volintsev.)

'I remain alone upon earth to devote myself, as you said to me this morning with bitter irony, to other interests more congenial to me. Alas! if I could really devote myself to these interests, if I could at last conquer my inertia.... But no! I shall remain to the end the incomplete creature I have always been.... The first obstacle, ... and I collapse entirely; what has passed with you has shown me that If I had but sacrificed my love to my future work, to my vocation; but I simply was afraid of the responsibility that had fallen upon me, and therefore I am, truly, unworthy of you. I do not deserve that you should be torn out of your sphere for me.... And indeed all this, perhaps, is for the best. I shall perhaps be the stronger and the purer for this experience.

'I wish you all happiness. Farewell! Think sometimes of me. I hope that you may still hear of me.

'RUDIN.'

Natalya let Rudin's letter drop on to her lap, and sat a long time motionless, her eyes fixed on the ground. This letter proved to her clearer than all possible arguments that she had been right, when in the morning, at her parting with Rudin, she had involuntarily cried out that he did not love her! But that made things no easier for her. She sat perfectly still; it seemed as though waves of darkness without a ray of light had closed over her head, and she had gone down cold and dumb to the depths. The first disillusionment is painful for every one; but for a sincere heart, averse to self-deception and innocent of frivolity or exaggeration, it is almost unendurable. Natalya remembered her childhood, how, when walking in the evening, she always tried to go in the direction of the setting sun, where there was light in the sky, and not toward the darkened half of the heavens. Life now stood in darkness before her, and she had turned her back on the light for ever....

Tears started into Natalya's eyes. Tears do not always bring relief. They are comforting and salutary when, after being long pent up in the breast, they flow at last—at first with violence, and then more easily, more softly; the dumb agony of sorrow is over with the tears. ... But there are cold tears, tears that flow sparingly, wrung out drop by drop from the heart by the immovable, weary weight of pain laid upon it: they are not comforting, and bring no relief. Poverty weeps such tears; and the man has not yet been unhappy who has not shed them. Natalya knew them on that day.

Two hours passed. Natalya pulled herself together, got up, wiped her eyes, and, lighting a candle, she burnt Rudin's letter in the flame, and threw the ash out of window. Then she opened Pushkin at random, and read the first lines that met her. (She often made it her oracle in this way.) This is what she saw:

'When he has known its pang, for him
The torturing ghost of days that are no more,
For him no more illusion, but remorse
And memory's serpent gnawing at his heart.'

She stopped, and with a cold smile looked at herself in the glass, slightly nodded her head, and went down to the drawing-room.

Darya Mihailovna, directly she saw her, called her into her study, made her sit near her, and caressingly stroked her cheek. Meanwhile she gazed attentively, almost with curiosity, into her eyes. Darya Mihailovna was secretly perplexed; for the first time it struck her that she did not really understand her daughter. When she had heard from Pandalevsky of her meeting with Rudin, she was not so much displeased as amazed that her sensible Natalya could resolve upon such a step. But when she had sent for her, and fell to upbraiding her—not at all as one would have expected from a lady of European renown, but with loud and vulgar abuse—Natalya's firm replies, and the resolution of her looks and movements, had confused and even intimidated her.

Rudin's sudden, and wholly unexplained, departure had taken a great load off her heart, but she had expected tears, and hysterics.... Natalya's outward composure threw her out of her reckoning again.

'Well, child,' began Darya Mihailovna, 'how are you to-day?' Natalya looked at her mother. 'He is gone, you see... your hero. Do you know why he decided on going so quickly?'

'Mamma!' said Natalya in a low voice, 'I give you my word, if you will not mention him, you shall never hear his name from me.'

'Then you acknowledge how wrongly you behaved to me?'

Natalya looked down and repeated:

'You shall never hear his name from me.'

'Well, well,' answered Darya Mihailovna with a smile, 'I believe you. But the day before yesterday, do you remember how—There, we will pass that over. It is all over and buried and forgotten. Isn't it? Come, I know you again now; but I was altogether puzzled then. There, kiss me like a sensible girl!'

Natalya lifted Darya Mihailovna's hand to her lips, and Darya Mihailovna kissed her stooping head.

'Always listen to my advice. Do not forget that you are a Lasunsky and my daughter,' she added, 'and you will be happy. And now you may go.'

Natalya went away in silence. Darya Mihailovna looked after her and thought: 'She is like me—she too will let herself be carried away by her feelings; *mais ella aura moins d'abandon*.' And Darya Mihailovna fell to musing over memories of the past... of the distant past.

Then she summoned Mlle. Boncourt and remained a long while closeted with her.

When she had dismissed her she sent for Pandalevsky. She wanted at all hazards to discover the real cause of Rudin's departure... but Pandalevsky succeeded in completely satisfying her. It was what he was there for.

The next day Volintsev and his sister came to dinner. Darya Mihailovna was always very affable to him, but this time she was especially cordial to him. Natalya felt unbearably miserable; but Volintsev was so respectful, and addressed her so timidly, that she could not but be grateful to him in her heart. The day passed quietly, rather tediously, but all felt as they separated that they had fallen back into the old order of things; and that means much, very much.

Yes, all had fallen back into their old order—all except Natalya. When at last she was able to be alone, she dragged herself with difficulty into her bed, and, weary and worn out, fell with her face on the pillow. Life seemed so cruel, so hateful, and so sordid, she was so ashamed of herself, her love, and her sorrow, that at that moment she would have been glad to die.... There were many sorrowful days in store for her, and sleepless nights and torturing emotions; but she was young—life had scarcely begun for her, and sooner or later life asserts its claims. Whatever blow has fallen on a man, he must—forgive the coarseness of the expression—eat that day or at least the next, and that is the first step to consolation.

Natalya suffered terribly, she suffered for the first time.... But the first sorrow, like first love, does not come again—and thank God for it!

XII

About two years had passed. The first days of May had come. Alexandra Pavlovna, no longer Lipin but Lezhnyov, was sitting on the balcony of her house; she had been married to Mihailo Mihailitch for more than a year. She was as charming as ever, and had only grown a little stouter of late. In front of the balcony, from which there were steps leading into the garden, a nurse was walking about carrying a rosy-cheeked baby in her arms, in a white cloak, with a white cap on his head. Alexandra Pavlovna kept her eyes constantly on him. The baby did not cry, but sucked his thumb gravely and looked about him. He was already showing himself a worthy son of Mihailo Mihailitch.

On the balcony, near Alexandra Pavlovna, was sitting our old friend, Pigasov. He had grown noticeably greyer since we parted from him, and was bent and thin, and he lisped when he spoke; one of his front teeth had gone; and this lisp gave still greater asperity to his words.... His spitefulness had not decreased with years, but his sallies were less lively, and he more frequently repeated himself. Mihailo Mihailitch was not at home; they were expecting him in to tea. The sun had already set. Where it had gone down, a streak of pale gold and of lemon colour stretched across the distant horizon; on the opposite quarter of the sky was a stretch of dove-colour below and crimson lilac above. Light clouds seemed melting away overhead. There was every promise of prolonged fine weather.

Suddenly Pigasov burst out laughing.

'What is it, African Semenitch?' inquired Alexandra Pavlovna.

'Oh, yesterday I heard a peasant say to his wife—she had been chattering away—"don't squeak!" I liked that immensely. And after all, what can a woman talk about? I never, you know, speak of present company. Our ancestors were wiser than we. The beauty in their stories always sits at the window with a star on her brow and never utters a syllable. That's how it ought to be. Think of it! the day before yesterday, our marshal's wife—she might have sent a pistol-shot into my head!—says to me she doesn't like my tendencies! Tendencies! Come, wouldn't it be better for her and for every one if by some beneficent ordinance of nature she were suddenly deprived of the use of her tongue?'

'Oh, you are always like that, African Semenitch; you are always attacking us poor... Do you know it's a misfortune of a sort, really? I am sorry for you.'

'A misfortune! Why do you say that? To begin with, in my opinion, there are only three misfortunes: to live in winter in cold lodgings, in summer to wear tight shoes, and to spend the night in a room where a baby cries whom you can't get rid of with Persian powder; and secondly, I am now the most peaceable of men. Why, I'm a model! You know how properly I behave!'

'Fine behaviour, indeed! Only yesterday Elena Antonovna complained to me of you.'

'Well! And what did she tell you, if I may know?'

'She told me that far one whole morning you would make no reply to all her questions but "what? what?" and always in the same squeaking voice.'

Pigasov laughed.

'But that was a happy idea, you'll allow, Alexandra Pavlovna, eh?'

'Admirable, indeed! Can you really have behaved so rudely to a lady, African Semenitch?'

'What! Do you regard Elena Antonovna as a lady?'

'What do you regard her as?'

'A drum, upon my word, an ordinary drum such as they beat with sticks.'

'Oh,' interrupted Alexandra Pavlovna, anxious to change the conversation, 'they tell me one may congratulate you.'

'Upon what?'

'The end of your lawsuit. The Glinovsky meadows are yours.'

'Yes, they are mine,' replied Pigasov gloomily.

'You have been trying to gain this so many years, and now you seem discontented.'

'I assure you, Alexandra Pavlovna,' said Pigasov slowly, 'nothing can be worse and more injurious than good-fortune that comes too late. It cannot give you pleasure in any way, and it deprives you of the right—the precious right—of complaining and cursing Providence. Yes, madam, it's a cruel and insulting trick—belated fortune.'

Alexandra Pavlovna only shrugged her shoulders.

'Nurse,' she began, 'I think it's time to put Misha to bed. Give him to me.'

While Alexandra Pavlovna busied herself with her son, Pigasov walked off muttering to the other corner of the balcony.

Suddenly, not far off on the road that ran the length of the garden, Mihailo Mihailitch made his appearance driving his racing droshky. Two huge house-dogs ran before the horse, one yellow, the other grey, both only lately obtained. They incessantly quarrelled, and were inseparable companions. An old pug-dog came out of the gate to meet them. He opened his mouth as if he were going to bark, but ended by yawning and turning back again with a friendly wag of the tail.

'Look here, Sasha,' cried Lezhnyov, from the distance, to his wife, 'whom I am bringing you.'

Alexandra Pavlovna did not at once recognise the man who was sitting behind her husband's back.

'Ah! Mr. Bassistoff!' she cried at last

'It's he,' answered Lezhnyov; 'and he has brought such glorious news. Wait a minute, you shall know directly.'

And he drove into the courtyard.

Some minutes later he came with Bassistoff into the balcony.

'Hurrah!' he cried, embracing his wife, 'Serezha is going to be married.'

'To whom?' asked Alexandra Pavlovna, much agitated.

'To Natalya, of course. Our friend has brought the news from Moscow, and there is a letter for you.'

'Do you hear, Misha,' he went on, snatching his son into his arms, 'your uncle's going to be married? What criminal indifference! he only blinks his eyes!'

'He is sleepy,' remarked the nurse.

'Yes,' said Bassistoff, going up to Alexandra Pavlovna, 'I have come to-day from Moscow on business for Darya Mihailovna—to go over the accounts on the estate. And here is the letter.'

Alexandra Pavlovna opened her brother's letter in haste. It consisted of a few lines only. In the first transport of joy he informed his sister that he had made Natalya an offer, and received her consent and Darya Mihailovna's; and he promised to write more by the next post, and sent embraces and kisses to all. It was clear he was writing in a state of delirium.

Tea was served, Bassistoff sat down. Questions were showered upon him. Every one, even Pigasov, was delighted at the news he had brought.

'Tell me, please,' said Lezhnyov among the rest, 'rumours reached us of a certain Mr. Kortchagin. That was all nonsense, I suppose?'

Kortchagin was a handsome young man, a society lion, excessively conceited and important; he behaved with extraordinary dignity, just as if he had not been a living man, but his own statue set up by public subscription.

'Well, no, not altogether nonsense,' replied Bassistoff with a smile; 'Darya Mihailovna was very favourable to him; but Natalya Alexyevna would not even hear of him.'

'I know him,' put in Pigasov, 'he's a double dummy, a noisy dummy, if you like! If all people were like that, it would need a large sum of money to induce one to consent to live—upon my word!'

'Very likely,' answered Bassistoff; 'but he plays a leading part in society.'

'Well, never mind him!' cried Alexandra Pavlovna. 'Peace be with him! Ah! how glad I am for my brother I And Natalya, is she bright and happy?'

'Yes. She is quiet, as she always is. You know her—but she seems contented.'

The evening was spent in friendly and lively talk. They sat down to supper.

'Oh, by the way,' inquired Lezhnyov of Bassistoff, as he poured him out some Lafitte, 'do you know where Rudin is?'

'I don't know for certain now. He came last winter to Moscow for a short time, and then went with a family to Simbirsk. I corresponded with him for some time; in his last letter he informed me he was leaving Simbirsk—he did not say where he was going—and since then I have heard nothing of him.'

'He is all right!' put in Pigasov. 'He is staying somewhere sermonising. That gentleman will always find two or three adherents everywhere, to listen to him open-mouthed and lend him money. You will see he will end by dying in some out-of-the-way corner in the arms of an old maid in a wig, who will believe he is the greatest genius in the world.'

'You speak very harshly of him,' remarked Bassistoff, in a displeased undertone.

'Not a bit harshly,' replied Pigasov; 'but perfectly fairly. In my opinion, he is simply nothing else than a sponge. I forgot to tell you,' he continued, turning to Lezhnyov, 'that I have made the acquaintance of that Terlahov, with whom Rudin travelled abroad. Yes! Yes! What he told me of him, you cannot imagine—it's simply screaming! It's a remarkable fact that all Rudin's friends and admirers become in time his enemies.'

'I beg you to except me from the number of such friends!' interposed Bassistoff warmly.

'Oh, you—that's a different thing! I was not speaking of you.'

'But what did Terlahov tell you?' asked Alexandra Pavlovna.

'Oh, he told me a great deal; there's no remembering it all. But the best of all was an anecdote of what happened to Rudin. As he was incessantly developing (these gentlemen always are developing; other people simply sleep and eat; but they manage their sleeping and eating in the intervals of development; isn't that it, Mr. Bassistoff?' Bassistoff made no reply.) 'And so, as he was continually developing, Rudin arrived at the conclusion, by means of philosophy, that he ought to fall in love. He began to look about for a sweetheart worthy of such an astonishing conclusion. Fortune smiled upon him. He made the acquaintance of a very pretty French dressmaker. The whole incident occurred in a German town on the Rhine, observe. He began to go and see her, to take her various books, to talk to her of Nature and Hegel. Can you fancy the position of the dressmaker? She took him for an astronomer. However, you know he's not a bad-looking fellow—and a foreigner, a Russian, of course—he took her fancy. Well, at last he invited her to a rendezvous, and a very poetical rendezvous, in a boat on the river. The Frenchwoman agreed; dressed herself in her best and went out with him in a boat. So they spent two hours. How do you think he was occupied all that time? He patted the Frenchwoman on the head, gazed thoughtfully at the sky, and frequently repeated that he felt for her the tenderness of a father. The Frenchwoman went back home in a fury, and she herself told the story to Terlahov afterwards! That's the kind of fellow he is.'

And Pigasov broke into a loud laugh.

'You old cynic!' said Alexandra Pavlovna in a tone of annoyance, 'but I am more and more convinced that even those who attack Rudin cannot find any harm to say of him.'

'No harm? Upon my word! and his perpetual living at other people's expense, his borrowing money.... Mihailo Mihailitch, he borrowed of you too, no doubt, didn't he?'

'Listen, African Semenitch!' began Lezhnyov, and his face assumed a serious expression, 'listen; you know, and my wife knows, that the last time I saw him I felt no special attachment for Rudin, and I even often blamed him. For all that (Lezhnyov filled up the glasses with champagne) this is what I suggest to you now; we have just drunk to the health of my dear brother and his future bride; I propose that you drink now to the health of Dmitri Rudin!'

Alexandra Pavlovna and Pigasov looked in astonishment at Lezhnyov, but Bassistoff sat wide-eyed, blushing and trembling all over with delight.

'I know him well,' continued Lezhnyov, 'I am well aware of his faults. They are the more conspicuous because he himself is not on a small scale.'

'Rudin has character, genius!' cried Bassistoff.

'Genius, very likely he has!' replied Lezhnyov, 'but as for character ... That's just his misfortune, that there's no character in him... But that's not the point. I want to speak of what is good, of what is rare in him. He has enthusiasm; and believe me, who am a phlegmatic person enough, that is the most precious quality in our times. We have all become insufferably reasonable, indifferent, and slothful; we are asleep and cold, and thanks to any one who will wake us up and warm us! It is high time! Do you remember, Sasha, once when I was talking to you about him, I blamed him for coldness? I was right, and wrong too, then. The coldness is in his blood—that is not his fault—and not in his head. He is not an actor, as I called him, nor a cheat, nor a scoundrel; he lives at other people's expense, not like a swindler, but like a child.... Yes; no doubt he will die somewhere in poverty and want; but are we to throw stones at him for that? He never does anything himself precisely, he has no vital force, no blood; but who has the right to say that he has not been of use? that his words have not scattered good seeds in young hearts, to whom nature has not denied, as she has to him, powers for action, and the faculty of carrying out their own ideas? Indeed, I myself, to begin with, have gained all that from him.... Sasha knows what Rudin did for me in my youth. I also maintained, I recollect, that Rudin's words could not produce an effect on men; but I was speaking then of men like myself, at my present age, of men who have already lived and been broken in by life. One false note in a man's eloquence, and the whole harmony is spoiled for us; but a young man's ear, happily, is not so over-fine, not so trained. If the substance of what he hears seems fine to him, what does he care about the intonation! The intonation he will supply for himself!'

'Bravo, bravo!' cried Bassistoff, 'that is justly spoken! And as regards Rudin's influence, I swear to you, that man not only knows how to move you, he lifts you up, he does not let you stand still, he stirs you to the depths and sets you on fire!'

'You hear?' continued Lezhnyov, turning to Pigasov; 'what further proof do you want? You attack philosophy; speaking of it, you cannot find words contemptuous enough. I myself am not excessively devoted to it, and I know little enough about it; but our principal misfortunes do not come from philosophy! The Russian will never be infected with philosophical hair-splittings and nonsense; he has too much common-sense for that; but we must not let every sincere effort after truth and knowledge be attacked under the name of philosophy. Rudin's misfortune is that he does not understand Russia, and that, certainly, is a great misfortune. Russia can do without every one of us, but not one of us can do without her. Woe to him who thinks he can, and woe twofold to him who actually does do without her! Cosmopolitanism is all twaddle, the cosmopolitan is a nonentity—worse than a nonentity; without nationality is no art, nor truth, nor life, nor anything. You cannot even have an ideal face without individual expression; only a vulgar face can be devoid of it. But I say again, that is not Rudin's fault; it is his fate—a cruel and unhappy fate—for which we cannot blame him. It would take us too far if we tried to trace why Rudins spring up among us. But for what is fine in him, let us be grateful to him. That is pleasanter than being unfair to him, and we have been unfair to him. It's not our business to punish him, and it's not needed; he has punished himself far more cruelly than he deserved. And God grant that unhappiness may have blotted out all the harm there was in him, and left only what was fine! I drink to the health of Rudin! I drink to the comrade of my best years, I drink to youth, to its hopes, its endeavours, its faith, and its honesty, to all that our hearts beat for at twenty; we have known, and shall know, nothing better than that in life.... I drink to that golden time—to the health of Rudin!'

All clinked glasses with Lezhnyov. Bassistoff, in his enthusiasm, almost cracked his glass and drained it off at a draught. Alexandra Pavlovna pressed Lezhnyov's hand.

'Why, Mihailo Mihailitch, I did not suspect you were an orator,' remarked Pigasov; 'it was equal to Mr. Rudin himself; even I was moved by it.'

'I am not at all an orator,' replied Lezhnyov, not without annoyance, 'but to move you, I fancy, would be difficult. But enough of Rudin; let us talk of something else. What of—what's his name—Pandalevsky? is he still living at Darya Mihailovna's?' he concluded, turning to Bassistoff.

'Oh yes, he is still there. She has managed to get him a very profitable place.'

Lezhnyov smiled.

'That's a man who won't die in want, one can count upon that.'

Supper was over. The guests dispersed. When she was left alone with her husband, Alexandra Pavlovna looked smiling into his face.

'How splendid you were this evening, Misha,' she said, stroking his forehead, 'how cleverly and nobly you spoke! But confess, you exaggerated a little in Rudin's praise, as in old days you did in attacking him.'

'I can't let them hit a man when he's down. And in those days I was afraid he was turning your head.'

'No,' replied Alexandra Pavlovna naively, 'he always seemed too learned for me. I was afraid of him, and never knew what to say in his presence. But wasn't Pigasov nasty in his ridicule of him to-day?'

'Pigasov?' responded Lezhnyov. 'That was just why I stood up for Rudin so warmly, because Pigasov was here. He dare to call Rudin a sponge indeed! Why, I consider the part he plays—Pigasov I mean—is a hundred times worse! He has an independent property, and he sneers at every one, and yet see how he fawns upon wealthy or distinguished people! Do you know that that fellow, who abuses everything and every one with such scorn, and attacks philosophy and women, do you know that when he was in the service, he took bribes and that sort of thing! Ugh! That's what he is!'

'Is it possible?' cried Alexandra Pavlovna, 'I should never have expected that! Misha,' she added, after a short pause, 'I want to ask you——'

'What?'

'What do you think, will my brother be happy with Natalya?'

'How can I tell you?... there's every likelihood of it. She will take the lead... there's no reason to hide the fact between us... she is cleverer than he is; but he's a capital fellow, and loves her with all his soul. What more would you have? You see we love one another and are happy, aren't we?'

Alexandra Pavlovna smiled and pressed his hand.

On the same day on which all that has been described took place in Alexandra Pavlovna's house, in one of the remote districts of Russia, a wretched little covered cart, drawn by three village horses was crawling along the high road in the sultry heat. On the front seat was perched a grizzled peasant in a ragged cloak, with his legs hanging slanting on the shaft; he kept flicking with the reins, which were of cord, and shaking the whip. Inside the cart there was sitting on a shaky portmanteau a tall man in a cap and old dusty cloak. It was Rudin. He sat with bent head, the peak of his cap pulled over his eyes. The jolting of the cart threw him from side to side; but he seemed utterly unconscious, as though he were asleep. At last he drew himself up.

'When are we coming to a station?' he inquired of the peasant sitting in front.

'Just over the hill, little father,' said the peasant, with a still more violent shaking of the reins. 'There's a mile and a half farther to go, not more.... Come! there! look about you.... I'll teach you,' he added in a shrill voice, setting to work to whip the right-hand horse.

'You seem to drive very badly,' observed Rudin; 'we have been crawling along since early morning, and we have not succeeded in getting there yet. You should have sung something.'

'Well, what would you have, little father? The horses, you see yourself, are overdone... and then the heat; and I can't sing. I'm not a coachman.... Hullo, you little sheep!' cried the peasant, suddenly turning to a man coming along in a brown smock and bark shoes downtrodden at heel. 'Get out of the way!'

'You're a nice driver!' muttered the man after him, and stood still. 'You wretched Muscovite,' he added in a voice full of contempt, shook his head and limped away.

'What are you up to?' sang out the peasant at intervals, pulling at the shaft-horse. 'Ah, you devil! Get on!'

The jaded horses dragged themselves at last up to the posting-station. Rudin crept out of the cart, paid the peasant (who did not bow to him, and kept shaking the coins in the palm of his hand a long while—evidently there was too little drink-money) and himself carried the portmanteau into the posting-station.

A friend of mine who has wandered a great deal about Russia in his time made the observation that if the pictures hanging on the walls of a posting-station represent scenes from 'the Prisoner of the Caucasus,' or Russian generals, you may get horses soon; but if the pictures depict the life of the well-known gambler George de Germany, the traveller need not hope to get off quickly; he will have time to admire to the full the hair *a la cockatoo*, the white open waistcoat, and the exceedingly short and narrow trousers of the gambler in his youth, and his exasperated physiognomy, when in his old age he kills his son, waving a chair above him, in a cottage with a narrow staircase. In the room into which Rudin walked precisely these pictures were hanging out of 'Thirty Years, or the Life of a Gambler.' In response to his call the superintendent appeared, who had just waked up (by the way, did any one ever see a superintendent who had not just been asleep?), and without even waiting for Rudin's question, informed him in a sleepy voice that there were no horses.

'How can you say there are no horses,' said Rudin, 'when you don't even know where I am going? I came here with village horses.'

'We have no horses for anywhere,' answered the superintendent. 'But where are you going?'

'To Sk——.'

'We have no horses,' repeated the superintendent, and he went away.

Rudin, vexed, went up to the window and threw his cap on the table. He was not much changed, but had grown rather yellow in the last two years; silver threads shone here and there in his curls, and his eyes, still magnificent, seemed somehow dimmed, fine lines, the traces of bitter and disquieting emotions, lay about his lips and on his temples. His clothes were shabby and old, and he had no linen visible anywhere. His best days were clearly over: as the gardeners say, he had gone to seed.

He began reading the inscriptions on the walls—the ordinary distraction of weary travellers; suddenly the door creaked and the superintendent came in.

'There are no horses for Sk——, and there won't be any for a long time,' he said, 'but here are some ready to go to V——.'

'To V——?' said Rudin. 'Why, that's not on my road at all. I am going to Penza, and V—— lies, I think, in the direction of Tamboff.'

'What of that? you can get there from Tamboff, and from V—— you won't be at all out of your road.'

Rudin thought a moment.

'Well, all right,' he said at last, 'tell them to put the horses to. It is the same to me; I will go to Tamboff.'

The horses were soon ready. Rudin carried his own portmanteau, climbed into the cart, and took his seat, his head hanging as before. There was something helpless and pathetically submissive in his bent figure.... And the three horses went off at a slow trot.

EPILOGUE

Some years had passed by.

It was a cold autumn day. A travelling carriage drew up at the steps of the principal hotel of the government town of C——; a gentleman yawning and stretching stepped out of it. He was not elderly, but had had time to acquire that fulness of figure which habitually commands respect. He went up the staircase to the second story, and stopped at the entrance to a wide corridor. Seeing no one before him he called out in a loud voice asking for a room. A door creaked somewhere, and a long waiter jumped up from behind a low screen, and came forward with a quick flank movement, an apparition of a glossy back and tucked-up sleeves in the half-dark corridor. The traveller went into the room and at once throwing off his cloak and scarf, sat down on the sofa, and with his fists propped on his knees, he first looked round as though he were hardly awake yet, and then gave the order to send up his servant. The hotel waiter made a bow and disappeared. The traveller was no other than Lezhnyov. He had come from the country to C—— about some conscription business.

Lezhnyov's servant, a curly-headed, rosy-cheeked youth in a grey cloak, with a blue sash round the waist, and soft felt shoes, came into the room.

'Well, my boy, here we are,' Lezhnyov said, 'and you were afraid all the while that a wheel would come off.'

'We are here,' replied the boy, trying to smile above the high collar of his cloak, 'but the reason why the wheel did not come off——'

'Is there no one in here?' sounded a voice in the corridor.

Lezhnyov started and listened.

'Eh? who is there?' repeated the voice.

Lezhnyov got up, walked to the door, and quickly threw it open.

Before him stood a tall man, bent and almost completely grey, in an old frieze coat with bronze buttons.

'Rudin!' he cried in an excited voice.

Rudin turned round. He could not distinguish Lezhnyov's features, as he stood with his back to the light, and he looked at him in bewilderment.

'You don't know me?' said Lezhnyov.

'Mihailo Mihailitch!' cried Rudin, and held out his hand, but drew it back again in confusion. Lezhnyov made haste to snatch it in both of his.

'Come, come in!' he said to Rudin, and drew him into the room.

'How you have changed!' exclaimed Lezhnyov after a brief silence, involuntarily dropping his voice.

'Yes, they say so!' replied Rudin, his eyes straying about the room. 'The years... and you not much. How is Alexandra—your wife?'

'She is very well, thank you. But what fate brought you here?'

'It is too long a story. Strictly speaking, I came here by chance. I was looking for a friend. But I am very glad...'

'Where are you going to dine?'

'Oh, I don't know. At some restaurant. I must go away from here to-day.'

'You must.'

Rudin smiled significantly.

'Yes, I must. They are sending me off to my own place, to my home.'

'Dine with me.'

Rudin for the first time looked Lezhnyov straight in the face.

'You invite me to dine with you?' he said.

'Yes, Rudin, for the sake of old times and old comradeship. Will you? I did not expect to meet you, and God only knows when we shall see each other again. I cannot part from you like this!'

'Very well, I agree!'

Lezhnyov pressed Rudin's hand, and calling his servant, ordered dinner, and told him to have a bottle of champagne put in ice.

In the course of dinner, Lezhnyov and Rudin, as though by agreement, kept talking of their student days, recalling many things and many friends—dead and living. At first Rudin spoke with little interest, but when he had drunk a few glasses of wine his blood grew warmer. At last the waiter took away the last dish, Lezhnyov got up, closed the door, and coming back to the table, sat down facing Rudin, and quietly rested his chin on his hands.

'Now, then,' he began, 'tell me all that has happened to you since I saw you last.'

Rudin looked at Lezhnyov.

'Good God!' thought Lezhnyov, 'how he has changed, poor fellow!'

Rudin's features had undergone little change since we saw him last at the posting-station, though approaching old age had had time to set its mark upon them; but their expression had become different. His eyes had a changed look; his whole being, his movements, which were at one time slow, at another abrupt and disconnected, his crushed, benumbed manner of speaking, all showed an utter exhaustion, a quiet and secret dejection, very different from the half-assumed melancholy which he had affected once, as it is generally affected by youth, when full of hopes and confident vanity.

'Tell you all that has happened to me?' he said; 'I could not tell you all, and it is not worth while. I am worn out; I have wandered far—in spirit as well as in flesh. What friends I have made—good God! How many things, how many men I have lost faith in! Yes, how many!' repeated Rudin, noticing that Lezhnyov was looking in his face with a kind of special sympathy. 'How many times have my own words grown hateful to me! I don't mean now on my own lips, but on the lips of those who had adopted my opinions! How many times have I passed from the petulance of a child to the dull insensibility of a horse who does not lash his tail when the whip cuts him!... How many times I have been happy and hopeful, and have made enemies and humbled myself for nothing! How many times I have taken flight like an eagle—and returned crawling like a snail whose shell has been crushed!... Where have I not been! What roads have I not travelled!... And the roads are often dirty,' added Rudin, slightly turning away. 'You know ...' he was continuing.... 'Listen,' interrupted Lezhnyov. 'We used once to say "Dmitri and Mihail" to one another. Let us revive the old habit,... will you? Let us drink to those days!'

Rudin started and drew himself up a little, and there was a gleam in his eyes of something no word can express.

'Let us drink to them,' he said. 'I thank you, brother, we will drink to them!'

Lezhnyov and Rudin drained their glasses.

'You know, Mihail,' Rudin began again with a smile and a stress on the name, 'there is a worm in me which gnaws and worries me and never lets me be at peace till the end. It brings me into collision with people,—at first they fall under my influence, but afterwards...'

Rudin waved his hand in the air.

'Since I parted from you, Mihail, I have seen much, have experienced many changes.... I have begun life, have started on something new twenty times—and here—you see!'

'You had no stability,' said Lezhnyov, as though to himself.

'As you say, I had no stability. I never was able to construct anything; and it's a difficult thing, brother, to construct when one has to create the very ground under one's feet, to make one's own foundation for one's self! All my adventures—that is, speaking accurately, all my failures, I will not describe. I will tell of two or three incidents—those incidents of my life when it seemed as if success were smiling on me, or rather when I began to hope for success—which is not altogether the same thing...'

Rudin pushed back his grey and already sparse locks with the same gesture which he used once to toss back his thick, dark curls.

'Well, I will tell you, Mihail,' he began. 'In Moscow I came across a rather strange man. He was very wealthy and was the owner of extensive estates. His chief and only passion was love of science, universal science. I have never yet been able to arrive at how this passion arose in him! It fitted him about as well as a saddle on a cow. He managed with difficulty to maintain himself at his mental elevation, he was almost without the power of speech, he only rolled his eyes with expression and shook his head significantly. I never met, brother, a poorer and less gifted nature than his.... In the Smolensk province there are places like that—nothing but sand and a few tufts of grass which no animal can eat. Nothing succeeded in his hands; everything seemed to slip away from him; but he was still mad on making everything plain complicated. If it had depended on his arrangements, his people would have eaten standing on their heads. He worked, and wrote, and read indefatigably. He devoted himself to science with a kind of stubborn perseverance, a terrible patience; his vanity was immense, and he had a will of iron. He lived alone, and had the reputation of an eccentric. I made friends with him... and he liked me. I quickly, I must own, saw through him; but his zeal attracted me. Besides, he was the master of such resources; so much good might be done, so much real usefulness through him.... I was installed in his house and went with him to the country. My plans, brother, were on a vast scale; I dreamed of various reforms, innovations...'

'Just as at the Lasunsky's, do you remember, Dmitri?' responded Lezhnyov, with an indulgent smile.

'Ah, but then I knew in my heart that nothing would come of my words; but this time... an altogether different field of activity lay open before me.... I took with me books on agriculture... to tell the truth, I did not read one of them through.... Well, I set to work. At first it did not progress as I had expected; but afterwards it did get on in a way. My new friend looked on and said nothing; he did not interfere with me, at least not to any noticeable extent. He accepted my suggestions, and carried them out, but with a stubborn sullenness, a secret want of faith; and he bent everything his own way. He prized extremely every idea of his own. He got to it with difficulty, like a ladybird on a blade of grass, and he would sit and sit upon it, as though pluming his wings and getting ready for a flight, and suddenly he would fall off and begin crawling again.... Don't be surprised at these comparisons; at that time they were always crowding on my imagination. So I struggled on there for two years. The work did not progress much in spite of all my efforts. I began to be tired of it, my friend bored me; I had come to sneer at him, and he stifled me like a featherbed; his want of faith had changed into a dumb resentment; a feeling of hostility had laid hold of both of us; we could scarcely now speak of anything; he quietly but incessantly tried to show me that he was not under my influence; my arrangements were either set aside or altogether transformed. I realised, at last, that I was playing the part of a toady in the noble landowner's house by providing him with intellectual amusement. It was very bitter to me to have wasted my time and strength for nothing, most bitter to feel that I had again and again been deceived in my expectations. I knew very well what I was losing if I went away; but I could not control myself, and one day after a painful and revolting scene of which I was a witness, and which showed my friend in a most disadvantageous light, I quarrelled with him finally, went away, and threw up this newfangled pedant, made of a queer compound of our native flour kneaded up with German treacle.'

'That is, you threw up your daily bread, Dmitri,' said Lezhnyov, laying both hands on Rudin's shoulders.

'Yes, and again I was turned adrift, empty-handed and penniless, to fly whither I listed. Ah! let us drink!'

'To your health!' said Lezhnyov, getting up and kissing Rudin on the forehead. 'To your health and to the memory of Pokorsky. He, too, knew how to be poor.'

'Well, that was number one of my adventures,' began Rudin, after a short pause. 'Shall I go on?'

'Go on, please.'

'Ah! I have no wish for talking. I am tired of talking, brother.... However, so be it. After knocking about in various parts—by the way, I might tell you how I became the secretary of a benevolent dignitary, and what came of that; but that would take me too long.... After knocking about in various parts, I resolved to become at last—don't smile, please—a practical business man. The opportunity came in this way. I became friendly with—he was much talked of at one time—a man called Kurbyev.'

'Oh, I never heard of him. But, really, Dmitri, with your intelligence, how was it you did not suspect that to be a business man was not the business for you?'

'I know, brother, that it was not; but, then, what is the business for me? But if you had seen Kurbyev! Do not, pray, fancy him as some empty-headed chatterer. They say I was eloquent once. I was simply nothing beside him. He was a man of wonderful learning and knowledge,—an intellect, brother, a creative intellect, for business and commercial enterprises. His brain seemed seething with the boldest, the most unexpected schemes. I joined him and we decided to turn our powers to a work of public utility.'

'What was it, may I know?'

Rudin dropped his eyes.

'You will laugh at it, Mihail.

'Why should I? No, I will not laugh.'

'We resolved to make a river in the K—— province fit for navigation,' said Rudin with an embarrassed smile.

'Really! This Kurbyev was a capitalist, then?'

'He was poorer than I,' responded Rudin, and his grey head sank on his breast.

Lezhnyov began to laugh, but he stopped suddenly and took Rudin by the hand.

'Pardon me, brother, I beg,' he said, 'but I did not expect that. Well, so I suppose your enterprise did not get further than paper?'

'Not so. A beginning was made. We hired workmen, and set to work. But then we were met by various obstacles. In the first place the millowners would not meet us favourably at all; and more than that, we could not turn the water out of its course without machinery, and we had not money enough for machinery. For six months we lived in mud huts. Kurbyev lived on dry bread, and I, too, had not much to eat. However, I don't complain of that; the scenery there is something magnificent. We struggled and struggled on, appealing to merchants, writing letters and circulars. It ended in my spending my last farthing on the project.'

'Well!' observed Lezhnyov, 'I imagine to spend your last farthing, Dmitri, was not a difficult matter?'

'It was not difficult, certainly.'

Rudin looked out of the window.

'But the project really was not a bad one, and it might have been of immense service.'

'And where did Kurbyev go to?' asked Lezhnyov.

'Oh, he is now in Siberia, he has become a gold-digger. And you will see he will make himself a position; he will get on.'

'Perhaps; but then you will not be likely to make a position for yourself, it seems.'

'Well, that can't be helped! But I know I was always a frivolous creature in your eyes.'

'Hush, brother; there was a time, certainly, when I saw your weak side; but now, believe me, I have learnt to value you. You will not make yourself a position. And I love you, Dmitri, for that, indeed I do!'

Rudin smiled faintly.

'Truly?'

'I respect you for it!' repeated Lezhnyov. 'Do you understand me?'

Both were silent for a little.

'Well, shall I proceed to number three?' asked Rudin.

'Please do.'

'Very well. The third and last. I have only now got clear of number three. But am I not boring you, Mihail?'

'Go on, go on.'

'Well,' began Rudin, 'once the idea occurred to me at some leisure moment—I always had plenty of leisure moments—the idea occurred to me; I have knowledge enough, my intentions are good. I suppose even you will not deny me good intentions?'

'I should think not!'

'In all other directions I had failed more or less... why should I not become an instructor, or speaking simply a teacher... rather than waste my life?'

Rudin stopped and sighed.

'Rather than waste my life, would it not be better to try to pass on to others what I know; perhaps they may extract at least some use from my knowledge. My abilities are above the ordinary anyway, I am a master of language. So I resolved to devote myself to this new work. I had difficulty in obtaining a post; I did not want to give private lessons; there was nothing I could do in the lower schools. At last I succeeded in getting an appointment as professor in the gymnasium here.'

'As professor of what?' asked Lezhnyov.

'Professor of literature. I can tell you I never started on any work with such zest as I did on this. The thought of producing an effect upon the young inspired me. I spent three weeks over the composition of my opening lecture.'

'Have you got it, Dmitri?' interrupted Lezhnyov.

'No! I lost it somewhere. It went off fairly well, and was liked. I can see now the faces of my listeners—good young faces, with an expression of pure-souled attention and sympathy, and even of amazement. I mounted the platform and read my lecture in a fever; I thought it would fill more than an hour, but I had finished it in twenty minutes. The inspector was sitting there—a dry old man in silver spectacles and a short wig—he sometimes turned his head in my direction. When I had finished, he jumped up from his seat and said to me, "Good, but rather over their heads, obscure, and too little said about the subject." But the pupils followed me with appreciation in their looks—indeed they did. Ah, that is how youth is so precious! I gave a second written lecture, and a third. After that I began to lecture extempore.'

'And you had success?' asked Lezhnyov.

'I had a great success. I gave my audience all that was in my soul. Among them were two or three really remarkable boys; the rest did not understand me much. I must confess though that even those who did understand me sometimes embarrassed me by their questions. But I did not lose heart. They all loved me; I gave them all full marks in examinations. But then an intrigue was started against me—or no! it was not an intrigue at all; it simply was, that I was not in my proper place. I was a hindrance to the others, and they were a hindrance to me. I lectured to the gymnasium pupils in a way lectures are not given every day, even to students; they carried away very little from my lectures.... I myself did not know the facts enough. Besides, I was not satisfied with the limited sphere assigned to me—you know that is always my weakness. I wanted radical reforms, and I swear to you that these reforms were both sensible and easy to carry out. I hoped to carry them through the director, a good and honest man, over whom I had at first some influence. His wife aided me. I have not, brother, met many women like her in my life. She was about forty; but she believed in goodness, and loved everything fine with the enthusiasm of a girl of fifteen, and was not afraid to give utterance to her convictions before any one whatever. I shall never forget her generous enthusiasm and goodness. By her advice I drew up a plan.... But then my influence was undermined, I was misrepresented to her. My chief enemy was the professor of mathematics, a little sour, bilious man who believed in nothing, a character like Pigasov, but far more able than he was.... By the way, how is Pigasov, is he living?'

'Oh, yes; and only fancy, he is married to a peasant woman, who, they say, beats him.'

'Serve him right! And Natalya Alexyevna—is she well?'

'Yes.'

'Is she happy?'

'Yes.'

Rudin was silent for a little.

'What was I talking about?... Oh yes! about the professor of mathematics. He perfectly hated me; he compared my lectures to fireworks, pounced upon every expression of mine that was not altogether clear, once even put me to confusion over some monument of the sixteenth century.... But the most important thing was, he suspected my intentions; my last soap-bubble struck on him as on a spike, and burst. The inspector, whom I had not got on with from the first, set the director against me. A scene followed. I was not ready to give in; I got hot; the matter came to the knowledge of the authorities; I was forced to resign. I did not stop there; I wanted to prove that they could not treat me like that.... But they could treat me as they liked.... Now I am forced to leave the town.'

A silence followed. Both the friends sat with bowed heads.

Rudin was the first to speak.

'Yes, brother,' he began, 'I can say now, in the words of Koltsov, "Thou hast led me astray, my youth, till there is nowhere I can turn my steps."... And yet can it be that I was fit for nothing, that for me there was, as it were, no work on earth to do? I have often put myself this question, and, however much I tried to humble myself in my own eyes, I could not but feel the existence of faculties within me which are not given to every one! Why have these faculties remained fruitless? And let me say more; you know, when I was with you abroad, Mihail, I was conceited and full of erroneous ideas.... Certainly I did not then realise clearly what I wanted; I lived upon words, and believed in phantoms. But now, I swear to you, I could speak out before all men every desire I feel. I have absolutely nothing to hide; I am absolutely, in the fullest meaning of the word, a well-intentioned man. I am humble, I am ready to adapt myself to circumstances; I want little; I want to do the good that lies nearest, to be even a little use. But no! I never succeed. What does it mean? What hinders me from living and working like others?... I am only dreaming of it now. But no sooner do I get into any definite position when fate throws the dice from me. I have come to dread it—my destiny.... Why is it so? Explain this enigma to me!'

'An enigma!' repeated Lezhnyov. 'Yes, that's true; you have always been an enigma for me. Even in our young days, when, after some trifling prank, you would suddenly speak as though you were pierced to the heart, and then you would begin again... well you know what I mean... even then I did not understand. That is why I grew apart from you.... You have so much power, such unwearying striving after the ideal.'

'Words, all words! There was nothing done!' Rudin broke in.

'Nothing done! What is there to do?'

'What is there to do! To keep an old blind woman and all her family by one's work, as, do you remember, Mihail, Pryazhentsov did... That's doing something.'

'Yes, but a good word—is also something done.'

Rudin looked at Lezhnyov without speaking and faintly shook his head.

Lezhnyov wanted to say something, and he passed his hand over his face.

'And so you are going to your country place?' he asked at last

'Yes.'

'There you have some property left?'

'Something is left me there. Two souls and a half. It is a corner to die in. You are thinking perhaps at this moment: "Even now he cannot do without fine words!" Words indeed have been my ruin; they have consumed me, and to the end I cannot be free of them. But what I have said was not mere words. These white hairs, brother, these wrinkles, these ragged elbows—they are not mere words. You have always been hard on me, Mihail, and you were right; but now is not a time to be hard, when all is over, when there's no oil left in the lamp, and the lamp itself is broken, and the wick is just smouldering out. Death, brother, should reconcile at last...'

Lezhnyov jumped up.

'Rudin!' he cried, 'why do you speak like that to me? How have I deserved it from you? Am I such a judge, and what kind of a man should I be, if at the sight of your hollow cheeks and wrinkles, "mere words" could occur to my mind? Do you want to know what I think of you, Dmitri? Well! I think: here is a man—with his abilities, what might he not have attained to, what worldly advantages might he not have possessed by now, if he had liked!... and I meet him hungry and homeless....'

'I rouse your compassion,' Rudin murmured in a choked voice.

'No, you are wrong. You inspire respect in me—that is what I feel. Who prevented you from spending year after year at that landowner's, who was your friend, and who would, I am fully persuaded, have made provision for you, if you had only been willing to humour him? Why could you not live harmoniously at the gymnasium, why have you—strange man!—with whatever ideas you have entered upon an undertaking, infallibly every time ended by sacrificing your personal interests, ever refusing to take root in any but good ground, however profitable it might be?'

'I was born a rolling stone,' Rudin said, with a weary smile. 'I cannot stop myself.'

'That is true; but you cannot stop, not because there is a worm gnawing you, as you said to me at first.... It is not a worm, not the spirit of idle restlessness—it is the fire of the love of truth that burns in you, and clearly, in spite of your failings; it burns in you more hotly than in many who do not consider themselves egoists and dare to call you a humbug perhaps. I, for one, in your place should long ago have succeeded in silencing that worm in me, and should have given in to everything; and you have not even been embittered by it, Dmitri. You are ready, I am sure, to-day, to set to some new work again like a boy.'

'No, brother, I am tired now,' said Rudin. 'I have had enough.'

'Tired! Any other man would have been dead long ago. You say that death reconciles; but does not life, don't you think, reconcile? A man who has lived and has not grown tolerant towards others does not deserve to meet with tolerance himself. And who can say he does not need tolerance? You have done what you could, Dmitri... you have struggled so long as you could... what more? Our paths lay apart,'...

'You were utterly different from me,' Rudin put in with a sigh.

'Our paths lay apart,' continued Lezhnyov, 'perhaps exactly because, thanks to my position, my cool blood, and other fortunate circumstances, nothing hindered me from being a stay-at-home, and remaining a spectator with folded hands; but you had to go out into the world, to turn up your shirt-sleeves, to toil and labour. Our paths lay apart—but see how near one another we are. We speak almost the same language, with half a hint we understand one another, we grew up on the same ideas. There is little left us now, brother; we are the last of the Mohicans! We might differ and even quarrel in old days, when so much life still remained before us; but now, when the ranks are thinned about us, when the younger generation is coming upon us with other aims than ours, we ought to keep close to one another! Let us clink glasses, Dmitri, and sing as of old, *Gaudeamus igitur*!'

The friends clinked their glasses, and sang the old student song in strained voices, all out of tune, in the true Russian style.

'So you are going now to your country place,' Lezhnyov began again. 'I don't think you will stay there long, and I cannot imagine where and how you will end.... But remember, whatever happens to you, you have always a place, a nest where you can hide yourself. That is my home,—do you hear, old fellow? Thought, too, has its veterans; they, too, ought to have their home.'

Rudin got up.

'Thanks, brother,' he said, 'thanks! I will not forget this in you. Only I do not deserve a home. I have wasted my life, and have not served thought, as I ought.'

'Hush!' said Lezhnyov. 'Every man remains what Nature has made him, and one cannot ask more of him! You have called yourself the Wandering Jew.... But how do you know,—perhaps it was right for you to be ever wandering, perhaps in that way you are fulfilling a higher calling than you know; popular wisdom says truly that we are all in God's hands. You are going, Dmitri,' continued Lezhnyov, seeing that Rudin was taking his hat 'You will not stop the night?'

'Yes, I am going! Good-bye. Thanks.... I shall come to a bad end.'

'God only knows.... You are resolved to go?'

'Yes, I am going. Good-bye. Do not remember evil against me.'

'Well, do not remember evil against me either,—and don't forget what I said to you. Good-bye.'...

The friends embraced one another. Rudin went quickly away.

Lezhnyov walked up and down the room a long while, stopped before the window thinking, and murmured half aloud, 'Poor fellow!' Then sitting down to the table, he began to write a letter to his wife.

But outside a wind had risen, and was howling with ill-omened moans, and wrathfully shaking the rattling window-panes. The long autumn night came on. Well for the man on such a night who sits under the shelter of home, who has a warm corner in safety.... And the Lord help all homeless wanderers!

On a sultry afternoon on the 26th of July in 1848 in Paris, when the Revolution of the *ateliers nationaux* had already been almost suppressed, a line battalion was taking a barricade in one of the narrow alleys of the Faubourg St Antoine. A few gunshots had already broken it; its surviving defenders abandoned it, and were only thinking of their own safety, when suddenly on the very top of the barricade, on the frame of an overturned omnibus, appeared a tall man in an old overcoat, with a red sash, and a straw hat on his grey dishevelled hair. In one hand he held a red flag, in the other a blunt curved sabre, and as he scrambled up, he shouted something in a shrill strained voice, waving his flag and sabre. A Vincennes tirailleur took aim at him—fired. The tall man dropped the flag—and like a sack he toppled over face downwards, as though he were falling at some one's feet. The bullet had passed through his heart.

'*Tiens*!' said one of the escaping revolutionists to another, '*on vient de tuer le Polonais*!

'*Bigre*!' answered the other, and both ran into the cellar of a house, the shutters of which were all closed, and its wall streaked with traces of powder and shot.

This 'Polonais' was Dmitri Rudin.

The Torrents of Spring

'Years of gladness,
Days of joy,
Like the torrents of spring
They hurried away.'
—*From an Old Ballad.*

... At two o'clock in the night he had gone back to his study. He had dismissed the servant after the candles were lighted, and throwing himself into a low chair by the hearth, he hid his face in both hands.

Never had he felt such weariness of body and of spirit. He had passed the whole evening in the company of charming ladies and cultivated men; some of the ladies were beautiful, almost all the men were distinguished by intellect or talent; he himself had talked with great success, even with brilliance ... and, for all that, never yet had the *taedium vitae* of which the Romans talked of old, the 'disgust for life,' taken hold of him with such irresistible, such suffocating force. Had he been a little younger, he would have cried with misery, weariness, and exasperation: a biting, burning bitterness, like the bitter of wormwood, filled his whole soul. A sort of clinging repugnance, a weight of loathing closed in upon him on all sides like a dark night of autumn; and he did not know how to get free from this darkness, this bitterness. Sleep it was useless to reckon upon; he knew he should not sleep.

He fell to thinking ... slowly, listlessly, wrathfully. He thought of the vanity, the uselessness, the vulgar falsity of all things human. All the stages of man's life passed in order before his mental gaze (he had himself lately reached his fifty-second year), and not one found grace in his eyes. Everywhere the same ever-lasting pouring of water into a sieve, the ever-lasting beating of the air, everywhere the same self-deception—half in good faith, half conscious—any toy to amuse the child, so long as it keeps him from crying. And then, all of a sudden, old age drops down like snow on the head, and with it the ever-growing, ever-gnawing, and devouring dread of death ... and the plunge into the abyss! Lucky indeed if life works out so to the end! May be, before the end, like rust on iron, sufferings, infirmities come.... He did not picture life's sea, as the poets depict it, covered with tempestuous waves; no, he thought of that sea as a smooth, untroubled surface, stagnant and transparent to its darkest depths. He himself sits in a little tottering boat, and down below in those dark oozy depths, like prodigious fishes, he can just make out the shapes of hideous monsters: all the ills of life, diseases, sorrows, madness, poverty, blindness.... He gazes, and behold, one of these monsters separates itself off from the darkness, rises higher and higher, stands out more and more distinct, more and more loathsomely distinct.... An instant yet, and the boat that bears him will be overturned! But behold, it grows dim again, it withdraws, sinks down to the bottom, and there it lies, faintly stirring in the slime.... But the fated day will come, and it will overturn the boat.

He shook his head, jumped up from his low chair, took two turns up and down the room, sat down to the writing-table, and opening one drawer after another, began to rummage among his papers, among old letters, mostly from women. He could not have said why he was doing it; he was not looking for anything—he simply wanted by some kind of external occupation to get away from the thoughts oppressing him. Opening several letters at random (in one of them there was a withered flower tied with a bit of faded ribbon), he merely shrugged his shoulders, and glancing at the hearth, he tossed them on one side, probably with the idea of burning all this useless rubbish. Hurriedly, thrusting his hands first into one, and then into another drawer, he suddenly opened his eyes wide, and slowly bringing out a little octagonal box of old-fashioned make, he slowly raised its lid. In the box, under two layers of cotton wool, yellow with age, was a little garnet cross. For a few instants he looked in perplexity at this cross—suddenly he gave a faint cry.... Something between regret and delight was expressed in his features. Such an expression a man's face wears when he suddenly meets some one whom he has long lost sight of, whom he has at one time tenderly loved, and who suddenly springs up before his eyes, still the same, and utterly transformed by the years.

He got up, and going back to the hearth, he sat down again in the arm-chair, and again hid his face in his hands.... 'Why to-day? just to-day?' was his thought, and he remembered many things, long since past.

This is what he remembered....

But first I must mention his name, his father's name and his surname.

He was called Dimitri Pavlovitch Sanin.

Here follows what he remembered.

I

It was the summer of 1840. Sanin was in his twenty-second year, and he was in Frankfort on his way home from Italy to Russia. He was a man of small property, but independent, almost without family ties. By the death of a distant relative, he had come into a few thousand roubles, and he had decided to spend this sum abroad before entering the service, before finally putting on the government yoke, without which he could not obtain a secure livelihood. Sanin had carried out this intention, and had fitted things in to such a nicety that on the day of his arrival in Frankfort he had only just enough money left to take him back to Petersburg. In the year 1840 there were few railroads in existence; tourists travelled by diligence. Sanin had taken a place in the '*bei-wagon*'; but the diligence did not start till eleven o'clock in the evening. There was a great deal of time to be got through before then. Fortunately it was lovely weather, and Sanin after dining at a hotel, famous in those days, the White Swan, set off to stroll about the town. He went in to look at Danneker's Ariadne, which he did not much care for, visited the house of Goethe, of whose works he had, however, only read *Werter*, and that in the French translation. He walked along the bank of the Maine, and was bored as a well-conducted tourist should be; at last at six o'clock in the evening, tired, and with dusty boots, he found himself in one of the least remarkable streets in Frankfort. That street he was fated not to forget long, long after. On one of its few houses he saw a signboard: 'Giovanni Roselli, Italian confectionery,' was announced upon it. Sanin went into it to get a glass of lemonade; but in the shop, where, behind the modest counter, on the shelves of a stained cupboard, recalling a chemist's shop, stood a few bottles with gold labels, and as many glass jars of biscuits, chocolate cakes, and sweetmeats—in this room, there was not a soul; only a grey cat blinked and purred, sharpening its claws on a tall wicker chair near the window and a bright patch of colour was made in the evening sunlight, by a big ball of red wool lying on the floor beside a carved wooden basket turned upside down. A confused noise was audible in the next room. Sanin stood a moment, and making the bell on the door ring its loudest, he called, raising his voice, 'Is there no one here?' At that instant the door from an inner room was thrown open, and Sanin was struck dumb with amazement.

II

A young girl of nineteen ran impetuously into the shop, her dark curls hanging in disorder on her bare shoulders, her bare arms stretched out in front of her. Seeing Sanin, she rushed up to him at once, seized him by the hand, and pulled him after her, saying in a breathless voice, 'Quick, quick, here, save him!' Not through disinclination to obey, but simply from excess of amazement, Sanin did not at once follow the girl. He stood, as it were, rooted to the spot; he had never in his life seen such a beautiful creature. She turned towards him, and with such despair in her voice, in her eyes, in the gesture of her clenched hand, which was lifted with a spasmodic movement to her pale cheek, she articulated, 'Come, come!' that he at once darted after her to the open door.

In the room, into which he ran behind the girl, on an old-fashioned horse-hair sofa, lay a boy of fourteen, white all over—white, with a yellowish tinge like wax or old marble—he was strikingly like the girl, obviously her brother. His eyes were closed, a patch of shadow fell from his thick black hair on a forehead like stone, and delicate, motionless eyebrows; between the blue lips could be seen clenched teeth. He seemed not to be breathing; one arm hung down to the floor, the other he had tossed above his head. The boy was dressed, and his clothes were closely buttoned; a tight cravat was twisted round his neck.

The girl rushed up to him with a wail of distress. 'He is dead, he is dead!' she cried; 'he was sitting here just now, talking to me—and all of a sudden he fell down and became rigid.... My God! can nothing be done to help him? And mamma not here! Pantaleone, Pantaleone, the doctor!' she went on suddenly in Italian. 'Have you been for the doctor?'

'Signora, I did not go, I sent Luise,' said a hoarse voice at the door, and a little bandy-legged old man came hobbling into the room in a lavender frock coat with black buttons, a high white cravat, short nankeen trousers, and blue worsted stockings. His diminutive little face was positively lost in a mass of iron-grey hair. Standing up in all directions, and falling back in ragged tufts, it gave the old man's figure a resemblance to a crested hen—a resemblance the more striking, that under the dark-grey mass nothing could be distinguished but a beak nose and round yellow eyes.
'Luise will run fast, and I can't run,' the old man went on in Italian, dragging his flat gouty feet, shod in high slippers with knots of ribbon. 'I've brought some water.'
In his withered, knotted fingers, he clutched a long bottle neck.
'But meanwhile Emil will die!' cried the girl, and holding out her hand to Sanin, 'O, sir, O *mein Herr*! can't you do something for him?'
'He ought to be bled—it's an apoplectic fit,' observed the old man addressed as Pantaleone.
Though Sanin had not the slightest notion of medicine, he knew one thing for certain, that boys of fourteen do not have apoplectic fits.
'It's a swoon, not a fit,' he said, turning to Pantaleone. 'Have you got any brushes?'
The old man raised his little face. 'Eh?'
'Brushes, brushes,' repeated Sanin in German and in French. 'Brushes,' he added, making as though he would brush his clothes.
The little old man understood him at last.
'Ah, brushes! *Spazzette*! to be sure we have!'
'Bring them here; we will take off his coat and try rubbing him.'
'Good … *Benone*! And ought we not to sprinkle water on his head?'
'No … later on; get the brushes now as quick as you can.'
Pantaleone put the bottle on the floor, ran out and returned at once with two brushes, one a hair-brush, and one a clothes-brush. A curly poodle followed him in, and vigorously wagging its tail, it looked up inquisitively at the old man, the girl, and even Sanin, as though it wanted to know what was the meaning of all this fuss.
Sanin quickly took the boy's coat off, unbuttoned his collar, and pushed up his shirt-sleeves, and arming himself with a brush, he began brushing his chest and arms with all his might. Pantaleone as zealously brushed away with the other—the hair-brush—at his boots and trousers. The girl flung herself on her knees by the sofa, and, clutching her head in both hands, fastened her eyes, not an eyelash quivering, on her brother.
Sanin rubbed on, and kept stealing glances at her. Mercy! what a beautiful creature she was!

III

Her nose was rather large, but handsome, aquiline-shaped; her upper lip was shaded by a light down; but then the colour of her face, smooth, uniform, like ivory or very pale milky amber, the wavering shimmer of her hair, like that of the Judith of Allorio in the Palazzo-Pitti; and above all, her eyes, dark-grey, with a black ring round the pupils, splendid, triumphant eyes, even now, when terror and distress dimmed their lustre…. Sanin could not help recalling the marvellous country he had just come from…. But even in Italy he had never met anything like her! The girl drew slow, uneven breaths; she seemed between each breath to be waiting to see whether her brother would not begin to breathe.
Sanin went on rubbing him, but he did not only watch the girl. The original figure of Pantaleone drew his attention too. The old man was quite exhausted and panting; at every movement of the brush he hopped up and down and groaned noisily, while his immense tufts of hair, soaked with perspiration, flapped heavily from side to side, like the roots of some strong plant, torn up by the water.
'You'd better, at least, take off his boots,' Sanin was just saying to him.
The poodle, probably excited by the unusualness of all the proceedings, suddenly sank on to its front paws and began barking.

'*Tartaglia—canaglia*!' the old man hissed at it. But at that instant the girl's face was transformed. Her eyebrows rose, her eyes grew wider, and shone with joy.
Sanin looked round ... A flush had over-spread the lad's face; his eyelids stirred ... his nostrils twitched. He drew in a breath through his still clenched teeth, sighed....
'Emil!' cried the girl ... 'Emilio mio!'
Slowly the big black eyes opened. They still had a dazed look, but already smiled faintly; the same faint smile hovered on his pale lips. Then he moved the arm that hung down, and laid it on his chest.
'Emilio!' repeated the girl, and she got up. The expression on her face was so tense and vivid, that it seemed that in an instant either she would burst into tears or break into laughter.
'Emil! what is it? Emil!' was heard outside, and a neatly-dressed lady with silvery grey hair and a dark face came with rapid steps into the room.
A middle-aged man followed her; the head of a maid-servant was visible over their shoulders.
The girl ran to meet them.
'He is saved, mother, he is alive!' she cried, impulsively embracing the lady who had just entered.
'But what is it?' she repeated. 'I come back ... and all of a sudden I meet the doctor and Luise ...'
The girl proceeded to explain what had happened, while the doctor went up to the invalid who was coming more and more to himself, and was still smiling: he seemed to be beginning to feel shy at the commotion he had caused.
'You've been using friction with brushes, I see,' said the doctor to Sanin and Pantaleone, 'and you did very well.... A very good idea ... and now let us see what further measures ...'
He felt the youth's pulse. 'H'm! show me your tongue!'
The lady bent anxiously over him. He smiled still more ingenuously, raised his eyes to her, and blushed a little.
It struck Sanin that he was no longer wanted; he went into the shop. But before he had time to touch the handle of the street-door, the girl was once more before him; she stopped him.
'You are going,' she began, looking warmly into his face; 'I will not keep you, but you must be sure to come to see us this evening: we are so indebted to you—you, perhaps, saved my brother's life, we want to thank you—mother wants to. You must tell us who you are, you must rejoice with us ...'
'But I am leaving for Berlin to-day,' Sanin faltered out.
'You will have time though,' the girl rejoined eagerly. 'Come to us in an hour's time to drink a cup of chocolate with us. You promise? I must go back to him! You will come?'
What could Sanin do?
'I will come,' he replied.
The beautiful girl pressed his hand, fluttered away, and he found himself in the street.

IV

When Sanin, an hour and a half later, returned to the Rosellis' shop he was received there like one of the family. Emilio was sitting on the same sofa, on which he had been rubbed; the doctor had prescribed him medicine and recommended 'great discretion in avoiding strong emotions' as being a subject of nervous temperament with a tendency to weakness of the heart. He had previously been liable to fainting-fits; but never had he lost consciousness so completely and for so long. However, the doctor declared that all danger was over. Emil, as was only suitable for an invalid, was dressed in a comfortable dressing-gown; his mother wound a blue woollen wrap round his neck; but he had a cheerful, almost a festive air; indeed everything had a festive air. Before the sofa, on a round table, covered with a clean cloth, towered a huge china coffee-pot, filled with fragrant chocolate, and encircled by cups, decanters of liqueur, biscuits and rolls, and even flowers; six slender wax candles were burning in two old-fashioned silver chandeliers; on one side of the sofa, a comfortable lounge-chair offered its soft embraces, and in this chair they made Sanin sit. All the inhabitants of the confectioner's shop, with whom he had made acquaintance that day, were present, not excluding the poodle, Tartaglia, and the cat; they all seemed happy beyond expression; the poodle positively sneezed with delight, only the cat was coy and blinked sleepily as before. They made Sanin tell them who he was, where he came from, and what was his name; when he said he was a Russian, both the ladies were a little surprised, uttered ejaculations of wonder, and declared with one voice that he spoke German splendidly; but if he preferred to speak French, he might make use of that language, as they both understood it and spoke it well. Sanin at once availed himself of this suggestion. 'Sanin! Sanin!' The ladies would never have expected that a Russian surname could be so easy to pronounce. His Christian name—'Dimitri'—they liked very much too. The elder lady observed that in her youth she had heard a fine opera—Demetrio e Polibio'—but that 'Dimitri' was much nicer than 'Demetrio.' In this way Sanin talked for about an hour. The ladies on their side initiated him into all the details of their own life. The talking was mostly done by the mother, the lady with grey hair. Sanin learnt from her that her name was Leonora Roselli; that she had lost her husband, Giovanni Battista Roselli, who had settled in Frankfort as a confectioner twenty—five years ago; that Giovanni Battista had come from Vicenza and had been a most excellent, though fiery and irascible man, and a republican withal! At those words Signora Roselli pointed to his portrait, painted in oil-colours, and hanging over the sofa. It must be presumed that the painter, 'also a republican!' as Signora Roselli observed with a sigh, had not fully succeeded in catching a likeness, for in his portrait the late Giovanni Battista appeared as a morose and gloomy brigand, after the style of Rinaldo Rinaldini! Signora Roselli herself had come from 'the ancient and splendid city of Parma where there is the wonderful cupola, painted by the immortal Correggio!' But from her long residence in Germany she had become almost completely Germanised. Then she added, mournfully shaking her head, that all she had left was *this* daughter and *this* son (pointing to each in turn with her finger); that the daughter's name was Gemma, and the son's Emilio; that they were both very good and obedient children—especially Emilio ... ('Me not obedient!' her daughter put in at that point. 'Oh, you're a republican, too!' answered her mother). That the business, of course, was not what it had been in the days of her husband, who had a great gift for the confectionery line ... ('*Un grand uomo*!' Pantaleone confirmed with a severe air); but that still, thank God, they managed to get along!

V

Gemma listened to her mother, and at one minute laughed, then sighed, then patted her on the shoulder, and shook her finger at her, and then looked at Sanin; at last, she got up, embraced her mother and kissed her in the hollow of her neck, which made the latter laugh extremely and shriek a little. Pantaleone too was presented to Sanin. It appeared he had once been an opera singer, a baritone, but had long ago given up the theatre, and occupied in the Roselli family a position between that of a family friend and a servant. In spite of his prolonged residence in Germany, he had learnt very little German, and only knew how to swear in it, mercilessly distorting even the terms of abuse. '*Ferroflucto spitchebubbio*' was his favourite epithet for almost every German. He spoke Italian with a perfect accent—for was he not by birth from Sinigali, where may be heard '*lingua toscana in bocca romana*'! Emilio, obviously, played the invalid and indulged himself in the pleasant sensations of one who has only just escaped a danger or is returning to health after illness; it was evident, too, that the family spoiled him. He thanked Sanin bashfully, but devoted himself chiefly to the biscuits and sweetmeats. Sanin was compelled to drink two large cups of excellent chocolate, and to eat a considerable number of biscuits; no sooner had he swallowed one than Gemma offered him another—and to refuse was impossible! He soon felt at home: the time flew by with incredible swiftness. He had to tell them a great deal—about Russia in general, the Russian climate, Russian society, the Russian peasant—and especially about the Cossacks; about the war of 1812, about Peter the Great, about the Kremlin, and the Russian songs and bells. Both ladies had a very faint conception of our vast and remote fatherland; Signora Roselli, or as she was more often called, Frau Lenore, positively dumfoundered Sanin with the question, whether there was still existing at Petersburg the celebrated house of ice, built last century, about which she had lately read a very curious article in one of her husband's books, '*Bettezze delle arti*.' And in reply to Sanin's exclamation, 'Do you really suppose that there is never any summer in Russia?' Frau Lenore replied that till then she had always pictured Russia like this—eternal snow, every one going about in furs, and all military men, but the greatest hospitality, and all the peasants very submissive! Sanin tried to impart to her and her daughter some more exact information. When the conversation touched on Russian music, they begged him at once to sing some Russian air and showed him a diminutive piano with black keys instead of white and white instead of black. He obeyed without making much ado and accompanying himself with two fingers of the right hand and three of the left (the first, second, and little finger) he sang in a thin nasal tenor, first 'The Sarafan,' then 'Along a Paved Street.' The ladies praised his voice and the music, but were more struck with the softness and sonorousness of the Russian language and asked for a translation of the text. Sanin complied with their wishes—but as the words of 'The Sarafan,' and still more of 'Along a Paved Street' (*sur une rue pavée une jeune fille allait à l'eau* was how he rendered the sense of the original) were not calculated to inspire his listeners with an exalted idea of Russian poetry, he first recited, then translated, and then sang Pushkin's, 'I remember a marvellous moment,' set to music by Glinka, whose minor bars he did not render quite faithfully. Then the ladies went into ecstasies. Frau Lenore positively discovered in Russian a wonderful likeness to the Italian. Even the names Pushkin (she pronounced it Pussekin) and Glinka sounded somewhat familiar to her. Sanin on his side begged the ladies to sing something; they too did not wait to be pressed. Frau Lenore sat down to the piano and sang with Gemma some duets and 'stornelle.' The mother had once had a fine contralto; the daughter's voice was not strong, but was pleasing.

VI

But it was not Gemma's voice—it was herself Sanin was admiring. He was sitting a little behind and on one side of her, and kept thinking to himself that no palm-tree, even in the poems of Benediktov—the poet in fashion in those days—could rival the slender grace of her figure. When, at the most emotional passages, she raised her eyes upwards—it seemed to him no heaven could fail to open at such a look! Even the old man, Pantaleone, who with his shoulder propped against the doorpost, and his chin and mouth tucked into his capacious cravat, was listening solemnly with the air of a connoisseur—even he was admiring the girl's lovely face and marvelling at it, though one would have thought he must have been used to it! When she had finished the duet with her daughter, Frau Lenore observed that Emilio had a fine voice, like a silver bell, but that now he was at the age when the voice changes—he did, in fact, talk in a sort of bass constantly falling into falsetto—and that he was therefore forbidden to sing; but that Pantaleone now really might try his skill of old days in honour of their guest! Pantaleone promptly put on a displeased air, frowned, ruffled up his hair, and declared that he had given it all up long ago, though he could certainly in his youth hold his own, and indeed had belonged to that great period, when there were real classical singers, not to be compared to the squeaking performers of to-day! and a real school of singing; that he, Pantaleone Cippatola of Varese, had once been brought a laurel wreath from Modena, and that on that occasion some white doves had positively been let fly in the theatre; that among others a Russian prince Tarbusky—'*il principe Tarbusski*'—with whom he had been on the most friendly terms, had after supper persistently invited him to Russia, promising him mountains of gold, mountains!... but that he had been unwilling to leave Italy, the land of Dante—*il paese del Dante!* Afterward, to be sure, there came ... unfortunate circumstances, he had himself been imprudent.... At this point the old man broke off, sighed deeply twice, looked dejected, and began again talking of the classical period of singing, of the celebrated tenor Garcia, for whom he cherished a devout, unbounded veneration. 'He was a man!' he exclaimed. 'Never had the great Garcia (*il gran Garcia*) demeaned himself by singing falsetto like the paltry tenors of to-day—*tenoracci*; always from the chest, from the chest, *voce di petto, si!*' and the old man aimed a vigorous blow with his little shrivelled fist at his own shirt-front! 'And what an actor! A volcano, *signori miei*, a volcano, *un Vesuvio*! I had the honour and the happiness of singing with him in the *opera dell' illustrissimo maestro* Rossini—in Otello! Garcia was Otello,—I was Iago—and when he rendered the phrase':—here Pantaleone threw himself into an attitude and began singing in a hoarse and shaky, but still moving voice:

"L'i ... ra daver ... so daver ... so il fato
lo più no ... no ... no ... non temerò!"

The theatre was all a-quiver, *signori miei*! though I too did not fall short, I too after him.

"L'i ra daver ... so daver ... so il fato
Temèr più non davro!"

And all of a sudden, he crashed like lightning, like a tiger: *Morro!... ma vendicato* ... Again when he was singing ... when he was singing that celebrated air from "*Matrimonio segreto*," *Pria che spunti* ... then he, *il gran Garcia*, after the words, "*I cavalli di galoppo*"—at the words, "*Senza posa cacciera*,"—listen, how stupendous, *come è stupendo*! At that point he made ...' The old man began a sort of extraordinary flourish, and at the tenth note broke down, cleared his throat, and with a wave of his arm turned away, muttering, 'Why do you torment me?' Gemma jumped up at once and clapping loudly and shouting, bravo!... bravo!... she ran to the poor old super-annuated Iago and with both hands patted him affectionately on the shoulders. Only Emil laughed ruthlessly. *Cet âge est sans pitié*—that age knows no mercy—Lafontaine has said already.

Sanin tried to soothe the aged singer and began talking to him in Italian—(he had picked up a smattering during his last tour there)—began talking of '*paese del Dante, dove il si suona*.' This phrase, together with '*Lasciate ogni speranza*,' made up the whole stock of poetic Italian of the young tourist; but Pantaleone was not won over by his blandishments. Tucking his chin deeper than ever into his cravat and sullenly rolling his eyes, he was once more like a bird, an angry one too,—a crow or a kite. Then Emil, with a faint momentary blush, such as one so often sees in spoilt children, addressing his sister, said if she wanted to entertain their guest, she could do nothing better than read him one of those little comedies of Malz, that she read so nicely. Gemma laughed, slapped her brother on the arm, exclaimed that he 'always had such ideas!' She went promptly, however, to her room, and returning thence with a small book in her hand, seated herself at the table before the lamp, looked round, lifted one finger as much as to say, 'hush!'—a typically Italian gesture—and began reading.

VII

Malz was a writer flourishing at Frankfort about 1830, whose short comedies, written in a light vein in the local dialect, hit off local Frankfort types with bright and amusing, though not deep, humour. It turned out that Gemma really did read excellently—quite like an actress in fact. She indicated each personage, and sustained the character capitally, making full use of the talent of mimicry she had inherited with her Italian blood; she had no mercy on her soft voice or her lovely face, and when she had to represent some old crone in her dotage, or a stupid burgomaster, she made the drollest grimaces, screwing up her eyes, wrinkling up her nose, lisping, squeaking.... She did not herself laugh during the reading; but when her audience (with the exception of Pantaleone: he had walked off in indignation so soon as the conversation turned *o quel ferroflucto Tedesco*) interrupted her by an outburst of unanimous laughter, she dropped the book on her knee, and laughed musically too, her head thrown back, and her black hair dancing in little ringlets on her neck and her shaking shoulders. When the laughter ceased, she picked up the book at once, and again resuming a suitable expression, began the reading seriously. Sanin could not get over his admiration; he was particularly astonished at the marvellous way in which a face so ideally beautiful assumed suddenly a comic, sometimes almost a vulgar expression. Gemma was less successful in the parts of young girls—of so-called '*jeunes premières*'; in the love-scenes in particular she failed; she was conscious of this herself, and for that reason gave them a faint shade of irony as though she did not quite believe in all these rapturous vows and elevated sentiments, of which the author, however, was himself rather sparing—so far as he could be.

Sanin did not notice how the evening was flying by, and only recollected the journey before him when the clock struck ten. He leaped up from his seat as though he had been stung.

'What is the matter?' inquired Frau Lenore.

'Why, I had to start for Berlin to-night, and I have taken a place in the diligence!'

'And when does the diligence start?'

'At half-past ten!'

'Well, then, you won't catch it now,' observed Gemma; 'you must stay ... and I will go on reading.'

'Have you paid the whole fare or only given a deposit?' Frau Lenore queried.

'The whole fare!' Sanin said dolefully with a gloomy face.

Gemma looked at him, half closed her eyes, and laughed, while her mother scolded her:

'The young gentleman has paid away his money for nothing, and you laugh!'

'Never mind,' answered Gemma; 'it won't ruin him, and we will try and amuse him. Will you have some lemonade?'
Sanin drank a glass of lemonade, Gemma took up Malz once more; and all went merrily again.
The clock struck twelve. Sanin rose to take leave.
'You must stay some days now in Frankfort,' said Gemma: 'why should you hurry away? It would be no nicer in any other town.' She paused. 'It wouldn't, really,' she added with a smile. Sanin made no reply, and reflected that considering the emptiness of his purse, he would have no choice about remaining in Frankfort till he got an answer from a friend in Berlin, to whom he proposed writing for money.
'Yes, do stay,' urged Frau Lenore too. 'We will introduce you to Mr. Karl Klüber, who is engaged to Gemma. He could not come to-day, as he was very busy at his shop ... you must have seen the biggest draper's and silk mercer's shop in the *Zeile*. Well, he is the manager there. But he will be delighted to call on you himself.'
Sanin—heaven knows why—was slightly disconcerted by this piece of information. 'He's a lucky fellow, that fiancé!' flashed across his mind. He looked at Gemma, and fancied he detected an ironical look in her eyes.
He began saying good-bye.
'Till to-morrow? Till to-morrow, isn't it?' queried Frau Lenore.
'Till to-morrow!' Gemma declared in a tone not of interrogation, but of affirmation, as though it could not be otherwise.
'Till to-morrow!' echoed Sanin.
Emil, Pantaleone, and the poodle Tartaglia accompanied him to the corner of the street. Pantaleone could not refrain from expressing his displeasure at Gemma's reading.
'She ought to be ashamed! She mouths and whines, *una caricatura*! She ought to represent Merope or Clytemnaestra—something grand, tragic—and she apes some wretched German woman! I can do that ... *merz, kerz, smerz*,' he went on in a hoarse voice poking his face forward, and brandishing his fingers.
Tartaglia began barking at him, while Emil burst out laughing. The old man turned sharply back.
Sanin went back to the White Swan (he had left his things there in the public hall) in a rather confused frame of mind. All the talk he had had in French, German, and Italian was ringing in his ears.
'Engaged!' he whispered as he lay in bed, in the modest apartment assigned to him. 'And what a beauty! But what did I stay for?'
Next day he sent a letter to his friend in Berlin.

VIII

He had not finished dressing, when a waiter announced the arrival of two gentlemen. One of them turned out to be Emil; the other, a good-looking and well-grown young man, with a handsome face, was Herr Karl Klüber, the betrothed of the lovely Gemma.
One may safely assume that at that time in all Frankfort, there was not in a single shop a manager as civil, as decorous, as dignified, and as affable as Herr Klüber. The irreproachable perfection of his get-up was on a level with the dignity of his deportment, with the elegance—a little affected and stiff, it is true, in the English style (he had spent two years in England)—but still fascinating, elegance of his manners! It was clear from the first glance that this handsome, rather severe, excellently brought-up and superbly washed young man was accustomed to obey his superior and to command his inferior, and that behind the counter of his shop he must infallibly inspire respect even in his customers! Of his supernatural honesty there could never be a particle of doubt: one had but to look at his stiffly starched collars! And his voice, it appeared, was just what one would expect; deep, and of a self-confident richness, but not too loud, with positively a certain caressing note in its timbre. Such a voice was peculiarly fitted to give orders to assistants under his control: 'Show the crimson Lyons velvet!' or, 'Hand the lady a chair!'
Herr Klüber began with introducing himself; as he did so, he bowed with such loftiness, moved his legs with such an agreeable air, and drew his heels together with such polished courtesy that no one could fail to feel, 'that man has both linen and moral principles of the first quality!' The finish of his bare right hand—(the left, in a suede glove, held a hat shining like a looking-glass, with the right glove placed within it)—the finish of the right hand, proffered modestly but resolutely to Sanin, surpassed all belief; each finger-nail was a

perfection in its own way! Then he proceeded to explain in the choicest German that he was anxious to express his respect and his indebtedness to the foreign gentleman who had performed so signal a service to his future kinsman, the brother of his betrothed; as he spoke, he waved his left hand with the hat in it in the direction of Emil, who seemed bashful and turning away to the window, put his finger in his mouth. Herr Klüber added that he should esteem himself happy should he be able in return to do anything for the foreign gentleman. Sanin, with some difficulty, replied, also in German, that he was delighted … that the service was not worth speaking of … and he begged his guests to sit down. Herr Klüber thanked him, and lifting his coat-tails, sat down on a chair; but he perched there so lightly and with such a transitory air that no one could fail to realise, 'this man is sitting down from politeness, and will fly up again in an instant.' And he did in fact fly up again quickly, and advancing with two discreet little dance-steps, he announced that to his regret he was unable to stay any longer, as he had to hasten to his shop—business before everything! but as the next day was Sunday, he had, with the consent of Frau Lenore and Fräulein Gemma, arranged a holiday excursion to Soden, to which he had the honour of inviting the foreign gentleman, and he cherished the hope that he would not refuse to grace the party with his presence. Sanin did not refuse so to grace it; and Herr Klüber repeating once more his complimentary sentiments, took leave, his pea-green trousers making a spot of cheerful colour, and his brand-new boots squeaking cheerfully as he moved.

IX

Emil, who had continued to stand with his face to the window, even after Sanin's invitation to him to sit down, turned round directly his future kinsman had gone out, and with a childish pout and blush, asked Sanin if he might remain a little while with him. 'I am much better to-day,' he added, 'but the doctor has forbidden me to do any work.'

'Stay by all means! You won't be in the least in my way,' Sanin cried at once. Like every true Russian he was glad to clutch at any excuse that saved him from the necessity of doing anything himself.

Emil thanked him, and in a very short time he was completely at home with him and with his room; he looked at all his things, asked him about almost every one of them, where he had bought it, and what was its value. He helped him to shave, observing that it was a mistake not to let his moustache grow; and finally told him a number of details about his mother, his sister, Pantaleone, the poodle Tartaglia, and all their daily life. Every semblance of timidity vanished in Emil; he suddenly felt extraordinarily attracted to Sanin—not at all because he had saved his life the day before, but because he was such a nice person! He lost no time in confiding all his secrets to Sanin. He expatiated with special warmth on the fact that his mother was set on making him a shopkeeper, while he *knew*, knew for certain, that he was born an artist, a musician, a singer; that Pantaleone even encouraged him, but that Herr Klüber supported mamma, over whom he had great influence; that the very idea of his being a shopkeeper really originated with Herr Klüber, who considered that nothing in the world could compare with trade! To measure out cloth—and cheat the public, extorting from it '*Narren—oder Russen Preise*' (fools'—or Russian prices)—that was his ideal! [Footnote: In former days—and very likely it is not different now—when, from May onwards, a great number of Russians visited Frankfort, prices rose in all the shops, and were called 'Russians',' or, alas! 'fools' prices.']

'Come! now you must come and see us!' he cried, directly Sanin had finished his toilet and written his letter to Berlin.

'It's early yet,' observed Sanin.

'That's no matter,' replied Emil caressingly. 'Come along! We'll go to the post—and from there to our place. Gemma will be so glad to see you! You must have lunch with us.… You might say a word to mamma about me, my career.…'

'Very well, let's go,' said Sanin, and they set off.

X

Gemma certainly was delighted to see him, and Frau Lenore gave him a very friendly welcome; he had obviously made a good impression on both of them the evening before. Emil ran to see to getting lunch ready, after a preliminary whisper, 'don't forget!' in Sanin's ear.

'I won't forget,' responded Sanin.

Frau Lenore was not quite well; she had a sick headache, and, half-lying down in an easy chair, she tried to keep perfectly still. Gemma wore a full yellow blouse, with a black leather belt round the waist; she too seemed exhausted, and was rather pale; there were dark rings round her eyes, but their lustre was not the less for it; it added something of charm and mystery to the classical lines of her face. Sanin was especially struck that day by the exquisite beauty of her hands; when she smoothed and put back her dark, glossy tresses he could not take his eyes off her long supple fingers, held slightly apart from one another like the hand of Raphael's Fornarina.

It was very hot out-of-doors; after lunch Sanin was about to take leave, but they told him that on such a day the best thing was to stay where one was, and he agreed; he stayed. In the back room where he was sitting with the ladies of the household, coolness reigned supreme; the windows looked out upon a little garden overgrown with acacias. Multitudes of bees, wasps, and humming beetles kept up a steady, eager buzz in their thick branches, which were studded with golden blossoms; through the half-drawn curtains and the lowered blinds this never-ceasing hum made its way into the room, telling of the sultry heat in the air outside, and making the cool of the closed and snug abode seem the sweeter.

Sanin talked a great deal, as on the day before, but not of Russia, nor of Russian life. Being anxious to please his young friend, who had been sent off to Herr Klüber's immediately after lunch, to acquire a knowledge of book-keeping, he turned the conversation on the comparative advantages and disadvantages of art and commerce. He was not surprised at Frau Lenore's standing up for commerce—he had expected that; but Gemma too shared her opinion.

'If one's an artist, and especially a singer,' she declared with a vigorous downward sweep of her hand, 'one's got to be first-rate! Second-rate's worse than nothing; and who can tell if one will arrive at being first-rate?'

Pantaleone, who took part too in the conversation—(as an old servant and an old man he had the privilege of sitting down in the presence of the ladies of the house; Italians are not, as a rule, strict in matters of etiquette)—Pantaleone, as a matter of course, stood like a rock for art. To tell the truth, his arguments were somewhat feeble; he kept expatiating for the most part on the necessity, before all things, of possessing '*un certo estro d'inspirazione*'—a certain force of inspiration! Frau Lenore remarked to him that he had, to be sure, possessed such an '*estro*'—and yet ... 'I had enemies,' Pantaleone observed gloomily. 'And how do you know that Emil will not have enemies, even if this "*estro*" is found in him?' 'Very well, make a tradesman of him, then,' retorted Pantaleone in vexation; 'but Giovan' Battista would never have done it, though he was a confectioner himself!' 'Giovan' Battista, my husband, was a reasonable man, and even though he was in his youth led away ...' But the old man would hear nothing more, and walked away, repeating reproachfully, 'Ah! Giovan' Battista!...' Gemma exclaimed that if Emil felt like a patriot, and wanted to devote all his powers to the liberation of Italy, then, of course, for such a high and holy cause he might sacrifice the security of the future—but not for the theatre! Thereupon Frau Lenore became much agitated, and began to implore her daughter to refrain at least from turning her brother's head, and to content herself with being such a desperate republican herself! Frau Lenore groaned as she uttered these words, and began complaining of her head, which was 'ready to split.' (Frau Lenore, in deference to their guest, talked to her daughter in French.)

Gemma began at once to wait upon her; she moistened her forehead with eau-de-Cologne, gently blew on it, gently kissed her cheek, made her lay her head on a pillow, forbade her to speak, and kissed her again. Then, turning to Sanin, she began telling him in a half-joking, half-tender tone what a splendid mother she had, and what a beauty she had been. '"Had been," did I say? she is charming now! Look, look, what eyes!'

Gemma instantly pulled a white handkerchief out of her pocket, covered her mother's face with it, and slowly drawing it downwards, gradually uncovered Frau Lenore's forehead, eyebrows, and eyes; she waited a moment and asked her to open them. Her mother obeyed; Gemma cried out in ecstasy (Frau Lenore's eyes really were very beautiful), and rapidly sliding the handkerchief over the lower, less regular part of the face, fell to kissing her again. Frau Lenore laughed, and turning a little away, with a pretence of violence, pushed her daughter away. She too pretended to struggle with her mother, and lavished caresses on her—not like a cat, in the French manner, but with that special Italian grace in which is always felt the presence of power. At last Frau Lenore declared she was tired out ... Then Gemma at once advised her to have a little nap, where she was, in her chair, 'and I and the Russian gentleman—"*avec le monsieur russe*"—will be as quiet, as quiet ... as little mice ... "*comme des petites souris*."' Frau Lenore smiled at her in reply, closed her eyes, and after a few sighs began to doze. Gemma quickly dropped down on a bench beside her and did not stir again, only from time to time she put a finger of one hand to her lips—with the other hand she was holding up a pillow behind her mother's head—and said softly, 'sh-sh!' with a sidelong look at Sanin, if he permitted himself the smallest movement. In the end he too sank into a kind of dream, and sat motionless as though spell-bound, while all his faculties were absorbed in admiring the picture presented him by the half-dark room, here and there spotted with patches of light crimson, where fresh, luxuriant roses stood in the old-fashioned green glasses, and the sleeping woman with demurely folded hands and kind, weary face, framed in the snowy whiteness of the pillow, and the young, keenly-alert and also kind, clever, pure, and unspeakably beautiful creature with such black, deep, overshadowed, yet shining eyes.... What was it? A dream? a fairy tale? And how came *he* to be in it?

XI

The bell tinkled at the outer door. A young peasant lad in a fur cap and a red waistcoat came into the shop from the street. Not one customer had looked into it since early morning ... 'You see how much business we do!' Frau Lenore observed to Sanin at lunch-time with a sigh. She was still asleep; Gemma was afraid to take her arm from the pillow, and whispered to Sanin: 'You go, and mind the shop for me!' Sanin went on tiptoe into the shop at once. The boy wanted a quarter of a pound of peppermints. 'How much must I take?' Sanin whispered from the door to Gemma. 'Six kreutzers!' she answered in the same whisper. Sanin weighed out a quarter of a pound, found some paper, twisted it into a cone, tipped the peppermints into it, spilt them, tipped them in again, spilt them again, at last handed them to the boy, and took the money.... The boy gazed at him in amazement, twisting his cap in his hands on his stomach, and in the next room, Gemma was stifling with suppressed laughter. Before the first customer had walked out, a second appeared, then a third.... 'I bring luck, it's clear!' thought Sanin. The second customer wanted a glass of orangeade, the third, half-a-pound of sweets. Sanin satisfied their needs, zealously clattering the spoons, changing the saucers, and eagerly plunging his fingers into drawers and jars. On reckoning up, it appeared that he had charged too little for the orangeade, and taken two kreutzers too much for the sweets. Gemma did not cease laughing softly, and Sanin too was aware of an extraordinary lightness of heart, a peculiarly happy state of mind. He felt as if he had for ever been standing behind the counter and dealing in orangeade and sweetmeats, with that exquisite creature looking at him through the doorway with affectionately mocking eyes, while the summer sun, forcing its way through the sturdy leafage of the chestnuts that grew in front of the windows, filled the whole room with the greenish-gold of the midday light and shade, and the heart grew soft in the sweet languor of idleness, carelessness, and youth—first youth!

A fourth customer asked for a cup of coffee; Pantaleone had to be appealed to. (Emil had not yet come back from Herr Klüber's shop.) Sanin went and sat by Gemma again. Frau Lenore still went on sleeping, to her daughter's great delight. 'Mamma always sleeps off her sick headaches,' she observed. Sanin began talking—in a whisper, of course, as before—of his minding the shop; very seriously inquired the price of various articles of confectionery; Gemma just as seriously told him these prices, and meanwhile both of them were inwardly laughing together, as though conscious they were playing in a very amusing farce. All of a sudden, an organ-grinder in the street began playing an air from the Freischütz: '*Durch die Felder, durch die Auen ...*' The dance tune fell shrill and quivering on the motionless air. Gemma started ... 'He will wake mamma!' Sanin promptly darted out into the street, thrust a few kreutzers into the organ-grinder's hand, and made him cease playing and move away. When he came back, Gemma thanked him with a little nod of the head, and with a pensive smile she began herself just audibly humming the beautiful melody of Weber's, in which Max expresses all the perplexities of first love. Then she asked Sanin whether he knew 'Freischütz,' whether he was fond of Weber, and added that though she was herself an Italian, she liked *such* music best of all. From

Weber the conversation glided off on to poetry and romanticism, on to Hoffmann, whom every one was still reading at that time.
And Frau Lenore still slept, and even snored just a little, and the sunbeams, piercing in narrow streaks through the shutters, were incessantly and imperceptibly shifting and travelling over the floor, the furniture, Gemma's dress, and the leaves and petals of the flowers.

XII

It appeared that Gemma was not very fond of Hoffmann, that she even thought him ... tedious! The fantastic, misty northern element in his stories was too remote from her clear, southern nature. 'It's all fairy-tales, all written for children!' she declared with some contempt. She was vaguely conscious, too, of the lack of poetry in Hoffmann. But there was one of his stories, the title of which she had forgotten, which she greatly liked; more precisely speaking, it was only the beginning of this story that she liked; the end she had either not read or had forgotten. The story was about a young man who in some place, a sort of restaurant perhaps, meets a girl of striking beauty, a Greek; she is accompanied by a mysterious and strange, wicked old man. The young man falls in love with the girl at first sight; she looks at him so mournfully, as though beseeching him to deliver her.... He goes out for an instant, and, coming back into the restaurant, finds there neither the girl nor the old man; he rushes off in pursuit of her, continually comes upon fresh traces of her, follows them up, and can never by any means come upon her anywhere. The lovely girl has vanished for him for ever and ever, and he is never able to forget her imploring glance, and is tortured by the thought that all the happiness of his life, perhaps, has slipped through his fingers.
Hoffmann does not end his story quite in that way; but so it had taken shape, so it had remained, in Gemma's memory.
'I fancy,' she said, 'such meetings and such partings happen oftener in the world than we suppose.'
Sanin was silent ... and soon after he began talking ... of Herr Klüber. It was the first time he had referred to him; he had not once remembered him till that instant.
Gemma was silent in her turn, and sank into thought, biting the nail of her forefinger and fixing her eyes away. Then she began to speak in praise of her betrothed, alluded to the excursion he had planned for the next day, and, glancing swiftly at Sanin, was silent again.
Sanin did not know on what subject to turn the conversation.
Emil ran in noisily and waked Frau Lenore ... Sanin was relieved by his appearance.
Frau Lenore got up from her low chair. Pantaleone came in and announced that dinner was ready. The friend of the family, ex-singer, and servant also performed the duties of cook.

XIII

Sanin stayed on after dinner too. They did not let him go, still on the same pretext of the terrible heat; and when the heat began to decrease, they proposed going out into the garden to drink coffee in the shade of the acacias. Sanin consented. He felt very happy. In the quietly monotonous, smooth current of life lie hid great delights, and he gave himself up to these delights with zest, asking nothing much of the present day, but also thinking nothing of the morrow, nor recalling the day before. How much the mere society of such a girl as Gemma meant to him! He would shortly part from her and, most likely, for ever; but so long as they were borne, as in Uhland's song, in one skiff over the sea of life, untossed by tempest, well might the traveller rejoice and be glad. And everything seemed sweet and delightful to the happy voyager. Frau Lenore offered to play against him and Pantaleone at 'tresette,' instructed him in this not complicated Italian game, and won a few kreutzers from him, and he was well content. Pantaleone, at Emil's request, made the poodle, Tartaglia, perform all his tricks, and Tartaglia jumped over a stick 'spoke,' that is, barked, sneezed, shut the door with his nose, fetched his master's trodden-down slippers; and, finally, with an old cap on his head, he portrayed

Marshal Bernadotte, subjected to the bitterest upbraidings by the Emperor Napoleon on account of his treachery. Napoleon's part was, of course, performed by Pantaleone, and very faithfully he performed it: he folded his arms across his chest, pulled a cocked hat over his eyes, and spoke very gruffly and sternly, in French—and heavens! what French! Tartaglia sat before his sovereign, all huddled up, with dejected tail, and eyes blinking and twitching in confusion, under the peak of his cap which was stuck on awry; from time to time when Napoleon raised his voice, Bernadotte rose on his hind paws. '*Fuori, traditore!*' cried Napoleon at last, forgetting in the excess of his wrath that he had to sustain his rôle as a Frenchman to the end; and Bernadotte promptly flew under the sofa, but quickly darted out again with a joyful bark, as though to announce that the performance was over. All the spectators laughed, and Sanin more than all.

Gemma had a particularly charming, continual, soft laugh, with very droll little shrieks.... Sanin was fairly enchanted by that laugh—he could have kissed her for those shrieks!

Night came on at last. He had in decency to take leave! After saying good-bye several times over to every one, and repeating several times to all, 'till to-morrow!'—Emil he went so far as to kiss—Sanin started home, carrying with him the image of the young girl, at one time laughing, at another thoughtful, calm, and even indifferent—but always attractive! Her eyes, at one time wide open, clear and bright as day, at another time half shrouded by the lashes and deep and dark as night, seemed to float before his eyes, piercing in a strange sweet way across all other images and recollections.

Of Herr Klüber, of the causes impelling him to remain in Frankfort—in short, of everything that had disturbed his mind the evening before—he never thought once.

XIV

We must, however, say a few words about Sanin himself.

In the first place, he was very, very good-looking. A handsome, graceful figure, agreeable, rather unformed features, kindly bluish eyes, golden hair, a clear white and red skin, and, above all, that peculiar, naïvely-cheerful, confiding, open, at the first glance, somewhat foolish expression, by which in former days one could recognise directly the children of steady-going, noble families, 'sons of their fathers,' fine young landowners, born and reared in our open, half-wild country parts,—a hesitating gait, a voice with a lisp, a smile like a child's the minute you looked at him ... lastly, freshness, health, softness, softness, softness,—there you have the whole of Sanin. And secondly, he was not stupid and had picked up a fair amount of knowledge. Fresh he had remained, for all his foreign tour; the disturbing emotions in which the greater part of the young people of that day were tempest-tossed were very little known to him.

Of late years, in response to the assiduous search for 'new types,' young men have begun to appear in our literature, determined at all hazards to be 'fresh'... as fresh as Flensburg oysters, when they reach Petersburg.... Sanin was not like them. Since we have had recourse already to simile, he rather recalled a young, leafy, freshly-grafted apple-tree in one of our fertile orchards—or better still, a well-groomed, sleek, sturdy-limbed, tender young 'three-year-old' in some old-fashioned seignorial stud stable, a young horse that they have hardly begun to break in to the traces.... Those who came across Sanin in later years, when life had knocked him about a good deal, and the sleekness and plumpness of youth had long vanished, saw in him a totally different man.

* * * * *

Next day Sanin was still in bed when Emil, in his best clothes, with a cane in his hand and much pomade on his head, burst into his room, announcing that Herr Klüber would be here directly with the carriage, that the weather promised to be exquisite, that they had everything ready by now, but that mamma was not going, as her head was bad again. He began to hurry Sanin, telling him that there was not a minute to lose.... And Herr Klüber did, in fact, find Sanin still at his toilet. He knocked at the door, came in, bowed with a bend from the waist, expressed his readiness to wait as long as might be desired, and sat down, his hat balanced elegantly on his knees. The handsome shop-manager had got himself up and perfumed himself to excess: his every action was accompanied by a powerful whiff of the most refined aroma. He arrived in a comfortable open carriage—one of the kind called landau—drawn by two tall and powerful but not well-shaped horses. A quarter of an hour later Sanin, Klüber, and Emil, in this same carriage, drew up triumphantly at the steps of

the confectioner's shop. Madame Roselli resolutely refused to join the party; Gemma wanted to stay with her mother; but she simply turned her out.
'I don't want any one,' she declared; 'I shall go to sleep. I would send Pantaleone with you too, only there would be no one to mind the shop.'
'May we take Tartaglia?' asked Emil.
'Of course you may.'
Tartaglia immediately scrambled, with delighted struggles, on to the box and sat there, licking himself; it was obviously a thing he was accustomed to. Gemma put on a large straw hat with brown ribbons; the hat was bent down in front, so as to shade almost the whole of her face from the sun. The line of shadow stopped just at her lips; they wore a tender maiden flush, like the petals of a centifoil rose, and her teeth gleamed stealthily—innocently too, as when children smile. Gemma sat facing the horses, with Sanin; Klüber and Emil sat opposite. The pale face of Frau Lenore appeared at the window; Gemma waved her handkerchief to her, and the horses started.

XV

Soden is a little town half an hour's distance from Frankfort. It lies in a beautiful country among the spurs of the Taunus Mountains, and is known among us in Russia for its waters, which are supposed to be beneficial to people with weak lungs. The Frankforters visit it more for purposes of recreation, as Soden possesses a fine park and various 'wirthschaften,' where one may drink beer and coffee in the shade of the tall limes and maples. The road from Frankfort to Soden runs along the right bank of the Maine, and is planted all along with fruit trees. While the carriage was rolling slowly along an excellent road, Sanin stealthily watched how Gemma behaved to her betrothed; it was the first time he had seen them together. *She* was quiet and simple in her manner, but rather more reserved and serious than usual; *he* had the air of a condescending schoolmaster, permitting himself and those under his authority a discreet and decorous pleasure. Sanin saw no signs in him of any marked attentiveness, of what the French call '*empressement*,' in his demeanour to Gemma. It was clear that Herr Klüber considered that it was a matter settled once for all, and that therefore he saw no reason to trouble or excite himself. But his condescension never left him for an instant! Even during a long ramble before dinner about the wooded hills and valleys behind Soden, even when enjoying the beauties of nature, he treated nature itself with the same condescension, through which his habitual magisterial severity peeped out from time to time. So, for example, he observed in regard to one stream that it ran too straight through the glade, instead of making a few picturesque curves; he disapproved, too, of the conduct of a bird—a chaffinch—for singing so monotonously. Gemma was not bored, and even, apparently, was enjoying herself; but Sanin did not recognise her as the Gemma of the preceding days; it was not that she seemed under a cloud—her beauty had never been more dazzling—but her soul seemed to have withdrawn into herself. With her parasol open and her gloves still buttoned up, she walked sedately, deliberately, as well-bred young girls walk, and spoke little. Emil, too, felt stiff, and Sanin more so than all. He was somewhat embarrassed too by the fact that the conversation was all the time in German. Only Tartaglia was in high spirits! He darted, barking frantically, after blackbirds, leaped over ravines, stumps and roots, rushed headlong into the water, lapped at it in desperate haste, shook himself, whining, and was off like an arrow, his red tongue trailing after him almost to his shoulder. Herr Klüber, for his part, did everything he supposed conducive to the mirthfulness of the company; he begged them to sit down in the shade of a spreading oak-tree, and taking out of a side pocket a small booklet entitled, '*Knallerbsen; oder du sollst und wirst lachen!*' (Squibs; or you must and shall laugh!) began reading the funny anecdotes of which the little book was full. He read them twelve specimens; he aroused very little mirth, however; only Sanin smiled, from politeness, and he himself, Herr Klüber, after each anecdote, gave vent to a brief, business-like, but still condescending laugh. At twelve o'clock the whole party returned to Soden to the best tavern there.
They had to make arrangements about dinner. Herr Klüber proposed that the dinner should be served in a summer-house closed in on all sides—'*im Gartensalon*'; but at this point Gemma rebelled and declared that she would have dinner in the open air, in the garden, at one of the little tables set before the tavern; that she

was tired of being all the while with the same faces, and she wanted to see fresh ones. At some of the little tables, groups of visitors were already sitting.
While Herr Klüber, yielding condescendingly to 'the caprice of his betrothed,' went off to interview the head waiter, Gemma stood immovable, biting her lips and looking on the ground; she was conscious that Sanin was persistently and, as it were, inquiringly looking at her—it seemed to enrage her. At last Herr Klüber returned, announced that dinner would be ready in half an hour, and proposed their employing the interval in a game of skittles, adding that this was very good for the appetite, he, he, he! Skittles he played in masterly fashion; as he threw the ball, he put himself into amazingly heroic postures, with artistic play of the muscles, with artistic flourish and shake of the leg. In his own way he was an athlete—and was superbly built! His hands, too, were so white and handsome, and he wiped them on such a sumptuous, gold-striped, Indian bandana!
The moment of dinner arrived, and the whole party seated themselves at the table.

XVI

Who does not know what a German dinner is like? Watery soup with knobby dumplings and pieces of cinnamon, boiled beef dry as cork, with white fat attached, slimy potatoes, soft beetroot and mashed horseradish, a bluish eel with French capers and vinegar, a roast joint with jam, and the inevitable '*Mehlspeise*,' something of the nature of a pudding with sourish red sauce; but to make up, the beer and wine first-rate! With just such a dinner the tavernkeeper at Soden regaled his customers. The dinner, itself, however, went off satisfactorily. No special liveliness was perceptible, certainly; not even when Herr Klüber proposed the toast 'What we like!' (Was wir lieben!) But at least everything was decorous and seemly. After dinner, coffee was served, thin, reddish, typically German coffee. Herr Klüber, with true gallantry, asked Gemma's permission to smoke a cigar.... But at this point suddenly something occurred, unexpected, and decidedly unpleasant, and even unseemly!
At one of the tables near were sitting several officers of the garrison of the Maine. From their glances and whispering together it was easy to perceive that they were struck by Gemma's beauty; one of them, who had probably stayed in Frankfort, stared at her persistently, as at a figure familiar to him; he obviously knew who she was. He suddenly got up, and glass in hand—all the officers had been drinking hard, and the cloth before them was crowded with bottles—approached the table at which Gemma was sitting. He was a very young flaxen-haired man, with a rather pleasing and even attractive face, but his features were distorted with the wine he had drunk, his cheeks were twitching, his blood-shot eyes wandered, and wore an insolent expression. His companions at first tried to hold him back, but afterwards let him go, interested apparently to see what he would do, and how it would end. Slightly unsteady on his legs, the officer stopped before Gemma, and in an unnaturally screaming voice, in which, in spite of himself, an inward struggle could be discerned, he articulated, 'I drink to the health of the prettiest confectioner in all Frankfort, in all the world (he emptied his glass), and in return I take this flower, picked by her divine little fingers!' He took from the table a rose that lay beside Gemma's plate. At first she was astonished, alarmed, and turned fearfully white ... then alarm was replaced by indignation; she suddenly crimsoned all over, to her very hair—and her eyes, fastened directly on the offender, at the same time darkened and flamed, they were filled with black gloom, and burned with the fire of irrepressible fury. The officer must have been confused by this look; he muttered something unintelligible, bowed, and walked back to his friends. They greeted him with a laugh, and faint applause.
Herr Klüber rose spasmodically from his seat, drew himself up to his full height, and putting on his hat pronounced with dignity, but not too loud, 'Unheard of! Unheard of! Unheard of impertinence!' and at once calling up the waiter, in a severe voice asked for the bill ... more than that, ordered the carriage to be put to, adding that it was impossible for respectable people to frequent the establishment if they were exposed to insult! At those words Gemma, who still sat in her place without stirring—her bosom was heaving violently—Gemma raised her eyes to Herr Klüber ... and she gazed as intently, with the same expression at him as at the officer. Emil was simply shaking with rage.

'Get up, *mein Fräulein,*' Klüber admonished her with the same severity, 'it is not proper for you to remain here. We will go inside, in the tavern!'

Gemma rose in silence; he offered her his arm, she gave him hers, and he walked into the tavern with a majestic step, which became, with his whole bearing, more majestic and haughty the farther he got from the place where they had dined. Poor Emil dragged himself after them.

But while Herr Klüber was settling up with the waiter, to whom, by way of punishment, he gave not a single kreutzer for himself, Sanin with rapid steps approached the table at which the officers were sitting, and addressing Gemma's assailant, who was at that instant offering her rose to his companions in turns to smell, he uttered very distinctly in French, 'What you have just done, sir, is conduct unworthy of an honest man, unworthy of the uniform you wear, and I have come to tell you you are an ill-bred cur!' The young man leaped on to his feet, but another officer, rather older, checked him with a gesture, made him sit down, and turning to Sanin asked him also in French, 'Was he a relation, brother, or betrothed of the girl?'

'I am nothing to her at all,' cried Sanin, 'I am a Russian, but I cannot look on at such insolence with indifference; but here is my card and my address; *monsieur l'officier*can find me.'

As he uttered these words, Sanin threw his visiting-card on the table, and at the same moment hastily snatched Gemma's rose, which one of the officers sitting at the table had dropped into his plate. The young man was again on the point of jumping up from the table, but his companion again checked him, saying, 'Dönhof, be quiet! Dönhof, sit still.' Then he got up himself, and putting his hand to the peak of his cap, with a certain shade of respectfulness in his voice and manner, told Sanin that to-morrow morning an officer of the regiment would have the honour of calling upon him. Sanin replied with a short bow, and hurriedly returned to his friends.

Herr Klüber pretended he had not noticed either Sanin's absence nor his interview with the officers; he was urging on the coachman, who was putting in the horses, and was furiously angry at his deliberateness. Gemma too said nothing to Sanin, she did not even look at him; from her knitted brows, from her pale and compressed lips, from her very immobility it could be seen that she was suffering inwardly. Only Emil obviously wanted to speak to Sanin, wanted to question him; he had seen Sanin go up to the officers, he had seen him give them something white—a scrap of paper, a note, or a card.... The poor boy's heart was beating, his cheeks burned, he was ready to throw himself on Sanin's neck, ready to cry, or to go with him at once to crush all those accursed officers into dust and ashes! He controlled himself, however, and did no more than watch intently every movement of his noble Russian friend.

The coachman had at last harnessed the horses; the whole party seated themselves in the carriage. Emil climbed on to the box, after Tartaglia; he was more comfortable there, and had not Klüber, whom he could hardly bear the sight of, sitting opposite to him.

* * * * *

The whole way home Herr Klüber discoursed ... and he discoursed alone; no one, absolutely no one, opposed him, nor did any one agree with him. He especially insisted on the point that they had been wrong in not following his advice when he suggested dining in a shut-up summer-house. There no unpleasantness could have occurred! Then he expressed a few decided and even liberal sentiments on the unpardonable way in which the government favoured the military, neglected their discipline, and did not sufficiently consider the civilian element in society (*das bürgerliche Element in der Societät*!), and foretold that in time this cause would give rise to discontent, which might well pass into revolution, of which (here he dropped a sympathetic though severe sigh) France had given them a sorrowful example! He added, however, that he personally had the greatest respect for authority, and never ... no, never!... could be a revolutionist—but he could not but express his ... disapprobation at the sight of such licence! Then he made a few general observations on morality and immorality, good-breeding, and the sense of dignity.

During all these lucubrations, Gemma, who even while they were walking before dinner had not seemed quite pleased with Herr Klüber, and had therefore held rather aloof from Sanin, and had been, as it were, embarrassed by his presence—Gemma was unmistakably ashamed of her betrothed! Towards the end of the drive she was positively wretched, and though, as before, she did not address a word to Sanin, she suddenly flung an imploring glance at him.... He, for his part, felt much more sorry for her than indignant with Herr Klüber; he was even secretly, half-consciously, delighted at what had happened in the course of that day, even though he had every reason to expect a challenge next morning.

This miserable *partie de plaisir* came to an end at last. As he helped Gemma out of the carriage at the confectionery shop, Sanin without a word put into her hand the rose he had recovered. She flushed crimson, pressed his hand, and instantly hid the rose. He did not want to go into the house, though the evening was

only just beginning. She did not even invite him. Moreover Pantaleone, who came out on the steps, announced that Frau Lenore was asleep. Emil took a shy good-bye of Sanin; he felt as it were in awe of him; he greatly admired him. Klüber saw Sanin to his lodging, and took leave of him stiffly. The well-regulated German, for all his self-confidence, felt awkward. And indeed every one felt awkward.
But in Sanin this feeling of awkwardness soon passed off. It was replaced by a vague, but pleasant, even triumphant feeling. He walked up and down his room, whistling, and not caring to think about anything, and was very well pleased with himself.

XVII

'I will wait for the officer's visit till ten o'clock,' he reflected next morning, as he dressed,' and then let him come and look for me!' But Germans rise early: it had not yet struck nine when the waiter informed Sanin that the Herr Seconde Lieutenant von Richter wished to see him. Sanin made haste to put on his coat, and told him to ask him up. Herr Richter turned out, contrary to Sanin's expectation, to be a very young man, almost a boy. He tried to give an expression of dignity to his beardless face, but did not succeed at all: he could not even conceal his embarrassment, and as he sat down on a chair, he tripped over his sword, and almost fell. Stammering and hesitating, he announced to Sanin in bad French that he had come with a message from his friend, Baron von Dönhof; that this message was to demand from Herr von Sanin an apology for the insulting expressions used by him on the previous day; and in case of refusal on the part of Herr von Sanin, Baron von Dönhof would ask for satisfaction. Sanin replied that he did not mean to apologise, but was ready to give him satisfaction. Then Herr von Richter, still with the same hesitation, asked with whom, at what time and place, should he arrange the necessary preliminaries. Sanin answered that he might come to him in two hours' time, and that meanwhile, he, Sanin, would try and find a second. ('Who the devil is there I can have for a second?' he was thinking to himself meantime.) Herr von Richter got up and began to take leave … but at the doorway he stopped, as though stung by a prick of conscience, and turning to Sanin observed that his friend, Baron von Dönhof, could not but recognise … that he had been … to a certain extent, to blame himself in the incident of the previous day, and would, therefore, be satisfied with slight apologies ('*des exghizes léchères*.') To this Sanin replied that he did not intend to make any apology whatever, either slight or considerable, since he did not consider himself to blame. 'In that case,' answered Herr von Richter, blushing more than ever,' you will have to exchange friendly shots—*des goups de bisdolet à l'amiaple*!'
'I don't understand that at all,' observed Sanin; 'are we to fire in the air or what?'
'Oh, not exactly that,' stammered the sub-lieutenant, utterly disconcerted, 'but I supposed since it is an affair between men of honour … I will talk to your second,' he broke off, and went away.
Sanin dropped into a chair directly he had gone, and stared at the floor. 'What does it all mean? How is it my life has taken such a turn all of a sudden? All the past, all the future has suddenly vanished, gone,—and all that's left is that I am going to fight some one about something in Frankfort.' He recalled a crazy aunt of his who used to dance and sing:

'O my lieutenant!
My little cucumber!
My little love!
Dance with me, my little dove!'

And he laughed and hummed as she used to: 'O my lieutenant! Dance with me, little dove!' 'But I must act, though, I mustn't waste time,' he cried aloud—jumped up and saw Pantaleone facing him with a note in his hand.
'I knocked several times, but you did not answer; I thought you weren't at home,' said the old man, as he gave him the note. 'From Signorina Gemma.'
Sanin took the note, mechanically, as they say, tore it open, and read it. Gemma wrote to him that she was very anxious—about he knew what—and would be very glad to see him at once.
'The Signorina is anxious,' began Pantaleone, who obviously knew what was in the note, 'she told me to see what you are doing and to bring you to her.'

Sanin glanced at the old Italian, and pondered. A sudden idea flashed upon his brain. For the first instant it struck him as too absurd to be possible.

'After all ... why not?' he asked himself.

'M. Pantaleone!' he said aloud.

The old man started, tucked his chin into his cravat and stared at Sanin.

'Do you know,' pursued Sanin,' what happened yesterday?'

Pantaleone chewed his lips and shook his immense top-knot of hair.

'Yes.'

(Emil had told him all about it directly he got home.)

'Oh, you know! Well, an officer has just this minute left me. That scoundrel challenges me to a duel. I have accepted his challenge. But I have no second. Will *you* be my second?'

Pantaleone started and raised his eyebrows so high that they were lost under his overhanging hair.

'You are absolutely obliged to fight?' he said at last in Italian; till that instant he had made use of French.

'Absolutely. I can't do otherwise—it would mean disgracing myself for ever.'

'H'm. If I don't consent to be your second you will find some one else.'

'Yes ... undoubtedly.'

Pantaleone looked down. 'But allow me to ask you, Signor de Tsanin, will not your duel throw a slur on the reputation of a certain lady?'

'I don't suppose so; but in any case, there's no help for it.'

'H'm!' Pantaleone retired altogether into his cravat. 'Hey, but that *ferroflucto Klüberio*—what's he about?' he cried all of a sudden, looking up again.

'He? Nothing.'

'*Che*!' Pantaleone shrugged his shoulders contemptuously. 'I have, in any case, to thank you,' he articulated at last in an unsteady voice 'that even in my present humble condition you recognise that I am a gentleman—*un galant'uomo*! In that way you have shown yourself to be a real *galant'uomo*. But I must consider your proposal.'

'There's no time to lose, dear Signor Ci ... cippa ...'

'Tola,' the old man chimed in. 'I ask only for one hour for reflection.... The daughter of my benefactor is involved in this.... And, therefore, I ought, I am bound, to reflect!... In an hour, in three-quarters of an hour, you shall know my decision.'

'Very well; I will wait.'

'And now ... what answer am I to give to Signorina Gemma?'

Sanin took a sheet of paper, wrote on it, 'Set your mind at rest, dear friend; in three hours' time I will come to you, and everything shall be explained. I thank you from my heart for your sympathy,' and handed this sheet to Pantaleone.

He put it carefully into his side-pocket, and once more repeating 'In an hour!' made towards the door; but turning sharply back, ran up to Sanin, seized his hand, and pressing it to his shirt-front, cried, with his eyes to the ceiling: 'Noble youth! Great heart! (*Nobil giovanotto! Gran cuore!*) permit a weak old man (*a un vecchiotto!*) to press your valorous right hand (*la vostra valorosa destra!*)' Then he skipped back a pace or two, threw up both hands, and went away.

Sanin looked after him ... took up the newspaper and tried to read.

But his eyes wandered in vain over the lines: he understood nothing.

XVIII

An hour later the waiter came in again to Sanin, and handed him an old, soiled visiting-card, on which were the following words: 'Pantaleone Cippatola of Varese, court singer (*cantante di camera*) to his Royal Highness the Duke of Modena'; and behind the waiter in walked Pantaleone himself. He had changed his clothes from top to toe. He had on a black frock coat, reddish with long wear, and a white piqué waistcoat, upon which a pinch-beck chain meandered playfully; a heavy cornelian seal hung low down on to his narrow black trousers. In his right hand he carried a black beaver hat, in his left two stout chamois gloves; he had tied his cravat in a taller and broader bow than ever, and had stuck into his starched shirt-front a pin with a stone, a so-called 'cat's eye.' On his forefinger was displayed a ring, consisting of two clasped hands with a burning heart between them. A smell of garments long laid by, a smell of camphor and of musk hung about the whole person of the old man; the anxious solemnity of his deportment must have struck the most casual spectator! Sanin rose to meet him.

'I am your second,' Pantaleone announced in French, and he bowed bending his whole body forward, and turning out his toes like a dancer. 'I have come for instructions. Do you want to fight to the death?'

'Why to the death, my dear Signor Cippatola? I will not for any consideration take back my words—but I am not a bloodthirsty person!... But come, wait a little, my opponent's second will be here directly. I will go into the next room, and you can make arrangements with him. Believe me I shall never forget your kindness, and I thank you from my heart.'

'Honour before everything!' answered Pantaleone, and he sank into an arm-chair, without waiting for Sanin to ask him to sit down. 'If that *ferroflucto spitchebubbio*,' he said, passing from French into Italian, 'if that counter-jumper Klüberio could not appreciate his obvious duty or was afraid, so much the worse for him!... A cheap soul, and that's all about it!... As for the conditions of the duel, I am your second, and your interests are sacred to me!... When I lived in Padua there was a regiment of the white dragoons stationed there, and I was very intimate with many of the officers!... I was quite familiar with their whole code. And I used often to converse on these subjects with your principe Tarbuski too.... Is this second to come soon?'

'I am expecting him every minute—and here he comes,' added Sanin, looking into the street.

Pantaleone got up, looked at his watch, straightened his topknot of hair, and hurriedly stuffed into his shoe an end of tape which was sticking out below his trouser-leg, and the young sub-lieutenant came in, as red and embarrassed as ever.

Sanin presented the seconds to each other. 'M. Richter, sous-lieutenant, M. Cippatola, artiste!' The sub-lieutenant was slightly disconcerted by the old man's appearance ... Oh, what would he have said had any one whispered to him at that instant that the 'artist' presented to him was also employed in the culinary art! But Pantaleone assumed an air as though taking part in the preliminaries of duels was for him the most everyday affair: probably he was assisted at this juncture by the recollections of his theatrical career, and he played the part of second simply as a part. Both he and the sub-lieutenant were silent for a little.

'Well? Let us come to business!' Pantaleone spoke first, playing with his cornelian seal.

'By all means,' responded the sub-lieutenant, 'but ... the presence of one of the principals ...'

'I will leave you at once, gentlemen,' cried Sanin, and with a bow he went away into the bedroom and closed the door after him.

He flung himself on the bed and began thinking of Gemma ... but the conversation of the seconds reached him through the shut door. It was conducted in the French language; both maltreated it mercilessly, each after his own fashion. Pantaleone again alluded to the dragoons in Padua, and Principe Tarbuski; the sub-lieutenant to '*exghizes léchères*' and '*goups de bistolet à l'amiaple*.' But the old man would not even hear of any *exghizes*! To Sanin's horror, he suddenly proceeded to talk of a certain young lady, an innocent maiden, whose little finger was worth more than all the officers in the world ... (*oune zeune damigella innoucenta, qu'a elle sola dans soun péti doa vale pin que tout le zouffissié del mondo*.'), and repeated several times with heat: 'It's shameful! it's shameful!' (*E ouna onta, ouna onta*!) The sub-lieutenant at first made him no reply, but presently an angry quiver could be heard in the young man's voice, and he observed that he had not come there to listen to sermonising.

'At your age it is always a good thing to hear the truth!' cried
Pantaleone.

The debate between the seconds several times became stormy; it lasted over an hour, and was concluded at last on the following conditions: 'Baron von Dönhof and M. de Sanin to meet the next day at ten o'clock in a small wood near Hanau, at the distance of twenty paces; each to have the right to fire twice at a signal given by the seconds, the pistols to be single-triggered and not rifle-barrelled.' Herr von Richter withdrew, and Pantaleone solemnly opened the bedroom door, and after communicating the result of their deliberations, cried again: '*Bravo Russo*! *Bravo giovanotto*! You will be victor!'

A few minutes later they both set off to the Rosellis' shop. Sanin, as a preliminary measure, had exacted a promise from Pantaleone to keep the affair of the duel a most profound secret. In reply, the old man had merely held up his finger, and half closing his eyes, whispered twice over, *Segredezza*! He was obviously in good spirits, and even walked with a freer step. All these unusual incidents, unpleasant though they might be, carried him vividly back to the time when he himself both received and gave challenges—only, it is true, on the stage. Baritones, as we all know, have a great deal of strutting and fuming to do in their parts.

XIX

Emil ran out to meet Sanin—he had been watching for his arrival over an hour—and hurriedly whispered into his ear that his mother knew nothing of the disagreeable incident of the day before, that he must not even hint of it to her, and that he was being sent to Klüber's shop again!... but that he wouldn't go there, but would hide somewhere! Communicating all this information in a few seconds, he suddenly fell on Sanin's shoulder, kissed him impulsively, and rushed away down the street. Gemma met Sanin in the shop; tried to say something and could not. Her lips were trembling a little, while her eyes were half-closed and turned away. He made haste to soothe her by the assurance that the whole affair had ended ... in utter nonsense.

'Has no one been to see you to-day?' she asked.

'A person did come to me and we had an explanation, and we ... we came to the most satisfactory conclusion.'

Gemma went back behind the counter.

'She does not believe me!' he thought ... he went into the next room, however, and there found Frau Lenore. Her sick headache had passed off, but she was in a depressed state of mind. She gave him a smile of welcome, but warned him at the same time that he would be dull with her to-day, as she was not in a mood to entertain him. He sat down beside her, and noticed that her eyelids were red and swollen.

'What is wrong, Frau Lenore? You've never been crying, surely?'

'Oh!' she whispered, nodding her head towards the room where her daughter was.

'Don't speak of it ... aloud.'

'But what have you been crying for?'

'Ah, M'sieu Sanin, I don't know myself what for!'

'No one has hurt your feelings?'

'Oh no!... I felt very low all of a sudden. I thought of Giovanni Battista ... of my youth ... Then how quickly it had all passed away. I have grown old, my friend, and I can't reconcile myself to that anyhow. I feel I'm just the same as I was ... but old age—it's here! it is here!' Tears came into Frau Lenore's eyes. 'You look at me, I see, and wonder.... But you will get old too, my friend, and will find out how bitter it is!'

Sanin tried to comfort her, spoke of her children, in whom her own youth lived again, even attempted to scoff at her a little, declaring that she was fishing for compliments ... but she quite seriously begged him to leave off, and for the first time he realised that for such a sorrow, the despondency of old age, there is no comfort or cure; one has to wait till it passes off of itself. He proposed a game of tresette, and he could have thought of nothing better. She agreed at once and seemed to get more cheerful.

Sanin played with her until dinner-time and after dinner Pantaleone too took a hand in the game. Never had his topknot hung so low over his forehead, never had his chin retreated so far into his cravat! Every movement was accompanied by such intense solemnity that as one looked at him the thought involuntarily arose, 'What secret is that man guarding with such determination?' But *segredezza*! *segredezza*!

During the whole of that day he tried in every possible way to show the profoundest respect for Sanin; at table, passing by the ladies, he solemnly and sedately handed the dishes first to him; when they were at cards he intentionally gave him the game; he announced, apropos of nothing at all, that the Russians were the most great-hearted, brave, and resolute people in the world!

'Ah, you old flatterer!' Sanin thought to himself.

And he was not so much surprised at Signora Roselli's unexpected state of mind, as at the way her daughter behaved to him. It was not that she avoided him ... on the contrary she sat continually a little distance from him, listened to what he said, and looked at him; but she absolutely declined to get into conversation with him, and directly he began talking to her, she softly rose from her place, and went out for some instants. Then she came in again, and again seated herself in some corner, and sat without stirring, seeming meditative and perplexed ... perplexed above all. Frau Lenore herself noticed at last, that she was not as usual, and asked her twice what was the matter.

'Nothing,' answered Gemma; 'you know I am sometimes like this.'
'That is true,' her mother assented.
So passed all that long day, neither gaily nor drearily—neither cheerfully nor sadly. Had Gemma been different—Sanin … who knows?… might not perhaps have been able to resist the temptation for a little display—or he might simply have succumbed to melancholy at the possibility of a separation for ever…. But as he did not once succeed in getting a word with Gemma, he was obliged to confine himself to striking minor chords on the piano for a quarter of an hour before evening coffee.
Emil came home late, and to avoid questions about Herr Klüber, beat a hasty retreat. The time came for Sanin too to retire.
He began saying good-bye to Gemma. He recollected for some reason Lensky's parting from Olga in *Oniegin*. He pressed her hand warmly, and tried to get a look at her face, but she turned a little away and released her fingers.

XX

It was bright starlight when he came out on the steps. What multitudes of stars, big and little, yellow, red, blue and white were scattered over the sky! They seemed all flashing, swarming, twinkling unceasingly. There was no moon in the sky, but without it every object could be clearly discerned in the half-clear, shadowless twilight. Sanin walked down the street to the end … He did not want to go home at once; he felt a desire to wander about a little in the fresh air. He turned back and had hardly got on a level with the house, where was the Rosellis' shop, when one of the windows looking out on the street, suddenly creaked and opened; in its square of blackness—there was no light in the room—appeared a woman's figure, and he heard his name—'Monsieur Dimitri!'
He rushed at once up to the window … Gemma! She was leaning with her elbows on the window-sill, bending forward.
'Monsieur Dimitri,' she began in a cautious voice, 'I have been wanting all day long to give you something … but I could not make up my mind to; and just now, seeing you, quite unexpectedly again, I thought that it seems it is fated' …
Gemma was forced to stop at this word. She could not go on; something extraordinary happened at that instant.
All of a sudden, in the midst of the profound stillness, over the perfectly unclouded sky, there blew such a violent blast of wind, that the very earth seemed shaking underfoot, the delicate starlight seemed quivering and trembling, the air went round in a whirlwind. The wind, not cold, but hot, almost sultry, smote against the trees, the roof of the house, its walls, and the street; it instantaneously snatched off Sanin's hat, crumpled up and tangled Gemma's curls. Sanin's head was on a level with the window-sill; he could not help clinging close to it, and Gemma clutched hold of his shoulders with both hands, and pressed her bosom against his head. The roar, the din, and the rattle lasted about a minute…. Like a flock of huge birds the revelling whirlwind darted revelling away. A profound stillness reigned once more.
Sanin raised his head and saw above him such an exquisite, scared, excited face, such immense, large, magnificent eyes—it was such a beautiful creature he saw, that his heart stood still within him, he pressed his lips to the delicate tress of hair, that had fallen on his bosom, and could only murmur, 'O Gemma!'
'What was that? Lightning?' she asked, her eyes wandering afar, while she did not take her bare arms from his shoulder.
'Gemma!' repeated Sanin.
She sighed, looked around behind her into the room, and with a rapid movement pulling the now faded rose out of her bodice, she threw it to Sanin.
'I wanted to give you this flower.'
He recognised the rose, which he had won back the day before….
But already the window had slammed-to, and through the dark pane nothing could be seen, no trace of white.
Sanin went home without his hat…. He did not even notice that he had lost it.

It was quite morning when he fell asleep. And no wonder! In the blast of that instantaneous summer hurricane, he had almost as instantaneously felt, not that Gemma was lovely, not that he liked her—that he had known before ... but that he almost ... loved her! As suddenly as that blast of wind, had love pounced down upon him. And then this senseless duel! He began to be tormented by mournful forebodings. And even suppose they didn't kill him.... What could come of his love for this girl, another man's betrothed? Even supposing this 'other man' was no danger, that Gemma herself would care for him, or even cared for him already ... What would come of it? How ask what! Such a lovely creature!...

He walked about the room, sat down to the table, took a sheet of paper, traced a few lines on it, and at once blotted them out.... He recalled Gemma's wonderful figure in the dark window, in the starlight, set all a-fluttering by the warm hurricane; he remembered her marble arms, like the arms of the Olympian goddesses, felt their living weight on his shoulders.... Then he took the rose she had thrown him, and it seemed to him that its half-withered petals exhaled a fragrance of her, more delicate than the ordinary scent of the rose.

'And would they kill him straight away or maim him?'

He did not go to bed, and fell asleep in his clothes on the sofa.

Some one slapped him on the shoulder.... He opened his eyes, and saw Pantaleone.

'He sleeps like Alexander of Macedon on the eve of the battle of Babylon!' cried the old man.

'What o'clock is it?' inquired Sanin.

'A quarter to seven; it's a two hours' drive to Hanau, and we must be the first on the field. Russians are always beforehand with their enemies! I have engaged the best carriage in Frankfort!'

Sanin began washing. 'And where are the pistols?'

'That *ferroflucto Tedesco* will bring the pistols. He'll bring a doctor too.'

Pantaleone was obviously putting a good face on it as he had done the day before; but when he was seated in the carriage with Sanin, when the coachman had cracked his whip and the horses had started off at a gallop, a sudden change came over the old singer and friend of Paduan dragoons. He began to be confused and positively faint-hearted. Something seemed to have given way in him, like a badly built wall.

'What are we doing, my God, *Santissima Madonna!*' he cried in an unexpectedly high pipe, and he clutched at his head. 'What am I about, old fool, madman, *frenetico*?'

Sanin wondered and laughed, and putting his arm lightly round Pantaleone's waist, he reminded him of the French proverb: '*Le vin est tiré—il faut le boire*.'

'Yes, yes,' answered the old man, 'we will drain the cup together to the dregs—but still I'm a madman! I'm a madman! All was going on so quietly, so well ... and all of a sudden: ta-ta-ta, tra-ta-ta!'

'Like the *tutti* in the orchestra,' observed Sanin with a forced smile. 'But it's not your fault.'

'I know it's not. I should think not indeed! And yet ... such insolent conduct! *Diavolo, diavolo*!' repeated Pantaleone, sighing and shaking his topknot.

The carriage still rolled on and on.

It was an exquisite morning. The streets of Frankfort, which were just beginning to show signs of life, looked so clean and snug; the windows of the houses glittered in flashes like tinfoil; and as soon as the carriage had driven beyond the city walls, from overhead, from a blue but not yet glaring sky, the larks' loud trills showered down in floods. Suddenly at a turn in the road, a familiar figure came from behind a tall poplar, took a few steps forward and stood still. Sanin looked more closely.... Heavens! it was Emil!

'But does he know anything about it?' he demanded of Pantaleone.

'I tell you I'm a madman,' the poor Italian wailed despairingly, almost in a shriek. 'The wretched boy gave me no peace all night, and this morning at last I revealed all to him!'

'So much for your *segredezza*!' thought Sanin. The carriage had got up to Emil. Sanin told the coachman to stop the horses, and called the 'wretched boy' up to him. Emil approached with hesitating steps, pale as he had been on the day he fainted. He could scarcely stand.

'What are you doing here?' Sanin asked him sternly. 'Why aren't you at home?'

'Let ... let me come with you,' faltered Emil in a trembling voice, and he clasped his hands. His teeth were chattering as in a fever. 'I won't get in your way—only take me.'

'If you feel the very slightest affection or respect for me,' said Sanin, 'you will go at once home or to Herr Klüber's shop, and you won't say one word to any one, and will wait for my return!'
'Your return,' moaned Emil—and his voice quivered and broke, 'but if you're—'
'Emil!' Sanin interrupted—and he pointed to the coachman, 'do control yourself! Emil, please, go home! Listen to me, my dear! You say you love me. Well, I beg you!' He held out his hand to him. Emil bent forward, sobbed, pressed it to his lips, and darting away from the road, ran back towards Frankfort across country.
'A noble heart too,' muttered Pantaleone; but Sanin glanced severely at him.... The old man shrank into the corner of the carriage. He was conscious of his fault; and moreover, he felt more and more bewildered every instant; could it really be he who was acting as second, who had got horses, and had made all arrangements, and had left his peaceful abode at six o'clock? Besides, his legs were stiff and aching.
Sanin thought it as well to cheer him up, and he chanced on the very thing, he hit on the right word.
'Where is your old spirit, Signor Cippatola? Where is *il antico valor*?'
Signor Cippatola drew himself up and scowled '*Il antico valor*?' he boomed in a bass voice. '*Non è ancora spento* (it's not all lost yet), *il antico valor!*'
He put himself in a dignified attitude, began talking of his career, of the opera, of the great tenor Garcia—and arrived at Hanau a hero.
After all, if you think of it, nothing is stronger in the world ... and weaker—than a word!

XXII

The copse in which the duel was to take place was a quarter of a mile from Hanau. Sanin and Pantaleone arrived there first, as the latter had predicted; they gave orders for the carriage to remain outside the wood, and they plunged into the shade of the rather thick and close-growing trees. They had to wait about an hour. The time of waiting did not seem particularly disagreeable to Sanin; he walked up and down the path, listened to the birds singing, watched the dragonflies in their flight, and like the majority of Russians in similar circumstances, tried not to think. He only once dropped into reflection; he came across a young lime-tree, broken down, in all probability by the squall of the previous night. It was unmistakably dying ... all the leaves on it were dead. 'What is it? an omen?' was the thought that flashed across his mind; but he promptly began whistling, leaped over the very tree, and paced up and down the path. As for Pantaleone, he was grumbling, abusing the Germans, sighing and moaning, rubbing first his back and then his knees. He even yawned from agitation, which gave a very comic expression to his tiny shrivelled-up face. Sanin could scarcely help laughing when he looked at him.
They heard, at last, the rolling of wheels along the soft road. 'It's they!' said Pantaleone, and he was on the alert and drew himself up, not without a momentary nervous shiver, which he made haste, however, to cover with the ejaculation 'B-r-r!' and the remark that the morning was rather fresh. A heavy dew drenched the grass and leaves, but the sultry heat penetrated even into the wood.
Both the officers quickly made their appearance under its arched avenues; they were accompanied by a little thick-set man, with a phlegmatic, almost sleepy, expression of face—the army doctor. He carried in one hand an earthenware pitcher of water—to be ready for any emergency; a satchel with surgical instruments and bandages hung on his left shoulder. It was obvious that he was thoroughly used to such excursions; they constituted one of the sources of his income; each duel yielded him eight gold crowns—four from each of the combatants. Herr von Richter carried a case of pistols, Herr von Dönhof—probably considering it the thing—was swinging in his hand a little cane.
'Pantaleone!' Sanin whispered to the old man; 'if ... if I'm killed—anything may happen—take out of my side pocket a paper—there's a flower wrapped up in it—and give the paper to Signorina Gemma. Do you hear? You promise?'
The old man looked dejectedly at him, and nodded his head affirmatively.... But God knows whether he understood what Sanin was asking him to do.
The combatants and the seconds exchanged the customary bows; the doctor alone did not move as much as an eyelash; he sat down yawning on the grass, as much as to say, 'I'm not here for expressions of chivalrous courtesy.' Herr von Richter proposed to Herr 'Tshibadola' that he should select the place; Herr 'Tshibadola'

responded, moving his tongue with difficulty—'the wall' within him had completely given way again. 'You act, my dear sir; I will watch....'
And Herr von Richter proceeded to act. He picked out in the wood close by a very pretty clearing all studded with flowers; he measured out the steps, and marked the two extreme points with sticks, which he cut and pointed. He took the pistols out of the case, and squatting on his heels, he rammed in the bullets; in short, he fussed about and exerted himself to the utmost, continually mopping his perspiring brow with a white handkerchief. Pantaleone, who accompanied him, was more like a man frozen. During all these preparations, the two principals stood at a little distance, looking like two schoolboys who have been punished, and are sulky with their tutors.
The decisive moment arrived.... 'Each took his pistol....'
But at this point Herr von Richter observed to Pantaleone that it was his duty, as the senior second, according to the rules of the duel, to address a final word of advice and exhortation to be reconciled to the combatants, before uttering the fatal 'one! two! three!'; that although this exhortation had no effect of any sort and was, as a rule, nothing but an empty formality, still, by the performance of this formality, Herr Cippatola would be rid of a certain share of responsibility; that, properly speaking, such an admonition formed the direct duty of the so-called 'impartial witness' (*unpartheiischer Zeuge*) but since they had no such person present, he, Herr von Richter, would readily yield this privilege to his honoured colleague. Pantaleone, who had already succeeded in obliterating himself behind a bush, so as not to see the offending officer at all, at first made out nothing at all of Herr von Richter's speech, especially, as it had been delivered through the nose, but all of a sudden he started, stepped hurriedly forward, and convulsively thumping at his chest, in a hoarse voice wailed out in his mixed jargon: '*A la la la ... Che bestialita! Deux zeun ommes comme ça que si battono—perchè? Che diavolo? An data a casa!*'
'I will not consent to a reconciliation,' Sanin intervened hurriedly.
'And I too will not,' his opponent repeated after him.
'Well, then shout one, two, three!' von Richter said, addressing the distracted Pantaleone. The latter promptly ducked behind the bush again, and from there, all huddled together, his eyes screwed up, and his head turned away, he shouted at the top of his voice: '*Una ... due ... tre!*'
The first shot was Sanin's, and he missed. His bullet went ping against a tree. Baron von Dönhof shot directly after him—intentionally, to one side, into the air.
A constrained silence followed.... No one moved. Pantaleone uttered a faint moan.
'Is it your wish to go on?' said Dönhof.
'Why did you shoot in the air?' inquired Sanin.
'That's nothing to do with you.'
'Will you shoot in the air the second time?' Sanin asked again.
'Possibly: I don't know.'
'Excuse me, excuse me, gentlemen ...' began von Richter; 'duellists have not the right to talk together. That's out of order.'
'I decline my shot,' said Sanin, and he threw his pistol on the ground.
'And I too do not intend to go on with the duel,' cried Dönhof, and he too threw his pistol on the ground. 'And more than that, I am prepared to own that I was in the wrong—the day before yesterday.'
He moved uneasily, and hesitatingly held out his hand. Sanin went rapidly up to him and shook it. Both the young men looked at each other with a smile, and both their faces flushed crimson.
'*Bravi! bravi!*' Pantaleone roared suddenly as if he had gone mad, and clapping his hands, he rushed like a whirlwind from behind the bush; while the doctor, who had been sitting on one side on a felled tree, promptly rose, poured the water out of the jug and walked off with a lazy, rolling step out of the wood.
'Honour is satisfied, and the duel is over!' von Richter announced.
'*Fuori!*' Pantaleone boomed once more, through old associations.
* * * * *
When he had exchanged bows with the officers, and taken his seat in the carriage, Sanin certainly felt all over him, if not a sense of pleasure, at least a certain lightness of heart, as after an operation is over; but there was another feeling astir within him too, a feeling akin to shame.... The duel, in which he had just played his part, struck him as something false, a got-up formality, a common officers' and students' farce. He recalled the phlegmatic doctor, he recalled how he had grinned, that is, wrinkled up his nose when he saw him coming out of the wood almost arm-in-arm with Baron Dönhof. And afterwards when Pantaleone had paid him the four crowns due to him ... Ah! there was something nasty about it!

Yes, Sanin was a little conscience-smitten and ashamed … though, on the other hand, what was there for him to have done? Could he have left the young officer's insolence unrebuked? could he have behaved like Herr Klüber? He had stood up for Gemma, he had championed her … that was so; and yet, there was an uneasy pang in his heart, and he was conscience—smitten, and even ashamed.
Not so Pantaleone—he was simply in his glory! He was suddenly possessed by a feeling of pride. A victorious general, returning from the field of battle he has won, could not have looked about him with greater self-satisfaction. Sanin's demeanour during the duel filled him with enthusiasm. He called him a hero, and would not listen to his exhortations and even his entreaties. He compared him to a monument of marble or of bronze, with the statue of the commander in Don Juan! For himself he admitted he had been conscious of some perturbation of mind, 'but, of course, I am an artist,' he observed; 'I have a highly-strung nature, while you are the son of the snows and the granite rocks.'
Sanin was positively at a loss how to quiet the jubilant artist.
* * * * *
Almost at the same place in the road where two hours before they had come upon Emil, he again jumped out from behind a tree, and, with a cry of joy upon his lips, waving his cap and leaping into the air, he rushed straight at the carriage, almost fell under the wheel, and, without waiting for the horses to stop, clambered up over the carriage-door and fairly clung to Sanin.
'You are alive, you are not wounded!' he kept repeating. 'Forgive me, I did not obey you, I did not go back to Frankfort … I could not! I waited for you here … Tell me how was it? You … killed him?'
Sanin with some difficulty pacified Emil and made him sit down.
With great verbosity, with evident pleasure, Pantaleone communicated to him all the details of the duel, and, of course, did not omit to refer again to the monument of bronze and the statue of the commander. He even rose from his seat and, standing with his feet wide apart to preserve his equilibrium, folding his arm on his chest and looking contemptuously over his shoulder, gave an ocular representation of the commander—Sanin! Emil listened with awe, occasionally interrupting the narrative with an exclamation, or swiftly getting up and as swiftly kissing his heroic friend.
The carriage wheels rumbled over the paved roads of Frankfort, and stopped at last before the hotel where Sanin was living.
Escorted by his two companions, he went up the stairs, when suddenly a woman came with hurried steps out of the dark corridor; her face was hidden by a veil, she stood still, facing Sanin, wavered a little, gave a trembling sigh, at once ran down into the street and vanished, to the great astonishment of the waiter, who explained that 'that lady had been for over an hour waiting for the return of the foreign gentleman.'
Momentary as was the apparition, Sanin recognised Gemma. He recognised her eyes under the thick silk of her brown veil.
'Did Fräulein Gemma know, then?'… he said slowly in a displeased voice in German, addressing Emil and Pantaleone, who were following close on his heels.
Emil blushed and was confused.
'I was obliged to tell her all,' he faltered; 'she guessed, and I could not help it…. But now that's of no consequence,' he hurried to add eagerly, 'everything has ended so splendidly, and she has seen you well and uninjured!'
Sanin turned away.
'What a couple of chatterboxes you are!' he observed in a tone of annoyance, as he went into his room and sat down on a chair.
'Don't be angry, please,' Emil implored.
'Very well, I won't be angry'—(Sanin was not, in fact, angry—and, after all, he could hardly have desired that Gemma should know nothing about it). 'Very well … that's enough embracing. You get along now. I want to be alone. I'm going to sleep. I'm tired.'
'An excellent idea!' cried Pantaleone. 'You need repose! You have fully earned it, noble signor! Come along, Emilio! On tip-toe! On tip-toe! Sh—sh—sh!'
When he said he wanted to go to sleep, Sanin had simply wished to get rid of his companions; but when he was left alone, he was really aware of considerable weariness in all his limbs; he had hardly closed his eyes all the preceding night, and throwing himself on his bed he fell immediately into a sound sleep.

XXIII

He slept for some hours without waking. Then he began to dream that he was once more fighting a duel, that the antagonist standing facing him was Herr Klüber, and on a fir-tree was sitting a parrot, and this parrot was Pantaleone, and he kept tapping with his beak: one, one, one!
'One ... one ... one!' he heard the tapping too distinctly; he opened his eyes, raised his head ... some one was knocking at his door.
'Come in!' called Sanin.
The waiter came in and answered that a lady very particularly wished to see him.
'Gemma!' flashed into his head ... but the lady turned out to be her mother, Frau Lenore.
Directly she came in, she dropped at once into a chair and began to cry.
'What is the matter, my dear, good Madame Roselli?' began Sanin, sitting beside her and softly touching her hand. 'What has happened? calm yourself, I entreat you.'
'Ah, Herr Dimitri, I am very ... very miserable!'
'You are miserable?'
'Ah, very! Could I have foreseen such a thing? All of a sudden, like thunder from a clear sky ...'
She caught her breath.
'But what is it? Explain! Would you like a glass of water?'
'No, thank you.' Frau Lenore wiped her eyes with her handkerchief and began to cry with renewed energy. 'I know all, you see! All!'
'All? that is to say?'
'Everything that took place to-day! And the cause ... I know that too! You acted like an honourable man; but what an unfortunate combination of circumstances! I was quite right in not liking that excursion to Soden ... quite right!' (Frau Lenore had said nothing of the sort on the day of the excursion, but she was convinced now that she had foreseen 'all' even then.) 'I have come to you as to an honourable man, as to a friend, though I only saw you for the first time five days ago.... But you know I am a widow, a lonely woman.... My daughter ...'
Tears choked Frau Lenore's voice. Sanin did not know what to think.
'Your daughter?' he repeated.
'My daughter, Gemma,' broke almost with a groan from Frau Lenore, behind the tear-soaked handkerchief, 'informed me to-day that she would not marry Herr Klüber, and that I must refuse him!'
Sanin positively started back a little; he had not expected that.
'I won't say anything now,' Frau Lenore went on, 'of the disgrace of it, of its being something unheard of in the world for a girl to jilt her betrothed; but you see it's ruin for us, Herr Dimitri!' Frau Lenore slowly and carefully twisted up her handkerchief in a tiny, tiny little ball, as though she would enclose all her grief within it. 'We can't go on living on the takings of our shop, Herr Dimitri! and Herr Klüber is very rich, and will be richer still. And what is he to be refused for? Because he did not defend his betrothed? Allowing that was not very handsome on his part, still, he's a civilian, has not had a university education, and as a solid business man, it was for him to look with contempt on the frivolous prank of some unknown little officer. And what sort of insult was it, after all, Herr Dimitri?'
'Excuse me, Frau Lenore, you seem to be blaming me.'
'I am not blaming you in the least, not in the least! You're quite another matter; you are, like all Russians, a military man ...'
'Excuse me, I'm not at all ...'
'You're a foreigner, a visitor, and I'm grateful to you,' Frau Lenore went on, not heeding Sanin. She sighed, waved her hands, unwound her handkerchief again, and blew her nose. Simply from the way in which her distress expressed itself, it could be seen that she had not been born under a northern sky.
'And how is Herr Klüber to look after his shop, if he is to fight with his customers? It's utterly inconsistent! And now I am to send him away! But what are we going to live on? At one time we were the only people that made angel cakes, and nougat of pistachio nuts, and we had plenty of customers; but now all the shops make angel cakes! Only consider; even without this, they'll talk in the town about your duel ... it's impossible to keep it secret. And all of a sudden, the marriage broken off! It will be a scandal, a scandal! Gemma is a splendid girl, she loves me; but she's an obstinate republican, she doesn't care for the opinion of others. You're the only person that can persuade her!'

Sanin was more amazed than ever. 'I, Frau Lenore?'
'Yes, you alone … you alone. That's why I have come to you; I could not think of anything else to do! You are so clever, so good! You have fought in her defence. She will trust you! She is bound to trust you—why, you have risked your life on her account! You will make her understand, for I can do nothing more; you make her understand that she will bring ruin on herself and all of us. You saved my son—save my daughter too! God Himself sent you here … I am ready on my knees to beseech you….' And Frau Lenore half rose from her seat as though about to fall at Sanin's feet…. He restrained her.
'Frau Lenore! For mercy's sake! What are you doing?'
She clutched his hand impulsively. 'You promise …'
'Frau Lenore, think a moment; what right have I …'
'You promise? You don't want me to die here at once before your eyes?'
Sanin was utterly nonplussed. It was the first time in his life he had had to deal with any one of ardent Italian blood.
'I will do whatever you like,' he cried. 'I will talk to Fräulein Gemma….'
Frau Lenore uttered a cry of delight.
'Only I really can't say what result will come of it …'
'Ah, don't go back, don't go back from your words!' cried Frau Lenore in an imploring voice; 'you have already consented! The result is certain to be excellent. Any way, *I* can do nothing more! She won't listen to *me*!'
'Has she so positively stated her disinclination to marry Herr Klüber?' Sanin inquired after a short silence.
'As if she'd cut the knot with a knife! She's her father all over, Giovanni Battista! Wilful girl!'
'Wilful? Is she!' … Sanin said slowly. 'Yes … yes … but she's an angel too. She will mind you. Are you coming soon? Oh, my dear Russian friend!' Frau Lenore rose impulsively from her chair, and as impulsively clasped the head of Sanin, who was sitting opposite her. 'Accept a mother's blessing—and give me some water!'
Sanin brought Signora Roselli a glass of water, gave her his word of honour that he would come directly, escorted her down the stairs to the street, and when he was back in his own room, positively threw up his arms and opened his eyes wide in his amazement.
'Well,' he thought, 'well, *now* life is going round in a whirl! And it's whirling so that I'm giddy.' He did not attempt to look within, to realise what was going on in himself: it was all uproar and confusion, and that was all he knew! What a day it had been! His lips murmured unconsciously: 'Wilful … her mother says … and I have got to advise her … her! And advise her what?'
Sanin, really, was giddy, and above all this whirl of shifting sensations and impressions and unfinished thoughts, there floated continually the image of Gemma, the image so ineffaceably impressed on his memory on that hot night, quivering with electricity, in that dark window, in the light of the swarming stars!

XXIV

With hesitating footsteps Sanin approached the house of Signora Roselli. His heart was beating violently; he distinctly felt, and even heard it thumping at his side. What should he say to Gemma, how should he begin? He went into the house, not through the shop, but by the back entrance. In the little outer room he met Frau Lenore. She was both relieved and scared at the sight of him.
'I have been expecting you,' she said in a whisper, squeezing his hand with each of hers in turn. 'Go into the garden; she is there. Mind, I rely on you!'
Sanin went into the garden.
Gemma was sitting on a garden-seat near the path, she was sorting a big basket full of cherries, picking out the ripest, and putting them on a dish. The sun was low—it was seven o'clock in the evening—and there was more purple than gold in the full slanting light with which it flooded the whole of Signora Roselli's little

garden. From time to time, faintly audibly, and as it were deliberately, the leaves rustled, and belated bees buzzed abruptly as they flew from one flower to the next, and somewhere a dove was cooing a never-changing, unceasing note. Gemma had on the same round hat in which she had driven to Soden. She peeped at Sanin from under its turned-down brim, and again bent over the basket.

Sanin went up to Gemma, unconsciously making each step shorter, and ... and ... and nothing better could he find to say to her than to ask why was she sorting the cherries.

Gemma was in no haste to reply.

'These are riper,' she observed at last, 'they will go into jam, and those are for tarts. You know the round sweet tarts we sell?'

As she said those words, Gemma bent her head still lower, and her right hand with two cherries in her fingers was suspended in the air between the basket and the dish.

'May I sit by you?' asked Sanin.

'Yes.' Gemma moved a little along on the seat. Sanin placed himself beside her. 'How am I to begin?' was his thought. But Gemma got him out of his difficulty.

'You have fought a duel to-day,' she began eagerly, and she turned all her lovely, bashfully flushing face to him—and what depths of gratitude were shining in those eyes! 'And you are so calm! I suppose for you danger does not exist?'

'Oh, come! I have not been exposed to any danger. Everything went off very satisfactorily and inoffensively.'

Gemma passed her finger to right and to left before her eyes ... Also an Italian gesture. 'No! no! don't say that! You won't deceive me! Pantaleone has told me everything!'

'He's a trustworthy witness! Did he compare me to the statue of the commander?'

'His expressions may be ridiculous, but his feeling is not ridiculous, nor is what you have done to-day. And all that on my account ... for me ... I shall never forget it.'

'I assure you, Fräulein Gemma ...'

'I shall never forget it,' she said deliberately; once more she looked intently at him, and turned away.

He could now see her delicate pure profile, and it seemed to him that he had never seen anything like it, and had never known anything like what he was feeling at that instant. His soul was on fire.

'And my promise!' flashed in among his thoughts.

'Fräulein Gemma ...' he began after a momentary hesitation.

'What?'

She did not turn to him, she went on sorting the cherries, carefully taking them by their stalks with her finger-tips, assiduously picking out the leaves.... But what a confiding caress could be heard in that one word,

'What?'

'Has your mother said nothing to you ... about ...'

'About?'

'About me?'

Gemma suddenly flung back into the basket the cherries she had taken.

'Has she been talking to you?' she asked in her turn.

'Yes.'

'What has she been saying to you?'

'She told me that you ... that you have suddenly decided to change ... your former intention.' Gemma's head was bent again. She vanished altogether under her hat; nothing could be seen but her neck, supple and tender as the stalk of a big flower.

'What intentions?'

'Your intentions ... relative to ... the future arrangement of your life.'

'That is ... you are speaking ... of Herr Klüber?'

'Yes.'

'Mamma told you I don't want to be Herr Klüber's wife?'

'Yes.'

Gemma moved forward on the seat. The basket tottered, fell ... a few cherries rolled on to the path. A minute passed by ... another.

'Why did she tell you so?' he heard her voice saying. Sanin as before could only see Gemma's neck. Her bosom rose and fell more rapidly than before.

'Why? Your mother thought that as you and I, in a short time, have become, so to say, friends, and you have some confidence in me, I am in a position to give you good advice—and you would mind what I say.'
Gemma's hands slowly slid on to her knees. She began plucking at the folds of her dress.
'What advice will you give me, Monsieur Dimitri?' she asked, after a short pause.
Sanin saw that Gemma's fingers were trembling on her knees.... She was only plucking at the folds of her dress to hide their trembling. He softly laid his hand on those pale, shaking fingers.
'Gemma,' he said, 'why don't you look at me?' She instantly tossed her hat back on to her shoulder, and bent her eyes upon him, confiding and grateful as before. She waited for him to speak.... But the sight of her face had bewildered, and, as it were, dazed him. The warm glow of the evening sun lighted up her youthful head, and the expression of that head was brighter, more radiant than its glow.
'I will mind what you say, Monsieur Dimitri,' she said, faintly smiling, and faintly arching her brows; 'but what advice do you give me?'
'What advice?' repeated Sanin. 'Well, you see, your mother considers that to dismiss Herr Klüber simply because he did not show any special courage the day before yesterday ...'
'Simply because?' said Gemma. She bent down, picked up the basket, and set it beside her on the garden seat.
'That ... altogether ... to dismiss him, would be, on your part ... unreasonable; that it is a step, all the consequences of which ought to be thoroughly weighed; that in fact the very position of your affairs imposes certain obligations on every member of your family ...'
'All that is mamma's opinion,' Gemma interposed; 'those are her words; but what is your opinion?'
'Mine?' Sanin was silent for a while. He felt a lump rising in his throat and catching at his breath. 'I too consider,' he began with an effort ...
Gemma drew herself up. 'Too? You too?'
'Yes ... that is ...' Sanin was unable, positively unable to add a single word more.
'Very well,' said Gemma. 'If you, as a friend, advise me to change my decision—that is, not to change my former decision—I will think it over.' Not knowing what she was doing, she began to tip the cherries back from the plate into the basket.... 'Mamma hopes that I will mind what you say. Well ... perhaps I really will mind what you say.'
'But excuse me, Fräulein Gemma, I should like first to know what reason impelled you ...'
'I will mind what you say,' Gemma repeated, her face right up to her brows was working, her cheeks were white, she was biting her lower lip. 'You have done so much for me, that I am bound to do as you wish; bound to carry out your wishes. I will tell mamma ... I will think again. Here she is, by the way, coming here.'
Frau Lenore did in fact appear in the doorway leading from the house to the garden. She was in an agony of impatience; she could not keep still. According to her calculations, Sanin must long ago have finished all he had to say to Gemma, though his conversation with her had not lasted a quarter of an hour.
'No, no, no, for God's sake, don't tell her anything yet,' Sanin articulated hurriedly, almost in alarm. 'Wait a little ... I will tell you, I will write to you ... and till then don't decide on anything ... wait!'
He pressed Gemma's hand, jumped up from the seat, and to Frau Lenore's great amazement, rushed past her, and raising his hat, muttered something unintelligible—and vanished.
She went up to her daughter.
'Tell me, please, Gemma...'
The latter suddenly got up and hugged her. 'Dear mamma, can you wait a little, a tiny bit ... till to-morrow? Can you? And till to-morrow not a word?... Ah!...'
She burst into sudden happy tears, incomprehensible to herself. This surprised Frau Lenore, the more as the expression of Gemma's face was far from sorrowful,—rather joyful in fact.
'What is it?' she asked. 'You never cry and here, all at once ...'
'Nothing, mamma, never mind! you only wait. We must both wait a little. Don't ask me anything till to-morrow—and let us sort the cherries before the sun has set.'
'But you will be reasonable?'
'Oh, I'm very reasonable!' Gemma shook her head significantly. She began to make up little bunches of cherries, holding them high above her flushed face. She did not wipe away her tears; they had dried of themselves.

XXV

Almost running, Sanin returned to his hotel room. He felt, he knew that only there, only by himself, would it be clear to him at last what was the matter, what was happening to him. And so it was; directly he had got inside his room, directly he had sat down to the writing-table, with both elbows on the table and both hands pressed to his face, he cried in a sad and choked voice, 'I love her, love her madly!' and he was all aglow within, like a fire when a thick layer of dead ash has been suddenly blown off. An instant more ... and he was utterly unable to understand how he could have sat beside her ... her!—and talked to her and not have felt that he worshipped the very hem of her garment, that he was ready as young people express it 'to die at her feet.' The last interview in the garden had decided everything. Now when he thought of her, she did not appear to him with blazing curls in the shining starlight; he saw her sitting on the garden-seat, saw her all at once tossing back her hat, and gazing at him so confidingly ... and the tremor and hunger of love ran through all his veins. He remembered the rose which he had been carrying about in his pocket for three days: he snatched it out, and pressed it with such feverish violence to his lips, that he could not help frowning with the pain. Now he considered nothing, reflected on nothing, did not deliberate, and did not look forward; he had done with all his past, he leaped forward into the future; from the dreary bank of his lonely bachelor life he plunged headlong into that glad, seething, mighty torrent—and little he cared, little he wished to know, where it would carry him, or whether it would dash him against a rock! No more the soft-flowing currents of the Uhland song, which had lulled him not long ago ... These were mighty, irresistible torrents! They rush flying onwards and he flies with them....

He took a sheet of paper, and without blotting out a word, almost with one sweep of the pen, wrote as follows:—

'DEAR GEMMA,—You know what advice I undertook to give you, what your mother desired, and what she asked of me; but what you don't know and what I must tell you now is, that I love you, love you with all the ardour of a heart that loves for the first time! This passion has flamed up in me suddenly, but with such force that I can find no words for it! When your mother came to me and asked me, it was still only smouldering in me, or else I should certainly, as an honest man, have refused to carry out her request.... The confession I make you now is the confession of an honest man. You ought to know whom you have to do with—between us there should exist no misunderstandings. You see that I cannot give you any advice.... I love you, love you, love you—and I have nothing else—either in my head or in my heart!!

'DM. SANIN.'

When he had folded and sealed this note, Sanin was on the point of ringing for the waiter and sending it by him.... 'No!' he thought, 'it would be awkward.... By Emil? But to go to the shop, and seek him out there among the other employés, would be awkward too. Besides, it's dark by now, and he has probably left the shop.' Reflecting after this fashion, Sanin put on his hat, however, and went into the street; he turned a corner, another, and to his unspeakable delight, saw Emil before him. With a satchel under his arm, and a roll of papers in his hand, the young enthusiast was hurrying home.

'They may well say every lover has a lucky star,' thought Sanin, and he called to Emil.

The latter turned and at once rushed to him.

Sanin cut short his transports, handed him the note, and explained to whom and how he was to deliver it.... Emil listened attentively.

'So that no one sees?' he inquired, assuming an important and mysterious air, that said, 'We understand the inner meaning of it all!'

'Yes, my friend,' said Sanin and he was a little disconcerted; however, he patted Emil on the cheek.... 'And if there should be an answer.... You will bring me the answer, won't you? I will stay at home.'

'Don't worry yourself about that!' Emil whispered gaily; he ran off, and as he ran nodded once more to him.

Sanin went back home, and without lighting a candle, flung himself on the sofa, put his hands behind his head, and abandoned himself to those sensations of newly conscious love, which it is no good even to describe. One who has felt them knows their languor and sweetness; to one who has felt them not, one could never make them known.

The door opened—Emil's head appeared.

'I have brought it,' he said in a whisper: 'here it is—the answer!'

He showed and waved above his head a folded sheet of paper.
Sanin leaped up from the sofa and snatched it out of Emil's hand. Passion was working too powerfully within him: he had no thought of reserve now, nor of the observance of a suitable demeanour—even before this boy, her brother. He would have been scrupulous, he would have controlled himself—if he could!
He went to the window, and by the light of a street lamp which stood just opposite the house, he read the following lines:—
I beg you, I beseech you—*don't come to see us, don't show yourself all day to-morrow*. It's necessary, absolutely necessary for me, and then everything shall be settled. I know you will not say no, because …

'GEMMA.'

Sanin read this note twice through. Oh, how touchingly sweet and beautiful her handwriting seemed to him! He thought a little, and turning to Emil, who, wishing to give him to understand what a discreet young person he was, was standing with his face to the wall, and scratching on it with his finger-nails, he called him aloud by name.
Emil ran at once to Sanin. 'What do you want me to do?'
'Listen, my young friend…'
'Monsieur Dimitri,' Emil interrupted in a plaintive voice, 'why do you address me so formally?'
Sanin laughed. 'Oh, very well. Listen, my dearest boy—(Emil gave a little skip of delight)—listen; *there* you understand, there, you will say, that everything shall be done exactly as is wished—(Emil compressed his lips and nodded solemnly)—and as for me … what are you doing to-morrow, my dear boy?'
'I? what am I doing? What would you like me to do?'
'If you can, come to me early in the morning—and we will walk about the country round Frankfort till evening…. Would you like to?'
Emil gave another little skip. 'I say, what in the world could be jollier? Go a walk with you—why, it's simply glorious! I'll be sure to come!'
'And if they won't let you?'
'They will let me!'
'Listen … Don't say *there* that I asked you to come for the whole day.'
'Why should I? But I'll get away all the same! What does it matter?'
Emil warmly kissed Sanin, and ran away.
Sanin walked up and down the room a long while, and went late to bed. He gave himself up to the same delicate and sweet sensations, the same joyous thrill at facing a new life. Sanin was very glad that the idea had occurred to him to invite Emil to spend the next day with him; he was like his sister. 'He will recall her,' was his thought.
But most of all, he marvelled how he could have been yesterday other than he was to-day. It seemed to him that he had loved Gemma for all time; and that he had loved her just as he loved her to-day.

XXVI

At eight o'clock next morning, Emil arrived at Sanin's hotel leading Tartaglia by a string. Had he sprung of German parentage, he could not have shown greater practicality. He had told a lie at home; he had said he was going for a walk with Sanin till lunch-time, and then going to the shop. While Sanin was dressing, Emil began to talk to him, rather hesitatingly, it is true, about Gemma, about her rupture with Herr Klüber; but Sanin preserved an austere silence in reply, and Emil, looking as though he understood why so serious a matter should not be touched on lightly, did not return to the subject, and only assumed from time to time an intense and even severe expression.
After drinking coffee, the two friends set off together—on foot, of course—to Hausen, a little village lying a short distance from Frankfort, and surrounded by woods. The whole chain of the Taunus mountains could be seen clearly from there. The weather was lovely; the sunshine was bright and warm, but not blazing hot; a fresh wind rustled briskly among the green leaves; the shadows of high, round clouds glided swiftly and

smoothly in small patches over the earth. The two young people soon got out of the town, and stepped out boldly and gaily along the well-kept road. They reached the woods, and wandered about there a long time; then they lunched very heartily at a country inn; then climbed on to the mountains, admired the views, rolled stones down and clapped their hands, watching the queer droll way in which the stones hopped along like rabbits, till a man passing below, unseen by them, began abusing them in a loud ringing voice. Then they lay full length on the short dry moss of yellowish-violet colour; then they drank beer at another inn; ran races, and tried for a wager which could jump farthest. They discovered an echo, and began to call to it; sang songs, hallooed, wrestled, broke up dry twigs, decked their hats with fern, and even danced. Tartaglia, as far as he could, shared in all these pastimes; he did not throw stones, it is true, but he rolled head over heels after them; he howled when they were singing, and even drank beer, though with evident aversion; he had been trained in this art by a student to whom he had once belonged. But he was not prompt in obeying Emil—not as he was with his master Pantaleone—and when Emil ordered him to 'speak,' or to 'sneeze,' he only wagged his tail and thrust out his tongue like a pipe.
The young people talked, too. At the beginning of the walk, Sanin, as the elder, and so more reflective, turned the conversation on fate and predestination, and the nature and meaning of man's destiny; but the conversation quickly took a less serious turn. Emil began to question his friend and patron about Russia, how duels were fought there, and whether the women there were beautiful, and whether one could learn Russian quickly, and what he had felt when the officer took aim at him. Sanin, on his side, questioned Emil about his father, his mother, and in general about their family affairs, trying every time not to mention Gemma's name—and thinking only of her. To speak more precisely, it was not of her he was thinking, but of the morrow, the mysterious morrow which was to bring him new, unknown happiness! It was as though a veil, a delicate, bright veil, hung faintly fluttering before his mental vision; and behind this veil he felt … felt the presence of a youthful, motionless, divine image, with a tender smile on its lips, and eyelids severely—with affected seventy—downcast. And this image was not the face of Gemma, it was the face of happiness itself! For, behold, at last *his* hour had come, the veil had vanished, the lips were parting, the eyelashes are raised—his divinity has looked upon him—and at once light as from the sun, and joy and bliss unending! He dreamed of this morrow—and his soul thrilled with joy again in the melting torture of ever-growing expectation!
And this expectation, this torture, hindered nothing. It accompanied every action, and did not prevent anything. It did not prevent him from dining capitally at a third inn with Emil; and only occasionally, like a brief flash of lightning, the thought shot across him, What if any one in the world knew? This suspense did not prevent him from playing leap-frog with Emil after dinner. The game took place on an open green lawn. And the confusion, the stupefaction of Sanin may be imagined! At the very moment when, accompanied by a sharp bark from Tartaglia, he was flying like a bird, with his legs outspread over Emil, who was bent double, he suddenly saw on the farthest border of the lawn two officers, in whom he recognised at once his adversary and his second, Herr von Dönhof and Herr von Richter! Each of them had stuck an eyeglass in his eye, and was staring at him, chuckling!… Sanin got on his feet, turned away hurriedly, put on the coat he had flung down, jerked out a word to Emil; the latter, too, put on his jacket, and they both immediately made off.
It was late when they got back to Frankfort. 'They'll scold me,' Emil said to Sanin as he said good-bye to him. 'Well, what does it matter? I've had such a splendid, splendid day!'
When he got home to his hotel, Sanin found a note there from Gemma. She fixed a meeting with him for next day, at seven o'clock in the morning, in one of the public gardens which surround Frankfort on all sides. How his heart throbbed! How glad he was that he had obeyed her so unconditionally! And, my God, what was promised … what was not promised, by that unknown, unique, impossible, and undubitably certain morrow!
He feasted his eyes on Gemma's note. The long, elegant tail of the letter G, the first letter of her name, which stood at the bottom of the sheet, reminded him of her lovely fingers, her hand…. He thought that he had not once touched that hand with his lips…. 'Italian women,' he mused, 'in spite of what's said of them, are modest and severe…. And Gemma above all! Queen … goddess … pure, virginal marble….'
'But the time will come; and it is not far off….' There was that night in Frankfort one happy man…. He slept; but he might have said of himself in the words of the poet:
'I sleep … but my watchful heart sleeps not.'
And it fluttered as lightly as a butterfly flutters his wings, as he stoops over the flowers in the summer sunshine.

At five o'clock Sanin woke up, at six he was dressed, at half-past six he was walking up and down the public garden within sight of the little arbour which Gemma had mentioned in her note. It was a still, warm, grey morning. It sometimes seemed as though it were beginning to rain; but the outstretched hand felt nothing, and only looking at one's coat-sleeve, one could see traces of tiny drops like diminutive beads, but even these were soon gone. It seemed there had never been a breath of wind in the world. Every sound moved not, but was shed around in the stillness. In the distance was a faint thickening of whitish mist; in the air there was a scent of mignonette and white acacia flowers.

In the streets the shops were not open yet, but there were already some people walking about; occasionally a solitary carriage rumbled along … there was no one walking in the garden. A gardener was in a leisurely way scraping the path with a spade, and a decrepit old woman in a black woollen cloak was hobbling across the garden walk. Sanin could not for one instant mistake this poor old creature for Gemma; and yet his heart leaped, and he watched attentively the retreating patch of black.

Seven! chimed the clock on the tower. Sanin stood still. Was it possible she would not come? A shiver of cold suddenly ran through his limbs. The same shiver came again an instant later, but from a different cause. Sanin heard behind him light footsteps, the light rustle of a woman's dress.... He turned round: she!

Gemma was coming up behind him along the path. She was wearing a grey cape and a small dark hat. She glanced at Sanin, turned her head away, and catching him up, passed rapidly by him.

'Gemma,' he articulated, hardly audibly.

She gave him a little nod, and continued to walk on in front. He followed her.

He breathed in broken gasps. His legs shook under him.

Gemma passed by the arbour, turned to the right, passed by a small flat fountain, in which the sparrows were splashing busily, and, going behind a clump of high lilacs, sank down on a bench. The place was snug and hidden. Sanin sat down beside her.

A minute passed, and neither he nor she uttered a word. She did not even look at him; and he gazed not at her face, but at her clasped hands, in which she held a small parasol. What was there to tell, what was there to say, which could compare, in importance, with the simple fact of their presence there, together, alone, so early, so close to each other.

'You … are not angry with me?' Sanin articulated at last.

It would have been difficult for Sanin to have said anything more foolish than these words … he was conscious of it himself.... But, at any rate, the silence was broken.

'Angry?' she answered. 'What for? No.'

'And you believe me?' he went on.

'In what you wrote?'

'Yes.'

Gemma's head sank, and she said nothing. The parasol slipped out of her hands. She hastily caught it before it dropped on the path.

'Ah, believe me! believe what I wrote to you!' cried Sanin; all his timidity suddenly vanished, he spoke with heat; 'if there is truth on earth—sacred, absolute truth—it's that I love, love you passionately, Gemma.'

She flung him a sideway, momentary glance, and again almost dropped the parasol.

'Believe me! believe me!' he repeated. He besought her, held out his hands to her, and did not dare to touch her. 'What do you want me to do … to convince you?'

She glanced at him again.

'Tell me, Monsieur Dimitri,' she began; 'the day before yesterday, when you came to talk to me, you did not, I imagine, know then … did not feel …'

'I felt it,' Sanin broke in; 'but I did not know it. I have loved you from the very instant I saw you; but I did not realise at once what you had become to me! And besides, I heard that you were solemnly betrothed.... As far as your mother's request is concerned—in the first place, how could I refuse?—and secondly, I think I carried out her request in such a way that you could guess....'

They heard a heavy tread, and a rather stout gentleman with a knapsack over his shoulder, apparently a foreigner, emerged from behind the clump, and staring, with the unceremoniousness of a tourist, at the couple sitting on the garden-seat, gave a loud cough and went on.

'Your mother,' Sanin began, as soon as the sound of the heavy footsteps had ceased, 'told me your breaking off your engagement would cause a scandal'—Gemma frowned a little—that I was myself in part responsible for unpleasant gossip, and that ... consequently ... I was, to some extent, under an obligation to advise you not to break with your betrothed, Herr Klüber....'

'Monsieur Dimitri,' said Gemma, and she passed her hand over her hair on the side turned towards Sanin, 'don't, please, call Herr Klüber my betrothed. I shall never be his wife. I have broken with him.'

'You have broken with him? when?'

'Yesterday.'

'You saw him?'

'Yes. At our house. He came to see us.'

'Gemma? Then you love me?'

She turned to him.

'Should ... I have come here, if not?' she whispered, and both her hands fell on the seat.

Sanin snatched those powerless, upturned palms, and pressed them to his eyes, to his lips.... Now the veil was lifted of which he had dreamed the night before! Here was happiness, here was its radiant form!

He raised his head, and looked at Gemma, boldly and directly. She, too, looked at him, a little downwards. Her half-shut eyes faintly glistened, dim with light, blissful tears. Her face was not smiling ... no! it laughed, with a blissful, noiseless laugh.

He tried to draw her to him, but she drew back, and never ceasing to laugh the same noiseless laugh, shook her head. 'Wait a little,' her happy eyes seemed to say.

'O Gemma!' cried Sanin: 'I never dreamed that you would love me!'

'I did not expect this myself,' Gemma said softly.

'How could I ever have dreamed,' Sanin went on, 'when I came to Frankfort, where I only expected to remain a few hours, that I should find here the happiness of all my life!'

'All your life? Really?' queried Gemma.

'All my life, for ever and ever!' cried Sanin with fresh ardour.

The gardener's spade suddenly scraped two paces from where they were sitting.

'Let's go home,' whispered Gemma: 'we'll go together—will you?'

If she had said to him at that instant 'Throw yourself in the sea, will you?' he would have been flying headlong into the ocean before she had uttered the last word.

They went together out of the garden and turned homewards, not by the streets of the town, but through the outskirts.

XXVIII

Sanin walked along, at one time by Gemma's side, at another time a little behind her. He never took his eyes off her and never ceased smiling. She seemed to hasten ... seemed to linger. As a matter of fact, they both—he all pale, and she all flushed with emotion—were moving along as in a dream. What they had done together a few instants before—that surrender of each soul to another soul—was so intense, so new, and so moving; so suddenly everything in their lives had been changed and displaced that they could not recover themselves, and were only aware of a whirlwind carrying them along, like the whirlwind on that night, which had almost flung them into each other's arms. Sanin walked along, and felt that he even looked at Gemma with other eyes; he instantly noted some peculiarities in her walk, in her movements,—and heavens! how infinitely sweet and precious they were to him! And she felt that that was how he was looking at her.

Sanin and she were in love for the first time; all the miracles of first love were working in them. First love is like a revolution; the uniformly regular routine of ordered life is broken down and shattered in one instant; youth mounts the barricade, waves high its bright flag, and whatever awaits it in the future—death or a new life—all alike it goes to meet with ecstatic welcome.

'What's this? Isn't that our old friend?' said Sanin, pointing to a muffled-up figure, which hurriedly slipped a little aside as though trying to remain unobserved. In the midst of his abundant happiness he felt a need to talk to Gemma, not of love—that was a settled thing and holy—but of something else.

'Yes, it's Pantaleone,' Gemma answered gaily and happily. 'Most likely he has been following me ever since I left home; all day yesterday he kept watching every movement I made … He guesses!'
'He guesses!' Sanin repeated in ecstasy. What could Gemma have said at which he would not have been in ecstasy?
Then he asked her to tell him in detail all that had passed the day before.
And she began at once telling him, with haste, and confusion, and smiles, and brief sighs, and brief bright looks exchanged with Sanin. She said that after their conversation the day before yesterday, mamma had kept trying to get out of her something positive; but that she had put off Frau Lenore with a promise to tell her her decision within twenty-four hours; how she had demanded this limit of time for herself, and how difficult it had been to get it; how utterly unexpectedly Herr Klüber had made his appearance more starched and affected than ever; how he had given vent to his indignation at the childish, unpardonable action of the Russian stranger—'he meant your duel, Dimitri,'—which he described as deeply insulting to him, Klüber, and how he had demanded that 'you should be at once refused admittance to the house, Dimitri.' 'For,' he had added—and here Gemma slightly mimicked his voice and manner—'"it casts a slur on my honour; as though I were not able to defend my betrothed, had I thought it necessary or advisable! All Frankfort will know by to-morrow that an outsider has fought a duel with an officer on account of my betrothed—did any one ever hear of such a thing! It tarnishes my honour!" Mamma agreed with him—fancy!—but then I suddenly told him that he was troubling himself unnecessarily about his honour and his character, and was unnecessarily annoyed at the gossip about his betrothed, for I was no longer betrothed to him and would never be his wife! I must own, I had meant to talk to you first … before breaking with him finally; but he came … and I could not restrain myself. Mamma positively screamed with horror, but I went into the next room and got his ring—you didn't notice, I took it off two days ago—and gave it to him. He was fearfully offended, but as he is fearfully self-conscious and conceited, he did not say much, and went away. Of course I had to go through a great deal with mamma, and it made me very wretched to see how distressed she was, and I thought I had been a little hasty; but you see I had your note, and even apart from it I knew …'
'That I love you,' put in Sanin.
'Yes … that you were in love with me.'
So Gemma talked, hesitating and smiling and dropping her voice or stopping altogether every time any one met them or passed by. And Sanin listened ecstatically, enjoying the very sound of her voice, as the day before he had gloated over her handwriting.
'Mamma is very much distressed,' Gemma began again, and her words flew very rapidly one after another; 'she refuses to take into consideration that I dislike Herr Klüber, that I never was betrothed to him from love, but only because of her urgent entreaties…. She suspects—you, Dimitri; that's to say, to speak plainly, she's convinced I'm in love with you, and she is more unhappy about it because only the day before yesterday nothing of the sort had occurred to her, and she even begged you to advise me…. It was a strange request, wasn't it? Now she calls you … Dimitri, a hypocrite and a cunning fellow, says that you have betrayed her confidence, and predicts that you will deceive me….'
'But, Gemma,' cried Sanin, 'do you mean to say you didn't tell her?…'
'I told her nothing! What right had I without consulting you?'
Sanin threw up his arms. 'Gemma, I hope that now, at least, you will tell all to her and take me to her…. I want to convince your mother that I am not a base deceiver!'
Sanin's bosom fairly heaved with the flood of generous and ardent emotions.
Gemma looked him full in the face. 'You really want to go with me now to mamma? to mamma, who maintains that … all this between us is impossible—and can never come to pass?' There was one word Gemma could not bring herself to utter…. It burnt her lips; but all the more eagerly Sanin pronounced it.
'Marry you, Gemma, be your husband—I can imagine no bliss greater!'
To his love, his magnanimity, his determination—he was aware of no limits now.
When she heard those words, Gemma, who had stopped still for an instant, went on faster than ever…. She seemed trying to run away from this too great and unexpected happiness! But suddenly her steps faltered. Round the corner of a turning, a few paces from her, in a new hat and coat, straight as an arrow and curled like a poodle—emerged Herr Klüber. He caught sight of Gemma, caught sight of Sanin, and with a sort of inward snort and a backward bend of his supple figure, he advanced with a dashing swing to meet them. Sanin felt a pang; but glancing at Klüber's face, to which its owner endeavoured, as far as in him lay, to give an expression of scornful amazement, and even commiseration, glancing at that red-cheeked, vulgar face, he felt a sudden rush of anger, and took a step forward.

Gemma seized his arm, and with quiet decision, giving him hers, she looked her former betrothed full in the face.... The latter screwed up his face, shrugged his shoulders, shuffled to one side, and muttering between his teeth, 'The usual end to the song!' (Das alte Ende vom Liede!)—walked away with the same dashing, slightly skipping gait.
'What did he say, the wretched creature?' asked Sanin, and would have rushed after Klüber; but Gemma held him back and walked on with him, not taking away the arm she had slipped into his.
The Rosellis' shop came into sight. Gemma stopped once more.
'Dimitri, Monsieur Dimitri,' she said, 'we are not there yet, we have not seen mamma yet.... If you would rather think a little, if ... you are still free, Dimitri!'
In reply Sanin pressed her hand tightly to his bosom, and drew her on.
'Mamma,' said Gemma, going with Sanin to the room where Frau Lenore was sitting, 'I have brought the real one!'

XXIX

If Gemma had announced that she had brought with her cholera or death itself, one can hardly imagine that Frau Lenore could have received the news with greater despair. She immediately sat down in a corner, with her face to the wall, and burst into floods of tears, positively wailed, for all the world like a Russian peasant woman on the grave of her husband or her son. For the first minute Gemma was so taken aback that she did not even go up to her mother, but stood still like a statue in the middle of the room; while Sanin was utterly stupefied, to the point of almost bursting into tears himself! For a whole hour that inconsolable wail went on—a whole hour! Pantaleone thought it better to shut the outer door of the shop, so that no stranger should come; luckily, it was still early. The old man himself did not know what to think, and in any case, did not approve of the haste with which Gemma and Sanin had acted; he could not bring himself to blame them, and was prepared to give them his support in case of need: he greatly disliked Klüber! Emil regarded himself as the medium of communication between his friend and his sister, and almost prided himself on its all having turned out so splendidly! He was positively unable to conceive why Frau Lenore was so upset, and in his heart he decided on the spot that women, even the best of them, suffer from a lack of reasoning power! Sanin fared worst of all. Frau Lenore rose to a howl and waved him off with her hands, directly he approached her; and it was in vain that he attempted once or twice to shout aloud, standing at a distance, 'I ask you for your daughter's hand!' Frau Lenore was particularly angry with herself. 'How could she have been so blind—have seen nothing? Had my Giovann' Battista been alive,' she persisted through her tears, 'nothing of this sort would have happened!' 'Heavens, what's it all about?' thought Sanin; 'why, it's positively senseless!' He did not dare to look at Gemma, nor could she pluck up courage to lift her eyes to him. She restricted herself to waiting patiently on her mother, who at first repelled even her....
At last, by degrees, the storm abated. Frau Lenore gave over weeping, permitted Gemma to bring her out of the corner, where she sat huddled up, to put her into an arm-chair near the window, and to give her some orange-flower water to drink. She permitted Sanin—not to approach ... oh, no!—but, at any rate, to remain in the room—she had kept clamouring for him to go away—and did not interrupt him when he spoke. Sanin immediately availed himself of the calm as it set in, and displayed an astounding eloquence. He could hardly have explained his intentions and emotions with more fire and persuasive force even to Gemma herself. Those emotions were of the sincerest, those intentions were of the purest, like Almaviva's in the *Barber of Seville*. He did not conceal from Frau Lenore nor from himself the disadvantageous side of those intentions; but the disadvantages were only apparent! It is true he was a foreigner; they had not known him long, they knew nothing positive about himself or his means; but he was prepared to bring forward all the necessary evidence that he was a respectable person and not poor; he would refer them to the most unimpeachable testimony of his fellow-countrymen! He hoped Gemma would be happy with him, and that he would be able to make up to her for the separation from her own people!... The allusion to 'separation'—the mere word 'separation'—almost spoiled the whole business.... Frau Lenore began to tremble all over and move about uneasily.... Sanin hastened to observe that the separation would only be temporary, and that, in fact, possibly it would not take place at all!

Sanin's eloquence was not thrown away. Frau Lenore began to glance at him, though still with bitterness and reproach, no longer with the same aversion and fury; then she suffered him to come near her, and even to sit down beside her (Gemma was sitting on the other side); then she fell to reproaching him,—not in looks only, but in words, which already indicated a certain softening of heart; she fell to complaining, and her complaints became quieter and gentler; they were interspersed with questions addressed at one time to her daughter, and at another to Sanin; then she suffered him to take her hand and did not at once pull it away … then she wept again, but her tears were now quite of another kind…. Then she smiled mournfully, and lamented the absence of Giovanni Battista, but quite on different grounds from before…. An instant more and the two criminals, Sanin and Gemma, were on their knees at her feet, and she was laying her hands on their heads in turn; another instant and they were embracing and kissing her, and Emil, his face beaming rapturously, ran into the room and added himself to the group so warmly united.
Pantaleone peeped into the room, smiled and frowned at the same time, and going into the shop, opened the front door.

XXX

The transition from despair to sadness, and from that to 'gentle resignation,' was accomplished fairly quickly in Frau Lenore; but that gentle resignation, too, was not slow in changing into a secret satisfaction, which was, however, concealed in every way and suppressed for the sake of appearances. Sanin had won Frau Lenore's heart from the first day of their acquaintance; as she got used to the idea of his being her son-in-law, she found nothing particularly distasteful in it, though she thought it her duty to preserve a somewhat hurt, or rather careworn, expression on her face. Besides, everything that had happened the last few days had been so extraordinary…. One thing upon the top of another. As a practical woman and a mother, Frau Lenore considered it her duty also to put Sanin through various questions; and Sanin, who, on setting out that morning to meet Gemma, had not a notion that he should marry her—it is true he did not think of anything at all at that time, but simply gave himself up to the current of his passion—Sanin entered, with perfect readiness, one might even say with zeal, into his part—the part of the betrothed lover, and answered all her inquiries circumstantially, exactly, with alacrity. When she had satisfied herself that he was a real nobleman by birth, and had even expressed some surprise that he was not a prince, Frau Lenore assumed a serious air and 'warned him betimes' that she should be quite unceremoniously frank with him, as she was forced to be so by her sacred duty as a mother! To which Sanin replied that he expected nothing else from her, and that he earnestly begged her not to spare him!
Then Frau Lenore observed that Herr Klüber—as she uttered the name, she sighed faintly, tightened her lips, and hesitated—Herr Klüber, Gemma's former betrothed, already possessed an income of eight thousand guldens, and that with every year this sum would rapidly be increased; and what was his, Herr Sanin's income? 'Eight thousand guldens,' Sanin repeated deliberately…. 'That's in our money … about fifteen thousand roubles…. My income is much smaller. I have a small estate in the province of Tula…. With good management, it might yield—and, in fact, it could not fail to yield—five or six thousand … and if I go into the government service, I can easily get a salary of two thousand a year.'
'Into the service in Russia?' cried Frau Lenore, 'Then I must part with Gemma!'
'One might be able to enter in the diplomatic service,' Sanin put in; 'I have some connections…. There one's duties lie abroad. Or else, this is what one might do, and that's much the best of all: sell my estate and employ the sum received for it in some profitable undertaking; for instance, the improvement of your shop.' Sanin was aware that he was saying something absurd, but he was possessed by an incomprehensible recklessness! He looked at Gemma, who, ever since the 'practical' conversation began, kept getting up, walking about the room, and sitting down again—he looked at her—and no obstacle existed for him, and he was ready to arrange everything at once in the best way, if only she were not troubled!
'Herr Klüber, too, had intended to give me a small sum for the improvement of the shop,' Lenore observed after a slight hesitation.
'Mother! for mercy's sake, mother!' cried Gemma in Italian.

'These things must be discussed in good time, my daughter,' Frau Lenore replied in the same language. She addressed herself again to Sanin, and began questioning him as to the laws existing in Russia as to marriage, and whether there were no obstacles to contracting marriages with Catholics as in Prussia. (At that time, in 1840, all Germany still remembered the controversy between the Prussian Government and the Archbishop of Cologne upon mixed marriages.) When Frau Lenore heard that by marrying a Russian nobleman, her daughter would herself become of noble rank, she evinced a certain satisfaction. 'But, of course, you will first have to go to Russia?'
'Why?'
'Why? Why, to obtain the permission of your Tsar.'
Sanin explained to her that that was not at all necessary ... but that he might certainly have to go to Russia for a very short time before his marriage—(he said these words, and his heart ached painfully, Gemma watching him, knew it was aching, and blushed and grew dreamy)—and that he would try to take advantage of being in his own country to sell his estate ... in any case he would bring back the money needed.
'I would ask you to bring me back some good Astrakhan lambskin for a cape,' said Frau Lenore. 'They're wonderfully good, I hear, and wonderfully cheap!'
'Certainly, with the greatest pleasure, I will bring some for you and for Gemma!' cried Sanin.
'And for me a morocco cap worked in silver,' Emil interposed, putting his head in from the next room.
'Very well, I will bring it you ... and some slippers for Pantaleone.'
'Come, that's nonsense, nonsense,' observed Frau Lenore. 'We are talking now of serious matters. But there's another point,' added the practical lady. 'You talk of selling your estate. But how will you do that? Will you sell your peasants then, too?'
Sanin felt something like a stab at his heart. He remembered that in a conversation with Signora Roselli and her daughter about serfdom, which, in his own words, aroused his deepest indignation, he had repeatedly assured them that never on any account would he sell his peasants, as he regarded such a sale as an immoral act.
'I will try and sell my estate to some man I know something of,' he articulated, not without faltering, 'or perhaps the peasants themselves will want to buy their freedom.'
'That would be best of all,' Frau Lenore agreed. 'Though indeed selling live people ...'
'*Barbari*!' grumbled Pantaleone, who showed himself behind Emil in the doorway, shook his topknot, and vanished.
'It's a bad business!' Sanin thought to himself, and stole a look at Gemma. She seemed not to have heard his last words. 'Well, never mind!' he thought again. In this way the practical talk continued almost uninterruptedly till dinner-time. Frau Lenore was completely softened at last, and already called Sanin 'Dimitri,' shook her finger affectionately at him, and promised she would punish him for his treachery. She asked many and minute questions about his relations, because 'that too is very important'; asked him to describe the ceremony of marriage as performed by the ritual of the Russian Church, and was in raptures already at Gemma in a white dress, with a gold crown on her head.
'She's as lovely as a queen,' she murmured with motherly pride,' indeed there's no queen like her in the world!'
'There is no one like Gemma in the world!' Sanin chimed in.
'Yes; that's why she is Gemma!' (Gemma, as every one knows, means in Italian a precious stone.)
Gemma flew to kiss her mother.... It seemed as if only then she breathed freely again, and the load that had been oppressing her dropped from off her soul.
Sanin felt all at once so happy, his heart was filled with such childish gaiety at the thought, that here, after all, the dreams had come true to which he had abandoned himself not long ago in these very rooms, his whole being was in such a turmoil that he went quickly out into the shop. He felt a great desire, come what might, to sell something in the shop, as he had done a few days before.... 'I have a full right to do so now!' he felt. 'Why, I am one of the family now!' And he actually stood behind the counter, and actually kept shop, that is, sold two little girls, who came in, a pound of sweets, giving them fully two pounds, and only taking half the price from them.
At dinner he received an official position, as betrothed, beside Gemma. Frau Lenore pursued her practical investigations. Emil kept laughing and urging Sanin to take him with him to Russia. It was decided that Sanin should set off in a fortnight. Only Pantaleone showed a somewhat sullen face, so much so that Frau Lenore reproached him. 'And he was his second!' Pantaleone gave her a glance from under his brows.

Gemma was silent almost all the time, but her face had never been lovelier or brighter. After dinner she called Sanin out a minute into the garden, and stopping beside the very garden-seat where she had been sorting the cherries two days before, she said to him. 'Dimitri, don't be angry with me; but I must remind you once more that you are not to consider yourself bound …'
He did not let her go on….
Gemma turned away her face. 'And as for what mamma spoke of, do you remember, the difference of our religion—see here!…'
She snatched the garnet cross that hung round her neck on a thin cord, gave it a violent tug, snapped the cord, and handed him the cross.
'If I am yours, your faith is my faith!' Sanin's eyes were still wet when he went back with Gemma into the house.
By the evening everything went on in its accustomed way. They even played a game of *tresette*.

XXXI

Sanin woke up very early. He found himself at the highest pinnacle of human happiness; but it was not that prevented him from sleeping; the question, the vital, fateful question—how he could dispose of his estate as quickly and as advantageously as possible—disturbed his rest. The most diverse plans were mixed up in his head, but nothing had as yet come out clearly. He went out of the house to get air and freshen himself. He wanted to present himself to Gemma with a project ready prepared and not without.
What was the figure, somewhat ponderous and thick in the legs, but well-dressed, walking in front of him, with a slight roll and waddle in his gait? Where had he seen that head, covered with tufts of flaxen hair, and as it were set right into the shoulders, that soft cushiony back, those plump arms hanging straight down at his sides? Could it be Polozov, his old schoolfellow, whom he had lost sight of for the last five years? Sanin overtook the figure walking in front of him, turned round…. A broad, yellowish face, little pig's eyes, with white lashes and eyebrows, a short flat nose, thick lips that looked glued together, a round smooth chin, and that expression, sour, sluggish, and mistrustful—yes; it was he, it was Ippolit Polozov!
'Isn't my lucky star working for me again?' flashed through Sanin's mind.
'Polozov! Ippolit Sidorovitch! Is it you?'
The figure stopped, raised his diminutive eyes, waited a little, and ungluing his lips at last, brought out in a rather hoarse falsetto, 'Dimitri Sanin?'
'That's me!' cried Sanin, and he shook one of Polozov's hands; arrayed in tight kid-gloves of an ashen-grey colour, they hung as lifeless as before beside his barrel-shaped legs. 'Have you been here long? Where have you come from? Where are you stopping?'
'I came yesterday from Wiesbaden,' Polozov replied in deliberate tones, 'to do some shopping for my wife, and I'm going back to Wiesbaden to-day.'
'Oh, yes! You're married, to be sure, and they say, to such a beauty!'
Polozov turned his eyes away. 'Yes, they say so.'
Sanin laughed. 'I see you're just the same … as phlegmatic as you were at school.'
'Why should I be different?'
'And they do say,' Sanin added with special emphasis on the word 'do,' 'that your wife is very rich.'
'They say that too.'
'Do you mean to say, Ippolit Sidorovitch, you are not certain on that point?'
'I don't meddle, my dear Dimitri … Pavlovitch? Yes, Pavlovitch!—in my wife's affairs.'
'You don't meddle? Not in any of her affairs?'
Polozov again shifted his eyes. 'Not in any, my boy. She does as she likes, and so do I.'
'Where are you going now?' Sanin inquired.
'I'm not going anywhere just now; I'm standing in the street and talking to you; but when we've finished talking, I'm going back to my hotel, and am going to have lunch.'
'Would you care for my company?'
'You mean at lunch?'

'Yes.'
'Delighted, it's much pleasanter to eat in company. You're not a great talker, are you?'
'I think not.'
'So much the better.'
Polozov went on. Sanin walked beside him. And Sanin speculated—Polozov's lips were glued together, again he snorted heavily, and waddled along in silence—Sanin speculated in what way had this booby succeeded in catching a rich and beautiful wife. He was not rich himself, nor distinguished, nor clever; at school he had passed for a dull, slow-witted boy, sleepy, and greedy, and had borne the nickname 'driveller.' It was marvellous!
'But if his wife is very rich, they say she's the daughter of some sort of a contractor, won't she buy my estate? Though he does say he doesn't interfere in any of his wife's affairs, that passes belief, really! Besides, I will name a moderate, reasonable price! Why not try? Perhaps, it's all my lucky star.... Resolved! I'll have a try!'
Polozov led Sanin to one of the best hotels in Frankfort, in which he was, of course, occupying the best apartments. On the tables and chairs lay piles of packages, cardboard boxes, and parcels. 'All purchases, my boy, for Maria Nikolaevna!' (that was the name of the wife of Ippolit Sidorovitch). Polozov dropped into an arm-chair, groaned, 'Oh, the heat!' and loosened his cravat. Then he rang up the head-waiter, and ordered with intense care a very lavish luncheon. 'And at one, the carriage is to be ready! Do you hear, at one o'clock sharp!'
The head-waiter obsequiously bowed, and cringingly withdrew.
Polozov unbuttoned his waistcoat. From the very way in which he raised his eyebrows, gasped, and wrinkled up his nose, one could see that talking would be a great labour to him, and that he was waiting in some trepidation to see whether Sanin was going to oblige him to use his tongue, or whether he would take the task of keeping up the conversation on himself.
Sanin understood his companion's disposition of mind, and so he did not burden him with questions; he restricted himself to the most essential. He learnt that he had been for two years in the service (in the Uhlans! how nice he must have looked in the short uniform jacket!) that he had married three years before, and had now been for two years abroad with his wife, 'who is now undergoing some sort of cure at Wiesbaden,' and was then going to Paris. On his side too, Sanin did not enlarge much on his past life and his plans; he went straight to the principal point—that is, he began talking of his intention of selling his estate.
Polozov listened to him in silence, his eyes straying from time to time to the door, by which the luncheon was to appear. The luncheon did appear at last. The head-waiter, accompanied by two other attendants, brought in several dishes under silver covers.
'Is the property in the Tula province?' said Polozov, seating himself at the table, and tucking a napkin into his shirt collar.
'Yes.'
'In the Efremovsky district ... I know it.'
'Do you know my place, Aleksyevka?' Sanin asked, sitting down too at the table.
'Yes, I know it.' Polozov thrust in his mouth a piece of omelette with truffles. 'Maria Nikolaevna, my wife, has an estate in that neighbourhood.... Uncork that bottle, waiter! You've a good piece of land, only your peasants have cut down the timber. Why are you selling it?'
'I want the money, my friend. I would sell it cheap. Come, you might as well buy it ... by the way.'
Polozov gulped down a glass of wine, wiped his lips with the napkin, and again set to work chewing slowly and noisily.
'Oh,' he enunciated at last.... 'I don't go in for buying estates; I've no capital. Pass the butter. Perhaps my wife now would buy it. You talk to her about it. If you don't ask too much, she's not above thinking of that.... What asses these Germans are, really! They can't cook fish. What could be simpler, one wonders? And yet they go on about "uniting the Fatherland." Waiter, take away that beastly stuff!'
'Does your wife really manage ... business matters herself?' Sanin inquired.
'Yes. Try the cutlets—they're good. I can recommend them. I've told you already, Dimitri Pavlovitch, I don't interfere in any of my wife's concerns, and I tell you so again.'
Polozov went on munching.
'H'm.... But how can I have a talk with her, Ippolit Sidorovitch?'
'It's very simple, Dimitri Pavlovitch. Go to Wiesbaden. It's not far from here. Waiter, haven't you any English mustard? No? Brutes! Only don't lose any time. We're starting the day after to-morrow. Let me pour you out a glass of wine; it's wine with a bouquet—no vinegary stuff.'

Polozov's face was flushed and animated; it was never animated but when he was eating—or drinking.
'Really, I don't know, how that could be managed,' Sanin muttered.
'But what makes you in such a hurry about it all of a sudden?'
'There is a reason for being in a hurry, brother.'
'And do you need a lot of money?'
'Yes, a lot. I … how can I tell you? I propose … getting married.'
Polozov set the glass he had been lifting to his lips on the table.
'Getting married!' he articulated in a voice thick with astonishment, and he folded his podgy hands on his stomach. 'So suddenly?'
'Yes … soon.'
'Your intended is in Russia, of course?'
'No, not in Russia.'
'Where then?'
'Here in Frankfort.'
'And who is she?'
'A German; that is, no—an Italian. A resident here.'
'With a fortune?'
'No, without a fortune.'
'Then I suppose your love is very ardent?'
'How absurd you are! Yes, very ardent.'
'And it's for that you must have money?'
'Well, yes … yes, yes.'
Polozov gulped down his wine, rinsed his mouth, and washed his hands, carefully wiped them on the napkin, took out and lighted a cigar. Sanin watched him in silence.
'There's one means,' Polozov grunted at last, throwing his head back, and blowing out the smoke in a thin ring. 'Go to my wife. If she likes, she can take all the bother off your hands.'
'But how can I see your wife? You say you are starting the day after to-morrow?'
Polozov closed his eyes.
'I'll tell you what,' he said at last, rolling the cigar in his lips, and sighing. 'Go home, get ready as quick as you can, and come here. At one o'clock I am going, there's plenty of room in my carriage. I'll take you with me. That's the best plan. And now I'm going to have a nap. I must always have a nap, brother, after a meal. Nature demands it, and I won't go against it And don't you disturb me.'
Sanin thought and thought, and suddenly raised his head; he had made up his mind.
'Very well, agreed, and thank you. At half-past twelve I'll be here, and we'll go together to Wiesbaden. I hope your wife won't be angry….'
But Polozov was already snoring. He muttered, 'Don't disturb me!' gave a kick, and fell asleep, like a baby. Sanin once more scanned his clumsy figure, his head, his neck, his upturned chin, round as an apple, and going out of the hotel, set off with rapid strides to the Rosellis' shop. He had to let Gemma know.

XXXII

He found her in the shop with her mother. Frau Lenore was stooping down, measuring with a big folding foot-rule the space between the windows. On seeing Sanin, she stood up, and greeted him cheerfully, though with a shade of embarrassment.
'What you said yesterday,' she began, 'has set my head in a whirl with ideas as to how we could improve our shop. Here, I fancy we might put a couple of cupboards with shelves of looking-glass. You know, that's the fashion nowadays. And then …'
'Excellent, excellent,' Sanin broke in, 'we must think it all over…. But come here, I want to tell you something.' He took Frau Lenpre and Gemma by the arm, and led them into the next room. Frau Lenore was alarmed, and the foot-rule slipped out of her hands. Gemma too was almost frightened, but she took an intent look at Sanin, and was reassured. His face, though preoccupied, expressed at the same time keen self-

confidence and determination. He asked both the women to sit down, while he remained standing before them, and gesticulating with his hands and ruffling up his hair, he told them all his story; his meeting with Polozov, his proposed expedition to Wiesbaden, the chance of selling the estate. 'Imagine my happiness,' he cried in conclusion: 'things have taken such a turn that I may even, perhaps, not have to go to Russia! And we can have our wedding much sooner than I had anticipated!'

'When must you go?' asked Gemma.

'To-day, in an hour's time; my friend has ordered a carriage—he will take me.'

'You will write to us?'

'At once! directly I have had a talk with this lady, I will write.'

'This lady, you say, is very rich?' queried the practical Frau Lenore.

'Exceedingly rich! her father was a millionaire, and he left everything to her.'

'Everything—to her alone? Well, that's so much the better for you. Only mind, don't let your property go too cheap! Be sensible and firm. Don't let yourself be carried away! I understand your wishing to be Gemma's husband as soon as possible … but prudence before everything! Don't forget: the better price you get for your estate, the more there will be for you two, and for your children.'

Gemma turned away, and Sanin gave another wave of his hand. 'You can rely on my prudence, Frau Lenore! Indeed, I shan't do any bargaining with her. I shall tell her the fair price; if she'll give it—good; if not, let her go.'

'Do you know her—this lady?' asked Gemma.

'I have never seen her.'

'And when will you come back?'

'If our negotiations come to nothing—the day after to-morrow; if they turn out favourably, perhaps I may have to stay a day or two longer. In any case I shall not linger a minute beyond what's necessary. I am leaving my heart here, you know! But I have said what I had to say to you, and I must run home before setting off too…. Give me your hand for luck, Frau Lenore—that's what we always do in Russia.'

'The right or the left?'

'The left, it's nearer the heart. I shall reappear the day after to-morrow with my shield or on it! Something tells me I shall come back in triumph! Good-bye, my good dear ones….'

He embraced and kissed Frau Lenore, but he asked Gemma to follow him into her room—for just a minute—as he must tell her something of great importance. He simply wanted to say good-bye to her alone. Frau Lenore saw that, and felt no curiosity as to the matter of such great importance.

Sanin had never been in Gemma's room before. All the magic of love, all its fire and rapture and sweet terror, seemed to flame up and burst into his soul, directly he crossed its sacred threshold…. He cast a look of tenderness about him, fell at the sweet girl's feet and pressed his face against her waist….

'You are mine,' she whispered: 'you will be back soon?'

'I am yours. I will come back,' he declared, catching his breath.

'I shall be longing for you back, my dear one!'

A few instants later Sanin was running along the street to his lodging. He did not even notice that Pantaleone, all dishevelled, had darted out of the shop-door after him, and was shouting something to him and was shaking, as though in menace, his lifted hand.

* * * * *

Exactly at a quarter to one Sanin presented himself before Polozov. The carriage with four horses was already standing at the hotel gates. On seeing Sanin, Polozov merely commented, 'Oh! you've made up your mind?' and putting on his hat, cloak, and over-shoes, and stuffing cotton-wool into his ears, though it was summer-time, went out on to the steps. The waiters, by his directions, disposed all his numerous purchases in the inside of the carriage, lined the place where he was to sit with silk cushions, bags, and bundles, put a hamper of provisions for his feet to rest on, and tied a trunk on to the box. Polozov paid with a liberal hand, and supported by the deferential door-keeper, whose face was still respectful, though he was unseen behind him, he climbed gasping into the carriage, sat down, disarranged everything about him thoroughly, took out and lighted a cigar, and only then extended a finger to Sanin, as though to say, 'Get in, you too!' Sanin placed himself beside him. Polozov sent orders by the door-keeper to the postillion to drive carefully—if he wanted drinks; the carriage steps grated, the doors slammed, and the carriage rolled off.

XXXIII

It takes less than an hour in these days by rail from Frankfort to Wiesbaden; at that time the extra post did it in three hours. They changed horses five times. Part of the time Polozov dozed and part of the time he simply shook from side to side, holding a cigar in his teeth; he talked very little; he did not once look out of the window; picturesque views did not interest them; he even announced that 'nature was the death of him!' Sanin did not speak either, nor did he admire the scenery; he had no thought for it. He was all absorbed in reflections and memories. At the stations Polozov paid with exactness, took the time by his watch, and tipped the postillions—more or less—according to their zeal. When they had gone half way, he took two oranges out of the hamper of edibles, and choosing out the better, offered the other to Sanin. Sanin looked steadily at his companion, and suddenly burst out laughing.

'What are you laughing at?' the latter inquired, very carefully peeling his orange with his short white nails.

'What at?' repeated Sanin. 'Why, at our journey together.'

'What about it?' Polozov inquired again, dropping into his mouth one of the longitudinal sections into which an orange parts.

'It's so very strange. Yesterday I must confess I thought no more of you than of the Emperor of China, and to-day I'm driving with you to sell my estate to your wife, of whom, too, I have not the slightest idea.'

'Anything may happen,' responded Polozov. 'When you've lived a bit longer, you won't be surprised at anything. For instance, can you fancy me riding as an orderly officer? But I did, and the Grand Duke Mihail Pavlovitch gave the order, 'Trot! let him trot, that fat cornet! Trot now! Look sharp!'

Sanin scratched behind his ear.

'Tell me, please, Ippolit Sidorovitch, what is your wife like? What is her character? It's very necessary for me to know that, you see.'

'It was very well for him to shout, "Trot!"' Polozov went on with sudden vehemence, 'But me! how about me? I thought to myself, "You can take your honours and epaulettes—and leave me in peace!" But ... you asked about my wife? What my wife is? A person like any one else. Don't wear your heart upon your sleeve with her—she doesn't like that. The great thing is to talk a lot to her ... something for her to laugh at. Tell her about your love, or something ... but make it more amusing, you know.'

'How more amusing?'

'Oh, you told me, you know, that you were in love, wanting to get married. Well, then, describe that.'

Sanin was offended. 'What do you find laughable in that?'

Polozov only rolled his eyes. The juice from the orange was trickling down his chin.

'Was it your wife sent you to Frankfort to shop for her?' asked Sanin after a short time.

'Yes, it was she.'

'What are the purchases?'

'Toys, of course.'

'Toys? have you any children?'

Polozov positively moved away from Sanin.

'That's likely! What do I want with children? Feminine fallals ... finery. For the toilet.'

'Do you mean to say you understand such things?'

'To be sure I do.'

'But didn't you tell me you didn't interfere in any of your wife's affairs?'

'I don't in any other. But this ... is no consequence. To pass the time—one may do it. And my wife has confidence in my taste. And I'm a first-rate hand at bargaining.'

Polozov began to speak by jerks; he was exhausted already. 'And is your wife very rich?'

'Rich; yes, rather! Only she keeps the most of it for herself.'

'But I expect you can't complain either?'

'Well, I'm her husband. I'm hardly likely not to get some benefit from it! And I'm of use to her. With me she can do just as she likes! I'm easy-going!'

Polozov wiped his face with a silk handkerchief and puffed painfully, as though to say, 'Have mercy on me; don't force me to utter another word. You see how hard it is for me.'

Sanin left him in peace, and again sank into meditation.

* * * * *

The hotel in Wiesbaden, before which the carriage stopped, was exactly like a palace. Bells were promptly set ringing in its inmost recesses; a fuss and bustle arose; men of good appearance in black frock-coats skipped out at the principal entrance; a door-keeper who was a blaze of gold opened the carriage doors with a flourish.
Like some triumphant general Polozov alighted and began to ascend a staircase strewn with rugs and smelling of agreeable perfumes. To him flew up another man, also very well dressed but with a Russian face—his valet. Polozov observed to him that for the future he should always take him everywhere with him, for the night before at Frankfort, he, Polozov, had been left for the night without hot water! The valet portrayed his horror on his face, and bending down quickly, took off his master's goloshes.
'Is Maria Nikolaevna at home?' inquired Polozov.
'Yes, sir. Madam is pleased to be dressing. Madam is pleased to be dining to-night at the Countess Lasunsky's.'
'Ah! there?... Stay! There are things there in the carriage; get them all yourself and bring them up. And you, Dmitri Pavlovitch,' added Polozov, 'take a room for yourself and come in in three-quarters of an hour. We will dine together.'
Polozov waddled off, while Sanin asked for an inexpensive room for himself; and after setting his attire to rights, and resting a little, he repaired to the immense apartment occupied by his Serenity (Durchlaucht) Prince von Polozov.
He found this 'prince' enthroned in a luxurious velvet arm-chair in the middle of a most magnificent drawing-room. Sanin's phlegmatic friend had already had time to have a bath and to array himself in a most sumptuous satin dressing-gown; he had put a crimson fez on his head. Sanin approached him and scrutinised him for some time. Polozov was sitting rigid as an idol; he did not even turn his face in his direction, did not even move an eyebrow, did not utter a sound. It was truly a sublime spectacle! After having admired him for a couple of minutes, Sanin was on the point of speaking, of breaking this hallowed silence, when suddenly the door from the next room was thrown open, and in the doorway appeared a young and beautiful lady in a white silk dress trimmed with black lace, and with diamonds on her arms and neck—Maria Nikolaevna Polozov. Her thick fair hair fell on both sides of her head, braided, but not fastened up into a knot.

XXXIV

'Ah, I beg your pardon!' she said with a smile half-embarrassed, half-ironical, instantly taking hold of one end of a plait of her hair and fastening on Sanin her large, grey, clear eyes.
'I did not think you had come yet.'
'Sanin, Dmitri Pavlovitch—known him from a boy,' observed Polozov, as before not turning towards him and not getting up, but pointing at him with one finger.
'Yes.... I know.... You told me before. Very glad to make your acquaintance. But I wanted to ask you, Ippolit Sidorovitch.... My maid seems to have lost her senses to-day ...'
'To do your hair up?'
'Yes, yes, please. I beg your pardon,' Maria Nikolaevna repeated with the same smile. She nodded to Sanin, and turning swiftly, vanished through the doorway, leaving behind her a fleeting but graceful impression of a charming neck, exquisite shoulders, an exquisite figure.
Polozov got up, and rolling ponderously, went out by the same door.
Sanin did not doubt for a single second that his presence in 'Prince Polozov's' drawing-room was a fact perfectly well known to its mistress; the whole point of her entry had been the display of her hair, which was certainly beautiful. Sanin was inwardly delighted indeed at this freak on the part of Madame Polozov; if, he thought, she is anxious to impress me, to dazzle me, perhaps, who knows, she will be accommodating about the price of the estate. His heart was so full of Gemma that all other women had absolutely no significance for him; he hardly noticed them; and this time he went no further than thinking, 'Yes, it was the truth they told me; that lady's really magnificent to look at!'
But had he not been in such an exceptional state of mind he would most likely have expressed himself differently; Maria Nikolaevna Polozov, by birth Kolishkin, was a very striking personality. And not that she

was of a beauty to which no exception could be taken; traces of her plebeian origin were rather clearly apparent in her. Her forehead was low, her nose rather fleshy and turned up; she could boast neither of the delicacy of her skin nor of the elegance of her hands and feet—but what did all that matter? Any one meeting her would not, to use Pushkin's words, have stood still before 'the holy shrine of beauty,' but before the sorcery of a half-Russian, half-Gipsy woman's body in its full flower and full power … and he would have been nothing loath to stand still!

But Gemma's image preserved Sanin like the three-fold armour of which the poets sing.

Ten minutes later Maria Nikolaevna appeared again, escorted by her husband. She went up to Sanin … and her walk was such that some eccentrics of that—alas!—already, distant day, were simply crazy over her walk alone. 'That woman, when she comes towards one, seems as though she is bringing all the happiness of one's life to meet one,' one of them used to say. She went up to Sanin, and holding out her hand to him, said in her caressing and, as it were, subdued voice in Russian, 'You will wait for me, won't you? I'll be back soon.' Sanin bowed respectfully, while Maria Nikolaevna vanished behind the curtain over the outside door; and as she vanished turned her head back over her shoulder, and smiled again, and again left behind her the same impression of grace.

When she smiled, not one and not two, but three dimples came out on each cheek, and her eyes smiled more than her lips—long, crimson, juicy lips with two tiny moles on the left side of them.

Polozov waddled into the room and again established himself in the arm-chair. He was speechless as before; but from time to time a queer smile puffed out his colourless and already wrinkled cheeks. He looked like an old man, though he was only three years older than Sanin.

The dinner with which he regaled his guest would of course have satisfied the most exacting gourmand, but to Sanin it seemed endless, insupportable! Polozov ate slowly, 'with feeling, with judgment, with deliberation,' bending attentively over his plate, and sniffing at almost every morsel. First he rinsed his mouth with wine, then swallowed it and smacked his lips…. Over the roast meat he suddenly began to talk—but of what? Of merino sheep, of which he was intending to order a whole flock, and in such detail, with such tenderness, using all the while endearing pet names for them. After drinking a cup of coffee, hot to boiling point (he had several times in a voice of tearful irritation mentioned to the waiter that he had been served the evening before with coffee, cold—cold as ice!) and bitten off the end of a Havannah cigar with his crooked yellow teeth, he dropped off, as his habit was, into a nap, to the intense delight of Sanin, who began walking up and down with noiseless steps on the soft carpet, and dreaming of his life with Gemma and of what news he would bring back to her. Polozov, however, awoke, as he remarked himself, earlier than usual—he had slept only an hour and a half—and after drinking a glass of iced seltzer water, and swallowing eight spoonfuls of jam, Russian jam, which his valet brought him in a dark-green genuine 'Kiev' jar, and without which, in his own words, he could not live, he stared with his swollen eyes at Sanin and asked him wouldn't he like to play a game of 'fools' with him. Sanin agreed readily; he was afraid that Polozov would begin talking again about lambs and ewes and fat tails. The host and the visitor both adjourned to the drawing-room, the waiter brought in the cards, and the game began, not,—of course, for money.

At this innocent diversion Maria Nikolaevna found them on her return from the Countess Lasunsky's. She laughed aloud directly she came into the room and saw the cards and the open card-table. Sanin jumped up, but she cried, 'Sit still; go on with the game. I'll change my dress directly and come back to you,' and vanished again with a swish of her dress, pulling off her gloves as she went.

She did in fact return very soon. Her evening dress she had exchanged for a full lilac silk tea-gown, with open hanging sleeves; a thick twisted cord was fastened round her waist. She sat down by her husband, and, waiting till he was left 'fool,' said to him, 'Come, dumpling, that's enough!' (At the word 'dumpling' Sanin glanced at her in surprise, and she smiled gaily, answering his look with a look, and displaying all the dimples on her cheeks.) 'I see you are sleepy; kiss my hand and get along; and Monsieur Sanin and I will have a chat together alone.'

'I'm not sleepy,' observed Polozov, getting up ponderously from his easy-chair; 'but as for getting along, I'm ready to get along and to kiss your hand.' She gave him the palm of her hand, still smiling and looking at Sanin.

Polozov, too, looked at him, and went away without taking leave of him.

'Well, tell me, tell me,' said Maria Nikolaevna eagerly, setting both her bare elbows on the table and impatiently tapping the nails of one hand against the nails of the other, 'Is it true, they say, you are going to be married?'

As she said these words, Maria Nikolaevna positively bent her head a little on one side so as to look more intently and piercingly into Sanin's eyes.

XXXV

The free and easy deportment of Madame Polozov would probably for the first moment have disconcerted Sanin—though he was not quite a novice and had knocked about the world a little—if he had not again seen in this very freedom and familiarity a good omen for his undertaking. 'We must humour this rich lady's caprices,' he decided inwardly; and as unconstrainedly as she had questioned him he answered, 'Yes; I am going to be married.'

'To whom? To a foreigner?'

'Yes.'

'Did you get acquainted with her lately? In Frankfort?'

'Yes.'

'And what is she? May I know?'

'Certainly. She is a confectioner's daughter.'

Maria Nikolaevna opened her eyes wide and lifted her eyebrows.

'Why, this is delightful,' she commented in a drawling voice; 'this is exquisite! I imagined that young men like you were not to be met with anywhere in these days. A confectioner's daughter!'

'I see that surprises you,' observed Sanin with some dignity; 'but in the first place, I have none of these prejudices …'

'In the first place, it doesn't surprise me in the least,' Maria Nikolaevna interrupted; 'I have no prejudices either. I'm the daughter of a peasant myself. There! what can you say to that? What does surprise and delight me is to have come across a man who's not afraid to love. You do love her, I suppose?'

'Yes.'

'Is she very pretty?'

Sanin was slightly stung by this last question.... However, there was no drawing back.

'You know, Maria Nikolaevna,' he began, 'every man thinks the face of his beloved better than all others; but my betrothed is really beautiful.'

'Really? In what style? Italian? antique?'

'Yes; she has very regular features.'

'You have not got her portrait with you?'

'No.' (At that time photography was not yet talked off. Daguerrotypes had hardly begun to be common.)

'What's her name?'

'Her name is Gemma.'

'And yours?'

'Dimitri.'

'And your father's?'

'Pavlovitch.'

'Do you know,' Maria Nikolaevna said, still in the same drawling voice, 'I like you very much, Dimitri Pavlovitch. You must be an excellent fellow. Give me your hand. Let us be friends.'

She pressed his hand tightly in her beautiful, white, strong fingers. Her hand was a little smaller than his hand, but much warmer and smoother and whiter and more full of life.

'Only, do you know what strikes me?'

'What?'

'You won't be angry? No? You say she is betrothed to you. But was that … was that quite necessary?'

Sanin frowned. 'I don't understand you, Maria Nikolaevna.'

Maria Nikolaevna gave a soft low laugh, and shaking her head tossed back the hair that was falling on her cheeks. 'Decidedly—he's delightful,' she commented half pensively, half carelessly. 'A perfect knight! After that, there's no believing in the people who maintain that the race of idealists is extinct!'

Maria Nikolaevna talked Russian all the time, an astonishingly pure true Moscow Russian, such as the people, not the nobles speak.
'You've been brought up at home, I expect, in a God-fearing, old orthodox family?' she queried. 'You're from what province?'
'Tula.'
'Oh! so we're from the same part. My father … I daresay you know who my father was?'
'Yes, I know.'
'He was born in Tula…. He was a Tula man. Well … well. Come, let us get to business now.'
'That is … how come to business? What do you mean to say by that?'
Maria Nikolaevna half-closed her eyes. 'Why, what did you come here for?' (when she screwed up her eyes, their expression became very kindly and a little bantering, when she opened them wide, into their clear, almost cold brilliancy, there came something-ill-natured … something menacing. Her eyes gained a peculiar beauty from her eyebrows, which were thick, and met in the centre, and had the smoothness of sable fur).
'Don't you want me to buy your estate? You want money for your nuptials? Don't you?'
'Yes.'
'And do you want much?'
'I should be satisfied with a few thousand francs at first. Your husband knows my estate. You can consult him—I would take a very moderate price.'
Maria Nikolaevna tossed her head from left to right. '*In the first place,*' she began in deliberate tones, drumming with the tips of her fingers on the cuff of Sanin's coat, 'I am not in the habit of consulting my husband, except about matters of dress—he's my right hand in that; *and in the second place*, why do you say that you will fix a low price? I don't want to take advantage of your being very much in love at the moment, and ready to make any sacrifices…. I won't accept sacrifices of any kind from you. What? Instead of encouraging you … come, how is one to express it properly?—in your noble sentiments, eh? am I to fleece you? that's not my way. I can be hard on people, on occasion—only not in that way.'
Sanin was utterly unable to make out whether she was laughing at him or speaking seriously, and only said to himself: 'Oh, I can see one has to mind what one's about with you!'
A man-servant came in with a Russian samovar, tea-things, cream, biscuits, etc., on a big tray; he set all these good things on the table between Sanin and Madame Polozov, and retired.
She poured him out a cup of tea. 'You don't object?' she queried, as she put sugar in his cup with her fingers … though sugar-tongs were lying close by.
'Oh, please!… From such a lovely hand …'
He did not finish his phrase, and almost choked over a sip of tea, while she watched him attentively and brightly.
'I spoke of a moderate price for my land,' he went on, 'because as you are abroad just now, I can hardly suppose you have a great deal of cash available, and in fact, I feel myself that the sale … the purchase of my land, under such conditions is something exceptional, and I ought to take that into consideration.'
Sanin got confused, and lost the thread of what he was saying, while Maria Nikolaevna softly leaned back in her easy-chair, folded her arms, and watched him with the same attentive bright look. He was silent at last.
'Never mind, go on, go on,' she said, as it were coming to his aid;
'I'm listening to you. I like to hear you; go on talking.'
Sanin fell to describing his estate, how many acres it contained, and where it was situated, and what were its agricultural advantages, and what profit could be made from it … he even referred to the picturesque situation of the house; while Maria Nikolaevna still watched him, and watched more and more intently and radiantly, and her lips faintly stirred, without smiling: she bit them. He felt awkward at last; he was silent a second time.
'Dimitri Pavlovitch' began Maria Nikolaevna, and sank into thought again…. 'Dimitri Pavlovitch,' she repeated…. 'Do you know what: I am sure the purchase of your estate will be a very profitable transaction for me, and that we shall come to terms; but you must give me two days…. Yes, two days' grace. You are able to endure two days' separation from your betrothed, aren't you? Longer I won't keep you against your will—I give you my word of honour. But if you want five or six thousand francs at once, I am ready with great pleasure to let you have it as a loan, and then we'll settle later.'
Sanin got up. 'I must thank you, Maria Nikolaevna, for your kindhearted and friendly readiness to do a service to a man almost unknown to you. But if that is your decided wish, then I prefer to await your decision about my estate—I will stay here two days.'

'Yes; that is my wish, Dimitri Pavlovitch. And will it be very hard for you? Very? Tell me.'
'I love my betrothed, Maria Nikolaevna, and to be separated from her is hard for me.'
'Ah! you're a heart of gold!' Maria Nikolaevna commented with a sigh.
'I promise not to torment you too much. Are you going?'
'It is late,' observed Sanin.
'And you want to rest after your journey, and your game of "fools" with my husband. Tell me, were you a great friend of Ippolit Sidorovitch, my husband?'
'We were educated at the same school.'
'And was he the same then?'
'The same as what?' inquired Sanin. Maria Nikolaevna burst out laughing, and laughed till she was red in the face; she put her handkerchief to her lips, rose from her chair, and swaying as though she were tired, went up to Sanin, and held out her hand to him.
He bowed over it, and went towards the door.
'Come early to-morrow—do you hear?' she called after him. He looked back as he went out of the room, and saw that she had again dropped into an easy-chair, and flung both arms behind her head. The loose sleeves of her tea-gown fell open almost to her shoulders, and it was impossible not to admit that the pose of the arms, that the whole figure, was enchantingly beautiful.

XXXVI

Long after midnight the lamp was burning in Sanin's room. He sat down to the table and wrote to 'his Gemma.' He told her everything; he described the Polozovs—husband and wife—but, more than all, enlarged on his own feelings, and ended by appointing a meeting with her in three days!!! (with three marks of exclamation). Early in the morning he took this letter to the post, and went for a walk in the garden of the Kurhaus, where music was already being played. There were few people in it as yet; he stood before the arbour in which the orchestra was placed, listened to an adaptation of airs from 'Robert le Diable,' and after drinking some coffee, turned into a solitary side walk, sat down on a bench, and fell into a reverie. The handle of a parasol gave him a rapid, and rather vigorous, thump on the shoulder. He started.... Before him in a light, grey-green barége dress, in a white tulle hat, and *suède* gloves, stood Maria Nikolaevna, fresh and rosy as a summer morning, though the languor of sound unbroken sleep had not yet quite vanished from her movements and her eyes.
'Good-morning,' she said. 'I sent after you to-day, but you'd already gone out. I've only just drunk my second glass—they're making me drink the water here, you know—whatever for, there's no telling ... am I not healthy enough? And now I have to walk for a whole hour. Will you be my companion? And then we'll have some coffee.'
'I've had some already,' Sanin observed, getting up; 'but I shall be very glad to have a walk with you.'
'Very well, give me your arm then; don't be afraid: your betrothed is not here—she won't see you.'
Sanin gave a constrained smile. He experienced a disagreeable sensation every time Maria Nikolaevna referred to Gemma. However, he made haste to bend towards her obediently.... Maria Nikolaevna's arm slipped slowly and softly into his arm, and glided over it, and seemed to cling tight to it.
'Come—this way,' she said to him, putting up her open parasol over her shoulder. 'I'm quite at home in this park; I will take you to the best places. And do you know what? (she very often made use of this expression), we won't talk just now about that sale, we'll have a thorough discussion of that after lunch; but you must tell me now about yourself ... so that I may know whom I have to do with. And afterwards, if you like, I will tell you about myself. Do you agree?'
'But, Maria Nikolaevna, what interest can there be for you ...'
'Stop, stop. You don't understand me. I don't want to flirt with you.' Maria Nikolaevna shrugged her shoulders. 'He's got a betrothed like an antique statue, is it likely I am going to flirt with him? But you've something to sell, and I'm the purchaser. I want to know what your goods are like. Well, of course, you must show what they are like. I don't only want to know what I'm buying, but whom I'm buying from. That was

my father's rule. Come, begin … come, if not from childhood—come now, have you been long abroad? And where have you been up till now? Only don't walk so fast, we're in no hurry.'

'I came here from Italy, where I spent several months.'

'Ah, you feel, it seems, a special attraction towards everything Italian. It's strange you didn't find your lady-love there. Are you fond of art? of pictures? or more of music?'

'I am fond of art.… I like everything beautiful.'

'And music?'

'I like music too.'

'Well, I don't at all. I don't care for anything but Russian songs—and that in the country and in the spring—with dancing, you know … red shirts, wreaths of beads, the young grass in the meadows, the smell of smoke … delicious! But we weren't talking of me. Go on, tell me.'

Maria Nikolaevna walked on, and kept looking at Sanin. She was tall—her face was almost on a level with his face.

He began to talk—at first reluctantly, unskilfully—but afterwards he talked more freely, chattered away in fact. Maria Nikolaevna was a very good listener; and moreover she seemed herself so frank, that she led others unconsciously on to frankness. She possessed that great gift of 'intimateness'—*le terrible don de la familiarité*—to which Cardinal Retz refers. Sanin talked of his travels, of his life in Petersburg, of his youth.… Had Maria Nikolaevna been a lady of fashion, with refined manners, he would never have opened out so; but she herself spoke of herself as a 'good fellow,' who had no patience with ceremony of any sort; it was in those words that she characterised herself to Sanin. And at the same time this 'good fellow' walked by his side with feline grace, slightly bending towards him, and peeping into his face; and this 'good fellow' walked in the form of a young feminine creature, full of the tormenting, fiery, soft and seductive charm, of which—for the undoing of us poor weak sinful men—only Slav natures are possessed, and but few of them, and those never of pure Slav blood, with no foreign alloy. Sanin's walk with Maria Nikolaevna, Sanin's talk with Maria Nikolaevna lasted over an hour. And they did not stop once; they kept walking about the endless avenues of the park, now mounting a hill and admiring the view as they went, and now going down into the valley, and getting hidden in the thick shadows,—and all the while arm-in-arm. At times Sanin felt positively irritated; he had never walked so long with Gemma, his darling Gemma … but this lady had simply taken possession of him, and there was no escape! 'Aren't you tired?' he said to her more than once. 'I never get tired,' she answered. Now and then they met other people walking in the park; almost all of them bowed—some respectfully, others even cringingly. To one of them, a very handsome, fashionably dressed dark man, she called from a distance with the best Parisian accent, '*Comte, vous savez, il ne faut pas venir me voir—ni aujourd'hui ni demain.*' The man took off his hat, without speaking, and dropped a low bow.

'Who's that?' asked Sanin with the bad habit of asking questions characteristic of all Russians.

'Oh, a Frenchman, there are lots of them here … He's dancing attendance on me too. It's time for our coffee, though. Let's go home; you must be hungry by this time, I should say. My better half must have got his eye-peeps open by now.'

'Better half! Eye-peeps!' Sanin repeated to himself … 'And speaks French so well … what a strange creature!'

* * * * *

Maria Nikolaevna was not mistaken. When she went back into the hotel with Sanin, her 'better half or 'dumpling' was already seated, the invariable fez on his head, before a table laid for breakfast.

'I've been waiting for you!' he cried, making a sour face. 'I was on the point of having coffee without you.'

'Never mind, never mind,' Maria Nikolaevna responded cheerfully. 'Are you angry? That's good for you; without that you'd turn into a mummy altogether. Here I've brought a visitor. Make haste and ring! Let us have coffee—the best coffee—in Saxony cups on a snow-white cloth!'

She threw off her hat and gloves, and clapped her hands.

Polozov looked at her from under his brows.

'What makes you so skittish to-day, Maria Nikolaevna?' he said in an undertone.

'That's no business of yours, Ippolit Sidoritch! Ring! Dimitri Pavlovitch, sit down and have some coffee for the second time. Ah, how nice it is to give orders! There's no pleasure on earth like it!'

'When you're obeyed,' grumbled her husband again.

'Just so, when one's obeyed! That's why I'm so happy! Especially with you. Isn't it so, dumpling? Ah, here's the coffee.'

On the immense tray, which the waiter brought in, there lay also a playbill. Maria Nikolaevna snatched it up at once.
'A drama!' she pronounced with indignation, 'a German drama. No matter; it's better than a German comedy. Order a box for me—*baignoire*—or no … better the*Fremden-Loge*,' she turned to the waiter. 'Do you hear: the *Fremden-Loge* it must be!'
'But if the *Fremden-Loge* has been already taken by his excellency, the director of the town (*seine Excellenz der Herr Stadt-Director*),' the waiter ventured to demur.
'Give his excellency ten *thalers*, and let the box be mine! Do you hear!'
The waiter bent his head humbly and mournfully.
'Dimitri Pavlovitch, you will go with me to the theatre? the German actors are awful, but you will go … Yes? Yes? How obliging you are! Dumpling, are you not coming?
'You settle it,' Polozov observed into the cup he had lifted to his lips.
'Do you know what, you stay at home. You always go to sleep at the theatre, and you don't understand much German. I'll tell you what you'd better do, write an answer to the overseer—you remember, about our mill … about the peasants' grinding. Tell him that I won't have it, and I won't and that's all about it! There's occupation for you for the whole evening.'
'All right,' answered Polozov.
'Well then, that's first-rate. You're a darling. And now, gentlemen, as we have just been speaking of my overseer, let's talk about our great business. Come, directly the waiter has cleared the table, you shall tell me all, Dimitri Pavlovitch, about your estate, what price you will sell it for, how much you want paid down in advance, everything, in fact! (At last, thought Sanin, thank God!) You have told me something about it already, you remember, you described your garden delightfully, but dumpling wasn't here…. Let him hear, he may pick a hole somewhere! I'm delighted to think that I can help you to get married, besides, I promised you that I would go into your business after lunch, and I always keep my promises, isn't that the truth, Ippolit Sidoritch?'
Polozov rubbed his face with his open hand. 'The truth's the truth.
You don't deceive any one.'
'Never! and I never will deceive any one. Well, Dimitri Pavlovitch, expound the case as we express it in the senate.'

XXXVII

Sanin proceeded to expound his case, that is to say, again, a second time, to describe his property, not touching this time on the beauties of nature, and now and then appealing to Polozov for confirmation of his 'facts and figures.' But Polozov simply gasped and shook his head, whether in approval or disapproval, it would have puzzled the devil, one might fancy, to decide. However, Maria Nikolaevna stood in no need of his aid. She exhibited commercial and administrative abilities that were really astonishing! She was familiar with all the ins-and-outs of farming; she asked questions about everything with great exactitude, went into every point; every word of hers went straight to the root of the matter, and hit the nail on the head. Sanin had not expected such a close inquiry, he had not prepared himself for it. And this inquiry lasted for fully an hour and a half. Sanin experienced all the sensations of the criminal on his trial, sitting on a narrow bench confronted by a stern and penetrating judge. 'Why, it's a cross-examination!' he murmured to himself dejectedly. Maria Nikolaevna kept laughing all the while, as though it were a joke; but Sanin felt none the more at ease for that; and when in the course of the 'cross-examination' it turned out that he had not clearly realised the exact meaning of the words 'repartition' and 'tilth,' he was in a cold perspiration all over.
'Well, that's all right!' Maria Nikolaevna decided at last. 'I know your estate now … as well as you do. What price do you suggest per soul?' (At that time, as every one knows, the prices of estates were reckoned by the souls living as serfs on them.)
'Well … I imagine … I could not take less than five hundred roubles for each,' Sanin articulated with difficulty. O Pantaleone, Pantaleone, where were you! This was when you ought to have cried again, 'Barbari!'

Maria Nikolaevna turned her eyes upwards as though she were calculating.
'Well?' she said at last. 'I think there's no harm in that price. But I reserved for myself two days' grace, and you must wait till to-morrow. I imagine we shall come to an arrangement, and then you will tell me how much you want paid down. And now, *basta cosi*!' she cried, noticing Sanin was about to make some reply. 'We've spent enough time over filthy lucre … *à demain les affaires*. Do you know what, I'll let you go now … (she glanced at a little enamelled watch, stuck in her belt) … till three o'clock … I must let you rest. Go and play roulette.'
'I never play games of chance,' observed Sanin.
'Really? Why, you're a paragon. Though I don't either. It's stupid throwing away one's money when one's no chance. But go into the gambling saloon, and look at the faces. Very comic ones there are there. There's one old woman with a rustic headband and a moustache, simply delicious! Our prince there's another, a good one too. A majestic figure with a nose like an eagle's, and when he puts down a *thaler*, he crosses himself under his waistcoat. Read the papers, go a walk, do what you like, in fact. But at three o'clock I expect you … *de pied ferme*. We shall have to dine a little earlier. The theatre among these absurd Germans begins at half-past six. She held out her hand. '*Sans rancune, n'est-ce pas?*'
'Really, Maria Nikolaevna, what reason have I to be annoyed?'
'Why, because I've been tormenting you. Wait a little, you'll see. There's worse to come,' she added, fluttering her eyelids, and all her dimples suddenly came out on her flushing cheeks. 'Till we meet!'
Sanin bowed and went out. A merry laugh rang out after him, and in the looking-glass which he was passing at that instant, the following scene was reflected: Maria Nikolaevna had pulled her husband's fez over his eyes, and he was helplessly struggling with both hands.

XXXVIII

Oh, what a deep sigh of delight Sanin heaved, when he found himself in his room! Indeed, Maria Nikolaevna had spoken the truth, he needed rest, rest from all these new acquaintances, collisions, conversations, from this suffocating atmosphere which was affecting his head and his heart, from this enigmatical, uninvited intimacy with a woman, so alien to him! And when was all this taking place? Almost the day after he had learnt that Gemma loved him, after he had become betrothed to her. Why, it was sacrilege! A thousand times he mentally asked forgiveness of his pure chaste dove, though he could not really blame himself for anything; a thousand times over he kissed the cross she had given him. Had he not the hope of bringing the business, for which he had come to Wiesbaden, to a speedy and successful conclusion, he would have rushed off headlong, back again, to sweet Frankfort, to that dear house, now his own home, to her, to throw himself at her loved feet…. But there was no help for it! The cup must be drunk to the dregs, he must dress, go to dinner, and from there to the theatre…. If only she would let him go to-morrow!
One other thing confounded him, angered him; with love, with tenderness, with grateful transport he dreamed of Gemma, of their life together, of the happiness awaiting him in the future, and yet this strange woman, this Madame Polozov persistently floated—no! not floated, poked herself, so Sanin with special vindictiveness expressed it—*poked herself* in and faced his eyes, and he could not rid himself of her image, could not help hearing her voice, recalling her words, could not help being aware even of the special scent, delicate, fresh and penetrating, like the scent of yellow lilies, that was wafted from her garments. This lady was obviously fooling him, and trying in every way to get over him … what for? what did she want? Could it be merely the caprice of a spoiled, rich, and most likely unprincipled woman? And that husband! What a creature he was! What were his relations with her? And why would these questions keep coming into his head, when he, Sanin, had really no interest whatever in either Polozov or his wife? Why could he not drive away that intrusive image, even when he turned with his whole soul to another image, clear and bright as God's sunshine? How, through those almost divine features, dare *those others* force themselves upon him? And not only that; those other features smiled insolently at him. Those grey, rapacious eyes, those dimples, those snake-like tresses, how was it all that seemed to cleave to him, and to shake it all off, and fling it away, he was unable, had not the power?

Nonsense! nonsense! to-morrow it would all vanish and leave no trace.... But would she let him go to-morrow?
Yes.... All these question he put to himself, but the time was moving on to three o'clock, and he put on a black frockcoat and after a turn in the park, went in to the Polozovs!
* * * * *
He found in their drawing-room a secretary of the legation, a very tall light-haired German, with the profile of a horse, and his hair parted down the back of his head (at that time a new fashion), and ... oh, wonder! whom besides? Von Dönhof, the very officer with whom he had fought a few days before! He had not the slightest expectation of meeting him there and could not help being taken aback. He greeted him, however.
'Are you acquainted?' asked Maria Nikolaevna who had not failed to notice Sanin's embarrassment.
'Yes ... I have already had the honour,' said Dönhof, and bending a little aside, in an undertone he added to Maria Nikolaevna, with a smile, 'The very man ... your compatriot ... the Russian ...'
'Impossible!' she exclaimed also in an undertone; she shook her finger at him, and at once began to bid good-bye both to him and the long secretary, who was, to judge by every symptom, head over ears in love with her; he positively gaped every time he looked at her. Dönhof promptly took leave with amiable docility, like a friend of the family who understands at half a word what is expected of him; the secretary showed signs of restiveness, but Maria Nikolaevna turned him out without any kind of ceremony.
'Get along to your sovereign mistress,' she said to him (there was at that time in Wiesbaden a certain princess di Monaco, who looked surprisingly like a *cocotte* of the poorer sort); 'what do you want to stay with a plebeian like me for?'
'Really, dear madam,' protested the luckless secretary,' all the princesses in the world....'
But Maria Nikolaevna was remorseless, and the secretary went away, parting and all.
Maria Nikolaevna was dressed that day very much 'to her advantage,' as our grandmothers used to say. She wore a pink glacé silk dress, with sleeves *à la Fontange*, and a big diamond in each ear. Her eyes sparkled as much as her diamonds; she seemed in a good humour and in high spirits.
She made Sanin sit beside her, and began talking to him about Paris, where she was intending to go in a few days, of how sick she was of Germans, how stupid they were when they tried to be clever, and how inappropriately clever sometimes when they were stupid; and suddenly, point-blank, as they say—*à brûle pourpoint*—asked him, was it true that he had fought a duel with the very officer who had been there just now, only a few days ago, on account of a lady?
'How did you know that?' muttered Sanin, dumfoundered.
'The earth is full of rumours, Dimitri Pavlovitch; but anyway, I know you were quite right, perfectly right, and behaved like a knight. Tell me, was that lady your betrothed?'
Sanin slightly frowned ...
'There, I won't, I won't,' Maria Nikolaevna hastened to say. 'You don't like it, forgive me, I won't do it, don't be angry!' Polozov came in from the next room with a newspaper in his hand. 'What do you want? Or is dinner ready?'
'Dinner'll be ready directly, but just see what I've read in the *Northern Bee* ... Prince Gromoboy is dead.'
Maria Nikolaevna raised her head.
'Ah! I wish him the joys of Paradise! He used,' she turned to Sanin, 'to fill all my rooms with camellias every February on my birthday, But it wasn't worth spending the winter in Petersburg for that. He must have been over seventy, I should say?' she said to her husband.
'Yes, he was. They describe his funeral in the paper. All the court were present. And here's a poem too, of Prince Kovrizhkin's on the occasion.'
'That's nice!'
'Shall I read them? The prince calls him the good man of wise counsel.'
'No, don't. The good man of wise counsel? He was simply the goodman of Tatiana Yurevna. Come to dinner. Life is for the living. Dimitri Pavlovitch, your arm.'
* * * * *
The dinner was, as on the day before, superb, and the meal was a very lively one. Maria Nikolaevna knew how to tell a story ... a rare gift in a woman, and especially in a Russian one! She did not restrict herself in her expressions; her countrywomen received particularly severe treatment at her hands. Sanin was more than once set laughing by some bold and well-directed word. Above all, Maria Nikolaevna had no patience with hypocrisy, cant, and humbug. She discovered it almost everywhere. She, as it were, plumed herself on and boasted of the humble surroundings in which she had begun life. She told rather queer anecdotes of her

relations in the days of her childhood, spoke of herself as quite as much of a clodhopper as Natalya Kirilovna Narishkin. It became apparent to Sanin that she had been through a great deal more in her time than the majority of women of her age.
Polozov ate meditatively, drank attentively, and only occasionally cast first on his wife, then on Sanin, his lightish, dim-looking, but, in reality, very keen eyes.
'What a clever darling you are!' cried Maria Nikolaevna, turning to him; 'how well you carried out all my commissions in Frankfort! I could give you a kiss on your forehead for it, but you're not very keen after kisses.'
'I'm not,' responded Polozov, and he cut a pine-apple with a silver knife.
Maria Nikolaevna looked at him and drummed with her fingers on the table. 'So our bet's on, isn't it?' she said significantly. 'Yes, it's on.'
'All right. You'll lose it.'
Polozov stuck out his chin. 'Well, this time you mustn't be too sanguine, Maria Nikolaevna, maybe you will lose.'
'What is the bet? May I know?' asked Sanin.
'No … not now,' answered Maria Nikolaevna, and she laughed.
It struck seven. The waiter announced that the carriage was ready.
Polozov saw his wife out, and at once waddled back to his easy-chair.
'Mind now! Don't forget the letter to the overseer,' Maria Nikolaevna shouted to him from the hall.
'I'll write, don't worry yourself. I'm a business-like person.'

XXXIX

In the year 1840, the theatre at Wiesbaden was a poor affair even externally, and its company, for affected and pitiful mediocrity, for studious and vulgar commonplaceness, not one hair's-breadth above the level, which might be regarded up to now as the normal one in all German theatres, and which has been displayed in perfection lately by the company in Carlsruhe, under the 'illustrious' direction of Herr Devrient. At the back of the box taken for her 'Serenity Madame von Polozov' (how the waiter devised the means of getting it, God knows, he can hardly have really bribed the stadt-director!) was a little room, with sofas all round it; before she went into the box, Maria Nikolaevna asked Sanin to draw up the screen that shut the box off from the theatre.
'I don't want to be seen,' she said, 'or else they'll be swarming round directly, you know.' She made him sit down beside her with his back to the house so that the box seemed to be empty. The orchestra played the overture from the *Marriage of Figaro*. The curtain rose, the play began.
It was one of those numerous home-raised products in which well-read but talentless authors, in choice, but dead language, studiously and cautiously enunciated some 'profound' or 'vital and palpitating' idea, portrayed a so-called tragic conflict, and produced dulness … an Asiatic dulness, like Asiatic cholera. Maria Nikolaevna listened patiently to half an act, but when the first lover, discovering the treachery of his mistress (he was dressed in a cinnamon-coloured coat with 'puffs' and a plush collar, a striped waistcoat with mother-of-pearl buttons, green trousers with straps of varnished leather, and white chamois leather gloves), when this lover pressed both fists to his bosom, and poking his two elbows out at an acute angle, howled like a dog, Maria Nikolaevna could not stand it.
'The humblest French actor in the humblest little provincial town acts better and more naturally than the highest German celebrity,' she cried in indignation; and she moved away and sat down in the little room at the back. 'Come here,' she said to Sanin, patting the sofa beside her. 'Let's talk.'
Sanin obeyed.
Maria Nikolaevna glanced at him. 'Ah, I see you're as soft as silk! Your wife will have an easy time of it with you. That buffoon,' she went on, pointing with her fan towards the howling actor (he was acting the part of a tutor), 'reminded me of my young days; I, too, was in love with a teacher. It was my first … no, my second passion. The first time I fell in love with a young monk of the Don monastery. I was twelve years old. I only saw him on Sundays. He used to wear a short velvet cassock, smelt of lavender water, and as he made his

way through the crowd with the censer, used to say to the ladies in French, "*Pardon, excusez*" but never lifted his eyes, and he had eyelashes like that!' Maria Nikolaevna marked off with the nail of her middle finger quite half the length of the little finger and showed Sanin. 'My tutor was called—Monsieur Gaston! I must tell you he was an awfully learned and very severe person, a Swiss,—and with such an energetic face! Whiskers black as pitch, a Greek profile, and lips that looked like cast iron! I was afraid of him! He was the only man I have ever been afraid of in my life. He was tutor to my brother, who died ... was drowned. A gipsy woman has foretold a violent death for me too, but that's all moonshine. I don't believe in it. Only fancy Ippolit Sidoritch with a dagger!'

'One may die from something else than a dagger,' observed Sanin.

'All that's moonshine! Are you superstitious? I'm not a bit. What is to be, will be. Monsieur Gaston used to live in our house, in the room over my head. Sometimes I'd wake up at night and hear his footstep—he used to go to bed very late—and my heart would stand still with veneration, or some other feeling. My father could hardly read and write himself, but he gave us an excellent education. Do you know, I learnt Latin!'

'You? learnt Latin?'

'Yes; I did. Monsieur Gaston taught me. I read the *Æneid* with him.
It's a dull thing, but there are fine passages. Do you remember when
Dido and Æneas are in the forest?...'

'Yes, yes, I remember,' Sanin answered hurriedly. He had long ago forgotten all his Latin, and had only very faint notions about the *Æneid.*

Maria Nikolaevna glanced at him, as her way was, a little from one side and looking upwards. 'Don't imagine, though, that I am very learned. Mercy on us! no; I'm not learned, and I've no talents of any sort. I scarcely know how to write ... really; I can't read aloud; nor play the piano, nor draw, nor sew—nothing! That's what I am—there you have me!'

She threw out her hands. 'I tell you all this,' she said, 'first, so as not to hear those fools (she pointed to the stage where at that instant the actor's place was being filled by an actress, also howling, and also with her elbows projecting before her) and secondly, because I'm in your debt; you told me all about yourself yesterday.'

'It was your pleasure to question me,' observed Sanin.

Maria Nikolaevna suddenly turned to him. 'And it's not your pleasure to know just what sort of woman I am? I can't wonder at it, though,' she went on, leaning back again on the sofa cushions. 'A man just going to be married, and for love, and after a duel.... What thoughts could he have for anything else?'

Maria Nikolaevna relapsed into dreamy silence, and began biting the handle of her fan with her big, but even, milkwhite teeth.

And Sanin felt mounting to his head again that intoxication which he had not been able to get rid of for the last two days.

The conversation between him and Maria Nikolaevna was carried on in an undertone, almost in a whisper, and this irritated and disturbed him the more....

When would it all end?

Weak people never put an end to things themselves—they always wait for the end.

Some one sneezed on the stage; this sneeze had been put into the play by the author as the 'comic relief' or 'element'; there was certainly no other comic element in it; and the audience made the most of it; they laughed.

This laugh, too, jarred upon Sanin.

There were moments when he actually did not know whether he was furious or delighted, bored or amused. Oh, if Gemma could have seen him!

'It's really curious,' Maria Nikolaevna began all at once. 'A man informs one and in such a calm voice, "I am going to get married"; but no one calmly says to one, "I'm going to throw myself in the water." And yet what difference is there? It's curious, really.'

Annoyance got the upper hand of Sanin. 'There's a great difference, Maria Nikolaevna! It's not dreadful at all to throw oneself in the water if one can swim; and besides ... as to the strangeness of marriages, if you come to that ...'

He stopped short abruptly and bit his tongue.

Maria Nikolaevna slapped her open hand with her fan.

'Go on, Dimitri Pavlovitch, go on—I know what you were going to say. "If it comes to that, my dear madam, Maria Nikolaevna Polozov," you were going to say, "anything more curious than *your* marriage it would be

impossible to conceive.... I know your husband well, from a child!" That's what you were going to say, you who can swim!'
'Excuse me,' Sanin was beginning....
'Isn't it the truth? Isn't it the truth?' Maria Nikolaevna pronounced insistently.
'Come, look me in the face and tell me I was wrong!'
Sanin did not know what to do with his eyes. 'Well, if you like; it's the truth, if you absolutely insist upon it,' he said at last.
Maria Nikolaevna shook her head. 'Quite so, quite so. Well, and did you ask yourself, you who can swim, what could be the reason of such a strange ... step on the part of a woman, not poor ... and not a fool ... and not ugly? All that does not interest you, perhaps, but no matter. I'll tell you the reason not this minute, but directly the*entr'acte* is over. I am in continual uneasiness for fear some one should come in....'
Maria Nikolaevna had hardly uttered this last word when the outer door actually was half opened, and into the box was thrust a head—red, oily, perspiring, still young, but toothless; with sleek long hair, a pendent nose, huge ears like a bat's, with gold spectacles on inquisitive dull eyes, and a *pince-nez* over the spectacles. The head looked round, saw Maria Nikolaevna, gave a nasty grin, nodded.... A scraggy neck craned in after it....
Maria Nikolaevna shook her handkerchief at it. 'I'm not at home! *Ich bin nicht zu Hause, Herr P....! Ich bin nicht zu Hause.... Ksh-sk! ksh-sh-sh!*'
The head was disconcerted, gave a forced laugh, said with a sort of sob, in imitation of Liszt, at whose feet he had once reverently grovelled, '*Sehr gut, sehr gut!*' and vanished.
'What is that object?' inquired Sanin.
'Oh, a Wiesbaden critic. A literary man or a flunkey, as you like. He is in the pay of a local speculator here, and so is bound to praise everything and be ecstatic over every one, though for his part he is soaked through and through with the nastiest venom, to which he does not dare to give vent. I am afraid he's an awful scandalmonger; he'll run at once to tell every one I'm in the theatre. Well, what does it matter?'
The orchestra played through a waltz, the curtain floated up again....
The grimacing and whimpering began again on the stage.
'Well,' began Maria Nikolaevna, sinking again on to the sofa. 'Since you are here and obliged to sit with me, instead of enjoying the society of your betrothed—don't turn away your eyes and get cross—I understand you, and have promised already to let you go to the other end of the earth—but now hear my confession. Do you care to know what I like more than anything?'
'Freedom,' hazarded Sanin.
Maria Nikolaevna laid her hand on his hand.
'Yes, Dimitri Pavlovitch,' she said, and in her voice there was a note of something special, a sort of unmistakable sincerity and gravity, 'freedom, more than all and before all. And don't imagine I am boasting of this—there is nothing praiseworthy in it; only it's *so* and always will be *so* with me to the day of my death. I suppose it must have been that I saw a great deal of slavery in my childhood and suffered enough from it. Yes, and Monsieur Gaston, my tutor, opened my eyes too. Now you can, perhaps, understand why I married Ippolit Sidoritch: with him I'm free, perfectly free as air, as the wind.... And I knew that before marriage; I knew that with him I should be a free Cossack!'
Maria Nikolaevna paused and flung her fan aside.
'I will tell you one thing more; I have no distaste for reflection ... it's amusing, and indeed our brains are given us for that; but on the consequences of what I do I never reflect, and if I suffer I don't pity myself—not a little bit; it's not worth it. I have a favourite saying: *Cela ne tire pas à conséquence*,—I don't know how to say that in Russian. And after all, what does *tire à consequence*? I shan't be asked to give an account of myself here, you see—in this world; and up there (she pointed upwards with her finger), well, up there—let them manage as best they can. When they come to judge me up there, *I* shall not be *I*! Are you listening to me? Aren't you bored?'
Sanin was sitting bent up. He raised his head. 'I'm not at all bored, Maria Nikolaevna, and I am listening to you with curiosity. Only I ... confess ... I wonder why you say all this to me?'
Maria Nikolaevna edged a little away on the sofa.
'You wonder?... Are you slow to guess? Or so modest?'
Sanin lifted his head higher than before.
'I tell you all this,' Maria Nikolaevna continued in an unmoved tone, which did not, however, at all correspond with the expression of her face, 'because I like you very much; yes, don't be surprised, I'm not

joking; because since I have met you, it would be painful to me that you had a disagreeable recollection of me ... not disagreeable even, that I shouldn't mind, but untrue. That's why I have made you come here, and am staying alone with you and talking to you so openly.... Yes, yes, openly. I'm not telling a lie. And observe, Dimitri Pavlovitch, I know you're in love with another woman, that you're going to be married to her.... Do justice to my disinterestedness! Though indeed it's a good opportunity for you to say in your turn: *Cela ne tire pas à conséquence*!'

She laughed, but her laugh suddenly broke off, and she stayed motionless, as though her own words had suddenly struck her, and in her eyes, usually so gay and bold, there was a gleam of something like timidity, even like sadness.

'Snake! ah, she's a snake!' Sanin was thinking meanwhile; 'but what a lovely snake!'

'Give me my opera-glass,' Maria Nikolaevna said suddenly. 'I want to see whether this *jeune première* really is so ugly. Upon my word, one might fancy the government appointed her in the interests of morality, so that the young men might not lose their heads over her.'

Sanin handed her the opera-glass, and as she took it from him, swiftly, but hardly audibly, she snatched his hand in both of hers.

'Please don't be serious,' she whispered with a smile. 'Do you know what, no one can put fetters on me, but then you see I put no fetters on others. I love freedom, and I don't acknowledge duties—not only for myself. Now move to one side a little, and let us listen to the play.'

Maria Nikolaevna turned her opera-glass upon the stage, and Sanin proceeded to look in the same direction, sitting beside her in the half dark of the box, and involuntarily drinking in the warmth and fragrance of her luxurious body, and as involuntarily turning over and over in his head all she had said during the evening—especially during the last minutes.

XL

The play lasted over an hour longer, but Maria Nikolaevna and Sanin soon gave up looking at the stage. A conversation sprang up between them again, and went on the same lines as before; only this time Sanin was less silent. Inwardly he was angry with himself and with Maria Nikolaevna; he tried to prove to her all the inconsistency of her 'theory,' as though she cared for theories! He began arguing with her, at which she was secretly rejoiced; if a man argues, it means that he is giving in or will give in. He had taken the bait, was giving way, had left off keeping shyly aloof! She retorted, laughed, agreed, mused dreamily, attacked him ... and meanwhile his face and her face were close together, his eyes no longer avoided her eyes.... Those eyes of hers seemed to ramble, seemed to hover over his features, and he smiled in response to them—a smile of civility, but still a smile. It was so much gained for her that he had gone off into abstractions, that he was discoursing upon truth in personal relations, upon duty, the sacredness of love and marriage.... It is well known that these abstract propositions serve admirably as a beginning ... as a starting-point....

People who knew Maria Nikolaevna well used to maintain that when her strong and vigorous personality showed signs of something soft and modest, something almost of maidenly shamefacedness, though one wondered where she could have got it from ... then ... then, things were taking a dangerous turn.

Things had apparently taken such a turn for Sanin.... He would have felt contempt for himself, if he could have succeeded in concentrating his attention for one instant; but he had not time to concentrate his mind nor to despise himself.

She wasted no time. And it all came from his being so very good-looking! One can but exclaim, No man knows what may be his making or his undoing!

The play was over. Maria Nikolaevna asked Sanin to put on her shawl and did not stir, while he wrapped the soft fabric round her really queenly shoulders. Then she took his arm, went out into the corridor, and almost cried out aloud. At the very door of the box Dönhof sprang up like some apparition; while behind his back she got a glimpse of the figure of the Wiesbaden critic. The 'literary man's' oily face was positively radiant with malignancy.

'Is it your wish, madam, that I find you your carriage?' said the young officer addressing Maria Nikolaevna with a quiver of ill-disguised fury in his voice.

'No, thank you,' she answered … 'my man will find it. Stop!' she added in an imperious whisper, and rapidly withdrew drawing Sanin along with her.
'Go to the devil! Why are you staring at me?' Dönhof roared suddenly at the literary man. He had to vent his feelings upon some one!
'*Sehr gut! sehr gut!*' muttered the literary man, and shuffled off.
Maria Nikolaevna's footman, waiting for her in the entrance, found her carriage in no time. She quickly took her seat in it; Sanin leapt in after her. The doors were slammed to, and Maria Nikolaevna exploded in a burst of laughter.
'What are you laughing at?' Sanin inquired.
'Oh, excuse me, please … but it struck me: what if Dönhof were to have another duel with you … on my account…. wouldn't that be wonderful?'
'Are you very great friends with him?' Sanin asked.
'With him? that boy? He's one of my followers. You needn't trouble yourself about him!'
'Oh, I'm not troubling myself at all.'
Maria Nikolaevna sighed. 'Ah, I know you're not. But listen, do you know what, you're such a darling, you mustn't refuse me one last request. Remember in three days' time I am going to Paris, and you are returning to Frankfort…. Shall we ever meet again?'
'What is this request?'
'You can ride, of course?'
'Yes.'
'Well, then, to-morrow morning I'll take you with me, and we'll go a ride together out of the town. We'll have splendid horses. Then we'll come home, wind up our business, and amen! Don't be surprised, don't tell me it's a caprice, and I'm a madcap—all that's very likely—but simply say, I consent.'
Maria Nikolaevna turned her face towards him. It was dark in the carriage, but her eyes glittered even in the darkness.
'Very well, I consent,' said Sanin with a sigh.
'Ah! You sighed!' Maria Nikolaevna mimicked him. 'That means to say, as you've begun, you must go on to the bitter end. But no, no…. You're charming, you're good, and I'll keep my promise. Here's my hand, without a glove on it, the right one, for business. Take it, and have faith in its pressure. What sort of a woman I am, I don't know; but I'm an honest fellow, and one can do business with me.'
Sanin, without knowing very well what he was doing, lifted the hand to his lips. Maria Nikolaevna softly took it, and was suddenly still, and did not speak again till the carriage stopped.
She began getting out…. What was it? Sanin's fancy? or did he really feel on his cheek a swift burning kiss?
'Till to-morrow!' whispered Maria Nikolaevna on the steps, in the light of the four tapers of a candelabrum, held up on her appearance by the gold-laced door-keeper. She kept her eyes cast down. 'Till to-morrow!'
When he got back to his room, Sanin found on the table a letter from Gemma. He felt a momentary dismay, and at once made haste to rejoice over it to disguise his dismay from himself. It consisted of a few lines. She was delighted at the 'successful opening of negotiations,' advised him to be patient, and added that all at home were well, and were already rejoicing at the prospect of seeing him back again. Sanin felt the letter rather stiff, he took pen and paper, however … and threw it all aside again. 'Why write? I shall be back myself to-morrow … it's high time!'
He went to bed immediately, and tried to get to sleep as quickly as possible. If he had stayed up and remained on his legs, he would certainly have begun thinking about Gemma, and he was for some reason … ashamed to think of her. His conscience was stirring within him. But he consoled himself with the reflection that to-morrow it would all be over for ever, and he would take leave for good of this feather-brained lady, and would forget all this rotten idiocy!…
Weak people in their mental colloquies, eagerly make use of strong expressions.
Et puis ... cela ne tire pas à consequence!

XLI

Such were Sanin's thoughts, as he went to bed; but what he thought next morning when Maria Nikolaevna knocked impatiently at his door with the coral handle of her riding-whip, when he saw her in the doorway, with the train of a dark-blue riding habit over her arm, with a man's small hat on her thickly coiled curls, with a veil thrown back over her shoulder, with a smile of invitation on her lips, in her eyes, over all her face—what he thought then—history does not record.

'Well? are you ready?' rang out a joyous voice.

Sanin buttoned his coat, and took his hat in silence. Maria Nikolaevna flung him a bright look, nodded to him, and ran swiftly down the staircase. And he ran after her.

The horses were already waiting in the street at the steps. There were three of them, a golden chestnut thorough-bred mare, with a thin-lipped mouth, that showed the teeth, with black prominent eyes, and legs like a stag's, rather thin but beautifully shaped, and full of fire and spirit, for Maria Nikolaevna; a big, powerful, rather thick-set horse, raven black all over, for Sanin; the third horse was destined for the groom. Maria Nikolaevna leaped adroitly on to her mare, who stamped and wheeled round, lifting her tail, and sinking on to her haunches. But Maria Nikolaevna, who was a first-rate horse-woman, reined her in; they had to take leave of Polozov, who in his inevitable fez and in an open dressing-gown, came out on to the balcony, and from there waved a *batiste* handkerchief, without the faintest smile, rather a frown, in fact, on his face. Sanin too mounted his horse; Maria Nikolaevna saluted Polozov with her whip, then gave her mare a lash with it on her arched and flat neck. The mare reared on her hind legs, made a dash forward, moving with a smart and shortened step, quivering in every sinew, biting the air and snorting abruptly. Sanin rode behind, and looked at Maria Nikolaevna; her slender supple figure, moulded by close-fitting but easy stays, swayed to and fro with self-confident grace and skill. She turned her head and beckoned him with her eyes alone. He came alongside of her.

'See now, how delightful it is,' she said. 'I tell you at the last, before parting, you are charming, and you shan't regret it.'

As she uttered those last words, she nodded her head several times as if to confirm them and make him feel their full weight.

She seemed so happy that Sanin was simply astonished; her face even wore at times that sedate expression which children sometimes have when they are very ... very much pleased.

They rode at a walking pace for the short distance to the city walls, but then started off at a vigorous gallop along the high road. It was magnificent, real summer weather; the wind blew in their faces, and sang and whistled sweetly in their ears. They felt very happy; the sense of youth, health and life, of free eager onward motion, gained possession of both; it grew stronger every instant.

Maria Nikolaevna reined in her mare, and again went at a walking pace;

Sanin followed her example.

'This,' she began with a deep blissful sigh, 'this now is the only thing worth living for. When you succeed in doing what you want to, what seemed impossible—come, enjoy it, heart and soul, to the last drop!' She passed her hand across her throat. 'And how good and kind one feels oneself then! I now, at this moment ... how good I feel! I feel as if I could embrace the whole world! No, not the whole world.... That man now I couldn't.' She pointed with her whip at a poorly dressed old man who was stealing along on one side. 'But I am ready to make him happy. Here, take this,' she shouted loudly in German, and she flung a net purse at his feet. The heavy little bag (leather purses were not thought of at that time) fell with a ring on to the road. The old man was astounded, stood still, while Maria Nikolaevna chuckled, and put her mare into a gallop.

'Do you enjoy riding so much?' Sanin asked, as he overtook her.

Maria Nikolaevna reined her mare in once more: only in this way could she bring her to a stop.

'I only wanted to get away from thanks. If any one thanks me, he spoils my pleasure. You see I didn't do that for his sake, but for my own. How dare he thank me? I didn't hear what you asked me.'

'I asked ... I wanted to know what makes you so happy to-day.'

'Do you know what,' said Maria Nikolaevna; either she had again not heard Sanin's question, or she did not consider it necessary to answer it. 'I'm awfully sick of that groom, who sticks up there behind us, and most likely does nothing but wonder when we gentlefolks are going home again. How shall we get rid of him?' She hastily pulled a little pocket-book out of her pocket. 'Send him back to the town with a note? No ... that won't do. Ah! I have it! What's that in front of us? Isn't it an inn?'

Sanin looked in the direction she pointed. 'Yes, I believe it is an inn.'
'Well, that's first-rate. I'll tell him to stop at that inn and drink beer till we come back.'
'But what will he think?'
'What does it matter to us? Besides, he won't think at all; he'll drink beer—that's all. Come, Sanin (it was the first time she had used his surname alone), on, gallop!'
When they reached the inn, Maria Nikolaevna called the groom up and told him what she wished of him. The groom, a man of English extraction and English temperament, raised his hand to the beak of his cap without a word, jumped off his horse, and took him by the bridle.
'Well, now we are free as the birds of the air!' cried Maria Nikolaevna. 'Where shall we go. North, south, east, or west? Look—I'm like the Hungarian king at his coronation (she pointed her whip in each direction in turn). All is ours! No, do you know what: see, those glorious mountains—and that forest! Let's go there, to the mountains, to the mountains!'
'*In die Berge wo die Freiheit thront!*'
She turned off the high-road and galloped along a narrow untrodden track, which certainly seemed to lead straight to the hills. Sanin galloped after her.

XLII

This track soon changed into a tiny footpath, and at last disappeared altogether, and was crossed by a stream. Sanin counselled turning back, but Maria Nikolaevna said, 'No! I want to get to the mountains! Let's go straight, as the birds fly,' and she made her mare leap the stream. Sanin leaped it too. Beyond the stream began a wide meadow, at first dry, then wet, and at last quite boggy; the water oozed up everywhere, and stood in pools in some places. Maria Nikolaevna rode her mare straight through these pools on purpose, laughed, and said, 'Let's be naughty children.'
'Do you know,' she asked Sanin, 'what is meant by pool-hunting?'
'Yes,' answered Sanin.
'I had an uncle a huntsman,' she went on.
'I used to go out hunting with him—in the spring. It was delicious! Here we are now, on the pools with you. Only, I see, you're a Russian, and yet mean to marry an Italian. Well, that's your sorrow. What's that? A stream again! Gee up!'
The horse took the leap, but Maria Nikolaevna's hat fell off her head, and her curls tumbled loose over her shoulders. Sanin was just going to get off his horse to pick up the hat, but she shouted to him, 'Don't touch it, I'll get it myself,' bent low down from the saddle, hooked the handle of her whip into the veil, and actually did get the hat. She put it on her head, but did not fasten up her hair, and again darted off, positively holloaing. Sanin dashed along beside her, by her side leaped trenches, fences, brooks, fell in and scrambled out, flew down hill, flew up hill, and kept watching her face. What a face it was! It was all, as it were, wide open: wide-open eyes, eager, bright, and wild; lips, nostrils, open too, and breathing eagerly; she looked straight before her, and it seemed as though that soul longed to master everything it saw, the earth, the sky, the sun, the air itself; and would complain of one thing only—that dangers were so few, and all she could overcome. 'Sanin!' she cried, 'why, this is like Bürger's Lenore! Only you're not dead—eh? Not dead … I am alive!' She let her force and daring have full fling. It seemed not an Amazon on a galloping horse, but a young female centaur at full speed, half-beast and half-god, and the sober, well-bred country seemed astounded, as it was trampled underfoot in her wild riot!
Maria Nikolaevna at last drew up her foaming and bespattered mare; she was staggering under her, and Sanin's powerful but heavy horse was gasping for breath.
'Well, do you like it?' Maria Nikolaevna asked in a sort of exquisite whisper.
'I like it!' Sanin echoed back ecstatically. And his blood was on fire.
'This isn't all, wait a bit.' She held out her hand. Her glove was torn across.
'I told you I would lead you to the forest, to the mountains…. Here they are, the mountains!' The mountains, covered with tall forest, rose about two hundred feet from the place they had reached in their wild ride.

'Look, here is the road; let us turn into it—and forwards. Only at a walk. We must let our horses get their breath.'

They rode on. With one vigorous sweep of her arm Maria Nikolaevna flung back her hair. Then she looked at her gloves and took them off. 'My hands will smell of leather,' she said, 'you won't mind that, eh?' ... Maria Nikolaevna smiled, and Sanin smiled too. Their mad gallop together seemed to have finally brought them together and made them friends.

'How old are you?' she asked suddenly.

'Twenty-two.'

'Really? I'm twenty-two too. A nice age. Add both together and you're still far off old age. It's hot, though. Am I very red, eh?'

'Like a poppy!'

Maria Nikolaevna rubbed her face with her handkerchief. 'We've only to get to the forest and there it will be cool. Such an old forest is like an old friend. Have you any friends?'

Sanin thought a little. 'Yes ... only few. No real ones.'

'I have; real ones—but not old ones. This is a friend too—a horse. How carefully it carries one! Ah, but it's splendid here! Is it possible I am going to Paris the day after to-morrow?'

'Yes ... is it possible?' Sanin chimed in.

'And you to Frankfort?'

'I am certainly going to Frankfort.'

'Well, what of it? Good luck go with you! Anyway, to-day's ours ... ours ... ours!'

* * * * *

The horses reached the forest's edge and pushed on into the forest.

The broad soft shade of the forest wrapt them round on all sides.

'Oh, but this is paradise!' cried Maria Nikolaevna. 'Further, deeper into the shade, Sanin!'

The horses moved slowly on, 'deeper into the shade,' slightly swaying and snorting. The path, by which they had come in, suddenly turned off and plunged into a rather narrow gorge. The smell of heather and bracken, of the resin of the pines, and the decaying leaves of last year, seemed to hang, close and drowsy, about it. Through the clefts of the big brown rocks came strong currents of fresh air. On both sides of the path rose round hillocks covered with green moss.

'Stop!' cried Maria Nikolaevna, 'I want to sit down and rest on this velvet. Help me to get off.'

Sanin leaped off his horse and ran up to her. She leaned on both his shoulders, sprang instantly to the ground, and seated herself on one of the mossy mounds. He stood before her, holding both the horses' bridles in his hand.

She lifted her eyes to him.... 'Sanin, are you able to forget?'

Sanin recollected what had happened yesterday ... in the carriage.

'What is that—a question ... or a reproach?'

'I have never in my life reproached any one for anything. Do you believe in magic?'

'What?'

'In magic?—you know what is sung of in our ballads—our Russian peasant ballads?'

'Ah! That's what you're speaking of,' Sanin said slowly.

'Yes, that's it. I believe in it ... and you will believe in it.'

'Magic is sorcery ...' Sanin repeated, 'Anything in the world is possible. I used not to believe in it—but I do now. I don't know myself.'

Maria Nikolaevna thought a moment and looked about her. 'I fancy this place seems familiar to me. Look, Sanin, behind that bushy oak—is there a red wooden cross, or not?'

Sanin moved a few steps to one side. 'Yes, there is.' Maria Nikolaevna smiled. 'Ah, that's good! I know where we are. We haven't got lost as yet. What's that tapping? A wood-cutter?'

Sanin looked into the thicket. 'Yes ... there's a man there chopping up dry branches.'

'I must put my hair to rights,' said Maria Nikolaevna. 'Else he'll see me and be shocked.' She took off her hat and began plaiting up her long hair, silently and seriously. Sanin stood facing her ... All the lines of her graceful limbs could be clearly seen through the dark folds of her habit, dotted here and there with tufts of moss.

One of the horses suddenly shook itself behind Sanin's back; he himself started and trembled from head to foot. Everything was in confusion within him, his nerves were strung up like harpstrings. He might well say

he did not know himself.... He really was bewitched. His whole being was filled full of one thing ... one idea, one desire. Maria Nikolaevna turned a keen look upon him.
'Come, now everything's as it should be,' she observed, putting on her hat. 'Won't you sit down? Here! No, wait a minute ... don't sit down! What's that?'
Over the tree-tops, over the air of the forest, rolled a dull rumbling.
'Can it be thunder?'
'I think it really is thunder,' answered Sanin.
'Oh, this is a treat, a real treat! That was the only thing wanting!' The dull rumble was heard a second time, rose, and fell in a crash. 'Bravo! Bis! Do you remember I spoke of the *Æneid* yesterday? They too were overtaken by a storm in the forest, you know. We must be off, though.' She rose swiftly to her feet. 'Bring me my horse.... Give me your hand. There, so. I'm not heavy.'
She hopped like a bird into the saddle. Sanin too mounted his horse.
'Are you going home?' he asked in an unsteady voice.
'Home indeed!' she answered deliberately and picked up the reins. 'Follow me,' she commanded almost roughly. She came out on to the road and passing the red cross, rode down into a hollow, clambered up again to a cross road, turned to the right and again up the mountainside.... She obviously knew where the path led, and the path led farther and farther into the heart of the forest. She said nothing and did not look round; she moved imperiously in front and humbly and submissively he followed without a spark of will in his sinking heart. Rain began to fall in spots. She quickened her horse's pace, and he did not linger behind her. At last through the dark green of the young firs under an overhanging grey rock, a tumbledown little hut peeped out at him, with a low door in its wattle wall.... Maria Nikolaevna made her mare push through the fir bushes, leaped off her, and appearing suddenly at the entrance to the hut, turned to Sanin, and whispered 'Æneas.'
* * * * *
Four hours later, Maria Nikolaevna and Sanin, accompanied by the groom, who was nodding in the saddle, returned to Wiesbaden, to the hotel. Polozov met his wife with the letter to the overseer in his hand. After staring rather intently at her, he showed signs of some displeasure on his face, and even muttered, 'You don't mean to say you've won your bet?'
Maria Nikolaevna simply shrugged her shoulders.
* * * * *
The same day, two hours later, Sanin was standing in his own room before her, like one distraught, ruined....
'Where are you going, dear?' she asked him. 'To Paris, or to Frankfort?'
'I am going where you will be, and will be with you till you drive me away,' he answered with despair and pressed close to him the hands of his sovereign. She freed her hands, laid them on his head, and clutched at his hair with her fingers. She slowly turned over and twisted the unresisting hair, drew herself up, her lips curled with triumph, while her eyes, wide and clear, almost white, expressed nothing but the ruthlessness and glutted joy of conquest. The hawk, as it clutches a captured bird, has eyes like that.

XLIII

This was what Dimitri Sanin remembered when in the stillness of his room turning over his old papers he found among them a garnet cross. The events we have described rose clearly and consecutively before his mental vision.... But when he reached the moment when he addressed that humiliating prayer to Madame Polozov, when he grovelled at her feet, when his slavery began, he averted his gaze from the images he had evoked, he tried to recall no more. And not that his memory failed him, oh no! he knew only too well what followed upon that moment, but he was stifled by shame, even now, so many years after; he dreaded that feeling of self-contempt, which he knew for certain would overwhelm him, and like a torrent, flood all other feelings if he did not bid his memory be still. But try as he would to turn away from these memories, he could not stifle them entirely. He remembered the scoundrelly, tearful, lying, pitiful letter he had sent to Gemma, that never received an answer.... See her again, go back to her, after such falsehood, such treachery, no! no! he could not, so much conscience and honesty was left in him. Moreover, he had lost every trace of confidence in himself, every atom of self-respect; he dared not rely on himself for anything. Sanin recollected too how he had later on—oh, ignominy!—sent the Polozovs' footman to Frankfort for his things, what cowardly terror he had felt, how he had had one thought only, to get away as soon as might be to Paris—to Paris; how in obedience to Maria Nikolaevna, he had humoured and tried to please Ippolit Sidoritch and been amiable to Dönhof, on whose finger he noticed just such an iron ring as Maria Nikolaevna had given him!!! Then followed memories still worse, more ignominious … the waiter hands him a visiting card, and on it is the name, 'Pantaleone Cippatola, court singer to His Highness the Duke of Modena!' He hides from the old man, but cannot escape meeting him in the corridor, and a face of exasperation rises before him under an upstanding topknot of grey hair; the old eyes blaze like red-hot coals, and he hears menacing cries and curses: '*Maledizione!*' hears even the terrible words: '*Codardo! Infame traditore!*' Sanin closes his eyes, shakes his head, turns away again and again, but still he sees himself sitting in a travelling carriage on the narrow front seat … In the comfortable places facing the horses sit Maria Nikolaevna and Ippolit Sidoritch, the four horses trotting all together fly along the paved roads of Wiesbaden to Paris! to Paris! Ippolit Sidoritch is eating a pear which Sanin has peeled for him, while Maria Nikolaevna watches him and smiles at him, her bondslave, that smile he knows already, the smile of the proprietor, the slave-owner…. But, good God, out there at the corner of the street not far from the city walls, wasn't it Pantaleone again, and who with him? Can it be Emilio? Yes, it was he, the enthusiastic devoted boy! Not long since his young face had been full of reverence before his hero, his ideal, but now his pale handsome face, so handsome that Maria Nikolaevna noticed him and poked her head out of the carriage window, that noble face is glowing with anger and contempt; his eyes, so like *her* eyes! are fastened upon Sanin, and the tightly compressed lips part to revile him….

And Pantaleone stretches out his hand and points Sanin out to Tartaglia standing near, and Tartaglia barks at Sanin, and the very bark of the faithful dog sounds like an unbearable reproach….

Hideous!

And then, the life in Paris, and all the humiliations, all the loathsome tortures of the slave, who dare not be jealous or complain, and who is cast aside at last, like a worn-out garment….

Then the going home to his own country, the poisoned, the devastated life, the petty interests and petty cares, bitter and fruitless regret, and as bitter and fruitless apathy, a punishment not apparent, but of every minute, continuous, like some trivial but incurable disease, the payment farthing by farthing of the debt, which can never be settled….

The cup was full enough.

* * * * *

How had the garnet cross given Sanin by Gemma existed till now, why had he not sent it back, how had it happened that he had never come across it till that day? A long, long while he sat deep in thought, and taught as he was by the experience of so many years, he still could not comprehend how he could have deserted Gemma, so tenderly and passionately loved, for a woman he did not love at all…. Next day he surprised all his friends and acquaintances by announcing that he was going abroad.

The surprise was general in society. Sanin was leaving Petersburg, in the middle of the winter, after having only just taken and furnished a capital flat, and having even secured seats for all the performances of the Italian Opera, in which Madame Patti … Patti, herself, herself, was to take part! His friends and acquaintances wondered; but it is not human nature as a rule to be interested long in other people's affairs, and when Sanin set off for abroad, none came to the railway station to see him off but a French tailor, and he only in the hope of securing an unpaid account '*pour un saute-en-barque en velours noir tout à fait chic.*'

XLIV

Sanin told his friends he was going abroad, but he did not say where exactly: the reader will readily conjecture that he made straight for Frankfort. Thanks to the general extension of railways, on the fourth day after leaving Petersburg he was there. He had not visited the place since 1840. The hotel, the White Swan, was standing in its old place and still flourishing, though no longer regarded as first class. The *Zeile*, the principal street of Frankfort was little changed, but there was not only no trace of Signora Roselli's house, the very street in which it stood had disappeared. Sanin wandered like a man in a dream about the places once so familiar, and recognised nothing; the old buildings had vanished; they were replaced by new streets of huge continuous houses and fine villas; even the public garden, where that last interview with Gemma had taken place, had so grown up and altered that Sanin wondered if it really were the same garden. What was he to do? How and where could he get information? Thirty years, no little thing! had passed since those days. No one to whom he applied had even heard of the name Roselli; the hotel-keeper advised him to have recourse to the public library, there, he told him, he would find all the old newspapers, but what good he would get from that, the hotel-keeper owned he didn't see. Sanin in despair made inquiries about Herr Klüber. That name the hotel-keeper knew well, but there too no success awaited him. The elegant shop-manager, after making much noise in the world and rising to the position of a capitalist, had speculated, was made bankrupt, and died in prison.... This piece of news did not, however, occasion Sanin the slightest regret. He was beginning to feel that his journey had been rather precipitate.... But, behold, one day, as he was turning over a Frankfort directory, he came on the name: Von Dönhof, retired major. He promptly took a carriage and drove to the address, though why was this Von Dönhof certain to be that Dönhof, and why even was the right Dönhof likely to be able to tell him any news of the Roselli family? No matter, a drowning man catches at straws.

Sanin found the retired major von Dönhof at home, and in the grey-haired gentleman who received him he recognised at once his adversary of bygone days. Dönhof knew him too, and was positively delighted to see him; he recalled to him his young days, the escapades of his youth. Sanin heard from him that the Roselli family had long, long ago emigrated to America, to New York; that Gemma had married a merchant; that he, Dönhof, had an acquaintance also a merchant, who would probably know her husband's address, as he did a great deal of business with America. Sanin begged Dönhof to consult this friend, and, to his delight, Dönhof brought him the address of Gemma's husband, Mr. Jeremy Slocum, New York, Broadway, No. 501. Only this address dated from the year 1863.

'Let us hope,' cried Dönhof, 'that our Frankfort belle is still alive and has not left New York! By the way,' he added, dropping his voice, 'what about that Russian lady, who was staying, do you remember, about that time at Wiesbaden—Madame von Bo ... von Bolozov, is she still living?'

'No,' answered Sanin, 'she died long ago.' Dönhof looked up, but observing that Sanin had turned away and was frowning, he did not say another word, but took his leave.

* * * * *

That same day Sanin sent a letter to Madame Gemma Slocum, at New York. In the letter he told her he was writing to her from Frankfort, where he had come solely with the object of finding traces of her, that he was very well aware that he was absolutely without a right to expect that she would answer his appeal; that he had not deserved her forgiveness, and could only hope that among happy surroundings she had long ago forgotten his existence. He added that he had made up his mind to recall himself to her memory in consequence of a chance circumstance which had too vividly brought back to him the images of the past; he described his life, solitary, childless, joyless; he implored her to understand the grounds that had induced him to address her, not to let him carry to the grave the bitter sense of his own wrongdoing, expiated long since by suffering, but never forgiven, and to make him happy with even the briefest news of her life in the new world to which she had gone away. 'In writing one word to me,' so Sanin ended his letter, 'you will be doing a good action worthy of your noble soul, and I shall thank you to my last breath. I am stopping here at the *White Swan* (he underlined those words) and shall wait, wait till spring, for your answer.'

He despatched this letter, and proceeded to wait. For six whole weeks he lived in the hotel, scarcely leaving his room, and resolutely seeing no one. No one could write to him from Russia nor from anywhere; and that just suited his mood; if a letter came addressed to him he would know at once that it was the one he was waiting for. He read from morning till evening, and not journals, but serious books—historical works. These prolonged studies, this stillness, this hidden life, like a snail in its shell, suited his spiritual condition to perfection; and for this, if nothing more, thanks to Gemma! But was she alive? Would she answer?

At last a letter came, with an American postmark, from New York, addressed to him. The handwriting of the address on the envelope was English.... He did not recognise it, and there was a pang at his heart. He could not at once bring himself to break open the envelope. He glanced at the signature—Gemma! The tears positively gushed from his eyes: the mere fact that she signed her name, without a surname, was a pledge to him of reconciliation, of forgiveness! He unfolded the thin sheet of blue notepaper: a photograph slipped out. He made haste to pick it up—and was struck dumb with amazement: Gemma, Gemma living, young as he had known her thirty years ago! The same eyes, the same lips, the same form of the whole face! On the back of the photograph was written, 'My daughter Mariana.' The whole letter was very kind and simple. Gemma thanked Sanin for not having hesitated to write to her, for having confidence in her; she did not conceal from him that she had passed some painful moments after his disappearance, but she added at once that for all that she considered—and had always considered—her meeting him as a happy thing, seeing that it was that meeting which had prevented her from becoming the wife of Mr. Klüber, and in that way, though indirectly, had led to her marriage with her husband, with whom she had now lived twenty-eight years, in perfect happiness, comfort, and prosperity; their house was known to every one in New York. Gemma informed Sanin that she was the mother of five children, four sons and one daughter, a girl of eighteen, engaged to be married, and her photograph she enclosed as she was generally considered very like her mother. The sorrowful news Gemma kept for the end of the letter. Frau Lenore had died in New York, where she had followed her daughter and son-in-law, but she had lived long enough to rejoice in her children's happiness and to nurse her grandchildren. Pantaleone, too, had meant to come out to America, but he had died on the very eve of leaving Frankfort. 'Emilio, our beloved, incomparable Emilio, died a glorious death for the freedom of his country in Sicily, where he was one of the "Thousand" under the leadership of the great Garibaldi; we all bitterly lamented the loss of our priceless brother, but, even in the midst of our tears, we were proud of him—and shall always be proud of him—and hold his memory sacred! His lofty, disinterested soul was worthy of a martyr's crown!' Then Gemma expressed her regret that Sanin's life had apparently been so unsuccessful, wished him before everything peace and a tranquil spirit, and said that she would be very glad to see him again, though she realised how unlikely such a meeting was....

We will not attempt to describe the feelings Sanin experienced as he read this letter. For such feelings there is no satisfactory expression; they are too deep and too strong and too vague for any word. Only music could reproduce them.

Sanin answered at once; and as a wedding gift to the young girl, sent to 'Mariana Slocum, from an unknown friend,' a garnet cross, set in a magnificent pearl necklace. This present, costly as it was, did not ruin him; during the thirty years that had elapsed since his first visit to Frankfort, he had succeeded in accumulating a considerable fortune. Early in May he went back to Petersburg, but hardly for long. It is rumoured that he is selling all his lands and preparing to go to America.

FIRST LOVE

The party had long ago broken up. The clock struck half-past twelve.

There was left in the room only the master of the house and Sergei Nikolaevitch and Vladimir Petrovitch.

The master of the house rang and ordered the remains of the supper to be cleared away. 'And so it's settled,' he observed, sitting back farther in his easy-chair and lighting a cigar; 'each of us is to tell the story of his first love. It's your turn, Sergei Nikolaevitch.'

Sergei Nikolaevitch, a round little man with a plump, light-complexioned face, gazed first at the master of the house, then raised his eyes to the ceiling. 'I had no first love,' he said at last; 'I began with the second.'

'How was that?'

'It's very simple. I was eighteen when I had my first flirtation with a charming young lady, but I courted her just as though it were nothing new to me; just as I courted others later on. To speak accurately, the first and last time I was in love was with my nurse when I was six years old; but that's in the remote past. The details of our relations have slipped out of my memory, and even if I remembered them, whom could they interest?'

'Then how's it to be?' began the master of the house. 'There was nothing much of interest about my first love either; I never fell in love with any one till I met Anna Nikolaevna, now my wife,—and everything went as smoothly as possible with us; our parents arranged the match, we were very soon in love with each other, and got married without loss of time. My story can be told in a couple of words. I must confess, gentlemen, in bringing up the subject of first love, I reckoned upon you, I won't say old, but no longer young, bachelors. Can't you enliven us with something, Vladimir Petrovitch?'

'My first love, certainly, was not quite an ordinary one,' responded, with some reluctance, Vladimir Petrovitch, a man of forty, with black hair turning grey.
'Ah!' said the master of the house and Sergei Nikolaevitch with one voice: 'So much the better.... Tell us about it.'
'If you wish it ... or no; I won't tell the story; I'm no hand at telling a story; I make it dry and brief, or spun out and affected. If you'll allow me, I'll write out all I remember and read it you.'
His friends at first would not agree, but Vladimir Petrovitch insisted on his own way. A fortnight later they were together again, and Vladimir Petrovitch kept his word.
His manuscript contained the following story:—

I

I was sixteen then. It happened in the summer of 1833.
I lived in Moscow with my parents. They had taken a country house for the summer near the Kalouga gate, facing the Neskutchny gardens. I was preparing for the university, but did not work much and was in no hurry.
No one interfered with my freedom. I did what I liked, especially after parting with my last tutor, a Frenchman who had never been able to get used to the idea that he had fallen 'like a bomb' (*comme une bombe*) into Russia, and would lie sluggishly in bed with an expression of exasperation on his face for days together. My father treated me with careless kindness; my mother scarcely noticed me, though she had no children except me; other cares completely absorbed her. My father, a man still young and very handsome, had married her from mercenary considerations; she was ten years older than he. My mother led a melancholy life; she was for ever agitated, jealous and angry, but not in my father's presence; she was very much afraid of him, and he was severe, cold, and distant in his behaviour.... I have never seen a man more elaborately serene, self-confident, and commanding.
I shall never forget the first weeks I spent at the country house. The weather was magnificent; we left town on the 9th of May, on St. Nicholas's day. I used to walk about in our garden, in the Neskutchny gardens, and beyond the town gates; I would take some book with me—Keidanov's Course, for instance—but I rarely looked into it, and more often than anything declaimed verses aloud; I knew a great deal of poetry by heart; my blood was in a ferment and my heart ached—so sweetly and absurdly; I was all hope and anticipation, was a little frightened of something, and full of wonder at everything, and was on the tiptoe of expectation; my imagination played continually, fluttering rapidly about the same fancies, like martins about a bell-tower at dawn; I dreamed, was sad, even wept; but through the tears and through the sadness, inspired by a musical verse, or the beauty of evening, shot up like grass in spring the delicious sense of youth and effervescent life.
I had a horse to ride; I used to saddle it myself and set off alone for long rides, break into a rapid gallop and fancy myself a knight at a tournament. How gaily the wind whistled in my ears! or turning my face towards the sky, I would absorb its shining radiance and blue into my soul, that opened wide to welcome it.
I remember that at that time the image of woman, the vision of love, scarcely ever arose in definite shape in my brain; but in all I thought, in all I felt, lay hidden a half-conscious, shamefaced presentiment of something new, unutterably sweet, feminine....
This presentiment, this expectation, permeated my whole being; I breathed in it, it coursed through my veins with every drop of blood ... it was destined to be soon fulfilled.
The place, where we settled for the summer, consisted of a wooden manor-house with columns and two small lodges; in the lodge on the left there was a tiny factory for the manufacture of cheap wall-papers.... I had more than once strolled that way to look at about a dozen thin and dishevelled boys with greasy smocks and worn faces, who were perpetually jumping on to wooden levers, that pressed down the square blocks of the press, and so by the weight of their feeble bodies struck off the variegated patterns of the wall-papers. The lodge on the right stood empty, and was to let. One day—three weeks after the 9th of May—the blinds in the windows of this lodge were drawn up, women's faces appeared at them—some family had installed themselves in it. I remember the same day at dinner, my mother inquired of the butler who were our new

neighbours, and hearing the name of the Princess Zasyekin, first observed with some respect, 'Ah! a princess!' ... and then added, 'A poor one, I suppose?'

'They arrived in three hired flies,' the butler remarked deferentially, as he handed a dish: 'they don't keep their own carriage, and the furniture's of the poorest.'

'Ah,' replied my mother, 'so much the better.'

My father gave her a chilly glance; she was silent.

Certainly the Princess Zasyekin could not be a rich woman; the lodge she had taken was so dilapidated and small and low-pitched that people, even moderately well-off in the world, would hardly have consented to occupy it. At the time, however, all this went in at one ear and out at the other. The princely title had very little effect on me; I had just been reading Schiller's *Robbers*.

II

I was in the habit of wandering about our garden every evening on the look-out for rooks. I had long cherished a hatred for those wary, sly, and rapacious birds. On the day of which I have been speaking, I went as usual into the garden, and after patrolling all the walks without success (the rooks knew me, and merely cawed spasmodically at a distance), I chanced to go close to the low fence which separated our domain from the narrow strip of garden stretching beyond the lodge to the right, and belonging to it. I was walking along, my eyes on the ground. Suddenly I heard a voice; I looked across the fence, and was thunder-struck.... I was confronted with a curious spectacle.

A few paces from me on the grass between the green raspberry bushes stood a tall slender girl in a striped pink dress, with a white kerchief on her head; four young men were close round her, and she was slapping them by turns on the forehead with those small grey flowers, the name of which I don't know, though they are well known to children; the flowers form little bags, and burst open with a pop when you strike them against anything hard. The young men presented their foreheads so eagerly, and in the gestures of the girl (I saw her in profile), there was something so fascinating, imperious, caressing, mocking, and charming, that I almost cried out with admiration and delight, and would, I thought, have given everything in the world on the spot only to have had those exquisite fingers strike me on the forehead. My gun slipped on to the grass, I forgot everything, I devoured with my eyes the graceful shape and neck and lovely arms and the slightly disordered fair hair under the white kerchief, and the half-closed clever eye, and the eyelashes and the soft cheek beneath them....

'Young man, hey, young man,' said a voice suddenly near me: 'is it quite permissible to stare so at unknown young ladies?'

I started, I was struck dumb.... Near me, the other side of the fence, stood a man with close-cropped black hair, looking ironically at me. At the same instant the girl too turned towards me.... I caught sight of big grey eyes in a bright mobile face, and the whole face suddenly quivered and laughed, there was a flash of white teeth, a droll lifting of the eyebrows.... I crimsoned, picked up my gun from the ground, and pursued by a musical but not ill-natured laugh, fled to my own room, flung myself on the bed, and hid my face in my hands. My heart was fairly leaping; I was greatly ashamed and overjoyed; I felt an excitement I had never known before.

After a rest, I brushed my hair, washed, and went downstairs to tea. The image of the young girl floated before me, my heart was no longer leaping, but was full of a sort of sweet oppression.

'What's the matter?' my father asked me all at once: 'have you killed a rook?'

I was on the point of telling him all about it, but I checked myself, and merely smiled to myself. As I was going to bed, I rotated—I don't know why—three times on one leg, pomaded my hair, got into bed, and slept like a top all night. Before morning I woke up for an instant, raised my head, looked round me in ecstasy, and fell asleep again.

III

'How can I make their acquaintance?' was my first thought when I waked in the morning. I went out in the garden before morning tea, but I did not go too near the fence, and saw no one. After drinking tea, I walked several times up and down the street before the house, and looked into the windows from a distance.... I fancied her face at a curtain, and I hurried away in alarm.
'I must make her acquaintance, though,' I thought, pacing distractedly about the sandy plain that stretches before Neskutchny park ... 'but how, that is the question.' I recalled the minutest details of our meeting yesterday; I had for some reason or other a particularly vivid recollection of how she had laughed at me.... But while I racked my brains, and made various plans, fate had already provided for me.
In my absence my mother had received from her new neighbour a letter on grey paper, sealed with brown wax, such as is only used in notices from the post-office or on the corks of bottles of cheap wine. In this letter, which was written in illiterate language and in a slovenly hand, the princess begged my mother to use her powerful influence in her behalf; my mother, in the words of the princess, was very intimate with persons of high position, upon whom her fortunes and her children's fortunes depended, as she had some very important business in hand. 'I address myself to you,' she wrote, 'as one gentlewoman to another gentlewoman, and for that reason am glad to avail myself of the opportunity.' Concluding, she begged my mother's permission to call upon her. I found my mother in an unpleasant state of indecision; my father was not at home, and she had no one of whom to ask advice. Not to answer a gentlewoman, and a princess into the bargain, was impossible. But my mother was in a difficulty as to how to answer her. To write a note in French struck her as unsuitable, and Russian spelling was not a strong point with my mother herself, and she was aware of it, and did not care to expose herself. She was overjoyed when I made my appearance, and at once told me to go round to the princess's, and to explain to her by word of mouth that my mother would always be glad to do her excellency any service within her powers, and begged her to come to see her at one o'clock. This unexpectedly rapid fulfilment of my secret desires both delighted and appalled me. I made no sign, however, of the perturbation which came over me, and as a preliminary step went to my own room to put on a new necktie and tail coat; at home I still wore short jackets and lay-down collars, much as I abominated them.

IV

In the narrow and untidy passage of the lodge, which I entered with an involuntary tremor in all my limbs, I was met by an old grey-headed servant with a dark copper-coloured face, surly little pig's eyes, and such deep furrows on his forehead and temples as I had never beheld in my life. He was carrying a plate containing the spine of a herring that had been gnawed at; and shutting the door that led into the room with his foot, he jerked out, 'What do you want?'
'Is the Princess Zasyekin at home?' I inquired.
'Vonifaty!' a jarring female voice screamed from within.
The man without a word turned his back on me, exhibiting as he did so the extremely threadbare hindpart of his livery with a solitary reddish heraldic button on it; he put the plate down on the floor, and went away.
'Did you go to the police station?' the same female voice called again. The man muttered something in reply.
'Eh.... Has some one come?' I heard again.... 'The young gentleman from next door. Ask him in, then.'
'Will you step into the drawing-room?' said the servant, making his appearance once more, and picking up the plate from the floor. I mastered my emotions, and went into the drawing-room.
I found myself in a small and not over clean apartment, containing some poor furniture that looked as if it had been hurriedly set down where it stood. At the window in an easy-chair with a broken arm was sitting a woman of fifty, bareheaded and ugly, in an old green dress, and a striped worsted wrap about her neck. Her small black eyes fixed me like pins.
I went up to her and bowed.
'I have the honour of addressing the Princess Zasyekin?'

'I am the Princess Zasyekin; and you are the son of Mr. V.?'
'Yes. I have come to you with a message from my mother.'
'Sit down, please. Vonifaty, where are my keys, have you seen them?'
I communicated to Madame Zasyekin my mother's reply to her note. She heard me out, drumming with her fat red fingers on the window-pane, and when I had finished, she stared at me once more.
'Very good; I'll be sure to come,' she observed at last. 'But how young you are! How old are you, may I ask?'
'Sixteen,' I replied, with an involuntary stammer.
The princess drew out of her pocket some greasy papers covered with writing, raised them right up to her nose, and began looking through them.
'A good age,' she ejaculated suddenly, turning round restlessly on her chair. 'And do you, pray, make yourself at home. I don't stand on ceremony.'
'No, indeed,' I thought, scanning her unprepossessing person with a disgust I could not restrain.
At that instant another door flew open quickly, and in the doorway stood the girl I had seen the previous evening in the garden. She lifted her hand, and a mocking smile gleamed in her face.
'Here is my daughter,' observed the princess, indicating her with her elbow. 'Zinotchka, the son of our neighbour, Mr. V. What is your name, allow me to ask?'
'Vladimir,' I answered, getting up, and stuttering in my excitement.
'And your father's name?'
'Petrovitch.'
'Ah! I used to know a commissioner of police whose name was Vladimir Petrovitch too. Vonifaty! don't look for my keys; the keys are in my pocket.'
The young girl was still looking at me with the same smile, faintly fluttering her eyelids, and putting her head a little on one side.
'I have seen Monsieur Voldemar before,' she began. (The silvery note of her voice ran through me with a sort of sweet shiver.) 'You will let me call you so?'
'Oh, please,' I faltered.
'Where was that?' asked the princess.
The young princess did not answer her mother.
'Have you anything to do just now?' she said, not taking her eyes off me.
'Oh, no.'
'Would you like to help me wind some wool? Come in here, to me.'
She nodded to me and went out of the drawing-room. I followed her.
In the room we went into, the furniture was a little better, and was arranged with more taste. Though, indeed, at the moment, I was scarcely capable of noticing anything; I moved as in a dream and felt all through my being a sort of intense blissfulness that verged on imbecility.
The young princess sat down, took out a skein of red wool and, motioning me to a seat opposite her, carefully untied the skein and laid it across my hands. All this she did in silence with a sort of droll deliberation and with the same bright sly smile on her slightly parted lips. She began to wind the wool on a bent card, and all at once she dazzled me with a glance so brilliant and rapid, that I could not help dropping my eyes. When her eyes, which were generally half closed, opened to their full extent, her face was completely transfigured; it was as though it were flooded with light.
'What did you think of me yesterday, M'sieu Voldemar?' she asked after a brief pause. 'You thought ill of me, I expect?'
'I ... princess ... I thought nothing ... how can I?...' I answered in confusion.
'Listen,' she rejoined. 'You don't know me yet. I'm a very strange person; I like always to be told the truth. You, I have just heard, are sixteen, and I am twenty-one: you see I'm a great deal older than you, and so you ought always to tell me the truth ... and to do what I tell you,' she added. 'Look at me: why don't you look at me?'
I was still more abashed; however, I raised my eyes to her. She smiled, not her former smile, but a smile of approbation. 'Look at me,' she said, dropping her voice caressingly: 'I don't dislike that ... I like your face; I have a presentiment we shall be friends. But do you like me?' she added slyly.
'Princess ...' I was beginning.
'In the first place, you must call me Zinaïda Alexandrovna, and in the second place it's a bad habit for children'—(she corrected herself) 'for young people—not to say straight out what they feel. That's all very well for grown-up people. You like me, don't you?'

Though I was greatly delighted that she talked so freely to me, still I was a little hurt. I wanted to show her that she had not a mere boy to deal with, and assuming as easy and serious an air as I could, I observed, 'Certainly. I like you very much, Zinaïda Alexandrovna; I have no wish to conceal it.'
She shook her head very deliberately. 'Have you a tutor?' she asked suddenly.
'No; I've not had a tutor for a long, long while.'
I told a lie; it was not a month since I had parted with my Frenchman.
'Oh! I see then—you are quite grown-up.'
She tapped me lightly on the fingers. 'Hold your hands straight!' And she applied herself busily to winding the ball.
I seized the opportunity when she was looking down and fell to watching her, at first stealthily, then more and more boldly. Her face struck me as even more charming than on the previous evening; everything in it was so delicate, clever, and sweet. She was sitting with her back to a window covered with a white blind, the sunshine, streaming in through the blind, shed a soft light over her fluffy golden curls, her innocent neck, her sloping shoulders, and tender untroubled bosom. I gazed at her, and how dear and near she was already to me! It seemed to me I had known her a long while and had never known anything nor lived at all till I met her.... She was wearing a dark and rather shabby dress and an apron; I would gladly, I felt, have kissed every fold of that dress and apron. The tips of her little shoes peeped out from under her skirt; I could have bowed down in adoration to those shoes.... 'And here I am sitting before her,' I thought; 'I have made acquaintance with her ... what happiness, my God!' I could hardly keep from jumping up from my chair in ecstasy, but I only swung my legs a little, like a small child who has been given sweetmeats.
I was as happy as a fish in water, and I could have stayed in that room for ever, have never left that place. Her eyelids were slowly lifted, and once more her clear eyes shone kindly upon me, and again she smiled.
'How you look at me!' she said slowly, and she held up a threatening finger.
I blushed ... 'She understands it all, she sees all,' flashed through my mind. 'And how could she fail to understand and see it all?'
All at once there was a sound in the next room—the clink of a sabre.
'Zina!' screamed the princess in the drawing-room, 'Byelovzorov has brought you a kitten.'
'A kitten!' cried Zinaïda, and getting up from her chair impetuously, she flung the ball of worsted on my knees and ran away.
I too got up and, laying the skein and the ball of wool on the window-sill, I went into the drawing-room and stood still, hesitating. In the middle of the room, a tabby kitten was lying with outstretched paws; Zinaïda was on her knees before it, cautiously lifting up its little face. Near the old princess, and filling up almost the whole space between the two windows, was a flaxen curly-headed young man, a hussar, with a rosy face and prominent eyes.
'What a funny little thing!' Zinaïda was saying; 'and its eyes are not grey, but green, and what long ears! Thank you, Viktor Yegoritch! you are very kind.'
The hussar, in whom I recognised one of the young men I had seen the evening before, smiled and bowed with a clink of his spurs and a jingle of the chain of his sabre.
'You were pleased to say yesterday that you wished to possess a tabby kitten with long ears ... so I obtained it. Your word is law.' And he bowed again.
The kitten gave a feeble mew and began sniffing the ground.
'It's hungry!' cried Zinaïda. 'Vonifaty, Sonia! bring some milk.'
A maid, in an old yellow gown with a faded kerchief at her neck, came in with a saucer of milk and set it before the kitten. The kitten started, blinked, and began lapping.
'What a pink little tongue it has!' remarked Zinaïda, putting her head almost on the ground and peeping at it sideways under its very nose.
The kitten having had enough began to purr and move its paws affectedly. Zinaïda got up, and turning to the maid said carelessly, 'Take it away.'
'For the kitten—your little hand,' said the hussar, with a simper and a shrug of his strongly-built frame, which was tightly buttoned up in a new uniform.
'Both,' replied Zinaïda, and she held out her hands to him. While he was kissing them, she looked at me over his shoulder.
I stood stockstill in the same place and did not know whether to laugh, to say something, or to be silent. Suddenly through the open door into the passage I caught sight of our footman, Fyodor. He was making signs to me. Mechanically I went out to him.

'What do you want?' I asked.
'Your mamma has sent for you,' he said in a whisper. 'She is angry that you have not come back with the answer.'
'Why, have I been here long?'
'Over an hour.'
'Over an hour!' I repeated unconsciously, and going back to the drawing-room I began to make bows and scrape with my heels.
'Where are you off to?' the young princess asked, glancing at me from behind the hussar.
'I must go home. So I am to say,' I added, addressing the old lady, 'that you will come to us about two.'
'Do you say so, my good sir.'
The princess hurriedly pulled out her snuff-box and took snuff so loudly that I positively jumped. 'Do you say so,' she repeated, blinking tearfully and sneezing.
I bowed once more, turned, and went out of the room with that sensation of awkwardness in my spine which a very young man feels when he knows he is being looked at from behind.
'Mind you come and see us again, M'sieu Voldemar,' Zinaïda called, and she laughed again.
'Why is it she's always laughing?' I thought, as I went back home escorted by Fyodor, who said nothing to me, but walked behind me with an air of disapprobation. My mother scolded me and wondered what ever I could have been doing so long at the princess's. I made her no reply and went off to my own room. I felt suddenly very sad.... I tried hard not to cry.... I was jealous of the hussar.

V

The princess called on my mother as she had promised and made a disagreeable impression on her. I was not present at their interview, but at table my mother told my father that this Prince Zasyekin struck her as a *femme très vulgaire*, that she had quite worn her out begging her to interest Prince Sergei in their behalf, that she seemed to have no end of lawsuits and affairs on hand—*de vilaines affaires d'argent*—and must be a very troublesome and litigious person. My mother added, however, that she had asked her and her daughter to dinner the next day (hearing the word 'daughter' I buried my nose in my plate), for after all she was a neighbour and a person of title. Upon this my father informed my mother that he remembered now who this lady was; that he had in his youth known the deceased Prince Zasyekin, a very well-bred, but frivolous and absurd person; that he had been nicknamed in society '*le Parisien*,' from having lived a long while in Paris; that he had been very rich, but had gambled away all his property; and for some unknown reason, probably for money, though indeed he might have chosen better, if so, my father added with a cold smile, he had married the daughter of an agent, and after his marriage had entered upon speculations and ruined himself utterly.
'If only she doesn't try to borrow money,' observed my mother.
'That's exceedingly possible,' my father responded tranquilly. 'Does she speak French?'
'Very badly.'
'H'm. It's of no consequence anyway. I think you said you had asked the daughter too; some one was telling me she was a very charming and cultivated girl.'
'Ah! Then she can't take after her mother.'
'Nor her father either,' rejoined my father. 'He was cultivated indeed, but a fool.'
My mother sighed and sank into thought. My father said no more. I felt very uncomfortable during this conversation.
After dinner I went into the garden, but without my gun. I swore to myself that I would not go near the Zasyekins' garden, but an irresistible force drew me thither, and not in vain. I had hardly reached the fence when I caught sight of Zinaïda. This time she was alone. She held a book in her hands, and was coming slowly along the path. She did not notice me.
I almost let her pass by; but all at once I changed my mind and coughed.
She turned round, but did not stop, pushed back with one hand the broad blue ribbon of her round straw hat, looked at me, smiled slowly, and again bent her eyes on the book.

I took off my cap, and after hesitating a moment, walked away with a heavy heart. '*Que suis-je pour elle?*' I thought (God knows why) in French.
Familiar footsteps sounded behind me; I looked round, my father came up to me with his light, rapid walk.
'Is that the young princess?' he asked me.
'Yes.'
'Why, do you know her?'
'I saw her this morning at the princess's.'
My father stopped, and, turning sharply on his heel, went back. When he was on a level with Zinaïda, he made her a courteous bow. She, too, bowed to him, with some astonishment on her face, and dropped her book. I saw how she looked after him. My father was always irreproachably dressed, simple and in a style of his own; but his figure had never struck me as more graceful, never had his grey hat sat more becomingly on his curls, which were scarcely perceptibly thinner than they had once been.
I bent my steps toward Zinaïda, but she did not even glance at me; she picked up her book again and went away.

VI

The whole evening and the following day I spent in a sort of dejected apathy. I remember I tried to work and took up Keidanov, but the boldly printed lines and pages of the famous text-book passed before my eyes in vain. I read ten times over the words: 'Julius Caesar was distinguished by warlike courage.' I did not understand anything and threw the book aside. Before dinner-time I pomaded myself once more, and once more put on my tail-coat and necktie.
'What's that for?' my mother demanded. 'You're not a student yet, and God knows whether you'll get through the examination. And you've not long had a new jacket! You can't throw it away!'
'There will be visitors,' I murmured almost in despair.
'What nonsense! fine visitors indeed!'
I had to submit. I changed my tail-coat for my jacket, but I did not take off the necktie. The princess and her daughter made their appearance half an hour before dinner-time; the old lady had put on, in addition to the green dress with which I was already acquainted, a yellow shawl, and an old-fashioned cap adorned with flame-coloured ribbons. She began talking at once about her money difficulties, sighing, complaining of her poverty, and imploring assistance, but she made herself at home; she took snuff as noisily, and fidgeted and lolled about in her chair as freely as ever. It never seemed to have struck her that she was a princess. Zinaïda on the other hand was rigid, almost haughty in her demeanour, every inch a princess. There was a cold immobility and dignity in her face. I should not have recognised it; I should not have known her smiles, her glances, though I thought her exquisite in this new aspect too. She wore a light barége dress with pale blue flowers on it; her hair fell in long curls down her cheek in the English fashion; this style went well with the cold expression of her face. My father sat beside her during dinner, and entertained his neighbour with the finished and serene courtesy peculiar to him. He glanced at her from time to time, and she glanced at him, but so strangely, almost with hostility. Their conversation was carried on in French; I was surprised, I remember, at the purity of Zinaïda's accent. The princess, while we were at table, as before made no ceremony; she ate a great deal, and praised the dishes. My mother was obviously bored by her, and answered her with a sort of weary indifference; my father faintly frowned now and then. My mother did not like Zinaïda either. 'A conceited minx,' she said next day. 'And fancy, what she has to be conceited about, *avec sa mine de grisette*!'
'It's clear you have never seen any grisettes,' my father observed to her.
'Thank God, I haven't!'
'Thank God, to be sure ... only how can you form an opinion of them, then?'
To me Zinaïda had paid no attention whatever. Soon after dinner the princess got up to go.
'I shall rely on your kind offices, Maria Nikolaevna and Piotr Vassilitch,' she said in a doleful sing-song to my mother and father.

'I've no help for it! There were days, but they are over. Here I am,
an excellency, and a poor honour it is with nothing to eat!'
My father made her a respectful bow and escorted her to the door of the hall. I was standing there in my short jacket, staring at the floor, like a man under sentence of death. Zinaïda's treatment of me had crushed me utterly. What was my astonishment, when, as she passed me, she whispered quickly with her former kind expression in her eyes: 'Come to see us at eight, do you hear, be sure....' I simply threw up my hands, but already she was gone, flinging a white scarf over her head.

VII

At eight o'clock precisely, in my tail-coat and with my hair brushed up into a tuft on my head, I entered the passage of the lodge, where the princess lived. The old servant looked crossly at me and got up unwillingly from his bench. There was a sound of merry voices in the drawing-room. I opened the door and fell back in amazement. In the middle of the room was the young princess, standing on a chair, holding a man's hat in front of her; round the chair crowded some half a dozen men. They were trying to put their hands into the hat, while she held it above their heads, shaking it violently. On seeing me, she cried, 'Stay, stay, another guest, he must have a ticket too,' and leaping lightly down from the chair she took me by the cuff of my coat 'Come along,' she said, 'why are you standing still? *Messieurs*, let me make you acquainted: this is M'sieu Voldemar, the son of our neighbour. And this,' she went on, addressing me, and indicating her guests in turn, 'Count Malevsky, Doctor Lushin, Meidanov the poet, the retired captain Nirmatsky, and Byelovzorov the hussar, whom you've seen already. I hope you will be good friends.' I was so confused that I did not even bow to any one; in Doctor Lushin I recognised the dark man who had so mercilessly put me to shame in the garden; the others were unknown to me.
'Count!' continued Zinaïda, 'write M'sieu Voldemar a ticket.'
'That's not fair,' was objected in a slight Polish accent by the count, a very handsome and fashionably dressed brunette, with expressive brown eyes, a thin little white nose, and delicate little moustaches over a tiny mouth. 'This gentleman has not been playing forfeits with us.'
'It's unfair,' repeated in chorus Byelovzorov and the gentleman described as a retired captain, a man of forty, pock-marked to a hideous degree, curly-headed as a negro, round-shouldered, bandy-legged, and dressed in a military coat without epaulets, worn unbuttoned.
'Write him a ticket, I tell you,' repeated the young princess. 'What's this mutiny? M'sieu Voldemar is with us for the first time, and there are no rules for him yet. It's no use grumbling—write it, I wish it.'
The count shrugged his shoulders but bowed submissively, took the pen in his white, ring-bedecked fingers, tore off a scrap of paper and wrote on it.
'At least let us explain to Mr. Voldemar what we are about,' Lushin began in a sarcastic voice, 'or else he will be quite lost. Do you see, young man, we are playing forfeits? the princess has to pay a forfeit, and the one who draws the lucky lot is to have the privilege of kissing her hand. Do you understand what I've told you?'
I simply stared at him, and continued to stand still in bewilderment, while the young princess jumped up on the chair again, and again began waving the hat. They all stretched up to her, and I went after the rest.
'Meidanov,' said the princess to a tall young man with a thin face, little dim-sighted eyes, and exceedingly long black hair, 'you as a poet ought to be magnanimous, and give up your number to M'sieu Voldemar so that he may have two chances instead of one.'
But Meidanov shook his head in refusal, and tossed his hair. After all the others I put my hand into the hat, and unfolded my lot.... Heavens! what was my condition when I saw on it the word, Kiss!
'Kiss!' I could not help crying aloud.
'Bravo! he has won it,' the princess said quickly. 'How glad I am!' She came down from the chair and gave me such a bright sweet look, that my heart bounded. 'Are you glad?' she asked me.
'Me?' ... I faltered.
'Sell me your lot,' Byelovzorov growled suddenly just in my ear. 'I'll give you a hundred roubles.'
I answered the hussar with such an indignant look, that Zinaïda clapped her hands, while Lushin cried, 'He's a fine fellow!'

'But, as master of the ceremonies,' he went on, 'it's my duty to see that all the rules are kept. M'sieu Voldemar, go down on one knee. That is our regulation.'
Zinaïda stood in front of me, her head a little on one side as though to get a better look at me; she held out her hand to me with dignity. A mist passed before my eyes; I meant to drop on one knee, sank on both, and pressed my lips to Zinaïda's fingers so awkwardly that I scratched myself a little with the tip of her nail.
'Well done!' cried Lushin, and helped me to get up.
The game of forfeits went on. Zinaïda sat me down beside her. She invented all sorts of extraordinary forfeits! She had among other things to represent a 'statue,' and she chose as a pedestal the hideous Nirmatsky, told him to bow down in an arch, and bend his head down on his breast. The laughter never paused for an instant. For me, a boy constantly brought up in the seclusion of a dignified manor-house, all this noise and uproar, this unceremonious, almost riotous gaiety, these relations with unknown persons, were simply intoxicating. My head went round, as though from wine. I began laughing and talking louder than the others, so much so that the old princess, who was sitting in the next room with some sort of clerk from the Tversky gate, invited by her for consultation on business, positively came in to look at me. But I felt so happy that I did not mind anything, I didn't care a straw for any one's jeers, or dubious looks. Zinaïda continued to show me a preference, and kept me at her side. In one forfeit, I had to sit by her, both hidden under one silk handkerchief: I was to tell her *my secret*. I remember our two heads being all at once in a warm, half-transparent, fragrant darkness, the soft, close brightness of her eyes in the dark, and the burning breath from her parted lips, and the gleam of her teeth and the ends of her hair tickling me and setting me on fire. I was silent. She smiled slyly and mysteriously, and at last whispered to me, 'Well, what is it?' but I merely blushed and laughed, and turned away, catching my breath. We got tired of forfeits—we began to play a game with a string. My God! what were my transports when, for not paying attention, I got a sharp and vigorous slap on my fingers from her, and how I tried afterwards to pretend that I was absent-minded, and she teased me, and would not touch the hands I held out to her! What didn't we do that evening! We played the piano, and sang and danced and acted a gypsy encampment. Nirmatsky was dressed up as a bear, and made to drink salt water. Count Malevsky showed us several sorts of card tricks, and finished, after shuffling the cards, by dealing himself all the trumps at whist, on which Lushin 'had the honour of congratulating him.' Meidanov recited portions from his poem 'The Manslayer' (romanticism was at its height at this period), which he intended to bring out in a black cover with the title in blood-red letters; they stole the clerk's cap off his knee, and made him dance a Cossack dance by way of ransom for it; they dressed up old Vonifaty in a woman's cap, and the young princess put on a man's hat.... I could not enumerate all we did. Only Byelovzorov kept more and more in the background, scowling and angry.... Sometimes his eyes looked bloodshot, he flushed all over, and it seemed every minute as though he would rush out upon us all and scatter us like shavings in all directions; but the young princess would glance at him, and shake her finger at him, and he would retire into his corner again.
We were quite worn out at last. Even the old princess, though she was ready for anything, as she expressed it, and no noise wearied her, felt tired at last, and longed for peace and quiet. At twelve o'clock at night, supper was served, consisting of a piece of stale dry cheese, and some cold turnovers of minced ham, which seemed to me more delicious than any pastry I had ever tasted; there was only one bottle of wine, and that was a strange one; a dark-coloured bottle with a wide neck, and the wine in it was of a pink hue; no one drank it, however. Tired out and faint with happiness, I left the lodge; at parting Zinaïda pressed my hand warmly, and again smiled mysteriously.
The night air was heavy and damp in my heated face; a storm seemed to be gathering; black stormclouds grew and crept across the sky, their smoky outlines visibly changing. A gust of wind shivered restlessly in the dark trees, and somewhere, far away on the horizon, muffled thunder angrily muttered as it were to itself.
I made my way up to my room by the back stairs. My old man-nurse was asleep on the floor, and I had to step over him; he waked up, saw me, and told me that my mother had again been very angry with me, and had wished to send after me again, but that my father had prevented her. (I had never gone to bed without saying good-night to my mother, and asking her blessing. There was no help for it now!)
I told my man that I would undress and go to bed by myself, and I put out the candle. But I did not undress, and did not go to bed.
I sat down on a chair, and sat a long while, as though spell-bound. What I was feeling was so new and so sweet.... I sat still, hardly looking round and not moving, drew slow breaths, and only from time to time laughed silently at some recollection, or turned cold within at the thought that I was in love, that this was she, that this was love. Zinaïda's face floated slowly before me in the darkness—floated, and did not float away;

her lips still wore the same enigmatic smile, her eyes watched me, a little from one side, with a questioning, dreamy, tender look ... as at the instant of parting from her. At last I got up, walked on tiptoe to my bed, and without undressing, laid my head carefully on the pillow, as though I were afraid by an abrupt movement to disturb what filled my soul.... I lay down, but did not even close my eyes. Soon I noticed that faint glimmers of light of some sort were thrown continually into the room.... I sat up and looked at the window. The window-frame could be clearly distinguished from the mysteriously and dimly-lighted panes. It is a storm, I thought; and a storm it really was, but it was raging so very far away that the thunder could not be heard; only blurred, long, as it were branching, gleams of lightning flashed continually over the sky; it was not flashing, though, so much as quivering and twitching like the wing of a dying bird. I got up, went to the window, and stood there till morning.... The lightning never ceased for an instant; it was what is called among the peasants a *sparrow night*. I gazed at the dumb sandy plain, at the dark mass of the Neskutchny gardens, at the yellowish façades of the distant buildings, which seemed to quiver too at each faint flash.... I gazed, and could not turn away; these silent lightning flashes, these gleams seemed in response to the secret silent fires which were aglow within me. Morning began to dawn; the sky was flushed in patches of crimson. As the sun came nearer, the lightning grew gradually paler, and ceased; the quivering gleams were fewer and fewer, and vanished at last, drowned in the sobering positive light of the coming day....

And my lightning flashes vanished too. I felt great weariness and peace ... but Zinaïda's image still floated triumphant over my soul. But it too, this image, seemed more tranquil: like a swan rising out of the reeds of a bog, it stood out from the other unbeautiful figures surrounding it, and as I fell asleep, I flung myself before it in farewell, trusting adoration....

Oh, sweet emotions, gentle harmony, goodness and peace of the softened heart, melting bliss of the first raptures of love, where are they, where are they?

VIII

The next morning, when I came down to tea, my mother scolded me—less severely, however, than I had expected—and made me tell her how I had spent the previous evening. I answered her in few words, omitting many details, and trying to give the most innocent air to everything.

'Anyway, they're people who're not *comme il faut*,' my mother commented, 'and you've no business to be hanging about there, instead of preparing yourself for the examination, and doing your work.'

As I was well aware that my mother's anxiety about my studies was confined to these few words, I did not feel it necessary to make any rejoinder; but after morning tea was over, my father took me by the arm, and turning into the garden with me, forced me to tell him all I had seen at the Zasyekins'.

A curious influence my father had over me, and curious were the relations existing between us. He took hardly any interest in my education, but he never hurt my feelings; he respected my freedom, he treated me—if I may so express it—with courtesy,... only he never let me be really close to him. I loved him, I admired him, he was my ideal of a man—and Heavens! how passionately devoted I should have been to him, if I had not been continually conscious of his holding me off! But when he liked, he could almost instantaneously, by a single word, a single gesture, call forth an unbounded confidence in him. My soul expanded, I chattered away to him, as to a wise friend, a kindly teacher ... then he as suddenly got rid of me, and again he was keeping me off, gently and affectionately, but still he kept me off.

Sometimes he was in high spirits, and then he was ready to romp and frolic with me, like a boy (he was fond of vigorous physical exercise of every sort); once—it never happened a second time!—he caressed me with such tenderness that I almost shed tears.... But high spirits and tenderness alike vanished completely, and what had passed between us, gave me nothing to build on for the future—it was as though I had dreamed it all. Sometimes I would scrutinise his clever handsome bright face ... my heart would throb, and my whole being yearn to him ... he would seem to feel what was going on within me, would give me a passing pat on the cheek, and go away, or take up some work, or suddenly freeze all over as only he knew how to freeze, and I shrank into myself at once, and turned cold too. His rare fits of friendliness to me were never called forth by my silent, but intelligible entreaties: they always occurred unexpectedly. Thinking over my father's character later, I have come to the conclusion that he had no thoughts to spare for me and for family life; his heart was in other things, and found complete satisfaction elsewhere. 'Take for yourself what you can, and don't be ruled by others; to belong to oneself—the whole savour of life lies in that,' he said to me one day. Another time, I, as a young democrat, fell to airing my views on liberty (he was 'kind,' as I used to call it, that day; and at such times I could talk to him as I liked). 'Liberty,' he repeated; 'and do you know what can give a man liberty?'

'What?'

'Will, his own will, and it gives power, which is better than liberty.

Know how to will, and you will be free, and will lead.'

'My father, before all, and above all, desired to live, and lived.... Perhaps he had a presentiment that he would not have long to enjoy the 'savour' of life: he died at forty-two.

I described my evening at the Zasyekins' minutely to my father. Half attentively, half carelessly, he listened to me, sitting on a garden seat, drawing in the sand with his cane. Now and then he laughed, shot bright, droll glances at me, and spurred me on with short questions and assents. At first I could not bring myself even to utter the name of Zinaïda, but I could not restrain myself long, and began singing her praises. My father still laughed; then he grew thoughtful, stretched, and got up. I remembered that as he came out of the house he had ordered his horse to be saddled. He was a splendid horseman, and, long before Rarey, had the secret of breaking in the most vicious horses.

'Shall I come with you, father?' I asked.

'No,' he answered, and his face resumed its ordinary expression of friendly indifference. 'Go alone, if you like; and tell the coachman I'm not going.'

He turned his back on me and walked rapidly away. I looked after him; he disappeared through the gates. I saw his hat moving along beside the fence; he went into the Zasyekins'.

He stayed there not more than an hour, but then departed at once for the town, and did not return home till evening.

After dinner I went myself to the Zasyekins'. In the drawing-room I found only the old princess. On seeing me she scratched her head under her cap with a knitting-needle, and suddenly asked me, could I copy a petition for her.

'With pleasure,' I replied, sitting down on the edge of a chair.

'Only mind and make the letters bigger,' observed the princess, handing me a dirty sheet of paper; 'and couldn't you do it to-day, my good sir?'

'Certainly, I will copy it to-day.'

The door of the next room was just opened, and in the crack I saw the face of Zinaïda, pale and pensive, her hair flung carelessly back; she stared at me with big chilly eyes, and softly closed the door.

'Zina, Zina!' called the old lady. Zinaïda made no response. I took home the old lady's petition and spent the whole evening over it.

IX

My 'passion' dated from that day. I felt at that time, I recollect, something like what a man must feel on entering the service: I had ceased now to be simply a young boy; I was in love. I have said that my passion dated from that day; I might have added that my sufferings too dated from the same day. Away from Zinaïda I pined; nothing was to my mind; everything went wrong with me; I spent whole days thinking intensely about her ... I pined when away,... but in her presence I was no better off. I was jealous; I was conscious of my insignificance; I was stupidly sulky or stupidly abject, and, all the same, an invincible force drew me to her, and I could not help a shudder of delight whenever I stepped through the doorway of her room. Zinaïda guessed at once that I was in love with her, and indeed I never even thought of concealing it. She amused herself with my passion, made a fool of me, petted and tormented me. There is a sweetness in being the sole source, the autocratic and irresponsible cause of the greatest joy and profoundest pain to another, and I was like wax in Zinaïda's hands; though, indeed, I was not the only one in love with her. All the men who visited the house were crazy over her, and she kept them all in leading-strings at her feet. It amused her to arouse their hopes and then their fears, to turn them round her finger (she used to call it knocking their heads together), while they never dreamed of offering resistance and eagerly submitted to her. About her whole being, so full of life and beauty, there was a peculiarly bewitching mixture of slyness and carelessness, of artificiality and simplicity, of composure and frolicsomeness; about everything she did or said, about every action of hers, there clung a delicate, fine charm, in which an individual power was manifest at work. And her face was ever changing, working too; it expressed, almost at the same time, irony, dreaminess, and passion. Various emotions, delicate and quick-changing as the shadows of clouds on a sunny day of wind, chased one another continually over her lips and eyes.

Each of her adorers was necessary to her. Byelovzorov, whom she sometimes called 'my wild beast,' and sometimes simply 'mine,' would gladly have flung himself into the fire for her sake. With little confidence in his intellectual abilities and other qualities, he was for ever offering her marriage, hinting that the others were merely hanging about with no serious intention. Meidanov responded to the poetic fibres of her nature; a man of rather cold temperament, like almost all writers, he forced himself to convince her, and perhaps himself, that he adored her, sang her praises in endless verses, and read them to her with a peculiar enthusiasm, at once affected and sincere. She sympathised with him, and at the same time jeered at him a little; she had no great faith in him, and after listening to his outpourings, she would make him read Pushkin, as she said, to clear the air. Lushin, the ironical doctor, so cynical in words, knew her better than any of them, and loved her more than all, though he abused her to her face and behind her back. She could not help respecting him, but made him smart for it, and at times, with a peculiar, malignant pleasure, made him feel that he too was at her mercy. 'I'm a flirt, I'm heartless, I'm an actress in my instincts,' she said to him one day in my presence; 'well and good! Give me your hand then; I'll stick this pin in it, you'll be ashamed of this young man's seeing it, it will hurt you, but you'll laugh for all that, you truthful person.' Lushin crimsoned, turned away, bit his lips, but ended by submitting his hand. She pricked it, and he did in fact begin to laugh,… and she laughed, thrusting the pin in pretty deeply, and peeping into his eyes, which he vainly strove to keep in other directions….

I understood least of all the relations existing between Zinaïda and Count Malevsky. He was handsome, clever, and adroit, but something equivocal, something false in him was apparent even to me, a boy of sixteen, and I marvelled that Zinaïda did not notice it. But possibly she did notice this element of falsity really and was not repelled by it. Her irregular education, strange acquaintances and habits, the constant presence of her mother, the poverty and disorder in their house, everything, from the very liberty the young girl enjoyed, with the consciousness of her superiority to the people around her, had developed in her a sort of half-contemptuous carelessness and lack of fastidiousness. At any time anything might happen; Vonifaty might announce that there was no sugar, or some revolting scandal would come to her ears, or her guests would fall to quarrelling among themselves—she would only shake her curls, and say, 'What does it matter?' and care little enough about it.

But my blood, anyway, was sometimes on fire with indignation when Malevsky approached her, with a sly, fox-like action, leaned gracefully on the back of her chair, and began whispering in her ear with a self-satisfied and ingratiating little smile, while she folded her arms across her bosom, looked intently at him and smiled too, and shook her head.

'What induces you to receive Count Malevsky?' I asked her one day.

'He has such pretty moustaches,' she answered. 'But that's rather beyond you.'

'You needn't think I care for him,' she said to me another time. 'No; I can't care for people I have to look down upon. I must have some one who can master me…. But, merciful heavens, I hope I may never come across any one like that! I don't want to be caught in any one's claws, not for anything.'

'You'll never be in love, then?'

'And you? Don't I love you?' she said, and she flicked me on the nose with the tip of her glove.

Yes, Zinaïda amused herself hugely at my expense. For three weeks I saw her every day, and what didn't she do with me! She rarely came to see us, and I was not sorry for it; in our house she was transformed into a young lady, a young princess, and I was a little overawed by her. I was afraid of betraying myself before my mother; she had taken a great dislike to Zinaïda, and kept a hostile eye upon us. My father I was not so much afraid of; he seemed not to notice me. He talked little to her, but always with special cleverness and significance. I gave up working and reading; I even gave up walking about the neighbourhood and riding my horse. Like a beetle tied by the leg, I moved continually round and round my beloved little lodge. I would gladly have stopped there altogether, it seemed … but that was impossible. My mother scolded me, and sometimes Zinaïda herself drove me away. Then I used to shut myself up in my room, or go down to the very end of the garden, and climbing into what was left of a tall stone greenhouse, now in ruins, sit for hours with

my legs hanging over the wall that looked on to the road, gazing and gazing and seeing nothing. White butterflies flitted lazily by me, over the dusty nettles; a saucy sparrow settled not far off on the half crumbling red brickwork and twittered irritably, incessantly twisting and turning and preening his tail-feathers; the still mistrustful rooks cawed now and then, sitting high, high up on the bare top of a birch-tree; the sun and wind played softly on its pliant branches; the tinkle of the bells of the Don monastery floated across to me from time to time, peaceful and dreary; while I sat, gazed, listened, and was filled full of a nameless sensation in which all was contained: sadness and joy and the foretaste of the future, and the desire and dread of life. But at that time I understood nothing of it, and could have given a name to nothing of all that was passing at random within me, or should have called it all by one name—the name of Zinaïda.
Zinaïda continued to play cat and mouse with me. She flirted with me, and I was all agitation and rapture; then she would suddenly thrust me away, and I dared not go near her—dared not look at her.
I remember she was very cold to me for several days together; I was completely crushed, and creeping timidly to their lodge, tried to keep close to the old princess, regardless of the circumstance that she was particularly scolding and grumbling just at that time; her financial affairs had been going badly, and she had already had two 'explanations' with the police officials.
One day I was walking in the garden beside the familiar fence, and I caught sight of Zinaïda; leaning on both arms, she was sitting on the grass, not stirring a muscle. I was about to make off cautiously, but she suddenly raised her head and beckoned me imperiously. My heart failed me; I did not understand her at first. She repeated her signal. I promptly jumped over the fence and ran joyfully up to her, but she brought me to a halt with a look, and motioned me to the path two paces from her. In confusion, not knowing what to do, I fell on my knees at the edge of the path. She was so pale, such bitter suffering, such intense weariness, was expressed in every feature of her face, that it sent a pang to my heart, and I muttered unconsciously, 'What is the matter?'
Zinaïda stretched out her head, picked a blade of grass, bit it and flung it away from her.
'You love me very much?' she asked at last. 'Yes.'
I made no answer—indeed, what need was there to answer?
'Yes,' she repeated, looking at me as before. 'That's so. The same eyes,'—she went on; sank into thought, and hid her face in her hands. 'Everything's grown so loathsome to me,' she whispered, 'I would have gone to the other end of the world first—I can't bear it, I can't get over it.... And what is there before me!... Ah, I am wretched.... My God, how wretched I am!'
'What for?' I asked timidly.
Zinaïda made no answer, she simply shrugged her shoulders. I remained kneeling, gazing at her with intense sadness. Every word she had uttered simply cut me to the heart. At that instant I felt I would gladly have given my life, if only she should not grieve. I gazed at her—and though I could not understand why she was wretched, I vividly pictured to myself, how in a fit of insupportable anguish, she had suddenly come out into the garden, and sunk to the earth, as though mown down by a scythe. It was all bright and green about her; the wind was whispering in the leaves of the trees, and swinging now and then a long branch of a raspberry bush over Zinaïda's head. There was a sound of the cooing of doves, and the bees hummed, flying low over the scanty grass, Overhead the sun was radiantly blue—while I was so sorrowful....
'Read me some poetry,' said Zinaïda in an undertone, and she propped herself on her elbow; 'I like your reading poetry. You read it in sing-song, but that's no matter, that comes of being young. Read me "On the Hills of Georgia." Only sit down first.'
I sat down and read 'On the Hills of Georgia.'
'"That the heart cannot choose but love,"' repeated Zinaïda. 'That's where poetry's so fine; it tells us what is not, and what's not only better than what is, but much more like the truth, "cannot choose but love,"—it might want not to, but it can't help it.' She was silent again, then all at once she started and got up. 'Come along. Meidanov's indoors with mamma, he brought me his poem, but I deserted him. His feelings are hurt too now ... I can't help it! you'll understand it all some day ... only don't be angry with me!'
Zinaïda hurriedly pressed my hand and ran on ahead. We went back into the lodge. Meidanov set to reading us his 'Manslayer,' which had just appeared in print, but I did not hear him. He screamed and drawled his four-foot iambic lines, the alternating rhythms jingled like little bells, noisy and meaningless, while I still watched Zinaïda and tried to take in the import of her last words.

'Perchance some unknown rival
Has surprised and mastered thee?'

Meidanov bawled suddenly through his nose—and my eyes and Zinaïda's met. She looked down and faintly blushed. I saw her blush, and grew cold with terror. I had been jealous before, but only at that instant the idea of her being in love flashed upon my mind. 'Good God! she is in love!'

X

My real torments began from that instant. I racked my brains, changed my mind, and changed it back again, and kept an unremitting, though, as far as possible, secret watch on Zinaïda. A change had come over her, that was obvious. She began going walks alone—and long walks. Sometimes she would not see visitors; she would sit for hours together in her room. This had never been a habit of hers till now. I suddenly became—or fancied I had become—extraordinarily penetrating.

'Isn't it he? or isn't it he?' I asked myself, passing in inward agitation from one of her admirers to another. Count Malevsky secretly struck me as more to be feared than the others, though, for Zinaïda's sake, I was ashamed to confess it to myself.

My watchfulness did not see beyond the end of my nose, and its secrecy probably deceived no one; any way, Doctor Lushin soon saw through me. But he, too, had changed of late; he had grown thin, he laughed as often, but his laugh seemed more hollow, more spiteful, shorter, an involuntary nervous irritability took the place of his former light irony and assumed cynicism.

'Why are you incessantly hanging about here, young man?' he said to me one day, when we were left alone together in the Zasyekins' drawing-room. (The young princess had not come home from a walk, and the shrill voice of the old princess could be heard within; she was scolding the maid.) 'You ought to be studying, working—while you're young—and what are you doing?'

'You can't tell whether I work at home,' I retorted with some haughtiness, but also with some hesitation.

'A great deal of work you do! that's not what you're thinking about! Well, I won't find fault with that ... at your age that's in the natural order of things. But you've been awfully unlucky in your choice. Don't you see what this house is?'

'I don't understand you,' I observed.

'You don't understand? so much the worse for you. I regard it as a duty to warn you. Old bachelors, like me, can come here, what harm can it do us! we're tough, nothing can hurt us, what harm can it do us; but your skin's tender yet—this air is bad for you—believe me, you may get harm from it.'

'How so?'

'Why, are you well now? Are you in a normal condition? Is what you're feeling—beneficial to you—good for you?'

'Why, what am I feeling?' I said, while in my heart I knew the doctor was right.

'Ah, young man, young man,' the doctor went on with an intonation that suggested that something highly insulting to me was contained in these two words, 'what's the use of your prevaricating, when, thank God, what's in your heart is in your face, so far? But there, what's the use of talking? I shouldn't come here myself, if ... (the doctor compressed his lips) ... if I weren't such a queer fellow. Only this is what surprises me; how it is, you, with your intelligence, don't see what is going on around you?'

'And what is going on?' I put in, all on the alert.

The doctor looked at me with a sort of ironical compassion.

'Nice of me!' he said as though to himself, 'as if he need know anything of it. In fact, I tell you again,' he added, raising his voice, 'the atmosphere here is not fit for you. You like being here, but what of that! it's nice and sweet-smelling in a greenhouse—but there's no living in it. Yes! do as I tell you, and go back to your Keidanov.'

The old princess came in, and began complaining to the doctor of her toothache. Then Zinaïda appeared.

'Come,' said the old princess, 'you must scold her, doctor. She's drinking iced water all day long; is that good for her, pray, with her delicate chest?'

'Why do you do that?' asked Lushin.

'Why, what effect could it have?'

'What effect? You might get a chill and die.'

'Truly? Do you mean it? Very well—so much the better.'
'A fine idea!' muttered the doctor. The old princess had gone out.
'Yes, a fine idea,' repeated Zinaïda. 'Is life such a festive affair? Just look about you.... Is it nice, eh? Or do you imagine I don't understand it, and don't feel it? It gives me pleasure—drinking iced water; and can you seriously assure me that such a life is worth too much to be risked for an instant's pleasure—happiness I won't even talk about.'
'Oh, very well,' remarked Lushin, 'caprice and irresponsibility.... Those two words sum you up; your whole nature's contained in those two words.'
Zinaïda laughed nervously.
'You're late for the post, my dear doctor. You don't keep a good look-out; you're behind the times. Put on your spectacles. I'm in no capricious humour now. To make fools of you, to make a fool of myself ... much fun there is in that!—and as for irresponsibility ... M'sieu Voldemar,' Zinaïda added suddenly, stamping, 'don't make such a melancholy face. I can't endure people to pity me.' She went quickly out of the room.
'It's bad for you, very bad for you, this atmosphere, young man,'
Lushin said to me once more.

XI

On the evening of the same day the usual guests were assembled at the
Zasyekins'. I was among them.
The conversation turned on Meidanov's poem. Zinaïda expressed genuine admiration of it. 'But do you know what?' she said to him. 'If I were a poet, I would choose quite different subjects. Perhaps it's all nonsense, but strange ideas sometimes come into my head, especially when I'm not asleep in the early morning, when the sky begins to turn rosy and grey both at once. I would, for instance ... You won't laugh at me?'
'No, no!' we all cried, with one voice.
'I would describe,' she went on, folding her arms across her bosom and looking away, 'a whole company of young girls at night in a great boat, on a silent river. The moon is shining, and they are all in white, and wearing garlands of white flowers, and singing, you know, something in the nature of a hymn.'
'I see—I see; go on,' Meidanov commented with dreamy significance.
'All of a sudden, loud clamour, laughter, torches, tambourines on the bank.... It's a troop of Bacchantes dancing with songs and cries. It's your business to make a picture of it, Mr. Poet;... only I should like the torches to be red and to smoke a great deal, and the Bacchantes' eyes to gleam under their wreaths, and the wreaths to be dusky. Don't forget the tiger-skins, too, and goblets and gold—lots of gold....'
'Where ought the gold to be?' asked Meidanov, tossing back his sleek hair and distending his nostrils.
'Where? on their shoulders and arms and legs—everywhere. They say in ancient times women wore gold rings on their ankles. The Bacchantes call the girls in the boat to them. The girls have ceased singing their hymn—they cannot go on with it, but they do not stir, the river carries them to the bank. And suddenly one of them slowly rises.... This you must describe nicely: how she slowly gets up in the moonlight, and how her companions are afraid.... She steps over the edge of the boat, the Bacchantes surround her, whirl her away into night and darkness.... Here put in smoke in clouds and everything in confusion. There is nothing but the sound of their shrill cry, and her wreath left lying on the bank.'
Zinaïda ceased. ('Oh! she is in love!' I thought again.)
'And is that all?' asked Meidanov.
'That's all.'
'That can't be the subject of a whole poem,' he observed pompously, 'but I will make use of your idea for a lyrical fragment.'
'In the romantic style?' queried Malevsky.
'Of course, in the romantic style—Byronic.'
'Well, to my mind, Hugo beats Byron,' the young count observed negligently; 'he's more interesting.'
'Hugo is a writer of the first class,' replied Meidanov; 'and my friend, Tonkosheev, in his Spanish romance, *El Trovador* ...'

'Ah! is that the book with the question-marks turned upside down?'
Zinaïda interrupted.
'Yes. That's the custom with the Spanish. I was about to observe that
Tonkosheev ...'
'Come! you're going to argue about classicism and romanticism again,'
Zinaïda interrupted him a second time.' We'd much better play ...
'Forfeits?' put in Lushin.
'No, forfeits are a bore; at comparisons.' (This game Zinaïda had invented herself. Some object was mentioned, every one tried to compare it with something, and the one who chose the best comparison got a prize.)
She went up to the window. The sun was just setting; high up in the sky were large red clouds.
'What are those clouds like?' questioned Zinaïda; and without waiting for our answer, she said, 'I think they are like the purple sails on the golden ship of Cleopatra, when she sailed to meet Antony. Do you remember, Meidanov, you were telling me about it not long ago?'
All of us, like Polonius in *Hamlet*, opined that the clouds recalled nothing so much as those sails, and that not one of us could discover a better comparison.
'And how old was Antony then?' inquired Zinaïda.
'A young man, no doubt,' observed Malevsky.
'Yes, a young man,' Meidanov chimed in in confirmation.
'Excuse me,' cried Lushin, 'he was over forty.'
'Over forty,' repeated Zinaïda, giving him a rapid glance....
I soon went home. 'She is in love,' my lips unconsciously repeated....
'But with whom?'

XII

The days passed by. Zinaïda became stranger and stranger, and more and more incomprehensible. One day I went over to her, and saw her sitting in a basket-chair, her head pressed to the sharp edge of the table. She drew herself up ... her whole face was wet with tears.
'Ah, you!' she said with a cruel smile. 'Come here.'
I went up to her. She put her hand on my head, and suddenly catching hold of my hair, began pulling it.
'It hurts me,' I said at last.
'Ah! does it? And do you suppose nothing hurts me?' she replied.
'Ai!' she cried suddenly, seeing she had pulled a little tuft of hair out. 'What have I done? Poor M'sieu Voldemar!'
She carefully smoothed the hair she had torn out, stroked it round her finger, and twisted it into a ring.
'I shall put your hair in a locket and wear it round my neck,' she said, while the tears still glittered in her eyes. 'That will be some small consolation to you, perhaps ... and now good-bye.'
I went home, and found an unpleasant state of things there. My mother was having a scene with my father; she was reproaching him with something, while he, as his habit was, maintained a polite and chilly silence, and soon left her. I could not hear what my mother was talking of, and indeed I had no thought to spare for the subject; I only remember that when the interview was over, she sent for me to her room, and referred with great displeasure to the frequent visits I paid the princess, who was, in her words, *une femme capable de tout*. I kissed her hand (this was what I always did when I wanted to cut short a conversation) and went off to my room. Zinaïda's tears had completely overwhelmed me; I positively did not know what to think, and was ready to cry myself; I was a child after all, in spite of my sixteen years. I had now given up thinking about Malevsky, though Byelovzorov looked more and more threatening every day, and glared at the wily count like a wolf at a sheep; but I thought of nothing and of no one. I was lost in imaginings, and was always seeking seclusion and solitude. I was particularly fond of the ruined greenhouse. I would climb up on the high wall, and perch myself, and sit there, such an unhappy, lonely, and melancholy youth, that I felt sorry for myself—and how consolatory where those mournful sensations, how I revelled in them!...

One day I was sitting on the wall looking into the distance and listening to the ringing of the bells.... Suddenly something floated up to me—not a breath of wind and not a shiver, but as it were a whiff of fragrance—as it were, a sense of some one's being near.... I looked down. Below, on the path, in a light greyish gown, with a pink parasol on her shoulder, was Zinaïda, hurrying along. She caught sight of me, stopped, and pushing back the brim of her straw hat, she raised her velvety eyes to me.
'What are you doing up there at such a height?' she asked me with a rather queer smile. 'Come,' she went on, 'you always declare you love me; jump down into the road to me if you really do love me.'
Zinaïda had hardly uttered those words when I flew down, just as though some one had given me a violent push from behind. The wall was about fourteen feet high. I reached the ground on my feet, but the shock was so great that I could not keep my footing; I fell down, and for an instant fainted away. When I came to myself again, without opening my eyes, I felt Zinaïda beside me. 'My dear boy,' she was saying, bending over me, and there was a note of alarmed tenderness in her voice, 'how could you do it, dear; how could you obey?... You know I love you.... Get up.'
Her bosom was heaving close to me, her hands were caressing my head, and suddenly—what were my emotions at that moment—her soft, fresh lips began covering my face with kisses ... they touched my lips.... But then Zinaïda probably guessed by the expression of my face that I had regained consciousness, though I still kept my eyes closed, and rising rapidly to her feet, she said: 'Come, get up, naughty boy, silly, why are you lying in the dust?' I got up. 'Give me my parasol,' said Zinaïda, 'I threw it down somewhere, and don't stare at me like that ... what ridiculous nonsense! you're not hurt, are you? stung by the nettles, I daresay? Don't stare at me, I tell you.... But he doesn't understand, he doesn't answer,' she added, as though to herself.... 'Go home, M'sieu' Voldemar, brush yourself, and don't dare to follow me, or I shall be angry, and never again ...'
She did not finish her sentence, but walked rapidly away, while I sat down by the side of the road ... my legs would not support me. The nettles had stung my hands, my back ached, and my head was giddy; but the feeling of rapture I experienced then has never come a second time in my life. It turned to a sweet ache in all my limbs and found expression at last in joyful hops and skips and shouts. Yes, I was still a child.

XIII

I was so proud and light-hearted all that day, I so vividly retained on my face the feeling of Zinaïda's kisses, with such a shudder of delight I recalled every word she had uttered, I so hugged my unexpected happiness that I felt positively afraid, positively unwilling to see her, who had given rise to these new sensations. It seemed to me that now I could ask nothing more of fate, that now I ought to 'go, and draw a deep last sigh and die.' But, next day, when I went into the lodge, I felt great embarrassment, which I tried to conceal under a show of modest confidence, befitting a man who wishes to make it apparent that he knows how to keep a secret. Zinaïda received me very simply, without any emotion, she simply shook her finger at me and asked me, whether I wasn't black and blue? All my modest confidence and air of mystery vanished instantaneously and with them my embarrassment. Of course, I had not expected anything particular, but Zinaïda's composure was like a bucket of cold water thrown over me. I realised that in her eyes I was a child, and was extremely miserable! Zinaïda walked up and down the room, giving me a quick smile, whenever she caught my eye, but her thoughts were far away, I saw that clearly.... 'Shall I begin about what happened yesterday myself,' I pondered; 'ask her, where she was hurrying off so fast, so as to find out once for all' ... but with a gesture of despair, I merely went and sat down in a corner.
Byelovzorov came in; I felt relieved to see him.
'I've not been able to find you a quiet horse,' he said in a sulky voice; 'Freitag warrants one, but I don't feel any confidence in it, I am afraid.'
'What are you afraid of?' said Zinaïda; 'allow me to inquire?'
'What am I afraid of? Why, you don't know how to ride. Lord save us, what might happen! What whim is this has come over you all of a sudden?'
'Come, that's my business, Sir Wild Beast. In that case I will ask
Piotr Vassilievitch.' ... (My father's name was Piotr Vassilievitch.

I was surprised at her mentioning his name so lightly and freely, as though she were confident of his readiness to do her a service.)
'Oh, indeed,' retorted Byelovzorov, 'you mean to go out riding with him then?'
'With him or with some one else is nothing to do with you. Only not with you, anyway.'
'Not with me,' repeated Byelovzorov. 'As you wish. Well, I shall find you a horse.'
'Yes, only mind now, don't send some old cow. I warn you I want to gallop.'
'Gallop away by all means … with whom is it, with Malevsky, you are going to ride?'
'And why not with him, Mr. Pugnacity? Come, be quiet,' she added, 'and don't glare. I'll take you too. You know that to my mind now Malevsky's—ugh!' She shook her head.
'You say that to console me,' growled Byelovzorov.
Zinaïda half closed her eyes. 'Does that console you? O … O … O … Mr. Pugnacity!' she said at last, as though she could find no other word. 'And you, M'sieu' Voldemar, would you come with us?'
'I don't care to … in a large party,' I muttered, not raising my eyes.
'You prefer a *tête-à-tête*?… Well, freedom to the free, and heaven to the saints,' she commented with a sigh.
'Go along, Byelovzorov, and bestir yourself. I must have a horse for to-morrow.'
'Oh, and where's the money to come from?' put in the old princess.
Zinaïda scowled.
'I won't ask you for it; Byelovzorov will trust me.'
'He'll trust you, will he?' … grumbled the old princess, and all of a sudden she screeched at the top of her voice, 'Duniashka!'
'Maman, I have given you a bell to ring,' observed Zinaïda.
'Duniashka!' repeated the old lady.
Byelovzorov took leave; I went away with him. Zinaïda did not try to detain me.

XIV

The next day I got up early, cut myself a stick, and set off beyond the town-gates. I thought I would walk off my sorrow. It was a lovely day, bright and not too hot, a fresh sportive breeze roved over the earth with temperate rustle and frolic, setting all things a-flutter and harassing nothing. I wandered a long while over hills and through woods; I had not felt happy, I had left home with the intention of giving myself up to melancholy, but youth, the exquisite weather, the fresh air, the pleasure of rapid motion, the sweetness of repose, lying on the thick grass in a solitary nook, gained the upper hand; the memory of those never-to-be-forgotten words, those kisses, forced itself once more upon my soul. It was sweet to me to think that Zinaïda could not, anyway, fail to do justice to my courage, my heroism….' Others may seem better to her than I,' I mused, 'let them! But others only say what they would do, while I have done it. And what more would I not do for her?' My fancy set to work. I began picturing to myself how I would save her from the hands of enemies; how, covered with blood I would tear her by force from prison, and expire at her feet. I remembered a picture hanging in our drawing-room—Malek-Adel bearing away Matilda—but at that point my attention was absorbed by the appearance of a speckled woodpecker who climbed busily up the slender stem of a birch-tree and peeped out uneasily from behind it, first to the right, then to the left, like a musician behind the bass-viol.
Then I sang 'Not the white snows,' and passed from that to a song well known at that period: 'I await thee, when the wanton zephyr,' then I began reading aloud Yermak's address to the stars from Homyakov's tragedy. I made an attempt to compose something myself in a sentimental vein, and invented the line which was to conclude each verse: 'O Zinaïda, Zinaïda!' but could get no further with it. Meanwhile it was getting on towards dinner-time. I went down into the valley; a narrow sandy path winding through it led to the town. I walked along this path…. The dull thud of horses' hoofs resounded behind me. I looked round instinctively, stood still and took off my cap. I saw my father and Zinaïda. They were riding side by side. My father was saying something to her, bending right over to her, his hand propped on the horses' neck, he was smiling. Zinaïda listened to him in silence, her eyes severely cast down, and her lips tightly pressed together. At first I saw them only; but a few instants later, Byelovzorov came into sight round a bend in the glade, he was

wearing a hussar's uniform with a pelisse, and riding a foaming black horse. The gallant horse tossed its head, snorted and pranced from side to side, his rider was at once holding him in and spurring him on. I stood aside. My father gathered up the reins, moved away from Zinaïda, she slowly raised her eyes to him, and both galloped off … Byelovzorov flew after them, his sabre clattering behind him. 'He's as red as a crab,' I reflected, 'while she … why's she so pale? out riding the whole morning, and pale?'
I redoubled my pace, and got home just at dinner-time. My father was already sitting by my mother's chair, dressed for dinner, washed and fresh; he was reading an article from the *Journal des Débats* in his smooth musical voice; but my mother heard him without attention, and when she saw me, asked where I had been to all day long, and added that she didn't like this gadding about God knows where, and God knows in what company. 'But I have been walking alone,' I was on the point of replying, but I looked at my father, and for some reason or other held my peace.

XV

For the next five or six days I hardly saw Zinaïda; she said she was ill, which did not, however, prevent the usual visitors from calling at the lodge to pay—as they expressed it, their duty—all, that is, except Meidanov, who promptly grew dejected and sulky when he had not an opportunity of being enthusiastic. Byelovzorov sat sullen and red-faced in a corner, buttoned up to the throat; on the refined face of Malevsky there flickered continually an evil smile; he had really fallen into disfavour with Zinaïda, and waited with special assiduity on the old princess, and even went with her in a hired coach to call on the Governor-General. This expedition turned out unsuccessful, however, and even led to an unpleasant experience for Malevsky; he was reminded of some scandal to do with certain officers of the engineers, and was forced in his explanations to plead his youth and inexperience at the time. Lushin came twice a day, but did not stay long; I was rather afraid of him after our last unreserved conversation, and at the same time felt a genuine attraction to him. He went a walk with me one day in the Neskutchny gardens, was very good-natured and nice, told me the names and properties of various plants and flowers, and suddenly, *à propos* of nothing at all, cried, hitting himself on his forehead, 'And I, poor fool, thought her a flirt! it's clear self-sacrifice is sweet for some people!'
'What do you mean by that?' I inquired.
'I don't mean to tell you anything,' Lushin replied abruptly.
Zinaïda avoided me; my presence—I could not help noticing it—affected her disagreeably. She involuntarily turned away from me … involuntarily; that was what was so bitter, that was what crushed me! But there was no help for it, and I tried not to cross her path, and only to watch her from a distance, in which I was not always successful. As before, something incomprehensible was happening to her; her face was different, she was different altogether. I was specially struck by the change that had taken place in her one warm still evening. I was sitting on a low garden bench under a spreading elderbush; I was fond of that nook; I could see from there the window of Zinaïda's room. I sat there; over my head a little bird was busily hopping about in the darkness of the leaves; a grey cat, stretching herself at full length, crept warily about the garden, and the first beetles were heavily droning in the air, which was still clear, though it was not light. I sat and gazed at the window, and waited to see if it would open; it did open, and Zinaïda appeared at it. She had on a white dress, and she herself, her face, shoulders, and arms, were pale to whiteness. She stayed a long while without moving, and looked out straight before her from under her knitted brows. I had never known such a look on her. Then she clasped her hands tightly, raised them to her lips, to her forehead, and suddenly pulling her fingers apart, she pushed back her hair behind her ears, tossed it, and with a sort of determination nodded her head, and slammed-to the window.
Three days later she met me in the garden. I was turning away, but she stopped me of herself.
'Give me your arm,' she said to me with her old affectionateness, 'it's a long while since we have had a talk together.'
I stole a look at her; her eyes were full of a soft light, and her face seemed as it were smiling through a mist.
'Are you still not well?' I asked her.
'No, that's all over now,' she answered, and she picked a small red rose. 'I am a little tired, but that too will pass off.'

'And will you be as you used to be again?' I asked.
Zinaïda put the rose up to her face, and I fancied the reflection of its bright petals had fallen on her cheeks.
'Why, am I changed?' she questioned me.
'Yes, you are changed,' I answered in a low voice.
'I have been cold to you, I know,' began Zinaïda, 'but you mustn't pay attention to that ... I couldn't help it.... Come, why talk about it!'
'You don't want me to love you, that's what it is!' I cried gloomily, in an involuntary outburst.
'No, love me, but not as you did.'
'How then?'
'Let us be friends—come now!' Zinaïda gave me the rose to smell. 'Listen, you know I'm much older than you—I might be your aunt, really; well, not your aunt, but an older sister. And you ...'
'You think me a child,' I interrupted.
'Well, yes, a child, but a dear, good clever one, whom I love very much. Do you know what? From this day forth I confer on you the rank of page to me; and don't you forget that pages have to keep close to their ladies. Here is the token of your new dignity,' she added, sticking the rose in the buttonhole of my jacket, 'the token of my favour.'
'I once received other favours from you,' I muttered.
'Ah!' commented Zinaïda, and she gave me a sidelong look, 'What a memory he has! Well? I'm quite ready now ...' And stooping to me, she imprinted on my forehead a pure, tranquil kiss.
I only looked at her, while she turned away, and saying, 'Follow me, my page,' went into the lodge. I followed her—all in amazement. 'Can this gentle, reasonable girl,' I thought, 'be the Zinaïda I used to know?' I fancied her very walk was quieter, her whole figure statelier and more graceful ...
And, mercy! with what fresh force love burned within me!

XVI

After dinner the usual party assembled again at the lodge, and the young princess came out to them. All were there in full force, just as on that first evening which I never forgot; even Nirmatsky had limped to see her; Meidanov came this time earliest of all, he brought some new verses. The games of forfeits began again, but without the strange pranks, the practical jokes and noise—the gipsy element had vanished. Zinaïda gave a different tone to the proceedings. I sat beside her by virtue of my office as page. Among other things, she proposed that any one who had to pay a forfeit should tell his dream; but this was not successful. The dreams were either uninteresting (Byelovzorov had dreamed that he fed his mare on carp, and that she had a wooden head), or unnatural and invented. Meidanov regaled us with a regular romance; there were sepulchres in it, and angels with lyres, and talking flowers and music wafted from afar. Zinaïda did not let him finish. 'If we are to have compositions,' she said, 'let every one tell something made up, and no pretence about it.' The first who had to speak was again Byelovzorov.
The young hussar was confused. 'I can't make up anything!' he cried.
'What nonsense!' said Zinaïda. 'Well, imagine, for instance, you are married, and tell us how you would treat your wife. Would you lock her up?'
'Yes, I should lock her up.'
'And would you stay with her yourself?'
'Yes, I should certainly stay with her myself.'
'Very good. Well, but if she got sick of that, and she deceived you?'
'I should kill her.'
'And if she ran away?'
'I should catch her up and kill her all the same.'
'Oh. And suppose now I were your wife, what would you do then?'
Byelovzorov was silent a minute. 'I should kill myself....'
Zinaïda laughed. 'I see yours is not a long story.'

The next forfeit was Zinaïda's. She looked at the ceiling and considered. 'Well, listen, she began at last, 'what I have thought of.... Picture to yourselves a magnificent palace, a summer night, and a marvellous ball. This ball is given by a young queen. Everywhere gold and marble, crystal, silk, lights, diamonds, flowers, fragrant scents, every caprice of luxury.'

'You love luxury?' Lushin interposed. 'Luxury is beautiful,' she retorted; 'I love everything beautiful.'

'More than what is noble?' he asked.

'That's something clever, I don't understand it. Don't interrupt me. So the ball is magnificent. There are crowds of guests, all of them are young, handsome, and brave, all are frantically in love with the queen.'

'Are there no women among the guests?' queried Malevsky.

'No—or wait a minute—yes, there are some.'

'Are they all ugly?'

'No, charming. But the men are all in love with the queen. She is tall and graceful; she has a little gold diadem on her black hair.'

I looked at Zinaïda, and at that instant she seemed to me so much above all of us, there was such bright intelligence, and such power about her unruffled brows, that I thought: 'You are that queen!'

'They all throng about her,' Zinaïda went on, 'and all lavish the most flattering speeches upon her.'

'And she likes flattery?' Lushin queried.

'What an intolerable person! he keeps interrupting ... who doesn't like flattery?'

'One more last question,' observed Malevsky, 'has the queen a husband?'

'I hadn't thought about that. No, why should she have a husband?'

'To be sure,' assented Malevsky, 'why should she have a husband?'

'*Silence!*' cried Meidanov in French, which he spoke very badly.

'*Merci!*' Zinaïda said to him. 'And so the queen hears their speeches, and hears the music, but does not look at one of the guests. Six windows are open from top to bottom, from floor to ceiling, and beyond them is a dark sky with big stars, a dark garden with big trees. The queen gazes out into the garden. Out there among the trees is a fountain; it is white in the darkness, and rises up tall, tall as an apparition. The queen hears, through the talk and the music, the soft splash of its waters. She gazes and thinks: you are all, gentlemen, noble, clever, and rich, you crowd round me, you treasure every word I utter, you are all ready to die at my feet, I hold you in my power ... but out there, by the fountain, by that splashing water, stands and waits he whom I love, who holds me in his power. He has neither rich raiment nor precious stones, no one knows him, but he awaits me, and is certain I shall come—and I shall come—and there is no power that could stop me when I want to go out to him, and to stay with him, and be lost with him out there in the darkness of the garden, under the whispering of the trees, and the splash of the fountain ...' Zinaïda ceased.

'Is that a made-up story?' Malevsky inquired slyly. Zinaïda did not even look at him.

'And what should we have done, gentlemen?' Lushin began suddenly, 'if we had been among the guests, and had known of the lucky fellow at the fountain?'

'Stop a minute, stop a minute,' interposed Zinaïda, 'I will tell you myself what each of you would have done. You, Byelovzorov, would have challenged him to a duel; you, Meidanov, would have written an epigram on him ... No, though, you can't write epigrams, you would have made up a long poem on him in the style of Barbier, and would have inserted your production in the *Telegraph*. You, Nirmatsky, would have borrowed ... no, you would have lent him money at high interest; you, doctor,...' she stopped. 'There, I really don't know what you would have done....'

'In the capacity of court physician,' answered Lushin, 'I would have advised the queen not to give balls when she was not in the humour for entertaining her guests....'

'Perhaps you would have been right. And you, Count?...'

'And I?' repeated Malevsky with his evil smile....

'You would offer him a poisoned sweetmeat.' Malevsky's face changed slightly, and assumed for an instant a Jewish expression, but he laughed directly.

'And as for you, Voldemar,...' Zinaïda went on, 'but that's enough, though; let us play another game.'

'M'sieu Voldemar, as the queen's page, would have held up her train when she ran into the garden,' Malevsky remarked malignantly.

I was crimson with anger, but Zinaïda hurriedly laid a hand on my shoulder, and getting up, said in a rather shaky voice: 'I have never given your excellency the right to be rude, and therefore I will ask you to leave us.' She pointed to the door.

'Upon my word, princess,' muttered Malevsky, and he turned quite pale.

'The princess is right,' cried Byelovzorov, and he too rose.
'Good God, I'd not the least idea,' Malevsky went on, 'in my words there was nothing, I think, that could … I had no notion of offending you…. Forgive me.'
Zinaïda looked him up and down coldly, and coldly smiled. 'Stay, then, certainly,' she pronounced with a careless gesture of her arm.
'M'sieu Voldemar and I were needlessly incensed. It is your pleasure to sting … may it do you good.'
'Forgive me,' Malevsky repeated once more; while I, my thoughts dwelling on Zinaïda's gesture, said to myself again that no real queen could with greater dignity have shown a presumptuous subject to the door.
The game of forfeits went on for a short time after this little scene; every one felt rather ill at ease, not so much on account of this scene, as from another, not quite definite, but oppressive feeling. No one spoke of it, but every one was conscious of it in himself and in his neighbour. Meidanov read us his verses; and Malevsky praised them with exaggerated warmth. 'He wants to show how good he is now,' Lushin whispered to me. We soon broke up. A mood of reverie seemed to have come upon Zinaïda; the old princess sent word that she had a headache; Nirmatsky began to complain of his rheumatism….
I could not for a long while get to sleep. I had been impressed by Zinaïda's story. 'Can there have been a hint in it?' I asked myself: 'and at whom and at what was she hinting? And if there really is anything to hint at … how is one to make up one's mind? No, no, it can't be,' I whispered, turning over from one hot cheek on to the other…. But I remembered the expression of Zinaïda's face during her story…. I remembered the exclamation that had broken from Lushin in the Neskutchny gardens, the sudden change in her behaviour to me, and I was lost in conjectures. 'Who is he?' These three words seemed to stand before my eyes traced upon the darkness; a lowering malignant cloud seemed hanging over me, and I felt its oppressiveness, and waited for it to break. I had grown used to many things of late; I had learned much from what I had seen at the Zasyekins; their disorderly ways, tallow candle-ends, broken knives and forks, grumpy Vonifaty, and shabby maid-servants, the manners of the old princess—all their strange mode of life no longer struck me…. But what I was dimly discerning now in Zinaïda, I could never get used to…. 'An adventuress!' my mother had said of her one day. An adventuress—she, my idol, my divinity? This word stabbed me, I tried to get away from it into my pillow, I was indignant—and at the same time what would I not have agreed to, what would I not have given only to be that lucky fellow at the fountain!… My blood was on fire and boiling within me. 'The garden … the fountain,' I mused…. 'I will go into the garden.' I dressed quickly and slipped out of the house. The night was dark, the trees scarcely whispered, a soft chill air breathed down from the sky, a smell of fennel trailed across from the kitchen garden. I went through all the walks; the light sound of my own footsteps at once confused and emboldened me; I stood still, waited and heard my heart beating fast and loudly. At last I went up to the fence and leaned against the thin bar. Suddenly, or was it my fancy, a woman's figure flashed by, a few paces from me … I strained my eyes eagerly into the darkness, I held my breath. What was that? Did I hear steps, or was it my heart beating again? 'Who is here?' I faltered, hardly audibly. What was that again, a smothered laugh … or a rustling in the leaves … or a sigh just at my ear? I felt afraid … 'Who is here?' I repeated still more softly.
The air blew in a gust for an instant; a streak of fire flashed across the sky; it was a star falling. 'Zinaïda?' I wanted to call, but the word died away on my lips. And all at once everything became profoundly still around, as is often the case in the middle of the night…. Even the grasshoppers ceased their churr in the trees—only a window rattled somewhere. I stood and stood, and then went back to my room, to my chilled bed. I felt a strange sensation; as though I had gone to a tryst, and had been left lonely, and had passed close by another's happiness.

XVII

The following day I only had a passing glimpse of Zinaïda: she was driving somewhere with the old princess in a cab. But I saw Lushin, who, however, barely vouchsafed me a greeting, and Malevsky. The young count grinned, and began affably talking to me. Of all those who visited at the lodge, he alone had succeeded in forcing his way into our house, and had favourably impressed my mother. My father did not take to him, and treated him with a civility almost insulting.

'Ah, *monsieur le page*,' began Malevsky, 'delighted to meet you. What is your lovely queen doing?'
His fresh handsome face was so detestable to me at that moment, and he looked at me with such contemptuous amusement that I did not answer him at all.
'Are you still angry?' he went on. 'You've no reason to be. It wasn't
I who called you a page, you know, and pages attend queens especially.
But allow me to remark that you perform your duties very badly.'
'How so?'
'Pages ought to be inseparable from their mistresses; pages ought to know everything they do, they ought, indeed, to watch over them,' he added, lowering his voice, 'day and night.'
'What do you mean?'
'What do I mean? I express myself pretty clearly, I fancy. Day and night. By day it's not so much matter; it's light, and people are about in the daytime; but by night, then look out for misfortune. I advise you not to sleep at nights and to watch, watch with all your energies. You remember, in the garden, by night, at the fountain, that's where there's need to look out. You will thank me.'
Malevsky laughed and turned his back on me. He, most likely, attached no great importance to what he had said to me, he had a reputation for mystifying, and was noted for his power of taking people in at masquerades, which was greatly augmented by the almost unconscious falsity in which his whole nature was steeped.... He only wanted to tease me; but every word he uttered was a poison that ran through my veins. The blood rushed to my head. 'Ah! so that's it!' I said to myself; 'good! So there was reason for me to feel drawn into the garden! That shan't be so!' I cried aloud, and struck myself on the chest with my fist, though precisely what should not be so I could not have said. 'Whether Malevsky himself goes into the garden,' I thought (he was bragging, perhaps; he has insolence enough for that), 'or some one else (the fence of our garden was very low, and there was no difficulty in getting over it), anyway, if any one falls into my hands, it will be the worse for him! I don't advise any one to meet me! I will prove to all the world and to her, the traitress (I actually used the word 'traitress') that I can be revenged!'
I returned to my own room, took out of the writing-table an English knife I had recently bought, felt its sharp edge, and knitting my brows with an air of cold and concentrated determination, thrust it into my pocket, as though doing such deeds was nothing out of the way for me, and not the first time. My heart heaved angrily, and felt heavy as a stone. All day long I kept a scowling brow and lips tightly compressed, and was continually walking up and down, clutching, with my hand in my pocket, the knife, which was warm from my grasp, while I prepared myself beforehand for something terrible. These new unknown sensations so occupied and even delighted me, that I hardly thought of Zinaïda herself. I was continually haunted by Aleko, the young gipsy—'Where art thou going, young handsome man? Lie there,' and then, 'thou art all besprent with blood.... Oh, what hast thou done?... Naught!' With what a cruel smile I repeated that 'Naught!' My father was not at home; but my mother, who had for some time past been in an almost continual state of dumb exasperation, noticed my gloomy and heroic aspect, and said to me at supper, 'Why are you sulking like a mouse in a meal-tub?' I merely smiled condescendingly in reply, and thought, 'If only they knew!' It struck eleven; I went to my room, but did not undress; I waited for midnight; at last it struck. 'The time has come!' I muttered between my teeth; and buttoning myself up to the throat, and even pulling my sleeves up, I went into the garden.
I had already fixed on the spot from which to keep watch. At the end of the garden, at the point where the fence, separating our domain from the Zasyekins,' joined the common wall, grew a pine-tree, standing alone. Standing under its low thick branches, I could see well, as far as the darkness of the night permitted, what took place around. Close by, ran a winding path which had always seemed mysterious to me; it coiled like a snake under the fence, which at that point bore traces of having been climbed over, and led to a round arbour formed of thick acacias. I made my way to the pine-tree, leaned my back against its trunk, and began my watch.
The night was as still as the night before, but there were fewer clouds in the sky, and the outlines of bushes, even of tall flowers, could be more distinctly seen. The first moments of expectation were oppressive, almost terrible. I had made up my mind to everything. I only debated how to act; whether to thunder, 'Where goest thou? Stand! show thyself—or death!' or simply to strike.... Every sound, every whisper and rustle, seemed to me portentous and extraordinary.... I prepared myself.... I bent forward.... But half-an-hour passed, an hour passed; my blood had grown quieter, colder; the consciousness that I was doing all this for nothing, that I was even a little absurd, that Malevsky had been making fun of me, began to steal over me. I left my ambush, and walked all about the garden. As if to taunt me, there was not the smallest sound to be heard

anywhere; everything was at rest. Even our dog was asleep, curled up into a ball at the gate. I climbed up into the ruins of the greenhouse, saw the open country far away before me, recalled my meeting with Zinaïda, and fell to dreaming....

I started.... I fancied I heard the creak of a door opening, then the faint crack of a broken twig. In two bounds I got down from the ruin, and stood still, all aghast. Rapid, light, but cautious footsteps sounded distinctly in the garden. They were approaching me. 'Here he is ... here he is, at last!' flashed through my heart. With spasmodic haste, I pulled the knife out of my pocket; with spasmodic haste, I opened it. Flashes of red were whirling before my eyes; my hair stood up on my head in my fear and fury.... The steps were coming straight towards me; I bent—I craned forward to meet him.... A man came into view.... My God! it was my father! I recognised him at once, though he was all muffled up in a dark cloak, and his hat was pulled down over his face. On tip-toe he walked by. He did not notice me, though nothing concealed me; but I was so huddled up and shrunk together that I fancy I was almost on the level of the ground. The jealous Othello, ready for murder, was suddenly transformed into a school-boy.... I was so taken aback by my father's unexpected appearance that for the first moment I did not notice where he had come from or in what direction he disappeared. I only drew myself up, and thought, 'Why is it my father is walking about in the garden at night?' when everything was still again. In my horror I had dropped my knife in the grass, but I did not even attempt to look for it; I was very much ashamed of myself. I was completely sobered at once. On my way to the house, however, I went up to my seat under the elder-tree, and looked up at Zinaïda's window. The small slightly-convex panes of the window shone dimly blue in the faint light thrown on them by the night sky. All at once—their colour began to change.... Behind them—I saw this, saw it distinctly—softly and cautiously a white blind was let down, let down right to the window-frame, and so stayed.

'What is that for?' I said aloud almost involuntarily when I found myself once more in my room. 'A dream, a chance, or ...' The suppositions which suddenly rushed into my head were so new and strange that I did not dare to entertain them.

XVIII

I got up in the morning with a headache. My emotion of the previous day had vanished. It was replaced by a dreary sense of blankness and a sort of sadness I had not known till then, as though something had died in me.

'Why is it you're looking like a rabbit with half its brain removed?' said Lushin on meeting me. At lunch I stole a look first at my father, then at my mother: he was composed, as usual; she was, as usual, secretly irritated. I waited to see whether my father would make some friendly remarks to me, as he sometimes did.... But he did not even bestow his everyday cold greeting upon me. 'Shall I tell Zinaïda all?' I wondered.... 'It's all the same, anyway; all is at an end between us.' I went to see her, but told her nothing, and, indeed, I could not even have managed to get a talk with her if I had wanted to. The old princess's son, a cadet of twelve years old, had come from Petersburg for his holidays; Zinaïda at once handed her brother over to me. 'Here,' she said,' my dear Volodya,'—it was the first time she had used this pet-name to me—'is a companion for you. His name is Volodya, too. Please, like him; he is still shy, but he has a good heart. Show him Neskutchny gardens, go walks with him, take him under your protection. You'll do that, won't you? you're so good, too!' She laid both her hands affectionately on my shoulders, and I was utterly bewildered. The presence of this boy transformed me, too, into a boy. I looked in silence at the cadet, who stared as silently at me. Zinaïda laughed, and pushed us towards each other. 'Embrace each other, children!' We embraced each other. 'Would you like me to show you the garden?' I inquired of the cadet. 'If you please,' he replied, in the regular cadet's hoarse voice. Zinaïda laughed again.... I had time to notice that she had never had such an exquisite colour in her face before. I set off with the cadet. There was an old-fashioned swing in our garden. I sat him down on the narrow plank seat, and began swinging him. He sat rigid in his new little uniform of stout cloth, with its broad gold braiding, and kept tight hold of the cords. 'You'd better unbutton your collar,' I said to him. 'It's all right; we're used to it,' he said, and cleared his throat. He was like his sister. The eyes especially recalled her, I liked being nice to him; and at the same time an aching sadness was gnawing at my heart. 'Now I certainly am a child,' I thought; 'but yesterday....' I remembered where I had dropped my knife

the night before, and looked for it. The cadet asked me for it, picked a thick stalk of wild parsley, cut a pipe out of it, and began whistling. Othello whistled too.
But in the evening how he wept, this Othello, in Zinaïda's arms, when, seeking him out in a corner of the garden, she asked him why he was so depressed. My tears flowed with such violence that she was frightened. 'What is wrong with you? What is it, Volodya?' she repeated; and seeing I made no answer, and did not cease weeping, she was about to kiss my wet cheek. But I turned away from her, and whispered through my sobs, 'I know all. Why did you play with me?... What need had you of my love?'
'I am to blame, Volodya ...' said Zinaïda. 'I am very much to blame ...' she added, wringing her hands. 'How much there is bad and black and sinful in me!... But I am not playing with you now. I love you; you don't even suspect why and how.... But what is it you know?'
What could I say to her? She stood facing me, and looked at me; and I belonged to her altogether from head to foot directly she looked at me.... A quarter of an hour later I was running races with the cadet and Zinaïda. I was not crying, I was laughing, though my swollen eyelids dropped a tear or two as I laughed. I had Zinaïda's ribbon round my neck for a cravat, and I shouted with delight whenever I succeeded in catching her round the waist. She did just as she liked with me.

XIX

I should be in a great difficulty, if I were forced to describe exactly what passed within me in the course of the week after my unsuccessful midnight expedition. It was a strange feverish time, a sort of chaos, in which the most violently opposed feelings, thoughts, suspicions, hopes, joys, and sufferings, whirled together in a kind of hurricane. I was afraid to look into myself, if a boy of sixteen ever can look into himself; I was afraid to take stock of anything; I simply hastened to live through every day till evening; and at night I slept ... the light-heartedness of childhood came to my aid. I did not want to know whether I was loved, and I did not want to acknowledge to myself that I was not loved; my father I avoided—but Zinaïda I could not avoid.... I burnt as in a fire in her presence ... but what did I care to know what the fire was in which I burned and melted—it was enough that it was sweet to burn and melt. I gave myself up to all my passing sensations, and cheated myself, turning away from memories, and shutting my eyes to what I foreboded before me.... This weakness would not most likely have lasted long in any case ... a thunderbolt cut it all short in a moment, and flung me into a new track altogether.
Coming in one day to dinner from a rather long walk, I learnt with amazement that I was to dine alone, that my father had gone away and my mother was unwell, did not want any dinner, and had shut herself up in her bedroom. From the faces of the footmen, I surmised that something extraordinary had taken place.... I did not dare to cross-examine them, but I had a friend in the young waiter Philip, who was passionately fond of poetry, and a performer on the guitar. I addressed myself to him. From him I learned that a terrible scene had taken place between my father and mother (and every word had been overheard in the maids' room; much of it had been in French, but Masha the lady's-maid had lived five years' with a dressmaker from Paris, and she understood it all); that my mother had reproached my father with infidelity, with an intimacy with the young lady next door, that my father at first had defended himself, but afterwards had lost his temper, and he too had said something cruel, 'reflecting on her age,' which had made my mother cry; that my mother too had alluded to some loan which it seemed had been made to the old princess, and had spoken very ill of her and of the young lady too, and that then my father had threatened her. 'And all the mischief,' continued Philip, 'came from an anonymous letter; and who wrote it, no one knows, or else there'd have been no reason whatever for the matter to have come out at all.'
'But was there really any ground,' I brought out with difficulty, while my hands and feet went cold, and a sort of shudder ran through my inmost being.
Philip winked meaningly. 'There was. There's no hiding those things; for all that your father was careful this time—but there, you see, he'd, for instance, to hire a carriage or something ... no getting on without servants, either.'
I dismissed Philip, and fell on to my bed. I did not sob, I did not give myself up to despair; I did not ask myself when and how this had happened; I did not wonder how it was I had not guessed it before, long ago; I

did not even upbraid my father.... What I had learnt was more than I could take in; this sudden revelation stunned me.... All was at an end. All the fair blossoms of my heart were roughly plucked at once, and lay about me, flung on the ground, and trampled underfoot.

XX

My mother next day announced her intention of returning to the town. In the morning my father had gone into her bedroom, and stayed there a long while alone with her. No one had overheard what he said to her; but my mother wept no more; she regained her composure, and asked for food, but did not make her appearance nor change her plans. I remember I wandered about the whole day, but did not go into the garden, and never once glanced at the lodge, and in the evening I was the spectator of an amazing occurrence: my father conducted Count Malevsky by the arm through the dining-room into the hall, and, in the presence of a footman, said icily to him: 'A few days ago your excellency was shown the door in our house; and now I am not going to enter into any kind of explanation with you, but I have the honour to announce to you that if you ever visit me again, I shall throw you out of window. I don't like your handwriting.' The count bowed, bit his lips, shrank away, and vanished.

Preparations were beginning for our removal to town, to Arbaty Street, where we had a house. My father himself probably no longer cared to remain at the country house; but clearly he had succeeded in persuading my mother not to make a public scandal. Everything was done quietly, without hurry; my mother even sent her compliments to the old princess, and expressed her regret that she was prevented by indisposition from seeing her again before her departure. I wandered about like one possessed, and only longed for one thing, for it all to be over as soon as possible. One thought I could not get out of my head: how could she, a young girl, and a princess too, after all, bring herself to such a step, knowing that my father was not a free man, and having an opportunity of marrying, for instance, Byelovzorov? What did she hope for? How was it she was not afraid of ruining her whole future? Yes, I thought, this is love, this is passion, this is devotion ... and Lushin's words came back to me: to sacrifice oneself for some people is sweet. I chanced somehow to catch sight of something white in one of the windows of the lodge.... 'Can it be Zinaïda's face?' I thought ... yes, it really was her face. I could not restrain myself. I could not part from her without saying a last good-bye to her. I seized a favourable instant, and went into the lodge.

In the drawing-room the old princess met me with her usual slovenly and careless greetings.

'How's this, my good man, your folks are off in such a hurry?' she observed, thrusting snuff into her nose. I looked at her, and a load was taken off my heart. The word 'loan,' dropped by Philip, had been torturing me. She had no suspicion ... at least I thought so then. Zinaïda came in from the next room, pale, and dressed in black, with her hair hanging loose; she took me by the hand without a word, and drew me away with her.

'I heard your voice,' she began, 'and came out at once. Is it so easy for you to leave us, bad boy?'

'I have come to say good-bye to you, princess,' I answered, 'probably for ever. You have heard, perhaps, we are going away.'

Zinaïda looked intently at me.

'Yes, I have heard. Thanks for coming. I was beginning to think I should not see you again. Don't remember evil against me. I have sometimes tormented you, but all the same I am not what you imagine me.' She turned away, and leaned against the window.

'Really, I am not like that. I know you have a bad opinion of me.'

'I?'

'Yes, you ... you.'

'I?' I repeated mournfully, and my heart throbbed as of old under the influence of her overpowering, indescribable fascination. 'I? Believe me, Zinaïda Alexandrovna, whatever you did, however you tormented me, I should love and adore you to the end of my days.'

She turned with a rapid motion to me, and flinging wide her arms, embraced my head, and gave me a warm and passionate kiss. God knows whom that long farewell kiss was seeking, but I eagerly tasted its sweetness. I knew that it would never be repeated. 'Good-bye, good-bye,' I kept saying ...

She tore herself away, and went out. And I went away. I cannot describe the emotion with which I went away. I should not wish it ever to come again; but I should think myself unfortunate had I never experienced such an emotion.

We went back to town. I did not quickly shake off the past; I did not quickly get to work. My wound slowly began to heal; but I had no ill-feeling against my father. On the contrary he had, as it were, gained in my eyes ... let psychologists explain the contradiction as best they can. One day I was walking along a boulevard, and to my indescribable delight, I came across Lushin. I liked him for his straightforward and unaffected character, and besides he was dear to me for the sake of the memories he aroused in me. I rushed up to him.

'Aha!' he said, knitting his brows,' so it's you, young man. Let me have a look at you. You're still as yellow as ever, but yet there's not the same nonsense in your eyes. You look like a man, not a lap-dog. That's good. Well, what are you doing? working?'

I gave a sigh. I did not like to tell a lie, while I was ashamed to tell the truth.

'Well, never mind,' Lushin went on, 'don't be shy. The great thing is to lead a normal life, and not be the slave of your passions. What do you get if not? Wherever you are carried by the tide—it's all a bad look-out; a man must stand on his own feet, if he can get nothing but a rock to stand on. Here, I've got a cough ... and Byelovzorov—have you heard anything of him?'

'No. What is it?'

'He's lost, and no news of him; they say he's gone away to the Caucasus. A lesson to you, young man. And it's all from not knowing how to part in time, to break out of the net. You seem to have got off very well. Mind you don't fall into the same snare again. Good-bye.'

'I shan't,' I thought.... 'I shan't see her again.' But I was destined to see Zinaïda once more.

XXI

My father used every day to ride out on horse-back. He had a splendid English mare, a chestnut piebald, with a long slender neck and long legs, an inexhaustible and vicious beast. Her name was Electric. No one could ride her except my father. One day he came up to me in a good humour, a frame of mind in which I had not seen him for a long while; he was getting ready for his ride, and had already put on his spurs. I began entreating him to take me with him.

'We'd much better have a game of leap-frog,' my father replied.

'You'll never keep up with me on your cob.'

'Yes, I will; I'll put on spurs too.'

'All right, come along then.'

We set off. I had a shaggy black horse, strong, and fairly spirited. It is true it had to gallop its utmost, when Electric went at full trot, still I was not left behind. I have never seen any one ride like my father; he had such a fine carelessly easy seat, that it seemed that the horse under him was conscious of it, and proud of its rider. We rode through all the boulevards, reached the 'Maidens' Field,' jumped several fences (at first I had been afraid to take a leap, but my father had a contempt for cowards, and I soon ceased to feel fear), twice crossed the river Moskva, and I was under the impression that we were on our way home, especially as my father of his own accord observed that my horse was tired, when suddenly he turned off away from me at the Crimean ford, and galloped along the river-bank. I rode after him. When he had reached a high stack of old timber, he slid quickly off Electric, told me to dismount, and giving me his horse's bridle, told me to wait for him there at the timber-stack, and, turning off into a small street, disappeared. I began walking up and down the river-bank, leading the horses, and scolding Electric, who kept pulling, shaking her head, snorting and neighing as she went; and when I stood still, never failed to paw the ground, and whining, bite my cob on the neck; in fact she conducted herself altogether like a spoilt thorough-bred. My father did not come back. A disagreeable damp mist rose from the river; a fine rain began softly blowing up, and spotting with tiny dark flecks the stupid grey timber-stack, which I kept passing and repassing, and was deadly sick of by now. I was

terribly bored, and still my father did not come. A sort of sentry-man, a Fin, grey all over like the timber, and with a huge old-fashioned shako, like a pot, on his head, and with a halberd (and how ever came a sentry, if you think of it, on the banks of the Moskva!) drew near, and turning his wrinkled face, like an old woman's, towards me, he observed, 'What are you doing here with the horses, young master? Let me hold them.'
I made him no reply. He asked me for tobacco. To get rid of him (I was in a fret of impatience, too), I took a few steps in the direction in which my father had disappeared, then walked along the little street to the end, turned the corner, and stood still. In the street, forty paces from me, at the open window of a little wooden house, stood my father, his back turned to me; he was leaning forward over the window-sill, and in the house, half hidden by a curtain, sat a woman in a dark dress talking to my father; this woman was Zinaïda.
I was petrified. This, I confess, I had never expected. My first impulse was to run away. 'My father will look round,' I thought, 'and I am lost ...' but a strange feeling—a feeling stronger than curiosity, stronger than jealousy, stronger even than fear—held me there. I began to watch; I strained my ears to listen. It seemed as though my father were insisting on something. Zinaïda would not consent. I seem to see her face now—mournful, serious, lovely, and with an inexpressible impress of devotion, grief, love, and a sort of despair—I can find no other word for it. She uttered monosyllables, not raising her eyes, simply smiling—submissively, but without yielding. By that smile alone, I should have known my Zinaïda of old days. My father shrugged his shoulders, and straightened his hat on his head, which was always a sign of impatience with him.... Then I caught the words: '*Vous devez vous séparer de cette...*' Zinaïda sat up, and stretched out her arm....
Suddenly, before my very eyes, the impossible happened. My father suddenly lifted the whip, with which he had been switching the dust off his coat, and I heard a sharp blow on that arm, bare to the elbow. I could scarcely restrain myself from crying out; while Zinaïda shuddered, looked without a word at my father, and slowly raising her arm to her lips, kissed the streak of red upon it. My father flung away the whip, and running quickly up the steps, dashed into the house.... Zinaïda turned round, and with outstretched arms and downcast head, she too moved away from the window.
My heart sinking with panic, with a sort of awe-struck horror, I rushed back, and running down the lane, almost letting go my hold of Electric, went back to the bank of the river. I could not think clearly of anything. I knew that my cold and reserved father was sometimes seized by fits of fury; and all the same, I could never comprehend what I had just seen.... But I felt at the time that, however long I lived, I could never forget the gesture, the glance, the smile, of Zinaïda; that her image, this image so suddenly presented to me, was imprinted for ever on my memory. I stared vacantly at the river, and never noticed that my tears were streaming. 'She is beaten,' I was thinking,... 'beaten ... beaten....'
'Hullo! what are you doing? Give me the mare!' I heard my father's voice saying behind me.
Mechanically I gave him the bridle. He leaped on to Electric ... the mare, chill with standing, reared on her haunches, and leaped ten feet away ... but my father soon subdued her; he drove the spurs into her sides, and gave her a blow on the neck with his fist.... 'Ah, I've no whip,' he muttered.
I remembered the swish and fall of the whip, heard so short a time before, and shuddered.
'Where did you put it?' I asked my father, after a brief pause.
My father made no answer, and galloped on ahead. I overtook him. I felt that I must see his face.
'Were you bored waiting for me?' he muttered through his teeth.
'A little. Where did you drop your whip?' I asked again.
My father glanced quickly at me. 'I didn't drop it,' he replied; 'I threw it away.' He sank into thought, and dropped his head ... and then, for the first, and almost for the last time, I saw how much tenderness and pity his stern features were capable of expressing.
He galloped on again, and this time I could not overtake him; I got home a quarter-of-an-hour after him.
'That's love,' I said to myself again, as I sat at night before my writing-table, on which books and papers had begun to make their appearance; 'that's passion!... To think of not revolting, of bearing a blow from any one whatever ... even the dearest hand! But it seems one can, if one loves.... While I ... I imagined ...'
I had grown much older during the last month; and my love, with all its transports and sufferings, struck me myself as something small and childish and pitiful beside this other unimagined something, which I could hardly fully grasp, and which frightened me like an unknown, beautiful, but menacing face, which one strives in vain to make out clearly in the half-darkness....
A strange and fearful dream came to me that same night. I dreamed I went into a low dark room.... My father was standing with a whip in his hand, stamping with anger; in the corner crouched Zinaïda, and not on her arm, but on her forehead, was a stripe of red ... while behind them both towered Byelovzorov, covered with blood; he opened his white lips, and wrathfully threatened my father.

Two months later, I entered the university; and within six months my father died of a stroke in Petersburg, where he had just moved with my mother and me. A few days before his death he received a letter from Moscow which threw him into a violent agitation.... He went to my mother to beg some favour of her: and, I was told, he positively shed tears—he, my father! On the very morning of the day when he was stricken down, he had begun a letter to me in French. 'My son,' he wrote to me, 'fear the love of woman; fear that bliss, that poison....' After his death, my mother sent a considerable sum of money to Moscow.

XXII

Four years passed. I had just left the university, and did not know exactly what to do with myself, at what door to knock; I was hanging about for a time with nothing to do. One fine evening I met Meidanov at the theatre. He had got married, and had entered the civil service; but I found no change in him. He fell into ecstasies in just the same superfluous way, and just as suddenly grew depressed again.
'You know,' he told me among other things, 'Madame Dolsky's here.'
'What Madame Dolsky?'
'Can you have forgotten her?—the young Princess Zasyekin whom we were all in love with, and you too. Do you remember at the country-house near Neskutchny gardens?'
'She married a Dolsky?'
'Yes.'
'And is she here, in the theatre?'
'No: but she's in Petersburg. She came here a few days ago. She's going abroad.'
'What sort of fellow is her husband?' I asked.
'A splendid fellow, with property. He's a colleague of mine in Moscow. You can well understand—after the scandal ... you must know all about it ...' (Meidanov smiled significantly) 'it was no easy task for her to make a good marriage; there were consequences ... but with her cleverness, everything is possible. Go and see her; she'll be delighted to see you. She's prettier than ever.'
Meidanov gave me Zinaïda's address. She was staying at the Hotel Demut. Old memories were astir within me.... I determined next day to go to see my former 'flame.' But some business happened to turn up; a week passed, and then another, and when at last I went to the Hotel Demut and asked for Madame Dolsky, I learnt that four days before, she had died, almost suddenly, in childbirth.
I felt a sort of stab at my heart. The thought that I might have seen her, and had not seen her, and should never see her—that bitter thought stung me with all the force of overwhelming reproach. 'She is dead!' I repeated, staring stupidly at the hall-porter. I slowly made my way back to the street, and walked on without knowing myself where I was going. All the past swam up and rose at once before me. So this was the solution, this was the goal to which that young, ardent, brilliant life had striven, all haste and agitation! I mused on this; I fancied those dear features, those eyes, those curls—in the narrow box, in the damp underground darkness—lying here, not far from me—while I was still alive, and, maybe, a few paces from my father.... I thought all this; I strained my imagination, and yet all the while the lines:

'From lips indifferent of her death I heard,
Indifferently I listened to it, too,'

were echoing in my heart. O youth, youth! little dost thou care for anything; thou art master, as it were, of all the treasures of the universe—even sorrow gives thee pleasure, even grief thou canst turn to thy profit; thou art self-confident and insolent; thou sayest, 'I alone am living—look you!'—but thy days fly by all the while, and vanish without trace or reckoning; and everything in thee vanishes, like wax in the sun, like snow.... And, perhaps, the whole secret of thy charm lies, not in being able to do anything, but in being able to think thou wilt do anything; lies just in thy throwing to the winds, forces which thou couldst not make other use of; in each of us gravely regarding himself as a prodigal, gravely supposing that he is justified in saying, 'Oh, what might I not have done if I had not wasted my time!'
I, now ... what did I hope for, what did I expect, what rich future did I foresee, when the phantom of my first love, rising up for an instant, barely called forth one sigh, one mournful sentiment?

And what has come to pass of all I hoped for? And now, when the shades of evening begin to steal over my life, what have I left fresher, more precious, than the memories of the storm—so soon over—of early morning, of spring?

But I do myself injustice. Even then, in those light-hearted young days, I was not deaf to the voice of sorrow, when it called upon me, to the solemn strains floating to me from beyond the tomb. I remember, a few days after I heard of Zinaïda's death, I was present, through a peculiar, irresistible impulse, at the death of a poor old woman who lived in the same house as we. Covered with rags, lying on hard boards, with a sack under her head, she died hardly and painfully. Her whole life had been passed in the bitter struggle with daily want; she had known no joy, had not tasted the honey of happiness. One would have thought, surely she would rejoice at death, at her deliverance, her rest. But yet, as long as her decrepit body held out, as long as her breast still heaved in agony under the icy hand weighing upon it, until her last forces left her, the old woman crossed herself, and kept whispering, 'Lord, forgive my sins'; and only with the last spark of consciousness, vanished from her eyes the look of fear, of horror of the end. And I remember that then, by the death-bed of that poor old woman, I felt aghast for Zinaïda, and longed to pray for her, for my father—and for myself.

MUMU

In one of the outlying streets of Moscow, in a grey house with white columns and a balcony, warped all askew, there was once living a lady, a widow, surrounded by a numerous household of serfs. Her sons were in the government service at Petersburg; her daughters were married; she went out very little, and in solitude lived through the last years of her miserly and dreary old age. Her day, a joyless and gloomy day, had long been over; but the evening of her life was blacker than night.

Of all her servants, the most remarkable personage was the porter, Gerasim, a man full twelve inches over the normal height, of heroic build, and deaf and dumb from his birth. The lady, his owner, had brought him up from the village where he lived alone in a little hut, apart from his brothers, and was reckoned about the most punctual of her peasants in the payment of the seignorial dues. Endowed with extraordinary strength, he did the work of four men; work flew apace under his hands, and it was a pleasant sight to see him when he was ploughing, while, with his huge palms pressing hard upon the plough, he seemed alone, unaided by his poor horse, to cleave the yielding bosom of the earth, or when, about St. Peter's Day, he plied his scythe with a. furious energy that might have mown a young birch copse up by the roots, or swiftly and untiringly wielded a flail over two yards long; while the hard oblong muscles of his shoulders rose and fell like a lever. His perpetual silence lent a solemn dignity to his unwearying labour. He was a splendid peasant, and, except for his affliction, any girl would have been glad to marry him.... But now they had taken Gerasim to Moscow, bought him boots, had him made a full-skirted coat for summer, a sheepskin for winter, put into his hand a broom and a spade, and appointed him porter.

At first he intensely disliked his new mode of life. From his childhood he had been used to field labour, to village life. Shut off by his affliction from the society of men, he had grown up, dumb and mighty, as a tree grows on a fruitful soil. When he was transported to the town, he could not understand what was being done with him; he was miserable and stupefied, with the stupefaction of some strong young bull, taken straight from the meadow, where the rich grass stood up to his belly, taken and put in the truck of a railway train, and there, while smoke and sparks and gusts of steam puff out upon the sturdy beast, he is whirled onwards, whirled along with loud roar and whistle, whither—God knows! What Gerasim had to do in his new duties seemed a mere trifle to him after his hard toil as a peasant; in half-an-hour, all his work was done, and he would once more stand stock-still in the middle of the courtyard, staring open-mouthed at all the passers-by, as though trying to wrest from them the explanation of his perplexing position; or he would suddenly go off into some corner, and flinging a long way off the broom or the spade, throw himself on his face on the ground, and lie for hours together without stirring, like a caged beast. But man gets used to anything, and Gerasim got used at last to living in town. He had little work to do; his whole duty consisted in keeping the courtyard clean, bringing in a barrel of water twice a day, splitting and dragging in wood for the kitchen and the house, keeping out strangers, and watching at night. And it must be said he did his duty zealously. In his courtyard there was never a shaving lying about, never a speck of dust; if sometimes, in the muddy season, the wretched nag, put under his charge for fetching water, got stuck in the road, he would simply give it a shove with his shoulder, and set not only the cart but the horse itself moving. If he set to chopping wood, the axe fairly rang like glass, and chips and chunks flew in all directions. And as for strangers, after he had one night caught two thieves and knocked their heads together—knocked them so that there was not the slightest need to take them to the police-station afterwards—every one in the neighbourhood began to feel a great respect for him; even those who came in the day-time, by no means robbers, but simply unknown persons, at the sight of the terrible porter, waved and shouted to him as though he could hear their shouts. With all the rest of the servants, Gerasim was on terms, hardly friendly—they were afraid of him—but familiar; he regarded them as his fellows. They explained themselves to him by signs, and he understood them, and exactly carried out all orders, but knew his own rights too, and soon no one dared to take his seat at the table. Gerasim was altogether of a strict and serious temper, he liked order in everything; even the cocks did not dare to fight in his presence, or woe betide them! directly he caught sight of them, he would seize them by the legs, swing them ten times round in the air like a wheel, and throw them in different directions. There were geese, too, kept in the yard; but the goose, as is well known, is a dignified and reasonable bird; Gerasim felt a respect for them, looked after them, and fed them; he was himself not unlike a gander of the steppes. He was assigned a little garret over the kitchen; he arranged it himself to his own liking, made a bedstead in it of oak boards on four stumps of wood for legs—a truly Titanic bedstead; one might have put a ton or two on it—it would not have bent under the load; under the bed was a solid chest; in a corner stood a little table of the same strong kind, and near the table a three-legged stool, so solid and squat that Gerasim himself would sometimes pick it up and drop it again with a smile of delight. The garret was locked up by means of a padlock that looked like a kalatch or basket-shaped loaf, only black; the key of this padlock Gerasim always carried about him in his girdle. He did not like people to come to his garret.

So passed a year, at the end of which a little incident befell
Gerasim.

The old lady, in whose service he lived as porter, adhered in everything to the ancient ways, and kept a large number of servants. In her house were not only laundresses, sempstresses, carpenters, tailors and tailoresses, there was even a harness-maker—he was reckoned as a veterinary surgeon, too,—and a doctor for the servants; there was a household doctor for the mistress; there was, lastly, a shoemaker, by name Kapiton Klimov, a sad drunkard. Klimov regarded himself as an injured creature, whose merits were unappreciated, a cultivated man from Petersburg, who ought not to be living in Moscow without occupation—in the wilds, so to speak; and if he drank, as he himself expressed it emphatically, with a blow on his chest, it was sorrow drove him to it. So one day his mistress had a conversation about him with her head steward, Gavrila, a man whom, judging solely from his little yellow eyes and nose like a duck's beak, fate itself, it seemed, had marked out as a person in authority. The lady expressed her regret at the corruption of the morals of Kapiton, who had, only the evening before, been picked up somewhere in the street.

'Now, Gavrila,' she observed, all of a sudden, 'now, if we were to marry him, what do you think, perhaps he would be steadier?'

'Why not marry him, indeed, 'm? He could be married, 'm,' answered
Gavrila, 'and it would be a very good thing, to be sure, 'm.'

'Yes; only who is to marry him?'

'Ay, 'm. But that's at your pleasure, 'm. He may, any way, so to say, be wanted for something; he can't be turned adrift altogether.'

'I fancy he likes Tatiana.'

Gavrila was on the point of making some reply, but he shut his lips tightly.

'Yes!… let him marry Tatiana,' the lady decided, taking a pinch of snuff complacently, 'Do you hear?'

'Yes, 'm,' Gavrila articulated, and he withdrew.

Returning to his own room (it was in a little lodge, and was almost filled up with metal-bound trunks), Gavrila first sent his wife away, and then sat down at the window and pondered. His mistress's unexpected arrangement had clearly put him in a difficulty. At last he got up and sent to call Kapiton. Kapiton made his appearance…. But before reporting their conversation to the reader, we consider it not out of place to relate in few words who was this Tatiana, whom it was to be Kapiton's lot to marry, and why the great lady's order had disturbed the steward.

Tatiana, one of the laundresses referred to above (as a trained and skilful laundress she was in charge of the fine linen only), was a woman of twenty-eight, thin, fair-haired, with moles on her left cheek. Moles on the left cheek are regarded as of evil omen in Russia—a token of unhappy life…. Tatiana could not boast of her good luck. From her earliest youth she had been badly treated; she had done the work of two, and had never known affection; she had been poorly clothed and had received the smallest wages. Relations she had practically none; an uncle she had once had, a butler, left behind in the country as useless, and other uncles of hers were peasants—that was all. At one time she had passed for a beauty, but her good looks were very soon over. In disposition, she was very meek, or, rather, scared; towards herself, she felt perfect indifference; of others, she stood in mortal dread; she thought of nothing but how to get her work done in good time, never talked to any one, and trembled at the very name of her mistress, though the latter scarcely knew her by sight. When Gerasim was brought from the country, she was ready to die with fear on seeing his huge figure, tried all she could to avoid meeting him, even dropped her eyelids when sometimes she chanced to run past him, hurrying from the house to the laundry. Gerasim at first paid no special attention to her, then he used to smile when she came his way, then he began even to stare admiringly at her, and at last he never took his eyes off her. She took his fancy, whether by the mild expression of her face or the timidity of her movements, who can tell? So one day she was stealing across the yard, with a starched dressing-jacket of her mistress's carefully poised on her outspread fingers ... some one suddenly grasped her vigorously by the elbow; she turned round and fairly screamed; behind her stood Gerasim. With a foolish smile, making inarticulate caressing grunts, he held out to her a gingerbread cock with gold tinsel on his tail and wings. She was about to refuse it, but he thrust it forcibly into her hand, shook his head, walked away, and turning round, once more grunted something very affectionately to her. From that day forward he gave her no peace; wherever she went, he was on the spot at once, coming to meet her, smiling, grunting, waving his hands; all at once he would pull a ribbon out of the bosom of his smock and put it in her hand, or would sweep the dust out of her way. The poor girl simply did not know how to behave or what to do. Soon the whole household knew of the dumb porter's wiles; jeers, jokes, sly hints were showered upon Tatiana. At Gerasim, however, it was not every one who would dare to scoff; he did not like jokes; indeed, in his presence, she, too, was left in peace. Whether she liked it or not, the girl found herself to be under his protection. Like all deaf-mutes, he was very suspicious, and very readily perceived when they were laughing at him or at her. One day, at dinner, the wardrobe-keeper, Tatiana's superior, fell to nagging, as it is called, at her, and brought the poor thing to such a state that she did not know where to look, and was almost crying with vexation. Gerasim got up all of a sudden, stretched out his gigantic hand, laid it on the wardrobe-maid's head, and looked into her face with such grim ferocity that her head positively flopped upon the table. Every one was still. Gerasim took up his spoon again and went on with his cabbage-soup. 'Look at him, the dumb devil, the wood-demon!' they all muttered in under-tones, while the wardrobe-maid got up and went out into the maids' room. Another time, noticing that Kapiton—the same Kapiton who was the subject of the conversation reported above—was gossiping somewhat too attentively with Tatiana, Gerasim beckoned him to him, led him into the cartshed, and taking up a shaft that was standing in a corner by one end, lightly, but most significantly, menaced him with it. Since then no one addressed a word to Tatiana. And all this cost him nothing. It is true the wardrobe-maid, as soon as she reached the maids' room, promptly fell into a fainting-fit, and behaved altogether so skilfully that Gerasim's rough action reached his mistress's knowledge the same day. But the capricious old lady only laughed, and several times, to the great offence of the wardrobe-maid, forced her to repeat 'how he bent your head down with his heavy hand,' and next day she sent Gerasim a rouble. She looked on him with favour as a strong and faithful watchman. Gerasim stood in considerable awe of her, but, all the same, he had hopes of her favour, and was preparing to go to her with a petition for leave to marry Tatiana. He was only waiting for a new coat, promised him by the steward, to present a proper appearance before his mistress, when this same mistress suddenly took it into her head to marry Tatiana to Kapiton.

The reader will now readily understand the perturbation of mind that overtook the steward Gavrila after his conversation with his mistress. 'My lady,' he thought, as he sat at the window, 'favours Gerasim, to be sure'—(Gavrila was well aware of this, and that was why he himself looked on him with an indulgent eye)—'still he is a speechless creature. I could not, indeed, put it before the mistress that Gerasim's courting Tatiana. But, after all, it's true enough; he's a queer sort of husband. But on the other hand, that devil, God forgive me, has only got to find out they're marrying Tatiana to Kapiton, he'll smash up everything in the house, 'pon my soul! There's no reasoning with him; why, he's such a devil, God forgive my sins, there's no getting over him no how ... 'pon my soul!'

Kapiton's entrance broke the thread of Gavrila's reflections. The dissipated shoemaker came in, his hands behind him, and lounging carelessly against a projecting angle of the wall, near the door, crossed his right foot in front of his left, and tossed his head, as much as to say, 'What do you want?'

Gavrila looked at Kapiton, and drummed with his fingers on the window-frame. Kapiton merely screwed up his leaden eyes a little, but he did not look down, he even grinned slightly, and passed his hand over his whitish locks which were sticking up in all directions. 'Well, here I am. What is it?'
'You're a pretty fellow,' said Gavrila, and paused. 'A pretty fellow you are, there's no denying!'
Kapiton only twitched his little shoulders.
'Are you any better, pray?' he thought to himself.
'Just look at yourself, now, look at yourself,' Gavrila went on reproachfully; 'now, what ever do you look like?'
Kapiton serenely surveyed his shabby tattered coat, and his patched trousers, and with special attention stared at his burst boots, especially the one on the tip-toe of which his right foot so gracefully poised, and he fixed his eyes again on the steward.
'Well?'
'Well?' repeated Gavrila. 'Well? And then you say well? You look like old Nick himself, God forgive my saying so, that's what you look like.'
Kapiton blinked rapidly.
'Go on abusing me, go on, if you like, Gavrila Andreitch,' he thought to himself again.
'Here you've been drunk again,' Gavrila began, 'drunk again, haven't you? Eh? Come, answer me!'
'Owing to the weakness of my health, I have exposed myself to spirituous beverages, certainly,' replied Kapiton.
'Owing to the weakness of your health!… They let you off too easy, that's what it is; and you've been apprenticed in Petersburg…. Much you learned in your apprenticeship! You simply eat your bread in idleness.'
'In that matter, Gavrila Andreitch, there is one to judge me, the Lord God Himself, and no one else. He also knows what manner of man I be in this world, and whether I eat my bread in idleness. And as concerning your contention regarding drunkenness, in that matter, too, I am not to blame, but rather a friend; he led me into temptation, but was diplomatic and got away, while I….'
'While you were left, like a goose, in the street. Ah, you're a dissolute fellow! But that's not the point,' the steward went on, 'I've something to tell you. Our lady…' here he paused a minute, 'it's our lady's pleasure that you should be married. Do you hear? She imagines you may be steadier when you're married. Do you understand?'
'To be sure I do.'
'Well, then. For my part I think it would be better to give you a good hiding. But there—it's her business. Well? are you agreeable?' Kapiton grinned.
'Matrimony is an excellent thing for any one, Gavrila Andreitch; and, as far as I am concerned, I shall be quite agreeable.'
'Very well, then,' replied Gavrila, while he reflected to himself: 'there's no denying the man expresses himself very properly. Only there's one thing,' he pursued aloud: 'the wife our lady's picked out for you is an unlucky choice.'
'Why, who is she, permit me to inquire?'
'Tatiana.'
'Tatiana?'
And Kapiton opened his eyes, and moved a little away from the wall.
'Well, what are you in such a taking for?… Isn't she to your taste, hey?'
'Not to my taste, do you say, Gavrila Andreitch! She's right enough, a hard-working steady girl…. But you know very well yourself, Gavrila Andreitch, why that fellow, that wild man of the woods, that monster of the steppes, he's after her, you know….'
'I know, mate, I know all about it,' the butler cut him short in a tone of annoyance: 'but there, you see….'
'But upon my soul, Gavrila Andreitch! why, he'll kill me, by God, he will, he'll crush me like some fly; why, he's got a fist—why, you kindly look yourself what a fist he's got; why, he's simply got a fist like Minin Pozharsky's. You see he's deaf, he beats and does not hear how he's beating! He swings his great fists, as if he's asleep. And there's no possibility of pacifying him; and for why? Why, because, as you know yourself, Gavrila Andreitch, he's deaf, and what's more, has no more wit than the heel of my foot. Why, he's a sort of beast, a heathen idol, Gavrila Andreitch, and worse … a block of wood; what have I done that I should have to suffer from him now? Sure it is, it's all over with me now; I've knocked about, I've had enough to put up with, I've been battered like an earthenware pot, but still I'm a man, after all, and not a worthless pot.'

'I know, I know, don't go talking away....'
'Lord, my God!' the shoemaker continued warmly, 'when is the end? when, O Lord! A poor wretch I am, a poor wretch whose sufferings are endless! What a life, what a life mine's been, come to think of it! In my young days, I was beaten by a German I was 'prentice to; in the prime of life beaten by my own countrymen, and last of all, in ripe years, see what I have been brought to....'
'Ugh, you flabby soul!' said Gavrila Andreitch. 'Why do you make so many words about it?'
'Why, do you say, Gavrila Andreitch? It's not a beating I'm afraid of, Gavrila Andreitch. A gentleman may chastise me in private, but give me a civil word before folks, and I'm a man still; but see now, whom I've to do with....'
'Come, get along,' Gavrila interposed impatiently. Kapiton turned away and staggered off.
'But, if it were not for him,' the steward shouted after him, 'you would consent for your part?'
'I signify my acquiescence,' retorted Kapiton as he disappeared.
His fine language did not desert him, even in the most trying positions.
The steward walked several times up and down the room.
'Well, call Tatiana now,' he said at last.
A few instants later, Tatiana had come up almost noiselessly, and was standing in the doorway.
'What are your orders, Gavrila Andreitch?' she said in a soft voice.
The steward looked at her intently.
'Well, Taniusha,' he said, 'would you like to be married? Our lady has chosen a husband for you.'
'Yes, Gavrila Andreitch. And whom has she deigned to name as a husband for me?' she added falteringly.
'Kapiton, the shoemaker.'
'Yes, sir.'
'He's a feather-brained fellow, that's certain. But it's just for that the mistress reckons upon you.'
'Yes, sir.'
'There's one difficulty ... you know the deaf man, Gerasim, he's courting you, you see. How did you come to bewitch such a bear? But you see, he'll kill you, very like, he's such a bear....'
'He'll kill me, Gavrila Andreitch, he'll kill me, and no mistake.'
'Kill you.... Well, we shall see about that. What do you mean by saying he'll kill you? Has he any right to kill you? tell me yourself.'
'I don't know, Gavrila Andreitch, about his having any right or not.'
'What a woman! why, you've made him no promise, I suppose....'
'What are you pleased to ask of me?'
The steward was silent for a little, thinking, 'You're a meek soul! Well, that's right,' he said aloud; 'we'll have another talk with you later, now you can go, Taniusha; I see you're not unruly, certainly.'
Tatiana turned, steadied herself a little against the doorpost, and went away.
'And, perhaps, our lady will forget all about this wedding by to-morrow,' thought the steward; 'and here am I worrying myself for nothing! As for that insolent fellow, we must tie him down, if it comes to that, we must let the police know' ... 'Ustinya Fyedorovna!' he shouted in a loud voice to his wife, 'heat the samovar, my good soul....' All that day Tatiana hardly went out of the laundry. At first she had started crying, then she wiped away her tears, and set to work as before. Kapiton stayed till late at night at the ginshop with a friend of his, a man of gloomy appearance, to whom he related in detail how he used to live in Petersburg with a gentleman, who would have been all right, except he was a bit too strict, and he had a slight weakness besides, he was too fond of drink; and, as to the fair sex, he didn't stick at anything. His gloomy companion merely said yes; but when Kapiton announced at last that, in a certain event, he would have to lay hands on himself to-morrow, his gloomy companion remarked that it was bedtime. And they parted in surly silence.
Meanwhile, the steward's anticipations were not fulfilled. The old lady was so much taken up with the idea of Kapiton's wedding, that even in the night she talked of nothing else to one of her companions, who was kept in her house solely to entertain her in case of sleeplessness, and, like a night cabman, slept in the day. When Gavrila came to her after morning tea with his report, her first question was: 'And how about our wedding—is it getting on all right?' He replied, of course, that it was getting on first rate, and that Kapiton would appear before her to pay his reverence to her that day. The old lady was not quite well; she did not give much time to business. The steward went back to his own room, and called a council. The matter certainly called for serious consideration. Tatiana would make no difficulty, of course; but Kapiton had declared in the hearing of all that he had but one head to lose, not two or three.... Gerasim turned rapid sullen looks on every one, would not budge from the steps of the maids' quarters, and seemed to guess that some mischief was being

hatched against him. They met together. Among them was an old sideboard waiter, nicknamed Uncle Tail, to whom every one looked respectfully for counsel, though all they got out of him was, 'Here's a pretty pass! to be sure, to be sure, to be sure!' As a preliminary measure of security, to provide against contingencies, they locked Kapiton up in the lumber-room where the filter was kept; then considered the question with the gravest deliberation, It would, to be sure, be easy to have recourse to force. But Heaven save us! there would be an uproar, the mistress would be put out—it would be awful! What should they do? They thought and thought, and at last thought out a solution. It had many a time been observed that Gerasim could not bear drunkards.... As he sat at the gates, he would always turn away with disgust when some one passed by intoxicated, with unsteady steps and his cap on one side of his ear. They resolved that Tatiana should be instructed to pretend to be tipsy, and should pass by Gerasim staggering and reeling about. The poor girl refused for a long while to agree to this, but they persuaded her at last; she saw, too, that it was the only possible way of getting rid of her adorer. She went out. Kapiton was released from the lumber-room; for, after all, he had an interest in the affair. Gerasim was sitting on the curb-stone at the gates, scraping the ground with a spade.... From behind every corner, from behind every window-blind, the others were watching him.... The trick succeeded beyond all expectations. On seeing Tatiana, at first, he nodded as usual, making caressing, inarticulate sounds; then he looked carefully at her, dropped his spade, jumped up, went up to her, brought his face close to her face.... In her fright she staggered more than ever, and shut her eyes.... He took her by the arm, whirled her right across the yard, and going into the room where the council had been sitting, pushed her straight at Kapiton. Tatiana fairly swooned away.... Gerasim stood, looked at her, waved his hand, laughed, and went off, stepping heavily, to his garret.... For the next twenty-four hours, he did not come out of it. The postillion Antipka said afterwards that he saw Gerasim through a. crack in the wall, sitting on his bedstead, his face in his hand. From time to time he uttered soft regular sounds; he was wailing a dirge, that is, swaying backwards and forwards with his eyes shut, and shaking his head as drivers or bargemen do when they chant their melancholy songs. Antipka could not bear it, and he came away from the crack. When Gerasim came out of the garret next day, no particular change could be observed in him. He only seemed, as it were, more morose, and took not the slightest notice of Tatiana or Kapiton. The same evening, they both had to appear before their mistress with geese under their arms, and in a week's time they were married. Even on the day of the wedding Gerasim showed no change of any sort in his behaviour. Only, he came back from the river without water, he had somehow broken the barrel on the road; and at night, in the stable, he washed and rubbed down his horse so vigorously, that it swayed like a blade of grass in the wind, and staggered from one leg to the other under his fists of iron.

All this had taken place in the spring. Another year passed by, during which Kapiton became a hopeless drunkard, and as being absolutely of no use for anything, was sent away with the store waggons to a distant village with his wife. On the day of his departure, he put a very good face on it at first, and declared that he would always be at home, send him where they would, even to the other end of the world; but later on he lost heart, began grumbling that he was being taken to uneducated people, and collapsed so completely at last that he could not even put his own hat on. Some charitable soul stuck it on his forehead, set the peak straight in front, and thrust it on with a slap from above. When everything was quite ready, and the peasants already held the reins in their hands, and were only waiting for the words 'With God's blessing!' to start, Gerasim came out of his garret, went up to Tatiana, and gave her as a parting present a red cotton handkerchief he had bought for her a year ago. Tatiana, who had up to that instant borne all the revolting details of her life with great indifference, could not control herself upon that; she burst into tears, and as she took her seat in the cart, she kissed Gerasim three times like a good Christian. He meant to accompany her as far as the town-barrier, and did walk beside her cart for a while, but he stopped suddenly at the Crimean ford, waved his hand, and walked away along the riverside.

It was getting towards evening. He walked slowly, watching the water. All of a sudden he fancied something was floundering in the mud close to the bank. He stooped over, and saw a little white-and-black puppy, who, in spite of all its efforts, could not get out of the water; it was struggling, slipping back, and trembling all over its thin wet little body. Gerasim looked at the unlucky little dog, picked it up with one hand, put it into the bosom of his coat, and hurried with long steps homewards. He went into his garret, put the rescued puppy on his bed, covered it with his thick overcoat, ran first to the stable for straw, and then to the kitchen for a cup of milk. Carefully folding back the overcoat, and spreading out the straw, he set the milk on the bedstead. The poor little puppy was not more than three weeks old, its eyes were only just open—one eye still seemed rather larger than the other; it did not know how to lap out of a cup, and did nothing but shiver and blink. Gerasim took hold of its head softly with two fingers, and dipped its little nose into the milk. The pup suddenly began lapping greedily, sniffing, shaking itself, and choking. Gerasim watched and watched it, and all at once he laughed outright.... All night long he was waiting on it, keeping it covered, and rubbing it dry. He fell asleep himself at last, and slept quietly and happily by its side.

No mother could have looked after her baby as Gerasim looked after his little nursling. At first, she—for the pup turned out to be a bitch—was very weak, feeble, and ugly, but by degrees she grew stronger and improved in looks, and thanks to the unflagging care of her preserver, in eight months' time she was transformed into a very pretty dog of the spaniel breed, with long ears, a bushy spiral tail, and large expressive eyes. She was devotedly attached to Gerasim, and was never a yard from his side; she always followed him about wagging her tail. He had even given her a name—the dumb know that their inarticulate noises call the attention of others. He called her Mumu. All the servants in the house liked her, and called her Mumu, too. She was very intelligent, she was friendly with every one, but was only fond of Gerasim. Gerasim, on his side, loved her passionately, and he did not like it when other people stroked her; whether he was afraid for her, or jealous—God knows! She used to wake him in the morning, pulling at his coat; she used to take the reins in her mouth, and bring him up the old horse that carried the water, with whom she was on very friendly terms. With a face of great importance, she used to go with him to the river; she used to watch his brooms and spades, and never allowed any one to go into his garret. He cut a little hole in his door on purpose for her, and she seemed to feel that only in Gerasim's garret she was completely mistress and at home; and directly she went in, she used to jump with a satisfied air upon the bed. At night she did not sleep at all, but she never barked without sufficient cause, like some stupid house-dog, who, sitting on its hind-legs, blinking, with its nose in the air, barks simply from dulness, at the stars, usually three times in succession. No! Mumu's delicate little voice was never raised without good reason; either some stranger was passing close to the fence, or there was some suspicious sound or rustle somewhere.... In fact, she was an excellent watch-dog. It is true that there was another dog in the yard, a tawny old dog with brown spots, called Wolf, but he was never, even at night, let off the chain; and, indeed, he was so decrepit that he did not even wish for freedom. He used to lie curled up in his kennel, and only rarely uttered a sleepy, almost noiseless bark, which broke off at once, as though he were himself aware of its uselessness. Mumu never went into the mistress's house; and when Gerasim carried wood into the rooms, she always stayed behind, impatiently waiting for him at the steps, pricking up her ears and turning her head to right and to left at the slightest creak of the door....

So passed another year. Gerasim went on performing his duties as house-porter, and was very well content with his lot, when suddenly an unexpected incident occurred.... One fine summer day the old lady was walking up and down the drawing-room with her dependants. She was in high spirits; she laughed and made jokes. Her servile companions laughed and joked too, but they did not feel particularly mirthful; the household did not much like it, when their mistress was in a lively mood, for, to begin with, she expected from every one prompt and complete participation in her merriment, and was furious if any one showed a face that did not beam with delight, and secondly, these outbursts never lasted long with her, and were usually followed by a sour and gloomy mood. That day she had got up in a lucky hour; at cards she took the four knaves, which means the fulfilment of one's wishes (she used to try her fortune on the cards every morning), and her tea struck her as particularly delicious, for which her maid was rewarded by words of praise, and by twopence in money. With a sweet smile on her wrinkled lips, the lady walked about the drawing-room and went up to the window. A flower-garden had been laid out before the window, and in the very middle bed, under a rose-bush, lay Mumu busily gnawing a bone. The lady caught sight of her.

'Mercy on us!' she cried suddenly; 'what dog is that?'

The companion, addressed by the old lady, hesitated, poor thing, in that wretched state of uneasiness which is common in any person in a dependent position who doesn't know very well what significance to give to the exclamation of a superior.

'I d ... d ... don't know,' she faltered: 'I fancy it's the dumb man's dog.'

'Mercy!' the lady cut her short: 'but it's a charming little dog! order it to be brought in. Has he had it long? How is it I've never seen it before?... Order it to be brought in.'

The companion flew at once into the hall.

'Boy, boy!' she shouted: 'bring Mumu in at once! She's in the flower-garden.'

'Her name's Mumu then,' observed the lady: 'a very nice name.'

'Oh, very, indeed!' chimed in the companion. 'Make haste, Stepan!'

Stepan, a sturdily-built young fellow, whose duties were those of a footman, rushed headlong into the flower-garden, and tried to capture Mumu, but she cleverly slipped from his fingers, and with her tail in the air, fled full speed to Gerasim, who was at that instant in the kitchen, knocking out and cleaning a barrel, turning it upside down in his hands like a child's drum. Stepan ran after her, and tried to catch her just at her master's feet; but the sensible dog would not let a stranger touch her, and with a bound, she got away. Gerasim looked on with a smile at all this ado; at last, Stepan got up, much amazed, and hurriedly explained to him by signs that the mistress wanted the dog brought in to her. Gerasim was a little astonished; he called Mumu, however, picked her up, and handed her over to Stepan. Stepan carried her into the drawing-room, and put her down on the parquette floor. The old lady began calling the dog to her in a coaxing voice. Mumu, who had never in her life been in such magnificent apartments, was very much frightened, and made a rush for the door, but, being driven back by the obsequious Stepan, she began trembling, and huddled close up against the wall.

'Mumu, Mumu, come to me, come to your mistress,' said the lady; 'come, silly thing … don't be afraid.'

'Come, Mumu, come to the mistress,' repeated the companions. 'Come along!'

But Mumu looked round her uneasily, and did not stir.

'Bring her something to eat,' said the old lady. 'How stupid she is! she won't come to her mistress. What's she afraid of?'

'She's not used to your honour yet,' ventured one of the companions in a timid and conciliatory voice.

Stepan brought in a saucer of milk, and set it down before Mumu, but Mumu would not even sniff at the milk, and still shivered, and looked round as before.

'Ah, what a silly you are!' said the lady, and going up to her, she stooped down, and was about to stroke her, but Mumu turned her head abruptly, and showed her teeth. The lady hurriedly drew back her hand….

A momentary silence followed. Mumu gave a faint whine, as though she would complain and apologise….

The old lady moved back, scowling. The dog's sudden movement had frightened her.

'Ah!' shrieked all the companions at once, 'she's not bitten you, has she? Heaven forbid! (Mumu had never bitten any one in her life.) Ah! ah!'

'Take her away,' said the old lady in a changed voice. 'Wretched little dog! What a spiteful creature!'

And, turning round deliberately, she went towards her boudoir. Her companions looked timidly at one another, and were about to follow her, but she stopped, stared coldly at them, and said, 'What's that for, pray? I've not called you,' and went out.

The companions waved their hands to Stepan in despair. He picked up Mumu, and flung her promptly outside the door, just at Gerasim's feet, and half-an-hour later a profound stillness reigned in the house, and the old lady sat on her sofa looking blacker than a thunder-cloud.

What trifles, if you think of it, will sometimes disturb any one!

Till evening the lady was out of humour; she did not talk to any one, did not play cards, and passed a bad night. She fancied the eau-de-Cologne they gave her was not the same as she usually had, and that her pillow smelt of soap, and she made the wardrobe-maid smell all the bed linen—in fact she was very upset and cross altogether. Next morning she ordered Gavrila to be summoned an hour earlier than usual.

'Tell me, please,' she began, directly the latter, not without some inward trepidation, crossed the threshold of her boudoir, 'what dog was that barking all night in our yard? It wouldn't let me sleep!'

'A dog, 'm … what dog, 'm … may be, the dumb man's dog, 'm,' he brought out in a rather unsteady voice.

'I don't know whether it was the dumb man's or whose, but it wouldn't let me sleep. And I wonder what we have such a lot of dogs for! I wish to know. We have a yard dog, haven't we?'

'Oh yes, 'm, we have, 'm. Wolf, 'm.'

'Well, why more, what do we want more dogs for? It's simply introducing disorder. There's no one in control in the house—that's what it is. And what does the dumb man want with a dog? Who gave him leave to keep dogs in my yard? Yesterday I went to the window, and there it was lying in the flower—garden; it had dragged in some nastiness it was gnawing, and my roses are planted there….'

The lady ceased.

'Let her be gone from to-day … do you hear?'

'Yes, 'm.'

'To-day. Now go. I will send for you later for the report.'

Gavrila went away.

As he went through the drawing-room, the steward by way of maintaining order moved a bell from one table to another; he stealthily blew his duck-like nose in the hall, and went into the outer-hall. In the outer-hall, on a locker was Stepan asleep in the attitude of a slain warrior in a battalion picture, his bare legs thrust out below the coat which served him for a blanket. The steward gave him a shove, and whispered some instructions to him, to which Stepan responded with something between a yawn and a laugh. The steward went away, and Stepan got up, put on his coat and his boots, went out and stood on the steps. Five minutes had not passed before Gerasim made his appearance with a huge bundle of hewn logs on his back, accompanied by the inseparable Mumu. (The lady had given orders that her bedroom and boudoir should be heated at times even in the summer.) Gerasim turned sideways before the door, shoved it open with his shoulder, and staggered into the house with his load. Mumu, as usual, stayed behind to wait for him. Then Stepan, seizing his chance, suddenly pounced on her, like a kite on a chicken, held her down to the ground, gathered her up in his arms, and without even putting on his cap, ran out of the yard with her, got into the first fly he met, and galloped off to a market-place. There he soon found a purchaser, to whom he sold her for a shilling, on condition that he would keep her for at least a week tied up; then he returned at once. But before he got home, he got off the fly, and going right round the yard, jumped over the fence into the yard from a back street. He was afraid to go in at the gate for fear of meeting Gerasim.

His anxiety was unnecessary, however; Gerasim was no longer in the yard. On coming out of the house he had at once missed Mumu. He never remembered her failing to wait for his return, and began running up and down, looking for her, and calling her in his own way.... He rushed up to his garret, up to the hay-loft, ran out into the street, this way and that.... She was lost! He turned to the other serfs, with the most despairing signs, questioned them about her, pointing to her height from the ground, describing her with his hands.... Some of them really did not know what had become of Mumu, and merely shook their heads, others did know, and smiled to him for all response, while the steward assumed an important air, and began scolding the coachmen. Then Gerasim ran right away out of the yard.

It was dark by the time he came back. From his worn-out look, his unsteady walk, and his dusty clothes, it might be surmised that he had been running over half Moscow. He stood still opposite the windows of the mistress' house, took a searching look at the steps where a group of house-serfs were crowded together, turned away, and uttered once more his inarticulate 'Mumu.' Mumu did not answer. He went away. Every one looked after him, but no one smiled or said a word, and the inquisitive postillion Antipka reported next morning in the kitchen that the dumb man had been groaning all night.

All the next day Gerasim did not show himself, so that they were obliged to send the coachman Potap for water instead of him, at which the coachman Potap was anything but pleased. The lady asked Gavrila if her orders had been carried out. Gavrila replied that they had. The next morning Gerasim came out of his garret, and went about his work. He came in to his dinner, ate it, and went out again, without a greeting to any one. His face, which had always been lifeless, as with all deaf-mutes, seemed now to be turned to stone. After dinner he went out of the yard again, but not for long; he came back, and went straight up to the hay-loft. Night came on, a clear moonlight night. Gerasim lay breathing heavily, and incessantly turning from side to side. Suddenly he felt something pull at the skirt of his coat. He started, but did not raise his head, and even shut his eyes tighter. But again there was a pull, stronger than before; he jumped up ... before him, with an end of string round her neck, was Mumu, twisting and turning. A prolonged cry of delight broke from his speechless breast; he caught up Mumu, and hugged her tight in his arms, she licked his nose and eyes, and beard and moustache, all in one instant.... He stood a little, thought a minute, crept cautiously down from the hay-loft, looked round, and having satisfied himself that no one could see him, made his way successfully to his garret. Gerasim had guessed before that his dog had not got lost by her own doing, that she must have been taken away by the mistress' orders; the servants had explained to him by signs that his Mumu had snapped at her, and he determined to take his own measures. First he fed Mumu with a bit of bread, fondled her, and put her to bed, then he fell to meditating, and spent the whole night long in meditating how he could best conceal her. At last he decided to leave her all day in the garret, and only to come in now and then to see her, and to take her out at night. The hole in the door he stopped up effectually with his old overcoat, and almost before it was light he was already in the yard, as though nothing had happened, even—innocent guile!—the same expression of melancholy on his face. It did not even occur to the poor deaf man that Mumu would betray herself by her whining; in reality, every one in the house was soon aware that the dumb man's dog had come back, and was locked up in his garret, but from sympathy with him and with her, and partly, perhaps, from dread of him, they did not let him know that they had found out his secret. The steward scratched his hand, and gave a despairing wave of his hand, as much as to say, 'Well, well, God have mercy on him! If only it doesn't come to the mistress' ears!'

But the dumb man had never shown such energy as on that day; he cleaned and scraped the whole courtyard, pulled up every single weed with his own hand, tugged up every stake in the fence of the flower-garden, to satisfy himself that they were strong enough, and unaided drove them in again; in fact, he toiled and laboured so that even the old lady noticed his zeal. Twice in the course of the day Gerasim went stealthily in to see his prisoner when night came on, he lay down to sleep with her in the garret, not in the hay-loft, and only at two o'clock in the night he went out to take her a turn in the fresh air. After walking about the courtyard a good while with her, he was just turning back, when suddenly a rustle was heard behind the fence on the side of the back street. Mumu pricked up her ears, growled—went up to the fence, sniffed, and gave vent to a loud shrill bark. Some drunkard had thought fit to take refuge under the fence for the night. At that very time the old lady had just fallen asleep after a prolonged fit of 'nervous agitation'; these fits of agitation always overtook her after too hearty a supper. The sudden bark waked her up: her heart palpitated, and she felt faint. 'Girls, girls!' she moaned. 'Girls!' The terrified maids ran into her bedroom. 'Oh, oh, I am dying!' she said, flinging her arms about in her agitation. 'Again, that dog again!... Oh, send for the doctor. They mean to be the death of me.... The dog, the dog again! Oh!' And she let her head fall back, which always signified a swoon. They rushed for the doctor, that is, for the household physician, Hariton. This doctor, whose whole qualification consisted in wearing soft-soled boots, knew how to feel the pulse delicately. He used to sleep fourteen hours out of the twenty-four, but the rest of the time he was always sighing, and continually dosing the old lady with cherrybay drops. This doctor ran up at once, fumigated the room with burnt feathers, and when the old lady opened her eyes, promptly offered her a wineglass of the hallowed drops on a silver tray. The old lady took them, but began again at once in a tearful voice complaining of the dog, of Gavrila, and of her fate, declaring that she was a poor old woman, and that every one had forsaken her, no one pitied her, every one wished her dead. Meanwhile the luckless Mumu had gone on barking, while Gerasim tried in vain to call her away from the fence. 'There ... there ... again,' groaned the old lady, and once more she turned up the whites of her eyes. The doctor whispered to a maid, she rushed into the outer-hall, and shook Stepan, he ran to wake Gavrila, Gavrila in a fury ordered the whole household to get up.

Gerasim turned round, saw lights and shadows moving in the windows, and with an instinct of coming trouble in his heart, put Mumu under his arm, ran into his garret, and locked himself in. A few minutes later five men were banging at his door, but feeling the resistance of the bolt, they stopped. Gavrila ran up in a fearful state of mind, and ordered them all to wait there and watch till morning. Then he flew off himself to the maids' quarter, and through an old companion, Liubov Liubimovna, with whose assistance he used to steal tea, sugar, and other groceries and to falsify the accounts, sent word to the mistress that the dog had unhappily run back from somewhere, but that to-morrow she should be killed, and would the mistress be so gracious as not to be angry and to overlook it. The old lady would probably not have been so soon appeased, but the doctor had in his haste given her fully forty drops instead of twelve. The strong dose of narcotic acted; in a quarter of an hour the old lady was in a sound and peaceful sleep; while Gerasim was lying with a white face on his bed, holding Mumu's mouth tightly shut.

Next morning the lady woke up rather late. Gavrila was waiting till she should be awake, to give the order for a final assault on Gerasim's stronghold, while he prepared himself to face a fearful storm. But the storm did not come off. The old lady lay in bed and sent for the eldest of her dependent companions.

'Liubov Liubimovna,' she began in a subdued weak voice—she was fond of playing the part of an oppressed and forsaken victim; needless to say, every one in the house was made extremely uncomfortable at such times—'Liubov Liubimovna, you see my position; go, my love to Gavrila Andreitch, and talk to him a little Can he really prize some wretched cur above the repose—the very life—of his mistress? I could not bear to think so,' she added, with an expression of deep feeling. 'Go, my love; be so good as to go to Gavrila Andreitch for me.'

Liubov Liubimovna went to Gavrila's room. What conversation passed between them is not known, but a short time after, a whole crowd of people was moving across the yard in the direction of Gerasim's garret. Gavrila walked in front, holding his cap on with his hand, though there was no wind. The footmen and cooks were close behind him; Uncle Tail was looking out of a window, giving instructions, that is to say, simply waving his hands. At the rear there was a crowd of small boys skipping and hopping along; half of them were outsiders who had run up. On the narrow staircase leading to the garret sat one guard; at the door were standing two more with sticks. They began to mount the stairs, which they entirely blocked up. Gavrila went up to the door, knocked with his fist, shouting, 'Open the door!'

A stifled bark was audible, but there was no answer.

'Open the door, I tell you,' he repeated.

'But, Gavrila Andreitch,' Stepan observed from below, 'he's deaf, you know—he doesn't hear.'

They all laughed.

'What are we to do?' Gavrila rejoined from above.

'Why, there's a hole there in the door,' answered Stepan, 'so you shake the stick in there.'
Gavrila bent down.
'He's stuffed it up with a coat or something.'
'Well, you just push the coat in.'
At this moment a smothered bark was heard again.
'See, see—she speaks for herself,' was remarked in the crowd, and again they laughed.
Gavrila scratched his ear.
'No, mate,' he responded at last, 'you can poke the coat in yourself, if you like.'
'All right, let me.'
And Stepan scrambled up, took the stick, pushed in the coat, and began waving the stick about in the opening, saying, 'Come out, come out!' as he did so. He was still waving the stick, when suddenly the door of the garret was flung open; all the crowd flew pell-mell down the stairs instantly, Gavrila first of all. Uncle Tail locked the window.
'Come, come, come,' shouted Gavrila from the yard, 'mind what you're about.'
Gerasim stood without stirring in his doorway. The crowd gathered at the foot of the stairs. Gerasim, with his arms akimbo, looked down at all these poor creatures in German coats; in his red peasant's shirt he looked like a giant before them. Gavrila took a step forward.
'Mind, mate,' said he, 'don't be insolent.'
And he began to explain to him by signs that the mistress insists on having his dog; that he must hand it over at once, or it would be the worse for him.
Gerasim looked at him, pointed to the dog, made a motion with his hand round his neck, as though he were pulling a noose tight, and glanced with a face of inquiry at the steward.
'Yes, yes,' the latter assented, nodding; 'yes, just so.'
Gerasim dropped his eyes, then all of a sudden roused himself and pointed to Mumu, who was all the while standing beside him, innocently wagging her tail and pricking up her ears inquisitively. Then he repeated the strangling action round his neck and significantly struck himself on the breast, as though announcing he would take upon himself the task of killing Mumu.
'But you'll deceive us,' Gavrila waved back in response.
Gerasim looked at him, smiled scornfully, struck himself again on the breast, and slammed-to the door.
They all looked at one another in silence.
'What does that mean?' Gavrila began. 'He's locked himself in.'
'Let him be, Gavrila Andreitch,' Stepan advised; 'he'll do it if he's promised. He's like that, you know.... If he makes a promise, it's a certain thing. He's not like us others in that. The truth's the truth with him. Yes, indeed.'
'Yes,' they all repeated, nodding their heads, 'yes—that's so—yes.'
Uncle Tail opened his window, and he too said, 'Yes.'
'Well, may be, we shall see,' responded Gavrila; 'any way, we won't take off the guard. Here you, Eroshka!' he added, addressing a poor fellow in a yellow nankeen coat, who considered himself to be a gardener, 'what have you to do? Take a stick and sit here, and if anything happens, run to me at once!'
Eroshka took a stick, and sat down on the bottom stair. The crowd dispersed, all except a few inquisitive small boys, while Gavrila went home and sent word through Liubov Liubimovna to the mistress, that everything had been done, while he sent a postillion for a policeman in case of need. The old lady tied a knot in her handkerchief, sprinkled some eau-de-Cologne on it, sniffed at it, and rubbed her temples with it, drank some tea, and, being still under the influence of the cherrybay drops, fell asleep again.
An hour after all this hubbub the garret door opened, and Gerasim showed himself. He had on his best coat; he was leading Mumu by a string. Eroshka moved aside and let him pass. Gerasim went to the gates. All the small boys in the yard stared at him in silence. He did not even turn round; he only put his cap on in the street. Gavrila sent the same Eroshka to follow him and keep watch on him as a spy. Eroshka, seeing from a distance that he had gone into a cookshop with his dog, waited for him to come out again.
Gerasim was well known at the cookshop, and his signs were understood. He asked for cabbage soup with meat in it, and sat down with his arms on the table. Mumu stood beside his chair, looking calmly at him with her intelligent eyes. Her coat was glossy; one could see she had just been combed down. They brought Gerasim the soup. He crumbled some bread into it, cut the meat up small, and put the plate on the ground. Mumu began eating in her usual refined way, her little muzzle daintily held so as scarcely to touch her food. Gerasim gazed a long while at her; two big tears suddenly rolled from his eyes; one fell on the dog's brow,

the other into the soup. He shaded his face with his hand. Mumu ate up half the plateful, and came away from it, licking her lips. Gerasim got up, paid for the soup, and went out, followed by the rather perplexed glances of the waiter. Eroshka, seeing Gerasim, hid round a corner, and letting him get in front, followed him again.

Gerasim walked without haste, still holding Mumu by a string. When he got to the corner of the street, he stood still as though reflecting, and suddenly set off with rapid steps to the Crimean Ford. On the way he went into the yard of a house, where a lodge was being built, and carried away two bricks under his arm. At the Crimean Ford, he turned along the bank, went to a place where there were two little rowing-boats fastened to stakes (he had noticed them there before), and jumped into one of them with Mumu. A lame old man came out of a shed in the corner of a kitchen-garden and shouted after him; but Gerasim only nodded, and began rowing so vigorously, though against stream, that in an instant he had darted two hundred yards away. The old man stood for a while, scratched his back first with the left and then with the right hand, and went back hobbling to the shed.

Gerasim rowed on and on. Moscow was soon left behind. Meadows stretched each side of the bank, market gardens, fields, and copses; peasants' huts began to make their appearance. There was the fragrance of the country. He threw down his oars, bent his head down to Mumu, who was sitting facing him on a dry cross seat—the bottom of the boat was full of water—and stayed motionless, his mighty hands clasped upon her back, while the boat was gradually carried back by the current towards the town. At last Gerasim drew himself up hurriedly, with a sort of sick anger in his face, he tied up the bricks he had taken with string, made a running noose, put it round Mumu's neck, lifted her up over the river, and for the last time looked at her.... she watched him confidingly and without any fear, faintly wagging her tail. He turned away, frowned, and wrung his hands.... Gerasim heard nothing, neither the quick shrill whine of Mumu as she fell, nor the heavy splash of the water; for him the noisiest day was soundless and silent as even the stillest night is not silent to us. When he opened his eyes again, little wavelets were hurrying over the river, chasing one another; as before they broke against the boat's side, and only far away behind wide circles moved widening to the bank.

Directly Gerasim had vanished from Eroshka's sight, the latter returned home and reported what he had seen.

'Well, then,' observed Stepan, 'he'll drown her. Now we can feel easy about it. If he once promises a thing....'

No one saw Gerasim during the day. He did not have dinner at home. Evening came on; they were all gathered together to supper, except him.

'What a strange creature that Gerasim is!' piped a fat laundrymaid; 'fancy, upsetting himself like that over a dog.... Upon my word!'

'But Gerasim has been here,' Stepan cried all at once, scraping up his porridge with a spoon.

'How? when?'

'Why, a couple of hours ago. Yes, indeed! I ran against him at the gate; he was going out again from here; he was coming out of the yard. I tried to ask him about his dog, but he wasn't in the best of humours, I could see. Well, he gave me a shove; I suppose he only meant to put me out of his way, as if he'd say, "Let me go, do!" but he fetched me such a crack on my neck, so seriously, that—oh! oh!' And Stepan, who could not help laughing, shrugged up and rubbed the back of his head. 'Yes,' he added; 'he has got a fist; it's something like a fist, there's no denying that!'

They all laughed at Stepan, and after supper they separated to go to bed.

Meanwhile, at that very time, a gigantic figure with a bag on his shoulders and a stick in his hand, was eagerly and persistently stepping out along the T—— highroad. It was Gerasim. He was hurrying on without looking round; hurrying homewards, to his own village, to his own country. After drowning poor Mumu, he had run back to his garret, hurriedly packed a few things together in an old horsecloth, tied it up in a bundle, tossed it on his shoulder, and so was ready. He had noticed the road carefully when he was brought to Moscow; the village his mistress had taken him from lay only about twenty miles off the highroad. He walked along it with a sort of invincible purpose, a desperate and at the same time joyous determination. He walked, his shoulders thrown back and his chest expanded; his eyes were fixed greedily straight before him. He hastened as though his old mother were waiting for him at home, as though she were calling him to her after long wanderings in strange parts, among strangers. The summer night, that was just drawing in, was still and warm; on one side, where the sun had set, the horizon was still light and faintly flushed with the last glow of the vanished day; on the other side a blue-grey twilight had already risen up. The night was coming up from that quarter. Quails were in hundreds around; corncrakes were calling to one another in the thickets.... Gerasim could not hear them; he could not hear the delicate night-whispering of the trees, by which his strong legs carried him, but he smelt the familiar scent of the ripening rye, which was wafted from the dark fields; he felt the wind, flying to meet him—the wind from home—beat caressingly upon his face, and play with his hair and his beard. He saw before him the whitening road homewards, straight as an arrow. He saw in the sky stars innumerable, lighting up his way, and stepped out, strong and bold as a lion, so that when the rising sun shed its moist rosy light upon the still fresh and unwearied traveller, already thirty miles lay between him and Moscow.

In a couple of days he was at home, in his little hut, to the great astonishment of the soldier's wife who had been put in there. After praying before the holy pictures, he set off at once to the village elder. The village elder was at first surprised; but the haycutting had just begun; Gerasim was a first-rate mower, and they put a scythe into his hand on the spot, and he went to mow in his old way, mowing so that the peasants were fairly astounded as they watched his wide sweeping strokes and the heaps he raked together....

In Moscow the day after Gerasim's flight they missed him. They went to his garret, rummaged about in it, and spoke to Gavrila. He came, looked, shrugged his shoulders, and decided that the dumb man had either run away or had drowned himself with his stupid dog. They gave information to the police, and informed the lady. The old lady was furious, burst into tears, gave orders that he was to be found whatever happened, declared she had never ordered the dog to be destroyed, and, in fact, gave Gavrila such a rating that he could do nothing all day but shake his head and murmur, 'Well!' until Uncle Tail checked him at last, sympathetically echoing 'We-ell!' At last the news came from the country of Gerasim's being there. The old lady was somewhat pacified; at first she issued a mandate for him to be brought back without delay to Moscow; afterwards, however, she declared that such an ungrateful creature was absolutely of no use to her. Soon after this she died herself; and her heirs had no thought to spare for Gerasim; they let their mother's other servants redeem their freedom on payment of an annual rent.

And Gerasim is living still, a lonely man in his lonely hut; he is strong and healthy as before, and does the work of four men as before, and as before is serious and steady. But his neighbours have observed that ever since his return from Moscow he has quite given up the society of women; he will not even look at them, and does not keep even a single dog. 'It's his good luck, though,' the peasants reason; 'that he can get on without female folk; and as for a dog—what need has he of a dog? you wouldn't get a thief to go into his yard for any money!' Such is the fame of the dumb man's Titanic strength.

THE JEW

...'Tell us a story, colonel,' we said at last to Nikolai Ilyitch.

The colonel smiled, puffed out a coil of tobacco smoke between his moustaches, passed his hand over his grey hair, looked at us and considered. We all had the greatest liking and respect for Nikolai Ilyitch, for his good-heartedness, common sense, and kindly indulgence to us young fellows. He was a tall, broad-shouldered, stoutly-built man; his dark face, 'one of the splendid Russian faces,' [Footnote: Lermontov in the *Treasurer's Wife*.—AUTHOR'S NOTE.] straight-forward, clever glance, gentle smile, manly and mellow voice—everything about him pleased and attracted one.

'All right, listen then,' he began.

It happened in 1813, before Dantzig. I was then in the E—— regiment of cuirassiers, and had just, I recollect, been promoted to be a cornet. It is an exhilarating occupation—fighting; and marching too is good enough in its way, but it is fearfully slow in a besieging army. There one sits the whole blessed day within some sort of entrenchment, under a tent, on mud or straw, playing cards from morning till night. Perhaps, from simple boredom, one goes out to watch the bombs and redhot bullets flying.

At first the French kept us amused with sorties, but they quickly subsided. We soon got sick of foraging expeditions too; we were overcome, in fact, by such deadly dulness that we were ready to howl for sheer *ennui*. I was not more than nineteen then; I was a healthy young fellow, fresh as a daisy, thought of nothing but getting all the fun I could out of the French... and in other ways too... you understand what I mean... and this is what happened. Having nothing to do, I fell to gambling. All of a sudden, after dreadful losses, my luck turned, and towards morning (we used to play at night) I had won an immense amount. Exhausted and sleepy, I came out into the fresh air, and sat down on a mound. It was a splendid, calm morning; the long lines of our fortifications were lost in the mist; I gazed till I was weary, and then began to doze where I was sitting.

A discreet cough waked me: I opened my eyes, and saw standing before me a Jew, a man of forty, wearing a long-skirted grey wrapper, slippers, and a black smoking-cap. This Jew, whose name was Girshel, was continually hanging about our camp, offering his services as an agent, getting us wine, provisions, and other such trifles. He was a thinnish, red-haired, little man, marked with smallpox; he blinked incessantly with his diminutive little eyes, which were reddish too; he had a long crooked nose, and was always coughing.

He began fidgeting about me, bowing obsequiously.

'Well, what do you want?' I asked him at last.

'Oh, I only—I've only come, sir, to know if I can't be of use to your honour in some way...'

'I don't want you; you can go.'

'At your honour's service, as you desire.... I thought there might be, sir, something....'

'You bother me; go along, I tell you.'

'Certainly, sir, certainly. But your honour must permit me to congratulate you on your success....'

'Why, how did you know?'

'Oh, I know, to be sure I do.... An immense sum... immense....Oh! how immense....'

Girshel spread out his fingers and wagged his head.

'But what's the use of talking,' I said peevishly; 'what the devil's the good of money here?'

'Oh! don't say that, your honour; ay, ay, don't say so. Money's a capital thing; always of use; you can get anything for money, your honour; anything! anything! Only say the word to the agent, he'll get you anything, your honour, anything! anything!'

'Don't tell lies, Jew.'

'Ay! ay!' repeated Girshel, shaking his side-locks. 'Your honour doesn't believe me.... Ay... ay....' The Jew closed his eyes and slowly wagged his head to right and to left.... 'Oh, I know what his honour the officer would like.... I know,... to be sure I do!'

The Jew assumed an exceedingly knowing leer.

'Really!'

The Jew glanced round timorously, then bent over to me.

'Such a lovely creature, your honour, lovely!...' Girshel again closed his eyes and shot out his lips.

'Your honour, you've only to say the word... you shall see for yourself... whatever I say now, you'll hear... but you won't believe... better tell me to show you... that's the thing, that's the thing!'

I did not speak; I gazed at the Jew.

'Well, all right then; well then, very good; so I'll show you then....'

Thereupon Girshel laughed and slapped me lightly on the shoulder, but skipped back at once as though he had been scalded.

'But, your honour, how about a trifle in advance?'

'But you 're taking me in, and will show me some scarecrow?'

'Ay, ay, what a thing to say!' the Jew pronounced with unusual warmth, waving his hands about. 'How can you! Why... if so, your honour, you order me to be given five hundred... four hundred and fifty lashes,' he added hurriedly....' You give orders—'

At that moment one of my comrades lifted the edge of his tent and called me by name. I got up hurriedly and flung the Jew a gold coin.

'This evening, this evening,' he muttered after me.

I must confess, my friends, I looked forward to the evening with some impatience. That very day the French made a sortie; our regiment marched to the attack. The evening came on; we sat round the fires... the soldiers cooked porridge. My comrades talked. I lay on my cloak, drank tea, and listened to my comrades' stories. They suggested a game of cards—I refused to take part in it. I felt excited. Gradually the officers dispersed to their tents; the fires began to die down; the soldiers too dispersed, or went to sleep on the spot; everything was still. I did not get up. My orderly squatted on his heels before the fire, and was beginning to nod. I sent him away. Soon the whole camp was hushed. The sentries were relieved. I still lay there, as it were waiting for something. The stars peeped out. The night came on. A long while I watched the dying flame.... The last fire went out. 'The damned Jew was taking me in,' I thought angrily, and was just going to get up.

'Your honour,'... a trembling voice whispered close to my ear.

I looked round: Girshel. He was very pale, he stammered, and whispered something.

'Let's go to your tent, sir.' I got up and followed him. The Jew shrank into himself, and stepped warily over the short, damp grass. I observed on one side a motionless, muffled-up figure. The Jew beckoned to her—she went up to him. He whispered to her, turned to me, nodded his head several times, and we all three went into the tent. Ridiculous to relate, I was breathless.

'You see, your honour,' the Jew whispered with an effort, 'you see. She's a little frightened at the moment, she's frightened; but I've told her his honour the officer's a good man, a splendid man.... Don't be frightened, don't be frightened,' he went on—'don't be frightened....'

The muffled-up figure did not stir. I was myself in a state of dreadful confusion, and didn't know what to say. Girshel too was fidgeting restlessly, and gesticulating in a strange way....

'Any way,' I said to him, 'you get out....' Unwillingly, as it seemed, Girshel obeyed.

I went up to the muffled-up figure, and gently took the dark hood off her head. There was a conflagration in Dantzig: by the faint, reddish, flickering glow of the distant fire I saw the pale face of a young Jewess. Her beauty astounded me. I stood facing her, and gazed at her in silence. She did not raise her eyes. A slight rustle made me look round. Girshel was cautiously poking his head in under the edge of the tent. I waved my hand at him angrily,... he vanished.

'What's your name?' I said at last.

'Sara,' she answered, and for one instant I caught in the darkness the gleam of the whites of her large, long-shaped eyes and little, even, flashing teeth.

I snatched up two leather cushions, flung them on the ground, and asked her to sit down. She slipped off her shawl, and sat down. She was wearing a short Cossack jacket, open in front, with round, chased silver buttons, and full sleeves. Her thick black hair was coiled twice round her little head. I sat down beside her and took her dark, slender hand. She resisted a little, but seemed afraid to look at me, and there was a catch in her breath. I admired her Oriental profile, and timidly pressed her cold, shaking fingers.

'Do you know Russian?'

'Yes... a little.'

'And do you like Russians?'

'Yes, I like them.'

'Then, you like me too?'

'Yes, I like you.'

I tried to put my arm round her, but she moved away quickly....

'No, no, please, sir, please...'

'Oh, all right; look at me, any way.'

She let her black, piercing eyes rest upon me, and at once turned away with a smile, and blushed.

I kissed her hand ardently. She peeped at me from under her eyelids and softly laughed.

'What is it?'

She hid her face in her sleeve and laughed more than before.

Girshel showed himself at the entrance of the tent and shook his finger at her. She ceased laughing.

'Go away!' I whispered to him through my teeth; 'you make me sick!'

Girshel did not go away.

I took a handful of gold pieces out of my trunk, stuffed them in his hand and pushed him out.

'Your honour, me too....' she said.

I dropped several gold coins on her lap; she pounced on them like a cat.

'Well, now I must have a kiss.'

'No, please, please,' she faltered in a frightened and beseeching voice.

'What are you frightened of?'

'I'm afraid.'

'Oh, nonsense....'

'No, please.'

She looked timidly at me, put her head a little on one side and clasped her hands. I let her alone.

'If you like... here,' she said after a brief silence, and she raised her hand to my lips. With no great eagerness, I kissed it. Sara laughed again.

My blood was boiling. I was annoyed with myself and did not know what to do. Really, I thought at last, what a fool I am.

I turned to her again.

'Sara, listen, I'm in love with you.'

'I know.'

'You know? And you're not angry? And do you like me too?'

Sara shook her head.

'No, answer me properly.'

'Well, show yourself,' she said.

I bent down to her. Sara laid her hands on my shoulders, began scrutinising my face, frowned, smiled.... I could not contain myself, and gave her a rapid kiss on her cheek. She jumped up and in one bound was at the entrance of the tent.

'Come, what a shy thing you are!'

She did not speak and did not stir.

'Come here to me....'

'No, sir, good-bye. Another time.'

Girshel again thrust in his curly head, and said a couple of words to her; she bent down and glided away, like a snake.

I ran out of the tent in pursuit of her, but could not get another glimpse of her nor of Girshel.

The whole night long I could not sleep a wink.

The next night we were sitting in the tent of our captain; I was playing, but with no great zest. My orderly came in.

'Some one's asking for you, your honour.'

'Who is it?'

'A Jew.'

'Can it be Girshel?' I wondered. I waited till the end of the rubber, got up and went out. Yes, it was so; I saw Girshel.

'Well,' he questioned me with an ingratiating smile, 'your honour, are you satisfied?'

'Ah, you———!' (Here the colonel glanced round. 'No ladies present, I believe.... Well, never mind, any way.') 'Ah, bless you!' I responded, 'so you're making fun of me, are you?'

'How so?'

'How so, indeed! What a question!'

'Ay, ay, your honour, you 're too bad,' Girshel said reproachfully, but never ceasing smiling. 'The girl is young and modest.... You frightened her, indeed, you did.'

'Queer sort of modesty! why did she take money, then?'

'Why, what then? If one's given money, why not take it, sir?'

'I say, Girshel, let her come again, and I '11 let you off... only, please, don't show your stupid phiz inside my tent, and leave us in peace; do you hear?'

Girshel's eyes sparkled.

'What do you say? You like her?'

'Well, yes.'

'She's a lovely creature! there's not another such anywhere. And have you something for me now?'

'Yes, here, only listen; fair play is better than gold. Bring her and then go to the devil. I'll escort her home myself.'

'Oh, no, sir, no, that's impossible, sir,' the Jew rejoined hurriedly. 'Ay, ay, that's impossible. I'll walk about near the tent, your honour, if you like; I'll... I'll go away, your honour, if you like, a little.... I'm ready to do your honour a service.... I'll move away... to be sure, I will.'

'Well, mind you do.... And bring her, do you hear?'

'Eh, but she's a beauty, your honour, eh? your honour, a beauty, eh?'

Girshel bent down and peeped into my eyes.

'She's good-looking.'

'Well, then, give me another gold piece.'

I threw him a coin; we parted.

The day passed at last. The night came on. I had been sitting for a long while alone in my tent. It was dark outside. It struck two in the town. I was beginning to curse the Jew.... Suddenly Sara came in, alone. I jumped up took her in my arms... put my lips to her face.... It was cold as ice. I could scarcely distinguish her features.... I made her sit down, knelt down before her, took her hands, touched her waist.... She did not speak, did not stir, and suddenly she broke into loud, convulsive sobbing. I tried in vain to soothe her, to persuade her.... She wept in torrents.... I caressed her, wiped her tears; as before, she did not resist, made no answer to my questions and wept—wept, like a waterfall. I felt a pang at my heart; I got up and went out of the tent.

Girshel seemed to pop up out of the earth before me.

'Girshel,' I said to him, 'here's the money I promised you. Take Sara away.'

The Jew at once rushed up to her. She left off weeping, and clutched hold of him.

'Good-bye, Sara,'I said to her. 'God bless you, good-bye. We'll see each other again some other time.'

Girshel was silent and bowed humbly. Sara bent down, took my hand and pressed it to her lips; I turned away....

For five or six days, my friends, I kept thinking of my Jewess. Girshel did not make his appearance, and no one had seen him in the camp. I slept rather badly at nights; I was continually haunted by wet, black eyes, and long eyelashes; my lips could not forget the touch of her cheek, smooth and fresh as a downy plum. I was sent out with a foraging party to a village some distance away. While my soldiers were ransacking the houses, I remained in the street, and did not dismount from my horse. Suddenly some one caught hold of my foot....

'Mercy on us, Sara!'

She was pale and excited.

'Your honour... help us, save us, your soldiers are insulting us.... Your honour....'

She recognised me and flushed red.

'Why, do you live here?'

'Yes.'

'Where?'

Sara pointed to a little, old house. I set spurs to my horse and galloped up. In the yard of the little house an ugly and tattered Jewess was trying to tear out of the hands of my long sergeant, Siliavka, three hens and a duck. He was holding his booty above his head, laughing; the hens clucked and the duck quacked.... Two other cuirassiers were loading their horses with hay, straw, and sacks of flour. Inside the house I heard shouts and oaths in Little-Russian.... I called to my men and told them to leave the Jews alone, not to take anything from them. The soldiers obeyed, the sergeant got on his grey mare, Proserpina, or, as he called her, 'Prozherpila,' and rode after me into the street.

'Well,' I said to Sara, 'are you pleased with me?'

She looked at me with a smile.

'What has become of you all this time?'

She dropped her eyes.

'I will come to you to-morrow.'

'In the evening?'

'No, sir, in the morning.'

'Mind you do, don't deceive me.'

'No... no, I won't.'

I looked greedily at her. By daylight she seemed to me handsomer than ever. I remember I was particularly struck by the even, amber tint of her face and the bluish lights in her black hair.... I bent down from my horse and warmly pressed her little hand.

'Good-bye, Sara... mind you come.'

'Yes.'

She went home; I told the sergeant to follow me with the party, and galloped off.

The next day I got up very early, dressed, and went out of the tent. It was a glorious morning; the sun had just risen and every blade of grass was sparkling in the dew and the crimson glow. I clambered on to a high breastwork, and sat down on the edge of an embrasure. Below me a stout, cast-iron cannon stuck out its black muzzle towards the open country. I looked carelessly about me... and all at once caught sight of a bent figure in a grey wrapper, a hundred paces from me. I recognised Girshel. He stood without moving for a long while in one place, then suddenly ran a little on one side, looked hurriedly and furtively round... uttered a cry, squatted down, cautiously craned his neck and began looking round again and listening. I could see all his actions very clearly. He put his hand into his bosom, took out a scrap of paper and a pencil, and began writing or drawing something. Girshel continually stopped, started like a hare, attentively scrutinised everything around him, and seemed to be sketching our camp. More than once he hid his scrap of paper, half closed his eyes, sniffed at the air, and again set to work. At last, the Jew squatted down on the grass, took off his slipper, and stuffed the paper in it; but he had not time to regain his legs, when suddenly, ten steps from him, there appeared from behind the slope of an earthwork the whiskered countenance of the sergeant Siliavka, and gradually the whole of his long clumsy figure rose up from the ground. The Jew stood with his back to him. Siliavka went quickly up to him and laid his heavy paw on his shoulder. Girshel seemed to shrink into himself. He shook like a leaf and uttered a feeble cry, like a hare's. Siliavka addressed him threateningly, and seized him by the collar. I could not hear their conversation, but from the despairing gestures of the Jew, and his supplicating appearance, I began to guess what it was. The Jew twice flung himself at the sergeant's feet, put his hand in his pocket, pulled out a torn check handkerchief, untied a knot, and took out gold coins.... Siliavka took his offering with great dignity, but did not leave off dragging the Jew by the collar. Girshel made a sudden bound and rushed away; the sergeant sped after him in pursuit. The Jew ran exceedingly well; his legs, clad in blue stockings, flashed by, really very rapidly; but Siliavka after a short run caught the crouching Jew, made him stand up, and carried him in his arms straight to the camp. I got up and went to meet him.

'Ah! your honour!' bawled Siliavka,—'it's a spy I'm bringing you—a spy!...' The sturdy Little-Russian was streaming with perspiration. 'Stop that wriggling, devilish Jew—now then... you wretch! you'd better look out, I'll throttle you!'

The luckless Girshel was feebly prodding his elbows into Siliavka's chest, and feebly kicking.... His eyes were rolling convulsively....

'What's the matter?' I questioned Siliavka.

'If your honour'll be so good as to take the slipper off his right foot,—I can't get at it.' He was still holding the Jew in his arms.

I took off the slipper, took out of it a carefully folded piece of paper, unfolded it, and found an accurate map of our camp. On the margin were a number of notes written in a fine hand in the Jews' language.

Meanwhile Siliavka had set Girshel on his legs. The Jew opened his eyes, saw me, and flung himself on his knees before me.

Without speaking, I showed him the paper.

'What's this?'

'It's—-nothing, your honour. I was only....' His voice broke.

'Are you a spy?'

He did not understand me, muttered disconnected words, pressed my knees in terror....

'Are you a spy?'

'I!' he cried faintly, and shook his head. 'How could I? I never did; I'm not at all. It's not possible; utterly impossible. I'm ready—I'll—this minute—I've money to give... I'll pay for it,' he whispered, and closed his eyes.

The smoking-cap had slipped back on to his neck; his reddish hair was soaked with cold sweat, and hung in tails; his lips were blue, and working convulsively; his brows were contracted painfully; his face was drawn....

Soldiers came up round us. I had at first meant to give Girshel a good fright, and to tell Siliavka to hold his tongue, but now the affair had become public, and could not escape 'the cognisance of the authorities.'

'Take him to the general,' I said to the sergeant.

'Your honour, your honour!' the Jew shrieked in a voice of despair. 'I am not guilty... not guilty.... Tell him to let me go, tell him...'

'His Excellency will decide about that,' said Siliavka. 'Come along.'

'Your honour!' the Jew shrieked after me—'tell him! have mercy!'

His shriek tortured me; I hastened my pace. Our general was a man of German extraction, honest and good-hearted, but strict in his adherence to military discipline. I went into the little house that had been hastily put up for him, and in a few words explained the reason of my visit. I knew the severity of the military regulations, and so I did not even pronounce the word 'spy,' but tried to put the whole affair before him as something quite trifling and not worth attention. But, unhappily for Girshel, the general put doing his duty higher than pity.

'You, young man,' he said to me in his broken Russian, 'inexperienced are. You in military matters yet inexperienced are. The matter, of which you to me reported have, is important, very important.... And where is this man who taken was? this Jew? where is he?'

I went out and told them to bring in the Jew. They brought in the Jew. The wretched creature could scarcely stand up.

'Yes,' pronounced the general, turning to me; 'and where's the plan which on this man found was?'

I handed him the paper. The general opened it, turned away again, screwed up his eyes, frowned....

'This is most as-ton-ish-ing...' he said slowly. 'Who arrested him?'

'I, your Excellency!' Siliavka jerked out sharply.

'Ah! good! good!... Well, my good man, what do you say in your defence?'

'Your... your... your Excellency,' stammered Girshel, 'I... indeed,... your Excellency... I'm not guilty... your Excellency; ask his honour the officer.... I'm an agent, your Excellency, an honest agent.'

'He ought to be cross-examined,' the general murmured in an undertone, wagging his head gravely. 'Come, how do you explain this, my friend?' 'I'm not guilty, your Excellency, I'm not guilty.'

'That is not probable, however. You were—how is it said in Russian?—taken on the fact, that is, in the very facts!'

'Hear me, your Excellency; I am not guilty.'

'You drew the plan? you are a spy of the enemy?'

'It wasn't me!' Girshel shrieked suddenly; 'not I, your Excellency!'

The general looked at Siliavka.

'Why, he's raving, your Excellency. His honour the officer here took the plan out of his slipper.'

The general looked at me. I was obliged to nod assent.

'You are a spy from the enemy, my good man....'

'Not I... not I...' whispered the distracted Jew.

'You have the enemy with similar information before provided? Confess....'

'How could I?'

'You will not deceive me, my good man. Are you a spy?'

The Jew closed his eyes, shook his head, and lifted the skirts of his gown.

'Hang him,' the general pronounced expressively after a brief silence,'according to the law. Where is Mr. Fiodor Schliekelmann?'

They ran to fetch Schliekelmann, the general's adjutant. Girshel began to turn greenish, his mouth fell open, his eyes seemed starting out of his head. The adjutant came in. The general gave him the requisite instructions. The secretary showed his sickly, pock-marked face for an instant. Two or three officers peeped into the room inquisitively.

'Have pity, your Excellency,' I said to the general in German as best I could; 'let him off....'

'You, young man,' he answered me in Russian, 'I was saying to you, are inexperienced, and therefore I beg you silent to be, and me no more to trouble.'

Girshel with a shriek dropped at the general's feet.

'Your Excellency, have mercy; I will never again, I will not, your Excellency; I have a wife... your Excellency, a daughter... have mercy....'

'It's no use!'

'Truly, your Excellency, I am guilty... it's the first time, your Excellency, the first time, believe me!'

'You furnished no other documents?'

'The first time, your Excellency,... my wife... my children... have mercy....'

'But you are a spy.'

'My wife... your Excellency... my children....'

The general felt a twinge, but there was no getting out of it.

'According to the law, hang the Hebrew,' he said constrainedly, with the air of a man forced to do violence to his heart, and sacrifice his better feelings to inexorable duty—'hang him! Fiodor Karlitch, I beg you to draw up a report of the occurrence....'

A horrible change suddenly came over Girshel. Instead of the ordinary timorous alarm peculiar to the Jewish nature, in his face was reflected the horrible agony that comes before death. He writhed like a wild beast trapped, his mouth stood open, there was a hoarse rattle in his throat, he positively leapt up and down, convulsively moving his elbows. He had on only one slipper; they had forgotten to put the other on again... his gown fell open... his cap had fallen off....

We all shuddered; the general stopped speaking.

'Your Excellency,' I began again, 'pardon this wretched creature.'

'Impossible! It is the law,' the general replied abruptly, and not without emotion, 'for a warning to others.'

'For pity's sake....'

'Mr. Cornet, be so good as to return to your post,' said the general, and he motioned me imperiously to the door.

I bowed and went out. But seeing that in reality I had no post anywhere, I remained at no great distance from the general's house.

Two minutes later Girshel made his appearance, conducted by Siliavka and three soldiers. The poor Jew was in a state of stupefaction, and could hardly move his legs. Siliavka went by me to the camp, and soon returned with a rope in his hands. His coarse but not ill-natured face wore a look of strange, exasperated commiseration. At the sight of the rope the Jew flung up his arms, sat down, and burst into sobs. The soldiers stood silently about him, and stared grimly at the earth. I went up to Girshel, addressed him; he sobbed like a baby, and did not even look at me. With a hopeless gesture I went to my tent, flung myself on a rug, and closed my eyes....

Suddenly some one ran hastily and noisily into my tent. I raised my head and saw Sara; she looked beside herself. She rushed up to me, and clutched at my hands.

'Come along, come along,' she insisted breathlessly.

'Where? what for? let us stop here.'

'To father, to father, quick... save him... save him!'

'To what father?'

'My father; they are going to hang him....'

'What! is Girshel...?'

'My father... I '11 tell you all about it later,' she added, wringing her hands in despair: 'only come... come....'

We ran out of the tent. In the open ground, on the way to a solitary birch-tree, we could see a group of soldiers.... Sara pointed to them without speaking....

'Stop,' I said to her suddenly: 'where are we running to? The soldiers won't obey me.'

Sara still pulled me after her.... I must confess, my head was going round.

'But listen, Sara,' I said to her; 'what sense is there in running here? It would be better for me to go to the general again; let's go together; who knows, we may persuade him.'

Sara suddenly stood still and gazed at me, as though she were crazy.

'Understand me, Sara, for God's sake. I can't do anything for your father, but the general can. Let's go to him.'

'But meanwhile they'll hang him,' she moaned....

I looked round. The secretary was standing not far off.

'Ivanov,' I called to him; 'run, please, over there to them, tell them to wait a little, say I've gone to petition the general.'

'Yes, sir.'

Ivanov ran off.

We were not admitted to the general's presence. In vain I begged, persuaded, swore even, at last... in vain, poor Sara tore her hair and rushed at the sentinels; they would not let us pass.

Sara looked wildly round, clutched her head in both hands, and ran at breakneck pace towards the open country, to her father. I followed her. Every one stared at us, wondering.

We ran up to the soldiers. They were standing in a ring, and picture it, gentlemen! they were laughing, laughing at poor Girshel. I flew into a rage and shouted at them. The Jew saw us and fell on his daughter's neck. Sara clung to him passionately.

The poor wretch imagined he was pardoned.... He was just beginning to thank me... I turned away.

'Your honour,' he shrieked and wrung his hands; 'I'm not pardoned?'

I did not speak.

'No?'

'No.'

'Your honour,' he began muttering; 'look, your honour, look... she, this girl, see—you know—she's my daughter.'

'I know,' I answered, and turned away again.

'Your honour,' he shrieked, 'I never went away from the tent! I wouldn't for anything...'

He stopped, and closed his eyes for an instant.... 'I wanted your money, your honour, I must own... but not for anything....'

I was silent. Girshel was loathsome to me, and she too, his accomplice....

'But now, if you save me,' the Jew articulated in a whisper, 'I'll command her... I... do you understand?... everything... I'll go to every length....'

He was trembling like a leaf, and looking about him hurriedly. Sara silently and passionately embraced him.

The adjutant came up to us.

'Cornet,' he said to me; 'his Excellency has given me orders to place you under arrest. And you...' he motioned the soldiers to the Jew... 'quickly.'

Siliavka went up to the Jew.

'Fiodor Karlitch,' I said to the adjutant (five soldiers had come with him); 'tell them, at least, to take away that poor girl....'

'Of course. Certainly.'

The unhappy girl was scarcely conscious. Girshel was muttering something to her in Yiddish....

The soldiers with difficulty freed Sara from her father's arms, and carefully carried her twenty steps away. But all at once she broke from their arms and rushed towards Girshel.... Siliavka stopped her. Sara pushed him away; her face was covered with a faint flush, her eyes flashed, she stretched out her arms.

'So may you be accursed,' she screamed in German; 'accursed, thrice accursed, you and all the hateful breed of you, with the curse of Dathan and Abiram, the curse of poverty and sterility and violent, shameful death! May the earth open under your feet, godless, pitiless, bloodthirsty dogs....'

Her head dropped back... she fell to the ground.... They lifted her up and carried her away.

The soldiers took Girshel under his arms. I saw then why it was they had been laughing at the Jew when I ran up from the camp with Sara. He was really ludicrous, in spite of all the horror of his position. The intense anguish of parting with life, his daughter, his family, showed itself in the Jew in such strange and grotesque gesticulations, shrieks, and wriggles that we all could not help smiling, though it was horrible—intensely horrible to us too. The poor wretch was half dead with terror....

'Oy! oy! oy!' he shrieked: 'oy... wait! I've something to tell you... a lot to tell you. Mr. Under-sergeant, you know me. I'm an agent, an honest agent. Don't hold me; wait a minute, a little minute, a tiny minute—wait! Let me go; I'm a poor Hebrew. Sara... where is Sara? Oh, I know, she's at his honour the quarter-lieutenant's.' (God knows why he bestowed such an unheard-of grade upon me.) 'Your honour the quarter-lieutenant, I'm not going away from the tent.' (The soldiers were taking hold of Girshel... he uttered a deafening shriek, and wriggled out of their hands.) 'Your Excellency, have pity on the unhappy father of a family. I'll give you ten golden pieces, fifteen I'll give, your Excellency!...' (They dragged him to the birch-tree.) 'Spare me! have mercy! your honour the quarter-lieutenant! your Excellency, the general and commander-in-chief!'

They put the noose on the Jew.... I shut my eyes and rushed away.

I remained for a fortnight under arrest. I was told that the widow of the luckless Girshel came to fetch away the clothes of the deceased. The general ordered a hundred roubles to be given to her. Sara I never saw again. I was wounded; I was taken to the hospital, and by the time I was well again, Dantzig had surrendered, and I joined my regiment on the banks of the Rhine.

AN UNHAPPY GIRL

Yes, yes, began Piotr Gavrilovitch; those were painful days... and I would rather not recall them.... But I have made you a promise; I shall have to tell you the whole story. Listen.

I

I was living at that time (the winter of 1835) in Moscow, in the house of my aunt, the sister of my dead mother. I was eighteen; I had only just passed from the second into the third course in the faculty 'of Language' (that was what it was called in those days) in the Moscow University. My aunt was a gentle, quiet woman—a widow. She lived in a big, wooden house in Ostozhonka, one of those warm, cosy houses such as, I fancy, one can find nowhere else but in Moscow. She saw hardly any one, sat from morning till night in the drawing-room with two companions, drank the choicest tea, played patience, and was continually requesting that the room should be fumigated. Thereupon her companions ran into the hall; a few minutes later an old servant in livery would bring in a copper pan with a bunch of mint on a hot brick, and stepping hurriedly upon the narrow strips of carpet, he would sprinkle the mint with vinegar. White fumes always puffed up about his wrinkled face, and he frowned and turned away, while the canaries in the dining-room chirped their hardest, exasperated by the hissing of the smouldering mint.

I was fatherless and motherless, and my aunt spoiled me. She placed the whole of the ground floor at my complete disposal. My rooms were furnished very elegantly, not at all like a student's rooms in fact: there were pink curtains in the bedroom, and a muslin canopy, adorned with blue rosettes, towered over my bed. Those rosettes were, I'll own, rather an annoyance to me; to my thinking, such 'effeminacies' were calculated to lower me in the eyes of my companions. As it was, they nicknamed me 'the boarding-school miss.' I could never succeed in forcing myself to smoke. I studied—why conceal my shortcomings?—very lazily, especially at the beginning of the course. I went out a great deal. My aunt had bestowed on me a wide sledge, fit for a general, with a pair of sleek horses. At the houses of 'the gentry' my visits were rare, but at the theatre I was quite at home, and I consumed masses of tarts at the restaurants. For all that, I permitted myself no breach of decorum, and behaved very discreetly, *en jeune homme de bonne maison*. I would not for anything in the world have pained my kind aunt; and besides I was naturally of a rather cool temperament.

II

From my earliest years I had been fond of chess; I had no idea of the science of the game, but I didn't play badly. One day in a café, I was the spectator of a prolonged contest at chess, between two players, of whom one, a fair-haired young man of about five-and-twenty, struck me as playing well. The game ended in his favour; I offered to play a match with him. He agreed,... and in the course of an hour, beat me easily, three times running.

'You have a natural gift for the game,' he pronounced in a courteous tone, noticing probably that my vanity was suffering; 'but you don't know the openings. You ought to study a chess-book—Allgacir or Petrov.'

'Do you think so? But where can I get such a book?'

'Come to me; I will give you one.'

He gave me his name, and told me where he was living. Next day I went to see him, and a week later we were almost inseparable.

III

My new acquaintance was called Alexander Davidovitch Fustov. He lived with his mother, a rather wealthy woman, the widow of a privy councillor, but he occupied a little lodge apart and lived quite independently, just as I did at my aunt's. He had a post in the department of Court affairs. I became genuinely attached to him. I had never in my life met a young man more 'sympathetic.' Everything about him was charming and attractive: his graceful figure, his bearing, his voice, and especially his small, delicate face with the golden-blue eyes, the elegant, as it were coquettishly moulded little nose, the unchanging amiable smile on the crimson lips, the light curls of soft hair over the rather narrow, snow-white brow. Fustov's character was remarkable for exceptional serenity, and a sort of amiable, restrained affability; he was never pre-occupied, and was always satisfied with everything; but on the other hand he was never ecstatic over anything. Every excess, even in a good feeling, jarred upon him; 'that's savage, savage,' he would say with a faint shrug, half closing his golden eyes. Marvellous were those eyes of Fustov's! They invariably expressed sympathy, good-will, even devotion. It was only at a later period that I noticed that the expression of his eyes resulted solely from their setting, that it never changed, even when he was sipping his soup or smoking a cigar. His preciseness became a byword between us. His grandmother, indeed, had been a German. Nature had endowed him with all sorts of talents. He danced capitally, was a dashing horseman, and a first-rate swimmer; did carpentering, carving and joinery, bound books and cut out silhouettes, painted in watercolours nosegays of flowers or Napoleon in profile in a blue uniform; played the zither with feeling; knew a number of tricks, with cards and without; and had a fair knowledge of mechanics, physics, and chemistry; but everything only up to a certain point. Only for languages he had no great facility: even French he spoke rather badly. He spoke in general little, and his share in our students' discussions was mostly limited to the bright sympathy of his glance and smile. To the fair sex Fustov was attractive, undoubtedly, but on this subject, of such importance among young people, he did not care to enlarge, and fully deserved the nickname given him by his comrades, 'the discreet Don Juan.' I was not dazzled by Fustov; there was nothing in him to dazzle, but I prized his affection, though in reality it was only manifested by his never refusing to see me when I called. To my mind Fustov was the happiest man in the world. His life ran so very smoothly. His mother, brothers, sisters, aunts, and uncles all adored him, he was on exceptionally good terms with all of them, and enjoyed the reputation of a paragon in his family.

IV

One day I went round to him rather early and did not find him in his study. He called to me from the next room; sounds of panting and splashing reached me from there. Every morning Fustov took a cold shower-bath and afterwards for a quarter of an hour practised gymnastic exercises, in which he had attained remarkable proficiency. Excessive anxiety about one's physical health he did not approve of, but he did not neglect necessary care. ('Don't neglect yourself, don't over-excite yourself, work in moderation,' was his precept.) Fustov had not yet made his appearance, when the outer door of the room where I was waiting flew wide open, and there walked in a man about fifty, wearing a bluish uniform. He was a stout, squarely-built man with milky-whitish eyes in a dark-red face and a perfect cap of thick, grey, curly hair. This person stopped short, looked at me, opened his mouth wide, and with a metallic chuckle, he gave himself a smart slap on his haunch, kicking his leg up in front as he did so.

'Ivan Demianitch?' my friend inquired through the door.

'The same, at your service,' the new comer responded. 'What are you up to? At your toilette? That's right! that's right!' (The voice of the man addressed as Ivan Demianitch had the same harsh, metallic note as his laugh.) 'I've trudged all this way to give your little brother his lesson; and he's got a cold, you know, and does nothing but sneeze. He can't do his work. So I've looked in on you for a bit to warm myself.'

Ivan Demianitch laughed again the same strange guffaw, again dealt himself a sounding smack on the leg, and pulling a check handkerchief out of his pocket, blew his nose noisily, ferociously rolling his eyes, spat into the handkerchief, and ejaculated with the whole force of his lungs: 'Tfoo-o-o!'

Fustov came into the room, and shaking hands with both of us, asked us if we were acquainted.

'Not a bit of it!' Ivan Demianitch boomed at once: 'the veteran of the year twelve has not that honour!'

Fustov mentioned my name first, then, indicating the 'veteran of the year twelve,' he pronounced: 'Ivan Demianitch Ratsch, professor of... various subjects.'

'Precisely so, various they are, precisely,' Mr. Ratsch chimed in. 'Come to think of it, what is there I haven't taught, and that I'm not teaching now, for that matter! Mathematics and geography and statistics and

Italian book-keeping, ha-ha ha-ha! and music! You doubt it, my dear sir?'—he pounced suddenly upon me—'ask Alexander Daviditch if I'm not first-rate on the bassoon. I should be a poor sort of Bohemian—Czech, I should say—if I weren't! Yes, sir, I'm a Czech, and my native place is ancient Prague! By the way, Alexander Daviditch, why haven't we seen you for so long! We ought to have a little duet... ha-ha! Really!'

'I was at your place the day before yesterday, Ivan Demianitch,' replied Fustov.

'But I call that a long while, ha-ha!'

When Mr. Ratsch laughed, his white eyes shifted from side to side in a strange, restless way.

'You're surprised, young man, I see, at my behaviour,' he addressed me again. 'But that's because you don't understand my temperament. You must just ask our good friend here, Alexander Daviditch, to tell you about me. What'll he tell you? He'll tell you old Ratsch is a simple, good-hearted chap, a regular Russian, in heart, if not in origin, ha-ha! At his christening named Johann Dietrich, but always called Ivan Demianitch! What's in my mind pops out on my tongue; I wear my heart, as they say, on my sleeve. Ceremony of all sorts I know naught about and don't want to neither! Can't bear it! You drop in on me one day of an evening, and you'll see for yourself. My good woman—my wife, that is—has no nonsense about her either; she'll cook and bake you... something wonderful! Alexander Daviditch, isn't it the truth I'm telling?'

Fustov only smiled, and I remained silent.

'Don't look down on the old fellow, but come round,' pursued Mr. Ratsch. 'But now...' (he pulled a fat silver watch out of his pocket and put it up to one of his goggle eyes)'I'd better be toddling on, I suppose. I've another chick expecting me.... Devil knows what I'm teaching him,... mythology, by God! And he lives a long way off, the rascal, at the Red Gate! No matter; I'll toddle off on foot. Thanks to your brother's cutting his lesson, I shall be the fifteen kopecks for sledge hire to the good! Ha-ha! A very good day to you, gentlemen, till we meet again!... Eh?... We must have a little duet!' Mr. Ratsch bawled from the passage putting on his goloshes noisily, and for the last time we heard his metallic laugh.

V

'What a strange man!' I said, turning to Fustov, who had already set to work at his turning-lathe. 'Can he be a foreigner? He speaks Russian so fluently.'

'He is a foreigner; only he's been thirty years in Russia. As long ago as 1802, some prince or other brought him from abroad... in the capacity of secretary... more likely, valet, one would suppose. He does speak Russian fluently, certainly.'

'With such go, such far-fetched turns and phrases,' I put in.

'Well, yes. Only very unnaturally too. They're all like that, these Russianised Germans.'

'But he's a Czech, isn't he?'

'I don't know; may be. He talks German with his wife.'

'And why does he call himself a veteran of the year twelve? Was he in the militia, or what?'

'In the militia! indeed! At the time of the fire he remained in Moscow and lost all his property.... That was all he did.'

'But what did he stay in Moscow for?'

Fustov still went on with his turning.

'The Lord knows. I have heard that he was a spy on our side; but that must be nonsense. But it's a fact that he received compensation from the treasury for his losses.'

'He wears some sort of uniform.... I suppose he's in government service then?'

'Yes. Professor in the cadet's corps. He has the rank of a petty councillor.'

'What's his wife like?'

'A German settled here, daughter of a sausagemaker... or butcher....'

'And do you often go to see him?'

'Yes.'

'What, is it pleasant there?'

'Rather pleasant.'

'Has he any children?'

'Yes. Three by the German, and a son and daughter by his first wife.'

'And how old is the eldest daughter?'

'About five-and-twenty,'

I fancied Fustov bent lower over his lathe, and the wheel turned more rapidly, and hummed under the even strokes of his feet.

'Is she good-looking?'

'That's a matter of taste. She has a remarkable face, and she's altogether... a remarkable person.'

'Aha!' thought I. Fustov continued his work with special earnestness, and to my next question he only responded by a grunt.

'I must make her acquaintance,' I decided.

VI

A few days later, Fustov and I set off to Mr. Ratsch's to spend the evening. He lived in a wooden house with a big yard and garden, in Krivoy Place near the Pretchistensky boulevard. He came out into the passage, and meeting us with his characteristic jarring guffaw and noise, led us at once into the drawing-room, where he presented me to a stout lady in a skimpy canvas gown, Eleonora Karpovna, his wife. Eleonora Karpovna had most likely in her first youth been possessed of what the French for some unknown reason call *beauté du diable*, that is to say, freshness; but when I made her acquaintance, she suggested involuntarily to the mind a good-sized piece of meat, freshly laid by the butcher on a clean marble table. Designedly I used the word 'clean'; not only our hostess herself seemed a model of cleanliness, but everything about her, everything in the house positively shone, and glittered; everything had been scoured, and polished, and washed: the samovar on the round table flashed like fire; the curtains before the windows, the table-napkins were crisp with starch, as were also the little frocks and shirts of Mr. Ratsch's four children sitting there, stout, chubby little creatures, exceedingly like their mother, with coarsely moulded, sturdy faces, curls on their foreheads, and red, shapeless fingers. All the four of them had rather flat noses, large, swollen-looking lips, and tiny, light-grey eyes.

'Here's my squadron!' cried Mr. Ratsch, laying his heavy hand on the children's heads one after another. 'Kolia, Olga, Sashka and Mashka! This one's eight, this one's seven, that one's four, and this one's only two! Ha! ha! ha! As you can see, my wife and I haven't wasted our time! Eh, Eleonora Karpovna?'

'You always say things like that,' observed Eleonora Karpovna and she turned away.

'And she's bestowed such Russian names on her squallers!' Mr. Ratsch pursued. 'The next thing, she'll have them all baptized into the Orthodox Church! Yes, by Jove! She's so Slavonic in her sympathies, 'pon my soul, she is, though she is of German blood! Eleonora Karpovna, are you Slavonic?'

Eleonora Karpovna lost her temper.

'I'm a petty councillor's wife, that's what I am! And so I'm a Russian lady and all you may say....'

'There, the way she loves Russia, it's simply awful!' broke in Ivan Demianitch. 'A perfect volcano, ho, ho!'

'Well, and what of it?' pursued Eleonora Karpovna. 'To be sure I love Russia, for where else could I obtain noble rank? And my children too are nobly born, you know. Kolia, sitze ruhig mit den Füssen!'

Ratsch waved his hand to her.

'There, there, princess, don't excite yourself! But where's the nobly born Viktor? To be sure, he's always gadding about! He'll come across the inspector one of these fine days! He'll give him a talking-to! Das ist ein Bummler, Fiktor!'

'Dem Fiktov kann ich nicht kommandiren, Ivan Demianitch. Sie wissen wohl!' grumbled Eleonora Karpovna.

I looked at Fustov, as though wishing finally to arrive at what induced him to visit such people... but at that instant there came into the room a tall girl in a black dress, the elder daughter of Mr. Ratsch, to whom Fustov had referred.... I perceived the explanation of my friend's frequent visits.

VII

There is somewhere, I remember, in Shakespeare, something about 'a white dove in a flock of black crows'; that was just the impression made on me by the girl, who entered the room. Between the world surrounding her and herself there seemed to be too little in common; she herself seemed secretly bewildered and wondering how she had come there. All the members of Mr. Ratsch's family looked self-satisfied, simple-hearted, healthy creatures; her beautiful, but already careworn, face bore the traces of depression, pride and morbidity. The others, unmistakable plebeians, were unconstrained in their manners, coarse perhaps, but simple; but a painful uneasiness was manifest in all her indubitably aristocratic nature. In her very exterior there was no trace of the type characteristic of the German race; she recalled rather the children of the south. The excessively thick, lustreless black hair, the hollow, black, lifeless but beautiful eyes, the low, prominent brow, the aquiline nose, the livid pallor of the smooth skin, a certain tragic line near the delicate lips, and in the slightly sunken cheeks, something abrupt, and at the same time helpless in the movements, elegance without gracefulness... in Italy all this would not have struck me as exceptional, but in Moscow, near the Pretchistensky boulevard, it simply astonished me! I got up from my seat on her entrance; she flung me a swift, uneasy glance, and dropping her black eyelashes, sat down near the window 'like Tatiana.' (Pushkin's *Oniegin* was then fresh in every one's mind.) I glanced at Fustov, but my friend was standing with his back to me, taking a cup of tea from the plump hands of Eleonora Karpovna. I noticed further that the girl as she came in seemed to bring with her a breath of slight physical chillness.... 'What a statue!' was my thought.

VIII

'Piotr Gavrilitch,' thundered Mr. Ratsch, turning to me, 'let me introduce you to my... to my... my number one, ha, ha, ha! to Susanna Ivanovna!'

I bowed in silence, and thought at once: 'Why, the name too is not the same sort as the others,' while Susanna rose slightly, without smiling or loosening her tightly clasped hands.

'And how about the duet?' Ivan Demianitch pursued: 'Alexander Daviditch? eh? benefactor! Your zither was left with us, and I've got the bassoon out of its case already. Let us make sweet music for the honourable company!' (Mr. Ratsch liked to display his Russian; he was continually bursting out with expressions, such as those which are strewn broadcast about the ultra-national poems of Prince Viazemsky.) 'What do you say? Carried?' cried Ivan Demianitch, seeing Fustov made no objection. 'Kolka, march into the study, and look sharp with the music-stand! Olga, this way with the zither! And oblige us with candles for the stands, better-half!' (Mr. Ratsch turned round and round in the room like a top.) 'Piotr Gavrilitch, you like music, hey? If you don't care for it, you must amuse yourself with conversation, only mind, not above a whisper! Ha, ha ha! But what ever's become of that silly chap, Viktor? He ought to be here to listen too! You spoil him completely, Eleonora Karpovna.'

Eleonora Karpovna fired up angrily.

'Aber was kann ich denn, Ivan Demianitch...'

'All right, all right, don't squabble! Bleibe ruhig, hast verstanden? Alexander Daviditch! at your service, sir!'

The children had promptly done as their father had told them. The music-stands were set up, the music began. I have already mentioned that Fustov played the zither extremely well, but that instrument has always produced the most distressing impression upon me. I have always fancied, and I fancy still, that there is imprisoned in the zither the soul of a decrepit Jew money-lender, and that it emits nasal whines and complaints against the merciless musician who forces it to utter sounds. Mr. Ratsch's performance, too, was not calculated to give me much pleasure; moreover, his face became suddenly purple, and assumed a malignant expression, while his whitish eyes rolled viciously, as though he were just about to murder some one with his bassoon, and were swearing and threatening by way of preliminary, puffing out chokingly husky, coarse notes one after another. I placed myself near Susanna, and waiting for a momentary pause, I asked her if she were as fond of music as her papa.

She turned away, as though I had given her a shove, and pronounced abruptly, 'Who?'

'Your father,' I repeated,'Mr. Ratsch.'

'Mr. Ratsch is not my father.'

'Not your father! I beg your pardon... I must have misunderstood... But I remember, Alexander Daviditch...'

Susanna looked at me intently and shyly.

'You misunderstood Mr. Fustov. Mr. Ratsch is my stepfather.'

I was silent for a while.

'And you don't care for music?' I began again.

Susanna glanced at me again. Undoubtedly there was something suggesting a wild creature in her eyes. She obviously had not expected nor desired the continuation of our conversation.

'I did not say that,' she brought out slowly. 'Troo-too-too-too-too-oo-oo...' the bassoon growled with startling fury, executing the final flourishes. I turned round, caught sight of the red neck of Mr. Ratsch, swollen like a boa-constrictor's, beneath his projecting ears, and very disgusting I thought him.

'But that... instrument you surely do not care for,' I said in an undertone.

'No... I don't care for it,' she responded, as though catching my secret hint.

'Oho!' thought I, and felt, as it were, delighted at something.

'Susanna Ivanovna,' Eleonora Karpovna announced suddenly in her German Russian, 'music greatly loves, and herself very beautifully plays the piano, only she likes not to play the piano when she is greatly pressed to play.'

Susanna made Eleonora Karpovna no reply—she did not even look at her—only there was a faint movement of her eyes, under their dropped lids, in her direction. From this movement alone—this movement of her pupils—I could perceive what was the nature of the feeling Susanna cherished for the second wife of her stepfather.... And again I was delighted at something.

Meanwhile the duet was over. Fustov got up and with hesitating footsteps approached the window, near which Susanna and I were sitting, and asked her if she had received from Lengold's the music that he had promised to order her from Petersburg.

'Selections from *Robert le Diable,*' he added, turning to me, 'from that new opera that every one's making such a fuss about.'

'No, I haven't got it yet,' answered Susanna, and turning round with her face to the window she whispered hurriedly. 'Please, Alexander Daviditch, I entreat you, don't make me play to-day. I don't feel in the mood a bit.'

'What's that? Robert le Diable of Meyer-beer?' bellowed Ivan Demianitch, coming up to us: 'I don't mind betting it's a first-class article! He's a Jew, and all Jews, like all Czechs, are born musicians. Especially Jews. That's right, isn't it, Susanna Ivanovna? Hey? Ha, ha, ha, ha!'

In Mr. Ratsch's last words, and this time even in his guffaw, there could be heard something more than his usual bantering tone—the desire to wound was evident. So, at least, I fancied, and so Susanna understood him. She started instinctively, flushed red, and bit her lower lip. A spot of light, like the gleam of a tear, flashed on her eyelash, and rising quickly, she went out of the room.

'Where are you off to, Susanna Ivanovna?' Mr. Ratsch bawled after her.

'Let her be, Ivan Demianitch, 'put in Eleonora Karpovna. 'Wenn sie einmal so et was im Kopfe hat...'

'A nervous temperament,'Ratsch pronounced, rotating on his heels, and slapping himself on the haunch, 'suffers with the *plexus solaris.*Oh! you needn't look at me like that, Piotr Gavrilitch! I've had a go at anatomy too, ha, ha! I'm even a bit of a doctor! You ask Eleonora Karpovna... I cure all her little ailments! Oh, I'm a famous hand at that!'

'You must for ever be joking, Ivan Demianitch,' the latter responded with displeasure, while Fustov, laughing and gracefully swaying to and fro, looked at the husband and wife.

'And why not be joking, mein Mütterchen?' retorted Ivan Demianitch. 'Life's given us for use, and still more for beauty, as some celebrated poet has observed. Kolka, wipe your nose, little savage!'

IX

'I was put in a very awkward position this evening through your doing,' I said the same evening to Fustov, on the way home with him. 'You told me that that girl—what's her name?—Susanna, was the daughter of Mr. Ratsch, but she's his stepdaughter.'

'Really! Did I tell you she was his daughter? But... isn't it all the same?'

'That Ratsch,' I went on.... 'O Alexander, how I detest him! Did you notice the peculiar sneer with which he spoke of Jews before her? Is she... a Jewess?'

Fustov walked ahead, swinging his arms; it was cold, the snow was crisp, like salt, under our feet.

'Yes, I recollect, I did hear something of the sort,' he observed at last.... 'Her mother, I fancy, was of Jewish extraction.'

'Then Mr. Ratsch must have married a widow the first time?'

'Probably.'

'H'm!... And that Viktor, who didn't come in this evening, is his stepson too?'

'No... he's his real son. But, as you know, I don't enter into other people's affairs, and I don't like asking questions. I'm not inquisitive.'

I bit my tongue. Fustov still pushed on ahead. As we got near home, I overtook him and peeped into his face.

'Oh!' I queried, 'is Susanna really so musical?'

Fustov frowned.

'She plays the piano well, 'he said between his teeth. 'Only she's very shy, I warn you!' he added with a slight grimace. He seemed to be regretting having made me acquainted with her.

I said nothing and we parted.

X

Next morning I set off again to Fustov's. To spend my mornings at his rooms had become a necessity for me. He received me cordially, as usual, but of our visit of the previous evening—not a word! As though he had taken water into his mouth, as they say. I began turning over the pages of the last number of the *Telescope.*

A person, unknown to me, came into the room. It turned out to be Mr. Ratsch's son, the Viktor whose absence had been censured by his father the evening before.

He was a young man, about eighteen, but already looked dissipated and unhealthy, with a mawkishly insolent grin on his unclean face, and an expression of fatigue in his swollen eyes. He was like his father, only his features were smaller and not without a certain prettiness. But in this very prettiness there was something offensive. He was dressed in a very slovenly way; there were buttons off his undergraduate's coat, one of his boots had a hole in it, and he fairly reeked of tobacco.

'How d'ye do,' he said in a sleepy voice, with those peculiar twitchings of the head and shoulders which I have always noticed in spoilt and conceited young men. 'I meant to go to the University, but here I am. Sort of oppression on my chest. Give us a cigar.' He walked right across the room, listlessly dragging his feet, and keeping his hands in his trouser-pockets, and sank heavily upon the sofa.

'Have you caught cold?' asked Fustov, and he introduced us to each other. We were both students, but were in different faculties.

'No!... Likely! Yesterday, I must own...' (here Ratsch junior smiled, again not without a certain prettiness, though he showed a set of bad teeth) 'I was drunk, awfully drunk. Yes'—he lighted a cigar and cleared his throat—'Obihodov's farewell supper.'

'Where's he going?'

'To the Caucasus, and taking his young lady with him. You know the black-eyed girl, with the freckles. Silly fool!'

'Your father was asking after you yesterday,' observed Fustov.

Viktor spat aside. 'Yes, I heard about it. You were at our den yesterday. Well, music, eh?'

'As usual.'

'And *she*... with a new visitor' (here he pointed with his head in my direction) 'she gave herself airs, I'll be bound. Wouldn't play, eh?'

'Of whom are you speaking?' Fustov asked.

'Why, of the most honoured Susanna Ivanovna, of course!'

Viktor lolled still more comfortably, put his arm up round his head, gazed at his own hand, and cleared his throat hoarsely.

I glanced at Fustov. He merely shrugged his shoulders, as though giving me to understand that it was no use talking to such a dolt.

XI

Viktor, staring at the ceiling, fell to talking, deliberately and through his nose, of the theatre, of two actors he knew, of a certain Serafrina Serafrinovna, who had 'made a fool' of him, of the new professor, R., whom he called a brute. 'Because, only fancy, what a monstrous notion! Every lecture he begins with calling over the students' names, and he's reckoned a liberal too! I'd have all your liberals locked up in custody!' and turning at last his full face and whole body towards Fustov, he brought out in a half-plaintive, half-ironical voice: 'I wanted to ask you something, Alexander Daviditch.... Couldn't you talk my governor round somehow?... You play duets with him, you know.... Here he gives me five miserable blue notes a month.... What's the use of that! Not enough for tobacco. And then he goes on about my not making debts! I should like to put him in my place, and then we should see! I don't come in for pensions, not like *some people*.' (Viktor pronounced these last words with peculiar emphasis.) 'But he's got a lot of tin, I know! It's no use his whining about hard times, there's no taking me in. No fear! He's made a snug little pile!'

Fustov looked dubiously at Victor.

'If you like,' he began, 'I'll speak to your father. Or, if you like... meanwhile... a trifling sum....'

'Oh, no! Better get round the governor... Though,' added Viktor, scratching his nose with all his fingers at once, 'you might hand over five-and-twenty roubles, if it's the same to you.... What's the blessed total I owe you?'

'You've borrowed eighty-five roubles of me.'

'Yes.... Well, that's all right, then... make it a hundred and ten. I'll pay it all in a lump.'

Fustov went into the next room, brought back a twenty-five-rouble note and handed it in silence to Viktor. The latter took it, yawned with his mouth wide open, grumbled thanks, and, shrugging and stretching, got up from the sofa.

'Foo! though... I'm bored,' he muttered, 'might as well turn in to the "Italie."'

He moved towards the door.

Fustov looked after him. He seemed to be struggling with himself.

'What pension were you alluding to just now, Viktor Ivanitch?' he asked at last.

Viktor stopped in the doorway and put on his cap.

'Oh, don't you know? Susanna Ivanovna's pension.... She gets one. An awfully curious story, I can tell you! I'll tell it you one of these days. Quite an affair, 'pon my soul, a queer affair. But, I say, the governor, you won't forget about the governor, please! His hide is thick, of course—German, and it's had a Russian tanning too, still you can get through it. Only, mind my step-mother Elenorka's nowhere about! Dad's afraid of her, and she wants to keep everything for her brats! But there, you know your way about! Good-bye!'

'Ugh, what a low beast that boy is!' cried Fustov, as soon as the door had slammed-to.

His face was burning, as though from the fire, and he turned away from me. I did not question him, and soon retired.

XII

All that day I spent in speculating about Fustov, about Susanna, and about her relations. I had a vague feeling of something like a family drama. As far as I could judge, my friend was not indifferent to Susanna. But she? Did she care for him? Why did she seem so unhappy? And altogether, what sort of creature was she? These questions were continually recurring to my mind. An obscure but strong conviction told me that it would be no use to apply to Fustov for the solution of them. It ended in my setting off the next day alone to Mr. Ratsch's house.

I felt all at once very uncomfortable and confused directly I found myself in the dark little passage. 'She won't appear even, very likely,' flashed into my mind. 'I shall have to stop with the repulsive veteran and his cook of a wife.... And indeed, even if she does show herself, what of it? She won't even take part in the conversation.... She was anything but warm in her manner to me the other day. Why ever did I come?' While I was making these reflections, the little page ran to announce my presence, and in the adjoining room, after two or three wondering 'Who is it? Who, do you say?' I heard the heavy shuffling of slippers, the folding-door was slightly opened, and in the crack between its two halves was thrust the face of Ivan Demianitch, an unkempt and grim-looking face. It stared at me and its expression did not immediately change.... Evidently, Mr. Ratsch did not at once recognise me; but suddenly his cheeks grew rounder, his eyes narrower, and from his opening mouth, there burst, together with a guffaw, the exclamation: 'Ah! my dear sir! Is it you? Pray walk in!'

I followed him all the more unwillingly, because it seemed to me that this affable, good-humoured Mr. Ratsch was inwardly wishing me at the devil. There was nothing to be done, however. He led me into the drawing-room, and in the drawing-room who should be sitting but Susanna, bending over an account-book? She glanced at me with her melancholy eyes, and very slightly bit the finger-nails of her left hand.... It was a habit of hers, I noticed, a habit peculiar to nervous people. There was no one else in the room.

'You see, sir,' began Mr. Ratsch, dealing himself a smack on the haunch, 'what you've found Susanna Ivanovna and me busy upon: we're at our accounts. My spouse has no great head for arithmetic, and I, I must own, try to spare my eyes. I can't read without spectacles, what am I to do? Let the young people exert themselves, ha-ha! That's the proper thing. But there's no need of haste.... More haste, worse speed in catching fleas, he-he!'

Susanna closed the book, and was about to leave the room.

'Wait a bit, wait a bit,' began Mr. Ratsch. 'It's no great matter if you're not in your best dress....' (Susanna was wearing a very old, almost childish, frock with short sleeves.) 'Our dear guest is not a stickler for ceremony, and I should like just to clear up last week.... You don't mind?'—he addressed me. 'We needn't stand on ceremony with you, eh?'

'Please don't put yourself out on my account!' I cried.

'To be sure, my good friend. As you're aware, the late Tsar Alexey Nikolavitch Romanoff used to say, "Time is for business, but a minute for recreation!" We'll devote one minute only to that same business... ha-ha! What about that thirteen roubles and thirty kopecks?' he added in a low voice, turning his back on me.

'Viktor took it from Eleonora Karpovna; he said that it was with your leave,' Susanna replied, also in a low voice.

'He said... he said... my leave...' growled Ivan Demianitch. 'I'm on the spot myself, I fancy. Might be asked. And who's had that seventeen roubles?'

'The upholsterer.'

'Oh... the upholsterer. What's that for?' 'His bill.'

'His bill. Show me!' He pulled the book away from Susanna, and planting a pair of round spectacles with silver rims on his nose, he began passing his finger along the lines. 'The upholsterer,.. the upholsterer... You'd chuck all the money out of doors! Nothing pleases you better!... Wie die Croaten! A bill indeed! But, after all,' he added aloud, and he turned round facing me again, and pulled the spectacles off his nose, 'why do this now? I can go into these wretched details later. Susanna Ivanovna, be so good as to put away that account-book, and come back to us and enchant our kind guest's ears with your musical accomplishments, to wit, playing on the pianoforte... Eh?'

Susanna turned away her head.

'I should be very happy,' I hastily observed; 'it would be a great pleasure for me to hear Susanna Ivanovna play. But I would not for anything in the world be a trouble...'

'Trouble, indeed, what nonsense! Now then, Susanna Ivanovna, eins, zwei, drei!'

Susanna made no response, and went out.

XIII

I had not expected her to come back; but she quickly reappeared. She had not even changed her dress, and sitting down in a corner, she looked twice intently at me. Whether it was that she was conscious in my manner to her of the involuntary respect, inexplicable to myself, which, more than curiosity, more even than sympathy, she aroused in me, or whether she was in a softened frame of mind that day, any way, she suddenly went to the piano, and laying her hand irresolutely on the keys, and turning her head a little over her shoulder towards me, she asked what I would like her to play. Before I had time to answer she had seated herself, taken up some music, hurriedly opened it, and begun to play. I loved music from childhood, but at that time I had but little comprehension of it, and very slight knowledge of the works of the great masters, and if Mr. Ratsch had not grumbled with some dissatisfaction, 'Aha! wieder dieser Beethoven!' I should not have guessed what Susanna had chosen. It was, as I found out afterwards, the celebrated sonata in F minor, opus 57. Susanna's playing impressed me more than I can say; I had not expected such force, such fire, such bold execution. At the very first bars of the intensely passionate allegro, the beginning of the sonata, I felt that numbness, that chill and sweet terror of ecstasy, which instantaneously enwrap the soul when beauty bursts with sudden flight upon it. I did not stir a limb till the very end. I kept, wanting—and not daring—to sigh. I was sitting behind Susanna; I could not see her face; I saw only from time to time her long dark hair tossed up and down on her shoulders, her figure swaying impulsively, and her delicate arms and bare elbows swiftly, and rather angularly, moving. The last notes died away. I sighed at last. Susanna still sat before the piano.

'Ja, ja,' observed Mr. Ratsch, who had also, however, listened with attention; 'romantische Musik! That's all the fashion nowadays. Only, why not play correctly? Eh? Put your finger on two notes at once—what's that for? Eh? To be sure, all we care for is to go quickly, quickly! Turns it out hotter, eh? Hot pancakes!' he bawled like a street seller.

Susanna turned slightly towards Mr. Ratsch. I caught sight of her face in profile. The delicate eyebrow rose high above the downcast eyelid, an unsteady flush overspread the cheek, the little ear was red under the lock pushed behind it.

'I have heard all the best performers with my own ears,' pursued Mr. Ratsch, suddenly frowning, 'and compared with the late Field they were all—tfoo! nil! zero!! Das war ein Kerl! Und ein so reines Spiel! And his own compositions the finest things! But all those now "tloo-too-too," and "tra-ta-ta," are written, I suppose, more for beginners. Da braucht man keine Delicatesse! Bang the keys anyhow... no matter! It'll turn out some how! Janitscharen Musik! Pugh!' (Ivan Demianitch wiped his forehead with his handkerchief.) 'But I don't say that for you, Susanna Ivanovna; you played well, and oughtn't to be hurt by my remarks.'

'Every one has his own taste,' Susanna said in a low voice, and her lips were trembling; 'but your remarks, Ivan Demianitch, you know, cannot hurt me.'

'Oh! of course not! Only don't you imagine'—Mr. Ratsch turned to me—'don't you imagine, my young friend, that that comes from our excessive good-nature and meekness of spirit; it's simply that we fancy ourselves so highly exalted that—oo-oo!—we can't keep our cap on our head, as the Russian proverb says, and, of course, no criticism can touch us. The conceit, my dear sir, the conceit!'

I listened in surprise to Mr. Ratsch. Spite, the bitterest spite, seemed as it were boiling over in every word he uttered.... And long it must have been rankling! It choked him. He tried to conclude his tirade with his usual laugh, and fell into a husky, broken cough instead. Susanna did not let drop a syllable in reply to him, only she shook her head, raised her face, and clasping her elbows with her hands, stared straight at him. In the depths of her fixed, wide-open eyes the hatred of long years lay smouldering with dim, unquenchable fire. I felt ill at ease.

'You belong to two different musical generations,' I began, with an effort at lightness, wishing by this lightness to suggest that I noticed nothing, 'and so it is not surprising that you do not agree in your opinions.... But, Ivan Demianitch, you must allow me to take rather... the side of the younger generation. I'm an outsider, of course; but I must confess nothing in music has ever made such an impression on me as the... as what Susanna Ivanovna has just played us.'

Ratsch pounced at once upon me.

'And what makes you suppose,' he roared, still purple from the fit of coughing, 'that we want to enlist you on our side? We don't want that at all! Freedom for the free, salvation for the saved! But as to the two generations, that's right enough; we old folks find it hard to get on with you young people, very hard! Our ideas don't agree in anything: neither in art, nor in life, nor even in morals; do they, Susanna Ivanovna?'

Susanna smiled a contemptuous smile.

'Especially in regard to morals, as you say, our ideas do not agree, and cannot agree,' she responded, and something menacing seemed to flit over her brows, while her lips were faintly trembling as before.

'Of course! of course!' Ratsch broke in, 'I'm not a philosopher! I'm not capable of... rising so superior! I'm a plain man, swayed by prejudices—oh yes!'

Susanna smiled again.

'I think, Ivan Demianitch, you too have sometimes been able to place yourself above what are called prejudices.'

'Wie so? How so, I mean? I don't know what you mean.'

'You don't know what I mean? Your memory's so bad!'

Mr. Ratsch seemed utterly taken aback.

'I... I...' he repeated, 'I...'

'Yes, you, Mr. Ratsch.'

There followed a brief silence.

'Really, upon my word...' Mr. Ratsch was beginning; 'how dare you... such insolence...'

Susanna all at once drew herself up to her full height, and still holding her elbows, squeezing them tight, drumming on them with her fingers, she stood still facing Ratsch. She seemed to challenge him to conflict, to stand up to meet him. Her face was changed; it became suddenly, in one instant, extraordinarily beautiful, and terrible too; a sort of bright, cold brilliance—the brilliance of steel—gleamed in her lustreless eyes; the lips that had been quivering were compressed in one straight, mercilessly stern line. Susanna challenged Ratsch, but he gazed blankly, and suddenly subsiding into silence, all of a heap, so to say, drew his head in, even stepped back a pace. The veteran of the year twelve was afraid; there could be no mistake about that.

Susanna slowly turned her eyes from him to me, as though calling upon me to witness her victory, and the humiliation of her foe, and, smiling once more, she walked out of the room.

The veteran remained a little while motionless in his arm-chair; at last, as though recollecting a forgotten part, he roused himself, got up, and, slapping me on the shoulder, laughed his noisy guffaw.

'There, 'pon my soul! fancy now, it's over ten years I've been living with that young lady, and yet she never can see when I'm joking, and when I'm in earnest! And you too, my young friend, are a little puzzled, I do believe.... Ha-ha-ha! That's because you don't know old Ratsch!'

'No.... I do know you now,' I thought, not without a feeling of some alarm and disgust.

'You don't know the old fellow, you don't know him,' he repeated, stroking himself on the stomach, as he accompanied me into the passage. 'I may be a tiresome person, knocked about by life, ha-ha! But I'm a good-hearted fellow, 'pon my soul, I am!'

I rushed headlong from the stairs into the street. I longed with all speed to get away from that good-hearted fellow.

XIV

'They hate one another, that's clear,' I thought, as I returned homewards; 'there's no doubt either that he's a wretch of a man, and she's a good girl. But what has there been between them? What is the reason of this continual exasperation? What was the meaning of those hints? And how suddenly it broke out! On such a trivial pretext!'

Next day Fustov and I had arranged to go to the theatre, to see Shtchepkin in 'Woe from Wit.' Griboyedov's comedy had only just been licensed for performance after being first disfigured by the censors' mutilations. We warmly applauded Famusov and Skalozub. I don't remember what actor took the part of Tchatsky, but I well remember that he was indescribably bad. He made his first appearance in a Hungarian jacket, and boots with tassels, and came on later in a frockcoat of the colour 'flamme du punch,' then in fashion, and the frockcoat looked about as suitable as it would have done on our old butler. I recollect too that we were all in ecstasies over the ball in the third act. Though, probably, no one ever executed such steps in reality, it was accepted as correct and I believe it is acted in just the same way to-day. One of the guests hopped excessively high, while his wig flew from side to side, and the public roared with laughter. As we were coming out of the theatre, we jostled against Viktor in a corridor.

'You were in the theatre!' he cried, flinging his arms about. 'How was it I didn't see you? I'm awfully glad I met you. You must come and have supper with me. Come on; I'll stand the supper!'

Young Ratsch seemed in an excited, almost ecstatic, frame of mind. His little eyes darted to and fro; he was grinning, and there were spots of red on his face.

'Why this gleefulness?' asked Fustov.

'Why? Wouldn't you like to know, eh?' Viktor drew us a little aside, and pulling out of his trouser-pocket a whole bundle of the red and blue notes then in use waved them in the air.

Fustov was surprised.

'Has your governor been so liberal?'

Viktor chuckled.

'He liberal! You just try it on!... This morning, relying on your intercession, I asked him for cash. What do you suppose the old skinflint answered? "I'll pay your debts," says he, "if you like. Up to twenty-five roubles inclusive!" Do you hear, inclusive! No, sir, this was a gift from God in my destitution. A lucky chance.'

'Been robbing someone?' Fustov hazarded carelessly.

Viktor frowned.

'Robbing, no indeed! I won it, won it from an officer, a guardsman. He only arrived from Petersburg yesterday. Such a chain of circumstances! It's worth telling... only this isn't the place. Come along to Yar's; not a couple of steps. I'll stand the show, as I said!'

We ought, perhaps, to have refused; but we followed without making any objection.

XV

At Yar's we were shown into a private room; supper was served, champagne was brought. Viktor related to us, omitting no detail, how he had in a certain 'gay' house met this officer of the guards, a very nice chap and of good family, only without a hap'orth of brains; how they had made friends, how he, the officer that is, had suggested as a joke a game of 'fools' with Viktor with some old cards, for next to nothing, and with the condition that the officer's winnings should go to the benefit of Wilhelmina, but Viktor's to his own benefit; how afterwards they had got on to betting on the games.

'And I, and I,' cried Viktor, and he jumped up and clapped his hands, 'I hadn't more than six roubles in my pocket all the while. Fancy! And at first I was completely cleaned out.... A nice position! Only then—in answer to whose prayers I can't say—fortune smiled. The other fellow began to get hot and kept showing all his cards.... In no time he'd lost seven hundred and fifty roubles! He began begging me to go on playing, but I'm not quite a fool, I fancy; no, one mustn't abuse such luck; I popped on my hat and cut away. So now I've no need to eat humble pie with the governor, and can treat my friends.... Hi waiter! Another bottle! Gentlemen, let's clink glasses!'

We did clink glasses with Viktor, and continued drinking and laughing with him, though his story was by no means to our liking, nor was his society a source of any great satisfaction to us either. He began being very affable, playing the buffoon, unbending, in fact, and was more loathsome than ever. Viktor noticed at last the impression he was making on us, and began to get sulky; his remarks became more disconnected and his looks gloomier. He began yawning, announced that he was sleepy, and after swearing with his characteristic coarseness at the waiter for a badly cleaned pipe, he suddenly accosted Fustov, with a challenging expression on his distorted face.

'I say, Alexander Daviditch,' said he, 'you tell me, if you please, what do you look down on me for?'

'How so?' My friend was momentarily at a loss for a reply.

'I'll tell you how.... I'm very well aware that you look down on me, and that person does too' (he pointed at me with his finger), 'so there! As though you were yourself remarkable for such high and exalted principles, and weren't just as much a sinner as the rest of us. Worse even. Still waters... you know the proverb?'

Fustov turned rather red.

'What do you mean by that?' he asked.

'Why, I mean that I'm not blind yet, and I see very clearly everything that's going on under my nose.... And I have nothing against it: first it's not my principle to interfere, and secondly, my sister Susanna Ivanovna hasn't always been so exemplary herself.... Only, why look down on me?'

'You don't understand what you're babbling there yourself! You're drunk,' said Fustov, taking his overcoat from the wall. 'He's swindled some fool of his money, and now he's telling all sorts of lies!'

Viktor continued reclining on the sofa, and merely swung his legs, which were hanging over its arm.

'Swindled! Why did you drink the wine, then? It was paid for with the money I won, you know. As for lies, I've no need for lying. It's not my fault that in her past Susanna Ivanovna...'

'Hold your tongue!' Fustov shouted at him, 'hold your tongue... or...'

'Or what?'

'You'll find out what. Come along, Piotr.'

'Aha!' pursued Viktor; 'our noble-hearted knight takes refuge in flight. He doesn't care to hear the truth, that's evident! It stings—the truth does, it seems!'

'Come along, Piotr,' Fustov repeated, completely losing his habitual coolness and self-possession.

'Let's leave this wretch of a boy!'

'The boy's not afraid of you, do you hear,' Viktor shouted after us, 'he despises you, the boy does! Do you hear!'

Fustov walked so quickly along the street that I had difficulty in keeping up with him. All at once he stopped short and turned sharply back.

'Where are you going?' I asked.

'Oh, I must find out what the idiot.... He's drunk, no doubt, God knows what.... Only don't you follow me... we shall see each other to-morrow. Good-bye!'

And hurriedly pressing my hand, Fustov set off towards Yar's hotel.

Next day I missed seeing Fustov; and on the day after that, on going to his rooms, I learned that he had gone into the country to his uncle's, near Moscow. I inquired if he had left no note for me, but no note was forth-coming. Then I asked the servant whether he knew how long Alexander Daviditch would be away in the country. 'A fortnight, or a little more, probably,' replied the man. I took at any rate Fustov's exact address, and sauntered home, meditating deeply. This unexpected absence from Moscow, in the winter, completed my utter perplexity. My good aunt observed to me at dinner that I seemed continually expecting something, and gazed at the cabbage pie as though I were beholding it for the first time in my life. 'Pierre, vous n'êtes pas amoureux?' she cried at last, having previously got rid of her companions. But I reassured her: no, I was not in love.

XVI

Three days passed. I had a secret prompting to go to the Ratschs'. I fancied that in their house I should be sure to find a solution of all that absorbed my mind, that I could not make out.... But I should have had to meet the veteran.... That thought pulled me up. One tempestuous evening—the February wind was howling angrily outside, the frozen snow tapped at the window from time to time like coarse sand flung by a mighty hand—I was sitting in my room, trying to read. My servant came, and, with a mysterious air, announced that a lady wished to see me. I was surprised... ladies did not visit me, especially at such a late hour; however, I told him to show her in. The door opened and with swift step there walked in a woman, muffled up in a light summer cloak and a yellow shawl. Abruptly she cast off the cloak and the shawl, which were covered with snow, and I saw standing before me Susanna. I was so astonished that I did not utter a word, while she went up to the window, and leaning her shoulder against the wall, remained motionless; only her bosom heaved convulsively and her eyes moved restlessly, and the breath came with a faint moan from her white lips. I realised that it was no slight trouble that had brought her to me; I realised, for all my youth and shallowness, that at that instant before my eyes the fate of a whole life was being decided—a bitter and terrible fate.

'Susanna Ivanovna,' I began, 'how...'

She suddenly clutched my hand in her icy fingers, but her voice failed her. She gave a broken sigh and looked down. Her heavy coils of black hair fell about her face.... The snow had not melted from off it.

'Please, calm yourself, sit down,' I began again, 'see here, on the sofa. What has happened? Sit down, I entreat you.'

'No,' she articulated, scarcely audibly, and she sank on to the window-seat. 'I am all right here.... Let me be.... You could not expect... but if you knew... if I could... if...'

She tried to control herself, but the tears flowed from her eyes with a violence that shook her, and sobs, hurried, devouring sobs, filled the room. I felt a tightness at my heart.... I was utterly stupefied. I had seen Susanna only twice; I had conjectured that she had a hard life, but I had regarded her as a proud girl, of strong character, and all at once these violent, despairing tears.... Mercy! Why, one only weeps like that in the presence of death!

I stood like one condemned to death myself.

'Excuse me,' she said at last, several times, almost angrily, wiping first one eye, then the other. 'It'll soon be over. I've come to you....' She was still sobbing, but without tears. 'I've come.... You know that Alexander Daviditch has gone away?'

In this single question Susanna revealed everything, and she glanced at me, as though she would say: 'You understand, of course, you will have pity, won't you?' Unhappy girl! There was no other course left her then!

I did not know what answer to make....

'He has gone away, he has gone away... he believed him!' Susanna was saying meanwhile. 'He did not care even to question me; he thought I should not tell him all the truth, he could think that of me! As though I had ever deceived him!'

She bit her lower lip, and bending a little, began to scratch with her nail the patterns of ice that covered the window-pane. I went hastily into the next room, and sending my servant away, came back at once and lighted another candle. I had no clear idea why I was doing all this.... I was greatly overcome. Susanna was sitting as before on the window-seat, and it was at this moment that I noticed how lightly she was dressed: a grey gown with white buttons and a broad leather belt, that was all. I went up to her, but she did not take any notice of me.

'He believed it,... he believed it,' she whispered, swaying softly from side to side. 'He did not hesitate, he dealt me this last... last blow!' She turned suddenly to me. 'You know his address?'

'Yes, Susanna Ivanovna.. I learnt it from his servants... at his house. He told me nothing of his intention; I had not seen him for two days—went to inquire and he had already left Moscow.'

'You know his address?' she repeated. 'Well, write to him then that he has killed me. You are a good man, I know. He did not talk to you of me, I dare say, but he talked to me about you. Write... ah, write to him to come back quickly, if he wants to find me alive!... No! He will not find me!...'

Susanna's voice grew quieter at each word, and she was quieter altogether. But this calm seemed to me more awful than the previous sobs.

'He believed him,...' she said again, and rested her chin on her clasped hands.

A sudden squall of wind beat upon the window with a sharp whistle and a thud of snow. A cold draught passed over the room.... The candles flickered.... Susanna shivered. Again I begged her to sit on the sofa.

'No, no, let me be,' she answered, 'I am all right here. Please.' She huddled up to the frozen pane, as though she had found herself a refuge in the recesses of the window. 'Please.'

'But you're shivering, you're frozen,' I cried, 'Look, your shoes are soaked.'

'Let me be... please...' she whispered,. and closed her eyes.

A panic seized me.

'Susanna Ivanovna!' I almost screamed: 'do rouse yourself, I entreat you! What is the matter with you? Why such despair? You will see, every thing will be cleared up, some misunderstanding... some unlooked-for chance.... You will see, he will soon be back. I will let him know.... I will write to him to-day.... But I will not repeat your words.... Is it possible!'

'He will not find me,' Susanna murmured, still in the same subdued voice. 'Do you suppose I would have come here, to you, to a stranger, if I had not known I should not long be living? Ah, all my past has been swept away beyond return! You see, I could not bear to die so, in solitude, in silence, without saying to some one, "I've lost every thing... and I'm dying.... Look!"'

She drew back into her cold little corner.... Never shall I forget that head, those fixed eyes with their deep, burnt-out look, those dark, disordered tresses against the pale window-pane, even the grey, narrow gown, under every fold of which throbbed such young, passionate life!

Unconsciously I flung up my hands.

'You... you die, Susanna Ivanovna! You have only to live.... You must live!'

She looked at me.... My words seemed to surprise her.

'Ah, you don't know,' she began, and she softly dropped both her hands. 'I cannot live, Too much, too much I have had to suffer, too much! I lived through it.... I hoped... but now... when even this is shattered... when...'

She raised her eyes to the ceiling and seemed to sink into thought. The tragic line, which I had once noticed about her lips, came out now still more clearly; it seemed to spread across her whole face. It seemed as though some relentless hand had drawn it immutably, had set a mark for ever on this lost soul.

She was still silent.

'Susanna Ivanovna,' I said, to break that awful silence with anything; 'he will come back, I assure you!'

Susanna looked at me again.

'What do you say?' she enunciated with visible effort.

'He will come back, Susanna Ivanovna, Alexander will come back!'

'He will come back?' she repeated. 'But even if he did come back, I cannot forgive him this humiliation, this lack of faith....'

She clutched at her head.

'My God! my God! what am I saying, and why am I here? What is it all? What... what did I come to ask... and whom? Ah, I am going mad!...'

Her eyes came to a rest.

'You wanted to ask me to write to Alexander,' I made haste to remind her.

She started.

'Yes, write, write to him... what you like.... And here...' She hurriedly fumbled in her pocket and brought out a little manuscript book. 'This I was writing for him... before he ran away.... But he believed... he believed him!'

I understood that her words referred to Viktor; Susanna would not mention him, would not utter his detested name.

'But, Susanna Ivanovna, excuse me,' I began, 'what makes you suppose that Alexander Daviditch had any conversation... with that person?'

'What? Why, he himself came to me and told me all about it, and bragged of it... and laughed just as his father laughs! Here, here, take it,' she went on, thrusting the manuscript into my hand, 'read it, send it to him, burn it, throw it away, do what you like, as you please.... But I can't die like this with no one knowing.... Now it is time.... I must go.'

She got up from the window-seat.... I stopped her.

'Where are you going, Susanna Ivanovna, mercy on us! Listen, what a storm is raging! You are so lightly dressed.... And your home is not near here. Let me at least go for a carriage, for a sledge....'

'No, no, I want nothing,' she said resolutely, repelling me and taking up her cloak and shawl. 'Don't keep me, for God's sake! or... I can't answer for anything! I feel an abyss, a dark abyss under my feet.... Don't come near me, don't touch me!' With feverish haste she put on her cloak, arranged her shawl.... 'Good-bye... good-bye.... Oh, my unhappy people, for ever strangers, a curse lies upon us! No one has ever cared for me, was it likely he...' She suddenly ceased. 'No; one man loved me,' she began again, wringing her hands, 'but death is all about me, death and no escape! Now it is my turn.... Don't come after me,' she cried shrilly. 'Don't come! don't come!'

I was petrified, while she rushed out; and an instant later, I heard the slam downstairs of the heavy street door, and the window panes shook again under the violent onslaught of the blast.

I could not quickly recover myself. I was only beginning life in those days: I had had no experience of passion nor of suffering, and had rarely witnessed any manifestation of strong feeling in others.... But the sincerity of this suffering, of this passion, impressed me. If it had not been for the manuscript in my hands, I might have thought that I had dreamed it all—it was all so unlikely, and swooped by like a passing storm. I was till midnight reading the manuscript. It consisted of several sheets of letter-paper, closely covered with a large, irregular writing, almost without an erasure. Not a single line was quite straight, and one seemed in every one of them to feel the excited trembling of the hand that held the pen. Here follows what was in the manuscript. I have kept it to this day.

XVII

MY STORY

I am this year twenty-eight years old. Here are my earliest recollections; I was living in the Tambov province, in the country house of a rich landowner, Ivan Matveitch Koltovsky, in a small room on the second storey. With me lived my mother, a Jewess, daughter of a dead painter, who had come from abroad, a woman always ailing, with an extraordinarily beautiful face, pale as wax, and such mournful eyes, that sometimes when she gazed long at me, even without looking at her, I was aware of her sorrowful, sorrowful eyes, and I would burst into tears and rush to embrace her. I had tutors come to me; I had music lessons, and was called 'miss.' I dined at the master's table together with my mother. Mr. Koltovsky was a tall, handsome old man with a stately manner; he always smelt of *ambre*. I stood in mortal terror of him, though he called me Suzon and gave me his dry, sinewy hand to kiss under its lace-ruffles. With my mother he was elaborately courteous, but he talked little even with her. He would say two or three affable words, to which she promptly made a hurried answer; and he would be silent and sit looking about him with dignity, and slowly picking up a pinch of Spanish snuff from his round, golden snuff-box with the arms of the Empress Catherine on it.

My ninth year has always remained vivid in my memory.... I learnt then, from the maids in the servants' room, that Ivan Matveitch Koltovsky was my father, and almost on the same day, my mother, by his command, was married to Mr. Ratsch, who was something like a steward to him. I was utterly unable to comprehend the possibility of such a thing, I was bewildered, I was almost ill, my brain suffered under the strain, my mind was overclouded. 'Is it true, is it true, mamma,' I asked her, 'that scented bogey' (that was my name for Ivan Matveitch) 'is my father?' My mother was terribly scared, she shut my mouth.... 'Never speak to any one of that, do you hear, Susanna, do you hear, not a word!'... she repeated in a shaking voice, pressing my head to her bosom.... And I never did speak to any one of it.... That prohibition of my mother's I understood.... I understood that I must be silent, that my mother begged my forgiveness!

My unhappiness began from that day. Mr. Ratsch did not love my mother, and she did not love him. He married her for money, and she was obliged to submit. Mr. Koltovsky probably considered that in this way everything had been arranged for the best, *la position était régularisée*. I remember the day before the marriage my mother and I—both locked in each other's arms—wept almost the whole morning—bitterly, bitterly—and silently. It is not strange that she was silent.... What could she say to me? But that I did not question her shows that unhappy children learn wisdom sooner than happy ones... to their cost.

Mr. Koltovsky continued to interest himself in my education, and even by degrees put me on a more intimate footing. He did not talk to me... but morning and evening, after flicking the snuff from his jabot with two fingers, he would with the same two fingers—always icy cold—pat me on the cheek and give me some sort of dark-coloured sweetmeats, also smelling of *ambre*, which I never ate. At twelve years old I became his reader—*sa petite lectrice*. I read him French books of the last century, the memoirs of Saint Simon, of Mably, Renal, Helvetius, Voltaire's correspondence, the encyclopedists, of course without understanding a word, even when, with a smile and a grimace, he ordered me, 'relire ce dernier paragraphe, qui est bien remarquable!' Ivan Matveitch was completely a Frenchman. He had lived in Paris till the Revolution, remembered Marie Antoinette, and had received an invitation to Trianon to see her. He had also seen Mirabeau, who, according to his account, wore very large buttons—*exagéré en tout*, and was altogether a man of *mauvais ton, en dépit de sa naissance!* Ivan Matveitch, however, rarely talked of that time; but two or three times a year, addressing himself to the crooked old emigrant whom he had taken into his house, and called for some unknown reason 'M. le Commandeur,' he recited in his deliberate, nasal voice, the impromptu he had once delivered at a soiree of the Duchesse de Polignac. I remember only the first two lines.... It had reference to a comparison between the Russians and the French:

'L'aigle se plait aux regions austères
Ou le ramier ne saurait habiter...'

'Digne de M. de Saint Aulaire!' M. le Commandeur would every time exclaim.

Ivan Matveitch looked youngish up to the time of his death: his cheeks were rosy, his teeth white, his eyebrows thick and immobile, his eyes agreeable and expressive, clear, black eyes, perfect agate. He was not at all unreasonable, and was very courteous with every one, even with the servants.... But, my God! how wretched I was with him, with what joy I always left him, what evil thoughts confounded me in his presence! Ah, I was not to blame for them!... I was not to blame for what they had made of me....

Mr. Ratsch was, after his marriage, assigned a lodge not far from the big house. I lived there with my mother. It was a cheerless life I led there. She soon gave birth to a son, Viktor, this same Viktor whom I have every right to think and to call my enemy. From the time of his birth my mother never regained her health, which had always been weak. Mr. Ratsch did not think fit in those days to keep up such a show of good spirits as he maintains now: he always wore a morose air and tried to pass for a busy, hard-working person. To me he was cruel and rude. I felt relief when I retired from Ivan Matveitch's presence; but my own home too I was glad to leave.... Unhappy was my youth! For ever tossed from one shore to the other, with no desire to anchor at either! I would run across the courtyard in winter, through the deep snow, in a thin frock—run to the big house to read to Ivan Matveitch, and as it were be glad to go.... But when I was there, when I saw those great cheerless rooms, the bright-coloured, upholstered furniture, that courteous and heartless old man in the open silk wadded jacket, in the white jabot and white cravat, with lace ruffles falling over his fingers, with a *soupçon* of powder (so his valet expressed it) on his combed-back hair, I felt choked by the stifling scent of *ambre*, and my heart sank. Ivan Matveitch usually sat in a large low chair; on the wall behind his head hung a picture, representing a young woman, with a bright and bold expression of face, dressed in a sumptuous Hebrew costume, and simply covered with precious stones, with diamonds.... I often stole a glance at this picture, but only later on I learned that it was the portrait of my mother, painted by her father at Ivan Matveitch's request. She had changed indeed since those days! Well had he succeeded in subduing and crushing her! 'And she loved him! Loved that old man!' was my thought.... 'How could it be! Love him!' And yet, when I recalled some of my mother's glances, some half-uttered phrases and unconscious gestures.... 'Yes, yes, she did love him!' I repeated with horror. Ah, God, spare others from knowing aught of such feelings!

Every day I read to Ivan Matveitch, sometimes for three or four hours together.... So much reading in such a loud voice was harmful to me. Our doctor was anxious about my lungs and even once communicated his fears to Ivan Matveitch. But the old man only smiled—no; he never smiled, but somehow sharpened and moved forward his lips—and told him: 'Vous ne savez pas ce qu'il y a de ressources dans cette jeunesse.' 'In former years, however, M. le Commandeur,'... the doctor ventured to observe. Ivan Matveitch smiled as before. 'Vous rêvez, mon cher,' he interposed: 'le commandeur n'a plus de dents, et il crache à chaque mot. J'aime les voix jeunes.'

And I still went on reading, though my cough was very troublesome in the mornings and at night.... Sometimes Ivan Matveitch made me play the piano. But music always had a soporific influence on his nerves. His eyes closed at once, his head nodded in time, and only rarely I heard, 'C'est du Steibelt, n'est-ce pas? Jouez-moi du Steibelt!' Ivan Matveitch looked upon Steibelt as a great genius, who had succeeded in overcoming in himself 'la grossière lourdeur des Allemands,' and only found fault with him for one thing: 'trop de fougue! trop d'imagination!'... When Ivan Matveitch noticed that I was tired from playing he would offer me 'du cachou de Bologne.' So day after day slipped by....

And then one night—a night never to be forgotten!—a terrible calamity fell upon me. My mother died almost suddenly. I was only just fifteen. Oh, what a sorrow that was, with what cruel violence it swooped down upon me! How terrified I was at that first meeting with death! My poor mother! Strange were our relations; we passionately loved each other... passionately and hopelessly; we both as it were treasured up and hid from each other our common secret, kept obstinately silent about it, though we knew all that was passing at the bottom of our hearts! Even of the past, of her own early past, my mother never spoke to me, and she never complained in words, though her whole being was nothing but one dumb complaint. We avoided all conversation of any seriousness. Alas! I kept hoping that the hour would come, and she would open her heart at last, and I too should speak out, and both of us would be more at ease.... But the daily little cares, her irresolute, shrinking temper, illnesses, the presence of Mr. Ratsch, and most of all the eternal question,—what is the use? and the relentless, unbroken flowing away of time, of life.... All was ended as though by a clap of thunder, and the words which would have loosed us from the burden of our secret—even the last dying words of leave-taking—I was not destined to hear from my mother! All that is left in my memory is Mr. Ratsch's calling, 'Susanna Ivanovna, go, please, your mother wishes to give you her blessing!' and then the pale hand stretched out from the heavy counterpane, the agonised breathing, the dying eyes.... Oh, enough! enough!

With what horror, with what indignation and piteous curiosity I looked next day, and on the day of the funeral, into the face of my father... yes, my father! In my dead mother's writing-case were found his letters. I fancied he looked a little pale and drawn... but no! Nothing was stirring in that heart of stone. Exactly as before, he summoned me to his room, a week later; exactly in the same voice he asked me to read: 'Si vous le voulez bien, les observations sur l'histoire de France de Mably, à la page 74... là où nous avons èté interrompus.' And he had not even had my mother's portrait moved! On dismissing me, he did indeed call me to him, and giving me his hand to kiss a second time, he observed: 'Suzanne, la mort de votre mère vous a privée de votre appui naturel; mais vous pourrez toujours compter sur ma protection,' but with the other hand he gave me at once a slight push on the shoulder, and, with the sharpening of the corners of the mouth habitual with him, he added, 'Allez, mon enfant.' I longed to shriek at him: 'Why, but you know you're my father!' but I said nothing and left the room.

Next morning, early, I went to the graveyard. May had come in all its glory of flowers and leaves, and a long while I sat on the new grave. I did not weep, nor grieve; one thought was filling my brain: 'Do you hear, mother? He means to extend his protection to me, too!' And it seemed to me that my mother ought not to be wounded by the smile which it instinctively called up on my lips.

At times I wonder what made me so persistently desire to wring—not a confession... no, indeed! but, at least, one warm word of kinship from Ivan Matveitch? Didn't I know what he was, and how little he was like all that I pictured in my dreams as a *father*!... But I was so lonely, so alone on earth! And then, that thought, ever recurring, gave me no rest: 'Did not she love him? She must have loved him for something?'

Three years more slipped by. Nothing changed in the monotonous round of life, marked out and arranged for us. Viktor was growing into a boy. I was eight years older and would gladly have looked after him, but Mr. Ratsch opposed my doing so. He gave him a nurse, who had orders to keep strict watch that the child was not 'spoilt,' that is, not to allow me to go near him. And Viktor himself fought shy of me. One day Mr. Ratsch came into my room, perturbed, excited, and angry. On the previous evening unpleasant rumours had reached me about my stepfather; the servants were talking of his having been caught embezzling a considerable sum of money, and taking bribes from a merchant.

'You can assist me,' he began, tapping impatiently on the table with his fingers. 'Go and speak for me to Ivan Matveitch.'

'Speak for you? On what ground? What about?'

'Intercede for me.... I'm not like a stranger any way... I'm accused... well, the fact is, I may be left without bread to eat, and you, too.'

'But how can I go to him? How can I disturb him?'

'What next! You have a right to disturb him!'

'What right, Ivan Demianitch?'

'Come, no humbug.... He cannot refuse you, for many reasons. Do you mean to tell me you don't understand that?'

He looked insolently into my eyes, and I felt my cheeks simply burning. Hatred, contempt, rose up within me, surged in a rush upon me, drowning me.

'Yes, I understand you, Ivan Demianitch,' I answered at last—my own voice seemed strange to me—'and I am not going to Ivan Matveitch, and I will not ask him for anything. Bread, or no bread!'

Mr. Ratsch shivered, ground his teeth, and clenched his fists.

'All right, wait a bit, your highness!' he muttered huskily. 'I won't forget it!' That same day, Ivan Matveitch sent for him, and, I was told, shook his cane at him, the very cane which he had once exchanged with the Due de la Rochefoucauld, and cried, 'You be a scoundrel and extortioner! I put you outside!' Ivan Matveitch could hardly speak Russian at all, and despised our 'coarse jargon,' *ce jargon vulgaire et rude*. Some one once said before him, 'That same's self-understood.' Ivan Matveitch was quite indignant, and often afterwards quoted the phrase as an example of the senselessness and absurdity of the Russian tongue. 'What does it mean, that same's self-understood?' he would ask in Russian, with emphasis on each syllable. 'Why not simply that's understood, and why same and self?'

Ivan Matveitch did not, however, dismiss Mr. Ratsch, he did not even deprive him of his position. But my stepfather kept his word: he never forgot it.

I began to notice a change in Ivan Matveitch. He was low-spirited, depressed, his health broke down a little. His fresh, rosy face grew yellow and wrinkled; he lost a front tooth. He quite ceased going out, and gave up the reception-days he had established for the peasants, without the assistance of the priest, *sans le concours du clergé*. On such days Ivan Matveitch had been in the habit of going in to the peasants in the hall or on the balcony, with a rose in his buttonhole, and putting his lips to a silver goblet of vodka, he would make them a speech something like this: 'You are content with my actions, even as I am content with your zeal, whereat I rejoice truly. We are all *brothers*; at our birth we are equal; I drink your health!' He bowed to them, and the peasants bowed to him, but only from the waist, no prostrating themselves to the ground, that was strictly forbidden. The peasants were entertained with good cheer as before, but Ivan Matveitch no longer showed himself to his subjects. Sometimes he interrupted my reading with exclamations: 'La machine se détraque! Cela se gâte!' Even his eyes—those bright, stony eyes—began to grow dim and, as it were, smaller; he dozed oftener than ever and breathed hard in his sleep. His manner with me was unchanged; only a shade of chivalrous deference began to be perceptible in it. He never failed to get up—though with difficulty—from his chair when I came in, conducted me to the door, supporting me with his hand under my elbow, and instead of Suzon began to call me sometimes, 'ma chère demoiselle,' sometimes, 'mon Antigone.' M. le Commandeur died two years after my mother's death; his death seemed to affect Ivan Matveitch far more deeply. A contemporary had disappeared: that was what distressed him. And yet in later years M. le Commandeur's sole service had consisted in crying, 'Bien joué, mal réussi!' every time Ivan Matveitch missed a stroke, playing billiards with Mr. Ratsch; though, indeed, too, when Ivan Matveitch addressed him at table with some such question as: 'N'est-ce pas, M. le Commandeur, c'est Montesquieu qui a dit cela dans ses *Lettres Persanes*?' he had still, sometimes dropping a spoonful of soup on his ruffle, responded profoundly: 'Ah, Monsieur de Montesquieu? Un grand écrivain, monsieur, un grand écrivain!' Only once, when Ivan Matveitch told him that 'les théophilanthropes ont eu pourtant du bon!' the old man cried in an excited voice, 'Monsieur de Kolontouskoi' (he hadn't succeeded in the course of twenty years in learning to pronounce his patron's name correctly), 'Monsieur de Kolontouskoi! Leur fondateur, l'instigateur de cette secte, ce La Reveillère Lepeaux était un bonnet rouge!' 'Non, non,' said Ivan Matveitch, smiling and rolling together a pinch of snuff: 'des fleurs, des jeunes vierges, le culte de la Nature... ils out eu du bon, ils out eu du bon!'...I was always surprised at the extent of Ivan Matveitch's knowledge, and at the uselessness of his knowledge to himself.

Ivan Matveitch was perceptibly failing, but he still put a good face on it. One day, three weeks before his death, he had a violent attack of giddiness just after dinner. He sank into thought, said, 'C'est la fin,' and pulling himself together with a sigh, he wrote a letter to Petersburg to his sole heir, a brother with whom he had had no intercourse for twenty years. Hearing that Ivan Matveitch was unwell, a neighbour paid him a visit—a German, a Catholic—once a distinguished physician, who was living in retirement in his little place in the country. He was very rarely at Ivan Matveitch's, but the latter always received him with special deference, and in fact had a great respect for him. He was almost the only person in the world he did respect. The old man advised Ivan Matveitch to send for a priest, but Ivan Matveitch responded that 'ces messieurs et moi, nous n'avons rien à nous dire,' and begged him to change the subject. On the neighbour's departure, he gave his valet orders to admit no one in future.

Then he sent for me. I was frightened when I saw him; there were blue patches under his eyes, his face looked drawn and stiff, his jaw hung down. 'Vous voila grande, Suzon,' he said, with difficulty articulating the consonants, but still trying to smile (I was then nineteen), 'vous allez peut-être bientót rester seule. Soyez toujours sage et vertueuse. C'est la dernière récommandation d'un'—he coughed—'d'un vieillard qui vous veut du bien. Je vous ai recommandé à mon frère et je ne doute pas qu'il ne respecte mes volontés....' He coughed again, and anxiously felt his chest. 'Du reste, j'esèpre encore pouvoir faire quelque chose pour vous... dans mon testament.' This last phrase cut me to the heart, like a knife. Ah, it was really too... too contemptuous and insulting! Ivan Matveitch probably ascribed to some other feeling—to a feeling of grief or gratitude—what was expressed in my face, and as though wishing to comfort me, he patted me on the shoulder, at the same time, as usual, gently repelling me, and observed: 'Voyons, mon enfant, du courage! Nous sommes tous mortels! Et puis il n'y a pas encore de danger. Ce n'est qu'une précaution que j'ai cru devoir prendre.... Allez!'

Again, just as when he had summoned me after my mother's death, I longed to shriek at him, 'But I'm your daughter! your daughter!' But I thought in those words, in that cry of the heart, he would doubtless hear nothing but a desire to assert my rights, my claims on his property, on his money.... Oh, no, for nothing in the world would I say a word to this man, who had not once mentioned my mother's name to me, in whose eyes I was of so little account that he did not even trouble himself to ascertain whether I was aware of my parentage! Or, perhaps, he suspected, even knew it, and did not wish 'to raise a dust' (a favourite saying of his, almost the only Russian expression he ever used), did not care to deprive himself of a good reader with a young voice! No! no! Let him go on wronging his daughter, as he had wronged her mother! Let him carry both sins to the grave! I swore it, I swore he should not hear from my lips the word which must have something of a sweet and holy sound in every ear! I would not say to him father! I would not forgive him for my mother and myself! He felt no need of that forgiveness, of that name.... It could not be, it could not be that he felt no need of it! But he should not have forgiveness, he should not, he should not!

God knows whether I should have kept my vow, and whether my heart would not have softened, whether I should not have overcome my shyness, my shame, and my pride... but it happened with Ivan Matveitch just as with my mother. Death carried him off suddenly, and also in the night. It was again Mr. Ratsch who waked me, and ran with me to the big house, to Ivan Matveitch's bedroom.... But I found not even the last dying gestures, which had left such a vivid impression on my memory at my mother's bedside. On the embroidered, lace-edged pillows lay a sort of withered, dark-coloured doll, with sharp nose and ruffled grey eyebrows.... I shrieked with horror, with loathing, rushed away, stumbled in doorways against bearded peasants in smocks with holiday red sashes, and found myself, I don't remember how, in the fresh air....

I was told afterwards that when the valet ran into the bedroom, at a violent ring of the bell, he found Ivan Matveitch not in the bed, but a few feet from it. And that he was sitting huddled up on the floor, and that twice over he repeated, 'Well, granny, here's a pretty holiday for you!' And that these were his last words. But I cannot believe that. Was it likely he would speak Russian at such a moment, and such a homely old Russian saying too!

For a whole fortnight afterwards we were awaiting the arrival of the new master, Semyon Matveitch Koltovsky. He sent orders that nothing was to be touched, no one was to be discharged, till he had looked into everything in person. All the doors, all the furniture, drawers, tables—all were locked and sealed up. All the servants were downcast and apprehensive. I became suddenly one of the most important persons in the house, perhaps the most important. I had been spoken of as 'the young lady' before; but now this expression seemed to take a new significance, and was pronounced with a peculiar emphasis. It began to be whispered that 'the old master had died suddenly, and hadn't time to send for a priest, indeed and he hadn't been at confession for many a long day; but still, a will doesn't take long to make.'

Mr. Ratsch, too, thought well to change his mode of action. He did not affect good-nature and friendliness; he knew he would not impose upon me, but his face wore an expression of sulky resignation. 'You see, I give in,' he seemed to say. Every one showed me deference, and tried to please me... while I did not know what to do or how to behave, and could only marvel that people failed to perceive how they were hurting me. At last Semyon Matveitch arrived.

Semyon Matveitch was ten years younger than Ivan Matveitch, and his whole life had taken a completely different turn. He was a government official in Petersburg, filling an important position.... He had married and been left early a widower; he had one son. In face Semyon Matveitch was like his brother, only he was shorter and stouter, and had a round bald head, bright black eyes, like Ivan Matveitch's, only more prominent, and full red lips. Unlike his brother, whom he spoke of even after his death as a French philosopher, and sometimes bluntly as a queer fish, Semyon Matveitch almost invariably talked Russian, loudly and fluently, and he was constantly laughing, completely closing his eyes as he did so and shaking all over in an unpleasant way, as though he were shaking with rage. He looked after things very sharply, went into everything himself, exacted the strictest account from every one. The very first day of his arrival he ordered a service with holy water, and sprinkled everything with water, all the rooms in the house, even the lofts and the cellars, in order, as he put it, 'radically to expel the Voltairean and Jacobin spirit.' In the first week several of Ivan Matveitch's favourites were sent to the right-about, one was even banished to a settlement, corporal punishment was inflicted on others; the old valet—he was a Turk, knew French, and had been given to Ivan Matveitch by the late field-marshal Kamensky—received his freedom, indeed, but with it a command to be gone within twenty-four hours, 'as an example to others.' Semyon Matveitch turned out to be a harsh master; many probably regretted the late owner.

'With the old master, Ivan Matveitch,' a butler, decrepit with age, wailed in my presence, 'our only trouble was to see that the linen put out was clean, and that the rooms smelt sweet, and that the servants' voices weren't heard in the passages—God forbid! For the rest, you might do as you pleased. The old master never hurt a fly in his life! Ah, it's hard times now! It's time to die!'

Rapid, too, was the change in my position, that is to say in the position in which I had been placed for a few days against my own will.... No sort of will was found among Ivan Matveitch's papers, not a line written for my benefit. At once every one seemed in haste to avoid me.... I am not speaking of Mr. Ratsch... every one else, too, was angry with me, and tried to show their anger, as though I had deceived them.

One Sunday after matins, in which he invariably officiated at the altar, Semyon Matveitch sent for me. Till that day I had seen him by glimpses, and he seemed not to have noticed me. He received me in his study, standing at the window. He was wearing an official uniform with two stars. I stood still, near the door; my heart was beating violently from fear and from another feeling, vague as yet, but still oppressive. 'I wish to see you, young lady,' began Semyon Matveitch, glancing first at my feet, and then suddenly into my eyes. The look was like a slap in the face. 'I wished to see you to inform you of my decision, and to assure you of my unhesitating inclination to be of service to you.' He raised his voice. 'Claims, of course, you have none, but as... my brother's reader you may always reckon on my... my consideration. I am... of course convinced of your good sense and of your principles. Mr. Ratsch, your stepfather, has already received from me the necessary instructions. To which I must add that your attractive exterior seems to me a pledge of the excellence of your sentiments.' Semyon Matveitch went off into a thin chuckle, while I... I was not offended exactly... but I suddenly felt very sorry for myself... and at that moment I fully realised how utterly forsaken and alone I was. Semyon Matveitch went with short, firm steps to the table, took a roll of notes out of the drawer, and putting it in my hand, he added: 'Here is a small sum from me for pocket-money. I won't forget you in future, my pretty; but good-bye for the present, and be a good girl.' I took the roll mechanically: I should have taken anything he had offered me, and going back to my own room, a long while I wept, sitting on my bed. I did not notice that I had dropped the roll of notes on the floor. Mr. Ratsch found it and picked it up, and, asking me what I meant to do with it, kept it for himself.

An important change had taken place in his fortunes too in those days. After a few conversations with Semyon Matveitch, he became a great favourite, and soon after received the position of head steward. From that time dates his cheerfulness, that eternal laugh of his; at first it was an effort to adapt himself to his patron... in the end it became a habit. It was then, too, that he became a Russian patriot. Semyon Matveitch was an admirer of everything national, he called himself 'a true Russian bear,' and ridiculed the European dress, which he wore however. He sent away to a remote village a cook, on whose training Ivan Matveitch had spent vast sums: he sent him away because he had not known how to prepare pickled giblets.

Semyon Matveitch used to stand at the altar and join in the responses with the deacons, and when the serf-girls were brought together to dance and sing choruses, he would join in their songs too, and beat time with his feet, and pinch their cheeks.... But he soon went back to Petersburg, leaving my stepfather practically in complete control of the whole property.

Bitter days began for me.... My one consolation was music, and I gave myself up to it with my whole soul. Fortunately Mr. Ratsch was very fully occupied, but he took every opportunity to make me feel his hostility; as he had promised, he 'did not forget' my refusal. He ill-treated me, made me copy his long and lying reports to Semyon Matveitch, and correct for him the mistakes in spelling. I was forced to obey him absolutely, and I did obey him. He announced that he meant to tame me, to make me as soft as silk. 'What do you mean by those mutinous eyes?' he shouted sometimes at dinner, drinking his beer, and slapping the table with his hand. 'You think, maybe, you're as silent as a sheep, so you must be all right.... Oh, no! You'll please look at me like a sheep too!' My position became a torture, insufferable,... my heart was growing bitter. Something dangerous began more and more frequently to stir within it. I passed nights without sleep and without a light, thinking, thinking incessantly; and in the darkness without and the gloom within, a fearful determination began to shape itself. The arrival of Semyon Matveitch gave another turn to my thoughts.

No one had expected him. It turned out that he was retiring in unpleasant circumstances; he had hoped to receive the Alexander ribbon, and they had presented him with a snuff-box. Discontented with the government, which had failed to appreciate his talents, and with Petersburg society, which had shown him little sympathy, and did not share his indignation, he determined to settle in the country, and devote himself to the management of his property. He arrived alone. His son, Mihail Semyonitch, arrived later, in the holidays for the New Year. My stepfather was scarcely ever out of Semyon Matveitch's room; he still stood high in his good graces. He left me in peace; he had no time for me then... Semyon Matveitch had taken it into his head to start a paper factory. Mr. Ratsch had no knowledge whatever of manufacturing work, and Semyon Matveitch was aware of the fact; but then my stepfather was an active man (the favourite expression just then), an 'Araktcheev!' That was just what Semyon Matveitch used to call him—'my Araktcheev!' 'That's all I want,' Semyon Matveitch maintained; 'if there is zeal, I myself will direct it.' In the midst of his numerous occupations—he had to superintend the factory, the estate, the foundation of a counting-house, the drawing up of counting-house regulations, the creation of new offices and duties—Semyon Matveitch still had time to attend to me.

I was summoned one evening to the drawing-room, and set to play the piano. Semyon Matveitch cared for music even less than his brother; he praised and thanked me, however, and next day I was invited to dine at the master's table. After dinner Semyon Matveitch had rather a long conversation with me, asked me questions, laughed at some of my replies, though there was, I remember, nothing amusing in them, and stared at me so strangely... I felt uncomfortable. I did not like his eyes, I did not like their open expression, their clear glance.... It always seemed to me that this very openness concealed something evil, that under that clear brilliance it was dark within in his soul. 'You shall not be my reader,' Semyon Matveitch announced to me at last, prinking and setting himself to rights in a repulsive way. 'I am, thank God, not blind yet, and can read myself; but coffee will taste better to me from your little hands, and I shall listen to your playing with pleasure.' From that day I always went over to the big house to dinner, and sometimes remained in the drawing-room till evening. I too, like my stepfather, was in favour: it was not a source of joy for me. Semyon Matveitch, I am bound to own, showed me a certain respect, but in the man there was, I felt it, something that repelled and alarmed me. And that 'something' showed itself not in words, but in his eyes, in those wicked eyes, and in his laugh. He never spoke to me of my father, of his brother, and it seemed to me that he avoided the subject, not because he did not want to excite ambitious ideas or pretensions in me, but from another cause, to which I could not give a definite shape, but which made me blush and feel bewildered.... Towards Christmas came his son, Mihail Semyonitch.

Ah, I feel I cannot go on as I have begun; these memories are too painful. Especially now I cannot tell my story calmly.... But what is the use of concealment? I loved Michel, and he loved me.

How it came to pass—I am not going to describe that either. From the very evening when he came into the drawing-room—I was at the piano, playing a sonata of Weber's when he came in—handsome and slender, in a velvet coat lined with sheepskin and high gaiters, just as he was, straight from the frost outside, and shaking his snow-sprinkled, sable cap, before he had greeted his father, glanced swiftly at me, and wondered—I knew that from that evening I could never forget him—I could never forget that good, young face. He began to speak... and his voice went straight to my heart.... A manly and soft voice, and in every sound such a true, honest nature!

Semyon Matveitch was delighted at his son's arrival, embraced him, but at once asked, 'For a fortnight, eh? On leave, eh?' and sent me away.

I sat a long while at my window, and gazed at the lights flitting to and fro in the rooms of the big house. I watched them, I listened to the new, unfamiliar voices; I was attracted by the cheerful commotion, and something new, unfamiliar, bright, flitted into my soul too.... The next day before dinner I had my first conversation with him. He had come across to see my stepfather with some message from Semyon Matveitch, and he found me in our little sitting-room. I was getting up to go; he detained me. He was very lively and unconstrained in all his movements and words, but of superciliousness or arrogance, of the tone of Petersburg superiority, there was not a trace in him, and nothing of the officer, of the guardsman.... On the contrary, in the very freedom of his manner there was something appealing, almost shamefaced, as though he were begging you to overlook something. Some people's eyes are never laughing, even at the moment of laughter; with *him* it was the lips that almost never changed their beautiful line, while his eyes were almost always smiling. So we chatted for about an hour... what about I don't remember; I remember only that I looked him straight in the face all the while, and oh, how delightfully at ease I felt with him!

In the evening I played on the piano. He was very fond of music, and he sat down in a low chair, and laying his curly head on his arm, he listened intently. He did not once praise me, but I felt that he liked my playing, and I played with ardour. Semyon Matveitch, who was sitting near his son, looking through some plans, suddenly frowned. 'Come, madam,' he said, smoothing himself down and buttoning himself up, as his manner was, 'that's enough; why are you trilling away like a canary? It's enough to make one's head ache. For us old folks you wouldn't exert yourself so, no fear...' he added in an undertone, and again he sent me away. Michel followed me to the door with his eyes, and got up from his seat. 'Where are you off to? Where are you off to?' cried Semyon Matveitch, and he suddenly laughed, and then said something more... I could not catch his words; but Mr. Ratsch, who was present, sitting in a corner of the drawing-room (he was always 'present,' and that time he had brought in the plans), laughed, and his laugh reached my ears.... The same thing, or almost the same thing, was repeated the following evening... Semyon Matveitch grew suddenly cooler to me.

Four days later I met Michel in the corridor that divided the big house in two. He took me by the hand, and led me to a room near the dining-room, which was called the portrait gallery. I followed him, not without emotion, but with perfect confidence. Even then, I believe, I would have followed him to the end of the world, though I had as yet no suspicion of all that he was to me. Alas, I loved him with all the passion, all the despair of a young creature who not only has no one to love, but feels herself an uninvited and unnecessary guest among strangers, among enemies!... Michel said to me—and it was strange! I looked boldly, directly in his face, while he did not look at me, and flushed slightly—he said to me that he understood my position, and sympathised with me, and begged me to forgive his father.... 'As far as I'm concerned,' he added, 'I beseech you always to trust me, and believe me, to me you 're a sister—yes, a sister.' Here he pressed my hand warmly. I was confused, it was my turn to look down; I had somehow expected something else, some other word. I began to thank him. 'No, please,'—he cut me short—'don't talk like that.... But remember, it's a brother's duty to defend his sister, and if you ever need protection, against any one whatever, rely upon me. I have not been here long, but I have seen a good deal already... and among other things, I see through your stepfather.' He squeezed my hand again, and left me.

I found out later that Michel had felt an aversion for Mr. Ratsch from his very first meeting with him. Mr. Ratsch tried to ingratiate himself with him too, but becoming convinced of the uselessness of his efforts, promptly took up himself an attitude of hostility to him, and not only did not disguise it from Semyon Matveitch, but, on the contrary, lost no opportunity of showing it, expressing, at the same time, his regret that he had been so unlucky as to displease the young heir. Mr. Ratsch had carefully studied Semyon Matveitch's character; his calculations did not lead him astray. 'This man's devotion to me admits of no doubt, for the very reason that after I am gone he will be ruined; my heir cannot endure him.'... This idea grew and strengthened in the old man's head. They say all persons in power, as they grow old, are readily caught by that bait, the bait of exclusive personal devotion....

Semyon Matveitch had good reason to call Mr. Ratsch his Araktcheev.... He might well have called him another name too. 'You're not one to make difficulties,' he used to say to him. He had begun in this condescendingly familiar tone with him from the very first, and my stepfather would gaze fondly at Semyon Matveitch, let his head droop deprecatingly on one side, and laugh with good-humoured simplicity, as though to say, 'Here I am, entirely in your hands.'

Ah, I feel my hands shaking, and my heart's thumping against the table on which I write at this moment. It's terrible for me to recall those days, and my blood boils.... But I will tell everything to the end... to the end!

A new element had come into Mr. Ratsch's treatment of me during my brief period of favour. He began to be deferential to me, to be respectfully familiar with me, as though I had grown sensible, and become more on a level with him. 'You've done with your airs and graces,' he said to me one day, as we were going back from the big house to the lodge. 'Quite right too! All those fine principles and delicate sentiments—moral precepts in fact—are not for us, young lady, they're not for poor folks.'

When I had fallen out of favour, and Michel did not think it necessary to disguise his contempt for Mr. Ratsch and his sympathy with me, the latter suddenly redoubled his severity with me; he was continually following me about, as though I were capable of any crime, and must be sharply looked after. 'You mind what I say,' he shouted, bursting without knocking into my room, in muddy boots and with his cap on his head; 'I won't put up with such goings on! I won't stand your stuck-up airs! You're not going to impose on me. I'll break your proud spirit.'

And accordingly, one morning he informed me that the decree had gone forth from Semyon Matveitch that I was not to appear at the dinner-table for the future without special invitation.... I don't know how all this would have ended if it had not been for an event which was the final turning-point of my destiny....

Michel was passionately fond of horses. He took it into his head to break in a young horse, which went well for a while, then began kicking and flung him out of the sledge.... He was brought home unconscious, with a broken arm and bruises on his chest. His father was panic-stricken; he sent for the best doctors from the town. They did a great deal for Michel; but he had to lie down for a month. He did not play cards, the doctor forbade him to talk, and it was awkward for him to read, holding the book up in one hand all the while. It ended by Semyon Matveitch sending me in to his son, in my old capacity of reader.

Then followed hours I can never forget! I used to go in to Michel directly after dinner, and sit at a little round table in the half-darkened window. He used to be lying down in a little room out of the drawing-room, at the further end, on a broad leather sofa in the Empire style, with a gold bas-relief on its high, straight back. The bas-relief represented a marriage procession among the ancients. Michel's head, thrown a little back on the pillow, always moved at once, and his pale face turned towards me: he smiled, his whole face brightened, he flung back his soft, damp curls, and said to me softly, 'Good-morning, my kind sweet girl.' I took up the book—Walter Scott's novels were at the height of their fame in those days—the reading of Ivanhoe has left a particularly vivid recollection in my mind.... I could not help my voice thrilling and quivering as I gave utterance to Rebecca's speeches. I, too, had Jewish blood, and was not my lot like hers? Was I not, like Rebecca, waiting on a sick man, dear to me? Every time I removed my eyes from the page and lifted them to him, I met his eyes with the same soft, bright smile over all his face. We talked very little; the door into the drawing-room was invariably open and some one was always sitting there; but whenever it was quiet there, I used, I don't know why, to cease reading and look intently at Michel, and he looked at me, and we both felt happy then and, as it were, glad and shamefaced, and everything, everything we told each other then without a gesture or a word! Alas! our hearts came together, ran to meet each other, as underground streams flow together, unseen, unheard... and irresistibly.

'Can you play chess or draughts?' he asked me one day.

'I can play chess a little,' I answered.

'That's good. Tell them to bring a chess-board and push up the table.'

I sat down beside the sofa, my heart was throbbing, I did not dare glance at Michel,... Yet from the window, across the room, how freely I had gazed at him!

I began to set the chessmen... My fingers shook.

'I suggested it... not for the game,'... Michel said in an undertone, also setting the pieces, 'but to have you nearer me.'

I made no answer, but, without asking which should begin, moved a pawn... Michel did not move in reply... I looked at him. His head was stretched a little forward; pale all over, with imploring eyes he signed towards my hand...

Whether I understood him... I don't remember, but something instantaneously whirled into my head.... Hesitating, scarcely breathing, I took up the knight and moved it right across the board. Michel bent down swiftly, and catching my fingers with his lips, and pressing them against the board, he began noiselessly and passionately kissing them.... I had no power, I had no wish to draw them back; with my other hand I hid my face, and tears, as I remember now, cold but blissful... oh, what blissful tears!... dropped one by one on the table. Ah, I knew, with my whole heart I felt at that moment, all that he was who held my hand in his power! I knew that he was not a boy, carried away by a momentary impulse, not a Don Juan, not a military Lovelace, but one of the noblest, the best of men... and he loved me!

'Oh, my Susanna!' I heard Michel whisper, 'I will never make you shed other tears than these.'

He was wrong... he did.

But what use is there in dwelling on such memories... especially, especially now?

Michel and I swore to belong to each other. He knew that Semyon Matveitch would never let him marry me, and he did not conceal it from me. I had no doubt about it myself and I rejoiced, not that he did not deceive me—he *could not* deceive—but that he did not try to delude himself. For myself I asked for nothing, and would have followed where and how he chose. 'You shall be my wife,' he repeated to me. 'I am not Ivanhoe; I know that happiness is not with Lady Rowena.'

Michel soon regained his health. I could not continue going to see him, but everything was decided between us. I was already entirely absorbed in the future; I saw nothing of what was passing around me, as though I were floating on a glorious, calm, but rushing river, hidden in mist. But we were watched, we were being spied upon. Once or twice I noticed my stepfather's malignant eyes, and heard his loathsome laugh.... But that laugh, those eyes as it were emerged for an instant from the mist... I shuddered, but forgot it directly, and surrendered myself again to the glorious, swift river...

On the day before the departure of Michel—we had planned together that he was to turn back secretly on the way and fetch me—I received from him through his trusted valet a note, in which he asked me to meet him at half-past nine in the summer billiard-room, a large, low-pitched room, built on to the big house in the garden. He wrote to me that he absolutely must speak with me and arrange things. I had twice already met Michel in the billiard-room... I had the key of the outer door. As soon as it struck half-past nine I threw a warm wrap over my shoulders, stepped quietly out of the lodge, and made my way successfully over the crackling snow to the billiard-room. The moon, wrapped in vapour, stood a dim blur just over the ridge of the roof, and the wind whistled shrilly round the corner of the wall. A shiver passed over me, but I put the key into the lock, went into the room, closed the door behind me, turned round... A dark figure became visible against one of the walls, took a couple of steps forward, stopped...

'Michel,' I whispered.

'Michel is locked up by my orders, and this is I!' answered a voice, which seemed to rend my heart...

Before me stood Semyon Matveitch!

I was rushing to escape, but he clutched at my arm.

'Where are you off to, vile hussy?' he hissed. 'You 're quite equal to stolen interviews with young fools, so you'll have to be equal to the consequences.'

I was numb with horror, but still struggled towards the door... In vain! Like iron hooks the ringers of Semyon Matveitch held me tight.

'Let me go, let me go,' I implored at last.

'I tell you you shan't stir!'

Semyon Matveitch forced me to sit down. In the half-darkness I could not distinguish his face. I had turned away from him too, but I heard him breathing hard and grinding his teeth. I felt neither fear nor despair, but a sort of senseless amazement... A captured bird, I suppose, is numb like that in the claws of the kite... and Semyon Matveitch's hand, which still held me as fast, crushed me like some wild, ferocious claw....

'Aha!' he repeated; 'aha! So this is how it is... so it's come to this... Ah, wait a bit!'

I tried to get up, but he shook me with such violence that I almost shrieked with pain, and a stream of abuse, insult, and menace burst upon me...

'Michel, Michel, where are you? save me,' I moaned.

Semyon Matveitch shook me again... That time I could not control myself... I screamed.

That seemed to have some effect on him. He became a little quieter, let go my arm, but remained where he was, two steps from me, between me and the door.

A few minutes passed... I did not stir; he breathed heavily as before.

'Sit still,' he began at last, 'and answer me. Let me see that your morals are not yet utterly corrupt, and that you are still capable of listening to the voice of reason. Impulsive folly I can overlook, but stubborn obstinacy—never! My son...' there was a catch in his breath... 'Mihail Semyonitch has promised to marry you? Hasn't he? Answer me! Has he promised, eh?'

I answered, of course, nothing. Semyon Matveitch was almost flying into fury again.

'I take your silence as a sign of assent,' he went on, after a brief pause. 'And so you were plotting to be my daughter-in-law? A pretty notion! But you're not a child of four years old, and you must be fully aware that young boobies are never sparing of the wildest promises, if only they can gain their ends... but to say nothing of that, could you suppose that I—a noble gentleman of ancient family, Semyon Matveitch Koltovsky—would ever give my consent to such a marriage? Or did you mean to dispense with the parental blessing?... Did you mean to run away, get married in secret, and then come back, go through a nice little farce, throw yourself at my feet, in the hope that the old man will be touched.... Answer me, damn you!'

I only bent my head. He could kill me, but to force me to speak—that was not in his power.

He walked up and down a little.

'Come, listen to me,' he began in a calmer voice. 'You mustn't think... don't imagine... I see one must talk to you in a different manner. Listen; I understand your position. You are frightened, upset.... Pull yourself together. At this moment I must seem to you a monster... a despot. But put yourself in my position too; how could I help being indignant, saying too much? And for all that I have shown you that I am not a monster, that I too have a heart. Remember how I treated you on my arrival here and afterwards till... till lately... till the illness of Mihail Semyonitch. I don't wish to boast of my beneficence, but I should have thought simple gratitude ought to have held you back from the slippery path on which you were determined to enter!'

Semyon Matveitch walked to and fro again, and standing still patted me lightly on the arm, on the very arm which still ached from his violence, and was for long after marked with blue bruises.

'To be sure,' he began again, 'we're headstrong... just a little headstrong! We don't care to take the trouble to think, we don't care to consider what our advantage consists in and where we ought to seek it. You ask me: where that advantage lies? You've no need to look far.... It's, maybe, close at hand.... Here am I now. As a father, as head of the family I am bound to be particular.... It's my duty. But I'm a man at the same time, and you know that very well. Undoubtedly I'm a practical person and of course cannot tolerate any sentimental nonsense; expectations that are quite inconsistent with everything, you must of course dismiss from your mind for really what sense is there in them?—not to speak of the immorality of such a proceeding.... You will assuredly realise all this yourself, when you have thought it over a little. And I say, simply and straightforwardly, I wouldn't confine myself to what I have done for you. I have always been prepared—and I am still prepared—to put your welfare on a sound footing, to guarantee you a secure position, because I know your value, I do justice to your talents, and your intelligence, and in fact... (here Semyon Matveitch stooped down to me a little)... you have such eyes that, I confess... though I am not a young man, yet to see them quite unmoved... I understand... is not an easy matter, not at all an easy matter.'

These words sent a chill through me. I could scarcely believe my ears. For the first minute I fancied that Semyon Matveitch meant to bribe me to break with Michel, to pay me 'compensation.'... But what was he saying? My eyes had begun to get used to the darkness and I could make out Semyon Matveitch's face. It was smiling, that old face, and he was walking to and fro with little steps, fidgeting restlessly before me....

'Well, what do you say,' he asked at last, 'does my offer please you?'

'Offer?'... I repeated unconsciously,... I simply did not understand a word.

Semyon Matveitch laughed... actually laughed his revolting thin laugh.

'To be sure,' he cried, 'you're all alike you young women'—he corrected himself—'young ladies... young ladies... you all dream of nothing else... you must have young men! You can't live without love! Of course not. Well, well! Youth's all very well! But do you suppose that it's only young men that can love?... There are some older men, whose hearts are warmer... and when once an old man does take a fancy to any one, well—he's simply like a rock! It's for ever! Not like these beardless, feather-brained young fools! Yes, yes; you mustn't look down on old men! They can do so much! You've only to take them the right way! Yes... yes! And as for kissing, old men know all about that too, he-he-he...' Semyon Matveitch laughed again. 'Come, please... your little hand... just as a proof... that's all....'

I jumped up from the chair, and with all my force I gave him a blow in the chest. He tottered, he uttered a sort of decrepit, scared sound, he almost fell down. There are no words in human language to express how loathsome and infinitely vile he seemed to me. Every vestige of fear had left me.

'Get away, despicable old man,' broke from my lips; 'get away, Mr. Koltovsky, you noble gentleman of ancient family! I, too, am of your blood, the blood of the Koltovskys, and I curse the day and the hour when I was born of that ancient family!'

'What!... What are you saying!... What!' stammered Semyon Matveitch, gasping for breath. 'You dare... at the very minute when I've caught you... when you came to meet Misha... eh? eh? eh?'

But I could not stop myself.... Something relentless, desperate was roused up within me.

'And you, you, the brother... of your brother, you had the insolence, you dared... What did you take me for? Can you be so blind as not to have seen long ago the loathing you arouse in me?... You dare use the word offer!... Let me out at once, this instant!'

I moved towards the door.

'Oh, indeed! oh, oh! so this is what she says!' Semyon Matveitch piped shrilly, in a fit of violent fury, but obviously not able to make up his mind to come near me.... 'Wait a bit, Mr. Ratsch, Ivan Demianitch, come here!'

The door of the billiard-room opposite the one I was near flew wide open, and my stepfather appeared, with a lighted candelabrum in each hand. His round, red face, lighted up on both sides, was beaming with the triumph of satisfied revenge, and slavish delight at having rendered valuable service.... Oh, those loathsome white eyes! when shall I cease to behold them?

'Be so good as to take this girl at once,' cried Semyon Matveitch, turning to my stepfather and imperiously pointing to me with a shaking hand. 'Be so good as to take her home and put her under lock and key... so that she... can't stir a finger, so that not a fly can get in to her! Till further orders from me! Board up the windows if need be! You'll answer for her with your head!'

Mr. Ratsch set the candelabra on the billiard-table, made Semyon Matveitch a low bow, and with a slight swagger and a malignant smile, moved towards me. A cat, I imagine, approaches a mouse who has no chance of escape in that way. All my daring left me in an instant. I knew the man was capable of... beating me. I began to tremble; yes; oh, shame! oh ignominy! I shivered.

'Now, then, madam,' said Mr. Ratsch, 'kindly come along.'

He took me, without haste, by the arm above the elbow.... He saw that I should not resist. Of my own accord I pushed forward towards the door; at that instant I had but one thought in my mind, to escape as quickly as possible from the presence of Semyon Matveitch.

But the loathsome old man darted up to us from behind, and Ratsch stopped me and turned me round face to face with his patron.

'Ah!' the latter shouted, shaking his fist; 'ah! So I'm the brother... of my brother, am I? Ties of blood! eh? But a cousin, a first cousin you could marry? You could? eh? Take her, you!' he turned to my stepfather. 'And remember, keep a sharp look-out! The slightest communication with her—and no punishment will be too severe.... Take her!'

Mr. Ratsch conducted me to my room. Crossing the courtyard, he said nothing, but kept laughing noiselessly to himself. He closed the shutters and the doors, and then, as he was finally returning, he bowed low to me as he had to Semyon Matveitch, and went off into a ponderous, triumphant guffaw!

'Good-night to your highness,' he gasped out, choking: 'she didn't catch her fairy prince! What a pity! It wasn't a bad idea in its way! It's a lesson for the future: not to keep up correspondence! Ho-ho-ho! How capitally it has all turned out though!' He went out, and all of a sudden poked his head in at the door. 'Well? I didn't forget you, did I? Hey? I kept my promise, didn't I? Ho-ho!' The key creaked in the lock. I breathed freely. I had been afraid he would tie my hands... but they were my own, they were free! I instantly wrenched the silken cord off my dressing-gown, made a noose, and was putting it on my neck, but I flung the cord aside again at once. 'I won't please you!' I said aloud. 'What madness, really! Can I dispose of my life without Michel's leave, my life, which I have surrendered into his keeping? No, cruel wretches! No! You have not won your game yet! He will save me, he will tear me out of this hell, he... my Michel!'

But then I remembered that he was shut up just as I was, and I flung myself, face downwards, on my bed, and sobbed... and sobbed.... And only the thought that my tormentor was perhaps at the door, listening and triumphing, only that thought forced me to swallow my tears....

I am worn out. I have been writing since morning, and now it is evening; if once I tear myself from this sheet of paper, I shall not be capable of taking up the pen again.... I must hasten, hasten to the finish! And besides, to dwell on the hideous things that followed that dreadful day is beyond my strength!

Twenty-four hours later I was taken in a closed cart to an isolated hut, surrounded by peasants, who were to watch me, and kept shut up for six whole weeks! I was not for one instant alone.... Later on I learnt that my stepfather had set spies to watch both Michel and me ever since his arrival, that he had bribed the servant, who had given me Michel's note. I ascertained too that an awful, heart-rending scene had taken place the next morning between the son and the father.... The father had cursed him. Michel for his part had sworn he would never set foot in his father's house again, and had set off to Petersburg. But the blow aimed at me by my stepfather rebounded upon himself. Semyon Matveitch announced that he could not have him remaining there, and managing the estate any longer. Awkward service, it seems, is an unpardonable offence, and some one must be fixed upon to bear the brunt of the *scandal*. Semyon Matveitch recompensed Mr. Ratsch liberally, however: he gave him the necessary means to move to Moscow and to establish himself there. Before the departure for Moscow, I was brought back to the lodge, but kept as before under the strictest guard. The loss of the 'snug little berth,' of which he was being deprived 'thanks to me,' increased my stepfather's vindictive rage against me more than ever.

'Why did you make such a fuss?' he would say, almost snorting with indignation; 'upon my word! The old chap, of course, got a little too hot, was a little too much in a hurry, and so he made a mess of it; now, of course, his vanity's hurt, there's no setting the mischief right again now! If you'd only waited a day or two, it'd all have been right as a trivet; you wouldn't have been kept on dry bread, and I should have stayed what I was! Ah, well, women's hair is long... but their wit is short! Never mind; I'll be even with you yet, and that pretty young gentleman shall smart for it too!'

I had, of course, to bear all these insults in silence. Semyon Matveitch I did not once see again. The separation from his son had been a shock to him too. Whether he felt remorse or—which is far more likely—wished to bind me for ever to my home, to my family—my family!—anyway, he assigned me a pension, which was to be paid into my stepfather's hands, and to be given to me till I married.... This humiliating alms, this pension I still receive... that is to say, Mr. Ratsch receives it for me....

We settled in Moscow. I swear by the memory of my poor mother, I would not have remained two days, not two hours, with my stepfather, after once reaching the town... I would have gone away, not knowing where... to the police; I would have flung myself at the feet of the governor-general, of the senators; I don't know what I would have done, if it had not happened, at the very moment of our starting from the country, that the girl who had been our maid managed to give me a letter from Michel! Oh, that letter! How many times I read over each line, how many times I covered it with kisses! Michel besought me not to lose heart, to go on hoping, to believe in his unchanging love; he swore that he would never belong to any one but me; he called me his wife, he promised to overcome all hindrances, he drew a picture of our future, he asked of me only one thing, to be patient, to wait a little....

And I resolved to wait and be patient. Alas! what would I not have agreed to, what would I not have borne, simply to do his will! That letter became my holy thing, my guiding star, my anchor. Sometimes when my stepfather would begin abusing and insulting me, I would softly lay my hand on my bosom (I wore Michel's letter sewed into an amulet) and only smile. And the more violent and abusive was Mr. Ratsch, the easier, lighter, and sweeter was the heart within me.... I used to see, at last, by his eyes, that he began to wonder whether I was going out of my mind.... Following on this first letter came a second, still more full of hope.... It spoke of our meeting soon.

Alas! instead of that meeting there came a morning... I can see Mr. Ratsch coming in—and triumph again, malignant triumph, in his face—and in his hands a page of the *Invalid*, and there the announcement of the death of the Captain of the Guards—Mihail Koltovsky.

What can I add? I remained alive, and went on living in Mr. Ratsch's house. He hated me as before—more than before—he had unmasked his black soul too much before me, he could not pardon me that. But that was of no consequence to me. I became, as it were, without feeling; my own fate no longer interested me. To think of him, to think of him! I had no interest, no joy, but that. My poor Michel died with my name on his lips.... I was told so by a servant, devoted to him, who had been with him when he came into the country. The same year my stepfather married Eleonora Karpovna. Semyon Matveitch died shortly after. In his will he secured to me and increased the pension he had allowed me.... In the event of my death, it was to pass to Mr. Ratsch....

Two—three—years passed... six years, seven years.... Life has been passing, ebbing away... while I merely watched how it was ebbing. As in childhood, on some river's edge one makes a little pond and dams it up, and tries in all sorts of ways to keep the water from soaking through, from breaking in. But at last the water breaks in, and then you abandon all your vain efforts, and you are glad instead to watch all that you had guarded ebbing away to the last drop....

So I lived, so I existed, till at last a new, unhoped-for ray of warmth and light....'

The manuscript broke off at this word; the following leaves had been torn off, and several lines completing the sentence had been crossed through and blotted out.

XVIII

The reading of this manuscript so upset me, the impression made by Susanna's visit was so great, that I could not sleep all night, and early in the morning I sent an express messenger to Fustov with a letter, in which I besought him to come to Moscow as soon as possible, as his absence might have the most terrible results. I mentioned also my interview with Susanna, and the manuscript she had left in my hands. After having sent off the letter, I did not go out of the house all day, and pondered all the time on what might be happening at the Ratsches'. I could not make up my mind to go there myself. I could not help noticing though that my aunt was in a continual fidget; she ordered pastilles to be burnt every minute, and dealt the game of patience, known as 'the traveller,' which is noted as a game in which one can never succeed. The visit of an unknown lady, and at such a late hour, had not been kept secret from her: her imagination at once pictured a yawning abyss on the edge of which I was standing, and she was continually sighing and moaning and murmuring French sentences, quoted from a little manuscript book entitled *Extraits de Lecture*. In the evening I found on the little table at my bedside the treatise of De Girando, laid open at the chapter: On the evil influence of the passions. This book had been put in my room, at my aunt's instigation of course, by the elder of her companions, who was called in the household Amishka, from her resemblance to a little poodle of that name, and was a very sentimental, not to say romantic, though elderly, maiden lady. All the following day was spent in anxious expectation of Fustov's coming, of a letter from him, of news from the Ratsches' house... though on what ground could they have sent to me? Susanna would be more likely to expect me to visit her.... But I positively could not pluck up courage to see her without first talking to Fustov. I recalled every expression in my letter to him.... I thought it was strong enough; at last, late in the evening, he appeared.

XIX

He came into my room with his habitual, rapid, but deliberate step. His face struck me as pale, and though it showed traces of the fatigue of the journey, there was an expression of astonishment, curiosity, and dissatisfaction—emotions of which he had little experience as a rule. I rushed up to him, embraced him, warmly thanked him for obeying me, and after briefly describing my conversation with Susanna, handed him the manuscript. He went off to the window, to the very window in which Susanna had sat two days before, and without a word to me, he fell to reading it. I at once retired to the opposite corner of the room, and for appearance' sake took up a book; but I must own I was stealthily looking over the edge of the cover all the while at Fustov. At first he read rather calmly, and kept pulling with his left hand at the down on his lip; then he let his hand drop, bent forward and did not stir again. His eyes seemed to fly along the lines and his mouth slightly opened. At last he finished the manuscript, turned it over, looked round, thought a little, and began reading it all through a second time from beginning to end. Then he got up, put the manuscript in his pocket and moved towards the door; but he turned round and stopped in the middle of the room.

'Well, what do you think?' I began, not waiting for him to speak.

'I have acted wrongly towards her,' Fustov declared thickly. 'I have behaved... rashly, unpardonably, cruelly. I believed that... Viktor—'

'What!' I cried; 'that Viktor whom you despise so! But what could he say to you?'

Fustov crossed his arms and stood obliquely to me. He was ashamed, I saw that.

'Do you remember,' he said with some effort, 'that... Viktor alluded to... a pension. That unfortunate word stuck in my head. It's the cause of everything. I began questioning him.... Well, and he—'

'What did he say?'

'He told me that the old man... what's his name?... Koltovsky, had allowed Susanna that pension because... on account of... well, in fact, by way of damages.'

I flung up my hands.

'And you believed him?'

Fustov nodded.

'Yes! I believed him.... He said, too, that with the young one... In fact, my behaviour is unjustifiable.'

'And you went away so as to break everything off?'

'Yes; that's the best way... in such cases. I acted savagely, savagely,' he repeated.

We were both silent. Each of us felt that the other was ashamed; but it was easier for me; I was not ashamed of myself.

XX

'I would break every bone in that Viktor's body now,' pursued Fustov, clenching his teeth, 'if I didn't recognise that I'm in fault. I see now what the whole trick was contrived for, with Susanna's marriage they would lose the pension.... Wretches!'

I took his hand.

'Alexander,' I asked him, 'have you been to her?'

'No; I came straight to you on arriving. I'll go to-morrow... early to-morrow. Things can't be left so. On no account!'

'But you... love her, Alexander?'

Fustov seemed offended.

'Of course I love her. I am very much attached to her.'

'She's a splendid, true-hearted girl!' I cried.

Fustov stamped impatiently.

'Well, what notion have you got in your head? I was prepared to marry her—she's been baptized—I'm ready to marry her even now, I'd been thinking of it, though she's older than I am.'

At that instant I suddenly fancied that a pale woman's figure was seated in the window, leaning on her arms. The lights had burnt down; it was dark in the room. I shivered, looked more intently, and saw nothing, of course, in the window seat; but a strange feeling, a mixture of horror, anguish and pity, came over me.

'Alexander!' I began with sudden intensity, 'I beg you, I implore you, go at once to the Ratsches', don't put it off till to-morrow! An inner voice tells me that you really ought to see Susanna to-day!'

Fustov shrugged his shoulders.

'What are you talking about, really! It's eleven o'clock now, most likely they're all in bed.'

'No matter.... Do go, for goodness' sake! I have a presentiment.... Please do as I say! Go at once, take a sledge....'

'Come, what nonsense!' Fustov responded coolly; 'how could I go now? To-morrow morning I will be there, and everything will be cleared up.'

'But, Alexander, remember, she said that she was dying, that you would not find her... And if you had seen her face! Only think, imagine, to make up her mind to come to me... what it must have cost her....'

'She's a little high-flown,' observed Fustov, who had apparently regained his self-possession completely. 'All girls are like that... at first. I repeat, everything will be all right to-morrow. Meanwhile, good-bye. I'm tired, and you're sleepy too.'

He took his cap, and went out of the room.

'But you promise to come here at once, and tell me all about it?' I called after him.

'I promise.... Good-bye!'

I went to bed, but in my heart I was uneasy, and I felt vexed with my friend. I fell asleep late and dreamed that I was wandering with Susanna along underground, damp passages of some sort, and crawling along narrow, steep staircases, and continually going deeper and deeper down, though we were trying to get higher up out into the air. Some one was all the while incessantly calling us in monotonous, plaintive tones.

XXI

Some one's hand lay on my shoulder and pushed it several times.... I opened my eyes and in the faint light of the solitary candle, I saw Fustov standing before me. He frightened me. He was staggering; his face was yellow, almost the same colour as his hair; his lips seemed hanging down, his muddy eyes were staring senselessly away. What had become of his invariably amiable, sympathetic expression? I had a cousin who from epilepsy was sinking into idiocy.... Fustov looked like him at that moment.

I sat up hurriedly.

'What is it? What is the matter? Heavens!'

He made no answer.

'Why, what has happened? Fustov! Do speak! Susanna?...'

Fustov gave a slight start.

'She...' he began in a hoarse voice, and broke off.

'What of her? Have you seen her?'

He stared at me.

'She's no more.'

'No more?'

'No. She is dead.'

I jumped out of bed.

'Dead? Susanna? Dead?'

Fustov turned his eyes away again.

'Yes; she is dead; she died at midnight.'

'He's raving!' crossed my mind.

'At midnight! And what's the time now?'

'It's eight o'clock in the morning now.

They sent to tell me. She is to be buried to-morrow.'

I seized him by the hand.

'Alexander, you're not delirious? Are you in your senses?'

'I am in my senses,' he answered. 'Directly I heard it, I came straight to you.'

My heart turned sick and numb, as always happens on realising an irrevocable misfortune.

'My God! my God! Dead!' I repeated. 'How is it possible? So suddenly! Or perhaps she took her own life?'

'I don't know,' said Fustov, 'I know nothing. They told me she died at midnight. And to-morrow she will be buried.'

'At midnight!' I thought.... 'Then she was still alive yesterday when I fancied I saw her in the window, when I entreated him to hasten to her....'

'She was still alive yesterday, when you wanted to send me to Ivan Demianitch's,' said Fustov, as though guessing my thought.

'How little he knew her!' I thought again. 'How little we both knew her! "High-flown," said he, "all girls are like that."... And at that very minute, perhaps, she was putting to her lips... Can one love any one and be so grossly mistaken in them?'

Fustov stood stockstill before my bed, his hands hanging, like a guilty man.

XXII

I dressed hurriedly.

'What do you mean to do now, Alexander?' I asked.

He gazed at me in bewilderment, as though marvelling at the absurdity of my question. And indeed what was there to do?

'You simply must go to them, though,' I began. 'You're bound to ascertain how it happened; there is, possibly, a crime concealed. One may expect anything of those people.... It is all to be thoroughly investigated. Remember the statement in her manuscript, the pension was to cease on her marriage, but in event of her death it was to pass to Ratsch. In any case, one must render her the last duty, pay homage to her remains!'

I talked to Fustov like a preceptor, like an elder brother. In the midst of all that horror, grief, bewilderment, a sort of unconscious feeling of superiority over Fustov had suddenly come to the surface in me.... Whether from seeing him crushed by the consciousness of his fault, distracted, shattered, whether that a misfortune befalling a man almost always humiliates him, lowers him in the opinion of others, 'you can't be much,' is felt, 'if you hadn't the wit to come off better than that!' God knows! Any way, Fustov seemed to me almost like a child, and I felt pity for him, and saw the necessity of severity. I held out a helping hand to him, stooping down to him from above. Only a woman's sympathy is free from condescension.

But Fustov continued to gaze with wild and stupid eyes at me—my authoritative tone obviously had no effect on him, and to my second question, 'You're going to them, I suppose?' he replied—

'No, I'm not going.'

'What do you mean, really? Don't you want to ascertain for yourself, to investigate, how, and what? Perhaps, she has left a letter... a document of some sort....'

Fustov shook his head.

'I can't go there,' he said. 'That's what I came to you for, to ask you to go... for me... I can't... I can't....'

Fustov suddenly sat down to the table, hid his face in both hands, and sobbed bitterly.

'Alas, alas!' he kept repeating through his tears; 'alas, poor girl... poor girl... I loved... I loved her... alas!'

I stood near him, and I am bound to confess, not the slightest sympathy was excited in me by those incontestably sincere sobs. I simply marvelled that Fustov could cry *like that*, and it seemed to me that *now* I knew what a small person he was, and that I should, in his place, have acted quite differently. What's one to make of it? If Fustov had remained quite unmoved, I should perhaps have hated him, have conceived an aversion for him, but he would not have sunk in my esteem.... He would have kept his prestige. Don Juan would have remained Don Juan! Very late in life, and only after many experiences, does a man learn, at the sight of a fellow-creature's real failing or weakness, to sympathise with him, and help him without a secret self-congratulation at his own virtue and strength, but on the contrary, with every humility and comprehension of the naturalness, almost the inevitableness, of sin.

XXIII

I was very bold and resolute in sending Fustov to the Ratsches'; but when I set out there myself at twelve o'clock (nothing would induce Fustov to go with me, he only begged me to give him an exact account of everything), when round the corner of the street their house glared at me in the distance with a yellowish blur from the coffin candles at one of the windows, an indescribable panic made me hold my breath, and I would gladly have turned back.... I mastered myself, however, and went into the passage. It smelt of incense and wax; the pink cover of the coffin, edged with silver lace, stood in a corner, leaning against the wall. In one of the adjoining rooms, the dining-room, the monotonous muttering of the deacon droned like the buzzing of a bee. From the drawing-room peeped out the sleepy face of a servant girl, who murmured in a subdued voice, 'Come to do homage to the dead?' She indicated the door of the dining-room. I went in. The coffin stood with the head towards the door; the black hair of Susanna under the white wreath, above the raised lace of the pillow, first caught my eyes. I went up sidewards, crossed myself, bowed down to the ground, glanced... Merciful God! what a face of agony! Unhappy girl! even death had no pity on her, had denied her—beauty, that would be little—even that peace, that tender and impressive peace which is often seen on the faces of the newly dead. The little, dark, almost brown, face of Susanna recalled the visages on old, old holy pictures. And the expression on that face! It looked as though she were on the point of shrieking—a shriek of despair—and had died so, uttering no sound... even the line between the brows was not smoothed out, and the fingers on the hands were bent back and clenched. I turned away my eyes involuntarily; but, after a brief interval, I forced myself to look, to look long and attentively at her. Pity filled my soul, and not pity alone. 'That girl died by violence,' I decided inwardly; 'that's beyond doubt.' While I was standing looking at the dead girl, the deacon, who on my entrance had raised his voice and uttered a few disconnected sounds, relapsed into droning again, and yawned twice. I bowed to the ground a second time, and went out into the passage.

In the doorway of the drawing-room Mr. Ratsch was already on the look-out for me, dressed in a gay-coloured dressing-gown. Beckoning to me with his hand, he led me to his own room—I had almost said, to his lair. The room, dark and close, soaked through and through with the sour smell of stale tobacco, suggested a comparison with the lair of a wolf or a fox.

XXIV

'Rupture! rupture of the external... of the external covering.... You understand.., the envelopes of the heart!' said Mr. Ratsch, directly the door closed. 'Such a misfortune! Only yesterday evening there was nothing to notice, and all of a sudden, all in a minute, all was over! It's a true saying, "heute roth, morgen todt!" It's true; it's what was to be expected. I always expected it. At Tambov the regimental doctor, Galimbovsky, Vikenty Kasimirovitch.... you've probably heard of him... a first-rate medical man, a specialist—'

'It's the first time I've heard the name,' I observed.

'Well, no matter; any way he was always,' pursued Mr. Ratsch, at first in a low voice, and then louder and louder, and, to my surprise, with a perceptible German accent, 'he was always warning me: "Ay, Ivan Demianitch! ay! my dear boy, you must be careful! Your stepdaughter has an organic defect in the heart—hypertrophia cordialis! The least thing and there'll be trouble! She must avoid all exciting emotions above all.... You must appeal to her reason."... But, upon my word, with a young lady... can one appeal to reason? Ha... ha... ha...'

Mr. Ratsch was, through long habit, on the point of laughing, but he recollected himself in time, and changed the incipient guffaw into a cough.

And this was what Mr. Ratsch said! After all that I had found out about him!... I thought it my duty, however, to ask him whether a doctor was called in.

Mr. Ratsch positively bounced into the air.

'To be sure there was.... Two were summoned, but it was already over—abgemacht! And only fancy, both, as though they were agreeing' (Mr. Ratsch probably meant, as though they had agreed), 'rupture! rupture of the heart! That's what, with one voice, they cried out. They proposed a post-mortem; but I... you understand, did not consent to that.'

'And the funeral's to-morrow?' I queried.

'Yes, yes, to-morrow, to-morrow we bury our dear one! The procession will leave the house precisely at eleven o'clock in the morning.... From here to the church of St. Nicholas on Hen's Legs... what strange names your Russian churches do have, you know! Then to the last resting-place in mother earth. You will come! We have not been long acquainted, but I make bold to say, the amiability of your character and the elevation of your sentiments!...'

I made haste to nod my head.

'Yes, yes, yes,' sighed Mr. Ratsch. 'It... it really has been, as they say, a thunderbolt from a clear sky! Ein Blitz aus heiterem Himmel!'

'And Susanna Ivanovna said nothing before her death, left nothing?'

'Nothing, positively! Not a scrap of anything! Not a bit of paper! Only fancy, when they called me to her, when they waked me up—she was stiff already! Very distressing it was for me; she has grieved us all terribly! Alexander Daviditch will be sorry too, I dare say, when he knows.... They say he is not in Moscow.'

'He did leave town for a few days...' I began.

'Viktor Ivanovitch is complaining they're so long getting his sledge harnessed,' interrupted a servant girl coming in—the same girl I had seen in the passage. Her face, still looking half-awake, struck me this time by the expression of coarse insolence to be seen in servants when they know that their masters are in their power, and that they do not dare to find fault or be exacting with them.

'Directly, directly,' Ivan Demianitch responded nervously. 'Eleonora Karpovna! Leonora! Lenchen! come here!'

There was a sound of something ponderous moving the other side of the door, and at the same instant I heard Viktor's imperious call: 'Why on earth don't they put the horses in? You don't catch me trudging off to the police on foot!'

'Directly, directly,' Ivan Demianitch faltered again. 'Eleonora Karpovna, come here!'

'But, Ivan Demianitch,' I heard her voice, 'ich habe keine Toilette gemacht!'

'Macht nichts. Komm herein!'

Eleonora Karpovna came in, holding a kerchief over her neck with two fingers. She had on a morning wrapper, not buttoned up, and had not yet done her hair. Ivan Demianitch flew up to her.

'You hear, Viktor's calling for the horses,' he said, hurriedly pointing his finger first to the door, then to the window. 'Please, do see to it, as quick as possible! Der Kerl schreit so!'

'Der Viktor schreit immer, Ivan Demianitch, Sie wissen wohl,' responded Eleonora Karpovna, 'and I have spoken to the coachman myself, but he's taken it into his head to give the horses oats. Fancy, what a calamity to happen so suddenly,' she added, turning to me; 'who could have expected such a thing of Susanna Ivanovna?'

'I was always expecting it, always!' cried Ratsch, and threw up his arms, his dressing-gown flying up in front as he did so, and displaying most repulsive unmentionables of chamois leather, with buckles on the belt. 'Rupture of the heart! rupture of the external membrane! Hypertrophy!'

'To be sure,' Eleonora Karpovna repeated after him, 'hyper... Well, so it is. Only it's a terrible, terrible grief to me, I say again...' And her coarse-featured face worked a little, her eyebrows rose into the shape of triangles, and a tiny tear rolled over her round cheek, that looked varnished like a doll's.... 'I'm very sorry that such a young person who ought to have lived and enjoyed everything... everything... And to fall into despair so suddenly!'

'Na! gut, gut... geh, alte!' Mr. Ratsch cut her short.

'Geh' schon, geh' schon,' muttered Eleonora Karpovna, and she went away, still holding the kerchief with her fingers, and shedding tears.

And I followed her. In the passage stood Viktor in a student's coat with a beaver collar and a cap stuck jauntily on one side. He barely glanced at me over his shoulder, shook his collar up, and did not nod to me, for which I mentally thanked him.

I went back to Fustov.

XXV

I found my friend sitting in a corner of his room with downcast head and arms folded across his breast. He had sunk into a state of numbness, and he gazed around him with the slow, bewildered look of a man who has slept very heavily and has only just been waked. I told him all about my visit to Ratsch's, repeated the veteran's remarks and those of his wife, described the impression they had made on me and informed him of my conviction that the unhappy girl had taken her own life.... Fustov listened to me with no change of expression, and looked about him with the same bewildered air.

'Did you see her?' he asked me at last.

'Yes.'

'In the coffin?'

Fustov seemed to doubt whether Susanna were really dead.

'In the coffin.'

Fustov's face twitched and he dropped his eyes and softly rubbed his hands.

'Are you cold?' I asked him.

'Yes, old man, I'm cold,' he answered hesitatingly, and he shook his head stupidly.

I began to explain my reasons for thinking that Susanna had poisoned herself or perhaps had been poisoned, and that the matter could not be left so....

Fustov stared at me.

'Why, what is there to be done?' he said, slowly opening his eyes wide and slowly closing them. 'Why, it'll be worse... if it's known about. They won't bury her. We must let things... alone.'

This idea, simple as it was, had never entered my head. My friend's practical sense had not deserted him.

'When is... her funeral?' he went on.

'To-morrow.'

'Are you going?'

'Yes.'

'To the house or straight to the church?'

'To the house and to the church too; and from there to the cemetery.'

'But I shan't go... I can't, I can't!' whispered Fustov and began crying. It was at these same words that he had broken into sobs in the morning. I have noticed that it is often so with weeping; as though to certain words, for the most of no great meaning,—but just to these words and to no others—it is given to open the fount of tears in a man, to break him down, and to excite in him the feeling of pity for others and himself... I remember a peasant woman was once describing before me the sudden death of her daughter, and she fairly dissolved and could not go on with her tale as soon as she uttered the phrase, 'I said to her, Fekla. And she says, "Mother, where have you put the salt... the salt... sa-alt?"' The word 'salt' overpowered her.

But again, as in the morning, I was but little moved by Fustov's tears. I could not conceive how it was he did not ask me if Susanna had not left something for him. Altogether their love for one another was a riddle to me; and a riddle it remained to me.

After weeping for ten minutes Fustov got up, lay down on the sofa, turned his face to the wall, and remained motionless. I waited a little, but seeing that he did not stir, and made no answer to my questions, I made up my mind to leave him. I am perhaps doing him injustice, but I almost believe he was asleep. Though indeed that would be no proof that he did not feel sorrow... only his nature was so constituted as to be unable to support painful emotions for long... His nature was too awfully well-balanced!

XXVI

The next day exactly at eleven o'clock I was at the place. Fine hail was falling from the low-hanging sky, there was a slight frost, a thaw was close at hand, but there were cutting, disagreeable gusts of wind flitting across in the air.... It was the most thoroughly Lenten, cold-catching weather. I found Mr. Ratsch on the steps of his house. In a black frock-coat adorned with crape, with no hat on his head, he fussed about, waved his arms, smote himself on the thighs, shouted up to the house, and then down into the street, in the direction of the funeral car with a white catafalque, already standing there with two hired carriages. Near it four garrison soldiers, with mourning capes over their old coats, and mourning hats pulled over their screwed-up eyes, were pensively scratching in the crumbling snow with the long stems of their unlighted torches. The grey shock of hair positively stood up straight above the red face of Mr. Ratsch, and his voice, that brazen voice, was cracking from the strain he was putting on it. 'Where are the pine branches? pine branches! this way! the branches of pine!' he yelled. 'They'll be bearing out the coffin directly! The pine! Hand over those pine branches! Look alive!' he cried once more, and dashed into the house. It appeared that in spite of my punctuality, I was late: Mr. Ratsch had thought fit to hurry things forward. The service in the house was already over; the priests—of whom one wore a calotte, and the other, rather younger, had most carefully combed and oiled his hair—appeared with all their retinue on the steps. The coffin too appeared soon after, carried by a coachman, two door-keepers, and a water-carrier. Mr. Ratsch walked behind, with the tips of his fingers on the coffin lid, continually repeating, 'Easy, easy!' Behind him waddled Eleonora Karpovna in a black dress, also adorned with crape, surrounded by her whole family; after all of them, Viktor stepped out in a new uniform with a sword with crape round the handle. The coffin-bearers, grumbling and altercating among themselves, laid the coffin on the hearse; the garrison soldiers lighted their torches, which at once began crackling and smoking; a stray old woman, who had joined herself on to the party, raised a wail; the deacons began to chant, the fine snow suddenly fell faster and whirled round like 'white flies.' Mr. Ratsch bawled, 'In God's name! start!' and the procession started. Besides Mr. Ratsch's family, there were in all five men accompanying the hearse: a retired and extremely shabby officer of roads and highways, with a faded Stanislas ribbon—not improbably hired—on his neck; the police superintendent's assistant, a diminutive man with a meek face and greedy eyes; a little old man in a fustian smock; an extremely fat fishmonger in a tradesman's bluejacket, smelling strongly of his calling, and I. The absence of the female sex (for one could hardly count as such two aunts of Eleonora Karpovna, sisters of the sausagemaker, and a hunchback old maiden lady with blue spectacles on her blue nose), the absence of girl friends and acquaintances struck me at first; but on thinking it over I realised that Susanna, with her character, her education, her memories, could not have made friends in the circle in which she was living. In the church there were a good many people assembled, more outsiders than acquaintances, as one could see by the expression of their faces. The service did not last long. What surprised me was that Mr. Ratsch crossed himself with great fervour, quite as though he were of the orthodox faith, and even chimed in with the deacons in the responses, though only with the notes not with the words. When at last it came to taking leave of the dead, I bowed low, but did not give the last kiss. Mr. Ratsch, on the contrary, went through this terrible ordeal with the utmost composure, and with a deferential inclination of his person invited the officer of the Stanislas ribbon to the coffin, as though offering him entertainment, and picking his children up under the arms swung them up in turn and held them up to the body. Eleonora Karpovna, on taking farewell of Susanna, suddenly broke into a roar that filled the church; but she was soon soothed and continually asked in an exasperated whisper, 'But where's my reticule?' Viktor held himself aloof, and seemed to be trying by his whole demeanour to convey that he was out of sympathy with all such customs and was only performing a social duty. The person who showed the most sympathy was the little old man in the smock, who had been, fifteen years before, a land surveyor in the Tambov province, and had not seen Ratsch since then. He did not know Susanna at all, but had drunk a couple of glasses of spirits at the sideboard before starting. My aunt had also come to the church. She had somehow or other found out that the deceased woman was the very lady who had paid me a visit, and had been thrown into a state of indescribable agitation! She could not bring herself to suspect me of any sort of misconduct, but neither could she explain such a strange chain of circumstances.... Not improbably she imagined that Susanna had been led by love for me to commit suicide, and attired in her darkest garments, with an aching heart and tears, she prayed on her knees for the peace of the soul of the departed, and put a rouble candle before the picture of the Consolation of Sorrow.... 'Amishka' had come with her too, and she too prayed, but was for the most part gazing at me, horror-stricken.... That elderly spinster, alas! did not regard me with indifference. On leaving the church, my aunt distributed all her money, more than ten roubles, among the poor.

At last the farewell was over. They began closing the coffin. During the whole service I had not courage to look straight at the poor girl's distorted face; but every time that my eyes passed by it—'he did not come, he did not come,' it seemed to me that it wanted to say. They were just going to lower the lid upon the coffin. I could not restrain myself: I turned a rapid glance on to the dead woman. 'Why did you do it?' I was unconsciously asking.... 'He did not come!' I fancied for the last time.... The hammer was knocking in the nails, and all was over.

XXVII

We followed the hearse towards the cemetery. We were forty in number, of all sorts and conditions, nothing else really than an idle crowd. The wearisome journey lasted more than an hour. The weather became worse and worse. Halfway there Viktor got into a carriage, but Mr. Ratsch stepped gallantly on through the sloppy snow; just so must he have stepped through the snow when, after the fateful interview with Semyon Matveitch, he led home with him in triumph the girl whose life he had ruined for ever. The 'veteran's' hair and eyebrows were edged with snow; he kept blowing and uttering exclamations, or manfully drawing deep breaths and puffing out his round, dark-red cheeks.... One really might have thought he was laughing. 'On my death the pension was to pass to Ivan Demianitch'; these words from Susanna's manuscript recurred again to my mind. We reached the cemetery at last; we moved up to a freshly dug grave. The last ceremony was quickly performed; all were chilled through, all were in haste. The coffin slid on cords into the yawning hole; they began to throw earth on it. Mr. Ratsch here too showed the energy of his spirit, so rapidly, with such force and vigour, did he fling clods of earth on to the coffin lid, throwing himself into an heroic pose, with one leg planted firmly before him... he could not have shown more energy if he had been stoning his bitterest foe. Viktor, as before, held himself aloof; he kept muffling himself up in his coat, and rubbing his chin in the fur of his collar. Mr. Ratsch's other children eagerly imitated their father. Flinging sand and earth was a source of great enjoyment to them, for which, of course, they were in no way to blame. A mound began to rise up where the hole had been; we were on the point of separating, when Mr. Ratsch, wheeling round to the left in soldierly fashion, and slapping himself on the thigh, announced to all of us 'gentlemen present,' that he invited us, and also the 'reverend clergy,' to a 'funeral banquet,' which had been arranged at no great distance from the cemetery, in the chief saloon of an extremely superior restaurant, 'thanks to the kind offices of our honoured friend Sigismund Sigismundovitch.'... At these words he indicated the assistant of the police superintendent, and added that for all his grief and his Lutheran faith, he, Ivan Demianitch Ratsch, as a genuine Russian, put the old Russian usages before everything. 'My spouse,' he cried, 'with the ladies that have accompanied her, may go home, while we gentlemen commemorate in a modest repast the shade of Thy departed servant!' Mr. Ratsch's proposal was received with genuine sympathy; 'the reverend clergy' exchanged expressive glances with one another, while the officer of roads and highways slapped Ivan Demianitch on the shoulder, and called him a patriot and the soul of the company.

We set off all together to the restaurant. In the restaurant, in the middle of a long, wide, and quite empty room on the first storey, stood two tables laid for dinner, covered with bottles and eatables, and surrounded by chairs. The smell of whitewash, mingled with the odours of spirits and salad oil, was stifling and oppressive. The police superintendent's assistant, as the organiser of the banquet, placed the clergy in the seats of honour, near which the Lenten dishes were crowded together conspicuously; after the priests the other guests took their seats; the banquet began. I would not have used such a festive word as banquet by choice, but no other word would have corresponded with the real character of the thing. At first the proceedings were fairly quiet, even slightly mournful; jaws munched busily, and glasses were emptied, but sighs too were audible—possibly sighs of digestion, but possibly also of feeling. There were references to death, allusions to the brevity of human life, and the fleeting nature of earthly hopes. The officer of roads and highways related a military but still edifying anecdote. The priest in the calotte expressed his approval, and himself contributed an interesting fact from the life of the saint, Ivan the Warrior. The priest with the superbly arranged hair, though his attention was chiefly engrossed by the edibles, gave utterance to something improving on the subject of chastity. But little by little all this changed. Faces grew redder, and voices grew louder, and laughter reasserted itself; one began to hear disconnected exclamations, caressing appellations, after the manner of 'dear old boy,' 'dear heart alive,' 'old cock,' and even 'a pig like that'—everything, in fact, of which the Russian nature is so lavish, when, as they say, 'it comes unbuttoned.' By the time that the corks of home-made champagne were popping, the party had become noisy; some one even crowed like a cock, while another guest was offering to bite up and swallow the glass out of which he had just been drinking. Mr. Ratsch, no longer red but purple, suddenly rose from his seat; he had been guffawing and making a great noise before, but now he asked leave to make a speech. 'Speak! Out with it!' every one roared; the old man in the smock even bawled 'bravo!' and clapped his hands... but he was already sitting on the floor. Mr. Ratsch lifted his glass high above his head, and announced that he proposed in brief but 'impressionable' phrases to refer to the qualities of the noble soul which,'leaving here, so to say, its earthly husk (die irdische Hülle) has soared to heaven, and plunged...' Mr. Ratsch corrected himself: 'and plashed....' He again corrected himself: 'and plunged...'

'Father deacon! Reverend sir! My good soul!' we heard a subdued but insistent whisper, 'they say you've a devilish good voice; honour us with a song, strike up: "We live among the fields!"'

'Sh! sh!... Shut up there!' passed over the lips of the guests.

...'Plunged all her devoted family,' pursued Mr. Ratsch, turning a severe glance in the direction of the lover of music, 'plunged all her family into the most irreplaceable grief! Yes!' cried Ivan Demianitch, 'well may the Russian proverb say, "Fate spares not the rod."...'

'Stop! Gentlemen!' shouted a hoarse voice at the end of the table, 'my purse has just been stolen!...'

'Ah, the swindler!' piped another voice, and slap! went a box on the ear.

Heavens! What followed then! It was as though the wild beast, till then only growling and faintly stirring within us, had suddenly broken from its chains and reared up, ruffled and fierce in all its hideousness. It seemed as though every one had been secretly expecting 'a scandal,' as the natural outcome and sequel of a banquet, and all, as it were, rushed to welcome it, to support it.... Plates, glasses clattered and rolled about, chairs were upset, a deafening din arose, hands were waving in the air, coat-tails were flying, and a fight began in earnest.

'Give it him! give it him!' roared like mad my neighbour, the fishmonger, who had till that instant seemed to be the most peaceable person in the world; it is true he had been silently drinking some dozen glasses of spirits. 'Thrash him!...'

Who was to be thrashed, and what he was to be thrashed for, he had no idea, but he bellowed furiously.

The police superintendent's assistant, the officer of roads and highways, and Mr. Ratsch, who had probably not expected such a speedy termination to his eloquence, tried to restore order... but their efforts were unavailing. My neighbour, the fishmonger, even fell foul of Mr. Ratsch himself.

'He's murdered the young woman, the blasted German,' he yelled at him, shaking his fists; 'he's bought over the police, and here he's crowing over it!!'

At this point the waiters ran in.... What happened further I don't know; I snatched up my cap in all haste, and made off as fast as my legs would carry me! All I remember is a fearful crash; I recall, too, the remains of a herring in the hair of the old man in the smock, a priest's hat flying right across the room, the pale face of Viktor huddled up in a corner, and a red beard in the grasp of a muscular hand.... Such were the last impressions I carried away of the 'memorial banquet,' arranged by the excellent Sigismund Sigismundovitch in honour of poor Susanna.

After resting a little, I set off to see Fustov, and told him all of which I had been a witness during that day. He listened to me, sitting still, and not raising his head, and putting both hands under his legs, he murmured again, 'Ah! my poor girl, my poor girl!' and again lay down on the sofa and turned his back on me.

A week later he seemed to have quite got over it, and took up his life as before. I asked him for Susanna's manuscript as a keepsake: he gave it me without raising any objection.

XXVIII

Several years passed by. My aunt was dead; I had left Moscow and settled in Petersburg. Fustov too had moved to Petersburg. He had entered the department of the Ministry of Finance, but we rarely met and I saw nothing much in him then. An official like every one else, and nothing more! If he is still living and not married, he is, most likely, unchanged to this day; he carves and carpenters and uses dumb-bells, and is as much a lady-killer as ever, and sketches Napoleon in a blue uniform in the albums of his lady friends. It happened that I had to go to Moscow on business. In Moscow I learned, with considerable surprise, that the fortunes of my former acquaintance, Mr. Ratsch, had taken an adverse turn. His wife had, indeed, presented him with twins, two boys, whom as a true Russian he had christened Briacheslav and Viacheslav, but his house had been burnt down, he had been forced to retire from his position, and worst of all, his eldest son, Viktor, had become practically a permanent inmate of the debtors' prison. During my stay in Moscow, among a company at a friendly gathering, I chanced to hear an allusion made to Susanna, and a most slighting, most insulting allusion! I did all I could to defend the memory of the unhappy girl, to whom fate had denied even the charity of oblivion, but my arguments did not make much impression on my audience. One of them, a young student poet, was, however, a little moved by my words. He sent me next day a poem, which I have forgotten, but which ended in the following four lines:

'Her tomb lies cold, forlorn, but even death
Her gentle spirit's memory cannot save
From the sly voice of slander whispering on,
Withering the flowers on her forsaken tomb....'

I read these lines and unconsciously sank into musing. Susanna's image rose before me; once more I seemed to see the frozen window in my room; I recalled that evening and the blustering snowstorm, and those words, those sobs.... I began to ponder how it was possible to explain Susanna's love for Fustov, and why she had so quickly, so impulsively given way to despair, as soon as she saw herself forsaken. How was it she had had no desire to wait a little, to hear the bitter truth from the lips of the man she loved, to write to him, even? How could she fling herself at once headlong into the abyss? Because she was passionately in love with Fustov, I shall be told; because she could not bear the slightest doubt of his devotion, of his respect for her. Perhaps; or perhaps because she was not at all so passionately in love with Fustov; that she did not deceive herself about him, but simply rested her last hopes on him, and could not get over the thought that even this man had at once, at the first breath of slander, turned away from her with contempt! Who can say what killed her; wounded pride, or the wretchedness of her helpless position, or the very memory of that first, noble, true-hearted nature to whom she had so joyfully pledged herself in the morning of her early days, who had so deeply trusted her, and so honoured her? Who knows; perhaps at the very instant when I fancied that her dead lips were murmuring, 'he did not come!' her soul was rejoicing that she had gone herself to him, to her Michel? The secrets of human life are great, and love itself, the most impenetrable of those secrets.... Anyway, to this day, whenever the image of Susanna rises before me, I cannot overcome a feeling of pity for her, and of angry reproach against fate, and my lips whisper instinctively, 'Unhappy girl! unhappy girl!'

1868.

THE DUELLIST

I

A regiment of cuirassiers was quartered in 1829 in the village of Kirilovo, in the K—- province. That village, with its huts and hay-stacks, its green hemp-patches, and gaunt willows, looked from a distance like an island in a boundless sea of ploughed, black-earth fields. In the middle of the village was a small pond, invariably covered with goose feathers, with muddy, indented banks; a hundred paces from the pond, on the other side of the road, rose the wooden manor-house, long, empty, and mournfully slanting on one side. Behind the house stretched the deserted garden; in the garden grew old apple-trees that bore no fruit, and tall birch-trees, full of rooks' nests. At the end of the principal garden-walk, in a little house, once the bath-house, lived a decrepit old steward. Every morning, gasping and groaning, he would, from years of habit, drag himself across the garden to the seignorial apartments, though there was nothing to take care of in them except a dozen white arm-chairs, upholstered in faded stuff, two podgy chests on carved legs with copper handles, four pictures with holes in them, and one black alabaster Arab with a broken nose. The owner of the house, a careless young man, lived partly at Petersburg, partly abroad, and had completely forgotten his estate. It had come to him eight years before, from a very old uncle, once noted all over the countryside for his excellent liqueurs. The empty, dark-green bottles are to this day lying about in the storeroom, in company with rubbish of all sorts, old manuscript books in parti-coloured covers, scantily filled with writing, old-fashioned glass lustres, a nobleman's uniform of the Catherine period, a rusty sabre with a steel handle and so forth. In one of the lodges of the great house the colonel himself took up his abode. He was a married man, tall, sparing of his words, grim and sleepy. In another lodge lived the regimental adjutant, an emotional person of fine sentiments and many perfumes, fond of flowers and female society. The social life of the officers of this regiment did not differ from any other kind of society. Among their number were good people and bad, clever and silly.... One of them, a certain Avdey Ivanovitch Lutchkov, staff captain, had a reputation as a duellist. Lutchkov was a short and not thick-set man; he had a small, yellowish, dry face, lank, black hair, unnoticeable features, and dark, little eyes. He had early been left an orphan, and had grown up among privations and hardships. For weeks together he would be quiet enough,... and then all at once—as though he were possessed by some devil—he would let no one alone, annoying everybody, staring every one insolently in the face; trying, in fact, to pick a quarrel. Avdey Ivanovitch did not, however, hold aloof from intercourse with his comrades, but he was not on intimate terms with any one but the perfumed adjutant. He did not play cards, and did not drink spirits.

In the May of 1829, not long before the beginning of the manoeuvres, there joined the regiment a young cornet, Fyodor Fedorovitch Kister, a Russian nobleman of German extraction, very fair-haired and very modest, cultivated and well read. He had lived up to his twentieth year in the home of his fathers, under the wings of his mother, his grandmother, and his two aunts. He was going into the army in deference solely to the wishes of his grandmother, who even in her old age could not see a white plumed helmet without emotion.... He served with no special enthusiasm but with energy, as it were conscientiously doing his duty. He was not a dandy, but was always cleanly dressed and in good taste. On the day of his arrival Fyodor Fedoritch paid his respects to his superior officers, and then proceeded to arrange his quarters. He had brought with him some cheap furniture, rugs, shelves, and so forth. He papered all the walls and the doors, put up some screens, had the yard cleaned, fixed up a stable, and a kitchen, even arranged a place for a bath.... For a whole week he was busily at work; but it was a pleasure afterwards to go into his room. Before the window stood a neat table, covered with various little things; in one corner was a set of shelves for books, with busts of Schiller and Goethe; on the walls hung maps, four Grevedon heads, and guns; near the table was an elegant row of pipes with clean mouthpieces; there was a rug in the outer room; all the doors shut and locked; the windows were hung with curtains. Everything in Fyodor Fedoritch's room had a look of cleanliness and order.

It was quite a different thing in his comrades' quarters. Often one could scarcely make one's way across the muddy yard; in the outer room, behind a canvas screen, with its covering peeling off it, would lie stretched the snoring orderly; on the floor rotten straw; on the stove, boots and a broken jam-pot full of blacking; in the room itself a warped card-table, marked with chalk; on the table, glasses, half-full of cold, dark-brown tea; against the wall, a wide, rickety, greasy sofa; on the window-sills, tobacco-ash.... In a podgy, clumsy arm-chair one would find the master of the place in a grass-green dressing-gown with crimson plush facings and an embroidered smoking-cap of Asiatic extraction, and a hideously fat, unpleasant dog in a stinking brass collar would be snoring at his side.... All the doors always ajar....

Fyodor Fedoritch made a favourable impression on his new comrades. They liked him for his good-nature, modesty, warm-heartedness, and natural inclination for everything beautiful, for everything, in fact, which in another officer they might, very likely, have thought out of place. They called Kister a young lady, and were kind and gentle in their manners with him. Avdey Ivanovitch was the only one who eyed him dubiously. One day after drill Lutchkov went up to him, slightly pursing up his lips and inflating his nostrils:

'Good-morning, Mr. Knaster.'

Kister looked at him in some perplexity.

'A very good day to you, Mr. Knaster,' repeated Lutchkov.

'My name's Kister, sir.'

'You don't say so, Mr. Knaster.'

Fyodor Fedoritch turned his back on him and went homewards. Lutchkov looked after him with a grin.

Next day, directly after drill he went up to Kister again.

'Well, how are you getting on, Mr. Kinderbalsam?'

Kister was angry, and looked him straight in the face. Avdey Ivanovitch's little bilious eyes were gleaming with malignant glee.

'I'm addressing you, Mr. Kinderbalsam!'

'Sir,' Fyodor Fedoritch replied, 'I consider your joke stupid and ill-bred—do you hear?—stupid and ill-bred.'

'When shall we fight?' Lutchkov responded composedly.

'When you like,... to-morrow.'

Next morning they fought a duel. Lutchkov wounded Kister slightly, and to the extreme astonishment of the seconds went up to the wounded man, took him by the hand and begged his pardon. Kister had to keep indoors for a fortnight. Avdey Ivanovitch came several times to ask after him and on Fyodor Fedoritch's recovery made friends with him. Whether he was pleased by the young officer's pluck, or whether a feeling akin to remorse was roused in his soul—it's hard to say... but from the time of his duel with Kister, Avdey Ivanovitch scarcely left his side, and called him first Fyodor, and afterwards simply Fedya. In his presence he became quite another man and—strange to say!—the change was not in his favour. It did not suit him to be gentle and soft. Sympathy he could not call forth in any one anyhow; such was his destiny! He belonged to that class of persons to whom has somehow been granted the privilege of authority over others; but nature had denied him the gifts essential for the justification of such a privilege. Having received no education, not being distinguished by intelligence, he ought not to have revealed himself; possibly his malignancy had its origin in his consciousness of the defects of his bringing up, in the desire to conceal himself altogether under one unchanging mask. Avdey Ivanovitch had at first forced himself to despise people, then he began to notice that it was not a difficult matter to intimidate them, and he began to despise them in reality. Lutchkov enjoyed cutting short by his very approach all but the most vulgar conversation. 'I know nothing, and have learned nothing, and I have no talents,' he said to himself; 'and so you too shall know nothing and not show off your talents before me....' Kister, perhaps, had made Lutchkov abandon the part he had taken up—just because before his acquaintance with him, the bully had never met any one genuinely idealistic, that is to say, unselfishly and simple-heartedly absorbed in dreams, and so, indulgent to others, and not full of himself.

Avdey Ivanovitch would come sometimes to Kister, light a pipe and quietly sit down in an arm-chair. Lutchkov was not in Kister's company abashed by his own ignorance; he relied—and with good reason—on his German modesty.

'Well,' he would begin, 'what did you do yesterday? Been reading, I'll bet, eh?'

'Yes, I read....'

'Well, and what did you read? Come, tell away, old man, tell away.' Avdey Ivanovitch kept up his bantering tone to the end.

'I read Kleist's *Idyll*. Ah, what a fine thing it is! If you don't mind, I'll translate you a few lines....' And Kister translated with fervour, while Lutchkov, wrinkling up his forehead and compressing his lips, listened attentively.... 'Yes, yes,' he would repeat hurriedly, with a disagreeable smile,'it's fine... very fine... I remember, I've read it... very fine.'

'Tell me, please,' he added affectedly, and as it were reluctantly, 'what's your view of Louis the Fourteenth?'

And Kister would proceed to discourse upon Louis the Fourteenth, while Lutchkov listened, totally failing to understand a great deal, misunderstanding a part... and at last venturing to make a remark.... This threw him into a cold sweat; 'now, if I'm making a fool of myself,' he thought. And as a fact he often did make a fool of himself. But Kister was never off-hand in his replies; the good-hearted youth was inwardly rejoicing that, as he thought, the desire for enlightenment was awakened in a fellow-creature. Alas! it was from no desire for enlightenment that Avdey Ivanovitch questioned Kister; God knows why he did! Possibly he wished to ascertain for himself what sort of head he, Lutchkov, had, whether it was really dull, or simply untrained. 'So I really am stupid,' he said to himself more than once with a bitter smile; and he would draw himself up instantly and look rudely and insolently about him, and smile malignantly to himself if he caught some comrade dropping his eyes before his glance. 'All right, my man, you're so learned and well educated,...' he would mutter between his teeth. 'I'll show you... that's all....'

The officers did not long discuss the sudden friendship of Kister and Lutchkov; they were used to the duellist's queer ways. 'The devil's made friends with the baby,' they said.... Kister was warm in his praises of his friend on all hands; no one disputed his opinion, because they were afraid of Lutchkov; Lutchkov himself never mentioned Kister's name before the others, but he dropped his intimacy with the perfumed adjutant.

II

The landowners of the South of Russia are very keen on giving balls, inviting officers to their houses, and marrying off their daughters.

About seven miles from the village of Kirilovo lived just such a country gentleman, a Mr. Perekatov, the owner of four hundred souls, and a fairly spacious house. He had a daughter of eighteen, Mashenka, and a wife, Nenila Makarievna. Mr. Perekatov had once been an officer in the cavalry, but from love of a country life and from indolence he had retired and had begun to live peaceably and quietly, as landowners of the middling sort do live. Nenila Makarievna owed her existence in a not perfectly legitimate manner to a distinguished gentleman of Moscow.

Her protector had educated his little Nenila very carefully, as it is called, in his own house, but got her off his hands rather hurriedly, at the first offer, as a not very marketable article. Nenila Makarievna was ugly; the distinguished gentleman was giving her no more than ten thousand as dowry; she snatched eagerly at Mr. Perekatov. To Mr. Perekatov it seemed extremely gratifying to marry a highly educated, intellectual young lady... who was, after all, so closely related to so illustrious a personage. This illustrious personage extended his patronage to the young people even after the marriage, that is to say, he accepted presents of salted quails from them and called Perekatov 'my dear boy,' and sometimes simply, 'boy.' Nenila Makarievna took complete possession of her husband, managed everything, and looked after the whole property—very sensibly, indeed; far better, any way, than Mr. Perekatov could have done. She did not hamper her partner's liberty too much; but she kept him well in hand, ordered his clothes herself, and dressed him in the English style, as is fitting and proper for a country gentleman. By her instructions, Mr. Perekatov grew a little Napoleonic beard on his chin, to cover a large wart, which looked like an over-ripe raspberry. Nenila Makarievna, for her part, used to inform visitors that her husband played the flute, and that all flute-players always let the beard grow under the lower lip; they could hold their instrument more comfortably. Mr. Perekatov always, even in the early morning, wore a high, clean stock, and was well combed and washed. He was, moreover, well content with his lot; he dined very well, did as he liked, and slept all he could. Nenila Makarievna had introduced into her household 'foreign ways,' as the neighbours used to say; she kept few servants, and had them neatly dressed. She was fretted by ambition; she wanted at least to be the wife of the marshal of the nobility of the district; but the gentry of the district, though they dined at her house to their hearts' content, did not choose her husband, but first the retired premier-major Burkolts, and then the retired second major Burundukov. Mr. Perekatov seemed to them too extreme a product of the capital.

Mr. Perekatov's daughter, Mashenka, was in face like her father. Nenila Makarievna had taken the greatest pains with her education. She spoke French well, and played the piano fairly. She was of medium height, rather plump and white; her rather full face was lighted up by a kindly and merry smile; her flaxen, not over-abundant hair, her hazel eyes, her pleasant voice—everything about her was gently pleasing, and that was all. On the other hand the absence of all affectation and conventionality, an amount of culture exceptional in a country girl, the freedom of her expressions, the quiet simplicity of her words and looks could not but be striking in her. She had developed at her own free will; Nenila Makarievna did not keep her in restraint.

One morning at twelve o'clock the whole family of the Perekatovs were in the drawing-room. The husband in a round green coat, a high check cravat, and pea-green trousers with straps, was standing at the window, very busily engaged in catching flies. The daughter was sitting at her embroidery frame; her small dimpled little hand rose and fell slowly and gracefully over the canvas. Nenila Makarievna was sitting on the sofa, gazing in silence at the floor.

'Did you send an invitation to the regiment at Kirilovo, Sergei Sergeitch?' she asked her husband.

'For this evening? To be sure I did, ma chère.' (He was under the strictest orders not to call her 'little mother.') 'To be sure!'

'There are positively no gentlemen,' pursued Nenila Makarievna. 'Nobody for the girls to dance with.'

Her husband sighed, as though crushed by the absence of partners.

'Mamma,' Masha began all at once, 'is Monsieur Lutchkov asked?'

'What Lutchkov?'

'He's an officer too. They say he's a very interesting person.'

'How's that?'

'Oh, he's not good-looking and he's not young, but every one's afraid of him. He's a dreadful duellist.' (Mamma frowned a little.) 'I should so like to see him.'

Sergei Sergeitch interrupted his daughter.

'What is there to see in him, my darling? Do you suppose he must look like Lord Byron?' (At that time we were only just beginning to talk about Lord Byron.) 'Nonsense! Why, I declare, my dear, there was a time when I had a terrible character as a fighting man.'

Masha looked wonderingly at her parent, laughed, then jumped up and kissed him on the cheek. His wife smiled a little, too... but Sergei Sergeitch had spoken the truth.

'I don't know if that gentleman is coming,' observed Nenila Makarievna. 'Possibly he may come too.'

The daughter sighed.

'Mind you don't go and fall in love with him,' remarked Sergei Sergeitch. 'I know you girls are all like that nowadays—so—what shall I say?—romantic...'

'No,' Masha responded simply.

Nenila Makarievna looked coldly at her husband. Sergei Sergeitch played with his watch-chain in some embarrassment, then took his wide-brimmed, English hat from the table, and set off to see after things on the estate.

His dog timidly and meekly followed him. As an intelligent animal, she was well aware that her master was not a person of very great authority in the house, and behaved herself accordingly with modesty and circumspection.

Nenila Makarievna went up to her daughter, gently raised her head, and looked affectionately into her eyes. 'Will you tell me when you fall in love?' she asked.

Masha kissed her mother's hand, smiling, and nodded her head several times in the affirmative.

'Mind you do,' observed Nenila Makarievna, stroking her cheek, and she went out after her husband. Masha leaned back in her chair, dropped her head on her bosom, interlaced her fingers, and looked long out of window, screwing up her eyes... A slight flush passed over her fresh cheeks; with a sigh she drew herself up, was setting to work again, but dropped her needle, leaned her face on her hand, and biting the tips of her nails, fell to dreaming... then glanced at her own shoulder, at her outstretched hand, got up, went to the window, laughed, put on her hat and went out into the garden.

That evening at eight o'clock, the guests began to arrive. Madame Perekatov with great affability received and 'entertained' the ladies, Mashenka the girls; Sergei Sergeitch talked about the crops with the gentlemen and continually glanced towards his wife. Soon there arrived the young dandies, the officers, intentionally a little late; at last the colonel himself, accompanied by his adjutants, Kister and Lutchkov. He presented them to the lady of the house. Lutchkov bowed without speaking, Kister muttered the customary 'extremely delighted'... Mr. Perekatov went up to the colonel, pressed his hand warmly and looked him in the face with great cordiality. The colonel promptly looked forbidding. The dancing began. Kister asked Mashenka for a dance. At that time the *Ecossaise* was still flourishing.

'Do tell me, please,' Masha said to him, when, after galloping twenty times to the end of the room, they stood at last, the first couple, 'why isn't your friend dancing?'

'Which friend?'

Masha pointed with the tip of her fan at Lutchkov.

'He never dances,' answered Kister.

'Why did he come then?'

Kister was a little disconcerted. 'He wished to have the pleasure...'

Mashenka interrupted him. 'You've not long been transferred into our regiment, I think?'

'Into your regiment,' observed Kister, with a smile: 'no, not long.'

'Aren't you dull here?'

'Oh no... I find such delightful society here... and the scenery!'... Kister launched into eulogies of the scenery. Masha listened to him, without raising her head. Avdey Ivanovitch was standing in a corner, looking indifferently at the dancers.

'How old is Mr. Lutchkov?' she asked suddenly.

'Oh... thirty-five, I fancy,' answered Kister.

'They say he's a dangerous man... hot-tempered,' Masha added hurriedly.

'He is a little hasty... but still, he's a very fine man.'

'They say every one's afraid of him.'

Kister laughed.

'And you?'

'I'm a friend of his.'

'Really?'

'Your turn, your turn,' was shrieked at them from all sides. They started and began galloping again right across the room.

'Well, I congratulate you,' Kister said to Lutchkov, going up to him after the dance; 'the daughter of the house does nothing but ask questions about you.'

'Really?' Lutchkov responded scornfully.

'On my honour! And you know she's extremely nice-looking; only look at her.'

'Which of them is she?'

Kister pointed out Masha.

'Ah, not bad.' And Lutchkov yawned.

'Cold-hearted person!' cried Kister, and he ran off to ask another girl to dance.

Avdey Ivanovitch was extremely delighted at the fact Kister had mentioned to him, though he did yawn, and even yawned loudly. To arouse curiosity flattered his vanity intensely: love he despised—in words—but inwardly he was himself aware that it would be a hard and difficult task for him to win love.... A hard and difficult task for him to win love, but easy and simple enough to wear a mask of indifference, of silent haughtiness. Avdey Ivanovitch was unattractive and no longer young; but on the other hand he enjoyed a terrible reputation—and consequently he had every right to pose. He was used to the bitter, unspoken enjoyment of grim loneliness. It was not the first time he had attracted the attention of women; some had even tried to get upon more friendly terms with him, but he repelled their advances with exasperated obstinacy; he knew that sentiment was not in his line (during tender interviews, avowals, he first became awkward and vulgar, and, through anger, rude to the point of grossness, of insult); he remembered that the two or three women with whom he had at different times been on a friendly footing had rapidly grown cool to him after the first moment of closer intimacy, and had of their own impulse made haste to get away from him... and so he had at last schooled himself to remain an enigma, and to scorn what destiny had denied him.... This is, I fancy, the only sort of scorn people in general do feel. No sort of frank, spontaneous, that is to say good, demonstration of passion suited Lutchkov; he was bound to keep a continual check on himself, even when he was angry. Kister was the only person who was not disgusted when Lutchkov broke into laughter; the kind-hearted German's eyes shone with the generous delight of sympathy, when he read Avdey his favourite passages from Schiller, while the bully would sit facing him with lowering looks, like a wolf.... Kister danced till he was worn out, Lutchkov never left his corner, scowled, glanced stealthily at Masha, and meeting her eyes, at once threw an expression of indifference into his own. Masha danced three times with Kister. The enthusiastic youth inspired her with confidence. She chatted with him gaily enough, but at heart she was not at ease. Lutchkov engrossed her thoughts.

A mazurka tune struck up. The officers fell to bounding up and down, tapping with their heels, and tossing the epaulettes on their shoulders; the civilians tapped with their heels too. Lutchkov still did not stir from his place, and slowly followed the couples with his eyes, as they whirled by. Some one touched his sleeve... he looked round; his neighbour pointed him out Masha. She was standing before him with downcast eyes, holding out her hand to him. Lutchkov for the first moment gazed at her in perplexity, then he carelessly took off his sword, threw his hat on the floor, picked his way awkwardly among the arm-chairs, took Masha by the hand, and went round the circle, with no capering up and down nor stamping, as it were unwillingly performing an unpleasant duty.... Masha's heart beat violently.

'Why don't you dance?' she asked him at last.

'I don't care for it,' answered Lutchkov.

'Where's your place?'

'Over there.'

Lutchkov conducted Masha to her chair, coolly bowed to her and coolly returned to his corner... but there was an agreeable stirring of the spleen within him.

Kister asked Masha for a dance.

'What a strange person your friend is!'

'He does interest you...' said Fyodor Fedoritch, with a sly twinkle of his blue and kindly eyes.

'Yes... he must be very unhappy.'

'He unhappy? What makes you suppose so?' And Fyodor Fedoritch laughed.

'You don't know... you don't know...' Masha solemnly shook her head with an important air.

'Me not know? How's that?'...

Masha shook her head again and glanced towards Lutchkov. Avdey Ivanovitch noticed the glance, shrugged his shoulders imperceptibly, and walked away into the other room.

III

Several months had passed since that evening. Lutchkov had not once been at the Perekatovs'. But Kister visited them pretty often. Nenila Makarievna had taken a fancy to him, but it was not she that attracted Fyodor Fedoritch. He liked Masha. Being an inexperienced person who had not yet talked himself out, he derived great pleasure from the interchange of ideas and feelings, and he had a simple-hearted faith in the possibility of a calm and exalted friendship between a young man and a young girl.

One day his three well-fed and skittish horses whirled him rapidly along to Mr. Perekatov's house. It was a summer day, close and sultry. Not a cloud anywhere. The blue of the sky was so thick and dark on the horizon that the eye mistook it for storm-cloud. The house Mr. Perekatov had erected for a summer residence had been, with the foresight usual in the steppes, built with every window directly facing the sun. Nenila Makarievna had every shutter closed from early morning. Kister walked into the cool, half-dark drawing-room. The light lay in long lines on the floor and in short, close streaks on the walls. The Perekatov family gave Fyodor Fedoritch a friendly reception. After dinner Nenila Makarievna went away to her own room to lie down; Mr. Perekatov settled himself on the sofa in the drawing-room; Masha sat near the window at her embroidery frame, Kister facing her. Masha, without opening her frame, leaned lightly over it, with her head in her hands. Kister began telling her something; she listened inattentively, as though waiting for something, looked from time to time towards her father, and all at once stretched out her hand.

'Listen, Fyodor Fedoritch... only speak a little more softly... papa's asleep.'

Mr. Perekatov had indeed as usual dropped asleep on the sofa, with his head hanging and his mouth a little open.

'What is it?' Kister inquired with curiosity.

'You will laugh at me.'

'Oh, no, really!...'

Masha let her head sink till only the upper part of her face remained uncovered by her hands and in a half whisper, not without hesitation, asked Kister why it was he never brought Mr. Lutchkov with him. It was not the first time Masha had mentioned him since the ball.... Kister did not speak. Masha glanced timorously over her interlaced fingers.

'May I tell you frankly what I think?' Kister asked her.

'Oh, why not? of course.'

'It seems to me that Lutchkov has made a great impression on you.'

'No!' answered Masha, and she bent over, as though wishing to examine the pattern more closely; a narrow golden streak of light lay on her hair; 'no... but...'

'Well, but?' said Kister, smiling.

'Well, don't you see,' said Masha, and she suddenly lifted her head, so that the streak of light fell straight in her eyes; 'don't you see... he...'

'He interests you....'

'Well... yes...' Masha said slowly; she flushed a little, turned her head a little away and in that position went on talking. 'There is something about him so... There, you're laughing at me,' she added suddenly, glancing swiftly at Fyodor Fedoritch.

Fyodor Fedoritch smiled the gentlest smile imaginable.

'I tell you everything, whatever comes into my head,' Masha went on: 'I know that you are a very'... (she nearly said great) 'good friend of mine.'

Kister bowed. Masha ceased speaking, and shyly held out her hand to him; Fyodor Fedoritch pressed the tips of her fingers respectfully.

'He must be a very queer person!' observed Masha, and again she propped her elbows on the frame.

'Queer?'

'Of course; he interests me just because he is queer!' Masha added slily.

'Lutchkov is a noble, a remarkable man,' Kister rejoined solemnly. 'They don't know him in our regiment, they don't appreciate him, they only see his external side. He's embittered, of course, and strange and impatient, but his heart is good.'

Masha listened greedily to Fyodor Fedoritch.

'I will bring him to see you, I'll tell him there's no need to be afraid of you, that it's absurd for him to be so shy... I'll tell him... Oh! yes, I know what to say... Only you mustn't suppose, though, that I would...' (Kister was embarrassed, Masha too was embarrassed.)... 'Besides, after all, of course you only... like him....'

'Of course, just as I like lots of people.'

Kister looked mischievously at her.

'All right, all right,' he said with a satisfied air; 'I'll bring him to you....'

'Oh, no....'

'All right, I tell you it will be all right.... I'll arrange everything.'

'You are so...' Masha began with a smile, and she shook her finger at him. Mr. Perekatov yawned and opened his eyes.

'Why, I almost think I've been asleep,' he muttered with surprise. This doubt and this surprise were repeated daily. Masha and Kister began discussing Schiller.

Fyodor Fedoritch was not however quite at ease; he felt something like a stir of envy within him... and was generously indignant with himself. Nenila Makarievna came down into the drawing-room. Tea was brought in. Mr. Perekatov made his dog jump several times over a stick, and then explained he had taught it everything himself, while the dog wagged its tail deferentially, licked itself and blinked. When at last the great heat began to lessen, and an evening breeze blew up, the whole family went out for a walk in the birch copse. Fyodor Fedoritch was continually glancing at Masha, as though giving her to understand that he would carry out her behests; Masha felt at once vexed with herself, and happy and uncomfortable. Kister suddenly, apropos of nothing, plunged into a rather high-flown discourse upon love in the abstract, and upon friendship... but catching Nenila Makarievna's bright and vigilant eye he, as abruptly, changed the subject. The sunset was brilliant and glowing. A broad, level meadow lay outstretched before the birch copse. Masha took it into her head to start a game of 'catch-catch.' Maid-servants and footmen came out; Mr. Perekatov stood with his wife, Kister with Masha. The maids ran with deferential little shrieks; Mr. Perekatov's valet had the temerity to separate Nenila Makarievna from her spouse; one of the servant-girls respectfully paired off with her master; Fyodor Fedoritch was not parted from Masha. Every time as he regained his place, he said two or three words to her; Masha, all flushed with running, listened to him with a smile, passing her hand over her hair. After supper, Kister took leave.

It was a still, starlight night. Kister took off his cap. He was excited; there was a lump in his throat. 'Yes,' he said at last, almost aloud; 'she loves him: I will bring them together; I will justify her confidence in me.' Though there was as yet nothing to prove a definite passion for Lutchkov on Masha's part, though, according to her own account, he only excited her curiosity, Kister had by this time made up a complete romance, and worked out his own duty in the matter. He resolved to sacrifice his feelings—the more readily as 'so far I have no other sentiment for her but sincere devotion,' thought he. Kister really was capable of sacrificing himself to friendship, to a recognised duty. He had read a great deal, and so fancied himself a person of experience and even of penetration; he had no doubt of the truth of his suppositions; he did not suspect that life is endlessly varied, and never repeats itself. Little by little, Fyodor Fedoritch worked himself into a state of ecstasy. He began musing with emotion on his mission. To be the mediator between a shy, loving girl and a man possibly embittered only because he had never once in his life loved and been loved; to bring them together; to reveal their own feelings to them, and then to withdraw, letting no one know the greatness of his sacrifice, what a splendid feat! In spite of the coolness of the night, the simple-hearted dreamer's face burned....

Next day he went round to Lutchkov early in the morning.

Avdey Ivanovitch was, as usual, lying on the sofa, smoking a pipe. Kister greeted him.
'I was at the Perekatovs yesterday,' he said with some solemnity.
'Ah!' Lutchkov responded indifferently, and he yawned.
'Yes. They are splendid people.'
'Really?'
'We talked about you.'
'Much obliged; with which of them was that?'
'With the old people... and the daughter too.'
'Ah! that... little fat thing?'
'She's a splendid girl, Lutchkov.'
'To be sure, they're all splendid.'
'No, Lutchkov, you don't know her. I have never met such a clever, sweet and sensitive girl.'
Lutchkov began humming through his nose:

'In the Hamburg Gazette,
You've read, I dare say,
How the year before last,
Munich gained the day....'

'But I assure you....'
'You 're in love with her, Fedya,' Lutchkov remarked sarcastically.
'Not at all. I never even thought of it.'
'Fedya, you're in love with her!'
'What nonsense! As if one couldn't...'
'You're in love with her, friend of my heart, beetle on my hearth,' Avdey Ivanovitch chanted drawling.
'Ah, Avdey, you really ought to be ashamed!' Kister said with vexation.
With any one else Lutchkov would thereupon have kept on more than before; Kister he did not tease. 'Well, well, sprechen Sie deutsch, Ivan Andreitch,' he muttered in an undertone, 'don't be angry.'
'Listen, Avdey,' Kister began warmly, and he sat down beside him. 'You know I care for you.' (Lutchkov made a wry face.) 'But there's one thing, I'll own, I don't like about you... it's just that you won't make friends with any one, that you will stick at home, and refuse all intercourse with nice people. Why, there are nice people in the world, hang it all! Suppose you have been deceived in life, have been embittered, what of it; there's no need to rush into people's arms, of course, but why turn your back on everybody? Why, you'll cast me off some day, at that rate, I suppose.'
Lutchkov went on smoking coolly.
'That's how it is no one knows you... except me; goodness knows what some people think of you... Avdey!' added Kister after a brief silence; 'do you disbelieve in virtue, Avdey?'
'Disbelieve... no, I believe in it,'... muttered Lutchkov.
Kister pressed his hand feelingly.
'I want,' he went on in a voice full of emotion, 'to reconcile you with life. You will grow happier, blossom out... yes, blossom out. How I shall rejoice then! Only you must let me dispose of you now and then, of your time. To-day it's—what? Monday... to-morrow's Tuesday... on Wednesday, yes, on Wednesday we'll go together to the Perekatovs'. They will be so glad to see you... and we shall have such a jolly time there... and now let me have a pipe.'
Avdey Ivanovitch lay without budging on the sofa, staring at the ceiling. Kister lighted a pipe, went to the window, and began drumming on the panes with his fingers.
'So they've been talking about me?' Avdey asked suddenly.
'They have,' Kister responded with meaning.
'What did they say?'
'Oh, they talked. There're very anxious to make your acquaintance.'
'Which of them's that?'
'I say, what curiosity!'
Avdey called his servant, and ordered his horse to be saddled.
'Where are you off to?'
'The riding-school.'

'Well, good-bye. So we're going to the Perekatovs', eh?'

'All right, if you like,' Lutchkov said lazily, stretching.

'Bravo, old man!' cried Kister, and he went out into the street, pondered, and sighed deeply.

IV

Masha was just approaching the drawing-room door when the arrival of Kister and Lutchkov was announced. She promptly returned to her own room, and went up to the looking-glass.... Her heart was throbbing violently. A girl came to summon her to the drawing-room. Masha drank a little water, stopped twice on the stairs, and at last went down. Mr. Perekatov was not at home. Nenila Makarievna was sitting on the sofa; Lutchkov was sitting in an easy-chair, wearing his uniform, with his hat on his knees; Kister was near him. They both got up on Masha's entrance—Kister with his usual friendly smile, Lutchkov with a solemn and constrained air. She bowed to them in confusion, and went up to her mother. The first ten minutes passed off favourably. Masha recovered herself, and gradually began to watch Lutchkov. To the questions addressed to him by the lady of the house, he answered briefly, but uneasily; he was shy, like all egoistic people. Nenila Makarievna suggested a stroll in the garden to her guests, but did not herself go beyond the balcony. She did not consider it essential never to lose sight of her daughter, and to be constantly hobbling after her with a fat reticule in her hands, after the fashion of many mothers in the steppes. The stroll lasted rather a long while. Masha talked more with Kister, but did not dare to look either at him or at Lutchkov. Avdey Ivanovitch did not address a remark to her; Kister's voice showed agitation. He laughed and chattered a little over-much.... They reached the stream. A couple of yards or so from the bank there was a water-lily, which seemed to rest on the smooth surface of the water, encircled by its broad, round leaves.

'What a beautiful flower!' observed Masha.

She had hardly uttered these words when Lutchkov pulled out his sword, clutched with one hand at the frail twigs of a willow, and, bending his whole body over the water, cut off the head of the flower. 'It's deep here, take care!' Masha cried in terror. Lutchkov with the tip of his sword brought the flower to the bank, at her very feet. She bent down, picked up the flower, and gazed with tender, delighted amazement at Avdey. 'Bravo!' cried Kister. 'And I can't swim...' Lutchkov observed abruptly. Masha did not like that remark. 'What made him say that?' she wondered.

Lutchkov and Kister remained at Mr. Perekatov's till the evening. Something new and unknown was passing in Masha's soul; a dreamy perplexity was reflected more than once in her face. She moved somehow more slowly, she did not flush on meeting her mother's eyes—on the contrary, she seemed to seek them, as though she would question her. During the whole evening, Lutchkov paid her a sort of awkward attention; but even this awkwardness gratified her innocent vanity. When they had both taken leave, with a promise to come again in a few days, she quietly went off to her own room, and for a long while, as it were, in bewilderment she looked about her. Nenila Makarievna came to her, kissed and embraced her as usual. Masha opened her lips, tried to say something—and did not utter a word. She wanted to confess—-she did not know what. Her soul was gently wandering in dreams. On the little table by her bedside the flower Lutchkov had picked lay in water in a clean glass. Masha, already in bed, sat up cautiously, leaned on her elbow, and her maiden lips softly touched the fresh white petals....

'Well,' Kister questioned his friend next day, 'do you like the Perekatovs? Was I right? eh? Tell me.'

Lutchkov did not answer.

'No, do tell me, do tell me!'

'Really, I don't know.'

'Nonsense, come now!'

'That... what's her name... Mashenka's all right; not bad-looking.'

'There, you see...' said Kister—and he said no more.

Five days later Lutchkov of his own accord suggested that they should call on the Perekatovs.

Alone he would not have gone to see them; in Fyodor Fedoritch's absence he would have had to keep up a conversation, and that he could not do, and as far as possible avoided.

On the second visit of the two friends, Masha was much more at her ease. She was by now secretly glad that she had not disturbed her mamma by an uninvited avowal. Before dinner, Avdey had offered to try a young horse, not yet broken in, and, in spite of its frantic rearing, he mastered it completely. In the evening he thawed, and fell into joking and laughing—and though he soon pulled himself up, yet he had succeeded in making a momentary unpleasant impression on Masha. She could not yet be sure herself what the feeling exactly was that Lutchkov excited in her, but everything she did not like in him she set down to the influence of misfortune, of loneliness.

V

The friends began to pay frequent visits to the Perekatovs'. Kister's position became more and more painful. He did not regret his action... no, but he desired at least to cut short the time of his trial. His devotion to Masha increased daily; she too felt warmly towards him; but to be nothing more than a go-between, a confidant, a friend even—it's a dreary, thankless business! Coldly idealistic people talk a great deal about the sacredness of suffering, the bliss of suffering... but to Kister's warm and simple heart his sufferings were not a source of any bliss whatever. At last, one day, when Lutchkov, ready dressed, came to fetch him, and the carriage was waiting at the steps, Fyodor Fedoritch, to the astonishment of his friend, announced point-blank that he should stay at home. Lutchkov entreated him, was vexed and angry... Kister pleaded a headache. Lutchkov set off alone.

The bully had changed in many ways of late. He left his comrades in peace, did not annoy the novices, and though his spirit had not 'blossomed out,' as Kister had foretold, yet he certainly had toned down a little. He could not have been called 'disillusioned' before—he had seen and experienced almost nothing—and so it is not surprising that Masha engrossed his thoughts. His heart was not touched though; only his spleen was satisfied. Masha's feelings for him were of a strange kind. She almost never looked him straight in the face; she could not talk to him.... When they happened to be left alone together, Masha felt horribly awkward. She took him for an exceptional man, and felt overawed by him and agitated in his presence, fancied she did not understand him, and was unworthy of his confidence; miserably, drearily—but continually—she thought of him. Kister's society, on the contrary, soothed her and put her in a good humour, though it neither overjoyed nor excited her. With him she could chatter away for hours together, leaning on his arm, as though he were her brother, looking affectionately into his face, and laughing with his laughter—and she rarely thought of him. In Lutchkov there was something enigmatic for the young girl; she felt that his soul was 'dark as a forest,' and strained every effort to penetrate into that mysterious gloom.... So children stare a long while into a deep well, till at last they make out at the very bottom the still, black water.

On Lutchkov's coming into the drawing-room alone, Masha was at first scared... but then she felt delighted. She had more than once fancied that there existed some sort of misunderstanding between Lutchkov and her, that he had not hitherto had a chance of revealing himself. Lutchkov mentioned the cause of Kister's absence; the parents expressed their regret, but Masha looked incredulously at Avdey, and felt faint with expectation. After dinner they were left alone; Masha did not know what to say, she sat down to the piano; her fingers flitted hurriedly and tremblingly over the keys; she was continually stopping and waiting for the first word... Lutchkov did not understand nor care for music. Masha began talking to him about Rossini (Rossini was at that time just coming into fashion) and about Mozart.... Avdey Ivanovitch responded: 'Quite so,' 'by no means,' 'beautiful,' 'indeed,' and that was all. Masha played some brilliant variations on one of Rossini's airs. Lutchkov listened and listened... and when at last she turned to him, his face expressed such unfeigned boredom, that Masha jumped up at once and closed the piano. She went up to the window, and for a long while stared into the garden; Lutchkov did not stir from his seat, and still remained silent. Impatience began to take the place of timidity in Masha's soul. 'What is it?' she wondered, 'won't you... or can't you?' It was Lutchkov's turn to feel shy. He was conscious again of his miserable, overwhelming diffidence; already he was raging!... 'It was the devil's own notion to have anything to do with the wretched girl,' he muttered to himself.... And all the while how easy it was to touch Masha's heart at that instant! Whatever had been said by such an extraordinary though eccentric man, as she imagined Lutchkov, she would have understood everything, have excused anything, have believed anything.... But this burdensome, stupid silence! Tears of vexation were standing in her eyes. 'If he doesn't want to be open, if I am really not worthy of his confidence, why does he go on coming to see us? Or perhaps it is that I don't set the right way to work to make him reveal himself?'... And she turned swiftly round, and glanced so inquiringly, so searchingly at him, that he could not fail to understand her glance, and could not keep silence any longer....

'Marya Sergievna,' he pronounced falteringly; 'I... I've... I ought to tell you something....'

'Speak,' Masha responded rapidly.

Lutchkov looked round him irresolutely.

'I can't now...'

'Why not?'

'I should like to speak to you... alone....'

'Why, we are alone now.'

'Yes... but... here in the house....'

Masha was at her wits' end.... 'If I refuse,' she thought, 'it's all over.'... Curiosity was the ruin of Eve....

'I agree,' she said at last.

'When then? Where?'

Masha's breathing came quickly and unevenly.

'To-morrow... in the evening. You know the copse above the Long Meadow?'...

'Behind the mill?'

Masha nodded.

'What time?'

'Wait...'

She could not bring out another word; her voice broke... she turned pale and went quickly out of the room.

A quarter of an hour later, Mr. Perekatov, with his characteristic politeness, conducted Lutchkov to the hall, pressed his hand feelingly, and begged him 'not to forget them'; then, having let out his guest, he observed with dignity to the footman that it would be as well for him to shave, and without awaiting a reply, returned with a careworn air to his own room, with the same careworn air sat down on the sofa, and guilelessly dropped asleep on the spot.

'You're a little pale to-day,' Nenila Makarievna said to her daughter, on the evening of the same day. 'Are you quite well?'

'Yes, mamma.'

Nenila Makarievna set straight the kerchief on the girl's neck.

'You are very pale; look at me,' she went on, with that motherly solicitude in which there is none the less audible a note of parental authority: 'there, now, your eyes look heavy too. You're not well, Masha.'

'My head does ache a little,' said Masha, to find some way of escape.

'There, I knew it.' Nenila Makarievna put some scent on Masha's forehead. 'You're not feverish, though.'

Masha stooped down, and picked a thread off the floor.

Nenila Makarievna's arms lay softly round Masha's slender waist.

'It seems to me you have something you want to tell me,' she said caressingly, not loosing her hands.

Masha shuddered inwardly.

'I? Oh, no, mamma.'

Masha's momentary confusion did not escape her mother's attention.

'Oh, yes, you do.... Think a little.'

But Masha had had time to regain her self-possession, and instead of answering, she kissed her mother's hand with a laugh.

'And so you've nothing to tell me?'

'No, really, nothing.'

'I believe you,' responded Nenila Makarievna, after a short silence. 'I know you keep nothing secret from me.... That's true, isn't it?'

'Of course, mamma.'

Masha could not help blushing a little, though.

'You do quite rightly. It would be wrong of you to keep anything from me.... You know how I love you, Masha.'

'Oh yes, mamma.'

And Masha hugged her.

'There, there, that's enough.' (Nenila Makarievna walked about the room.) 'Oh tell me,' she went on in the voice of one who feels that the question asked is of no special importance; 'what were you talking about with Avdey Ivanovitch to-day?'

'With Avdey Ivanovitch?' Masha repeated serenely. 'Oh, all sorts of things....'

'Do you like him?'

'Oh yes, I like him.'

'Do you remember how anxious you were to get to know him, how excited you were?'

Masha turned away and laughed.

'What a strange person he is!' Nenila Makarievna observed good-humouredly.

Masha felt an inclination to defend Lutchkov, but she held her tongue.
'Yes, of course,' she said rather carelessly; 'he is a queer fish, but still he's a nice man!'
'Oh, yes!... Why didn't Fyodor Fedoritch come?'
'He was unwell, I suppose. Ah! by the way, Fyodor Fedoritch wanted to make me a present of a puppy.... Will you let me?'
'What? Accept his present?'
'Yes.'
'Of course.'
'Oh, thank you!' said Masha, 'thank you, thank you!'
Nenila Makarievna got as far as the door and suddenly turned back again.
'Do you remember your promise, Masha?'
'What promise?'
'You were going to tell me when you fall in love.'
'I remember.'
'Well... hasn't the time come yet?' (Masha laughed musically.) 'Look into my eyes.'
Masha looked brightly and boldly at her mother.
'It can't be!' thought Nenila Makarievna, and she felt reassured. 'As if she could deceive me!... How could I think of such a thing!... She's still a perfect baby....'
She went away....
'But this is really wicked,' thought Masha.

VI

Kister had already gone to bed when Lutchkov came into his room. The bully's face never expressed *one* feeling; so it was now: feigned indifference, coarse delight, consciousness of his own superiority... a number of different emotions were playing over his features.
'Well, how was it? how was it?' Kister made haste to question him.
'Oh! I went. They sent you greetings.'
'Well? Are they all well?'
'Of course, why not?'
'Did they ask why I didn't come?'
'Yes, I think so.'
Lutchkov stared at the ceiling and hummed out of tune. Kister looked down and mused.
'But, look here,' Lutchkov brought out in a husky, jarring voice, 'you're a clever fellow, I dare say, you're a cultured fellow, but you're a good bit out in your ideas sometimes for all that, if I may venture to say so.'
'How do you mean?'
'Why, look here. About women, for instance. How you're always cracking them up! You're never tired of singing their praises! To listen to you, they're all angels.... Nice sort of angels!'
'I like and respect women, but———'
'Oh, of course, of course,' Avdey cut him short. 'I am not going to argue with you. That's quite beyond me! I'm a plain man.'
'I was going to say that... But why just to-day... just now,... are you talking about women?'
'Oh, nothing!' Avdey smiled with great meaning. 'Nothing!'
Kister looked searchingly at his friend. He imagined (simple heart!) that Masha had been treating him badly; had been torturing him, perhaps, as only women can....
'You are feeling hurt, my poor Avdey; tell me...'
Lutchkov went off into a chuckle.
'Oh, well, I don't fancy I've much to feel hurt about,' he said, in a drawling tone, complacently stroking his moustaches. 'No, only, look here, Fedya,' he went on with the manner of a preceptor, 'I was only going to point out that you're altogether out of it about women, my lad. You believe me, Fedya, they 're all alike. One's only got to take a little trouble, hang about them a bit, and you've got things in your own hands. Look at Masha Perekatov now....'
'Oh!'
Lutchkov tapped his foot on the floor and shook his head.

'Is there anything so specially attractive about me, hey? I shouldn't have thought there was anything. There isn't anything, is there? And here, I've a clandestine appointment for to-morrow.'

Kister sat up, leaned on his elbow, and stared in amazement at Lutchkov.

'For the evening, in a wood...' Avdey Ivanovitch continued serenely. 'Only don't you go and imagine it means much. It's only a bit of fun. It's slow here, don't you know. A pretty little girl,... well, says I, why not? Marriage, of course, I'm not going in for... but there, I like to recall my young days. I don't care for hanging about petticoats—but I may as well humour the baggage. We can listen to the nightingales together. Of course, it's really more in your line; but the wench has no eyes, you see. I should have thought I wasn't worth looking at beside you.'

Lutchkov talked on a long while. But Kister did not hear him. His head was going round. He turned pale and passed his hand over his face. Lutchkov swayed up and down in his low chair, screwed up his eyes, stretched, and putting down Kister's emotion to jealousy, was almost gasping with delight. But it was not jealousy that was torturing Kister; he was wounded, not by the fact itself, but by Avdey's coarse carelessness, his indifferent and contemptuous references to Masha. He was still staring intently at the bully, and it seemed as if for the first time he was thoroughly seeing his face. So this it was he had been scheming for! This for which he had sacrificed his own inclinations! Here it was, the blessed influence of love.

'Avdey... do you mean to say you don't care for her?' he muttered at last.

'O innocence! O Arcadia!' responded Avdey, with a malignant chuckle.

Kister in the goodness of his heart did not give in even then; perhaps, thought he, Avdey is in a bad temper and is 'humbugging' from old habit... he has not yet found a new language to express new feelings. And was there not in himself some other feeling lurking under his indignation? Did not Lutchkov's avowal strike him so unpleasantly simply because it concerned Masha? How could one tell, perhaps Lutchkov really was in love with her.... Oh, no! no! a thousand times no! That man in love?... That man was loathsome with his bilious, yellow face, his nervous, cat-like movements, crowing with conceit... loathsome! No, not in such words would Kister have uttered to a devoted friend the secret of his love.... In overflowing happiness, in dumb rapture, with bright, blissful tears in his eyes would he have flung himself on his bosom....

'Well, old man,' queried Avdey, 'own up now you didn't expect it, and now you feel put out. Eh? jealous? Own up, Fedya. Eh? eh?'

Kister was about to speak out, but he turned with his face to the wall. 'Speak openly... to him? Not for anything!' he whispered to himself. 'He wouldn't understand me... so be it! He supposes none but evil feelings in me—so be it!...'

Avdey got up.

'I see you're sleepy,' he said with assumed sympathy: 'I don't want to be in your way. Pleasant dreams, my boy... pleasant dreams!'

And Lutchkov went away, very well satisfied with himself.

Kister could not get to sleep before the morning. With feverish persistence he turned over and over and thought over and over the same single idea—an occupation only too well known to unhappy lovers.

'Even if Lutchkov doesn't care for her,' he mused, 'if she has flung herself at his head, anyway he ought not even with me, with his friend, to speak so disrespectfully, so offensively of her! In what way is she to blame? How could any one have no feeling for a poor, inexperienced girl?

'But can she really have a secret appointment with him? She has—yes, she certainly has. Avdey's not a liar, he never tells a lie. But perhaps it means nothing, a mere freak....

'But she does not know him.... He is capable, I dare say, of insulting her. After to-day, I wouldn't answer for anything.... And wasn't it I myself that praised him up and exalted him? Wasn't it I who excited her curiosity?... But who could have known this? Who could have foreseen it?...

'Foreseen what? Has he so long ceased to be my friend?... But, after all, was he ever my friend? What a disenchantment! What a lesson!'

All the past turned round and round before Kister's eyes. 'Yes, I did like him,' he whispered at last. 'Why has my liking cooled so suddenly?... And do I dislike him? No, why did I ever like him? I alone?'

Kister's loving heart had attached itself to Avdey for the very reason that all the rest avoided him. But the good-hearted youth did not know himself how great his good-heartedness was.

'My duty,' he went on, 'is to warn Marya Sergievna. But how? What right have I to interfere in other people's affairs, in other people's love? How do I know the nature of that love? Perhaps even in Lutchkov.... No, no!' he said aloud, with irritation, almost with tears, smoothing out his pillow, 'that man's stone....

'It is my own fault... I have lost a friend.... A precious friend, indeed! And she's not worth much either!... What a sickening egoist I am! No, no! from the bottom of my soul I wish them happiness.... Happiness! but he is laughing at her!... And why does he dye his moustaches? I do, really, believe he does.... Ah, how ridiculous I am!' he repeated, as he fell asleep.

VII

The next morning Kister went to call on the Perekatovs. When they met, Kister noticed a great change in Masha, and Masha, too, found a change in him, but neither spoke of it. The whole morning they both, contrary to their habit, felt uncomfortable. Kister had prepared at home a number of hints and phrases of double meaning and friendly counsels... but all this previous preparation turned out to be quite thrown away. Masha was vaguely aware that Kister was watching her; she fancied that he pronounced some words with intentional significance; but she was conscious, too, of her own excitement, and did not trust her own observations. 'If only he doesn't mean to stay till evening!' was what she was thinking incessantly, and she tried to make him realise that he was not wanted. Kister, for his part, took her awkwardness and her uneasiness for obvious signs of love, and the more afraid he was for her the more impossible he found it to speak of Lutchkov; while Masha obstinately refrained from uttering his name. It was a painful experience for poor Fyodor Fedoritch. He began at last to understand his own feelings. Never had Masha seemed to him more charming. She had, to all appearances, not slept the whole night. A faint flush stood in patches on her pale face; her figure was faintly drooping; an unconscious, weary smile never left her lips; now and then a shiver ran over her white shoulders; a soft light glowed suddenly in her eyes, and quickly faded away. Nenila Makarievna came in and sat with them, and possibly with intention mentioned Avdey Ivanovitch. But in her mother's presence Masha was armed *jusqu'aux dents,* as the French say, and she did not betray herself at all. So passed the whole morning.

'You will dine with us?' Nenila Makarievna asked Kister.

Masha turned away.

'No,' Kister said hurriedly, and he glanced towards Masha. 'Excuse me... duties of the service...'

Nenila Makarievna duly expressed her regret. Mr. Perekatov, following her lead, also expressed something or other. 'I don't want to be in the way,' Kister wanted to say to Masha, as he passed her, but he bowed down and whispered instead: 'Be happy... farewell... take care of yourself...' and was gone.

Masha heaved a sigh from the bottom of her heart, and then felt panic-stricken at his departure. What was it fretting her? Love or curiosity? God knows; but, we repeat, curiosity alone was enough to ruin Eve.

VIII

Long Meadow was the name of a wide, level stretch of ground on the right of the little stream Sniezhinka, nearly a mile from the Perekatovs' property. The left bank, completely covered by thick young oak bushes, rose steeply up over the stream, which was almost overgrown with willow bushes, except for some small 'breeding-places,' the haunts of wild ducks. Half a mile from the stream, on the right side of Long Meadow, began the sloping, undulating uplands, studded here and there with old birch-trees, nut bushes, and guelder-roses.

The sun was setting. The mill rumbled and clattered in the distance, sounding louder or softer according to the wind. The seignorial drove of horses was lazily wandering about the meadows; a shepherd walked, humming a tune, after a flock of greedy and timorous sheep; the sheepdogs, from boredom, were running after the crows. Lutchkov walked up and down in the copse, with his arms folded. His horse, tied up near by, more than once whinnied in response to the sonorous neighing of the mares and fillies in the meadow. Avdey was ill-tempered and shy, as usual. Not yet convinced of Masha's love, he felt wrathful with her and annoyed with himself... but his excitement smothered his annoyance. He stopped at last before a large nut bush, and began with his riding-whip switching off the leaves at the ends of the twigs....

He heard a light rustle... he raised his head.... Ten paces from him stood Masha, all flushed from her rapid walk, in a hat, but with no gloves, in a white dress, with a hastily tied kerchief round her neck. She dropped her eyes instantly, and softly nodded....

Avdey went awkwardly up to her with a forced smile.

'How happy I am...' he was beginning, scarcely audibly.

'I am very glad... to meet you...' Masha interrupted breathlessly. 'I usually walk here in the evening... and you...'

But Lutchkov had not the sense even to spare her modesty, to keep up her innocent deception.

'I believe, Marya Sergievna,' he pronounced with dignity, 'you yourself suggested...'

'Yes... yes...' rejoined Masha hurriedly. 'You wished to see me, you wanted...' Her voice died away.

Lutchkov did not speak. Masha timidly raised her eyes.

'Excuse me,' he began, not looking at her, 'I'm a plain man, and not used to talking freely... to ladies... I... I wished to tell you... but, I fancy, you 're not in the humour to listen to me....'

'Speak.'

'Since you tell me to... well, then, I tell you frankly that for a long while now, ever since I had the honour of making your acquaintance...'

Avdey stopped. Masha waited for the conclusion of his sentence.

'I don't know, though, what I'm telling you all this for.... There's no changing one's destiny...'

'How can one know?...'

'I know!' responded Avdey gloomily. 'I am used to facing its blows!'

It struck Masha that this was not exactly the befitting moment for Lutchkov to rail against destiny.

'There are kind-hearted people in the world,' she observed with a smile; 'some even too kind....'

'I understand you, Marya Sergievna, and believe me, I appreciate your friendliness... I... I... You won't be angry?'

'No.... What do you want to say?'

'I want to say... that I think you charming... Marya Sergievna, awfully charming....'

'I am very grateful to you,' Masha interrupted him; her heart was aching with anticipation and terror. 'Ah, do look, Mr. Lutchkov,' she went on—'look, what a view!'

She pointed to the meadow, streaked with long, evening shadows, and flushed red with the sunset.

Inwardly overjoyed at the abrupt change in the conversation, Lutchkov began admiring the view. He was standing near Masha....

'You love nature?' she asked suddenly, with a rapid turn of her little head, looking at him with that friendly, inquisitive, soft glance, which is a gift only vouchsafed to young girls.

'Yes... nature... of course...' muttered Avdey. 'Of course... a stroll's pleasant in the evening, though, I confess, I'm a soldier, and fine sentiments are not in my line.'

Lutchkov often repeated that he 'was a soldier.' A brief silence followed. Masha was still looking at the meadow.

'How about getting away?' thought Avdey. 'What rot it is, though! Come, more pluck!... Marya Sergievna...' he began, in a fairly resolute voice.

Masha turned to him.

'Excuse me,' he began, as though in joke, 'but let me on my side know what you think of me, whether you feel at all... so to say,... amiably disposed towards my person?'

'Mercy on us, how uncouth he is!' Masha said to herself. 'Do you know, Mr. Lutchkov,' she answered him with a smile, 'it's not always easy to give a direct answer to a direct question.'

'Still...'

'But what is it to you?'

'Oh, really now, I want to know...'

'But... Is it true that you are a great duellist? Tell me, is it true?' said Masha, with shy curiosity. 'They do say you have killed more than one man?'

'It has happened so,' Avdey responded indifferently, and he stroked his moustaches.

Masha looked intently at him.

'This hand then...' she murmured. Meanwhile Lutchkov's blood had caught fire. For more than a quarter of an hour a young and pretty girl had been moving before his eyes.

'Marya Sergievna,' he began again, in a sharp and strange voice, 'you know my feelings now, you know what I wanted to see you for.... You've been so kind.... You tell me, too, at last what I may hope for....'

Masha twisted a wildflower in her hands.... She glanced sideways at Lutchkov, flushed, smiled, said,' What nonsense you do talk,' and gave him the flower.

Avdey seized her hand.

'And so you love me!' he cried.

Masha turned cold all over with horror. She had not had the slightest idea of making a declaration of love to Avdey: she was not even sure herself as yet whether she did care for him, and here he was forestalling her, forcing her to speak out—he must be misunderstanding her then.... This idea flashed quicker than lightning into Masha's head. She had never expected such a speedy *dénouement*.... Masha, like an inquisitive child, had been asking herself all day: 'Can it be that Lutchkov cares for me?' She had dreamed of a delightful evening walk, a respectful and tender dialogue; she had fancied how she would flirt with him, make the wild creature feel at home with her, permit him at parting to kiss her hand... and instead of that...

Instead of that, she was suddenly aware of Avdey's rough moustaches on her cheek....

'Let us be happy,' he was whispering: 'there's no other happiness on earth!'

Masha shuddered, darted horror-stricken on one side, and pale all over, stopped short, one hand leaning on a birch-tree. Avdey was terribly confused.

'Excuse me,' he muttered, approaching her, 'I didn't expect really...'

Masha gazed at him, wide-eyed and speechless... A disagreeable smile twisted his lips... patches of red came out on his face....

'What are you afraid of?' he went on; 'it's no such great matter.... Why, we understand each other... and so....'

Masha did not speak.

'Come, stop that!... that's all nonsense! it's nothing but...' Lutchkov stretched out his hand to her.

Masha recollected Kister, his 'take care of yourself,' and, sinking with terror, in a rather shrill voice screamed, 'Taniusha!'

From behind a nutbush emerged the round face of her maid.... Avdey was completely disconcerted. Reassured by the presence of her hand-maiden, Masha did not stir. But the bully was shaking all over with rage; his eyes were half closed; he clenched his fists and laughed nervously.

'Bravo! bravo! Clever trick—no denying that!' he cried out.

Masha was petrified.

'So you took every care, I see, to be on the safe side, Marya Sergievna! Prudence is never thrown away, eh? Upon my word! Nowadays young ladies see further than old men. So this is all your love amounts to!'

'I don't know, Mr. Lutchkov, who has given you any right to speak about love... what love?'

'Who? Why, you yourself!' Lutchkov cut her short: 'what next!' He felt he was ship-wrecking the whole business, but he could not restrain himself.

'I have acted thoughtlessly,' said Masha.... 'I yielded to your request, relying upon your *délicatesse*... but you don't know French... on your courtesy, I mean....'

Avdey turned pale. Masha had stung him to the quick.

'I don't know French... may be; but I know... I know very well that you have been amusing yourself at my expense.'

'Not at all, Avdey Ivanovitch... indeed, I'm very sorry...'

'Oh, please, don't talk about being sorry for me,' Avdey cut her short peremptorily; 'spare me that, anyway!'

'Mr. Lutchkov...'

'Oh, you needn't put on those grand-duchess airs... It's trouble thrown away! you don't impress me.'

Masha stepped back a pace, turned swiftly round and walked away.

'Won't you give me a message for your friend, your shepherd lad, your tender sweet-heart, Kister,' Avdey shouted after her. He had lost his head. 'Isn't he the happy man?'...

Masha made him no reply, and hurriedly, gladly retreated. She felt light at heart, in spite of her fright and excitement. She felt as though she had waked up from a troubled sleep, had stepped out of a dark room into air and sunshine.... Avdey glared about him like a madman; in speechless frenzy he broke a young tree, jumped on to his mare, and so viciously drove the spurs into her, so mercilessly pulled and tugged at the reins that the wretched beast galloped six miles in a quarter of an hour and almost expired the same night.

Kister waited for Lutchkov in vain till midnight, and next morning he went round himself to see him. The orderly informed Fyodor Fedoritch that his master was lying down and had given orders that he would see no one. 'He won't see me even?'. 'Not even your honour.' Kister walked twice up and down the street, tortured by the keenest apprehensions, and then went home again. His servant handed him a note.

'From whom?'

'From the Perekatovs. Artiomka the postillion brought it.'

Kister's hands began to tremble.

'He had orders to give you their greetings. He had orders to wait for your answer. Am I to give Artiomka some vodka?'

Kister slowly unfolded the note, and read as follows:

'DEAR GOOD FYODOR FEDORITCH,—I want very, very much to see you. Come to-day, if you can. Don't refuse my request, I entreat you, for the sake of our old friendship. If only you knew... but you shall know everything. Good-bye for a little while,—eh?

MARIE.

'P.S.—Be sure to come to-morrow.'

'So your honour, am I to give Artiomka some vodka?'

Kister turned a long, bewildered stare at his servant's countenance, and went out without uttering a word.

'The master has told me to get you some vodka, and to have a drink with you,' said Kister's servant to Artiomka the postillion.

IX

Masha came with such a bright and grateful face to meet Kister, when he came into the drawing-room, she pressed his hand so warmly and affectionately, that his heart throbbed with delight, and a weight seemed rolled from his mind. Masha did not, however, say a single word, and she promptly left the room. Sergei Sergeitch was sitting on the sofa, playing patience. Conversation sprang up. Sergei Sergeitch had not yet succeeded with his usual skill in bringing the conversation round from all extraneous topics to his dog, when Masha reappeared, wearing a plaid silk sash, Kister's favourite sash. Nenila Makarievna came in and gave Fyodor Fedoritch a friendly greeting. At dinner they were all laughing and making jokes; even Sergei Sergeitch plucked up spirit and described one of the merriest pranks of his youthful days, hiding his head from his wife like an ostrich, as he told the story.

'Let us go for a walk, Fyodor Fedoritch,' Masha said to Kister after dinner with that note of affectionate authority in her voice which is, as it were, conscious that you will gladly submit to it. 'I want to talk to you about something very, very important,' she added with enchanting solemnity, as she put on her suede gloves. 'Are you coming with us, *maman*?'

'No,' answered Nenila Makarievna.

'But we are not going into the garden.'

'Where then?'

'To Long Meadow, to the copse.'

'Take Taniusha with you.'

'Taniusha, Taniusha!' Masha cried musically, flitting lightly as a bird from the room.

A quarter of an hour later Masha walked with Kister into the Long Meadow. As she passed the cattle, she gave a piece of bread to her favourite cow, patted it on the head and made Kister stroke it. Masha was in great good humour and chatted merrily. Kister responded willingly, though he awaited explanations with impatience.... Taniusha walked behind at a respectful distance, only from time to time stealing a sly glance at her young lady.

'You're not angry with me, Fyodor Fedoritch?' queried Masha.

'With you, Marya Sergievna? Why, whatever for?'

'The day before yesterday... don't you remember?'

'You were out of humour... that was all.'

'What are we walking in single file for? Give me your arm. That's right.... You were out of humour too.'

'Yes, I was too.'

'But to-day I'm in good humour, eh?'

'Yes, I think so, to-day...'

'And do you know why? Because...'

Masha nodded her head gravely. 'Well, I know why.... Because I am with you,' she added, not looking at Kister.

Kister softly pressed her hand.

'But why don't you question me?...' Masha murmured in an undertone.

'What about?'

'Oh, don't pretend... about my letter.'

'I was waiting for...'

'That's just why I am happy with you,' Masha interrupted him impulsively: 'because you are a gentle, good-hearted person, because you are incapable... *parceque vous avez de la délicatesse*. One can say that to you: you understand French.'

Kister did understand French, but he did not in the least understand Masha.

'Pick me that flower, that one... how pretty it is!' Masha admired it, and suddenly, swiftly withdrawing her hand from his arm, with an anxious smile she began carefully sticking the tender stalk in the buttonhole of Kister's coat. Her slender fingers almost touched his lips. He looked at the fingers and then at her. She nodded her head to him as though to say 'you may.'... Kister bent down and kissed the tips of her gloves.

Meanwhile they drew near the already familiar copse. Masha became suddenly more thoughtful, and at last kept silent altogether. They came to the very place where Lutchkov had waited for her. The trampled grass had not yet grown straight again; the broken sapling had not yet withered, its little leaves were only just beginning to curl up and fade. Masha stared about her, and turned quickly to Kister.

'Do you know why I have brought you here?'

'No, I don't.'

'Don't you know? Why is it you haven't told me anything about your friend Lutchkov to-day? You always praise him so...'

Kister dropped his eyes, and did not speak.

'Do you know,' Masha brought out with some effort, 'that I made... an appointment... to meet him here... yesterday?'

'I know that,' Kister rejoined hurriedly.

'You know it?... Ah! now I see why the day before yesterday... Mr. Lutchkov was in a hurry it seems to boast of his *conquest*.'

Kister was about to answer....

'Don't speak, don't say anything in opposition.... I know he's your friend. You are capable of taking his part. You knew, Kister, you knew.... How was it you didn't prevent me from acting so stupidly? Why didn't you box my ears, as if I were a child? You knew... and didn't you care?'

'But what right had I...'

'What right!... the right of a friend. But he too is your friend.... I'm ashamed, Kister.... He your friend.... That man behaved to me yesterday, as if...'

Masha turned away. Kister's eyes flamed; he turned pale.

'Oh, never mind, don't be angry.... Listen, Fyodor Fedoritch, don't be angry. It's all for the best. I am very glad of yesterday's explanation... yes, that's just what it was,' added Masha. 'What do you suppose I am telling you about it for? To complain of Mr. Lutchkov? Nonsense! I've forgotten about him. But I have done you a wrong, my good friend.... I want to speak openly to you, to ask your forgiveness... your advice. You have accustomed me to frankness; I am at ease with you.... You are not a Mr. Lutchkov!'

'Lutchkov is clumsy and coarse,' Kister brought out with difficulty; 'but...'

'Why *but*? Aren't you ashamed to say *but*? He is coarse, *and* clumsy, *and* ill-natured, *and* conceited.... Do you hear?—*and*, not *but*.'

'You are speaking under the influence of anger, Marya Sergievna,' Kister observed mournfully.

'Anger? A strange sort of anger! Look at me; are people like this when they 're angry? Listen,' pursued Masha; 'you may think what you like of me... but if you imagine I am flirting with you to-day from pique, well... well...' (tears stood in her eyes)'I shall be angry in earnest.'

'Do be open with me, Marya Sergievna...'

'O, silly fellow! how slow you are! Why, look at me, am I not open with you, don't you see right through me?'

'Oh, very well... yes; I believe you,' Kister said with a smile, seeing with what anxious insistence she tried to catch his eyes. 'But tell me, what induced you to arrange to meet Lutchkov?'

'What induced me? I really don't know. He wanted to speak to me alone. I fancied he had never had time, never had an opportunity to speak freely. He has spoken freely now! Do you know, he may be an extraordinary man, but he's a fool, really.... He doesn't know how to put two words together. He's simply an ignoramus. Though, indeed, I don't blame him much... he might suppose I was a giddy, mad, worthless girl. I hardly ever talked to him.... He did excite my curiosity, certainly, but I imagined that a man who was worthy of being your friend...'

'Don't, please, speak of him as my friend,' Kister interposed.

'No, no, I don't want to separate you.'

'Oh, my God, for you I'm ready to sacrifice more than a friend.... Everything is over between me and Mr. Lutchkov,' Kister added hurriedly.

Masha looked intently into his face.

'Well, enough of him,' she said. 'Don't let us talk of him. It's a lesson to me for the future. It's I that am to blame. For several months past I have almost every day seen a man who is good, clever, bright, friendly who...' (Masha was confused, and stammered) 'who, I think, cared... a little... for me too... and I like a fool,' she went on quickly, 'preferred to him... no, no, I didn't prefer him, but...'

She drooped her head, and ceased speaking in confusion.

Kister was in a sort of terror. 'It can't be!' he kept repeating to himself.

'Marya Sergievna!' he began at last.

Masha lifted her head, and turned upon him eyes heavy with unshed tears.

'You don't guess of whom I am speaking?' she asked.

Scarcely daring to breathe, Kister held out his hand. Masha at once clutched it warmly.

'You are my friend as before, aren't you?... Why don't you answer?'

'I am your friend, you know that,' he murmured.

'And you are not hard on me? You forgive me?... You understand me? You're not laughing at a girl who made an appointment only yesterday with one man, and to-day is talking to another, as I am talking to you.... You're not laughing at me, are you?...' Masha's face glowed crimson, she clung with both hands to Kister's hand....

'Laugh at you,' answered Kister: 'I... I... why, I love you... I love you,' he cried.

Masha hid her face.

'Surely you've long known that I love you, Marya Sergievna?'

X

Three weeks after this interview, Kister was sitting alone in his room, writing the following letter to his mother:—

Dearest Mother!—I make haste to share my great happiness with you; I am going to get married. This news will probably only surprise you from my not having, in my previous letters, even hinted at so important a change in my life—and you know that I am used to sharing all my feelings, my joys and my sorrows, with you. My reasons for silence are not easy to explain to you. To begin with, I did not know till lately that I was loved; and on my own side too, it is only lately that I have realised myself all the strength of my own feeling. In one of my first letters from here, I wrote to you of our neighbours, the Perekatovs; I am engaged to their only daughter, Marya. I am thoroughly convinced that we shall both be happy. My feeling for her is not a fleeting passion, but a deep and genuine emotion, in which friendship is mingled with love. Her bright, gentle disposition is in perfect harmony with my tastes. She is well-educated, clever, plays the piano splendidly.... If you could only see her! I enclose her portrait sketched by me. I need hardly say she is a hundred times better-looking than her portrait. Masha loves you already, like a daughter, and is eagerly looking forward to seeing you. I mean to retire, to settle in the country, and to go in for farming. Mr. Perekatov has a property of four hundred serfs in excellent condition. You see that even from the material point of view, you cannot but approve of my plans. I will get leave and come to Moscow and to you. Expect me in a fortnight, not later. My own dearest mother, how happy I am!... Kiss me...' and so on.

Kister folded and sealed the letter, got up, went to the window, lighted a pipe, thought a little, and returned to the table. He took out a small sheet of notepaper, carefully dipped his pen into the ink, but for a long while he did not begin to write, knitted his brows, lifted his eyes to the ceiling, bit the end of his pen.... At last he made up his mind, and in the course of a quarter of an hour he had composed the following:

'Dear Avdey Ivanovitch,—Since the day of your last visit (that is, for three weeks) you have sent me no message, have not said a word to me, and have seemed to avoid meeting me. Every one is, undoubtedly, free to act as he pleases; you have chosen to break off our acquaintance, and I do not, believe me, in addressing you intend to reproach you in any way. It is not my intention or my habit to force myself upon any one whatever; it is enough for me to feel that I am not to blame in the matter. I am writing to you now from a feeling of duty. I have made an offer to Marya Sergievna Perekatov, and have been accepted by her, and also by her parents. I inform *you* of this fact—directly and immediately—to avoid any kind of misapprehension or suspicion. I frankly confess, sir, that I am unable to feel great concern about the good opinion of a man who himself shows so little concern for the opinions and feelings of other people, and I am writing to you solely because I do not care in this matter even to appear to have acted or to be acting underhandedly. I make bold to say, you know me, and will not ascribe my present action to any other lower motive. Addressing you for the last time, I cannot, for the sake of our old friendship, refrain from wishing you all good things possible on earth.—I remain, sincerely, your obedient servant, Fyodor Kister.'

Fyodor Fedoritch despatched this note to the address, changed his uniform, and ordered his carriage to be got ready. Light-hearted and happy, he walked up and down his little room humming, even gave two little skips in the air, twisted a book of songs into a roll, and was tying it up with blue ribbon.... The door opened, and Lutchkov, in a coat without epaulettes, with a cap on his head, came into the room. Kister, astounded, stood still in the middle of the room, without finishing the bow he was tying.

'So you're marrying the Perekatov girl?' queried Avdey in a calm voice.

Kister fired up.

'Sir,' he began; 'decent people take off their caps and say good-morning when they come into another man's room.'

'Beg pardon,' the bully jerked out; and he took off his cap. 'Good-morning.'

'Good-morning, Mr. Lutchkov. You ask me if I am about to marry Miss Perekatov? Haven't you read my letter, then?'

'I have read your letter. You're going to get married. I congratulate you.'

'I accept your congratulation, and thank you for it. But I must be starting.'

'I should like to have a few words of explanation with you, Fyodor Fedoritch.'

'By all means, with pleasure,' responded the good-natured fellow. 'I must own I was expecting such an explanation. Your behaviour to me has been so strange, and I think, on my side, I have not deserved... at least, I had no reason to expect... But won't you sit down? Wouldn't you like a pipe?'

Lutchkov sat down. There was a certain weariness perceptible in his movements. He stroked his moustaches and lifted his eyebrows.

'I say, Fyodor Fedoritch,' he began at last; 'why did you keep it up with me so long?...'

'How do you mean?'

'Why did you pose as such... a disinterested being, when you were just such another as all the rest of us sinners all the while?'

'I don't understand you.... Can I have wounded you in some way?...'

'You don't understand me... all right. I'll try and speak more plainly. Just tell me, for instance, openly, Have you had a liking for the Perekatov girl all along, or is it a case of sudden passion?'

'I should prefer, Avdey Ivanitch, not to discuss with you my relations with Marya Sergievna,' Kister responded coldly.

'Oh, indeed! As you please. Only you'll kindly allow me to believe that you've been humbugging me.'

Avdey spoke very deliberately and emphatically.

'You can't believe that, Avdey Ivanitch; you know me.'

'I know you?... who knows you? The heart of another is a dark forest, and the best side of goods is always turned uppermost. I know you read German poetry with great feeling and even with tears in your eyes; I know that you've hung various maps on your walls; I know you keep your person clean; that I know,... but beyond that, I know nothing...'

Kister began to lose his temper.

'Allow me to inquire,' he asked at last, 'what is the object of your visit? You have sent no message to me for three weeks, and now you come to me, apparently with the intention of jeering at me. I am not a boy, sir, and I do not allow any one...'

'Mercy on us,' Lutchkov interrupted him; 'mercy on us, Fyodor Fedoritch, who would venture to jeer at you? It's quite the other way; I've come to you with a most humble request, that is, that you'd do me the favour to explain your behaviour to me. Allow me to ask you, wasn't it you who forced me to make the acquaintance of the Perekatov family? Didn't you assure your humble servant that it would make his soul blossom into flower? And lastly, didn't you throw me with the virtuous Marya Sergievna? Why am I not to presume that it's to *you* I'm indebted for that final agreeable scene, of which you have doubtless been informed in befitting fashion? An engaged girl, of course, tells her betrothed of everything, especially of her *innocent* indiscretions. How can I help supposing that it's thanks to you I've been made such a terrific fool of? You took such a mighty interest in my "blossoming out," you know!'

Kister walked up and down the room.

'Look here, Lutchkov,' he said at last; 'if you really—joking apart—are convinced of what you say, which I confess I don't believe, then let me tell you, it's shameful and wicked of you to put such an insulting construction on my conduct and intentions. I don't want to justify myself... I appeal to your own conscience, to your memory.'

'Yes; I remember you were continually whispering with Marya Sergievna. Besides that, let me ask you another question: Weren't you at the Perekatovs' after a certain conversation with me, after that evening when I like a fool chattered to you, thinking you my greatest friend, of the meeting she'd arranged?'

'What! you suspect me...'

'I suspect other people of nothing,' Avdey cut him short with cutting iciness, 'of which I would not suspect myself; but I have the weakness to suppose that other men are no better than I am.'

'You are mistaken,' Kister retorted emphatically; 'other men are better than you.'

'I congratulate them upon it,' Lutchkov dropped carelessly; 'but...'

'But remember,' broke in Kister, now in his turn thoroughly infuriated, 'in what terms you spoke of... of that meeting... of... But these explanations are leading to nothing, I see.... Think what you choose of me, and act as you think best.'

'Come, that's better,' observed Avdey. 'At last you're beginning to speak plainly.'

'As you think best,' repeated Kister.

'I understand your position, Fyodor Fedoritch,' Avdey went on with an affectation of sympathy; 'it's disagreeable, certainly. A man has been acting, acting a part, and no one has recognised him as a humbug; and all of a sudden...'

'If I could believe,' Kister interrupted, setting his teeth, 'that it was wounded love that makes you talk like this, I should feel sorry for you; I could excuse you.... But in your abuse, in your false charges, I hear nothing but the shriek of mortified pride... and I feel no sympathy for you.... You have deserved what you've got.'

'Ugh, mercy on us, how the fellow talks!' Avdey murmured. 'Pride,' he went on; 'may be; yes, yes, my pride, as you say, has been mortified intensely and insufferably. But who isn't proud? Aren't you? Yes, I'm proud, and for instance, I permit no one to feel sorry for me....'

'You don't permit it!' Kister retorted haughtily. 'What an expression, sir! Don't forget, the tie between us you yourself have broken. I must beg you to behave with me as with a complete outsider.'

'Broken! Broken the tie between us!' repeated Avdey. 'Understand me; I have sent you no message, and have not been to see you because I was sorry for you; you must allow me to be sorry for you, since you 're sorry for me!... I didn't want to put you in a false position, to make your conscience prick.... You talk of a tie between us... as though you could remain my friend as before your marriage! Rubbish! Why, you were only friendly with me before to gloat over your fancied superiority...'

Avdey's duplicity overwhelmed, confounded Kister.

'Let us end this unpleasant conversation!' he cried at last. 'I must own I don't see why you've been pleased to come to me.'

'You don't see what I've come to you for?' Avdey asked inquiringly.

'I certainly don't see why.'

'N—o?'

'No, I tell you...'

'Astonishing!... This is astonishing! Who'd have thought it of a fellow of your intelligence!'

'Come, speak plainly...'

'I have come, Mr. Kister,' said Avdey, slowly rising to his feet, 'I have come to challenge you to a duel. Do you understand now? I want to fight you. Ah! you thought you could get rid of me like that! Why, didn't you know the sort of man you have to do with? As if I'd allow...'

'Very good,' Kister cut in coldly and abruptly. 'I accept your challenge. Kindly send me your second.'

'Yes, yes,' pursued Avdey, who, like a cat, could not bear to let his victim go so soon: 'it'll give me great pleasure I'll own to put a bullet into your fair and idealistic countenance to-morrow.'

'You are abusive after a challenge, it seems,' Kister rejoined contemptuously. 'Be so good as to go. I'm ashamed of you.'

'Oh, to be sure, *délicatesse*!... Ah, Marya Sergievna, I don't know French!' growled Avdey, as he put on his cap. 'Till we meet again, Fyodor Fedoritch!'

He bowed and walked out.

Kister paced several times up and down the room. His face burned, his breast heaved violently. He felt neither fear nor anger; but it sickened him to think what this man really was that he had once looked upon as a friend. The idea of the duel with Lutchkov was almost pleasant to him.... Once get free from the past, leap over this rock in his path, and then to float on an untroubled tide... 'Good,' he thought, 'I shall be fighting to win my happiness.' Masha's image seemed to smile to him, to promise him success. 'I'm not going to be killed! not I!' he repeated with a serene smile. On the table lay the letter to his mother.... He felt a momentary pang at his heart. He resolved any way to defer sending it off. There was in Kister that quickening of the vital energies of which a man is aware in face of danger. He calmly thought over all the possible results of the duel, mentally placed Masha and himself in all the agonies of misery and parting, and looked forward to the future with hope. He swore to himself not to kill Lutchkov... He felt irresistibly drawn to Masha. He paused a second, hurriedly arranged things, and directly after dinner set off to the Perekatovs. All the evening Kister was in good spirits, perhaps in too good spirits.

Masha played a great deal on the piano, felt no foreboding of evil, and flirted charmingly with him. At first her unconsciousness wounded him, then he took Masha's very unconsciousness as a happy omen, and was rejoiced and reassured by it. She had grown fonder and fonder of him every day; happiness was for her a much more urgent need than passion. Besides, Avdey had turned her from all exaggerated desires, and she renounced them joyfully and for ever. Nenila Makarievna loved Kister like a son. Sergei Sergeitch as usual followed his wife's lead.

'Till we meet,' Masha said to Kister, following him into the hall and gazing at him with a soft smile, as he slowly and tenderly kissed her hands.

'Till we meet,' Fyodor Fedoritch repeated confidently; 'till we meet.'

But when he had driven half a mile from the Perekatovs' house, he stood up in the carriage, and with vague uneasiness began looking for the lighted windows.... All in the house was dark as in the tomb.

XI

Next day at eleven o'clock in the morning Kister's second, an old major of tried merit, came for him. The good old man growled to himself, bit his grey moustaches, and wished Avdey Ivanovitch everything unpleasant.... The carriage was brought to the door. Kister handed the major two letters, one for his mother, the other for Masha.

'What's this for?'

'Well, one can never tell...'

'Nonsense! we'll shoot him like a partridge...'

'Any way it's better...'

The major with vexation stuffed the two letters in the side pocket of his coat.

'Let us start.'

They set off. In a small copse, a mile and a half from the village of Kirilovo, Lutchkov was awaiting them with his former friend, the perfumed adjutant. It was lovely weather, the birds were twittering peacefully; not far from the copse a peasant was tilling the ground. While the seconds were marking out the distance, fixing the barrier, examining and loading the pistols, the opponents did not even glance at one another.... Kister walked to and fro with a careless air, swinging a flower he had gathered; Avdey stood motionless, with folded arms and scowling brow. The decisive moment arrived. 'Begin, gentlemen!' Kister went rapidly towards the barrier, but he had not gone five steps before Avdey fired, Kister started, made one more step forward, staggered. His head sank... His knees bent under him... He fell like a sack on the grass. The major rushed up to him.... 'Is it possible?' whispered the dying man.

Avdey went up to the man he had killed. On his gloomy and sunken face was a look of savage, exasperated regret.... He looked at the adjutant and the major, bent his head like a guilty man, got on his horse without a word, and rode slowly straight to the colonel's quarters.

Masha... is living to this day.

THREE PORTRAITS

'Neighbours' constitute one of the most serious drawbacks of life in the country. I knew a country gentleman of the Vologodsky district, who used on every suitable occasion to repeat the following words, 'Thank God, I have no neighbours,' and I confess I could not help envying that happy mortal. My own little place is situated in one of the most thickly peopled provinces of Russia. I am surrounded by a vast number of dear neighbours, from highly respectable and highly respected country gentlemen, attired in ample frockcoats and still more ample waistcoats, down to regular loafers, wearing jackets with long sleeves and a so-called shooting-bag on their back. In this crowd of gentlefolks I chanced, however, to discover one very pleasant fellow. He had served in the army, had retired and settled for good and all in the country. According to his story, he had served for two years in the B——— regiment. But I am totally unable to comprehend how that man could have performed any sort of duty, not merely for two years, but even for two days. He was born 'for a life of peace and country calm,' that is to say, for lazy, careless vegetation, which, I note parenthetically, is not without great and inexhaustible charms. He possessed a very fair property, and without giving too much thought to its management, spent about ten thousand roubles a year, had obtained an excellent cook—my friend was fond of good fare—and ordered too from Moscow all the newest French books and magazines. In Russian he read nothing but the reports of his bailiff, and that with great difficulty. He used, when he did not go out shooting, to wear a dressing-gown from morning till dinner-time and at dinner. He would look through plans of some sort, or go round to the stables or to the threshing barn, and joke with the peasant women, who, to be sure, in his presence wielded their flails in leisurely fashion. After dinner my friend would dress very carefully before the looking-glass, and drive off to see some neighbour possessed of two or three pretty daughters. He would flirt serenely and unconcernedly with one of them, play blind-man's-buff with them, return home rather late and promptly fall into a heroic sleep. He could never be bored, for he never gave himself up to complete inactivity; and in the choice of occupations he was not difficult to please, and was amused like a child with the smallest trifle. On the other hand, he cherished no particular attachment to life, and at times, when he chanced to get a glimpse of the track of a wolf or a fox, he would let his horse go at full gallop over such ravines that to this day I cannot understand how it was he did not break his neck a hundred times over. He belonged to that class of persons who inspire in one the idea that they do not know their own value, that under their appearance of indifference strong and violent passions lie concealed. But he would have laughed in one's face if he could have guessed that one cherished such an opinion of him. And indeed I must own I believe myself that even supposing my friend had had in youth some strong impulse, however vague, towards what is so sweetly called 'higher things,' that impulse had long, long ago died out. He was rather stout and enjoyed superb health. In our day one cannot help liking people who think little about themselves, because they are exceedingly rare... and my friend had almost forgotten his own personality. I fancy, though, that I have said too much about him already, and my prolixity is the more uncalled for as he is not the hero of my story. His name was Piotr Fedorovitch Lutchinov.

One autumn day there were five of us, ardent sportsmen, gathered together at Piotr Fedorovitch's. We had spent the whole morning out, had run down a couple of foxes and a number of hares, and had returned home in that supremely agreeable frame of mind which comes over every well-regulated person after a successful day's shooting. It grew dusk. The wind was frolicking over the dark fields and noisily swinging the bare tops of the birches and lime-trees round Lutchinov's house. We reached the house, got off our horses.... On the steps I stood still and looked round: long storm-clouds were creeping heavily over the grey sky; a dark-brown bush was writhing in the wind, and murmuring plaintively; the yellow grass helplessly and forlornly bowed down to the earth; flocks of thrushes were fluttering in the mountain-ashes among the bright, flame-coloured clusters of berries. Among the light brittle twigs of the birch-trees blue-tits hopped whistling. In the village there was the hoarse barking of dogs. I felt melancholy... but it was with a genuine sense of comfort that I walked into the dining-room. The shutters were closed; on a round table, covered with a tablecloth of dazzling whiteness, amid cut-glass decanters of red wine, there were eight lighted candles in silver candlesticks; a fire glowed cheerfully on the hearth, and an old and very stately-looking butler, with a huge bald head, wearing an English dress, stood before another table on which was pleasingly conspicuous a large soup-tureen, encircled by light savoury-smelling steam. In the hall we passed by another venerable man, engaged in icing champagne—'according to the strictest rules of the art.' The dinner was, as is usual in such cases, exceedingly pleasant. We laughed and talked of the incidents of the day's shooting, and recalled with enthusiasm two glorious 'runs.' After dining pretty heartily, we settled comfortably into ample arm-chairs round the fire; a huge silver bowl made its appearance on the table, and in a few minutes the white flame of the burning rum announced our host's agreeable intention 'to concoct a punch.' Piotr Fedoritch was a man of some taste; he was aware, for instance, that nothing has so fatal an influence on the fancy as the cold, steady, pedantic light of a lamp, and so he gave orders that only two candles should be left in the room. Strange half-shadows quivered on the walls, thrown by the fanciful play of the fire in the hearth and the flame of the punch... a soft, exceedingly agreeable sense of soothing comfort replaced in our hearts the somewhat boisterous gaiety that had reigned at dinner.

Conversations have their destinies, like books, as the Latin proverb says, like everything in the world. Our conversation that evening was particularly many-sided and lively. From details it passed to rather serious general questions, and lightly and casually came back to the daily incidents of life.... After chatting a good deal, we suddenly all sank into silence. At such times they say an angel of peace is flying over.

I cannot say why my companions were silent, but I held my tongue because my eyes had suddenly come to rest on three dusty portraits in black wooden frames. The colours were rubbed and cracked in places, but one could still make out the faces. The portrait in the centre was that of a young woman in a white gown with lace ruffles, her hair done up high, in the style of the eighties of last century. On her right, upon a perfectly black background, there stood out the full, round face of a good-natured country gentleman of five-and-twenty, with a broad, low brow, a thick nose, and a good-humoured smile. The French powdered coiffure was utterly out of keeping with the expression of his Slavonic face. The artist had portrayed him wearing a long loose coat of crimson colour with large paste buttons; in his hand he was holding some unlikely-looking flower. The third portrait, which was the work of some other more skilful hand, represented a man of thirty, in the green uniform, with red facings, of the time of Catherine, in a white shirt, with a fine cambric cravat. One hand leaned on a gold-headed cane, the other lay on his shirt front. His dark, thinnish face was full of insolent haughtiness. The fine long eyebrows almost grew together over the pitch-black eyes, about the thin, scarcely discernible lips played an evil smile.

'Why do you keep staring at those faces?' Piotr Fedoritch asked me.

'Oh, I don't know!' I answered, looking at him.

'Would you care to hear a whole story about those three persons?'

'Oh, please tell it,' we all responded with one voice.

Piotr Fedoritch got up, took a candle, carried it to the portraits, and in the tone of a showman at a wild beast show, 'Gentlemen!' he boomed, 'this lady was the adopted child of my great-grandfather, Olga Ivanovna N.N., called Lutchinov, who died forty years ago unmarried. This gentleman,' he pointed to the portrait of a man in uniform, 'served as a lieutenant in the Guards, Vassily Ivanovitch Lutchinov, expired by the will of God in the year seventeen hundred and ninety. And this gentleman, to whom I have not the honour of being related, is a certain Pavel Afanasiitch Rogatchov, serving nowhere, as far as I'm aware.... Kindly take note of the hole in his breast, just on the spot where the heart should be. That hole, you see, a regular three-sided hole, would be hardly likely to have come there by chance.... Now, 'he went on in his usual voice, 'kindly seat yourselves, arm yourselves with patience, and listen.'

Gentlemen! (he began) I come of a rather old family. I am not proud of my descent, seeing that my ancestors were all fearful prodigals. Though that reproach cannot indeed be made against my great-grandfather, Ivan Andreevitch Lutchinov; on the contrary, he had the character of being excessively careful, even miserly—at any rate, in the latter years of his life. He spent his youth in Petersburg, and lived through the reign of Elizabeth. In Petersburg he married, and had by his wife, my great-grandmother, four children, three sons, Vassily, Ivan, and Pavel, my grandfather, and one daughter, Natalia. In addition, Ivan Andreevitch took into his family the daughter of a distant relation, a nameless and destitute orphan—Olga Ivanovna, of whom I spoke just now. My great-grandfather's serfs were probably aware of his existence, for they used (when nothing particularly unlucky occurred) to send him a trifling rent, but they had never seen his face. The village of Lutchinovka, deprived of the bodily presence of its lord, was flourishing exceedingly, when all of a sudden one fine morning a cumbrous old family coach drove into the village and stopped before the elder's hut. The peasants, alarmed at such an unheard-of occurrence, ran up and saw their master and mistress and all their young ones, except the eldest, Vassily, who was left behind in Petersburg. From that memorable day down to the very day of his death, Ivan Andreevitch never left Lutchinovka. He built himself a house, the very house in which I have the pleasure of conversing with you at this moment. He built a church too, and began living the life of a country gentleman. Ivan Andreevitch was a man of immense height, thin, silent, and very deliberate in all his movements. He never wore a dressing-gown, and no one but his valet had ever seen him without powder. Ivan Andreevitch usually walked with his hands clasped behind his back, turning his head at each step. Every day he used to walk in a long avenue of lime-trees, which he had planted with his own hand; and before his death he had the pleasure of enjoying the shade of those trees. Ivan Andreevitch was exceedingly sparing of his words; a proof of his taciturnity is to be found in the remarkable fact that in the course of twenty years he had not said a single word to his wife, Anna Pavlovna. His relations with Anna Pavlovna altogether were of a very curious sort. She directed the whole management of the household; at dinner she always sat beside her husband—he would mercilessly have chastised any one who had dared to say a disrespectful word to her—and yet he never spoke to her, never touched her hand.

Anna Pavlovna was a pale, broken-spirited woman, completely crushed. She prayed every day on her knees in church, and she never smiled. There was a rumour that they had formerly, that is, before they came into the country, lived on very cordial terms with one another. They did say too that Anna Pavlovna had been untrue to her matrimonial vows; that her conduct had come to her husband's knowledge.... Be that as it may, any way Ivan Andreevitch, even when dying, was not reconciled to her. During his last illness, she never left him; but he seemed not to notice her. One night, Anna Pavlovna was sitting in Ivan Andreevitch's bedroom—he suffered from sleeplessness—a lamp was burning before the holy picture. My grandfather's servant, Yuditch, of whom I shall have to say a few words later, went out of the room. Anna Pavlovna got up, crossed the room, and sobbing flung herself on her knees at her husband's bedside, tried to say something—stretched out her hands... Ivan Andreevitch looked at her, and in a faint voice, but resolutely, called, 'Boy!' The servant went in; Anna Pavlovna hurriedly rose, and went back, tottering, to her place.

Ivan Andreevitch's children were exceedingly afraid of him. They grew up in the country, and were witnesses of Ivan Andreevitch's strange treatment of his wife. They all loved Anna Pavlovna passionately, but did not dare to show their love. She seemed of herself to hold aloof from them.... You remember my grandfather, gentlemen; to the day of his death he always walked on tiptoe, and spoke in a whisper... such is the force of habit! My grandfather and his brother, Ivan Ivanovitch, were simple, good-hearted people, quiet and depressed. My grand'tante Natalia married, as you are aware, a coarse, dull-witted man, and all her life she cherished an unutterable, slavish, sheep-like passion for him. But their brother Vassily was not of that sort. I believe I said that Ivan Andreevitch had left him in Petersburg. He was then twelve. His father confided him to the care of a distant kinsman, a man no longer young, a bachelor, and a terrible Voltairean.

Vassily grew up and went into the army. He was not tall, but was well-built and exceedingly elegant; he spoke French excellently, and was renowned for his skilful swordsmanship. He was considered one of the most brilliant young men of the beginning of the reign of Catherine. My father used often to tell me that he had known more than one old lady who could not refer to Vassily Ivanovitch Lutchinov without heartfelt emotion. Picture to yourselves a man endowed with exceptional strength of will, passionate and calculating, persevering and daring, reserved in the extreme, and—according to the testimony of all his contemporaries—fascinatingly, captivatingly attractive. He had no conscience, no heart, no principle, though no one could have called him positively a bad-hearted man. He was vain, but knew how to disguise his vanity, and passionately cherished his independence. When Vassily Ivanovitch would half close his black eyes, smiling affectionately, when he wanted to fascinate any one, they say it was impossible to resist him; and even people, thoroughly convinced of the coldness and hardness of his heart, were more than once vanquished by the bewitching power of his personal influence. He served his own interests devotedly, and made other people, too, work for his advantage; and he was always successful in everything, because he never lost his head, never disdained using flattery as a means, and well understood how to use it.

Ten years after Ivan Andreevitch had settled in the country, he came for a four months' visit to Lutchinovka, a brilliant officer of the Guards, and in that time succeeded positively in turning the head of the grim old man, his father. Strange to say, Ivan Andreevitch listened with enjoyment to his son's stories of some of his *conquests*. His brothers were speechless in his presence, and admired him as a being of a higher order. And Anna Pavlovna herself became almost fonder of him than any of her other children who were so sincerely devoted to her.

Vassily Ivanovitch had come down into the country primarily to visit his people, but also with the second object of getting as much money as possible from his father. He lived sumptuously in the glare of publicity in Petersburg, and had made a mass of debts. He had no easy task to get round his father's miserliness, and though Ivan Andreevitch gave him on this one visit probably far more money than he gave all his other children together during twenty years spent under his roof, Vassily followed the well-known Russian rule, 'Get what you can!'

Ivan Andreevitch had a servant called Yuditch, just such another tall, thin, taciturn person as his master. They say that this man Yuditch was partly responsible for Ivan Andreevitch's strange behaviour with Anna Pavlovna; they say he discovered my great-grandmother's guilty intrigue with one of my great-grandfather's dearest friends. Most likely Yuditch deeply regretted his ill-timed jealousy, for it would be difficult to conceive a more kind-hearted man. His memory is held in veneration by all my house-serfs to this day. My great-grandfather put unbounded confidence in Yuditch. In those days landowners used to have money, but did not put it into the keeping of banks, they kept it themselves in chests, under their floors, and so on. Ivan Andreevitch kept all his money in a great wrought-iron coffer, which stood under the head of his bed. The key of this coffer was intrusted to Yuditch. Every evening as he went to bed Ivan Andreevitch used to bid him open the coffer in his presence, used to tap in turn each of the tightly filled bags with a stick, and every Saturday he would untie the bags with Yuditch, and carefully count over the money. Vassily heard of all these doings, and burned with eagerness to overhaul the sacred coffer. In the course of five or six days he had *softened* Yuditch, that is, he had worked on the old man till, as they say, he worshipped the ground his young master trod on. Having thus duly prepared him, Vassily put on a careworn and gloomy air, for a long while refused to answer Yuditch's questions, and at last told him that he had lost at play, and should make an end of himself if he could not get money somehow. Yuditch broke into sobs, flung himself on his knees before him, begged him to think of God, not to be his own ruin. Vassily locked himself in his room without uttering a word. A little while after he heard some one cautiously knocking at his door; he opened it, and saw in the doorway Yuditch pale and trembling, with the key in his hand. Vassily took in the whole position at a glance. At first, for a long while, he refused to take it. With tears Yuditch repeated, 'Take it, your honour, graciously take it!'... Vassily at last agreed. This took place on Monday. The idea occurred to Vassily to replace the money taken out with broken bits of crockery. He reckoned on Ivan Andreevitch's tapping the bags with his stick, and not noticing the hardly perceptible difference in the sound, and by Saturday he hoped to obtain and to replace the sum in the coffer. As he planned, so he did. His father did not, in fact, notice anything. But by Saturday Vassily had not procured the money; he had hoped to win the sum from a rich neighbour at cards, and instead of that, he lost it all. Meantime, Saturday had come; it came at last to the turn of the bags filled with broken crocks. Picture, gentlemen, the amazement of Ivan Andreevitch!

'What does this mean?' he thundered. Yuditch was silent.

'You stole the money?'

'No, sir.'

'Then some one took the key from you?'

'I didn't give the key to any one.'

'Not to any one? Well then, you are the thief. Confess!'

'I am not a thief, Ivan Andreevitch.'

'Where the devil did these potsherds come from then? So you're deceiving me! For the last time I tell you—confess!' Yuditch bowed his head and folded his hands behind his back.

'Hi, lads!' shrieked Ivan Andreevitch in a voice of frenzy. 'A stick!'

'What, beat... me?' murmured Yuditch.

'Yes, indeed! Are you any better than the rest? You are a thief! O Yuditch! I never expected such dishonesty of you!'

'I have grown grey in your service, Ivan Andreevitch,' Yuditch articulated with effort.

'What have I to do with your grey hairs? Damn you and your service!'

The servants came in.

'Take him, do, and give it him thoroughly.' Ivan Andreevitch's lips were white and twitching. He walked up and down the room like a wild beast in a small cage.

The servants did not dare to carry out his orders.

'Why are you standing still, children of Ham? Am I to undertake him myself, eh?'

Yuditch was moving towards the door....

'Stay!' screamed Ivan Andreevitch. 'Yuditch, for the last time I tell you, I beg you, Yuditch, confess!'

'I can't!' moaned Yuditch.

'Then take him, the sly old fox! Flog him to death! His blood be on my head!' thundered the infuriated old man. The flogging began.... The door suddenly opened, and Vassily came in. He was almost paler than his father, his hands were shaking, his upper lip was lifted, and laid bare a row of even, white teeth.

'I am to blame,' he said in a thick but resolute voice. 'I took the money.'

The servants stopped.

'You! what? you, Vaska! without Yuditch's consent?'

'No!' said Yuditch, 'with my consent. I gave Vassily Ivanovitch the key of my own accord. Your honour, Vassily Ivanovitch! why does your honour trouble?'

'So this is the thief!' shrieked Ivan Andreevitch. 'Thanks, Vassily, thanks! But, Yuditch, I'm not going to forgive you anyway. Why didn't you tell me all about it directly? Hey, you there! why are you standing still? do you too resist my authority? Ah, I'll settle things with you, my pretty gentleman!' he added, turning to Vassily.

The servants were again laying hands on Yuditch....

'Don't touch him!' murmured Vassily through his teeth. The men did not heed him. 'Back!' he shrieked and rushed upon them.... They stepped back.

'Ah! mutiny!' moaned Ivan Andreevitch, and, raising his stick, he approached his son. Vassily leaped back, snatched at the handle of his sword, and bared it to half its length. Every one was trembling. Anna Pavlovna, attracted by the noise, showed herself at the door, pale and scared.

A terrible change passed over the face of Ivan Andreevitch. He tottered, dropped the stick, and sank heavily into an arm-chair, hiding his face in both hands. No one stirred, all stood rooted to the spot, Vassily like the rest. He clutched the steel sword-handle convulsively, and his eyes glittered with a weary, evil light....

'Go, all of you... all, out,' Ivan Andreevitch brought out in a low voice, not taking his hands from his face.

The whole crowd went out. Vassily stood still in the doorway, then suddenly tossed his head, embraced Yuditch, kissed his mother's hand... and two hours later he had left the place. He went back to Petersburg.

In the evening of the same day Yuditch was sitting on the steps of the house serfs' hut. The servants were all round him, sympathising with him and bitterly reproaching their young master.

'That's enough, lads,' he said to them at last, 'give over... why do you abuse him? He himself, the young master, I dare say is not very happy at his audacity....'

In consequence of this incident, Vassily never saw his father again. Ivan Andreevitch died without him, and died probably with such a load of sorrow on his heart as God grant none of us may ever know. Vassily Ivanovitch, meanwhile, went into the world, enjoyed himself in his own way, and squandered money recklessly. How he got hold of the money, I cannot tell for certain. He had obtained a French servant, a very smart and intelligent fellow, Bourcier, by name. This man was passionately attached to him and aided him in all his numerous manoeuvres. I do not intend to relate in detail all the exploits of my grand-uncle; he was possessed of such unbounded daring, such serpent-like resource, such inconceivable wiliness, such a fine and ready wit, that I must own I can understand the complete sway that unprincipled person exercised even over the noblest natures.

Soon after his father's death, in spite of his wiliness, Vassily Ivanovitch was challenged by an injured husband. He fought a duel, seriously wounded his opponent, and was forced to leave the capital; he was banished to his estate, and forbidden to leave it. Vassily Ivanovitch was thirty years old. You may easily imagine, gentlemen, with what feelings he left the brilliant life in the capital that he was used to, and came into the country. They say that he got out of the hooded cart several times on the road, flung himself face downwards in the snow and cried. No one in Lutchinovka would have known him as the gay and charming Vassily Ivanovitch they had seen before. He did not talk to any one; went out shooting from morning to night; endured his mother's timid caresses with undisguised impatience, and was merciless in his ridicule of his brothers, and of their wives (they were both married by that time)....

I have not so far, I think, told you anything about Olga Ivanovna. She had been brought as a tiny baby to Lutchinovka; she all but died on the road. Olga Ivanovna was brought up, as they say, in the fear of God and her betters. It must be admitted that Ivan Andreevitch and Anna Pavlovna both treated her as a daughter. But there lay hid in her soul a faint spark of that fire which burned so fiercely in Vassily Ivanovitch. While Ivan Andreevitch's own children did not dare even to wonder about the cause of the strange, dumb feud between their parents, Olga was from her earliest years disturbed and tormented by Anna Pavlovna's position. Like Vassily, she loved independence; any restriction fretted her. She was devoted with her whole soul to her benefactress; old Lutchinov she detested, and more than once, sitting at table, she shot such black looks at him, that even the servant handing the dishes felt uncomfortable. Ivan Andreevitch never noticed these glances, for he never took the slightest notice of his family.

At first Anna Pavlovna had tried to eradicate this hatred, but some bold questions of Olga's forced her to complete silence. The children of Ivan Andreevitch adored Olga, and the old lady too was fond of her, but not with a very ardent affection.

Long continued grieving had crushed all cheerfulness and every strong feeling in that poor woman; nothing is so clear a proof of Vassily's captivating charm as that he had made even his mother love him passionately. Demonstrations of tenderness on the part of children were not in the spirit of the age, and so it is not to be wondered at that Olga did not dare to express her devotion, though she always kissed Anna Pavlovna's hand with special reverence, when she said good-night to her. Twenty years later, Russian girls began to read romances of the class of *The Adventures of Marquis Glagol, Fanfan and Lolotta, Alexey or the Cottage in the Forest*; they began to play the clavichord and to sing songs in the style of the once very well-known:

'Men like butterflies in sunshine
Flutter round us opening blossoms,' etc.

But in the seventies of last century (Olga Ivanovna was born in 1757) our country beauties had no notion of such accomplishments. It is difficult for us now to form a clear conception of the Russian miss of those days. We can indeed judge from our grandmothers of the degree of culture of girls of noble family in the time of Catherine; but how is one to distinguish what they had gradually gained in the course of their long lives from what they were in the days of their youth?

Olga Ivanovna spoke French a little, but with a strong Russian accent: in her day there was as yet no talk of French emigrants. In fact, with all her fine qualities, she was still pretty much of a savage, and I dare say in the simplicity of her heart, she had more than once chastised some luckless servant girl with her own hands....

Some time before Vassily Ivanovitch's arrival, Olga Ivanovna had been betrothed to a neighbour, Pavel Afanasievitch Rogatchov, a very good-natured and straightforward fellow. Nature had forgotten to put any spice of ill-temper into his composition. His own serfs did not obey him, and would sometimes all go off, down to the least of them, and leave poor Rogatchov without any dinner... but nothing could trouble the peace of his soul. From his childhood he had been stout and indolent, had never been in the government service, and was fond of going to church and singing in the choir. Look, gentlemen, at this round, good-natured face; glance at this mild, beaming smile... don't you really feel it reassuring, yourselves? His father used at long intervals to drive over to Lutchinovka, and on holidays used to bring with him his Pavlusha, whom the little Lutchinovs teased in every possible way. Pavlusha grew up, began driving over to call on Ivan Andreevitch on his own account, fell in love with Olga Ivanovna, and offered her his hand and heart—not to her personally, but to her benefactors. Her benefactors gave their consent. They never even thought of asking Olga Ivanovna whether she liked Rogatchov. In those days, in the words of my grandmother, 'such refinements were not the thing.' Olga soon got used to her betrothed, however; it was impossible not to feel fond of such a gentle and amiable creature. Rogatchov had received no education whatever; his French consisted of the one word *bonjour*, and he secretly considered even that word improper. But some jocose person had taught him the following lines, as a French song: 'Sonitchka, Sonitchka! Ke-voole-voo-de-mwa—I adore you—me-je-ne-pyoo-pa....' This supposed song he always used to hum to himself when he felt in good spirits. His father was also a man of incredible good-nature, always wore a long nankin coat, and whatever was said to him he responded with a smile. From the time of Pavel Afanasievitch's betrothal, both the Rogatchovs, father and son, had been tremendously busy. They had been having their house entirely transformed adding various 'galleries,' talking in a friendly way with the workmen, encouraging them with drinks. They had not yet completed all these additions by the winter; they put off the wedding till the summer. In the summer Ivan Andreevitch died; the wedding was deferred till the following spring. In the winter Vassily Ivanovitch arrived. Rogatchov was presented to him; he received him coldly and contemptuously, and as time went on, he, so alarmed him by his haughty behaviour that poor Rogatchov trembled like a leaf at the very sight of him, was tongue-tied and smiled nervously. Vassily once almost annihilated him altogether—by making him a bet, that he, Rogatchov, was not able to stop smiling. Poor Pavel Afanasievitch almost cried with, embarrassment, but—actually!—a smile, a stupid, nervous smile refused to leave his perspiring face! Vassily toyed deliberately with the ends of his neckerchief, and looked at him with supreme contempt. Pavel Afanasievitch's father heard too of Vassily's presence, and after an interval of a few days—'for the sake of greater formality'—he sallied off to Lutchinovka with the object of 'felicitating our honoured guest on his advent to the halls of his ancestors.' Afanasey Lukitch was famed all over the countryside for his eloquence—that is to say, for his capacity for enunciating without faltering a rather long and complicated speech, with a sprinkling of bookish phrases in it. Alas! on this occasion he did not sustain his reputation; he was even more disconcerted than his son, Pavel Afanasievitch; he mumbled something quite inarticulate, and though he had never been used to taking vodka, he at once drained a glass 'to carry things off'—he found Vassily at lunch,—tried at least to clear his throat with some dignity, and did not succeed in making the slightest sound. On their way home, Pavel Afanasievitch whispered to his parent, 'Well, father?' Afanasey Lukitch responded angrily also in a whisper, 'Don't speak of it!'

The Rogatchovs began to be less frequent visitors at Lutchinovka. Though indeed they were not the only people intimidated by Vassily; he awakened in his own brothers, in their wives, in Anna Pavlovna herself, an instinctive feeling of uneasiness and discomfort... they tried to avoid him in every way they could. Vassily must have noticed this, but apparently had no intention of altering his behaviour to them. Suddenly, at the beginning of the spring, he became once more the charming, attractive person they had known of old...

The first symptom of this sudden transformation was Vassily's unexpected visit to the Rogatchovs. Afanasey Lukitch, in particular, was fairly disconcerted at the sight of Lutchinov's carriage, but his dismay very quickly vanished. Never had Vassily been more courteous and delightful. He took young Rogatchov by the arm, went with him to look at the new buildings, talked to the carpenters, made some suggestions, with his own hands chopped a few chips off with the axe, asked to be shown Afanasey Lukitch's stud horses, himself trotted them out on a halter, and altogether so affected the good-hearted children of the steppes by his gracious affability that they both embraced him more than once. At home, too, Vassily managed, in the course of a few days, to turn every one's head just as before. He contrived all sorts of laughable games, got hold of musicians, invited the ladies and gentlemen of the neighbourhood, told the old ladies the scandals of the town in the most amusing way, flirted a little with the young ones, invented unheard-of diversions, fireworks and such things, in short, he put life into every thing and every one. The melancholy, gloomy house of the Lutchinovs was suddenly converted into a noisy, brilliant, enchanted palace of which the whole countryside was talking. This sudden transformation surprised many and delighted all. All sorts of rumours began to be whispered about. Sagacious persons opined that Vassily Ivanovitch had till then been crushed under the weight of some secret trouble, that he saw chances of returning to the capital... but the true cause of Vassily Ivanovitch's metamorphosis was guessed by no one.

Olga Ivanovna, gentlemen, was rather pretty; though her beauty consisted rather in the extraordinary softness and freshness of her shape, in the quiet grace of her movements than in the strict regularity of her features. Nature had bestowed on her a certain independence; her bringing up—she had grown up without father or mother—had developed in her reserve and determination. Olga did not belong to the class of quiet and tame-spirited young ladies; but only one feeling had reached its full possibilities in her as yet—hatred for her benefactor. Other more feminine passions might indeed flare up in Olga Ivanovna's heart with abnormal and painful violence... but she had not the cold pride, nor the intense strength of will, nor the self-centred egoism, without which any passion passes quickly away.

The first rush of feeling in such half-active, half-passive natures is sometimes extremely violent; but they give way very quickly, especially when it is a question of relentless conformity with accepted principles; they are afraid of consequences.... And yet, gentlemen, I will frankly confess, women of that sort always make the strongest impression on me. ... (At these words the speaker drank a glass of water. Rubbish! rubbish! thought I, looking at his round chin; nothing in the world makes a strong impression on you, my dear fellow!)

Piotr Fedoritch resumed: Gentlemen, I believe in blood, in race. Olga Ivanovna had more blood than, for instance, her foster sister, Natalia. How did this blood show itself, do you ask? Why, in everything; in the lines of her hands, in her lips, in the sound of her voice, in her glance, in her carriage, in her hair, in the very folds of her gown. In all these trifles there lay hid something special, though I am bound to admit that the—how can one express it?—*la distinction*, which had fallen to Olga Pavlovna's share would not have attracted Vassily's notice had he met her in Petersburg. But in the country, in the wilds, she not only caught his attention, she was positively the sole cause of the transformation of which I have just been speaking.

Consider the position. Vassily Ivanovitch liked to enjoy life; he could not but be bored in the country; his brothers were good-natured fellows, but extremely limited people: he had nothing in common with them. His sister, Natalia, with the assistance of her husband, had brought into the world in the course of three years no less than four babies; between her and Vassily was a perfect gulf.... Anna Pavlovna went to church, prayed, fasted, and was preparing herself for death. There remained only Olga—a fresh, shy, pretty girl.... Vassily did not notice her at first... indeed, who does notice a dependant, an orphan girl kept from charity in the house?... One day, at the very beginning of spring, Vassily was walking about the garden, and with his cane slashing off the heads of the dandelions, those stupid yellow flowers, which come out first in such numbers in the meadows, as soon as they begin to grow green. He was walking in the garden in front of the house; he lifted his head, and caught sight of Olga Ivanovna.

She was sitting sideways at the window, dreamily stroking a tabby kitten, who, purring and blinking, nestled on her lap, and with great satisfaction held up her little nose into the rather hot spring sunshine. Olga Ivanovna was wearing a white morning gown, with short sleeves; her bare, pale-pink, girlish shoulders and arms were a picture of freshness and health. A little red cap discreetly restrained her thick, soft, silky curls. Her face was a little flushed; she was only just awake. Her slender, flexible neck bent forward so charmingly; there was such seductive negligence, such modesty in the restful pose of her figure, free from corsets, that

Vassily Ivanovitch (a great connoisseur!) halted involuntarily and peeped in. It suddenly occurred to him that Olga Ivanovna ought not to be left in her primitive ignorance; that she might with time be turned into a very sweet and charming woman. He stole up to the window, stretched up on tiptoe, and imprinted a silent kiss on Olga Ivanovna's smooth, white arm, a little below the elbow.

Olga shrieked and jumped up, the kitten put its tail in the air and leaped into the garden. Vassily Ivanovitch with a smile kept her by the arm.... Olga flushed all over, to her ears; he began to rally her on her alarm... invited her to come a walk with him. But Olga Ivanovna became suddenly conscious of the negligence of her attire, and 'swifter than the swift red deer' she slipped away into the next room.

The very same day Vassily set off to the Rogatchovs. He was suddenly happy and light-hearted. Vassily was not in love with Olga, no! the word 'love' is not to be used lightly.... He had found an occupation, had set himself a task, and rejoiced with the delight of a man of action. He did not even remember that she was his mother's ward, and another man's betrothed. He never for one instant deceived himself; he was fully aware that it was not for her to be his wife.... Possibly there was passion to excuse him—not a very elevated nor noble passion, truly, but still a fairly strong and tormenting passion. Of course he was not in love like a boy; he did not give way to vague ecstasies; he knew very well what he wanted and what he was striving for.

Vassily was a perfect master of the art of winning over, in the shortest time, any one however shy or prejudiced against him. Olga soon ceased to be shy with him. Vassily Ivanovitch led her into a new world. He ordered a clavichord for her, gave her music lessons (he himself played fairly well on the flute), read books aloud to her, had long conversations with her.... The poor child of the steppes soon had her head turned completely. Vassily dominated her entirely. He knew how to tell her of what had been till then unknown to her, and to tell her in a language she could understand. Olga little by little gained courage to express all her feelings to him: he came to her aid, helped her out with the words she could not find, did not alarm her, at one moment kept her back, at another encouraged her confidences.... Vassily busied himself with her education from no disinterested desire to awaken and develop her talents. He simply wanted to draw her a little closer to himself; and he knew too that an innocent, shy, but vain young girl is more easily seduced through the mind than the heart. Even if Olga had been an exceptional being, Vassily would never have perceived it, for he treated her like a child. But as you are aware, gentlemen, there was nothing specially remarkable in Olga. Vassily tried all he could to work on her imagination, and often in the evening she left his side with such a whirl of new images, phrases and ideas in her head that she could not sleep all night, but lay breathing uneasily and turning her burning cheeks from side to side on the cool pillows, or got up, went to the window and gazed fearfully and eagerly into the dark distance. Vassily filled every moment of her life; she could not think of any one else. As for Rogatchov, she soon positively ceased to notice his existence. Vassily had the tact and shrewdness not to talk to Olga in his presence; but he either made him laugh till he was ready to cry, or arranged some noisy entertainment, a riding expedition, a boating party by night with torches and music—he did not in fact let Pavel Afanasievitch have a chance to think clearly.

But in spite of all Vassily Ivanovitch's tact, Rogatchov dimly felt that he, Olga's betrothed and future husband, had somehow become as it were an outsider to her... but in the boundless goodness of his heart, he was afraid of wounding her by reproaches, though he sincerely loved her and prized her affection. When left alone with her, he did not know what to say, and only tried all he could to follow her wishes. Two months passed by. Every trace of self-reliance, of will, disappeared at last in Olga. Rogatchov, feeble and tongue-tied, could be no support to her. She had no wish even to resist the enchantment, and with a sinking heart she surrendered unconditionally to Vassily....

Olga Ivanovna may very likely then have known something of the bliss of love; but it was not for long. Though Vassily—for lack of other occupation—did not drop her, and even attached himself to her and looked after her fondly, Olga herself was so utterly distraught that she found no happiness even in love and yet could not tear herself away from Vassily. She began to be frightened at everything, did not dare to think, could talk of nothing, gave up reading, and was devoured by misery. Sometimes Vassily succeeded in carrying her along with him and making her forget everything and every one. But the very next day he would find her pale, speechless, with icy hands, and a fixed smile on her lips.... There followed a time of some difficulty for Vassily; but no difficulties could dismay him. He concentrated himself like a skilled gambler. He could not in the least rely upon Olga Ivanovna; she was continually betraying herself, turning pale, blushing, weeping... her new part was utterly beyond her powers. Vassily toiled for two: in his restless and boisterous gaiety, only an experienced observer could have detected something strained and feverish. He played his brothers, sisters, the Rogatchovs, the neighbours, like pawns at chess. He was everlastingly on the alert. Not a single glance, a single movement, was lost on him, yet he appeared the most heedless of men.

Every morning he faced the fray, and every evening he scored a victory. He was not the least oppressed by such a fearful strain of activity. He slept four hours out of the twenty-four, ate very little, and was healthy, fresh, and good-humoured.

Meantime the wedding-day was approaching. Vassily succeeded in persuading Pavel Afanasievitch himself of the necessity of delay. Then he despatched him to Moscow to make various purchases, while he was himself in correspondence with friends in Petersburg. He took all this trouble, not so much from sympathy for Olga Ivanovna, as from a natural bent and liking for bustle and agitation.... Besides, he was beginning to be sick of Olga Ivanovna, and more than once after a violent outbreak of passion for her, he would look at her, as he sometimes did at Rogatchov. Lutchinov always remained a riddle to every one. In the coldness of his relentless soul you felt the presence of a strange almost southern fire, and even in the wildest glow of passion a breath of icy chill seemed to come from the man.

Before other people he supported Olga Ivanovna as before. But when they were alone, he played with her like a cat with a mouse, or frightened her with sophistries, or was wearily, malignantly bored, or again flung himself at her feet, swept her away, like a straw in a hurricane... and there was no feigning at such moments in his passion... he really was moved himself.

One day, rather late in the evening, Vassily was sitting alone in his room, attentively reading over the last letters he had received from Petersburg, when suddenly he heard a faint creak at the door, and Olga Ivanovna's maid, Palashka, came in.

'What do you want?' Vassily asked her rather crossly.

'My mistress begs you to come to her.'

'I can't just now. Go along.... Well what are you standing there for?' he went on, seeing that Palashka did not go away.

'My mistress told me to say that she very particularly wants to see you,' she said.

'Why, what's the matter?'

'Would your honour please to see for yourself....'

Vassily got up, angrily flung the letters into a drawer, and went in to Olga Ivanovna. She was sitting alone in a corner, pale and passive.

'What do you want?' he asked her, not quite politely.

Olga looked at him and closed her eyes.

'What's the matter? what is it, Olga?'

He took her hand.... Olga Ivanovna's hand was cold as ice... She tried to speak... and her voice died away. The poor woman had no possible doubt of her condition left her.

Vassily was a little disconcerted. Olga Ivanovna's room was a couple of steps from Anna Pavlovna's bedroom. Vassily cautiously sat down by Olga, kissed and chafed her hands, comforted her in whispers. She listened to him, and silently, faintly, shuddered. In the doorway stood Palashka, stealthily wiping her eyes. In the next room they heard the heavy, even ticking of the clock, and the breathing of some one asleep. Olga Ivanovna's numbness dissolved at last into tears and stifled sobs. Tears are like a storm; after them one is always calmer. When Olga Ivanovna had quieted down a little, and only sobbed convulsively at intervals, like a child, Vassily knelt before her with caresses and tender promises, soothed her completely, gave her something to drink, put her to bed, and went away. He did not undress all night; wrote two or three letters, burnt two or three papers, took out a gold locket containing the portrait of a black-browed, black-eyed woman with a bold, voluptuous face, scrutinised her features slowly, and walked up and down the room pondering.

Next day, at breakfast, he saw with extreme displeasure poor Olga's red and swollen eyes and pale, agitated face. After breakfast he proposed a stroll in the garden to her. Olga followed Vassily, like a submissive sheep. When two hours afterwards she came in from the garden she quite broke down; she told Anna Pavlovna she was unwell, and went to lie down on her bed. During their walk Vassily had, with a suitable show of remorse, informed her that he was secretly married—he was really as much a bachelor as I am. Olga Ivanovna did not fall into a swoon—people don't fall into swoons except on the stage—but she turned all at once stony, though she herself was so far from hoping to marry Vassily Ivanovitch that she was even afraid to think about it. Vassily had begun to explain to her the inevitableness of her parting from him and marrying Rogatchov. Olga Ivanovna looked at him in dumb horror. Vassily talked in a cool, business-like, practical way, blamed himself, expressed his regret, but concluded all his remarks with the following words: 'There's no going back on the past; we've got to act.'

Olga was utterly overwhelmed; she was filled with terror and shame; a dull, heavy despair came upon her; she longed for death, and waited in agony for Vassily's decision.

'We must confess everything to my mother,' he said to her at last.

Olga turned deadly pale; her knees shook under her.

'Don't be afraid, don't be afraid,' repeated Vassily, 'trust to me, I won't desert you... I will make everything right... rely upon me.'

The poor woman looked at him with love... yes, with love, and deep, but hopeless devotion.

'I will arrange everything, everything,' Vassily said to her at parting... and for the last time he kissed her chilly hands....

Next morning—Olga Ivanovna had only just risen from her bed—her door opened... and Anna Pavlovna appeared in the doorway. She was supported by Vassily. In silence she got as far as an arm-chair, and in silence she sat down. Vassily stood at her side. He looked composed; his brows were knitted and his lips slightly parted. Anna Pavlovna, pale, indignant, angry, tried to speak, but her voice failed her. Olga Ivanovna glanced in horror from her benefactress to her lover, with a terrible sinking at her heart... she fell on her knees with a shriek in the middle of the room, and hid her face in her hands.

'Then it's true... is it true?' murmured Anna Pavlovna, and bent down to her.... 'Answer!' she went on harshly, clutching Olga by the arm.

'Mother!' rang out Vassily's brazen voice, 'you promised me not to be hard on her.'

'I want... confess... confess... is it true? is it true?'

'Mother... remember...' Vassily began deliberately.

This one word moved Anna Pavlovna greatly. She leaned back in her chair, and burst into sobs.

Olga Ivanovna softly raised her head, and would have flung herself at the old lady's feet, but Vassily kept her back, raised her from the ground, and led her to another arm-chair. Anna Pavlovna went on weeping and muttering disconnected words....

'Come, mother,' began Vassily, 'don't torment yourself, the trouble may yet be set right.... If Rogatchov...'

Olga Ivanovna shuddered, and drew herself up.

'If Rogatchov,' pursued Vassily, with a meaning glance at Olga Ivanovna, 'imagines that he can disgrace an honourable family with impunity...'

Olga Ivanovna was overcome with horror.

'In my house,' moaned Anna Pavlovna.

'Calm yourself, mother. He took advantage of her innocence, her youth, he—you wish to say something'—he broke off, seeing that Olga made a movement towards him....

Olga Ivanovna sank back in her chair.

'I will go at once to Rogatchov. I will make him marry her this very day. You may be sure I will not let him make a laughing-stock of us....'

'But... Vassily Ivanovitch... you...' whispered Olga.

He gave her a prolonged, cold stare. She sank into silence again.

'Mother, give me your word not to worry her before I return. Look, she is half dead. And you, too, must rest. Rely upon me; I answer for everything; in any case, wait till I return. I tell you again, don't torture her, or yourself, and trust to me.'

He went to the door and stopped. 'Mother,' said he, 'come with me, leave her alone, I beg of you.'

Anna Pavlovna got up, went up to the holy picture, bowed down to the ground, and slowly followed her son. Olga Ivanovna, without a word or a movement, looked after them.

Vassily turned back quickly, snatched her hand, whispered in her ear, 'Rely on me, and don't betray us,' and at once withdrew.... 'Bourcier!' he called, running swiftly down the stairs, 'Bourcier!'

A quarter of an hour later he was sitting in his carriage with his valet.

That day the elder Rogatchov was not at home. He had gone to the district town to buy cloth for the liveries of his servants. Pavel Afanasievitch was sitting in his own room, looking through a collection of faded butterflies. With lifted eyebrows and protruding lips, he was carefully, with a pin, turning over the fragile wings of a 'night sphinx' moth, when he was suddenly aware of a small but heavy hand on his shoulder. He looked round. Vassily stood before him.

'Good-morning, Vassily Ivanovitch,' he said in some amazement.

Vassily looked at him, and sat down on a chair facing him.

Pavel Afanasievitch was about to smile... but he glanced at Vassily, and subsided with his mouth open and his hands clasped.

'Tell me, Pavel Afanasievitch,' said Vassily suddenly, 'are you meaning to dance at your *wedding soon?*'

'I?... soon... of course... for my part... though as you and your sister ... I, for my part, am ready to-morrow even.'

'Very good, very good. You're a very impatient person, Pavel Afanasievitch.'

'How so?'

'Let me tell you,' pursued Vassily Ivanovitch, getting up, 'I know all; you understand me, and I order you without delay to-morrow to marry Olga.'

'Excuse me, excuse me,' objected Rogatchov, not rising from his seat; 'you order me. I sought Olga Ivanovna's hand of myself and there's no need to give me orders.... I confess, Vassily Ivanovitch, I don't quite understand you.'

'You don't understand me?'

'No, really, I don't understand you.'

'Do you give me your word to marry her to-morrow?'

'Why, mercy on us, Vassily Ivanovitch... haven't you yourself put off our wedding more than once? Except for you it would have taken place long ago. And now I have no idea of breaking it off. What is the meaning of your threats, your insistence?'

Pavel Afanasievitch wiped the sweat off his face.

'Do you give me your word? Say yes or no!' Vassily repeated emphatically.

'Excuse me... I will... but...'

'Very good. Remember then... She has confessed everything.'

'Who has confessed?'

'Olga Ivanovna.'

'Why, what has she confessed?'

'Why, what are you pretending to me for, Pavel Afanasievitch? I'm not a stranger to you.'

'What am I pretending? I don't understand you, I don't, I positively don't understand a word. What could Olga Ivanovna confess?'

'What? You are really too much! You know what.'

'May God slay me...'

'No, I'll slay you, if you don't marry her... do you understand?'

'What!...' Pavel Afanasievitch jumped up and stood facing Vassily. 'Olga Ivanovna... you tell me...'

'You're a clever fellow, you are, I must own'—Vassily with a smile patted him on the shoulder—'though you do look so innocent.'

'Good God!... You'll send me out of my mind.... What do you mean, explain, for God's sake!'

Vassily bent down and whispered something in his ear.

Rogatchov cried out, 'What!...!?'

Vassily stamped.

'Olga Ivanovna? Olga?...'

'Yes... your betrothed...'

'My betrothed... Vassily Ivanovitch... she... she... Why, I never wish to see her again,' cried Pavel Afanasievitch. 'Good-bye to her for ever! What do you take me for? I'm being duped... I'm being duped... Olga Ivanovna, how wrong of you, have you no shame?...' (Tears gushed from his eyes.) 'Thanks, Vassily Ivanovitch, thanks very much... I never wish to see her again now! no! no! don't speak of her.... Ah, merciful Heavens! to think I have lived to see this! Oh, very well, very well!'

'That's enough nonsense,' Vassily Ivanovitch observed coldly. 'Remember, you've given me your word: the wedding's to-morrow.'

'No, that it won't be! Enough of that, Vassily Ivanovitch. I say again, what do you take me for? You do me too much honour. I'm humbly obliged. Excuse me.'

'As you please!' retorted Vassily. 'Get your sword.'

'Sword... what for?'

'What for?... I'll show you what for.'

Vassily drew out his fine, flexible French sword and bent it a little against the floor.

'You want... to fight... me?'

'Precisely so.'

'But, Vassily Ivanovitch, put yourself in my place! How can I, only think, after what you have just told me.... I'm a man of honour, Vassily Ivanovitch, a nobleman.'

'You're a nobleman, you're a man of honour, so you'll be so good as to fight with me.'

'Vassily Ivanovitch!'

'You are frightened, I think, Mr. Rogatchov.'

'I'm not in the least frightened, Vassily Ivanovitch. You thought you would frighten me, Vassily Ivanovitch. I'll scare him, you thought, he's a coward, and he'll agree to anything directly... No, Vassily Ivanovitch, I am a nobleman as much as you are, though I've not had city breeding, and you won't succeed in frightening me into anything, excuse me.'

'Very good,' retorted Vassily; 'where is your sword then?'

'Eroshka!' shouted Pavel Afanasievitch. A servant came in.

'Get me the sword—there—you know, in the loft... make haste....'

Eroshka went out. Pavel Afanasievitch suddenly became exceedingly pale, hurriedly took off his dressing-gown, put on a reddish coat with big paste buttons... twisted a cravat round his neck... Vassily looked at him, and twiddled the fingers of his right hand.

'Well, are we to fight then, Pavel Afanasievitch?'

'Let's fight, if we must fight,' replied Rogatchov, and hurriedly buttoned up his shirt.

'Ay, Pavel Afanasievitch, you take my advice, marry her... what is it to you... And believe me, I'll...'

'No, Vassily Ivanovitch,' Rogatchov interrupted him. 'You'll kill me or maim me, I know, but I'm not going to lose my honour; if I'm to die then I must die.'

Eroshka came in, and trembling, gave Rogatchov a wretched old sword in a torn leather scabbard. In those days all noblemen wore swords with powder, but in the steppes they only put on powder twice a year. Eroshka moved away to the door and burst out crying. Pavel Afanasievitch pushed him out of the room.

'But, Vassily Ivanovitch,' he observed with some embarrassment, 'I can't fight with you on the spot: allow me to put off our duel till to-morrow. My father is not at home, and it would be as well for me to put my affairs in order to—to be ready for anything.'

'I see you're beginning to feel frightened again, sir.'

'No, no, Vassily Ivanovitch; but consider yourself...'

'Listen!' shouted Lutchinov, 'you drive me out of patience.... Either give me your word to marry her at once, or fight...or I'll thrash you with my cane like a coward,—do you understand?'

'Come into the garden,' Rogatchov answered through his teeth.

But all at once the door opened, and the old nurse, Efimovna, utterly distracted, broke into the room, fell on her knees before Rogatchov, and clasped his legs....

'My little master!' she wailed, 'my nursling... what is it you are about? Will you be the death of us poor wretches, your honour? Sure, he'll kill you, darling! Only you say the word, you say the word, and we'll make an end of him, the insolent fellow.... Pavel Afanasievitch, my baby-boy, for the love of God!'

A number of pale, excited faces showed in the door...there was even the red beard of the village elder...

'Let me go, Efimovna, let me go!' muttered Rogatchov.

'I won't, my own, I won't. What are you about, sir, what are you about? What'll Afanasey Lukitch say? Why, he'll drive us all out of the light of day.... Why are you fellows standing still? Take the uninvited guest in hand and show him out of the house, so that not a trace be left of him.'

'Rogatchov!' Vassily Ivanovitch shouted menacingly.

'You are crazy, Efimovna, you are shaming me, come, come...' said Pavel Afanasievitch. 'Go away, go away, in God's name, and you others, off with you, do you hear?...'

Vassily Ivanovitch moved swiftly to the open window, took out a small silver whistle, blew lightly... Bourcier answered from close by. Lutchinov turned at once to Pavel Afanasievitch.

'What's to be the end of this farce?'

'Vassily Ivanovitch, I will come to you to-morrow. What can I do with this crazy old woman?...'

'Oh, I see it's no good wasting words on you,' said Vassily, and he swiftly raised his cane...

Pavel Afanasievitch broke loose, pushed Efimovna away, snatched up the sword, and rushed through another door into the garden.

Vassily dashed after him. They ran into a wooden summerhouse, painted cunningly after the Chinese fashion, shut themselves in, and drew their swords. Rogatchov had once taken lessons in fencing, but now he was scarcely capable of drawing a sword properly. The blades crossed. Vassily was obviously playing with Rogatchov's sword. Pavel Afanasievitch was breathless and pale, and gazed in consternation into Lutchinov's face.

Meanwhile, screams were heard in the garden; a crowd of people were running to the summerhouse. Suddenly Rogatchov heard the heart-rending wail of old age...he recognised the voice of his father. Afanasey Lukitch, bare-headed, with dishevelled hair, was running in front of them all, frantically waving his hands....

With a violent and unexpected turn of the blade Vassily sent the sword flying out of Pavel Afanasievitch's hand.

'Marry her, my boy,' he said to him: 'give over this foolery!'

'I won't marry her,' whispered Rogatchov, and he shut his eyes, and shook all over.

Afanasey Lukitch began banging at the door of the summerhouse.

'You won't?' shouted Vassily.

Rogatchov shook his head.

'Well, damn you, then!'

Poor Pavel Afanasievitch fell dead: Lutchinov's sword stabbed him to the heart... The door gave way; old Rogatchov burst into the summerhouse, but Vassily had already jumped out of window...

Two hours later he went into Olga Ivanovna's room... She rushed in terror to meet him... He bowed to her in silence; took out his sword and pierced Pavel Afanasievitch's portrait in the place of the heart. Olga shrieked and fell unconscious on the floor... Vassily went in to Anna Pavlovna. He found her in the oratory. 'Mother,' said he, 'we are avenged.' The poor old woman shuddered and went on praying.

Within a week Vassily had returned to Petersburg, and two years later he came back stricken with paralysis—tongue-tied. He found neither Anna Pavlovna nor Olga living, and soon after died himself in the arms of Yuditch, who fed him like a child, and was the only one who could understand his incoherent stuttering.

1846.

ENOUGH

A FRAGMENT FROM THE NOTE-BOOK OF A DEAD ARTIST

I

II

III

'Enough,' I said to myself as I moved with lagging steps over the steep mountainside down to the quiet little brook. 'Enough,' I said again, as I drank in the resinous fragrance of the pinewood, strong and pungent in the freshness of falling evening. 'Enough,' I said once more, as I sat on the mossy mound above the little brook and gazed into its dark, lingering waters, over which the sturdy reeds thrust up their pale green blades.... 'Enough.'

No more struggle, no more strain, time to draw in, time to keep firm hold of the head and to bid the heart be silent. No more to brood over the voluptuous sweetness of vague, seductive ecstasy, no more to run after each fresh form of beauty, no more to hang over every tremour of her delicate, strong wings.

All has been felt, all has been gone through... I am weary. What to me now that at this moment, larger, fiercer than ever, the sunset floods the heavens as though aflame with some triumphant passion? What to me that, amid the soft peace and glow of evening, suddenly, two paces hence, hidden in a thick bush's dewy stillness, a nightingale has sung his heart out in notes magical as though no nightingale had been on earth before him, and he first sang the first song of first love? All this was, has been, has been again, and is a thousand times repeated—and to think that it will last on so to all eternity—as though decreed, ordained—it stirs one's wrath! Yes... wrath!

IV

Ah, I am grown old! Such thoughts would never have come to me once—in those happy days of old, when I too was aflame like the sunset and my heart sang like the nightingale.

There is no hiding it—everything has faded about me, all life has paled. The light that gives life's colours depth and meaning—the light that comes out of the heart of man—is dead within me.... No, not dead yet—it feebly smoulders on, giving no light, no warmth.

Once, late in the night in Moscow, I remember I went up to the grating window of an old church, and leaned against the faulty pane. It was dark under the low arched roof—a forgotten lamp shed a dull red light upon the ancient picture; dimly could be discerned the lips only of the sacred face—stern and sorrowful. The sullen darkness gathered about it, ready it seemed to crush under its dead weight the feeble ray of impotent light.... Such now in my heart is the light; and such the darkness.

V

And this I write to thee, to thee, my one never forgotten friend, to thee, my dear companion, whom I have left for ever, but shall not cease to love till my life's end.... Alas! thou knowest what parted us. But that I have no wish to speak of now. I have left thee... but even here, in these wilds, in this far-off exile, I am all filled through and through with thee; as of old I am in thy power, as of old I feel the sweet burden of thy hand on my bent head!

For the last time I drag myself from out the grave of silence in which I am lying now. I turn a brief and softened gaze on all my past... our past.... No hope and no return; but no bitterness is in my heart and no regret, and clearer than the blue of heaven, purer than the first snow on mountain tops, fair memories rise up before me like the forms of departed gods.... They come, not thronging in crowds, in slow procession they follow one another like those draped Athenian figures we admired so much—dost thou remember?—in the ancient bas-reliefs in the Vatican.

VI

I have spoken of the light that comes from the heart of man, and sheds brightness on all around him... I long to talk with thee of the time when in my heart too that light burned bright with blessing... Listen... and I will fancy thee sitting before me, gazing up at me with those eyes—so fond yet stern almost in their intentness. O eyes, never to be forgotten! On whom are they fastened now? Who folds in his heart thy glance—that glance that seems to flow from depths unknown even as mysterious springs—like ye, both clear and dark—that gush out into some narrow, deep ravine under the frowning cliffs.... Listen.

VII

It was at the end of March before Annunciation, soon after I had seen thee for the first time and—not yet dreaming of what thou wouldst be to me—already, silently, secretly, I bore thee in my heart. I chanced to cross one of the great rivers of Russia. The ice had not yet broken up, but looked swollen and dark; it was the fourth day of thaw. The snow was melting everywhere—steadily but slowly; there was the running of water on all sides; a noiseless wind strayed in the soft air. Earth and sky alike were steeped in one unvarying milky hue; there was not fog nor was there light; not one object stood out clear in the general whiteness, everything looked both close and indistinct. I left my cart far behind and walked swiftly over the ice of the river, and except the muffled thud of my own steps heard not a sound. I went on enfolded on all sides by the first breath, the first thrill, of early spring... and gradually gaining force with every step, with every movement forwards, a glad tremour sprang up and grew, all uncomprehended within me... it drew me on, it hastened me, and so strong was the flood of gladness within me, that I stood still at last and with questioning eyes looked round me, as I would seek some outer cause of my mood of rapture.... All was soft, white, slumbering, but I lifted my eyes; high in the heavens floated a flock of birds flying back to us.... 'Spring! welcome spring!' I shouted aloud: 'welcome, life and love and happiness!' And at that instance, with sweetly troubling shock, suddenly like a cactus flower thy image blossomed aflame within me, blossomed and grew, bewilderingly fair and radiant, and I knew that I love thee, thee only—that I am all filled full of thee....

VIII

I think of thee... and many other memories, other pictures float before me with thee everywhere, at every turn of my life I meet thee. Now an old Russian garden rises up before me on the slope of a hillside, lighted up by the last rays of the summer sun. Behind the silver poplars peeps out the wooden roof of the manor-house with a thin curl of reddish smoke above the white chimney, and in the fence a little gate stands just ajar, as though some one had drawn it to with faltering hand; and I stand and wait and gaze at that gate and the sand of the garden path—wonder and rapture in my heart. All that I behold seems new and different; over all a breath of some glad, brooding mystery, and already I catch the swift rustle of steps, and I stand intent and alert as a bird with wings folded ready to take flight anew, and my heart burns and shudders in joyous dread before the approaching, the alighting rapture....

IX

Then I see an ancient cathedral in a beautiful, far-off land. In rows kneel the close packed people; a breath of prayerful chill, of something grave and melancholy is wafted from the high, bare roof, from the huge, branching columns. Thou standest at my side, mute, apart, as though knowing me not. Each fold of thy dark cloak hangs motionless as carved in stone. Motionless, too, lie the bright patches cast by the stained windows at thy feet on the worn flags. And lo, violently thrilling the incense-clouded air, thrilling us within, rolled out the mighty flood of the organ's notes... and I saw thee paler, rigid—thy glance caressed me, glided higher and rose heavenwards—while to me it seemed none but an immortal soul could look so, with such eyes...

X

Another picture comes back to me.

No old-world temple subdues us with its stern magnificence; the low walls of a little snug room shut us off from the whole world. What am I saying? We are alone, alone in the whole world; except us two there is nothing living—outside these friendly walls darkness and death and emptiness... It is not the wind that howls without, not the rain streaming in floods; without, Chaos wails and moans, his sightless eyes are weeping. But with us all is peaceful and light and warm and welcoming; something droll, something of childish innocence, like a butterfly—isn't it so?—flutters about us. We nestle close to one another, we lean our heads together and both read a favourite book. I feel the delicate vein beating in thy soft forehead; I hear that thou livest, thou hearest that I am living, thy smile is born on my face before it is on thine, thou makest mute answer to my mute question, thy thoughts, my thoughts are like the two wings of one bird, lost in the infinite blue... the last barriers have fallen—and so soothed, so deepened is our love, so utterly has all apartness vanished that we have no need for word or look to pass between us.... Only to breathe, to breathe together is all we want, to be together and scarcely to be conscious that we are together....

XI

Or last of all, there comes before me that bright September when we walked through the deserted, still flowering garden of a forsaken palace on the bank of a great river—not Russian—under the soft brilliance of the cloudless sky. Oh, how put into words what we felt! The endlessly flowing river, the solitude and peace and bliss, and a kind of voluptuous melancholy, and the thrill of rapture, the unfamiliar monotonous town, the autumn cries of the jackdaws in the high sun-lit treetops, and the tender words and smiles and looks, long, soft, piercing to the very in-most soul, and the beauty, beauty in our lives, about us, on all sides—it is above words. Oh, the bench on which we sat in silence with heads bowed down under the weight of feeling—I cannot forget it till the hour I die! How delicious were those few strangers passing us with brief greetings and kind faces, and the great quiet boats floating by (in one—dost thou remember?—stood a horse pensively gazing at the gliding water), the baby prattle of the tiny ripples by the bank, and the very bark of the distant dogs across the water, the very shouts of the fat officer drilling the red-faced recruits yonder, with outspread arms and knees crooked like grasshoppers!... We both felt that better than those moments nothing in the world had been or would be for us, that all else... But why compare? Enough... enough... Alas! yes: enough.

XII

For the last time I give myself up to those memories and bid them farewell for ever. So a miser gloating over his hoard, his gold, his bright treasure, covers it over in the damp, grey earth; so the wick of a smouldering lamp flickers up in a last bright flare and sinks into cold ash. The wild creature has peeped out from its hole for the last time at the velvet grass, the sweet sun, the blue, kindly waters, and has huddled back into the depths, curled up, and gone to sleep. Will he have glimpses even in sleep of the sweet sun and the grass and the blue kindly water?...

XIII

Sternly, remorselessly, fate leads each of us, and only at the first, absorbed in details of all sorts, in trifles, in ourselves, we are not aware of her harsh hand. While one can be deceived and has no shame in lying, one can live and there is no shame in hoping. Truth, not the full truth, of that, indeed, we cannot speak, but even that little we can reach locks up our lips at once, ties our hands, leads us to 'the No.' Then one way is left a man to keep his feet, not to fall to pieces, not to sink into the mire of self-forgetfulness... of self-contempt,—calmly to turn away from all, to say 'enough!' and folding impotent arms upon the empty breast, to save the last, the sole honour he can attain to, the dignity of knowing his own nothingness; that dignity at which Pascal hints when calling man a thinking reed he says that if the whole universe crushed him, he, that reed, would be higher than the universe, because he would know it was crushing him, and it would know it not. A poor dignity! A sorry consolation! Try your utmost to be penetrated by it, to have faith in it, you, whoever you may be, my poor brother, and there's no refuting those words of menace:

'Life's but a walking shadow, a poor player,
That struts and frets his hour upon the stage
And then is heard no more: it is a tale
Told by an idiot, full of sound and fury
Signifying nothing.'

I quoted these lines from *Macbeth*, and there came back to my mind the witches, phantoms, apparitions.... Alas! no ghosts, no fantastic, unearthly powers are terrible; there are no terrors in the Hoffmann world, in whatever form it appears.... What is terrible is that there is nothing terrible, that the very essence of life is petty, uninteresting and degradingly inane. Once one is soaked through and through with that knowledge, once one has tasted of that bitter, no honey more seems sweet, and even the highest, sweetest bliss, the bliss of love, of perfect nearness, of complete devotion—even that loses all its magic; all its dignity is destroyed by its own pettiness, its brevity. Yes; a man loved, glowed with passion, murmured of eternal bliss, of undying raptures, and lo, no trace is left of the very worm that devoured the last relic of his withered tongue. So, on a frosty day in late autumn, when all is lifeless and dumb in the bleached grey grass, on the bare forest edge, if the sun but come out for an instant from the fog and turn one steady glance on the frozen earth, at once the gnats swarm up on all sides; they sport in the warm rays, bustle, flutter up and down, circle round one another... The sun is hidden—the gnats fall in a feeble shower, and there is the end of their momentary life.

XIV

But are there no great conceptions, no great words of consolation: patriotism, right, freedom, humanity, art? Yes; those words there are, and many men live by them and for them. And yet it seems to me that if Shakespeare could be born again he would have no cause to retract his Hamlet, his Lear. His searching glance would discover nothing new in human life: still the same motley picture—in reality so little complex—would unroll before him in its terrifying sameness. The same credulity and the same cruelty, the same lust of blood, of gold, of filth, the same vulgar pleasures, the same senseless sufferings in the name... why, in the name of the very same shams that Aristophanes jeered at two thousand years ago, the same coarse snares in which the many-headed beast, the multitude, is caught so easily, the same workings of power, the same traditions of slavishness, the same innateness of falsehood—in a word, the same busy squirrel's turning in the same old unchanged wheel.... Again Shakespeare would set Lear repeating his cruel: 'None doth offend,' which in other words means: 'None is without offence.' and he too would say 'enough!' he too would turn away. One thing perhaps, may be: in contrast to the gloomy tragic tyrant Richard, the great poet's ironic genius would want to paint a newer type, the tyrant of to-day, who is almost ready to believe in his own virtue, and sleeps well of nights, or finds fault with too sumptuous a dinner at the very time when his half-crushed victims try to find comfort in picturing him, like Richard, haunted by the phantoms of those he has ruined...

But to what end?

Why prove—picking out, too, and weighing words, smoothing and rounding off phrases—why prove to gnats that they are really gnats?

XV

But art?... beauty?... Yes, these are words of power; they are more powerful, may be, than those I have spoken before. Venus of Milo is, may be, more real than Roman law or the principles of 1789. It may be objected—how many times has the retort been heard!—that beauty itself is relative; that by the Chinese it is conceived as quite other than the European's ideal.... But it is not the relativity of art confounds me; its transitoriness, again its brevity, its dust and ashes—that is what robs me of faith and courage. Art at a given moment is more powerful, may be, than nature; for in nature is no symphony of Beethoven, no picture of Ruysdäel, no poem of Goethe, and only dull-witted pedants or disingenuous chatterers can yet maintain that art is the imitation of nature. But at the end of all, nature is inexorable; she has no need to hurry, and sooner or later she takes her own. Unconsciously and inflexibly obedient to laws, she knows not art, as she knows not freedom, as she knows not good; from all ages moving, from all ages changing, she suffers nothing immortal, nothing unchanging.... Man is her child; but man's work—art—is hostile to her, just because it strives to be unchanging and immortal. Man is the child of nature; but she is the universal mother, and she has no preferences; all that exists in her lap has arisen only at the cost of something else, and must in its time yield its place to something else. She creates destroying, and she cares not whether she creates or she destroys—so long as life be not exterminated, so long as death fall not short of his dues.... And so just as serenely she hides in mould the god-like shape of Phidias's Zeus as the simplest pebble, and gives the vile worm for food the priceless verse of Sophokles. Mankind, 'tis true, jealously aid her in her work of of slaughter; but is it not the same elemental force, the force of nature, that finds vent in the fist of the barbarian recklessly smashing the radiant brow of Apollo, in the savage yells with which he casts in the fire the picture of Apelles? How are we, poor folks, poor artists to be a match for this deaf, dumb, blind force who triumphs not even in her conquests, but goes onward, onward, devouring all things? How stand against those coarse and mighty waves, endlessly, unceasingly moving upward? How have faith in the value and dignity of the fleeting images, that in the dark, on the edge of the abyss, we shape out of dust for an instant?

XVI

All this is true,... but only the transient is beautiful, said Schiller; and nature in the incessant play of her rising, vanishing forms is not averse to beauty. Does not she carefully deck the most fleeting of her children—the petals of the flowers, the wings of the butterfly—in the fairest hues, does she not give them the most exquisite lines? Beauty needs not to live for ever to be eternal—one instant is enough for her. Yes; that may be is true—but only there where personality is not, where man is not, where freedom is not; the butterfly's wing spoiled appears again and again for a thousand years as the same wing of the same butterfly; there sternly, fairly, impersonally necessity completes her circle... but man is not repeated like the butterfly, and the work of his hands, his art, his spontaneous creation once destroyed is lost for ever.... To him alone is it vouchsafed to create... but strange and dreadful it is to pronounce: we are creators... for one hour—as there was, in the tale, a caliph for an hour. In this is our pre-eminence—and our curse; each of those 'creators' himself, even he and no other, even this *I* is, as it were, constructed with certain aim, on lines laid down beforehand; each more or less dimly is aware of his significance, is aware that he is innately something noble, eternal—and lives, and must live in the moment and for the moment.[1] Sit in the mud, my friend, and aspire to the skies! The greatest among us are just those who more deeply than all others have felt this rooted contradiction; though if so, it may be asked, can such words be used as greatest, great?

[Footnote 1: One cannot help recalling here Mephistopheles's words to Faust:—

'Er (Gott) findet sich in einem ewgen Glanze,
Uns hat er in die Finsterniss gebracht—
Und euch taugt einzig Tag und Nacht.'
—AUTHOR'S NOTE.]

XVII

What is to be said of those to whom, with all goodwill, one cannot apply such terms, even in the sense given them by the feeble tongue of man? What can one say of the ordinary, common, second-rate, third-rate toilers—whatsoever they may be—statesmen, men of science, artists—above all, artists? How conjure them to shake off their numb indolence, their weary stupor, how draw them back to the field of battle, if once the conception has stolen into their brains of the nullity of everything human, of every sort of effort that sets before itself a higher aim than the mere winning of bread? By what crowns can they be lured for whom laurels and thorns alike are valueless? For what end will they again face the laughter of 'the unfeeling crowd' or 'the judgment of the fool'—of the old fool who cannot forgive them from turning away from the old bogies—of the young fool who would force them to kneel with him, to grovel with him before the new, lately discovered idols? Why should they go back again into that jostling crowd of phantoms, to that market-place where seller and buyer cheat each other alike, where is noise and clamour, and all is paltry and worthless? Why 'with impotence in their bones' should they struggle back into that world where the peoples, like peasant boys on a holiday, are tussling in the mire for handfuls of empty nutshells, or gape in open-mouthed adoration before sorry tinsel-decked pictures, into that world where only that is living which has no right to live, and each, stifling self with his own shouting, hurries feverishly to an unknown, uncomprehended goal? No... no.... Enough... enough... enough!

The Diary of a Superfluous Man and Other Stories

VILLAGE OF SHEEP'S SPRINGS, *March* 20, 18—.

The doctor has just left me. At last I have got at something definite! For all his cunning, he had to speak out at last. Yes, I am soon, very soon, to die. The frozen rivers will break up, and with the last snow I shall, most likely, swim away … whither? God knows! To the ocean too. Well, well, since one must die, one may as well die in the spring. But isn't it absurd to begin a diary a fortnight, perhaps, before death? What does it matter? And by how much are fourteen days less than fourteen years, fourteen centuries? Beside eternity, they say, all is nothingness—yes, but in that case eternity, too, is nothing. I see I am letting myself drop into metaphysics; that's a bad sign—am I not rather faint-hearted, perchance? I had better begin a description of some sort. It's damp and windy out of doors.

I'm forbidden to go out. What can I write about, then? No decent man talks of his maladies; to write a novel is not in my line; reflections on elevated topics are beyond me; descriptions of the life going on around me could not even interest me; while I am weary of doing nothing, and too lazy to read. Ah, I have it, I will write the story of all my life for myself. A first-rate idea! Just before death it is a suitable thing to do, and can be of no harm to any one. I will begin.

I was born thirty years ago, the son of fairly well-to-do landowners. My father had a passion for gambling; my mother was a woman of character … a very virtuous woman. Only, I have known no woman whose moral excellence was less productive of happiness. She was crushed beneath the weight of her own virtues, and was a source of misery to every one, from herself upwards. In all the fifty years of her life, she never once took rest, or sat with her hands in her lap; she was for ever fussing and bustling about like an ant, and to absolutely no good purpose, which cannot be said of the ant. The worm of restlessness fretted her night and day. Only once I saw her perfectly tranquil, and that was the day after her death, in her coffin. Looking at her, it positively seemed to me that her face wore an expression of subdued amazement; with the half-open lips, the sunken cheeks, and meekly-staring eyes, it seemed expressing, all over, the words, 'How good to be at rest!' Yes, it is good, good to be rid, at last, of the wearing sense of life, of the persistent, restless consciousness of existence! But that's neither here nor there.

I was brought up badly and not happily. My father and mother both loved me; but that made things no better for me. My father was not, even in his own house, of the slightest authority or consequence, being a man openly abandoned to a shameful and ruinous vice; he was conscious of his degradation, and not having the strength of will to give up his darling passion, he tried at least, by his invariably amiable and humble demeanour and his unswerving submissiveness, to win the condescending consideration of his exemplary wife. My mother certainly did bear her trial with the superb and majestic long-suffering of virtue, in which there is so much of egoistic pride. She never reproached my father for anything, gave him her last penny, and paid his debts without a word. He exalted her as a paragon to her face and behind her back, but did not like to be at home, and caressed me by stealth, as though he were afraid of contaminating me by his presence. But at such times his distorted features were full of such kindness, the nervous grin on his lips was replaced by such a touching smile, and his brown eyes, encircled by fine wrinkles, shone with such love, that I could not help pressing my cheek to his, which was wet and warm with tears. I wiped away those tears with my handkerchief, and they flowed again without effort, like water from a brimming glass. I fell to crying, too, and he comforted me, stroking my back and kissing me all over my face with his quivering lips. Even now, more than twenty years after his death, when I think of my poor father, dumb sobs rise into my throat, and my heart beats as hotly and bitterly and aches with as poignant a pity as if it had long to go on beating, as if there were anything to be sorry for!

My mother's behaviour to me, on the contrary, was always the same, kind, but cold. In children's books one often comes across such mothers, sermonising and just. She loved me, but I did not love her. Yes! I fought shy of my virtuous mother, and passionately loved my vicious father.

But enough for to-day. It's a beginning, and as for the end, whatever it may be, I needn't trouble my head about it. That's for my illness to see to.

March 21.

To-day it is marvellous weather. Warm, bright; the sunshine frolicking gaily on the melting snow; everything shining, steaming, dripping; the sparrows chattering like mad things about the drenched, dark hedges.

Sweetly and terribly, too, the moist air frets my sick chest. Spring, spring is coming! I sit at the window and look across the river into the open country. O nature! nature! I love thee so, but I came forth from thy womb good for nothing—not fit even for life. There goes a cock-sparrow, hopping along with outspread wings; he chirrups, and every note, every ruffled feather on his little body, is breathing with health and strength....

What follows from that? Nothing. He is well and has a right to chirrup and ruffle his wings; but I am ill and must die—that's all. It's not worth while to say more about it. And tearful invocations to nature are mortally absurd. Let us get back to my story.

I was brought up, as I have said, very badly and not happily. I had no brothers or sisters. I was educated at home. And, indeed, what would my mother have had to occupy her, if I had been sent to a boarding-school or a government college? That's what children are for—that their parents may not be bored. We lived for the most part in the country, and sometimes went to Moscow. I had tutors and teachers, as a matter of course; one, in particular, has remained in my memory, a dried-up, tearful German, Rickmann, an exceptionally mournful creature, cruelly maltreated by destiny, and fruitlessly consumed by an intense pining for his far-off fatherland. Sometimes, near the stove, in the fearful stuffiness of the close ante-room, full of the sour smell of stale kvas, my unshaved man-nurse, Vassily, nicknamed Goose, would sit, playing cards with the coachman, Potap, in a new sheepskin, white as foam, and superb tarred boots, while in the next room Rickmann would sing, behind the partition—

Herz, mein Herz, warum so traurig?
Was bekümmert dich so sehr?
'Sist ja schön im fremden Lande—
Herz, mein Herz—was willst du mehr?'

After my father's death we moved to Moscow for good. I was twelve years old. My father died in the night from a stroke. I shall never forget that night. I was sleeping soundly, as children generally do; but I remember, even in my sleep, I was aware of a heavy gasping noise at regular intervals. Suddenly I felt some one taking hold of my shoulder and poking me. I opened my eyes and saw my nurse. 'What is it?' 'Come along, come along, Alexey Mihalitch is dying.' ... I was out of bed and away like a mad thing into his bedroom. I looked: my father was lying with his head thrown back, all red, and gasping fearfully. The servants were crowding round the door with terrified faces; in the hall some one was asking in a thick voice: 'Have they sent for the doctor?' In the yard outside, a horse was being led from the stable, the gates were creaking, a tallow candle was burning in the room on the floor, my mother was there, terribly upset, but not oblivious of the proprieties, nor of her own dignity. I flung myself on my father's bosom, and hugged him, faltering: 'Papa, papa...' He lay motionless, screwing up his eyes in a strange way. I looked into his face—an unendurable horror caught my breath; I shrieked with terror, like a roughly captured bird—they picked me up and carried me away. Only the day before, as though aware his death was at hand, he had caressed me so passionately and despondently.

A sleepy, unkempt doctor, smelling strongly of spirits, was brought. My father died under his lancet, and the next day, utterly stupefied by grief, I stood with a candle in my hands before a table, on which lay the dead man, and listened senselessly to the bass sing-song of the deacon, interrupted from time to time by the weak voice of the priest. The tears kept streaming over my cheeks, my lips, my collar, my shirt-front. I was dissolved in tears; I watched persistently, I watched intently, my father's rigid face, as though I expected something of him; while my mother slowly bowed down to the ground, slowly rose again, and pressed her fingers firmly to her forehead, her shoulders, and her chest, as she crossed herself. I had not a single idea in my head; I was utterly numb, but I felt something terrible was happening to me.... Death looked me in the face that day and took note of me.

We moved to Moscow after my father's death for a very simple cause: all our estate was sold up by auction for debts—that is, absolutely all, except one little village, the one in which I am at this moment living out my magnificent existence. I must admit that, in spite of my youth at the time, I grieved over the sale of our home, or rather, in reality, I grieved over our garden. Almost my only bright memories are associated with our garden. It was there that one mild spring evening I buried my best friend, an old bob-tailed, crook-pawed dog, Trix. It was there that, hidden in the long grass, I used to eat stolen apples—sweet, red, Novgorod apples they were. There, too, I saw for the first time, among the ripe raspberry bushes, the housemaid Klavdia, who, in spite of her turned-up nose and habit of giggling in her kerchief, aroused such a tender passion in me that I could hardly breathe, and stood faint and tongue-tied in her presence; and once at Easter, when it came to her turn to kiss my seignorial hand, I almost flung myself at her feet to kiss her down-trodden goat-skin slippers. My God! Can all that be twenty years ago? It seems not long ago that I used to ride on my shaggy chestnut pony along the old fence of our garden, and, standing up in the stirrups, used to pick the two-coloured poplar leaves. While a man is living he is not conscious of his own life; it becomes audible to him, like a sound, after the lapse of time.

Oh, my garden, oh, the tangled paths by the tiny pond! Oh, the little sandy spot below the tumbledown dike, where I used to catch gudgeons! And you tall birch-trees, with long hanging branches, from beyond which came floating a peasant's mournful song, broken by the uneven jolting of the cart, I send you my last farewell!... On parting with life, to you alone I stretch out my hands. Would I might once more inhale the fresh, bitter fragrance of the wormwood, the sweet scent of the mown buckwheat in the fields of my native place! Would I might once more hear far away the modest tinkle of the cracked bell of our parish church; once more lie in the cool shade under the oak sapling on the slope of the familiar ravine; once more watch the moving track of the wind, flitting, a dark wave over the golden grass of our meadow!... Ah, what's the good of all this? But I can't go on to-day. Enough till to-morrow.

March 22.

To-day it's cold and overcast again. Such weather is a great deal more suitable. It's more in harmony with my task. Yesterday, quite inappropriately, stirred up a multitude of useless emotions and memories within me. This shall not occur again. Sentimental out-breaks are like liquorice; when first you suck it, it's not bad, but afterwards it leaves a very nasty taste in the mouth. I will set to work simply and serenely to tell the story of my life. And so, we moved to Moscow....

But it occurs to me, is it really worth while to tell the story of my life?

No, it certainly is not.... My life has not been different in any respect from the lives of numbers of other people. The parental home, the university, the government service in the lower grades, retirement, a little circle of friends, decent poverty, modest pleasures, unambitious pursuits, moderate desires—kindly tell me, is that new to any one? And so I will not tell the story of my life, especially as I am writing for my own pleasure; and if my past does not afford even me any sensation of great pleasure or great pain, it must be that there is nothing in it deserving of attention. I had better try to describe my own character to myself. What manner of man am I?... It may be observed that no one asks me that question—admitted. But there, I'm dying, by Jove!—I'm dying, and at the point of death I really think one may be excused a desire to find out what sort of a queer fish one really was after all.

Thinking over this important question, and having, moreover, no need whatever to be too bitter in my expressions in regard to myself, as people are apt to be who have a strong conviction of their valuable qualities, I must admit one thing. I was a man, or perhaps I should say a fish, utterly superfluous in this world. And that I propose to show to-morrow, as I keep coughing to-day like an old sheep, and my nurse, Terentyevna, gives me no peace: 'Lie down, my good sir,' she says, 'and drink a little tea.'... I know why she keeps on at me: she wants some tea herself. Well! she's welcome! Why not let the poor old woman extract the utmost benefit she can from her master at the last ... as long as there is still the chance?

March 23.

Winter again. The snow is falling in flakes. Superfluous, superfluous.... That's a capital word I have hit on. The more deeply I probe into myself, the more intently I review all my past life, the more I am convinced of the strict truth of this expression. Superfluous—that's just it. To other people that term is not applicable.... People are bad, or good, clever, stupid, pleasant, and disagreeable; but superfluous ... no. Understand me, though: the universe could get on without those people too... no doubt; but uselessness is not their prime characteristic, their most distinctive attribute, and when you speak of them, the word 'superfluous' is not the first to rise to your lips. But I ... there's nothing else one can say about me; I'm superfluous and nothing more. A supernumerary, and that's all. Nature, apparently, did not reckon on my appearance, and consequently treated me as an unexpected and uninvited guest. A facetious gentleman, a great devotee of preference, said very happily about me that I was the forfeit my mother had paid at the game of life. I am speaking about myself calmly now, without any bitterness.... It's all over and done with! Throughout my whole life I was constantly finding my place taken, perhaps because I did not look for my place where I should have done. I was apprehensive, reserved, and irritable, like all sickly people. Moreover, probably owing to excessive self-consciousness, perhaps as the result of the generally unfortunate cast of my personality, there existed between my thoughts and feelings, and the expression of those feelings and thoughts, a sort of inexplicable, irrational, and utterly insuperable barrier; and whenever I made up my mind to overcome this obstacle by force, to break down this barrier, my gestures, the expression of my face, my whole being, took on an appearance of painful constraint. I not only seemed, I positively became unnatural and affected. I was conscious of this myself, and hastened to shrink back into myself. Then a terrible commotion was set up within me. I analysed myself to the last thread, compared myself with others, recalled the slightest glances, smiles, words of the people to whom I had tried to open myself out, put the worst construction on everything, laughed vindictively at my own pretensions to 'be like every one else,'—and suddenly, in the midst of my laughter, collapsed utterly into gloom, sank into absurd dejection, and then began again as before—went round and round, in fact, like a squirrel on its wheel. Whole days were spent in this harassing, fruitless exercise. Well now, tell me, if you please, to whom and for what is such a man of use? Why did this happen to me? what was the reason of this trivial fretting at myself?—who knows? who can tell?

I remember I was driving once from Moscow in the diligence. It was a good road, but the driver, though he had four horses harnessed abreast, hitched on another, alongside of them. Such an unfortunate, utterly useless, fifth horse—fastened somehow on to the front of the shaft by a short stout cord, which mercilessly cuts his shoulder, forces him to go with the most unnatural action, and gives his whole body the shape of a comma—always arouses my deepest pity. I remarked to the driver that I thought we might on this occasion have got on without the fifth horse.... He was silent a moment, shook his head, lashed the horse a dozen times across his thin back and under his distended belly, and with a grin responded: 'Ay, to be sure; why do we drag him along with us? What the devil's he for?' And here am I too dragged along. But, thank goodness, the station is not far off.

Superfluous.... I promised to show the justice of my opinion, and I will carry out my promise. I don't think it necessary to mention the thousand trifles, everyday incidents and events, which would, however, in the eyes of any thinking man, serve as irrefutable evidence in my support—I mean, in support of my contention. I had better begin straight away with one rather important incident, after which probably there will be no doubt left of the accuracy of the term superfluous. I repeat: I do not intend to indulge in minute details, but I cannot pass over in silence one rather serious and significant fact, that is, the strange behaviour of my friends (I too used to have friends) whenever I met them, or even called on them. They used to seem ill at ease; as they came to meet me, they would give a not quite natural smile, look, not into my eyes nor at my feet, as some people do, but rather at my cheeks, articulate hurriedly, 'Ah! how are you, Tchulkaturin!' (such is the surname fate has burdened me with) or 'Ah! here's Tchulkaturin!' turn away at once and positively remain stockstill for a little while after, as though trying to recollect something. I used to notice all this, as I am not devoid of penetration and the faculty of observation; on the whole I am not a fool; I sometimes even have ideas come into my head that are amusing, not absolutely commonplace. But as I am a superfluous man with a padlock on my inner self, it is very painful for me to express my idea, the more so as I know beforehand that I shall express it badly. It positively sometimes strikes me as extraordinary the way people manage to talk, and so simply and freely.... It's marvellous, really, when you think of it. Though, to tell the truth, I too, in spite of my padlock, sometimes have an itch to talk. But I did actually utter words only in my youth; in riper years I almost always pulled myself up. I would murmur to myself: 'Come, we'd better hold our tongue.' And I was still. We are all good hands at being silent; our women especially are great in that line. Many an exalted Russian young lady keeps silent so strenuously that the spectacle is calculated to produce a faint shudder and cold sweat even in any one prepared to face it. But that's not the point, and it's not for me to criticise others. I proceed to my promised narrative.

A few years back, owing to a combination of circumstances, very insignificant in themselves, but very important for me, it was my lot to spend six months in the district town O——. This town is all built on a slope, and very uncomfortably built, too. There are reckoned to be about eight hundred inhabitants in it, of exceptional poverty; the houses are hardly worthy of the name; in the chief street, by way of an apology for a pavement, there are here and there some huge white slabs of rough-hewn limestone, in consequence of which even carts drive round it instead of through it. In the very middle of an astoundingly dirty square rises a diminutive yellowish edifice with black holes in it, and in these holes sit men in big caps making a pretence of buying and selling. In this place there is an extraordinarily high striped post sticking up into the air, and near the post, in the interests of public order, by command of the authorities, there is kept a cartload of yellow hay, and one government hen struts to and fro. In short, existence in the town of O—— is truly delightful. During the first days of my stay in this town, I almost went out of my mind with boredom. I ought to say of myself that, though I am, no doubt, a superfluous man, I am not so of my own seeking; I'm morbid myself, but I can't bear anything morbid.... I'm not even averse to happiness— indeed, I've tried to approach it right and left.... And so it is no wonder that I too can be bored like any other mortal. I was staying in the town of O—— on official business.

Terentyevna has certainly sworn to make an end of me. Here's a specimen of our conversation:—

TERENTYEVNA. Oh—oh, my good sir! what are you for ever writing for? it's bad for you, keeping all on writing.

I. But I'm dull, Terentyevna.

SHE. Oh, you take a cup of tea now and lie down. By God's mercy you'll get in a sweat and maybe doze a bit.

I. But I'm not sleepy.
SHE. Ah, sir! why do you talk so? Lord have mercy on you! Come, lie down, lie down; it's better for you.
I. I shall die any way, Terentyevna!
SHE. Lord bless us and save us!... Well, do you want a little tea?
I. I shan't live through the week, Terentyevna!
SHE. Eh, eh! good sir, why do you talk so?... Well, I'll go and heat the samovar.
Oh, decrepit, yellow, toothless creature! Am I really, even in your eyes, not a man?
March 24. Sharp frost.
On the very day of my arrival in the town of O——, the official business, above referred to, brought me into contact with a certain Kirilla Matveitch Ozhogin, one of the chief functionaries of the district; but I became intimate, or, as it is called, 'friends' with him a fortnight later. His house was in the principal street, and was distinguished from all the others by its size, its painted roof, and the lions on its gates, lions of that species extraordinarily resembling unsuccessful dogs, whose natural home is Moscow. From those lions alone, one might safely conclude that Ozhogin was a man of property. And so it was; he was the owner of four hundred peasants; he entertained in his house all the best society of the town of O——, and had a reputation for hospitality. At his door was seen the mayor with his wide chestnut-coloured droshky and pair—an exceptionally bulky man, who seemed as though cut out of material that had been laid by for a long time. The other officials, too, used to drive to his receptions: the attorney, a yellowish, spiteful creature; the land surveyor, a wit—of German extraction, with a Tartar face; the inspector of means of communication—a soft soul, who sang songs, but a scandalmonger; a former marshal of the district—a gentleman with dyed hair, crumpled shirt front, and tight trousers, and that lofty expression of face so characteristic of men who have stood on trial. There used to come also two landowners, inseparable friends, both no longer young and indeed a little the worse for wear, of whom the younger was continually crushing the elder and putting him to silence with one and the same reproach. 'Don't you talk, Sergei Sergeitch! What have you to say? Why, you spell the word cork with two *k*'s in it.... Yes, gentlemen,' he would go on, with all the fire of conviction, turning to the bystanders, 'Sergei Sergeitch spells it not cork, but kork.' And every one present would laugh, though probably not one of them was conspicuous for special accuracy in orthography, while the luckless Sergei Sergeitch held his tongue, and with a faint smile bowed his head. But I am forgetting that my hours are numbered, and am letting myself go into too minute descriptions. And so, without further beating about the bush,—Ozhogin was married, he had a daughter, Elizaveta Kirillovna, and I fell in love with this daughter.
Ozhogin himself was a commonplace person, neither good-looking nor bad-looking; his wife resembled an aged chicken; but their daughter had not taken after her parents. She was very pretty and of a bright and gentle disposition. Her clear grey eyes looked out kindly and directly from under childishly arched brows; she was almost always smiling, and she laughed too, pretty often. Her fresh voice had a very pleasant ring; she moved freely, rapidly, and blushed gaily. She did not dress very stylishly, only plain dresses suited her. I did not make friends quickly as a rule, and if I were at ease with any one from the first—which, however, scarcely ever occurred—it said, I must own, a great deal for my new acquaintance. I did not know at all how to behave with women, and in their presence I either scowled and put on a morose air, or grinned in the most idiotic way, and in my embarrassment turned my tongue round and round in my mouth. With Elizaveta Kirillovna, on the contrary, I felt at home from the first moment. It happened in this way.
I called one day at Ozhogin's before dinner, asked, 'At home?' was told, 'The master's at home, dressing; please to walk into the drawing-room.' I went into the drawing-room; I beheld standing at the window, with her back to me, a girl in a white gown, with a cage in her hands. I was, as my way was, somewhat taken aback; however, I showed no sign of it, but merely coughed, for good manners. The girl turned round quickly, so quickly that her curls gave her a

slap in the face, saw me, bowed, and with a smile showed me a little box half full of seeds. 'You don't mind?' I, of course, as is the usual practice in such cases, first bowed my head, and at the same time rapidly crooked my knees, and straightened them out again (as though some one had given me a blow from behind in the legs, a sure sign of good breeding and pleasant, easy manners), and then smiled, raised my hand, and softly and carefully brandished it twice in the air. The girl at once turned away from me, took a little piece of board out of the cage, began vigorously scraping it with a knife, and suddenly, without changing her attitude, uttered the following words: 'This is papa's parrot.... Are you fond of parrots?' 'I prefer siskins,' I answered, not without some effort. 'I like siskins, too; but look at him, isn't he pretty? Look, he's not afraid.' (What surprised me was that I was not afraid.) 'Come closer. His name's Popka.' I went up, and bent down. 'Isn't he really sweet?' She turned her face to me; but we were standing so close together, that she had to throw her head back to get a look at me with her clear eyes. I gazed at her; her rosy young face was smiling all over in such a friendly way that I smiled too, and almost laughed aloud with delight. The door opened; Mr. Ozhogin came in. I promptly went up to him, and began talking to him very unconstrainedly. I don't know how it was, but I stayed to dinner, and spent the whole evening with them; and next day the Ozhogins' footman, an elongated, dull-eyed person, smiled upon me as a friend of the family when he helped me off with my overcoat.

To find a haven of refuge, to build oneself even a temporary nest, to feel the comfort of daily intercourse and habits, was a happiness I, a superfluous man, with no family associations, had never before experienced. If anything about me had had any resemblance to a flower, and if the comparison were not so hackneyed, I would venture to say that my soul blossomed from that day. Everything within me and about me was suddenly transformed! My whole life was lighted up by love, the whole of it, down to the paltriest details, like a dark, deserted room when a light has been brought into it. I went to bed, and got up, dressed, ate my breakfast, and smoked my pipe—differently from before. I positively skipped along as I walked, as though wings were suddenly sprouting from my shoulders. I was not for an instant, I remember, in uncertainty with regard to the feeling Elizaveta Kirillovna inspired in me. I fell passionately in love with her from the first day, and from the first day I knew I was in love. During the course of three weeks I saw her every day. Those three weeks were the happiest time in my life; but the recollection of them is painful to me. I can't think of them alone; I cannot help dwelling on what followed after them, and the intensest bitterness slowly takes possession of my softened heart.

When a man is very happy, his brain, as is well known, is not very active. A calm and delicious sensation, the sensation of satisfaction, pervades his whole being; he is swallowed up by it; the consciousness of personal life vanishes in him—he is in beatitude, as badly educated poets say. But when, at last, this 'enchantment' is over, a man is sometimes vexed and sorry that, in the midst of his bliss, he observed himself so little; that he did not, by reflection, by recollection, redouble and prolong his feelings ... as though the 'beatific' man had time, and it were worth his while to reflect on his sensations! The happy man is what the fly is in the sunshine. And so it is that, when I recall those three weeks, it is almost impossible for me to retain in my mind any exact and definite impression, all the more so as during that time nothing very remarkable took place between us.... Those twenty days are present to my imagination as something warm, and young, and fragrant, a sort of streak of light in my dingy, greyish life. My memory becomes all at once remorselessly clear and trustworthy, only from the instant when, to use the phrase of badly-educated writers, the blows of destiny began to fall upon me.

Yes, those three weeks.... Not but what they have left some images in my mind. Sometimes when it happens to me to brood a long while on that time, some memories suddenly float up out of the darkness of the past—like stars which suddenly come out against the evening sky to meet the eyes straining to catch sight of them. One country walk in a wood has remained particularly distinct in my memory. There were four of us, old Madame Ozhogin, Liza, I, and a certain Bizmyonkov, a petty official of the town of O——, a light-haired, good-natured, and harmless person. I shall have more to say of him later. Mr. Ozhogin had stayed at home; he had a headache, from sleeping too long. The day was exquisite; warm and soft. I must observe that pleasure-gardens and picnic-parties are not to the taste of the average Russian. In district towns, in the so-called public gardens, you never meet a living soul at any time of the year; at the most, some old woman sits sighing and moaning on a green garden seat, broiling in the sun, not far from a sickly tree—and that, only if there is no greasy little bench in the gateway near. But if there happens to be a scraggy birchwood in the neighbourhood of the town, tradespeople and even officials gladly make excursions thither on Sundays and holidays, with samovars, pies, and melons; set all this abundance on the dusty grass, close by the road, sit round, and eat and drink tea in the sweat of their brows till evening. Just such a wood there was at that time a mile and a half from the town of O—-. We repaired there after dinner, duly drank our fill of tea, and then all four began to wander about the wood. Bizmyonkov walked with Madame Ozhogin on his arm, I with Liza on mine. The day was already drawing to evening. I was at that time in the very fire of first love (not more than a fortnight had passed since our first meeting), in that condition of passionate and concentrated adoration, when your whole soul innocently and unconsciously follows every movement of the beloved being, when you can never have enough of her presence, listen enough to her voice, when you smile with the look of a child convalescent after sickness, and a man of the smallest experience cannot fail at the first glance to recognise a hundred yards off what is the matter with you. Till that day I had never happened to have Liza on my arm. We walked side by side, stepping slowly over the green grass. A light breeze, as it were, flitted about us between the white stems of the birches, every now and then flapping the ribbon of her hat into my face. I incessantly followed her eyes, until at last she turned gaily to me and we both smiled at each other. The birds were chirping approvingly above us, the blue sky peeped caressingly at us through the delicate foliage. My head was going round with excess of bliss. I hasten to remark, Liza was not a bit in love with me. She liked me; she was never shy with any one, but it was not reserved for me to trouble her childlike peace of mind. She walked arm in arm with me, as she would with a brother. She was seventeen then.... And meanwhile, that very evening, before my eyes, there began that soft inward ferment which precedes the metamorphosis of the child into the woman.... I was witness of that transformation of the whole being, that guileless bewilderment, that agitated dreaminess; I was the first to detect the sudden softness of the glance, the sudden ring in the voice—and oh, fool! oh, superfluous man! For a whole week I had the face to imagine that I, I was the cause of this transformation! This was how it happened.

We walked rather a long while, till evening, and talked little. I was silent, like all inexperienced lovers, and she, probably, had nothing to say to me. But she seemed to be pondering over something, and shook her head in a peculiar way, as she pensively nibbled a leaf she had picked. Sometimes she started walking ahead, so resolutely...then all at once stopped, waited for me, and looked round with lifted eyebrows and a vague smile. On the previous evening we had read together. *The Prisoner of the Caucasus*. With what eagerness she had listened to me, her face propped in both hands, and her bosom pressed against the table! I began to speak of our yesterday's reading; she flushed, asked me whether I had given the parrot any hemp-seed before starting, began humming some little song aloud, and all at once was silent again. The copse ended on one side in a rather high and abrupt precipice; below coursed a winding stream, and beyond it, over an immense expanse, stretched the boundless prairies, rising like waves, spreading wide like a table-cloth, and broken here and there by ravines. Liza and I were the first to come out at the edge of the wood; Bizmyonkov and the elder lady were behind. We came out, stood still, and involuntarily we both half shut our eyes; directly facing us, across a lurid mist, the vast, purple sun was setting. Half the sky was flushed and glowing; red rays fell slanting on the meadows, casting a crimson reflection even on the side of the ravines in shadow, lying in gleams of fire on the stream, where it was not hidden under the overhanging bushes, and, as it were, leaning on the bosom of the precipice and the copse. We stood, bathed in the blazing brilliance. I am not capable of describing all the impassioned solemnity of this scene. They say that by a blind man the colour red is imagined as the sound of a trumpet. I don't know how far this comparison is correct, but really there was something of a challenge in this glowing gold of the evening air, in the crimson flush on sky and earth. I uttered a cry of rapture and at once turned to Liza. She was looking straight at the sun. I remember the sunset glow was reflected in little points of fire in her eyes. She was overwhelmed, deeply moved. She made no response to my exclamation; for a long while she stood, not stirring, with drooping head.... I held out my hand to her; she turned away from me, and suddenly burst into tears. I looked at her with secret, almost delighted amazement.... The voice of Bizmyonkov was heard a couple of yards off. Liza quickly wiped her tears and looked with a faltering smile at me. The elder lady came out of the copse leaning on the arm of her flaxen-headed escort; they, in their turn, admired the view. The old lady addressed some question to Liza, and I could not help shuddering, I remember, when her daughter's broken voice, like cracked glass, sounded in reply. Meanwhile the sun had set, and the afterglow began to fade. We turned back. Again I took Liza's arm in mine. It was still light in the wood, and I could clearly distinguish her features. She was confused, and did not raise her eyes. The flush that overspread her face did not vanish; it was as though she were still standing in the rays of the setting sun.... Her hand scarcely touched my arm. For a long while I could not frame a sentence; my heart was beating so violently. Through the trees there was a glimpse of the carriage in the distance; the coachman was coming at a walking pace to meet us over the soft sand of the road.

'Lizaveta Kirillovna,' I brought out at last, 'what did you cry for?'

'I don't know,' she answered, after a short silence. She looked at me with her soft eyes still wet with tears—her look struck me as changed, and she was silent again.

'You are very fond, I see, of nature,' I pursued. That was not at all what I meant to say, and the last words my tongue scarcely faltered out to the end. She shook her head. I could not utter another word.... I was waiting for something ... not an avowal—how was that possible? I waited for a confiding glance, a question.... But Liza looked at the ground, and kept silent. I repeated once more in a whisper: 'Why was it?' and received no reply. She had grown, I saw that, ill at ease, almost ashamed.

A quarter of an hour later we were sitting in the carriage driving to the town. The horses flew along at an even trot; we were rapidly whirled along through the darkening, damp air. I suddenly began talking, more than once addressing first Bizmyonkov, and then Madame Ozhogin. I did not look at Liza, but I could see that from her corner in the carriage her eyes did not once rest on me. At home she roused herself, but would not read with me, and soon went off to bed. A turning-point, that turning-point I have spoken of, had been reached by her. She had ceased to be a little girl, she too had begun ... like me ... to wait for something. She had not long to wait.

But that night I went home to my lodgings in a state of perfect ecstasy. The vague half presentiment, half suspicion, which had been arising within me, had vanished. The sudden constraint in Liza's manner towards me I ascribed to maidenly bashfulness, timidity.... Hadn't I read a thousand times over in many books that the first appearance of love always agitates and alarms a young girl? I felt supremely happy, and was already making all sorts of plans in my head.

If some one had whispered in my ear then: 'You're raving, my dear chap! that's not a bit what's in store for you. What's in store for you is to die all alone, in a wretched little cottage, amid the insufferable grumbling of an old hag who will await your death with impatience to sell your boots for a few coppers...'!

Yes, one can't help saying with the Russian philosopher—'How's one to know what one doesn't know?'

Enough for to-day.

March 25. A white winter day.

I have read over what I wrote yesterday, and was all but tearing up the whole manuscript. I think my story's too spun out and too sentimental. However, as the rest of my recollections of that time presents nothing of a pleasurable character, except that peculiar sort of consolation which Lermontov had in view when he said there is pleasure and pain in irritating the sores of old wounds, why not indulge oneself? But one must know where to draw the line. And so I will continue without any sort of sentimentality.

During the whole of the week after the country excursion, my position was in reality in no way improved, though the change in Liza became more noticeable every day. I interpreted this change, as I have said before, in the most favourable way for me.... The misfortune of solitary and timid people—who are timid from self-consciousness—is just that, though they have eyes and indeed open them wide, they see nothing, or see everything in a false light, as though through coloured spectacles. Their own ideas and speculations trip them up at every step. At the commencement of our acquaintance, Liza behaved confidingly and freely with me, like a child; perhaps there may even have been in her attitude to me something more than mere childish liking.... But after this strange, almost instantaneous change had taken place in her, after a period of brief perplexity, she felt constrained in my presence; she unconsciously turned away from me, and was at the same time melancholy and dreamy.... She was waiting ... for what? She did not know ... while I ... I, as I have said above, was delighted at this change.... Yes, by God, I was ready to expire, as they say, with rapture. Though I am prepared to allow that any one else in my place might have been deceived.... Who is free from vanity? I need not say that all this was only clear to me in the course of time, when I had to lower my clipped and at no time over-powerful wings.

The misunderstanding that had arisen between Liza and me lasted a whole week—and there is nothing surprising in that: it has been my lot to be a witness of misunderstandings that have lasted for years and years. Who was it said, by the way, that truth alone is powerful? Falsehood is just as living as truth, if not more so. To be sure, I recollect that even during that week I felt from time to time an uneasy gnawing astir within me ... but solitary people like me, I say again, are as incapable of understanding what is going on within them as what is taking place before their eyes. And, besides, is love a natural feeling? Is it natural for man to love? Love is a sickness; and for sickness there is no law. Granting that there was at times an unpleasant pang in my heart; well, everything inside me was turned upside down. And how is one to know in such circumstances, what is all right and what is all wrong? and what is the cause, and what the significance, of each separate symptom? But, be that as it may, all these misconceptions, presentiments, and hopes were shattered in the following manner.

One day—it was in the morning about twelve o'clock—I had hardly entered Mr. Ozhogin's hall, when I heard an unfamiliar, mellow voice in the drawing-room, the door opened, and a tall and slim man of five-and-twenty appeared in the doorway, escorted by the master of the house. He rapidly put on a military overcoat which lay on the slab, and took cordial leave of Kirilla Matveitch. As he brushed past me, he carelessly touched his foraging cap, and vanished with a clink of his spurs.

'Who is that?' I asked Ozhogin.

'Prince N., 'the latter responded, with a preoccupied face; 'sent from Petersburg to collect recruits. But where are the servants?' he went on in a tone of annoyance; 'no one handed him his coat.'

We went into the drawing-room.

'Has he been here long?' I inquired.

'Arrived yesterday evening, I'm told. I offered him a room here, but he refused. He seems a very nice fellow, though.'

'Has he been long with you?'

'About an hour. He asked me to introduce him to Olimpiada Nikitishna.'

'And did you introduce him?'

'Of course.'

'And Lizaveta Kirillovna, too, did he ...'

'He made her acquaintance, too, of course.'

I was silent for a space.

'Has he come here for long, do you know?'

'Yes, I believe he has to be here for a fortnight.'

And Kirilla Matveitch hurried away to dress. I walked several times up and down the drawing-room. I don't recollect that Prince N.'s arrival made any special impression on me at the time, except that feeling of hostility which usually possesses us on the appearance of any new person in our domestic circle. Possibly there was mingled with this feeling something too of the nature of envy—of a shy and obscure person from Moscow towards a brilliant officer from Petersburg. 'The prince,' I mused, 'is an upstart from the capital; he'll look down upon us....' I had not seen him for more than an instant, but I had had time to perceive that he was good-looking, clever, and at his ease. After pacing the room for some time, I stopped at last before a looking-glass, pulled a comb out of my pocket, gave a picturesque carelessness to my hair, and, as sometimes happens, became suddenly absorbed in the contemplation of my own face. I remember my attention centred anxiously about my nose; the soft and undefined outlines of that feature afforded me no great satisfaction, when suddenly in the dark depths of the sloping mirror, which reflected almost the whole room, the door opened, and the slender figure of Liza appeared. I don't know why I did not stir, and kept the same expression on my face. Liza craned her head forward, looked intently at me, and raising her eyebrows, biting her lips, and holding her breath as any one does who is glad at not being noticed, she cautiously drew back and stealthily drew the door to after her. The door creaked slightly. Liza started and stood rooted to the spot... I still kept from stirring ... she pulled the handle again and vanished. There was no possibility of doubt: the expression of Liza's face at the sight of my figure, that expression in which nothing could be detected except a desire to get away again successfully, to escape a disagreeable interview, the quick flash of delight I had time to catch in her eyes when she fancied she really had managed to creep away unnoticed—it all spoke too clearly; that girl did not love me. For a long, long while I could not take my eyes off that motionless, dumb door, which was once more a patch of white in the looking-glass. I tried to smile at my own long face—dropped my head, went home again, and flung myself on the sofa. I felt extraordinarily heavy at heart, so much so that I could not cry ... and, besides, what was there to cry about...? 'Is it possible?' I repeated incessantly, lying, as though I were murdered, on my back with my hands folded on my breast—'is it possible?'...Don't you think that's rather good, that 'is it possible?'

March 26. Thaw.

When, next day, after long hesitation and with a low sinking at my heart, I went into the Ozhogins' familiar drawing-room, I was no longer the same man as they had known during the last three weeks. All my old peculiarities, which I had begun to get over, under the influence of a new feeling, reappeared and took possession of me, like proprietors returning to their house. People of my sort are usually guided, not so much by positive facts, as by their own impressions: I, who no longer ago than the day before had been dreaming of the 'raptures of love returned,' was that day no less convinced of my 'unhappiness,' and was absolutely despairing, though I was not myself able to find any rational ground for my despair. I could not as yet be jealous of Prince N., and whatever his qualities might be, his mere arrival was not sufficient to extinguish Liza's good-will towards me at once.... But stay, was there any good-will on her part? I recalled the past. 'What of the walk in the wood?' I asked myself. 'What of the expression of her face in the glass?' 'But,' I went on, 'the walk in the wood, I think ... Fie on me! my God, what a wretched creature I am!' I said at last, out loud. Of such sort were the unphrased, incomplete thoughts that went round and round a thousand times over in a monotonous whirl in my head. I repeat, I went back to the Ozhogins' the same hypersensitive, suspicious, constrained creature I had been from my childhood up....

I found the whole family in the drawing-room; Bizmyonkov was sitting there, too, in a corner. Every one seemed in high good-humour; Ozhogin, in particular, positively beamed, and his first word was to tell me that Prince N. had spent the whole of the previous evening with them. Liza gave me a tranquil greeting. 'Oh,' said I to myself; 'now I understand why you're in such spirits.' I must own the prince's second visit puzzled me. I had not anticipated it. As a rule fellows like me anticipate everything in the world, except what is bound to occur in the natural order of things; I sulked and put on the air of an injured but magnanimous person; I tried to punish Liza by showing my displeasure, from which one must conclude I was not yet completely desperate after all. They do say that in some cases when one is really loved, it's positively of use to torment the adored one; but in my position it was indescribably stupid. Liza, in the most innocent way, paid no attention to me. No one but Madame Ozhogin observed my solemn taciturnity, and she inquired anxiously after my health. I replied, of course, with a bitter smile, that I was thankful to say I was perfectly well. Ozhogin continued to expatiate on the subject of their visitor; but noticing that I responded reluctantly, he addressed himself principally to Bizmyonkov, who was listening to him with great attention, when a servant suddenly came in, announcing the arrival of Prince N. Our host jumped up and ran to meet him; Liza, upon whom I at once turned an eagle eye, flushed with delight, and made as though she would move from her seat. The prince came in, all agreeable perfume, gaiety, cordiality….

As I am not composing a romance for a gentle reader, but simply writing for my own amusement, it stands to reason I need not make use of the usual dodges of our respected authors. I will say straight out without further delay that Liza fell passionately in love with the prince from the first day she saw him, and the prince fell in love with her too—partly from having nothing to do, and partly from a propensity for turning women's heads, and also owing to the fact that Liza really was a very charming creature. There was nothing to be wondered at in their falling in love with each other. He had certainly never expected to find such a pearl in such a wretched shell (I am alluding to the God-forsaken town of O——), and she had never in her wildest dreams seen anything in the least like this brilliant, clever, fascinating aristocrat.

After the first courtesies, Ozhogin introduced me to the prince, who was very affable in his behaviour to me. He was as a rule very affable with every one; and in spite of the immeasurable distance between him and our obscure provincial circle, he was clever enough to avoid being a source of constraint to any one, and even to make a show of being on our level, and only living at Petersburg, as it were, by accident.

That first evening…. Oh, that first evening! In our happy days of childhood our teachers used to describe and set up before us as an example the manly fortitude of the young Spartan, who, having stolen a fox and hidden it under his tunic, without uttering one shriek let it devour all his entrails, and so preferred death itself to disgrace…. I can find no better comparison for my indescribable sufferings during the evening on which I first saw the prince by Liza's side. My continual forced smile and painful vigilance, my idiotic silence, my miserable and ineffectual desire to get away—all that was doubtless something truly remarkable in its own way. It was not one wild beast alone gnawing at my vitals; jealousy, envy, the sense of my own insignificance, and helpless hatred were torturing me. I could not but admit that the prince really was a very agreeable young man…. I devoured him with my eyes; I really believe I forgot to blink as usual, as I stared at him. He talked not to Liza alone, but all he said was of course really for her. He must have felt me a great bore. He most likely guessed directly that it was a discarded lover he had to deal with, but from sympathy for me, and also a profound sense of my absolute harmlessness, he treated me with extraordinary gentleness. You can fancy how this wounded me! In the course of the evening I tried, I remember, to smooth over my mistake. I positively (don't laugh at me, whoever you may be, who chance to look through these lines—especially as it was my last illusion…) … I, positively, in the midst of my different sufferings, imagined all of a sudden that Liza wanted to punish me for my haughty coldness at the beginning of my visit, that she was angry with me and only flirting with the prince from pique.... I seized my opportunity and with a meek but gracious smile, I went up to her, and muttered—'Enough, forgive me, not that I'm afraid ...' and suddenly, without awaiting her reply, I gave my features an extraordinarily cheerful and free-and-easy expression, with a set grin, passed my hand above my head in the direction of the ceiling (I wanted, I remember, to set my cravat straight), and was even on the point of pirouetting round on one foot, as though to say, 'All is over, I am happy, let's all be happy,'—I did not, however, execute this manoeuvre, as I was afraid of losing my balance, owing to an unnatural stiffness in my knees.... Liza failed absolutely to understand me; she looked in my face with amazement, gave a hasty smile, as though she wanted to get rid of me as quickly as possible, and again approached the prince. Blind and deaf as I was, I could not but be inwardly aware that she was not in the least angry, and was not annoyed with me at that instant: she simply never gave me a thought. The blow was a final one. My last hopes were shattered with a crash, just as a block of ice, thawed by the sunshine of spring, suddenly falls into tiny morsels. I was utterly defeated at the first skirmish, and, like the Prussians at Jena, lost everything at once in one day. No, she was not angry with me!...

Alas, it was quite the contrary! She too—I saw that—was being swept off her feet by the torrent. Like a young tree, already half torn from the bank, she bent eagerly over the stream, ready to abandon to it for ever the first blossom of her spring and her whole life. A man whose fate it has been to be the witness of such a passion, has lived through bitter moments if he has loved himself and not been loved. I shall for ever remember that devouring attention, that tender gaiety, that innocent self-oblivion, that glance, still a child's and already a woman's, that happy, as it were flowering smile that never left the half-parted lips and glowing cheeks.... All that Liza had vaguely foreshadowed during our walk in the wood had come to pass now—and she, as she gave herself up utterly to love, was at once stiller and brighter, like new wine, which ceases to ferment because its full maturity has come....

I had the fortitude to sit through that first evening and the subsequent evenings ... all to the end! I could have no hope of anything. Liza and the prince became every day more devoted to each other ... But I had absolutely lost all sense of personal dignity, and could not tear myself away from the spectacle of my own misery. I remember one day I tried not to go, swore to myself in the morning that I would stay at home, and at eight o'clock in the evening (I usually set off at seven) leaped up like a madman, put on my hat, and ran breathless into Kirilla Matveitch's drawing-room. My position was excessively absurd. I was obstinately silent; sometimes for whole days together I did not utter a sound. I was, as I have said already, never distinguished for eloquence; but now everything I had in my mind took flight, as it were, in the presence of the prince, and I was left bare and bereft. Besides, when I was alone, I set my wretched brain working so hard, slowly going over everything I had noticed or surmised during the preceding day, that when I went back to the Ozhogins' I scarcely had energy left to observe again. They treated me considerately, as a sick person; I saw that. Every morning I adopted some new, final resolution, for the most part painfully hatched in the course of a sleepless night. At one time I made up my mind to have it out with Liza, to give her friendly advice ... but when I chanced to be alone with her, my tongue suddenly ceased to work, froze as it were, and we both, in great discomfort, waited for the entrance of some third person. Another time I meant to run away, of course for ever, leaving my beloved a letter full of reproaches, and I even one day began this letter; but the sense of justice had not yet quite vanished in me. I realised that I had no right to reproach any one for anything, and I flung what I had written in the fire. Then I suddenly offered myself up wholly as a sacrifice, gave Liza my benediction, praying for her happiness, and smiled in meek and friendly fashion from my corner at the prince. But the cruel-hearted lovers not only never thanked me for my self-sacrifice, they never even noticed me, and were, apparently, quite ready to dispense with my smiles and my blessings....

Then, in wrath, I suddenly flew into quite the opposite mood. I swore to myself, wrapping my cloak about me like a Spaniard, to rush out from some dark corner and stab my lucky rival, and with brutal glee I imagined Liza's despair.... But, in the first place, such corners were few in the town of O——; and, secondly—the wooden fence, the street lamp, the policeman in the distance.... No! in such corners it was somehow far more suitable to sell buns and oranges than to shed human blood. I must own that, among other means of deliverance, as I very vaguely expressed it in my colloquies with myself, I did entertain the idea of having recourse to Ozhogin himself ... of calling the attention of that nobleman to the perilous situation of his daughter, and the mournful consequences of her indiscretion....

I even once began speaking to him on a certain delicate subject; but my remarks were so indirect and misty, that after listening and listening to me, he suddenly, as it were, waking up, rubbed his hand rapidly and vigorously all over his face, not sparing his nose, gave a snort, and walked away from me. It is needless to say that in resolving on this step I persuaded myself that I was acting from the most disinterested motives, was desirous of the general welfare, and was doing my duty as a friend of the house.... But I venture to think that even had Kirilla Matveitch not cut short my outpourings, I should in any case not have had courage to finish my monologue. At times I set to work with all the solemnity of some sage of antiquity, weighing the qualities of the prince; at times I comforted myself with the hope that it was all of no consequence, that Liza would recover her senses, that her love was not real love ... oh, no! In short, I know no idea that I did not worry myself with at that time. There was only one resource which never, I candidly admit, entered my head: I never once thought of taking my life. Why it did not occur to me I don't know.... Possibly, even then, I had a presentiment I should not have long to live in any case.

It will be readily understood that in such unfavourable circumstances my manner, my behaviour with people, was more than ever marked by unnaturalness and constraint. Even Madame Ozhogin—that creature dull-witted from her birth up—began to shun me, and at times did not know in what way to approach me. Bizmyonkov, always polite and ready to do services, avoided me. I fancied even at that time that I had in him a companion in misfortune—that he too loved Liza. But he never responded to my hints, and altogether showed a reluctance to converse with me. The prince behaved in a very friendly way to him; the prince, one might say, respected him. Neither Bizmyonkov nor I was any obstacle to the prince and Liza; but he did not shun them as I did, nor look savage nor injured—and readily joined them when they desired it. It is true that on such occasions he was not conspicuous for any special mirthfulness; but his good-humour had always been somewhat subdued in character.

In this fashion about a fortnight passed by. The prince was not only handsome and clever: he played the piano, sang, sketched fairly well, and was a good hand at telling stories. His anecdotes, drawn from the highest circles of Petersburg society, always made a great impression on his audience, all the more so from the fact that he seemed to attach no importance to them....

The consequence of this, if you like, simple accomplishment of the prince's was that in the course of his not very protracted stay in the town of O—— he completely fascinated all the neighbourhood. To fascinate us poor dwellers in the steppes is at all times a very easy task for any one coming from higher spheres. The prince's frequent visits to the Ozhogins (he used to spend his evenings there) of course aroused the jealousy of the other worthy gentry and officials of the town. But the prince, like a clever person and a man of the world, never neglected a single one of them; he called on all of them; to every married lady and every unmarried miss he addressed at least one flattering phrase, allowed them to feed him on elaborately solid edibles, and to make him drink wretched wines with magnificent names; and conducted himself, in short, like a model of caution and tact. Prince N—— was in general a man of lively manners, sociable and genial by inclination, and in this case incidentally from prudential motives also; he could not fail to be a complete success in everything.

Ever since his arrival, all in the house had felt that the time had flown by with unusual rapidity; everything had gone off beautifully. Papa Ozhogin, though he pretended that he noticed nothing, was doubtless rubbing his hands in private at the idea of such a son-in-law. The prince, for his part, managed matters with the utmost sobriety and discretion, when, all of a sudden, an unexpected incident….

Till to-morrow. To-day I'm tired. These recollections irritate me even at the edge of the grave. Terentyevna noticed to-day that my nose has already begun to grow sharp; and that, they say, is a bad sign.

March 27. Thaw continuing.

Things were in the position described above: the prince and Liza were in love with each other; the old Ozhogins were waiting to see what would come of it; Bizmyonkov was present at the proceedings—there was nothing else to be said of him. I was struggling like a fish on the ice, and watching with all my might,—I remember that at that time I set myself the task of preventing Liza at least from falling into the snares of a seducer, and consequently began paying particular attention to the maidservants and the fateful 'back stairs'—though, on the other hand, I often spent whole nights in dreaming with what touching magnanimity I would one day hold out a hand to the betrayed victim and say to her, 'The traitor has deceived thee; but I am thy true friend … let us forget the past and be happy!'—when sudden and glad tidings overspread the whole town. The marshal of the district proposed to give a great ball in honour of their respected guest, on his private estate Gornostaevka. All the official world, big and little, of the town of O—— received invitations, from the mayor down to the apothecary, an excessively emaciated German, with ferocious pretensions to a good Russian accent, which led him into continually and quite inappropriately employing racy colloquialisms…. Tremendous preparations were, of course, put in hand. One purveyor of cosmetics sold sixteen dark-blue jars of pomatum, which bore the inscription *à la jesmin.* The young ladies provided themselves with tight dresses, agonising in the waist and jutting out sharply over the stomach; the mammas put formidable erections on their heads by way of caps; the busy papas were half dead with the bustle. The longed-for day arrived at last. I was among those invited. From the town to Gornostaevka was reckoned between seven and eight miles. Kirilla Matveitch offered me a seat in his coach; but I refused…. In the same way children, who have been punished, wishing to pay their parents out, refuse their favourite dainties at table. Besides, I felt that my presence would be felt as a constraint by Liza. Bizmyonkov took my place. The prince drove in his own carriage, and I in a wretched little droshky, hired for an immense sum for this solemn occasion. I am not going to describe that ball. Everything about it was just as it always is. There was a band, with trumpets extraordinarily out of tune, in the gallery; there were country gentlemen, greatly flustered, with their inevitable families, mauve ices, viscous lemonade; servants in boots trodden down at heel and knitted cotton gloves; provincial lions with spasmodically contorted faces, and so on and so on. And all this little world was revolving round its sun—round the prince. Lost in the crowd, unnoticed even by the young ladies of eight-and-forty, with red pimples on their brows and blue flowers on the top of their heads, I stared incessantly, first at the prince, then at Liza. She was very charmingly dressed and very pretty that evening. They only twice danced together (it is true, he danced the mazurka with her); but it seemed, to me at least, that there was a sort of secret, continuous communication between them. Even while not looking at her, while not speaking to her, he was still, as it were, addressing her, and her alone. He was handsome and brilliant and charming with other people—for her sake only. She was apparently conscious that she was the queen of the ball, and that she was loved. Her face at once beamed with childlike delight and innocent pride, and was suddenly illuminated by another, deeper feeling. Happiness radiated from her. I observed all this…. It was not the first time I had watched them…. At first this wounded me intensely; afterwards it, as it were, touched me; but, finally, it infuriated me. I suddenly felt extraordinarily wrathful, and, I remember, was extraordinarily delighted at this new sensation, and even conceived a certain respect for myself. 'We'll show them we're not crushed yet,' I said to myself. When the first inviting notes of the mazurka sounded, I looked about me with composure, and with a cool and easy air approached a long-faced young lady with a red and shiny nose, a mouth that stood awkwardly open, as though it had come unbuttoned, and a scraggy neck that recalled the handle of a bass-viol. I went up to her, and, with a perfunctory scrape of my heels, invited her to the dance. She was wearing a dress of faded rosebud pink, not full-blown rose colour; on her head quivered a striped and dejected beetle of some sort on a thick bronze pin; and altogether this lady was, if one may so express it, soaked through and through with a sort of sour ennui and inveterate lack of success. From the very commencement of the evening she had not once stirred from her seat; no one had thought of asking her to dance. One flaxen-headed youth of sixteen had, through lack of a partner, been on the point of addressing this lady, and had taken a step in her direction, but had thought better of it, stared at her, and hurriedly dived into the crowd. You can fancy with what joyful amazement she agreed to my proposal! I led her in triumph right across the ballroom, picked out two chairs, and sat down with her in the ring of the mazurka, among ten couples, almost opposite the prince, who had, of course, been offered the first place. The prince, as I have said already, was dancing with Liza. Neither I nor my partner was disturbed by invitations; consequently, we had plenty of time for conversation. To tell the truth, my partner was not conspicuous for her capacity for the utterance of words in consecutive speech; she used her mouth principally for the achievement of a strange downward smile such as I had never till then beheld; while she raised her eyes upward, as though some unseen force were pulling her face in two. But I did not feel her lack of eloquence. Happily I felt full of wrath, and my partner did not make me shy. I fell to finding fault with everything and every one in the world, with especial emphasis on town-bred youngsters and Petersburg dandies; and went to such lengths at last, that my partner gradually ceased smiling, and instead of turning her eyes upward, began suddenly—from astonishment, I suppose—to squint, and that so strangely, as though she had for the first time observed the fact that she had a nose on her face. And one of the lions, referred to above, who was sitting next me, did not once take his eyes off me; he positively turned to me with the expression of an actor on the stage, who has waked up in an unfamiliar place, as though he would say, 'Is it really you!' While I poured forth this tirade, I still, however, kept watch on the prince and Liza. They were continually invited; but I suffered less when they were both dancing; and even when they were sitting side by side, and smiling as they talked to each other that sweet smile which hardly leaves the faces of happy lovers, even then I was not in such torture; but when Liza flitted across the room with some desperate dandy of an hussar, while the prince with her blue gauze scarf on his knees followed her dreamily with his eyes, as though delighting in his conquest;—then, oh! then, I went through intolerable agonies, and in my anger gave vent to such spiteful observations, that the pupils of my partner's eyes simply fastened on her nose!

Meanwhile the mazurka was drawing to a close. They were beginning the figure called *la confidente*. In this figure the lady sits in the middle of a circle, chooses another lady as her confidant, and whispers in her ear the name of the gentleman with whom she wishes to dance. Her partner conducts one after another of the dancers to her; but the lady, who is in the secret, refuses them, till at last the happy man fixed on beforehand arrives. Liza sat in the middle of the circle and chose the daughter of the host, one of those young ladies of whom one says, 'God help them!'... The prince proceeded to discover her choice. After presenting about a dozen young men to her in vain (the daughter of the house refused them all with the most amiable of smiles), he at last turned to me.

Something extraordinary took place within me at that instant; I, as it were, twitched all over, and would have refused, but got up and went along. The prince conducted me to Liza.... She did not even look at me; the daughter of the house shook her head in refusal, the prince turned to me, and, probably incited by the goose-like expression of my face, made me a deep bow. This sarcastic bow, this refusal, transmitted to me through my triumphant rival, his careless smile, Liza's indifferent inattention, all this lashed me to frenzy…. I moved up to the prince and whispered furiously, 'You think fit to laugh at me, it seems?'

The prince looked at me with contemptuous surprise, took my arm again, and making a show of re-conducting me to my seat, answered coldly, 'I?'

'Yes, you!' I went on in a whisper, obeying, however—that is to say, following him to my place; 'you; but I do not intend to permit any empty-headed Petersburg up-start——'

The prince smiled tranquilly, almost condescendingly, pressed my arm, whispered, 'I understand you; but this is not the place; we will have a word later,' turned away from me, went up to Bizmyonkov, and led him up to Liza. The pale little official turned out to be the chosen partner. Liza got up to meet him.

Sitting beside my partner with the dejected beetle on her head, I felt almost a hero. My heart beat violently, my breast heaved gallantly under my starched shirt front, I drew deep and hurried breaths, and suddenly gave the local lion near me such a magnificent glare that there was an involuntary quiver of his foot in my direction. Having disposed of this person, I scanned the whole circle of dancers…. I fancied two or three gentlemen were staring at me with some perplexity; but, in general, my conversation with the prince had passed unnoticed…. My rival was already back in his chair, perfectly composed, and with the same smile on his face. Bizmyonkov led Liza back to her place. She gave him a friendly bow, and at once turned to the prince, as I fancied, with some alarm. But he laughed in response, with a graceful wave of his hand, and must have said something very agreeable to her, for she flushed with delight, dropped her eyes, and then bent them with affectionate reproach upon him.

The heroic frame of mind, which had suddenly developed in me, had not disappeared by the end of the mazurka; but I did not indulge in any more epigrams or 'quizzing.' I contented myself with glancing occasionally with gloomy severity at my partner, who was obviously beginning to be afraid of me, and was utterly tongue-tied and continuously blinking by the time I placed her under the protection of her mother, a very fat woman with a red cap on her head. Having consigned the scared maiden lady to her natural belongings, I turned away to a window, folded my arms, and began to await what would happen. I had rather long to wait. The prince was the whole time surrounded by his host—surrounded, simply, as England is surrounded by the sea,—to say nothing of the other members of the marshal's family and the rest of the guests. And besides, he could hardly go up to such an insignificant person as me and begin to talk without arousing a general feeling of surprise. This insignificance, I remember, was positively a joy to me at the time. 'All right,' I thought, as I watched him courteously addressing first one and then another highly respected personage, honoured by his notice, if only for an 'instant's flash,' as the poets say;—'all right, my dear … you'll come to me soon—I've insulted you, anyway.' At last the prince, adroitly escaping from the throng of his adorers, passed close by me, looked somewhere between the window and my hair, was turning away, and suddenly stood still, as though he had recollected something. 'Ah, yes!' he said, turning to me with a smile, 'by the way, I have a little matter to talk to you about.'

Two country gentlemen, of the most persistent, who were obstinately pursuing the prince, probably imagined the 'little matter' to relate to official business, and respectfully fell back. The prince took my arm and led me apart. My heart was thumping at my ribs.

'You, I believe,' he began, emphasising the word *you,* and looking at my chin with a contemptuous expression, which, strange to say, was supremely becoming to his fresh and handsome face, 'you said something abusive to me?'

'I said what I thought,' I replied, raising my voice.

'Sh … quietly,' he observed; 'decent people don't bawl. You would like, perhaps, to fight me?'

'That's your affair,' I answered, drawing myself up.

'I shall be obliged to challenge you,' he remarked carelessly, 'if you don't withdraw your expressions….'

'I do not intend to withdraw from anything,' I rejoined with pride.

'Really?' he observed, with an ironical smile.
'In that case,' he continued, after a brief pause, 'I shall have the honour of sending my second to you to-morrow.'
'Very good, 'I said in a voice, if possible, even more indifferent.
The prince gave a slight bow.
'I cannot prevent you from considering me empty-headed,' he added, with a haughty droop of his eyelids; 'but the Princes N—— cannot be upstarts. Good-bye till we meet, Mr.... Mr. Shtukaturin.'
He quickly turned his back on me, and again approached his host, who was already beginning to get excited.
Mr. Shtukaturin!... My name is Tchulkaturin.... I could think of nothing to say to him in reply to this last insult, and could only gaze after him with fury. 'Till to-morrow,' I muttered, clenching my teeth, and I at once looked for an officer of my acquaintance, a cavalry captain in the Uhlans, called Koloberdyaev, a desperate rake, and a very good fellow. To him I related, in few words, my quarrel with the prince, and asked him to be my second. He, of course, promptly consented, and I went home.
I could not sleep all night—from excitement, not from cowardice. I am not a coward. I positively thought very little of the possibility confronting me of losing my life—that, as the Germans assure us, highest good on earth. I could think only of Liza, of my ruined hopes, of what I ought to do. 'Ought I to try to kill the prince?' I asked myself; and, of course, I wanted to kill him—not from revenge, but from a desire for Liza's good. 'But she will not survive such a blow,' I went on. 'No, better let him kill me!' I must own it was an agreeable reflection, too, that I, an obscure provincial person, had forced a man of such consequence to fight a duel with me.
The morning light found me still absorbed in these reflections; and, not long after it, appeared Koloberdyaev.
'Well,' he asked me, entering my room with a clatter, 'where's the prince's second?' 'Upon my word,' I answered with annoyance, 'it's seven o'clock at the most; the prince is still asleep, I should imagine.' 'In that case,' replied the cavalry officer, in nowise daunted, 'order some tea for me. My head aches from yesterday evening.... I've not taken my clothes off all night. Though, indeed,' he added with a yawn, 'I don't as a rule often take my clothes off.'
Some tea was given him. He drank off six glasses of tea and rum, smoked four pipes, told me he had on the previous day bought, for next to nothing, a horse the coachman refused to drive, and that he was meaning to drive her out with one of her fore legs tied up, and fell asleep, without undressing, on the sofa, with a pipe in his mouth. I got up and put my papers to rights. One note of invitation from Liza, the one note I had received from her, I was on the point of putting in my bosom, but on second thoughts I flung it in a drawer. Koloberdyaev was snoring feebly, with his head hanging from the leather pillow.... For a long while, I remember, I scrutinised his unkempt, daring, careless, and good-natured face. At ten o'clock the man announced the arrival of Bizmyonkov. The prince had chosen him as second.
We both together roused the soundly sleeping cavalry officer. He sat up, stared at us with dim eyes, in a hoarse voice demanded vodka. He recovered himself, and exchanging greetings with Bizmyonkov, he went with him into the next room to arrange matters. The consultation of the worthy seconds did not last long. A quarter of an hour later, they both came into my bedroom. Koloberdyaev announced to me that 'we're going to fight to-day at three o'clock with pistols.' In silence I bent my head, in token of my agreement. Bizmyonkov at once took leave of us, and departed. He was rather pale and inwardly agitated, like a man unused to such jobs, but he was, nevertheless, very polite and chilly. I felt, as it were, conscience-stricken in his presence, and did not dare look him in the face. Koloberdyaev began telling me about his horse. This conversation was very welcome to me. I was afraid he would mention Liza. But the good-natured cavalry officer was not a gossip, and, moreover, he despised all women, calling them, God knows why, green stuff. At two o'clock we had lunch, and at three we were

at the place fixed upon—the very birch copse in which I had once walked with Liza, a couple of yards from the precipice.

We arrived first; but the prince and Bizmyonkov did not keep us long waiting. The prince was, without exaggeration, as fresh as a rose; his brown eyes looked out with excessive cordiality from under the peak of his cap. He was smoking a cigar, and on seeing Koloberdyaev shook his hand in a friendly way.

Even to me he bowed very genially. I was conscious, on the contrary, of being pale, and my hands, to my terrible vexation, were slightly trembling … my throat was parched…. I had never fought a duel before. 'O God!' I thought; 'if only that ironical gentleman doesn't take my agitation for timidity!' I was inwardly cursing my nerves; but glancing, at last, straight in the prince's face, and catching on his lips an almost imperceptible smile, I suddenly felt furious again, and was at once at my ease. Meanwhile, our seconds were fixing the barrier, measuring out the paces, loading the pistols. Koloberdyaev did most; Bizmyonkov rather watched him. It was a magnificent day—as fine as the day of that ever-memorable walk. The thick blue of the sky peeped, as then, through the golden green of the leaves. Their lisping seemed to mock me. The prince went on smoking his cigar, leaning with his shoulder against the trunk of a young lime-tree….

'Kindly take your places, gentlemen; ready,' Koloberdyaev pronounced at last, handing us pistols.

The prince walked a few steps away, stood still, and, turning his head, asked me over his shoulder, 'You still refuse to take back your words, then?'

I tried to answer him; but my voice failed me, and I had to content myself with a contemptuous wave of the hand. The prince smiled again, and took up his position in his place. We began to approach one another. I raised my pistol, was about to aim at my enemy's chest—but suddenly tilted it up, as though some one had given my elbow a shove, and fired. The prince tottered, and put his left hand to his left temple—a thread of blood was flowing down his cheek from under the white leather glove, Bizmyonkov rushed up to him.

'It's all right,' he said, taking off his cap, which the bullet had pierced; 'since it's in the head, and I've not fallen, it must be a mere scratch.'

He calmly pulled a cambric handkerchief out of his pocket, and put it to his blood-stained curls.

I stared at him, as though I were turned to stone, and did not stir.

'Go up to the barrier, if you please!' Koloberdyaev observed severely.

I obeyed.

'Is the duel to go on?' he added, addressing Bizmyonkov.

Bizmyonkov made him no answer. But the prince, without taking the handkerchief from the wound, without even giving himself the satisfaction of tormenting me at the barrier, replied with a smile. 'The duel is at an end,' and fired into the air. I was almost crying with rage and vexation. This man by his magnanimity had utterly trampled me in the mud; he had completely crushed me. I was on the point of making objections, on the point of demanding that he should fire at me. But he came up to me, and held out his hand.

'It's all forgotten between us, isn't it?' he said in a friendly voice.

I looked at his blanched face, at the blood-stained handkerchief, and utterly confounded, put to shame, and annihilated, I pressed his hand.

'Gentlemen!' he added, turning to the seconds, 'everything, I hope, will be kept secret?'

'Of course!' cried Koloberdyaev; 'but, prince, allow me …'

And he himself bound up his head.

The prince, as he went away, bowed to me once more. But Bizmyonkov did not even glance at me. Shattered—morally shattered—went homewards with Koloberdyaev.

'Why, what's the matter with you?' the cavalry captain asked me. 'Set your mind at rest; the wound's not serious. He'll be able to dance by to-morrow, if you like. Or are you sorry you didn't kill him? You're wrong, if you are; he's a first-rate fellow.'

'What business had he to spare me!' I muttered at last.

'Oh, so that's it!' the cavalry captain rejoined tranquilly… 'Ugh, you writing fellows are too much for me!'

I don't know what put it into his head to consider me an author.

I absolutely decline to describe my torments during the evening following upon that luckless duel. My vanity suffered indescribably. It was not my conscience that tortured me; the consciousness of my imbecility crushed me. 'I have given myself the last decisive blow by my own act!' I kept repeating, as I strode up and down my room. 'The prince, wounded by me, and forgiving me… Yes, Liza is now his. Now nothing can save her, nothing can hold her back on the edge of the abyss.' I knew very well that our duel could not be kept secret, in spite of the prince's words; in any case, it could not remain a secret for Liza.

'The prince is not such a fool,' I murmured in a frenzy of rage, 'as not to profit by it.'… But, meanwhile, I was mistaken. The whole town knew of the duel and of its real cause next day, of course. But the prince had not blabbed of it; on the contrary, when, with his head bandaged and an explanation ready, he made his appearance before Liza, she had already heard everything…. Whether Bizmyonkov had betrayed me, or the news had reached her by other channels, I cannot say. Though, indeed, can anything ever be concealed in a little town? You can fancy how Liza received him, how all the family of the Ozhogins received him! As for me, I suddenly became an object of universal indignation and loathing, a monster, a jealous bloodthirsty madman. My few acquaintances shunned me as if I were a leper. The authorities of the town promptly addressed the prince, with a proposal to punish me in a severe and befitting manner. Nothing but the persistent and urgent entreaties of the prince himself averted the calamity that menaced me. That man was fated to annihilate me in every way. By his generosity he had shut, as it were, a coffin-lid down upon me. It's needless to say that the Ozhogins' doors were at once closed against me. Kirilla Matveitch even sent me back a bit of pencil I had left in his house. In reality, he, of all people, had no reason to be angry with me. My 'insane' (that was the expression current in the town) jealousy had pointed out, defined, so to speak, the relations of the prince to Liza. Both the old Ozhogins themselves and their fellow-citizens began to look on him almost as betrothed to her. This could not, as a fact, have been quite to his liking. But he was greatly attracted by Liza; and meanwhile, he had not at that time attained his aims. With all the adroitness of a clever man of the world, he took advantage of his new position, and promptly entered, as they say, into the spirit of his new part….

But I!… For myself, for my future, I renounced all hopes, at that time. When suffering reaches the point of making our whole being creak and groan, like an overloaded cart, it ought to cease to be ridiculous … but no! laughter not only accompanies tears to the end, to exhaustion, to the impossibility of shedding more—it even rings and echoes, where the tongue is dumb, and complaint itself is dead…. And so, as in the first place I don't intend to expose myself as ridiculous, even to myself, and secondly as I am fearfully tired, I will put off the continuation, and please God the conclusion, of my story till tomorrow….

_March 29.

A slight frost; yesterday it was thawing._

Yesterday I had not the strength to go on with my diary; like Poprishtchin, I lay, for the most part, on my bed, and talked to Terentyevna. What a woman! Sixty years ago she lost her first betrothed from the plague, she has outlived all her children, she is inexcusably old, drinks tea to her heart's desire, is well fed, and warmly clothed; and what do you suppose she was talking to me about, all day yesterday? I had sent another utterly destitute old woman the collar of an old livery, half moth-eaten, to put on her vest (she wears strips over the chest by way of vest) … and why wasn't it given to her? 'But I'm your nurse; I should think… Oh … oh, my good sir, it's too bad of you … after I've looked after you as I have!' … and so on. The merciless old woman utterly wore me out with her reproaches…. But to get back to my story.

And so, I suffered like a dog, whose hindquarters have been run over by a wheel. It was only then, only after my banishment from the Ozhogins' house, that I fully realised how much happiness a man can extract from the contemplation of his own unhappiness. O men! pitiful race, indeed!

... But, away with philosophical reflections.... I spent my days in complete solitude, and could only by the most roundabout and even humiliating methods find out what was passing in the Ozhogins' household, and what the prince was doing. My man had made friends with the cousin of the latter's coachman's wife. This acquaintance afforded me some slight relief, and my man soon guessed, from my hints and little presents, what he was to talk about to his master when he pulled his boots off every evening. Sometimes I chanced to meet some one of the Ozhogins' family, Bizmyonkov, or the prince in the street.... To the prince and to Bizmyonkov I bowed, but I did not enter into conversation with them. Liza I only saw three times: once, with her mamma, in a fashionable shop; once, in an open carriage with her father and mother and the prince; and once, in church. Of course, I was not impudent enough to approach her, and only watched her from a distance. In the shop she was very much preoccupied, but cheerful.... She was ordering something for herself, and busily matching ribbons. Her mother was gazing at her, with her hands folded on her lap, and her nose in the air, smiling with that foolish and devoted smile which is only permissible in adoring mothers. In the carriage with the prince, Liza was ... I shall never forget that meeting! The old people were sitting in the back seats of the carriage, the prince and Liza in the front. She was paler than usual; on her cheek two patches of pink could just be seen. She was half facing the prince; leaning on her straight right arm (in the left hand she was holding a sunshade), with her little head drooping languidly, she was looking straight into his face with her expressive eyes. At that instant she surrendered herself utterly to him, intrusted herself to him for ever. I had not time to get a good look at his face—the carriage galloped by too quickly,—but I fancied that he too was deeply touched.

The third time I saw her in church. Not more than ten days had passed since the day when I met her in the carriage with the prince, not more than three weeks since the day of my duel. The business upon which the prince had come to O—— was by now completed. But he still kept putting off his departure. At Petersburg, he was reported to be ill. In the town, it was expected every day that he would make a proposal in form to Kirilla Matveitch. I was myself only awaiting this final blow to go away for ever. The town of O—— had grown hateful to me. I could not stay indoors, and wandered from morning to night about the suburbs. One grey, gloomy day, as I was coming back from a walk, which had been cut short by the rain, I went into a church. The evening service had only just begun, there were very few people; I looked round me, and suddenly, near a window, caught sight of a familiar profile. For the first instant, I did not recognise it: that pale face, that spiritless glance, those sunken cheeks—could it be the same Liza I had seen a fortnight before? Wrapped in a cloak, without a hat on, with the cold light from the broad white window falling on her from one side, she was gazing fixedly at the holy image, and seemed striving to pray, striving to awake from a sort of listless stupor. A red-cheeked, fat little page with yellow trimmings on his chest was standing behind her, and, with his hands clasped behind his back, stared in sleepy bewilderment at his mistress. I trembled all over, was about to go up to her, but stopped short. I felt choked by a torturing presentiment. Till the very end of the evening service, Liza did not stir. All the people went out, a beadle began sweeping out the church, but still she did not move from her place. The page went up to her, said something to her, touched her dress; she looked round, passed her hand over her face, and went away. I followed her home at a little distance, and then returned to my lodging.

'She is lost!' I cried, when I had got into my room.

As a man, I don't know to this day what my sensations were at that moment. I flung myself, I remember, with clasped hands, on the sofa and fixed my eyes on the floor. But I don't know—in the midst of my woe I was, as it were, pleased at something.... I would not admit this for anything in the world, if I were not writing only for myself.... I had been tormented, certainly, by terrible, harassing suspicions ... and who knows, I should, perhaps, have been greatly disconcerted if they had not been fulfilled. 'Such is the heart of man!' some middle-aged Russian teacher would exclaim at this point in an expressive voice, while he raises a fat forefinger, adorned with a cornelian ring. But what have we to do with the opinion of a Russian teacher, with an expressive voice and a cornelian on his finger?

Be that as it may, my presentiment turned out to be well founded. Suddenly the news was all over the town that the prince had gone away, presumably in consequence of a summons from Petersburg; that he had gone away without making any proposal to Kirilla Matveitch or his wife, and that Liza would have to deplore his treachery till the end of her days. The prince's departure was utterly unexpected, for only the evening before his coachman, so my man assured me, had not the slightest suspicion of his master's intentions. This piece of news threw me into a perfect fever. I at once dressed, and was on the point of hastening to the Ozhogins', but on thinking the matter over I considered it more seemly to wait till the next day. I lost nothing, however, by remaining at home. The same evening, there came to see me in all haste a certain Pandopipopulo, a wandering Greek, stranded by some chance in the town of O——, a scandalmonger of the first magnitude, who had been more indignant with me than any one for my duel with the prince. He did not even give my man time to announce him; he fairly burst into my room, warmly pressed my hand, begged my pardon a thousand times, called me a paragon of magnanimity and courage, painted the prince in the darkest colours, censured the old Ozhogins, who, in his opinion, had been punished as they deserved, made a slighting reference to Liza in passing, and hurried off again, kissing me on my shoulder. Among other things, I learned from him that the prince, *en vrai grand seigneur*, on the eve of his departure, in response to a delicate hint from Kirilla Matveitch, had answered coldly that he had no intention of deceiving any one, and no idea of marrying, had risen, made his bow, and that was all.... Next day I set off to the Ozhogins'. The shortsighted footman leaped up from his bench on my appearance, with the rapidity of lightning. I bade him announce me; the footman hurried away and returned at once. 'Walk in,' he said; 'you are begged to go in.' I went into Kirilla Matveitch's study.... The rest to-morrow.

March 30. Frost.

And so I went into Kirilla Matveitch's study. I would pay any one handsomely, who could show me now my own face at the moment when that highly respected official, hurriedly flinging together his dressing-gown, approached me with outstretched arms. I must have been a perfect picture of modest triumph, indulgent sympathy, and boundless magnanimity.... I felt myself something in the style of Scipio Africanus. Ozhogin was visibly confused and cast down, he avoided my eyes, and kept fidgeting about. I noticed, too, that he spoke unnaturally loudly, and in general expressed himself very vaguely. Vaguely, but with warmth, he begged my forgiveness, vaguely alluded to their departed guest, added a few vague generalities about deception and the instability of earthly blessings, and, suddenly feeling the tears in his eyes, hastened to take a pinch of snuff, probably in order to deceive me as to the cause of his tearfulness.... He used the Russian green snuff, and it's well known that that article forces even old men to shed tears that make the human eye look dull and senseless for several minutes.

I behaved, of course, very cautiously with the old man, inquired after the health of his wife and daughter, and at once artfully turned the conversation on to the interesting subject of the rotation of crops. I was dressed as usual, but the feeling of gentle propriety and soft indulgence which filled me gave me a fresh and festive sensation, as though I had on a white waistcoat and a white cravat. One thing agitated me, the thought of seeing Liza.... Ozhogin, at last, proposed of his own accord to take me up to his wife. The kind-hearted but foolish woman was at first terribly embarrassed on seeing me; but her brain was not capable of retaining the same impression for long, and so she was soon at her ease. At last I saw Liza ... she came into the room....

I had expected to find in her a shamed and penitent sinner, and had assumed beforehand the most affectionate and reassuring expression of face.... Why lie about it? I really loved her and was thirsting for the happiness of forgiving her, of holding out a hand to her; but to my unutterable astonishment, in response to my significant bow, she laughed coldly, observed carelessly, 'Oh, is that you?' and at once turned away from me. It is true that her laugh struck me as forced, and in any case did not accord well with her terribly thin face ... but, all the same, I had not expected such a reception.... I looked at her with amazement ... what a change had taken place in her! Between the child she had been and the woman before me, there was nothing in common. She had, as it were, grown up, straightened out; all the features of her face, especially her lips, seemed defined ... her gaze had grown deeper, harder, and gloomier. I stayed on at the Ozhogins' till dinner-time. She got up, went out of the room, and came back again, answered questions with composure, and designedly took no notice of me. She wanted, I saw, to make me feel that I was not worth her anger, though I had been within an ace of killing her lover. I lost patience at last; a malicious allusion broke from my lips.... She started, glanced swiftly at me, got up, and going to the window, pronounced in a rather shaky voice, 'You can say anything you like, but let me tell you that I love that man, and always shall love him, and do not consider that he has done me any injury, quite the contrary.'... Her voice broke, she stopped ... tried to control herself, but could not, burst into tears, and went out of the room.... The old people were much upset.... I pressed the hands of both, sighed, turned my eyes heavenward, and withdrew.

I am too weak, I have too little time left, I am not capable of describing in the same detail the new range of torturing reflections, firm resolutions, and all the other fruits of what is called inward conflict, that arose within me after the renewal of my acquaintance with the Ozhogins. I did not doubt that Liza still loved, and would long love, the prince ... but as one reconciled to the inevitable, and anxious myself to conciliate, I did not even dream of her love. I desired only her affection, I desired to gain her confidence, her respect, which, we are assured by persons of experience, forms the surest basis for happiness in marriage.... Unluckily, I lost sight of one rather important circumstance, which was that Liza had hated me ever since the day of the duel. I found this out too late. I began, as before, to be a frequent visitor at the house of the Ozhogins. Kirilla Matveitch received me with more effusiveness and affability than he had ever done. I have even ground for believing that he would at that time have cheerfully given me his daughter, though I was certainly not a match to be coveted. Public opinion was very severe upon him and Liza, while, on the other hand, it extolled me to the skies. Liza's attitude to me was unchanged. She was, for the most part, silent; obeyed, when they begged her to eat, showed no outward signs of sorrow, but, for all that, was wasting away like a candle. I must do Kirilla Matveitch the justice to say that he spared her in every way. Old Madame Ozhogin only ruffled up her feathers like a hen, as she looked at her poor nestling. There was only one person Liza did not shun, though she did not talk much even to him, and that was Bizmyonkov. The old people were rather short, not to say rude, in their behaviour to him. They could not forgive him for having been second in the duel. But he went on going to see them, as though he did not notice their unamiability. With me he was very chilly, and—strange to say—I felt, as it were, afraid of him. This state of things went on for a fortnight. At last, after a sleepless night, I resolved to have it out with Liza, to open my heart to her, to tell her that, in spite of the past, in spite of all possible gossip and scandal, I should consider myself only too happy if she would give me her hand, and restore me her confidence. I really did seriously imagine that I was showing what they call in the school reading-books an unparalleled example of magnanimity, and that, from sheer amazement alone, she would consent. In any case, I resolved to have an explanation and to escape, at last, from suspense.

Behind the Ozhogins' house was a rather large garden, which ended in a little grove of lime-trees, neglected and overgrown. In the middle of this thicket stood an old summer-house in the Chinese style: a wooden paling separated the garden from a blind alley. Liza would sometimes walk, for hours together, alone in this garden. Kirilla Matveitch was aware of this, and forbade her being disturbed or followed; let her grief wear itself out, he said. When she could not be found indoors, they had only to ring a bell on the steps at dinner-time and she made her appearance at once, with the same stubborn silence on her lips and in her eyes, and some little leaf crushed up in her hand. So, noticing one day that she was not in the house, I made a show of going away, took leave of Kirilla Matveitch, put on my hat, and went out from the hall into the courtyard, and from the courtyard into the street, but promptly darted in at the gate again with extraordinary rapidity and hurried past the kitchen into the garden. Luckily no one noticed me. Without losing time in deliberation, I went with rapid steps into the grove. In a little path before me was standing Liza. My heart beat violently. I stood still, drew a deep sigh, and was just on the point of going up to her, when suddenly she lifted her hand without turning round, and began listening.... From behind the trees, in the direction of the blind alley, came a distinct sound of two knocks, as though some one were tapping at the paling. Liza clapped her hands together, there was heard the faint creak of the gate, and out of the thicket stepped Bizmyonkov. I hastily hid behind a tree. Liza turned towards him without speaking.... Without speaking, he drew her arm in his, and the two walked slowly along the path together. I looked after them in amazement. They stopped, looked round, disappeared behind the bushes, reappeared again, and finally went into the summer-house. This summer-house was a diminutive round edifice, with a door and one little window. In the middle stood an old one-legged table, overgrown with fine green moss; two discoloured deal benches stood along the sides, some distance from the damp and darkened walls. Here, on exceptionally hot days, in bygone times, perhaps once a year or so, they had drunk tea. The door did not quite shut, the window-frame had long ago come out of the window, and hung disconsolately, only attached at one corner, like a bird's broken wing. I stole up to the summer-house, and peeped cautiously through the chink in the window. Liza was sitting on one of the benches, with her head drooping. Her right hand lay on her knees, the left Bizmyonkov was holding in both his hands. He was looking sympathetically at her.

'How do you feel to-day?' he asked her in a low voice.

'Just the same,' she answered, 'not better, nor worse.—The emptiness, the fearful emptiness!' she added, raising her eyes dejectedly.

Bizmyonkov made her no answer.

'What do you think,' she went on: 'will he write to me once more?'

'I don't think so, Lizaveta Kirillovna!'

She was silent.

'And after all, why should he write? He told me everything in his first letter. I could not be his wife; but I have been happy ... not for long ... I have been happy ...'

Bizmyonkov looked down.

'Ah,' she went on quickly, 'if you knew how I loathe that Tchulkaturin ... I always fancy I see on that man's hands ... his blood.' (I shuddered behind my chink.) 'Though indeed,' she added, dreamily, 'who knows, perhaps, if it had not been for that duel.... Ah, when I saw him wounded I felt at once that I was altogether his.'

'Tchulkaturin loves you,' observed Bizmyonkov.

'What is that to me? I don't want any one's love.'... She stopped and added slowly, 'Except yours. Yes, my friend, your love is necessary to me; except for you, I should be lost. You have helped me to bear terrible moments ...'

She broke off ... Bizmyonkov began with fatherly tenderness stroking her hand.

'There's no help for it! What is one to do! what is one to do, Lizaveta Kirillovna!' he repeated several times.

'And now indeed,' she went on in a lifeless voice, 'I should die, I think, if it were not for you. It's you alone that keep me up; besides, you remind me of him.... You knew all about it, you see. Do you remember how fine he was that day.... But forgive me; it must be hard for you....'

'Go on, go on! Nonsense! Bless you!' Bizmyonkov interrupted her.

She pressed his hand.

'You are very good, Bizmyonkov,' she went on;' you are good as an angel. What can I do! I feel I shall love him to the grave. I have forgiven him, I am grateful to him. God give him happiness! May God give him a wife after his own heart'—and her eyes filled with tears—'if only he does not forget me, if only he will sometimes think of his Liza!—Let us go,' she added, after a brief silence.

Bizmyonkov raised her hand to his lips.

'I know,' she began again hotly, 'every one is blaming me now, every one is throwing stones at me. Let them! I wouldn't, any way, change my misery for their happiness … no! no!… He did not love me for long, but he loved me! He never deceived me, he never told me I should be his wife; I never dreamed of it myself. It was only poor papa hoped for it. And even now I am not altogether unhappy; the memory remains to me, and however fearful the results … I'm stifling here … it was here I saw him the last time…. Let's go into the air.'

They got up. I had only just time to skip on one side and hide behind a thick lime-tree. They came out of the summer-house, and, as far as I could judge by the sound of their steps, went away into the thicket. I don't know how long I went on standing there, without stirring from my place, plunged in a sort of senseless amazement, when suddenly I heard steps again. I started, and peeped cautiously out from my hiding-place. Bizmyonkov and Liza were coming back along the same path. Both were greatly agitated, especially Bizmyonkov.

I fancied he was crying. Liza stopped, looked at him, and distinctly uttered the following words: 'I do consent, Bizmyonkov. I would never have agreed if you were only trying to save me, to rescue me from a terrible position, but you love me, you know everything—and you love me. I shall never find a trustier, truer friend. I will be your wife.'

Bizmyonkov kissed her hand: she smiled at him mournfully and moved away towards the house. Bizmyonkov rushed into the thicket, and I went my way. Seeing that Bizmyonkov had apparently said to Liza precisely what I had intended to say to her, and she had given him precisely the reply I was longing to hear from her, there was no need for me to trouble myself further. Within a fortnight she was married to him. The old Ozhogins were thankful to get any husband for her.

Now, tell me, am I not a superfluous man? Didn't I play throughout the whole story the part of a superfluous person? The prince's part … of that it's needless to speak; Bizmyonkov's part, too, is comprehensible…. But I—with what object was I mixed up in it?… A senseless fifth wheel to the cart!… Ah, it's bitter, bitter for me!… But there, as the barge-haulers say, 'One more pull, and one more yet,'—one day more, and one more yet, and there will be no more bitter nor sweet for me.

March 31.

I'm in a bad way. I am writing these lines in bed. Since yesterday evening there has been a sudden change in the weather. To-day is hot, almost a summer day. Everything is thawing, breaking up, flowing away. The air is full of the smell of the opened earth, a strong, heavy, stifling smell. Steam is rising on all sides. The sun seems beating, seems smiting everything to pieces. I am very ill, I feel that I am breaking up.

I meant to write my diary, and, instead of that, what have I done? I have related one incident of my life. I gossiped on, slumbering reminiscences were awakened and drew me away. I have written, without haste, in detail, as though I had years before me. And here now, there's no time to go on. Death, death is coming. I can hear her menacing *crescendo*. The time is come … the time is come!…

And indeed, what does it matter? Isn't it all the same whatever I write? In sight of death the last earthly cares vanish. I feel I have grown calm; I am becoming simpler, clearer. Too late I've gained sense!… It's a strange thing! I have grown calm—certainly, and at the same time … I'm full of dread. Yes, I'm full of dread. Half hanging over the silent, yawning abyss, I shudder, turn away, with greedy intentness gaze at everything about me. Every object is doubly precious to me. I cannot gaze enough at my poor, cheerless room, saying farewell to each spot on my walls. Take your fill for the last time, my eyes. Life is retreating; slowly and smoothly she is flying away from me, as the shore flies from the eyes of one at sea. The old yellow face of my nurse, tied up in a dark kerchief, the hissing samovar on the table, the pot of geranium in the window, and you, my poor dog, Tresór, the pen I write these lines with, my own hand, I see you now … here you are, here…. Is it possible … can it be, to-day … I shall never see you again! It's hard for a live creature to part with life! Why do you fawn on me, poor dog? why do you come putting your forepaws on the bed, with your stump of a tail wagging so violently, and your kind, mournful eyes fixed on me all the while? Are you sorry for me? or do you feel already that your master will soon be gone? Ah, if I could only keep my thoughts, too, resting on all the objects in my room! I know these reminiscences are dismal and of no importance, but I have no other. 'The emptiness, the fearful emptiness!' as Liza said.

O my God, my God! Here I am dying…. A heart capable of loving and ready to love will soon cease to beat…. And can it be it will be still for ever without having once known happiness, without having once expanded under the sweet burden of bliss? Alas! it's impossible, impossible, I know…. If only now, at least, before death—for death after all is a sacred thing, after all it elevates any being—if any kind, sad, friendly voice would sing over me a farewell song of my own sorrow, I could, perhaps, be resigned to it. But to die stupidly, stupidly….

I believe I'm beginning to rave.

Farewell, life! farewell, my garden! and you, my lime-trees! When the summer comes, do not forget to be clothed with flowers from head to foot … and may it be sweet for people to lie in your fragrant shade, on the fresh grass, among the whispering chatter of your leaves, lightly stirred by the wind. Farewell, farewell! Farewell, everything and for ever!

Farewell, Liza! I wrote those two words, and almost laughed aloud. This exclamation strikes me as taken out of a book. It's as though I were writing a sentimental novel and ending up a despairing letter….

To-morrow is the first of April. Can I be going to die to-morrow? That would be really too unseemly. It's just right for me, though …

How the doctor did chatter to-day.

April 1.

It is over…. Life is over. I shall certainly die to-day. It's hot outside … almost suffocating … or is it that my lungs are already refusing to breathe? My little comedy is played out. The curtain is falling.

Sinking into nothing, I cease to be superfluous …

Ah, how brilliant that sun is! Those mighty beams breathe of eternity …

Farewell, Terentyevna!… This morning as she sat at the window she was crying … perhaps over me … and perhaps because she too will soon have to die. I have made her promise not to kill Tresór.

It's hard for me to write…. I will put down the pen…. It's high time; death is already approaching with ever-increasing rumble, like a carriage at night over the pavement; it is here, it is flitting about me, like the light breath which made the prophet's hair stand up on end.

I am dying…. Live, you who are living,

'And about the grave
May youthful life rejoice,
And nature heedless
Glow with eternal beauty.

Note by the Editor.—Under this last line was a head in profile with a big streak of hair and moustaches, with eyes *en face*, and eyelashes like rays; and under the head some one had written the following words:

'This manuscript was read
And the Contents of it Not Approved

By Peter Zudotyeshin
My My My
My dear Sir,
Peter Zudotyeshin,
Dear Sir.'

But as the handwriting of these lines was not in the least like the handwriting in which the other part of the manuscript was written, the editor considers that he is justified in concluding that the above lines were added subsequently by another person, especially since it has come to his (the editor's) knowledge that Mr. Tchulkaturin actually did die on the night between the 1st and 2nd of April in the year 18—, at his native place, Sheep's Springs.

* * * * *

A TOUR IN THE FOREST

FIRST DAY

The sight of the vast pinewood, embracing the whole horizon, the sight of the 'Forest,' recalls the sight of the ocean. And the sensations it arouses are the same; the same primaeval untouched force lies outstretched in its breadth and majesty before the eyes of the spectator. From the heart of the eternal forest, from the undying bosom of the waters, comes the same voice: 'I have nothing to do with thee,'—nature says to man, 'I reign supreme, while do thou bestir thyself to thy utmost to escape dying.' But the forest is gloomier and more monotonous than the sea, especially the pine forest, which is always alike and almost soundless. The ocean menaces and caresses, it frolics with every colour, speaks with every voice; it reflects the sky, from which too comes the breath of eternity, but an eternity as it were not so remote from us.... The dark, unchanging pine-forest keeps sullen silence or is filled with a dull roar—and at the sight of it sinks into man's heart more deeply, more irresistibly, the sense of his own nothingness. It is hard for man, the creature of a day, born yesterday, and doomed to death on the morrow, it is hard for him to bear the cold gaze of the eternal Isis, fixed without sympathy upon him: not only the daring hopes and dreams of youth are humbled and quenched within him, enfolded by the icy breath of the elements; no—his whole soul sinks down and swoons within him; he feels that the last of his kind may vanish off the face of the earth—and not one needle will quiver on those twigs; he feels his isolation, his feebleness, his fortuitousness;—and in hurried, secret panic, he turns to the petty cares and labours of life; he is more at ease in that world he has himself created; there he is at home, there he dares yet believe in his own importance and in his own power.

Such were the ideas that came into my mind, some years ago, when, standing on the steps of a little inn on the bank of the marshy little river Ressetta, I first gazed upon the forest. The bluish masses of fir-forest lay in long, continuous ridges before me; here and there was the green patch of a small birch-copse; the whole sky-line was hugged by the pine-wood; nowhere was there the white gleam of a church, nor bright stretches of meadow—it was all trees and trees, everywhere the ragged edge of the tree-tops, and a delicate dim mist, the eternal mist of the forest, hung over them in the distance. It was not indolent repose this immobility of life suggested; no—the absence of life, something dead, even in its grandeur, was what came to me from every side of the horizon. I remember big white clouds were swimming by, slowly and very high up, and the hot summer day lay motionless upon the silent earth. The reddish water of the stream glided without a splash among the thick reeds: at its bottom could be dimly discerned round cushions of pointed moss, and its banks sank away in the swampy mud, and sharply reappeared again in white hillocks of fine crumbling sand. Close by the little inn ran the trodden highroad.

On this road, just opposite the steps, stood a cart, loaded with boxes and hampers. Its owner, a thin pedlar with a hawk nose and mouse-like eyes, bent and lame, was putting in it his little nag, lame like himself. He was a gingerbread-seller, who was making his way to the fair at Karatchev. Suddenly several people appeared on the road, others straggled after them ... at last, quite a crowd came trudging into sight; all of them had sticks in their hands and satchels on their shoulders. From their fatigued yet swinging gait, and from their sun-burnt faces, one could see they had come from a long distance. They were leatherworkers and diggers coming back from working for hire.

An old man of seventy, white all over, seemed to be their leader. From time to time he turned round and with a quiet voice urged on those who lagged behind. 'Now, now, now, lads,' he said, 'no—ow.' They all walked in silence, in a sort of solemn hush. Only one of them, a little man with a wrathful air, in a sheepskin coat wide open, and a lambswool cap pulled right over his eyes, on coming up to the gingerbread man, suddenly inquired: 'How much is the gingerbread, you tomfool?'

'What sort of gingerbread will it be, worthy sir?' the disconcerted gingerbread—man responded in a thin, little voice. 'Some are a farthing—and others cost a halfpenny. Have you a halfpenny in your purse?'

'But I guess it will sweeten the belly too much,' retorted the sheepskin, and he retreated from the cart.

'Hurry up, lads, hurry up,' I heard the old man's voice: 'it's far yet to our night's rest.'

'An uneducated folk,' said the gingerbread-man, with a squint at me, directly all the crowd had trudged past: 'is such a dainty for the likes of them?'

And quickly harnessing his horse, he went down to the river, where a little wooden ferry could be seen. A peasant in a white felt 'schlik' (the usual headgear in the forest) came out of a low mud hut to meet him, and ferried him over to the opposite bank. The little cart, with one wheel creaking from time to time, crawled along the trodden and deeply rutted road.

I fed my horses, and I too was ferried over. After struggling for a couple of miles through the boggy prairie, I got at last on to a narrow raised wooden causeway to a clearing in the forest. The cart jolted unevenly over the round beams of the causeway: I got out and went along on foot. The horses moved in step snorting and shaking their heads from the gnats and flies. The forest took us into its bosom. On the outskirts, nearer to the prairie, grew birches, aspens, limes, maples, and oaks. Then they met us more rarely, the dense firwood moved down on us in an unbroken wall. Further on were the red, bare trunks of pines, and then again a stretch of mixed copse, overgrown with underwood of hazelnut, mountain ash, and bramble, and stout, vigorous weeds. The sun's rays threw a brilliant light on the tree-tops, and, filtering through the branches, here and there reached the ground in pale streaks and patches. Birds I scarcely heard—they do not like great forests. Only from time to time there came the doleful, thrice-repeated call of a hoopoe, and the angry screech of a nuthatch or a jay; a silent, always solitary bird kept fluttering across the clearing, with a flash of golden azure from its lovely feathers. At times the trees grew further apart, ahead of us the light broke in, the cart came out on a cleared, sandy, open space. Thin rye was growing over it in rows, noiselessly nodding its pale ears. On one side there was a dark, dilapidated little chapel, with a slanting cross over a well. An unseen brook was babbling peaceably with changing, ringing sounds, as though it were flowing into an empty bottle. And then suddenly the road was cut in half by a birch-tree recently fallen, and the forest stood around, so old, lofty, and slumbering, that the air seemed pent in. In places the clearing lay under water. On both sides stretched a forest bog, all green and dark, all covered with reeds and tiny alders. Ducks flew up in pairs—and it was strange to see those water-birds darting rapidly about among the pines. 'Ga, ga, ga, ga,' their drawn-out call kept rising unexpectedly. Then a shepherd drove a flock through the underwood: a brown cow with short, pointed horns broke noisily through the bushes and stood stockstill at the edge of the clearing, her big, dark eyes fixed on the dog running before me. A slight breeze brought the delicate, pungent smell of burnt wood. A white smoke in the distance crept in eddying rings over the pale, blue forest air, showing that a peasant was charcoal-burning for a glass-factory or for a foundry. The further we went on, the darker and stiller it became all round us. In the pine-forest it is always still; there is only, high overhead, a sort of prolonged murmur and subdued roar in the tree-tops. One goes on and on, and this eternal murmur of the forest never ceases, and the heart gradually begins to sink, and a man longs to come out quickly into the open, into the daylight; he longs to draw a full breath again, and is oppressed by the fragrant damp and decay....

For about twelve miles we drove on at a walking pace, rarely at a trot. I wanted to get by daylight to Svyatoe, a hamlet lying in the very heart of the forest. Twice we met peasants with stripped bark or long logs on carts.

'Is it far to Svyatoe?' I asked one of them.

'No, not far.'

'How far?'

'It'll be a little over two miles.'

Another hour and a half went by. We were still driving on and on. Again we heard the creak of a laden cart. A peasant was walking beside it.

'How far, brother, is it still to Svyatoe?'

'What?'

'How far to Svyatoe?'

'Six miles.'

The sun was already setting when at last I got out of the forest and saw facing me a little village. About twenty homesteads were grouped close about an old wooden church, with a single green cupola, and tiny windows, brilliantly red in the evening glow. This was Svyatoe. I drove into its outskirts. A herd returning homewards overtook my cart, and with lowing, grunting and bleating moved by us. Young girls and bustling peasant women came to meet their beasts. Whiteheaded boys with merry shrieks went in chase of refractory pigs. The dust swirled along the street in light clouds, flushed crimson as they rose higher in the air.

I stopped at the house of the village elder, a crafty and clever 'forester,' one of those foresters of whom they say he can see two yards into the ground. Early next morning, accompanied by the village elder's son, and another peasant called Yegor, I set off in a little cart with a pair of peasant's horses, to shoot woodcocks and moorhens. The forest formed a continuous bluish ring all round the sky-line; there was reckoned to be two hundred acres, no more, of ploughed land round Svyatoe; but one had to go some five miles to find good places for game. The elder's son was called Kondrat. He was a flaxen-haired, rosy-cheeked young fellow, with a good-natured, peaceable expression of face, obliging and talkative. He drove the horses. Yegor sat by my side. I want to say a few words about him.

He was considered the cleverest sportsman in the whole district. Every step of the ground for fifty miles round he had been over again and again. He seldom fired at a bird, for lack of powder and shot; but it was enough for him to decoy a moorhen or to detect the track of a grouse. Yegor had the character of being a straightforward fellow and 'no talker.' He did not care for talking and never exaggerated the number of birds he had taken—a trait rare in a sportsman. He was of medium height, thin, and had a pale, long face, and big, honest eyes. All his features, especially his straight and never-moving lips, were expressive of untroubled serenity. He gave a slight, as it were inward smile, whenever he uttered a word—very sweet was that quiet smile. He never drank spirits, and worked industriously; but nothing prospered with him. His wife was always ailing, his children didn't live; he got poorer and poorer and could never pick up again. And there is no denying that a passion for the chase is no good for a peasant, and any one who 'plays with a gun' is sure to be a poor manager of his land. Either from constantly being in the forest, face to face with the stern and melancholy scenery of that inhuman country, or from the peculiar cast and formation of his character, there was noticeable in every action of Yegor's a sort of modest dignity and stateliness—stateliness it was, and not melancholy—the stateliness of a majestic stag. He had in his time killed seven bears, lying in wait for them in the oats. The last he had only succeeded in killing on the fourth night of his ambush; the bear persisted in not turning sideways to him, and he had only one bullet. Yegor had killed him the day before my arrival. When Kondrat brought me to him, I found him in his back yard; squatting on his heels before the huge beast, he was cutting the fat out with a short, blunt knife.

'What a fine fellow you've knocked over there!' I observed.

Yegor raised his head and looked first at me, then at the dog, who had come with me.

'If it's shooting you've come after, sir, there are woodcocks at Moshnoy—three coveys, and five of moorhens,' he observed, and set to work again.

With Yegor and with Kondrat I went out the next day in search of sport. We drove rapidly over the open ground surrounding Svyatoe, but when we got into the forest we crawled along at a walking pace once more.

'Look, there's a wood-pigeon,' said Kondrat suddenly, turning to me: 'better knock it over!'

Yegor looked in the direction Kondrat pointed, but said nothing. The wood-pigeon was over a hundred paces from us, and one can't kill it at forty paces; there is such strength in its feathers. A few more remarks were made by the conversational Kondrat; but the forest hush had its influence even on him; he became silent. Only rarely exchanging a word or two, looking straight ahead, and listening to the puffing and snorting of the horses, we got at last to 'Moshnoy.' That is the name given to the older pine-forest, overgrown in places by fir saplings. We got out; Kondrat led the cart into the bushes, so that the gnats should not bite the horses. Yegor examined the cock of his gun and crossed himself: he never began anything without the sign of the cross.

The forest into which we had come was exceedingly old. I don't know whether the Tartars had wandered over it, but Russian thieves or Lithuanians, in disturbed times, might certainly have hidden in its recesses. At a respectful distance from one another stood the mighty pines with their slightly curved, massive, pale-yellow trunks. Between them stood in single file others, rather younger. The ground was covered with greenish moss, sprinkled all over with dead pine-needles; blueberries grew in dense bushes; the strong perfume of the berries, like the smell of musk, oppressed the breathing. The sun could not pierce through the high network of the pine-branches; but it was stiflingly hot in the forest all the same, and not dark; like big drops of sweat the heavy, transparent resin stood out and slowly trickled down the coarse bark of the trees. The still air, with no light or shade in it, stung the face. Everything was silent; even our footsteps were not audible; we walked on the moss as on a carpet. Yegor in particular moved as silently as a shadow; even the brushwood did not crackle under his feet. He walked without haste, from time to time blowing a shrill note on a whistle; a woodcock soon answered back, and before my eyes darted into a thick fir-tree. But in vain Yegor pointed him out to me; however much I strained my eyes, I could not make him out. Yegor had to take a shot at him. We came upon two coveys of moorhens also. The cautious birds rose at a distance with an abrupt, heavy sound. We succeeded, however, in killing three young ones.

At one *meidan* [Footnote 1: *Meidan* is the name given to a place where tar has been made.—Author's Note.] Yegor suddenly stopped and called me up.

'A bear has been trying to get water,' he observed, pointing to a broad, fresh scratch, made in the very middle of a hole covered with fine moss.

'Is that the print of his paw?' I inquired.

'Yes; but the water has dried up. That's the track of him too on that pine; he has been climbing after honey. He has cut into it with his claws as if with a knife.'

We went on making our way into the inner-most depths of the forest. Yegor only rarely looked upwards, and walked on serenely and confidently. I saw a high, round rampart, enclosed by a half-choked-up ditch.
'What's that? a *meidan* too?' I inquired.
'No,' answered Yegor; 'here's where the thieves' town stood.'
'Long ago?'
'Long ago; our grandfathers remember it. Here they buried their treasure. And they took a mighty oath: on human blood.'
We went on another mile and a half; I began to feel thirsty.
'Sit down a little while,' said Yegor: 'I will go for water; there is a well not far from here.'
He went away; I was left alone.
I sat down on a felled stump, leaned my elbows on my knees, and after a long stillness, raised my head and looked around me. Oh, how still and sullenly gloomy was everything around me—no, not gloomy even, but dumb, cold, and menacing at the same time! My heart sank. At that instant, at that spot, I had a sense of death breathing upon me, I felt I almost touched its perpetual closeness. If only one sound had vibrated, one momentary rustle had arisen, in the engulfing stillness of the pine-forest that hemmed me in on all sides! I let my head sink again, almost in terror; it was as though I had looked in, where no man ought to look.... I put my hand over my eyes—and all at once, as though at some mysterious bidding, I began to remember all my life....
There passed in a flash before me my childhood, noisy and peaceful, quarrelsome and good-hearted, with hurried joys and swift sorrows; then my youth rose up, vague, queer, self-conscious, with all its mistakes and beginnings, with disconnected work, and agitated indolence.... There came back, too, to my memory the comrades who shared those early aspirations ... then like lightning in the night there came the gleam of a few bright memories ... then the shadows began to grow and bear down on me, it was darker and darker about me, more dully and quietly the monotonous years ran by—and like a stone, dejection sank upon my heart. I sat without stirring and gazed, gazed with effort and perplexity, as though I saw all my life before me, as though scales had fallen from my eyes. Oh, what have I done! my lips involuntarily murmured in a bitter whisper. O life, life, where, how have you gone without a trace? How have you slipped through my clenched fingers? Have you deceived me, or was it that I knew not how to make use of your gifts? Is it possible? is this fragment, this poor handful of dusty ashes, all that is left of you? Is this cold, stagnant, unnecessary something—I, the I of old days? How? The soul was athirst for happiness so perfect, she rejected with such scorn all that was small, all that was insufficient, she waited: soon happiness would burst on her in a torrent—and has not one drop moistened the parched lips? Oh, my golden strings, you that once so delicately, so sweetly quivered,—I have never, it seems, heard your music ... you had but just sounded—when you broke. Or, perhaps, happiness, the true happiness of all my life, passed close by me, smiled a resplendent smile upon me—and I failed to recognise its divine countenance. Or did it really visit me, sit at my bedside, and is forgotten by me, like a dream? Like a dream, I repeated disconsolately. Elusive images flitted over my soul, awakening in it something between pity and bewilderment ... you too, I thought, dear, familiar, lost faces, you, thronging about me in this deadly solitude, why are you so profoundly and mournfully silent? From what abyss have you arisen? How am I to interpret your enigmatic glances? Are you greeting me, or bidding me farewell? Oh, can it be there is no hope, no turning back? Why are these heavy, belated drops trickling from my eyes? O heart, why, to what end, grieve more? try to forget if you would have peace, harden yourself to the meek acceptance of the last parting, to the bitter words 'good-bye' and 'for ever.' Do not look back, do not remember, do not strive to reach where it is light, where youth laughs, where hope is wreathed with the flowers of spring, where dovelike delight soars on azure wings, where love, like dew in the sunrise, flashes with tears of ecstasy; look not where is bliss, and faith and power—that is not our place!

'Here is water for you,' I heard Yegor's musical voice behind me: 'drink, with God's blessing.'
I could not help starting; this living speech shook me, sent a delightful tremor all through me. It was as though I had fallen into unknown, dark depths, where all was hushed about me, and nothing could be heard but the soft, persistent moan of some unending grief.... I was faint and could not struggle, and all at once there floated down to me a friendly voice, and some mighty hand with one pull drew me up into the light of day. I looked round, and with unutterable consolation saw the serene and honest face of my guide. He stood easily and gracefully before me, and with his habitual smile held out a wet flask full of clear liquid.... I got up.
'Let's go on; lead the way,' I said eagerly. We set off and wandered a long while, till evening. Directly the noonday heat was over, it became cold and dark so rapidly in the forest that one felt no desire to remain in it.
'Away, restless mortals,' it seemed whispering sullenly from each pine. We came out, but it was some time before we could find Kondrat. We shouted, called to him, but he did not answer. All of a sudden, in the profound stillness of the air, we heard his 'wo, wo,' sound distinctly in a ravine close to us.... The wind, which had suddenly sprung up, and as suddenly dropped again, had prevented him from hearing our calls. Only on the trees which stood some distance apart were traces of its onslaught to be seen; many of the leaves were blown inside out, and remained so, giving a variegated look to the motionless foliage. We got into the cart, and drove home. I sat, swaying to and fro, and slowly breathing in the damp, rather keen air; and all my recent reveries and regrets were drowned in the one sensation of drowsiness and fatigue, in the one desire to get back as soon as possible to the shelter of a warm house, to have a good drink of tea with cream, to nestle into the soft, yielding hay, and to sleep, to sleep, to sleep....

SECOND DAY

The next morning the three of us set off to the 'Charred Wood.' Ten years before, several thousand acres in the 'Forest' had been burnt down, and had not up to that time grown again; here and there, young firs and pines were shooting up, but for the most part there was nothing but moss and ashes. In this 'Charred Wood,' which is reckoned to be about nine miles from Svyatoe, there are all sorts of berries growing in great profusion, and it is a favourite haunt of grouse, who are very fond of strawberries and bilberries.
We were driving along in silence, when suddenly Kondrat raised his head.
'Ah!' he exclaimed: 'why, that's never Efrem standing yonder! 'Morning to you, Alexandritch,' he added, raising his voice, and lifting his cap.
A short peasant in a short, black smock, with a cord round the waist, came out from behind a tree, and approached the cart.
'Why, have they let you off?' inquired Kondrat.
'I should think so!' replied the peasant, and he grinned. 'You don't catch them keeping the likes of me.'
'And what did Piotr Filippitch say to it?'
'Filippov, is it? Oh, he's all right.'
'You don't say so! Why, I thought, Alexandritch—well, brother, thought I, now you 're the goose that must lie down in the frying-pan!'
'On account of Piotr Filippov, hey? Get along! We've seen plenty like him. He tries to pass for a wolf, and then slinks off like a dog.—Going shooting your honour, hey?' the peasant suddenly inquired, turning his little, screwed-up eyes rapidly upon me, and at once dropping them again.
'Yes.'

'And whereabouts, now?'

'To the Charred Wood,' said Kondrat.

'You 're going to the Charred Wood? mind you don't get into the fire.'

'Eh?'

'I've seen a lot of woodcocks,' the peasant went on, seeming all the while to be laughing, and making Kondrat no answer. 'But you'll never get there; as the crow flies it'll be fifteen miles. Why, even Yegor here—not a doubt but he's as at home in the forest as in his own back-yard, but even he won't make his way there. Hullo, Yegor, you honest penny halfpenny soul!' he shouted suddenly.

'Good morning, Efrem,' Yegor responded deliberately.

I looked with curiosity at this Efrem. It was long since I had seen such a queer face. He had a long, sharp nose, thick lips, and a scanty beard. His little blue eyes positively danced, like little imps. He stood in a free-and-easy pose, his arms akimbo, and did not touch his cap.

'Going home for a visit, eh?' Kondrat questioned him.

'Go on! on a visit! It's not the weather for that, my lad; it's set fair. It's all open and free, my dear; one may lie on the stove till winter time, not a dog will stir. When I was in the town, the clerk said: "Give us up," says he, "'Lexandritch; you just get out of the district, we'll let you have a passport, first-class one ..." but there, I'd pity on you Svyatoe fellows: you'd never get another thief like me.'

Kondrat laughed.

'You will have your joke, uncle, you will, upon my word,' he said, and he shook the reins. The horses started off.

'Wo,' said Efrem. The horses stopped. Kondrat did not like this prank.

'Enough of your nonsense, Alexandritch,' he observed in an undertone: 'don't you see we're out with a gentleman? You mind; he'll be angry.'

'Get on with you, sea-drake! What should he be angry about? He's a good-natured gentleman. You see, he'll give me something to drink. Hey, master, give a poor scoundrel a dram! Won't I drink it!' he added, shrugging his shoulder up to his ear, and grating his teeth.

I could not help smiling, gave him a copper, and told Kondrat to drive on.

'Much obliged, your honour,' Efrem shouted after us in soldierly fashion. 'And you'll know, Kondrat, for the future from whom to learn manners. Faint heart never wins; 'tis boldness gains the day. When you come back, come to my place, d'ye hear? There'll be drinking going on three days at home; there'll be some necks broken, I can tell you; my wife's a devil of a woman; our yard's on the side of a precipice.... Ay, magpie, have a good time till your tail gets pinched.' And with a sharp whistle, Efrem plunged into the bushes.

'What sort of man is he?' I questioned Kondrat, who, sitting in the front, kept shaking his head, as though deliberating with himself.

'That fellow?' replied Kondrat, and he looked down. 'That fellow?' he repeated.

'Yes. Is he of your village?'

'Yes, he's a Svyatoe man. He's a fellow.... You wouldn't find the like of him, if you hunted for a hundred miles round. A thief and cheat—good Lord, yes! Another man's property simply, as it were, takes his eye. You may bury a thing underground, and you won't hide it from him; and as to money, you might sit on it, and he'd get it from under you without your noticing it.'

'What a bold fellow he is!'

'Bold? Yes, he's not afraid of any one. But just look at him; he's a beast by his physiognomy; you can see by his nose.' (Kondrat often used to drive with gentlemen, and had been in the chief town of the province, and so liked on occasion to show off his attainments.) 'There's positively no doing anything with him. How many times they've taken him off to put him in the prison!—it's simply trouble thrown away. They start tying him up, and he'll say, "Come, why don't you fasten that leg? fasten that one too, and a little tighter: I'll have a little sleep meanwhile; and I shall get home before your escort." And lo and behold! there he is back again, yes, back again, upon my soul! Well as we all about here know the forest, being used to it from childhood, we're no match for him there. Last summer he came at night straight across from Altuhin to Svyatoe, and no one had ever been known to walk it—it'll be over thirty miles. And he steals honey too; no one can beat him at that; and the bees don't sting him. There's not a hive he hasn't plundered.'

'I expect he doesn't spare the wild bees either?'

'Well, no, I won't lay a false charge against him. That sin's never been observed in him. The wild bees' nest is a holy thing with us. A hive is shut in by fences; there's a watch kept; if you get the honey—it's your luck; but the wild bee is a thing of God's, not guarded; only the bear touches it.'

'Because he is a bear,' remarked Yegor.

'Is he married?'

'To be sure. And he has a son. And won't he be a thief too, the son! He's taken after his father. And he's training him now too. The other day he took a pot with some old coppers in it, stolen somewhere, I've no doubt, went and buried it in a clearing in the forest, and went home and sent his son to the clearing. "Till you find the pot," says he, "I won't give you anything to eat, or let you into the place." The son stayed the whole day in the forest, and spent the night there, but he found the pot. Yes, he's a smart chap, that Efrem. When he's at home, he's a civil fellow, presses every one; you may eat and drink as you will, and there'll be dancing got up at his place and merry-making of all sorts. And when he comes to the meeting—we have a parish meeting, you know, in our village—well, no one talks better sense than he does; he'll come up behind, listen, say a word as if he chopped it off, and away again; and a weighty word it'll be, too. But when he's about in the forest, ah! that means trouble! We've to look out for mischief. Though, I must say, he doesn't touch his own people unless he's in a fix. If he meets a Svyatoe man: "Go along with you, brother," he'll shout, a long way away; "the forest devil's upon me: I shall kill you!"—it's a bad business!'

'What can you all be thinking about? A whole district can't get even with one man?'

'Well, that's just how it is, any way.'

'Is he a sorcerer, then?'

'Who can say! Here, some days ago, he crept round at night to the deacon's near, after the honey, and the deacon was watching the hive himself. Well, he caught him, and in the dark he gave him a good hiding. When he'd done, Efrem, he says to him: "But d'you know who it is you've been beating?" The deacon, when he knew him by his voice, was fairly dumfoundered. "Well, my good friend," says Efrem, "you won't get off so easily for this." The deacon fell down at his feet. "Take," says he, "what you please." "No," says he. "I'll take it from you at my own time and as I choose." And what do you think? Since that day the deacon's as though he'd been scalded; he wanders about like a ghost. "It's taken," says he, "all the heart out of me; it was a dreadful, powerful saying, to be sure, the brigand fastened upon me." That's how it is with him, with the deacon.'

'That deacon must be a fool,' I observed.

'A fool? Well, but what do you say to this? There was once an order issued to seize this fellow, Efrem. We had a police commissary then, a sharp man. And so a dozen chaps went off into the forest to take Efrem. They look, and there he is coming to meet them.... One of them shouts, "Here he is, hold him, tie him!" But Efrem stepped into the forest and cut himself a branch, two fingers' thickness, like this, and then out he skips into the road again, looking so frightful, so terrible, and gives the command like a general at a review: "On your knees!" All of them fairly fell down. "But who," says he, "shouted hold him, tie him? You, Seryoga?" The fellow simply jumped up and ran ... and Efrem after him, and kept swinging his branch at his heels.... For nearly a mile he stroked him down. And afterwards he never ceased to regret: "Ah," he'd say, "it is annoying I didn't lay him up for the confession." For it was just before St. Philip's day. Well, they changed the police commissary soon after, but it all ended the same way.'

'Why did they all give in to him?'

'Why! well, it is so….'

'He has frightened you all, and now he does as he likes with you.'

'Frightened, yes…. He'd frighten any one. And he's a wonderful hand at contrivances, my goodness, yes! I once came upon him in the forest; there was a heavy rain falling; I was for edging away…. But he looked at me, and beckoned to me with his hand like this. "Come along," says he, "Kondrat, don't be afraid. Let me show you how to live in the forest, and to keep dry in the rain." I went up to him, and he was sitting under a fir-tree, and he'd made a fire of damp twigs: the smoke hung about in the fir-tree, and kept the rain from dripping through. I was astonished at him then. And I'll tell you what he contrived one time' (and Kondrat laughed); 'he really did do a funny thing. They'd been thrashing the oats at the thrashing-floor, and they hadn't finished; they hadn't time to rake up the last heap; well, they 'd set two watch-men by it for the night, and they weren't the boldest-hearted of the chaps either. Well, they were sitting and gossiping, and Efrem takes and stuffs his shirt-sleeves full of straw, ties up the wrist-bands, and puts the shirt up over his head. And so he steals up in that shape to the thrashing-floor, and just pops out from behind the corner and gives them a peep of his horns. One chap says to the other: "Do you see?" "Yes," says the other, and didn't he give a screech all of a sudden … and then the fences creaked and nothing more was seen of them. Efrem shovelled up the oats into a bag and dragged it off home. He told the story himself afterwards. He put them to shame, he did, the chaps…. He did really!'

Kondrat laughed again. And Yegor smiled. 'So the fences creaked and that was all?' he commented. 'There was nothing more seen of them,' Kondrat assented. 'They were simply gone in a flash.'

We were all silent again. Suddenly Kondrat started and sat up.

'Eh, mercy upon us!' he ejaculated; 'surely it's never a fire!'

'Where, where?' we asked.

'Yonder, see, in front, where we 're going…. A fire it is! Efrem there, Efrem—why, he foretold it! If it's not his doing, the damned fellow!…'

I glanced in the direction Kondrat was pointing. Two or three miles ahead of us, behind a green strip of low fir saplings, there really was a thick column of dark blue smoke slowly rising from the ground, gradually twisting and coiling into a cap-shaped cloud; to the right and left of it could be seen others, smaller and whiter.

A peasant, all red and perspiring, in nothing but his shirt, with his hair hanging dishevelled about his scared face, galloped straight towards us, and with difficulty stopped his hastily bridled horse.

'Mates,' he inquired breathlessly, 'haven't you seen the foresters?'

'No, we haven't. What is it? is the forest on fire?'

'Yes. We must get the people together, or else if it gets to Trosnoe …'

The peasant tugged with his elbows, pounded with his heels on the horse's sides…. It galloped off.

Kondrat, too, whipped up his pair. We drove straight towards the smoke, which was spreading more and more widely; in places it suddenly grew black and rose up high. The nearer we moved to it, the more indefinite became its outlines; soon all the air was clouded over, there was a strong smell of burning, and here and there between the trees, with a strange, weird quivering in the sunshine, gleamed the first pale red tongues of flame.

'Well, thank God,' observed Kondrat, 'it seems it's an overground fire.'

'What's that?'

'Overground? One that runs along over the earth. With an underground fire, now, it's a difficult job to deal. What's one to do, when the earth's on fire for a whole yard's depth? There's only one means of safety—digging ditches,—and do you suppose that's easy? But an overground fire's nothing. It only scorches the grasses and burns the dry leaves! The forest will be all the better for it. Ouf, though, mercy on us, look how it flares!'

We drove almost up to the edge of the fire. I got down and went to meet it. It was neither dangerous nor difficult. The fire was running over the scanty pine-forest against the wind; it moved in an uneven line, or, to speak more accurately, in a dense jagged wall of curved tongues. The smoke was carried away by the wind. Kondrat had told the truth; it really was an overground fire, which only scorched the grass and passed on without finishing its work, leaving behind it a black and smoking, but not even smouldering, track. At times, it is true, when the fire came upon a hole filled with dry wood and twigs, it suddenly and with a kind of peculiar, rather vindictive roar, rose up in long, quivering points; but it soon sank down again and ran on as before, with a slight hiss and crackle. I even noticed, more than once, an oak-bush, with dry hanging leaves, hemmed in all round and yet untouched, except for a slight singeing at its base. I must own I could not understand why the dry leaves were not burned. Kondrat explained to me that it was owing to the fact that the fire was overground, 'that's to say, not angry.' 'But it's fire all the same,' I protested. 'Overground fire,' repeated Kondrat. However, overground as it was, the fire, none the less, produced its effect: hares raced up and down with a sort of disorder, running back with no sort of necessity into the neighbourhood of the fire; birds fell down in the smoke and whirled round and round; horses looked back and neighed, the forest itself fairly hummed—and man felt discomfort from the heat suddenly beating into his face....

'What are we looking at?' said Yegor suddenly, behind my back. 'Let's go on.'

'But where are we to go?' asked Kondrat.

'Take the left, over the dry bog; we shall get through.'

We turned to the left, and got through, though it was sometimes difficult for both the horses and the cart.

The whole day we wandered over the Charred Wood. At evening—the sunset had not yet begun to redden in the sky, but the shadows from the trees already lay long and motionless, and in the grass one could feel that chill that comes before the dew—I lay down by the roadside near the cart in which Kondrat, without haste, was harnessing the horses after their feed, and I recalled my cheerless reveries of the day before. Everything around was as still as the previous evening, but there was not the forest, stifling and weighing down the spirit. On the dry moss, on the crimson grasses, on the soft dust of the road, on the slender stems and pure little leaves of the young birch-trees, lay the clear soft light of the no longer scorching, sinking sun. Everything was resting, plunged in soothing coolness; nothing was yet asleep, but everything was getting ready for the restoring slumber of evening and night-time. Everything seemed to be saying to man: 'Rest, brother of ours; breathe lightly, and grieve not, thou too, at the sleep close before thee.' I raised my head and saw at the very end of a delicate twig one of those large flies with emerald head, long body, and four transparent wings, which the fanciful French call 'maidens,' while our guileless people has named them 'bucket-yokes.' For a long while, more than an hour, I did not take my eyes off her. Soaked through and through with sunshine, she did not stir, only from time to time turning her head from side to side and shaking her lifted wings ... that was all. Looking at her, it suddenly seemed to me that I understood the life of nature, understood its clear and unmistakable though, to many, still mysterious significance. A subdued, quiet animation, an unhasting, restrained use of sensations and powers, an equilibrium of health in each separate creature—there is her very basis, her unvarying law, that is what she stands upon and holds to. Everything that goes beyond this level, above or below—it makes no difference—she flings away as worthless. Many insects die as soon as they know the joys of love, which destroy the equilibrium. The sick beast plunges into the thicket and expires there alone: he seems to feel that he no longer has the right to look upon the sun that is common to all, nor to breathe the open air; he has not the right to live;—and the man who from his own fault or from the fault of others is faring ill in the world—ought, at least, to know how to keep silence.

'Well, Yegor!' cried Kondrat all at once. He had already settled himself on the box of the cart and was shaking and playing with the reins. 'Come, sit down. What are you so thoughtful about? Still about the cow?'
'About the cow? What cow?' I repeated, and looked at Yegor: calm and stately as ever, he certainly did seem thoughtful, and was gazing away into the distance towards the fields already beginning to get dark.
'Don't you know?' answered Kondrat; 'his last cow died last night. He has no luck.—What are you going to do?'....
Yegor sat down on the box, without speaking, and we drove off. 'That man knows how to bear in silence,' I thought.

YAKOV PASINKOV

I

It happened in Petersburg, in the winter, on the first day of the carnival. I had been invited to dinner by one of my schoolfellows, who enjoyed in his youth the reputation of being as modest as a maiden, and turned out in the sequel a person by no means over rigid in his conduct. He is dead now, like most of my schoolfellows. There were to be present at the dinner, besides me, Konstantin Alexandrovitch Asanov, and a literary celebrity of those days. The literary celebrity kept us waiting for him, and finally sent a note that he was not coming, and in place of him there turned up a little light-haired gentleman, one of the everlasting uninvited guests with whom Petersburg abounds.
The dinner lasted a long while; our host did not spare the wine, and by degrees our heads were affected. Everything that each of us kept hidden in his heart—and who is there that has not something hidden in his heart?—came to the surface. Our host's face suddenly lost its modest and reserved expression; his eyes shone with a brazen-faced impudence, and a vulgar grin curved his lips; the light-haired gentleman laughed in a feeble way, with a senseless crow; but Asanov surprised me more than any one. The man had always been conspicuous for his sense of propriety, but now he began by suddenly rubbing his hand over his forehead, giving himself airs, boasting of his connections, and continually alluding to a certain uncle of his, a very important personage.... I positively should not have known him; he was unmistakably jeering at us ... he all but avowed his contempt for our society. Asanov's insolence began to exasperate me.
'Listen,' I said to him; 'if we are such poor creatures to your thinking, you'd better go and see your illustrious uncle. But possibly he's not at home to you.'
Asanov made me no reply, and went on passing his hand across his forehead.
'What a set of people!' he said again; 'they've never been in any decent society, never been acquainted with a single decent woman, while I have here,' he cried, hurriedly pulling a pocket-book out of his side-pocket and tapping it with his hand, 'a whole pack of letters from a girl whom you wouldn't find the equal of in the whole world.'
Our host and the light-haired gentleman paid no attention to Asanov's last words; they were holding each other by their buttons, and both relating something; but I pricked up my ears.
'Oh, you 're bragging, Mr. nephew of an illustrious personage,' I said, going up to Asanov; 'you haven't any letters at all.'
'Do you think so?' he retorted, and he looked down loftily at me; 'what's this, then?' He opened the pocket-book, and showed me about a dozen letters addressed to him.... A familiar handwriting, I fancied.... I feel the flush of shame mounting to my cheeks ... my self-love is suffering horribly.... No one likes to own to a mean action.... But there is nothing for it:

when I began my story, I knew I should have to blush to my ears in the course of it. And so, I am bound to harden my heart and confess that....

Well, this was what passed: I took advantage of the intoxicated condition of Asanov, who had carelessly dropped the letters on the champagne-stained tablecloth (my own head was dizzy enough too), and hurriedly ran my eyes over one of the letters....

My heart stood still.... Alas! I was myself in love with the girl who had written to Asanov, and I could have no doubt now that she loved him. The whole letter, which was in French, expressed tenderness and devotion....

'Mon cher ami Constantin!' so it began ... and it ended with the words: 'be careful as before, and I will be yours or no one's.'

Stunned as by a thunderbolt, I sat for a few instants motionless; at last I regained my self-possession, jumped up, and rushed out of the room.

A quarter of an hour later I was back at home in my own lodgings.

* * * * *

The family of the Zlotnitskys was one of the first whose acquaintance I made on coming to Petersburg from Moscow. It consisted of a father and mother, two daughters, and a son. The father, a man already grey, but still vigorous, who had been in the army, held a fairly important position, spent the morning in a government office, went to sleep after dinner, and in the evening played cards at his club.... He was seldom at home, spoke little and unwillingly, looked at one from under his eyebrows with an expression half surly, half indifferent, and read nothing except books of travels and geography. Sometimes he was unwell, and then he would shut himself up in his own room, and paint little pictures, or tease the old grey parrot, Popka. His wife, a sickly, consumptive woman, with hollow black eyes and a sharp nose, did not leave her sofa for days together, and was always embroidering cushion-covers in canvas. As far as I could observe, she was rather afraid of her husband, as though she had somehow wronged him at some time or other. The elder daughter, Varvara, a plump, rosy, fair-haired girl of eighteen, was always sitting at the window, watching the people that passed by. The son, who was being educated in a government school, was only seen at home on Sundays, and he, too, did not care to waste his words. Even the younger daughter, Sophia, the girl with whom I was in love, was of a silent disposition. In the Zlotnitskys' house there reigned a perpetual stillness; it was only broken by the piercing screams of Popka, but visitors soon got used to these, and were conscious again of the burden and oppression of the eternal stillness. Visitors, however, seldom looked in upon the Zlotnitskys; their house was a dull one. The very furniture, the red paper with yellow patterns in the drawing-room, the numerous rush-bottomed chairs in the dining-room, the faded wool-work cushions, embroidered with figures of girls and dogs, on the sofa, the branching lamps, and the gloomy-looking portraits on the walls—everything inspired an involuntary melancholy, about everything there clung a sense of chill and flatness. On my arrival in Petersburg, I had thought it my duty to call on the Zlotnitskys. They were relations of my mother's. I managed with difficulty to sit out an hour with them, and it was a long while before I went there again. But by degrees I took to going oftener and oftener. I was drawn there by Sophia, whom I had not cared for at first, and with whom I finally fell in love.

She was a slender, almost thin, girl of medium height, with a pale face, thick black hair, and big brown eyes, always half closed. Her severe and well-defined features, especially her tightly shut lips, showed determination and strength of will. At home they knew her to be a girl with a will of her own....

'She's like her eldest sister, like Katerina,' Madame Zlotnitsky said one day, as she sat alone with me (in her husband's presence she did not dare to mention the said Katerina). 'You don't know her; she's in the Caucasus, married. At thirteen, only fancy, she fell in love with her husband, and announced to us at the time that she would never marry any one else. We did everything we could—nothing was of any use. She waited till she was three-and-twenty, and braved her father's anger, and so married her idol. There is no saying what Sonitchka might not do! The Lord preserve her from such stubbornness! But I am afraid for her; she's only sixteen now, and there's no turning her….'

Mr. Zlotnitsky came in, and his wife was instantly silent.

What had captivated me in Sophia was not her strength of will—no; but with all her dryness, her lack of vivacity and imagination, she had a special charm of her own, the charm of straightforwardness, genuine sincerity, and purity of heart. I respected her as much as I loved her…. It seemed to me that she too looked with friendly eyes on me; to have my illusions as to her feeling for me shattered, and her love for another man proved conclusively, was a blow to me.

The unlooked-for discovery I had made astonished me the more as Asanov was not often at the Zlotnitskys' house, much less so than I, and had shown no marked preference for Sonitchka. He was a handsome, dark fellow, with expressive but rather heavy features, with brilliant, prominent eyes, with a large white forehead, and full red lips under fine moustaches. He was very discreet, but severe in his behaviour, confident in his criticisms and utterances, and dignified in his silence. It was obvious that he thought a great deal of himself. Asanov rarely laughed, and then with closed teeth, and he never danced. He was rather loosely and clumsily built. He had at one time served in the —th regiment, and was spoken of as a capable officer.

'A strange thing!' I ruminated, lying on the sofa; 'how was it I noticed nothing?' … 'Be careful as before': those words in Sophia's letter suddenly recurred to my memory. 'Ah!' I thought: 'that's it! What a sly little hussy! And I thought her open and sincere…. Wait a bit, that's all; I'll let you know….'

But at this point, if I can trust my memory, I began weeping bitterly, and could not get to sleep all night.

* * * * *

Next day at two o'clock I set off to the Zlotnitskys'. The father was not at home, and his wife was not sitting in her usual place; after the pancake festival of the preceding day, she had a headache, and had gone to lie down in her bedroom. Varvara was standing with her shoulder against the window, looking into the street; Sophia was walking up and down the room with her arms folded across her bosom; Popka was shrieking.

'Ah! how do you do?' said Varvara lazily, directly I came into the room, and she added at once in an undertone, 'There goes a peasant with a tray on his head.' … (She had the habit of keeping up a running commentary on the passers-by to herself.)

'How do you do?' I responded; 'how do you do, Sophia Nikolaevna? Where is Tatiana Vassilievna?'

'She has gone to lie down,' answered Sophia, still pacing the room.

'We had pancakes,' observed Varvara, without turning round. 'Why didn't you come? … Where can that clerk be going?' 'Oh, I hadn't time.' ('Present arms!' the parrot screeched shrilly.) 'How Popka is shrieking to-day!'

'He always does shriek like that,' observed Sophia.

We were all silent for a time.

'He has gone in at the gate,' said Varvara, and she suddenly got up on the window-sill and opened the window.

'What are you about?' asked Sophia.

'There's a beggar,' responded Varvara. She bent down, picked up a five-copeck piece from the window; the remains of a fumigating pastille still stood in a grey heap of ashes on the copper coin, as she flung it into the street; then she slammed the window to and jumped heavily down to the floor….

'I had a very pleasant time yesterday,' I began, seating myself in an arm-chair. 'I dined with a friend of mine; Konstantin Alexandritch was there…. (I looked at Sophia; not an eyebrow quivered on her face.) 'And I must own,' I continued, 'we'd a good deal of wine; we emptied eight bottles between the four of us.'

'Really!' Sophia articulated serenely, and she shook her head.
'Yes,' I went on, slightly irritated at her composure: 'and do you know what, Sophia Nikolaevna, it's a true saying, it seems, that in wine is truth.'
'How so?'
'Konstantin Alexandritch made us laugh. Only fancy, he began all at once passing his hand over his forehead like this, and saying: "I'm a fine fellow! I've an uncle a celebrated man!"….'
'Ha, ha!' came Varvara's short, abrupt laugh.
….'Popka! Popka! Popka!' the parrot dinned back at her.
Sophia stood still in front of me, and looked me straight in the face.
'And you, what did you say?' she asked; 'don't you remember?'
I could not help blushing.
'I don't remember! I expect I was pretty absurd too. It certainly is dangerous to drink,' I added with significant emphasis; 'one begins chattering at once, and one's apt to say what no one ought to know. One's sure to be sorry for it afterwards, but then it's too late.'
'Why, did you let out some secret?' asked Sophia.
'I am not referring to myself.'
Sophia turned away, and began walking up and down the room again. I stared at her, raging inwardly. 'Upon my word,' I thought, 'she is a child, a baby, and how she has herself in hand! She's made of stone, simply. But wait a bit….'
'Sophia Nikolaevna …' I said aloud.
Sophia stopped.
'What is it?'
'Won't you play me something on the piano? By the way, I've something I want to say to you,' I added, dropping my voice.
Sophia, without saying a word, walked into the other room; I followed her. She came to a standstill at the piano.
'What am I to play you?' she inquired.
'What you like … one of Chopin's nocturnes.'
Sophia began the nocturne. She played rather badly, but with feeling. Her sister played nothing but polkas and waltzes, and even that very seldom. She would go sometimes with her indolent step to the piano, sit down, let her coat slip from her shoulders down to her elbows (I never saw her without a coat), begin playing a polka very loud, and without finishing it, begin another, then she would suddenly heave a sigh, get up, and go back again to the window. A queer creature was that Varvara!
I sat down near Sophia.
'Sophia Nikolaevna,' I began, watching her intently from one side. 'I ought to tell you a piece of news, news disagreeable to me.'
'News? what is it?'
'I'll tell you…. Up till now I have been mistaken in you, completely mistaken.'
'How was that?' she rejoined, going on playing, and keeping her eyes fixed on her fingers.
'I imagined you to be open; I imagined that you were incapable of hypocrisy, of hiding your feelings, deceiving….'
Sophia bent her face closer over the music.
'I don't understand you.'
'And what's more,' I went on; 'I could never have conceived that you, at your age, were already quite capable of acting a part in such masterly fashion.'
Sophia's hands faintly trembled above the keys. 'Why are you saying this?' she said, still not looking at me; 'I play a part?'
'Yes, you do.' (She smiled … I was seized with spiteful fury.) … 'You pretend to be indifferent to a man and … and you write letters to him,' I added in a whisper.
Sophia's cheeks grew white, but she did not turn to me: she played the nocturne through to the end, got up, and closed the piano.

'Where are you going?' I asked her in some perplexity. 'You have no answer to make me?'
'What answer can I make you? I don't know what you 're talking about…. And I am not good at pretending….'
She began putting by the music.
The blood rushed to my head. 'No; you know what I am talking about,' I said, and I too got up from my seat; 'or if you like, I will remind you directly of some of your expressions in one letter: "be as careful as before"….'
Sophia gave a faint start.
'I never should have expected this of you,' she said at last.
'I never should have expected,' I retorted, 'that you, Sophia Nikolaevna, would have deigned to notice a man who …'
Sophia turned with a rapid movement to me; I instinctively stepped back a little from her; her eyes, always half closed, were so wide open that they looked immense, and they glittered wrathfully under her frowning brows.
'Oh! if that's it,' she said, 'let me tell you that I love that man, and that it's absolutely no consequence to me what you think about him or about my love for him. And what business is it of yours? … What right have you to speak of this? If I have made up my mind …'
She stopped speaking, and went hurriedly out of the room. I stood still. I felt all of a sudden so uncomfortable and so ashamed that I hid my face in my hands. I realised all the impropriety, all the baseness of my behaviour, and, choked with shame and remorse, I stood as it were in disgrace. 'Mercy,' I thought, 'what I've done!'
'Anton Nikititch,' I heard the maid-servant saying in the outer-room, 'get a glass of water, quick, for Sophia Nikolaevna.'
'What's wrong?' answered the man.
'I fancy she's crying….'
I started up and went into the drawing-room for my hat.
'What were you talking about to Sonitchka?' Varvara inquired indifferently, and after a brief pause she added in an undertone, 'Here's that clerk again.'
I began saying good-bye.
'Why are you going? Stay a little; mamma is coming down directly.'
'No; I can't now,' I said: 'I had better call and see her another time.'
At that instant, to my horror, to my positive horror, Sophia walked with resolute steps into the drawing-room. Her face was paler than usual, and her eyelids were a little red. She never even glanced at me.
'Look, Sonia,' observed Varvara; 'there's a clerk keeps continually passing our house.'
'A spy, perhaps…' Sophia remarked coldly and contemptuously.
This was too much. I went away, and I really don't know how I got home.
I felt very miserable, wretched and miserable beyond description. In twenty-four hours two such cruel blows! I had learned that Sophia loved another man, and I had for ever forfeited her respect. I felt myself so utterly annihilated and disgraced that I could not even feel indignant with myself. Lying on the sofa with my face turned to the wall, I was revelling in the first rush of despairing misery, when I suddenly heard footsteps in the room. I lifted my head and saw one of my most intimate friends, Yakov Pasinkov.
I was ready to fly into a rage with any one who had come into my room that day, but with Pasinkov I could never be angry. Quite the contrary; in spite of the sorrow devouring me, I was inwardly rejoiced at his coming, and I nodded to him. He walked twice up and down the room, as his habit was, clearing his throat, and stretching out his long limbs; then he stood a minute facing me in silence, and in silence he seated himself in a corner.
I had known Pasinkov a very long while, almost from childhood. He had been brought up at the same private school, kept by a German, Winterkeller, at which I had spent three years. Yakov's father, a poor major on the retired list, a very honest man, but a little deranged mentally, had brought him, when a boy of seven, to this German; had paid for him for a year

in advance, and had then left Moscow and been lost sight of completely.... From time to time there were dark, strange rumours about him. Eight years later it was known as a positive fact that he had been drowned in a flood when crossing the Irtish. What had taken him to Siberia, God knows. Yakov had no other relations; his mother had long been dead. He was simply left stranded on Winterkeller's hands. Yakov had, it is true, a distant relation, a great-aunt; but she was so poor, that she was afraid at first to go to her nephew, for fear she should have the care of him thrust upon her. Her fears turned out to be groundless; the kind-hearted German kept Yakov with him, let him study with his other pupils, fed him (dessert, however, was not offered him except on Sundays), and rigged him out in clothes cut out of the cast-off morning-gowns—usually snuff-coloured—of his mother, an old Livonian lady, still alert and active in spite of her great age. Owing to all these circumstances, and owing generally to Yakov's inferior position in the school, his schoolfellows treated him in rather a casual fashion, looked down upon him, and used to call him 'mammy's dressing-gown,' the 'nephew of the mob-cap' (his aunt invariably wore a very peculiar mob-cap with a bunch of yellow ribbons sticking straight upright, like a globe artichoke, upon it), and sometimes the 'son of Yermak' (because his father had, like that hero, been drowned in the Irtish). But in spite of those nicknames, in spite of his ridiculous garb, and his absolute destitution, every one was fond of him, and indeed it was impossible not to be fond of him; a sweeter, nobler nature, I imagine, has never existed upon earth. He was very good at lessons too.

When I saw him first, he was sixteen years old, and I was only just thirteen. I was an exceedingly selfish and spoilt boy; I had grown up in a rather wealthy house, and so, on entering the school, I lost no time in making friends with a little prince, an object of special solicitude to Winterkeller, and with two or three other juvenile aristocrats; while I gave myself great airs with all the rest. Pasinkov I did not deign to notice at all. I regarded the long, gawky lad, in a shapeless coat and short trousers, which showed his coarse thread stockings, as some sort of page-boy, one of the house-serfs—at best, a person of the working class. Pasinkov was extremely courteous and gentle to everybody, though he never sought the society of any one. If he were rudely treated, he was neither humiliated nor sullen; he simply withdrew and held himself aloof, with a sort of regretful look, as it were biding his time. This was just how he behaved with me. About two months passed. One bright summer day I happened to go out of the playground after a noisy game of leap-frog, and walking into the garden I saw Pasinkov sitting on a bench under a high lilac-bush. He was reading. I glanced at the cover of the book as I passed, and read *Schiller's Werke* on the back. I stopped short.

'Do you mean to say you know German?' I questioned Pasinkov....

I feel ashamed to this day as I recall all the arrogance there was in the very sound of my voice.... Pasinkov softly raised his small but expressive eyes and looked at me.

'Yes,' he answered; 'do you?'

'I should hope so!' I retorted, feeling insulted at the question, and I was about to go on my way, but something held me back.

'What is it you are reading of Schiller?' I asked, with the same haughty insolence.

'At this moment I am reading "Resignation," a beautiful poem. Would you like me to read it to you? Come and sit here by me on the bench.'

I hesitated a little, but I sat down. Pasinkov began reading. He knew

German far better than I did. He had to explain the meaning of several lines for me. But already I felt no shame at my ignorance and his superiority to me. From that day, from the very hour of our reading together in the garden, in the shade of the lilac-bush, I loved Pasinkov with my whole soul, I attached myself to him and fell completely under his sway.

I have a vivid recollection of his appearance in those days. He changed very little, however, later on. He was tall, thin, and rather awkwardly built, with a long back, narrow shoulders, and a hollow chest, which made him look rather frail and delicate, although as a fact he had nothing to complain of on the score of health. His large, dome-shaped head was carried a little on one side; his soft, flaxen hair straggled in lank locks about his slender neck. His face was not handsome, and might even have struck one as absurd, owing to the long, full, and reddish nose, which seemed almost to overhang his wide, straight mouth. But his open brow was splendid; and when he smiled, his little grey eyes gleamed with such mild and affectionate goodness, that every one felt warmed and cheered at heart at the very sight of him. I remember his voice too, soft and even, with a peculiar sort of sweet huskiness in it. He spoke, as a rule, little, and with noticeable difficulty. But when he warmed up, his words flowed freely, and—strange to say!—his voice grew still softer, his glance seemed turned inward and lost its fire, while his whole face faintly glowed. On his lips the words 'goodness,' 'truth,' 'life,' 'science,' 'love,' however enthusiastically they were uttered, never rang with a false note. Without strain, without effort, he stepped into the realm of the ideal; his pure soul was at any moment ready to stand before the 'holy shrine of beauty'; it awaited only the welcoming call, the contact of another soul.... Pasinkov was an idealist, one of the last idealists whom it has been my lot to come across. Idealists, as we all know, are all but extinct in these days; there are none of them, at any rate, among the young people of to day. So much the worse for the young people of to-day!

About three years I spent with Pasinkov, 'soul in soul,' as the saying is.

I was the confidant of his first love. With what grateful sympathy and intentness I listened to his avowal! The object of his passion was a niece of Winterkeller's, a fair-haired, pretty little German, with a chubby, almost childish little face, and confidingly soft blue eyes. She was very kind and sentimental: she loved Mattison, Uhland, and Schiller, and repeated their verses very sweetly in her timid, musical voice. Pasinkov's love was of the most platonic. He only saw his beloved on Sundays, when she used to come and play at forfeits with the Winterkeller children, and he had very little conversation with her. But once, when she said to him, 'mein lieber, lieber Herr Jacob!' he did not sleep all night from excess of bliss. It never even struck him at the time that she called all his schoolfellows 'mein lieber.' I remember, too, his grief and dejection when the news suddenly reached us that Fräulein Frederike—that was her name—was going to be married to Herr Kniftus, the owner of a prosperous butcher's shop, a very handsome man, and well educated too; and that she was marrying him, not simply in submission to parental authority, but positively from love. It was a bitter blow for Pasinkov, and his sufferings were particularly severe on the day of the young people's first visit. The former Fräulein, now Frau, Frederike presented him, once more addressing him as 'lieber Herr Jacob,' to her husband, who was all splendour from top to toe; his eyes, his black hair brushed up into a tuft, his forehead and his teeth, and his coat buttons, and the chain on his waistcoat, everything, down to the boots on his rather large, turned-out feet, shone brilliantly. Pasinkov pressed Herr Kniftus's hand, and wished him (and the wish was sincere, that I am certain) complete and enduring happiness. This took place in my presence. I remember with what admiration and sympathy I gazed at Yakov. I thought him a hero!.... And afterwards, what mournful conversations passed between us. 'Seek consolation in art,' I said to him. 'Yes,' he answered me; 'and in poetry.' 'And in friendship,' I added. 'And in friendship,' he repeated. Oh, happy days!...

It was a grief to me to part from Pasinkov. Just before I left school, he had, after prolonged efforts and difficulties, after a correspondence often amusing, succeeded in obtaining his certificates of birth and baptism and his passport, and had entered the university. He still went on living at Winterkeller's expense; but instead of home-made jackets and breeches, he was provided now with ordinary attire, in return for lessons on various subjects, which he gave the younger pupils. Pasinkov was unchanged in his behaviour to me up to the end of my time at the school, though the difference in our ages began to be more noticeable, and I, I remember, grew jealous of some of his new student friends. His influence on me was most beneficial. It was a pity it did not last longer. To give a single instance: as a child I was in the habit of telling lies.... In Yakov's presence I could not bring my tongue to utter an untruth. What I particularly loved was walking alone with him, or pacing by his side up and down the room, listening while he, not looking at me, read poetry in his soft, intense voice. It positively seemed to me that we were slowly, gradually, getting away from the earth, and soaring away to some radiant, glorious land of mystery.... I remember one night. We were sitting together under the same lilac-bush; we were fond of that spot. All our companions were asleep; but we had softly got up, dressed, fumbling in the dark, and stealthily stepped out 'to dream.' It was fairly warm out of doors, but a fresh breeze blew now and then and made us huddle closer together. We talked, we talked a lot, and with much warmth—so much so, that we positively interrupted each other, though we did not argue. In the sky gleamed stars innumerable. Yakov raised his eyes, and pressing my hand he softly cried out:

'Above our heads
The sky with the eternal stars....
Above the stars their Maker....'

A thrill of awe ran through me; I felt cold all over, and sank on his shoulder.... My heart was full.... Where are those raptures? Alas! where youth is.

In Petersburg I met Yakov again eight years after. I had only just been appointed to a position in the service, and some one had got him a little post in some department. Our meeting was most joyful. I shall never forget the moment when, sitting alone one day at home, I suddenly heard his voice in the passage....

How I started; with what throbbing at the heart I leaped up and flung myself on his neck, without giving him time to take off his fur overcoat and unfasten his scarf! How greedily I gazed at him through bright, involuntary tears of tenderness! He had grown a little older during those seven years; lines, delicate as if they had been traced by a needle, furrowed his brow here and there, his cheeks were a little more hollow, and his hair was thinner; but he had hardly more beard, and his smile was just the same as ever; and his laugh, a soft, inward, as it were breathless laugh, was the same too....

Mercy on us! what didn't we talk about that day! ... The favourite poems we read to one another! I began begging him to move and come and live with me, but he would not consent. He promised, however, to come every day to see me, and he kept his word.

In soul, too, Pasinkov was unchanged. He showed himself just the same idealist as I had always known him. However rudely life's chill, the bitter chill of experience, had closed in about him, the tender flower that had bloomed so early in my friend's heart had kept all its pure beauty untouched. There was no trace of sadness even, no trace even of melancholy in him; he was quiet, as he had always been, but everlastingly glad at heart.

In Petersburg he lived as in a wilderness, not thinking of the future, and knowing scarcely any one. I took him to the Zlotnitskys'. He used to go and see them rather often. Not being self-conscious, he was not shy, but in their house, as everywhere, he said very little; they liked him, however. Even the tedious old man, Tatiana Vassilievna's husband, was friendly to him, and both the silent girls were soon quite at home with him.

Sometimes he would arrive, bringing with him in the back pocket of his coat some book that had just come out, and for a long time would not make up his mind to read, but would keep stretching his neck out on one side, like a bird, looking about him as though inquiring, 'could he?' At last he would establish himself in a corner (he always liked sitting in corners), would pull out a book and set to reading, at first in a whisper, then louder and louder, occasionally interrupting himself with brief criticisms or exclamations. I noticed that Varvara was readier to sit by him and listen than her sister, though she certainly did not understand much; literature was not in her line. She would sit opposite Pasinkov, her chin in her hands, staring at him—not into his eyes, but into his whole face—and would not utter a syllable, but only heave a noisy, sudden sigh. Sometimes in the evenings we used to play forfeits, especially on Sundays and holidays. We were joined on these occasions by two plump, short young ladies, sisters, and distant relations of the Zlotnitskys, terribly given to giggling, and a few lads from the military school, very good-natured, quiet fellows. Pasinkov always used to sit beside Tatiana Vassilievna, and with her, judge what was to be done to the one who had to pay a forfeit.

Sophia did not like the kisses and such demonstrations, with which forfeits are often paid, while Varvara used to be cross if she had to look for anything or guess something. The young ladies giggled incessantly—laughter seemed to bubble up by some magic in them,—I sometimes felt positively irritated as I looked at them, but Pasinkov only smiled and shook his head. Old Zlotnitsky took no part in our games, and even looked at us rather disapprovingly from the door of his study. Only once, utterly unexpectedly, he came in to us, and proposed that whoever had next to pay a forfeit should waltz with him; we, of course, agreed. It happened to be Tatiana Vassilievna who had to pay the forfeit. She crimsoned all over, and was confused and abashed like a girl of fifteen; but her husband at once told Sophia to go to the piano, while he went up to his wife, and waltzed two rounds with her of the old-fashioned *trois temps* waltz. I remember how his bilious, gloomy face, with its never-smiling eyes, kept appearing and disappearing as he slowly turned round, his stern expression never relaxing. He waltzed with a long step and a hop, while his wife pattered rapidly with her feet, and huddled up with her face close to his chest, as though she were in terror. He led her to her place, bowed to her, went back to his room and shut the door. Sophia was just getting up, but Varvara asked her to go on, went up to Pasinkov, and holding out her hand, with an awkward smile, said, 'Will you like a turn?' Pasinkov was surprised, but he jumped up—he was always distinguished by the most delicate courtesy—and took Varvara by the waist, but he slipped down at the first step, and leaving hold of his partner at once, rolled right under the pedestal on which the parrot's cage was standing.... The cage fell, the parrot was frightened and shrieked, 'Present arms!' Every one laughed.... Zlotnitsky appeared at his study door, looked grimly at us, and slammed the door to. From that time forth, one had only to allude to this incident before Varvara, and she would go off into peals of laughter at once, and look at Pasinkov, as though anything cleverer than his behaviour on that occasion it was impossible to conceive.

Pasinkov was very fond of music. He used often to beg Sophia to play him something, and to sit on one side listening, and now and then humming in a thin voice the most pathetic passages. He was particularly fond of Schubert's Constellation. He used to declare that when he heard the air played he could always fancy that with the sounds long rays of azure light came pouring down from on high, straight upon him. To this day, whenever I look upon a cloudless sky at night, with the softly quivering stars, I always recall Schubert's melody and Pasinkov.... An excursion into the country comes back to my mind. We set out, a whole party of us, in two hired four-wheel carriages, to Pargolovo. I remember we took the carriages from the Vladimirsky; they were very old, and painted blue, with round springs, and a wide box-seat, and bundles of hay inside; the brown, broken-winded horses that drew us along at a slow trot were each lame in a different leg. We strolled a long while about the pinewoods round Pargolovo, drank milk out of earthenware pitchers, and ate wild strawberries and sugar. The weather was exquisite. Varvara did not care for long walks: she used soon to get tired; but this time she did not lag behind us. She took off her hat, her hair came down, her heavy features lighted up, and her cheeks were flushed. Meeting two peasant girls in the wood, she sat down suddenly on the ground, called them to her, did not patronise them, but made them sit down beside her. Sophia looked at them from some distance with a cold smile, and did not go up to them. She was walking with Asanov. Zlotnitsky observed that Varvara was a regular hen for sitting. Varvara got up and walked away. In the course of the walk she several times went up to Pasinkov, and said to him, 'Yakov Ivanitch, I want to tell you something,' but what she wanted to tell him—remained unknown.

But it's high time for me to get back to my story.

* * * * *

I was glad to see Pasinkov; but when I recalled what I had done the day before, I felt unutterably ashamed, and I hurriedly turned away to the wall again. After a brief pause, Yakov asked me if I were unwell.

'I'm quite well,' I answered through my teeth; 'only my head aches.'

Yakov made no reply, and took up a book. More than an hour passed by; I was just coming to the point of confessing everything to Yakov ... suddenly there was a ring at the outer bell of my flat.

The door on to the stairs was opened.... I listened.... Asanov was asking my servant if I were at home.

Pasinkov got up; he did not care for Asanov, and telling me in a whisper that he would go and lie down on my bed, he went into my bedroom.

A minute later Asanov entered.

From the very sight of his flushed face, from his brief, cool bow, I guessed that he had not come to me without some set purpose in his mind. 'What is going to happen?' I wondered.

'Sir,' he began, quickly seating himself in an armchair, 'I have come to you for you to settle a matter of doubt for me.'

'And that is?'

'That is: I wish to know whether you are an honest man.'

I flew into a rage. 'What's the meaning of that?' I demanded.

'I'll tell you what's the meaning of it,' he retorted, underlining as it were each word. 'Yesterday I showed you a pocket-book containing letters from a certain person to me.... To-day you repeated to that person, with reproach—with reproach, observe—some expressions from those letters, without having the slightest right to do so. I should like to know what explanation you can give of this?'

'And I should like to know what right you have to cross-examine me,' I answered, trembling with fury and inward shame.

'You chose to boast of your uncle, of your correspondence; I'd nothing to do with it. You've got all your letters all right, haven't you?'

'The letters are all right; but I was yesterday in a condition in which you could easily——'

'In short, sir,' I began, speaking intentionally as loud as I could, 'I beg you to leave me alone, do you hear? I don't want to know anything about it, and I'm not going to give you any explanation. You can go to that person for explanations!' I felt that my head was beginning to go round.

Asanov turned upon me a look to which he obviously tried to impart an air of scornful penetration, pulled his moustaches, and got up slowly.

'I know now what to think,' he observed; 'your face is the best evidence against you. But I must tell you that that's not the way honourable people behave.... To read a letter on the sly, and then to go and worry an honourable girl....'

'Will you go to the devil!' I shouted, stamping, 'and send me a second; I don't mean to talk to you.'

'Kindly refrain from telling me what to do,' Asanov retorted frigidly; 'but I certainly will send a second to you.'

He went away. I fell on the sofa and hid my face in my hands. Some one touched me on the shoulder; I moved my hands—before me was standing Pasinkov.

'What's this? is it true?' ... he asked me. 'You read another man's letter?'

I had not the strength to answer, but I nodded in assent.

Pasinkov went to the window, and standing with his back to me, said slowly: 'You read a letter from a girl to Asanov. Who was the girl?'

'Sophia Zlotnitsky,' I answered, as a prisoner on his trial answers the judge.

For a long while Pasinkov did not utter a word.

'Nothing but passion could to some extent excuse you,' he began at last. 'Are you in love then with the younger Zlotnitsky?'

'Yes.'

Pasinkov was silent again for a little.

'I thought so. And you went to her to-day and began reproaching her?...'

'Yes, yes, yes!...' I articulated desperately. 'Now you can despise me....'

Pasinkov walked a couple of times up and down the room.
'And she loves him?' he queried.
'She loves him….'
Pasinkov looked down, and gazed a long while at the floor without moving.
'Well, it must be set right,' he began, raising his head,' things can't be left like this.'
And he took up his hat.
'Where are you going?'
'To Asanov.'
I jumped up from the sofa.
'But I won't let you. Good heavens! how can you! what will he think?'
Pasinkov looked at me.
'Why, do you think it better to keep this folly up, to bring ruin on yourself, and disgrace on the girl?'
'But what are you going to say to Asanov?'
'I'll try and explain things to him, I'll tell him you beg his forgiveness …'
'But I don't want to apologise to him!'
'You don't? Why, aren't you in fault?'
I looked at Pasinkov; the calm and severe, though mournful, expression of his face impressed me; it was new to me. I made no reply, and sat down on the sofa.
Pasinkov went out.
In what agonies of suspense I waited for his return! With what cruel slowness the time lingered by! At last he came back—late.
'Well?' I queried in a timid voice.
'Thank goodness!' he answered; 'it's all settled.'
'You have been at Asanov's?'
'Yes.'
'Well, and he?—made a great to-do, I suppose?' I articulated with an effort.
'No, I can't say that. I expected more … He … he's not such a vulgar fellow as I thought.'
'Well, and have you seen any one else besides?' I asked, after a brief pause.
'I've been at the Zlotnitskys'.'
'Ah!…' (My heart began to throb. I did not dare look Pasinkov in the face.) 'Well, and she?'
'Sophia Nikolaevna is a reasonable, kind-hearted girl…. Yes, she is a kind-hearted girl. She felt awkward at first, but she was soon at ease. But our whole conversation only lasted five minutes.'
'And you … told her everything … about me … everything?'
'I told her what was necessary.'
'I shall never be able to go and see them again now!' I pronounced dejectedly….
'Why? No, you can go occasionally. On the contrary, you are absolutely bound to go and see them, so that nothing should be thought….'
'Ah, Yakov, you will despise me now!' I cried, hardly keeping back my tears.
'Me! Despise you? …' (His affectionate eyes glowed with love.) 'Despise you … silly fellow! Don't I see how hard it's been for you, how you're suffering?'
He held out his hand to me; I fell on his neck and broke into sobs.
After a few days, during which I noticed that Pasinkov was in very low spirits, I made up my mind at last to go to the Zlotnitskys'. What I felt, as I stepped into their drawing-room, it would be difficult to convey in words; I remember that I could hardly distinguish the persons in the room, and my voice failed me. Sophia was no less ill at ease; she obviously forced herself to address me, but her eyes avoided mine as mine did hers, and every movement she made, her whole being, expressed constraint, mingled … why conceal the truth? with secret aversion. I tried, as far as possible, to spare her and myself from such painful sensations. This meeting was happily our last—before her marriage. A sudden change in my fortunes carried

me off to the other end of Russia, and I bade a long farewell to Petersburg, to the Zlotnitsky family, and, what was most grievous of all for me, to dear Yakov Pasinkov.

II

Seven years had passed by. I don't think it necessary to relate all that happened to me during that period. I moved restlessly about over Russia, and made my way into the remotest wilds, and thank God I did! The wilds are not so much to be dreaded as some people suppose, and in the most hidden places, under the fallen twigs and rotting leaves in the very heart of the forest, spring up flowers of sweet fragrance.

One day in spring, as I was passing on some official duties through a small town in one of the outlying provinces of Eastern Russia, through the dim little window of my coach I saw standing before a shop in the square a man whose face struck me as exceedingly familiar. I looked attentively at the man, and to my great delight recognised him as Elisei, Pasinkov's servant.

I at once told the driver to stop, jumped out of the coach, and went up to Elisei.

'Hullo, friend!' I began, with difficulty concealing my excitement; 'are you here with your master?'

'Yes, I'm with my master,' he responded slowly, and then suddenly cried out: 'Why, sir, is it you? I didn't know you.'

'Are you here with Yakov Ivanitch?'

'Yes, sir, with him, to be sure … whom else would I be with?'

'Take me to him quickly.'

'To be sure! to be sure! This way, please, this way … we're stopping here at the tavern.' Elisei led me across the square, incessantly repeating—'Well, now, won't Yakov Ivanitch be pleased!'

This man, of Kalmuck extraction, and hideous, even savage appearance, but the kindest-hearted creature and by no means a fool, was passionately devoted to Pasinkov, and had been his servant for ten years.

'Is Yakov Ivanitch quite well?' I asked him.

Elisei turned his dusky, yellow little face to me.

'Ah, sir, he's in a poor way … in a poor way, sir! You won't know his honour…. He's not long for this world, I'm afraid. That's how it is we've stopped here, or we had been going on to Odessa for his health.'

'Where do you come from?'

'From Siberia, sir.'

'From Siberia?'

'Yes, sir. Yakov Ivanitch was sent to a post out there. It was there his honour got his wound.'

'Do you mean to say he went into the military service?'

'Oh no, sir. He served in the civil service.'

'What a strange thing!' I thought.

Meanwhile we had reached the tavern, and Elisei ran on in front to announce me. During the first years of our separation, Pasinkov and I had written to each other pretty often, but his last letter had reached me four years before, and since then I had heard nothing of him.

'Please come up, sir!' Elisei shouted to me from the staircase; 'Yakov Ivanitch is very anxious to see you.'

I ran hurriedly up the tottering stairs, went into a dark little room—and my heart sank…. On a narrow bed, under a fur cloak, pale as a corpse, lay Pasinkov, and he was stretching out to me a bare, wasted hand. I rushed up to him and embraced him passionately.

'Yasha!' I cried at last; 'what's wrong with you?'

'Nothing,' he answered in a faint voice; 'I'm a bit feeble. What chance brought you here?'

I sat down on a chair beside Pasinkov's bed, and, never letting his hands out of my hands, I began gazing into his face. I recognised the features I loved; the expression of the eyes and the smile were unchanged; but what a wreck illness had made of him!

He noticed the impression he was making on me.

'It's three days since I shaved,' he observed; 'and, to be sure, I've not been combed and brushed, but except for that … I'm not so bad.'

'Tell me, please, Yasha,' I began; 'what's this Elisei's been telling me … you were wounded?'

'Ah! yes, it's quite a history,' he replied. 'I'll tell you it later. Yes, I was wounded, and only fancy what by?—an arrow.'

'An arrow?'

'Yes, an arrow; only not a mythological one, not Cupid's arrow, but a real arrow of very flexible wood, with a sharply-pointed tip at one end.... A very unpleasant sensation is produced by such an arrow, especially when it sticks in one's lungs.'

'But however did it come about? upon my word!...'

'I'll tell you how it happened. You know there always was a great deal of the absurd in my life. Do you remember my comical correspondence about getting my passport? Well, I was wounded in an absurd fashion too. And if you come to think of it, what self-respecting person in our enlightened century would permit himself to be wounded by an arrow? And not accidentally—observe—not at sports of any sort, but in a battle.'

'But you still don't tell me …'

'All right, wait a minute,' he interrupted. 'You know that soon after you left Petersburg I was transferred to Novgorod. I was a good time at Novgorod, and I must own I was bored there, though even there I came across one creature....' (He sighed.) … 'But no matter about that now; two years ago I got a capital little berth, some way off, it's true, in the Irkutsk province, but what of that! It seems as though my father and I were destined from birth to visit Siberia. A splendid country, Siberia! Rich, fertile—every one will tell you the same. I liked it very much there. The natives were put under my rule; they're a harmless lot of people; but as my ill-luck would have it, they took it into their heads, a dozen of them, not more, to smuggle in contraband goods. I was sent to arrest them. Arrest them I did, but one of them, crazy he must have been, thought fit to defend himself, and treated me to the arrow.... I almost died of it; however, I got all right again. Now, here I am going to get completely cured.... The government—God give them all good health!—have provided the cash.'

Pasinkov let his head fall back on the pillow, exhausted, and ceased speaking. A faint flush suffused his cheeks. He closed his eyes.

'He can't talk much,' Elisei, who had not left the room, murmured in an undertone.

A silence followed; nothing was heard but the sick man's painful breathing.

'But here,' he went on, opening his eyes, 'I've been stopping a fortnight in this little town.... I caught cold, I suppose. The district doctor here is attending me—you'll see him; he seems to know his business. I'm awfully glad it happened so, though, or how should we have met?' (And he took my hand. His hand, which had just before been cold as ice, was now burning hot.) 'Tell me something about yourself,' he began again, throwing the cloak back off his chest. 'You and I haven't seen each other since God knows when.'

I hastened to carry out his wish, so as not to let him talk, and started giving an account of myself. He listened to me at first with great attention, then asked for drink, and then began closing his eyes again and turning his head restlessly on the pillow. I advised him to have a little nap, adding that I should not go on further till he was well again, and that I should establish myself in a room beside him. 'It's very nasty here …' Pasinkov was beginning, but I stopped his mouth, and went softly out. Elisei followed me.

'What is it, Elisei? Why, he's dying, isn't he?' I questioned the faithful servant.

Elisei simply made a gesture with his hand, and turned away.

Having dismissed my driver, and rapidly moved my things into the next room, I went to see whether Pasinkov was asleep. At the door I ran up against a tall man, very fat and heavily

built. His face, pock-marked and puffy, expressed laziness—and nothing else; his tiny little eyes seemed, as it were, glued up, and his lips looked polished, as though he were just awake.
'Allow me to ask,' I questioned him, 'are you not the doctor?'
The fat man looked at me, seeming with an effort to lift his overhanging forehead with his eyebrows.
'Yes, sir,' he responded at last.
'Do me the favour, Mr. Doctor, won't you, please, to come this way into my room? Yakov Ivanitch, is, I believe, now asleep. I am a friend of his and should like to have a little talk with you about his illness, which makes me very uneasy.'
'Very good,' answered the doctor, with an expression which seemed to try and say, 'Why talk so much? I'd have come anyway,' and he followed me.
'Tell me, please,' I began, as soon as he had dropped into a chair, 'is my friend's condition serious? What do you think?'
'Yes,' answered the fat man, tranquilly.
'And… is it very serious?'
'Yes, it's serious.'
'So that he may…even die?'
'He may.'
I confess I looked almost with hatred at the fat man.
'Good heavens!' I began; 'we must take some steps, call a consultation, or something. You know we can't… Mercy on us!'
'A consultation?—quite possible; why not? It's possible. Call in Ivan Efremitch….'
The doctor spoke with difficulty, and sighed continually. His stomach heaved perceptibly when he spoke, as it were emphasising each word.
'Who is Ivan Efremitch?'
'The parish doctor.'
'Shouldn't we send to the chief town of the province? What do you think? There are sure to be good doctors there.'
'Well! you might.'
'And who is considered the best doctor there?'
'The best? There was a doctor Kolrabus there … only I fancy he's been transferred somewhere else. Though I must own there's no need really to send.'
'Why so?'
'Even the best doctor will be of no use to your friend.'
'Why, is he so bad?'
'Yes, he's run down.' 'In what way precisely is he ill?'
'He received a wound…. The lungs were affected in consequence … and then he's taken cold too, and fever was set up … and so on. And there's no reserve force; a man can't get on, you know yourself, with no reserve force.'
We were both silent for a while.
'How about trying homoeopathy?…' said the fat man, with a sidelong glance at me.
'Homoeopathy? Why, you're an allopath, aren't you?'
'What of that? Do you think I don't understand homoeopathy? I understand it as well as the other! Why, the chemist here among us treats people homeopathically, and he has no learned degree whatever.'
'Oh,' I thought, 'it's a bad look-out!…'
'No, doctor,' I observed, 'you had better treat him according to your usual method.'
'As you please.'
The fat man got up and heaved a sigh.
'You are going to him? 'I asked.
'Yes, I must have a look at him.'

And he went out.
I did not follow him; to see him at the bedside of my poor, sick friend was more than I could stand. I called my man and gave him orders to drive at once to the chief town of the province, to inquire there for the best doctor, and to bring him without fail. There was a slight noise in the passage. I opened the door quickly.
The doctor was already coming out of Pasinkov's room.
'Well?' I questioned him in a whisper.
'It's all right. I have prescribed a mixture.'
'I have decided, doctor, to send to the chief town. I have no doubt of your skill, but as you're aware, two heads are better than one.'
'Well, that's very praiseworthy!' responded the fat man, and he began to descend the staircase. He was obviously tired of me.
I went in to Pasinkov.
'Have you seen the local Aesculapius?' he asked.
'Yes,' I answered.
'What I like about him,' remarked Pasinkov, 'is his astounding composure. A doctor ought to be phlegmatic, oughtn't he? It's so encouraging for the patient.'
I did not, of course, try to controvert this.
Towards the evening, Pasinkov, contrary to my expectations, seemed better. He asked Elisei to set the samovar, announced that he was going to regale me with tea, and drink a small cup himself, and he was noticeably more cheerful. I tried, though, not to let him talk, and seeing that he would not be quiet, I asked him if he would like me to read him something. 'Just as at Winterkeller's—do you remember?' he answered. 'If you will, I shall be delighted. What shall we read? Look, there are my books in the window.'...
I went to the window and took up the first book that my hand chanced upon....
'What is it?' he asked.
'Lermontov.'
'Ah, Lermontov! Excellent! Pushkin is greater, no doubt.... Do you remember: "Once more the storm-clouds gather close Above me in the perfect calm" ... or, "For the last time thy image sweet in thought I dare caress." Ah! marvellous! marvellous! But Lermontov's fine too. Well, I'll tell you what, dear boy: you take the book, open it by chance, and read what you find!'
I opened the book, and was disconcerted; I had chanced upon 'The Last Will.' I tried to turn over the page, but Pasinkov noticed my action and said hurriedly: 'No, no, no, read what turned up.'
There was no getting out of it; I read 'The Last Will.'
[Footnote: THE LAST WILL

Alone with thee, brother,
I would wish to be;
On earth, so they tell me,
I have not long to stay,
Soon you will go home:
See that ... But nay! for my fate
To speak the truth, no one
Is very greatly troubled.

But if any one asks ...

Well, whoever may ask,
Tell them that through the breast
I was shot by a bullet;
That I died honourably for the Tsar,
That our doctors are not much good,

And that to my native land
I send a humble greeting.
My father and mother, hardly
Will you find living….
I'll own I should be sorry
That they should grieve for me.]

'Splendid thing!' said Pasinkov, directly I had finished the last verse. 'Splendid thing! But, it's queer,' he added, after a brief pause, 'it's queer you should have chanced just on that…. Queer.'

I began to read another poem, but Pasinkov was not listening to me; he looked away, and twice he repeated again: 'Queer!'

I let the book drop on my knees.

'"There is a girl, their neighbour,"' he whispered, and turning to me he asked—'I say, do you remember Sophia Zlotnitsky?'

I turned red.

'I should think I did!'

'She was married, I suppose?…'

'To Asanov, long, long ago. I wrote to you about it.'

* * * * *

But if either of them is living,
Say I am lazy about writing,
That our regiment has been sent forward,
And that they must not expect me home.
There is a girl, their neighbour….
As you remember, it's long
Since we parted…. She will not
Ask for me…. All the same,
You tell her all the truth,
Don't spare her empty heart—
Let her weep a little….
It will not hurt her much!

'To be sure, to be sure, so you did. Did her father forgive her in the end?'

'He forgave her; but he would not receive Asanov.'

'Obstinate old fellow! Well, and are they supposed to be happy?'

'I don't know, really… I fancy they 're happy. They live in the country, in —— province. I've never seen them, though I have been through their parts.'

'And have they any children?'

'I think so…. By the way, Pasinkov?…' I began questioningly.

He glanced at me.

'Confess—do you remember, you were unwilling to answer my question at the time—did you tell her I cared for her?'

'I told her everything, the whole truth…. I always told her the truth. To be hypocritical with her would have been a sin!'

Pasinkov was silent for a while.

'Come, tell me,' he began again: 'did you soon get over caring for her, or not?'

'Not very soon, but I got over it. What's the good of sighing in vain?'

Pasinkov turned over, facing me.

'Well, I, brother,' he began—and his lips were quivering—'am no match for you there; I've not got over caring for her to this day.'

'What!' I cried in indescribable amazement; 'did you love her?'

'I loved her,' said Pasinkov slowly, and he put both hands behind his head. 'How I loved her, God only knows. I've never spoken of it to any one, to any one in the world, and I never

meant to … but there! "On earth, so they tell me, I have not long to stay." … What does it matter?'
Pasinkov's unexpected avowal so utterly astonished me that I could positively say nothing. I could only wonder, 'Is it possible? how was it I never suspected it?'
'Yes,' he went on, as though speaking to himself, 'I loved her. I never ceased to love her even when I knew her heart was Asanov's. But how bitter it was for me to know that! If she had loved you, I should at least have rejoiced for you; but Asanov…. How did he make her care for him? It was just his luck! And change her feelings, cease to care, she could not! A true heart does not change….'
I recalled Asanov's visit after the fatal dinner, Pasinkov's intervention, and I could not help flinging up my hands in astonishment.
'You learnt it all from me, poor fellow!' I cried; 'and you undertook to go and see her then!'
'Yes,' Pasinkov began again; 'that explanation with her … I shall never forget it.' It was then I found out, then I realised the meaning of the word I had chosen for myself long before: resignation. But still she has remained my constant dream, my ideal…. And he's to be pitied who lives without an ideal!'
I looked at Pasinkov; his eyes, fastened, as it were, on the distance, shone with feverish brilliance.
'I loved her,' he went on, 'I loved her, her, calm, true, unapproachable, incorruptible; when she went away, I was almost mad with grief…. Since then I have never cared for any one.'…
And suddenly turning, he pressed his face into the pillow, and began quietly weeping.
I jumped up, bent over him, and began trying to comfort him….
'It's no matter,' he said, raising his head and shaking back his hair; 'it's nothing; I felt a little bitter, a little sorry … for myself, that is…. But it's all no matter. It's all the fault of those verses. Read me something else, more cheerful.'
I took up Lermontov and began hurriedly turning over the pages; but, as fate would have it, I kept coming across poems likely to agitate Pasinkov again. At last I read him 'The Gifts of Terek.'
'Jingling rhetoric!' said my poor friend, with the tone of a preceptor; 'but there are fine passages. Since I saw you, brother, I've tried my hand at poetry, and began one poem—"The Cup of Life"—but it didn't come off! It's for us, brother, to appreciate, not to create…. But I'm rather tired; I'll sleep a little—what do you say? What a splendid thing sleep is, come to think of it! All our life's a dream, and the best thing in it is dreaming too.'
'And poetry?' I queried.
'Poetry's a dream too, but a dream of paradise.'
Pasinkov closed his eyes.
I stood for a little while at his bedside. I did not think he would get to sleep quickly, but soon his breathing became more even and prolonged. I went away on tiptoe, turned into my own room, and lay down on the sofa. For a long while I mused on what Pasinkov had told me, recalled many things, wondered; at last I too fell asleep….
Some one touched me; I started up; before me stood Elisei.
'Come in to my master,' he said.
I got up at once.
'What's the matter with him?'
'He's delirious.'
'Delirious? And hasn't it ever been so before with him?'
'Yes, he was delirious last night, too; only to-day it is something terrible.'
I went to Pasinkov's room. He was not lying down, but sitting up in bed, his whole body bent forward. He was slowly gesticulating with his hands, smiling and talking, talking all the time in a weak, hollow voice, like the whispering of rushes. His eyes were wandering. The gloomy light of a night light, set on the floor, and shaded off by a book, lay, an unmoving patch on the ceiling; Pasinkov's face seemed paler than ever in the half darkness.

I went up to him, called him by his name—he did not answer. I began listening to his whispering: he was talking of Siberia, of its forests. From time to time there was sense in his ravings.

'What trees!' he whispered; 'right up to the sky. What frost on them! Silver ... snowdrifts.... And here are little tracks ... that's a hare's leaping, that's a white weasel... No, it's my father running with my papers. Here he is!... Here he is! Must go; the moon is shining. Must go, look for my papers.... Ah! A flower, a crimson flower—there's Sophia.... Oh, the bells are ringing, the frost is crackling.... Ah, no; it's the stupid bullfinches hopping in the bushes, whistling.... See, the redthroats! Cold.... Ah! here's Asanov.... Oh yes, of course, he's a cannon, a copper cannon, and his gun-carriage is green. That's how it is he's liked. Is it a star has fallen? No, it's an arrow flying.... Ah, how quickly, and straight into my heart!... Who shot it? You, Sonitchka?'

He bent his head and began muttering disconnected words. I glanced at Elisei; he was standing, his hands clasped behind his back, gazing ruefully at his master.

'Ah, brother, so you've become a practical person, eh?' he asked suddenly, turning upon me such a clear, such a fully conscious glance, that I could not help starting and was about to reply, but he went on at once: 'But I, brother, have not become a practical person, I haven't, and that's all about it! A dreamer I was born, a dreamer! Dreaming, dreaming.... What is dreaming? Sobakevitch's peasant—that's dreaming. Ugh!...'

Almost till morning Pasinkov wandered in delirium; at last he gradually grew quieter, sank back on the pillow, and dozed off. I went back into my room. Worn out by the cruel night, I slept soundly.

Elisei again waked me.

'Ah, sir!' he said in a shaking voice, 'I do believe Yakov Ivanitch is dying....'

I ran in to Pasinkov. He was lying motionless. In the light of the coming day he looked already a corpse. He recognised me.

'Good-bye,' he whispered; 'greet her for me, I'm dying....'

'Yasha!' I cried; 'nonsense! you are going to live....'

'No, no! I am dying.... Here, take this as a keepsake.' ... (He pointed to his breast.) ...

'What's this?' he began suddenly; 'look: the sea ... all golden, and blue isles upon it, marble temples, palm-trees, incense....'

He ceased speaking ... stretched....

Within half an hour he was no more. Elisei flung himself weeping at his feet. I closed his eyes.

On his neck there was a little silken amulet on a black cord. I took it.

Three days afterwards he was buried.... One of the noblest hearts was hidden for ever in the grave. I myself threw the first handful of earth upon him.

III

Another year and a half passed by. Business obliged me to visit Moscow. I took up my quarters in one of the good hotels there. One day, as I was passing along the corridor, I glanced at the black-board with the list of visitors staying in the hotel, and almost cried out aloud with astonishment. Opposite the number 12 stood, distinctly written in chalk, the name, Sophia Nikolaevna Asanova. Of late I had chanced to hear a good deal that was bad about her husband. I had learned that he was addicted to drink and to gambling, had ruined himself, and was generally misconducting himself. His wife was spoken of with respect.... In some excitement I went back to my room. The passion, that had long long ago grown cold, began as it were to stir within my heart, and it throbbed. I resolved to go and see Sophia Nikolaevna. 'Such a long time has passed since the day we parted,' I thought, 'she has, most likely, forgotten everything there was between us in those days.'

I sent Elisei, whom I had taken into my service after the death of Pasinkov, with my visiting-card to her door, and told him to inquire whether she was at home, and whether I might see her. Elisei quickly came back and announced that Sophia Nikolaevna was at home and would see me.
I went at once to Sophia Nikolaevna. When I went in, she was standing in the middle of the room, taking leave of a tall stout gentleman.
'As you like,' he was saying in a rich, mellow voice; 'he is not a harmless person, he's a useless person; and every useless person in a well-ordered society is harmful, harmful, harmful!'
With those words the tall gentleman went out. Sophia Nikolaevna turned to me.
'How long it is since we met!' she said. 'Sit down, please....'
We sat down. I looked at her.... To see again after long absence the features of a face once dear, perhaps beloved, to recognise them, and not recognise them, as though across the old, unforgotten countenance a new one, like, but strange, were looking out at one; instantaneously, almost unconsciously, to note the traces time has laid upon it;—all this is rather melancholy. 'I too must have changed in the same way,' each is inwardly thinking....
Sophia Nikolaevna did not, however, look much older; though, when I had seen her last, she was sixteen, and that was nine years ago.
Her features had become still more correct and severe; as of old, they expressed sincerity of feeling and firmness; but in place of her former serenity, a sort of secret ache and anxiety could be discerned in them. Her eyes had grown deeper and darker. She had begun to show a likeness to her mother....
Sophia Nikolaevna was the first to begin the conversation.
'We are both changed,' she began. 'Where have you been all this time?'
'I've been a rolling stone,' I answered. 'And have you been living in the country all the while?'
'For the most part I've been in the country. I'm only here now for a little time.'
'How are your parents?'
'My mother is dead, but my father is still in Petersburg; my brother's in the service; Varia lives with him.'
'And your husband?'
'My husband,' she said in a rather hurried voice—'he's just now in South Russia for the horse fairs. He was always very fond of horses, you know, and he has started stud stables ... and so, on that account ... he's buying horses now.'
At that instant there walked into the room a little girl of eight years old, with her hair in a pigtail, with a very keen and lively little face, and large dark grey eyes. On seeing me, she at once drew back her little foot, dropped a hasty curtsey, and went up to Sophia Nikolaevna.
'This is my little daughter; let me introduce her to you,' said Sophia
Nikolaevna, putting one finger under the little girl's round chin; 'she would not stop at home—she persuaded me to bring her with me.'
The little girl scanned me with her rapid glance and faintly dropped her eyelids.
'She is a capital little person,' Sophia Nikolaevna went on: 'there's nothing she's afraid of. And she's good at her lessons; I must say that for her.'
'Comment se nomme monsieur?' the little girl asked in an undertone, bending over to her mother.
Sophia Nikolaevna mentioned my name.
The little girl glanced at me again.
'What is your name?' I asked her.
'My name is Lidia,' answered the little girl, looking me boldly in the face.
'I expect they spoil you,' I observed.
'Who spoil me?'
'Who? everyone, I expect; your parents to begin with.'

(The little girl looked, without a word, at her mother.) 'I can fancy Konstantin Alexandritch,' I was going on ...
'Yes, yes,' Sophia Nikolaevna interposed, while her little daughter kept her attentive eyes fastened upon her; 'my husband, of course—he is very fond of children....'
A strange expression flitted across Lidia's clever little face. There was a slight pout about her lips; she hung her head.
'Tell me,' Sophia Nikolaevna added hurriedly; 'you are here on business, I expect?'
'Yes, I am here on business.... And are you too?'
'Yes.... In my husband's absence, you understand, I'm obliged to look after business matters.'
'Maman!' Lidia was beginning.
'Quoi, mon enfant?'
'Non—rien.... Je te dirai après.'
Sophia Nikolaevna smiled and shrugged her shoulders.
'Tell me, please,' Sophia Nikolaevna began again; 'do you remember, you had a friend ... what was his name? he had such a good-natured face ... he was always reading poetry; such an enthusiastic—'
'Not Pasinkov?'
'Yes, yes, Pasinkov ... where is he now?'
'He is dead.'
'Dead?' repeated Sophia Nikolaevna; 'what a pity!...'
'Have I seen him?' the little girl asked in a hurried whisper.
'No, Lidia, you've never seen him.—What a pity!' repeated Sophia Nikolaevna.
'You regret him ...' I began; 'what if you had known him, as I knew him?... But, why did you speak of him, may I ask?'
'Oh, I don't know....' (Sophia Nikolaevna dropped her eyes.) 'Lidia,' she added; 'run away to your nurse.'
'You'll call me when I may come back?' asked the little girl.
'Yes.'
The little girl went away. Sophia Nikolaevna turned to me.
'Tell me, please, all you know about Pasinkov.' I began telling her his story. I sketched in brief words the whole life of my friend; tried, as far as I was able, to give an idea of his soul; described his last meeting with me and his end.
'And a man like that,' I cried, as I finished my story—'has left us, unnoticed, almost unappreciated! But that's no great loss. What is the use of man's appreciation? What pains me, what wounds me, is that such a man, with such a loving and devoted heart, is dead without having once known the bliss of love returned, without having awakened interest in one woman's heart worthy of him!... Such as I may well know nothing of such happiness; we don't deserve it; but Pasinkov!... And yet haven't I met thousands of men in my life, who could not compare with him in any respect, who were loved? Must one believe that some faults in a man—conceit, for instance, or frivolity—are essential to gain a woman's devotion? Or does love fear perfection, the perfection possible on earth, as something strange and terrible?'
Sophia Nikolaevna heard me to the end, without taking her stern, searching eyes off me, without moving her lips; only her eyebrows contracted from time to time.
'What makes you suppose,' she observed after a brief silence, 'that no woman ever loved your friend?'
'Because I know it, know it for a fact.'
Sophia Nikolaevna seemed about to say something, but she stopped. She seemed to be struggling with herself.

'You are mistaken,' she began at last; 'I know a woman who loved your dead friend passionately; she loves him and remembers him to this day … and the news of his death will be a fearful blow for her.'

'Who is this woman? may I know?'

'My sister, Varia.'

'Varvara Nikolaevna!' I cried in amazement.

'Yes.'

'What? Varvara Nikolaevna?' I repeated, 'that…'

'I will finish your sentence,' Sophia Nikolaevna took me up; 'that girl you thought so cold, so listless and indifferent, loved your friend; that is why she has never married and never will marry. Till this day no one has known of this but me; Varia would die before she would betray her secret. In our family we know how to suffer in silence.'

I looked long and intently at Sophia Nikolaevna, involuntarily pondering on the bitter significance of her last words.

'You have surprised me,' I observed at last. 'But do you know, Sophia Nikolaevna, if I were not afraid of recalling disagreeable memories, I might surprise you too….'

'I don't understand you,' she rejoined slowly, and with some embarrassment.

'You certainly don't understand me,' I said, hastily getting up; 'and so allow me, instead of verbal explanation, to send you something …'

'But what is it?' she inquired.

'Don't be alarmed, Sophia Nikolaevna, it's nothing to do with me.'

I bowed, and went back to my room, took out the little silken bag I had taken off Pasinkov, and sent it to Sophia Nikolaevna with the following note—

'This my friend wore always on his breast and died with it on him. In it is the only note you ever wrote him, quite insignificant in its contents; you can read it. He wore it because he loved you passionately; he confessed it to me only the day before his death. Now, when he is dead, why should you not know that his heart too was yours?'

Elisei returned quickly and brought me back the relic.

'Well?' I queried; 'didn't she send any message?'

'No.'

I was silent for a little.

'Did she read my note?'

'No doubt she did; the maid took it to her.'

'Unapproachable,' I thought, remembering Pasinkov's last words. 'All right, you can go,' I said aloud.

Elisei smiled somewhat queerly and did not go.

'There's a girl …' he began, 'here to see you.'

'What girl?'

Elisei hesitated.

'Didn't my master say anything to you?'

'No…. What is it?'

'When my master was in Novgorod,' he went on, fingering the door-post, 'he made acquaintance, so to say, with a girl. So here is this girl, wants to see you. I met her the other day in the street. I said to her, "Come along; if the master allows it, I'll let you see him."

'Ask her in, ask her in, of course. But … what is she like?'

'An ordinary girl… working class… Russian.'

'Did Yakov Ivanitch care for her?'

'Well, yes … he was fond of her. And she…when she heard my master was dead, she was terribly upset. She's a good sort of girl.'

'Ask her in, ask her in.'

Elisei went out and at once came back. He was followed by a girl in a striped cotton gown, with a dark kerchief on her head, that half hid her face. On seeing me, she was much taken aback and turned away.

'What's the matter?' Elisei said to her; 'go on, don't be afraid.'

I went up to her and took her by the hand.

'What is your name?' I asked her.

'Masha,' she replied in a soft voice, stealing a glance at me.

She looked about two- or three-and-twenty; she had a round, rather simple-looking, but pleasant face, soft cheeks, mild blue eyes, and very pretty and clean little hands. She was tidily dressed.

'You knew Yakov Ivanitch?' I pursued.

'I used to know him,' she said, tugging at the ends of her kerchief, and the tears stood in her eyes.

I asked her to sit down.

She sat down at once on the edge of a chair, without any affectation of ceremony. Elisei went out.

'You became acquainted with him in Novgorod?'

'Yes, in Novgorod,' she answered, clasping her hands under her kerchief. 'I only heard the day before yesterday, from Elisei Timofeitch, of his death. Yakov Ivanitch, when he went away to Siberia, promised to write to me, and twice he did write, and then he wrote no more. I would have followed him out to Siberia, but he didn't wish it.'

'Have you relations in Novgorod?'

'Yes.'

'Did you live with them?'

'I used to live with mother and my married sister; but afterwards mother was cross with me, and my sister was crowded up, too; she has a lot of children: and so I moved. I always rested my hopes on Yakov Ivanitch, and longed for nothing but to see him, and he was always good to me—you can ask Elisei Timofeitch.'

Masha paused.

'I have his letters,' she went on. 'Here, look.' She took several letters out of her pocket, and handed them to me. 'Read them,' she added.

I opened one letter and recognised Pasinkov's hand.

'Dear Masha!' (he wrote in large, distinct letters) 'you leaned your little head against my head yesterday, and when I asked why you do so, you told me—"I want to hear what you are thinking." I'll tell you what I was thinking; I was thinking how nice it would be for Masha to learn to read and write! She could make out this letter ...'

Masha glanced at the letter.

'That he wrote me in Novgorod,' she observed, 'when he was just going to teach me to read. Look at the others. There's one from Siberia. Here, read this.'

I read the letters. They were very affectionate, even tender. In one of them, the first one from Siberia, Pasinkov called Masha his best friend, promised to send her the money for the journey to Siberia, and ended with the following words—'I kiss your pretty little hands; the girls here have not hands like yours; and their heads are no match for yours, nor their hearts either.... Read the books I gave you, and think of me, and I'll not forget you. You are the only, only girl that ever cared for me; and so I want to belong only to you....'

'I see he was very much attached to you,' I said, giving the letters back to her.

'He was very fond of me,' replied Masha, putting the letters carefully into her pocket, and the tears flowed slowly down her cheeks. 'I always trusted in him; if the Lord had vouchsafed him long life, he would not have abandoned me. God grant him His heavenly peace!'...

She wiped her eyes with a corner of her kerchief.

'Where are you living now?' I inquired.

'I'm here now, in Moscow; I came here with my mistress, but now I'm out of a place. I did go to Yakov Ivanitch's aunt, but she is very poor herself. Yakov Ivanitch used often to talk of you,' she added, getting up and bowing; 'he always loved you and thought of you. I met Elisei Timofeitch the day before yesterday, and wondered whether you wouldn't be willing to assist me, as I'm out of a place just now….'

'With the greatest pleasure, Maria … let me ask, what's your name from your father?'

'Petrovna,' answered Masha, and she cast down her eyes.

'I will do anything for you I can, Maria Petrovna,' I continued; 'I am only sorry that I am a visitor here, and know few good families.'

Masha sighed.

'If I could get a situation of some sort … I can't cut out, but I can sew, so I'm always doing sewing … and I can look after children too.'

'Give her money,' I thought; 'but how's one to do it?'

'Listen, Maria Petrovna,' I began, not without faltering; 'you must, please, excuse me, but you know from Pasinkov's own words what a friend of his I was … won't you allow me to offer you—for the immediate present—a small sum?' …

Masha glanced at me.

'What?' she asked.

'Aren't you in want of money?' I said.

Masha flushed all over and hung her head.

'What do I want with money?' she murmured; 'better get me a situation.'

'I will try to get you a situation, but I can't answer for it for certain; but you ought not to make any scruple, really … I'm not like a stranger to you, you know…. Accept this from me, in memory of our friend….'

I turned away, hurriedly pulled a few notes out of my pocket-book, and handed them to her.

Masha was standing motionless, her head still more downcast.

'Take it,' I persisted.

She slowly raised her eyes to me, looked me in the face mournfully, slowly drew her pale hand from under her kerchief and held it out to me.

I laid the notes in her cold fingers. Without a word, she hid the hand again under her kerchief, and dropped her eyes.

'In future, Maria Petrovna,' I resumed, 'if you should be in want of anything, please apply directly to me. I will give you my address.'

'I humbly thank you,' she said, and after a short pause she added: 'He did not speak to you of me?'

'I only met him the day before his death, Maria Petrovna. But I'm not sure … I believe he did say something.'

Masha passed her hand over her hair, pressed her cheek lightly, thought a moment, and saying 'Good-bye,' walked out of the room.

I sat at the table and fell into bitter musings. This Masha, her relations with Pasinkov, his letters, the hidden love of Sophia Nikolaevna's sister for him…. 'Poor fellow! poor fellow!' I whispered, with a catching in my breath. I thought of all Pasinkov's life, his childhood, his youth, Fräulein Frederike…. 'Well,' I thought, 'much fate gave to thee! much cause for joy!'

Next day I went again to see Sophia Nikolaevna. I was kept waiting in the ante-room, and when I entered, Lidia was already seated by her mother. I understood that Sophia Nikolaevna did not wish to renew the conversation of the previous day.

We began to talk—I really don't remember what about—about the news of the town, public affairs…. Lidia often put in her little word, and looked slily at me. An amusing air of importance had suddenly become apparent on her mobile little visage…. The clever little girl must have guessed that her mother had intentionally stationed her at her side.

I got up and began taking leave. Sophia Nikolaevna conducted me to the door.

'I made you no answer yesterday,' she said, standing still in the doorway; 'and, indeed, what answer was there to make? Our life is not in our own hands; but we all have one anchor, from which one can never, without one's own will, be torn—a sense of duty.'

Without a word I bowed my head in sign of assent, and parted from the youthful Puritan.

All that evening I stayed at home, but I did not think of her; I kept thinking and thinking of my dear, never-to-be-forgotten Pasinkov—the last of the idealists; and emotions, mournful and tender, pierced with sweet anguish into my soul, rousing echoes on the strings of a heart not yet quite grown old.... Peace to your ashes, unpractical man, simple-hearted idealist! and God grant to all practical men—to whom you were always incomprehensible, and who, perhaps, will laugh even now over you in the grave—God grant to them to experience even a hundredth part of those pure delights in which, in spite of fate and men, your poor and unambitious life was so rich!

ANDREI KOLOSOV

In a small, decently furnished room several young men were sitting before the fire. The winter evening was only just beginning; the samovar was boiling on the table, the conversation had hardly taken a definite turn, but passed lightly from one subject to another. They began discussing exceptional people, and in what way they differed from ordinary people. Every one expounded his views to the best of his abilities; they raised their voices and began to be noisy. A small, pale man, after listening long to the disquisitions of his companions, sipping tea and smoking a cigar the while, suddenly got up and addressed us all (I was one of the disputants) in the following words:—

'Gentlemen! all your profound remarks are excellent in their own way, but unprofitable.

Every one, as usual, hears his opponent's views, and every one retains his own convictions. But it's not the first time we have met, nor the first time we have argued, and so we have probably by now had ample opportunity for expressing our own views and learning those of others. Why, then, do you take so much trouble?'

Uttering these words, the small man carelessly flicked the ash off his cigar into the fireplace, dropped his eyelids, and smiled serenely. We all ceased speaking.

'Well, what are we to do then, according to you?' said one of us; 'play cards, or what? go to sleep? break up and go home?'

'Playing cards is agreeable, and sleep's always salutary,' retorted the small man; 'but it's early yet to break up and go home. You didn't understand me, though. Listen: I propose, if it comes to that, that each of you should describe some exceptional personality, tell us of any meeting you may have had with any remarkable man. I can assure you even the feeblest description has far more sense in it than the finest argument.'

We pondered.

'It's a strange thing,' observed one of us, an inveterate jester; 'except myself I don't know a single exceptional person, and with my life you are all, I fancy, familiar already. However, if you insist—'

'No!' cried another, 'we don't! But, I tell you what,' he added, addressing the small man, 'you begin. You have put a stopper on all of us, you're the person to fill the gap. Only mind, if we don't care for your story, we shall hiss you.'

'If you like,' answered the small man. He stood close to the fire; we sat round him and kept quiet. The small man looked at all of us, glanced at the ceiling, and began as follows:—

'Ten years ago, my dear friends, I was a student at Moscow. My father, a virtuous landowner of the steppes, had handed me over to a retired German professor, who, for a hundred roubles a month, undertook to lodge and board me, and to watch over my morals. This German was the fortunate possessor of an exceedingly solemn and decorous manner; at first I went in considerable awe of him. But on returning home one evening, I saw, with indescribable emotion, my preceptor sitting with three or four companions at a round table, on which there stood a fair-sized collection of empty bottles and half-full glasses. On seeing me, my revered preceptor got up, and, waving his arms and stammering, presented me to the honourable company, who all promptly offered me a glass of punch. This agreeable spectacle had a most illuminating effect on my intelligence; my future rose before me in the most seductive images. And, as a fact, from that memorable day I enjoyed unbounded freedom, and all but worried my preceptor to death. He had a wife who always smelt of smoke and pickled cucumbers; she was still youngish, but had not a single front tooth in her head. All German women, as we know, very quickly lose those indispensable ornaments of the human frame. I mention her, solely because she fell passionately in love with me and fed me almost into my grave.'

'To the point, to the point,' we shouted. 'Surely it's not your own adventures you're going to tell us?'

'No, gentlemen!' the small man replied composedly. 'I am an ordinary mortal. And so I lived at my German's, as the saying is, in clover. I did not attend lectures with too much assiduity, while at home I did positively nothing. In a very short time, I had got to know all my comrades and was on intimate terms with all of them. Among my new friends was one rather decent and good-natured fellow, the son of a town provost on the retired list. His name was Bobov. This Bobov got in the habit of coming to see me, and seemed to like me. I, too … do you know, I didn't like him, nor dislike him; I was more or less indifferent…. I must tell I hadn't in all Moscow a single relation, except an old uncle, who used sometimes to ask me for money. I never went anywhere, and was particularly afraid of women; I also avoided all acquaintance with the parents of my college friends, ever after one such parent (in my presence) pulled his son's hair—because a button was off his uniform, while at the very time I hadn't more than six buttons on my whole coat. In comparison with many of my comrades, I passed for being a person of wealth; my father used to send me every now and then small packets of faded blue notes, and consequently I not only enjoyed a position of independence, but I was continually surrounded by toadies and flatterers…. What am I saying?—why, for that matter, so was my bobtail dog Armishka, who, in spite of his setter pedigree, was so frightened of a shot, that the very sight of a gun reduced him to indescribable misery. Like every young man, however, I was not without that vague inward fermentation which usually, after bringing forth a dozen more or less shapeless poems, passes off in a peaceful and propitious manner. I wanted something, strove towards something, and dreamed of something; I'll own I didn't know precisely what it was I dreamed of. Now I understand what was lacking:—I felt my loneliness, thirsted for the society of so-called live people; the word Life waked echoes in my heart, and with a vague ache I listened to the sound of it…. Valerian Nikitich, pass me a cigarette.'

Lighting the cigarette, the small man continued:

'One fine morning Bobov came running to me, out of breath: "Do you know, old man, the great news? Kolosov has arrived." "Kolosov? and who on earth is Mr. Kolosov?"

'"You don't know him? Andriusha Kolosov! Come, old boy, let's go to him directly. He came back last night from a holiday engagement." "But what sort of fellow is he?" "An exceptional man, my boy, let me assure you!" "An exceptional man," I answered; "then you go alone. I'll stop at home. I know your exceptional men! A half-tipsy rhymester with an everlastingly ecstatic smile!" … "Oh no! Kolosov's not like that." I was on the point of observing that it was for Mr. Kolosov to call on me; but, I don't know why, I obeyed Bobov and went. Bobov conducted me to one of the very dirtiest, crookedest, and narrowest streets in Moscow…. The house in which Kolosov lodged was built in the old-fashioned style, rambling and uncomfortable. We went into the courtyard; a fat peasant woman was hanging out clothes on a line stretched from the house to the fence.... Children were squalling on the wooden staircase...'

'Get on! get on!' we objected plaintively.

'I see, gentlemen, you don't care for the agreeable, and cling solely to the profitable. As you please! We groped our way through a dark and narrow passage to Kolosov's room; we went in. You have most likely an approximate idea of what a poor student's room is like. Directly facing the door Kolosov was sitting on a chest of drawers, smoking a pipe. He gave his hand to Bobov in a friendly way, and greeted me affably. I looked at Kolosov and at once felt irresistibly drawn to him. Gentlemen! Bobov was right: Kolosov really was a remarkable person. Let me describe a little more in detail.... He was rather tall, slender, graceful, and exceedingly good-looking. His face... I find it very difficult to describe his face. It is easy to describe all the features one by one; but how is one to convey to any one else what constitutes the distinguishing characteristic, the essence of just *that* face?'

'What Byron calls "the music of the face,"' observed a tightly buttoned-up, pallid gentleman.

'Quite so.... And therefore I will confine myself to a single remark: the especial "something" to which I have just referred consisted in Kolosov's case in a carelessly gay and fearless expression of face, and also in an exceedingly captivating smile. He did not remember his parents, and had had a wretched bringing-up in the house of a distant relative, who had been degraded from the service for taking bribes. Up to the age of fifteen, he had lived in the country; then he found his way into Moscow, and after two years spent in the care of an old deaf priest's wife, he entered the university and began to get his living by lessons. He gave instruction in history, geography, and Russian grammar, though he had only a dim notion of these branches of science; but in the first place, there is an abundance of 'textbooks' among us in Russia, of the greatest usefulness to teachers; and secondly, the requirements of the respectable merchants, who confided their children's education to Kolosov, were exceedingly limited. Kolosov was neither a wit nor a humorist; but you cannot imagine how readily we all fell under that fellow's sway. We felt a sort of instinctive admiration of him; his words, his looks, his gestures were all so full of the charm of youth that all his comrades were head over ears in love with him. The professors considered him as a fairly intelligent lad, but 'of no marked abilities,' and lazy.

Kolosov's presence gave a special harmony to our evening reunions. Before him, our liveliness never passed into vulgar riotousness; if we were all melancholy—this half childlike melancholy, in his presence, led on to quiet, sometimes fairly sensible, conversation, and never ended in dejected boredom. You are smiling, gentlemen—I understand your smile; no doubt, many of us since then have turned out pretty cads! But youth ... youth....'

'Oh, talk not to me of a name great in story!
The days of our youth are the days of our glory....'

commented the same pallid gentleman.

'By Jove, what a memory he's got! and all from Byron!' observed the storyteller. 'In one word, Kolosov was the soul of our set. I was attached to him by a feeling stronger than any I have ever felt for any woman. And yet, I don't feel ashamed even now to remember that strange love—yes, love it was, for I recollect I went through at that time all the tortures of that passion, jealousy, for instance. Kolosov liked us all equally, but was particularly friendly with a silent, flaxen-haired, and unobtrusive youth, called Gavrilov. From Gavrilov he was almost inseparable; he would often speak to him in a whisper, and used to disappear with him out of Moscow, no one knew where, for two or three days at a time.... Kolosov did not care to be questioned, and I was lost in surmises. It was not simple curiosity that disturbed me. I longed to become the friend, the attendant squire of Kolosov; I was jealous of Gavrilov; I envied him; I could never find an explanation to satisfy me of Kolosov's strange absences. Meanwhile he had none of that air of mysteriousness about him, which is the proud possession of youths endowed with vanity, pallor, black hair, and 'expressive' eyes, nor had he anything of that studied carelessness under which we are given to understand that vast forces are slumbering; no, he was quite open and free; but when he was possessed by passion, an intense, impulsive energy was apparent in everything about him; only he did not waste his energies in vain, and never under any circumstances became high-flown or affected. By the way … tell me the truth, hasn't it happened to you to sit smoking a pipe with an air of as weary solemnity as if you had just resolved on a grand achievement, while you were simply pondering on what colour to choose for your next pair of trousers?… But the point is, that I was the first to observe in Kolosov, always cheerful and friendly as he was, these instinctive, passionate impulses…. They may well say that love is penetrating. I made up my mind at all hazards to get into his confidence. It was no use for me to lay myself out to please Kolosov; I had such a childlike adoration for him that he could have no doubt of my devotion … but to my indescribable vexation, I had, at last, to yield to the conviction that Kolosov avoided closer intimacy with me, that he was as it were oppressed by my uninvited attachment. Once, when with obvious displeasure he asked me to lend him money—the very next day he returned me the loan with ironical gratitude. During the whole winter my relations with Kolosov were utterly unchanged; I often compared myself with Gavrilov, and could not make out in what respect he was better than I…. But suddenly everything was changed. In the middle of April, Gavrilov fell ill, and died in the arms of Kolosov, who never left his room for an instant, and went nowhere for a whole week afterwards. We were all grieved for poor Gavrilov; the pale, silent lad seemed to have had a foreboding of his end. I too grieved sincerely for him, but my heart ached with expectation of something…. One ever memorable evening … I was alone, lying on the sofa, gazing idly at the ceiling … some one rapidly opened the door of my room and stood still in the doorway; I raised my head; before me stood Kolosov.

He slowly came in and sat down beside me. 'I have come to you,' he began in a rather thick voice, 'because you care more for me than any of the others do…. I have lost my best friend'—his voice shook a little—'and I feel lonely…. None of you knew Gavrilov … none of you knew….' He got up, paced up and down the room, came rapidly towards me again…. 'Will you take his place?' he said, and gave me his hand. I leaped up and flung myself on his breast. My genuine delight touched him…. I did not know what to say, I was choking…. Kolosov looked at me and softly laughed. We had tea. At tea he talked of Gavrilov; I heard that that timid, gentle boy had saved Kolosov's life, and I could not but own to myself that in Gavrilov's place I couldn't have resisted chattering about it—boasting of my luck. It struck eight. Kolosov got up, went to the window, drummed on the panes, turned swiftly round to me, tried to say something … and sat down on a chair without a word. I took his hand. 'Kolosov, truly, truly I deserve your confidence!' He looked straight into my eyes. 'Well, if so,' he brought out at last, 'take your cap and come along.' 'Where to?' 'Gavrilov did not ask me.' I was silent at once. 'Can you play at cards?' 'Yes.'

We went out, took a cab to one of the gates of the town. At the gate we got out. Kolosov went on in front very quickly; I followed him. We walked along the highroad. After we had gone three-quarters of a mile, Kolosov turned off. Meanwhile night had come on. On the right in the fog were the twinkling lights, the innumerable church-spires of the immense city; on the left, two white horses were grazing in a meadow skirting the forest: before us stretched fields covered with greyish mists. I followed Kolosov in silence. He stopped all at once, stretched his hand out in front of him, and said: 'Here, this is where we are going.' I saw a small dark house; two little windows showed a dim light in the fog. 'In this house,' Kolosov went on, 'lives a man called Sidorenko, a retired lieutenant, with his sister, an old maid, and his daughter. I shall pass you off as a relation of mine—you must sit down and play at cards with him.' I nodded without a word.

I wanted to show Kolosov that I could be as silent as Gavrilov…. But I will own I was suffering agonies of curiosity. As we went up to the steps of the house, I caught sight, at a lighted window, of the slender figure of a girl…. She seemed waiting for us and vanished at once. We went into a dark and narrow passage. A crooked, hunchback old woman came to meet us, and looked at me with astonishment. 'Is Ivan Semyonitch at home?' inquired Kolosov. 'He is at home.'... 'He is at home!' called a deep masculine voice from within. We went into the dining-room, if dining-room one can call the long, rather dirty room; a small old piano huddled unassumingly in a corner beside the stove; a few chairs stood out along the walls which had once been yellow. In the middle of the room stood a tall, stooping man of fifty, in a greasy dressing-gown. I looked at him more attentively: a morose looking countenance, hair standing up like a brush, a low forehead, grey eyes, immense whiskers, thick lips.... 'A nice customer!' I thought. 'It's a longish time since we've seen you, Andrei Nikolaevitch,' he observed, holding out his hideous red hand, 'a longish time it is! And where's Sevastian Sevastianovitch?' 'Gavrilov is dead,' answered Kolosov mournfully. 'Dead! you don't say so! And who's this?' 'My relation—I have the honour to present to you Nikolai Alexei....' 'All right, all right,' Ivan Semyonitch cut him short, 'delighted, delighted. And does he play cards?' 'Play, of course he does!' 'Ah, then, that's capital; we'll sit down directly. Hey! Matrona Semyonovna—where are you? the card-table—quick!... And tea!' With these words Mr. Sidorenko walked into the next room. Kolosov looked at me. 'Listen,' he said, 'you can't think how ashamed I am!'... I shut him up. 'Come, you there, what's your name, this way,' called Ivan Semyonitch. I went into the drawing-room. The drawing-room was even smaller than the dining-room. On the walls hung some monstrosities of portraits; in front of the sofa, of which the stuffing protruded in several places, stood a green table; on the sofa sat Ivan Semyonitch, already shuffling the cards. Near him on the extreme edge of a low chair sat a spare woman in a white cap and a black gown, yellow and wrinkled, with short-sighted eyes and thin cat-like lips. 'Here,' said Ivan Semyonitch, 'let me introduce him; the first man's dead; Andrei Nikolaevitch has brought us another; let's see how he plays!' The old lady bowed awkwardly and cleared her throat. I looked round; Kolosov was no longer in the room. 'Stop that coughing, Matrona Semyonovna; sheep cough,' grumbled Sidorenko. I sat down; the game began. Mr. Sidorenko got fearfully hot and furious at my slightest mistake; he pelted his sister with abusive epithets, but she had apparently had time to get used to her brother's amenities, and only blinked in response. But when he announced to Matrona Semyonovna that she was 'Antichrist,' the poor old woman fired up. 'Ivan Semyonitch,' she protested with heat, 'you were the death of your wife, Anfisa Karpovna, but you shan't worry me into my grave!' 'Indeed?' 'No! you shan't.' 'Indeed?' 'No! you shan't.' They kept it up in this fashion for some time. My position was, as you perceive, not merely an unenviable one: it was positively idiotic. I couldn't conceive what had induced Kolosov to bring me.... I have never been a good card-player; but on that occasion I was aware myself that I was playing excruciatingly badly. 'No!' the retired lieutenant repeated continually,' you can't hold a candle to Sevastianovitch! No! you play carelessly!' I, you may be sure, was inwardly wishing him at the devil. This torture continued for two hours; they beat me hollow. Before the end of the last rubber, I heard a slight sound behind my chair—I looked round and saw Kolosov; beside him stood a girl of seventeen, who was watching me with a scarcely perceptible smile. 'Fill me my pipe, Varia,' muttered Ivan Semyonitch. The girl promptly flew off into the other room. She was not very pretty, rather pale, rather thin; but never before or since have I seen such hair, such eyes. We finished the rubber somehow; I paid up, Sidorenko lighted his pipe and grumbled:

'Well, now it's time for supper!' Kolosov presented me to Varia, that is, to Varvara Ivanovna, the daughter of Ivan Semyonitch. Varia was embarrassed; I too was embarrassed. But in a few minutes Kolosov, as usual, had got everything and everyone into full swing; he sat Varia down to the piano, begged her to play a dance tune, and proceeded to dance a Cossack dance in competition with Ivan Semyonitch. The lieutenant uttered little shrieks, stamped and cut such incredible capers that even Matrona Semyonovna burst out laughing and retreated to her own room upstairs. The hunchback old woman laid the table; we sat down to supper. At supper Kolosov told all sorts of nonsensical stories; the lieutenant's guffaws were deafening; I peeped from under my eyelids at Varia. She never took her eyes off Kolosov ... and from the expression of her face alone, I could divine that she both loved him and was loved by him. Her lips were slightly parted, her head bent a little forward, a faint colour kept flitting across her whole face; from time to time she sighed deeply, suddenly dropped her eyes, and softly laughed to herself.... I rejoiced for Kolosov.... But at the same time, deuce take it, I was envious....

After supper, Kolosov and I promptly took up our caps, which did not, however, prevent the lieutenant from saying, with a yawn: 'You've paid us a long visit, gentlemen; it's time to say good-bye.' Varia accompanied Kolosov into the passage: 'When are you coming, Andrei Nikolaevitch?' she whispered to him. 'In a few days, for certain.' 'Bring him too,' she added, with a very sly smile. 'Of course, of course.' ... 'Your humble servant!' thought I....

On the way home, I heard the following story. Six months before, Kolosov had become acquainted with Mr. Sidorenko in a rather queer way. One rainy evening, Kolosov was returning home from shooting, and had reached the gate of the city, when suddenly, at no great distance from the highroad, he heard groans, interspersed with curses. He had a gun; without thinking long, he made straight for the sound, and found a man lying on the ground with a dislocated ankle. This man was Mr. Sidorenko. With great difficulty he got him home, handed him over to the care of his frightened sister and his daughter, and ran for the doctor.... Meantime it was nearly morning; Kolosov was almost dropping with fatigue. With the permission of Matrona Semyonovna, he lay down on the sofa in the parlour, and slept till eight o'clock. On waking up he would at once have gone home; but they kept him and gave him some tea. In the night he had twice succeeded in catching a glimpse of the pale face of Varvara Ivanovna; he had not particularly noticed her, but in the morning she made a decidedly agreeable impression on him. Matrona Semyonovna garrulously praised and thanked Kolosov; Varvara sat silent, pouring out the tea, glanced at him now and then, and with timid shame-faced attentiveness handed him first a cup of tea, then the cream, then the sugar-basin. Meanwhile the lieutenant waked up, loudly called for his pipe, and after a short pause bawled: 'Sister! hi, sister!' Matrona Semyonovna went to his bedroom. 'What about that...what the devil's his name? is he gone?' 'No, I'm still here,' answered Kolosov, going up to the door; 'are you better now?' 'Yes,' answered the lieutenant; 'come in here, my good sir.' Kolosov went in. Sidorenko looked at him, and reluctantly observed: 'Well, thanks; come sometimes and see me—what's your name? who the devil's to know?' 'Kolosov,' answered Andrei. 'Well, well, come and see us; but it's no use your sticking on here now, I daresay they're expecting you at home.' Kolosov retreated, said good-bye to Matrona Semyonovna, bowed to Varvara Ivanovna, and returned home. From that day he began to visit Ivan Semyonitch, at first at long intervals, then more and more frequently. The summer came on; he would sometimes take his gun, put on his knapsack, and set off as if he were going shooting. He would go to the retired lieutenant's, and stay on there till evening.

Varvara Ivanovna's father had served twenty-five years in the army, had saved a small sum of money, and bought himself a few acres of land a mile and a half from Moscow. He could scarcely read and write; but in spite of his external clumsiness and coarseness, he was shrewd and cunning, and even, on occasion, capable of sharp practice, like many Little Russians. He was a fearful egoist, obstinate as an ox, and in general exceedingly impolite, especially with strangers; I even detected in him something like a contempt for the whole human race. He indulged himself in every caprice, like a spoilt child; would know no one, and lived for his own pleasure. We were once somehow or other talking about marriages with him; 'Marriage ... marriage,' said he; 'whom the devil would I let my daughter marry? Eh? what should I do it for? for her husband to knock her about as I used to my wife? Besides, whom should I be left with?' Such was the retired lieutenant, Ivan Semyonitch. Kolosov used to go and see him, not on his account, of course, but for the sake of his daughter. One fine evening, Andrei was sitting in the garden with her, chatting about something; Ivan Semyonitch went up to him, looked sullenly at Varia, and called Andrei away. 'Listen, my dear fellow,' he said to him; 'you find it good fun, I see, gossiping with my only child, but I'm dull in my old age; bring some one with you, or I've nobody to deal a card to; d'ye hear? I shan't give admittance to you by yourself.' The next day Kolosov turned up with Gavrilov, and poor Sevastian Sevastianovitch had for a whole autumn and winter been playing cards in the evenings with the retired lieutenant; that worthy treated him without ceremony, as it is called—in other words, fearfully rudely. You now probably realise why it was that, after Gavrilov's death, Kolosov took me with him to Ivan Semyonitch's. As he communicated all these details, Kolosov added, 'I love Varia, she is the dearest girl; she liked you.'

I have forgotten, I fancy, to make known to you that up to that time I had been afraid of women and avoided them, though I would sometimes, in solitude, spend whole hours in dreaming of tender interviews, of love, of mutual love, and so on. Varvara Ivanovna was the first girl with whom I was forced to talk, by necessity—by necessity it really was. Varia was an ordinary girl, and yet there are very few such girls in holy Russia. You will ask me—why so? Because I never noticed in her anything strained, unnatural, affected; because she was a simple, candid, rather melancholy creature, because one could never call her 'a young lady.' I liked her soft smile; I liked her simple-hearted, ringing little voice, her light and mirthful laugh, her attentive though by no means 'profound' glances. The child promised nothing; but you could not help admiring her, as you admire the sudden, soft cry of the oriole at evening, in the lofty, dark birch-wood. I must confess that at the present time I should pass by such a creature with some indifference; I've no taste now for solitary evening strolls, and orioles; but in those days …

I've no doubt, gentlemen, that, like all well-educated persons, you have been in love at least once in the course of your life, and have learnt from your own experience how love springs up and develops in the human heart, and therefore I'm not going to enlarge too much on what took place with me at that time. Kolosov and I used to go pretty often to Ivan Semyonitch's; and though those damned cards often drove me to utter despair, still, in the mere proximity of the woman one loves (I had fallen in love with Varia) there is a sort of strange, sweet, tormenting joy. I made no effort to suppress this growing feeling; besides, by the time I had at last brought myself to call the emotion by its true name, it was already too strong.... I cherished my love in silence, and jealously and shyly concealed it. I myself enjoyed this agonising ferment of silent passion. My sufferings did not rob me of my sleep, nor of my appetite; but for whole days together I was conscious of that peculiar physical sensation in my breast which is a symptom of the presence of love. I am incapable of depicting the conflict of various sensations which took place within me when, for example, Kolosov came in from the garden with Varia, and her whole face was aglow with ecstatic devotion, exhaustion from excess of bliss.... She so completely lived in his life, was so completely taken up with him, that unconsciously she adopted his ways, looked as he looked, laughed as he laughed.... I can imagine the moments she passed with Andrei, the raptures she owed to him.... While he … Kolosov did not lose his freedom; in her absence he did not, I suppose, even think of her; he was still the same unconcerned, gay, and happy fellow we had always known him.

And, as I have already told you, we used, Kolosov and I, to go pretty often to Ivan Semyonitch's. Sometimes, when he was out of humour, the retired lieutenant did not make me sit down to cards; on such occasions, he would shrink into a corner in silence, scowling and looking crossly at every one. The first time I was delighted at his letting me off so easily; but afterwards I would sometimes begin myself begging him to sit down to whist, the part of third person was so insupportable! I was so unpleasantly in Kolosov's and Varia's way, though they did assure each other that there was no need to mind me!...

Meanwhile time went on.... They were happy.... I have no great fondness for describing other people's happiness. But then I began to notice that Varia's childish ecstasy had gradually given way to a more womanly, more restless feeling. I began to surmise that the new song was being sung to the old tune—that is, that Kolosov was...little by little...cooling. This discovery, I must own, delighted me; I did not feel, I must confess, the slightest indignation against Andrei.

The intervals between our visits became longer and longer.... Varia began to meet us with tear-stained eyes. Reproaches were heard ... Sometimes I asked Kolosov with affected indifference, 'Well, shall we go to Ivan Semyonitch's to-day?' ... He looked coldly at me, and answered quietly, 'No, we're not going.' I sometimes fancied that he smiled slily when he spoke to me of Varia.... I failed generally to fill Gavrilov's place with him.... Gavrilov was a thousand times more good-natured and foolish than I.

Now allow me a slight digression.... When I spoke of my university comrades, I did not mention a certain Mr. Shtchitov. He was five-and-thirty; he had been a student for ten years already. I can see even now his rather long pale face, his little brown eyes, his long hawk nose crooked at the end, his thin sarcastic lips, his solemn upstanding shock of hair, and his chin that lost itself complacently in the wide striped cravat of the colour of a raven's wing, the shirt front with bronze buttons, the open blue frock-coat and striped waistcoat.... I can hear his unpleasantly jarring laugh.... He went everywhere, was conspicuous at all possible kinds of 'dancing classes.' ... I remember I could not listen to his cynical stories without a peculiar shudder.... Kolosov once compared him to an unswept Russian refreshment bar ... a horrible comparison! And with all that, there was a lot of intelligence, common sense, observation, and wit in the man.... He sometimes impressed us by some saying so apt, so true and cutting, that we were all involuntarily reduced to silence and looked at him with amazement. But, to be sure, it is just the same to a Russian whether he has uttered an absurdity or a clever thing. Shtchitov was especially dreaded by those self-conscious, dreamy, and not particularly gifted youths who spend whole days in painfully hatching a dozen trashy lines of verse and reading them in sing-song to their 'friends,' and who despise every sort of positive science. One such he simply drove out of Moscow, by continually repeating to him two of his own lines. Yet all the while Shtchitov himself did nothing and learnt nothing.... But that's all in the natural order of things. Well, Shtchitov, God only knows why, began jeering at my romantic attachment to Kolosov. The first time, with noble indignation, I told him to go to the devil; the second time, with chilly contempt, I informed him that he was not capable of judging of our friendship—but I did not send him away; and when, on taking leave of me, he observed that without Kolosov's permission I didn't even dare to praise him, I felt annoyed; Shtchitov's last words sank into my heart.—For more than a fortnight I had not seen Varia.... Pride, love, a vague anticipation, a number of different feelings were astir within me ... with a wave of the hand and a fearful sinking at my heart, I set off alone to Ivan Semyonitch's.

I don't know how I made my way to the familiar little house; I remember I sat down several times by the road to rest, not from fatigue, but from emotion. I went into the passage, and had not yet had time to utter a single word when the door of the drawing-room flew open and Varia ran to meet me. 'At last,' she said, in a quavering voice; 'where's Andrei Nikolaevitch?' 'Kolosov has not come,' I muttered with an effort. 'Not come!' she repeated. 'Yes ... he told me to tell you that ... he was detained....' I positively did not know what I was saying, and I did not dare to raise my eyes. Varia stood silent and motionless before me. I glanced at her: she turned away her head; two big tears rolled slowly down her cheeks. In the expression of her face there was such sudden, bitter suffering; the conflict between bashfulness, sorrow, and confidence in me was so simply, so touchingly apparent in the unconscious movement of her poor little head that it sent a pang to my heart. I bent a little forward ... she gave a hurried start and ran away. In the parlour I was met by Ivan Semyonitch. 'How's this, my good sir, are you alone?' he asked me, with a queer twitch of his left eyelid. 'Yes, I've come alone,' I stammered. Sidorenko went off into a sudden guffaw and departed into the next room.

I had never been in such a foolish position; it was too devilishly disgusting! But there was nothing to be done. I began walking up and down the room. 'What was the fat pig laughing at?' I wondered. Matrona Semyonovna came into the room with a stocking in her hands and sat down in the window. I began talking to her. Meanwhile tea was brought in. Varia came downstairs, pale and sorrowful. The retired lieutenant made jokes about Kolosov. 'I know,' said he, 'what sort of customer he is; you couldn't tempt him here with lollipops now, I expect!' Varia hurriedly got up and went away. Ivan Semyonitch looked after her and gave a sly whistle. I glanced at him in perplexity. 'Can it be,' I wondered, 'that he knows all about it?' And the lieutenant, as though divining my thoughts, nodded his head affirmatively. Directly after tea I got up and took leave. 'You, my good sir, we shall see again,' observed the lieutenant. I did not say a word in reply.... I began to feel simply frightened of the man.

On the steps a cold and trembling hand clutched at mine; I looked round: Varia. 'I must speak to you,' she whispered. 'Come to-morrow rather earlier, straight into the garden. After dinner papa is asleep; no one will interfere with us.' I pressed her hand without a word, and we parted.

Next day, at three o'clock in the afternoon, I was in Ivan Semyonitch's garden. In the morning I had not seen Kolosov, though he had come to see me. It was a grey autumn day, but soft and warm. Delicate yellow blades of grass nodded over the blanching turf; the nimble tomtits were hopping about the bare dark-brown twigs; some belated larks were hurriedly running about the paths; a hare was creeping cautiously about among the greens; a herd of cattle wandered lazily over the stubble. I found Varia in the garden under the apple-tree on the little garden-seat; she was wearing a dark dress, rather creased; her weary eyes, the dejected droop of her hair, seemed to express genuine suffering.

I sat down beside her. We were both silent. For a long while she kept twisting a twig in her hand; she bent her head, and uttered: 'Andrei Nikolaevitch....' I noticed at once, by the twitching of her lips, that she was getting ready to cry, and began consoling her, assuring her hotly of Andrei's devotion.... She heard me, nodded her head mournfully, articulated some indistinct words, and then was silent but did not cry. The first moments I had dreaded most of all had gone off fairly well. She began little by little to talk about Andrei. 'I know that he does not love me now,' she repeated: 'God be with him! I can't imagine how I am to live without him.... I don't sleep at nights, I keep weeping.... What am I to do! What am I to do! ...' Her eyes filled with tears. 'I thought him so kind ... and here ...' Varia wiped her eyes, cleared her throat, and sat up. 'It seems such a little while ago,' she went on: 'he was reading to me out of Pushkin, sitting with me on this bench....' Varia's naïve communicativeness touched me. I listened in silence to her confessions; my soul was slowly filled with a bitter, torturing bliss; I could not take my eyes off that pale face, those long, wet eyelashes, and half-parted, rather parched lips.... And meanwhile I felt ... Would you care to hear a slight psychological analysis of my emotions at that moment? in the first place I was tortured by the thought that it was not I that was loved, not I that as making Varia suffer: secondly, I was delighted at her confidence; I knew she would be grateful to me for giving her an opportunity of expressing her sorrow: thirdly, I was inwardly vowing to myself to bring Kolosov and Varia together again, and was deriving consolation from the consciousness of my magnanimity ... in the fourth place, I hoped, by my self-sacrifice, to touch Varia's heart; and then ... You see I do not spare myself; no, thank God! it's high time!

But from the bell-tower of the monastery near it struck five o'clock; the evening was coming on rapidly. Varia got up hastily, thrust a little note into my hand, and went off towards the house. I overtook her, promised to bring Andrei to her, and stealthily, like a happy lover, crept out by the little gate into the field. On the note was written in an unsteady hand the words: To Andrei Nikolaevitch.

Next day I set off early in the morning to Kolosov's. I'm bound to confess that, although I assured myself that my intentions were not only honourable, but positively brimful of great-hearted self-sacrifice, I was yet conscious of a certain awkwardness, even timidity. I arrived at Kolosov's. There was with him a fellow called Puzyritsin, a former student who had never taken his degree, one of those authors of sensational novels of the so-called 'Moscow' or 'grey' school. Puzyritsin was a very good-natured and shy person, and was always preparing to be an hussar, in spite of his thirty-three years. He belonged to that class of people who feel it absolutely necessary, once in the twenty-four hours, to utter a phrase after the pattern of, 'The beautiful always falls into decay in the flower of its splendour; such is the fate of the beautiful in the world,' in order to smoke his pipe with redoubled zest all the rest of the day in a circle of 'good comrades.' On this account he was called an idealist. Well, so Puzyritsin was sitting with Kolosov reading him some 'fragment.' I began to listen; it was all about a youth, who loves a maiden, kills her, and so on. At last Puzyritsin finished and retreated. His absurd production, solemnly bawling voice, his presence altogether, had put Kolosov into a mood of sarcastic irritability. I felt that I had come at an unlucky moment, but there was nothing to be done for it; without any kind of preface, I handed Andrei Varia's note.

Kolosov looked at me in perplexity, tore open the note, ran his eyes over it, said nothing, but smiled composedly. 'Oh, ho!' he said at last; 'so you've been at Ivan Semyonitch's?'

'Yes, I was there yesterday, alone,' I answered abruptly and resolutely.

'Ah!...' observed Kolosov ironically, and he lighted his pipe. 'Andrei,' I said to him, 'aren't you sorry for her?... If you had seen her tears...'

And I launched into an eloquent description of my visit of the previous day. I was genuinely moved. Kolosov did not speak, and smoked his pipe.

'You sat with her under the apple-tree in the garden,' he said at last. 'I remember in May I, too, used to sit with her on that seat.... The apple-tree was in blossom, the fresh white flowers fell upon us sometimes; I held both Varia's hands... we were happy then.... Now the apple-blossom is over, and the apples on the tree are sour.'

I flew into a passion of noble indignation, began reproaching Andrei for coldness, for cruelty, argued with him that he had no right to abandon a girl so suddenly, after awakening in her a multitude of new emotions; I begged him at least to go and say good-bye to Varia. Kolosov heard me to the end.

'Admitting,' he said to me, when, agitated and exhausted, I flung myself into an armchair, 'that you, as my friend, may be allowed to criticise me. But hear my defence, at least, though...'

Here he paused for a little while and smiled curiously. 'Varia's an excellent girl,' he went on, 'and has done me no wrong whatever.... On the contrary, I am greatly, very greatly indebted to her. I have left off going to see her for a very simple reason—I have left off caring for her....'

'But why? why?' I interrupted him.

'Goodness knows why. While I loved her, I was entirely hers; I never thought of the future, and everything, my whole life, I shared with her ... now this passion has died out in me.... Well, you would tell me to be a humbug, to play at being in love, wouldn't you? But what for? from pity for her? If she's a decent girl, she won't care for such charity herself, but if she is glad to be consoled by my ... my sympathy, well, she's not good for much!'

Kolosov's carelessly offhand expressions offended me, perhaps, the more because they were applied to the woman with whom I was secretly in love.... I fired up. 'Stop,' I said to him; 'stop! I know why you have given up going to see Varia.'

'Why?'

'Taniusha has forbidden you to.'

In uttering these words, I fancied I was dealing a most cutting blow at Andrei. Taniusha was a very 'easy-going' young lady, black-haired, dark, five-and-twenty, free in her manners, and devilishly clever, a Shtchitov in petticoats. Kolosov quarrelled with her and made it up again half a dozen times in a month. She was passionately fond of him, though sometimes, during their misunderstandings, she would vow and declare that she thirsted for his blood.... And Andrei, too, could not get on without her. Kolosov looked at me, and responded serenely, 'Perhaps so.'

'Not perhaps so,' I shouted, 'but certainly!'

Kolosov at last got sick of my reproaches.... He got up and put on his cap.

'Where are you going?'

'For a walk; you and Puzyritsin have given me a headache between you.'

'You are angry with me?'

'No,' he answered, smiling his sweet smile, and holding out his hand to me.

'Well, anyway, what do you wish me to tell Varia?'
'Eh?' ... He thought a little. 'She told you,' he said, 'that we had read Pushkin together.... Remind her of one line of Pushkin's.' 'What line? what line?' I asked impatiently. 'This one: "What has been will not be again."'
With those words he went out of the room. I followed him; on the stairs he stopped.
'And is she very much upset?' he asked me, pulling his cap over his eyes.
'Very, very much!...'
'Poor thing! Console her, Nikolai; you love her, you know.'
'Yes, I have grown fond of her, certainly....'
'You love her,' repeated Kolosov, and he looked me straight in the face. I turned away without a word, and we separated.
On reaching home, I was in a perfect fever.
'I have done my duty,' I thought; 'I have overcome my own egoism; I have urged Andrei to go back to Varia!... Now I am in the right; he that will not when he may...!' At the same time Andrei's indifference wounded me. He had not been jealous of me, he told me to console her.... But is Varia such an ordinary girl, is she not even worthy of sympathy?... There are people who know how to appreciate what you despise, Andrei Nikolaitch!... But what's the good? She does not love me.... No, she does not love me now, while she has not quite lost hope of Kolosov's return.... But afterwards...who knows, my devotion will touch her. I will make no claims.... I will give myself up to her wholly, irrevocably.... Varia! is it possible you will not love me?...never!...never!...
Such were the speeches your humble servant was rehearsing in the city of Moscow, in the year 1833, in the house of his revered preceptor. I wept... I felt faint... The weather was horrible...a fine rain trickled down the window panes with a persistent, thin, little patter; damp, dark-grey storm-clouds hung stationary over the town. I dined hurriedly, made no response to the anxious inquiries of the kind German woman, who whimpered a little herself at the sight of my red, swollen eyes (Germans—as is well known—are always glad to weep). I behaved very ungraciously to my preceptor...and at once after dinner set off to Ivan Semyonitch... Bent double in a jolting droshky, I kept asking myself whether I should tell Varia all as it was, or go on deceiving her, and little by little turn her heart from Andrei... I reached Ivan Semyonitch's without knowing what to decide upon... I found all the family in the parlour. On seeing me, Varia turned fearfully white, but did not move from her place; Sidorenko began talking to me in a peculiarly jeering way. I responded as best I could, looking from time to time at Varia, and almost unconsciously giving a dejected and pensive expression to my features. The lieutenant started whist again. Varia sat near the window and did not stir. 'You're dull now, I suppose?' Ivan Semyonitch asked her twenty times over.
At last I succeeded in seizing a favourable opportunity.
'You are alone again,' Varia whispered to me.
'Yes,' I answered gloomily; 'and probably for long.'
She swiftly drew in her head.
'Did you give him my letter?' she asked in a voice hardly audible.
'Yes.'
'Well?'... she gasped for breath. I glanced at her.... There was a sudden flash of spiteful pleasure within me.
'He told me to tell you,' I pronounced deliberately, 'that "what has been will not be again...."'
Varia pressed her left hand to her heart, stretched her right hand out in front, staggered, and went quickly out of the room. I tried to overtake her.... Ivan Semyonitch stopped me. I stayed another two hours with him, but Varia did not appear. On the way back I felt ashamed ... ashamed before Varia, before Andrei, before myself; though they say it is better to cut off an injured limb at once than to keep the patient in prolonged suffering; but who gave me a right to deal such a merciless blow at the heart of a poor girl?... For a long while I could not sleep ... but I fell asleep at last. In general I must repeat that 'love' never once deprived me of sleep.

I began to go pretty often to Ivan Semyonitch's. I used to see Kolosov as before, but neither he nor I ever referred to Varia. My relations with her were of a rather curious kind. She became attached to me with that sort of attachment which excludes every possibility of love. She could not help noticing my warm sympathy, and talked eagerly with me … of what, do you suppose?… of Kolosov, nothing but Kolosov! The man had taken such possession of her that she did not, as it were, belong to herself. I tried in vain to arouse her pride … she was either silent or, if she talked—chattered on about Kolosov. I did not even suspect in those days that sorrow of that kind—talkative sorrow—is in reality far more genuine than any silent suffering. I must own I passed many bitter moments at that time. I was conscious that I was not capable of filling Kolosov's place; I was conscious that Varia's past was so full, so rich … and her present so poor…. I got to the point of an involuntary shudder at the words 'Do you remember' … with which almost every sentence of hers began. She grew a little thinner during the first days of our acquaintance … but afterwards got better again, and even grew cheerful; she might have been compared then with a wounded bird, not yet quite recovered. Meanwhile my position had become insupportable; the lowest passions gradually gained possession of my soul; it happened to me to slander Kolosov in Varia's presence. I resolved to cut short such unnatural relations. But how? Part from Varia—I could not…. Declare my love to her—I did not dare; I felt that I could not, as yet, hope for a return. Marry her…. This idea alarmed me; I was only eighteen; I felt a dread of putting all my future into bondage so early; I thought of my father, I could hear the jeering comments of Kolosov's comrades…. But they say every thought is like dough; you have only to knead it well—you can make anything you like of it. I began, for whole days together, to dream of marriage…. I imagined what gratitude would fill Varia's heart when I, the friend and confidant of Kolosov, should offer her my hand, knowing her to be hopelessly in love with another. Persons of experience, I remembered, had told me that marriage for love is a complete absurdity; I began to indulge my fancy; I pictured to myself our peaceful life together in some snug corner of South Russia; an mentally I traced the gradual transition in Varia's heart from gratitude to affection, from affection to love…. I vowed to myself at once to leave Moscow, the university, to forget everything and every one. I began to avoid meeting Kolosov.

At last, one bright winter day (Varia had been somehow peculiarly enchanting the previous evening), I dressed myself in my best, slowly and solemnly sallied out from my room, took a first-rate sledge, and drove down to Ivan Semyonitch's. Varia was sitting alone in the drawing-room reading Karamzin. On seeing me she softly laid the book down on her knees, and with agitated curiosity looked into my face; I had never been to see them in the morning before…. I sat down beside her; my heart beat painfully. 'What are you reading?' I asked her at last. 'Karamzin.' 'What, are you taking up Russian literature?…' She suddenly cut me short. 'Tell me, haven't you come from Andrei?' That name, that trembling, questioning voice, the half-joyful, half-timid expression of her face, all these unmistakable signs of persistent love, pierced to my heart like arrows. I resolved either to part from Varia, or to receive from her herself the right to chase the hated name of Andrei from her lips for ever. I do not remember what I said to her; at first I must have expressed myself in rather confused fashion, as for a long while she did not understand me; at last I could stand it no longer, and almost shouted, 'I love you, I want to marry you.' 'You love me?' said Varia in bewilderment. I fancied she meant to get up, to go away, to refuse me. 'For God's sake,' I whispered breathlessly, 'don't answer me, don't say yes or no; think it over; to-morrow I will come again for a final answer…. I have long loved you. I don't ask of you love, I want to be your champion, your friend; don't answer me now, don't answer…. Till to-morrow.' With these words I rushed out of the room. In the passage Ivan Semyonitch met me, and not only showed no surprise at my visit, but positively, with an agreeable smile, offered me an apple. Such unexpected amiability so struck me that I was simply dumb with amazement. 'Take the apple, it's a nice apple, really!' persisted Ivan Semyonitch. Mechanically I took the apple at last, and drove all the way home with it in my hand.

You may easily imagine how I passed all that day and the following morning. That night I slept rather badly. 'My God! my God!' I kept thinking; 'if she refuses me! … I shall die…. I shall die….' I repeated wearily. 'Yes, she will certainly refuse me…. And why was I in such a hurry!'… Wishing to turn my thoughts, I began to write a letter to my father—a desperate, resolute letter. Speaking of myself, I used the expression 'your son.' Bobov came in to see me. I began weeping on his shoulder, which must have surprised poor Bobov not a little…. I afterwards learned that he had come to me to borrow money (his landlord had threatened to turn him out of the house); he had no choice but to hook it, as the students say….

At last the great moment arrived. On going out of my room, I stood still in the doorway. 'With what feelings,' thought I, 'shall I cross this threshold again to-day?' … My emotion at the sight of Ivan Semyonitch's little house was so great that I got down, picked up a handful of snow and pressed it to my face. 'Oh, heavens!' I thought, 'if I find Varia alone—I am lost!' My legs were giving way under me; I could hardly get to the steps. Things were as I had hoped. I found Varia in the parlour with Matrona Semyonovna. I made my bows awkwardly, and sat down by the old lady. Varia's face was rather paler than usual…. I fancied that she tried to avoid my eyes…. But what were my feelings when Matrona Semyonovna suddenly got up and went into the next room!… I began looking out of the window—I was trembling inwardly like an autumn leaf. Varia did not speak…. At last I mastered my timidity, went up to her, bent my head….

'What are you going to say to me?' I articulated in a breaking voice.

Varia turned away—the tears were glistening on her eyelashes.

'I see,' I went on, 'it's useless for me to hope.'…

Varia looked shyly round and gave me her hand without a word.

'Varia!' I cried involuntarily…and stopped, as though frightened at my own hopes.

'Speak to papa,' she articulated at last.

'You permit me to speak to Ivan Semyonitch?' …

'Yes.'… I covered her hands with kisses.

'Don't, don't,' whispered Varia, and suddenly burst into tears.

I sat down beside her, talked soothingly to her, wiped away her tears…. Luckily, Ivan Semyonitch was not at home, and Matrona Semyonovna had gone up to her own little room. I made vows of love, of constancy to Varia.

…'Yes,' she said, suppressing her sobs and continually wiping her eyes; 'I know you are a good man, an honest man; you are not like Kolosov.'… 'That name again!' thought I. But with what delight I kissed those warm, damp little hands! with what subdued rapture I gazed into that sweet face!… I talked to her of the future, walked about the room, sat down on the floor at her feet, hid my eyes in my hands, and shuddered with happiness…. Ivan Semyonitch's heavy footsteps cut short our conversation. Varia hurriedly got up and went off to her own room—without, however, pressing my hand or glancing at me. Mr. Sidorenko was even more amiable than on the previous day: he laughed, rubbed his stomach, made jokes about Matrona Semyonovna, and so on. I was on the point of asking for his blessing there and then, but I thought better of it and deferred doing so till the next day. His ponderous jokes jarred upon me; besides I was exhausted…. I said good-bye to him and went away.

I am one of those persons who love brooding over their own sensations, though I cannot endure such persons myself. And so, after the first transport of heartfelt joy, I promptly began to give myself up to all sorts of reflections. When I had got half a mile from the house of the retired lieutenant, I flung my hat up in the air, in excessive delight, and shouted 'Hurrah!' But while I was being jolted through the long, crooked streets of Moscow, my thoughts gradually took another turn. All sorts of rather sordid doubts began to crowd upon my mind. I recalled my conversation with Ivan Semyonitch about marriage in general … and unconsciously I murmured to myself, 'So he was putting it on, the old humbug!' It is true that I continually repeated, 'but then Varia is mine! mine!' … Yet that 'but'—alas, that *but*!—and then, too, the words, 'Varia is mine!' aroused in me not a deep, overwhelming rapture, but a sort of paltry, egoistic triumph.... If Varia had refused me point-blank, I should have been burning with furious passion; but having received her consent, I was like a man who has just said to a guest, 'Make yourself at home,' and sees the guest actually beginning to settle into his room, as if he were at home. 'If she had loved Kolosov,' I thought, 'how was it she consented so soon? It's clear she's glad to marry any one.... Well, what of it? all the better for me.'... It was with such vague and curious feelings that I crossed the threshold of my room. Possibly, gentlemen, my story does not strike you as sounding true.

I don't know whether it sounds true or not, but I know that all I have told is the absolute and literal truth. However, I gave myself up all that day to a feverish gaiety, assured myself that I simply did not deserve such happiness; but next morning....

A wonderful thing is sleep! It not only renews one's body: in a way it renews one's soul, restoring it to primaeval simplicity and naturalness. In the course of the day you succeed in *tuning* yourself, in soaking yourself in falsity, in false ideas ... sleep with its cool wave washes away all such pitiful trashiness; and on waking up, at least for the first few instants, you are capable of understanding and loving truth. I waked up, and, reflecting on the previous day, I felt a certain discomfort.... I was, as it were, ashamed of all my own actions. With instinctive uneasiness I thought of the visit to be made that day, of my interview with Ivan Semyonitch.... This uneasiness was acute and distressing; it was like the uneasiness of the hare who hears the barking of the dogs and is bound at last to run out of his native forest into the open country...and there the sharp teeth of the harriers are awaiting him.... 'Why was I in such a hurry?' I repeated, just as I had the day before, but in quite a different sense. I remember the fearful difference between yesterday and to-day struck myself; for the first time it occurred to me that in human life there lie hid secrets—strange secrets.... With childish perplexity I gazed into this new, not fantastic, real world. By the word 'real' many people understand 'trivial.' Perhaps it sometimes is so; but I must own that the first appearance of *reality* before me shook me profoundly, scared me, impressed me....

What fine-sounding phrases all about love that didn't come off, to use Gogol's expression! ... I come back to my story. In the course of that day I assured myself again that I was the most blissful of mortals. I drove out of the town to Ivan Semyonitch's. He received me very gleefully; he had been meaning to go and see a neighbour, but I myself stopped him. I was afraid to be left alone with Varia. The evening was cheerful, but not reassuring. Varia was neither one thing nor the other, neither cordial nor melancholy ... neither pretty nor plain. I looked at her, as the philosophers say, objectively—that is to say, as the man who has dined looks at the dishes. I thought her hands were rather red. Sometimes, however, my heart warmed, and watching her I gave way to other dreams and reveries. I had only just made her an offer, as it is called, and here I was already feeling as though we were living as husband and wife ... as though our souls already made up one lovely whole, belonged to one another, and consequently were trying each to seek out a separate path for itself....

'Well, have you spoken to papa?' Varia said to me, as soon as we were left alone.

This inquiry impressed me most disagreeably.... I thought to myself, 'You're pleased to be in a desperate hurry, Varvara Ivanovna.'

'Not yet,' I answered, rather shortly, 'but I will speak to him.'

Altogether I behaved rather casually with her. In spite of my promise, I said nothing definite to Ivan Semyonitch. As I was leaving, I pressed his hand significantly, and informed him that I wanted to have a little talk with him ... that was all.... 'Good-bye!' I said to Varia.

'Till we meet!' said she.

I will not keep you long in suspense, gentlemen; I am afraid of exhausting your patience.... We never met again. I never went back to Ivan Semyonitch's. The first days, it is true, of my voluntary separation from Varia did not pass without tears, self-reproach, and emotion; I was frightened myself at the rapid drooping of my love; twenty times over I was on the point of starting off to see her. Vividly I pictured to myself her amazement, her grief, her wounded feelings; but—I never went to Ivan Semyonitch's again. In her absence I begged her forgiveness, fell on my knees before her, assured her of my profound repentance—and once, when I met a girl in the street slightly resembling her, I took to my heels without looking back, and only breathed freely in a cook-shop after the fifth jam-puff. The word 'to-morrow' was invented for irresolute people, and for children; like a baby, I lulled myself with that magic word. 'To-morrow I will go to her, whatever happens,' I said to myself, and ate and slept well to-day. I began to think a great deal more about Kolosov than about Varia ... everywhere, continually, I saw his open, bold, careless face. I began going to see him as before. He gave me the same welcome as ever. But how deeply I felt his superiority to me! How ridiculous I thought all my fancies, my pensive melancholy, during the period of Kolosov's connection with Varia, my magnanimous resolution to bring them together again, my anticipations, my raptures, my remorse!... I had played a wretched, drawn-out part of screaming farce, but he had passed so simply, so well, through it all....

You will say, 'What is there wonderful in that? your Kolosov fell in love with a girl, then fell out of love again, and threw her over.... Why, that happens with everybody....' Agreed; but which of us knows just when to break with our past? Which of us, tell me, is not afraid of the reproaches—I don't mean of the woman—the reproaches of every chance fool? Which of us is proof against the temptation of making a display of magnanimity, or of playing egoistically with another devoted heart? Which of us, in fact, has the force of character to be superior to petty vanity, to *petty fine feelings*, sympathy and self-reproach?... Oh, gentlemen, the man who leaves a woman at that great and bitter moment when he is forced to recognise that his heart is not altogether, not fully, hers, that man, believe me, has a truer and deeper comprehension of the sacredness of love than the faint-hearted creatures who, from dulness or weakness, go on playing on the half-cracked strings of their flabby and sentimental hearts! At the beginning of my story I told you that we all considered Andrei Kolosov an extraordinary man. And if a clear, simple outlook upon life, if the absence of every kind of cant in a young man, can be called an extraordinary thing, Kolosov deserved the name. At a certain age, to be natural is to be extraordinary.... It is time to finish, though. I thank you for your attention.... Oh, I forgot to tell you that three months after my last visit I met the old humbug Ivan Semyonitch. I tried, of course, to glide hurriedly and unnoticed by him, but yet I could not help overhearing the words, 'Feather-headed scoundrels!' uttered angrily.

'And what became of Varia?' asked some one.

'I don't know,' answered the story-teller.

We all got up and separated.

1864.

A CORRESPONDENCE

A few years ago I was in Dresden. I was staying at an hotel. From early morning till late evening I strolled about the town, and did not think it necessary to make acquaintance with my neighbours; at last it reached my ears in some chance way that there was a Russian in the hotel—lying ill. I went to see him, and found a man in galloping consumption. I had begun to be tired of Dresden; I stayed with my new acquaintance. It's dull work sitting with a sick man, but even dulness is sometimes agreeable; moreover, my patient was not low-spirited and was very ready to talk. We tried to kill time in all sorts of ways; We played 'Fools,' the two of us together, and made fun of the doctor. My compatriot used to tell this very bald-headed German all sorts of fictions about himself, which the doctor had always 'long ago anticipated.' He used to mimic his astonishment at any new, exceptional symptom, to throw his medicines out of window, and so on. I observed more than once, however, to my friend that it would be as well to send for a good doctor before it was too late, that his complaint was not to be trifled with, and so on. But Alexey (my new friend's name was Alexey Petrovitch S——) always turned off my advice with jests at the expense of doctors in general, and his own in particular; and at last one rainy autumn evening he answered my urgent entreaties with such a mournful look, he shook his head so sorrowfully and smiled so strangely, that I felt somewhat disconcerted. The same night Alexey was worse, and the next day he died. Just before his death his usual cheerfulness deserted him; he tossed about uneasily in his bed, sighed, looked round him in anguish … clutched at my hand, and whispered with an effort, 'But it's hard to die, you know … dropped his head on the pillow, and shed tears. I did not know what to say to him, and sat in silence by his bed. But Alexey soon got the better of these last, late regrets…. 'I say,' he said to me, 'our doctor'll come to-day and find me dead…. I can fancy his face.'… And the dying man tried to mimic him. He asked me to send all his things to Russia to his relations, with the exception of a small packet which he gave me as a souvenir.

This packet contained letters—a girl's letters to Alexey, and copies of his letters to her. There were fifteen of them. Alexey Petrovitch S—— had known Marya Alexandrovna B—— long before, in their childhood, I fancy. Alexey Petrovitch had a cousin, Marya Alexandrovna had a sister. In former years they had all lived together; then they had been separated, and had not seen each other for a long while. Later on, they had chanced one summer to be all together again in the country, and they had fallen in love—Alexey's cousin with Marya Alexandrovna, and Alexey with her sister. The summer had passed by, the autumn came; they parted. Alexey, like a sensible person, soon came to the conclusion that he was not in love at all, and had effected a very satisfactory parting from his charmer. His cousin had continued writing to Marya Alexandrovna for nearly two years longer … but he too perceived at last that he was deceiving her and himself in an unconscionable way, and he too dropped the correspondence.

I could tell you something about Marya Alexandrovna, gentle reader, but you will find out what she was from her letters. Alexey wrote his first letter to her soon after she had finally broken with his cousin. He was at that time in Petersburg; he went suddenly abroad, fell ill, and died at Dresden. I resolved to print his correspondence with Marya Alexandrovna, and trust the reader will look at it with indulgence, as these letters are not love-letters—Heaven forbid! Love-letters are as a rule only read by two persons (they read them over a thousand times to make up), and to a third person they are unendurable, if not ridiculous.

I

FROM ALEXEY PETROVITCH TO MARYA ALEXANDROVNA

ST. PETERSBURG, *March* 7, 1840.

DEAR MARYA ALEXANDROVNA,—

I fancy I have never written to you before, and here I am writing to you now…. I have chosen a curious time to begin, haven't I? I'll tell you what gave me the impulse. Mon cousin Théodore was with me to-day, and…how shall I put it?…and he confided to me as the greatest secret (he never tells one anything except as a great secret), that he was in love with the daughter of a gentleman here, and that this time he is firmly resolved to be married, and that he has already taken the first step—he has declared himself! I made haste, of course, to congratulate him on an event so agreeable for him; he has been longing to declare himself for a great while…but inwardly, I must own, I was rather astonished. Although I knew that everything was over between you, still I had fancied…. In short, I was surprised. I had made arrangements to go out to see friends to-day, but I have stopped at home and mean to have a little gossip with you. If you do not care to listen to me, fling this letter forthwith into the fire. I warn you I mean to be frank, though I feel you are fully justified in taking me for a rather impertinent person. Observe, however, that I would not have taken up my pen if I had not known your sister was not with you; she is staying, so Théodore told me, the whole summer with your aunt, Madame B—-. God give her every blessing!

And so, this is how it has all worked out.... But I am not going to offer you my friendship and all that; I am shy as a rule of high-sounding speeches and 'heartfelt' effusions. In beginning to write this letter, I simply obeyed a momentary impulse. If there is another feeling latent within me, let it remain hidden under a bushel for the time.

I'm not going to offer you sympathy either. In sympathising with others, people for the most part want to get rid, as quick as they can, of an unpleasant feeling of involuntary, egoistic regret.... I understand genuine, warm sympathy ... but such sympathy you would not accept from just any one.... Do, please, get angry with me.... If you're angry, you'll be sure to read my missive to the end.

But what right have I to write to you, to talk of my friendship, of my feelings, of consolation? None, absolutely none; that I am bound to admit, and I can only throw myself on your kindness.

Do you know what the preface of my letter's like? I'll tell you: some Mr. N. or M. walking into the drawing-room of a lady who doesn't in the least expect him, and who does, perhaps, expect some one else.... He realises that he has come at an unlucky moment, but there's no help for it.... He sits down, begins talking...goodness knows what about: poetry, the beauties of nature, the advantages of a good education...talks the most awful rot, in fact. But, meanwhile, the first five minutes have gone by, he has settled himself comfortably; the lady has resigned herself to the inevitable, and so Mr. N. or M. regains his self-possession, takes breath, and begins a real conversation—to the best of his ability.

In spite, though, of all this rigmarole, I don't still feel quite comfortable. I seem to see your bewildered—even rather wrathful—face; I feel that it will be almost impossible you should not ascribe to me some hidden motives, and so, like a Roman who has committed some folly, I wrap myself majestically in my toga, and await in silence your final sentence....

The question is: Will you allow me to go on writing to you?—I remain sincerely and warmly devoted to you,

ALEXEY S.

II
FROM MARYA ALEXANDROVNA TO ALEXEY PETROVITCH

VILLAGE OF X——, *March* 22, 1840.

DEAR SIR,
ALEXEY PETROVITCH,

I have received your letter, and I really don't know what to say to you. I should not even have answered you at all, if it had not been that I fancied that under your jesting remarks there really lies hid a feeling of some friendliness. Your letter made an unpleasant impression on me. In answer to your rigmarole, as you call it, let me too put to you one question: *What for?* What have I to do with you, or you with me? I do not ascribe to you any bad motives ... on the contrary, I'm grateful for your sympathy ... but we are strangers to each other, and I, just now at least, feel not the slightest inclination for greater intimacy with any one whatever.—With sincere esteem, I remain, etc.,

MARYA B.

III

FROM ALEXEY PETROVITCH TO MARYA ALEXANDROVNA

ST. PETERSBURG, *March* 30.

Thank you, Marya Alexandrovna, thank you for your note, brief as it was. All this time I have been in great suspense; twenty times a day I have thought of you and my letter. You can't imagine how bitterly I laughed at myself; but now I am in an excellent frame of mind, and very much pleased with myself. Marya Alexandrovna, I am going to begin a correspondence with you! Confess, this was not at all what you expected after your answer; I'm surprised myself at my boldness.... Well, I don't care, here goes! But don't be uneasy; I want to talk to you, not of you, but of myself. It's like this, do you see: it's absolutely needful for me, in the old-fashioned phraseology, to open my heart to some one. I have not the slightest right to select you for my confidant—agreed.

But listen: I won't demand of you an answer to my letters; I don't even want to know whether you read my 'rigmarole'; but, in the name of all that's holy, don't send my letters back to me!

Let me tell you, I am utterly alone on earth. In my youth I led a solitary life, though I never, I remember, posed as a Byronic hero; but first, circumstances, and secondly, a faculty of imaginative dreaming and a love for dreaming, rather cool blood, pride, indolence—a number of different causes, in fact, cut me off from the society of men. The transition from dream-life to real life took place in me late...perhaps too late, perhaps it has not fully taken place up to now. So long as I found entertainment in my own thoughts and feelings, so long as I was capable of abandoning myself to causeless and unuttered transports and so on, I did not complain of my solitude. I had no associates; I had what are called friends. Sometimes I needed their presence, as an electrical machine needs a discharger—and that was all. Love... of that subject we will not speak for the present. But now, I will own, now solitude weighs heavy on me; and at the same time, I see no escape from my position. I do not blame fate; I alone am to blame and am deservedly punished. In my youth I was absorbed by one thing—my precious self; I took my simple-hearted self-love for modesty; I avoided society—and here I am now, a fearful bore to myself. What am I to do with myself? There is no one I love; all my relations with other people are somehow strained and false.

And I've no memories either, for in all my past life I can find nothing but my own personality. Save me. To you I have made no passionate protestations of love. You I have never smothered in a flood of aimless babble. I passed by you rather coldly, and it is just for that reason I make up my mind to have recourse to you now. (I have had thoughts of doing so before this, but at that time you were not free....) Among all my self-created sensations, pleasures and sufferings, the one genuine feeling was the not great, but instinctive attraction to you, which withered up at the time, like a single ear of wheat in the midst of worthless weeds.... Let me just for once look into another face, into another soul—my own face has grown hateful to me. I am like a man who should have been condemned to live all his life in a room with walls of looking-glass.... I do not ask of you any sort of confessions—oh mercy, no! Bestow on me a sister's unspoken sympathy, or at least the simple curiosity of a reader. I will entertain you, I will really.

Meanwhile I have the honour to be your sincere friend,

A. S.

IV

FROM ALEXEY PETROVITCH TO MARYA ALEXANDROVNA

ST. PETERSBURG, *April* 7.

I am writing to you again, though I foresee that without your approval I shall soon cease writing. I must own that you cannot but feel some distrust of me. Well, perhaps you are right too. In old days I should have triumphantly announced to you (and very likely I should have quite believed my own words myself) that I had 'developed,' made progress, since the time when we parted. With condescending, almost affectionate, contempt I should have referred to my past, and with touching self-conceit have initiated you into the secrets of my real, present life ... but, now, I assure you, Marya Alexandrovna, I'm positively ashamed and sick to remember the capers and antics cut at times by my paltry egoism. Don't be afraid: I am not going to force upon you any great truths, any profound views. I have none of them—of those truths and views. I have become a simple good fellow—really. I am bored, Marya Alexandrovna, I'm simply bored past all enduring. That is why I am writing to you.... I really believe we may come to be friends....

But I'm positively incapable of talking to you, till you hold out a hand to me, till I get a note from you with the one word 'Yes.' Marya Alexandrovna, are you willing to listen to me? That's the question.—Yours devotedly,

A. S.

V

FROM MARYA ALEXANDROVNA TO ALEXEY PETROVITCH

VILLAGE OF X——, *April* 14.

What a strange person you are! Very well, then.—Yes!

MARYA B.

VI

FROM ALEXEY PETROVITCH TO MARYA ALEXANDROVNA

ST. PETERSBURG, *May* 2, 1840.

Hurrah! Thanks, Marya Alexandrovna, thanks! You are a very kind and indulgent creature.

I will begin according to my promise to talk about myself, and I shall talk with a relish approaching to appetite.... That's just it. Of anything in the world one may speak with fire, with enthusiasm, with ecstasy, but with appetite one talks only of oneself.

Let me tell you, during the last few days a very strange experience has befallen me. I have for the first time taken an all-round view of my past. You understand me. Every one of us often recalls what is over—with regret, or vexation, or simply from nothing to do. But to bend a cold, clear gaze over all one's past life—as a traveller turns and looks from a high mountain on the plain he has passed through—is only possible at a certain age ... and a secret chill clutches at a man's heart when it happens to him for the first time. Mine, anyway, felt a sick pang. While we are young, *such* an all-round view is impossible. But my youth is over, and, like one who has climbed on to a mountain, everything lies clear before me.

Yes, my youth is gone, gone never to return!... Here it lies before me, as it were in the palm of my hand.

A sorry spectacle! I will confess to you, Marya Alexandrovna, I am very sorry for myself. My God! my God! Can it be that I have myself so utterly ruined my life, so mercilessly embroiled and tortured myself!... Now I have come to my senses, but it's too late. Has it ever happened to you to save a fly from a spider? Has it? You remember, you put it in the sun; its wings and legs were stuck together, glued.... How awkwardly it moved, how clumsily it attempted to get clear!... After prolonged efforts, it somehow gets better, crawls, tries to open its wings ... but there is no more frolicking for it, no more light-hearted buzzing in the sunshine, as before, when it was flying through the open window into the cool room and out again, freely winging its way into the hot air.... The fly, at least, fell through none of its own doing into the dreadful web ... but I!

I have been my own spider!

And, at the same time, I cannot greatly blame myself. Who, indeed, tell me, pray, is ever to blame for anything—alone? Or, to put it better, we are all to blame, and yet we can't be blamed. Circumstances determine us; they shove us into one road or another, and then they punish us for it. Every man has his destiny.... Wait a bit, wait a bit! A cleverly worked-out but true comparison has just come into my head. As the clouds are first condensed from the vapours of earth, rise from out of her bosom, then separate, move away from her, and at last bring her prosperity or ruin: so, about every one of us, and out of ourselves, is fashioned—how is one to express it?—is fashioned a sort of element, which has afterwards a destructive or saving influence on us. This element I call destiny.... In other words, and speaking simply, every one makes his own destiny and destiny makes every one....

Every one makes his destiny—yes!... but people like us make it too much—that's what's wrong with us! Consciousness is awakened too early in us; too early we begin to keep watch on ourselves.... We Russians have set ourselves no other task in life but the cultivation of our own personality, and when we're children hardly grown-up we set to work to cultivate it, this luckless personality! Receiving no definite guidance from without, with no real respect for anything, no strong belief in anything, we are free to make what we choose of ourselves ... one can't expect every one to understand on the spot the uselessness of intellect 'seething in vain activity' ... and so we get again one monster the more in the world, one more of those worthless creatures in whom habits of self-ccnsciousness distort the very striving for truth, and a ludicrous simplicity exists side by side with a pitiful duplicity ... one of those beings of impotent, restless thought who all their lives know neither the satisfaction of natural activity, nor genuine suffering, nor the genuine thrill of conviction.... Mixing up together in ourselves the defects of all ages, we rob each defect of its good redeeming side ... we are as silly as children, but we are not sincere as they are; we are cold as old people, but we have none of the good sense of old age.... To make up, we are psychologists. Oh yes, we are great psychologists! But our psychology is akin to pathology; our psychology is that subtle study of the laws of morbid condition and morbid development, with which healthy people have nothing to do.... And, what is the chief point, we are not young, even in our youth we are not young!

And at the same time—why libel ourselves? Were we never young, did we never know the play, the fire, the thrill of life's forces? We too have been in Arcady, we too have strayed about her bright meadows!... Have you chanced, strolling about a copse, to come across those dark grasshoppers which, jumping up from under your very feet, suddenly with a whirring sound expand bright red wings, fly a few yards, and then drop again into the grass? So our dark youth at times spread its particoloured wings for a few moments and for no long flight.... Do you remember our silent evening walks, the four of us together, beside your garden fence, after some long, warm, spirited conversation? Do you remember those blissful moments? Nature, benign and stately, took us to her bosom. We plunged, swooning, into a flood of bliss. All around, the sunset with a sudden and soft flush, the glowing sky, the earth bathed in light, everything on all sides seemed full of the fresh and fiery breath of youth, the joyous triumph of some deathless happiness. The sunset flamed; and, like it, our rapturous hearts burned with soft and passionate fire, and the tiny leaves of the young trees quivered faintly and expectantly over our heads, as though in response to the inward tremor of vague feelings and anticipations in us. Do you remember the purity, the goodness and trustfulness of ideas, the softening of noble hopes, the silence of full hearts? Were we not really then worth something better than what life has brought us to? Why was it ordained for us only at rare moments to see the longed-for shore, and never to stand firmly on it, never to touch it:

'Never to weep with joy, like the first Jew
Upon the border of the promised land'!

These two lines of Fet's remind me of others, also his.... Do you remember once, as we stood in the highroad, we saw in the distance a cloud of pink dust, blown up by the light breeze against the setting sun? 'In an eddying cloud,' you began, and we were all still at once to listen:

'In an eddying cloud
Dust rises in the distance ...
Rider or man on foot
Is seen not in the dust.
I see some one trotting
On a gallant steed ...
Friend of mine, friend far away,
Think! oh, think of me!'

You ceased ... we all felt a shudder pass over us, as though the breath of love had flitted over our hearts, and each of us—I am sure of it—felt irresistibly drawn into the distance, the unknown distance, where the phantom of bliss rises and lures through the mist. And all the while, observe the strangeness; why, one wonders, should we have a yearning for the far away? Were we not in love with each other? Was not happiness 'so close, so possible'? As I asked you just now: why was it we did not touch the longed-for shore? Because falsehood walked hand in hand with us; because it poisoned our best feelings; because everything in us was artificial and strained; because we did not love each other at all, but were only trying to love, fancying we loved....

But enough, enough! why inflame one's wounds? Besides, it is all over and done with. What was good in our past moved me, and on that good I will take leave of you for a while. It's time to make an end of this long letter. I am going out for a breath here of the May air, in which spring is breaking through the dry fastness of winter with a sort of damp, keen warmth. Farewell.—Yours,

A. S.
VII

FROM MARYA ALEXANDROVNA TO ALEXEY PETROVITCH

VILLAGE OF X——,*May* 1840.

I have received your letter, Alexey Petrovitch, and do you know what feeling t aroused in me?—indignation ... yes, indignation ... and I will explain to you at once why it aroused just that feeling in me. It's only a pity I'm not a great hand with my pen; I rarely write, and am not good at expressing my thoughts precisely and in few words. But you will, I hope, come to my aid. You must try, on your side, to understand me, if only to find out why I am indignant with you.

Tell me—you have brains—have you ever asked yourself what sort of creature a Russian woman is? what is her destiny? her position in the world—in short, what is her life? I don't know if you have had time to put this question to yourself; I can't picture to myself how you would answer it.... I should, perhaps, in conversation be capable of giving you my ideas on the subject, but on paper I am scarcely equal to it. No matter, though. This is the point: you will certainly agree with me that we women, those of us at least who are not satisfied with the common interests of domestic life, receive our final education, in any case, from you men: you have a great and powerful influence on us. Now, consider what you do to us. I am talking about young girls, especially those who, like me, live in the wilds, and there are very many such in Russia. Besides, I don't know anything of others and cannot judge of them. Picture to yourself such a girl. Her education, suppose, is finished; she begins to live, to enjoy herself. But enjoyment alone is not much to her. She demands much from life, she reads, and dreams ... of love. Always nothing but love! you will say.... Suppose so; but that word means a great deal to her. I repeat that I am not speaking of a girl to whom thinking is tiresome and boring.... She looks round her, is waiting for the time when he will come for whom her soul yearns.... At last he makes his appearance—she is captivated; she is wax in his hands. All—happiness and love and thought—all have come with a rush together with him; all her tremors are soothed, all her doubts solved by him. Truth itself seems speaking by his lips. She venerates him, is over-awed at her own happiness, learns, loves. Great is his power over her at that time!... If he were a hero, he would fire her, would teach her to sacrifice herself, and all sacrifices would be easy to her! But there are no heroes in our times.... Anyway, he directs her as he pleases. She devotes herself to whatever interests him, every word of his sinks into her soul. She has not yet learned how worthless and empty and false a word may be, how little it costs him who utters it, and how little it deserves belief! After these first moments of bliss and hope there usually comes—through circumstances—(circumstances are always to blame)—there comes a parting. They say there have been instances of two kindred souls, on getting to know one another, becoming at once inseparably united; I have heard it said, too, that things did not always go smoothly with them in consequence ... but of what I have not seen myself I will not speak,—and that the pettiest calculation, the most pitiful prudence, can exist in a youthful heart, side by side with the most passionate enthusiasm—of that I have to my sorrow had practical experience. And so, the parting comes.... Happy the girl who realises at once that it is the end of everything, who does not beguile herself with expectations! But you, valorous, just men, for the most part, have not the pluck, nor even the desire, to tell us the truth.... It is less disturbing for you to deceive us.... However, I am ready to believe that you deceive yourselves together with us.... Parting! To bear separation is both hard and easy. If only there be perfect, untouched faith in him whom one loves, the soul can master the anguish of parting.... I will say more. It is only then, when she is left alone, that she finds out the sweetness of solitude—not fruitless, but filled with memories and ideas. It is only then that she finds out herself, comes to her true self, grows strong.... In the letters of her friend far away she finds a support for herself; in her own, she, very likely for the first time, finds full self-expression.... But as two people who start from a stream's source, along opposite banks, at first can touch hands, then only communicate by voice, and finally lose sight of each other altogether; so two natures grow apart at last by separation. Well, what then? you will say; it's clear they were not destined to be together.... But herein the difference between a man and a woman comes out. For a man it means nothing to begin a new life, to shake off all his past; a woman cannot do this. No, she cannot fling off her past, she cannot break away from her roots—no, a thousand times no! And now begins a pitiful and ludicrous spectacle.... Gradually losing hope and faith in herself—and how bitter that is you cannot even imagine!—she pines and wears herself out alone, obstinately clinging to her memories and turning away from everything that the life around offers her.... But he? Look for him! where is he? And is it worth his while to stand still? When has he time to look round? Why, it's all a thing of the past for him. Or else this is what happens: it happens that he feels a sudden inclination to meet the former object of his feelings, that he even makes an excursion with that aim.... But, mercy on us! the pitiful conceit that leads him into doing that! In his gracious sympathy, in his would-be friendly advice, in his indulgent explanation of the past, such consciousness of his superiority is manifest! It is so agreeable and cheering for him to let himself feel every instant—what a clever person he is, and how kind! And how little he understands what he has done! How clever he is at not even guessing what is passing in a woman's heart, and how offensive is his compassion if he does guess it!... Tell me, please, where is she to get strength to bear all this? Recollect this, too: for the most part, a girl in whose brain—to her misfortune—thought has begun to stir, such a girl, when she begins to love, and falls under a man's influence, inevitably grows apart from her family, her circle of friends. She was not, even before then, satisfied with their life, though she moved in step with them, while she treasured all her secret dreams in her soul.... But the discrepancy soon becomes apparent.... They cease to comprehend her, and are ready to look askance at everything she does.... At first this is nothing to her, but afterwards, afterwards ... when she is left alone, when what she was striving towards, for which she had sacrificed everything—when heaven is not gained while everything near, everything possible, is lost—what is there to support her? Jeers, sly hints, the vulgar triumph of coarse commonsense, she could still endure somehow ... but what is she to do, what is to be her refuge, when an inner voice begins to whisper to her that all of them are right and she was wrong, that life, whatever it may be, is better than dreams, as health is better than sickness ... when her favourite pursuits, her favourite books, grow hateful to her, books out of which there is no reading happiness—what, tell me, is to be her support? Must she not inevitably succumb in such a struggle? how is she to live and to go on living in such a desert? To know oneself beaten and to hold out one's hand, like a beggar, to persons quite indifferent, for them to bestow the sympathy which the proud heart had once fancied it could well dispense with—all that would be nothing! But to feel yourself ludicrous at the very instant when you are shedding bitter, bitter tears ... O God, spare such suffering!...

My hands are trembling, and I am quite in a fever.... My face burns. It is time to stop.... I'll send off this letter quickly, before I'm ashamed of its feebleness. But for God's sake, in your answer not a word—do you hear?—not a word of sympathy, or I'll never write to you again. Understand me: I should not like you to take this letter as the outpouring of a misunderstood soul, complaining.... Ah! I don't care!—Good-bye.

M.

VIII

FROM ALEXEY PETROVITCH TO MARYA ALEXANDROVNA

ST. PETERSBURG, *May* 28, 1840.

Marya Alexandrovna, you are a splendid person ... you ... your letter revealed the truth to me at last! My God! what suffering! A man is constantly thinking that now at last he has reached simplicity, that he's no longer showing off, humbugging, lying ... but when you come to look at him more attentively, he's become almost worse than before. And this, too, one must remark: the man himself, alone that is, never attains this self-recognition, try as he will; his eyes cannot see his own defects, just as the compositor's wearied eyes cannot see the slips he makes; another fresh eye is needed for that. My thanks to you, Marya Alexandrovna.... You see, I speak to you of myself; of you I dare not speak.... Ah, how absurd my last letter seems to me now, so flowery and sentimental! I beg you earnestly, go on with your confession. I fancy you, too, will be the better for it, and it will do me great good. It's a true saying: 'A woman's wit's better than many a reason,' and a woman's heart's far and away—by God, yes! If women knew how much better, nobler, and wiser they are than men—yes, wiser—they would grow conceited and be spoiled. But happily they don't know it; they don't know it because their intelligence isn't in the habit of turning incessantly upon themselves, as with us. They think very little about themselves—that's their weakness and their strength; that's the whole secret—I won't say of our superiority, but of our power. They lavish their soul, as a prodigal heir does his father's gold, while we exact a percentage on every worthless morsel.... How are they to hold their own with us?... All this is not compliments, but the simple truth, proved by experience. Once more, I beseech you, Marya Alexandrovna, go on writing to me.... If you knew all that is coming into my brain! ... But I have no wish now to speak, I want to listen to you. My turn will come later. Write, write.—Your devoted,

IX
FROM MARYA ALEXANDROVNA TO ALEXEY PETROVITCH

VILLAGE OF X——, *June* 12, 1840.

I had hardly sent off my last letter to you, Alexey Petrovitch, when I regretted it; but there was no help for it then. One thing reassures me somewhat: I am sure you realised that it was under the influence of feelings long ago suppressed that it was written, and you excused me. I did not even read through, at the time, what I had written to you; I remember my heart beat so violently that the pen shook in my fingers. However, though I should probably have expressed myself differently if I had allowed myself time to reflect, I don't mean, all the same, to disavow my own words, or the feelings which I described to you as best I could. To-day I am much cooler and far more self-possessed.

I remember at the end of my letter I spoke of the painful position of a girl who is conscious of being solitary, even among her own people.... I won't expatiate further upon them, but will rather tell you a few instances; I think I shall bore you less in that way. In the first place, then, let me tell you that all over the country-side I am never called anything but the female philosopher. The ladies especially honour me with that name. Some assert that I sleep with a Latin book in my hand, and in spectacles; others declare that I know how to extract cube roots, whatever they may be. Not a single one of them doubts that I wear manly apparel on the sly, and instead of 'good-morning', address people spasmodically with 'Georges Sand!'—and indignation grows apace against the female philosopher. We have a neighbour, a man of five-and-forty, a great wit ... at least, he is reputed a great wit ... for him my poor personality is an inexhaustible subject of jokes. He used to tell of me that directly the moon rose I could not take my eyes off it, and he will mimic the way in which I gaze at it; and declares that I positively take my coffee with moonshine instead of with milk—that's to say, I put my cup in the moonlight. He swears that I use phrases of this kind—'It is easy because it is difficult, though on the other hand it is difficult because it is easy'.... He asserts that I am always looking for a word, always striving 'thither,' and with comic rage inquires: 'whither-thither? whither?' He has also circulated a story about me that I ride at night up and down by the river, singing Schubert's Serenade, or simply moaning, 'Beethoven, Beethoven!' She is, he will say, such an impassioned old person, and so on, and so on. Of course, all this comes straight to me. This surprises you, perhaps. But do not forget that four years have passed since your stay in these parts. You remember how every one frowned upon us in those days. Their turn has come now. And all that, too, is no consequence. I have to hear many things that wound my heart more than that. I won't say anything about my poor, good mother's never having been able to forgive me for your cousin's indifference to me. But my whole life is burning away like a house on fire, as my nurse expresses it. 'Of course,' I am constantly hearing, 'we can't keep pace with you! we are plain people, we are guided by nothing but common-sense. Though, when you come to think of it, what have all these metaphysics, and books, and intimacies with learned folks brought you to?' You perhaps remember my sister—not the one to whom you were once not indifferent—but the other elder one, who is married. Her husband, if you recollect, is a simple and rather comic person; you often used to make fun of him in those days. But she's happy, after all; she's the mother of a family, she's fond of her husband, her husband adores her.... 'I am like every one else,' she says to me sometimes, 'but you!' And she's right; I envy her....

And yet, I feel I should not care to change with her, all the same. Let them call me a female philosopher, a queer fish, or what they choose—I will remain true to the end ... to what? to an ideal, or what? Yes, to my ideal. Yes, I will be faithful to the end to what first set my heart throbbing—to what I have recognised, and recognise still, as truth, and good.... If only my strength does not fail me, if only my divinity does not turn out to be a dumb and soulless idol!...

If you really feel any friendship for me, if you have really not forgotten me, you ought to aid me, you ought to solve my doubts, and strengthen my convictions....

Though after all, what help can you give me? 'All that's rubbish, fiddle-faddle,' was said to me yesterday by my uncle—I think you don't know him—a retired naval officer, a very sensible man; 'husband, children, a pot of soup; to look after the husband and children and keep an eye on the pot—that's what a woman wants.'... Tell me, is he right?

If he really is right, I can still make up for the past, I can still get into the common groove. Why should I wait any longer? what have I to hope for? In one of your letters you spoke of the wings of youth. How often—how long they are tied! And later on comes the time when they fall off, and there is no rising above earth, no flying to heaven any more. Write to me.—Yours,

M.

X

FROM ALEXEY PETROVITCH TO MARYA ALEXANDROVNA

ST. PETERSBURG, *June* 16, 1840.

I hasten to answer your letter, dear Marya Alexandrovna. I will confess to you that if it were not ... I can't say for business, for I have none ... if it were not that I am stupidly accustomed to this place, I should have gone off to see you again, and should have talked to my heart's content, but on paper it all comes out cold and dead....

Marya Alexandrovna, I tell you again, women are better than men, and you ought to prove this in practice. Let such as us fling away our convictions, like cast-off clothes, or abandon them for a crust of bread, or lull them into an untroubled sleep, and put over them—as over the dead, once dear to us—a gravestone, at which to come at rare intervals to pray—let us do all this; but you women must not be false to yourselves, you must not be false to your ideal.... That word has become ridiculous.... To fear being ridiculous—is not to love truth. It happens, indeed, that the senseless laughter of the fool drives even good men into giving up a great deal ... as, for instance, the defence of an absent friend.... I have been guilty of that myself. But, I repeat, you women are better than we.... In trifling matters you give in sooner than we; but you know how to face fearful odds better than we. I don't want to give you either advice or help—how should I? besides, you have no need of it. But I hold out my hand to you; I say to you, Have patience, struggle on to the end; and let me tell you, that, as a sentiment, the consciousness of an honestly sustained struggle is almost higher than the triumph of victory.... Victory does not depend on ourselves. Of course your uncle is right from a certain point of view; family life is everything for a woman; for her there is no other life.

But what does that prove? None but Jesuits will maintain that any means are good if only they attain the end. It's false! it's false! Feet sullied with the mud of the road are unworthy to go into a holy temple. At the end of your letter is a phrase I do not like; you want to get into the common groove; take care, don't make a false step! Besides—do not forget,—there is no erasing the past; and however much you try, whatever pressure you put on yourself, you will not turn into your sister. You have reached a higher level than she; but your soul has been scorched in the fire, hers is untouched. Descend to her level, stoop to her, you can; but nature will not give up her rights, and the burnt place will not grow again....

You are afraid—let us speak plainly—you are afraid of being left an old maid. You are, I know, already twenty-six. Certainly the position of old maids is an unenviable one; every one is so ready to laugh at them, every one comments with such ungenerous amusement on their peculiarities and weaknesses. But if you scrutinise with a little attention any old bachelor, one may just as well point the finger of scorn at him; one will find plenty in him, too, to laugh at. There's no help for it. There is no getting happiness by struggling for it. But we must not forget that it's not happiness, but human dignity, that's the chief aim in life.

You describe your position with great humour. I well understand all the bitterness of it; your position one may really call tragic. But let me tell you you are not alone in it; there is scarcely any quite modern person who isn't placed in it. You will say that that makes it no better for you; but I am of opinion that suffering in company with thousands is quite a different matter from suffering alone. It is not a matter of egoism, but a sense of a general inevitability which comes in.

All this is very fine, granted, you will say … but not practicable in reality. Why not practicable? I have hitherto imagined, and I hope I shall never cease to imagine, that in God's world everything honest, good, and true is practicable, and will sooner or later come to pass, and not only will be realised, but is already being realised. Let each man only hold firm in his place, not lose patience, nor desire the impossible, but do all in his power. But I fancy I have gone off too much into abstractions. I will defer the continuation of my reflections till the next letter; but I cannot lay down my pen without warmly, most warmly, pressing your hand, and wishing you from my soul all that is good on earth.

Yours, A. S.

P.S.—By the way, you say it's useless for you to wait, that you have nothing to hope for; how do you know that, let me ask?

XI

FROM MARYA ALEXANDROVNA TO ALEXEY PETROVITCH

VILLAGE OF X——, *June* 30, 1840.

How grateful I am to you for your letter, Alexey Petrovitch! How much good it did me! I see you really are a good and trustworthy man, and so I shall not be reserved with you. I trust you. I know you would make no unkind use of my openness, and will give me friendly counsel. Here is the question.

You noticed at the end of my letter a phrase which you did not quite like. I will tell what it had reference to. There is one of the neighbours here … he was not here when you were, and you have not seen him. He … I could marry him if I liked; he is still young, well-educated, and has property. There are no difficulties on the part of my parents; on the contrary, they—I know for a fact—desire this marriage. He is a good man, and I think he loves me … but he is so spiritless and narrow, his aspirations are so limited, that I cannot but be conscious of my superiority to him. He is aware of this, and as it were rejoices in it, and that is just what sets me against him. I cannot respect him, though he has an excellent heart. What am I to do? tell me! Think for me and write me your opinion sincerely.

But how grateful I am to you for your letter!… Do you know, I have been haunted at times by such bitter thoughts…. Do you know, I had come to the point of being almost ashamed of every feeling—not of enthusiasm only, but even of faith; I used to shut a book with vexation whenever there was anything about hope or happiness in it, and turned away from a cloudless sky, from the fresh green of the trees, from everything that was smiling and joyful. What a painful condition it was! I say, *was* … as though it were over!

I don't know whether it is over; I know hat if it does not return I am indebted to you for it. Do you see, Alexey Petrovitch, how much good you have done, perhaps, without suspecting it yourself! By the way, do you know I feel very sorry for you? We are now in the full blaze of summer, the days are exquisite, the sky blue and brilliant…. It couldn't be lovelier in Italy even, and you are staying in the stifling, baking town, and walking on the burning pavement. What induces you to do so? You might at least move into some summer villa out of town. They say there are bright spots at Peterhof, on the sea-coast.

I should like to write more to you, but it's impossible. Such a sweet fragrance comes in from the garden that I can't stay indoors. I am going to put on my hat and go for a walk.
... Good-bye till another time, good Alexey Petrovitch. Yours devotedly, M. B.
P.S.—I forgot to tell you ... only fancy, that witty gentleman, about whom I wrote to you the other day, has made me a declaration of love, and in the most ardent terms. I thought at first he was laughing at me; but he finished up with a formal proposal—what do you think of him, after all his libels! But he is positively too old. Yesterday evening, to tease him, I sat down to the piano before the open window, in the moonlight, and played Beethoven. It was so nice to feel its cold light on my face, so delicious to fill the fragrant night air with the sublime music, through which one could hear at times the singing of a nightingale. It is long since I have been so happy. But write to me about what I asked you at the beginning of my letter; it is very important.

XII

FROM ALEXEY PETROVITCH TO MARYA ALEXANDROVNA

ST. PETERSBURG, *July* 8, 1840.
DEAR MARYA ALEXANDROVNA,—Here is my opinion in a couple of words: both the old bachelor and the young suitor—overboard with them both! There is no need even to consider it. Neither of them is worthy of you—that's as clear as that twice two makes four. The young neighbour is very likely a good-natured person, but that's enough about him! I am convinced that there is nothing in common between him and you, and you can fancy how amusing it would be for you to live together! Besides, why be in a hurry? Is it a possible thing that a woman like you—I don't want to pay compliments, and that's why I don't expatiate further—that such a woman should meet no one who would be capable of appreciating her? No, Marya Alexandrovna, listen to me, if you really believe that I am your friend, and that my advice is of use. But confess, it was agreeable to see the old scoffer at your feet.... If I had been in your place, I'd have kept him singing Beethoven's Adelaïda and gazing at the moon the whole night long.
Enough of them, though,—your adorers! It's not of them I want to talk to you to-day. I am in a strange, half-irritated, half-emotional state of mind to-day, in consequence of a letter I got yesterday. I am enclosing a copy of it to you. This letter was written by one of my friends of long ago, a colleague in the service, a good-natured but rather limited person. He went abroad two years ago, and till now has not written to me once. Here is his letter.—*N.B.* He is very good-looking.
'CHER ALEXIS,—I am in Naples, sitting at the window in my room, in Chiaja. The weather is superb. I have been staring a long while at the sea, then I was seized with impatience, and suddenly the brilliant idea entered my head of writing a letter to you. I always felt drawn to you, my dear boy—on my honour I did. And so now I feel an inclination to pour out my soul into your bosom ... that's how one expresses it, I believe, in your exalted language. And why I've been overcome with impatience is this. I'm expecting a friend—a woman; we're going together to Baiae to eat oysters and oranges, and see the tanned shepherds in red caps dance the tarantella, to bask in the sun, like lizards—in short, to enjoy life to the utmost. My dear boy, I am more happy than I can possibly tell you.
If only I had your style—oh! what a picture I would draw for you! But unfortunately, as you are aware, I'm an illiterate person. The woman I am expecting, and who has kept me now more than a hour continually starting and looking at the door, loves me—but how I love her I fancy even your fluent pen could not describe.
'I must tell you that it is three months since I got to know her, and from the very first day of our acquaintance my love mounts continually *crescendo*, like a chromatic scale, higher and higher, and at the present moment I am simply in the seventh heaven. I jest, but in reality my

devotion to this woman is something extraordinary, supernatural. Fancy, I scarcely talk to her, I can do nothing but stare at her, and laugh like a fool. I sit at her feet, I feel that I'm awfully silly and happy, simply inexcusably happy. It sometimes happens that she lays her hand on my head.... Well, I tell you, simply ... But there, you can't understand it; you 're a philosopher and always were a philosopher. Her name is Nina, Ninetta, as you like; she's the daughter of a rich merchant here. Fine as any of your Raphaels; fiery as gunpowder, gay, so clever that it's amazing how she can care for a fool like me; she sings like a bird, and her eyes ...

'Please excuse this unintentional break.... I fancied the door creaked.... No, she's not coming yet, the heartless wretch! You will ask me how all this is going to end, and what I intend to do with myself, and whether I shall stay here long? I know nothing about it, my boy, and I don't want to. What will be, will be.... Why, if one were to be for ever stopping and considering ...

'She! ... she's running up the staircase, singing.... She is here. Well, my boy, good-bye.... I've no time for you now, I'm so sorry. She has bespattered the whole letter; she slapped a wet nosegay down on the paper. For the first moment, she thought I was writing to a woman; when she knew that it was to a friend, she told me to send her greetings, and ask you if you have any flowers, and whether they are sweet? Well, good-bye. ... If you could hear her laughing. Silver can't ring like it; and the good-nature in every note of it—you want to kiss her little feet for it. We are going, going. Don't mind the untidy smudges, and envy yours, M.'

The letter was in fact bespattered all over, and smelt of orange-blossom ... two white petals had stuck to the paper. This letter has agitated me.... I remember my stay in Naples.... The weather was magnificent then too—May was just beginning; I had just reached twenty-two; but I knew no Ninetta. I sauntered about alone, consumed with a thirst for bliss, at once torturing and sweet, so sweet that it was, as it were, like bliss itself. ... Ah, what is it to be young! ... I remember I went out once for a row in the bay. There were two of us; the boatman and I ... what did you imagine? What a night it was, and what a sky, what stars, how they quivered and broke on the waves! with what delicate flame the water flashed and glimmered under the oars, what delicious fragrance filled the whole sea—cannot describe this, 'eloquent' though my style may be. In the harbour was a French ship of the line. It was all red with lights; long streaks of red, the reflection of the lighted windows, stretched over the dark sea. The captain of the ship was giving a ball. The gay music floated across to me in snatches at long intervals. I recall in particular the trill of a little flute in the midst of the deep blare of the trumpets; it seemed to flit, like a butterfly, about my boat. I bade the man row to the ship; twice he took me round it. ... I caught glimpses at the windows of women's figures, borne gaily round in the whirl-wind of the waltz.... I told the boatman to row away, far away, straight into the darkness.... I remember a long while the music persistently pursued me.... At last the sounds died away. I stood up in the boat, and in the dumb agony of desire stretched out my arms to the sea.... Oh! how my heart ached at that moment! How bitter was my loneliness to me! With what rapture would I have abandoned myself utterly then, utterly ... utterly, if there had been any one to abandon myself to! With what a bitter emotion in my soul I flung myself down in the bottom of the boat and, like Repetilov, asked to be taken anywhere, anywhere away! But my friend here has experienced nothing like that. And why should he? He has managed things far more wisely than I. He is living ... while I ... He may well call me a philosopher.... Strange! they call you a philosopher too.... What has brought this calamity on both of us?

I am not living.... But who is to blame for that? Why am I staying on here, in Petersburg? what am I doing here? why am I wearing away day after day? why don't I go into the country? What is amiss with our steppes? has not one free breathing space in them? is one cramped in them? A strange craze to pursue dreams, when happiness is perhaps within reach! Resolved! I am going, going to-morrow, if I can. I am going home—that is, to you,—it's just the same; we're only twenty versts from one another. Why, after all, grow stale here! And how was it this idea did not strike me sooner? Dear Marya Alexadrovna, we shall soon see each other. It's

extraordinary, though, that this idea never entered my head before! I ought to have gone long, long ago. Good-bye till we meet, Marya Alexandrovna.
July 9.
I purposely gave myself twenty-four hours for reflection, and am now absolutely convinced that I have no reason to stay here. The dust in the streets is so penetrating that my eyes are bad. To-day I am beginning to pack, the day after to-morrow I shall most likely start, and within ten days I shall have the pleasure of seeing you. I trust you will welcome me as in old days. By the way, your sister is still staying at your aunt's, isn't she?
Marya Alexandrovna, let me press your hand warmly, and say from my heart, Good-bye till we meet. I had been getting ready to go away, but that letter has hastened my project. Supposing the letter proves nothing, supposing even Ninetta would not please any one else, me for instance, still I am going; that's decided now. Till we meet, yours,

A. S.

XIII

FROM MARYA ALEXANDROVNA TO ALEXEY PETROVITCH

VILLAGE OF X——-,*July* 16, 1840.
You are coming here, Alexey Petrovitch, you will soon be with us, eh? I will not conceal from you that this news both rejoices and disturbs me.... How shall we meet? Will the spiritual tie persist which, as it seems to me, has sprung up between us? Will it not be broken by our meeting? I don't know; I feel somehow afraid. I will not answer your last letter, though I could say much; I am putting it all off till our meeting. My mother is very much pleased at your coming.... She knew I was corresponding with you. The weather is delicious; we will go a great many walks, and I will show you some new places I have discovered.... I especially like one long, narrow valley; it lies between hillsides covered with forest.... It seems to be hiding in their windings. A little brook courses through it, scarcely seeming to move through the thick grass and flowers.... You shall see. Come: perhaps you will not be bored.

M.B.

P.S.—I think you will not see my sister; she is still staying at my aunt's. I fancy (but this is between ourselves) she is going to marry a very agreeable young man—an officer. Why did you send me that letter from Naples? Life here cannot help seeming dingy and poor in contrast with that luxuriance and splendour. But Mademoiselle Ninetta is wrong; flowers grow and smell sweet—with us too.

XIV

FROM MARYA ALEXANDROVNA TO ALEXEY PETROVITCH

VILLAGE OF X——, *January* 1841.
I have written to you several times, Alexey Petrovitch ... you have not answered. Are you living? Or perhaps you are tired of our correspondence; perhaps you have found yourself some diversion more agreeable than what can be afforded for you by the letters of a provincial young lady. You remembered me, it is easy to see, simply from want of anything better to do. If that's so, I wish you all happiness. If you do not even now answer me, I will not trouble you further. It only remains for me to regret my indiscretion in having allowed myself to be agitated for nothing, in having held out a hand to a friend, and having come for one minute

out of my lonely corner. I must remain in it for ever, must lock myself up—that is my apportioned lot, the lot of all old maids. I ought to accustom myself to this idea. It's useless to come out into the light of day, needless to wish for fresh air, when the lungs cannot bear it. By the way, we are now hemmed in all round by deadly drifts of snow. For the future I will be wiser.... People don't die of dreariness; but of misery, perhaps, one might perish. If I am wrong, prove it to me. But I fancy I am not wrong. In any case, good-bye. I wish you all happiness.

M. B.

XV

FROM ALEXEY PETROVITCH TO MARYA ALEXANDROVNA

DRESDEN, *September* 1842.

I am writing to you, my dear Marya Alexandrovna, and I am writing only because I do not want to die without saying good-bye to you, without recalling myself to your memory. I am given up by the doctors ... and I feel myself that my life is ebbing away. On my table stands a rose: before it withers, I shall be no more. This comparison is not, however, altogether an apt one. A rose is far more interesting than I.

I am, as you see, abroad. It is now six months since I have been in Dresden. I received your last letters—I am ashamed to confess—more than a year ago. I lost some of them and never answered them.... I will tell you directly why. But it seems you were always dear to me; to no one but you have I any wish to say good-bye, and perhaps I have no one else to take leave of.

Soon after my last letter to you (I was on the very point of going down to your neighbourhood, and had made various plans in advance) an incident occurred which had, one may truly say, a great influence on my fate, so great an influence that here I am dying, thanks to that incident. I went to the theatre to see a ballet. I never cared for ballets; and for every sort of actress, singer, and dancer I had always had a secret feeling of repulsion.... But it is clear there's no changing one's fate, and no one knows himself, and one cannot foresee the future. In reality, in life it's only the unexpected that happens, and we do nothing in a whole lifetime but accommodate ourselves to facts.... But I seem to be rambling off into philosophising again. An old habit! In brief, I fell in love with a dancing-girl.

This was the more curious as one could not even call her a beauty. It is true she had marvellous hair of ashen gold colour, and great clear eyes, with a dreamy, and at the same time daring, look in them.... Could I fail to know the expression of those eyes? For a whole year I was pining and swooning in the light—of them! She was splendidly well-made, and when she danced her national dance the audience would stamp and shout with delight.... But, I fancy, no one but I fell in love with her,—at least, no one was in love with her as I was. From the very minute when I saw her for the first time (would you believe it, I have only to close my eyes, and at once the theatre is before me, the almost empty stage, representing the heart of a forest, and she running in from the wing on the right, with a wreath of vine on her head and a tiger-skin over her shoulders)—from that fatal moment I have belonged to her utterly, just as a dog belongs to its master; and if, now that I am dying, I do not belong to her, it is only because she has cast me off.

To tell the truth, she never troubled herself particularly about me. She scarcely noticed me, though she was very good-natured in making use of my money. I was for her, as she expressed it in her broken French, 'oun Rousso, boun enfant,' and nothing more. But I ... I could not live where she was not living; I tore myself away once for all from everything dear to me, from my country even, and followed that woman.

You will suppose, perhaps, that she had brains. Not in the least! One had only to glance at her low brow, one needed only one glimpse of her lazy, careless smile, to feel certain at once of the scantiness of her intellectual endowments. And I never imagined her to be an exceptional woman. In fact, I never for one instant deceived myself about her. But that was of no avail to me. Whatever I thought of her in her absence, in her presence I felt nothing but slavish adoration.... In German fairy-tales, the knights often fall under such an enchantment. I could not take my eyes off her features, I could never tire of listening to her talk, of admiring all her gestures; I positively drew my breath as she breathed. However, she was good-natured, unconstrained—too unconstrained indeed,—did not give herself airs, as actresses generally do. There was a lot of life in her—that is, a lot of blood, that splendid southern blood, into which the sun of those parts must have infused some of its beams. She slept nine hours out of the twenty-four, enjoyed her dinner, never read a single line of print, except, perhaps, the newspaper articles in which she was mentioned; and almost the only tender feeling in her life was her devotion to il Signore Carlino, a greedy little Italian, who waited on her in the capacity of secretary, and whom, later on, she married. And such a woman I could fall in love with—I, a man, versed in all sorts of intellectual subtleties, and no longer young! ... Who could have anticipated it? I, at least, never anticipated it. I never anticipated the part I was to play. I never anticipated that I should come to hanging about rehearsals, waiting, bored and frozen, behind the scenes, breathing in the smut and grime of the theatre, making friends with all sorts of utterly unpresentable persons.... Making friends, did I say?— cringing slavishly upon them. I never anticipated that I should carry a ballet-dancer's shawl; buy her her new gloves, clean her old ones with bread-crumbs (I did even that, alas!), carry home her bouquets, hang about the offices of journalists and editors, waste my substance, give serenades, catch colds, wear myself out.... I never expected in a little German town to receive the jeering nickname 'der Kunst-barbar.'... And all this for nothing, in the fullest sense of the word, for nothing. That's just it.

... Do you remember how we used, in talk and by letter, to reason together about love and indulge in all sort of subtleties? But in actual life it turns out that real love is a feeling utterly unlike what we pictured to ourselves. Love, indeed, is not a feeling at all, it's a malady, a certain condition of soul and body. It does not develop gradually. One cannot doubt about it, one cannot outwit it, though it does not always come in the same way. Usually it takes possession of a person without question, suddenly, against his will—for all the world like cholera or fever.... It clutches him, poor dear, as the hawk pounces on the chicken, and bears him off at its will, however he struggles or resists.... In love, there's no equality, none of the so-called free union of souls, and such idealisms, concocted at their leisure by German professors.... No, in love, one person is slave, and the other master; and well may the poets talk of the fetters put on by love. Yes, love is a fetter, and the heaviest to bear. At least I have come to this conviction, and have come to it by the path of experience; I have bought this conviction at the cost of my life, since I am dying in my slavery.

What a life mine has been, if you think of it! In my first youth nothing would satisfy me but to take heaven by storm for myself.... Then I fell to dreaming of the good of all humanity, of the good of my country. Then that passed too. I was thinking of nothing but making a home, family life for myself ... and so tripped over an ant-heap—and plop, down into the grave.... Ah, we're great hands, we Russians, at making such a finish!

But it's time to turn away from all that, it's long been time! May this burden be loosened from off my soul together with life! I want, for the last time, if only for an instant, to enjoy the sweet and gentle feeling which is shed like a soft light within me, directly I think of you. Your image is now doubly precious to me.... With it, rises up before me the image of my country, and I send to it and to you a farewell greeting. Live, live long and happily, and remember one thing: whether you remain in the wilds of the steppes—where you have sometimes been so sorrowful, but where I should so like to spend my last days—or whether you enter upon a different career, remember life deceives all but him who does not reflect upon her, and, demanding nothing of her, accepts serenely her few gifts and serenely makes the most of them. Go forward while you can. But if your strength fails you, sit by the wayside and watch those that pass by without anger or envy. They, too, have not far to go. In old days, I did not tell you this, but death will teach any one. Though who says what is life, what is truth? Do you remember who it was made no reply to that question? … Farewell, Marya Alexandrovna, farewell for the last time, and do not remember evil against poor ALEXEY.

CPSIA information can be obtained at www.ICGtesting.com
Printed in the USA
LVOW10s2012020814
397264LV00017B/695/P